The Oxford *Color* Dictionary

Second Edition

Edited by
Angus Stevenson

With
Julia Ell
Richard J

OXFORD
UNIVERSITY PRESS

OXFORD

UNIVERSITY PRESS

Great Clarendon Street, Oxford OX2 6DP

Oxford University Press is a department of the University of Oxford.
It furthers the University's objective of excellence in research, scholarship,
and education by publishing worldwide in

Oxford New York

Athens Auckland Bangkok Bogotá Buenos Aires
Cape Town Chennai Dar es Salaam Delhi Florence Hong Kong Istanbul
Karachi Kolkata Kuala Lumpur Madrid Melbourne Mexico City Mumbai
Nairobi Paris São Paulo Shanghai Singapore Taipei Tokyo Toronto Warsaw

with associated companies in Berlin Ibadan

Oxford is a registered trade mark of Oxford University Press
in the UK and in certain other countries

Published in the United States
by Oxford University Press Inc., New York

First edition 1995, first published as the *Little Oxford Dictionary,*
seventh edition, in 1994

Revised edition 1998

Second edition 2001

British Library Cataloguing in Publication Data

Data available

Library of Congress Cataloging in Publication Data

Data available

ISBN 0–19–8603754
ISBN 0–19–8603762 (US edition)
ISBN 0–19–8604092 (Educational edition)

10 9 8 7 6 5 4 3 2 1

Typeset in Nimrod and Arial
by Interactive Sciences Ltd, Gloucester
Printed and bound in Spain by Bookprint S. L, Barcelona

Oxford Color Dictionary

The *Oxford Color Dictionary* is the clearest and most helpful small English dictionary available today. The definitions are easier to understand than ever before, and there is extra help with spelling, grammar, and pronunciation. The special color type and attractive page layout make it easy to find the word or phrase that you are looking for. The dictionary will be particularly useful for school students.

The *Oxford Color Dictionary* is part of the new range of dictionaries based on the *New Oxford Dictionary of English* (*NODE*), which was first published in 1998. For *NODE* we analysed hundreds of millions of words of English to find out how the language is really used today.

Definitions focus on the most important meanings of words and avoid the use of difficult vocabulary and abbreviations. In addition, there are notes giving clear guidance on points of spelling and good English. Special boxes deal with grammar and punctuation, and show some of the main elements that make up English words.

Pronunciations are given using a simple system which is easy to understand for anyone who can read and speak English. This is outlined below, along with the other dictionary terms and symbols that are used.

Guide to the Dictionary

Headword

Part of speech

Verb inflections

accuse verb (**accuses, accusing, accused**) (often **accuse of**) **1** charge someone with an offence or crime. **2** claim that someone has done something wrong.

Typical use

Sense number

desperate adjective **1** feeling, showing, or involving despair. **2** extremely serious: *a desperate shortage*. **3** very violent or dangerous. ■ **desperately** adverb **desperation** noun.

Example of use

Derivatives (in alphabetical order)

Spelling note

✓ desperate, not -*parate*.

whale noun (plural **whale** or **whales**) a very large sea mammal with a blow-hole on top of the head for breathing. □ **have a whale of a time** informal enjoy yourself very much.

Plural form

Phrases and compounds

Label showing how term is used

Adjective inflections

nervy adjective (**nervier, nerviest**) Brit. nervous or tense.

Label showing where term is used

aloud adverb not silently; audibly.

Usage note

ⓘ don't confuse **aloud**, meaning 'out loud', with **allowed**, meaning 'permitted'.

Homonym number (indicates different word with the same spelling)

bail[2] noun Cricket either of the two small pieces of wood that rest on the stumps.

Label showing subject the entry deals with

Different spelling of headword (both are allowed)

bosun or **bo'sun** /boh-suhn/ = **BOATSWAIN**.

Pronunciation (given for difficult and problem words)

Cross reference to another dictionary entry

Labels

Unless otherwise stated, the words and senses in this dictionary are all part of standard English. Some words, however, are appropriate only to certain situations or are found only in certain contexts, and where this is the case a label (or a combination of labels) is used.

Register labels

These refer to the particular level of use in the language—indicating where a term is informal or formal, historical or old-fashioned, and so on.

formal: normally used only in writing, such as in official documents

informal: normally used only in speaking, or informal writing

dated: no longer used by most people

old use: not in ordinary use today, though sometimes used to give an old-fashioned effect and also found in the literature of the past

historical: only used today to refer to things that are no longer part of modern life, e.g. *blunderbuss*

literary: found only or mainly in literature

technical: normally used only in technical language

humorous: used to sound funny or playful

dialect: used only in certain local regions of the English-speaking world

disapproving: intended to convey a low opinion or cause personal offence

offensive: likely to cause offence, whether the speaker means to or not

vulgar: informal language referring to sexual activity or other bodily functions, which may cause offence.

Geographical labels

The label Brit. implies that the word or phrase is used in standard British English but is not in American English, though it may be found in other varieties such as Australian English. The labels US and N. Amer., on the other hand, imply that the use is typically American and is not standard in British English, though it may be found elsewhere.

Subject labels

These are used to indicate that a word or sense is associated with a particular subject field or specialist activity, such as Music, Chemistry, or Soccer.

Cross References

Cross references are indicated by an arrow (⇨) or an equals sign (=). The arrow means that the term is an alternative spelling of the one referred to, whereas the equals sign indicates that the term means the same as the one referred to.

Pronunciations

Pronunciations are given for any word which might cause difficulty, but not for everyday words assumed to be familiar to everyone, such as *table* or *large*. The part of the pronunciation printed in bold is the syllable that is stressed.

List of Symbols

Vowels	Examples	Vowels	Examples
a	as in **cat**	oh	as in **most**
ah	as in **calm**	oi	as in **join**
air	as in **hair**	oo	as in **soon**
ar	as in **bar**	oor	as in **poor**
aw	as in **law**	or	as in **corn**
ay	as in **say**	ow	as in **cow**
e	as in **bed**	oy	as in **boy**
ee	as in **meet**	u	as in **cup**
eer	as in **beer**	uh	as in **along**
er	as in **her**	uu	as in **book**
ew	as in **few**	y	as in **cry**
i	as in **pin**	yoo	as in **unit**
I	as in **eye**	yoor	as in **Europe**
o	as in **top**	yr	as in **fire**

Consonants	Examples	Consonants	Examples
b	as in **bat**	nk	as in **thank**
ch	as in **chin**	p	as in **pen**
d	as in **day**	r	as in **red**
f	as in **fat**	s	as in **sit**
g	as in **get**	sh	as in **shop**
h	as in **hat**	t	as in **top**
j	as in **jam**	th	as in **thin**
k	as in **king**	*th*	as in **this**
kh	as in **loch**	v	as in **van**
l	as in **leg**	w	as in **will**
m	as in **man**	y	as in **yes**
n	as in **not**	z	as in **zebra**
ng	as in **sing**, **finger**	*zh*	as in **vision**

Note on trademarks and proprietary status

This dictionary includes some words which have, or are asserted to have, proprietary status as trademarks or otherwise. Their inclusion does not imply that they have acquired for legal purposes a non-proprietary or general significance, nor any other judgement concerning their legal status. In cases where the editorial staff have some evidence that a word has proprietary status this is indicated in the entry for that word by the label trademark, but no judgement concerning the legal status of such words is made or implied thereby.

A or **a** noun (plural **As** or **A's**) the first letter of the alphabet. **abbreviation 1** amperes. **2** (Å) angstroms. □ **A-bomb** an atom bomb. **A level** (in the UK except Scotland) the higher of the two main levels of the GCE examination.

a determiner **1** used when mentioning someone or something for the first time; the indefinite article. **2** one single. **3** per.

AA abbreviation **1** Alcoholics Anonymous. **2** Automobile Association.

aardvark /ard-vark/ noun an African mammal with a long snout, that eats ants and termites.

aback adverb (**be taken aback**) be shocked or surprised.

abacus /a-buh-kuhss/ noun (plural **abacuses**) a device used for counting, consisting of a frame with rows of wires along which you slide beads.

abaft adverb & preposition Nautical at the back of, or behind, a ship.

abandon verb **1** leave a place or person permanently. **2** give up a practice completely. **3** (**abandon yourself to**) give in to a desire. noun complete lack of self-consciousness or self-control. ■ **abandonment** noun.

abase verb (**abases**, **abasing**, **abased**) (**abase yourself**) behave in a very humble way. ■ **abasement** noun.

abashed adjective embarrassed or ashamed.

abate verb (**abates**, **abating**, **abated**) become less severe or widespread. ■ **abatement** noun.

abattoir /a-buh-twar/ noun a slaughterhouse.

abbess noun a woman who is the head of an abbey of nuns.

abbey noun (plural **abbeys**) a building occupied by a community of monks or nuns.

abbot noun a man who is the head of an abbey of monks.

abbreviate verb (**abbreviates**, **abbreviating**, **abbreviated**) shorten a word or phrase.

abbreviation noun a shortened form of a word or phrase.

ABC noun **1** the alphabet. **2** the basic facts of a subject.

abdicate verb (**abdicates**, **abdicating**, **abdicated**) **1** give up being king or queen. **2** fail to carry out a duty. ■ **abdication** noun.

abdomen /ab-duh-muhn/ noun **1** the part of the body that contains the organs used for digestion and reproduction; the belly. **2** the rear part of the body of an insect, spider, or crustacean. ■ **abdominal** adjective.

abduct verb take someone away by force or trickery. ■ **abduction** noun **abductor** noun.

aberrant /uh-berr-uhnt/ adjective not normal or acceptable.

aberration /a-buh-ray-sh'n/ noun **1** an action or event which is not normal or acceptable. **2** an unexpected silly mistake.

abet verb (**abets**, **abetting**, **abetted**) encourage or help someone to do something wrong.

abeyance /uh-bay-uhnss/ noun (**in** or **into abeyance**) temporarily not occurring or in use.

abhor /uhb-hor/ verb (**abhors**, **abhorring**, **abhorred**) detest; hate.

abhorrent adjective very unappealing. ■ **abhorrence** noun.

abide verb (**abides**, **abiding**, **abided**) **1** (**abide by**) accept or obey a rule or decision. **2** informal put up with. **3** (of a feeling or memory) last for a long time.

ability noun (plural **abilities**) **1** the power or capacity to do something. **2** skill or talent.

abject /ab-jekt/ adjective **1** extremely

unpleasant and wretched. **2** completely without pride or dignity. ■ **abjectly** adverb.

abjure /uhb-**joor**/ verb (abjures, abjuring, abjured) formal swear that you will give up a belief or claim.

ablaze adjective burning fiercely.

able adjective (abler, ablest) **1** having the power, skill, or means to do something. **2** skilful and capable. □ **able-bodied** physically fit; not disabled. ■ **ably** adverb.

ablutions /uh-**bloo**-shuhnz/ plural noun the act of washing yourself.

abnegate /**ab**-ni-gayt/ verb (abnegates, abnegating, abnegated) formal give up or refuse something that you want or that is your duty. ■ **abnegation** noun.

abnormal adjective different from what is usual or expected in a bad or worrying way. ■ **abnormality** noun **abnormally** adverb.

aboard adverb & preposition on or into a ship, train, or other vehicle.

abode noun a house or home.

abolish verb put an end to a custom or law.

abolition noun the abolishing of a custom or law.

abolitionist noun a person who supports the abolition of something.

abominable adjective **1** morally wrong; wicked or disgusting. **2** informal very bad; terrible. □ **Abominable Snowman** a large, hairy manlike animal said to exist in the Himalayas; a yeti. ■ **abominably** adverb.

abominate verb (abominates, abominating, abominated) hate; detest.

abomination noun **1** something that you hate or find disgusting. **2** a feeling of hatred.

aboriginal adjective **1** existing in a country from the earliest times. **2** (Aboriginal) having to do with the Australian Aboriginals. noun (Aboriginal) a member of one of the native peoples of Australia.

Aborigine /ab-uh-**ri**-ji-nee/ noun an Australian aboriginal.

abort verb **1** end a pregnancy early to stop the baby from developing and being born. **2** undergo a natural abortion. **3** end something early because of a problem or fault.

abortion noun **1** the deliberate ending of a human pregnancy. **2** the natural ending of a pregnancy before the fetus is able to survive on its own.

abortionist noun disapproving a person who carries out abortions.

abortive adjective failing to achieve the intended result; unsuccessful.

abound verb **1** exist in large numbers or amounts. **2** (abound in or with) have a specified thing in large numbers or amounts.

about preposition & adverb **1** on the subject of; concerning. **2** here and there within a particular area. **3** approximately. □ **about-turn** Brit. **1** Military a turn made so as to face the opposite direction. **2** informal a complete change of opinion or policy.

above preposition & adverb **1** at a higher level than. **2** rather or more than. **3** (in printed text) mentioned earlier. □ **above board** lawful and honest.

abracadabra exclamation a word said by magicians when performing a trick.

abrade verb (abrades, abrading, abraded) scrape or wear away.

abrasion /uh-**bray**-zh'n/ noun **1** the process of scraping or wearing away. **2** an area of scraped skin.

abrasive /uh-**bray**-siv/ adjective **1** able to polish or clean a surface by rubbing or grinding. **2** harsh or rough in manner. ■ **abrasively** adverb.

abreast adverb **1** side by side and facing the same way. **2** (abreast of) up to date with.

abridge verb (abridges, abridging, abridged) shorten a text or film. ■ **abridgement** noun.

abroad adverb **1** in or to a foreign country or countries. **2** over a wide area. **3** at large. **4** old use outdoors.

abrogate /**ab**-ruh-gayt/ verb (abrogates, abrogating, abrogated) formal cancel or do away with a law or agreement. ■ **abrogation** noun.

abrupt adjective **1** sudden and unexpected. **2** rudely brief. ■ **abruptly** adverb **abruptness** noun.

abscess noun a swelling that contains pus.

> ☑ remember the *s* and *c*: ab**sc**ess.

abscond /uhb-**skond**/ verb leave quickly and secretly to escape from custody or avoid arrest.

abseil /**ab**-sayl/ verb climb down a rock face using a rope wrapped round the body and fixed at a higher point.

absence noun **1** the state of being away from a place or person. **2** (**absence of**) the lack of.

absent adjective /**ab**-s'nt/ **1** not present. **2** not paying attention. verb /uhb-**sent**/ (**absent yourself**) go away. □ **absent-minded** forgetful, or not paying attention. ■ **absently** adverb.

absentee noun a person who is absent.

absenteeism noun frequent absence from work or school without good reason.

absinthe /**ab**-sinth/ noun a green aniseed-flavoured liqueur.

absolute adjective **1** complete; total. **2** having unlimited power. **3** independent; not related or compared to anything else. □ **absolute zero** the lowest temperature theoretically possible ($-273.15°C$). ■ **absolutely** adverb.

absolution noun formal forgiveness of a person's sins.

absolutism noun the principle that the government or ruler should have unlimited power. ■ **absolutist** noun & adjective.

absolve /uhb-**zolv**/ verb (**absolves, absolving, absolved**) formally declare that someone is free from guilt, blame, or sin.

absorb verb **1** soak up or another substance. **2** take in information. **3** take over something less powerful. **4** use up time or resources. **5** reduce the effect or strength of sound or an impact. **6** hold the atten-

tion of.

absorbent adjective able to soak up liquid easily. ■ **absorbency** noun.

absorption noun the process of absorbing, or of being absorbed.

abstain verb **1** (**abstain from**) stop yourself from doing something pleasant. **2** formally choose not to vote.

abstemious /uhb-**stee**-mi-uhss/ adjective not letting yourself have much food, alcohol, or enjoyment.

abstention /uhb-**sten**-sh'n/ noun **1** a choice not to vote. **2** abstinence.

abstinence /**ab**-sti-nuhnss/ noun the avoidance of doing or indulging in something. ■ **abstinent** adjective.

abstract adjective /**ab**-strakt/ **1** having to do with ideas or qualities rather than physical or concrete things. **2** (of art) using colour and shapes to create an effect rather than attempting to represent real life accurately. verb /uhb-**strakt**/ take out or remove. noun /**ab**-strakt/ a summary of a book or article. ■ **abstractly** adverb.

abstracted adjective not paying attention to what is happening; preoccupied. ■ **abstractedly** adverb.

abstraction noun **1** the quality of being abstract. **2** something which exists only as an idea. **3** the state of being preoccupied.

abstruse /uhb-**strooss**/ adjective difficult to understand.

absurd adjective completely unreasonable or inappropriate. ■ **absurdity** noun **absurdly** adverb.

abundance noun a very large quantity or amount of something.

abundant adjective **1** existing in large quantities; plentiful. **2** (**abundant in**) having plenty of. ■ **abundantly** adverb.

abuse verb /uh-**byooz**/ (**abuses, abusing, abused**) **1** use something wrongly or badly. **2** treat someone cruelly or violently. **3** speak to someone in an insulting way. noun /uh-**byooss**/ **1** the wrong or harmful use of something. **2** cruel and violent treatment. **3** insulting language. ■ **abuser** noun.

abusive adjective **1** extremely insulting. **2** involving cruelty and violence. ■ **abusively** adverb.

abut /uh-**but**/ verb (**abuts, abutting, abutted**) be next to or touching.

abysmal /uh-**biz**-m'l/ adjective extremely bad; terrible. ■ **abysmally** adverb.

abyss /uh-**biss**/ noun a very deep hole.

AC abbreviation alternating current.

acacia /uh-**kay**-shuh/ noun a tree or shrub with yellow or white flowers.

academia /a-kuh-**dee**-mi-uh/ noun the academic environment or community.

academic adjective **1** having to do with education or study. **2** not of practical relevance. noun a teacher or scholar in a university or college. ■ **academically** adverb.

academy noun (plural **academies**) **1** a place where people study or are trained in a particular field. **2** a society of scholars, artists, or scientists. □ **Academy Award** an Oscar.

acanthus /uh-**kan**-thuhss/ noun a plant or shrub with spiny leaves.

a cappella /a kuh-**pel**-luh/ adjective & adverb (of music) sung without being accompanied by instruments.

accede verb (**accedes, acceding, acceded**) (usu. **accede to**) formal **1** agree to a demand or request. **2** take up an office or position.

accelerate verb (**accelerates, accelerating, accelerated**) **1** begin to move more quickly. **2** begin to happen more quickly or intensely. ■ **acceleration** noun.

accelerator noun **1** a foot pedal which controls the speed of a vehicle. **2** a machine that makes charged particles move at high speeds.

accent noun **1** a way of pronouncing a language. **2** an emphasis given to a syllable, word, or note. **3** a mark on a letter or word showing how a sound is pronounced or stressed. **4** a particular emphasis. verb /**ak**-sent/ **1** (**ac-cented**) spoken with a particular accent. **2** stress or emphasize.

accentuate /uhk-**sen**-tyuu-ayt/ verb (**accentuates, accentuating, accentuated**) make a feature more noticeable. ■ **accentuation** noun.

accept verb **1** agree to receive or do something that is offered or proposed. **2** regard someone favourably or with approval. **3** believe that something said is valid or correct. **4** take on a responsibility or liability. **5** tolerate or submit to. ■ **acceptance** noun.

acceptable adjective **1** able to be accepted. **2** adequate. ■ **acceptability** noun **acceptably** adverb.

access noun **1** a way of approaching or entering a place. **2** the right or opportunity to use something or see someone. verb approach or enter a place.

accessible adjective **1** able to be reached or used. **2** friendly and easy to talk to. **3** easily understood or enjoyed. ■ **accessibility** noun **accessibly** adverb.

accession noun **1** the gaining of an important position or rank. **2** a new item added to a library or museum collection.

accessory noun (plural **accessories**) **1** a thing which can be added to or worn with something else to make it more useful or attractive. **2** Law a person who helps someone commit a crime without taking part in it.

accident noun **1** something harmful that happens unexpectedly or without being intended. **2** an incident that happens by chance or without apparent cause.

accidental adjective happening by chance. ■ **accidentally** adverb.

acclaim verb praise enthusiastically and publicly. noun enthusiastic public praise.

acclamation noun enthusiastic approval or praise.

acclimatize or **acclimatise** verb (**acclimatizes, acclimatizing, acclimatized**) get used to a new climate or conditions. ■ **acclimatization** noun.

accolade /**ak**-kuh-layd/ noun something given as a special honour or as a

GRAMMAR

Accent

A person's accent is the way he or she pronounces words. People from
different regions and groups in society have different accents. For instance,
most people in northern England say *path* with a 'short' *a*, while most
people in southern England say it with a 'long' *a*; in America and Canada
the *r* in *far* is generally pronounced, while in south-eastern England it is
not. Everyone speaks with an accent, although some accents may be
regarded as more prestigious or socially acceptable, such as 'received
pronunciation' (the accent of educated people in southern England) in the
UK.

An accent on a letter is a mark added to it to alter the sound it stands for.
In French, for example, there are

- ´ (acute), as in *état*
- ` (grave), as in *mère*
- ^ (circumflex), as in *guêpe*
- ¨ (diaeresis), as in *Noël*
- ¸ (cedilla), as in *français*

and German has ¨ (umlaut), as in *München*.

There are no accents on native English words, but some words borrowed
from other languages still have them, such as *blasé*.

a reward for excellence.

accommodate verb (accommodates, accommodating, accommodated) **1** provide lodging or space for. **2** adapt to or fit in with.

☑ double c, double m: accommodate.

accommodating adjective willing to fit in with someone's wishes.

accommodation noun a room, building, or space where someone may live or stay.

accompaniment noun **1** a musical part which accompanies an instrument, voice, or group. **2** something that accompanies something else.

accompany verb (accompanies, accompanying, accompanied) **1** go somewhere with someone. **2** be present or occur at the same time as. **3** play musical backing for an instrument or voice. ■ **accompanist** noun.

accomplice noun a person who helps another commit a crime.

accomplish verb achieve or complete something successfully.

accomplished adjective highly trained or skilled.

accomplishment noun **1** an activity that you can do well. **2** something that has been achieved. **3** the successful achievement of a task.

accord verb **1** give power or recognition to. **2** (**accord with**) be consistent or in agreement with. noun **1** agreement in opinion or feeling. **2** an official agreement or treaty. □ **of your own accord** willingly.

accordance noun (**in accordance with**) in a way that fits in with.

according adverb **1** (**according to**) as stated by. **2** (**according to**) in a way that corresponds to. **3** (**according as**) depending on whether.

accordingly adverb **1** appropriately. **2** therefore.

accordion noun a musical instrument that you play by stretching and squeezing it with the hands and pressing buttons or keys. ■ **accordionist** noun.

accost verb approach someone and speak to them boldly or aggressively.

account noun **1** a description of an event. **2** a record of money that has been spent and received. **3** an arrangement by which you can keep money in a bank or buy things from a business on credit. **4** importance. **verb** consider or regard in a particular way. □ **account for 1** supply or make up an amount. **2** give an explanation of. **on someone's account** for someone's benefit. **on account of** because of. **on no account** under no circumstances. **take account of** take into consideration.

accountable adjective expected to explain actions or decisions. ■ **accountability** noun.

accountant noun a person who keeps or inspects financial accounts. ■ **accountancy** noun.

accoutrement /uh-**koo**-truh-muhnt/ (US spelling **accouterment**) **noun** an extra item of dress or equipment.

accredit verb (**accredits**, **accrediting**, **accredited**) **1** (**accredit to**) give someone the credit for something. **2** officially authorize.

accretion noun **1** growth or increase by a gradual build-up. **2** something formed or added gradually.

accrue verb (**accrues**, **accruing**, **accrued**) **1** (of money) be received in regular or increasing amounts. **2** collect or receive payments or benefits. ■ **accrual** noun.

accumulate verb (**accumulates**, **accumulating**, **accumulated**) **1** gather together a number or quantity of. **2** increase. ■ **accumulation** noun **accumulative** adjective.

> two c's, one *m*: ac**cum**ulate.

accumulator noun Brit. **1** a large rechargeable electric cell. **2** a bet placed on a series of events, the winnings from each being placed on the next.

accurate adjective **1** correct in all details. **2** reaching an intended target. ■ **accuracy** noun **accurately** adverb.

accursed /uh-**ker**-sid, uh-**kerst**/ adjective **1** literary under a curse. **2** informal horrible.

accusation noun a claim that someone has done something illegal or wrong.

accusative noun Grammar (in some languages) the case used for the object of a verb.

accuse verb (**accuses**, **accusing**, **accused**) (often **accuse of**) **1** charge someone with an offence or crime. **2** claim that someone has done something wrong. ■ **accusatory** adjective **accuser** noun.

accustom verb **1** (**accustom to**) make used to. **2** (**be accustomed to**) be used to.

accustomed adjective customary; usual.

AC/DC adjective alternating current/direct current.

ace noun **1** a playing card with a single spot on it, the highest card in its suit in most games. **2** informal a person who is very good at a particular activity. **3** Tennis a service that an opponent is unable to return. adjective informal very good.

acerbic /uh-**ser**-bik/ adjective sharp and direct. ■ **acerbically** adverb **acerbity** noun.

acetate /a-si-tayt/ noun **1** a kind of chemical compound made from acetic acid. **2** fibre or plastic made of cellulose acetate.

acetic acid /uh-**see**-tik/ noun the acid that gives vinegar its taste.

acetone /a-si-tohn/ noun a colourless liquid used as a solvent.

acetylene /uh-**set**-i-leen/ noun a gas which burns with a bright flame, used in welding.

ache noun a continuous or long-lasting dull pain. verb (**aches**, **aching**, **ached**) **1** suffer from an ache. **2** (**ache for or to do**) want very much to have or do something. ■ **achy** adjective.

achieve verb (**achieves**, **achieving**, **achieved**) manage to do something by effort, skill, or courage. ■ **achievable** adjective **achiever** noun.

> 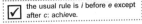 the usual rule is *i* before *e* except after *c*: ach**ie**ve.

achievement noun **1** a thing that is

achieved. **2** the process of achieving something.

Achilles heel /uh-**kil**-leez/ **noun** a weak point.

Achilles tendon **noun** the tendon connecting calf muscles to the heel.

acid **noun 1** a substance that turns litmus red, neutralizes alkalis, and dissolves some metals. **2** informal the drug LSD. **adjective 1** sharp-tasting or sour. **2** (of a remark) bitter or cutting. □ **acid rain** rainfall that has been made acidic by pollution. **acid test** a decisive test of something. ■ **acidic** adjective **acidity** noun **acidly** adverb.

acidify **verb** (acidifies, acidifying, acidified) make or become acid.

acknowledge **verb** (acknowledges, acknowledging, acknowledged) **1** accept that something exists or is true. **2** confirm that you have received something. **3** greet someone with words or gestures.

acknowledgement or **acknowledgment** **noun 1** the action of acknowledging. **2** something done or given as thanks to someone. **3** a mention of someone in a book thanking them for work they have done.

acme /**ak**-mi/ **noun** the highest point of achievement or excellence.

acne **noun** a skin condition causing red pimples.

acolyte /**ak**-uh-lyt/ **noun** an assistant or follower.

acorn **noun** the fruit of the oak, a smooth oval nut in a cup-like base.

acoustic **adjective 1** having to do with sound or hearing. **2** not electrically amplified. **noun** (acoustics) **1** the aspects of a room or building that affect how well it transmits sound. **2** the branch of physics concerned with sound. ■ **acoustically** adverb.

acquaint **verb 1** (acquaint with) make someone aware of or familiar with. **2** (be acquainted with) know someone personally.

> ☑ **acquaint, acquiesce, acquire, acquit,** and related words have a *c* before the *qu*: *acquaint*.

acquaintance **noun 1** familiarity with someone or something. **2** a person you know slightly.

acquiesce /ak-wi-**ess**/ **verb** (acquiesces, acquiescing, acquiesced) accept something without protest.

acquiescent **adjective** ready to accept or do something without protest. ■ **acquiescence** noun.

acquire **verb** (acquires, acquiring, acquired) **1** buy or obtain an article. **2** learn or develop a skill or quality.

acquisition **noun 1** something that you have recently acquired. **2** the action of acquiring.

acquisitive **adjective** too interested in gaining money or material things.

acquit **verb** (acquits, acquitting, acquitted) **1** formally state that someone is not guilty of a criminal charge. **2** (acquit yourself) behave or perform in a particular way. ■ **acquittal** noun.

acre **noun** a unit of land area equal to 4,840 square yards (0.405 hectare). ■ **acreage** noun.

acrid **adjective** unpleasantly bitter or sharp.

acrimonious **adjective** angry and bitter. ■ **acrimoniously** adverb.

acrimony **noun** feelings of anger and bitterness.

acrobat **noun** an entertainer who performs spectacular gymnastic feats.

acrobatic **adjective** involving or performing spectacular gymnastic feats. **noun** (acrobatics) spectacular gymnastic feats. ■ **acrobatically** adverb.

acronym /**ak**-ruh-nim/ **noun** a word formed from the first letters of other words (e.g. *Aids*).

across **preposition & adverb** from one side to the other of something. □ **across the board** applying to all.

acrylic **adjective** (of paint, fabric, etc.) made using acrylic acid.

act **verb 1** take action; do something. **2** have a particular effect. **3** behave in a particular way. **4** (act as) perform the function of. **5** (acting) temporarily doing the duties of another. **6** perform a role in a play or film. **noun 1** a thing done. **2** a law passed formally by a parliament. **3** a pretence. **4** a main division of a play, ballet, or opera. **5** a set performance, or a performing group. □ **act of God** an occurrence which is the result of uncontrollable natural forces.

action noun 1 the process of doing something to achieve an aim. **2** a thing done. **3** the effect of something such as a chemical. **4** a lawsuit. **5** armed conflict. **6** the way in which something works or moves. **7** *informal* exciting activity. **verb** deal with a particular matter. □ **action stations** the positions taken up by soldiers in preparation for action.

actionable adjective Law giving cause for legal action.

activate verb (**activates, activating, activated**) make a device, chemical process, etc. work. ■ **activation noun**.

active adjective 1 moving about often or energetically. **2** participating in a particular area of activity. **3** working; functioning. **4** (of a volcano) erupting or having erupted in the past. **5** Grammar (of a verb) having as its subject the person or thing performing the action (e.g. *she loved him* as opposed to the passive form *he was loved*). □ **active service** military service in wartime. ■ **actively adverb**.

activist noun a person who campaigns for political or social change. ■ **activism noun**.

activity noun (plural **activities**) **1** a condition in which things are happening or being done. **2** busy or energetic action or movement. **3** an action or pursuit.

actor noun a person whose profession is acting.

actress noun a female actor.

actual adjective existing in fact or reality.

actuality noun (plural **actualities**) actual reality or fact.

actualize or **actualise verb** (**actualizes, actualizing, actualized**) make something real or actual.

actually adverb in truth; in reality.

actuary noun (plural **actuaries**) a person who calculates insurance risks and premiums. ■ **actuarial adjective**.

actuate verb 1 cause a machine to function. **2** motivate someone to act in a particular way.

acuity /uh-**kyoo**-i-ti/ **noun** sharpness of thought, vision, or hearing.

acumen /**ak**-yoo-muhn/ **noun** the ability to make good judgements and take quick decisions.

acupuncture noun the insertion of very thin needles into the skin as a medical treatment. ■ **acupuncturist noun**.

acute adjective 1 (of something bad) critical; serious. **2** sharp-witted; shrewd. **3** (of a physical sense or faculty) highly developed. **4** (of an angle) less than 90°. □ **acute accent** a mark (´) placed over certain letters in some languages to indicate pronunciation (e.g. in *fiancée*). ■ **acutely adverb acuteness noun**.

AD abbreviation used to indicate that a date comes the specified number of years after the traditional date of Jesus's birth.

> ℹ️ short for *Anno Domini* ('in the year of our Lord' in Latin). Write AD **before** the numerals, e.g. AD *375*, unless the date is spelled out, as in *the third century AD*.

adage /**ad**-ij/ **noun** a proverb or saying expressing a general truth.

adagio /uh-**dah**-ji-oh/ **noun** (plural **adagios**) a piece of music to be played in slow time.

adamant adjective refusing to be persuaded or to change your mind. ■ **adamantly adverb**.

Adam's apple noun a projection at the front of the neck, more prominent in men than women.

adapt verb 1 make something suitable for a new use or purpose. **2** become adjusted to new conditions.

adaptable adjective able to adjust to, or be altered for, new conditions or uses. ■ **adaptability** noun **adaptably** adverb.

adaptation or **adaption** noun **1** the process of adapting. **2** a film or play adapted from a written work.

adaptor or **adapter** noun **1** a device for connecting pieces of equipment. **2** Brit. a device for connecting a plug or plugs to an electrical socket.

add verb **1** put something together with something else. **2** put together two or more numbers or amounts to find their total value. **3** (**add up**) increase in amount, number, or degree. **4** say as a further remark. **5** (**add up**) informal make sense.

addendum /uh-**den**-duhm/ noun (plural **addenda**) an extra item added at the end of a book or text.

adder noun a poisonous snake with a dark zigzag pattern on its back.

addict noun a person who is addicted to something.

addicted adjective (usu. **addicted to**) **1** physically dependent on a particular substance. **2** very keen on a particular interest or activity.

addiction noun the condition of being addicted to something. ■ **addictive** adjective.

addition noun **1** the action of adding. **2** a person or thing that is added.

additional adjective added; extra. ■ **additionally** adverb.

additive noun a substance added to improve or preserve something.

addled adjective **1** humorous confused or puzzled. **2** (of an egg) rotten.

address noun **1** the details of where a building is or where someone lives. **2** a string of characters identifying a destination for email messages. **3** a formal speech. verb **1** write a name and address on an envelope or parcel. **2** speak formally to. **3** think about a task and begin to deal with it.

> ✓ two d's: add**ress**.

adduce verb (**adduces**, **adducing**, **adduced**) formal refer to something as evidence.

adenoids /**ad**-uh-noydz/ plural noun a mass of tissue between the back of the nose and the throat.

adept adjective /a-**dept**, uh-**dept**/ very skilled or able. noun /**ad**-ept/ an adept person. ■ **adeptly** adverb.

adequate adjective satisfactory or acceptable; good enough. ■ **adequacy** noun **adequately** adverb.

adhere verb (**adheres**, **adhering**, **adhered**) (**adhere to**) stick firmly to. ■ **adherence** noun.

adherent noun a person who supports a particular party, person, or set of ideas. adjective sticking firmly to an object or surface.

adhesion noun the action or process of adhering.

adhesive adjective sticky. noun a substance which causes things to stick.

ad hoc adjective & adverb created or done for a particular purpose only.

adieu /uh-**dyoo**/ exclamation old use goodbye.

ad infinitum /ad in-fi-**ny**-tuhm/ adverb endlessly; forever.

adjacent /uh-**jay**-s'nt/ adjective near or next to something else.

adjective noun Grammar a word used to describe a noun or to make its meaning clearer, such as *sweet* or *red*. ■ **adjectival** adjective.

adjoin verb be next to and joined with.

adjourn /uh-**jern**/ verb **1** break off a meeting until later. **2** postpone a decision. ■ **adjournment** noun.

adjudge verb (**adjudges**, **adjudging**, **adjudged**) (of a law court or judge) formally decide.

adjudicate /uh-**joo**-di-kayt/ verb (**adjudicates**, **adjudicating**, **adjudicated**) **1** make a formal judgement. **2** judge a competition. ■ **adjudication** noun **adjudicator** noun.

adjunct noun an additional part or thing.

adjure verb (**adjures**, **adjuring**, **adjured**) formal urge someone to do something.

adjust verb **1** alter something slightly.

GRAMMAR [i]

Adjective

An adjective is a word that describes a noun or pronoun, e.g.

red, clever, German, depressed, battered, sticky, shining

Most can be used either before a noun, e.g.

the red house   *a clever woman*

or after a verb like *be, seem,* or *call,* e.g.

the house is red   *she seems very* clever

Some can be used only before a noun, e.g.

the chief *reason (you cannot say* the reason is chief*)*

Some can be used only after a verb, e.g.

the ship is still afloat *(you cannot say* an afloat ship*).*

A few can be used only immediately after a noun, e.g.

the president elect *(you cannot say either* an elect president *or the president is elect).*

---

2 become used to a new situation. **3** decide the amount to be paid when settling an insurance claim. ∎ **adjustable** adjective **adjustment** noun.

adjutant /a-juu-tuhnt/ noun a military officer who helps a senior officer with administrative work.

ad-lib verb (**ad-libs, ad-libbing, ad-libbed**) speak or perform in public without preparing first. noun an unprepared remark or speech.

administer verb (**administers, administering, administered**) **1** organize or put into effect. **2** give out or apply a drug or remedy.

administrate verb (**administrates, administrating, administrated**) manage the affairs of an organization or company. ∎ **administrative** adjective **administrator** noun.

administration noun **1** the running of a business or system. **2** the action of giving out or applying something. **3** the government in power.

admirable /ad-mi-ruh-b'l/ adjective deserving respect and approval. ∎ **admirably** adverb.

admiral noun **1** the most senior commander of a fleet or navy. **2** (**Admiral**) a naval officer of the second most senior rank.

admire verb (**admires, admiring, admired**) **1** greatly approve of or respect. **2** look at with pleasure. ∎ **admiration** noun **admirer** noun.

admissible adjective **1** acceptable or valid. **2** allowed to enter a place.

admission noun **1** a confession. **2** the process of being allowed in to a place.

admit verb (**admits, admitting, admitted**) **1** confess that something is true or is the case. **2** allow someone to enter a place. **3** accept that something is valid.

admittance noun the process of entering, or of being allowed to enter.

admonish verb **1** firmly tell someone off. **2** seriously urge or warn. ∎ **admonition** noun **admonitory** adjective.

ad nauseam /ad naw-zi-am/ adverb to a tiresomely excessive degree.

ado noun trouble; fuss.

adolescent adjective in the process of developing from a child into an adult. noun an adolescent boy or girl. ∎ **adolescence** noun.

Adonis /uh-doh-nis/ noun an extremely handsome young man.

adopt verb **1** legally take someone else's child and bring it up as your own. **2** choose an option or course of action. ■ **adoption** noun.

adoptive adjective (of a parent) having adopted a child.

adorable adjective very lovable or charming. ■ **adorably** adverb.

adore verb (adores, adoring, adored) love and respect deeply. ■ **adoration** noun.

adorn verb make more attractive; decorate. ■ **adornment** noun.

adrenal /uh-**dree**-nuhl/ adjective having to do with the **adrenal glands**, a pair of glands above the kidneys.

adrenalin or **adrenaline** /uh-**dre**-nuh-lin/ noun a hormone produced by the adrenal glands in response to stress, that makes the body's natural processes work more quickly.

adrift adjective & adverb **1** (of a boat) drifting without control. **2** Brit. informal no longer fixed in position.

adroit adjective clever or skilful. ■ **adroitly** adverb.

adulation noun excessive admiration. ■ **adulatory** adjective.

adult noun a person who is fully grown and developed. adjective **1** fully grown and developed. **2** suitable for or typical of adults. ■ **adulthood** noun.

adulterate verb (adulterates, adulterating, adulterated) make something poorer in quality by adding another substance. ■ **adulteration** noun.

adulterer noun (feminine **adulteress**) a person who has committed adultery.

adultery noun sex between a married person and a person who is not their husband or wife. ■ **adulterous** adjective.

adumbrate /ad-um-brayt/ verb (adumbrates, adumbrating, adumbrated) formal **1** give a faint or general idea of. **2** be a warning of.

advance verb (advances, advancing, advanced) **1** move forwards. **2** put forward a theory or suggestion. **3** hand over payment to someone as a loan or before it is due. noun **1** a forward movement. **2** a development or improvement. **3** an amount of money advanced. **4** an approach made with the aim of beginning a sexual or romantic relationship. adjective done, sent, or supplied beforehand.

advanced adjective **1** far on in progress or life. **2** complex; not basic. □ **advanced level** an A level.

advancement noun **1** the furthering of a cause or plan. **2** the raising of a person to a higher rank or status. **3** a development or improvement.

advantage noun **1** something that puts you in a favourable position. **2** Tennis a score marking a point between deuce and winning the game. verb (advantages, advantaging, advantaged) be of benefit to. □ **take advantage of 1** make unfair use of someone. **2** make good use of an opportunity. ■ **advantageous** adjective.

advent noun **1** the arrival of an important person or thing. **2** (Advent) (in Christian belief) the coming or second coming of Jesus. **3** (Advent) the time leading up to Christmas.

adventitious /ad-vuhn-ti-shuhss/ adjective formal happening by chance.

adventure noun **1** an unusual, exciting, and daring experience. **2** excitement resulting from danger or risk.

adventurer noun **1** a person willing to take risks or do dishonest things for personal gain. **2** a person who seeks adventure.

adventurous adjective **1** involving new or daring methods or experiences. **2** willing to take risks and try new things. ■ **adventurously** adverb.

adverb noun Grammar a word that makes the meaning of an adjective, verb, or other adverb more specific (e.g. *gently*, *very*). ■ **adverbial** adjective.

adversarial /ad-ver-sair-i-uhl/ adjective having to do with conflict or opposition.

adversary /ad-ver-suh-ri/ noun (plural **adversaries**) an opponent or enemy.

adverse adjective harmful; unfavourable. ■ **adversely** adverb.

GRAMMAR   i

Adverb

An adverb is used:

1 with a verb, to say:
- how something happens, e.g. *he walks* quickly
- where something happens, e.g. *I live* here
- when something happens, e.g. *they visited us* yesterday.

2 to strengthen or weaken the meaning of:
- a verb, e.g. *he* really *meant it; I almost* fell asleep
- an adjective, e.g. *she is* very *clever; this is a* slightly *better result*
- another adverb, e.g. *the boys* nearly *always get home late.*

3 to add to the meaning of a whole sentence, e.g.

he is probably *our best player;* luckily, *no one was hurt*

In writing or formal speech it is wrong to use an adjective instead of an adverb. For example, use

    do it properly   *and not*   *do it* proper

but note that many words are both an adjective and an adverb, e.g.

    a fast *horse (adjective)*   *he ran* fast *(adverb)*
    a long *time (adjective)*   *have you been here* long? *(adverb).*

---

i   don't confuse **adverse** with **averse**, which means 'strongly disliking or opposed to', as in *I am not averse to helping out.*

adversity noun (plural **adversities**) difficulty; misfortune.

advert noun Brit. informal an advertisement.

advertise verb (**advertises, advertising, advertised**) **1** describe a product, service, or event in a publication or on television in order to increase sales. **2** try to fill a job vacancy by publishing details of it. **3** make a quality or fact known. ■ **advertiser** noun.

advertisement noun a notice or display advertising something.

advice noun guidance or recommendations about what someone should do in the future.

advisable adjective to be recommended; sensible. ■ **advisability** noun.

advise verb (**advises, advising, advised**) **1** recommend a course of action. **2** inform someone about a fact

or situation. **3** offer advice to. ■ **adviser** (or **advisor**) noun.

advised adjective behaving as others would recommend; sensible. ■ **advisedly** adverb.

advisory adjective having the power to make recommendations but not to make sure that they are carried out.

advocaat /ad-vuh-kah/ noun a liqueur made with eggs, sugar, and brandy.

advocate noun /ad-vuh-kuht/ **1** a person who publicly supports or recommends a cause or policy. **2** a person who argues a case on someone else's behalf. **3** Scottish a barrister. verb /ad-vuh-kayt/ (**advocates, advocating, advocated**) publicly recommend or support. ■ **advocacy** noun.

adze /adz/ (US spelling **adz**) noun a tool like an axe, with an arched blade.

aegis /ee-jiss/ noun the protection, backing, or support of someone.

aeon /ee-on/ (US spelling **eon**) noun an extremely long period of time.

aerate verb introduce air into. ■ **aeration** noun.

aerial noun a device that sends out or receives radio or television signals. adjective **1** existing or taking place in the air. **2** involving the use of aircraft.

aerie US spelling of **EYRIE**.

aerobatics noun exciting and daring flying performed for display. ■ **aerobatic** adjective.

aerobic /air-**oh**-bik/ adjective (of exercise) intended to increase the amount of oxygen you breathe in and make it move around the body more quickly. ■ **aerobically** adverb.

aerobics noun exercises intended to strengthen the heart and lungs.

aerodrome noun Brit. an airfield.

aerodynamic adjective **1** relating to aerodynamics. **2** having a shape which moves through the air quickly. noun (**aerodynamics**) the science concerned with the movement of solid bodies through the air. ■ **aerodynamically** adverb.

aerofoil noun Brit. a curved structure, such as a wing, designed to give an aircraft lift.

aeronautics noun the study or practice of travel through the air. ■ **aeronautical** adjective.

aeroplane noun chiefly Brit. a powered flying vehicle with fixed wings.

aerosol noun a substance sealed in a container under pressure and released as a fine spray.

aerospace noun the technology and industry concerned with flight.

aesthete /**eess**-theet/ (US spelling **esthete**) noun a person who appreciates art and beauty.

aesthetic /eess-**thet**-ik/ (US spelling **esthetic**) adjective **1** concerned with beauty. **2** having a pleasant appearance. noun a set of principles behind the work of an artist or artistic movement. ■ **aesthetically** adverb.

aesthetics (US spelling **esthetics**) noun **1** a set of principles concerned with beauty. **2** the branch of philosophy which deals with questions of beauty and artistic taste.

afar adverb at or to a distance.

affable adjective good-natured and friendly. ■ **affability** noun **affably** adverb.

affair noun **1** an event or series of events. **2** a matter that is a particular person's responsibility. **3** a love affair. **4** (**affairs**) matters of public interest and importance.

affect verb **1** make a difference to; have an effect on. **2** make someone feel sadness, pity, etc. **3** pretend to have a particular feeling. **4** wear something or behave in a particular way in an attempt to impress people.

> **i** don't confuse **affect** and **effect**. *Affect* chiefly means 'make a difference to', as in *the changes will affect everyone*. As a verb *effect* means 'bring about a result', as in *she effected a cost-cutting exercise*.

affectation noun behaviour that is designed to impress people.

affected adjective designed to impress people. ■ **affectedly** adverb.

affection noun a feeling of fondness or liking.

affectionate adjective readily showing affection. ■ **affectionately** adverb.

affidavit /af-fi-**day**-vit/ noun a written statement that a person swears is true and that can be used as evidence in a law court.

affiliate verb /uh-**fil**-i-ayt/ (**affiliates, affiliating, affiliated**) officially link a person or group to an organization. noun /uh-**fil**-i-uht/ an affiliated person or group. ■ **affiliation** noun.

affinity noun (plural **affinities**) **1** a natural liking or understanding. **2** a close relationship between people or things with similar qualities.

affirm verb state firmly or publicly. ■ **affirmation** noun.

affirmative adjective agreeing with a statement, or consenting to a request. ■ **affirmatively** adverb.

affix verb /uh-**fiks**/ attach or fasten

something to something else. **noun** /af-fiks/ Grammar a prefix or suffix.

afflict **verb** cause pain or suffering to. ■ **affliction** noun.

affluent **adjective** wealthy; rich. ■ **affluence** noun.

afford **verb** **1** have enough money or time for. **2** provide an opportunity or facility. ■ **affordable** adjective.

affray **noun** Law, dated a breach of the peace by fighting in a public place.

affront **noun** an action or remark that offends someone. **verb** offend.

aficionado /uh-fi-shuh-**nah**-doh/ **noun** (plural **aficionados**) a person who knows a lot about an activity or subject and is very keen on it.

afield **adverb** to or at a distance.

aflame **adjective** in flames.

afloat **adjective & adverb** **1** floating in water. **2** out of debt or difficulty.

afoot **adverb & adjective** in preparation or progress.

aforementioned **adjective** previously mentioned.

afraid **adjective** feeling fear.

afresh **adverb** in a new or different way.

African **noun** a person from Africa, especially a black person. **adjective** relating to Africa or Africans.

Afrikaans /af-ri-**kahns**/ **noun** a language of southern Africa derived from Dutch.

aft **adverb & adjective** at or towards the rear of a ship or an aircraft.

after **preposition** **1** in the time following an event or another period of time. **2** behind. **3** in pursuit of. **4** next to and following in order or importance. **5** in reference to. **conjunction & adverb** in the time following an event. □ **after-effect** an effect that occurs after its cause has gone.

afterbirth **noun** the placenta and other material discharged from the womb after a birth.

afterlife **noun** life after death.

aftermath **noun** the consequences of an unpleasant or disastrous event.

afternoon **noun** the time from noon or lunchtime to evening.

aftershave **noun** a scented lotion that men apply to their skin after shaving.

afterthought **noun** something that is thought of or added later.

afterwards (US spelling **afterward**) **adverb** at a later or future time.

afterword **noun** a section at the end of a book, usually by a person other than the author.

again **adverb** **1** once more. **2** returning to a previous position or condition. **3** in addition.

against **preposition** **1** in opposition to. **2** in resistance to. **3** in contrast to. **4** in or into contact with.

agape **adjective** (of a person's mouth) wide open.

agate /**ag**-uht/ **noun** an ornamental stone marked with bands of colour.

age **noun** **1** the length of time that a person or thing has existed. **2** a particular stage in someone's life. **3** old age. **4** a distinct period of history. **verb** (**ages**, **ageing** or **aging**, **aged**) grow old or older. □ **age of consent** the age at which a person can legally have sex. **come of age** reach adult status.

aged **adjective** **1** /ayjd/ of a specified age. **2** /**ay**-jid/ old.

ageism **noun** prejudice or discrimination on the grounds of a person's age. ■ **ageist** adjective & noun.

ageless **adjective** not ageing or appearing to age.

agency **noun** **1** an organization providing a particular service. **2** action or intervention.

agenda **noun** **1** a list of items to be discussed at a meeting. **2** a list of matters to be dealt with.

agent **noun** **1** a person who provides a particular service. **2** a spy. **3** a person or thing that takes an active role or produces a particular effect.

agent provocateur /a-zhon pruh-vo-kuh-**ter**/ **noun** (plural **agents provocateurs** /a-zhon pruh-vo-kuh-**ter**/) a person who tempts suspected criminals to commit a crime and therefore be convicted.

agglomeration noun a mass or collection of things.

aggrandize or **aggrandise** verb (aggrandizes, aggrandizing, aggrandized) make more powerful, important, or impressive. ■ **aggrandizement** noun.

aggravate verb (aggravates, aggravating, aggravated) **1** make worse. **2** informal annoy or exasperate. ■ **aggravation** noun.

aggregate noun /ag-gri-guht/ **1** a whole formed by combining several different elements. **2** the total score of a player or team in a fixture that is made up of more than one game or round. adjective /ag-gri-guht/ formed by combining many separate items. verb /ag-gri-gayt/ (aggregates, aggregating, aggregated) combine into a whole.

aggression noun hostile or violent behaviour or attitudes.

aggressive adjective **1** very angry or hostile. **2** too forceful. ■ **aggressively** adverb.

 ✓ double g, double s: *aggressive*.

aggressor noun a person or country that attacks another without being provoked.

aggrieved adjective resentful because you feel you have been treated unfairly.

aghast /uh-**gahst**/ adjective filled with horror or shock.

agile adjective **1** able to move quickly and easily. **2** quick-witted or shrewd. ■ **agilely** adverb **agility** noun.

agitate verb (agitates, agitating, agitated) **1** make someone troubled or nervous. **2** try to arouse public concern about an issue. **3** stir or disturb a liquid briskly. ■ **agitation** noun.

agitator noun a person who urges others to protest or rebel.

AGM abbreviation annual general meeting.

agnostic noun a person who believes it is impossible to know whether or not God exists. ■ **agnosticism** noun.

ago adverb before the present.

agog adjective very eager to hear or see something.

agonize or **agonise** verb (agonizes, agonizing, agonized) **1** worry greatly about something. **2** (agonizing) very painful or worrying. ■ **agonizingly** adverb.

agony noun (plural **agonies**) extreme suffering. □ **agony column** Brit. informal a column in a newspaper or magazine offering advice on readers' personal problems.

agoraphobia /ag-uh-ruh-**foh**-bi-uh/ noun abnormal fear of open or public places. ■ **agoraphobic** adjective & noun.

agrarian /uh-**grair**-i-uhn/ adjective having to do with agriculture.

agree verb (agrees, agreeing, agreed) **1** have the same opinion about something. **2** (agree to) say that you will do something that has been suggested by someone else. **3** (agree with) be consistent with. **4** (agree with) be good for.

agreeable adjective **1** pleasant. **2** willing to agree to something. **3** acceptable. ■ **agreeably** adverb.

agreement noun **1** the sharing of opinion or feeling. **2** an arrangement that has been made between people. **3** consistency between two things.

agriculture noun the science or practice of farming. ■ **agricultural** adjective **agriculturally** adverb.

aground adjective & adverb (of a ship) touching the bottom in shallow water.

ague /**ay**-gyoo/ noun old use malaria or some other illness involving fever and shivering.

ahead adverb **1** further forward. **2** in advance. **3** in the lead.

ahoy exclamation a call used by people in ships or boats to attract attention.

aid noun **1** help or support. **2** food or money given to a country in need of help. verb give help to.

aide /ayd/ noun an assistant to a political leader.

Aids noun a disease, caused by the HIV virus and transmitted in body fluids, which breaks down the sufferer's natural defences against infection.

> i short for *acquired immune deficiency syndrome*.

aikido /ɪ-kee-doh/ noun a Japanese martial art.

ail verb old use cause someone to suffer or have problems.

ailing adjective in poor health.

ailment noun a minor illness.

aim verb 1 point a weapon, camera, etc. at a target. 2 try to achieve something. noun 1 a purpose or intention. 2 the aiming of a weapon or missile.

aimless adjective having no direction or purpose. ■ **aimlessly** adverb.

ain't short form informal 1 am not; are not; is not. 2 has not; have not.

> i do not use **ain't** when writing or speaking in a formal situation.

air noun 1 the invisible mixture of gases surrounding the earth. 2 the open space above the surface of the earth. 3 (**an air of**) an impression of. 4 (**airs**) a pretentious, condescending manner. 5 a short, tuneful piece of music; a tune. verb 1 express an opinion or complaint publicly. 2 broadcast a programme on radio or television. 3 expose something to fresh or warm air. □ **air conditioning** a system that cools the air in a building or vehicle. **air force** the branch of the armed forces concerned with fighting in the air. **air gun** a gun which uses compressed air to fire pellets. **air hostess** Brit. a stewardess in a passenger aircraft. **on the air** being broadcast on radio or television. **up in the air** unresolved. ■ **airing** noun **airless** adjective.

airbase noun a base for military aircraft.

airborne adjective 1 carried or spread through the air. 2 (of an aircraft) in the air; flying.

airbrush noun a device for spraying paint by means of compressed air. verb paint with an airbrush.

aircraft noun (plural **aircraft**) an aeroplane, helicopter, or other machine capable of flight. ■ **aircraft carrier** a large warship from which aircraft can take off and land.

airfield noun an area of ground where aircraft can take off and land.

airlift noun an act of transporting supplies by aircraft.

airline noun a company that provides regular flights for the public to use.

airliner noun a large passenger aircraft.

airlock noun 1 a stoppage of the flow in a pump or pipe, caused by an air bubble. 2 a compartment which allows people to move between areas that are at different pressures.

airmail noun a system of transporting mail overseas by air.

airman noun a pilot or crew member in a military aircraft.

airplane noun N. Amer. an aeroplane.

airport noun a complex of runways and buildings where non-military aircraft can take off and land.

airship noun a large aircraft filled with gas which is lighter than air.

airspace noun the part of the air above a particular country.

airstrip noun a strip of ground where aircraft can take off and land.

airtight adjective 1 not allowing air to escape or pass through. 2 unable to be proved false.

airwaves plural noun the radio frequencies used for broadcasting.

airway noun 1 the passage by which air reaches the lungs. 2 a recognized route followed by aircraft.

airworthy adjective (of an aircraft) safe to fly.

airy adjective (**airier**, **airiest**) 1 spacious and well ventilated. 2 light as air; delicate. 3 casual; dismissive. ■ **airily** adverb.

airy-fairy adjective informal vague and unrealistic or impractical.

aisle /rhymes with mile/ **noun** a passage between rows of seats in a church or other public building or between shelves in a shop.

ajar **adverb & adjective** (of a door or window) slightly open.

aka **abbreviation** also known as.

akimbo /uh-**kim**-boh/ **adverb** with hands on the hips and elbows turned outwards.

akin **adjective 1** of similar character. **2** related by blood.

alabaster /**al**-uh-bass-ter/ **noun** a white, semi-transparent mineral that is carved into ornaments.

à la carte /ah lah **kart**/ **adjective & adverb** (of a menu) offering dishes that are separately priced, rather than part of a set meal.

alacrity **noun** brisk eagerness or enthusiasm.

alarm **noun 1** anxiety or fear caused by being aware of danger. **2** a warning of danger. **3** a sound or device that gives a warning of danger. **verb 1** frighten or disturb. **2** (be alarmed) be fitted or protected with an alarm. □ **alarm clock** a clock set to sound at a particular time to wake you up.

alarmist **noun** a person who exaggerates a danger and causes needless alarm.

alas **exclamation** literary or humorous an expression of grief, pity, or concern.

albatross /**al**-buh-tross/ **noun** (plural **albatrosses**) a very large white seabird with long, narrow wings.

albeit /awl-**bee**-it/ **conjunction** though.

albino /al-**bee**-noh/ **noun** (plural **albinos**) a person or animal born with white skin and hair and pink eyes.

album **noun 1** a blank book for displaying photographs, stamps, etc. **2** a collection of musical recordings issued as a single item.

albumen /**al**-byuu-muhn/ **noun** egg white.

alchemy /**al**-kuh-mi/ **noun** a medieval form of chemistry concerned particularly with attempts to convert ordinary metals into gold. ■ **alchemical**

adjective **alchemist** noun.

alcohol **noun 1** a colourless liquid found in intoxicating drinks such as wine, beer, and spirits. **2** drink containing alcohol.

alcoholic **adjective** relating to alcohol. **noun** a person suffering from alcoholism.

alcoholism **noun** addiction to alcoholic drink.

alcove **noun** a recess in the wall of a room.

alder **noun** a tree of the birch family, which bears catkins.

alderman **noun** chiefly historical a member of a council below the rank of mayor.

ale **noun** chiefly Brit. beer other than lager, stout, or porter.

alert **adjective 1** quick to notice and respond to danger or change. **2** quickthinking; intelligent. **noun 1** a watchful state. **2** a warning of danger. **verb** warn someone of a danger or problem. ■ **alertly** adverb **alertness** noun.

alfalfa /al-**fal**-fuh/ **noun** a plant with clover-like leaves and bluish flowers, used as food for animals.

alfresco /al-**fress**-koh/ **adverb & adjective** in the open air.

algae /**al**-jee, **al**-gee/ **plural noun** simple plants that do not have true stems, roots, and leaves, e.g. seaweed.

algebra /**al**-ji-bruh/ **noun** the branch of mathematics in which letters and other symbols are used to represent numbers and quantities. ■ **algebraic** /al-ji-**bray**-ik/ adjective.

algorithm /**al**-guh-ri-th'm/ **noun** a process or set of rules used in calculations.

alias /**ay**-li-uhss/ **adverb** also known as. **noun** a false identity.

alibi /**a**-li-bI/ **noun** (plural **alibis**) a piece of evidence that someone was elsewhere when a crime was committed.

alien **adjective 1** belonging to a foreign country. **2** unfamiliar and unappealing. **3** from another world. **noun 1** a foreigner. **2** a being from another world.

alienate verb (alienates, alienating, alienated) **1** make someone feel isolated. **2** lose the support or sympathy of. ■ alienation noun.

alight¹ verb **1** get down from a vehicle. **2** (alight on) happen to notice.

alight² adverb & adjective **1** on fire. **2** shining brightly.

align verb **1** place something in a straight line or in the correct position in relation to others. **2** (align yourself with) be on the side of. ■ alignment noun.

alike adjective similar. adverb in a similar way.

alimentary canal noun the passage along which food passes through the body.

alimony /a-li-muh-ni/ noun chiefly N. Amer. financial support for a husband or wife after separation or divorce.

alive adjective **1** living; not dead. **2** continuing in existence or use. **3** alert and active. **4** (alive with) teeming with.

alkali /al-kuh-lI/ noun (plural alkalis) a substance whose chemical properties include turning litmus blue and neutralizing acids. ■ alkaline adjective.

all determiner **1** the whole quantity or extent of. **2** any whatever. **3** the greatest possible. pronoun everything or everyone. adverb **1** completely. **2** indicating an equal score: one-all. □ all and sundry everyone. the all clear a signal that danger is over. all in informal exhausted. all-in Brit. (of a price) including everything. all out trying as hard as you can. all-rounder Brit. a person with a wide range of skills. all told in total. on all fours on hands and knees.

Allah /al-luh/ noun the name of God among Muslims.

allay /uh-lay/ verb reduce or end fear, concern, or difficulty.

allegation noun a claim that someone has done something illegal or wrong.

allege verb (alleges, alleging, alleged) claim that someone has done something illegal or wrong. ■ alleged adjective allegedly adverb.

allegiance noun loyalty to a person, group, or cause.

allegory noun (plural allegories) a story, poem, or picture which contains a hidden meaning. ■ allegorical adjective.

allegro /uh-lay-groh/ noun (plural allegros) a piece of music that is to be played at a brisk speed.

alleluia ⇒ HALLELUJAH.

allergic adjective **1** caused by an allergy. **2** having an allergy.

allergy noun (plural allergies) a medical condition that makes you feel unwell when you eat or come into contact with a particular substance.

alleviate verb (alleviates, alleviating, alleviated) make a pain or problem less severe. ■ alleviation noun.

alley noun (plural alleys) **1** (also alleyway) a narrow passageway between or behind buildings. **2** a path in a park or garden. **3** a long, narrow area in which skittles and bowling are played.

alliance noun **1** the state of being joined or associated. **2** an agreement made between countries or organizations to work together. **3** a relationship or connection.

allied adjective **1** joined by an alliance. **2** (Allied) relating to Britain and its allies in the First and Second World Wars. **3** (allied to or with) combined with.

alligator noun a large reptile similar to a crocodile.

alliteration noun the occurrence of the same letter or sound at the beginning of words that are next to or close to each other. ■ alliterative adjective.

allocate verb (allocates, allocating, allocated) assign or give to. ■ allocation noun.

allot verb (allots, allotting, allotted) give out as a share, or assign to.

allotment noun **1** Brit. a small plot of rented land for growing vegetables or flowers. **2** the action of allotting, or an amount of something alloted.

allow verb **1** permit someone to do something. **2** (allow for) take into consideration. **3** provide or set aside. **4** admit that something is true. ■ **allowable** adjective.

> ℹ don't confuse **allowed**, meaning 'permitted', with **aloud**, meaning 'out loud'.

allowance noun **1** the amount of something that is allowed. **2** a sum of money paid regularly to a person. **3** an amount of money that can be earned free of tax. □ **make allowances for 1** take into consideration. **2** treat someone less harshly because they are in difficult circumstances.

alloy noun /al-loy/ **1** a mixture of two or more metals. **2** an inferior metal mixed with a precious one. verb /uh-loy/ **1** mix metals to make an alloy. **2** spoil by adding something inferior.

all right adjective **1** satisfactory; acceptable. **2** permitted. adverb fairly well.

> ℹ use the spelling **all right** rather than **alright**.

allude verb (alludes, alluding, alluded) (allude to) **1** hint at. **2** mention in passing.

allure noun powerful attractiveness or charm.

alluring adjective very attractive or tempting. ■ **alluringly** adverb.

allusion noun an indirect reference to something.

alluvial adjective made of clay, silt, and sand that is left by flood water.

ally /al-lI/ noun (plural allies) **1** a person, organization, or country that co-operates with another. **2** (the Allies) the countries that fought with Britain in the First and Second World Wars. verb /uh-lI/ (allies, allying, allied) **1** (ally to or with) combine one resource with another in a way that benefits both. **2** (ally yourself with) side with.

alma mater /al-muh **mah**-ter (or **may**-ter)/ noun the school, college, or university that a person once attended.

almanac or **almanack** /al-muh-nak/ noun **1** a calendar that gives important dates and also information about the sun, moon, tides, etc. **2** a book published yearly and containing useful information for that year.

almighty adjective **1** having unlimited or very great power. **2** informal enormous. noun (the Almighty) God.

almond noun an oval nut with a woody shell, growing on a tree found in warm climates.

almost adverb very nearly.

alms /ahmz/ plural noun historical charitable donations of money or food to the poor.

almshouse noun a house built for poor people to live in.

aloe /a-loh/ noun a tropical plant with succulent leaves, whose bitter juice is used in medicine.

aloe vera /veer-uh/ noun a jelly-like substance obtained from a kind of aloe, used to soothe the skin.

aloft adjective & adverb up in or into the air.

alone adjective & adverb **1** on your own. **2** isolated and lonely. **3** only; exclusively.

along preposition & adverb **1** moving on a surface in a constant direction. **2** extending on a surface in a horizontal line. **3** in company with others.

alongside preposition **1** close to the side of; next to. **2** at the same time as.

aloof adjective cool and distant. ■ **aloofness** noun.

alopecia /a-luh-**pee**-shuh/ noun abnormal loss of hair.

aloud adverb not silently; audibly.

> ℹ don't confuse **aloud**, meaning 'out loud', with **allowed**, meaning 'permitted'.

alp noun **1** a high mountain. **2** (the Alps) a high range of mountains in Switzerland and adjoining countries.

alpaca /al-**pak**-uh/ noun (plural alpaca

or **alpacas**) a long-haired South American mammal related to the llama.

alpha noun the first letter of the Greek alphabet (A, α). □ **alpha particle** Physics a helium nucleus, emitted by some radioactive substances.

alphabet noun a set of letters or symbols used to represent the basic speech sounds of a language.

alphabetical adjective in the order of the letters of the alphabet. ■ **alphabetically** adverb.

alpine adjective **1** relating to, or found on, high mountains. **2** (**Alpine**) relating to the Alps.

already adverb **1** before the time in question. **2** as surprisingly soon or early as this.

alright = **ALL RIGHT**.

Alsatian noun Brit. a German shepherd dog.

also adverb in addition. □ **also-ran** a loser in a race or contest.

altar noun **1** the table in a Christian church at which bread and wine are made sacred. **2** a table or block on which offerings are made to a god or goddess.

alter verb make or become different; change. ■ **alteration** noun.

altercation noun a noisy argument or disagreement.

alter ego /awl-ter ee-goh/ noun **1** a person's secondary or alternative personality. **2** a close friend who is very like yourself.

alternate verb /awl-ter-nayt/ (**alternates, alternating, alternated**) **1** (of two things or people) repeatedly follow one another in turn. **2** keep changing between two states. adjective /awl-**ter**-nuht/ **1** every other. **2** (of two things) each following and succeeded by the other in a regular pattern. □ **alternating current** an electric current that reverses its direction many times a second. ■ **alternately** adverb **alternation** noun.

alternative adjective **1** (of one or more things) available as another possibility. **2** different from what is usual or traditional: *alternative therapy.* noun one of two or more available possibilities. ■ **alternatively** adverb.

alternator noun a dynamo that generates an alternating current.

although conjunction **1** in spite of the fact that. **2** but.

altimeter /al-ti-mee-ter/ noun an instrument which indicates the altitude that has been reached.

altitude noun the height of an object or point above sea level or ground level.

alto noun (plural **altos**) the highest adult male or lowest female singing voice.

altogether adverb **1** completely. **2** in total. **3** on the whole.

altruism /al-troo-iz'm/ noun unselfish concern for others. ■ **altruist** noun **altruistic** adjective.

alum /a-luhm/ noun a compound of aluminium and potassium, used in dyeing and tanning.

aluminium /al-yoo-**min**-i-uhm/ (US spelling **aluminum** /uh-**loo**-mi-nuhm/) noun a lightweight silvery-grey metal.

alumnus /uh-**lum**-nuhss/ noun (plural **alumni** /uh-**lum**-nl/) a former student of a particular school, college, or university.

always adverb **1** at all times. **2** forever. **3** repeatedly. **4** failing all else.

Alzheimer's disease /alts-hy-merz/ noun a disease of older people, which affects the functioning of the brain.

AM abbreviation amplitude modulation.

am 1st person singular present of **BE**.

a.m. abbreviation before noon.

> ℹ️ short for Latin *ante meridiem*.

amalgam noun **1** a mixture or blend of two or more things. **2** an alloy of mercury with another metal.

amalgamate verb (**amalgamates, amalgamating, amalgamated**) combine two or more things to form one organization or structure. ■ **amalgamation** noun.

amanuensis /uh-man-yoo-**en**-siss/ noun (plural **amanuenses** /uh-man-yoo-en-seez/) a person who helps a writer or composer with their work.

amass verb build up over time.

amateur noun **1** a person who takes part in a sport or other activity without being paid. **2** an incompetent person. adjective **1** non-professional. **2** incompetent. ■ **amateurism** noun.

 -eur, not *-uer*: amateur.

amateurish adjective incompetent; unskilful.

amatory /**am**-uh-tuh-ri/ adjective having to do with love or desire.

amaze verb (**amazes, amazing, amazed**) surprise someone greatly; astonish. ■ **amazement** noun **amazing** adjective **amazingly** adverb.

Amazon noun **1** a member of a legendary race of female warriors. **2** a very tall, strong woman. ■ **Amazonian** adjective.

ambassador noun **1** a person sent by a state as its permanent representative in a foreign country. **2** a person who represents or promotes a particular activity.

amber noun **1** a hard, clear yellowish substance used in jewellery. **2** a yellowish colour.

ambergris /**am**-ber-greess/ noun a wax-like substance produced by sperm whales, used in making perfume.

ambidextrous /am-bi-**deks**-truhss/ adjective able to use the right and left hands equally well.

ambience or **ambiance** noun the character and atmosphere of a place.

ambient adjective **1** relating to the surroundings of something. **2** (of music) quiet and relaxing.

ambiguity noun (plural **ambiguities**) uncertain or inexact meaning.

ambiguous adjective **1** having more than one meaning. **2** not clear or decided. ■ **ambiguously** adverb.

ambit noun the scope or extent of something.

ambition noun **1** a strong desire to do or achieve something. **2** desire for success, wealth, or fame.

ambitious adjective **1** having or showing determination to succeed. **2** intended to reach a high standard and therefore difficult to achieve. ■ **ambitiously** adverb.

ambivalent /am-**biv**-uh-luhnt/ adjective having mixed feelings about something or someone. ■ **ambivalence** noun **ambivalently** adverb.

amble verb (**ambles, ambling, ambled**) walk at a leisurely pace. noun a leisurely walk.

ambrosia noun **1** Greek & Roman Mythology the food of the gods. **2** something very pleasing to taste or smell.

ambulance noun a vehicle for taking sick or injured people to and from hospital.

ambulatory adjective relating to walking, or able to walk or move.

ambush noun a surprise attack by people lying in wait in a hidden position. verb make a surprise attack on someone from a hidden position.

ameba US spelling of **AMOEBA**.

ameliorate /uh-**mee**-li-uh-rayt/ verb (**ameliorates, ameliorating, ameliorated**) formal make something better.

amen /**ah**-men, **ay**-men/ exclamation a word said at the end of a prayer or hymn, meaning 'so be it'.

amenable /uh-**meen**-uh-b'l/ adjective **1** willing to be persuaded. **2** (**amenable to**) able to be affected by.

amend verb change or make minor improvements to.

amendment noun a minor change or improvement.

amends plural noun (**make amends**) make up for a wrongdoing.

amenity noun (plural **amenities**) a useful or desirable feature of a place.

American adjective relating to the United States or to the continents of America. noun a person from the United States or any of the countries of North, South, or Central America. ◻ **American football** a kind of football played with an oval ball on a field marked with parallel lines. **American Indian** a member of one of the native peoples of America.

amethyst /**am**-uh-thist/ **noun** a violet or purple precious stone.

amiable **adjective** friendly and pleasant in manner. ■ **amiability** noun **amiably** adverb.

amicable **adjective** friendly and without disagreement. ■ **amicably** adverb.

amid or **amidst** **preposition** in the middle of.

amidships **adverb & adjective** in the middle of a ship.

amino acid /uh-**mee**-noh/ **noun** any of the natural substances which combine to form proteins.

amir ⇨ **EMIR.**

amiss **adjective** not quite right; inappropriate. ◻ **take amiss** be offended by.

amity **noun** friendly relations.

ammeter **noun** an instrument for measuring electric current.

ammo **noun** informal ammunition.

ammonia **noun** a colourless, strong-smelling gas which can be used to make a cleaning fluid.

ammonite **noun** an extinct sea creature with a spiral shell.

ammunition **noun** **1** a supply of bullets and shells. **2** points used to support your case in an argument.

amnesia /am-**nee**-zi-uh/ **noun** loss of memory. ■ **amnesiac** adjective.

amnesty **noun** (plural **amnesties**) **1** a pardon given to people who have committed an offence against the government. **2** a period during which people who admit to committing an offence are not punished.

amniotic fluid **noun** the fluid surrounding an unborn baby in the womb.

amoeba /uh-**mee**-buh/ (US spelling **ameba**) **noun** (plural **amoebas** or **amoebae** /uh-**mee**-bee/) a microscopic creature that is made up of a single

cell and can change its shape.

amok /uh-**mok**/ or **amuck** /uh-**muk**/ **adverb** (**run amok**) behave in an uncontrolled way.

among or **amongst** **preposition** **1** surrounded by. **2** included or occurring in. **3** shared by; between.

amoral /ay-**mo**-ruhl/ **adjective** not concerned with doing what is right. ■ **amorality** noun.

amorous **adjective** showing or feeling sexual desire. ■ **amorously** adverb.

amorphous /uh-**mor**-fuhss/ **adjective** without a clear shape or form.

amount **noun** **1** the total number, size, or value of something. **2** a quantity. **verb** (**amount to**) **1** add up to. **2** be the same as.

ampere /**am**-pair/ **noun** a basic unit of electric current.

ampersand /**am**-per-sand/ **noun** the sign &, which means *and*.

amphetamine /am-**fet**-uh-meen/ **noun** a drug used as a stimulant.

amphibian **noun** an animal such as a frog or toad, which lives in the water when young and on the land as an adult. ■ **amphibious** adjective.

amphitheatre (US spelling **amphitheater**) **noun** a round building without a roof, in which tiers of seats surround a central space used for performing plays or for sports.

ample **adjective** (**ampler, amplest**) **1** enough or more than enough; plentiful. **2** large. ■ **amply** adverb.

amplifier **noun** a device that makes sounds or radio signals louder.

amplify **verb** (**amplifies, amplifying, amplified**) **1** increase the strength of a sound or an electrical signal. **2** explain something in more detail. ■ **amplification** noun.

amplitude **noun** **1** the maximum amount by which a vibration such as an alternating current varies from its average intensity. **2** great size, range, or extent.

ampoule **noun** a small glass capsule containing liquid used in giving an injection.

amputate verb (amputates, amputating, amputated) cut off a limb. ■ amputation noun.

amputee noun a person who has had a limb cut off.

amuck ⇨ **AMOK**.

amulet noun a small piece of jewellery worn as protection against evil.

amuse verb (amuses, amusing, amused) **1** make someone laugh or smile. **2** give someone something enjoyable to do.

amusement noun **1** the feeling that you have when something is funny or amusing. **2** Brit. a fairground ride or machine for playing games on.

an determiner the form of the indefinite article 'a' used before words beginning with a vowel sound.

anabolic steroid /an-uh-**bol**-ik/ noun a synthetic hormone used to build up muscle.

anachronism /uh-**nak**-ruh-ni-z'm/ noun **1** something which seems to belong to another time. **2** something which is wrongly placed in a particular period. ■ anachronistic adjective.

anaconda /an-uh-**kon**-duh/ noun a very large snake of the boa family, found in South America.

anaemia /uh-**nee**-mi-uh/ (US spelling anemia) noun a shortage of red cells or haemoglobin in the blood, causing tiredness. ■ anaemic adjective.

anaesthetic /an-iss-**thet**-ik/ (US spelling anesthetic) noun a drug or gas that stops you feeling pain.

anaesthetize or **anaesthetise** /uh-**neess**-thuh-tyz/ (US spelling anesthetize) verb (anaesthetizes, anaesthetizing, anaesthetized) give an anaesthetic to. ■ anaesthetist noun.

anagram noun a word or phrase formed by rearranging the letters of another.

anal /**ay**-nuhl/ adjective having to do with the anus.

analgesic /an-uhl-**jee**-zik/ noun a pain-relieving drug.

analogous /uh-**nal**-uh-guhss/ adjective similar to and able to be compared with something else.

analogue /**an**-uh-log/ (US spelling analog) noun something that is similar to and can be compared with something else. adjective using a variable physical property, such as voltage, to represent information, rather than binary digits.

analogy /uh-**nal**-uh-ji/ noun (plural analogies) a way of explaining something by comparing it to something else. ■ analogical adjective.

analyse (US spelling analyze) verb (analyses, analysing, analysed) **1** examine in detail to explain it or to find out its structure or composition. **2** psychoanalyse.

analysis /uh-**nal**-i-siss/ noun (plural analyses /uh-**nal**-i-seez/) **1** a detailed examination of the elements or structure of something. **2** psychoanalysis.

analyst noun a person who carries out analysis.

analytical or **analytic** adjective using analysis. ■ analytically adverb.

anarchic /uh-**nar**-kik/ adjective not controlled or governed by any rules or principles.

anarchist noun a person who believes that all government and laws should be abolished. ■ anarchism noun anarchistic adjective.

anarchy noun **1** a situation in which no rules or principles are being followed and there is complete disorder. **2** a society with no government.

anathema /uh-**na**-thuh-muh/ noun something that you hate.

anatomy noun (plural anatomies) **1** the scientific study of the structure of the human body. **2** the structure of a person, animal, or plant. **3** a detailed examination or analysis. ■ anatomical adjective anatomically adverb anatomist noun.

ancestor noun **1** a person from whom you are descended. **2** something from which a later species or version has developed.

ancestral /an-**sess**-truhl/ adjective inherited from your ancestors.

ancestry noun (plural ancestries) your

ancestors or ethnic origins.

anchor noun a heavy object that is attached to a boat by a rope or chain and is dropped to the sea bed to stop the boat from drifting. verb **1** hold with an anchor. **2** secure or fix firmly in position.

anchorage noun a place where ships may anchor safely.

anchorite /**ang**-kuh-ryt/ noun (in the past) a person who lived apart from others for religious reasons.

anchorman noun a person who presents a live television or radio programme.

anchovy /**an**-chuh-vi/ noun (plural **anchovies**) a small fish of the herring family, with a strong flavour.

ancien régime /on-si-an ray-*zheem*/ noun (plural **anciens régimes** /on-si-an ray-*zheem*/) a political or social system that has been replaced by a more modern one.

ancient adjective **1** belonging to the very distant past. **2** very old. noun (**the ancients**) the people of ancient times. ∎ **anciently** adverb.

ancillary adjective **1** providing support. **2** additional; extra.

and conjunction **1** used to connect words, clauses, or sentences. **2** (connecting two numbers) plus.

andante /an-**dan**-tay/ adverb & adjective Music at a moderately slow pace.

androgynous /an-**dro**-ji-nuhss/ adjective partly male and partly female. ∎ **androgyny** noun.

android /**an**-droyd/ noun (in science fiction) a robot with a human appearance.

anecdotal /an-ik-**doh**-t'l/ adjective (of a story) not backed up by facts.

anecdote /**an**-ik-doht/ noun a short entertaining story about a real incident or person.

anemia US spelling of **ANAEMIA**.

anemometer noun an instrument for measuring the speed of the wind.

anemone /uh-**nem**-uh-nï/ noun **1** a plant with brightly coloured flowers. **2** a sea anemone.

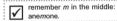
✓ remember *m* in the middle: ane*m*one.

anesthetic US spelling of **ANAESTHETIC**.

aneurysm or **aneurism** /**an**-yuu-ri-z'm/ noun a swelling of the wall of an artery.

anew adverb **1** in a new or different way. **2** once more; again.

angel noun **1** a messenger of God, pictured as being of human form but with wings. **2** a very beautiful or good person. ∎ **angelic** adjective.

angelica /an-**jel**-li-kuh/ noun a plant whose stalks are preserved in sugar and used in cake decoration.

anger noun a strong feeling of extreme displeasure. verb (**angers, angering, angered**) make someone angry.

angina /an-**jy**-nuh/ or **angina pectoris** /**pek**-tuh-riss/ noun severe pain in the chest caused by an inadequate supply of blood to the heart.

angle¹ noun **1** the space between two lines or surfaces that meet. **2** a position from which something is viewed. **3** a way of thinking about something. verb (**angles, angling, angled**) **1** place something in a slanting position. **2** present information from a particular point of view.

angle² verb (**angles, angling, angled**) **1** fish with a rod and line. **2** try to get something without asking for it directly. ∎ **angler** noun.

Anglican adjective relating to the Church of England. noun a member of the Church of England. ∎ **Anglicanism** noun.

anglicize or **anglicise** verb (**anglicizes, anglicizing, anglicized**) make something English. ∎ **anglicization** noun.

Anglophile noun a person who admires England or Britain.

Anglo-Saxon noun **1** a person living in England between the 5th century and the Norman Conquest, whose ancestors came from north and west Europe. **2** the Old English language.

angora /ang-**gor**-uh/ noun **1** a breed of cat, goat, or rabbit with long, soft hair. **2** fabric made from the hair of the angora goat or rabbit.

angostura /ang-guh-**styoor**-uh/ noun the bitter bark of a South American tree, used as a flavouring.

angry adjective (**angrier, angriest**) **1** feeling or showing anger. **2** (of a wound or sore) red and inflamed. ■ **angrily** adverb.

angst noun a strong feeling of anxiety about life in general.

angstrom /**ang**-struhm/ noun a unit of length equal to one hundred-millionth of a centimetre.

anguish noun severe pain or suffering. ■ **anguished** adjective.

angular /**ang**-gyuu-ler/ adjective **1** having angles or sharp corners. **2** (of a person) lean and bony. **3** placed or directed at an angle. ■ **angularity** noun.

animal noun **1** a living being that can move about of its own accord and has specialized sense organs and nervous system. **2** a mammal, as opposed to a bird, reptile, fish, or insect. adjective **1** having to do with animals. **2** physical rather than spiritual or intellectual. ■ **animality** noun.

animate verb /**an**-i-mayt/ (**animates, animating, animated**) **1** bring life or energy to. **2** make drawings or models into an animated film. adjective /**an**-i-muht/ living. ■ **animator** noun.

animated adjective **1** lively. **2** (of a film) made using animation. ■ **animatedly** adverb.

animation noun **1** liveliness. **2** the technique of filming a sequence of drawings or positions of models to give the appearance of movement. **3** the creation of moving images by means of a computer.

animism /**an**-i-mi-z'm/ noun the belief that all things in nature have a soul. ■ **animist** noun.

animosity noun (plural **animosities**) strong hatred or dislike; hostility.

animus noun hatred or dislike.

anion /**an**-I-uhn/ noun an ion with a negative charge.

aniseed noun the seed of the **anise** plant, used as a flavouring.

ankle noun the joint connecting the foot with the leg.

anklet noun a chain or band worn round the ankle.

annals plural noun a historical record of events made year by year.

anneal /uh-**neel**/ verb heat metal or glass and allow it to cool slowly, so as to toughen it.

annex verb /an-**neks**/ **1** take possession of another country's land. **2** add something as an extra part. noun (also **annexe**) /**an**-neks/ (plural **annexes**) **1** a building attached or near to a main building. **2** an addition to a document. ■ **annexation** noun.

annihilate /uh-**ny**-i-layt/ verb (**annihilates, annihilating, annihilated**) destroy completely. ■ **annihilation** noun.

anniversary noun (plural **anniversaries**) the date on which an event took place in a previous year.

annotate verb (**annotates, annotating, annotated**) add explanatory notes to. ■ **annotation** noun.

announce verb (**announces, announcing, announced**) **1** make a public statement about. **2** be a sign of. ■ **announcer** noun.

announcement noun a public statement.

annoy verb **1** make someone a little angry. **2** trouble or harass someone. ■ **annoyance** noun.

annual adjective **1** happening once a year. **2** calculated over or covering a year. **3** (of a plant) living for a year or less. noun a book published once a year. ■ **annually** adverb.

annuity /uh-**nyoo**-i-ti/ noun (plural **annuities**) a fixed sum of money paid to someone each year.

annul /uh-**nul**/ verb (**annuls, annulling, annulled**) declare a law, marriage, or other legal contract to be no longer valid. ■ **annulment** noun.

annular /an-yuu-ler/ **adjective** technical ring-shaped.

annunciation **noun** (**the Annunciation**) (in Christian belief) the announcement by the angel Gabriel to the Virgin Mary that she was to be the mother of Jesus.

anode /an-ohd/ **noun** an electrode with a positive charge.

anodized or **anodised** **adjective** (of metal) coated with a protective layer by the action of an electric current.

anodyne **adjective** unlikely to cause offence or disagreement; bland. **noun** a painkilling drug.

anoint **verb** dab or smear water or oil on someone as part of a religious ceremony.

anomalous **adjective** differing from what is standard or normal.

anomaly /uh-**nom**-uh-li/ **noun** (plural **anomalies**) something that is different from what is normal or expected.

anon **adverb** old use soon; shortly.

anonymous **adjective** 1 having a name that is not publicly known. 2 having no outstanding or individual features. ■ **anonymity** **noun** anonymously **adverb**.

anorak **noun** a waterproof jacket with a hood.

anorexia or **anorexia nervosa** **noun** a disorder in which a person refuses to eat because they are afraid of becoming fat. ■ **anorexic** **adjective** & **noun**.

another **determiner** & **pronoun** 1 one more. 2 different from the one already mentioned.

answer **noun** 1 something said or written in reaction to a question or statement. 2 the solution to a problem. **verb** (**answers, answering, answered**) 1 give an answer. 2 (**answer back**) give a cheeky reply. 3 (**answer to**) have to explain your actions or decisions to someone. 4 (**answer for**) be responsible for the things you do. 5 meet a need. □ **answering machine** a device attached to a telephone which gives a prerecorded reply to an incoming call and can record a message from the caller.

answerable **adjective** 1 (**answerable to**) having to explain to someone why you have done the things you have done. 2 (**answerable for**) responsible for something.

ant **noun** a small insect that lives with many others in an organized group.

antacid /an-**tass**-id/ **adjective** (of a medicine) reducing excess acid in the stomach.

antagonism /an-**tag**-uh-ni-z'm/ **noun** the expression of hostile feelings.

antagonist **noun** an opponent or enemy. ■ **antagonistic** **adjective**.

antagonize or **antagonise** **verb** (**antagonizes, antagonizing, antagonized**) make someone feel hostile.

Antarctic **adjective** relating to the region surrounding the South Pole.

anteater **noun** a mammal with a long snout and sticky tongue, that feeds on ants and termites.

antecedent **noun** 1 a thing that comes before another. 2 (**antecedents**) a person's ancestors. **adjective** coming before in time or order.

antedate **verb** (**antedates, antedating, antedated**) come or exist before something else.

antediluvian /an-ti-di-**loo**-vi-uhn/ **adjective** 1 belonging to the time before the biblical Flood. 2 ridiculously old-fashioned.

antelope **noun** a swift deer-like animal found in Africa and Asia.

antenatal **adjective** before birth; during or relating to pregnancy.

antenna /an-**ten**-nuh/ **noun** 1 (plural **antennae** /an-**ten**-nee/) each of a pair of long, thin feelers on the heads of some insects and shellfish. 2 (plural **antennae** or **antennas**) an aerial.

anterior **adjective** at or near the front.

ante-room **noun** a small room leading to a more important one.

anthem **noun** 1 a song chosen by a country to express patriotic feelings. 2 a musical setting of a religious text that is sung by a choir during a church service.

anther noun the part of a flower's stamen that contains the pollen.

anthill noun a mound of earth made by ants when they build a nest.

anthology noun (plural **anthologies**) a collection of poems or other pieces of writing or music.

anthracite noun hard coal that burns with little flame and smoke.

anthrax noun a serious disease of sheep and cattle, that can be transmitted to humans.

anthropoid adjective having to do with apes that resemble human beings in form, such as gorillas or chimpanzees.

anthropology noun the study of human origins, societies, and cultures. ■ **anthropological** adjective **anthropologist** noun.

anthropomorphic /an-thruh-puh-**mor**-fik/ adjective (of a god, animal, or object) treated as if it was human.

antibiotic noun a medicine that kills bacteria.

antibody noun (plural **antibodies**) a protein produced in the blood to react against harmful substances.

Antichrist noun an enemy of Christ that some people believe will appear before the end of the world.

anticipate verb (**anticipates**, **anticipating**, **anticipated**) **1** be aware of and prepared for a future event. **2** look forward to. **3** do something earlier than someone else. ■ **anticipation** noun **anticipatory** adjective.

anticlimax noun a disappointing end to an exciting series of events. ■ **anticlimactic** adjective.

anticlockwise adverb & adjective Brit. in the opposite direction to the way in which a clock's hands move round.

antics plural noun foolish or amusing behaviour.

anticyclone noun an area of high atmospheric pressure around which air slowly circulates, usually resulting in calm, fine weather.

antidote noun a medicine taken to undo the effect of a poison.

antifreeze noun a liquid added to water to prevent it from freezing, used in car radiators.

antigen /**an**-ti-jen/ noun a harmful substance which causes the body to produce antibodies.

anti-hero noun a central character in a story, film, or play who is either ordinary or unpleasant.

antihistamine noun a drug that is used in treating allergies.

antimacassar /an-ti-muh-**kass**-er/ noun a decorative piece of cloth put over the back of a chair to protect it from grease and dirt.

antimatter noun matter consisting of particles with the same mass as those of normal matter but opposite electric or magnetic properties.

antimony /**an**-ti-muh-ni/ noun a brittle silvery-white metallic element.

antipathy /an-**ti**-puh-thi/ noun (plural **antipathies**) a strong feeling of dislike. ■ **antipathetic** adjective.

antiperspirant noun a substance applied to the skin to prevent or reduce sweating.

antiphonal adjective sung or recited alternately by two groups.

Antipodes /an-**ti**-puh-deez/ plural noun (**the Antipodes**) Australia and New Zealand. ■ **Antipodean** adjective & noun.

antiquarian /an-ti-**kwair**-i-uhn/ adjective relating to the collection or study of antiques or rare books.

antiquated adjective very old-fashioned or out of date.

antique noun an object or piece of furniture that is valuable because of its age. adjective having value because of its age.

antiquity noun (plural **antiquities**) **1** the distant past. **2** an object from the distant past.

anti-Semitism noun hostility to or prejudice against Jews. ■ **anti-Semite** noun **anti-Semitic** adjective.

antiseptic adjective preventing the

---

anti-

anti- is used in words meaning:

■ opposed to or against, e.g. *anti-aircraft*
■ preventing or relieving, as in *antibacterial*
■ the opposite of, such as *anticlimax*.

anti- is not the same as **ante-**, which is found in words such as *antechamber* and *antecedent* and means 'before, preceding'.

---

growth of germs that cause disease or infection. **noun** an antiseptic substance.

antisocial adjective 1 behaving in a way that is unacceptable or annoying to others. **2** not wanting to mix with other people.

antithesis /an-ti-thuh-siss/ **noun** (plural **antitheses** /an-ti-thuh-seez/) **1** a person or thing that is the direct opposite of another. **2** the putting together of contrasting ideas or words to produce an effect in writing or speaking.

antithetical /an-ti-**thet**-i-k'l/ **adjective** opposed to each other.

antler noun each of a pair of branched horns on the head of an adult male deer.

antonym /**an**-tuh-nim/ **noun** a word opposite in meaning to another.

anus /**ay**-nuhss/ **noun** the opening through which solid waste matter leaves the body.

anvil noun an iron block on which metal is hammered and shaped.

anxiety noun (plural **anxieties**) an anxious feeling or state.

anxious adjective 1 experiencing worry or unease. **2** very eager. ■ **anxiously** adverb.

any determiner & pronoun 1 one or some, no matter how much or how many. **2** whichever or whatever you choose. **adverb** at all.

anybody pronoun anyone.

anyhow adverb 1 anyway. **2** in a careless or haphazard way.

anyone pronoun any person or people.

anything pronoun a thing of any kind.

anyway adverb 1 said to emphasize something just said or to change the subject. **2** nevertheless.

anywhere adverb in or to any place. **pronoun** any place.

aorta /ay-**or**-tuh/ **noun** the main artery supplying blood from the heart to the rest of the body.

apace adverb literary quickly.

apart adverb 1 separated by a distance. **2** into pieces. ▫ **apart from 1** except for. **2** as well as.

apartheid /uh-**par**-tayt/ **noun** the official system of racial segregation formerly in force in South Africa.

apartment noun 1 a flat. **2** (**apartments**) a private set of rooms in a large house.

 only one *p*: apartment.

apathetic adjective not interested or enthusiastic.

apathy noun general lack of interest or enthusiasm.

ape noun an animal related to the monkeys but with no tail, such as a chimpanzee or gorilla. **verb** (**apes, aping, aped**) imitate someone.

aperitif /uh-**pe**-ri-teef/ **noun** an alcoholic drink taken before a meal.

aperture noun 1 an opening, hole, or gap. **2** the variable opening by which light enters a camera.

apex /**ay**-peks/ **noun** (plural **apexes** or **apices** /**ay**-pi-seez/) the top or highest point of something.

aphid /**ay**-fid/ **noun** a small insect that

feeds on the sap of plants.

aphorism noun a short witty remark which contains a general truth.

aphrodisiac /af-ruh-**diz**-i-ak/ noun a food, drink, or drug that makes people want to have sex.

apiary /**ay**-pee-uh-ri/ noun (plural **apiaries**) a place where bees are kept.

apiece adverb for or by each one.

aplenty adjective in large amounts.

aplomb /uh-**plom**/ noun calm self-confidence.

apocalypse noun a terrible event in which everything is destroyed.

apocalyptic adjective having far-reaching or disastrous consequences.

apocryphal adjective (of information) widely circulated but unlikely to be true.

apogee /**ap**-uh-jee/ noun **1** the point in the orbit of the moon or a satellite at which it is furthest from the earth. **2** the highest point reached.

apolitical adjective not interested or involved in politics.

apologetic adjective showing that you are sorry for making a mistake or doing something wrong. ■ **apologetically** adverb.

apologia /ap-uh-**loh**-ji-uh/ noun a formal defence of opinions or actions.

apologist noun a person who defends something controversial.

apologize or **apologise** verb (**apologizes**, **apologizing**, **apologized**) say you are sorry for making a mistake or doing something wrong.

apology noun (plural **apologies**) **1** a statement in which someone apologizes for a mistake made or for harm done. **2** (**an apology for**) a very poor example of.

apoplectic /a-puh-**plek**-tik/ adjective **1** informal extremely angry. **2** old use relating to apoplexy (a stroke).

apoplexy /**a**-puh-plek-si/ noun (plural **apoplexies**) old use a stroke.

apostasy /uh-**poss**-tuh-si/ noun abandonment of a belief or principle.

apostate /**a**-puh-stayt/ noun a person who abandons a belief or principle.

apostle noun **1** (**Apostle**) each of the twelve chief disciples of Jesus Christ. **2** a person who strongly supports a policy, cause, etc.

apostrophe /uh-**poss**-truh-fi/ noun a punctuation mark (') used to show that something belongs to someone or to show that letters or numbers have been missed out.

apothecary /uh-**poth**-uh-kuh-ri/ noun (plural **apothecaries**) old use a person who prepared and sold medicines.

apotheosis /uh-po-thi-**oh**-siss/ noun (plural **apotheoses** /uh-po-thi-**oh**-seez/) the highest level in the development of something.

appal (US spelling **appall**) verb (**appals**, **appalling**, **appalled**) **1** make someone feel horror and dismay. **2** (**appalling**) informal very bad. ■ **appallingly** adverb.

apparatus noun (plural **apparatuses**) the equipment needed for a particular activity or task.

apparel /uh-**pa**-ruhl/ noun formal clothing.

apparent adjective **1** clearly seen or understood; obvious. **2** seeming real, but not necessarily so. ■ **apparently** adverb.

apparition noun a remarkable thing making a sudden appearance, especially a ghost.

appeal verb **1** ask earnestly or formally for something. **2** be attractive or interesting. **3** ask a higher court of law to reverse the decision of a lower court. noun **1** an act of appealing. **2** attractiveness or interest.

appealing adjective attractive or interesting. ■ **appealingly** adverb.

appear verb **1** come into view or start to exist. **2** seem. **3** present yourself as a performer or in a law court.

appearance noun **1** the way that someone or something looks or seems. **2** an act of appearing.

appease verb (**appeases**, **appeasing**, **appeased**) make someone calm or less hostile by agreeing to their

---

PUNCTUATION | i |

Apostrophe

An apostrophe is used:

1 to indicate possession:
- with a singular noun: *a boy's book*; *a week's work*; *the boss's salary*
- with a plural already ending with *s*: *a girls' school*; *two weeks' newspapers*; *the bosses' salaries*
- with a plural not already ending with *s*: *the children's books*; *women's liberation*
- with a singular name: *Bill's book*; *Nicholas' (or Nicholas's) coat*
- with a name ending in *-es* that is pronounced *-is* or *-eez*: *Moses' mother*
- but it is often omitted in a business name: *Barclays Bank*.

2 to show that one or more letters or numbers have been omitted:

he's (*he is* or *he has*)	*haven't* (*have not*)
can't (*cannot*)	*we'll* (*we shall*)
won't (*will not*)	*o'clock* (*of the clock*)
the summer of '68 (*1968*)	

3 when letters or numbers are referred to in plural form:

mind your p's and q's; *find all the number 7's*

but it is unnecessary in, for example, *MPs*; *the 1940s*.
It is also unnecessary when forming the plural of a regular noun: write *two dogs* rather than *two dog's*.

---

demands. ■ **appeasement** noun.

appellation noun formal a name or title.

append verb add something to the end of a document.

appendage noun a thing that is attached to something larger or more important.

appendicitis noun inflammation of the appendix.

appendix noun (plural **appendices** or **appendixes**) **1** a small tube of tissue attached to the lower end of the large intestine. **2** a section of additional information at the end of a book.

appertain verb **1** (**appertain to**) relate to. **2** be applicable.

appetite noun **1** a natural desire and physical need for food. **2** a liking or desire for something.

appetizer or **appetiser** noun a small dish of food or a drink taken before a meal to stimulate the appetite.

appetizing or **appetising** adjective stimulating the appetite.

applaud verb **1** show approval by clapping. **2** say that you approve of or admire something.

applause noun clapping.

apple noun a round fruit with green or red skin and crisp flesh. □ **the apple of your eye** a person who you are very fond of and proud of.

appliance noun an electrically operated machine for use in the home.

applicable adjective able to be applied to something; relevant. ■ **applicability** noun.

applicant noun a person who applies for something.

application noun **1** a formal request to an authority. **2** the action of applying something. **3** practical use or relevance. **4** continued effort.

applicator noun a device for putting something into or on to something.

applied adjective (of a subject of study) used in a practical way.

appliqué /uh-**plee**-kay/ noun decorative needlework in which fabric shapes are fixed on to a background.

apply verb (applies, applying, applied) **1** make a formal request for something. **2** bring into operation or use. **3** be relevant. **4** put a substance on a surface. **5** (apply yourself) concentrate on what you are doing.

appoint verb **1** give someone a job or role. **2** decide on a time for something. **3** (appointed) equipped or furnished in a particular way.

appointment noun **1** an arrangement to meet. **2** the appointing of someone to a job. **3** (appointments) furniture or fittings.

apportion verb share out. ■ apportionment noun.

apposite adjective appropriate.

appraisal noun **1** an assessment of the quality or value of something. **2** a formal assessment of an employee's performance.

appraise verb (appraises, appraising, appraised) assess the quality or value of something.

appreciable adjective large or important enough to be noticed. ■ appreciably adverb.

appreciate verb (appreciates, appreciating, appreciated) **1** recognize the value of. **2** understand a situation fully. **3** be grateful for. **4** rise in value or price.

appreciation noun **1** recognition of the value of something. **2** gratitude for something. **3** a piece of writing in which the qualities of a person are discussed. **4** an increase in value.

appreciative adjective feeling or showing gratitude or pleasure. ■ appreciatively adverb.

apprehend verb **1** arrest someone for doing something wrong. **2** grasp the meaning of; understand.

apprehension noun **1** a feeling of worry or fear about what might happen. **2** understanding.

apprehensive adjective worried or afraid about what might happen. ■ apprehensively adverb.

apprentice noun a person learning a skilled trade from an employer. verb (be apprenticed) be employed as an apprentice. ■ apprenticeship noun.

apprise verb (apprises, apprising, apprised) (apprise of) make someone aware of.

approach verb **1** come near to. **2** go to someone with a proposal or request. **3** deal with something in a certain way. noun **1** a way of dealing with something. **2** a proposal or request. **3** the action of approaching. **4** a way leading to a place.

approachable adjective **1** friendly and easy to talk to. **2** able to be reached from a particular direction.

approbation noun approval.

appropriate adjective /uh-**proh**-pri-uht/ acceptable and right; suitable. verb /uh-**proh**-pri-ayt/ (appropriates, appropriating, appropriated) **1** take something for your own use without permission. **2** set money aside for a special purpose. ■ appropriately adverb appropriation noun.

approval noun **1** a feeling that something is good or acceptable. **2** official acceptance. □ on approval (of goods) able to be returned to a supplier if unsatisfactory.

approve verb (approves, approving, approved) **1** feel that something is good or acceptable. **2** officially accept something as satisfactory.

approximate adjective /uh-**prok**-si-muht/ almost but not completely accurate. verb /uh-**prok**-si-mayt/ (approximates, approximating, approximated) come close or be similar to. ■ approximately adverb approximation noun.

appurtenances /uh-**per**-ti-nuhn-siz/ plural noun the things you need for a particular activity.

après-ski /ap-ray **skee**/ noun parties and entertainments which take place after a day's skiing.

apricot noun an orange-yellow fruit resembling a small peach.

April noun the fourth month of the year.

a priori /ay pry-**or**-I/ **adjective & adverb** using facts that are known to be true in order to decide what an unknown effect or result will be.

apron noun **1** a garment tied over the front of clothes to keep them clean. **2** an area on an airfield used for manoeuvring or parking aircraft. **3** a strip of stage extending in front of the curtain.

apropos /a-pruh-**poh**/ **preposition** (**apropos of**) with reference to.

apse noun a recess with a domed or arched roof at the end of a church.

apt adjective **1** fitting for the occasion; appropriate. **2** (**apt to**) tending to. **3** quick to learn. ■ **aptly** adverb.

aptitude noun a natural ability.

aqualung noun a breathing apparatus for divers.

aquamarine noun **1** a bluish-green precious stone. **2** a light bluish-green colour.

aquaplane verb (**aquaplanes, aquaplaning, aquaplaned**) (of a vehicle) slide uncontrollably on a wet surface.

aquarium noun (plural **aquaria** or **aquariums**) a water-filled glass tank in which fish and other sea creatures are kept.

Aquarius /uh-**kwair**-i-uhss/ noun a sign of the zodiac (the Water Carrier), 21 January–20 February.

aquatic /uh-**kwat**-ik/ adjective **1** relating to water. **2** living in or near water.

aqueduct /**ak**-wuh-dukt/ noun a long channel or bridge-like structure for carrying water across country.

aqueous /**ay**-kwee-uhss/ adjective relating to or containing water.

aquiline /**ak**-wi-lyn/ adjective **1** (of a nose) curved like an eagle's beak. **2** like an eagle.

Arab noun a member of a people inhabiting much of the Middle East and North Africa. ■ **Arabian** noun & adjective.

arabesque noun **1** a ballet posture in which one leg is extended horizon-

tally backwards and the arms are outstretched. **2** an ornamental design of intertwined flowing lines.

Arabic noun the language of the Arabs, written from right to left. **adjective** relating to the Arabs or Arabic. □ **Arabic numeral** any of the numerals 0, 1, 2, 3, 4, 5, 6, 7, 8, and 9.

arable adjective (of land) able to be used for growing crops.

arachnid /uh-**rak**-nid/ noun a creature of a class including spiders, scorpions, mites, and ticks.

arachnophobia /uh-rak-nuh-**foh**-bi-uh/ noun extreme fear of spiders.

arbiter /**ar**-bi-ter/ noun **1** a person who settles a dispute. **2** a person who has influence in a particular area.

arbitrary adjective **1** not seeming to be based on any plan or system. **2** (of power) used without restraint. ■ **arbitrarily** adverb.

arbitrate verb (**arbitrates, arbitrating, arbitrated**) act as an arbitrator to settle a dispute. ■ **arbitration** noun.

arbitrator noun a person or body appointed to settle a dispute.

arboreal /ar-**bor**-i-uhl/ adjective **1** relating to trees. **2** living in trees.

arboretum /ar-buh-**ree**-tuhm/ noun (plural **arboretums** or **arboreta**) a garden in which trees are grown for study and display to the public.

arbour (US spelling **arbor**) noun a shady place in a garden, with a canopy of trees or climbing plants.

arc noun **1** a curve forming part of the circumference of a circle. **2** a curving movement through the air. **3** a glowing electrical discharge between two points. verb (**arcs, arcing, arced**) move in an arc.

arcade noun **1** a series of arches supporting a roof or wall. **2** a covered walk with shops along the sides.

Arcadian adjective literary relating to an idyllic rural scene or way of life.

arcane adjective secret and mysterious.

arch[1] noun **1** a curved structure spanning an opening or supporting the

WORD FORMATION

arch-, -archy

1 arch- is used in nouns meaning:
- chief or principal: *archbishop*
- most extreme: *an arch-enemy*.

The *arch-* in **archaeology** and **archaic** is from a different root, which means 'ancient'.

2 -archy is used with the meaning 'rule or government' to form nouns such as:

anarchy	disorder or lack of government
matriarchy	a society in which the mother is head of the family
monarchy	rule by a king or queen
oligarchy	rule by a small group of people.

weight of a bridge or roof. **2** the inner side of the foot. **verb** form an arch.

arch² adjective suggesting in a playful way that you know more than you are revealing. ■ **archly** adverb.

archaeology (US spelling **archeology**) noun the study of ancient history through the examination of objects, structures, and materials dug up from old sites. ■ **archaeological** adjective **archaeologist** noun.

archaeopteryx /ar-ki-**op**-tuh-riks/ noun the oldest known fossil bird, which had teeth like a dinosaur.

archaic /ar-**kay**-ik/ adjective **1** very old or old-fashioned. **2** belonging to an earlier period. ■ **archaism** noun.

archangel /**ark**-ayn-j'l/ noun an angel of high rank.

archbishop noun a bishop of the highest rank.

archdeacon noun a senior Christian priest.

archer noun a person who shoots with a bow and arrows. ■ **archery** noun.

archetype /**ar**-ki-typ/ noun **1** a very typical example. **2** a model which others follow. ■ **archetypal** adjective.

archipelago /ar-ki-**pel**-uh-goh/ noun (plural **archipelagos** or **archipelagoes**) a group of many islands and the sea surrounding them.

architect noun **1** a person who designs buildings. **2** the person responsible for something: *the architect of the reforms*.

architecture noun **1** the design and construction of buildings. **2** the complex structure of something. ■ **architectural** adjective.

architrave /ar-ki-trayv/ noun **1** (in classical architecture) a beam resting across the tops of columns. **2** the frame around a doorway or window.

archive /**ar**-kyv/ noun a collection of historical documents or records. **verb** (**archives**, **archiving**, **archived**) place in an archive. ■ **archival** adjective.

archivist /**ar**-ki-vist/ noun a person who is in charge of archives.

archway noun a curved structure forming a passage or entrance.

Arctic adjective relating to the regions around the North Pole.

 remember the c: Arctic.

ardent adjective **1** feeling passionate about something. **2** old use burning; glowing. ■ **ardently** adverb.

ardour (US spelling **ardor**) noun passionate feelings.

arduous adjective difficult and tiring. ■ **arduously** adverb.

are 2nd person singular present and 1st, 2nd, and 3rd person plural present of **BE**.

> ℹ️ don't confuse **are** with **our**.

area noun **1** a part of a place, object, or surface. **2** the extent or measurement of a surface. **3** a subject or range of activity.

arena noun **1** a level area surrounded by seating, in which sports and other events are held. **2** an area of activity.

aren't short form **1** are not. **2** am not (only in questions).

areola /uh-**ree**-uh-luh/ noun (plural **areolae** /uh-**ree**-uh-lee/) the circular area of darker skin surrounding a human nipple.

argon noun an inert gaseous element, present in small amounts in the air.

argot /**ar**-goh/ noun the jargon or slang of a particular group.

arguable adjective able to be argued or disagreed with. ■ **arguably** adverb.

argue verb (**argues**, **arguing**, **argued**) **1** discuss something in a serious or angry way with someone who disagrees with you. **2** make statements in support of something.

argument noun **1** a serious or angry discussion between people who disagree with each other. **2** a set of reasons given in support of an action or opinion.

argumentative adjective tending to argue.

aria /**ah**-ri-uh/ noun a song for a solo voice in an opera.

arid adjective **1** very dry because having little or no rain. **2** dull and boring. ■ **aridity** noun.

Aries /**air**-eez/ noun a sign of the zodiac (the Ram), 20 March–20 April.

arise verb (**arises**, **arising**, **arose**; past participle **arisen**) **1** start to exist or be noticed. **2** (**arise from** or **out of**) occur as a result of. **3** formal stand up.

aristocracy noun (plural **aristocracies**) the highest social class, consisting of people whose families hold a title such as *lord* or *duke*. ■ **aristocrat** noun **aristocratic** adjective.

arithmetic noun the use of numbers in counting and calculation. ■ **arith-**

metical adjective.

ark noun **1** (in the Bible) the ship built by Noah to save two of every kind of animal from the Flood. **2** a chest or cupboard housing the holy scrolls in a synagogue. **3** (**Ark of the Covenant**) the chest which contained the laws of the ancient Israelites.

arm¹ noun **1** each of the two upper limbs of the human body from the shoulder to the hand. **2** a side part of a chair supporting a sitter's arm. **3** a strip of water or land. **4** a branch or division of an organization.

arm² verb **1** supply with weapons. **2** make a bomb ready to explode. **3** provide with essential equipment or information.

armada noun a fleet of warships.

armadillo noun (plural **armadillos**) an insect-eating mammal of Central and South America, with a body covered in bony plates.

Armageddon /ar-muh-**ged**-duhn/ noun **1** (in the Bible) the final battle between good and evil before the Last Judgement. **2** a terrible war with a catastrophic ending.

armament noun **1** (also **armaments**) military weapons and equipment. **2** the equipping of military forces.

armature noun **1** the rotating coil of a dynamo or electric motor. **2** a piece of iron placed across the poles of a magnet to preserve its power.

armchair noun an upholstered chair with side supports for the sitter's arms.

armed adjective carrying a weapon. □ **armed forces** a country's army, navy, and air force.

armistice /**ar**-miss-tiss/ noun an agreement to stop fighting.

armorial adjective relating to coats of arms.

armour (US spelling **armor**) noun **1** metal coverings worn in the past to protect the body in battle. **2** (also **armour plate**) the tough metal layer covering a military vehicle or ship. ■ **armoured** adjective.

armourer (US spelling **armorer**) noun

a person who makes, supplies, or looks after weapons or armour.

armoury (US spelling **armory**) noun (plural **armouries**) a store of arms.

armpit noun a hollow under the arm at the shoulder.

arms plural noun **1** guns and other weapons. **2** the emblems on a coat of arms. □ **up in arms** protesting vigorously.

army noun (plural **armies**) **1** a military force that fights on land. **2** a large number.

aroma noun a pleasant smell. ■ **aromatic** adjective.

aromatherapy noun the use of aromatic oils for healing or to give pleasant feelings. ■ **aromatherapist** noun.

arose past of **ARISE**.

around adverb & preposition **1** on every side of something. **2** in or to many places throughout an area. adverb **1** so as to face in the opposite direction. **2** approximately; generally. **3** available or present.

arouse verb (**arouses**, **arousing**, **aroused**) **1** bring about a feeling or response in someone. **2** excite someone sexually. **3** awaken someone from sleep. ■ **arousal** noun.

arpeggio /ar-**pej**-ji-oh/ noun (plural **arpeggios**) the notes of a musical chord played in rapid succession.

arraign /uh-**rayn**/ verb call someone before a court to answer a criminal charge. ■ **arraignment** noun.

arrange verb (**arranges**, **arranging**, **arranged**) **1** put tidily or in a particular order. **2** organize or plan. **3** adapt a piece of music for performance. ■ **arranger** noun.

arrangement noun **1** something made up of things arranged in a particular way. **2** a plan for a future event. **3** an arranged piece of music.

arrant /**ar**-ruhnt/ adjective utter; complete.

array noun **1** an impressive display or range. **2** an ordered arrangement of troops. **3** literary elaborate clothing. verb **1** (**be arrayed**) be displayed or ar-

ranged in a neat or impressive way. **2** (**be arrayed in**) be clothed in.

arrears plural noun money owed that should already have been paid. □ **in arrears 1** behind with paying money that is owed. **2** (of wages or rent) paid at the end of each period of work or occupation.

arrest verb **1** seize someone and take them into custody. **2** stop the progress of something. **3** (**arresting**) attracting attention. noun **1** the action of arresting someone. **2** a sudden stop.

arrival noun **1** the process of arriving somewhere. **2** a person or thing that has just arrived.

arrive verb (**arrives**, **arriving**, **arrived**) **1** reach a destination. **2** (of a particular moment) come about. **3** (**arrive at**) reach a conclusion or decision.

arrogant adjective behaving in an unpleasant way because you think that you are better than other people. ■ **arrogance** noun **arrogantly** adverb.

arrogate /ar-ruh-gayt/ verb (**arrogates**, **arrogating**, **arrogated**) formal take or claim something that you have no right to.

arrow noun **1** a stick with a sharp point, shot from a bow. **2** a symbol resembling this, used to show direction or position.

arrowroot noun a starch obtained from a plant and used as a thickener in cookery.

arse noun Brit. vulgar a person's bottom.

arsenal noun a store of weapons and ammunition.

arsenic noun a brittle grey element from which a highly poisonous white powder is obtained.

arson noun the criminal act of deliberately setting fire to property. ■ **arsonist** noun.

art noun **1** the expression of creative skill in a visual form such as painting or sculpture. **2** paintings, drawings, and sculpture as a whole. **3** (**the arts**) creative activities such as painting, music, and drama. **4** (**arts**) subjects of study concerned with human culture. **5** a skill.

artefact /**ar**-ti-fakt/ (US spelling **arti-fact**) noun a useful or decorative man-made object.

 in British English it has an e in the middle: artefact.

artery noun (plural **arteries**) **1** any of the tubes through which blood flows from the heart around the body. **2** an important transport route. ■ **arterial** adjective.

artesian well /ar-**tee**-zh'n/ noun a well in which water comes to the surface through natural pressure.

artful adjective cunningly clever. ■ **artfully** adverb.

arthritis /ar-**thry**-tiss/ noun painful inflammation and stiffness of the joints. ■ **arthritic** adjective & noun.

arthropod /**ar**-thruh-pod/ noun an animal with a body that is divided into segments, such as an insect, spider, etc.

artichoke noun a vegetable consisting of the unopened flower head of a thistle-like plant.

article noun **1** a particular object. **2** a piece of writing in a newspaper or magazine. **3** an item in a legal document. **4** (**articles**) a period of training in a company as a solicitor, accountant, etc. verb (**be articled**) (of a solicitor, accountant, etc.) be employed as a trainee.

articulate adjective /ar-**tik**-yuu-luht/ **1** fluent and clear in speech. **2** having joints or jointed segments. verb /ar-**tik**-yuu-layt/ (**articulates, articulating, articulated**) **1** pronounce words distinctly. **2** clearly express an idea or feeling. **3** (**articulated**) having sections connected by a flexible joint or joints. ■ **articulacy** noun **articulately** adverb **articulation** noun.

artifact US spelling of **ARTEFACT**.

artifice noun the clever use of tricks to deceive someone.

artificer noun a person skilled in making or planning things.

artificial adjective **1** made as a copy of something natural. **2** not sincere. □ **artificial insemination** the injec-tion of semen through a syringe into the vagina or womb. **artificial intelligence** the performance by computers of tasks normally requiring human intelligence. **artificial respiration** the forcing of air into and out of a person's lungs to make them begin breathing again. ■ **artificiality** noun **artificially** adverb.

artillery noun **1** large guns used in warfare on land. **2** a branch of the armed forces that uses artillery.

artisan noun a skilled worker who makes things by hand.

artist noun **1** a person who paints or draws. **2** a person who practises or performs any of the creative arts.

artiste /ar-**teest**/ noun a professional singer or dancer.

artistic adjective **1** having creative skill. **2** having to do with art or artists. ■ **artistically** adverb.

artistry noun creative or accomplished skill.

artless adjective straightforward and sincere. ■ **artlessly** adverb.

artwork noun illustrations to be included in a publication.

arty (US spelling **artsy**) adjective informal displaying an obvious interest in the arts. ■ **artiness** noun.

Aryan /**air**-i-uhn/ noun **1** a member of an ancient people of Europe and Asia. **2** (in Nazi thinking) a white person not of Jewish descent. adjective relating to Aryans.

as adverb used in comparisons to refer to extent or amount. conjunction **1** while. **2** in the way that. **3** because. **4** even though. preposition **1** in the role of; being. **2** while; when.

asap abbreviation as soon as possible.

asbestos noun a fibrous grey-white mineral that does not burn.

ascend verb go up; climb or rise.

ascendant adjective **1** rising in power or status. **2** (of a planet or sign of the zodiac) just above the eastern horizon. ■ **ascendancy** noun.

ascension noun **1** the action of reaching a higher position or status.

2 (the Ascension) the ascent of Jesus into heaven after the Resurrection.

ascent noun **1** the action of going up. **2** an upward slope.

ascertain /ass-er-**tayn**/ verb find something out for certain. ■ **ascertainable** adjective.

ascetic /uh-**set**-ik/ adjective choosing to live without pleasures and luxuries. noun an ascetic person. ■ **asceticism** noun.

ascorbic acid /uh-**skor**-bik/ noun vitamin C.

ascribe verb (**ascribes, ascribing, ascribed**) (**ascribe to**) regard as being caused by. ■ **ascription** noun.

aseptic /ay-**sep**-tik/ adjective free from germs.

asexual adjective **1** without sex or sexual organs. **2** not having sexual feelings. ■ **asexually** adverb.

ash¹ noun **1** the powder remaining after something has been burned. **2 (ashes)** the remains of a human body after cremation.

ash² noun a tree with winged fruits and hard pale wood.

ashamed adjective feeling embarrassed or guilty.

ashen adjective very pale from shock, fear, or illness.

ashore adverb to or on the shore or land.

ashram /**ash**-ruhm/ noun a Hindu religious retreat or community.

Asian noun a person from Asia, or whose family originally came from Asia. adjective relating to Asia.

Asiatic adjective relating to Asia.

aside adverb **1** to one side; out of the way. **2** in reserve. noun **1** an actor's remark spoken to the audience. **2** a remark not directly related to the subject being discussed.

asinine /**ass**-i-nyn/ adjective extremely stupid or foolish.

ask verb **1** say something so as to get an answer or some information. **2** say that you want someone to do, give, or allow something. **3 (ask for)** say that you want to speak to. **4** expect something of someone. **5** invite someone to a social occasion.

askance /uh-**skanss**/ adverb with a suspicious or disapproving look.

askew /uh-**skyoo**/ adverb & adjective not straight or level.

aslant adverb & preposition at a slant or crossing something at a slant.

asleep adjective & adverb **1** in or into a state of sleep. **2** not alert. **3** (of a limb) numb.

asp noun a small viper with an upturned snout.

asparagus /uh-**spa**-ruh-guhss/ noun a vegetable consisting of the tender young shoots of a tall plant.

aspect noun **1** a particular part or feature of something. **2** a particular appearance or quality. **3** the side of a building facing a particular direction.

aspen noun a poplar tree with small rounded leaves.

asperity /uh-**spe**-ri-ti/ noun harshness in the way you say or do something.

aspersion /uh-**sper**-sh'n/ noun (**cast aspersions on**) attack someone's character or reputation.

asphalt /**ass**-falt/ noun a tar-like substance used in surfacing roads or roofs.

> ☑️ just as-, not ash-: asphalt.

asphyxia /uh-**sfik**-si-uh/ noun a condition in which someone cannot get enough oxygen and becomes unconscious or dies.

asphyxiate verb (**asphyxiates, asphyxiating, asphyxiated**) kill or make unconscious by depriving of oxygen. ■ **asphyxiation** noun.

aspic noun a savoury jelly made with meat stock.

aspidistra /ass-pi-**diss**-truh/ noun a plant with broad tapering leaves.

aspirant noun a person with ambitions to do or be something.

aspiration noun a hope or ambition. ■ **aspirational** adjective.

aspire verb (aspires, aspiring, aspired) have a strong desire to achieve or become something.

aspirin noun (plural aspirin or aspirins) a medicine used to relieve pain and reduce fever and inflammation.

ass¹ noun 1 a donkey or related small wild horse. 2 informal a stupid person.

ass² US spelling of **ARSE**.

assail verb 1 attack someone violently. 2 (of an unpleasant feeling) come over someone strongly.

assailant noun an attacker.

assassin noun a person who assassinates someone.

assassinate verb (assassinates, assassinating, assassinated) murder a political or religious leader. ■ assassination noun.

assault noun 1 a violent attack. 2 a determined attempt. verb make an assault on. □ assault course Brit. an obstacle course used for training soldiers.

assay noun the testing of a metal to see how pure it is. verb test a metal.

assemblage noun 1 a collection or gathering of things or people. 2 something made of pieces fitted together.

assemble verb (assembles, assembling, assembled) 1 come or bring together. 2 construct something by fitting parts together.

assembly noun (plural assemblies) 1 a group of people gathered together. 2 a body of people with law-making powers. 3 the putting together of parts. □ assembly line a series of machines used in a factory to assemble a product in large numbers.

assent noun approval or agreement. verb agree to a request or suggestion.

assert verb 1 confidently state that something is true. 2 (assert yourself) be confident and forceful.

assertion noun a confident and forceful statement.

assertive adjective speaking and doing things in a confident and forceful way. ■ assertively adverb assertiveness noun.

assess verb make a judgement about the value or quality of something. ■ assessment noun assessor noun.

asset noun 1 a useful or valuable thing or person. 2 (assets) property owned by a person or company.

assiduity /ass-i-dyoo-i-ti/ noun (plural assiduities) careful attention to what you are doing.

assiduous /uh-sid-yoo-uhss/ adjective showing great care and thoroughness. ■ assiduously adverb.

assign verb 1 give someone a task or duty. 2 set something aside for a purpose. 3 say that something happened for a particular reason.

assignation noun a secret arrangement to meet.

assignment noun a piece of work that someone has been asked to do.

assimilate verb (assimilates, assimilating, assimilated) 1 take in and understand information. 2 absorb people or ideas into a society or culture. 3 regard something as similar to or fitting in with something else. ■ assimilation noun.

assist verb help someone.

assistance noun help or support.

assistant noun a person employed to help someone more senior.

assize /uh-syz/ or **assizes** noun historical a court which sat at intervals in each county of England and Wales.

associate verb (associates, associating, associated) (associate with) 1 mentally connect something with something else. 2 frequently meet or have dealings with. 3 (associate yourself with) be involved with. noun a work partner or colleague. adjective 1 connected with an organization. 2 belonging to an association but not having full membership.

association noun 1 a group of people organized for a joint purpose. 2 a connection or link. □ Association Football soccer.

assonance /ass-uh-nuhnss/ noun a rhyming of vowel sounds.

assorted adjective made up of various sorts.

assortment noun a varied collection.

assuage /uh-**swayj**/ verb (assuages, assuaging, assuaged) **1** make an unpleasant feeling less intense. **2** relieve thirst or an appetite or desire.

assume verb (assumes, assuming, assumed) **1** think that something must be true but have no proof. **2** take responsibility or control. **3** begin to have. **4** pretend to have or feel.

assumption noun **1** a feeling that something must be true. **2** the taking on of responsibility or control.

assurance noun **1** something said to make someone feel confident about something. **2** self-confidence. **3** Brit. life insurance.

assure verb (assures, assuring, assured) **1** make someone feel confident about something. **2** make certain. **3** Brit. cover with life insurance.

assured adjective **1** confident in yourself and your abilities. **2** certain; guaranteed. ■ **assuredly** adverb.

asterisk noun a symbol (*) used as a pointer to a note.

✓ | asterisk, not -ix (Astérix is a character in a cartoon strip).

astern adverb behind or towards the rear of a ship or aircraft.

asteroid /**ass**-tuh-royd/ noun a small rocky planet orbiting the sun.

asthma /**ass**-muh/ noun a medical condition that causes difficulty in breathing. ■ **asthmatic** adjective & noun.

astigmatism /uh-**stig**-muh-ti-z'm/ noun a fault in the shape of the eye which prevents clear vision.

astir adjective **1** in a state of excited movement. **2** awake and out of bed.

astonish verb surprise or impress someone greatly. ■ **astonishment** noun.

astound verb shock or greatly surprise. ■ **astoundingly** adverb.

astrakhan /ass-truh-**kan**/ noun the dark curly fleece of young lambs from central Asia, used to make coats and hats.

astral adjective relating to the stars.

astray adverb away from the correct course.

astride preposition & adverb with a leg on each side of. adverb (of a person's legs) apart.

astringent /uh-**strin**-juhnt/ adjective **1** causing body tissue to contract. **2** sharp or severe. noun an astringent lotion. ■ **astringency** noun.

astrolabe /**ass**-truh-layb/ noun an instrument formerly used in navigation and for measuring the altitude of the stars.

astrology noun the study of the supposed influence of the stars and planets on human affairs. ■ **astrologer** noun **astrological** adjective.

astronaut noun a person trained to travel in a spacecraft.

astronomical adjective **1** relating to astronomy. **2** informal very large. ■ **astronomic** adjective **astronomically** adverb.

astronomy noun the scientific study of stars, planets, and the universe. ■ **astronomer** noun.

astrophysics noun the study of the physical nature of stars and planets. ■ **astrophysicist** noun.

astute /uh-**styoot**/ adjective good at making accurate judgements. ■ **astutely** adverb.

asunder adverb apart or into pieces.

asylum noun **1** protection from danger. **2** protection given to someone who has fled their country for political reasons. **3** dated an institution for people who are mentally ill.

asymmetrical adjective lacking symmetry. ■ **asymmetric** adjective.

asymmetry noun (plural asymmetries) lack of symmetry.

at preposition used to express: **1** location, arrival, or time. **2** a value, rate, or point on a scale. **3** a state or condition. **4** direction towards. **5** the means by which something is done.

atavistic /at-uh-**viss**-tik/ adjective inherited from the earliest human beings. ∎ **atavism** noun.

ate past of **EAT**.

atheism /ay-thi-iz'm/ **noun** the belief that God does not exist. ∎ **atheist** noun **atheistic** adjective.

athlete noun **1** a person who is good at sports. **2** a person who competes in track and field events. □**athlete's foot** a form of ringworm infection affecting the feet.

athletic adjective **1** fit and good at sport. **2** relating to athletics. **noun** (**athletics**) Brit. the sport of competing in track and field events. ∎ **athletically** adverb **athleticism** noun.

athwart preposition across from side to side.

Atlantic adjective having to do with the Atlantic Ocean.

atlas noun a book of maps or charts.

atmosphere noun **1** the gases surrounding the earth or another planet. **2** the quality of the air in a place. **3** an overall tone or mood. **4** a unit of pressure equal to the pressure of the atmosphere at sea level.

atmospheric adjective **1** relating to the atmosphere of a planet. **2** creating a distinctive mood. **noun** (**atmospherics**) electrical disturbances in the atmosphere.

atoll noun a ring-shaped coral reef or chain of islands.

atom noun **1** the smallest particle of a chemical element that can exist. **2** a very small amount. □**atom bomb** (or **atomic bomb**) a bomb whose explosive power comes from the fission of atomic nuclei.

atomic adjective **1** relating to an atom or atoms. **2** relating to nuclear energy or weapons.

atomize or **atomise** verb (**atomizes**, **atomizing**, **atomized**) convert something into very fine particles or droplets. ∎ **atomizer** noun.

atonal /ay-toh-n'l/ adjective not written in any musical key.

atone verb (**atones**, **atoning**, **atoned**) (**atone for**) do something to show you

are sorry for something that happened in the past. ∎ **atonement** noun.

atrium /ay-tri-uhm/ **noun** (plural **atria** /ay-tri-uh/ or **atriums**) **1** a central hall rising through several storeys. **2** an open central court in an ancient Roman house. **3** each of the two upper cavities of the heart.

atrocious adjective **1** horrifyingly wicked. **2** informal very bad or unpleasant. ∎ **atrociously** adverb.

atrocity noun (plural **atrocities**) an extremely wicked or cruel act.

atrophy /a-truh-fi/ **verb** (**atrophies**, **atrophying**, **atrophied**) (of a part of the body) waste away. **noun** the condition or process of atrophying.

attach verb **1** fasten; join. **2** attribute significance or importance to. **3** (**be attached to**) be working with a group of people. **4** (**attached to**) very fond of. ∎ **attachable** adjective.

 -ach, not *-atch*: attach.

attaché /uh-tash-ay/ **noun** a person attached to an ambassador's staff. □**attaché case** a small, flat briefcase for carrying documents.

attachment noun an extra part that is attached to something.

attack verb **1** violently hurt or attempt to hurt. **2** have a harmful effect on. **3** fiercely criticize. **4** tackle something with determination. **5** (in sport) try to score goals or points. **noun 1** an instance of attacking. **2** a sudden spell of an illness. ∎ **attacker** noun.

attain verb **1** succeed in doing. **2** reach. ∎ **attainable** adjective.

attainment noun **1** the achieving of something. **2** an achievement.

attar /at-tar/ **noun** a sweet-smelling oil made from rose petals.

attempt verb make an effort to do something. **noun** an effort to do something.

attend verb **1** be present at or go regularly to. **2** (**attend to**) deal with or pay attention to. **3** accompany something as a result of. **4** escort and help someone.

WORD FORMATION   ℹ️

audio-

audio- means 'relating to hearing or sound' in words and phrases such as:

audio tape	magnetic tape on which sound can be recorded
audio typist	a person who types documents from recorded dictation
audio-visual	using both sight and sound.

audio- comes from the Latin word *audire*, meaning 'to hear'.

---

attendance noun **1** the action of attending. **2** the number of people present.

attendant noun **1** a person employed to help people in a public place. **2** an assistant to an important person. **adjective** accompanying.

attention noun **1** special care, notice, or consideration. **2** (**attentions**) things done to help someone or to express sexual interest. **3** a straight standing position taken by soldiers.

attentive adjective **1** paying close attention. **2** considerate and helpful. ■ **attentively** adverb.

attenuate verb (**attenuates**, **attenuating**, **attenuated**) **1** make something weaker. **2** make something thin or thinner. ■ **attenuation** noun.

attest verb **1** provide or act as clear evidence of something. **2** declare something to be true. ■ **attestation** noun.

attic noun a space or room inside the roof of a building.

attire noun clothes of a particular kind. **verb** (**be attired**) be dressed in clothes of a particular kind.

attitude noun **1** a way of thinking. **2** a way in which the body is held. **3** informal self-confident or aggressive behaviour.

attitudinize or **attitudinise** /at-ti-**tyoo**-di-nyz/ **verb** (**attitudinizes**, **attitudinizing**, **attitudinized**) adopt an attitude just for effect.

attorney /uh-**ter**-ni/ **noun** (plural **attorneys**) **1** a person who is appointed to act for someone else in legal matters. **2** chiefly US a lawyer.

attract verb **1** draw someone in by offering something interesting or appealing. **2** cause a particular reaction. **3** draw something closer by an unseen force.

attraction noun **1** the action or power of attracting. **2** something interesting or appealing.

attractive adjective **1** very pleasing to look at. **2** arousing interest. ■ **attractively** adverb **attractiveness** noun.

attribute verb /uh-**trib**-yoot/ (**attributes**, **attributing**, **attributed**) (**attribute to**) say or believe that something is the result of or belongs to. **noun** /**at**-tri-byoot/ a quality or feature. ■ **attributable** adjective **attribution** noun.

attrition noun gradual wearing down through prolonged attack, pressure, or friction.

attune verb (**attunes**, **attuning**, **attuned**) make someone familiar and comfortable with a new situation.

atypical adjective not typical.

aubergine /**oh**-ber-*zh*een/ **noun** a purple fruit eaten as a vegetable.

auburn noun a reddish-brown colour.

auction noun a public sale in which each item is sold to the person who offers most for it. **verb** sell something at an auction.

auctioneer noun a person who conducts auctions.

audacious adjective bold and daring. ■ **audaciously** adverb **audacity** noun.

audible adjective able to be heard. ■ **audibility** noun **audibly** adverb.

audience noun **1** the people gathered to see or listen to a play, concert, film, etc. **2** a formal interview with a person in authority.

audit noun an official inspection of an organization's accounts. verb (audits, auditing, audited) inspect the accounts of. ■ auditor noun.

audition noun an interview for a performer in which they give a practical demonstration of their skill. verb assess or be assessed by an audition.

auditorium noun (plural auditoriums or auditoria) the part of a theatre or hall in which the audience sits.

auditory adjective relating to hearing.

au fait /oh fay/ adjective (au fait with) completely familiar with.

auger noun a tool for boring holes.

aught pronoun old use anything at all.

augment verb increase the amount or value of. ■ augmentation noun.

augur /aw-ger/ verb be a sign of a likely outcome.

augury /aw-gyoo-ri/ noun (plural auguries) a sign of what will happen in the future.

August noun the eighth month of the year.

august /aw-gust/ adjective inspiring respect and admiration.

auk noun a black and white seabird with short wings.

aunt noun the sister of your father or mother or the wife of your uncle.

au pair /oh pair/ noun a foreign girl employed to look after children and help with housework.

aura /aw-ruh/ noun (plural aurae /aw-ree/ or auras) the distinctive feeling that seems to surround a particular place or person.

aural /aw-ruhl/ adjective having to do with the ear or hearing. ■ aurally adverb.

aureole /aw-ri-ohl/ noun a circle of light around the sun or moon.

au revoir /aw ruh-vwar/ exclamation goodbye.

aurora borealis /aw-raw-ruh bo-ri-ay-liss/ noun streamers of light sometimes seen in the sky near the North Pole; the northern lights.

auspice /awss-piss/ noun old use an omen. □ under the auspices of with the support or protection of.

auspicious /aw-spi-shuhss/ adjective suggesting that there is a good chance of success. ■ auspiciously adverb.

Aussie informal noun (plural Aussies) an Australian. adjective Australian.

austere adjective 1 severe or strict in appearance or manner. 2 lacking comforts, luxuries, or decoration. ■ austerely adverb austerity noun.

Australian noun a person from Australia. adjective relating to Australia.

authentic adjective known to be real; genuine. ■ authentically adverb authenticity noun.

authenticate verb (authenticates, authenticating, authenticated) prove or show that something is authentic. ■ authentication noun.

author noun 1 a writer of a book or article. 2 the inventor of something. ■ authorship noun.

authoritarian adjective demanding strict obedience of authority and rules. noun an authoritarian person.

authoritative adjective 1 true or accurate and so able to be trusted. 2 commanding and self-confident. 3 official. ■ authoritatively adverb.

authority noun (plural authorities) 1 the power to give orders and make people obey you. 2 a person or organization that has official power. 3 recognized knowledge or expertise. 4 a person or book that is trusted as a source of knowledge.

authorize or **authorise** verb (authorizes, authorizing, authorized) give official permission for. ■ authorization noun.

autism noun a mental condition characterized by great difficulty in communicating with others. ■ autistic adjective.

autobiography noun (plural autobiographies) an account of a person's life written by that person. ■ autobiographical adjective.

autocracy /aw-tok-ruh-si/ noun (plural autocracies) a system of government in which one person has total power.

WORD FORMATION

auto-

auto- is used in words with the meaning:

- automatic or spontaneous: *autofocusing*
- self: *automobile* (literally 'something that moves by itself')
- your own: *autograph* | *autobiography*.

It comes from the ancient Greek word *autos*, meaning 'self'.

auto- can also mean 'relating to cars', as in *the auto industry*.

autocrat noun **1** a ruler who has absolute power. **2** a person who expects obedience. ■ **autocratic** adjective.

autograph noun a celebrity's signature written for an admirer. verb write an autograph on.

automate verb (**automates, automating, automated**) convert a process or machine so that it can operate automatically. ■ **automation** noun.

automatic adjective **1** operating by itself without human control. **2** (of a gun) able to fire continuously until the bullets run out. **3** done without conscious thought. **4** (of a punishment) applied without question because of a fixed rule. □ **automatic pilot** a device for keeping an aircraft on course without the pilot having to control it. ■ **automatically** adverb.

automaton /aw-**tom**-uh-tuhn/ noun (plural **automata** /aw-**tom**-uh-tuh/ or **automatons**) a mechanical device that looks like a human being.

automobile noun N. Amer. a car.

automotive adjective having to do with motor vehicles.

autonomous /aw-**ton**-uh-muhss/ adjective self-governing or independent. ■ **autonomously** adverb.

autonomy noun **1** self-government. **2** freedom of action.

autopsy /**aw**-top-si/ noun (plural **autopsies**) an examination of a dead body to discover the cause of death.

autumn noun chiefly Brit. the season after summer and before winter. ■ **autumnal** adjective.

auxiliary adjective providing extra help and support. noun (plural **auxiliar-** ies) an auxiliary person or thing.

avail verb (**avail yourself of**) use or take advantage of. noun use or benefit.

available adjective **1** able to be used or obtained. **2** not occupied. ■ **availability** noun.

avalanche /**av**-uh-lahnsh/ noun **1** a mass of snow and ice falling rapidly down a mountainside. **2** an overwhelming amount of something.

avant-garde /a-von **gard**/ adjective (in the arts) new and experimental.

avarice noun extreme greed for wealth or material things.

avaricious adjective very greedy for wealth or material things.

avenge verb (**avenges, avenging, avenged**) repay something bad that has been done to you by harming the person that did it. ■ **avenger** noun.

avenue noun **1** a broad road or path. **2** a way of making progress towards achieving something.

aver /uh-**ver**/ verb (**avers, averring, averred**) formal declare that something is the case.

average noun **1** the result obtained by adding several amounts together and then dividing the total by the number of amounts. **2** a usual amount or level. adjective **1** being an average. **2** usual or ordinary. verb (**averages, averaging, averaged**) **1** amount to a particular figure as an average. **2** calculate the average of several amounts.

averse adjective (**averse to**) strongly disliking or opposed to.

Auxiliary Verb

An auxiliary verb is used in front of another verb to alter its meaning. Mainly, it expresses:

1 when something happens, by forming a tense of the main verb, e.g. *I* **shall** *go*, *he was* *going*

2 permission, obligation, or ability to do something, e.g. *they may go,* *you must go, I can't go*

3 the likelihood of something happening, e.g. *I might go, she would go if* *she could.*

The principal auxiliary verbs are:

be	*have*	*must*	*will*
can	*let*	*ought*	*would*
could	*may*	*shall*	
do	*might*	*should*	

don't confuse **averse** with **adverse**, which means 'harmful or unfavourable'.

aversion noun a strong dislike.

avert verb **1** turn away your eyes. **2** prevent something unpleasant happening.

avian /**ay**-vi-uhn/ **adjective** having to do with birds.

aviary noun (plural **aviaries**) a large enclosure for keeping birds in.

aviation noun the activity of operating and flying aircraft.

aviator noun dated a pilot.

avid adjective keenly interested or enthusiastic. ■ **avidly** adverb.

avionics plural noun electronics used in aviation.

avocado noun (plural **avocados**) a pear-shaped fruit with pale green flesh and a large stone.

avoid verb **1** keep away from, or stop yourself from doing. **2** prevent something from happening. **3** manage not to collide with. ■ **avoidable** adjective **avoidance** noun.

avoirdupois /av-war-dyoo-**pwah**/ **noun** the system of weights based on a pound of 16 ounces.

avow verb openly state or confess. ■ **avowed** adjective.

avuncular /uh-**vung**-kyuu-ler/ **adjective** kind and friendly towards a younger person.

await verb wait for.

awake verb (**awakes**, **awaking**, **awoke**; past participle **awoken**) **1** stop sleeping. **2** make or become active again. **adjective** not asleep.

awaken verb **1** stop sleeping; awake. **2** stir up a feeling.

award verb give an official prize or reward to. **noun 1** an official prize or reward. **2** the action of awarding.

aware adjective (usu. **aware of** or **that**) knowing about a situation or fact. ■ **awareness** noun.

awash adjective covered or flooded with water.

away adverb **1** to or at a distance. **2** into a place for storage. **3** out of existence. **4** constantly or continuously. **adjective** (of a sports match) played at the opponents' ground.

awe noun a feeling of great respect mixed with fear. verb (**awes**, **awing**, **awed**) inspire someone with awe.

awesome adjective **1** inspiring awe. **2** informal excellent. ■ **awesomely** adverb.

awful adjective **1** very bad or unpleasant. **2** used to emphasize something: *an awful lot.* ■ **awfully** adverb.

awhile adverb for a short time.

awkward adjective **1** hard to do or deal with. **2** causing or feeling embarrassment. **3** inconvenient. **4** clumsy. ■ **awkwardly** adverb.

awl noun a small pointed tool used for making holes.

awning noun a sheet of canvas on a frame, used for shelter.

awoke past of **AWAKE**.

awoken past participle of **AWAKE**.

AWOL /ay-wol/ adjective **(go AWOL)** informal go missing.

> i short for *absent without official leave*, a military expression.

awry /uh-rI/ adverb & adjective away from the expected course or position.

axe (US spelling **ax**) noun a tool with a heavy blade, used for chopping wood. verb (**axes, axing, axed**) suddenly and ruthlessly cancel or dismiss. □ **have an axe to grind** have a private reason

for doing something.

axiom /ak-si-uhm/ noun a statement regarded as being obviously true. ■ **axiomatic** adjective.

axis /ak-sis/ noun (plural **axes** /ak-seez/) **1** an imaginary line around which an object or shape rotates. **2** a fixed line against which points on a graph are measured. **3 (the Axis)** Germany and its allies in the Second World War.

axle noun a rod passing through the centre of a wheel or group of wheels.

ayatollah /I-uh-**tol**-luh/ noun a religious leader in Iran.

aye /rhymes with my/ exclamation old use or dialect yes.

azalea /uh-**zay**-li-uh/ noun a shrub with brightly coloured flowers.

azimuth /az-i-muhth/ noun Astronomy the direction of a star measured horizontally as an angle from due north or south.

azure /az-yuur/ noun a bright blue colour like a cloudless sky.

Bb

B or **b** noun (plural **Bs** or **B's**) the second letter of the alphabet.

BA abbreviation Bachelor of Arts.

baa verb (**baas, baaing, baaed**) (of a sheep or lamb) bleat.

babble verb talk rapidly in a thoughtless or confused way. noun thoughtless or confused talk.

babe noun **1** literary a baby. **2** informal an attractive young woman.

babel /bay-b'l/ noun a confused noise made by many people speaking together.

baboon noun a large monkey with a long snout and a pink rump.

baby noun (plural **babies**) **1** a child or animal that has recently been born. **2** a timid or childish person. adjective

small or very young. verb (**babies, babying, babied**) treat someone too protectively. ■ **babyhood** noun **babyish** adjective.

babysit verb (**babysits, babysat, babysitting**) look after a child or children while the parents are out. ■ **babysitter** noun.

baccalaureate /ba-kuh-**lor**-i-uht/ noun an examination taken in some countries to qualify for higher education.

baccarat /bak-kuh-rah/ noun a gambling card game.

bacchanalian /bak-kuh-**nay**-li-uhn/ adjective (of a party or celebration) drunken and wild.

bachelor noun **1** a man who has never been married. **2** a person who holds a first degree from a university.

bacillus /buh-**sil**-luhss/ noun (plural **bacilli** /buh-**sil**-lee/) a type of bacterium.

back noun **1** the rear surface of a person's body, or the upper part of an animal's body. **2** the side or part of something that is furthest from the front. **3** a defending player in a team game. adverb **1** in the opposite direction from the one in which you are facing or travelling. **2** so as to return to an earlier or normal position or state. **3** into the past. **4** in return. adjective **1** at or towards the back. **2** in a remote or less important position. **3** relating to the past. verb **1** give support to. **2** walk or drive backwards. **3** bet money on a person or animal to win a race or contest. **4** (**back on to**) (of a building) have its back facing or next to. **5** cover the back of an object. **6** provide musical accompaniment for a singer or musician. □ **the back of beyond** a very remote place. **back down** give in. **back off** stop opposing someone. **back out** withdraw from something you have promised to do. **back-pedal** go back on something previously said. **back up 1** support or reinforce. **2** Computing make a spare copy of data or a disk. **back-up 1** support. **2** a reserve or reinforcement. **put someone's back up** annoy someone. ■ **backer** noun.

backbencher noun an MP who does not hold a government or opposition post.

backbiting noun spiteful talk about a person who is not present.

backbone noun **1** the spine. **2** strength of character.

backchat noun Brit. informal rude or cheeky remarks.

backdate verb (**backdates**, **backdating**, **backdated**) Brit. make something valid from an earlier date.

backdrop noun **1** a painted cloth hung at the back of a theatre stage as part of the scenery. **2** the setting or background for a scene or event.

backfire verb (**backfires**, **backfiring**, **backfired**) **1** (of an engine) make a banging sound as a result of fuel igniting wrongly. **2** produce the opposite effect to what was intended.

backgammon noun a board game played with counters and a dice.

background noun **1** the part of a scene or picture behind the main figures. **2** information or circumstances that influence or explain something. **3** a person's education, experience, and early life.

backhand noun (in tennis and similar games) a stroke played with the back of the hand facing in the direction of the stroke.

backhanded adjective seeming favourable but not really so: *a backhanded compliment.*

backhander noun **1** a backhand stroke or blow. **2** Brit. informal a bribe.

backing noun **1** support. **2** a layer of material that forms or strengthens the back of something. **3** music or singing accompanying a pop singer.

backlash noun an angry reaction by a large number of people.

backlog noun a build-up of things needing to be dealt with.

backpack noun a rucksack. verb travel carrying your belongings in a rucksack. ■ **backpacker** noun.

backside noun informal a person's bottom.

backslapping noun the offering of hearty congratulations or praise.

backsliding noun a return to bad behaviour after an attempt to improve.

backstage adverb & adjective behind the stage in a theatre.

backstreet noun a less important street in a town or city.

backstroke noun a swimming stroke in which you lie on your back and lift your arms out of the water in a backward circular movement.

backtrack verb **1** retrace your steps. **2** change your opinion to the opposite of what it was.

backward adjective **1** directed towards the back. **2** having made less progress than is normal or expected. **adverb** (also **backwards**) **1** towards the back, or back towards the starting point. **2** opposite to the usual direction or order. □ **bend over backwards** informal try your hardest to be fair or helpful.

backwash noun waves flowing outwards behind a ship.

backwater noun **1** a stretch of stagnant water on a river. **2** a place where change happens very slowly.

backwoods plural noun a remote area or region.

bacon noun salted or smoked meat from the back or sides of a pig.

bacteria plural noun a group of microscopic organisms, many kinds of which can cause disease. ■ **bacterial** adjective.

> ℹ️ **bacteria** is actually a plural (the singular is **bacterium**), and should always be used with a plural verb, e.g. *the bacteria were multiplying.*

bad adjective (**worse**, **worst**) **1** poor in quality; well below standard. **2** unpleasant. **3** severe; serious. **4** wicked or evil. **5** (**bad for**) harmful to. **6** injured, ill, or diseased. **7** (of food) decayed. **8** N. Amer. informal good; excellent. ■ **badness** noun.

bade past of **BID²**.

badge noun a small flat object that a person pins to their clothing as an emblem or to show who they are.

badger noun a mammal with a black and white striped head which lives underground and is active at night. **verb** (**badgers**, **badgering**, **badgered**) pester someone to do something.

badinage /bad-i-nahzh/ noun witty conversation.

badlands plural noun poor land with very little soil.

badly adverb (**worse**, **worst**) **1** in a way that is not acceptable or pleasing. **2** severely; seriously. **3** very much. □ **badly off** poor.

badminton noun a game in which the players hit a shuttlecock across a high net with rackets.

baffle verb (**baffles**, **baffling**, **baffled**) make someone feel puzzled. noun a device for controlling the flow of sound, light, gas, or fluid. ■ **bafflement** noun.

bag noun **1** a flexible container with an opening at the top. **2** (**bags**) loose folds of skin under a person's eyes. **3** (**bags of**) Brit. informal plenty of. **4** informal an unpleasant or unattractive woman. **verb** (**bags**, **bagging**, **bagged**) **1** put in a bag. **2** manage to catch an animal. **3** informal manage to get.

bagatelle noun **1** a game in which you hit small balls into numbered holes on a board. **2** something unimportant or trivial.

bagel /bay-g'l/ noun a ring-shaped bread roll with a heavy texture.

baggage noun luggage packed with belongings for travelling.

baggy adjective (**baggier**, **baggiest**) loose and hanging in bulges or folds.

bagpipe or **bagpipes** noun a musical instrument with pipes that are sounded by wind squeezed from a bag. ■ **bagpiper** noun.

baguette /ba-get/ noun a long, narrow French loaf of bread.

bail¹ noun **1** the release of an accused person on condition that a sum of money is left with the court, which will be returned as long as the person attends their trial. **2** money paid to release an accused person. **verb** set someone free on payment of bail.

bail² noun Cricket either of the two small pieces of wood that rest on the stumps.

bail³ or Brit. **bale** verb **1** scoop water out of a ship or boat. **2** (**bail out**) make an emergency jump out of an aircraft, using a parachute. **3** (**bail out**) rescue someone who is in difficulties.

bailey noun (plural **baileys**) the outer wall of a castle.

bailiff noun chiefly Brit. a person who delivers writs and seizes the property of people who owe money for rent.

bailiwick noun a district over which a bailiff has authority.

bait noun food put on a hook or in a trap to attract fish or other animals. verb **1** taunt or tease. **2** set dogs on an animal that is tied up. **3** put bait on a hook or in a trap.

baize noun a thick green material used for covering billiard tables.

bake verb (**bakes**, **baking**, **baked**) **1** cook food in an oven. **2** heat something to dry or harden it. **3** (**baking**) informal (of weather) very hot. □ **baking soda** sodium bicarbonate.

baker noun a person whose job is making bread and cakes. □ **baker's dozen** a group of thirteen. ■ **bakery** noun (plural **bakeries**).

balaclava /ba-luh-**klah**-vuh/ noun a close-fitting woollen hat covering the head and neck except for the face.

balance noun **1** a state in which weight is evenly distributed, so that a person or object does not wobble or fall over. **2** a situation in which different parts are in the correct proportions. **3** a device for weighing. **4** an amount that is the difference between money received and money spent in an account. **5** an amount still owed when part of a debt has been paid. verb (**balances**, **balancing**, **balanced**) **1** put your body, or an object, in a steady position. **2** compare the value of one thing with another. **3** give equal importance to two or more things. □ **balance of payments** the difference between payments into and out of a country over a period. **balance sheet** a written statement of what a business owns and what it owes.

balcony noun (plural **balconies**) **1** a platform with a railing or low wall, projecting from the outside of a building. **2** the highest level of seats in a theatre or cinema.

bald adjective **1** having no hair on the head. **2** (of a tyre) having the tread worn away. **3** plain or blunt. ■ **baldly** adverb **baldness** noun.

balderdash noun nonsense.

balding adjective going bald.

bale¹ noun a large bundle of paper, hay, or cloth. verb (**bales**, **baling**, **baled**) make up into bales.

bale² ⇒ **BAIL³**.

baleen /buh-**leen**/ noun whalebone.

baleful adjective threatening to cause harm. ■ **balefully** adverb.

balk US spelling of **BAULK**.

ball¹ noun **1** a rounded object that is kicked, thrown, or hit in a game. **2** a single throw or kick of the ball in a game. **3** a rounded part or thing. verb squeeze or form something into a ball. □ **ball bearing 1** a ring of small metal balls which separate moving parts to reduce rubbing. **2** one of these balls.

ball² noun a formal gathering for dancing and meeting people. □ **have a ball** informal really enjoy yourself.

ballad noun **1** a poem or song telling a story. **2** a slow sentimental song.

ballast noun **1** a heavy substance carried by a ship or hot-air balloon to keep it stable. **2** stones used to form the base of a railway track or road.

ballcock noun a valve which automatically tops up a cistern when liquid is drawn from it.

ballerina noun a female ballet dancer.

ballet noun an artistic form of dancing performed to music, using set steps and gestures. ■ **balletic** adjective.

ballistic /buh-**liss**-tik/ adjective having to do with the flight of missiles, bullets, or similar objects. □ **ballistic missile** a missile which is fired into the air and falls on to its target.

balloon noun **1** a small rubber bag which is blown up and used as a toy or decoration. **2** a large bag filled with hot air or gas to make it rise in the air, with a basket for passengers attached to it. **3** a rounded outline in which the words of characters in a cartoon are written. verb **1** swell outwards. **2** increase rapidly. **3** (**ballooning**) travelling by hot-air balloon.

ballot noun **1** a way of voting on something secretly by putting paper slips in a box. **2** (**the ballot**) the total number of votes recorded. verb (**ballots**, balloting, balloted) ask people to vote secretly about something.

ballpoint pen noun a pen with a tiny ball as its writing point.

ballroom noun a large room for formal dancing. □ ballroom dancing formal dancing for couples.

balls plural noun vulgar **1** testicles. **2** courage. **3** Brit. nonsense.

ballyhoo noun informal a lot of fuss.

balm noun **1** a sweet-smelling ointment used to heal or soothe the skin. **2** something that soothes or heals.

balmy adjective (balmier, balmiest) (of the weather) pleasantly warm.

baloney noun informal nonsense.

balsa /bawl-suh/ noun very lightweight wood from a tropical American tree, used for making models.

balsam noun a scented resin obtained from some trees and shrubs, used in perfumes and medicines.

baluster noun a short pillar forming part of a series supporting a rail.

balustrade noun a railing supported by balusters.

bamboo noun a giant tropical grass with hollow woody stems.

bamboozle verb (bamboozles, bamboozling, bamboozled) informal **1** cheat or deceive. **2** confuse.

ban verb (bans, banning, banned) **1** officially forbid something. **2** forbid someone to do something. noun an official order forbidding something.

banal /buh-nahl/ adjective boring through being too ordinary and predictable. ■ banality noun (plural banalities) banally adverb.

banana noun a long curved fruit of a tropical tree, with yellow skin.

band[1] noun **1** a flat, thin strip or loop of material used for fastening, strengthening, or decoration. **2** a stripe or strip that is different from its surroundings. ■ banded adjective.

band[2] noun **1** a small group of musicians and singers who play pop, jazz, or rock music. **2** a group of musicians who play brass, wind, or percussion instruments. **3** a group of people with the same aim or a shared feature. verb form a group with other people.

bandage noun a strip of material used to tie around a wound or to protect an injury. verb (bandages, bandaging, bandaged) tie a bandage around.

bandanna noun a square of cloth tied round the head or neck.

B. & B. abbreviation bed and breakfast.

bandit noun a member of a gang of armed robbers. ■ banditry noun.

bandolier /ban-duh-leer/ noun a shoulder belt with loops or pockets for carrying bullets.

bandstand noun a covered outdoor platform for a band to play on.

bandwagon noun an activity or cause that has suddenly become fashionable or popular.

bandwidth noun **1** a range of frequencies used in telecommunications. **2** the ability of a computer network to transmit signals.

bandy[1] adjective (bandier, bandiest) (of a person's legs) curved outwards so that the knees are wide apart.

bandy[2] verb (bandies, bandying, bandied) use an idea or word frequently in casual talk. □ bandy words exchange angry remarks.

bane noun a cause of great distress or annoyance.

bang noun **1** a sudden loud noise. **2** a sudden painful blow. verb **1** hit or put down forcefully and noisily. **2** make a bang. adverb Brit. informal exactly: *bang on time.*

banger noun chiefly Brit. **1** informal a sausage. **2** informal an old car. **3** a loud explosive firework.

bangle noun a rigid band worn around the wrist as jewellery.

banish verb **1** make someone leave a place as a punishment. **2** get rid of; drive away. ■ banishment noun.

banister or **bannister** noun **1** the upright posts and handrail at the side of a staircase. **2** a single upright post at the side of a staircase.

banjo noun (plural **banjos** or **banjoes**) a musical instrument like a guitar, with a circular body.

bank[1] noun **1** the land alongside a river or lake. **2** a long, high slope, mound, or mass. **3** a set of similar things grouped together in rows. verb **1** form into a bank. **2** (of an aircraft) tilt sideways in making a turn.

bank[2] noun **1** an organization that makes loans and keeps customers' money for them. **2** a stock or supply of something. **3** a site or container where you can leave something for recycling. verb **1** put money in a bank. **2** have an account at a bank. **3** (**bank on**) rely on. □ **bank holiday** Brit. a public holiday, when banks are officially closed. **break the bank** informal cost more than you can afford. ■ **banker** noun **banking** noun.

bankable adjective certain to bring profit and success.

banknote noun a piece of paper money.

bankroll noun N. Amer. a roll of banknotes. verb informal give funds to.

bankrupt adjective officially declared not to have the money to pay your debts. noun a bankrupt person. verb make someone bankrupt. ■ **bankruptcy** noun (plural **bankruptcies**).

banner noun a long strip of cloth with a slogan or design, hung up or carried on poles.

bannister ⇒ **BANISTER**.

banns plural noun an announcement of an intended marriage read out in a church.

banquet noun an elaborate formal meal for many people. verb (**banquets**, **banqueting**, **banqueted**) attend a banquet.

banshee noun (in Irish legend) a female spirit whose wailing warns of a death.

bantam noun a kind of small chicken.

banter noun friendly teasing. verb (**banters**, **bantering**, **bantered**) make friendly teasing remarks.

bap noun Brit. a soft, round, flattish bread roll.

baptism noun the Christian ceremony of sprinkling a person with water or dipping them in it to show that they have entered the Church. □ **baptism of fire** a difficult new experience. ■ **baptismal** adjective.

Baptist noun a member of a Christian group believing that only adults, not babies, should be baptized.

baptize or **baptise** verb (**baptizes**, **baptizing**, **baptized**) **1** perform the baptism ceremony on someone. **2** give someone a name or nickname.

bar noun **1** a long rigid piece of wood, metal, etc. **2** a counter, room, or place where alcohol is served. **3** something that stops or delays progress. **4** any of the short units into which a piece of music is divided. **5** (**the bar**) the place in a court room where an accused person stands during a trial. **6** (**the Bar**) the profession of barrister. **7** Brit. a metal strip added to a medal as an additional honour. verb (**bars**, **barring**, **barred**) **1** fasten with a bar or bars. **2** forbid or prevent. preposition chiefly Brit. except for. □ **bar code** a row of printed stripes identifying a product and its price, able to be read by a computer.

barb noun **1** the backward-pointing part of an arrowhead, fish hook, etc. **2** a spiteful remark.

barbarian noun **1** (in ancient times) a person who did not belong to the Greek, Roman, or Christian civilizations. **2** a very uncivilized or cruel person.

barbaric adjective **1** savagely cruel. **2** lacking culture; coarse.

barbarism noun **1** great cruelty. **2** an uncivilized or primitive state. ■ **barbarity** noun (plural **barbarities**).

barbarous adjective **1** very cruel. **2** uncivilized or uncultured.

barbecue noun **1** an outdoor meal at which food is grilled over a charcoal fire. **2** a grill used at a barbecue. verb (**barbecues**, **barbecuing**, **barbecued**) cook food on a barbecue.

barbed adjective **1** having a barb or

barbs. **2** (of a remark) spiteful. ■ **barbed wire** wire with clusters of short, sharp spikes along it.

barbel noun **1** a long, thin growth hanging from the mouth or snout of some fish. **2** a freshwater fish with barbels.

barbell noun a long metal bar with discs of different weights attached at each end, used for weightlifting.

barber noun a person whose job is cutting men's hair and shaving or trimming their beards.

barbiturate noun a kind of sedative drug.

bard noun **1** old use a poet. **2** (the Bard) Shakespeare.

bare adjective **1** not wearing clothes. **2** without the usual covering or contents. **3** without detail; basic. **4** only just enough. verb (bares, baring, bared) uncover or reveal. ■ **barely** adverb **bareness** noun.

bareback adverb & adjective on a horse without a saddle.

barefaced adjective done openly and without shame.

bargain noun **1** an agreement made between people to do something for each other. **2** a thing sold at a low price. verb **1** discuss the terms of an agreement. **2** (bargain for or on) expect. □ **into the bargain** as well.

> ✓ remember the *a* at the end:
> bar*gain*.

barge noun a long flat-bottomed boat for carrying goods on canals and rivers. verb (barges, barging, barged) **1** move forcefully or roughly. **2** (barge in) burst in on someone rudely.

baritone noun a man's singing voice between tenor and bass.

barium noun a chemical element that is a soft white metal.

bark¹ noun the sharp sudden cry of a dog, fox, or seal. verb **1** give a bark. **2** say a command or question suddenly or fiercely. **3** (barking) Brit. informal completely mad.

bark² noun the tough outer covering of the trunk and branches of a tree.

verb scrape the skin off your shin by accidentally hitting it.

barley noun a type of cereal plant with a bristly head. □ **barley sugar** an orange sweet made of boiled sugar.

bar mitzvah /bar **mitz**-vuh/ noun a religious ceremony in which a Jewish boy aged 13 takes on the responsibilities of an adult.

barmy adjective (barmier, barmiest) Brit. informal mad.

barn noun a large farm building used for storing hay or crops or housing livestock. □ **barn dance** a party with country dancing.

barnacle noun a small shellfish which fixes itself to things.

barnstorming adjective flamboyantly energetic.

barnyard noun N. Amer. a farmyard.

barometer noun an instrument that measures the pressure of the atmosphere, used to forecast the weather.

baron noun **1** a man belonging to the lowest rank of the British nobility. **2** (in the Middle Ages) a man who held lands or property granted to him by the king or queen or a lord. ■ **baronial** adjective.

baroness noun **1** the wife or widow of a baron. **2** a woman holding the rank of baron.

baronet noun a man who holds a title below that of baron.

baroque /buh-**rok**/ adjective in a highly decorated style of European architecture, art, and music popular during the 17th and 18th centuries.

barrack verb Brit. shout loud insulting comments at a performer or speaker.

barracks noun a building or set of buildings for soldiers to live in.

barracuda /ba-ruh-**koo**-duh/ noun (plural barracuda or barracudas) a large predatory fish found in tropical seas.

barrage noun **1** a continuous attack by heavy guns. **2** an overwhelming number of questions or complaints. **3** Brit. a barrier placed across a river to control the water level.

barrel noun **1** a large cylindrical container bulging out in the middle and with flat ends. **2** a tube forming part of a gun, pen, etc. □ **barrel organ** a small organ that plays a tune when you turn a handle. **over a barrel** informal in a very weak position.

barren adjective **1** (of land) too poor to produce vegetation. **2** unable to bear young. **3** bleak.

barricade noun a makeshift barrier used to block a road or entrance. **verb (barricades, barricading, barricaded)** block or defend with a barricade.

barrier noun something that stops people entering a place or making progress.

barring preposition except for; if not for.

barrister noun Brit. a lawyer qualified to argue a case in court.

barrow¹ noun Brit. a two-wheeled handcart used by street traders.

barrow² noun an ancient burial mound.

bartender noun a person serving drinks at a bar.

barter verb **(barters, bartering, bartered)** exchange goods or services for other goods or services. noun trade by bartering.

basalt /ba-sawlt/ noun a dark volcanic rock.

base¹ noun **1** the lowest or supporting part of something. **2** the main place where a person works or stays. **3** a centre of operations: *a military base*. **4** a main element to which others are added. **5** Chemistry a substance able to react with an acid to form a salt and water. **6** Baseball each of the four points that you must reach in turn to score a run. verb **(bases, basing, based) 1 (base on)** use something as the foundation for. **2** station someone or something at a particular base.

base² adjective **1** bad or immoral. **2** old use of low social class. □ **base metal** a common non-precious metal.

baseball noun a game played with a bat and ball on a diamond-shaped circuit of four bases, which a batsman must run around to score. □ **baseball cap** a cotton cap with a large peak.

baseless adjective not based on fact; untrue.

baseline noun **1** a starting point for comparisons. **2** (in tennis, volleyball, etc.) the line marking each end of a court.

basement noun a room or floor below ground level.

bases plural of **BASE¹** and **BASIS**.

bash informal verb hit hard and violently. noun **1** a heavy blow. **2** a party. **3** Brit. an attempt.

bashful adjective shy and easily embarrassed. ■ **bashfully** adverb.

basic adjective **1** forming an essential foundation; fundamental. **2** of the simplest or lowest kind or standard. noun **(basics)** essential facts or principles. ■ **basically** adverb.

basil noun a herb used in cooking.

basilica /buh-zil-i-kuh/ noun a large church or hall having two rows of columns inside and a curved end with a dome.

basilisk /baz-i-lisk/ noun a mythical reptile that could kill people by looking at or breathing on them.

basin noun **1** a large bowl or open container for holding liquid. **2** a circular valley or natural depression. **3** an area drained by a river. **4** an enclosed area of water for mooring boats.

basis noun (plural bases /bay-seez/) **1** the foundation of a theory or process. **2** the reasons why something is done.

bask verb **1** lie in the sun for pleasure. **2 (bask in)** take great pleasure in.

basket noun **1** a container for carrying things, made from strips of cane or wire. **2** Basketball a net fixed on a hoop, used as the goal.

basketball noun a team game in which goals are scored by throwing a ball through a netted hoop.

bass¹ /bayss/ noun **1** the lowest adult male singing voice. **2** informal a bass guitar or double bass. **3** the deep, low-frequency part of sound. ■ **bassist** noun.

bass² /bass/ **noun** (plural **bass** or **basses**) a fish related to the perch that is used for food.

basset hound noun a breed of hunting dog with a long body, short legs, and long, drooping ears.

bassoon noun a large bass woodwind instrument of the oboe family. ■ **bassoonist** noun.

bastard noun 1 old use a person whose parents were not married. **2** informal an unpleasant person.

bastardize or **bastardise verb** (**bastardizes, bastardizing, bastardized**) make something less good by adding new elements.

baste verb (**bastes, basting, basted**) pour fat or juices over meat while it cooks.

bastion noun 1 a part of a fortification that sticks out. **2** something that protects or preserves particular principles or activities.

bat¹ noun a piece of wood with a handle and a solid surface, used in sports for hitting the ball. **verb** (**bats, batting, batted**) **1** (in sport) take the role of hitting rather than throwing the ball. **2** hit someone with the flat of your hand. □ **off your own bat** Brit. informal of your own accord.

bat² noun 1 a winged mammal that flies around at night. **2** (**old bat**) informal an unpleasant woman.

bat³ verb (**bats, batting, batted**) flutter your eyelashes.

batch noun a quantity of goods produced or dispatched at one time.

bated adjective (**with bated breath**) in great suspense.

 bated, not baited.

bath noun 1 a large tub that you fill with water and sit or lie in to wash your body. **2** an act of washing yourself in a bath. **3** (also **baths**) a building containing a public swimming pool or washing facilities. **verb** wash in a bath.

bathe verb (**bathes, bathing, bathed**) **1** wash by putting your body in water. **2** Brit. have a swim. **3** soak or wipe gently with liquid. **noun** Brit. a swim. ■ **bather** noun.

bathos /**bay**-thoss/ **noun** (in literature) a change from a serious mood to something trivial.

bathroom noun 1 a room containing a bath and usually also a washbasin and toilet. **2** N. Amer. a room containing a toilet.

batik /ba-**teek**/ **noun** a method of producing coloured designs on cloth using wax to resist the dye.

baton noun 1 a thin stick used to conduct an orchestra or choir. **2** a short stick passed from runner to runner in a relay race. **3** a stick carried and twirled by a drum major.

batsman noun a player who bats in cricket.

battalion noun a large body of troops, forming part of a brigade.

batten noun a long wooden or metal strip used for strengthening or securing something. □ **batten down the hatches** prepare for a crisis.

batter¹ verb (**batters, battering, battered**) hit repeatedly with hard blows.

batter² noun a mixture of flour, egg, and milk or water, used for making pancakes or coating food before frying.

battery noun (plural **batteries**) **1** a device containing one or more electrical cells, used as a source of power. **2** an extensive series: *a battery of tests.* **3** Brit. a series of small cages for keeping chickens in artificial conditions. **4** Law the infliction of unlawful personal violence on another person.

battle noun 1 a prolonged fight between organized armed forces. **2** a long and difficult struggle. **verb** (**battles, battling, battled**) fight or struggle with determination.

battleaxe noun 1 a large axe used in ancient warfare. **2** informal an aggressive older woman.

battledress noun clothing worn by soldiers for fighting.

battlefield noun the piece of ground where a battle is fought.

battlement noun a wall with gaps for firing through, forming part of a fortification.

battleship noun a heavily armoured warship with large guns.

batty adjective (**battier**, **battiest**) informal mad.

bauble noun a small, showy trinket or decoration.

baulk /bawlk/ (US spelling **balk**) verb 1 (**baulk at**) hesitate to accept an idea. 2 thwart or hinder.

bauxite noun a clay-like rock from which aluminium is obtained.

bawdy adjective (**bawdier**, **bawdiest**) rude in an amusing way.

bawl verb 1 shout out noisily. 2 (**bawl out**) criticize someone angrily. 3 weep noisily. noun a loud shout.

bay[1] noun an area of sea and coast forming a broad curve.

bay[2] noun a Mediterranean shrub whose leaves are used in cookery.

bay[3] noun 1 a window area that projects outwards from a wall. 2 an area for a particular purpose: *a loading bay*. □ **bay window** a window projecting out from a wall.

bay[4] adjective (of a horse) mainly reddish-brown in colour.

bay[5] verb (of a dog) bark or howl loudly. □ **at bay** trapped or cornered. **hold** (or **keep**) **at bay** prevent from approaching or having an effect.

bayonet noun a long blade fixed to a rifle for hand-to-hand fighting. verb (**bayonets**, **bayoneting**, **bayoneted**) stab someone with a bayonet.

bazaar noun 1 a market in a Middle Eastern country. 2 a sale of goods to raise funds.

bazooka noun a short-range rocket launcher used against tanks.

BBC abbreviation British Broadcasting Corporation.

BC abbreviation before Christ (used to indicate that a date is before the Christian era).

> [i] write BC **after** the numerals, as in 72 BC.

be verb (singular present **am**; **are**; **is**; plural present **are**; 1st and 3rd singular past **was**; 2nd singular past and plural past **were**; present participle **being**; past participle **been**) 1 exist; be present. 2 happen. 3 have the specified state, nature, or role. 4 come, go, or visit. **auxiliary verb** 1 used with a present participle to form continuous tenses. 2 used with a past participle to form the passive voice. 3 used to show something that is due to, may, or should happen. □ **the be-all and end-all** informal the most important aspect of something.

beach noun a shore of sand or pebbles at the edge of the sea. verb bring something on to a beach from the water.

beachcomber noun a person who searches beaches for valuable things.

beacon noun 1 a fire lit on the top of a hill as a signal. 2 a light acting as a signal for ships or aircraft.

bead noun 1 a small piece of glass, stone, etc., threaded with others to make a necklace. 2 a drop of a liquid on a surface. ■ **beaded** adjective.

beadle noun Brit. 1 an official of a church, college, etc. 2 historical a parish officer who dealt with minor offenders.

beady adjective (of a person's eyes) small, round, and observant.

beagle noun a small short-legged breed of hound.

beak noun a bird's hard projecting jaws; a bill.

beaker noun Brit. 1 a tall plastic cup. 2 a cylindrical glass container used in laboratories.

beam noun 1 a long piece of timber or metal used as a support in building. 2 a narrow length of timber for balancing on in gymnastics. 3 a ray of light or particles. 4 a radiant smile. 5 the width of a ship. verb 1 transmit a radio signal. 2 shine brightly. 3 smile radiantly. □ **off beam** informal on the wrong track.

bean noun **1** an edible seed growing in long pods on certain plants. **2** the hard seed of a coffee or cocoa plant. **3** informal a very small amount. □ **full of beans** informal in high spirits.

beanbag noun **1** a small bag filled with dried beans and used in children's games. **2** a large cushion filled with polystyrene beads, used as a seat.

bear¹ verb (**bears, bearing, bore**; past participle **borne**) **1** carry. **2** have a particular quality or visible mark. **3** support a weight. **4** (**bear yourself**) behave in a particular manner. **5** tolerate. **6** give birth to a child. **7** (of a tree or plant) produce fruit or flowers. **8** turn and proceed in a specified direction. □ **bear down on** approach in a purposeful or threatening manner. **bear in mind** remember and take into account. **bear out** support or confirm. **bear up** remain cheerful in difficult circumstances. **bear with** be patient with. ■ **bearable** adjective **bearably** adverb **bearer** noun.

bear² noun a large mammal with thick fur and a very short tail.

beard noun a growth of hair on a man's chin and lower cheeks. verb boldly confront or challenge someone formidable. ■ **bearded** adjective.

bearing noun **1** a person's way of standing, moving, or behaving. **2** relevance. **3** (**bearings**) a device that allows two parts to rotate or move in contact with each other. **4** direction or position in relation to a fixed point. **5** (**your bearings**) awareness of where you are.

beast noun **1** an animal, especially a large or dangerous mammal. **2** a very cruel or wicked person. □ **beast of burden** an animal used for carrying loads.

beastly adjective Brit. informal very unpleasant. ■ **beastliness** noun.

beat verb (**beats, beating, beat**; past participle **beaten**) **1** hit someone repeatedly and violently. **2** hit something repeatedly to flatten it or make a noise. **3** defeat or overcome. **4** informal baffle. **5** (of the heart) pulsate. **6** (of a bird)

move its wings up and down. **7** stir cooking ingredients vigorously. noun **1** a main accent in music or poetry. **2** a pulsation of the heart. **3** a movement of a bird's wings. **4** a brief pause or hesitation. **5** an area patrolled by a police officer. adjective informal completely exhausted. □ **beat about the bush** discuss a matter without coming to the point. **beat it** informal leave. **beat up** hit or kick someone repeatedly. **off the beaten track** isolated.

beatific /bee-uh-**tif**-ik/ adjective feeling or expressing blissful happiness. ■ **beatifically** adverb.

beatify /bi-**at**-i-fI/ verb (**beatifies, beatifying, beatified**) state officially that a dead person is very holy (the first step towards making them a saint).

beatnik noun a young person in the 1950s and early 1960s who rejected conventional society.

beau /boh/ noun (plural **beaux** or **beaus** /bohz, boh/) dated a boyfriend.

beautician noun a person whose job is to give beauty treatments.

beautiful adjective **1** very pleasing to the senses. **2** of a very high standard; excellent. ■ **beautifully** adverb.

remember the *u* before the *t*: beau**ti**ful.

beautify verb (**beautifies, beautifying, beautified**) make someone or something look more attractive.

beauty noun (plural **beauties**) **1** the quality of being very pleasing to the senses. **2** a beautiful woman. **3** an excellent example of something. **4** an attractive feature or advantage.

beaver noun (plural **beaver** or **beavers**) a large rodent that lives partly in water. verb (**beavers, beavering, beavered**) (**beaver away**) informal work hard.

becalm verb (**be becalmed**) (of a sailing ship) be unable to move owing to a lack of wind.

because conjunction for the reason that; since.

beck noun (**at someone's beck and**

call) always having to be ready to obey someone's orders.

beckon verb **1** make a movement encouraging someone to approach or follow. **2** seem appealing.

become verb (**becomes, becoming, became**; past participle **become**) **1** begin to be. **2** turn into. **3** (**become of**) happen to. **4** (of clothing) look good when worn by a particular person.

becquerel /bek-kuh-rel/ noun a unit of radioactivity.

bed noun **1** a piece of furniture for sleeping on. **2** an area of ground where flowers and shrubs are grown. **3** a flat base. verb (**beds, bedding, bedded**) **1** (**bed down**) sleep in an improvised place. **2** (**bed in**) fix something firmly.

bedclothes plural noun coverings for a bed, such as sheets and blankets.

bedding noun **1** bedclothes. **2** straw for animals to sleep on.

bedevil verb (**bedevils, bedevilling, bedevilled**; US spelling **bedevils, bedeviling, bedeviled**) cause continual trouble to.

bedlam noun a scene of great confusion and noise.

bedpan noun a container used as a toilet by a bedridden patient.

bedraggled adjective untidy.

bedridden adjective unable to get out of bed because of sickness or old age.

bedrock noun **1** a layer of solid rock under soil. **2** the central principles on which something is based.

bedroom noun a room for sleeping in.

bedsit or **bedsitter** noun Brit. informal a rented room consisting of a combined bedroom and living room, with cooking facilities.

bedsore noun a sore caused by lying in bed in one position for a long time.

bedspread noun a decorative cloth used to cover a bed.

bedstead noun the framework of a bed.

bee noun a winged insect which col-

lects nectar and pollen from flowers and produces wax and honey. □ **the bee's knees** informal an outstandingly good person or thing.

beech noun a large tree with grey bark and pale wood.

beef noun the flesh of a cow, bull, or ox, used as food. verb (**beef up**) informal make something stronger or larger.

beefburger noun a fried or grilled cake of minced beef eaten in a bun.

beefy adjective (**beefier, beefiest**) informal muscular or strong.

beehive noun a structure in which bees are kept.

beeline noun (**make a beeline for**) hurry straight to.

Beelzebub /bi-el-zi-bub/ noun the Devil.

been past participle of BE.

beep noun a short, high-pitched sound made by electronic equipment or the horn of a vehicle. verb produce a beep.

beer noun an alcoholic drink made from fermented malt flavoured with hops.

beeswax noun wax produced by bees to make honeycombs, used for wood polishes and candles.

beet noun a plant with a fleshy root, grown as food and for making into sugar.

beetle noun an insect with hard, shiny covers over its wings.

beetroot noun Brit. the edible dark-red root of a kind of beet.

befall verb (**befalls, befalling, befell**; past participle **befallen**) literary (of something bad) happen to.

befit verb (**befits, befitting, befitted**) be appropriate for. ■ **befitting** adjective.

before preposition, conjunction, & adverb **1** during the time preceding. **2** in front of. **3** rather than.

beforehand adverb in advance.

befriend verb become a friend to.

befuddled adjective muddled or confused.

beg verb (**begs, begging, begged**

1 humbly ask someone for something. **2** ask for food or money as charity. □ **beg the question 1** (of a fact or action) invite a question or point that has not been dealt with. **2** assume that something is true without discussing it. **go begging** be available because unwanted by others.

beget /bi-get/ **verb** (**begets**, **begetting**, **begot** or **begat**; past participle **begotten**) old use **1** produce a child. **2** cause something.

beggar **noun 1** a person who lives by begging for food or money. **2** informal a person of a certain type: *lucky beggar!* **verb** (**beggars**, **beggaring**, **beggared**) make someone very poor. □ **beggar belief** be too extraordinary to be believed. ■ **beggarly** adjective.

begin **verb** (**begins**, **beginning**, **began**; past participle **begun**) **1** carry out or experience the first part of an action or activity. **2** come into being. **3** have a particular starting point. **4** (**begin on**) set to work on. ■ **beginner** noun **beginning** noun.

begonia /bi-goh-ni-uh/ **noun** a plant with brightly coloured flowers.

begrudge **verb 1** feel envious that someone possesses something. **2** give something resentfully.

beguile **verb** charm or trick.

behalf **noun** (**on behalf of** or **on someone's behalf**) **1** in the interests of a particular person, group, or principle. **2** as a representative of.

behave **verb 1** act in a certain way. **2** (also **behave yourself**) act in a polite or proper way.

behaved **adjective** acting in a certain way: *a well-behaved child.*

behaviour (US spelling **behavior**) **noun** the way in which someone or something behaves.

behead **verb** execute someone by cutting off their head.

behemoth /bi-hee-moth/ **noun** a huge creature or monster.

behest /bi-hest/ **noun** (**at someone's behest**) in response to someone's order.

behind **preposition & adverb 1** at or to the back or far side of. **2** further back than other members of a group. **3** in support of. **4** responsible for an event or plan. **5** late in doing something.

behold **verb** (**behold**, **beholding**, **beheld**) old use see or observe.

beholden **adjective** (**beholden to**) owing something to someone because they have done you a favour.

behove **verb** (**it behoves someone to do**) formal it is right or appropriate for someone to do.

beige **noun** a pale sandy colour.

being **noun 1** existence. **2** the nature of a person. **3** a living creature.

bejewelled (US spelling **bejeweled**) **adjective** decorated with jewels.

belated **adjective** coming late or too late. ■ **belatedly** adverb.

belch **verb 1** noisily expel wind from the stomach through the mouth. **2** give out smoke or flames with great force. **noun** an act of belching.

beleaguered **adjective 1** under siege. **2** in difficulties; harassed.

belfry **noun** (plural **belfries**) the place in a bell tower or steeple in which the bells are housed.

belie **verb** (**belies**, **belying**, **belied**) **1** fail to give a true idea of. **2** show that something is untrue.

belief **noun 1** a feeling that something exists or is true. **2** a firmly held opinion. **3** (**belief in**) trust or confidence in. **4** religious faith.

believe **verb** (**believes**, **believing**, **believed**) **1** accept that something is true or someone is telling the truth. **2** (**believe in**) have faith that something is true or exists. **3** think or suppose. **4** have a religious faith. ■ **believable** adjective **believer** noun.

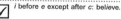 *i* before *e* except after *c*: beli**eve**.

belittle **verb** (**belittles**, **belittling**, **belittled**) dismiss as unimportant.

bell **noun 1** a deep metal cup that sounds a clear musical note when struck. **2** a device that buzzes or rings to give a signal. □ **ring a bell** informal sound vaguely familiar.

belladonna noun **1** deadly nightshade. **2** a drug made from deadly nightshade.

belle noun a beautiful woman.

bellicose adjective aggressive and ready to fight.

belligerence noun aggressive or warlike behaviour.

belligerent adjective **1** hostile and aggressive. **2** engaged in a war or conflict. ■ **belligerently** adverb.

bellow verb **1** give a deep roar of pain or anger. **2** shout or sing very loudly. noun a deep shout or noise.

bellows plural noun a device consisting of a bag with two handles, used for blowing air into a fire.

belly noun (plural **bellies**) **1** the front part of the body below the ribs, containing the stomach and bowels. **2** a person's stomach.

bellyache informal noun a stomach pain. verb complain noisily or often.

bellyflop noun informal a dive into water in which you land flat on your front.

belong verb **1** be rightly put into a particular position or class. **2** fit or be acceptable in a place or environment. **3** (**belong to**) be a member of. **4** (**belong to**) be the property of.

belongings plural noun a person's movable possessions.

beloved adjective dearly loved. noun a much loved person.

below preposition & adverb **1** at a lower level than. **2** (in printed text) mentioned further down.

belt noun **1** a strip of leather or fabric worn round the waist to support or hold in clothes or to carry weapons. **2** a continuous band in machinery that connects two wheels. **3** a strip or encircling area. verb **1** fasten or secure with a belt. **2** beat or hit very hard. **3** (**belt out**) informal sing or play something loudly and forcefully. **5** (**belt up**) informal be quiet. □ **tighten your belt** spend less money. **under your belt** achieved or acquired.

belying present participle of **BELIE**.

bemoan verb express sadness or regret about something.

bemused adjective confused or bewildered. ■ **bemusement** noun.

bench noun **1** a long seat for more than one person. **2** a long table for working at in a workshop or laboratory. **3** (**the bench**) the office of judge or magistrate. **4** (**the bench**) a seat at the side of a sports field for coaches and reserve players.

benchmark noun a standard or point of reference.

bend verb (**bends, bending, bent**) **1** give something a curved or angled shape, form, or course. **2** lean or curve the body downwards; stoop. **3** change a rule to suit yourself. noun **1** a curved or angled part or course. **2** (**the bends**) decompression sickness. □ **round the bend** informal mad.

bender noun informal a drinking bout.

beneath preposition & adverb extending or directly underneath. preposition of lower status or worth than.

benediction noun the speaking of a blessing.

benefactor noun a person who gives money or other help.

benefice /ben-i-fiss/ noun an arrangement by which a Christian priest is paid and given accommodation for being in charge of a parish.

beneficial adjective favourable or advantageous. ■ **beneficially** adverb.

beneficiary noun (plural **beneficiaries**) a person who benefits from something, especially a trust or will.

benefit noun **1** advantage or profit. **2** payment made by the state to someone in need: *unemployment benefit.* **3** a public performance to raise money for a charity. verb (**benefits, benefiting, benefited** or **benefitting, benefitted**) **1** get an advantage; profit. **2** bring advantage to.

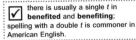 there is usually a single *t* in **benefited** and **benefiting**; spelling with a double *t* is commoner in American English.

benevolent adjective **1** well meaning

and kindly. **2** (of an organization) charitable rather than profit-making. ■ **benevolence** noun.

benighted adjective ignorant or primitive.

benign adjective **1** cheerful and kindly. **2** favourable; not harmful. **3** (of a tumour) not malignant.

bent past and past participle of **BEND. adjective 1** Brit. informal dishonest or corrupt. **2** (**bent on**) determined to do. noun a natural talent.

benzene noun a liquid present in coal tar and petroleum.

bequeath verb **1** leave property to someone by a will. **2** hand down or pass on.

bequest noun **1** something that is left to someone by a will. **2** the action of bequeathing.

berate verb (**berates, berating, berated**) angrily scold or criticize.

bereave verb (**bereaves, bereaving, bereaved**) (**be bereaved**) be deprived of a close relation or friend through their death. ■ **bereavement** noun.

bereft adjective **1** (**bereft of**) deprived of; without. **2** lonely and abandoned.

beret /be-ray/ noun a flat round cap of felt or cloth.

bergamot /ber-guh-mot/ noun an oily substance found in some oranges, used as a flavouring.

beriberi noun a disease caused by a lack of vitamin B₁.

berk noun Brit. informal a stupid person.

berry noun (plural **berries**) a small, juicy round fruit without a stone.

berserk adjective out of control; wild and frenzied.

berth noun **1** a place in a harbour where a boat can stay. **2** a bunk on a ship or train. verb moor a boat in a berth. □ **give a wide berth** to stay well away from.

beryllium noun a hard, grey, lightweight metallic element.

beseech verb (**beseeches, beseeching, besought** or **beseeched**) ask in a pleading way.

beset verb (**besets, besetting, beset**) continually trouble or worry.

beside preposition **1** at the side of. **2** compared with. **3** (also **besides**) as well as. adverb (**besides**) as well. □ **beside yourself** frantic with worry.

besiege verb (**besieges, besieging, besieged**) **1** surround a place so that no one can come or go. **2** overwhelm with requests or complaints.

> ✓ remember *i* before *e* except after *c*: besi**e**ge.

besmirch verb damage someone's reputation.

besotted adjective so much in love that you stop acting sensibly.

bespoke adjective Brit. made to a customer's requirements.

best adjective **1** of the highest quality. **2** most suitable or sensible. adverb **1** to the highest degree; most. **2** most suitably or sensibly. noun (**the best**) something which is of the highest quality. □ **best man** a male friend or relative who helps a bridegroom at his wedding. **best-seller** a book or other product that sells in very large numbers. **get the best of** overcome. **make the best of** get what advantage you can from.

bestial adjective savagely cruel.

bestiality noun **1** savagely cruel behaviour. **2** sex between a person and an animal.

bestir verb (**bestirs, bestirring, bestirred**) (**bestir yourself**) make yourself start to do something

bestow verb give an honour, right, or gift.

bestride verb (**bestrides, bestriding, bestrode**; past participle **bestridden**) put a leg on either side of.

bet verb (**bets, betting, bet** or **betted**) **1** risk money against someone else's on the basis of the outcome of an unpredictable event such as a race. **2** informal feel sure. noun an act of betting or the money betted.

beta /bee-tuh/ noun the second letter of the Greek alphabet (Β, β). □ **beta blocker** a drug used to treat high blood pressure and angina. **beta par-**

ticle a fast-moving electron given off by some radioactive substances.

bête noire /bet **nwar**/ noun (plural **bêtes noires** /bet **nwar**/) a person or thing that you particularly dislike.

betide verb (betide, betiding, betided) literary happen or happen to.

betimes adverb in good time; early.

betoken verb be a sign of.

betray verb 1 harm someone or something by giving information to an enemy. 2 be disloyal to someone. 3 reveal a secret without meaning to. ■ **betrayal** noun.

betrothed adjective engaged to be married. ■ **betrothal** noun.

better adjective 1 of a higher standard or quality. 2 partly or fully recovered from illness or injury. adverb 1 in a more satisfactory way. 2 to a greater degree; more. noun (**your betters**) people who have greater ability or are more important than you. verb 1 improve on something. 2 (**better yourself**) improve your social position. □ **better off** having more money or being in a more desirable situation. **get the better of** defeat.

betterment noun improvement.

between preposition & adverb 1 at, into, or across the space separating two things. 2 in the period separating two points in time. 3 indicating a connection or relationship. 4 shared by two or more people or things.

betwixt preposition & adverb old use between.

bevel noun an edge cut at an angle in wood or glass. verb (**bevels, bevelling, bevelled**; US spelling **bevels, beveling, beveled**) cut the edge of wood or glass at an angle.

beverage noun a drink.

bevy noun (plural **bevies**) a large group.

bewail verb be very sorry or sad about.

beware verb be aware of danger.

bewilder verb (**bewilders, bewildering, bewildered**) puzzle or confuse. ■ **bewilderment** noun.

bewitch verb 1 put a magic spell on. 2 attract and delight.

beyond preposition & adverb 1 at or to the further side of. 2 outside the range or limits of. 3 happening or continuing after. 4 except.

biannual adjective occurring twice a year.

bias noun 1 a feeling for or against a person or thing that is based on prejudice rather than sound reason. 2 a direction diagonal to the grain of a fabric. □ **bias binding** a strip of fabric cut on the bias, used to bind edges.

biased adjective having a bias; prejudiced.

biathlon noun a sporting event combining cross-country skiing and rifle shooting.

bib noun 1 a piece of cloth or plastic fastened under a baby's chin to protect its clothes when it is being fed. 2 the part of an apron or pair of dungarees that covers the chest.

Bible noun the book containing the writings of the Christian Church.

biblical adjective relating to the Bible.

bibliography noun (plural **bibliographies**) a list of books on a particular subject. ■ **bibliographer** noun **bibliographic** adjective.

bibliophile /**bib**-li-oh-fyl/ noun a person who collects books.

bibulous adjective fond of drinking alcohol.

bicameral adjective (of a parliament) having two separate parts.

bicarbonate of soda noun a soluble white powder used in fizzy drinks and in baking.

bicentenary noun (plural **bicentenaries**) a two-hundredth anniversary. ■ **bicentennial** noun & adjective.

biceps /**by**-seps/ noun (plural **biceps**) a large muscle in the upper arm which flexes the arm and forearm.

bicker verb (**bickers, bickering, bickered**) argue about unimportant things.

WORD FORMATION

bi-

bi- is used in words with the meaning 'two' or 'having two', as in *biathlon*, *bilingual*, and *biplane*. It comes from Latin.

Confusingly, when **bi-** refers to a period of time it can mean either 'twice in a particular period' or 'once in every two periods'. So, for example, **bimonthly** can mean either 'happening twice a month' or 'happening every two months'. The only way to make yourself clear is to use alternatives such as *every two months* and *twice a month*.

bicycle noun a two-wheeled vehicle that you ride by pushing the pedals with your feet. verb (**bicycles, bicycling, bicycled**) ride a bicycle.

bid¹ verb (**bids, bidding, bid**) **1** offer a price for something. **2** (**bid for**) offer to do work for a stated price. **3** (**bid for**) try to get. noun an act of bidding.

bid² verb (**bids, bidding, bid or bade**; past participle **bid**) **1** say a greeting. **2** old use command.

biddable adjective obedient.

biddy noun (plural **biddies**) informal an old woman.

bide verb (**bides, biding, bided**) old use or dialect stay in a place. □ **bide your time** wait patiently for an opportunity to do something.

bidet /bee-day/ noun a low basin that you sit on to wash your bottom.

biennial adjective **1** taking place every other year. **2** (of a plant) living for two years.

bier /beer/ noun a platform on which a coffin or dead body is placed before burial.

biff verb informal hit hard with the fist.

bifocal adjective (of a lens) made in two sections, one for distant and one for close vision. noun (**bifocals**) a pair of glasses with bifocal lenses.

big adjective (**bigger, biggest**) **1** large in size, amount, or extent. **2** very important or serious. **3** informal (of a brother or sister) older. □ **big bang** the rapid expansion of dense matter which is thought to have started the formation of the universe. **big-head** a conceited person. **big top** the main

tent in a circus.

bigamy noun the crime of marrying someone when you are already married to someone else. ■ **bigamist** noun **bigamous** adjective.

bigot /bi-guht/ noun a prejudiced and intolerant person. ■ **bigoted** adjective **bigotry** noun.

bigwig noun informal an important person.

bijou /bee-zhoo/ adjective small and elegant.

bike informal noun a bicycle or motorcycle. verb (**bikes, biking, biked**) ride a bicycle or motorcycle. ■ **biker** noun.

bikini noun (plural **bikinis**) a woman's two-piece swimsuit.

bilateral adjective involving two countries or groups of people.

bilberry noun (plural **bilberries**) a small blue edible berry.

bile noun **1** a bitter fluid which is produced by the liver and helps digestion. **2** anger.

bilge noun the bottom of a ship's hull.

bilingual adjective **1** speaking two languages fluently. **2** expressed in two languages.

bilious adjective **1** feeling sick. **2** relating to bile.

bilk verb informal cheat someone.

bill¹ noun **1** a note saying how much a person owes for something. **2** a written proposal for a new law, presented to parliament for discussion. **3** a programme of entertainment at a theatre or cinema. **4** an advertising poster. **5** N. Amer. a banknote. verb **1** list someone in a programme of entertainment. **2** (**bill as**) describe someone as. **3** send someone a bill saying what they owe. □ **fit the bill** be suitable.

bill² noun the beak of a bird.

billboard noun a large board for displaying advertising posters.

billet noun a private house used as lodgings for soldiers. **verb** (**be billeted**) (of a soldier) stay in a particular place.

billet-doux /bil-li-**doo**/ noun (plural **billets-doux** /bil-li-**dooz**/) a love letter.

billhook noun a tool with a curved blade, used for pruning.

billiards noun a game played on a table with pockets at the sides and corners, into which balls are struck with a cue.

billion cardinal number (plural **billions** or (with another word or number) **billion**) a thousand million; 1,000,000,000. ■ **billionth** ordinal number.

billionaire noun a person owning money and property worth at least a billion pounds or dollars.

billow verb **1** (of smoke, cloud, or steam) roll outward. **2** fill with air and swell out. **noun 1** a large rolling mass of cloud, smoke, or steam. **2** literary a large sea wave.

billy or **billycan** noun (plural **billies**) a metal cooking pot with a lid and handle, used in camping.

billy goat noun a male goat.

bimbo noun (plural **bimbos**) informal an attractive but unintelligent young woman.

bin Brit. **noun 1** a container for rubbish. **2** a large storage container. **verb** (**bins**, **binning**, **binned**) throw away.

binary /by-nuh-ri/ **adjective 1** composed of or involving two things. **2** relating to a system of numbers which has two as its base and uses only the digits 0 and 1.

bind verb (**binds**, **binding**, **bound**) **1** firmly tie, wrap, or fasten. **2** hold together in a united group or mass. **3** (**be bound by**) be hampered or restricted by. **4** require someone to do something by law or because of a contract. **5** (**bind over**) (of a court of law) require someone to do something. **6** enclose the pages of a book in a cover. **7** trim the edge of a piece of material with a fabric strip. **noun** informal an annoying or difficult situation.

binder noun **1** a cover for holding loose papers together. **2** a machine that binds grain into sheaves. **3** a bookbinder. ■ **bindery** noun (plural **binderies**).

binding noun **1** a strong covering holding the pages of a book together. **2** fabric in a strip, used for binding the edges of material. **adjective** (of an agreement) legally compelling someone to do what is stated.

bindweed noun a plant that twines itself round things.

binge informal **noun** a short period of uncontrolled eating or drinking. **verb** (**binges**, **bingeing**, **binged**) eat or drink in an uncontrolled way.

bingo noun a game in which players mark off on a card numbers called at random, the winner being the first to mark off all their numbers.

binocular adjective for or using both eyes. **noun** (**binoculars**) an instrument with a separate lens for each eye, for viewing distant objects.

biochemistry noun the study of the chemical processes that take place within living things. ■ **biochemical** adjective **biochemist** noun.

biodegradable adjective able to be decomposed by bacteria or other living things.

biodiversity noun the variety of plant and animal life in the world or in a particular environment.

biography noun (plural **biographies**) an account of a person's life written by someone else. ■ **biographer** noun **biographical** adjective.

biological adjective **1** relating to biology or living things. **2** (of a parent or child) related by blood. **3** relating to the use of germs as a weapon in war. **4** (of a detergent) containing enzymes. ■ **biologically** adverb.

biology noun the scientific study of the life and structure of plants and animals. ■ **biologist** noun.

bionic adjective **1** (of an artificial body part) electronically powered. **2** informal having superhuman powers.

biopsy noun (plural **biopsies**) an examination of tissue taken from the body, to discover the presence or cause of a disease.

biorhythm noun a recurring cycle in the functioning of an animal or plant.

bipartite adjective involving two separate parties.

biped /by-ped/ noun an animal that walks on two feet.

biplane noun an early type of aircraft with two pairs of wings, one above the other.

bipolar adjective having two poles or outer limits.

birch noun **1** a slender tree with thin, peeling bark. **2** (**the birch**) (in the past) the punishment of being beaten with a bundle of birch twigs.

bird noun **1** an animal with feathers, wings, and a beak, that lays eggs and is usually able to fly. **2** Brit. informal a young woman or girlfriend. □ **bird of prey** (plural **birds of prey**) a bird that eats small animals or birds, such as an eagle or hawk. **bird's-eye view** a view from above.

birdie noun (plural **birdies**) Golf a score of one stroke under par at a hole.

biro noun (plural **biros**) Brit. trademark a ballpoint pen.

birth noun **1** the process by which a baby or other young animal comes out of its mother's body. **2** the beginning of something. **3** a person's family origins. □ **birth control** the use of contraceptives to prevent unwanted pregnancies. **give birth** produce a baby or young animal.

birthday noun the day in each year which is the same as the day on which a person was born.

birthmark noun a coloured mark on the body which is there from birth.

birthright noun **1** a right or privilege that a person inherits. **2** a basic right belonging to all human beings.

biscuit noun **1** Brit. a small, flat, crisp cake. **2** a light brown colour.

> ✓ there's a *u* at the end: bisc*u*it.

bisect verb divide into two parts.

bisexual adjective **1** sexually attracted to both men and women. **2** Biology having both male and female organs. noun a bisexual person. ■ **bisexuality** noun.

bishop noun (in the Christian Church) a senior minister who is in charge of a diocese (a district).

bismuth noun a brittle reddish-grey metallic element resembling lead.

bison noun (plural **bison**) a wild ox with a humped back and shaggy hair.

bistro /bee-stroh/ noun (plural **bistros**) a small, inexpensive restaurant.

bit¹ noun **1** a small piece or quantity. **2** (**a bit**) a short time or distance. **3** (**a bit**) rather; slightly. □ **bit part** a small acting role in a play or a film.

bit² noun **1** a metal mouthpiece attached to a bridle, used to control a horse. **2** a tool or piece for boring or drilling. □ **get the bit between your teeth** make a determined effort.

bit³ noun Computing the smallest unit of information, expressed as either a 0 or a 1.

bitch noun **1** a female dog. **2** informal a spiteful or unpleasant woman. **3** (**a bitch**) informal something difficult or unpleasant. verb informal make spiteful comments.

bitchy adjective (**bitchier, bitchiest**) informal spiteful. ■ **bitchiness** noun.

bite verb (**bites, biting, bit**; past participle **bitten**) **1** cut into something with your teeth. **2** (of a tool, tyre, etc.) grip a surface. **3** take effect in an unwelcome way. noun **1** an act of biting or a piece bitten off. **2** informal a quick snack. **3** a feeling of cold in the air. □ **bite the bullet** make yourself do something difficult or unpleasant.

bite the dust informal die or be killed.

biting adjective **1** (of a wind) painfully cold. **2** (of something said) cruel.

bitter adjective **1** having a sharp or sour taste or smell; not sweet. **2** painful or distressing. **3** feeling deep resentment. **4** (of a conflict) intense and full of hatred. **5** intensely cold. noun **1** Brit. bitter-tasting beer that is strongly flavoured with hops. **2** (**bitters**) bitter-tasting liquor used in cocktails. ■ **bitterly** adverb **bitterness** noun.

bittersweet adjective **1** sweet with a bitter aftertaste. **2** bringing pleasure mixed with sadness.

bitty adjective (**bittier**, **bittiest**) informal made up of small unrelated parts.

bitumen noun a black sticky substance obtained from oil, used for covering roads and roofs. ■ **bituminous** adjective.

bivalve noun a creature with a hinged double shell, such as an oyster or mussel.

bivouac noun a makeshift open-air camp without tents. verb (**bivouacs**, **bivouacking**, **bivouacked**) stay overnight in such a camp.

bizarre adjective very strange or unusual. ■ **bizarrely** adverb.

 ✓ one z, two *rr*'s: bi**zarr**e.

blab verb (**blabs**, **blabbing**, **blabbed**) informal give away a secret.

blabber verb (**blabbers**, **blabbering**, **blabbered**) informal talk carelessly or in an annoying way.

black adjective **1** of the very darkest colour. **2** relating to people who have dark-coloured skin. **3** (of coffee or tea) without milk. **4** indicating that bad or unwelcome things are likely to happen. **5** (of a joke) making something bad or unwelcome seem funny. **6** full of anger or hatred. noun **1** black colour or material. **2** a black person. verb **1** make something black. **2** Brit. dated refuse to deal with someone or something as a form of industrial action. □ **black belt** a black belt awarded to an expert in judo, karate, and other martial arts. **black box** a machine that records what is happening to the controls in an aircraft during a flight. **black economy** illegal buying and selling of goods that takes place without being taxed. **black eye** an area of bruising around the eye. **black hole** an area in space where gravity is so strong that nothing, not even light, can escape. **black ice** a transparent coating of ice on a road. **black magic** magic in which evil spirits are called on. **black mark** a note that someone has behaved badly. **black market** an illegal trade in goods that are scarce or officially controlled. **black pudding** a pork sausage containing dried pig's blood. **black sheep** a person who is considered bad or embarrassing by the rest of their family. **black spot** a place that is dangerous or where problems arise. **black widow** a very poisonous American spider with a black body and red markings. **in the black** not owing any money. ■ **blackness** noun.

blackball verb prevent someone from joining a club.

blackberry noun (plural **blackberries**) a soft purple-black fruit that grows on a prickly bush.

blackbird noun a bird with black feathers and a yellow beak.

blackboard noun a board with a black surface for writing on with chalk.

blackcurrant noun a small round edible purple-black berry.

blacken verb **1** make or become black. **2** damage someone's reputation.

blackfly noun a small black fly which eats the young shoots of plants.

blackguard /**blag**-gerd/ noun dated a man who is dishonest or treats others badly.

blackhead noun a lump of oily matter blocking a pore in the skin.

blackleg noun Brit. disapproving a person who continues working when other workers are on strike.

blacklist noun a list of people who cannot be trusted or who are out of favour. **verb** put on a blacklist.

blackmail noun **1** the demanding of money from someone in return for not giving away secret information about them. **2** the use of threats or other pressure to influence someone. **verb** use blackmail on someone.

blackout noun **1** a period when all lights must be turned out during an enemy air raid. **2** a sudden failure of electric lights. **3** a short loss of consciousness. **4** an official restriction on the publishing of news. **verb** (black out) **1** make a building dark by switching off lights and covering windows. **2** faint.

blacksmith noun a person who makes and repairs things made of iron.

blackthorn noun a thorny bush that has blue-black fruits (called sloes).

bladder noun a bag-like organ in the abdomen in which urine collects before it is passed from the body.

blade noun **1** the flat cutting edge of a knife or other tool or weapon. **2** the broad flat part of an oar, leaf, or other object. **3** a long, narrow leaf of grass.

blag verb (blags, blagging, blagged) Brit. informal get something by clever talk or lying. ■ **blagger** noun.

blame verb (blames, blaming, blamed) say that someone is responsible for something bad. noun **1** responsibility for something bad. **2** criticism for doing something badly or wrongly. ■ **blameworthy** adjective.

blameless adjective having done nothing bad; innocent.

blanch verb **1** become white or pale. **2** prepare vegetables by putting them briefly in boiling water.

blancmange /bluh-**monzh**/ noun a dessert like a milky jelly, made with cornflour and milk.

bland adjective **1** lacking any interesting features or qualities. **2** showing no emotion or excitement.

blandishments plural noun nice things said to someone in order to persuade them to do something.

blank adjective **1** not marked or decorated. **2** not understanding or reacting. noun **1** a space left to be filled in in a form. **2** a situation in which you cannot understand or remember something. **3** a gun cartridge containing gunpowder but no bullet. **4** a plain or unfinished object. **verb 1** (blank out) hide or block out. **2** Brit. informal deliberately ignore someone. □ **blank verse** poetry that does not rhyme. ■ **blankly** adverb **blankness** noun.

blanket noun **1** a large piece of woollen material used as a warm covering. **2** a thick mass or layer. **verb** (blankets, blanketing, blanketed) cover with a thick layer.

blare verb (blares, blaring, blared) make a loud, harsh sound. noun a loud, harsh sound.

blarney noun talk that is friendly and charming but may not be truthful.

blasé /**blah**-zay/ adjective unimpressed by something because you have experienced it often before.

blaspheme verb (blasphemes, blaspheming, blasphemed) speak rudely about God or use the name of God as a swear word. ■ **blasphemous** adjective **blasphemy** noun (plural **blasphemies**).

blast noun **1** an explosion, or the rush of compressed air spreading outwards from it. **2** a strong gust of wind. **3** a single loud note of a horn or whistle. **verb 1** blow something up with explosives. **2** (blast off) (of a rocket or spacecraft) take off. **3** produce loud music or noise. **4** informal criticize fiercely. □ **blast furnace** a furnace for extracting metal from ore, using blasts of hot compressed air.

blatant adjective open and unashamed. ■ **blatancy** noun **blatantly** adverb.

 -ant, not *-ent*: blat*ant*.

blather verb (blathers, blathering, blathered) talk without making much sense. noun rambling talk.

blaze noun **1** a very large or fierce fire. **2** a very bright light or display of colour. **3** an outburst: *a blaze of glory*. **4** a white stripe down the face of a horse. verb (**blazes**, **blazing**, **blazed**) **1** burn or shine fiercely or brightly. **2** shoot repeatedly or wildly. **3** present a piece of information in a prominent or sensational way. □ **blaze a trail 1** mark out a path. **2** be the first to do something.

blazer noun **1** a jacket worn by schoolchildren or sports players as part of a uniform. **2** a man's smart jacket.

blazon /blay-zuhn/ verb display or proclaim something in a way that catches people's attention.

bleach verb lighten something by using a chemical or leaving it in sunlight. noun a chemical used to remove stains and also to sterilize drains, sinks, etc.

bleak adjective **1** bare and exposed to the weather. **2** dreary and unwelcoming. **3** (of a situation) not hopeful. ■ **bleakly** adverb **bleakness** noun.

bleary adjective (**blearier**, **bleariest**) (of the eyes) tired and not focusing properly. ■ **blearily** adverb.

bleat verb **1** (of a sheep or goat) make a weak, wavering cry. **2** speak or complain in a weak or foolish way. noun a bleating sound.

bleed verb (**bleeds**, **bleeding**, **bled**) **1** lose blood from the body. **2** (in the past) take blood from someone as a medical treatment. **3** *informal* drain something of money or resources. **4** (of dye or colour) seep into an adjoining colour or area. **5** allow fluid or gas to escape from a closed system through a valve. noun an instance of bleeding.

bleep noun a short high-pitched sound made by an electronic device. verb **1** make a bleep. **2** call someone with a device that makes a bleep. ■ **bleeper** noun.

blemish noun a small mark or flaw. verb spoil the appearance of.

blench verb flinch suddenly out of fear or pain.

blend verb **1** mix and combine with something else. **2** (**blend in**) become unnoticeable. noun a mixture.

blender noun an electric device for liquidizing or chopping food.

bless verb **1** call on God to protect. **2** make something holy by saying a prayer over it. **3** (**be blessed with**) be given something desired.

blessed /bless-id, blest/ adjective **1** holy and protected by God. **2** bringing welcome pleasure or relief. ■ **blessedly** adverb.

blessing noun **1** God's approval and protection. **2** a prayer asking for this. **3** something for which you are very grateful. **4** a person's approval or support.

blew past of **BLOW**¹.

blight noun **1** a plant disease caused by fungi. **2** a thing that spoils or damages something. verb **1** infect with blight. **2** spoil or damage.

blighter noun *Brit. informal* an annoying or unfortunate person: *poor blighter!*

blind adjective **1** not able to see. **2** done without being able to see or without certain information. **3** lacking awareness or judgement. **4** concealed, closed, or blocked off: *a blind alley*. verb **1** make someone blind. **2** stop someone thinking clearly or sensibly. **3** (**blind with**) confuse someone by presenting them with something hard to understand. noun a screen for a window. □ **blind date** a meeting between two people who have not met before, arranged in the hope that they will have a romantic relationship. **blind man's buff** a game in which a player tries to catch people while wearing a blindfold. **blind spot 1** a small area in the retina of the eye which is insensitive to light. **2** an area where someone's view is obstructed. **3** an inability to understand or judge something. **turn a blind eye** pretend not to notice. ■ **blindly** adverb **blindness** noun.

blindfold noun a piece of cloth covering someone's eyes, so that they cannot see. **verb** cover someone's eyes with a blindfold.

blinding adjective **1** (of light) very bright. **2** (of a situation) suddenly very obvious. ■ **blindingly** adverb.

blink verb **1** shut and open the eyes quickly. **2** (of a light) flash on and off. **noun** an act of blinking. □ **on the blink** informal no longer working properly.

blinker noun **1** (**blinkers**) a pair of flaps used to prevent a horse from seeing sideways. **2** a flashing vehicle indicator light. **verb 1** put blinkers on a horse. **2** (**be blinkered**) be reluctant to accept new ideas.

blip noun **1** a short high-pitched sound made by an electronic device. **2** a small flashing point of light on a radar screen. **3** a temporary change in a situation or process that is generally steady. **verb** (**blips, blipping, blipped**) make a blip.

bliss noun perfect happiness.

blissful adjective full of joy and happiness. ■ **blissfully** adverb.

blister noun **1** a small bubble on the skin filled with watery liquid. **2** a similar bubble on a surface. **verb** form blisters.

blistering adjective **1** (of heat) intense. **2** very fierce or forceful.

blithe adjective **1** without thought or care. **2** very happy. ■ **blithely** adverb.

blithering adjective informal thoroughly stupid.

blitz noun **1** a sudden fierce military attack. **2** informal a sudden and concentrated effort. **verb** make a sudden fierce attack on.

blizzard noun a snowstorm with high winds.

bloat verb cause something to swell with fluid or gas. ■ **bloated** adjective.

bloater noun a salted and smoked herring.

blob noun **1** a drop of a thick or sticky liquid. **2** a roundish mass or shape.

bloc noun a group of allied countries with similar political systems.

block noun **1** a large solid piece of material. **2** a large building divided into flats or offices. **3** a group of buildings bounded by four streets. **4** an obstacle. **verb** prevent movement, flow, or progress. □ **block capitals** plain capital letters.

blockade noun a blocking of the way in or out of a place to prevent people or goods from entering or leaving it. **verb** (**blockades, blockading, blockaded**) block the way in or out of.

blockage noun an obstruction.

blockbuster noun informal a film or book that is very successful.

bloke noun Brit. informal a man.

blonde adjective (also **blond**) **1** (of hair) pale yellow. **2** having pale yellow hair. **noun** a woman with blonde hair.

blood noun **1** the red liquid that flows through the arteries and veins. **2** family background. **verb** give someone their first experience of an activity. □ **blood-curdling** horrifying. **blood group** any of the various types into which human blood is classified for medical purposes. **blood pressure** the pressure created by blood as it moves around the body. **blood sport** a sport involving the hunting or killing of animals. **blood vessel** a vein, artery, or capillary carrying blood through the body. **in your blood** part of your character. **new** (or **fresh**) **blood** new people joining an established group.

bloodbath noun an event in which many people are violently killed.

bloodhound noun a large hound used for following scents.

bloodless adjective **1** without violence or killing. **2** (of the skin) drained of colour. **3** lacking in vitality; feeble.

bloodletting noun **1** violent conflict. **2** (in the past) the removal of some of a patient's blood, as a medical treatment.

bloodshed noun the killing or wounding of people.

bloodshot adjective (of the eyes) having tiny red blood vessels visible in the whites.

bloodstream noun the blood circulating through the body.

bloodthirsty adjective (**bloodthirstier**, **bloodthirstiest**) taking pleasure in killing and violence.

bloody adjective (**bloodier**, **bloodiest**) **1** covered with or containing blood. **2** involving violence or cruelty. verb (**bloodies**, **bloodying**, **bloodied**) cover or stain with blood. □ **bloody-minded** Brit. informal deliberately unhelpful.

bloom verb **1** produce flowers; be in flower. **2** be healthy and happy. noun **1** a flower. **2** a state or period of blooming. **3** a healthy glow in a person's complexion. **4** a filmy coating found on some fruits and leaves.

bloomers plural noun historical **1** women's baggy underpants. **2** women's loose-fitting trousers, used for sport.

blossom noun a flower or a mass of flowers on a tree. verb **1** produce blossom. **2** become strong and healthy.

blot noun **1** a spot of ink. **2** a thing that spoils something good. verb (**blots**, **blotting**, **blotted**) **1** dry something with an absorbent material. **2** mark or spoil. **3** (**blot out**) obscure a view. **4** (**blot out**) keep from your mind. □ **blotting paper** absorbent paper used for drying ink when writing. **blot your copybook** Brit. spoil your good reputation.

blotch noun an irregular mark. verb mark something with blotches. ■ **blotchy** adjective.

blotter noun a pad of blotting paper.

blouse noun a garment like a shirt that is shaped to fit a woman.

blouson /bloo-zon/ noun a short loose-fitting jacket.

blow[1] verb (**blows**, **blowing**, **blew**; past participle **blown**) **1** (of the wind) move. **2** send out air through pursed lips. **3** force air into a instrument through the mouth. **4** sound a horn. **5** break something open with explosives. **6** burst through pressure or overheating. **7** informal spend money recklessly. **8** informal ruin an opportunity. noun an act of blowing. □ **blow hot and cold** keep changing your mind. **blow over** (of trouble) fade away. **blow up 1** explode. **2** inflate. **3** enlarge an image.

blow[2] noun **1** a powerful stroke with a hand or weapon. **2** a sudden shock or disappointment.

blowfly noun a large fly which lays its eggs in meat.

blowhole noun the nostril of a whale or dolphin on the top of its head.

blowout noun the release of air or gas from a tyre, oil well, etc.

blowsy or **blowzy** /rhymes with drowsy/ adjective (of a woman) plump and untidy.

blowtorch or **blowlamp** noun a portable device producing a hot flame, used to burn off paint.

blowy adjective windy or windswept.

blub verb (**blubs**, **blubbing**, **blubbed**) informal sob noisily.

blubber[1] noun the fat of whales and seals. ■ **blubbery** adjective.

blubber[2] verb (**blubbers**, **blubbering**, **blubbered**) informal sob noisily.

bludgeon noun a thick, heavy stick used as a weapon. verb **1** hit someone with a thick, heavy stick. **2** bully someone into doing something.

blue adjective (**bluer**, **bluest**) **1** of the colour of the sky on a sunny day. **2** informal sad or depressed. **3** informal indecent or pornographic. noun a blue colour. □ **blue-blooded** from a royal or aristocratic family. **blue cheese** cheese having veins of mould in it. **blue-chip** (of an investment) safe and reliable. **blue-collar** relating to manual work. **out of the blue** unexpectedly.

bluebell noun a woodland plant with clusters of blue bell-shaped flowers.

blueberry noun (plural **blueberries**) a blue-black berry that grows on a North American bush.

bluebottle noun a large fly with a metallic blue body.

blueprint noun **1** a technical drawing or plan. **2** a model or prototype.

blues noun **1** slow, sad music of black

American origin. **2 (the blues)** informal feelings of sadness or depression. ■ **bluesy** adjective.

bluestocking noun a serious intellectual woman.

bluff[1] noun a pretence that you know or can do something when this is not true. verb pretend in this way. □ **call someone's bluff** challenge someone to prove something, in the belief that they are bluffing.

bluff[2] adjective frank and direct in a good-natured way.

bluff[3] noun a steep cliff or bank.

bluish or **blueish** adjective having a blue tinge.

blunder noun a clumsy mistake. verb **(blunders, blundering, blundered) 1** make a blunder. **2** move clumsily or as if unable to see.

blunderbuss noun historical a gun with a short, wide barrel.

blunt adjective **1** lacking a sharp edge or point. **2** frank and direct. verb make or become blunt. ■ **bluntly** adverb.

blur verb **(blurs, blurring, blurred)** make or become unclear or less distinct. noun something that cannot be seen, heard, or remembered clearly. ■ **blurry** adjective.

blurb noun a short description written to promote a book, film, or other product.

blurt verb **(blurt out)** say something suddenly and without thinking.

blush verb become red in the face through shyness or embarrassment. noun an instance of blushing.

blusher noun a cosmetic used to give a reddish tinge to the cheeks.

bluster verb **(blusters, blustering, blustered) 1** talk loudly or aggressively but without having any effect. **2** (of wind or rain) blow or beat fiercely and noisily. noun loud and empty talk. ■ **blustery** adjective.

boa noun **1** a large snake which winds itself round and crushes its prey. **2** a long, thin stole of feathers or fur.

boar noun (plural **boar** or **boars**) **1** (also **wild boar**) a wild pig with tusks. **2** a male pig.

board noun **1** a long, narrow, flat piece of wood used in building. **2** a rectangular piece of stiff material used as a surface for a particular purpose. **3** the people who control and direct an organization. **4** regular meals provided in return for payment. verb **1** get on a ship, aircraft, or other passenger vehicle. **2** have a bedroom and receive meals in return for payment. **3** (of a pupil) live in a school during term time. **4** (**board up** or **over**) seal something in with pieces of wood. □ **board game** a game in which counters are moved around a board. **boarding house** a private house providing rooms and meals for paying guests. **boarding school** a school in which the pupils live during term time. **go by the board** (of a plan or principle) be abandoned or rejected. **on board** on or in a ship, aircraft, or other vehicle.

boarder noun a pupil who lives in school during term time.

boardroom noun a room in which a board of directors regularly meets.

boast verb **1** talk about yourself with too much pride. **2** (of a place or organization) have something as an impressive feature. noun an act of boasting.

boastful adjective showing too much pride in yourself.

boat noun **1** a vehicle that travels on water and is smaller than a ship. **2** a flattish jug for sauce or gravy. □ **rock the boat** informal make a situation unsettled.

boater noun a flat-topped straw hat with a brim.

boatswain /boh-s'n/ noun an officer in charge of equipment and the crew on a ship.

bob[1] verb **(bobs, bobbing, bobbed) 1** make a quick, short movement up and down. **2** curtsy briefly. noun a bobbing movement.

bob[2] noun **1** a short hairstyle that hangs evenly all round. **2** a weight on a pendulum or plumb line. verb **(bobs, bobbing, bobbed)** cut hair in a bob.

bob³ noun (plural **bob**) Brit. informal, dated a shilling.

bobbin noun a reel for holding thread.

bobble noun a small ball made of strands of wool.

bobby noun (plural **bobbies**) Brit. informal, dated a police officer.

bobsleigh noun a sledge used for racing down an ice-covered run.

bode verb (**bodes**, **boding**, **boded**) (**bode well** or **ill**) be a sign of a good or bad outcome.

bodge verb (**bodges**, **bodging**, **bodged**) Brit. informal make or repair something badly or clumsily.

bodice noun **1** the upper part of a woman's dress. **2** a woman's sleeveless undergarment.

bodily adjective relating to the body. adverb by taking hold of a person's body with force.

bodkin noun a thick needle with a blunt, rounded end.

body noun (plural **bodies**) **1** a person's or animal's physical structure. **2** the main part of the body, apart from the head and limbs. **3** the main or central part of something. **4** a mass or collection. **5** a group of people organized for a particular purpose. □ **body blow 1** a heavy punch to the body. **2** a severe setback. **body language** the showing of your feelings through the way in which you move or hold your body. **body stocking** an all-in-one stretchy garment that covers the body.

bodybuilder noun a person who enlarges their muscles through exercise.

bodyguard noun a person paid to protect someone rich or famous.

bodywork noun the metal outer shell of a vehicle.

Boer /rhymes with more or mower/ noun a member of the Dutch people who settled in southern Africa.

boffin noun Brit. informal a scientist.

bog noun an area of soft, wet ground. verb (**bogs**, **bogging**, **bogged**) (**bog down**) hinder or confuse someone with a lot of complicated details. ■ **boggy** adjective.

bogey or **bogy** noun (plural **bogeys**) **1** an evil spirit. **2** a cause of fear or alarm. **3** Brit. informal a piece of mucus in the nose.

bogeyman or **bogyman** noun an evil spirit.

boggle verb (**boggles**, **boggling**, **boggled**) informal **1** be astonished or baffled. **2** (**boggle at**) hesitate to do.

bogie /boh-gi/ noun (plural **bogies**) a supporting frame with wheels, fitted beneath the end of a railway vehicle.

bogus adjective not genuine or true.

Bohemian noun an artistic and unconventional person. adjective unconventional.

boil¹ verb **1** (of a liquid) reach a temperature where it bubbles and turns to vapour. **2** cook food in boiling water. **3** (**boil down to**) amount to. noun the process of boiling.

boil² noun an inflamed pus-filled swelling on the skin.

boiler noun a fuel-burning device for heating water. □ **boiler suit** Brit. a pair of overalls worn for dirty work.

boiling adjective **1** (of a liquid) at or near the temperature at which it boils. **2** informal extremely hot.

boisterous adjective lively and high-spirited. ■ **boisterously** adverb.

bold adjective **1** brave and confident. **2** (of a colour or design) strong or vivid. **3** (of type) having thick strokes. ■ **boldly** adverb **boldness** noun.

bole noun a tree trunk.

bolero noun (plural **boleros**) **1** /buh-lair-oh/ a Spanish dance. **2** /bol-uh-roh/ a woman's short open jacket.

boll noun the rounded seed capsule of plants such as cotton or flax.

bollard noun **1** Brit. a short post used to prevent traffic from entering an area. **2** a short post on a ship or quayside for securing a rope.

bollocks plural noun Brit. vulgar **1** the testicles. **2** nonsense.

Bolshevik noun a member of the

group which seized power in the Russian Revolution of 1917. ■ **Bolshevism** noun.

bolshie or **bolshy** adjective Brit. informal bad-tempered and uncooperative.

bolster noun a long, firm pillow. verb (**bolsters, bolstering, bolstered**) support or strengthen.

bolt noun **1** a heavy metal pin with a head that screws into a nut, used to fasten things together. **2** a bar that slides into a socket to fasten a door or window. **3** a short, heavy arrow shot from a crossbow. **4** a flash of lightning. **5** a roll of fabric. verb **1** fasten with a bolt. **2** run away suddenly. **3** (of a plant) grow quickly upwards and stop flowering as seeds develop. **4** eat food quickly. □ **bolt hole** a place to escape to and hide in. **bolt upright** with the back very straight. **make a bolt for** run suddenly towards.

bomb noun **1** a device designed to explode and cause damage. **2** (**the bomb**) nuclear weapons. **3** (**a bomb**) Brit. informal a large sum of money. verb **1** attack with a bomb or bombs. **2** Brit. informal move very quickly. **3** informal fail badly. □ **go like a bomb** Brit. informal move very fast.

bombard verb **1** attack continuously with bombs or other missiles. **2** direct a continuous flow of questions or information at. ■ **bombardment** noun.

bombardier /bom-buh-**deer**/ noun **1** a rank of non-commissioned officer in some artillery regiments. **2** a member of a bomber crew in the US air force who is responsible for releasing the bombs.

bombast noun language that sounds impressive but has little meaning. ■ **bombastic** adjective.

bomber noun **1** an aircraft designed for dropping bombs. **2** a person who plants bombs.

bombshell noun **1** a great surprise or shock. **2** informal a very attractive woman.

bona fide /boh-nuh **fy**-di/ adjective genuine; real.

bonanza noun a sudden supply of riches or good luck.

bonbon noun a sweet.

bond noun **1** a thing used to tie or fasten things together. **2** (**bonds**) ropes or chains used to hold someone prisoner. **3** an instinct or feeling that draws people together. **4** a legally binding agreement. **5** a certificate issued by a government or public company promising to repay money lent to it at a fixed rate of interest and at a specified time. verb **1** join securely to something else. **2** feel connected to someone.

bondage noun **1** the state of being a slave or of having no freedom. **2** sexual activity that involves the tying up of one partner.

bone noun **1** any of the pieces of hard material that make up the skeleton in vertebrates. **2** a strip of stiffening inserted into a garment. verb (**bones, boning, boned**) remove the bones from. □ **bone china** white porcelain that contains a mineral derived from bone. **bone dry** completely dry. **bone idle** very idle. **bone of contention** something argued about. **close to the bone 1** (of a remark) accurate to the point of making you feel uncomfortable. **2** (of a joke or story) rather rude. **have a bone to pick with** informal have reason to quarrel with someone or to tell them off. **make no bones about** be direct in stating or dealing with. ■ **boneless** adjective.

bonemeal noun ground bones used as a fertilizer.

bonfire noun an open-air fire lit to burn rubbish or as a celebration.

bongo noun (plural **bongos** or **bongoes**) each of a pair of small drums that are held between the knees.

bonhomie /bon-uh-**mee**/ noun good-natured friendliness.

bonk informal verb **1** hit. **2** Brit. have sex. noun **1** a hit or knock. **2** Brit. an act of having sex.

bonkers adjective informal mad.

bonnet noun **1** a woman's or child's hat tied under the chin. **2** Brit. the hinged metal cover over the engine of a motor vehicle.

bonny or **bonnie** adjective (bonnier, bonniest) chiefly Scottish & N. English attractive and healthy-looking.

bonsai /bon-sI/ noun the art of growing miniature ornamental trees.

bonus noun **1** a sum of money added to a person's wages for good performance. **2** an unexpected and welcome thing.

bon voyage /bon voy-**yahzh**/ exclamation have a good journey.

bony adjective (bonier, boniest) **1** containing or resembling bones. **2** so thin that the bones can be seen.

boo exclamation **1** said suddenly to surprise someone. **2** said to show disapproval or contempt. verb (boos, booing, booed) say 'boo' to show disapproval or contempt.

boob[1] Brit. informal noun an embarrassing mistake. verb make an embarrassing mistake.

boob[2] noun informal a woman's breast.

booby noun (plural boobies) informal a stupid person. □ **booby prize** a prize given to someone who comes last in a contest. **booby trap** an object containing a hidden explosive device.

boogie verb (boogies, boogieing, boogied) informal dance to pop music.

book noun **1** a written or printed work consisting of pages fastened together along one side and bound in covers. **2** a main division of a literary work or of the Bible. **3** (books) a record of financial transactions. verb **1** reserve accommodation or a ticket. **2** (book in) register your arrival at a hotel. **3** engage a performer or guest for an event. **4** (be booked up) have all places or dates reserved. **5** record the name of someone who has broken a law or rule.

bookcase noun a cabinet containing shelves on which books are kept.

bookend noun a support placed at the end of a row of books to keep them upright.

bookie noun (plural bookies) informal a bookmaker.

bookish adjective devoted to reading and studying.

bookkeeping noun the keeping of records of financial transactions.

booklet noun a small, thin book with paper covers.

bookmaker noun a person who takes bets and pays out winnings.

bookmark noun a strip of leather or card used to mark a place in a book.

bookworm noun informal a person who loves reading.

boom[1] noun **1** a deep, loud sound. **2** a period of rapid economic growth. verb **1** make a deep, loud sound. **2** experience rapid economic growth.

boom[2] noun **1** a pivoted beam at the foot of a sail. **2** a movable arm carrying a microphone or film camera. **3** a beam used to form a barrier across the mouth of a harbour.

boomerang noun a curved flat piece of wood that follows a circle through the air and returns to you when you throw it.

boon noun a very helpful thing.

boor noun a rough and bad-mannered person. ■ **boorish** adjective.

boost verb help or encourage. noun a source of help or encouragement.

booster noun **1** a dose of a vaccine that increases or renews the effect of an earlier one. **2** the part of a rocket or spacecraft used to give acceleration after lift-off.

boot noun **1** an item of footwear covering the foot and the ankle or lower leg. **2** Brit. a space at the back of a car for carrying luggage. **3** (the boot) informal a hard kick. **4** (the boot) informal dismissal from a job. verb **1** informal kick someone hard. **2** (boot out) informal force someone to leave. **3** load a program that triggers the start-up program in a computer. □ **old boot** informal an unpleasant old woman. **to boot** as well.

bootee or **bootie** noun **1** a baby's woollen shoe. **2** a woman's short boot.

booth noun **1** a small temporary

structure used for selling goods or staging shows at a market or fair. **2** an enclosed compartment that gives you privacy when telephoning, voting, etc.

bootleg adjective made or distributed illegally. ∎ **bootlegger** noun **bootlegging** noun.

booty noun valuable stolen goods.

booze informal noun alcoholic drink. **verb** (**boozes, boozing, boozed**) drink a lot of alcohol. ∎ **boozer** noun **boozy** adjective.

bop[1] informal noun a dance to pop music. **verb** (**bops, bopping, bopped**) dance to pop music. ∎ **bopper** noun.

bop[2] verb (**bops, bopping, bopped**) informal hit or punch someone.

boracic adjective having to do with boric acid.

borage noun a plant with bright blue flowers and hairy leaves.

borax noun a white mineral used in making glass and in soldering or smelting.

border noun **1** a boundary between two countries or areas. **2** a decorative band around the edge of something. **3** a strip of ground along the edge of a lawn where flowers or shrubs are planted. **verb** (**borders, bordering, bordered**) **1** form a border around or along. **2** (of a country or area) be next to. **3** (**border on**) come near to.

borderline noun a boundary. adjective on the boundary between two qualities or categories.

bore[1] verb (**bores, boring, bored**) make a hole in something with a drill or other tool. noun the hollow part inside a gun barrel or other tube.

bore[2] noun a dull person or activity. **verb** (**bores, boring, bored**) make someone feel tired and unenthusiastic by being dull. ∎ **boring** adjective.

bore[3] past of **BEAR**[1].

bored adjective feeling tired and unenthusiastic because you have nothing interesting to do.

> **i** use **bored by** or **bored with** rather than **bored of**.

boredom noun the state of feeling bored.

borehole noun a deep hole in the ground made to find water or oil.

boric acid noun a substance made from boron, used as an antiseptic.

born adjective **1** having come out of your mother's body; having started life. **2** (**born of**) existing as a result of. **3** having a particular natural ability: *a born engineer.* ∎ **born-again** newly converted to Christianity or some other cause.

borne past participle of **BEAR**[1].

boron noun a chemical element used in making alloy steel and in nuclear reactors.

borough noun **1** Brit. a town with a corporation and privileges granted by a royal charter. **2** a part of London or New York City which has its own local council.

borrow verb take and use something belonging to someone else with the intention of returning it.

borstal noun Brit. historical a type of prison for young offenders.

bosom noun **1** a woman's breast or chest. **2** loving care: *he went home to the bosom of his family.* adjective (of a friend) very close.

boss[1] informal noun a person who is in charge of other people at work. **verb** tell someone what to do in an arrogant or annoying way.

boss[2] noun a knob at the centre of a shield, propeller, or similar object.

bossa nova /bos-suh **noh**-vuh/ noun a dance like the samba, from Brazil.

boss-eyed adjective Brit. informal cross-eyed.

bossy adjective (**bossier, bossiest**) tending to tell people what to do in an arrogant or annoying way.

bosun or **bo'sun** /**boh**-suhn/ = **BOATSWAIN**.

botany noun the scientific study of plants. ∎ **botanical** (or **botanic**) adjective **botanist** noun.

botch verb informal do something badly or carelessly.

both determiner & pronoun two people or things, considered together. adverb applying to each of two alternatives.

bother verb (**bothers, bothering, bothered**) **1** take the trouble to do something. **2** annoy, worry, or upset someone. **3** (**bother with** or **about**) feel concern about or interest in. noun **1** trouble and fuss. **2** (**a bother**) a cause of trouble or fuss.

bothersome adjective troublesome.

bottle noun **1** a container with a narrow neck, used for storing liquids. **2** Brit. informal courage. verb (**bottles, bottling, bottled**) **1** place in bottles for storage. **2** (**bottle up**) hide your feelings. **3** (**bottle out**) Brit. informal lose your nerve and decide not to do something. □ **bottle green** dark green.

bottleneck noun a narrow section of road where the flow of traffic is restricted.

bottom noun **1** the lowest or furthest point or part of something. **2** the lowest position in a competition or ranking. **3** a person's buttocks. **4** (also **bottoms**) the lower half of a two-piece garment. adjective in the lowest or furthest position. verb **1** (of a ship) touch the bottom of the sea. **2** (**bottom out**) (of a situation) reach the lowest point before becoming stable or improving. □ **get to the bottom of** find the underlying cause of. **the bottom line** informal the most important factor. ■ **bottomless** adjective.

botulism /bot-yuu-li-z'm/ noun a dangerous form of food poisoning.

boudoir /boo-dwar/ noun a woman's bedroom or small private room.

bouffant /boo-fon/ adjective (of hair) styled so as to stand out from the head in a rounded shape.

bougainvillea /boo-guhn-**vil**-li-uh/ noun a tropical climbing plant with brightly coloured bracts surrounding the flowers.

bough noun a large branch.

bought past and past participle of **BUY**.

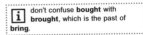
don't confuse **bought** with **brought**, which is the past of **bring**.

boulder noun a large rock.

boulevard /boo-luh-vard/ noun a wide street.

bounce verb (**bounces, bouncing, bounced**) **1** move quickly up or away from a surface after hitting it. **2** move or jump up and down repeatedly. **3** informal (of a cheque) be returned by a bank when there is not enough money in an account for it to be paid. noun **1** an act of bouncing. **2** lively confidence. **3** body in a person's hair.

bouncer noun a person employed by a nightclub to control or keep out troublemakers.

bouncy adjective (**bouncier, bounciest**) **1** able to bounce, or making something bounce. **2** confident and lively.

bound¹ verb move with leaping strides. noun a leaping movement.

bound² verb **1** form the boundary of. **2** restrict. noun a boundary or restriction. □ **out of bounds 1** (in sport) beyond the field of play. **2** beyond where you are allowed to go.

bound³ past and past participle of **BIND**. adjective **1** restricted to or by a place or situation: *his job kept him city-bound*. **2** going towards somewhere: *a train bound for Edinburgh*. **3** (**bound to**) certain to be, do, or have. **4** (**bound to**) obliged to do.

boundary noun (plural **boundaries**) a line marking the limits of an area.

boundless adjective unlimited.

bounteous adjective old use given or giving generously.

bountiful adjective **1** plentiful. **2** giving generously.

bounty noun (plural **bounties**) **1** a reward paid for killing or capturing someone. **2** something given in generous amounts. **3** generosity.

bouquet /boo-**kay**, boh-**kay**/ noun **1** a bunch of flowers. **2** the characteristic scent of a wine or perfume.

bourbon /**ber**-buhn/ noun an American whisky made from maize and rye.

bourgeois /**boor**-zhwah/ **adjective** having to do with the middle class, especially in being concerned with wealth and social status.

bourgeoisie /boor-zhwah-zee/ **noun** the middle class.

bout **noun 1** a short period of intense activity or of illness. **2** a wrestling or boxing match.

boutique /boo-**teek**/ **noun** a small shop selling fashionable clothes.

bovine /**boh**-vyn/ **adjective 1** having to do with cattle. **2** sluggish or stupid. **noun** an animal of the cattle group.

bow¹ /rhymes with toe/ **noun 1** a knot tied with two loops and two loose ends. **2** a weapon for shooting arrows, consisting of a string held taut by a strip of bent wood. **3** a rod with horsehair stretched along its length, used for playing some stringed instruments. □ **bow-legged** having legs that curve outwards at the knee. **bow tie** a necktie that is tied in a bow. **bow window** a curved bay window.

bow² /rhymes with cow/ **verb 1** bend the head and upper body as a sign of respect. **2** bend with age or under a heavy weight. **3** give in to pressure. **4** (**bow out**) withdraw from an activity. **noun** an act of bowing. □ **bow and scrape** try too hard to please someone.

bow³ /rhymes with cow/ or **bows** **noun** the front end of a ship.

bowdlerize or **bowdlerise** /**bowd**-luh-ryz/ **verb** (**bowdlerizes, bowdlerizing, bowdlerized**) remove parts of a text that might shock or offend people.

bowel **noun 1** (also **bowels**) the intestine. **2** (**bowels**) the innermost parts of something. □ **bowel movement** an act of emptying waste matter from the bowels.

bower **noun** a pleasant shady place under trees.

bowl¹ **noun 1** a round, deep dish or basin. **2** a rounded, hollow part of an object.

bowl² **verb 1** roll a round object along the ground. **2** Cricket (of a bowler) throw the ball towards the wicket. **3** move rapidly and smoothly. **4** (**bowl over**) knock down. **5** (**bowl over**) informal astonish. **noun** a heavy ball used in bowls or tenpin bowling.

bowler¹ **noun 1** Cricket a member of the fielding side who bowls. **2** a player at bowls or tenpin bowling.

bowler² **noun** a man's hard black felt hat that is rounded at the top and has a rim.

bowling **noun** bowls, tenpin bowling, or skittles.

bowls **noun** a game played with wooden balls called bowls, in which you roll your bowl as close as possible to a small white ball (the jack).

box¹ **noun 1** a square or rectangular container with a lid. **2** an enclosed area reserved for a group of people in a theatre or sports ground. **3** (**the box**) informal television. **verb 1** put something in a box. **2** (**box in**) restrict or confine. □ **box number** a number identifying a receptacle used for the delivery of mail. **box office** the place at a theatre or cinema where tickets are sold.

box² **verb** take part in boxing. **noun** a slap on the side of a person's head. □ **box someone's ears** slap someone on both sides of the head.

box³ **noun** a shrub with small, round glossy leaves.

boxer **noun 1** a person who boxes as a sport. **2** a breed of dog with a smooth brown coat and a flattened face. □ **boxer shorts** men's underpants that look like shorts.

boxing **noun** a sport in which contestants fight each other wearing big padded gloves.

Boxing Day **noun** Brit. a public holiday on the day after Christmas Day.

boxroom **noun** Brit. a small room used for storage.

boxy **adjective 1** roughly square in

PUNCTUATION

Brackets

Round brackets, also called parentheses, are used mainly to enclose explanations and extra information or comment, e.g.

> Zimbabwe (*formerly Rhodesia*)
> He is (*as he always was*) a rebel
> This is done using integrated circuits (*see page 38*).

Square brackets are used mainly to enclose:

- words added by someone other than the original writer or speaker, e.g.
  'He [*the police officer*] can't prove I did it.'
- various special types of information, such as stage directions, e.g.
  HEDLEY: Goodbye [*Exit*].

---

shape. **2** (of a room or space) cramped.

boy noun a male child or youth. ■ **boyhood** noun **boyish** adjective.

boycott verb **1** refuse to have dealings with. **2** refuse to buy goods as a protest. noun an act of boycotting.

boyfriend noun a person's regular male companion in a romantic or sexual relationship.

bra noun a woman's undergarment worn to support the breasts.

brace noun **1** (**braces**) Brit. a pair of straps that pass over the shoulders and fasten to the top of trousers to hold them up. **2** a strengthening or supporting part. **3** a wire device used to straighten the teeth. **4** (also **brace and bit**) a drilling tool with a crank handle and a socket to hold a bit. **5** (plural **brace**) a pair. verb (**braces, bracing, braced**) **1** make something stronger or firmer with a brace. **2** press your body firmly against something to stay balanced. **3** (**brace yourself**) prepare for something difficult or unpleasant.

bracelet noun an ornamental band or chain worn on the wrist or arm.

bracing adjective fresh and invigorating.

bracken noun a tall fern.

bracket noun **1** each of a pair of marks ( ) [ ] { } < > used to enclose words or figures. **2** a category of similar people or things. **3** a right-angled support that sticks out from a wall. verb (**brackets, bracketing, bracketed**) **1** enclose in brackets. **2** place in the same category.

brackish adjective (of water) slightly salty.

bract noun a leaf with a flower in the angle where it meets the stem.

brag verb (**brags, bragging, bragged**) speak boastfully. noun a simplified form of the card game poker.

braggart /brag-gert/ noun a boastful person.

braid noun **1** threads woven into a decorative band. **2** a length of hair made up of strands laced together. verb **1** form hair into a braid. **2** trim something with braid.

Braille noun a written language for blind people, using raised dots.

brain noun **1** an organ contained in the skull that controls thought and feeling and is the centre of the nervous system. **2** intellectual ability. **3** (**the brains**) informal the main organizer within a group. verb informal hit someone hard on the head.

brainchild noun informal an idea or invention thought up by a particular person.

brainless adjective very stupid.

brainstorm noun **1** informal a moment in which you are suddenly unable to think clearly. **2** a group discussion to produce ideas.

brainwash verb cause someone to change their attitudes and beliefs by putting pressure on them or repeating the same thing over and over.

brainwave noun **1** an electrical impulse in the brain. **2** informal a sudden clever idea.

brainy adjective (**brainier, brainiest**) informal intelligent.

braise verb (**braises, braising, braised**) fry food lightly and then stew it slowly in a closed container.

brake noun a device for slowing or stopping a moving vehicle. verb (**brakes, braking, braked**) slow or stop a vehicle with a brake.

bramble noun **1** a blackberry bush or similar prickly shrub. **2** Brit. the fruit of the blackberry.

bran noun pieces of the outer husk left when grain is made into flour.

branch noun **1** a part of a tree which grows out from the trunk. **2** a river, road, or railway extending out from a main one. **3** a division of a larger group. verb **1** divide into one or more branches. **2** (**branch out**) start doing a different sort of activity.

brand noun **1** a type of product made by a company under a particular name. **2** (also **brand name**) a name given to a product by its maker. **3** a mark burned on farm animals with a hot iron. **4** a piece of smouldering wood. verb **1** mark with a hot iron. **2** mark someone out as being bad in a particular way. **3** give a brand name to. □ **brand new** completely new.

brandish verb wave something as a threat or in anger or excitement.

brandy noun (plural **brandies**) a strong alcoholic drink made from wine or fermented fruit juice.

brash adjective confident in a rather rude or aggressive way. ■ **brashly** adverb **brashness** noun.

brass noun **1** a yellowish metal made by mixing copper and zinc. **2** (also **horse brass**) a flat brass ornament for a horse's harness. **3** Brit. a brass plate fixed in a church in memory of someone. **4** brass wind instruments forming a section of an orchestra. □ **brass band** a group of musicians playing brass instruments. **top brass** informal people in authority.

brasserie /brass-uh-ri/ noun (plural **brasseries**) an inexpensive French or French-style restaurant.

brassiere /braz-i-er/ noun a bra.

brassy adjective (**brassier, brassiest**) **1** resembling brass in colour. **2** harsh or blaring like a brass instrument. **3** tastelessly showy.

brat noun informal a badly behaved child.

bravado noun boldness intended to impress or intimidate people.

brave adjective having or showing courage. noun dated an American Indian warrior. verb (**braves, braving, braved**) face something frightening or unpleasant in a courageous way. ■ **bravely** adverb **bravery** noun.

bravo exclamation shouted to express approval for a performer.

bravura /bruh-vyoor-uh/ noun **1** great skill; brilliance. **2** the display of great daring.

brawl noun a noisy fight or quarrel. verb take part in a brawl.

brawn noun physical strength. ■ **brawny** adjective.

bray noun the loud, harsh cry of a donkey. verb make such a sound.

brazen adjective bold and shameless. verb (**brazen it out**) endure an awkward situation without seeming ashamed or embarrassed. ■ **brazenly** adverb.

brazier /bray-zi-er/ noun a portable heater holding lighted coals.

brazil nut noun the large three-sided nut of a South American forest tree.

breach verb **1** make a hole in; break through. **2** break a rule or agreement. noun **1** a gap made in a wall or barrier. **2** an action that breaks a rule or agreement. **3** a quarrel or disagreement. □ **step into the breach** replace someone who is suddenly unable to do a job.

bread noun **1** food made of flour, water, and yeast mixed together and baked. **2** informal money. □ **bread and butter** a person's main source of income. **on the breadline** Brit. very poor.

breadcrumb noun a small fragment of bread.

breaded adjective (of food) coated with breadcrumbs and fried.

breadth noun **1** the distance from side to side of something. **2** wide range.

breadwinner noun a person who supports their family with the money they earn.

break verb (**breaks, breaking, broke**; past participle **broken**) **1** separate into pieces as a result of a blow or strain. **2** stop working. **3** interrupt a sequence or course. **4** fail to obey a rule or agreement. **5** beat a record. **6** work out a code. **7** make a rush or dash. **8** soften a fall. **9** suddenly become public. **10** (of a person's voice) falter and change tone. **11** (of a teenage boy's voice) become deeper. **12** (of the weather) change suddenly. noun **1** a pause or gap. **2** a short rest. **3** an instance of breaking, or the point where something is broken. **4** a sudden rush or dash. **5** informal a chance. **6** Tennis the winning of a game against an opponent's serve. **7** Snooker & Billiards an uninterrupted series of successful shots. **8** a short solo in music. □ **break away** escape. **break down 1** stop working. **2** lose control of your emotions when upset. **break in 1** force your way into a building. **2** make a horse used to being ridden. **break off** stop suddenly. **break out 1** (of something undesirable) start suddenly. **2** escape. **break out in** suddenly be affected by. **break up** (of a gathering or relationship) end or part. **break wind** release gas from the anus. **break with 1** quarrel with. **2** go against a tradition. ■ **breakable** adjective.

breakage noun **1** the action of breaking something. **2** a thing that has been broken.

breakaway noun **1** a major change from something established. **2** a sudden attack or forward movement.

breakdown noun **1** a failure or collapse. **2** a careful examination.

breaker noun **1** a heavy sea wave that breaks on the shore. **2** a person that breaks up old machinery.

breakfast noun the first meal of the day. verb eat breakfast.

breakneck adjective dangerously fast.

breakthrough noun a sudden important development or success.

breakwater noun a barrier built out into the sea to protect a coast or harbour from waves.

bream noun (plural **bream**) a greenish-bronze freshwater fish.

breast noun **1** either of the two soft organs on a woman's chest which produce milk when she has had a baby. **2** a person's or animal's chest. verb **1** reach the top of a hill. **2** move forwards while pushing against something.

breastbone noun a bone running down the centre of the chest and connecting the ribs.

breastfeed verb (**breastfeeds, breastfeeding, breastfed**) feed a baby with milk from the breast.

breastplate noun a piece of armour covering the chest.

breaststroke noun a swimming stroke in which you push your arms forwards and then sweep them back while kicking your legs out.

breath noun **1** air taken into or sent out of the lungs. **2** an instance of breathing in or out. **3** a slight movement of air. **4** a sign or hint. ■ **breathable** adjective.

breathalyse (US spelling **breathalyze**) verb (**breathalyses, breathalysing, breathalysed**) test a driver's breath with a breathalyser.

breathalyser (US spelling **Breathalyzer** (trademark)) noun a device for measuring the amount of alcohol in a driver's breath.

breathe verb (**breathes, breathing, breathed**) **1** take air into the lungs and send it out again. **2** say quietly. **3** let air or moisture in or out.

breather noun informal a brief pause for rest.

breathless adjective **1** gasping for breath. **2** feeling or causing great excitement. ■ **breathlessly** adverb.

breathtaking adjective astonishing or awe-inspiring. ■ **breathtakingly** adverb.

breathy adjective (of speech or singing) having a noticeable sound of breathing.

breech noun the back part of a rifle or gun barrel.

breech birth noun a birth in which the baby's buttocks or feet are delivered first.

breeches plural noun short trousers fastened just below the knee.

breed verb (**breeds, breeding, bred**) **1** (of animals) mate and then produce young. **2** keep animals for the young that they produce. **3** produce or cause. noun a particular type of domestic or farm animal that has been specially developed. ■ **breeder** noun.

breeding noun upper-class good manners.

breeze noun **1** a gentle wind. **2** informal something easy to do. verb (**breezes, breezing, breezed**) informal come or go casually.

breeze block noun Brit. a lightweight building brick made from cinders, sand, and cement.

breezy adjective (**breezier, breeziest**) **1** pleasantly windy. **2** relaxed and cheerily brisk.

brethren plural noun **1** old-fashioned plural of **BROTHER**. **2** fellow Christians or members of a male religious order.

breve /rhymes with sleeve/ noun Music a note twice as long as a semibreve.

brevity noun **1** economical and exact use of words. **2** shortness of time.

brew verb **1** make beer. **2** make tea or coffee by mixing it with hot water. **3** begin to develop. noun something brewed. ■ **brewer** noun.

brewery noun (plural **breweries**) a place where beer is made.

briar or **brier** noun a prickly shrub.

bribe verb (**bribes, bribing, bribed**) pay someone to do something dishonest that helps you. noun an amount of money offered in an attempt to bribe someone. ■ **bribery** noun.

bric-a-brac noun various objects of little value.

brick noun **1** a small rectangular block of fired clay, used in building. **2** Brit. a child's toy building block. verb (**brick up**) block or enclose with a wall of bricks. □ **bricks and mortar** buildings or housing.

brickbat noun a critical remark.

bricklayer noun a person whose job is to build structures with bricks.

bridal adjective relating to a bride or a newly married couple.

bride noun a woman at the time of her wedding.

bridegroom noun a man at the time of his wedding.

bridesmaid noun a girl or woman who accompanies a bride at her wedding.

bridge noun **1** a structure that allows people or vehicles to cross a river, road, etc. **2** the platform on a ship where the captain and officers stand. **3** the upper bony part of a person's nose. **4** the part on a stringed instrument over which the strings are stretched. **5** a card game played by two teams of two players. verb (**bridges, bridging, bridged**) be or make a bridge over.

bridgehead noun a strong position gained by an army inside enemy territory.

bridle noun the harness used to control a horse. verb (**bridles, bridling, bridled**) **1** put a bridle on. **2** show resentment or anger.

bridleway noun Brit. a path along

which horse riders have right of way.

brief adjective 1 lasting a short time. **2** using few words. **3** (of clothing) not covering much of the body. **noun** chiefly Brit. **1** a summary of the facts in a case given to a barrister to argue in court. **2** informal a solicitor or barrister. **3** a set of instructions about a task. **verb** instruct someone about a task you want them to do. ■ **briefly** adverb.

briefcase noun a flat rectangular case for carrying documents.

briefing noun a meeting for giving information or instructions.

briefs plural noun short, close-fitting underpants.

brier ⇒ **BRIAR**.

brig noun a sailing ship with two masts.

brigade noun 1 a large body of troops, forming part of a division. **2** disapproving a particular group of people: *the anti-smoking brigade*.

brigadier /bri-guh-**deer**/ **noun** a rank of officer in the British army, above colonel.

brigand /**brig**-uhnd/ **noun** a member of a gang of bandits.

bright adjective 1 giving out light, or filled with light. **2** (of colour) vivid and bold. **3** intelligent and quick-witted. **4** (of sound) clear and high-pitched. **5** cheerfully lively. **6** (of prospects) good. ■ **brightly** adverb **brightness** noun.

brighten verb make or become brighter or more cheerful.

brilliant adjective 1 (of light or colour) very bright or vivid. **2** extremely clever or talented. **3** Brit. informal excellent; marvellous. ■ **brilliance** noun **brilliantly** adverb.

brim noun 1 the projecting edge around the bottom of a hat. **2** the lip of a cup, bowl, etc. **verb** (brims, brimming, brimmed) be full to the point of overflowing.

brimstone noun old use sulphur.

brindle or **brindled adjective** (of an animal) brownish with streaks of grey or black.

brine noun salt water.

bring verb (brings, bringing, brought) **1** carry or accompany to a place. **2** cause to be in a particular position or state. **3** cause someone to receive. **4** (bring yourself to do) force yourself to do something unpleasant. **5** begin legal action. □ **bring about** cause something to happen. **bring off** achieve something successfully. **bring on 1** help someone to improve. **2** cause something unpleasant to occur. **bring out 1** produce and launch. **2** emphasize a feature. **bring round 1** make someone conscious again. **2** persuade someone to adopt a point of view. **bring up 1** look after a child until it is an adult. **2** raise a matter for discussion. ■ **bringer** noun.

brink noun 1 the edge of land before a steep slope or a body of water. **2** the stage just before a new situation.

brinkmanship noun the pursuing of a dangerous course of action to the limits of safety before stopping.

briny adjective salty. **noun** (the briny) Brit. informal the sea.

brio /**bree**-oh/ **noun** energy or liveliness.

brioche /**bree**-osh/ **noun** a soft, sweet French roll.

brisk adjective 1 active and energetic. **2** slightly abrupt. ■ **briskly** adverb.

brisket noun meat from the chest of a cow.

bristle noun a short, stiff hair. **verb** (bristles, bristling, bristled) **1** (of hair or fur) stand upright away from the skin. **2** react angrily or defensively. **3** (bristle with) be covered with. ■ **bristly** adjective.

British adjective relating to Great Britain.

Briton noun a British person.

brittle adjective 1 hard but likely to break easily. **2** sharp or artificial: *a brittle laugh*.

broach verb 1 raise a subject for discussion. **2** pierce a container.

broad adjective 1 larger than usual from side to side; wide. **2** of a specified distance wide. **3** large in area or range. **4** without detail. **5** (of a hint) clear and unmistakable. **6** (of an accent) very strong. **noun** N. Amer. informal a woman. □ **broad bean** a large flat green bean. **broad-minded** tolerant and open-minded. ■ **broadly** adverb.

broadcast verb (broadcasts, broadcasting, broadcast; past participle broadcast or broadcasted) **1** transmit on radio or television. **2** tell to a lot of people. **noun** a radio or television programme. ■ **broadcaster** noun.

broaden verb make or become broader.

broadsheet noun a newspaper printed on large sheets of paper.

broadside noun 1 a strongly worded critical attack. **2** historical a firing of all the guns from one side of a warship.

brocade noun a rich fabric woven with a raised pattern.

broccoli /brok-kuh-li/ **noun** a vegetable with heads of small green or purplish flower buds.

 two c's, one l: broccoli.

brochure /broh-sher/ **noun** a booklet or magazine containing information about a product or service.

brogue noun 1 a strong outdoor shoe with perforated patterns in the leather. **2** a strong regional accent.

broil verb chiefly N. Amer. cook meat or fish using direct heat.

broke past of **BREAK**. **adjective** informal having no money.

broken past participle of **BREAK**. **adjective** (of a language) spoken hesitantly and with many mistakes. □ **broken home** a family in which the parents are divorced or separated.

broker noun a person who buys and sells things for others. **verb** arrange a deal or plan.

bromide noun a compound of bromine, used in medicine.

bromine noun a dark red liquid chemical element.

bronchial adjective relating to the tubes leading to the lungs.

bronchitis noun inflammation of the tubes that lead to the lungs.

bronco noun (plural broncos) a wild or half-tamed horse of the western US.

brontosaurus noun a huge plant-eating dinosaur with a long neck and tail.

bronze noun 1 a yellowish-brown metal made by mixing copper and tin. **2** a yellowish-brown colour. **3** (also **bronze medal**) a medal given for third place in a competition. **verb** (bronzes, bronzing, bronzed) **1** give something a bronze surface. **2** make someone suntanned. □ **Bronze Age** an ancient period when weapons and tools were made of bronze, following the Stone Age.

brooch noun an ornament fastened to clothing with a hinged pin.

brood noun a family of young animals born or hatched at one time. **verb 1** think deeply about an unpleasant subject. **2** (brooding) appearing darkly menacing. **3** (of a bird) sit on eggs to hatch them.

broody adjective (broodier, broodiest) **1** (of a hen) wishing to hatch eggs. **2** informal (of a woman) having a strong desire to have a baby. **3** thoughtful and unhappy.

brook[1] **noun** a small stream.

brook[2] **verb** formal tolerate.

broom noun 1 a long-handled brush used for sweeping. **2** a shrub with yellow flowers.

broomstick noun a brush with twigs at one end and a long handle, on which witches are said to fly.

Bros abbreviation brothers.

broth noun thin soup or stock, sometimes with chunks of meat or vegetables.

brothel noun a house where men visit prostitutes.

brother noun 1 a man or boy in relation to other children of his parents. **2** a male colleague or friend. **3** (plural brothers or brethren) a male fellow Christian or member of a religious order. □ **brother-in-law** (plural

brothers-in-law) 1 the brother of your wife or husband. **2** the husband of your sister or sister-in-law. ∎ **brotherly** adjective.

brotherhood noun **1** the relationship between brothers. **2** a feeling of friendliness and understanding between people. **3** a group of people linked by a shared interest.

brought past and past participle of **BRING**.

> ℹ️ don't confuse **brought** with **bought**, which is the past of buy.

brow noun **1** a person's forehead. **2** an eyebrow. **3** the highest point of a hill.

browbeat verb (**browbeats, browbeating, browbeat**; past participle **browbeaten**) bully someone with words.

brown adjective **1** of a colour produced by mixing red, yellow, and blue. **2** dark-skinned or suntanned. noun brown colour or material. verb **1** make or become brown by cooking. **2** (**be browned off**) informal be dissatisfied.

brownfield adjective (of a site) having had previous development on it.

Brownie noun (plural **Brownies**) **1** a member of the junior branch of the Guides Association. **2** (**brownie**) a small square of rich chocolate cake. **3** (**brownie**) a kind elf believed to do people's housework secretly.

browse verb (**browses, browsing, browsed**) **1** look at goods or text in a leisurely way. **2** look at information on a computer. **3** (of an animal) feed on leaves, twigs, etc. noun an act of browsing.

browser noun **1** a person or animal that browses. **2** a computer program for navigating the World Wide Web.

bruise noun **1** an area of discoloured skin on the body, caused by a blow. **2** a damaged area on a fruit or vegetable. verb (**bruises, bruising, bruised**) make a bruise appear on.

bruiser noun informal a tough, aggressive person.

brunch noun a late morning meal eaten instead of breakfast and lunch.

brunette noun a woman or girl with dark brown hair.

brunt noun the chief impact of something bad.

brush¹ noun **1** an object with a handle and a block of bristles, hair, or wire. **2** an act of brushing. **3** a slight, brief touch. **4** a brief encounter with something bad. **5** the bushy tail of a fox. verb **1** clean, smooth, or apply with a brush. **2** touch lightly. **3** (**brush off**) dismiss someone abruptly. **4** (**brush up**) work to improve a skill you have not used for a long time.

brush² noun undergrowth, small trees, and shrubs.

brushwood noun undergrowth, twigs, and small branches.

brusque /bruusk/ adjective rather rude and abrupt. ∎ **brusquely** adverb.

Brussels sprout noun a small green vegetable, the bud of a variety of cabbage.

brutal adjective **1** savagely violent. **2** not attempting to hide something unpleasant: *brutal honesty.* ∎ **brutality** noun **brutally** adverb.

brutalize or **brutalise** verb (**brutalizes, brutalizing, brutalized**) **1** make someone brutal by frequently exposing them to violence. **2** treat brutally.

brute noun a violent or savage person, or a large and unmanageable animal. adjective merely physical: *brute force.* ∎ **brutish** adjective.

BSE abbreviation bovine spongiform encephalopathy, a fatal brain disease in cattle.

BST abbreviation British Summer Time.

bubble noun **1** a thin ball of liquid enclosing a gas. **2** a ball filled with gas in a liquid or a material such as glass. **3** a transparent dome. verb (**bubbles, bubbling, bubbled**) **1** (of a liquid) contain rising bubbles of gas. **2** (**bubble with**) be filled with.

bubblegum noun chewing gum that can be blown into bubbles.

bubbly adjective (**bubblier, bubbliest**) **1** containing bubbles. **2** cheerful and high-spirited. noun informal champagne.

bubonic plague noun a form of plague passed on by rat fleas.

buccaneer noun **1** historical a pirate. **2** a recklessly adventurous person. ■ **buccaneering** adjective.

buck[1] noun **1** the male of some animals, e.g. deer and rabbits. **2** a vertical jump performed by a horse. **3** old use a fashionable young man. verb **1** (of a horse) perform a buck. **2** go against. **3** (**buck up**) informal make or become more cheerful. □ **buck teeth** teeth that stick out.

buck[2] noun N. Amer. & Austral./NZ informal a dollar.

buck[3] noun an object placed in front of a poker player whose turn it is to deal. □ **pass the buck** informal shift responsibility to someone else.

bucket noun **1** an open container with a handle used to carry liquids. **2** (**buckets**) informal large quantities. verb (**buckets, bucketing, bucketed**) (**bucket down**) Brit. informal rain very heavily.

buckle noun a flat frame with a hinged pin, used as a fastener. verb (**buckles, buckling, buckled**) **1** fasten with a buckle. **2** bend and give way under pressure. **3** (**buckle down**) tackle a task with determination.

buckwheat noun a grain used for flour or animal feed.

bucolic /byoo-**kol**-ik/ adjective relating to country life.

bud noun a growth on a plant which develops into a leaf, flower, or shoot. verb (**buds, budding, budded**) form a bud or buds.

Buddhism /**buud**-di-z'm/ noun a religion based on the teachings of Buddha (real name Siddhartha Gautama, c.563–c.460 BC). ■ **Buddhist** noun and adjective.

budding adjective beginning and showing signs of promise.

buddy noun (plural **buddies**) informal, chiefly N. Amer. a close friend.

budge verb (**budges, budging, budged**) **1** move very slightly. **2** change an opinion.

budgerigar noun a small Australian parakeet.

budget noun **1** an estimate of income and spending for a set period of time. **2** the amount of money needed or available for a purpose. **3** (**Budget**) a regular estimate of national income and spending put forward by a finance minister. verb (**budgets, budgeting, budgeted**) plan to spend a particular amount of money. adjective inexpensive. ■ **budgetary** adjective.

budgie noun a budgerigar.

buff[1] noun a yellowish-beige colour. verb polish something with a soft cloth. □ **in the buff** informal naked.

buff[2] noun informal a person who knows a lot about a particular subject.

buffalo noun (plural **buffalo** or **buffaloes**) **1** a heavily built wild ox with backward-curving horns. **2** the North American bison.

buffer noun **1** (**buffers**) Brit. shock absorbers at the end of a railway track or on a railway vehicle. **2** a person or thing that lessens the impact of harmful effects.

buffet[1] /**boo**-fay, **buf**-fay/ noun **1** a meal made up of several dishes from which you serve yourself. **2** a counter at which snacks are sold.

buffet[2] /**buf**-fit/ verb (**buffets, buffeting, buffeted**) (especially of wind or waves) strike repeatedly.

buffoon noun a ridiculous but amusing person. ■ **buffoonery** noun.

bug noun **1** a small insect. **2** informal a germ, or an illness caused by one. **3** informal an enthusiasm for something: *the sailing bug.* **4** a microphone used for secret recording. **5** an error in a computer program or system. verb (**bugs, bugging, bugged**) **1** hide a microphone in a room or telephone. **2** informal annoy; bother. □ **bug-eyed** with bulging eyes.

bugbear noun something that causes anxiety or irritation.

bugger vulgar, chiefly Brit. noun **1** disapproving a person who commits buggery. **2** a person regarded with contempt or pity. **3** an annoyingly awkward thing. verb **1** have anal sex with. **2** cause serious harm or trouble to. **3 (bugger off)** go away. **exclamation** used to express annoyance.

buggery noun anal sex.

buggy noun (plural **buggies**) **1** a small motor vehicle with an open top. **2** historical a light horse-drawn vehicle.

bugle noun a brass instrument like a small trumpet. ■ **bugler** noun.

build verb (**builds**, **building**, **built**) **1** construct something by putting parts together. **2 (build up)** increase over time. **3 (build on)** use as a basis for further development. **noun** the size or form of someone or something. □ **build-up 1** a gradual increase. **2** a period of preparation before an event. ■ **builder** noun.

building noun 1 a structure with a roof and walls. **2** the process or trade of building houses and other structures. □ **building society** Brit. a financial organization which pays interest on members' investments and lends money for mortgages.

built past and past participle of **BUILD**. **adjective** of a particular physical build. □ **built-in** included as part of a larger structure. **built-up** covered by many buildings.

bulb noun 1 the rounded base of the stem of some plants, from which the roots grow. **2** (also **light bulb**) a glass ball filled with gas, which provides light when an electric current is passed through it.

bulbous adjective 1 round or bulging in shape. **2** (of a plant) growing from a bulb.

bulge noun 1 a rounded swelling on a flat surface. **2** informal a temporary increase. **verb** (**bulges**, **bulging**, **bulged**) **1** swell or stick out unnaturally. **2 (bulge with)** be full of.

bulimia /buu-**lim**-mi-uh/ **noun** a disorder marked by bouts of overeating, followed by fasting or vomiting. ■ **bulimic** adjective & noun.

bulk noun 1 the mass or size of something large. **2** the greater part of something. **3** a large mass or shape. **4** roughage in food. **adjective** large in

quantity. □ **in bulk** (of goods) in large quantities.

bulkhead noun an internal wall or barrier in a ship or aircraft.

bulky adjective (**bulkier**, **bulkiest**) large and unwieldy.

bull¹ noun 1 an adult male animal of the cattle group. **2** a large male animal, e.g. a whale or elephant. □ **take the bull by the horns** deal decisively with a difficult situation.

bull² noun an order or announcement issued by the Pope.

bulldog noun a breed of dog with a flat wrinkled face and a broad chest.

bulldoze verb (**bulldozes**, **bulldozing**, **bulldozed**) clear or destroy with a bulldozer.

bulldozer noun a tractor with a broad curved blade at the front for clearing ground.

bullet noun a small piece of metal fired from a gun.

bulletin noun 1 a short official statement or summary of news. **2** a regular newsletter or report.

bullfighting noun the sport of baiting and killing a bull. ■ **bullfight** noun **bullfighter** noun.

bullfinch noun a finch with a pink breast.

bullfrog noun a very large frog with a deep croak.

bullion noun gold or silver in bulk before being made into coins.

bullish adjective aggressively confident.

bullock noun a castrated bull.

bullring noun an arena where bullfights are held.

bullseye noun the centre of the target in sports such as archery and darts.

bully noun (plural **bullies**) a person who intimidates weaker people. **verb** (**bullies**, **bullying**, **bullied**) intimidate.

bulrush or **bullrush noun** a tall reedlike waterside plant.

bulwark /**buul**-werk/ **noun 1** a defensive wall. **2** an extension of a ship's sides above deck level.

bum[1] noun Brit. informal a person's bottom.

bum[2] N. Amer. informal noun **1** a homeless person or beggar. **2** a lazy or worthless person. verb (**bums**, **bumming**, **bummed**) **1** get something by asking or begging. **2** (**bum around**) laze around. adjective bad.

bumble verb (**bumbles**, **bumbling**, **bumbled**) act or speak in an awkward or confused way.

bumblebee noun a large hairy bee with a loud hum.

bumf or **bumph** noun Brit. informal printed information.

bump noun **1** a light blow or collision. **2** a hump or projection on a level surface. verb **1** knock or run into with a jolt. **2** move with a lot of jolting. **3** (**bump into**) meet by chance. **4** (**bump off**) informal murder. **5** (**bump up**) informal increase. ■ **bumpy** (**bumpier**, **bumpiest**) adjective.

bumper noun a bar fixed across the front or back of a motor vehicle to reduce damage in a collision. adjective exceptionally large or successful.

bumpkin noun an unsophisticated person from the countryside.

bumptious adjective irritatingly forceful and confident.

bun noun **1** a small cake or bread roll. **2** a tight coil of hair at the back of the head.

bunch noun **1** a number of things grouped or held together. **2** informal a group of people. verb collect or form into a bunch.

bundle noun **1** a group of things tied or wrapped up together. **2** informal a large amount of money. verb (**bundles**, **bundling**, **bundled**) **1** tie or roll up in a bundle. **2** (**be bundled up**) be dressed in a lot of warm clothes. **3** informal push or carry forcibly.

bunfight noun Brit. humorous a grand tea party or other function.

bung noun a stopper for a hole in a container. verb **1** (**bung up**) block up. **2** Brit. informal put or throw somewhere casually.

bungalow noun a house with only one storey.

bungee jumping noun the sport of leaping from a high place to which you are attached with a long elastic cord tied to the ankles.

bungle verb (**bungles**, **bungling**, **bungled**) fail in performing a task. noun a mistake or failure. ■ **bungler** noun.

bunion noun a painful swelling on the big toe.

bunk[1] noun a narrow shelf-like bed.

bunk[2] verb Brit. informal play truant from school. □ **do a bunk** make a hurried departure.

bunker noun **1** a large container for storing fuel. **2** an underground shelter for use in wartime. **3** a hollow filled with sand on a golf course.

bunkum noun informal, dated nonsense.

bunny noun (plural **bunnies**) informal a rabbit.

Bunsen burner noun a small gas burner used in laboratories.

bunting[1] noun a small bird with brown streaked plumage.

bunting[2] noun flags and streamers used as decorations.

buoy noun an anchored float used to mark an area of water. verb (**be buoyed** or **buoyed up**) be cheered up and made more confident.

> ✓ the *u* comes before the *o* in buoy and buoyant.

buoyant adjective **1** able to keep afloat. **2** cheerful and optimistic. ■ **buoyancy** noun.

burble verb (**burbles**, **burbling**, **burbled**) **1** make a continuous murmuring noise. **2** speak for a long time in an unclear way; ramble. noun a continuous murmuring noise.

burden noun **1** a heavy load. **2** something that causes hardship, worry, or grief. **3** the main responsibility for a task. verb **1** load heavily. **2** cause someone worry, hardship, or grief.

burdensome adjective troublesome.

bureau /byoor-oh/ noun (plural **bureaux** or **bureaus**) **1** Brit. a writing desk with an angled top. **2** N. Amer. a chest of drawers. **3** an office for carrying out particular business. **4** a government department.

bureaucracy /byuu-**rok**-ruh-si/ noun (plural **bureaucracies**) **1** a system of government in which most decisions are taken by state officials. **2** excessively complicated administrative procedure.

bureaucrat noun a government official, especially one who follows guidelines rigidly. ■ **bureaucratic** adjective.

burgeon verb grow or increase rapidly.

burger noun a hamburger.

burgher /**ber**-guh/ noun old use a citizen of a town or city.

burglar noun a person who burgles a building.

burglary noun (plural **burglaries**) the action of burgling a building.

burgle verb (**burgles**, **burgling**, **burgled**) go into a building illegally to steal its contents.

burgundy /**ber**-guhn-di/ noun (plural **burgundies**) **1** a red wine from Burgundy in France. **2** a deep red colour.

burial noun the burying of a dead body.

burlesque /ber-**lesk**/ noun **1** a comically exaggerated imitation of something. **2** N. Amer. a variety show.

burly adjective (**burlier**, **burliest**) (of a man) large and strong.

burn[1] verb (**burns**, **burning**, **burned** or chiefly Brit. **burnt**) **1** (of a fire) produce flames and heat while using up a fuel. **2** harm or damage by fire. **3** (**be burning with**) be entirely possessed by a desire or emotion. **4** (**burn out**) become exhausted through overwork. noun an injury caused by burning. ▫ **burn your boats** (or **bridges**) do something which makes turning back impossible. **burn the candle at both ends** go to bed late and get up early.

burn[2] noun Scottish a small stream.

burner noun a part of a cooker, lamp, etc. that puts out a flame. ▫ **on the back burner** given a low priority.

burning adjective **1** very hot. **2** deeply felt. **3** important and urgent.

burnish verb polish something by rubbing it.

burnout noun physical or mental collapse.

burp informal verb belch. noun a belch.

burr noun **1** a strong pronunciation of the letter *r*. **2** a prickly seed case or flower head that clings to clothing and animal fur.

burrow noun a hole or tunnel dug by a small animal as a dwelling. verb **1** make a burrow. **2** hide underneath or delve into something.

bursar noun a person who manages the financial affairs of a college or school.

bursary noun (plural **bursaries**) a grant.

burst verb (**bursts**, **bursting**, **burst**) **1** break suddenly and violently apart. **2** (**be bursting**) be very full. **3** move or be opened suddenly and forcibly. **4** (**be bursting with**) feel full of an emotion. **5** (**burst out** or **into**) suddenly do something as a result of strong emotion. noun **1** an instance of bursting. **2** a sudden brief outbreak. **3** a period of continuous effort.

bury verb (**buries**, **burying**, **buried**) **1** place or hide something underground. **2** make something disappear or be hidden. **3** (**bury yourself**) involve yourself deeply in something.

bus noun (plural **buses**; US also **busses**) a large motor vehicle that carries customers along a fixed route. verb (**buses**, **busing**, **bused** or **busses**, **bussing**, **bussed**) transport or travel in a bus. ▫ **a busman's holiday** leisure time spent doing the same thing that you do at work.

busby noun (plural **busbies**) a tall fur hat worn by certain military regiments.

bush noun **1** a shrub or clump of shrubs. **2** (**the bush**) (in Australia and Africa) wild or uncultivated country.

bushbaby noun (plural **bushbabies**) a small African mammal with very large eyes.

bushel noun **1** Brit. a measure of capacity equal to 8 gallons (36.4 litres). **2** US a measure of capacity equal to 64 US pints (35.2 litres).

bushy adjective (**bushier**, **bushiest**) **1** growing thickly. **2** covered with bush or bushes.

business noun **1** a person's regular occupation. **2** work to be done or matters to be attended to. **3** a person's concern. **4** commercial activity. **5** a commercial organization.

businesslike adjective efficient and practical.

businessman or **businesswoman** noun a person who works in business.

busk verb play music in the street in the hope of being given money by passers-by. ■ **busker** noun.

bust[1] noun **1** a woman's breasts. **2** a sculpture of a person's head, shoulders, and chest.

bust[2] informal verb (**busts**, **busting**, **busted** or **bust**) **1** break, split, or burst. **2** chiefly N. Amer. strike violently. **3** chiefly N. Amer. raid, search, or arrest. noun **1** a period of economic difficulty. **2** a police raid. adjective **1** damaged; broken. **2** bankrupt. □ **bust-up** a serious quarrel or fight.

bustle[1] verb (**bustles**, **bustling**, **bustled**) **1** move energetically or noisily. **2** (of a place) be full of activity. noun excited activity and movement.

bustle[2] noun a pad or frame formerly worn by women under a skirt to puff it out behind.

busty adjective informal (of a woman) having large breasts.

busy adjective (**busier**, **busiest**) **1** having a lot to do. **2** occupied with an activity. **3** excessively detailed. verb (**busies**, **busying**, **busied**) (**busy yourself**) keep occupied. ■ **busily** adverb.

busybody noun an interfering or nosy person.

but conjunction **1** nevertheless. **2** on the contrary. **3** other than; otherwise than. **4** old use without it being the case that. preposition except; apart from. adverb only. □ **but for 1** except

for. **2** if it were not for.

butane /byoo-tayn/ noun a flammable gas present in petroleum and natural gas and used as a fuel.

butch adjective informal aggressively masculine.

butcher noun **1** a person who cuts up and sells meat as a trade. **2** a person who slaughters animals for food. **3** a person who kills brutally. verb (**butchers**, **butchering**, **butchered**) **1** slaughter or cut up an animal for food. **2** kill someone brutally. **3** ruin something. ■ **butchery** noun.

butler noun the chief male servant of a house.

butt[1] verb **1** hit with the head or horns. **2** (**butt in**) interrupt a conversation. noun a rough push with the head.

butt[2] noun **1** an object of criticism or ridicule. **2** a target in archery or shooting.

butt[3] noun **1** the thicker end of a tool or a weapon. **2** the stub of a cigar or a cigarette. **3** N. Amer. informal a person's bottom. verb meet end to end.

butter noun a pale yellow fatty substance made by churning cream. verb (**butters**, **buttering**, **buttered**) **1** spread with butter. **2** (**butter up**) informal flatter someone. □ **butter bean** a large flat edible bean.

buttercream noun a mixture of butter and icing sugar used to ice cakes.

buttercup noun a plant with bright yellow cup-shaped flowers.

butterfly noun **1** an insect with two pairs of large wings, which feeds on nectar. **2** a showy or frivolous person. **3** (**butterflies**) informal a fluttering sensation in the stomach when you are nervous. **4** a stroke in swimming in which you raise both arms out of the water together.

buttermilk noun the slightly sour liquid left after butter has been churned.

butterscotch noun a sweet made with butter and brown sugar.

buttery adjective containing, resembling, or covered with butter. noun (plural **butteries**) Brit. a room in a college where food is sold to students.

buttock noun either of the two round fleshy parts of the human body that form the bottom.

button noun **1** a small disc sewn on to a garment to fasten it by being pushed through a buttonhole. **2** a knob on a piece of equipment which is pressed to operate it. verb fasten with buttons.

buttonhole noun **1** a slit in a garment through which a button is pushed to fasten it. **2** Brit. a flower or spray worn in a lapel buttonhole. verb (**buttonholes, buttonholing, buttonholed**) informal seek out and hold someone in conversation.

buttress noun **1** a projecting support, built against a wall. **2** a projecting part of a hill or mountain. verb support or strengthen.

buxom adjective (of a woman) attractively plump and large-breasted.

buy verb (**buys, buying, bought**) **1** get something in return for payment. **2** get something by sacrifice or great effort. **3** informal accept that something is true. noun informal a purchase. □ **buy out** pay someone to give up a share in something. ■ **buyer** noun.

buzz noun **1** a low continuous humming sound. **2** the sound of a buzzer or telephone. **3** an atmosphere of excitement and activity. **4** informal a thrill. verb **1** make a humming sound. **2** signal with a buzzer. **3** move quickly. **4** (**buzz off**) informal go away. **5** have an air of excitement or activity.

buzzard noun a large bird of prey.

buzzer noun an electrical device that makes a buzzing noise to attract attention.

buzzword noun informal a technical word or phrase that has become fashionable.

by preposition **1** through the action of. **2** indicating an amount or the size of a margin. **3** indicating the end of a time period. **4** beside. **5** past and beyond. **6** during. **7** according to. adverb so as to go past. □ **by and by** before long. **by the by** in passing. **by and large** on the whole.

bye[1] noun **1** the moving of a competitor straight to the next round of a competition because they have no opponent. **2** Cricket a run scored from a ball that passes the batsman without being hit.

bye[2] exclamation informal goodbye.

by-election noun Brit. an election held during a government's term of office to fill a vacant seat.

bygone adjective belonging to an earlier time. □ **let bygones be bygones** forget past disagreements.

by-law or **bye-law** noun **1** Brit. a rule made by a local authority. **2** a rule made by a company or society.

byline noun **1** a line in a newspaper naming the writer of an article. **2** (in soccer) the part of the goal line to either side of the goal.

bypass noun **1** a road passing round a town. **2** an operation to help the circulation of blood by directing it through a new passage. verb go past or round.

by-product noun a product produced in the process of making something else.

byre noun Brit. a cowshed.

bystander noun a person who is present at an event but does not take part.

byte noun a unit of information stored in a computer, equal to eight bits.

byway noun a minor road or path.

byword noun **1** a notable example of something. **2** a saying.

Byzantine /bi-**zan**-tyn/ adjective **1** relating to Byzantium (now Istanbul) or the Eastern Orthodox Church. **2** excessively complicated and detailed. **3** very devious or underhand.

C or **c noun** (plural **Cs** or **C's**) **1** the third letter of the alphabet. **2** the Roman numeral for 100. **abbreviation 1** Celsius or centigrade. **2** (©) copyright. **3** (c) cents. **4** (c or ca.) circa. **5** (c.) century or centuries.

cab noun 1 a taxi. **2** the driver's compartment in a truck, bus, or train.

cabal /kuh-**bal**/ **noun** a secret political group.

cabaret /kab-uh-ray/ **noun** entertainment held in a nightclub or restaurant while the audience sit at tables.

cabbage noun 1 a vegetable with thick green or purple leaves. **2** informal a person with a very dull or limited life.

caber /**kay**-ber/ **noun** a tree trunk used in the Scottish Highland sport of tossing the caber.

cabin noun 1 a private compartment on a ship. **2** the passenger compartment in an aircraft. **3** a small wooden shelter or house.

cabinet noun 1 a cupboard with drawers or shelves for storage. **2** a piece of furniture housing a radio, speaker, etc. **3** (**Cabinet**) a committee of senior government ministers.

cabinetmaker noun a skilled joiner who makes furniture.

cable noun 1 a thick rope of wire or fibre. **2** a wire for transmitting electricity or telecommunication signals. □ **cable car** a small carriage that hangs from a moving cable and travels up and down a mountainside. **cable television** a system in which programmes are transmitted by cable.

caboodle noun (**the whole caboodle**) informal the whole number of people or things in question.

caboose /kuh-**booss**/ **noun** N. Amer. a guards' van on a goods train.

cabriolet /kab-ri-oh-lay/ **noun 1** a car with a roof that folds down. **2** a horse-drawn carriage with a hood.

cacao /kuh-**kah**-oh/ **noun** the seeds of a tropical American tree, from which cocoa and chocolate are made.

cache /kash/ **noun** a hidden store of things.

cachet /**ka**-shay/ **noun** prestige or renown.

cackle noun a noisy clucking cry. **verb** (**cackles, cackling, cackled**) give a cackle.

cacophony /kuh-**kof**-uh-ni/ **noun** (plural **cacophonies**) a clashing mixture of sounds. ■ **cacophonous** adjective.

cactus /**kak**-tuhss/ **noun** (plural **cacti** /**kak**-ty/ or **cactuses**) a plant with a thick fleshy stem bearing spines but no leaves.

cad noun dated or humorous a dishonourable man. ■ **caddish** adjective.

cadaver /kuh-**da**-ver, kuh-**dah**-ver/ **noun** Medicine or literary a dead body.

cadaverous adjective very pale and thin.

caddie or **caddy noun** (plural **caddies**) a person who carries a golfer's clubs. **verb** (**caddies, caddying, caddied**) work as a caddie.

caddy noun (plural **caddies**) a small storage container.

cadence /**kay**-duhnss/ **noun 1** the rise and fall in pitch of the voice. **2** the close of a musical phrase.

cadenza /kuh-**den**-zuh/ **noun** a difficult solo passage in a musical work.

cadet noun a young trainee in the armed services or police.

cadge verb (**cadges, cadging, cadged**) informal ask for or get something which you are not entitled to.

cadmium /**kad**-mi-uhm/ **noun** a silvery-white metallic element.

cadre /**kah**-der/ **noun** a small group of people trained for a particular purpose or at the centre of a political organization.

Caesar /**see**-zer/ noun a title of Roman emperors.

 -ae-, not *-ea-*: Caesar.

Caesarean section /si-**zair**-i-uhn/ noun an operation for delivering a child by cutting through the wall of the mother's abdomen.

cafe /**ka**-fay/ noun a small restaurant selling light meals and drinks.

cafeteria /ka-fuh-**teer**-i-uh/ noun a self-service restaurant.

cafetière /ka-fuh-**tyair**/ noun a coffee pot containing a plunger to push the grounds to the bottom.

caffeine /**kaf**-feen/ noun a stimulating substance found in tea and coffee.

caftan ⇒ **KAFTAN**.

cage noun a structure of bars or wires used for confining animals. verb (**cages**, **caging**, **caged**) enclose in a cage.

cagey adjective informal cautiously reluctant to speak. ■ **cagily** adverb.

cagoule /kuh-**gool**/ noun a lightweight hooded waterproof jacket.

cahoots /kuh-**hoots**/ plural noun (**in cahoots**) informal making secret plans together.

caiman /**kay**-muhn/ noun a tropical American reptile similar to an alligator.

Cain noun (**raise Cain**) informal create trouble or a commotion.

cairn noun a mound of rough stones built as a memorial or landmark.

cajole /kuh-**johl**/ verb (**cajoles**, **cajoling**, **cajoled**) persuade someone to do something by flattering them.

cake noun **1** an item of soft sweet food made from baking a mixture of flour, fat, eggs, and sugar. **2** a flat, round item of savoury food. verb (**cakes**, **caking**, **caked**) (of a thick or sticky substance) cover and become encrusted on. □ **a piece of cake** informal something easily achieved.

calabrese /**kal**-uh-breez/ noun a bright green variety of broccoli.

calamine /**kal**-uh-myn/ noun a pink powder used to make a soothing lotion or ointment.

calamity noun (plural **calamities**) an event causing great and sudden damage or distress. ■ **calamitous** adjective.

calcified /**kal**-si-fyd/ adjective hardened by the addition of calcium salts.

calcium noun a soft grey metallic substance. □ **calcium carbonate** a white compound found as chalk, limestone, and marble.

calculate verb (**calculates**, **calculating**, **calculated**) **1** work out a figure using mathematics. **2** intend an action to have a particular effect. ■ **calculable** adjective.

calculated adjective done with awareness of the likely effect.

calculating adjective selfishly scheming or devious.

calculation noun **1** a count or assessment done using mathematics. **2** an assessment of the risks or effects of a course of action.

calculator noun a small electronic device used for making mathematical calculations.

calculus /**kal**-kyuu-luhss/ noun (plural **calculi** /**kal**-kyuu-lII/ or **calculuses**) the branch of mathematics concerned with problems involving rates of change.

caldron US spelling of **CAULDRON**.

calendar noun **1** a chart showing the days, weeks, and months of a particular year. **2** a system by which the beginning and end of a year are fixed. **3** a list of special days or events.

calf¹ noun (plural **calves**) **1** a young cow or bull. **2** the young of some other large mammals, e.g. elephants.

calf² noun (plural **calves**) the fleshy part at the back of a person's leg below the knee.

calibrate verb (**calibrates**, **calibrating**, **calibrated**) **1** mark a gauge or instrument with units of measurement.

2 compare the readings of an instrument with those of a standard. ■ **calibration** noun.

calibre (US spelling **caliber**) noun **1** the diameter of the inside of a gun barrel, or of a bullet or shell. **2** quality or ability.

calico noun (plural **calicoes** or US **calicos**) **1** Brit. a type of plain white or unbleached cotton cloth. **2** N. Amer. printed cotton fabric.

caliper or **calliper** noun **1** (also **calipers**) a measuring instrument with two hinged legs. **2** a metal support for a person's leg.

caliph /kay-lif/ noun (in the past) the chief Muslim ruler.

calk US spelling of **CAULK**.

call verb **1** cry out to someone to summon them or attract their attention. **2** telephone. **3** (of a bird or animal) make its characteristic cry. **4** pay a brief visit. **5** name or describe. **6** predict the result of a vote or contest. noun **1** a cry made as a summons or to attract attention. **2** a telephone communication. **3** the cry of a bird or animal. **4** a brief visit. **5** (**call for**) demand or need for. □ **call centre** an office in which large numbers of telephone calls are handled for an organization. **call girl** a prostitute who accepts appointments by telephone. **call for** require. **call off** cancel. **call on** turn to for help. **call the shots** (or **tune**) be in charge of how something should be done. **call up** summon someone to serve in the army or to play in a team. ■ **caller** noun.

calligraphy /kuh-lig-ruh-fi/ noun decorative handwriting. ■ **calligrapher** noun **calligraphic** adjective.

calling noun **1** a profession or occupation. **2** a strong feeling that you are suitable for a particular occupation; a vocation.

callisthenics /kal-liss-**then**-iks/ (US spelling **calisthenics**) plural noun gymnastic exercises.

callous adjective insensitive and cruel. ■ **callously** adverb.

callow adjective (of a young person) inexperienced and immature.

callus or **callous** noun an area of thickened and hardened skin.

calm adjective **1** not nervous, angry, or excited. **2** peaceful and undisturbed. noun a calm state or period. verb (often **calm down**) make or become peaceful and calm. ■ **calmly** adverb **calmness** noun.

calorie noun (plural **calories**) **1** a unit for measuring how much energy food will produce. **2** a unit of heat.

calorific adjective relating to the amount of energy contained in food or fuel.

calumniate /kuh-**lum**-ni-ayt/ verb (**calumniates**, **calumniating**, **calumniated**) formal make false and damaging statements about.

calumny /**ka**-luhm-ni/ noun (plural **calumnies**) formal the making of false and damaging statements about someone.

calve verb (**calves**, **calving**, **calved**) give birth to a calf.

calves plural of **CALF**[1], **CALF**[2].

calypso noun (plural **calypsos**) a kind of West Indian song with improvised words on a topical theme.

calyx /**kay**-liks/ noun (plural **calyces** /**kay**-li-seez/ or **calyxes**) the ring of small leaves (sepals) which form a layer around the bud of a flower.

cam noun **1** a projecting part on a wheel or shaft, which comes into contact with another part while rotating and makes it move. **2** a camshaft.

camaraderie /kam-uh-**rah**-duh-ri/ noun trust and friendship between people.

camber noun a slightly curved shape of a horizontal surface such as a road.

cambric noun a lightweight white linen or cotton fabric.

camcorder noun a portable combined video camera and video recorder.

came past tense of **COME**.

camel noun a large, long-necked mammal with either one or two humps on its back.

camellia /kuh-**mee**-li-uh/ noun an evergreen shrub with bright flowers and shiny leaves.

cameo noun (plural **cameos**) **1** a piece of jewellery consisting of a carving of a head against a differently coloured background. **2** a short descriptive piece of writing. **3** a small part played by a well-known actor.

camera noun a device for taking photographs or recording moving images. □ **in camera** Law in a judge's private rooms, without the press and public being present.

camisole noun a woman's loose-fitting undergarment for the upper body.

camomile ⇒ **CHAMOMILE**.

camouflage /**kam**-uh-flah*zh*/ noun **1** the painting or covering of soldiers and military equipment to make them blend in with their surroundings. **2** clothing or materials used for such a purpose. **3** the natural appearance of an animal which allows it to blend in with its surroundings. verb (**camouflages, camouflaging, camouflaged**) disguise using camouflage.

camp¹ noun **1** a place where tents are temporarily set up. **2** a complex of buildings for soldiers, holiday-makers, or prisoners. **3** the supporters of a particular party or set of beliefs. verb live in a tent or caravan while on holiday. □ **camp bed** Brit. a folding portable bed. **camp follower 1** a civilian attached to a military camp. **2** a person who associates with a group. ∎ **camper** noun.

camp² informal adjective **1** (of a man) theatrically effeminate. **2** deliberately exaggerated and theatrical in style. noun camp behaviour or style. □ **camp it up** behave in a camp way.

campaign noun **1** a series of military operations in a particular area. **2** an organized course of action to achieve a goal. verb work towards a goal. ∎ **campaigner** noun.

campanology /kam-puh-**nol**-uh-ji/ noun the art of bell-ringing.

campfire noun an open-air fire in a camp.

camphor noun a white substance with a sweet smell and bitter taste, found in certain essential oils.

campus noun (plural **campuses**) the grounds and buildings of a university or college.

camshaft noun a shaft with one or more cams attached to it.

can¹ modal verb (3rd singular present **can**; past **could**) **1** be able to. **2** be permitted to.

> ℹ️ when you're asking to be allowed to do something, it is better to say **may** rather than **can** (*may we leave now?* rather than *can we leave now?*).

can² noun a cylindrical metal container. verb (**cans, canning, canned**) preserve in a can. □ **can of worms** a complicated matter that will prove difficult to manage.

Canadian noun a person from Canada. adjective relating to Canada.

canal noun **1** a water-filled channel made for boats to travel on or to convey water to fields. **2** a passage in a plant or animal carrying food, liquid, or air.

canapé /**kan**-uh-pay/ noun a small piece of bread or pastry with a savoury topping.

canard /ka-**nard**/ noun an unfounded rumour or story.

canary noun (plural **canaries**) a small bright yellow bird with a tuneful song.

canasta /kuh-**nass**-tuh/ noun a card game using two packs and usually played by two pairs of partners.

cancan noun a lively, high-kicking stage dance.

cancel verb (**cancels, cancelling, cancelled**; US spelling **cancels, canceling, canceled**) **1** decide that a planned event will not take place. **2** withdraw from or end an arrangement. **3** (**cancel out**) (of one thing) have an equal but opposite effect on another thing. **4** mark a stamp, ticket, etc. to show that it has been used. ∎ **cancellation** noun.

Cancer noun a sign of the zodiac (the Crab), 21 June–22 July.

cancer noun **1** a disease caused by an uncontrolled growth of abnormal cells in a part of the body. **2** a tumour. **3** something evil or destructive that is hard to contain or destroy. ■ **cancerous** adjective.

candela /kan-**dee**-luh/ noun the basic unit of luminous intensity.

candelabrum /kan-di-**lah**-bruhm/ noun (plural **candelabra** /kan-di-**lah**-bruh/) a large branched holder for several candles or lamps.

candid adjective truthful and straightforward; frank. ■ **candidly** adverb.

candidate noun **1** a person who applies for a job or is nominated for election. **2** a person taking an examination. **3** a person or thing seen as suitable for a particular treatment or position. ■ **candidacy** noun.

candied adjective (of fruit) preserved in a sugar syrup.

candle noun a stick of wax with a central wick that is lit to produce light as it burns.

candlestick noun a support or holder for a candle.

candlewick noun a thick, soft cotton fabric with a raised, tufted pattern.

candour (US spelling candor) noun the quality of being open and honest.

candy noun (plural **candies**) N. Amer. sweets.

candyfloss noun Brit. a mass of pink or white fluffy spun sugar wrapped round a stick.

cane noun **1** the hollow stem of tall reeds, grasses, etc. **2** a length of cane used as a walking stick, for beating someone, etc. verb (**canes, caning, caned**) beat someone with a cane as a punishment.

canine /**kay**-nyn/ adjective relating to or resembling a dog. noun a pointed tooth next to the incisors.

canister noun a round or cylindrical container.

canker noun **1** a disease of trees and plants. **2** a condition in animals that causes open sores.

cannabis noun a drug obtained from the hemp plant.

canned adjective preserved in a sealed can.

cannelloni /kan-nuh-**loh**-ni/ plural noun rolls of pasta stuffed with a meat or vegetable mixture and cooked in a cheese sauce.

cannery noun (plural **canneries**) a factory where food is canned.

cannibal noun a person who eats the flesh of other human beings. ■ **cannibalism** noun **cannibalistic** adjective.

cannibalize or **cannibalise** verb (**cannibalizes, cannibalizing, cannibalized**) use a machine as a source of spare parts for others.

cannon noun (plural **cannon** or **cannons**) **1** a large, heavy gun formerly used in warfare. **2** an automatic heavy gun that fires shells from an aircraft or tank. □ **cannon fodder** soldiers seen merely as a resource to be used up in war.

cannonball noun a metal or stone ball fired from a cannon.

cannot short form can not.

canny adjective (**cannier, canniest**) shrewd, especially in financial matters. ■ **cannily** adverb.

canoe noun a narrow boat with pointed ends, propelled with a paddle. verb (**canoes, canoeing, canoed**) travel in a canoe. ■ **canoeist** noun.

canon noun **1** a general rule or principle by which something is judged. **2** a Church decree or law. **3** the authentic works of a particular author or artist. **4** a list of literary works considered as being of the highest quality. **5** a Christian priest on the staff of a cathedral. **6** a piece of music in which a theme is taken up by two or more parts that overlap. □ **canon law** the laws of the Christian Church.

canonical /kuh-**non**-i-k'l/ adjective **1** according to canon law. **2** accepted as authentic or as a standard.

canonize or **canonise** verb (**canonizes, canonizing, canonized**) offi-

cially declare a dead person to be a saint. ■ **canonization** noun.

canoodle verb (**canoodles, canoodling, canoodled**) informal kiss and cuddle lovingly.

canopy noun (plural **canopies**) **1** a cloth covering over a throne or bed. **2** a roof-like covering or shelter. **3** the expanding, umbrella-like part of a parachute.

cant[1] /rhymes with rant/ noun **1** insincere talk about moral or religious matters. **2** disapproving the language typical of a particular group.

cant[2] /rhymes with rant/ verb tilt or slope. noun a slope or tilt.

can't short form cannot.

cantaloupe /kan-tuh-loop/ noun a small melon with orange flesh.

cantankerous adjective bad-tempered and uncooperative.

cantata /kan-**tah**-tuh/ noun a musical composition with a solo voice and usually a chorus and orchestra.

canteen noun **1** a restaurant in a workplace or educational establishment. **2** Brit. a case containing a set of cutlery. **3** a small water bottle used by soldiers or campers.

canter noun a pace of a horse between a trot and a gallop. verb (**canters, cantering, cantered**) move at this pace. □ **at a canter** Brit. easily.

canticle noun a hymn or chant forming part of a church service.

cantilever noun a long beam or girder fixed at only one end, used for supporting a bridge. ■ **cantilevered** adjective.

canto /kan-toh/ noun (plural **cantos**) a division of a long poem.

canton noun a political or administrative subdivision of a country, especially in Switzerland.

canvas noun (plural **canvases** or **canvasses**) **1** a strong, coarse cloth used to make sails, tents, etc. **2** an oil painting on canvas.

canvass verb **1** visit someone to ask for their vote in an election. **2** question someone to find out their opin-

ion. ■ **canvasser** noun.

canyon noun a deep gorge.

cap noun **1** a soft, flat hat with a peak. **2** a cap awarded to members of a national sports team. **3** a lid or cover. **4** an upper limit on spending or borrowing. **5** a small amount of explosive powder in a case that explodes when you hit it. **6** a contraceptive diaphragm. verb (**caps, capping, capped**) **1** put a cap on. **2** be a fitting end to. **3** impose a limit on. **4** (be **capped**) be chosen as a member of a national sports team. □ **cap in hand** humbly asking for a favour.

capability noun (plural **capabilities**) the power or ability to do something.

capable adjective **1** (**capable of**) having the ability to do something. **2** able to achieve what you need to do; competent. ■ **capably** adverb.

capacious adjective having a lot of space inside; roomy.

capacitance noun the ability to store electric charge.

capacitor noun a device used to store electric charge.

capacity noun (plural **capacities**) **1** the maximum amount that something can contain or produce. **2** the ability or power to do something. **3** a role or position.

cape[1] noun a short cloak.

cape[2] noun a piece of land that sticks out into the sea.

caper[1] verb (**capers, capering, capered**) skip or dance about in a lively or playful way. noun **1** a playful skipping movement. **2** informal a light-hearted or dishonest activity.

caper[2] noun the flower bud of a shrub, pickled and used in cooking.

capillarity noun capillary action.

capillary /kuh-**pil**-luh-ri/ noun **1** a very small blood vessel. **2** a tube with a very narrow diameter. □ **capillary action** the force which acts on a liquid in a narrow tube to push it up or down.

capital noun **1** the most important city or town of a country or region.

2 wealth that is owned or invested, lent, or borrowed. **3** a capital letter. **4** the top part of a pillar. **adjective** informal, dated excellent. □ **capital letter** a large size of letter used to begin sentences and names. **capital offence** an offence that is punished by death. **capital punishment** the punishment of a crime by death. **make capital out of** use to your own advantage.

capitalism noun a system in which a country's trade and industry are controlled by private owners for profit. ■ **capitalist** noun & adjective.

capitalize or **capitalise verb** (capitalizes, capitalizing, capitalized) **1** (capitalize on) take advantage of. **2** convert into or provide with financial capital. **3** write in capital letters or with a capital first letter. ■ **capitalization** noun.

capitulate verb (capitulates, capitulating, capitulated) give in to an opponent. ■ **capitulation** noun.

capon /**kay**-puhn/ **noun** a domestic cock that has been fattened up for eating.

cappuccino /kap-puh-**chee**-noh/ **noun** (plural **cappuccinos**) coffee made with milk that has been frothed up with pressurized steam.

caprice /kuh-**preess**/ **noun** a sudden change of mood or behaviour.

capricious /kuh-**pri**-shuhss/ **adjective** having sudden changes of mood. ■ **capriciously** adverb.

Capricorn noun a sign of the zodiac (the Goat), 21 December–20 January.

capsicum noun (plural **capsicums**) a sweet pepper or chilli pepper.

capsize verb (capsizes, capsizing, capsized) (of a boat) overturn in the water.

capstan noun a broad revolving cylinder for winding a heavy rope or cable.

capsule noun 1 a small case of gelatin containing a dose of medicine. **2** a small case or compartment.

captain noun 1 the person in command of a ship or commercial aircraft. **2** the rank of naval officer above

commander. **3** the rank of army officer above lieutenant. **4** the leader of a team. **verb** be the captain of. ■ **captaincy** noun.

caption noun 1 a title or explanation accompanying an illustration or cartoon. **2** a piece of text appearing as part of a film or television broadcast. **verb** provide a caption for.

captivate verb (captivates, captivating, captivated) attract and hold the interest of; charm.

captive noun a person who has been captured. **adjective** unable to escape. ■ **captivity** noun.

captor noun a person who captures another.

capture verb (captures, capturing, captured) **1** take prisoner, or forcibly get possession of. **2** record accurately in words or pictures. **3** cause data to be stored in a computer. **noun** the action of capturing.

capybara /ka-pi-**bah**-ruh/ **noun** (plural **capybara** or **capybaras**) a large South American rodent.

car noun 1 a powered road vehicle designed to carry a small number of people. **2** a railway carriage or wagon.

carafe /kuh-**raf**/ **noun** a wide-necked glass bottle for serving wine.

caramel noun 1 sugar or syrup heated until it turns brown. **2** soft toffee made with sugar and butter.

carapace /**ka**-ruh-payss/ **noun** the hard upper shell of a tortoise, lobster, etc.

carat /**ka**-ruht/ **noun 1** a unit of weight for precious stones and pearls. **2** a measure of the purity of gold.

caravan noun 1 a vehicle equipped for living in, designed to be towed by a vehicle. **2** historical a group of people travelling together across a desert.

caraway noun a Mediterranean plant whose seeds are used as a spice.

carbide noun a compound of carbon with a metal or other element.

carbine noun a light automatic rifle.

carbohydrate noun a substance (e.g.

sugar and starch) containing carbon, hydrogen, and oxygen, found in food and used to give energy.

carbolic or **carbolic acid** noun a kind of disinfectant.

carbon noun a chemical element with two main pure forms (diamond and graphite), found in all organic compounds. □ **carbon copy 1** a copy made with carbon paper. **2** a person or thing identical to another. **carbon dating** a method of finding out how old something is by measuring the amount of radioactive carbon-14. **carbon dioxide** a gas produced by people and animals breathing out, and also by burning carbon, which is absorbed by plants in photosynthesis. **carbon monoxide** a poisonous gas formed when carbon is incompletely burned. **carbon paper** thin paper coated with carbon, used for making a copy of a document.

carbonaceous adjective consisting of or containing carbon or its compounds.

carbonate noun a compound containing carbon and oxygen together with a metal.

carbonated adjective (of a drink) fizzy because it contains small bubbles of carbon dioxide.

carbonic acid noun a very weak acid formed from carbon dioxide and water.

carborundum noun a very hard black substance used for grinding and polishing.

carbuncle noun **1** a large abscess or boil in the skin. **2** a polished red gem.

carburettor (US spelling **carburetor**) noun a device in an engine that mixes the fuel with air.

carcass or **carcase** noun the dead body of an animal.

carcinogen /kar-**sin**-uh-juhn/ noun a substance that can cause cancer. ■ **carcinogenic** adjective.

carcinoma /kar-si-**noh**-muh/ noun (plural **carcinomas** or **carcinomata** /kar-si-**noh**-ma-tuh/) a cancer of the skin or of the internal organs.

card[1] noun **1** thick, stiff paper or thin cardboard. **2** a piece of card printed with information, greetings, etc. **3** a small rectangular piece of plastic used for obtaining money from a bank or paying for goods. **4** a playing card. **5** (**cards**) a game played with playing cards. □ **card sharp** a person who cheats at cards. **get your cards** be dismissed from employment. **on the cards** possible or likely.

card[2] verb disentangle the fibres of raw wool by combing with a sharp-toothed instrument.

cardamom noun the seed and pods of a SE Asian plant, used as a spice.

cardboard noun thin board made from paper pulp.

cardiac adjective having to do with the heart.

cardigan noun a sweater with buttons down the front.

cardinal noun an important Roman Catholic priest, having the power to elect the Pope. adjective most important; chief. □ **cardinal number** a number expressing quantity (one, two, three, etc.).

cardiograph noun an instrument for recording heart movements.

cardiology noun the branch of medicine concerned with the heart.

cardiovascular adjective having to do with the heart and blood vessels.

care noun **1** the providing of welfare and protection. **2** the bringing up of a child by a local authority rather than its parents. **3** special attention or effort made to avoid damage, risk, or error. **4** a cause for anxiety, or a worried feeling. verb (**cares**, **caring**, **cared**) **1** feel concern or interest. **2** feel affection or liking. **3** (**care for** or **to do**) like to have or be willing to do. **4** (**care for**) look after. □ **care of** at the address of someone who will look after or pass on mail. **take care of** look after or deal with.

careen /kuh-**reen**/ verb **1** (of a ship) tilt to one side. **2** move in an uncontrolled way; career.

career noun an occupation undertaken for a long period of a person's life. verb (careers, careering, careered) move swiftly and uncontrollably.

careerist noun a person whose only concern is to progress in their career. ■ careerism noun.

carefree adjective free from anxiety or responsibility.

careful adjective 1 taking care to avoid harm; cautious. 2 showing a lot of thought and attention. ■ carefully adverb.

careless adjective not giving enough attention to avoiding harm or mistakes. ■ carelessly adverb carelessness noun.

carer noun someone who looks after a sick, elderly, or disabled person.

caress verb touch or stroke gently or lovingly. noun a gentle or loving touch.

caretaker noun a person employed to look after a public building.

careworn adjective showing signs of prolonged worry.

cargo noun (plural cargoes or cargos) goods carried on a ship, aircraft, etc.

Caribbean /ka-rib-bee-uhn/ adjective relating to the Caribbean Sea and its islands.

> ✓ one r and two b's: Caribbean.

caribou /ka-ri-boo/ noun (plural caribou) N. Amer. a reindeer.

caricature /ka-ri-kuh-tyoor/ noun a picture in which a person's distinctive features are amusingly exaggerated. verb (caricatures, caricaturing, caricatured) make a caricature of.

caries /kair-eez/ noun decay of a tooth or bone.

carmine /kar-myn/ noun a vivid crimson colour.

carnage /kar-nij/ noun the killing of a large number of people.

carnal adjective relating to sexual needs and activities. ■ carnality noun.

carnation noun a plant with pink, white, or red flowers.

carnelian /kar-nee-li-uhn/ noun a dull red or pink semi-precious stone.

carnival noun a festival involving processions, music, and dancing.

carnivore /kar-ni-vor/ noun an animal that eats meat.

carnivorous /kar-niv-uh-ruhss/ adjective eating a diet of meat.

carob noun a substitute for chocolate made from the pod of an Arabian tree.

carol noun a religious song associated with Christmas. verb (carols, carolling, carolled; US spelling caroling, caroled) 1 sing carols in the streets. 2 sing or say happily.

carotene noun an orange or red substance found in carrots and other plants, important in the formation of vitamin A.

carotid artery /kuh-rot-id/ noun either of two main arteries carrying blood to the head.

carouse /kuh-rowz/ verb (carouses, carousing, caroused) drink alcohol and enjoy yourself with others in a noisy, lively way.

carousel noun 1 a merry-go-round at a fair. 2 a rotating device for baggage collection at an airport.

carp[1] noun (plural carp) an edible freshwater fish.

carp[2] verb complain or find fault.

carpal adjective relating to the bones in the wrist.

carpel noun the female reproductive organ of a flower.

carpenter noun a person who makes objects and structures out of wood. ■ carpentry noun.

carpet noun 1 a floor covering made from thick woven fabric. 2 a thick or soft layer of something. verb (carpets, carpeting, carpeted) 1 cover with a carpet. 2 informal tell someone off severely. □ carpet bag a travelling bag of a kind originally made of carpet-like fabric. carpet-bomb bomb an area intensively.

carport noun an open-sided shelter for a parked car.

carriage noun 1 a four-wheeled horse-drawn vehicle for passengers. 2 a passenger vehicle in a train. 3 the carrying of goods from one place to another. 4 the way in which a person moves or holds themselves. 5 a wheeled support for moving a gun. □ **carriage clock** a portable clock with a handle on top.

carriageway 1 each of the two sides of a dual carriageway or motorway. 2 the part of a road intended for vehicles.

carrier noun 1 a person or thing that carries or holds something. 2 a company that transports goods or people for payment. □ **carrier bag** a plastic or paper bag with handles. **carrier pigeon** a homing pigeon trained to carry messages.

carrion noun the decaying flesh of dead animals.

carrot noun 1 a tapering orange root vegetable. 2 something tempting offered as a means of persuasion.

carry verb (carries, carrying, carried) 1 move or take from one place to another. 2 support the weight of. 3 assume or accept responsibility or blame. 4 have a particular feature or result. 5 approve a proposal by a majority of votes. 6 publish or broadcast something. 7 (of a sound or voice) travel a long way. 8 (**carry yourself**) stand and move in a specified way. 9 be pregnant with. □ **be** (or **get**) **carried away** lose self-control. **carry the can** informal take responsibility for a mistake. **carry forward** transfer figures to a new page or account. **carry off** 1 take away by force. 2 succeed in doing. **carry on** 1 continue. 2 take part in. 3 informal have a love affair. **carry-on** informal 1 a fuss. 2 (also **carryings-on**) improper behaviour. **carry out** perform a task. **carry over** 1 keep something to use or deal with in a new situation. 2 postpone. **carry through** manage to complete.

carrycot noun a baby's small portable cot.

cart noun 1 an open horse-drawn vehicle for carrying goods or people. 2 a shallow open container on wheels, pulled or pushed by hand. verb 1 carry in a cart or similar vehicle. 2 informal carry a heavy object with difficulty.

carte blanche /kart **blahnsh**/ noun complete freedom to act as you wish.

cartel /kar-**tel**/ noun an association of manufacturers or suppliers formed to keep prices high.

carthorse noun a large, strong horse suitable for heavy work.

cartilage /**kar**-ti-lij/ noun firm, flexible tissue which covers the ends of joints and forms structures such as the external ear. ■ **cartilaginous** adjective.

cartography /kar-**tog**-ruh-fi/ noun the science or practice of drawing maps. ■ **cartographer** noun **cartographic** adjective.

carton noun a light cardboard box or container.

cartoon noun 1 a humorous drawing in a newspaper or magazine. 2 (also **cartoon strip**) a sequence of cartoon drawings that tell a story. 3 an animated film made from a sequence of drawings. 4 a full-size drawing made as a preliminary design for a work of art. ■ **cartoonist** noun.

cartridge noun 1 a container holding film, ink, etc., designed to be inserted into a mechanism. 2 a casing containing explosives and a bullet or shot for a gun. □ **cartridge paper** thick paper for drawing on.

cartwheel noun a sideways handspring performed with the arms and legs extended. verb perform cartwheels.

carve verb (carves, carving, carved) 1 cut into a hard material to produce an object or design. 2 cut cooked meat into slices for eating. 3 (**carve out**) develop a career, reputation, etc. through great effort. 4 (**carve up**) divide up ruthlessly.

carvery noun (plural **carveries**) a buffet or restaurant where cooked joints are carved as required.

carving noun an object or design carved from wood or stone.

Casanova /ka-suh-**noh**-vuh/ noun a man known for seducing many women.

casbah ⇒ **KASBAH**.

cascade noun **1** a small waterfall. **2** a mass of something that falls, hangs, or occurs in large quantities. verb (**cascades**, **cascading**, **cascaded**) pour downwards in large quantities.

case¹ noun **1** an instance of something occurring. **2** an incident being investigated by the police. **3** a legal action decided in a court of law. **4** a set of facts or arguments supporting one side of a debate or lawsuit. **5** a person or situation being given medical or welfare attention. **6** Grammar a form of a noun, adjective, or pronoun expressing the relationship of the word to others in the sentence. □ **in case** to provide for the possibility of something happening.

case² noun **1** a container or protective covering. **2** a suitcase. **3** a box containing twelve bottles of wine. verb (**cases**, **casing**, **cased**) **1** enclose in a case. **2** informal examine a place before robbing it.

casement noun a window hinged at the side so that it opens like a door.

cash noun **1** money in coins or notes. **2** money available for use. verb **1** give or obtain notes or coins for a cheque or money order. **2** (**cash in**) convert an insurance policy, savings account, etc. into money. **3** (**cash in on**) informal take advantage of. □ **cash crop** a crop produced for sale rather than for use by the grower. **cash flow** the total amount of money passing into and out of a business. **cash in your chips** informal die. **cash register** a machine used in shops for adding up and recording the amount of each sale and storing the money received.

cashew noun the edible kidney-shaped nut of a tropical American tree.

cashier noun a person responsible for

paying out and receiving money in a shop, bank, etc. verb (**cashiers**, **cashiering**, **cashiered**) dismiss someone from the armed forces.

cashmere noun fine, soft wool from a breed of Himalayan goat.

casing noun a cover that protects or encloses something.

casino noun (plural **casinos**) a public building or room for gambling.

cask noun a large barrel for storing alcoholic drinks.

casket noun **1** a small ornamental box or chest for holding valuable objects. **2** chiefly N. Amer. a coffin.

cassava /kuh-**sah**-vuh/ noun the root of a tropical American tree, used as food.

casserole noun **1** a large dish with a lid, used for cooking food slowly in an oven. **2** a kind of stew cooked slowly in an oven. verb (**casseroles**, **casseroling**, **casseroled**) cook food in a casserole.

cassette noun a sealed plastic case containing audio tape, videotape, film, etc., designed to be inserted into a player or camera.

cassock noun a long garment worn by Christian priests and members of church choirs.

cassowary /**kass**-uh-wuh-ri/ noun (plural **cassowaries**) a very large bird that cannot fly, found in New Guinea.

cast verb (**casts**, **casting**, **cast**) **1** throw forcefully. **2** cause light or shadow to appear on a surface. **3** direct your eyes or thoughts. **4** register a vote. **5** give a part to an actor, or allocate parts in a play or film. **6** shed or discard. **7** shape metal by pouring it into a mould while molten. **8** cause a magic spell to take effect. **9** throw a fishing line out into the water. noun **1** the actors taking part in a play or film. **2** (also **casting**) an object made by casting metal or other material. **3** a bandage stiffened with plaster of Paris to support and protect a broken limb. **4** form, appearance, or character. **5** a slight squint. □ **cast about** (or around or round) search far and wide. **casting vote** an extra vote used by a chairperson to decide an issue when votes on each side are equal. **cast iron** a hard alloy of iron and carbon which can be cast in a mould. **cast off** set a boat or ship free from its moorings. **cast-off** abandoned or discarded.

castanets plural noun a pair of small curved pieces of wood, clicked together by the fingers to accompany Spanish dancing.

castaway noun a person who has been shipwrecked in an isolated place.

caste noun each of the classes of Hindu society.

castellated adjective having battlements.

castigate verb (**castigates, castigating, castigated**) tell someone off severely. ■ **castigation** noun.

castle noun 1 a large fortified building of the medieval period. 2 Chess a rook. □ **castles in the air** schemes existing in the imagination that will never be achieved.

castor or **caster** noun 1 a small swivelling wheel fixed to the legs or base of a piece of furniture. 2 a small container with holes in the top, used for sprinkling salt, sugar, etc. □ **castor oil** oil from the seeds of an African shrub, used as a laxative. **castor sugar** white sugar in fine granules.

castrate verb (**castrates, castrating, castrated**) 1 remove the testicles of. 2 make something less powerful or vigorous. ■ **castration** noun.

casual adjective 1 relaxed and unconcerned. 2 done without enough attention or proper planning. 3 not regular or firmly established; occasional or temporary: *casual work.* 4 happening by chance; accidental. 5 informal. ■ **casually** adverb.

casualty noun (plural **casualties**) 1 a person killed or injured in a war or accident. 2 a person or thing badly affected by an event or situation.

casuistry /**kazh**-oo-iss-tri/ noun the use of clever but false reasoning.

cat noun 1 a small furry domesticated mammal. 2 a wild animal related to the domestic cat, such as a lion. 3 informal a spiteful woman. □ **cat burglar** a thief who enters a building by climbing to an upper storey. **cat's paw** a person used by another to carry out an unpleasant task. **the cat's whiskers** informal an excellent person or thing. **let the cat out of the bag** reveal a secret by mistake.

cataclysm /**kat**-uh-kli-z'm/ noun a violent upheaval or disaster. ■ **cataclysmic** adjective.

catacomb /**kat**-uh-koom/ noun an underground cemetery consisting of tunnels with recesses for tombs.

catalepsy /**kat**-uh-lep-si/ noun a condition in which a person becomes unconscious and goes rigid.

catalogue (US spelling **catalog**) noun 1 a list of items arranged in order. 2 a publication containing details of items for sale. 3 a series of bad things: *a catalogue of failures.* verb (**catalogues, cataloguing, catalogued**; US spelling **catalogs, cataloging, cataloged**) list in a catalogue.

catalyse /**kat**-uh-lyz/ (US spelling **catalyze**) verb (**catalyses, catalysing, catalysed**) cause or speed up a reaction by acting as a catalyst.

catalysis /**kuh-tal**-i-siss/ noun the speeding up of a chemical reaction by a catalyst.

catalyst /**kat**-uh-list/ noun 1 a substance that increases the rate of a chemical reaction while remaining unchanged itself. 2 a person or thing that triggers an event.

catalytic /**kat**-uh-**lit**-ik/ adjective involving catalysis. □ **catalytic converter** a device in a motor vehicle which converts exhaust gases into less polluting ones.

catamaran /**kat**-uh-muh-ran/ noun a boat with twin hulls in parallel.

catapult noun 1 a forked stick with elastic fastened to the two prongs, used for shooting small stones. 2 a military machine formerly used for hurling large stones. **3** a device for launching a glider or aircraft. verb **1** hurl or launch forcefully. **2** move suddenly or at great speed.

cataract noun **1** a large waterfall. **2** a condition in which the lens of the eye becomes cloudy, resulting in blurred vision.

catarrh /kuh-**tar**/ noun excessive mucus in the nose or throat.

catastrophe /kuh-**tass**-truh-fi/ noun a sudden event that causes great damage or suffering. ■ **catastrophic** adjective **catastrophically** adverb.

catatonia /kat-uh-**toh**-ni-uh/ noun a condition in which a person experiences periods of unconsciousness and overactivity. ■ **catatonic** adjective.

catcall noun a shrill whistle or shout of mockery or disapproval. verb make a catcall.

catch verb (**catches**, **catching**, **caught**) **1** seize and hold something moving. **2** capture a person or animal. **3** be in time to board a vehicle or to see a person or event. **4** entangle or become entangled. **5** surprise someone in the act of doing something wrong or embarrassing. **6** (**be caught in**) unexpectedly find yourself in an unwelcome situation. **7** see, hear, or understand. **8** hit or strike. **9** become infected with an illness. **10** (**catching**) informal (of a disease) infectious. noun **1** an act of catching. **2** a device for fastening a door, window, etc. **3** a hidden problem. **4** a break in a person's voice caused by emotion. **5** informal a person considered desirable as a husband or wife. □ **catch on** informal **1** become popular. **2** understand. **catch out** discover that someone has done something wrong. **catch-22** a difficult situation from which there is no escape because it involves conditions which conflict with each other. **catch up 1** succeed in reaching a person ahead. **2** do tasks which you should have done earlier.

catchment area noun **1** the area from which a hospital's patients or a school's pupils are drawn. **2** the area

from which rainfall flows into a river, lake, or reservoir.

catchphrase noun a well-known sentence or phrase.

catchword noun a word or phrase commonly used to sum up a concept.

catchy adjective (**catchier**, **catchiest**) (of a tune or phrase) appealing and easy to remember.

catechism /**kat**-i-ki-z'm/ noun a summary of the principles of Christian religion in the form of questions and answers, used for teaching.

categorical adjective completely clear and direct. ■ **categorically** adverb.

categorize or **categorise** verb (**categorizes**, **categorizing**, **categorized**) place in a category. ■ **categorization** noun.

category noun (plural **categories**) a class or group of people or things with shared characteristics.

cater verb **1** (**cater for**) provide food and drink at a social event. **2** (**cater for**) provide with what is needed. **3** (**cater for**) take into account. **4** (**cater to**) satisfy a need or demand. ■ **caterer** noun.

caterpillar noun a creature like a small worm with legs, which develops into a butterfly or moth.

caterwaul /**kat**-er-wawl/ verb make a shrill howling or wailing noise.

catgut noun material used for the strings of musical instruments, made of the dried intestines of sheep or horses.

catharsis /kuh-**thar**-siss/ noun the releasing of pent-up emotions through an experience like watching an exciting film. ■ **cathartic** adjective.

cathedral noun the principal church of a diocese (district).

Catherine wheel noun Brit. a firework in the form of a spinning coil.

catheter /**kath**-i-ter/ noun a tube that is inserted into a body cavity to drain fluid.

cathode /**kath**-ohd/ noun an electrode with a negative charge. □ **cath-**

ode ray tube a tube in which beams of electrons produce a luminous image on a screen, as in a television.

catholic adjective **1** including a wide variety of things. **2** (Catholic) Roman Catholic. noun (Catholic) a Roman Catholic. ■ **Catholicism** noun.

cation /kat-I-uhn/ noun an ion with a positive charge.

catkin noun a spike of small, soft flowers hanging from trees such as willow and hazel.

catnap noun a short sleep during the day.

catseye noun Brit. trademark each of a series of reflective studs marking the lanes or edges of a road.

catsuit noun a woman's close-fitting one-piece garment with trouser legs.

cattery noun (plural **catteries**) a place where cats are kept while their owners are away.

cattle plural noun cows, bulls, and oxen.

catty adjective (**cattier, cattiest**) spiteful.

catwalk noun **1** a narrow raised walkway. **2** a narrow platform along which models walk to display clothes.

Caucasian adjective **1** relating to peoples from Europe, western Asia, and parts of India and North Africa. **2** white-skinned. noun a Caucasian person.

caucus /kaw-kuhss/ noun (plural **caucuses**) **1** a meeting of a policy-making group of a political party. **2** a group of people within a larger organization.

caught past and past participle of **CATCH**.

caul /rhymes with ball/ noun a membrane that encloses an unborn baby in the womb.

cauldron (US spelling **caldron**) noun a large metal cooking pot.

cauliflower noun a vegetable with a large white edible flower head.

caulk (US spelling **calk**) noun a waterproof substance used to fill cracks and seal joins.

causal adjective relating to or being a cause. ■ **causally** adverb **causality** noun.

causation noun the process of causing an effect. ■ **causative** adjective.

cause noun **1** a person or thing that produces an effect. **2** a good reason for thinking or doing something. **3** a principle or movement. verb (**causes, causing, caused**) make something happen.

causeway noun a raised road or track across low or wet ground.

caustic adjective **1** able to burn through or wear away something by chemical action. **2** sarcastic in a hurtful way. □ caustic soda sodium hydroxide, used in industrial processes, such as soap-making.

cauterize or **cauterise** verb (**cauterizes, cauterizing, cauterized**) burn the area around a wound to stop bleeding or prevent infection.

caution noun **1** care taken to avoid danger or mistakes. **2** a warning to the public. **3** Law a formal warning given to someone who has committed a minor offence. verb **1** warn or advise someone. **2** give a legal caution to.

cautionary adjective acting as a warning.

cautious adjective taking care to avoid possible problems or dangers. ■ **cautiously** adverb.

cavalcade noun a procession of vehicles or people on horseback.

cavalier noun (Cavalier) a supporter of King Charles I in the English Civil War. adjective showing a lack of real concern.

cavalry noun (plural **cavalries**) (in the past) the part of the army that fought on horseback. ■ **cavalryman** noun.

cave noun a large natural hollow in the side of a hill or cliff, or underground. verb (**caves, caving, caved**) **1** (**caving**) exploration of caves as a sport. **2** (**cave in**) give way or collapse. **3** (**cave in**) give in to demands. ■ **caver** noun.

caveat /ka-vi-at/ noun a warning.

cavern noun a large cave.

cavernous /ka-ver-nuhss/ adjective huge, spacious, or gloomy.

caviar or **caviare** /ka-vi-ar/ noun the pickled roe of the sturgeon (a large fish).

cavil /ka-vuhl/ verb (cavils, cavilling, cavilled; US spelling cavils, caviling, caviled) make unnecessary complaints. noun an unnecessary complaint.

cavity noun (plural cavities) **1** a hollow space inside something solid. **2** a decayed part of a tooth.

cavort verb jump or dance around excitedly.

caw verb make a harsh cry.

cayenne /kay-en/ noun a hot-tasting red powder made from dried chillies.

CBE abbreviation Commander of the Order of the British Empire.

cc or **c.c.** abbreviation **1** carbon copy. **2** cubic centimetres.

CCTV abbreviation closed-circuit television.

CD abbreviation compact disc.

CD-ROM abbreviation a compact disc storing large amounts of information, used in a computer (*ROM* stands for 'read-only memory').

cease verb (ceases, ceasing, ceased) come or bring to an end; stop.

ceasefire noun a temporary period during a conflict when fighting stops.

ceaseless adjective not stopping. ■ **ceaselessly** adverb.

cedar noun a tall spreading evergreen tree.

cede verb (cedes, ceding, ceded) give up power or territory.

cedilla /si-dil-luh/ noun a mark (,) written under the letter c to show that it is pronounced like an s (e.g. *façade*).

ceilidh /kay-li/ noun a party with Scottish or Irish folk music and dancing.

ceiling noun **1** the top surface of a room. **2** a top limit set on prices, wages, or spending.

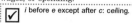
i before e except after c: ceiling.

celebrate verb (celebrates, celebrating, celebrated) mark an important occasion by doing something special. ■ **celebration** noun **celebratory** adjective.

celebrity noun (plural celebrities) **1** a famous person. **2** the state of being famous.

celeriac /suh-lair-i-ak/ noun a vegetable with a large edible root.

celerity /si-le-ri-ti/ noun old use speed of movement.

celery noun a vegetable with crisp juicy stalks.

celestial adjective **1** relating to heaven. **2** relating to the sky or outer space.

celibate /sel-i-buht/ adjective not married or in a sexual relationship. ■ **celibacy** noun.

cell noun **1** a small room for a prisoner, monk, or nun. **2** the smallest unit of a living organism. **3** a small political group that is part of a larger organization. **4** a device for producing electricity by chemical action or light.

cellar noun **1** a room below ground level, used for storage. **2** a stock of wine.

cello /chel-loh/ noun (plural cellos) an instrument like a large violin, held upright on the floor between the legs of the seated player. ■ **cellist** noun.

cellophane noun trademark a thin transparent wrapping material.

cellular adjective **1** relating to or made up of cells. **2** (of a mobile phone system) using a number of short-range radio stations to cover the area it serves.

cellulite noun fat that builds up under the skin, causing a dimpled effect.

celluloid noun a kind of transparent plastic formerly used for cinema film.

cellulose noun a substance found in all plant tissues, used in making paint, plastics, and fibres.

Celsius /**sel**-si-uhss/ noun a scale of temperature on which water freezes at 0° and boils at 100°.

Celt /kelt/ noun a member of a people who lived in Britain and elsewhere in Europe before the Romans arrived.

Celtic /**kel**-tik/ noun a group of languages including Irish, Scottish Gaelic, and Welsh. adjective relating to Celtic languages or to the Celts.

cement noun a powdery substance made by heating lime and clay, used in making mortar and concrete. verb **1** fix with cement. **2** strengthen.

cemetery noun (plural **cemeteries**) a large burial ground.

 -tery, not *-try* or *-tary*: cemetery.

cenotaph noun a monument built to honour soldiers killed in a war.

censer noun a container in which incense is burnt.

censor noun a person who examines material that is to be published and bans unacceptable parts. verb ban unacceptable parts of a document or film. ■ **censorship** noun.

censorious /sen-**sor**-i-uhss/ adjective severely critical.

censure verb (**censures**, **censuring**, **censured**) express strong disapproval of. noun strong disapproval or criticism.

ⓘ don't confuse **censure** with **censor**.

census noun (plural **censuses**) an official count of a population.

cent noun a unit of money equal to one hundredth of a dollar or other decimal currency unit.

centaur noun (in Greek mythology) a creature with a man's head, arms, and upper body and a horse's lower body and legs.

centenarian /sen-ti-**nair**-i-uhn/ noun a person who has reached one hundred years of age.

centenary /sen-**tee**-nuh-ri/ noun (plural **centenaries**) the hundredth anniversary of an event.

centennial adjective relating to a hundredth anniversary. noun a hundredth anniversary.

center US spelling of **CENTRE**.

centigrade adjective measured by the Celsius scale of temperature.

centilitre (US spelling **centiliter**) noun a metric unit equal to one hundredth of a litre.

centime /**son**-teem/ noun a unit of money equal to one hundredth of a franc.

centimetre (US spelling **centimeter**) noun a metric unit equal to one hundredth of a metre.

centipede noun an insect-like creature with a long, thin body and lots of legs.

central adjective **1** in or near the centre. **2** very important. □ **central heating** heating conducted from a boiler through pipes and radiators. **central nervous system** the system of nerve tissues in the brain and spinal cord in vertebrates. ■ **centrally** adverb.

centralize or **centralise** verb (**centralizes**, **centralizing**, **centralized**) bring under the control of a central authority. ■ **centralization** noun.

centre (US spelling **center**) noun **1** a point in the middle of something. **2** a place where an activity takes place. **3** a point from which something spreads or to which something is directed. verb (**centres**, **centring**, **centred**; US spelling **centers**, **centering**, **centered**) **1** place in the centre. **2** (**centre on** or **around**) have as a major concern or theme. □ **centre back** (or **centre half**) (in soccer) a defender who plays in the middle of the field. **centre forward** (in soccer) an attacker who plays in the middle of the field. **centre of gravity** the central point in an object, around which its mass is evenly distributed.

centrefold noun the two middle pages of a magazine, usually containing illustrations or a special feature.

centrepiece noun an item that is designed to have people's attention focused on it.

centrifugal force noun a force which appears to cause something travelling round a central point to fly outwards from its circular path.

centurion noun a commander of one hundred men in the army of ancient Rome.

century noun (plural **centuries**) **1** a period of one hundred years. **2** a batsman's score of a hundred runs in cricket. **3** a unit of a hundred men in the army of ancient Rome.

cephalic /si-**fal**-ik, ki-**fal**-ik/ adjective relating to the head.

ceramic adjective made of fired clay. noun (**ceramics**) the art of making ceramic articles.

cereal noun **1** a grass producing an edible grain, such as wheat, oats, maize, or rye. **2** a breakfast food made from the grain of cereals.

cerebellum /se-ri-**bel**-luhm/ noun (plural **cerebellums** or **cerebella**) the part of the brain at the back of the skull.

cerebral /**se**-ri-bruhl, suh-**ree**-bruhl/ adjective **1** relating to the brain. **2** intellectual rather than emotional or physical. □ **cerebral palsy** a condition in which a person has difficulty in controlling their muscles.

cerebrum /**se**-ri-bruhm/ noun (plural **cerebra**) the main, front, part of the brain.

ceremonial adjective relating to ceremonies. ■ **ceremonially** adverb.

ceremonious adjective done in a formal and grand way. ■ **ceremoniously** adverb.

ceremony noun (plural **ceremonies**) a formal occasion during which a set of special acts are performed. □ **stand on ceremony** behave formally.

cerise /suh-**reess**/ noun a light pinkish-red colour.

cerium /**seer**-i-uhm/ noun a silvery-white metallic element.

certain adjective **1** able to be relied on to happen or be the case. **2** completely sure about something. **3** specific but not directly named or stated. pronoun some but not all.

certainly adverb **1** without doubt; definitely. **2** yes.

certainty noun (plural **certainties**) **1** the state of being certain. **2** a fact that is true or an event that is definitely going to take place.

certifiable adjective **1** needing to be certified as insane. **2** able to be officially confirmed.

certificate noun **1** an official document recording a particular fact, event, or achievement. **2** an official classification given to a cinema film, saying which age group it is suitable for. ■ **certification** noun.

certify verb (**certifies, certifying, certified**) **1** declare or confirm in a certificate or other official document. **2** officially declare someone insane.

certitude noun a feeling of complete certainty.

cervical /**ser**-vi-k'l, ser-**vy**-k'l/ adjective relating to the cervix. □ **cervical smear** a specimen of cells taken from the neck of the womb and examined for signs of cancer.

cervix /**ser**-viks/ noun (plural **cervices** /**ser**-vi-seez/) the narrow neck-like passage between the lower end of the womb and the vagina.

Cesarean US spelling of **CAESAREAN**.

cessation noun the stopping of something.

cession noun the giving up of rights or territory by a state.

cesspool or **cesspit** noun an underground tank or covered pit where sewage is collected.

cetacean /si-**tay**-sh'n/ noun the name in zoology for a whale or dolphin.

cf abbreviation compare with.

> **i** short for Latin *confer*, meaning 'compare'.

CFC abbreviation chlorofluorocarbon, a gas used in refrigerators and aerosols that is harmful to the ozone layer.

CFE abbreviation College of Further Education.

chador /**chah**-dor/ noun a piece of dark cloth worn by Muslim women around the head and upper body.

chafe verb (**chafes, chafing, chafed**) **1** make something sore or worn by rubbing against it. **2** rub a part of the body to warm it. **3** become impatient because of restrictions.

chaff[1] noun husks of grain that have been separated from the seed.

chaff[2] verb tease someone.

chaffinch noun a finch with pink underparts and dark wings.

chagrin /sha-**grin**, **sha**-grin/ noun a feeling of disappointment or annoyance. verb (**be chagrined**) feel disappointed or annoyed.

chain noun **1** a series of connected metal links. **2** a connected series, set, or sequence. **3** a measure of length equal to 66 ft. verb fasten or restrain with a chain. □ **chain mail** armour made of small metal rings linked together. **chain reaction 1** a chemical reaction in which the products of the reaction cause further changes. **2** a series of events, each caused by the previous one. **chain-smoke** smoke cigarettes one after the other. **chain store** each of a series of shops owned by one firm.

chainsaw noun a power-driven saw with teeth set on a moving chain.

chair noun **1** a seat for one person, with a back and four legs. **2** the person in charge of a meeting or an organization. **3** a post as professor. verb act as chairperson of a meeting.

chairlift noun a lift for carrying skiers up and down a mountain, consisting of a series of chairs hung from a moving cable.

chairman or **chairwoman** noun a person in charge of a meeting or organization.

chairperson noun a person in charge of a meeting.

chaise longue /shayz **longg**/ noun (plural **chaises longues** /shayz **longg**/)

a sofa with a backrest at only one end.

chalet /**sha**-lay/ noun **1** a wooden house with overhanging eaves, found in the Swiss Alps. **2** a wooden cabin used by holidaymakers.

chalice /**cha**-liss/ noun a large cup or glass for wine.

chalk noun **1** a soft white limestone. **2** a similar substance made into sticks and used for drawing or writing. verb draw or write with chalk. □ **by a long chalk** by far. **chalk up 1** achieve something noteworthy. **2** (**chalk up to**) associate something with a particular cause. ■ **chalkiness** noun **chalky** adjective.

challenge noun **1** an invitation to someone to take part in a contest or to prove something. **2** a demanding task or situation. verb (**challenges, challenging, challenged**) **1** raise doubt as to whether something is true or genuine. **2** call on someone to fight or do something difficult. **3** (of a guard) call on someone to prove their identity. ■ **challenger** noun.

challenging adjective testing your abilities in an interesting way.

chamber noun **1** a large room used for formal or public events. **2** each of the houses of a parliament. **3** (**chambers**) rooms used by a barrister. **4** old use a bedroom. **5** a space or cavity inside something. **6** the part of a gun bore that contains the explosive. □ **chamber music** classical music played by a small group of musicians. **chamber pot** a bowl kept in a bedroom and used as a toilet.

chamberlain noun (in the past) a person who looked after the household of a king or queen, or a noble.

chambermaid noun a woman who cleans rooms in a hotel.

chameleon /kuh-**mee**-li-uhn/ noun a small lizard that can change colour to fit in with its surroundings.

chamfer /**sham**-fer/ verb (**chamfers, chamfering, chamfered**) (in carpentry) cut an angled edge on a piece of wood.

chamois /**sham**-wah/ noun (plural **chamois** /**sham**-wah, **sham**-wahz/) an antelope that lives in the mountains of southern Europe. □ **chamois leather** /**sham**-mi/ very soft leather made from the skin of sheep, goats, or deer.

chamomile or **camomile** /**kam**-uh-myl/ noun a plant with white and yellow flowers, used in herbal preparations and to flavour tea.

champ verb munch noisily. □ **champ at the bit** be very impatient.

champagne /sham-**payn**/ noun a white sparkling wine from the Champagne region of France.

champion noun **1** a person who has won a contest. **2** a person who argues or fights for a cause. verb argue or fight in support of a cause. adjective informal or dialect excellent.

championship noun a competition for the position of champion.

chance noun **1** (also **chances**) a possibility of something happening. **2** an opportunity. **3** occurrence without any obvious plan or cause: *they met by chance.* verb (**chances, chancing, chanced**) **1** happen to do something. **2** informal try something uncertain or dangerous. □ **on the off chance** just in case. **take a chance** (or **chances**) take a risk.

chancel /**chahn**-s'l/ noun the part of a church near the altar, where the choir sits.

chancellor noun **1** a senior state or legal official. **2** (**Chancellor**) the head of the government in some European countries. □ **Chancellor of the Exchequer** (in the UK) the government minister in charge of the country's finances.

chancer noun informal a person who makes the most of any opportunity.

chancy adjective (**chancier, chanciest**) informal uncertain and risky.

chandelier noun an ornamental hanging light with branches for candles or light bulbs.

chandler noun a dealer in supplies and equipment for ships and boats.

■ **chandlery** noun.

change verb (**changes, changing, changed**) **1** make or become different. **2** exchange a thing for something else. **3** (**change over**) move from one system or situation to another. **4** exchange a sum of money for the same sum in a different currency or different units. noun **1** a process through which something becomes different. **2** money returned as the balance of the sum paid or given in exchange for the same sum in larger units. **3** coins as opposed to banknotes. **4** replacement clothing. □ **change hands** pass to a different owner.

changeable adjective **1** tending to change in an unpredictable way. **2** able to be changed.

changeling noun a child believed to have been left by fairies in exchange for the parents' real child.

changeover noun a change from one system or situation to another.

channel noun **1** a wide stretch of water joining two seas. **2** a passage along which liquid flows. **3** a means of communication. **4** a band of frequencies used in radio and television broadcasting. **5** an electric circuit which acts as a path for a signal. **6** a passage that boats can pass through in a stretch of water. verb (**channels, channelling, channelled**; US spelling **channels, channeling, channeled**) **1** direct something towards a particular purpose. **2** cause to go along or through a particular channel.

chant noun **1** a repeated rhythmic phrase that is called out or sung to music. **2** a tune to which the words of psalms are fitted by singing several syllables or words to the same note. verb say, shout, or sing in a chant.

Chanukkah ⇒ **HANUKKAH**.

chaos noun complete confusion and disorder.

chaotic /kay-**ot**-ik/ adjective in a state of complete confusion and disorder.
■ **chaotically** adverb.

chap noun informal a man or boy.

chapatti /chuh-**pah**-ti, chuh-**pat**-ti/

noun (plural **chapattis**) (in Indian cookery) a flat cake of wholemeal bread.

chapel noun 1 a small building or room used for prayers. **2** a part of a large church with its own altar.

chaperone /shap-uh-rohn/ **noun** an older woman in charge of an unmarried girl at social occasions. **verb** (**chaperones, chaperoning, chaperoned**) accompany and look after.

chaplain noun a minister of the church attached to a chapel in an institution or military unit, or a private house. ■ **chaplaincy** noun.

chapped adjective (of the skin) cracked and sore through exposure to cold weather.

chapter noun 1 a main division of a book. **2** a particular period in history or in a person's life. **3** the group of people in charge of a cathedral or other religious community. **4** chiefly N. Amer. a local branch of a society.

char¹ verb (**chars, charring, charred**) partially burn something so as to blacken the surface.

char² noun a woman employed as a cleaner in a private house.

char³ noun informal tea.

character noun 1 the particular qualities that make a person or thing an individual and different from others. **2** strong personal qualities such as courage and determination. **3** a person's good reputation. **4** a person in a novel, play, or film. **5** informal an eccentric or amusing person. **6** a printed or written letter or symbol. ■ **characterful** adjective **characterless** adjective.

characteristic adjective typical of a particular person or thing. **noun** a quality typical of a person or thing. ■ **characteristically** adverb.

characterize or **characterise verb** (**characterizes, characterizing, characterized**) **1** describe the character of. **2** be typical of. ■ **characterization** noun.

charade /shuh-**rahd**/ **noun 1** a pretence that something is true when it is clearly not. **2** (**charades**) a game of guessing a word or phrase from clues that are acted out.

charcoal noun 1 a form of carbon obtained when wood is heated in the absence of air. **2** a dark grey–black colour.

chard noun a vegetable with large leaves and thick leaf stalks.

charge verb (**charges, charging, charged**) **1** ask an amount as a price. **2** formally accuse someone of something. **3** rush forward in an attack. **4** (**charge with**) give someone a task or responsibility. **5** store electrical energy in a battery. **6** load or fill a container, gun, etc. **7** fill with an emotion or quality. **noun 1** a price asked. **2** a formal accusation. **3** responsibility for care or control. **4** a person or thing handed over to someone's care. **5** a headlong rush forward. **6** the electricity naturally existing in a substance. **7** energy stored chemically in a battery. **8** a quantity of explosive needed to fire a gun. □ **charge card** a kind of credit card issued by a large shop. ■ **chargeable** adjective.

chargé d'affaires /shar-zhay da-**fair**/ **noun** (plural **chargés d'affaires** /shar-zhay da-**fair**/) **1** an ambassador's deputy. **2** the diplomatic representative of a state in a minor country.

charger noun 1 a device for charging a battery. **2** a strong horse formerly ridden by a knight or mounted soldier.

chargrill verb grill food quickly at a very high heat.

chariot noun a two-wheeled horse-drawn vehicle, used in ancient warfare and racing. ■ **charioteer** noun.

charisma /kuh-**riz**-muh/ **noun** attractiveness that inspires admiration or enthusiasm in other people. ■ **charismatic** adjective.

charitable adjective 1 relating to help given to people in need. **2** showing kindness and understanding when judging others. ■ **charitably** adverb.

charity noun (plural **charities**) **1** an organization set up to help people in need. **2** the giving of money or other help to people in need. **3** kindness and understanding shown when judging others.

charlatan /shar-luh-tuhn/ noun a person who claims to have knowledge or skills that they do not really have.

charm noun **1** the power or quality of delighting or fascinating others. **2** a small ornament worn on a necklace or bracelet. **3** an object or saying believed to have magic power. verb **1** delight someone greatly. **2** use your charm in order to influence someone. **3** (**charmed**) unusually lucky as if protected by magic. ■ **charmer** noun **charmless** adjective.

charming adjective **1** delightful; attractive. **2** very likeable. ■ **charmingly** adverb.

charnel house noun a place formerly used for keeping dead bodies and bones in.

chart noun **1** a sheet of paper on which information is displayed in the form of a table, graph, or diagram. **2** a map used for navigation by sea or air. **3** (**the charts**) a weekly listing of the current best-selling pop records. verb **1** make a map of. **2** follow progress or record something on a chart.

charter noun **1** an official document stating that a ruler or government allows an institution to exist and setting out its rights. **2** a document listing and describing the functions of an organization. **3** the hiring of an aircraft, ship, or vehicle. verb **1** hire an aircraft, ship, or vehicle. **2** grant a charter to. □ **charter flight** a flight by an aircraft that has been hired for a specific journey.

chartered adjective (of an accountant, engineer, etc.) qualified as a member of a professional institution that has a royal charter.

chary /chair-i/ adjective (**charier**, **chariest**) cautiously hesitating.

chase¹ verb (**chases**, **chasing**, **chased**) **1** go after someone in order to catch them. **2** rush or hurry. **3** try to make contact with or get hold of.

noun **1** an act of chasing. **2** (**the chase**) hunting as a sport.

chase² verb (**chases**, **chasing**, **chased**) engrave metal.

chaser noun informal a strong alcoholic drink taken after a weaker one.

chasm noun **1** a deep crack in the earth. **2** a very big difference between two people or their opinions.

chassis /sha-si/ noun (plural **chassis** /sha-siz/) the framework forming the base of a vehicle.

chaste adjective **1** having sex only with your husband or wife, or not at all. **2** not expressing sexual interest; demure and modest. ■ **chastely** adverb.

chasten /chay-s'n/ verb make someone subdued and less confident about something.

chastise verb (**chastises**, **chastising**, **chastised**) tell someone off in a very strict manner.

chastity noun the state of being chaste.

chasuble /chaz-yuu-b'l/ noun a long sleeveless garment worn by a priest over other robes.

chat verb (**chats**, **chatting**, **chatted**) **1** talk informally. **2** (**chat up**) informal talk flirtatiously to. noun an informal conversation.

chateau /sha-toh/ noun (plural **chateaux** /sha-toh, sha-tohz/) a large French country house or castle.

chattel /chat-t'l/ noun a personal possession.

chatter verb (**chatters**, **chattering**, **chattered**) **1** talk informally about unimportant matters. **2** (of a person's teeth) click together continuously from cold or fear. noun **1** unimportant talk. **2** a series of short high-pitched sounds. ■ **chatty** adjective.

chatterbox noun informal a person who likes to chatter.

chauffeur noun a person who is employed to drive someone around in a car. verb be a driver for.

chauvinism /shoh-vin-iz'm/ noun **1** an aggressive belief that your own country or group is better than others. **2** the belief held by some men that men are superior to women. ■ **chauvinist** adjective & noun **chauvinistic** adjective.

cheap adjective **1** low in price. **2** charging low prices. **3** inexpensive and of poor quality. **4** having no value because achieved in a bad way. ■ **cheaply** adverb **cheapness** noun.

cheapen verb lower the quality or value of something.

cheapskate noun informal a person who hates to spend money.

cheat verb **1** act dishonestly or unfairly to gain an advantage. **2** deprive someone of something by tricking them. noun **1** a person who cheats. **2** an act of cheating.

check¹ verb **1** examine the accuracy, quality, or condition of. **2** stop or slow the progress of. **3** Chess move a piece or pawn to a square where it directly attacks the opposing king. noun **1** an act of checking accuracy, quality, or condition. **2** a control or restraint. **3** Chess a position in which a king is directly threatened. **4** N. Amer. the bill in a restaurant. □ **check in** register at a hotel or airport. **check out 1** settle your hotel bill before leaving. **2** find out about. **check-up** an examination by a doctor or dentist. **check up on** investigate. **in check** under control.

check² noun a pattern of small squares. adjective (also **checked**) having a pattern of small squares.

check³ US spelling of **CHEQUE**.

checker US spelling of **CHEQUER**.

checklist noun a list of items to be considered or things to be done.

checkmate Chess noun a position of check from which a king cannot escape. verb put a king into checkmate.

checkout noun a point at which goods are paid for in a supermarket or large shop.

checkpoint noun a barrier where security checks are carried out on travellers.

Cheddar noun a kind of firm, smooth cheese.

cheek noun **1** the area on either side of the face below the eye. **2** either of the buttocks. **3** impertinent or bold behaviour. verb speak impertinently to. □ **cheek by jowl** close together. **turn the other cheek** stop yourself from fighting back.

cheekbone noun the rounded bone below the eye.

cheeky adjective (**cheekier**, **cheekiest**) showing a cheerful lack of respect. ■ **cheekily** adverb.

cheep noun a squeaky cry made by a young bird. verb make a cheep.

cheer verb **1** shout for joy or in praise or encouragement. **2** praise or encourage a person or group with shouts. **3** (**cheer up**) make or become less miserable. **4** give comfort to. noun **1** a shout of joy, encouragement, or praise. **2** (also **good cheer**) cheerfulness; optimism.

cheerful adjective **1** noticeably happy and optimistic. **2** bright and pleasant. ■ **cheerfully** adverb **cheerfulness** noun.

cheerleader noun (in North America) a girl belonging to a group that performs organized chanting and dancing at sporting events.

cheerless adjective gloomy; depressing.

cheers exclamation informal **1** said before having an alcoholic drink with other people. **2** said to express thanks or on parting.

cheery adjective (**cheerier**, **cheeriest**) happy and optimistic. ■ **cheerily** adverb.

cheese¹ noun a food made from the pressed curds of milk. □ **cheese-paring** excessive care with money; meanness.

cheese² verb (**be cheesed off**) informal be irritated or bored.

cheesecake noun a rich, sweet tart having a thick topping made with cream cheese.

cheesecloth noun thin, loosely woven cotton cloth.

cheesy adjective (**cheesier**, **cheesiest**) **1** resembling cheese. **2** informal sentimental or of poor quality.

cheetah noun a large spotted cat that can run very fast, found in Africa and parts of Asia.

chef noun a professional cook in a restaurant or hotel.

chemical adjective relating to chemistry or chemicals. noun a substance which has been artificially prepared or purified. ■ **chemically** adverb.

chemise /shuh-**meez**/ noun a woman's loose-fitting dress, nightdress, or undergarment.

chemist noun 1 a person who is authorized to give out or sell medicines. 2 a shop where medicines, toiletries, and cosmetics are sold. 3 a person who studies chemistry.

chemistry noun 1 the branch of science concerned with the nature of substances and how they react with each other. 2 attraction or interaction between two people.

chemotherapy noun the treatment of cancer with drugs.

chenille /shuh-**neel**/ noun a fabric with a long velvety pile.

cheque (US spelling **check**) noun a written order to a bank to pay a stated sum from an account to a specified person. □ **cheque card** a card issued by a bank to guarantee payment of a customer's cheques.

chequer (US spelling **checker**) noun 1 (**chequers**) a pattern of alternately coloured squares. 2 (**checkers**) N. Amer. the game of draughts. verb 1 (be **chequered**) be divided into or marked with chequers. 2 (**chequered**) marked by periods of varying fortune: *a chequered career.*

cherish verb 1 protect and care for someone lovingly. 2 keep a thought or memory in your mind.

cheroot /shuh-**root**/ noun a cigar with both ends open.

cherry noun (plural **cherries**) 1 a small, round red fruit with a stone. 2 a bright red colour.

cherub noun 1 (plural **cherubim** or **cherubs**) a type of angel, shown in art as a chubby child with wings. 2 (plural **cherubs**) a beautiful or innocent-looking child. ■ **cherubic** adjective /chuh-**roo**-bik/.

chervil noun a herb with an aniseed flavour.

chess noun a board game for two players, the object of which is to put the opponent's king under a direct attack, leading to checkmate.

chest noun 1 the front of a person's body between the neck and the stomach. 2 a large, strong box for storing or transporting things. □ **chest of drawers** a piece of furniture fitted with a set of drawers.

chesterfield noun a sofa with a back of the same height as the arms.

chestnut noun 1 an edible nut with a glossy brown shell. 2 a deep reddish-brown colour. 3 (**old chestnut**) a joke, story, or subject that has become uninteresting through being repeated too often.

chesty adjective informal having a lot of catarrh in the lungs.

chevron noun a V-shaped line or stripe, worn on the sleeve of a military uniform to show rank or length of service.

chew verb 1 grind food with the teeth to make it easier to swallow. 2 (**chew over**) discuss or consider something at length. noun 1 an act of chewing. 2 a sweet meant for chewing. □ **chewing gum** flavoured gum for chewing. **chew the fat** informal chat with someone in a leisurely way.

chewy adjective needing a lot of chewing.

chic /sheek/ adjective (**chicer, chicest**) smart and fashionable.

chicane /shi-**kayn**/ noun a sharp double bend in a motor-racing track.

chicanery noun the use of cunning tricks to get what you want.

chick noun 1 a newly hatched young bird. 2 informal a young woman.

chicken noun 1 a large domestic bird kept for its eggs or meat. 2 informal a coward. adjective informal cowardly. verb (**chicken out**) informal be too scared to do something.

chickenpox noun a disease causing itchy inflamed pimples.

chickpea noun a yellowish seed eaten as a pulse.

chickweed noun a small white-flowered plant that grows as a garden weed.

chicory noun (plural **chicories**) a plant whose leaves are eaten and whose root can be used instead of coffee.

chide verb (**chides**, **chiding**, **chided**) tell someone off.

chief noun a leader or ruler. adjective **1** having the highest rank or authority. **2** most important.

chiefly adverb mainly; mostly.

chieftain noun the leader of a people or clan.

chiffon noun a light, see-through fabric.

chignon /**sheen**-yon/ noun a knot or coil of hair arranged on the back of a woman's head.

chihuahua /chi-**wah**-wuh/ noun a very small breed of dog with smooth hair and large eyes.

chilblain noun a painful, itching swelling on a hand or foot caused by exposure to cold.

child noun (plural **children**) **1** a young human being below the age of full physical development. **2** a son or daughter of any age. ∎ **childhood** noun **childless** adjective.

childbirth noun the process of giving birth to a baby.

childish adjective **1** like a child. **2** silly and immature.

childlike adjective (of an adult) innocent and unsuspecting like a child.

childminder noun Brit. a person who is paid to look after other people's children.

chill noun **1** an unpleasant feeling of coldness. **2** a feverish cold. verb **1** make cold. **2** worry or frighten someone. **3** (usu. **chill out**) informal relax. adjective unpleasantly cold.

chilli noun (plural **chillies**) a small hot-tasting pepper, used in cookery and as a spice. □ **chilli con carne** a stew of minced beef and beans flavoured with chilli.

chilly adjective (**chillier**, **chilliest**) **1** too cold to be comfortable. **2** unfriendly.

chime noun **1** a tuneful ringing sound. **2** a bell, bar, or tube used in a set to produce chimes when struck. verb (**chimes**, **chiming**, **chimed**) **1** (of a bell or clock) make a tuneful ringing sound. **2** (**chime in**) interrupt a conversation with a remark.

chimera or **chimaera** /ky-**meer**-uh/ noun **1** (in Greek mythology) a female monster with a lion's head, a goat's body, and a serpent's tail. **2** an impossible hope or dream.

chimerical /ky-**merr**-i-k'l/ adjective not real or possible.

chimney noun (plural **chimneys**) a pipe or channel which takes smoke and gases up from a fire or furnace. □ **chimney breast** the part of an inside wall that surrounds a chimney.

chimpanzee noun an ape native to west and central Africa.

chin noun the part of the face below the mouth.

china noun **1** a fine white ceramic material. **2** household objects made from china. □ **china clay** a soft white clay used for making porcelain and china.

chinchilla /chin-**chil**-luh/ noun a small South American rodent with soft grey fur and a long bushy tail.

Chinese noun (plural **Chinese**) **1** the language of China. **2** a person from China. adjective relating to China.

chink[1] noun **1** a narrow opening or crack. **2** a beam of light entering through a chink.

chink[2] verb make a high-pitched ringing sound. noun a high-pitched ringing sound.

chinos /**chee**-nohz/ plural noun casual trousers made from a smooth cotton fabric.

chintz noun patterned cotton fabric with a glazed finish, used for curtains and upholstery.

chintzy adjective **1** resembling chintz. **2** colourful but fussy and tasteless.

chip noun **1** a small piece cut or broken off from something hard. **2** Brit. a long, thin piece of deep-fried potato. **3** (also **potato chip**) chiefly N. Amer. a potato crisp. **4** a microchip. **5** a counter used in some gambling games to represent money. verb (**chips**, **chipping**, **chipped**) **1** cut or break off a small piece from something hard. **2** (**chip away**) gradually make something smaller or weaker. **3** (**chip in**) add a contribution.

chipboard noun material made from compressed wood chips and resin.

chipmunk noun a burrowing squirrel with light and dark stripes running down the body.

chipolata noun Brit. a small, thin sausage.

chipper adjective informal cheerful and lively.

chipping noun Brit. a small fragment of stone, wood, or similar material.

chiropody /ki-**rop**-uh-di/ noun care and treatment of the feet. ■ **chiropodist** noun.

chiropractic /ky-roh-**prak**-tik/ noun a system of complementary medicine based on the manipulation of the joints, especially those of the spinal column. ■ **chiropractor** noun.

chirp verb (of a small bird) utter a short, high-pitched sound. noun a chirping sound.

chirpy adjective (**chirpier**, **chirpiest**) informal cheerful and lively.

chisel noun a hand tool with a narrow blade, used with a hammer to cut or shape wood, stone, or metal. verb (**chisels**, **chiselling**, **chiselled**; US spelling **chisels**, **chiseling**, **chiseled**) **1** cut or shape something with a chisel. **2** (**chiselled**) (of the features of a man's face) strongly defined.

chit noun a short note recording a sum of money owed.

chivalrous adjective acting in a polite and charming way towards women. ■ **chivalrously** adverb.

chivalry noun **1** an honourable code of behaviour adopted by knights in medieval times. **2** polite behaviour by a man towards women.

chives plural noun a plant with long, thin leaves that are used as a herb.

chivvy verb (**chivvies**, **chivvying**, **chivvied**) keep telling someone to do something.

chloride noun a compound of chlorine with another substance.

chlorinate verb (**chlorinates**, **chlorinating**, **chlorinated**) treat water with chlorine.

chlorine /**klor**-een/ noun a chemical element in the form of a green gas, which is sometimes added as a disinfectant to water.

chloroform noun a liquid used to dissolve things and formerly as an anaesthetic. verb use chloroform to make someone unconscious.

chlorophyll /**klo**-ruh-fil/ noun a green pigment in plants which allows them to absorb sunlight and use it in photosynthesis.

chloroplast noun a structure in green plant cells which contains chlorophyll and in which photosynthesis takes place.

chock noun a wedge or block placed against a wheel to prevent it from moving.

chock-a-block adjective informal crammed full.

chocolate noun **1** a dark brown sweet food made from roasted cacao seeds. **2** a drink made by mixing milk or water with chocolate.

choice noun **1** an act of choosing. **2** the right or ability to choose. **3** a range from which to choose. **4** something that has been chosen. adjective of very good quality.

choir noun **1** an organized group of singers. **2** the part of a church between the altar and the nave, used by the choir.

choirboy noun a boy who sings in a church choir.

choke verb (**chokes**, **choking**, **choked**) **1** prevent someone from breathing by blocking their throat or depriving them of air. **2** have trouble breathing. **3** (be choked with) be blocked or filled with. **noun** a valve used to reduce the amount of air in the fuel mixture of a petrol engine.

choker noun a close-fitting necklace or ornamental neckband.

cholera /ko-luh-ruh/ noun an infectious disease causing severe vomiting and diarrhoea.

choleric /ko-luh-rik/ adjective literary irritable.

cholesterol /kuh-less-tuh-rol/ noun a substance in the body which is believed to cause disease of the arteries when there is too much of it in the blood.

chomp verb munch or chew noisily or vigorously.

choose verb (chooses, choosing, chose; past participle chosen) pick something out as being the closest to what you want or need.

choosy adjective (choosier, choosiest) informal very careful in making a choice.

chop verb (chops, chopping, chopped) **1** cut something into pieces with a knife or axe. **2** hit with a short, downward stroke. noun **1** a downward cutting movement. **2** (the chop) Brit. informal the cancellation or end of something. **3** a thick slice of meat cut from or including the rib bone. □ **chop and change** Brit. informal keep changing your opinions or behaviour.

chopper noun **1** Brit. a short axe with a large blade. **2** informal a helicopter.

choppy adjective (of the sea) having many small waves.

chopstick noun each of a pair of thin, tapered sticks used by the Chinese and Japanese to eat with.

choral adjective sung by a choir or chorus.

chorale noun a simple, stately hymn tune.

chord noun a group of three or more notes sounded together in harmony.

chore noun an unpleasant or tedious job or task.

choreograph /ko-ri-uh-grahf/ verb compose the sequence of steps for a ballet or dance routine. ■ **choreographer** noun **choreography** noun.

chorister noun a choirboy or choirgirl.

chortle verb (chortles, chortling, chortled) chuckle merrily.

chorus noun (plural choruses) **1** a part of a song which is repeated after each verse. **2** something said at the same time by many people. **3** a group of singers or dancers performing together in a supporting role in an opera, musical, etc. verb (choruses, chorusing, chorused) (of a group of people) say the same thing at the same time.

chose past of **CHOOSE**.

chosen past participle of **CHOOSE**.

choux pastry /shoo/ noun very light pastry, used for eclairs and profiteroles.

Christ noun the title given to Jesus.

christen verb give a name to a baby while it is being baptized.

Christian adjective based on or believing in the life and teaching of Jesus Christ. noun a person who follows the religion based on the teachings of Jesus Christ. □ **Christian name** a person's first name.

Christianity noun the religion based on Jesus Christ and his teachings.

Christmas noun (plural Christmases) the annual Christian festival celebrating the birth of Jesus Christ, held on 25 December. □ **Christmas tree** an evergreen tree decorated with lights and ornaments at Christmas.

chromatic adjective **1** Music using notes that do not belong to the key in which the passage is written. **2** Music going up or down by semitones. **3** relating to or produced by colour.

chrome noun a hard, bright metal coating made from chromium.

chromium noun a hard white metallic element.

chromosome noun a thread-like

structure found in the nuclei of most living cells, carrying genetic information in the form of genes.

chronic adjective **1** (of an illness or problem) lasting for a long time. **2** having a long-lasting illness or bad habit. **3** Brit. informal very bad. ■ **chronically** adverb.

chronicle noun a record of historical events made in the order in which they happened. verb (**chronicles, chronicling, chronicled**) record a series of events in detail. ■ **chronicler** noun.

chronological adjective **1** relating to the time and order in which things happen. **2** (of a record of events) starting with the earliest and following the order in which they occurred. ■ **chronologically** adverb.

chronology /kruh-**nol**-uh-ji/ noun (plural **chronologies**) **1** the study of records to establish the dates of past events. **2** the arrangement of events or dates in the order of their occurrence.

chronometer noun an instrument for measuring time.

chrysalis /**kriss**-uh-liss/ noun (plural **chrysalises**) a butterfly or moth when it is changing from a larva to the adult form, inside a hard case.

chrysanthemum /kri-**santh**-i-muhm/ noun (plural **chrysanthemums**) a garden plant with brightly coloured flowers.

chub noun a thick-bodied river fish.

chubby adjective (**chubbier, chubbiest**) plump and rounded.

chuck[1] verb informal throw something carelessly or casually.

chuck[2] verb touch someone playfully under the chin.

chuckle verb (**chuckles, chuckling, chuckled**) laugh quietly or inwardly. noun a quiet laugh.

chuff verb (of a steam engine) move with a regular puffing sound.

chuffed adjective Brit. informal very pleased.

chug verb (**chugs, chugging, chugged**) (of a vehicle) move slowly with a loud, regular sound.

chum noun informal a close friend. ■ **chummy** adjective.

chump noun informal a silly person.

chunk noun a thick, solid piece. ■ **chunky** adjective.

church noun **1** a building where Christians go to worship. **2** (**Church**) a particular Christian organization. **3** (**the Church**) people within the Christian faith.

churchyard noun an enclosed area surrounding a church.

churlish adjective unfriendly and rude. ■ **churlishly** adverb.

churn noun **1** a machine for making butter by shaking milk or cream. **2** a large metal milk can. verb **1** shake milk or cream in a churn to produce butter. **2** (of liquid) move about vigorously. **3** (**churn out**) produce something mechanically and in large quantities.

chute noun **1** a sloping channel for moving things to a lower level. **2** a slide into a swimming pool.

chutney noun (plural **chutneys**) a spicy sauce made of fruits or vegetables with vinegar, spices, and sugar.

chutzpah /**khuuts**-puh/ noun informal shameless audacity.

CIA abbreviation (in the US) Central Intelligence Agency.

ciabatta /chuh-**bah**-tuh/ noun a flat Italian bread made with olive oil.

cicada /si-**kah**-duh/ noun an insect which makes a shrill droning noise.

CID abbreviation Criminal Investigation Department.

cider noun an alcoholic drink made from apple juice.

cigar noun a cylinder of tobacco rolled in tobacco leaves for smoking.

cigarette noun a cylinder of finely cut tobacco rolled in paper for smoking.

cilium /**sil**-i-uhm/ noun (plural **cilia** /**sil**-i-uh/) a microscopic hair-like structure, occurring on the surface of certain cells.

WORD FORMATION

-cide

-cide is used with the meaning:

1 'the killing of another', as in:

genocide	the killing of a large number of a particular people
homicide	the killing of a person; murder
infanticide	the killing of a baby
suicide	intentional killing of yourself.

2 'a substance used to destroy plant or animal life', for example:

fungicide	something used to destroy fungi
herbicide	something used to destroy vegetation
pesticide	something used to destroy pests.

-cide comes from the Latin word *caedere*, meaning 'to kill'.

cinch noun informal **1** a very easy task. **2** a certainty.

cinder noun a piece of partly burnt coal or wood.

cine adjective relating to or used for the making of films.

cinema noun Brit. **1** a theatre where films are shown. **2** the production of films as an art or industry.

cinematic adjective relating to the cinema, or like a film.

cinematography noun the skilled use of the camera in film-making. ∎ **cinematographer** noun.

cinnamon noun a spice made from the bark of an Asian tree.

cipher or **cypher** noun **1** a code. **2** a key to a code. **3** an unimportant person or thing. verb (**ciphers, ciphering, ciphered**) put a message into code.

circa /**ser**-kuh/ preposition approximately.

circadian /ser-**kay**-di-uhn/ adjective (of biological processes) happening on a twenty-four-hour cycle.

circle noun **1** a round flat shape of which the edge is at the same distance from the centre all the way round. **2** a group of people or things forming a circle. **3** a curved upper tier of seats in a theatre. verb (**circles, circling, circled**) **1** move or be placed all the way around. **2** draw a line around.

circuit noun **1** a roughly circular line, route, or movement. **2** Brit. a track used for motor racing. **3** a system of components forming a complete path for an electric current. **4** a series of sporting events or entertainments. verb move all the way around.

circuitous /ser-**kyoo**-i-tuhss/ adjective (of a route) long and indirect.

circuitry noun (plural **circuitries**) electric circuits collectively.

circular adjective **1** having the form of a circle. **2** (of a letter or advertisement) for distribution to a large number of people. noun a circular letter or advertisement.

circulate verb (**circulates, circulating, circulated**) **1** move continuously through a closed system or area. **2** pass from place to place or person to person.

circulation noun **1** movement through a system or area. **2** the continuous movement of blood round the body. **3** the spreading or passing of something from one person or place to another. **4** the number of copies of a newspaper or magazine sold.

circumcise verb (**circumcises, circumcising, circumcised**) **1** cut off a boy's or man's foreskin. **2** cut off a girl's or woman's clitoris. ∎ **circumcision** noun.

circumference noun **1** the boundary which encloses a circle. **2** the distance around something.

circumflex noun a mark (^) placed over a vowel in some languages to show a change in its sound.

circumlocution noun a way of saying something which uses more words than are necessary.

circumnavigate verb (circumnavigates, circumnavigating, circumnavigated) sail all the way around. ■ circumnavigation noun.

circumscribe verb (circumscribes, circumscribing, circumscribed) restrict the freedom or movements of.

circumspect adjective thoughtful and cautious about something.

circumstance noun **1** the facts and conditions that are connected with an event or action. **2** things that happen that are beyond your control. **3** (circumstances) the practical things that affect a person's life.

circumstantial adjective (of evidence) consisting of facts that make something seem likely but do not prove it. ■ circumstantially adverb.

circumvent /ser-kuhm-vent/ verb find a way around an obstacle.

circus noun (plural circuses) a travelling group of entertainers, including acrobats, clowns, and people who perform with trained animals.

cirrhosis /si-roh-siss/ noun a disease of the liver.

cirrus /sir-ruhss/ noun (plural cirri /sir-rI/) cloud forming wispy streaks high in the sky.

CIS abbreviation Commonwealth of Independent States.

cistern noun **1** a tank connected to a toilet, in which the water used for flushing it is stored. **2** an underground reservoir for rainwater.

citadel noun a fortress protecting or overlooking a city.

citation noun **1** a quotation from a book or author. **2** an official mention of someone who has done something deserving praise.

cite verb (cites, citing, cited) make a quotation from a book or author.

citizen noun **1** a person who is legally recognized as being a member of a country. **2** an inhabitant of a town or city. ■ citizenship noun.

citric acid noun a sharp-tasting acid present in the juice of lemons and other sour fruits.

citrus noun (plural citruses) a fruit of a group that includes the lemon, lime, orange, and grapefruit.

city noun (plural cities) **1** a large town, in particular (Brit.) a town that has been created a city by charter and contains a cathedral. **2** (the City) the part of London that is a centre of finance and business. □ city state a city that forms an independent state.

civet /siv-it/ noun **1** a cat native to Africa and Asia. **2** a strong perfume obtained from the civet.

civic adjective having to do with a city or town.

civil adjective **1** relating to the lives of ordinary people rather than to military or church matters. **2** (of a court) dealing with personal legal matters rather than criminal offences. **3** polite; courteous. □ civil engineer an engineer who designs public roads, bridges, dams, etc. civil liberties a person's rights to freedom of action and speech within the law. civil servant a person who works in the civil service. civil service the departments that carry out the work of the government. civil war a war between groups of people within the same country. ■ civilly adverb.

civilian noun a person who is not a member of the armed services or the police force. adjective relating to a civilian.

civility noun (plural civilities) politeness in behaviour or speech.

civilization or **civilisation** noun **1** an advanced stage of human development in which people in a society behave well towards each other and share a common culture. **2** the society, culture, and way of life of a particular area or period.

civilize or **civilise** verb (civilizes, civilizing, civilized) **1** bring a person or group to an advanced stage of social development. **2** (civilized) polite and good-mannered.

CJD abbreviation Creutzfeldt–Jakob disease, a fatal disease affecting the brain, possibly linked to BSE.

cl abbreviation centilitre.

clack verb make a sharp sound like that of a hard object striking another. noun a clacking sound.

clad adjective **1** clothed. **2** fitted with cladding.

cladding noun a protective or insulating covering or coating.

claim verb **1** say that something is true although you are not able to prove it. **2** request something that you believe you have a right to. **3** call for someone's attention. **4** ask for money under the terms of an insurance policy. **5** cause the loss of someone's life. noun **1** a statement that something is true. **2** a statement requesting something that you believe you have a right to. **3** a request for compensation under the terms of an insurance policy. ■ claimant noun.

clairvoyant noun a person who claims that they can see into the future or that they can communicate mentally with people who are dead or far away. adjective claiming to have these powers. ■ clairvoyance noun.

clam noun a large shellfish with a hinged shell. verb (clams, clamming, clammed) (clam up) informal suddenly stop talking about something.

clamber verb (clambers, clambering, clambered) climb or move using your hands and feet.

clammy adjective (clammier, clammiest) **1** unpleasantly damp and sticky. **2** (of air) cold and damp.

clamour (US spelling clamor) noun **1** a loud and confused noise. **2** a loud protest or demand. verb make a clamour. ■ clamorous adjective.

clamp noun **1** a brace, band, or clasp for holding something tightly. **2** a device placed around the wheel of an unlawfully parked car to prevent it being driven away. verb **1** fasten or hold with a clamp. **2** (clamp down) suppress or prevent something. **3** fit a wheel clamp to a car.

clan noun a group of families, especially in the Scottish Highlands.

clandestine /klan-**dess**-tin/ adjective done secretly. ■ clandestinely adverb.

clang noun a loud metallic sound. verb make a clang.

clank noun a sharp sound like that of pieces of metal being struck together. verb make a clank.

clannish adjective tending to exclude people outside the group.

clap verb (claps, clapping, clapped) **1** bring the palms of your hands together loudly and repeatedly to show that you approve of something. **2** slap someone encouragingly on the back. **3** suddenly place a hand over a part of your face as a gesture of dismay. noun **1** an act of clapping. **2** a sudden loud sound of thunder. □ clapped-out informal worn out from age or heavy use.

clapper noun the moving part inside a bell.

clapperboard noun a pair of hinged boards that are struck together at the beginning of filming so that the picture and sound can be matched.

claret /**kla**-ruht/ noun a red wine from Bordeaux in France.

clarify verb (clarifies, clarifying, clarified) **1** make easier to understand. **2** melt butter to separate out the impurities. ■ clarification noun.

clarinet noun a woodwind instrument with holes that are stopped by keys. ■ clarinettist (US spelling clarinetist) noun.

clarion /**kla**-ri-uhn/ noun historical a war trumpet. □ clarion call a loud, clear call for action.

clarity noun **1** the quality of being clear and easily understood. **2** transparency or purity.

clash verb **1** come into violent conflict. **2** disagree or be at odds. **3** (of colours) not go well together. **4** (of

Clause

A clause is a group of words that includes a verb. If it makes complete sense by itself, it is known as a main clause, e.g. *the sun came out.* Otherwise it must be attached to a main clause; it is then known as a subordinate clause, e.g. *when the sun came out,* we went outside.

events) occur inconveniently at the same time. **5** strike metal objects together, producing a loud harsh sound. **noun** an act or sound of clashing.

clasp verb 1 grasp tightly with your hand. **2** place your arms tightly around. **3** fasten with a clasp. **noun 1** a device with interlocking parts used for fastening. **2** an act of clasping. ☐ **clasp knife** a knife with a blade that folds into the handle.

class noun 1 a set or category of things that have something in common. **2** the division of people into different groups according to their social status. **3** a group of people of the same social status. **4** a group of students or pupils who are taught together. **5** a school or college lesson. **6** informal impressive stylishness. **verb** place something in a particular category. ∎ **classless** adjective.

classic adjective 1 judged over a period of time to be of the highest quality. **2** typical. **noun (Classics)** the study of ancient Greek and Latin language and culture.

classical adjective 1 relating to the cultures of ancient Greece and Rome. **2** representing the highest standard within a long-established form. **3** (of music) written in the tradition of formal European music. ∎ **classically** adverb.

classicism noun the use of a simple and elegant style characteristic of the art, architecture, or literature of ancient Greece and Rome.

classicist noun a person who studies Classics.

classification noun 1 the arrangement of things in categories. **2** a category into which something is put.

classified adjective 1 (of newspaper or magazine advertisements) organized in categories. **2** (of information or documents) officially secret.

classify verb (classifies, classifying, classified) 1 arrange things in groups according to features that they have in common. **2** put in a particular class or category. **3** make documents or information officially secret.

classroom noun a room in which a class of pupils or students is taught.

classy adjective (classier, classiest) informal stylish and sophisticated.

clatter noun a loud rattling sound like that of hard objects striking each other. **verb (clatters, clattering, clattered)** make a clatter.

clause noun 1 a group of words that includes a subject and a verb and forms part of a sentence. **2** a part of a treaty, bill, or contract.

claustrophobia /kloss-truh-**foh**-bi-uh/ **noun** an extreme fear of being in a small or enclosed space. ∎ **claustrophobic** adjective.

clavicle noun the collarbone.

claw noun 1 each of the horny nails on the feet of birds, lizards, and some mammals. **2** the pincer of a shellfish. **verb** scratch or tear at something with the claws or fingernails.

clay noun sticky earth that can be moulded when wet and baked to make bricks and pottery.

clean adjective 1 free from dirt or harmful substances. **2** not obscene. **3** not yet used or marked. **4** having no record of offences or crimes. **5** (of an action) smoothly and skilfully done. **verb** make something free from dirt or harmful substances. **noun** an act of cleaning. □ **clean-cut** (of a person) clean and neat. **clean-shaven** (of a man) without a beard or moustache. **come clean** informal fully confess something. ■ **cleaner** noun **cleanly** adverb.

cleanliness /klen-li-nuhss/ **noun** the quality of being clean.

cleanse **verb** (**cleanses**, **cleansing**, **cleansed**) make something thoroughly clean or pure. ■ **cleanser** noun.

clear **adjective 1** easy to see, hear, or understand. **2** leaving or feeling no doubt. **3** transparent; uncoloured. **4** free of obstructions or unwanted objects. **5** (of a period of time) free of commitments. **6** free from disease, contamination, or guilt. **7** (**clear of**) not touching. **verb 1** make or become clear. **2** get past or over something safely or without touching it. **3** show or state that someone is innocent. **4** give official approval to. **5** make people leave a place. **6** (of a cheque) be paid into someone's account. □ **clear-cut** sharply defined; easy to see or understand. **clear off** informal go away. **clear the air** ease a tense situation by talking about things. **clear up 1** tidy something by removing unwanted items. **2** solve or explain a mystery or misunderstanding. **3** (of an illness) become cured. **4** stop raining. **in the clear** no longer in danger or under suspicion. ■ **clearly** adverb.

clearance noun **1** the action of clearing. **2** official authorization for something to take place. **3** clear space allowed for a thing to move past or under another.

clearing **noun** an open space in a wood or forest.

clearway **noun** Brit. a main road other than a motorway on which vehicles are not allowed to stop.

cleat noun **1** a projection to which a rope can be attached. **2** a projecting wedge on a tool, the sole of a boot, etc., to prevent it slipping.

cleavage noun **1** a sharp division; a split. **2** the hollow between a woman's breasts.

cleave[1] **verb** (**cleaves**, **cleaving**, **clove** or **cleft** or **cleaved**; past participle **cloven** or **cleft** or **cleaved**) **1** split along a natural grain or line. **2** divide; split.

cleave[2] **verb** (**cleaves**, **cleaving**, **cleaved**) (**cleave to**) literary **1** stick fast to. **2** become strongly involved with.

cleaver **noun** a tool with a heavy broad blade, used for chopping meat.

clef **noun** Music a symbol placed next to the notes on a stave, to show their pitch.

cleft past participle of **CLEAVE**[1]. **adjective** split or divided into two. **noun** a split or indentation. □ **cleft palate** a split in the roof of the mouth which is present from birth.

clematis /klem-uh-tiss/ **noun** an ornamental climbing plant.

clement **adjective 1** (of weather) mild. **2** merciful. ■ **clemency** noun.

clementine **noun** a small citrus fruit with bright orange-red skin.

clench **verb 1** close your fist or hold your teeth or muscles together tightly in response to stress or anger. **2** grasp something tightly.

clerestory /kleer-stor-i/ **noun** (plural **clerestories**) a row of windows in the upper part of the wall of a church or other large building.

clergy /kler-ji/ **noun** (plural **clergies**) the priests and ministers who carry out religious duties in the Christian Church.

clergyman **noun** a Christian priest or minister.

cleric **noun** a priest or religious leader.

clerical **adjective 1** relating to the normal work of an office clerk. **2** relating to the priests and ministers of the Christian Church.

clerk noun **1** a person employed in an office or bank to keep records or accounts and do other routine work. **2** a person in charge of the records of a local council or court.

clever **adjective** (**cleverer**, **cleverest**)

1 quick to understand and learn. **2** skilled at doing something. ■ **cleverly** adverb **cleverness** noun.

cliché /klee-shay/ noun a phrase or idea that has been used too much and is no longer fresh or interesting. ■ **clichéd** adjective.

click noun a short, sharp sound as of two hard objects coming smartly into contact. verb **1** make a click. **2** move or become secured with a click. **3** Computing press a mouse button. **4** informal become suddenly clear.

client noun a person who uses the services of a professional person or organization.

clientele /klee-on-tel/ noun the clients or customers of a shop, restaurant, or professional service.

cliff noun a steep rock face at the edge of the sea.

cliffhanger noun a situation in a story which is exciting because you do not know what is going to happen next.

climacteric /kly-mak-tuh-rik/ noun the period in a person's life when their fertility has started to decline.

climactic /kly-mak-tik/ adjective forming an exciting climax.

> ℹ️ don't confuse **climactic**, 'forming a climax', with **climatic**, which means 'relating to climate'.

climate noun **1** the general weather conditions in an area over a long period. **2** a general attitude or feeling among people. ■ **climatic** adjective.

climax noun **1** the most intense, exciting, or important point of something. **2** an orgasm. verb reach a climax.

climb verb **1** go or come up to a higher position. **2** go up or scale a hill, rock face, etc. **3** (of a plant) grow up a structure by clinging to or twining round it. **4** move with effort into or out of a confined space. noun **1** an act of climbing. **2** a route up a mountain or cliff. □ **climb down** admit that you are wrong about something. **climbing frame** a structure consisting of joined

bars for children to climb on. ■ **climber** noun.

clime noun literary a place considered in terms of its climate: *sunnier climes.*

clinch verb **1** settle a contract or contest. **2** settle something that has been uncertain or undecided. noun **1** a tight hold in a struggle. **2** a tight embrace.

cling verb (**clings, clinging, clung**) (**cling to** or **on to**) **1** hold on tightly to. **2** stick to. **3** remain faithful to. **4** be emotionally dependent on. □ **cling film** Brit. thin plastic film used to wrap or cover food. ■ **clingy** adjective.

clinic noun a place where medical treatment or advice is given.

clinical adjective **1** relating to the observation and treatment of patients. **2** (of a place) bare, functional, and clean. **3** efficient and showing no emotion. ■ **clinically** adverb.

clink noun a sharp ringing sound. verb make a clink.

clinker noun the stony remains from burnt coal or from a furnace.

clip[1] noun **1** a flexible or spring-loaded device for holding objects together or in place. **2** a piece of jewellery that is fastened to a garment with a clip. verb (**clips, clipping, clipped**) fasten with a clip.

clip[2] verb (**clips, clipping, clipped**) **1** cut or trim with shears or scissors. **2** trim the hair or wool of an animal. **3** hit quickly or lightly. noun **1** an act of clipping. **2** a short sequence taken from a film or broadcast. **3** informal a quick or light blow.

clipboard noun a board with a clip at the top, for holding papers and writing on.

clipped adjective (of speech) having short, sharp vowel sounds and clear pronunciation.

clipper noun **1** (**clippers**) an instrument for clipping. **2** (in the past) a type of fast sailing ship.

clipping noun **1** a small piece trimmed from something. **2** an article cut from a newspaper or magazine.

clique /rhymes with seek/ noun a small group of people who do not allow others to join them. ■ **cliquey** adjective.

clitoris /**kli**-tuh-riss/ noun the small sensitive organ just in front of the vagina.

cloak noun 1 an outer garment that hangs loosely from the shoulders to the knees or ankles. 2 something that hides or covers. verb cover or hide something. □ **cloak-and-dagger** concealed or mysterious.

cloakroom noun 1 a room where coats and bags may be left. 2 Brit. a room that contains a toilet.

clobber[1] verb (**clobbers**, **clobbering**, **clobbered**) informal hit someone hard.

clobber[2] noun Brit. informal clothing and personal belongings.

cloche /klosh/ noun 1 a small cover for protecting young or tender plants. 2 a woman's bell-shaped hat.

clock noun 1 an instrument that indicates the time. 2 informal a measuring device resembling a clock, such as a speedometer. verb informal 1 reach a particular speed or distance. 2 (**clock in** or **out** or Brit. **on** or **off**) register the time you are arriving at or leaving work. 3 (**clock up**) reach a total. 4 Brit. see or watch.

clockwise adverb & adjective in the direction of the movement of the hands of a clock.

clockwork noun a mechanism with a spring and a system of interlocking wheels, used to drive a mechanical clock or other device. □ **like clockwork** very smoothly and easily.

clod noun 1 a lump of earth. 2 informal a stupid person.

clodhopper noun informal 1 a large, heavy shoe. 2 an awkward or clumsy person.

clog noun 1 a shoe with a thick wooden sole. verb (**clogs**, **clogging**, **clogged**) (often **clog up**) block or become blocked.

cloister noun a covered passage round an open court in a convent, monastery, cathedral, etc.

cloistered adjective 1 having a cloister. 2 protected from the outside world.

clomp verb walk with a heavy tread. noun the sound of a heavy tread.

clone noun an animal or plant created from the cells of another, to which it is genetically identical. verb (**clones**, **cloning**, **cloned**) 1 create something as a clone. 2 make an identical copy of something.

close[1] /rhymes with dose/ adjective 1 only a short distance away or apart in space or time. 2 (of a connection or likeness) strong. 3 (of two people) very affectionate or intimate. 4 (of observation or examination) done in a careful and thorough way. 5 so as to be very near; with very little space between. noun Brit. a street of houses that is closed at one end. □ **close-knit** (of a group of people) bound together by strong relationships. **at close quarters** (or **range**) from a position close to someone or something. **close shave** (or **close call**) informal a narrow escape from danger or disaster. **close-up** a photograph or sequence in a film that is taken from a very short distance. ■ **closely** adverb.

close[2] /rhymes with nose/ verb (**closes**, **closing**, **closed**) 1 move something so as to cover an opening. 2 (also **close up**) bring two parts of something together. 3 (**close on** or **in** on) gradually surround or get nearer to. 4 (**close around** or **over**) encircle and hold. 5 come or bring something to an end. 6 finish speaking or writing. 7 (often **close down** or **up**) stop trading or working. 8 bring a deal or arrangement to a conclusion. noun 1 the end of an event or of a period of time or activity. 2 a shut position. □ **close season** (or **closed season**) a period in the year when fishing or hunting is officially forbidden, or when a sport is not played.

closed adjective 1 not open or allowing people to go in. 2 not communicating with or influenced by other people. □ **closed-circuit television** a television system used to observe people within a building, shopping centre, etc. **closed shop** a place of work where all employees must belong to a particular trade union.

closet noun chiefly N. Amer. **1** a tall cupboard or wardrobe. **2** a small room. verb (**closets, closeting, closeted**) shut someone in a private room. □ **in** (or **out of**) **the closet** not open (or open) about being homosexual.

closure noun **1** the closing of something. **2** a device that closes or seals.

clot noun **1** a lump that is formed when a thick liquid substance dries or becomes thicker. **2** Brit. informal a foolish or clumsy person. verb (**clots, clotting, clotted**) form into clots. □ **clotted cream** thick cream obtained by heating and cooling milk slowly.

cloth noun (plural **cloths**) **1** fabric made from a soft fibre such as wool or cotton. **2** a piece of cloth for a particular purpose. **3** (**the cloth**) ministers of the Church.

clothe verb (**clothes, clothing, clothed**) **1** provide with clothes. **2** (**be clothed in**) be dressed in.

clothes plural noun things worn to cover the body. □ **clothes horse** a frame on which washed clothes are hung to dry.

clothing noun clothes.

cloud noun **1** a mass of vapour floating in the atmosphere. **2** a hazy or billowing mass of smoke, dust, etc. **3** a state or cause of gloom or anxiety. verb **1** (**cloud over**) (of the sky) become full of clouds. **2** become less clear. **3** (of someone's face or eyes) show sadness, anxiety, or anger. □ **cloud cuckoo land** a state of fantasy. **have your head in the clouds** have a lot of fantasies and unrealistic thoughts. **on cloud nine** extremely happy. **under a cloud** out of favour or suspected of something. ■ **cloudy** adjective.

cloudburst noun a sudden violent rainstorm.

clout informal noun **1** a heavy blow. **2** influence or power. verb hit someone hard.

clove[1] noun the dried flower bud of a tropical tree, used as a spice.

clove[2] noun any of the small bulbs making up a larger bulb of garlic.

clove[3] past of **CLEAVE**[1]. □ **clove hitch** a knot by which a rope is secured to a spar or another rope.

cloven past participle of **CLEAVE**[1]. □ **cloven hoof** the divided hoof of animals such as cattle, sheep, and deer.

clover noun a plant with white or pink flowers and a leaf with three lobes. □ **in clover** in ease and luxury.

clown noun **1** an entertainer who does silly things to make people laugh. **2** a playful or silly person. verb **1** perform as a clown. **2** behave in a funny or silly way. ■ **clownish** adjective.

cloying adjective **1** too sweet and making you feel slightly sick. **2** too sentimental.

club[1] noun **1** a group of people who meet regularly for a particular activity. **2** a place where members can relax, eat meals, or stay overnight. **3** a nightclub with dance music. verb (**clubs, clubbing, clubbed**) (**club together**) combine with others to do something. ■ **clubber** noun.

club[2] noun **1** a heavy stick used as a weapon. **2** a heavy stick with a thick head, used to hit the ball in golf. **3** (**clubs**) one of the four suits in a pack of playing cards, represented by a black trefoil. verb (**clubs, clubbing, clubbed**) beat someone with a club or similar heavy object. □ **club foot** a deformed foot which is twisted so that the sole cannot be placed flat on the ground.

clubhouse noun a building having a bar and other facilities for club members.

cluck noun the short, throaty sound made by a hen. verb make a cluck.

clue noun a fact or piece of evidence that helps to clear up a mystery or solve a problem. □ **not have a clue** informal have no idea about something. **clued up** informal well informed.

clueless adjective not able to understand or do something.

clump noun **1** a small group of trees or plants growing closely together. **2** a mass or lump of something. **3** the sound of a heavy tread. **verb 1** form into a clump or mass. **2** walk with a heavy tread.

clumpy adjective (of shoes or boots) thick and heavy.

clumsy adjective (**clumsier**, **clumsiest**) **1** awkward and badly coordinated. **2** tactless. ■ **clumsily** adverb **clumsiness** noun.

clung past and past participle of **CLING**.

clunk noun a dull, heavy sound. **verb** make a clunk.

cluster noun a group of similar things placed or occurring closely together. **verb** (**cluster**, **clustering**, **clustered**) form a cluster.

clutch[1] **verb** grasp something tightly. **noun 1** a tight grasp. **2** (**clutches**) power and control. **3** a mechanism in a vehicle that connects the engine with the axle and wheels.

clutch[2] **noun 1** a group of eggs fertilized at the same time and laid in a single session. **2** a group of chicks hatched from the same batch of eggs.

clutter noun **1** things lying about untidily. **2** an untidy state. **verb** (**clutters**, **cluttering**, **cluttered**) cover or fill with clutter.

cm abbreviation centimetres.

Co. abbreviation **1** company. **2** county.

co- prefix joint; mutual; together with another or others: *coexist* | *co-star.*

c/o abbreviation care of.

coach[1] noun **1** chiefly Brit. a comfortable single-decker bus used for longer journeys. **2** a railway carriage.

coach[2] noun **1** a person who trains someone in a sport. **2** a person who gives private lessons in a subject. **verb** give private lessons or training to someone.

coagulate /koh-**ag**-yoo-layt/ **verb** (**coagulates**, **coagulating**, **coagulated**) (of a liquid) thicken or become solid. ■ **coagulant** noun **coagulation** noun.

coal noun a black rock consisting mainly of carbonized plant matter and used as fuel. □ **coal tar** a thick black liquid distilled from coal.

coalesce /koh-uh-**less**/ verb (**coalesces**, **coalescing**, **coalesced**) come or bring together to form a single mass or whole.

coalface noun an exposed surface of coal in a mine.

coalfield noun a large area where there is a lot of coal underground.

coalition /koh-uh-**li**-sh'n/ noun a government made up of two political parties who have agreed to work together.

coarse adjective **1** rough or harsh in texture. **2** consisting of large grains or particles. **3** rude or vulgar. □ **coarse fish** Brit. any freshwater fish other than salmon and trout. ■ **coarsely** adverb.

coarsen verb make or become coarse.

coast noun a stretch of land next to or near the sea. **verb 1** move easily without using power. **2** do something without making much effort. □ **the coast is clear** there is no danger of being seen or caught. ■ **coastal** adjective.

coaster noun **1** a small mat for a glass. **2** a ship that sails along the coast from port to port.

coastguard noun an organization or person that keeps watch over coastal waters.

coastline noun the shape or appearance of the land along a coast.

coat noun **1** a full-length outer garment with sleeves. **2** an animal's covering of fur or hair. **3** an enclosing or covering layer or structure. **4** a single layer of paint. **verb** form or provide with a layer or covering. □ **coat of arms** a design used as a special symbol of a family, city, or organization.

coax verb **1** gently persuade someone to do something. **2** gently guide or move something.

coaxial /koh-**ak**-si-uhl/ adjective (of a cable) having two wires, one wrapped round the other but separated by insulation.

cob noun **1** Brit. a loaf of bread. **2** the central part of an ear of maize. **3** (also

cobnut) a hazelnut or filbert.

cobalt noun a silvery-white metallic element.

cobber noun Austral./NZ informal a companion or friend.

cobble[1] or **cobblestone** noun a small round stone used to cover road surfaces. ■ **cobbled** adjective.

cobble[2] verb (**cobbles**, **cobbling**, **cobbled**) (**cobble together**) make up something roughly from materials that happen to be available.

cobbler noun **1** a person whose job is mending shoes. **2** chiefly N. Amer. a fruit pie with a cake-like crust.

cobra noun a highly poisonous snake native to Africa and Asia.

cobweb noun a spider's web.

cocaine noun an addictive stimulant drug obtained from the leaves of a tropical plant.

coccyx /kok-siks/ noun (plural **coccyges** /kok-si-jeez/ or **coccyxes**) a small triangular bone at the base of the spine.

cochineal /koch-i-neel/ noun a scarlet dye used for colouring food.

cochlea /kok-li-uh/ noun (plural **cochleae** /kok-li-ee/) the spiral cavity of the inner ear.

cock noun **1** a male chicken or game bird. **2** vulgar a man's penis. verb **1** tilt or bend something in a particular direction. **2** raise the firing lever of a gun to make it ready to shoot. **3** (**cock up**) Brit. informal spoil something by doing it badly. □ **cock-a-hoop** extremely pleased. **cock and bull story** a very unlikely story. **cock-eyed 1** crooked. **2** absurd and impractical.

cockade noun a rosette or knot of ribbons worn on a hat as part of a uniform.

cockatoo noun a kind of parrot with a crest.

cockcrow noun literary dawn.

cockerel noun a young cock.

cocker spaniel noun a small breed of spaniel with a silky coat.

cockle noun an edible shellfish with a ribbed shell.

cockney noun (plural **cockneys**) **1** a person who was born in the East End of London. **2** the dialect or accent used in this area.

cockpit noun **1** a compartment for the pilot and crew in an aircraft or spacecraft. **2** the driver's compartment in a racing car.

cockroach noun a beetle-like insect with long antennae and legs.

cocksure adjective arrogantly confident.

cocktail noun **1** an alcoholic drink consisting of a spirit mixed with other ingredients. **2** a mixture.

cocky adjective (**cockier**, **cockiest**) conceited in a bold or cheeky way.

cocoa noun a drink made from powdered cacao seeds, mixed with hot milk.

coconut noun **1** the large brown seed of a tropical palm, consisting of a woody husk lined with edible white flesh. **2** the white flesh of a coconut. □ **coconut shy** a sideshow at a fair, in which you throw balls at a coconut and win it if you dislodge it.

> ✓ just -o-, not -oa-: coconut.

cocoon noun **1** a silky case spun by the larva of many insects, which protects it while it is turning into an adult. **2** something that envelops you in a protective or comforting way. verb wrap in a cocoon.

cod noun (plural **cod**) a large sea fish which is used for food. □ **cod liver oil** oil obtained from the liver of cod, rich in vitamins D and A.

coda /koh-duh/ noun an extra passage marking the end of a piece of music.

coddle verb (**coddles**, **coddling**, **coddled**) give someone too much care and attention.

code noun **1** a system of words, figures, or symbols used to represent others secretly or briefly. **2** (also **dialling code**) a sequence of numbers dialled to connect a telephone line with another exchange. **3** instructions for a computer program. **4** a set of laws or rules. **verb** (codes, coding, coded) **1** convert into a code. **2** (coded) expressed in an indirect way.

codeine /koh-deen/ **noun** a painkilling drug obtained from morphine.

codger **noun** informal an elderly man.

codicil /koh-di-sil/ **noun** a part added to a will that explains or alters an earlier part.

codify /koh-di-fl/ **verb** (codifies, codifying, codified) arrange a set of rules as a formal code.

codpiece **noun** (in the past) a pouch worn by a man over his trousers, covering the groin.

codswallop **noun** Brit. informal nonsense.

co-education **noun** the teaching of boys and girls together in the same schools. ■ **co-educational** adjective.

coefficient **noun 1** Mathematics a quantity which is placed before another which it multiplies (e.g. *4* in $4x^2$). **2** Physics a multiplier or factor that measures some property.

coerce /koh-erss/ **verb** (coerces, coercing, coerced) force someone to do something. ■ **coercion** noun **coercive** adjective.

coexist **verb 1** exist at the same time or in the same place. **2** be together in harmony. ■ **coexistence** noun.

C. of E. **abbreviation** Church of England.

coffee **noun** a hot drink made from the bean-like seeds of a tropical shrub. □ **coffee table** a small low table for putting cups, books, etc. on.

coffer **noun** a small chest for holding money or valuable items.

coffin **noun** a long box in which a dead body is buried or cremated.

cog **noun 1** a wheel or bar with projections on its edge, which transfers motion by engaging with projections on another wheel or bar. **2** a projection on a cog.

cogent /koh-juhnt/ **adjective** (of an argument) clear, logical, and convincing. ■ **cogency** noun **cogently** adverb.

cogitate /koj-i-tayt/ **verb** (cogitates, cogitating, cogitated) formal think carefully about something. ■ **cogitation** noun.

cognac /kon-yak/ **noun** brandy made in Cognac in western France.

cognition /kog-ni-sh'n/ **noun** the acquiring of knowledge through thought, experience, and the senses. ■ **cognitive** adjective.

cognizance or **cognisance** /kog-ni-zuhnss/ **noun** formal knowledge or awareness. □ **take cognizance of** take account of. ■ **cognizant** adjective.

cognoscenti /kon-yuh-shen-ti/ **plural noun** people who are well informed about a particular subject.

cohabit **verb** (cohabits, cohabiting, cohabited) live together and have a sexual relationship without being married. ■ **cohabitation** noun.

cohere **verb** (coheres, cohering, cohered) hold firmly together; form a whole.

coherent **adjective 1** (of an argument or theory) logical and consistent. **2** able to speak clearly and logically. ■ **coherence** noun **coherently** adverb.

cohesion /koh-hee-zh'n/ **noun** the holding together of something.

cohesive **adjective** holding or making something hold together.

cohort /koh-hort/ **noun 1** an ancient Roman military unit equal to one tenth of a legion. **2** a large band of people.

coif **noun** /koyf/ a close-fitting cap worn by nuns under a veil. **verb** /kwahf, kwof/ (coifs, coiffing, coiffed) arrange someone's hair.

coiffure /kwah-fyoor/ **noun** a person's hairstyle. ■ **coiffured** adjective.

coil **noun 1** a length of something wound in loops. **2** a contraceptive in the form of a small coil, fitted into the womb. **verb** arrange or form something into a coil.

coin **noun** a flat disc or piece of metal used as money. **verb 1** make coins by stamping metal. **2** invent a new word or phrase.

coinage noun **1** coins of a particular type. **2** a newly invented word or phrase.

coincide verb (coincides, coinciding, coincided) **1** happen at the same time or place. **2** be the same or similar; tally.

coincidence noun **1** a remarkable occurrence of events or circumstances at the same time. **2** a state in which things tally or are similar. ■ **coincidental** adjective **coincidentally** adverb.

coitus /koh-i-tuhss/ noun technical sexual intercourse. □ **coitus interruptus** sexual intercourse in which the man withdraws his penis before he ejaculates so that the woman does not become pregnant. ■ **coital** adjective.

coke[1] noun a solid fuel made by heating coal in the absence of air.

coke[2] noun informal cocaine.

colander noun a bowl with holes in it, used to strain off liquid from food.

cold adjective **1** at a low temperature. **2** not feeling or showing emotion. **3** (of a colour) containing a lot of blue or grey and giving no impression of warmth. **4** (of a scent or trail) no longer fresh and easy to follow. **5** without preparation. noun **1** cold weather. **2** an infection causing running at the nose and sneezing. □ **cold-blooded 1** (of reptiles and fish) having a body that is the same temperature as the surrounding air. **2** heartless and cruel. **the cold shoulder** unfriendliness or rejection. **cold sore** an inflamed blister beside the mouth, caused by a virus. **cold turkey** unpleasant feelings experienced by someone who has suddenly stopped taking a drug to which they are addicted. **cold war** a state of hostility between the countries of the Soviet bloc and the Western powers after the Second World War. **get cold feet** lose your nerve. **in cold blood** without feeling. ■ **coldly** adverb **coldness** noun.

coleslaw noun a dish of shredded raw cabbage and carrots mixed with mayonnaise.

colic noun severe pain in the abdomen caused by wind or obstruction in the intestines. ■ **colicky** adjective.

collaborate verb (collaborates, collaborating, collaborated) **1** work together on an activity. **2** cooperate with your country's enemy. ■ **collaboration** noun **collaborative** adjective **collaborator** noun.

collage /kol-lah*zh*/ noun a form of art in which various materials are arranged and stuck to a backing.

collapse verb (collapses, collapsing, collapsed) **1** suddenly fall down or give way. **2** fail and come to a sudden end. noun **1** the falling down or giving way of a structure. **2** a sudden failure.

collapsible adjective able to be folded down.

collar noun **1** a band of material around the neck of a shirt or other garment. **2** a band put around the neck of a dog or cat. verb informal seize someone.

collarbone noun either of the pair of bones joining the breastbone to the shoulder blades.

collate verb (collates, collating, collated) collect and combine texts or information. ■ **collation** noun.

collateral noun something that you promise to give up if you are unable to repay a loan. adjective additional but less important; secondary.

colleague noun a person that you work with.

collect verb **1** bring or gather things together. **2** come together and form a group. **3** find and keep items of a particular kind as a hobby. **4** go somewhere to fetch someone or something. ■ **collectable** (or **collectible**) adjective **collector** noun.

collected adjective **1** calm. **2** brought together in one volume or edition.

collection noun **1** the action of collecting. **2** a group of things collected or accumulated. **3** a time when mail is picked up from a postbox, or when rubbish is taken away.

collective adjective **1** done by or

PUNCTUATION   [i]

Colon

A colon is used:

1 between two main clauses, of which the second explains or follows from the first, e.g.

It was not easy: to begin with I had to find the right house.

2 to introduce a list of items, and after expressions such as *namely, for example, to resume, to sum up,* and *the following,* e.g.

You will need: a tent, a sleeping bag, cooking equipment, and a rucksack.

There is no need to add a dash after the colon.

3 before a quotation, e.g.

The poem begins: 'Earth has not anything to show more fair'.

---

belonging to all the members of a group. **2** taken as a whole. **noun** a small business or project owned by all the people who work for it. ■ **collectively** adverb.

college noun **1** a place providing higher education or specialized training. **2** (in Britain) any of the independent institutions into which some universities are separated.

collegiate /kuh-**lee**-ji-uht/ **adjective 1** having to do with a college or college students. **2** (of a university) composed of different colleges.

collide verb (**collides, colliding, collided**) move or bump into something.

collie noun (plural **collies**) a breed of sheepdog with long hair.

collier noun a coal miner.

colliery noun (plural **collieries**) a coal mine.

collision noun an instance when two or more things collide.

colloquial /kuh-**loh**-kwi-uhl/ **adjective** (of language) used in ordinary conversation. ■ **colloquialism** noun **colloquially** adverb.

colloquy /**kol**-luh-kwi/ noun (plural **colloquies**) formal a conference or conversation.

collude verb (**colludes, colluding, colluded**) have a secret plan with someone. ■ **collusion** noun.

collywobbles plural noun informal

1 queasiness. **2** great anxiety.

cologne /kuh-**lohn**/ noun a type of light perfume.

colon[1] noun a punctuation mark (:) used before a list of items, a quotation, or an expansion or explanation.

colon[2] noun the main part of the large intestine, which leads to the rectum. ■ **colonic** adjective.

colonel /**ker**-nuhl/ noun a rank of officer in the army and in the US air force, above a lieutenant colonel.

colonial adjective having to do with a colony or with colonialism. **noun** a person who lives in a colony.

colonialism noun the practice of acquiring and controlling another country and occupying it with settlers. ■ **colonialist** noun & adjective.

colonist noun an inhabitant of a colony.

colonize or **colonise** verb (**colonizes, colonizing, colonized**) **1** make a colony in. **2** take over a place for your own use. ■ **colonization** noun.

colonnade noun a row of evenly spaced columns supporting a roof.

colony noun (plural **colonies**) **1** a country or area under the control of another country and occupied by settlers from that country. **2** a group of people of one nationality or race living in a foreign place. **3** a place where a group of people with a common interest live together. **4** a community of animals or plants living close together.

coloration or **colouration** noun the colours and markings of a plant or animal.

colossal adjective extremely large. ■ **colossally** adverb.

colossus /kuh-**loss**-uh-suhss/ noun (plural **colossi** /kuh-**loss**-I/ or **colossuses**) a person or thing of enormous size.

colostomy /kuh-**loss**-tuh-mi/ noun (plural **colostomies**) a surgical operation in which the colon is shortened and the cut end is diverted to a new opening made in the wall of the abdomen.

colour (US spelling **color**) noun **1** an object's property of producing different sensations on the eye as a result of the way it reflects or gives out light. **2** one of the parts into which light can be separated. **3** the use of all colours in photography or television. **4** pigmentation of the skin as an indication of someone's race. **5** redness of the complexion. **6** interest and excitement. verb **1** give a colour to. **2** blush. **3** influence something. ▫ **colour-blind** not able to see certain colours.

coloured (US spelling **colored**) adjective **1** having a colour or colours. **2** dated or offensive not having white skin. **3** (in South Africa) having parents who are of different races. noun **1** dated or offensive a non-white person. **2** (in South Africa) a person with parents of different races.

colourful (US spelling **colorful**) adjective **1** having many or varied colours. **2** lively and exciting; vivid. ■ **colourfully** adverb.

colouring (US spelling **coloring**) noun **1** the process or art of applying colour. **2** visual appearance with regard to colour. **3** a substance used to colour something.

colourist (US spelling **colorist**) noun an artist or designer who uses colour in a special or skilful way.

colourless (US spelling **colorless**) adjective **1** without colour. **2** lacking character or interest; dull.

colt noun a young male horse.

coltish adjective energetic but awkward in movement or behaviour.

column noun **1** an upright pillar supporting a structure or standing alone as a monument. **2** a line of people or vehicles moving in the same direction. **3** a vertical division of a page or text. **4** a regular section of a newspaper or magazine on a particular subject or by a particular person.

columnist noun a journalist who writes a column in a newspaper or magazine.

coma noun a state of long-lasting deep unconsciousness.

comatose adjective in a state of coma.

comb noun **1** an object with a row of narrow teeth, used for smoothing and neatening the hair. **2** a device for separating and smoothing textile fibres. **3** the red fleshy crest on the head of a chicken. verb **1** neaten the hair by drawing a comb through it. **2** prepare wool, flax, or cotton for manufacture with a comb. **3** search systematically through.

combat noun fighting, especially between armed forces. verb (**combats, combating, combated** or **combats, combatting, combatted**) take action to prevent something undesirable.

combatant noun a person or group engaged in fighting a battle or war. adjective engaged in fighting.

combative adjective ready or eager to fight or argue.

combe /koom/ noun Brit. a short valley or hollow on a hillside or coastline.

combination noun **1** the action of combining two or more different things. **2** something that is made up of distinct parts. ▫ **combination lock** a lock that is opened using a sequence of letters or numbers.

combine verb /kuhm-**byn**/ (**combines, combining, combined**) **1** join or mix together. **2** join together to do something. noun /**kom**-byn/ a group acting together for a commercial purpose. □ **combine harvester** a farming machine that cuts a crop and separates out the grain in one operation.

combust verb catch fire or burn. ■ **combustion** noun.

combustible adjective able to catch fire and burn easily.

come verb (**comes**, **coming**, **came**; past participle **come**) **1** move towards or into a place near to the speaker. **2** arrive. **3** happen; take place. **4** have or achieve a certain position. **5** pass into a particular condition or state. **6** be sold or available in a particular form. **7** (**coming**) likely to be successful in the future. **8** informal have an orgasm. □ **come about** happen. **come across 1** give a particular impression. **2** meet or find by chance. **come by** manage to acquire. **come-hither** informal flirtatious. **come into** inherit. **come of** result from. **come off** succeed, or have a specified amount of success. **come on 1** (of a state or condition) begin. **2** (also **come upon**) meet or find by chance. **come out 1** (of a fact) become known. **2** say publicly that you are for or against something. **3** declare publicly that you are homosexual. **come round** Brit. **1** recover consciousness. **2** be converted to another person's opinion. **come to 1** recover consciousness. **2** (of an expense) amount to. **come up** occur.

comeback noun **1** a return to fame or popularity. **2** informal a quick reply to a remark.

comedian noun (feminine **comedienne**) an entertainer whose act is intended to make people laugh.

comedown noun informal **1** a loss of status or importance. **2** a feeling of disappointment or depression.

comedy noun (plural **comedies**) **1** a film, play, or other entertainment intended to make people laugh. **2** a light-hearted play in which the characters triumph over difficult situations.

comely /kum-li/ adjective (**comelier**, **comeliest**) old use pleasant to look at.

comestibles plural noun formal items of food.

comet noun a mass of ice and dust with a long tail, moving around the solar system.

comeuppance noun (**get your comeuppance**) informal get the punishment or fate that you deserve.

comfort noun **1** a pleasant state of ease and relaxation. **2** (**comforts**) things that contribute to comfort. **3** consolation for grief or anxiety. verb make someone less unhappy. ■ **comforter** noun.

comfortable adjective **1** giving or enjoying physical comfort. **2** free from financial worry. **3** (of a victory) easily achieved. ■ **comfortably** adverb.

comfy adjective (**comfier**, **comfiest**) informal comfortable.

comic adjective **1** causing laughter; amusing. **2** having to do with comedy. noun **1** a comedian. **2** a children's magazine that contains comic strips. □ **comic strip** a sequence of drawings that tell an amusing story.

comical adjective causing laughter, especially through being ridiculous. ■ **comically** noun.

comma noun a punctuation mark (,) showing a pause between parts of a sentence or separating items in a list.

command verb **1** give an order. **2** be in charge of a military unit. noun **1** an order. **2** authority. **3** a group of officers in control of a particular group or operation. **4** the ability to use or control something. **5** an instruction causing a computer to perform one of its basic functions.

commandant noun an officer in charge of a force or institution.

commandeer verb (**commandeers**, **commandeering**, **commandeered**) officially take possession of something for military purposes.

commander noun **1** a person in command. **2** the rank of naval officer below captain. □ **commander-in-chief** (plural **commanders-in-chief**) an officer in charge of all of the

PUNCTUATION

Comma

The comma marks a slight break between words, phrases, etc. In particular, it is used:

1 to separate items in a list, e.g.

> *We bought some shoes, socks, gloves, and handkerchiefs*
> *red, white, and blue (or red, white and blue)*
> *potatoes, peas, or carrots (or potatoes, peas or carrots).*

2 to separate adjectives that describe something in the same way, e.g.

> *It is a hot, dry, dusty place*

but not if they describe it in different ways, e.g.

> *a distinguished foreign author*

or if one adjective adds to or alters the meaning of another, e.g.

> *a bright red tie.*

3 to separate main clauses, e.g.

> *Cars will park here, and coaches will turn left.*

4 to separate a name or word used to address someone, e.g.

> *David, I'm here*
> *Well, Mr Jones, we meet again*
> *Have you seen this, my friend?*

5 to separate a phrase, e.g.

> *Having had lunch, we went back to work*

especially in order to clarify meaning, e.g.

> *In the valley below, the village looked very small.*

6 after words that introduce direct speech, or after direct speech where there is no question mark or exclamation mark, e.g.

> *They answered, 'Here we are'*
> *'Here we are,' they answered.*

7 after *Dear Sir*, *Dear Sara*, etc., and *Yours faithfully*, *Yours sincerely*, etc. in letters.

8 to separate a word, phrase, or clause that is secondary or adds information or a comment, e.g.

> *I am sure, however, that it will not happen*
> *Fred, who is bald, complained of the cold.*

but not with a relative clause (one usually beginning with *who*, *which*, or *that*) that restricts the meaning of the noun it follows, e.g.

> *Men who are bald should wear hats*

No comma is needed between a month and a year in dates, e.g.

> *in December 2001*

or between a number and a road in addresses, e.g.

> *23 Arnold Road.*

armed forces of a country.

commanding adjective **1** indicating authority; imposing. **2** having superior strength.

commandment noun a divine rule, especially one of the Ten Commandments.

commando noun (plural **commandos**) a soldier trained for carrying out raids.

commemorate verb (**commemorates, commemorating, commemorated**) honour the memory of. ■ **commemoration** noun **commemorative** adjective.

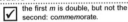 the first *m* is double, but not the second: com**mem**orate.

commence verb (**commences, commencing, commenced**) begin.

commencement noun the beginning of something.

commend verb **1** praise formally or officially. **2** present something as being suitable or good; recommend. ■ **commendation** noun.

commendable adjective deserving praise. ■ **commendably** adverb.

commensurable adjective **1** able to be measured by the same standard. **2** (**commensurable to**) proportionate to.

commensurate adjective (often **commensurate with**) corresponding or in proportion.

comment noun **1** a remark expressing an opinion or reaction. **2** discussion of an issue or event. verb express an opinion or reaction.

commentary noun (plural **commentaries**) **1** the expression of opinions about an event or situation. **2** a spoken description of an event as it happens. **3** a set of explanatory notes on a text.

commentate verb (**commentates, commentating, commentated**) provide a commentary on an event. ■ **commentator** noun.

commerce noun the activity of buying and selling; trade.

commercial adjective **1** concerned with commerce. **2** making or intended to make a profit. noun a television or radio advertisement. ■ **commercially** adverb.

commercialism noun emphasis on making as much profit as possible.

commercialize or **commercialise** verb (**commercializes, commercializing, commercialized**) manage something in a way designed to make a profit. ■ **commercialization** noun.

commiserate verb (**commiserates, commiserating, commiserated**) express sympathy or pity; sympathize. ■ **commiseration** noun.

commissar noun a Communist official responsible for political education.

commission noun **1** an instruction, command, or duty. **2** an order for something to be produced. **3** a group of people given official authority to do something. **4** payment made to someone for selling goods or services. **5** an officer's position in the armed forces. verb **1** order something to be produced. **2** bring something into working order. **3** (**commissioned**) having the rank of a military officer. ◻ **out of commission** not in working order.

commissionaire noun Brit. a uniformed door attendant at a hotel, theatre, etc.

commissioner noun **1** a member of a commission. **2** a representative of the supreme authority in an area.

commit verb (**commits, committing, committed**) **1** do something wrong or bad. **2** set aside something for a particular use. **3** (**commit yourself**) say that you will definitely do something. **4** entrust something to a safe place. **5** send someone to prison or psychiatric hospital.

commitment noun **1** dedication to a cause or policy. **2** a pledge or undertaking. **3** an engagement or obligation that restricts freedom of action.

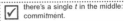 there's a single *t* in the middle: commitment.

committal noun the sending of someone to prison or psychiatric hospital, or for trial.

committed adjective dedicated to a cause, activity, job, etc.

committee noun a group of people appointed for a particular function by a larger group.

 double *m*, double *t*: committee.

commode noun a piece of furniture containing a concealed chamber pot.

commodious adjective formal roomy and comfortable.

commodity noun (plural **commodities**) **1** a raw material or agricultural product that can be bought and sold. **2** something useful or valuable.

commodore noun **1** the naval rank above captain. **2** the president of a yacht club.

common adjective (**commoner, commonest**) **1** occurring, found, or done often; not rare. **2** without special qualities or position; ordinary. **3** of the most familiar type. **4** lacking refinement in a way supposedly typical of the lower classes. **5** shared by two or more people or things. **6** belonging to or affecting the whole of a community. noun **1** a piece of open land for the public to use. **2** (**the Commons**) the House of Commons. □ **common denominator 1** Mathematics a number that can be divided exactly by all the numbers below the line in a set of fractions. **2** a feature shared by all members of a group. **common ground** views shared by each of two or more parties. **the common market** the European Union. **common or garden** Brit. informal of the usual or ordinary type. **common room** chiefly Brit. a room in a school or college for students or staff to use outside teaching hours. **common sense** good sense and judgement in practical matters. **in common** shared. ■ **commonly** adverb.

commoner noun an ordinary person as opposed to an aristocrat.

commonplace adjective ordinary. noun a trivial saying or topic.

commonsensical adjective having common sense.

commonwealth noun **1** an independent state or community. **2** (**the Commonwealth**) an association consisting of the UK together with countries that used to be part of the British Empire.

commotion noun a state of confused and noisy disturbance.

communal adjective shared or done by all members of a community. ■ **communally** adverb.

commune[1] /kom-myoon/ noun a group of people living together and sharing possessions.

commune[2] /kuh-myoon/ verb (**communes, communing, communed**) (**commune with**) share your intimate thoughts or feelings with.

communicable adjective (of a disease) able to be passed on to others.

communicant noun a person who receives Holy Communion.

communicate verb (**communicates, communicating, communicated**) **1** share or exchange information. **2** pass on or convey an emotion, disease, etc. **3** (**communicating**) (of two rooms) having a common connecting door.

communication noun **1** the action of communicating. **2** a letter or message. **3** (**communications**) means of travelling or of sending information.

communicative adjective willing or eager to talk or pass on information.

communion noun **1** the sharing of intimate thoughts and feelings. **2** (also **Holy Communion**) the service of Christian worship at which bread and wine are made holy and shared; the Eucharist.

communiqué /kuh-myoo-ni-kay/ noun an official announcement or statement.

communism noun **1** a political system in which all property is owned by the community. **2** a system of this kind derived from Marxism, followed in China and formerly in Russia. ■ **communist** noun & adjective.

community noun (plural **communities**) **1** a group of people living together in one place or having the same religion, race, etc. **2** (**the community**) the people of an area or country considered as a group; society. □ **community service** socially useful work that an offender is sentenced to do instead of going to prison.

commute verb (**commutes, commuting, commuted**) **1** regularly travel some distance between your home and place of work. **2** reduce a sentence given to an offender to a less severe one. ■ **commuter** noun.

compact[1] adjective /kuhm-**pakt**/ **1** closely and neatly packed together; dense. **2** having all the necessary parts fitted into a small space. verb /kuhm-**pakt**/ press something together into a small space. noun /**kom**-pakt/ a small case containing face powder, a mirror, and a powder puff. □ **compact disc** a small disc on which music or other digital information is stored.

compact[2] /**kom**-pakt/ noun a formal agreement between two or more parties.

companion noun **1** a person that you spend time or travel with. **2** each of a pair of things intended to complement or match each other. ■ **companionship** noun.

companionable adjective friendly and sociable. ■ **companionably** adverb.

company noun (plural **companies**) **1** a commercial business. **2** the fact of being with other people. **3** a guest or guests. **4** a number of people gathered together. **5** a body of soldiers. **6** a group of actors, singers, or dancers who perform together.

comparable adjective able to be likened to another; similar. ■ **comparably** adverb.

comparative adjective **1** measured or judged by comparison; relative. **2** involving comparison between two or more subjects. **3** (of an adjective or adverb) expressing a higher degree of a quality, but not the highest possible (e.g. *braver*). ■ **comparatively** adverb.

compar*ative*, not -*itive*.

compare verb (**compares, comparing, compared**) **1** (often **compare to** or **with**) estimate or measure the ways in which one thing is similar to or unlike another. **2** (**compare to**) point out the ways in which one thing is similar to another. **3** (usu. **compare with**) be similar to another.

comparison noun **1** the action of comparing. **2** the quality of being similar or equivalent.

compartment noun a separate section of a structure or container.

compartmentalize or **compartmentalise** verb (**compartmentalizes, compartmentalizing, compartmentalized**) divide into categories or sections.

compass noun **1** an instrument containing a pointer which shows the direction of magnetic north. **2** (also **compasses**) an instrument for drawing circles, consisting of two arms linked by a movable joint. **3** range or scope.

compassion noun sympathetic pity and concern for the sufferings of others.

compassionate adjective feeling or showing compassion. ■ **compassionately** adverb.

compatible adjective **1** able to exist or be used together. **2** (of two people) able to have a harmonious relationship; well suited. **3** (usu. **compatible with**) consistent or in keeping. ■ **compatibility** noun.

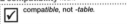
compat*ible*, not -*table*.

compatriot noun a person from the same country; a fellow citizen.

compel verb (**compels, compelling, compelled**) **1** force someone to do something. **2** make something happen.

compelling adjective powerfully gaining people's attention or admiration. ■ **compellingly** adverb.

compendium noun (plural **compendiums** or **compendia**) **1** a collection of information about a subject. **2** a collection of similar items.

compensate verb (**compensates, compensating, compensated**) **1** give someone something to reduce or balance the bad effect of loss, suffering, or injury. **2** (**compensate for**) do or provide something to reduce or balance something else.

compensation noun **1** something given to compensate for loss, suffering, or injury. **2** something that compensates for something bad.

compère /kom-pair/ Brit. noun a person who introduces the different acts that are performing in one show. verb (**compères, compèring, compèred**) act as a compère for.

compete verb (**competes, competing, competed**) try to gain or win something by defeating others.

competent adjective **1** having the necessary skill or knowledge to do something successfully. **2** satisfactory, though not outstanding. ■ **competence** (or **competency**) noun **competently** adverb.

competition noun **1** the activity of competing against others. **2** an event or contest in which people compete. **3** the person or people that you are competing with.

competitive adjective **1** characterized by competition. **2** strongly wanting to be more successful than others. **3** as good as or better than others of a similar nature. ■ **competitively** adverb.

competitor noun **1** a person who takes part in a sporting contest. **2** an organization that competes with others in business.

compilation noun **1** the action or process of compiling. **2** a thing compiled from different sources.

compile verb (**compiles, compiling, compiled**) produce a book, record, etc. by assembling material from other sources. ■ **compiler** noun.

complacent adjective smug and uncritically satisfied with yourself. ■ **complacency** noun **complacently** adverb.

complain verb **1** express dissatisfaction or annoyance. **2** (**complain of**) state that you are suffering from a particular symptom.

complainant noun Law a plaintiff.

complaint noun **1** an act of complaining. **2** a reason to be dissatisfied. **3** an illness or medical condition, especially a minor one.

complaisant /kuhm-**play**-z'nt/ adjective willing to please others or to accept their behaviour without protest.

complement noun /kom-pli-muhnt/ **1** a thing that contributes extra features to something else so as to improve it. **2** the number or quantity that makes something complete. verb /kom-pli-ment/ add to something in a way that improves it.

> [i] don't confuse **complement** and **compliment**. **Complement** means 'add to something in a way that improves', while **compliment** means 'politely congratulate or praise'.

complementary adjective combining so as to form a complete whole or to enhance each other. ■ **complementary medicine** medical therapy that is not part of scientific medicine, e.g. acupuncture.

complete adjective **1** having all the necessary parts; entire. **2** having run its course; finished. **3** to the greatest extent or degree; total. **4** skilled at every aspect of an activity. verb (**completes, completing, completed**) **1** finish making or doing. **2** make something complete. **3** write the required information on a form. ■ **completely** adverb **completion** noun.

complex adjective **1** consisting of many different and connected parts. **2** not easy to understand; complicated. noun **1** a group of similar buildings or facilities on the same site. **2** a network of linked things. **3** an abnormal mental state caused by repressed feelings. ■ **complexity** noun.

complexion noun **1** the condition of the skin of a person's face. **2** the general character of something.

compliance noun the action of complying.

compliant adjective **1** excessively obedient. **2** obeying rules.

complicate verb (**complicates, complicating, complicated**) make more intricate or confusing.

complicated adjective **1** consisting of many connected elements; intricate. **2** involving many different and confusing aspects.

complication noun **1** a circumstance that complicates something; a difficulty. **2** an involved or confused state. **3** an extra disease or condition which makes an existing one worse.

complicit adjective involved with others in an unlawful activity.

complicity noun involvement with others in an unlawful activity.

compliment noun /kom-pli-muhnt/ **1** a remark that expresses praise or admiration. **2** (**compliments**) formal greetings. verb /kom-pli-ment/ politely congratulate or praise.

> ℹ️ don't confuse **compliment** and **complement**: see the note at **COMPLEMENT**.

complimentary adjective **1** praising or approving. **2** given free of charge.

comply verb (**complies, complying, complied**) (**comply with**) **1** do what someone wants or tells you to do. **2** meet specified standards.

component noun a part of a larger whole.

comportment noun formal behaviour or bearing.

compose verb (**composes, composing, composed**) **1** create a work of art, especially music or poetry. **2** make up a whole. **3** arrange in an orderly or artistic way. **4** (**composed**) calm and in control of your feelings. ■ **composer** noun.

composite /kom-puh-zit/ adjective made up of various parts. noun a thing

made up of several parts.

composition noun **1** the way in which something is made up. **2** a work of music, literature, or art. **3** something made up of various elements. **4** the action of composing.

compositor noun a person who arranges type or keys text for printing.

compos mentis /kom-poss **men**-tiss/ adjective having full control of your mind.

compost noun decayed organic material added to soil as a fertilizer.

composure noun the state of being calm and self-controlled.

compound[1] noun /kom-pownd/ **1** a thing made up of two or more separate elements. **2** a substance formed from two or more elements chemically united in fixed proportions. adjective /kom-pownd/ made up or consisting of several parts. verb /kuhm-**pownd**/ **1** make up a whole from several elements. **2** make something bad worse. □ **compound fracture** an injury in which a broken bone pierces the skin.

compound[2] /kom-pownd/ noun a large open area enclosed by a fence.

comprehend verb grasp mentally; understand.

comprehensible adjective able to be understood; intelligible.

comprehension noun **1** the action of understanding. **2** the ability to understand.

comprehensive adjective **1** including or dealing with all or nearly all aspects of something. **2** Brit. (of secondary education) in which children of all abilities are educated in one school. **3** (of a victory or defeat) by a large margin. noun Brit. a comprehensive school.

compress verb /kuhm-**press**/ **1** flatten by pressure; force into less space. **2** squeeze or press two things together. noun /kom-press/ an absorbent pad pressed on to part of the body to relieve inflammation or stop bleeding. ■ **compression** noun.

compressor noun a machine used to

supply air at increased pressure.

comprise verb (**comprises, comprising, comprised**) **1** be made up of; consist of. **2** (also **be comprised of**) make up; constitute.

compromise noun **1** an agreement reached by each side giving way on some points. **2** an intermediate state between conflicting opinions. verb (**compromises, compromising, compromised**) **1** give way on some points in order to settle a dispute. **2** accept something that is less good than you would like. **3** cause someone danger or embarrassment by behaving in an indiscreet or reckless way.

comptroller /kuhn-**troh**-ler, komp-**troh**-ler/ noun a controller of financial affairs.

compulsion noun **1** pressure to do something. **2** an irresistible urge to behave in a certain way.

compulsive adjective **1** done because of an irresistible urge. **2** unable to stop yourself doing something. **3** irresistibly exciting. ■ **compulsively** adverb.

compulsory adjective required by law or a rule; obligatory.

compunction noun a feeling of guilt about doing something wrong.

computation noun **1** mathematical calculation. **2** the use of computers. ■ **computational** adjective.

compute verb (**computes, computing, computed**) reckon or calculate a figure or amount.

computer noun an electronic device capable of storing and processing information in accordance with a set of instructions. ■ **computing** noun.

computerize or **computerise** verb (**computerizes, computerizing, computerized**) convert to a system controlled by or stored on computer.

comrade noun **1** (among men) a person who shares your activities or is a fellow member of an organization. **2** a fellow soldier. ■ **comradeship** noun.

con¹ informal verb (**cons, conning, conned**) deceive someone into doing or believing something. noun a deception of this kind. □ **con man** a man who cheats people after gaining their trust.

con² noun (usu. in **pros and cons**) a disadvantage or argument against something.

concatenation noun a series of interconnected things.

concave adjective having an outline or surface that curves inwards.

conceal verb stop someone or something being seen or known. ■ **concealment** noun.

concede verb (**concedes, conceding, conceded**) **1** finally admit that something is true. **2** surrender a possession, advantage, or right. **3** admit defeat in a match or contest. **4** fail to prevent an opponent scoring a goal or point.

conceit noun **1** excessive pride in yourself. **2** an artistic effect. **3** a fanciful idea.

conceited adjective excessively proud of yourself.

conceivable adjective able to be imagined or understood. ■ **conceivably** adverb.

conceive verb (**conceives, conceiving, conceived**) **1** become pregnant with a child. **2** imagine.

✓ | *i* before *e* except after *c*: conc*ei*ve.

---

concentrate verb (**concentrates, concentrating, concentrated**) **1** (often **concentrate on**) focus all of your attention on something. **2** gather together in numbers or a mass at one point. **3** (**concentrated**) (of a solution) strong. noun a concentrated substance or solution.

concentration noun **1** the action or power of concentrating. **2** a close gathering of people or things. **3** the amount of a particular substance in a solution or mixture. □ **concentration camp** a camp for holding political prisoners.

concentric adjective (of circles or arcs) sharing the same centre.

concept noun an abstract idea.

conception noun **1** the conceiving of a child. **2** the devising of a plan or idea. **3** a concept. **4** ability to imagine or understand.

conceptual adjective having to do with concepts. ■ **conceptually** adverb.

conceptualize or **conceptualise** verb (**conceptualizes, conceptualizing, conceptualized**) form an idea of something in your mind.

concern verb **1** relate to; be about. **2** affect or involve. **3** make someone anxious or worried. noun **1** worry; anxiety. **2** a matter of interest or importance. **3** a business.

concerned adjective worried or anxious.

concerning preposition about.

concert noun **1** a musical performance given in public. **2** formal agreement or harmony.

concerted adjective **1** jointly arranged or carried out. **2** done in a determined way.

concertina noun a small musical instrument which you play by stretching and squeezing it and pressing buttons. verb (**concertinas, concertinaing, concertinaed**) compress in folds like those of a concertina.

concerto /kuhn-**cher**-toh/ noun (plural **concertos** or **concerti**) a musical composition for an orchestra and one or more solo instruments.

concession noun **1** something done or given up in order to settle a dispute. **2** a reduction allowed in the price of something. **3** the right to use land or other property for a particular purpose. **4** a stall or bar selling things within a larger business or shop. ■ **concessionary** adjective.

conch noun (plural **conches**) a shellfish with a spiral shell.

concierge /kon-si-**airzh**/ noun a resident caretaker of a block of flats or small hotel.

conciliate verb (**conciliates, conciliating, conciliated**) **1** make someone calm and content. **2** try to bring the two sides in a dispute together. ■ **conciliation** noun **conciliatory** adjective.

concise adjective giving a lot of information clearly and in few words. ■ **concisely** adverb **concision** noun.

conclave noun a private meeting.

conclude verb (**concludes, concluding, concluded**) **1** bring or come to an end. **2** arrive at an opinion by reasoning. **3** formally settle or arrange a treaty or agreement.

conclusion noun **1** an end or finish. **2** the summing up of an argument or text. **3** a decision reached by reasoning.

conclusive adjective decisive or convincing. ■ **conclusively** adverb.

concoct verb **1** make a dish by combining ingredients. **2** invent or devise a story or plan. ■ **concoction** noun.

concomitant /kuhn-**kom**-i-tuhnt/ adjective formal naturally accompanying or associated.

concord noun agreement; harmony.

concordance noun an alphabetical list of the important words in a text.

concordat /kuhn-**kor**-dat/ noun an agreement or treaty.

concourse noun a large open area inside or in front of a public building.

concrete adjective **1** existing in a material or physical form; not abstract. **2** specific; definite. noun a building material made from gravel, sand, cement, and water. verb (**concretes, concreting, concreted**) cover or fix solidly with concrete.

concretion noun a hard solid mass formed by accumulation of matter.

concubine /**kong**-kyuu-byn/ noun (in some societies) a woman who lives with a man but has lower status than his wife or wives.

concur verb (**concurs, concurring, concurred**) **1** (often **concur with**) agree. **2** happen at the same time.

concurrent adjective existing or happening at the same time. ■ **concurrently** adverb.

concussion noun **1** temporary unconsciousness or confusion caused by a blow on the head. **2** violent shock or shaking. ■ **concussed** adjective.

condemn verb 1 express complete disapproval of. 2 (usu. **condemn to**) sentence someone to a punishment. 3 (**condemn to**) force someone to endure something unpleasant. 4 officially declare something to be unfit for use. ■ **condemnation** noun.

condensation noun 1 water from humid air collecting as droplets on a cold surface. 2 the conversion of a vapour or gas to a liquid.

condense verb (**condenses, condensing, condensed**) 1 make more concentrated. 2 change from a gas or vapour to a liquid. 3 express a piece of writing or speech in fewer words. □ **condensed milk** milk that has been thickened and sweetened.

condescend verb 1 show that you feel superior to someone. 2 do something despite regarding it as beneath your dignity. 3 (**condescending**) patronizing in manner.

condescension noun a patronizing attitude or way of behaving.

condiment noun something such as salt or mustard that is added to food to bring out its flavour.

condition noun 1 the state that someone or something is in as regards appearance, fitness, or working order. 2 (**conditions**) circumstances that affect the way something works or exists. 3 a state of affairs that must exist before something else is possible. 4 an illness or medical problem. verb 1 (**be conditioned**) be influenced or determined by. 2 bring something into a good condition. 3 train or influence someone to behave in a certain way.

conditional adjective 1 subject to one or more conditions. 2 Grammar expressing something that must happen or be true before something else can happen or be true. ■ **conditionally** adverb.

conditioner noun a liquid added when washing hair or clothing, to make them softer.

condo = **CONDOMINIUM**.

condole verb (**condoles, condoling, condoled**) (**condole with**) express sympathy to.

condolence noun an expression of sympathy.

condom noun a rubber sheath that a man wears on his penis during sex to stop the woman getting pregnant.

condominium /kon-duh-**min**-i-uhm/ noun (plural **condominiums**) N. Amer. a building containing a number of individually owned flats.

condone verb (**condones, condoning, condoned**) accept or forgive an offence or wrong.

condor noun a very large South American vulture.

conducive adjective (**conducive to**) contributing or helping towards.

conduct noun /kon-dukt/ 1 the way in which a person behaves. 2 management or direction. verb /kuhn-**dukt**/ 1 organize and carry out. 2 direct the performance of a piece of music. 3 guide or lead someone to a place. 4 (**conduct yourself**) behave in a particular way. 5 transmit heat or electricity directly through a substance. ■ **conduction** noun.

conductance noun the degree to which a material conducts electricity.

conductive adjective conducting heat or electricity. ■ **conductivity** noun.

conductor noun 1 a person who conducts musicians. 2 a material or device that conducts heat or electricity. 3 a person who collects fares on a bus.

conduit /kon-dit, kon-dyuu-it/ noun 1 a channel for moving water from one place to another. 2 a tube protecting electric wiring.

cone noun 1 an object which tapers from a circular base to a point. 2 the hard, dry fruit of a pine or fir tree.

coney noun (plural **coneys**) a rabbit.

confect verb make something elaborate.

confection noun 1 an elaborate sweet dish or delicacy. 2 something put together elaborately.

confectionery noun (plural **confectioneries**) sweets and chocolates.

> ☑ the ending is *-ery*, not *-ary*: confectionery.

confederacy noun (plural **confederacies**) **1** an alliance of groups or states. **2** (**the Confederacy**) the Confederate states of the US.

confederate adjective /kuhn-**fed**-uh-ruht/ **1** joined by an agreement or treaty. **2** (**Confederate**) having to do with the southern states which separated from the US in 1860–1. verb /kuhn-**fed**-uh-rayt/ (**confederates, confederating, confederated**) unite in an alliance.

confederation noun an alliance of states or groups.

confer verb (**confers, conferring, conferred**) **1** formally give a title, benefit, or right. **2** have discussions.

conference noun a formal meeting to discuss something.

confess verb **1** admit that you have done something criminal or wrong. **2** acknowledge reluctantly. **3** formally declare your sins to a priest.

confession noun **1** an act of confessing. **2** formal declaration of your sins to a priest.

confessional noun **1** an enclosed box in a church, in which a priest sits to hear confessions. **2** a confession.

confessor noun a priest who hears confessions.

confetti noun small pieces of coloured paper traditionally thrown over a bride and groom after a marriage ceremony.

confidant noun (feminine **confidante**) a person that you confide in.

confide verb (**confides, confiding, confided**) (often **confide in**) tell someone about a secret or private matter.

confidence noun **1** faith in someone or something. **2** a positive feeling gained from a belief in your own ability to do things well. **3** a feeling of certainty about something. □ **confidence trick** an act of cheating someone after gaining their trust. **in confidence** as a secret.

confident adjective **1** feeling confidence in yourself. **2** feeling certain about something. ■ **confidently** noun.

confidential adjective intended to be kept secret. ■ **confidentiality** noun **confidentially** adverb.

configuration noun a particular arrangement of parts.

configure verb (**configures, configuring, configured**) arrange or set up in a particular way.

confine verb /kuhn-**fyn**/ (**confines, confining, confined**) **1** (**confine to**) restrict to certain limits. **2** (**be confined to**) be unable to leave a place due to illness or disability. noun (**confines**) /**kon**-fynz/ limits, boundaries, or restrictions.

confined adjective (of a space) enclosed; cramped.

confinement noun **1** the state of being confined. **2** dated the time around which a woman gives birth to a baby.

confirm verb **1** establish that something is true or correct. **2** state that something is definitely true. **3** make something definite or valid. **4** (**be confirmed**) go through the religious ceremony of confirmation.

confirmation noun **1** the action of confirming. **2** the rite at which a baptized person is admitted as a full member of the Christian Church.

confirmed adjective firmly established in a habit, belief, etc.

confiscate verb (**confiscates, confiscating, confiscated**) officially take or seize someone's property.

conflagration noun a large and destructive fire.

conflate verb (**conflates, conflating, conflated**) combine into one.

conflict noun /**kon**-flikt/ **1** a serious disagreement. **2** a long-lasting armed struggle. **3** a difference of opinions, principles, etc. verb /kuhn-**flikt**/ (of opinions, stories, etc.) disagree or be different.

confluence noun the junction of two rivers.

conform verb (often **conform to**) **1** obey a rule. **2** behave in an expected or conventional way. **3** be similar in form or type.

conformist noun a person who behaves in an expected or conventional way.

conformity noun **1** compliance with conventions, rules, or laws. **2** similarity in form or type.

confound verb **1** surprise or bewilder. **2** prove someone wrong. **3** defeat a plan, aim, or hope. **4** (**confounded**) informal, dated used to express annoyance.

confront verb **1** meet an enemy or opponent face to face. **2** face up to and deal with a problem. **3** make someone face up to a problem.

confrontation noun a hostile or argumentative situation. ■ **confrontational** adjective.

confuse verb (**confuses**, **confusing**, **confused**) **1** make someone bewildered or perplexed. **2** make something less easy to understand. **3** mistake one thing or person for another.

confused adjective **1** bewildered. **2** difficult to understand or distinguish.

confusion noun **1** uncertainty or bewilderment. **2** a situation of panic or disorder. **3** the mistaking of one person or thing for another.

confute verb (**confutes**, **confuting**, **confuted**) formal prove a person or argument to be wrong.

conga noun a Latin American dance performed by people in single file.

congeal /kuhn-jeel/ verb become semi-solid.

congenial /kuhn-jee-ni-uhl/ adjective suited or pleasing to your tastes.

congenital /kuhn-jen-i-t'l/ adjective **1** (of a disease or abnormality) present from birth. **2** having a particular characteristic as part of your character: *a congenital liar.*

conger eel /kong-ger/ noun a large eel found in coastal waters.

congested adjective **1** so crowded that it is difficult to move freely. **2** abnormally full of blood. **3** blocked with mucus. ■ **congestion** noun.

conglomerate noun /kuhn-glom-muh-ruht/ **1** something consisting of a number of different and distinct things. **2** a large corporation formed by the merging of separate firms. ■ **conglomeration** noun.

congratulate verb (**congratulates**, **congratulating**, **congratulated**) **1** tell someone that you are pleased at their success or good fortune. **2** (**congratulate yourself**) think that you are fortunate or clever. ■ **congratulatory** adjective.

congratulation noun **1** (**congratulations**) good wishes given to someone who has had success or good fortune. **2** the action of congratulating.

congregate verb (**congregates**, **congregating**, **congregated**) gather into a crowd or mass.

congregation noun **1** a group of people assembled for religious worship. **2** a gathering or collection of people or things.

congress noun **1** a formal meeting or series of meetings between representatives of different groups. **2** (**Congress**) (in the US and some other countries) the national law-making body. ■ **congressional** adjective.

congruent /kong-groo-uhnt/ adjective **1** in agreement or harmony. **2** Geometry (of figures) identical in form. ■ **congruence** noun.

conical adjective shaped like a cone.

conifer noun a tree that bears cones and evergreen needle-like leaves. ■ **coniferous** adjective.

conjecture noun an opinion based on incomplete information; a guess. verb (**conjectures**, **conjecturing**, **conjectured**) form a conjecture; guess. ■ **conjectural** adjective.

conjoin verb formal join; combine.

conjugal /kon-juu-g'l/ adjective relating to marriage or the relationship between husband and wife.

conjugate /kon-juu-gayt/ verb (conjugates, conjugating, conjugated) Grammar give the different forms of a verb. ■ conjugation noun.

conjunction noun 1 a word used to connect words or clauses (e.g. *and*, *if*). 2 an instance of two or more things happening at the same time or being in the same place.

conjunctivitis /kuhn-jungk-ti-vy-tiss/ noun inflammation of the eye.

conjure verb (conjures, conjuring, conjured) (usu. conjure up) 1 make something appear by magic, or as if by magic. 2 make something appear as an image in the mind.

conjuring noun entertainment in the form of seemingly magical tricks. ■ conjuror (or conjurer) noun.

conk informal verb (conk out) 1 (of a machine) break down. 2 faint or go to sleep. noun a person's nose.

conker noun Brit. the dark brown nut of a horse chestnut tree.

connect verb 1 join or bring together; link. 2 (be connected) be related in some way. 3 join telephone lines so that a caller can speak to the desired person. ■ connective adjective.

connection or Brit. **connexion** noun 1 a link or relationship. 2 the action of connecting. 3 (connections) influential people that you know or are related to. 4 a train, bus, etc. that you can catch to continue a journey.

connive /kuh-nyv/ verb (connives, conniving, connived) 1 (connive at or in) secretly allow something wrong to be done. 2 (often connive with) conspire to do something wrong. ■ connivance noun.

connoisseur /kon-nuh-ser/ noun a person with very good judgement in matters of taste.

connotation noun an idea or feeling that is suggested by a word in addition to its main meaning.

connote verb (connotes, connoting, connoted) (of a word) suggest something in addition to its main meaning.

connubial /kuh-nyoo-bi-uhl/ adjective having to do with marriage.

conquer verb (conquers, conquering, conquered) 1 take control of a country or its people by military force. 2 successfully overcome a problem. ■ conqueror noun.

conquest noun 1 the action of conquering. 2 a place that has been conquered. 3 a person whose affection you have won.

conscience noun a person's moral sense of right and wrong.

conscientious /kon-shi-en-shuhss/ adjective careful and thorough in carrying out your work or duty. □ conscientious objector a person who refuses to serve in the armed forces for moral reasons. ■ conscientiously adverb.

conscious adjective 1 aware of and responding to your surroundings. 2 (usu. conscious of) aware. 3 deliberate; intentional. ■ consciously adverb consciousness noun.

conscript verb /kuhn-skript/ call someone up for compulsory military service. noun /kon-skript/ a person who has been conscripted. ■ conscription noun.

consecrate verb (consecrates, consecrating, consecrated) 1 make or declare something holy. 2 officially make someone a priest. ■ consecration noun.

consecutive adjective following in unbroken or logical sequence. ■ consecutively adverb.

consensual adjective relating to or involving consent or consensus.

consensus noun general agreement.

☑ con*sens*us, not -*cen*-.

consent noun permission or agreement. verb 1 give permission. 2 agree to do.

consequence noun 1 a result or effect. 2 importance or relevance.

consequent adjective following as a consequence. ■ consequently adverb.

conservation noun 1 preservation

GRAMMAR

Conjunction

A conjunction is used to join parts of sentences which usually, but not always, contain their own verbs, e.g.

> He found it difficult but I helped him
> They made lunch for Alice and Mary
> I waited until you came.

The most common conjunctions are:

after	in order that	that
although	like	though
and	now	till
as	once	unless
because	or	until
before	since	when
but	so	where
for	so that	whether
if	than	while

---

or restoration of the natural environment. **2** preservation of historical sites and objects. **3** careful use of a resource. ■ **conservationist** noun.

conservative adjective **1** opposed to change and holding traditional values. **2** (in politics) favouring free enterprise and private ownership. **3** (**Conservative**) relating to the Conservative Party. **4** (of an estimate) deliberately low for the sake of caution. noun **1** a conservative person. **2** (**Conservative**) a supporter or member of the Conservative Party. ■ **conservatism** noun **conservatively** adverb.

conservatory noun (plural **conservatories**) Brit. a room with a glass roof and walls, attached to a house.

conserve /kuhn-**serv**/ verb (**conserves, conserving, conserved**) protect something from being harmed or overused. noun /kuhn-**serv**, **kon**-serv/ fruit jam.

consider verb (**considers, considering, considers**) **1** think carefully about. **2** believe or think. **3** take into account when making a judgement.

considerable adjective **1** notably large. **2** significant or notable. ■ **considerably** adverb.

considerate adjective careful not to harm or inconvenience others. ■ **considerately** adverb.

consideration noun **1** careful thought. **2** a fact taken into account when making a decision. **3** thoughtfulness towards others.

considering preposition & conjunction taking into consideration. adverb informal taking everything into account.

consign verb **1** deliver something to someone. **2** (**consign to**) put someone or something in a place so as to be rid of them.

consignment noun a batch of goods that are delivered.

consist verb **1** (**consist of**) be composed or made up of. **2** (**consist in**) have as an essential feature.

consistency noun (plural **consistencies**) **1** the state of being consistent. **2** the thickness of a liquid or semi-liquid substance.

consistent adjective **1** always behaving in the same way; unchanging. **2** (usu. **consistent with**) in agreement. ■ **consistently** adverb.

consolation noun **1** comfort received after a loss or disappointment. **2** a source of such comfort. ◻ **consola-**

tion prize a prize given to a competitor who just fails to win.

console[1] /kuhn-**sohl**/ verb (consoles, consoling, consoled) comfort someone who is unhappy or disappointed about something.

console[2] /**kon**-sohl/ noun **1** a panel or unit accommodating a set of controls. **2** a small machine for playing computerized video games.

consolidate verb (consolidates, consolidating, consolidated) **1** make stronger or more solid. **2** combine into a single unit. ∎ **consolidation** noun.

consommé /kuhn-**som**-may/ noun a clear soup made with concentrated stock.

consonance noun formal agreement or compatibility.

consonant noun a letter of the alphabet representing a sound in which the breath is completely or partly obstructed. **adjective (consonant with)** formal in agreement or harmony with.

consort formal noun /**kon**-sort/ a wife, husband, or companion. verb /kuhn-**sort**/ (consort with) habitually associate with.

consortium noun (plural consortia or consortiums) an association of several companies.

conspicuous /kuhn-**spik**-yoo-uhss/ adjective **1** clearly visible. **2** attracting notice. ∎ **conspicuously** adverb.

conspiracy noun (plural conspiracies) a secret plan by a group to do something unlawful or harmful.

conspire verb (conspires, conspiring, conspired) **1** jointly make secret plans to commit a wrongful act. **2** (of circumstances) seem to be working together to bring about something bad. ∎ **conspirator** noun **conspiratorial** adjective.

constable noun Brit. a police officer of the lowest rank.

constabulary /kuhn-**stab**-yuu-luh-ri/ noun (plural constabularies) Brit. a police force.

constant adjective **1** occurring continuously. **2** remaining the same.

3 faithful and dependable. noun **1** an unchanging situation. **2** Mathematics & Physics a number or quantity that does not change its value. ∎ **constancy** noun **constantly** adverb.

constellation noun a group of stars forming a recognized pattern.

consternation noun anxiety or dismay.

constipated adjective affected with constipation.

constipation noun difficulty in emptying the bowels.

constituency noun (plural constituencies) chiefly Brit. an area that elects a representative to a law-making body.

constituent adjective being a part of a whole. noun **1** a member of a constituency. **2** a part of a whole.

constitute verb (constitutes, constituting, constituted) **1** be a part of a whole. **2** be equivalent to. **3** establish by law.

constitution noun **1** a body of principles according to which a state or organization is governed. **2** composition or formation. **3** a person's physical or mental state.

constitutional adjective **1** relating to or in accordance with a constitution. **2** relating to a person's physical or mental state. noun dated a walk taken regularly to maintain good health. ∎ **constitutionally** adverb.

constrain verb **1** force someone to do a particular thing. **2** (constrained) appearing forced. **3** severely restrict or limit.

constraint noun a limitation or restriction.

constrict verb **1** make or become narrower; tighten. **2** stop someone moving or acting freely. ∎ **constriction** noun.

constrictor noun a snake that kills by squeezing and choking its prey.

construct verb /kuhn-**strukt**/ build or erect. noun /**kon**-strukt/ an idea or theory containing various elements.

construction noun **1** the process of constructing. **2** a building or other structure. **3** an interpretation of something.

constructive adjective having a useful and helpful effect. ■ **constructively** adverb.

construe verb (**construes, construing, construed**) interpret something in a particular way.

consul noun **1** an official who is based in a foreign city and protects their country's citizens and interests there. **2** (in ancient Rome) each of two elected officials who ruled the republic jointly for a year. ■ **consular** adjective.

consulate noun the place where a consul works.

consult verb **1** try to get information or advice from. **2** ask someone for permission or approval. ■ **consultation** noun **consultative** adjective.

consultancy noun (plural **consultancies**) a company that gives expert advice in a particular field.

consultant noun **1** a person who provides expert advice professionally. **2** Brit. a senior hospital doctor.

consume verb (**consumes, consuming, consumed**) **1** eat or drink. **2** use up. **3** (of a fire) completely destroy. **4** (of a feeling) absorb someone wholly.

consumer noun a person who buys a product or uses a service.

consumerism noun the preoccupation of society with acquiring goods. ■ **consumerist** adjective.

consummate verb /**kon**-syuu-mayt/ (**consummates, consummating, consummated**) **1** make a marriage or relationship complete by having sex. **2** complete a transaction. adjective /kuhn-**sum**-muht, **kon**-sum-muht/ showing great skill and flair. ■ **consummation** noun.

consumption noun **1** the process of consuming. **2** an amount consumed. **3** dated a wasting disease, especially tuberculosis. ■ **consumptive** adjective.

contact noun **1** physical touching. **2** communicating or meeting. **3** a person whom you can ask for information or help. **4** a connection for an electric current to pass from one thing to another. verb get in touch with. □ **contact lens** a plastic lens placed on the surface of the eye to help you see better.

contagion noun the passing of a disease from one person to another by close contact.

contagious adjective **1** (of a disease) spread by contact between people. **2** having a contagious disease.

contain verb **1** have or hold something inside. **2** control or restrain. **3** prevent a problem from becoming worse.

container noun **1** a box or similar object for holding something. **2** a large metal box for transporting goods.

containment noun the keeping of something harmful under control.

contaminate verb (**contaminates, contaminating, contaminated**) make something impure by exposing it to a poisonous or polluting substance. ■ **contamination** noun.

contemplate verb (**contemplates, contemplating, contemplated**) **1** look at thoughtfully. **2** think about. **3** think profoundly and at length. ■ **contemplation** noun **contemplative** adjective.

contemporaneous /kuhn-tem-puh-**ray**-ni-uhss/ adjective existing at or occurring in the same period of time. ■ **contemporaneously** adverb.

contemporary adjective **1** living or occurring at the same time. **2** belonging to or occurring in the present. **3** modern in style. noun (plural **contemporaries**) a person living or working in the same period as another.

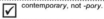 contem*porary*, not *-pory*.

contempt noun **1** the feeling that someone or something is worthless. **2** (also **contempt of court**) the offence of disobeying or being disrespectful to a court of law. □ **beneath contempt** utterly worthless or despicable.

contemptible adjective deserving contempt. ■ **contemptibly** adverb.

contemptuous adjective showing contempt. ■ **contemptuously** adverb.

contend verb **1** (**contend with** or **against**) struggle to deal with a difficulty. **2** (**contend for**) struggle to achieve. **3** put forward a view in an argument. ■ **contender** noun.

content[1] /kuhn-**tent**/ adjective peacefully happy or satisfied. verb satisfy or please. noun a state of happiness or satisfaction. ■ **contentment** noun.

content[2] /**kon**-tent/ noun **1** (**contents**) the things that are contained in something. **2** the amount of a particular thing occurring in a substance. **3** (**contents**) a list of chapters given at the front of a book or magazine. **4** the material in a piece of writing, as opposed to its form or style.

contented adjective **1** happy and at ease. **2** willing to accept something; satisfied. ■ **contentedly** adverb.

contention noun **1** heated disagreement. **2** a point of view that is expressed. □ **in contention** having a good chance of success in a contest.

contentious adjective causing disagreement or controversy; controversial. ■ **contentiously** adverb.

contest noun /**kon**-test/ an event in which people compete to see who is the best. verb /kuhn-**test**/ **1** take part in a competition or election. **2** challenge or dispute a decision or theory.

contestant noun a person who takes part in a contest.

context noun **1** the circumstances surrounding an event, statement, or idea. **2** the parts that come immediately before and after a word or passage and make its meaning clearer. ■ **contextual** adjective.

contiguous /kuhn-**tig**-yoo-uhss/ adjective **1** sharing a border. **2** next or together in sequence.

continent[1] noun **1** any of the world's main continuous expanses of land (Europe, Asia, Africa, North and South America, Australia, Antarctica). **2** (**the Continent**) the mainland of Europe as distinct from the British Isles.

continent[2] adjective **1** able to control movements of the bowels and bladder. **2** restrained; self-disciplined. ■ **continence** noun.

continental adjective **1** forming or belonging to a continent. **2** coming from or like mainland Europe. noun a person from mainland Europe. □ **continental breakfast** a light breakfast of coffee and bread rolls.

contingency noun (plural **contingencies**) **1** a future event which is possible but cannot be predicted with certainty. **2** a plan made in case a particular thing happens.

contingent adjective **1** depending on chance. **2** (**contingent on**) dependent on. noun a group of people forming part of a larger group.

continual adjective happening constantly or often, with intervals in between: *he met with continual delays.* ■ **continually** adverb.

> i note that **continual** and **continuous** don't mean exactly the same thing.

continuation noun **1** the action of continuing. **2** a part that is attached to something else and is an extension of it.

continue verb (**continues, continuing, continued**) **1** keep doing something; carry on with. **2** keep existing or happening. **3** carry on travelling in the same direction. **4** start doing something again; resume.

continuity noun (plural **continuities**) **1** unbroken existence or operation. **2** an unbroken connection or line of development. **3** organization of a film or television programme so that the plot makes sense and clothing, scenery, etc. remain the same in different scenes.

continuous adjective forming an unbroken whole or sequence without interruptions or exceptions: *it was a day of continuous rain.* ■ **continuously** adverb.

WORD FORMATION

contra-, counter-

contra- and **counter-** both come from the Latin word *contra*, meaning 'against'. Both are used in words that mean 'against or opposite', such as *contraception*, *contraflow*, *counter-attack*, and *counterproductive*.
counter- has the extra meaning 'corresponding', as in *counterpart*.

---

continuum noun (plural **continua**) a continuous sequence in which the elements change gradually.

contort verb twist or bend something out of its normal shape. ■ **contortion** noun.

contortionist noun an entertainer who twists and bends their body into unnatural positions.

contour noun **1** an outline of the shape or form of something. **2** (also **contour line**) a line on a map joining points of equal height. ■ **contoured** adjective.

contraband noun goods that have been imported or exported illegally.

contraception noun the use of contraceptives.

contraceptive adjective preventing a woman becoming pregnant. noun a device or drug used to prevent a woman becoming pregnant.

contract noun /kon-trakt/ **1** an official, legally binding agreement. **2** informal an arrangement for someone to be killed by a hired assassin. verb /kuhn-**trakt**/ **1** make or become smaller. **2** become shorter and tighter. **3** shorten a word or phrase. **4** enter into a formal and legally binding agreement. **5** catch or develop a disease. ■ **contractual** adjective.

contraction noun **1** the process of contracting. **2** a shortening of the muscles of the womb occurring at intervals during childbirth.

contractor noun a person who undertakes a contract to provide materials or labour for a job.

contradict verb **1** deny that a statement is true by saying the opposite. **2** challenge someone by making a statement opposing one made by them.

contradiction noun **1** a combination of statements, ideas, or features which are opposed to one another. **2** saying the opposite to something already said.

contradictory adjective **1** inconsistent with or opposing each other. **2** containing inconsistent elements.

contradistinction noun distinction made by contrasting two things.

contraflow noun Brit. an arrangement by which the lanes of a dual carriageway normally carrying traffic in one direction become two-directional.

contralto /kuhn-**tral**-toh/ noun (plural **contraltos**) the lowest female singing voice.

contraption noun a machine or device that appears strange or unnecessarily complicated.

contrapuntal /kon-truh-**pun**-t'l/ adjective Music of or in counterpoint.

contrariwise adverb in the opposite way.

contrary /**kon**-truh-ri/ adjective **1** opposite in nature, direction, or meaning. **2** (of two or more statements, beliefs, etc.) opposed to one another. **3** /kuhn-**trair**-i/ deliberately inclined to do the opposite of what is expected or desired. noun (**the contrary**) the opposite.

contrast noun /**kon**-trahst/ **1** the state of being noticeably different from something else. **2** a thing or person noticeably different from another. **3** the amount of difference between tones in a television picture, photograph, etc. verb /kuhn-**trahst**/ **1** be noticeably different. **2** compare two things to emphasize their differences.

contravene verb (**contravenes**, **contravening**, **contravened**) **1** do something that breaks a law, treaty, etc. **2** conflict with a right, principle, etc. ■ **contravention** noun.

contretemps /kon-truh-ton/ noun (plural **contretemps** /kon-truh-tonz/) a minor disagreement.

contribute verb (**contributes**, **contributing**, **contributed**) **1** give something in order to help an undertaking or effort. **2** (**contribute to**) help to cause or bring about. ■ **contribution** noun **contributor** noun.

contributory adjective **1** playing a part in bringing something about. **2** (of a pension or insurance scheme) operated by means of a fund into which people pay.

contrite adjective sorry for something that you have done. ■ **contritely** adverb **contrition** noun.

contrivance noun **1** the action of contriving. **2** an ingenious device or scheme.

contrive verb (**contrives**, **contriving**, **contrived**) **1** skilfully devise or plan something. **2** manage to do something foolish.

contrived adjective obviously created deliberately rather than arising spontaneously.

control noun **1** the power to influence people's behaviour or the course of events. **2** the restriction of an activity or phenomenon. **3** a way of limiting or regulating something. **4** a person or thing used as a standard of comparison for checking the results of a survey or experiment. verb (**controls**, **controlling**, **controlled**) **1** have control or command of. **2** limit or regulate. □ **control tower** a tall building at an airport from which the movements of aircraft are controlled. ■ **controllable** adjective **controller** noun.

controversial adjective causing or likely to cause controversy. ■ **controversially** adverb.

controversy /kon-truh-ver-si, kuhn-trov-er-si/ noun (plural **controversies**) debate or disagreement about a matter which arouses strong opinions.

contumely /kon-**tyoom**-li/ noun (plural **contumelies**) old use insulting language or treatment.

contusion noun a bruise.

conundrum /kuh-**nun**-druhm/ noun (plural **conundrums**) **1** a difficult problem or question. **2** a riddle.

conurbation /kon-er-**bay**-sh'n/ noun an area consisting of several towns merging together or with a city.

convalesce verb (**convalesces**, **convalescing**, **convalesced**) gradually get better after an illness or injury.

convalescent adjective recovering from an illness or injury. ■ **convalescence** noun.

convection noun the process by which heat moves through a gas or liquid as the warmer part rises and the cooler part sinks.

convector noun a heater that circulates warm air by convection.

convene verb (**convenes**, **convening**, **convened**) **1** call people together for a meeting. **2** come together for a meeting. ■ **convener** (or **convenor**) noun.

convenience noun **1** freedom from effort or difficulty. **2** a useful or helpful device or situation. **3** Brit. a public toilet.

convenient adjective **1** fitting in well with a person's needs, activities, and plans. **2** involving little trouble or effort. ■ **conveniently** adverb.

convent noun a building where nuns live together.

convention noun **1** a way in which something is usually done. **2** socially acceptable behaviour. **3** an agreement between countries. **4** a large meeting or conference.

conventional adjective **1** done in accordance with convention. **2** not individual or adventurous. **3** (of weapons or power) non-nuclear. ■ **conventionally** adverb.

converge verb (**converges**, **conver-**

ging, converged) 1 come together from different directions. **2 (converge on)** come from different directions and meet at. ■ **convergent** adjective.

conversant adjective (conversant with) familiar with or knowledgeable about.

conversation noun an informal spoken exchange. ■ **conversational** adjective **conversationalist** noun.

converse¹ verb /kuhn-verss/ **(converses, conversing, conversed)** hold a conversation.

converse² /kon-verss/ **noun** something that is the opposite of another. **adjective** opposite. ■ **conversely** adverb.

conversion noun 1 the action of converting. **2** Brit. a building that has been converted to a new purpose. **3** Rugby a successful kick at goal after a try.

convert verb /kuhn-**vert**/ **1** change the form, character, or function of something. **2** change money or units into others of a different kind. **3** adapt a building for a new purpose. **4** change your religious faith. **noun** /**kon**-vert/ a person who has changed their religious faith.

convertible adjective 1 able to be converted. **2** (of a car) having a folding or detachable roof. **noun** a convertible car.

convex adjective having an outline or surface that curves outwards.

convey verb 1 transport or carry to a place. **2** communicate an idea or feeling.

conveyance noun 1 the action of conveying. **2** formal a means of transport. **3** the legal process of transferring property from one owner to another. ■ **conveyancing** noun.

conveyor belt noun a continuous moving band used for transporting objects from one place to another.

convict verb /kuhn-**vikt**/ officially declare that someone is guilty of a criminal offence. **noun** /**kon**-vikt/ a person in prison after being convicted of a criminal offence.

conviction noun 1 an instance of being convicted of a criminal offence. **2** a firmly held belief or opinion. **3** the quality of showing that you believe strongly in what you are saying or doing.

convince verb (convinces, convincing, convinced) 1 cause someone to believe firmly that something is true. **2** persuade to do something.

convincing adjective 1 able to convince. **2** (of a victory or a winner) leaving no margin of doubt. ■ **convincingly** adverb.

convivial adjective 1 (of an atmosphere or event) friendly and lively. **2** (of a person) cheerfully sociable. ■ **conviviality** noun.

convoluted adjective 1 (of an argument or account) extremely complex. **2** intricately folded, twisted, or coiled.

convolution noun 1 a coil or twist. **2 (convolutions)** something complex and difficult to follow.

convoy noun a group of ships or vehicles travelling together under armed protection.

convulse verb (convulses, convulsing, convulsed) 1 suffer convulsions. **2 (be convulsed)** make sudden, uncontrollable movements because of emotion, laughter, etc. ■ **convulsive** adjective.

convulsion noun 1 a sudden, irregular movement of the body caused by the involuntary contraction of muscles. **2 (convulsions)** uncontrollable laughter. **3** a violent upheaval.

coo verb (coos, cooing, cooed) 1 (of a pigeon or dove) make a soft murmuring sound. **2** speak in a soft, gentle voice. **noun** a cooing sound.

cook verb 1 prepare food or a meal by heating the ingredients. **2** (of food) be heated so as to become edible. **3** informal alter accounts dishonestly. **4 (cook up)** informal concoct a story, excuse, or plan. **noun** a person who cooks.

cooker noun Brit. an appliance for cooking food.

cookery noun the practice or skill of preparing and cooking food.

cookie noun (plural **cookies**) **1** N. Amer. a sweet biscuit. **2** informal a person of a specified kind: *she's a tough cookie.*

cool adjective **1** at a fairly low temperature. **2** stopping you from becoming too hot. **3** unfriendly or unenthusiastic. **4** not anxious or excited. **5** informal fashionably attractive or impressive. **6** informal excellent. noun composure. verb (**cools, cooling, cooled**) make or become cool. ■ **cooler** noun **coolly** adverb **coolness** noun.

coolant noun a fluid used to cool an engine or other device.

coolie noun (plural **coolies**) dated an unskilled labourer in an Asian country.

coon noun N. Amer. a raccoon.

coop noun a cage or pen for poultry. verb (**coop up**) confine in a small space.

cooper noun a person who makes or repairs casks and barrels.

cooperate or **co-operate** verb (co-operates, cooperating, cooperated) **1** work together towards the same end. **2** do what someone wants. ■ **cooperation** noun.

cooperative or **co-operative** adjective **1** involving cooperation. **2** willing to be of assistance. **3** (of a business) owned and run jointly by its members. noun a cooperative organization. ■ **cooperatively** adverb.

co-opt verb **1** appoint someone as a member of a committee or other body. **2** adopt an idea or policy for your own use. ■ **co-option** noun.

coordinate or **co-ordinate** verb /koh-**or**-di-nayt/ (**coordinates, coordinating, coordinated**) **1** bring the different elements of something together so that it works well. **2** (co-ordinate with) negotiate with others to work together effectively. **3** match or harmonize different elements attractively. noun /koh-**or**-di-nuht/ Mathematics each of a group of numbers used to indicate the position of a point, line, or plane. ■ **coordinator** noun.

coordination or **co-ordination**

noun **1** the process of coordinating. **2** the ability to move different parts of the body smoothly and at the same time.

coot noun a waterbird with black plumage and a white bill.

cop informal noun a police officer. verb (**cops, copping, copped**) **1** arrest an offender. **2** receive or suffer something unwelcome. **3** (**cop out**) avoid doing something that you ought to do. □ **cop it** Brit. **1** get into trouble. **2** be killed. **not much cop** Brit. not very good.

cope[1] verb (**copes, coping, coped**) deal effectively with something difficult.

cope[2] noun a long cloak worn by a priest on ceremonial occasions.

copier noun a machine that makes exact copies of something.

co-pilot noun a second pilot in an aircraft.

coping noun the top line of bricks or stones in a wall.

copious adjective abundant; plentiful. ■ **copiously** adverb.

copper[1] noun **1** a reddish-brown metal. **2** (**coppers**) Brit. coins made of copper or bronze. **3** a reddish-brown colour. □ **copper-bottomed** Brit. thoroughly reliable.

copper[2] noun Brit. informal a police officer.

copperplate noun an elaborate style of handwriting.

coppice noun an area of woodland in which the trees or shrubs are periodically cut back to ground level.

copse noun a small group of trees.

copulate verb (**copulates, copulating, copulated**) mate or have sex. ■ **copulation** noun.

copy noun (plural **copies**) **1** a thing made to be similar or identical to another. **2** a single example of a particular book, record, etc. **3** material for a newspaper or magazine article. verb (**copies, copying, copied**) **1** make a copy of. **2** imitate the behaviour or style of. □ **copy-edit** check that text is consistent and accurate. ■ **copyist** noun.

copyright noun the exclusive right to publish, perform, film, or record literary, artistic, or musical material.

copywriter noun a person who writes the text of advertisements or publicity material.

coquette /ko-ket/ noun a flirtatious woman. ■ **coquetry** noun **coquettish** adjective.

coracle /ko-ruh-k'l/ noun a small round boat made of wickerwork covered with a watertight material.

coral noun 1 a hard substance found in warm seas which consists of the skeletons of small animals living together as a stationary group. 2 a pinkish-red colour.

cor anglais /kor ong-glay/ noun (plural **cors anglais** /kor ong-glay/) a woodwind instrument of the oboe family.

corbel noun a projection jutting out from a wall to support a structure above it.

cord noun 1 thin string or rope made from several twisted strands. 2 an electric flex. 3 corduroy. 4 (**cords**) trousers made of corduroy. ■ **cordless** adjective.

cordial adjective 1 warm and friendly. 2 sincere. noun 1 Brit. a sweet fruit-flavoured drink, sold in concentrated form. 2 chiefly N. Amer. a liqueur. ■ **cordiality** noun **cordially** adverb.

cordite noun a kind of explosive.

cordon noun a line or circle of police, soldiers, or guards forming a barrier. verb (**cordon off**) close off by means of a cordon.

cordon bleu /kor-don bler/ adjective Cookery of the highest class.

corduroy /kor-duh-roy/ noun a thick cotton fabric with velvety ridges.

core noun 1 the tough central part of a fruit. 2 the central or most important part of something. verb (**cores, coring, cored**) remove the core from a fruit.

co-respondent noun a person named in a divorce case as having committed adultery with the respondent.

corgi noun (plural **corgis**) a breed of dog with short legs and a pointed face.

coriander /ko-ri-an-der/ noun a plant used as a herb in cookery.

cork noun 1 a light, soft brown substance obtained from the bark of a tree. 2 a bottle stopper made of cork. verb 1 seal a bottle with a cork. 2 (**corked**) (of wine) spoilt by a faulty cork.

corker noun informal an excellent person or thing. ■ **corking** adjective.

corkscrew noun a device used for pulling corks from bottles. verb move or twist in a spiral.

corm noun an underground part of certain plants.

cormorant /kor-muh-ruhnt/ noun a diving seabird with a long hooked bill and black plumage.

corn[1] noun 1 Brit. the chief cereal crop of a district (in England, wheat). 2 N. Amer. & Austral./NZ maize. 3 informal something sentimental or overused. □ **corn on the cob** maize cooked and eaten straight from the cob.

corn[2] noun a painful area of thickened skin on the toes or foot.

cornea noun the transparent layer forming the front of the eye.

corned beef noun beef preserved with salt, often sold in tins.

corner noun 1 a place or angle where two or more sides or edges meet. 2 a place where two streets meet. 3 a secluded or remote area. 4 a difficult or awkward position. 5 Soccer a free kick taken by the attacking side from a corner of the field. verb (**corners, cornering, cornered**) 1 force someone into a place or situation from which it is hard to escape. 2 control the trade in a particular type of goods. 3 go round a bend in a road.

cornerstone noun 1 a stone that forms the base of a corner of a building. 2 a vital part.

cornet noun 1 a brass instrument resembling a trumpet but shorter and wider. **2** Brit. a cone-shaped wafer for holding ice cream.

cornflour noun Brit. ground maize flour, used for thickening sauces.

cornflower noun a plant with deep blue flowers.

cornice /**kor**-niss/ noun a decorative border round the wall of a room just below the ceiling.

cornucopia /kor-nyuu-**koh**-pi-uh/ noun a plentiful supply of good things.

corny adjective (**cornier, corniest**) informal sentimental or overused.

corolla /kuh-**rol**-luh/ noun the petals of a flower.

corollary /kuh-**rol**-luh-ri/ noun (plural **corollaries**) **1** a logical conclusion. **2** a direct consequence or result.

corona /kuh-**roh**-nuh/ noun (plural **coronae** /kuh-**roh**-nee/) **1** the gases surrounding the sun or a star. **2** a small circle of light around the sun or moon.

coronary /**ko**-ruh-nuh-ri/ adjective having to do with the heart, in particular with the arteries which supply it with blood. noun (plural **coronaries**) (also **coronary thrombosis**) a blockage of the flow of blood to the heart.

coronation noun the ceremony of crowning a sovereign.

coroner noun an official who holds inquests into violent, sudden, or suspicious deaths.

coronet noun **1** a small or simple crown. **2** a decorative band put around the head.

corpora plural of **CORPUS**.

corporal[1] noun a rank of officer in the army, below sergeant.

corporal[2] adjective relating to the human body. □ **corporal punishment** physical punishment, such as caning.

corporate adjective **1** relating to a business corporation. **2** of or shared by all members of a group.

corporation noun **1** a large company, or a group of companies acting as a single unit. **2** Brit. a group of people elected to govern a city, town, or borough.

corporeal /kor-**por**-i-uhl/ adjective relating to a person's body; physical rather than spiritual.

corps /kor/ noun (plural **corps** /korz/) **1** a large unit of an army. **2** a branch of an army with a particular kind of work. **3** a body of people engaged in a particular activity.

corpse noun a dead body, especially of a human.

corpulent /**kor**-pyuu-luhnt/ adjective (of a person) fat. ■ **corpulence** noun.

corpus /**kor**-puhss/ noun (plural **corpora** /**kor**-puh-ruh/ or **corpuses**) a collection of written texts.

corpuscle /**kor**-pus-s'l/ noun a red or white blood cell.

corral /kuh-**rahl**/ noun N. Amer. a pen for animals on a farm or ranch. verb (**corrals, corralling, corralled**) **1** N. Amer. drive animals into a corral. **2** gather a group together.

correct adjective **1** free from error; true or right. **2** behaving in accordance with accepted social standards. verb **1** put something right. **2** mark the errors in a text. **3** tell someone that they are wrong. ■ **correctly** adverb **correctness** noun.

correction noun **1** the process of correcting. **2** a change that corrects an error or inaccuracy.

corrective adjective designed to correct something undesirable.

correlate verb (**correlates, correlating, correlated**) place things together so that one thing affects or depends on another.

correlation noun **1** a situation in which one thing affects or depends on another. **2** the process of correlating two or more things.

correspond verb **1** match or agree almost exactly. **2** be comparable or equivalent. **3** communicate by exchanging letters.

correspondence noun **1** the fact of corresponding. **2** letters sent or received. □ **correspondence course** a course of study in which student and tutors communicate by post.

 -ence, not *-ance*: correspond**ence**.

correspondent noun **1** a person who writes letters. **2** a journalist who reports on a particular subject.

corridor noun **1** a passage in a building or train, with doors leading into rooms or compartments. **2** a belt of land linking two other areas.

 there is no *door*: corri**dor**.

corroborate verb (**corroborates, corroborating, corroborated**) confirm or give support to a statement or theory. ■ **corroboration** noun.

corrode verb (**corrodes, corroding, corroded**) **1** slowly wear away a hard material by the action of a chemical. **2** gradually weaken or destroy.

corrosion noun the process of corroding, or damage caused by it.

corrosive adjective tending to cause corrosion.

corrugate verb **1** contract into wrinkles or folds. **2** (**corrugated**) shaped into alternate ridges and grooves. ■ **corrugation** noun.

corrupt adjective **1** willing to act dishonestly in return for money or other reward. **2** evil or immoral. **3** (of a text or computer data) unreliable because of errors or alterations. verb make corrupt. ■ **corruptly** adverb.

corruption noun **1** dishonest or illegal behaviour. **2** the action of corrupting. **3** an alteration or error in a text or computer data.

corsage /kor-sah*zh*/ noun a small bunch of flowers worn pinned to a woman's clothes.

corset noun a tight-fitting undergarment worn to shape a woman's figure or to support a person's back.

cortège /kor-te*zh*/ noun a funeral procession.

cortex /kor-teks/ noun (plural **cortices** /kor-ti-seez/) the outer layer of an organ or structure, especially the outer layer of the brain.

coruscating /ko-ruh-skay-ting/ adjective literary flashing or sparkling.

corvette /kor-vet/ noun a small warship designed for escorting convoys.

cos abbreviation cosine.

cosh noun a thick, heavy stick or bar used as a weapon. verb hit someone on the head with a cosh.

cosine /koh-syn/ noun Mathematics (in a right-angled triangle) the ratio of the side next to a particular acute angle to the longest side.

cosmetic adjective **1** (of treatment) intended to improve a person's appearance. **2** improving something only outwardly. noun (**cosmetics**) substances put on the face and body to make them more attractive.

cosmic adjective relating to the universe.

cosmonaut noun a Russian astronaut.

cosmopolitan adjective **1** made up of people from many different countries and cultures. **2** familiar with many different countries.

cosmos noun the universe.

Cossack /koss-ak/ noun a member of a people of Russia and Ukraine famous for being good riders.

cosset verb (**cossets, cosseting, cosseted**) look after and protect someone in an excessively softhearted way.

cost verb (**costs, costing, cost**) **1** be able to be obtained in exchange for a specific price. **2** involve the loss of. **3** (**costs, costing, costed**) estimate the cost of work that needs to be done. noun **1** an amount given or required as payment. **2** the effort or loss necessary to achieve something. **3** (**costs**) legal expenses. □ **cost-effective** effective or productive in relation to its cost.

co-star noun a performer appearing with another or others of equal importance. verb **1** appear in a production as a co-star. **2** (of a production) include someone as a co-star.

costermonger noun dated a person who sells fruit and vegetables in the street.

costly adjective (**costlier, costliest**) **1** expensive. **2** causing suffering, loss, or disadvantage.

costume noun **1** a set of clothes in a style typical of a particular country or historical period. **2** a set of clothes worn by an actor or performer for a role. verb (**be costumed**) be dressed in a costume. □ **costume jewellery** jewellery made with inexpensive materials or imitation gems.

costumier /koss-**tyoo**-mi-er/ noun a person who makes or supplies theatrical or fancy-dress costumes.

cosy (US spelling **cozy**) adjective (**cosier, cosiest**) **1** comfortable, warm, and secure. **2** not difficult or demanding. noun (plural **cosies**) a cover to keep a teapot or a boiled egg hot. ■ **cosily** adverb **cosiness** noun.

cot noun a small bed with high barred sides for a baby or very young child. □ **cot death** the unexplained death of a baby in its sleep.

coterie /**koh**-tuh-ri/ noun (plural **coteries**) a small, close-knit group of people.

cottage noun a small house in the country. □ **cottage cheese** soft, lumpy white cheese.

cotter pin noun a metal pin used to fasten two parts of a mechanism together.

cotton noun **1** soft white fibres surrounding the seeds of a plant that grows in warm climates. **2** cloth or thread made from these fibres. verb (**cotton on**) informal begin to understand. □ **cotton wool** fluffy soft material used for wiping the skin.

cotyledon /ko-ti-**lee**-duhn/ noun the first leaf that grows from a seed.

couch noun a long upholstered piece of furniture for sitting or lying on. verb (**couch in**) express something in language of a particular style. □ **couch potato** informal a person who watches a lot of television.

cougar /**koo**-ger/ noun N. Amer. a puma.

cough verb **1** send out air from the lungs with a sudden sharp sound. **2** (**cough up**) informal reluctantly give money or information noun **1** an act of coughing. **2** an illness of the throat or lungs causing coughing.

could modal verb past of CAN¹.

couldn't short form could not.

coulomb /**koo**-lom/ noun a unit of electric charge.

council noun **1** an assembly of people that meets regularly to discuss or organize something. **2** a body of people elected to manage the affairs of a city, county, or district. □ **council house** a house owned by a local council and rented to tenants. **council tax** (in the UK) a tax charged on households by local authorities.

councillor noun a member of a council.

> ℹ note the difference between **councillor** and **counsellor**.

counsel noun **1** advice. **2** (plural **counsel**) a barrister or other lawyer involved in a case. verb (**counsels, counselling, counselled**; US spelling **counsels, counseling, counseled**) **1** advise or recommend. **2** give professional help and advice to someone with psychological or personal problems. □ **keep your own counsel** not reveal your plans or opinions.

counsellor (US spelling **counselor**) noun a person trained to give advice on personal or psychological problems.

count¹ verb **1** find the total number of. **2** recite numbers in ascending order. **3** take into account. **4** regard as being a specified thing. **5** be important. **6** (**count on**) rely on. **7** (**count in** or **out**) include (or not include) in an activity. noun **1** an act of counting. **2** a total found by counting. **3** a point to be discussed or considered. **4** Law each of the charges against an accused person. □ **out for the count 1** Boxing defeated by being knocked to the ground and unable to rise within ten seconds. **2** informal unconscious or asleep.

count² noun a foreign nobleman.

countdown noun an act of counting down to zero.

countenance noun a person's face or expression. verb (**countenances**, **countenancing**, **countenanced**) tolerate or allow.

counter¹ noun **1** a long flat surface over which goods are sold or served or across which business is conducted with customers. **2** a small disc used in board games or to represent a coin. **3** a person or thing that counts something. □**under the counter** bought or sold secretly and illegally.

counter² verb (**counters**, **countering**, **countered**) **1** argue against or reply to. **2** try to stop or prevent. adverb (**counter to**) **1** in the opposite direction to. **2** in opposition to.

counteract verb do something to reduce or prevent the bad effects of.

counter-attack noun an attack made in response to an attack. verb attack in response.

counterbalance noun **1** a weight that balances another. **2** something that has an equal but opposite effect to something else. verb (**counterbalances**, **counterbalancing**, **counterbalanced**) have an equal but opposite effect on.

counter-espionage noun activities designed to prevent or frustrate spying by an enemy.

counterfeit /kown-ter-fit/ adjective made in exact imitation of something valuable so as to deceive or cheat people. noun a forgery. verb imitate something dishonestly.

counterfoil noun the part of a cheque, ticket, etc. that you keep when you give the other part up.

countermand verb cancel an order.

countermeasure noun something done to deal with a danger or threat.

counterpane noun dated a bedspread.

counterpart noun a person or thing that corresponds to another.

counterpoint noun **1** the playing of two or more tunes at the same time. **2** a tune played at the same time as another.

counterproductive adjective having the opposite of the desired effect.

countersign verb sign a document that has already been signed by another person.

countersink verb (**countersinks**, **countersinking**, **countersunk**) insert a screw or bolt so that the head lies flat with the surface.

countertenor noun the highest male adult singing voice.

countervailing adjective having an equal but opposite effect.

countess noun **1** the wife or widow of a count or earl. **2** a woman holding the rank of count or earl.

counting preposition taking account of; including.

countless adjective too many to be counted; very many.

countrified adjective characteristic of the country or country life.

country noun (plural **countries**) **1** a nation with its own government. **2** areas outside large towns and cities. **3** an area of land with particular physical features: *hilly country.* □**country music** (or **country and western**) a kind of popular music from the rural southern US.

countryside noun land and scenery outside towns and cities.

county noun (plural **counties**) each of the main areas into which some countries are divided for the purposes of local government. □**county town** the main town of a county, where its council is based.

coup /koo/ noun (plural **coups** /kooz/) **1** (also **coup d'état** /koo day-**tah**/) a sudden violent seizing of power from a government. **2** an unexpected successful move.

coupe /koo-pay, koop/ noun a sports car with a fixed roof and a sloping rear.

couple noun **1** two individuals of the same sort considered together. **2** two people who are married or in a romantic or sexual relationship. **3** informal an unspecified small number. verb (**couples, coupling, coupled**) **1** connect or combine. **2** have sex.

couplet noun a pair of rhyming lines of poetry one after another.

coupling noun a device for connecting railway vehicles or parts of machinery together.

coupon noun **1** a voucher that gives you the right to claim a discount or buy something. **2** a form that can be sent off to ask for information or to enter a competition.

courage noun **1** the ability to do something frightening; bravery. **2** strength when faced with pain or grief.

courageous adjective having courage; brave. ■ **courageously** adverb.

courgette /koor-*zh*et/ noun Brit. a long, thin vegetable with green skin and soft white flesh.

courier noun **1** a person employed to deliver goods or documents quickly. **2** a person employed to guide and help a group of tourists.

course noun **1** a direction that is taken or intended. **2** the way in which something progresses or develops. **3** a procedure adopted to deal with a situation. **4** a dish forming one of the stages of a meal. **5** a series of lectures or lessons in a particular subject. **6** a series of repeated treatments or doses of a drug. **7** an area prepared for racing, golf, or another sport. verb (**courses, coursing, coursed**) **1** (of liquid) flow. **2** (**coursing**) hunting game, especially hares, with greyhounds. □ **of course 1** as expected. **2** certainly; yes.

court noun **1** the judge, jury, and lawyers who sit and hear legal cases. **2** the place where a law court meets. **3** an area marked out for ball games such as tennis. **4** (also **courtyard**) an open area surrounded by walls or buildings. **5** the home, advisers, and staff of a king or queen. verb **1** dated try to win the love of someone you want to marry. **2** try to win the support of someone. **3** behave in a way that might lead to something bad happening. □ **court shoe** a woman's plain shoe with a low-cut upper and no fastening. **hold court** be the centre of attention. **pay court to** give someone a lot of flattering attention.

courteous /ker-ti-uhss/ adjective polite and considerate. ■ **courteously** adverb.

courtesan /kor-ti-zan/ noun a prostitute with wealthy clients.

courtesy /ker-tuh-si/ noun (plural **courtesies**) **1** polite and considerate behaviour. **2** a polite speech or action. □ **(by) courtesy of** given or allowed by.

courtier /kor-ti-er/ noun a companion or adviser of a king or queen.

courtly adjective (**courtlier, courtliest**) very dignified and polite.

court martial noun (plural **courts martial** or **court martials**) a court for trying people accused of breaking military law. verb (**court-martial**) (**court-martials, court-martialling, court-martialled**) try someone in a court martial.

courtship noun **1** a period during which a couple develop a romantic relationship. **2** the process of trying to win someone's love or support.

couscous /kuuss-kuuss/ noun a North African dish of steamed or soaked semolina.

cousin noun (also **first cousin**) a child of your uncle or aunt. □ **second cousin** a child of your mother's or father's first cousin.

couture /koo-tyoor/ noun the design and making of fashionable clothes specially for a particular customer.

couturier /koo-tyoo-ri-ay/ noun a person who designs couture clothes.

cove noun a small sheltered bay.

coven /kuv-uhn/ noun a group of witches who meet regularly.

covenant /kuv-uh-nuhnt/ noun **1** a formal agreement. **2** an agreement to

cover verb (covers, covering, covered) **1** protect or conceal by putting something over or in front of. **2** spread or extend over. **3** deal with a subject. **4** travel a specified distance. **5** (of money) be enough to pay for. **6** (of insurance) protect against a loss or accident. **7** (cover up) try to conceal or deny a mistake or crime. **8** (cover for) temporarily take over the job of. **9** perform a cover version of a song. noun **1** something that covers or protects. **2** a thick protective outer part or page of a book or magazine. **3** shelter. **4** a means of concealing an illegal or secret activity. **5** protection by insurance. **6** a place setting in a restaurant. **7** (also cover version) a performance of a song previously recorded by a different artist. □ break cover suddenly leave shelter when being pursued. cover charge a charge per person added to the bill in a restaurant. covering letter a letter sent with a document or object to explain what it is. cover-up an attempt to conceal a mistake or crime.

coverage noun the extent to which something is covered.

coverlet noun a bedspread.

covert adjective /kuv-ert, koh-vert/ not done openly; secret. noun /kuv-ert/ an area of bushes and undergrowth where game can hide. ■ **covertly** adverb.

covet /kuv-it/ verb (covets, coveting, coveted) long to possess something belonging to someone else. ■ **covetous** adjective.

covey /kuv-i/ noun (plural coveys) a small flock of game birds.

cow[1] noun **1** a mature female animal of a domesticated breed of ox. **2** the female of certain other large animals. **3** informal an unpleasant woman.

cow[2] verb frighten someone so much that they do what you want.

coward noun a person who is too scared to do dangerous or unpleasant things.

cowardice noun lack of bravery.

cowardly adjective not brave; lacking courage.

cowboy noun **1** a man on horseback who herds cattle in the western US. **2** informal a dishonest or unqualified tradesman.

cower verb (cowers, cowering, cowered) crouch down or shrink back in fear.

cowl noun **1** a large, loose hood forming part of a monk's garment. **2** a hood-shaped covering for a chimney or ventilation shaft.

cowling noun a removable cover for a vehicle or aircraft engine.

cowrie noun (plural cowries) a shellfish that has a glossy shell with a long, narrow opening.

cowslip noun a wild plant with clusters of sweet-smelling yellow flowers.

cox noun the person who steers a rowing boat.

coxcomb noun old use a vain and conceited man; a dandy.

coxswain /kok-suhn/ = cox.

coy adjective (coyer, coyest) **1** pretending to be shy or modest. **2** reluctant to give details about something. ■ **coyly** adverb.

coyote /koy-oht, koy-oh-ti/ noun (plural coyote or coyotes) a wolf-like wild dog found in North America.

coypu /koy-pyoo/ noun (plural coypus) a large South American rodent resembling a beaver.

cozy US spelling of cosy.

crab noun a sea creature with a broad shell and five pairs of legs. □ crab apple a small, sour kind of apple.

crabbed adjective **1** (of writing) hard to read or understand. **2** bad-tempered.

crabby adjective (crabbier, crabbiest) informal bad-tempered.

crack noun **1** a narrow opening between two parts of something which has split or been broken. **2** a sudden sharp noise. **3** a sharp blow. **4** informal a joke. **5** informal an attempt or chance to do something. **6** (also crack cocaine) a very strong form of cocaine. verb

-cracy

-cracy comes from the ancient Greek word *kratia*, meaning 'power, rule'. Some of the more common words with this ending are:

aristocracy	government by the highest social class
autocracy	government by one person with total power
bureaucracy	government by state officials
democracy	government by the ordinary people
meritocracy	government by people selected according to merit.

Word endings related to **-cracy** are **-cratic**, which forms adjectives such as *bureaucratic*, and **-crat**, which forms nouns such as *aristocrat*.

1 break without dividing into separate parts. **2** give way under pressure or strain. **3** make a sudden sharp sound. **4** hit hard. **5** (of a person's voice) suddenly change in pitch. **6** informal solve or decipher. **adjective** very good or skilful: *a crack shot.* □ **crack down on** informal deal severely with. **crack of dawn** daybreak. **crack on** informal proceed or progress quickly. **crack up** informal **1** suffer an emotional breakdown. **2** (**be cracked up to be**) be said to be.

crackdown noun a series of severe measures against undesirable or illegal behaviour.

cracker noun 1 a paper cylinder which makes a sharp noise and releases a small toy when it is pulled apart. **2** a firework that explodes with a crack. **3** a thin, dry biscuit. **4** informal a very good example of something.

crackers or **cracked adjective** informal insane; mad.

cracking adjective informal **1** excellent. **2** fast: *a cracking pace.*

crackle verb (**crackles, crackling, crackled**) make a series of slight cracking noises. **noun** a crackling sound. ■ **crackly** adjective.

crackling noun the crisp fatty skin of roast pork.

crackpot noun informal an eccentric or foolish person.

cradle noun 1 a baby's bed on rockers. **2** a place or period in which something originates or flourishes: *the cradle of civilization.* **3** a supporting framework. **verb** (**cradles, cradling, cradled**) hold gently and protectively.

craft noun 1 an activity involving skill in making things by hand. **2** skill in carrying out work. **3** (**crafts**) things made by hand. **4** cunning. **5** (plural **craft**) a boat, ship, or aircraft. **verb** make skilfully.

craftsman noun a worker who is skilled in a particular craft. ■ **craftsmanship** noun.

crafty adjective (**craftier, craftiest**) clever at deceiving people; cunning. ■ **craftily** adverb.

crag noun a steep or rugged cliff or rock face. ■ **craggy** adjective.

cram verb (**crams, cramming, crammed**) **1** force too many people or things into a space. **2** fill something to the point of overflowing. **3** study hard just before an examination.

crammer noun a college that prepares students for examinations.

cramp noun 1 pain caused by a muscle or muscles tightening. **2** a tool for clamping two objects together. **verb** restrict the development of.

cramped adjective 1 uncomfortably small or crowded. **2** (of handwriting) small and difficult to read.

crampon noun a spiked plate fixed to a boot for climbing on ice or rock.

cranberry noun (plural **cranberries**) a small sour-tasting red berry.

crane noun 1 a tall machine used for moving heavy objects by suspending them from a projecting arm. 2 a wading bird with long legs and a long neck. verb (cranes, craning, craned) stretch out your neck to see something. □ crane fly a fly with very long legs; a daddy-long-legs.

cranium /kray-ni-uhm/ noun (plural craniums or crania /kray-ni-uh/) the part of the skull that encloses the brain. ■ cranial adjective.

crank noun 1 a part of an axle or shaft that is bent at right angles, turned to produce motion. 2 an eccentric person. verb 1 turn a crankshaft or handle. 2 (crank up) informal increase the intensity of. 3 (crank out) informal produce regularly and routinely.

crankshaft noun a shaft driven by a crank.

cranky adjective (crankier, crankiest) informal 1 odd; eccentric. 2 bad-tempered; irritable.

cranny noun (plural crannies) a small, narrow space or opening.

crap vulgar noun 1 excrement. 2 nonsense. verb (craps, crapping, crapped) defecate. adjective extremely poor in quality. ■ crappy adjective.

crape noun black silk, formerly used for mourning clothes.

craps noun a North American gambling game played with two dice.

crash verb 1 (of a vehicle) collide violently with an obstacle or another vehicle. 2 (of an aircraft) fall from the sky and hit the land or sea. 3 move or fall with a sudden loud noise. 4 (of shares) fall suddenly in value. 5 Computing fail suddenly. 6 (also crash out) informal fall deeply asleep. 7 (crashing) informal complete; total: *a crashing bore*. noun 1 an instance of crashing. 2 a sudden loud, deep noise. adjective rapid and concentrated: *a crash course in Italian*. □ crash helmet a helmet worn by a motorcyclist to protect the head. crash-land (of an aircraft) land roughly in an emergency.

crass adjective very thoughtless and stupid. ■ crassly adverb.

crate noun 1 a wooden case for transporting goods. 2 a square container divided into individual units for holding bottles. 3 informal an old and ramshackle vehicle. verb (crates, crating, crated) pack in a crate.

crater noun a large hollow caused by an explosion or impact or forming the mouth of a volcano.

cravat /kruh-vat/ noun a strip of fabric worn by men around the neck and tucked inside a shirt.

crave verb (craves, craving, craved) 1 feel a very strong desire for. 2 old use ask for.

craven adjective cowardly.

craving noun a very strong desire for something.

craw noun dated the part of a bird's throat where food is prepared for digestion.

crawl verb 1 move forward on the hands and knees or with the body close to the ground. 2 move very slowly along. 3 (be crawling with) be unpleasantly covered or crowded with. 4 feel an unpleasant sensation resembling something moving over the skin. 5 informal behave in an insincerely friendly or submissive way. noun 1 an act of crawling. 2 a very slow rate of movement. 3 a swimming stroke involving alternate overarm movements and rapid kicks of the legs.

crayfish noun (plural crayfish) a shellfish resembling a small lobster.

crayon noun a stick of coloured chalk or wax, used for drawing. verb draw with a crayon or crayons.

craze noun a widespread but short-lived enthusiasm for something.

crazed adjective 1 wildly insane. 2 covered with fine cracks.

crazy adjective (crazier, craziest) 1 insane. 2 (usu. crazy about) very enthusiastic about or fond of. 3 foolish or ridiculous. □ crazy paving paving made of irregular pieces of flat stone. ■ crazily adverb craziness noun.

creak verb make a harsh, high sound.

noun a creaking sound. ■ **creaky** adjective.

cream noun **1** the thick fatty liquid which rises to the top when milk is left to stand. **2** a food containing cream or having a creamy texture. **3** a thick liquid substance that is applied to the skin. **4** the very best of a group. **5** a very pale yellow or off-white colour. verb **1** mash a cooked vegetable with milk or cream. **2** (**cream off**) take away the best of. □ **cream cheese** a soft, rich kind of cheese. ■ **creamy** adjective.

creamery noun (plural **creameries**) a factory where butter and cheese are produced.

crease noun **1** a line or ridge produced on paper or cloth by folding or pressing it. **2** Cricket any of a number of lines marked on the pitch. verb (**creases, creasing, creased**) **1** make creases in. **2** (**crease up**) informal burst out laughing.

create verb (**creates, creating, created**) **1** bring into existence. **2** cause something to happen. **3** informal make a fuss; complain.

creation noun **1** the action of creating. **2** a thing which has been made or invented. **3** (**Creation**) literary the universe.

creative adjective involving the use of the imagination in order to create something. ■ **creatively** adverb **creativity** noun.

creator noun **1** a person or thing that creates. **2** (**the Creator**) God.

creature noun a living being, in particular an animal rather than a person. □ **creature comforts** things that make life comfortable.

crèche /kresh/ noun a place where babies and young children are looked after while their parents are at work.

credence /kree-duhnss/ noun belief that something is true.

credential /kri-**den**-sh'l/ noun **1** a qualification, achievement, or quality used to indicate how suitable a person is for something. **2** (**credentials**) documents that prove a person's identity or qualifications.

credible adjective able to be believed; convincing. ■ **credibility** noun **credibly** adverb.

> ⓘ don't confuse **credible** with **creditable**: **credible** means 'believable, convincing', whereas **creditable** means 'deserving recognition and praise'.

credit noun **1** the system of doing business by trusting that a customer will pay at a later date for goods or services supplied. **2** public recognition or praise given for an achievement or quality. **3** (**a credit to**) a source of pride to. **4** an entry in an account recording an amount received. **5** a written acknowledgement of a contributor's role displayed at the beginning or end of a film or programme. **6** a unit of study counting towards a degree or diploma. verb (**credits, crediting, credited**) **1** (**credit with**) feel that someone is responsible for something good. **2** believe something. **3** add an amount of money to an account. □ **be in credit** (of an account) have money in it. **credit card** a plastic card that allows you to buy goods and pay for them later.

creditable adjective deserving recognition and praise. ■ **creditably** adverb.

creditor noun a person or company to whom money is owed.

credo /**kree**-doh, **kray**-doh/ noun (plural **credos**) a statement of a person's beliefs or aims.

credulous adjective too ready to believe things. ■ **credulity** noun.

creed noun **1** a system of religious belief; a faith. **2** a set of beliefs or principles.

creek noun **1** a narrow stretch of water running inland from the coast. **2** N. Amer. & Austral./NZ a stream or small river. □ **up the creek** informal in severe difficulty.

creel noun a large basket for carrying fish.

creep verb (**creeps, creeping, crept**)

1 move slowly and cautiously. **2** progress or develop gradually. **noun 1** informal a person who is insincerely friendly or submissive. **2** slow and gradual movement. □ **give you the creeps** make you feel disgust or fear. **make your flesh creep** give you an unpleasant feeling, as if there is something crawling over your skin.

creeper noun a plant that grows along the ground or another surface.

creepy adjective (creepier, creepiest) informal causing an unpleasant feeling of fear or unease.

cremate verb (cremates, cremating, cremated) dispose of a dead body by burning it. ■ **cremation** noun.

crematorium /kre-muh-**tor**-i-uhm/ **noun** (plural **crematoria** or **crematoriums**) a building where dead people are cremated.

crème de la crème /krem duh la krem/ **noun** the best person or thing of a particular kind.

crenellations plural noun battlements. ■ **crenellated** adjective.

Creole /**kree**-ohl/ **noun 1** a person of mixed European and black descent. **2** a descendant of French settlers in the southern US. **3** a combination of a European language and an African language.

creosote /**kree**-uh-soht/ **noun** a dark brown oil obtained from coal tar, painted on to wood to preserve it.

crêpe /krayp/ **noun 1** a light, thin fabric with a wrinkled surface. **2** hardwearing wrinkled rubber used for the soles of shoes. **3** a thin pancake. □ **crêpe paper** thin, crinkled paper.

crept past and past participle of **CREEP**.

crepuscular /kri-**pus**-kyuu-ler/ **adjective** literary resembling twilight; dim and shadowy.

crescendo /kri-**shen**-doh/ **noun** (plural **crescendos** or **crescendi** /kri-**shen**-di/) **1** a gradual increase in loudness in a piece of music. **2** a climax.

crescent noun a narrow curved shape tapering to a point at each end.

cress noun a plant with hot-tasting leaves.

crest noun 1 a tuft or growth of feathers, fur, or skin on the head of a bird or animal. **2** a plume of feathers on a helmet. **3** the top of a ridge, wave, etc. **4** a distinctive design in heraldry representing a family or organization. **verb** reach the top of. ■ **crested** adjective.

crestfallen adjective sad and disappointed.

cretin noun a stupid person. ■ **cretinous** adjective.

crevasse /kri-**vass**/ **noun** a deep open crack in a glacier or ice field.

crevice noun a narrow opening or crack in a rock or wall.

crew¹ noun 1 a group of people who work on a ship, aircraft, or train. **2** the members of a crew other than the officers. **3** a group of people who work together: *a film crew.* **verb 1** provide with a crew. **2** act as a member of a crew. □ **crew cut** a very short haircut for men and boys. **crew neck** a close-fitting round neckline.

crew² past of **CROW²**.

crib noun 1 chiefly N. Amer. a child's cot. **2** informal a translation of a text for use by students. **3** the card game cribbage. **verb (cribs, cribbing, cribbed)** informal copy something dishonestly.

cribbage noun a card game for two players.

crick noun a painful stiff feeling in the neck or back. **verb** twist or strain the neck or back.

cricket¹ noun a team game played with a bat, ball, and wickets. ■ **cricketer** noun.

cricket² noun an insect like a grasshopper, the male of which produces a shrill chirping sound.

cried past and past participle of **CRY**.

crime noun 1 an action that is against the law. **2** illegal actions as a whole. **3** informal something disgraceful or very unfair.

criminal noun a person who has committed a crime. **adjective 1** relating to crime or a crime. **2** informal disgraceful or very unfair. ■ **criminality** noun **criminally** adverb.

crimp verb press into small folds or ridges.

crimson noun a deep red colour.

cringe verb (**cringes**, **cringing**, **cringed**) **1** shrink back or cower in fear. **2** have a sudden feeling of embarrassment or disgust.

crinkle verb (**crinkle**, **crinkling**, **crinkled**) form small creases or wrinkles. noun a small crease or wrinkle. ■ **crinkly** adjective.

crinoline /krin-uh-lin/ noun a petticoat stiffened with hoops, formerly worn to make a long skirt stand out.

cripple noun old use or offensive a person who is unable to walk or move properly because they are disabled or injured. **verb** (**cripples**, **crippling**, **crippled**) **1** make someone unable to move or walk properly. **2** severely damage or weaken.

crisis noun (plural **crises**) **1** a time of severe difficulty or danger. **2** a time when a difficult decision must be made.

crisp adjective **1** firm, dry, and brittle. **2** (of the weather) cool and fresh. **3** brisk and decisive. noun a thin, crisp slice of fried potato. ■ **crisply** adverb **crispy** adjective.

crispbread noun a thin, crisp biscuit made from rye or wheat.

criss-cross adjective with a pattern of crossing lines. verb **1** form a criss-cross pattern on. **2** repeatedly go back and forth around a place.

criterion /kry-teer-i-uhn/ noun (plural **criteria** /kry-teer-i-uh/) a standard by which something may be judged.

> ℹ️ the singular form is **criterion** and the plural form is **criteria**. It is wrong to use **criteria** as a singular, as in *a further criteria needs to be considered*.

critic noun **1** a person who finds fault with something. **2** a person who assesses literary or artistic works.

critical adjective **1** expressing disapproving comments. **2** assessing a literary or artistic work. **3** having a decisive importance. **4** at a point of danger or crisis. ■ **critically** adverb.

criticism noun **1** expression of disapproval. **2** the assessment of literary or artistic works.

criticize or **criticise** verb (**criticizes**, **criticizing**, **criticized**) **1** express disapproval of. **2** assess a literary or artistic work.

critique /kri-teek/ noun a critical assessment.

croak noun a deep, hoarse sound, like that made by a frog. verb **1** utter a croak. **2** informal die. ■ **croaky** adjective.

crochet /kroh-shay/ noun a craft in which yarn is made into fabric with a hooked needle. verb (**crochets**, **crocheting crocheted**) make an article by means of crochet.

crock[1] noun informal a feeble and useless old person.

crock[2] noun an earthenware pot or jar.

crockery noun plates, dishes, cups, etc. made of earthenware or china.

crocodile noun **1** a large reptile with long jaws, a long tail, and a thick skin. **2** Brit. informal a line of schoolchildren walking in pairs. □ **crocodile tears** insincere tears or sorrow.

crocus noun (plural **crocuses**) a small plant with bright yellow, purple, or white flowers.

croft noun a small rented farm in Scotland or northern England. ■ **crofter** noun.

croissant /krwass-on/ noun a flaky crescent-shaped bread roll.

crone noun an ugly old woman.

crony noun (plural **cronies**) informal a close friend or companion.

crook noun **1** a shepherd's or bishop's hooked staff. **2** a bend at a person's elbow. **3** informal a criminal or dishonest person. verb bend a finger or leg.

crooked adjective **1** bent or twisted out of shape or position. **2** informal dishonest or illegal.

croon verb hum, sing, or speak in a soft, low voice. ■ **crooner** noun.

crop noun **1** a plant grown for food or other use. **2** an amount of a crop harvested at one time. **3** a very short hairstyle. **4** a pouch in a bird's throat where food is stored or prepared for digestion. **5** a short flexible whip used by horse riders. verb (**crops, cropping, cropped**) **1** cut something very short. **2** (of an animal) bite off and eat the tops of plants. **3** (**crop up**) appear or occur unexpectedly.

cropper noun (**come a cropper**) informal fall or fail heavily.

croquet /kroh-kay/ noun a game in which wooden balls are driven through hoops with a mallet.

croquette /kroh-ket/ noun a small cake or roll of vegetables, meat, or fish, fried in breadcrumbs.

cross noun **1** a mark, object, or shape formed by two short intersecting lines or pieces (+ or ×). **2** a cross-shaped medal or monument. **3** (**the Cross**) the wooden cross on which Jesus was crucified. **4** an animal or plant resulting from cross-breeding. **5** a mixture of two things. verb **1** go or extend across or to the other side of. **2** pass in an opposite or different direction. **3** place crosswise. **4** mark with a cross. **5** Brit. mark a cheque with a pair of parallel lines to indicate that it must be paid into a named bank account. **6** Soccer pass the ball across the field towards the centre. **7** cause an animal to breed with another of a different species. **8** oppose or stand in the way of. adjective annoyed. □ **at cross purposes** misunderstanding or having different aims from one another. **cross-breed** produce an animal or plant by causing two different species, breeds, or varieties to breed. **cross-check** check figures or information by using an alternative source or method. **cross-country 1** across fields or countryside. **2** across a region or country. **cross-dressing** the wearing of clothing typical of the opposite sex. **cross-examine** question a witness called by the other party in a court of law. **cross-eyed** having one or both eyes turned inwards towards the nose. **cross-fertilize** (or **cross-fertilise**) fertilize a plant using pollen from another plant of the same species. **cross off** delete from a list. **cross out** delete a word or phrase by drawing a line through it. **cross-question** question in great detail. **cross reference** a reference to another text or part of a text, given to provide further information. **cross section 1** a surface exposed by making a straight cut through a solid object at right angles to its length. **2** a sample of a larger group. **cross swords** have an argument or dispute. **cross yourself** make the sign of the cross in front of your chest. ■ **crossly** adverb.

crossbar noun **1** a horizontal bar between the two upright posts of a football goal. **2** a bar between the handlebars and saddle on a bicycle.

crossbow noun a bow with a mechanism for drawing and releasing the string.

crossfire noun gunfire from two or more directions passing through the same area.

crossing noun **1** a place where roads or railway lines cross. **2** a place to cross a street or railway line.

crossroads noun a place where two or more roads cross each other.

crosswise or **crossways** adverb **1** in the form of a cross. **2** diagonally.

crossword noun a puzzle in which words crossing each other vertically and horizontally are written according to clues.

crotch noun the part of the human body between the legs.

crotchet noun a musical note that lasts half as long as a minim.

crotchety adjective irritable.

crouch verb bend the knees and bring the upper body forward and down. noun a crouching position.

croup[1] /kroop/ noun an illness of children, with coughing and breathing difficulties.

croup² /kroop/ **noun** the rump of a horse.

croupier /kroo-pi-ay, kroo-pi-er/ **noun** the person in charge of a gambling table in a casino.

crouton /kroo-ton/ **noun** a small piece of fried or toasted bread served with soup or used as a garnish.

crow¹ **noun** a large black bird with a harsh call. □ **as the crow flies** in a straight line across country. **crow's foot** a wrinkle at the outer corner of a person's eye. **crow's-nest** a platform at the top of a ship's mast to watch from.

crow² **verb** (**crows, crowing, crowed** or **crew**) **1** (of a cock) make its loud, shrill cry. **2** boastfully express pride or triumph. **noun** the cry of a cock.

crowbar **noun** an iron bar with a flattened end, used as a lever.

crowd **noun** **1** a large number of people gathered together. **2** informal a group of people with a shared quality. **verb** **1** fill a space almost completely. **2** move or come together as a crowd. **3** move or stand too close to.

crown **noun** **1** a circular headdress worn by a king or queen. **2** (**the Crown**) the reigning king or queen. **3** a wreath of leaves or flowers worn as an emblem of victory. **4** an award gained by a victory. **5** the top or highest part of something. **6** an artificial replacement or covering for the upper part of a tooth. **7** a former British coin worth five shillings (25 pence). **verb** **1** place a crown on the head of someone to declare them to be king or queen. **2** rest on or form the top of.

crozier /kroh-zi-er/ **noun** a hooked staff carried by a bishop.

crucial **adjective 1** decisive or critical. **2** informal very important. ■ **crucially** adverb.

crucible **noun** a container in which metals or other substances may be melted or heated.

crucifix **noun** a small cross with a fig-

ure of Jesus Christ on it.

crucifixion **noun 1** the execution of a person by crucifying them. **2** (**the Crucifixion**) the crucifixion of Jesus.

cruciform **adjective** having the shape of a cross.

crucify **verb** (**crucifies, crucifying, crucified**) **1** kill someone by nailing or binding them to a cross. **2** informal criticize someone severely.

crud **noun** informal **1** an unpleasantly dirty or messy substance. **2** nonsense. ■ **cruddy** adjective.

crude **adjective 1** in a natural state; not yet processed. **2** rough or simple. **3** coarse or vulgar. ■ **crudely** adverb **crudity** noun.

cruel **adjective** (**crueller, cruellest** or **crueler, cruelest**) **1** taking pleasure in the suffering of others. **2** causing pain or suffering. ■ **cruelly** adverb.

cruelty **noun** (plural **cruelties**) cruel behaviour or attitudes.

cruet **noun 1** a small container for salt, pepper, oil, or vinegar. **2** Brit. a stand holding such containers.

cruise **verb** (**cruises, cruising, cruised**) **1** move slowly around without a precise destination. **2** travel smoothly at a moderate speed. **noun** a voyage on a ship taken as a holiday.

cruiser **noun 1** a large, fast warship. **2** a yacht or motor boat with passenger accommodation.

crumb **noun 1** a small fragment of bread, cake, or biscuit. **2** a very small amount.

crumble **verb** (**crumbles, crumbling, crumbled**) **1** break or fall apart into small fragments. **2** gradually decline or fall apart. **noun** Brit. a baked pudding made with fruit and a crumbly topping. ■ **crumbly** adjective.

crummy **adjective** (**crummier, crummiest**) informal bad or unpleasant.

crumpet **noun 1** a soft, flat cake with an open texture, eaten toasted and buttered. **2** Brit. informal women regarded as objects of sexual desire.

crumple **verb** (**crumples, crumpling, crumpled**) **1** crease something by crushing it. **2** collapse.

crunch verb **1** crush something hard or brittle with the teeth. **2** move with a noisy grinding sound. noun **1** a crunching sound. **2** (the crunch) informal the crucial point of a situation. ■ **crunchy** adjective.

crusade noun **1** (the Crusades) a series of medieval military expeditions made by Europeans against Muslims in the Middle East. **2** an energetic organized campaign. verb (crusades, crusading, crusaded) take part in a crusade. ■ **crusader** noun.

crush verb **1** squash, crease, or break up something by pressing it. **2** defeat completely. noun **1** a crowd of people pressed closely together. **2** informal an intense infatuation.

crust noun **1** the tough outer part of a loaf of bread. **2** a hardened layer, coating, or deposit. **3** the outermost layer of the earth. **4** a layer of pastry covering a pie. verb form into a crust, or cover with a crust.

crustacean /kruss-tay-sh'n/ noun a hard-shelled creature such as a crab or lobster, usually living in water.

crusty adjective (crustier, crustiest) **1** having or consisting of a crust. **2** easily irritated.

crutch noun **1** a long stick with a crosspiece at the top, used as a support by a lame person. **2** a person's crotch.

crux noun (the crux) the most important point that is being discussed.

cry verb (cries, crying, cried) **1** shed tears. **2** shout or scream loudly. **3** (of an animal) make a distinctive call. **4** (cry out for) demand or require. **5** (cry off) informal fail to keep to an arrangement. noun (plural cries) **1** a spell of shedding tears. **2** a loud shout or scream. **3** a distinctive call of an animal. □ **a crying shame** a very unfortunate situation.

cryogenics /kry-uh-jen-iks/ noun the branch of physics concerned with very low temperatures. ■ **cryogenic** adjective.

crypt noun an underground room be-

neath a church, used as a chapel or burial place.

cryptic adjective mysterious or obscure in meaning. ■ **cryptically** adverb.

crystal noun **1** a transparent mineral, especially quartz. **2** a piece of a solid substance that is formed naturally and has flat sides arranged symmetrically. **3** very clear glass. □ **crystal ball** a globe of glass or crystal, used for predicting the future.

crystalline adjective **1** resembling a crystal. **2** literary very clear.

crystallize or **crystallise** verb (crystallizes, crystallizing, crystallized) **1** form crystals. **2** become definite and clear. **3** (crystallized) (of fruit) coated with and preserved in sugar.

cu. abbreviation cubic.

cub noun **1** the young of a fox, bear, lion, or other carnivorous mammal. **2** (also Cub Scout) a member of the junior branch of the Scout Association.

cubbyhole noun a small enclosed space or room.

cube noun **1** a three-dimensional shape with six equal square faces. **2** the result obtained when a number is multiplied by itself twice. verb **1** cut food into small cubes. **2** find the cube of a number. □ **cube root** the number which produces a given number when cubed.

cubic adjective **1** having the shape of a cube. **2** involving the cube of a quantity: *a cubic metre*.

cubicle noun a small area of a room that is separated off for privacy.

cubism noun a style of painting featuring regular lines and shapes. ■ **cubist** noun & adjective.

cubit noun an ancient measure of length, approximately equal to the length of a forearm.

cuckoo noun a bird known for laying its eggs in the nests of other birds. adjective informal crazy.

cucumber noun a long green fruit

which has watery flesh and is eaten in salads.

cud noun partly digested food returned from the first stomach of cattle or similar animals to the mouth for further chewing.

cuddle verb (**cuddles, cuddling, cuddled**) **1** hold closely and lovingly in your arms. **2** (often **cuddle up to**) lie or sit close. noun an affectionate hug.

cuddly adjective (**cuddlier, cuddliest**) pleasantly soft or plump.

cudgel noun a short, thick stick used as a weapon. verb (**cudgels, cudgelling, cudgelled**; US spelling **cudgels, cudgeling, cudgeled**) beat with a cudgel. □ **take up cudgels** start to defend someone or something strongly.

cue¹ noun **1** a signal to an actor to enter or to begin their speech or performance. **2** a signal or prompt for action. verb (**cues, cueing** or **cuing, cued**) **1** give a cue to. **2** set a piece of audio or video equipment to play a particular part of a recording.

cue² noun a long rod for striking the ball in snooker, billiards, or pool.

cuff¹ noun **1** the end part of a sleeve, where the material of the sleeve is turned back or a separate band is sewn on. **2** chiefly N. Amer. a trouser turn-up. □ **off the cuff** informal without preparation.

cuff² verb strike with an open hand. noun a blow with an open hand.

cufflink noun a device for fastening together the sides of a shirt cuff.

cuisine /kwi-**zeen**/ noun a particular style of cooking.

cul-de-sac /**kul**-duh-sak/ noun (plural **culs-de-sac** /**kul**-duh-sak/) a street or passage closed at one end.

culinary adjective having to do with cooking.

cull verb **1** reduce the numbers of animals by selective slaughter. **2** select a few things from a wide range. noun a selective slaughter of animals.

culminate verb (**culminates, culminating, culminated**) reach a climax or point of highest development. ■ **culmination** noun.

culottes /kyuu-**lots**/ plural noun women's wide-legged knee-length trousers.

culpable adjective deserving blame. ■ **culpability** noun.

culprit noun the person responsible for an offence.

cult noun **1** a system of religious worship directed towards a particular person or object. **2** a small, unconventional religious group. **3** something popular or fashionable among a particular group of people.

cultivate verb (**cultivates, cultivating, cultivated**) **1** prepare and use land for crops or gardening. **2** grow plants or crops. **3** try to develop or gain a particular quality. **4** try to win the friendship or favour of. **5** (**cultivated**) refined and well educated. ■ **cultivation** noun **cultivator** noun.

cultural adjective **1** relating to the culture of a society. **2** relating to the arts and intellectual achievements. ■ **culturally** adverb.

culture noun **1** the arts, customs, and institutions of a nation, people, or group. **2** the arts and intellectual achievements regarded as a whole. **3** a refined understanding or appreciation of culture. **4** a preparation of cells or bacteria grown in an artificial medium.

cultured adjective **1** refined and well educated. **2** (of a pearl) formed round a foreign body inserted into an oyster.

culvert noun a tunnel carrying a stream or open drain under a road or railway.

cum preposition combined with.

cumbersome adjective **1** difficult to carry or use on account of its size or weight. **2** complicated and time-consuming.

cumin /**kum**-in, **kyoo**-min/ noun the seeds of a plant, used as a spice.

cummerbund noun a sash worn around the waist as part of a man's formal evening suit.

cumulative adjective increasing by

successive additions. ■ **cumulatively** adverb.

cuneiform /**kyoo**-ni-form/ adjective (of ancient writing systems) using wedge-shaped characters.

cunning adjective **1** skilled at deceiving people. **2** skilful or clever. noun craftiness. ■ **cunningly** adverb.

cunt noun vulgar **1** a woman's genitals. **2** an unpleasant or stupid person.

cup noun **1** a small bowl-shaped container with a handle for drinking from. **2** a cup-shaped trophy awarded as a prize in a sports contest. **3** a sports contest in which the winner is awarded a cup. **4** either of the two parts of a bra shaped to contain one breast. verb (**cups**, **cupping**, **cupped**) **1** form your hand or hands into the curved shape of a cup. **2** place your curved hand or hands around.

cupboard noun a recess or piece of furniture with a door, used for storage. □ **cupboard love** false affection that is put on to obtain something.

Cupid noun **1** the Roman god of love. **2** (also **cupid**) a picture or statue of a naked winged child carrying a bow.

cupidity noun greed for money or possessions.

cupola noun a rounded dome that forms or decorates a roof.

cur noun an aggressive mongrel dog.

curate noun an assistant to a parish priest.

curative adjective able to cure disease.

curator noun a keeper of a museum or other collection.

curb noun **1** something that limits or restrains. **2** a type of bit with a strap or chain which passes under a horse's lower jaw. **3** US spelling of **KERB**. verb keep in check.

curd or **curds** noun a soft, white substance formed when milk coagulates.

curdle verb (**curdles**, **curdling**, **curdled**) form curds or lumps.

cure verb (**cures**, **curing**, **cured**) **1** make a person who is ill well again. **2** end a disease, condition, or problem by treatment or appropriate action. **3** preserve meat, fish, etc. by salting, drying, or smoking. noun **1** something that cures; a remedy. **2** the healing of a person who is ill. ■ **curable** adjective.

curfew noun **1** a regulation requiring people to remain indoors between specified hours of the night. **2** the time at which a curfew begins.

curie noun (plural **curies**) a unit of radioactivity.

curio /**kyoor**-i-oh/ noun (plural **curios**) an object that is interesting because it is rare or unusual.

curiosity noun (plural **curiosities**) **1** a strong desire to know or learn something. **2** a unusual or interesting object or fact.

curious adjective **1** eager to know or learn something. **2** strange; unusual. ■ **curiously** adverb.

curl verb form a curved or spiral shape. noun something in the shape of a spiral or coil. ■ **curly** adjective.

curler noun a roller or clasp around which you wrap hair to curl it.

curlew /**ker**-lyoo/ noun (plural **curlew** or **curlews**) a large wading bird with a long curved bill.

curling noun a game played on ice, in which you slide large circular flat stones towards a mark.

curmudgeon noun a bad-tempered person. ■ **curmudgeonly** adjective.

currant noun a dried fruit made from a small seedless variety of grape.

currency noun (plural **currencies**) **1** a system of money used in a country. **2** the state or period of being current.

current adjective **1** happening or being used or done now. **2** in common or general use. noun **1** a body of water or air moving in a particular direction. **2** a flow of electrically charged particles. □ **current account** Brit. a bank or building society account from which you may withdraw money at any time. ■ **currently** adverb.

curriculum noun (plural **curricula** or **curriculums**) the subjects that make up a course of study in a school or college. ■ curricular adjective.

curriculum vitae /kuh-**rik**-yuu-luhm **vee**-tI, **vy**-tee/ noun (plural curricula vitae) a brief account of a person's qualifications and previous occupations, sent with a job application.

curry[1] noun (plural curries) a dish of meat, vegetables, or fish, cooked in a hot, spicy sauce of Indian origin.

curry[2] verb (curries, currying, curried) chiefly N. Amer. groom a horse with a jagged device. □ curry favour try to win someone's approval by flattering them and being very helpful.

curse noun 1 an appeal to a supernatural power to harm someone or something. 2 a cause of harm or misery. 3 an offensive word or phrase used to express anger or annoyance. verb (curses, cursing, cursed) 1 use a curse against. 2 (be cursed with) be afflicted with. 3 utter offensive words; swear.

cursor noun 1 a mark on a computer screen identifying the point where typing or other input will take effect. 2 the sliding part used to locate points on a slide rule.

cursory adjective hasty and therefore not thorough.

curt adjective (of a person's speech) rudely brief. ■ curtly adverb.

curtail verb cut short or restrict. ■ curtailment noun.

curtain noun 1 a piece of material hung up to form a screen at a window or between the stage and the audience in a theatre. 2 (curtains) informal a disastrous end. verb provide or screen with a curtain or curtains. □ curtain call the appearance of a performer on stage after a performance to acknowledge applause. curtain-raiser an event happening just before a longer or more important one.

curtsy or curtsey noun (plural curtsies or curtseys) a woman's or girl's respectful greeting, made by bending the knees with one foot in front of the other. verb (curtsies, curtsying, curt-sied or curtseys, curtseying, curtseyed) perform a curtsy.

curvaceous adjective having an attractively curved shape.

curvature noun the fact of being curved; curved shape.

curve noun a line which gradually turns from a straight course. verb (curves, curving, curved) form a curve. ■ curvy adjective.

cushion noun 1 a bag of cloth stuffed with soft material, used to provide comfort when sitting. 2 something that gives protection against impact or something unpleasant. 3 the inner sides of a billiard table. verb 1 soften the effect of an impact on. 2 lessen the bad effects of.

cushy adjective (cushier, cushiest) informal easy and undemanding.

cusp noun 1 a pointed end where two curves meet. 2 a point in between two different states.

custard noun 1 a sweet sauce made with milk and eggs, or milk and flavoured cornflour. 2 a baked dessert made from eggs and milk.

custodial adjective having to do with custody.

custodian noun a person responsible for looking after something.

custody noun 1 protective care. 2 imprisonment.

custom noun 1 a traditional way of behaving or doing something. 2 regular dealings with a shop or business by customers. □ custom-built made to a particular customer's order.

customary adjective in accordance with custom; usual. ■ customarily adverb.

customer noun 1 a person who buys goods or services from a shop or business. 2 a person or thing that you have to deal with: a tough customer.

customize or customise verb (customizes, customizing, customized) modify something to suit a person or task.

customs plural noun 1 charges made by a government on imported goods.

WORD FORMATION

cyber-

Words that begin with **cyber-**, for example **cyberspace**, are related to computers. Some other examples are:

cybercafe   a cafe where people can log on to the Internet

cyberphobia   fear of computers or technology.

cyber- comes from *kubernētēs*, the ancient Greek word for the man who steered a sailing ship.

---

2 the official department that administers and collects customs charges.

cut verb **(cuts, cutting, cut) 1** make an opening or wound with something sharp. **2** shorten, divide, or remove with something sharp. **3** make or design a garment in a particular way. **4** reduce the amount or quantity of. **5** go across or through an area. **6** stop filming or recording. **7** divide a pack of playing cards by lifting a portion from the top. noun **1** a wound or opening resulting from cutting. **2** a reduction. **3** the style in which a garment or a person's hair is cut. **4** a piece of meat cut from a carcass. **5** informal a share of profits. **6** a version of a film after editing. □ **cut and dried** decided or planned in advance. **cut and thrust** a competitive atmosphere or environment. **cut both ways 1** (of a point) serve both sides of an argument. **2** have both good and bad effects. **cut corners** do something badly to save time or money. **cut glass** glass with decorative patterns cut into it. **cut in 1** interrupt. **2** pull in too closely in front of another vehicle. **3** (of a machine) begin operating automatically. **cut the mustard** informal reach the required standard. **cut no ice** informal have no influence or effect. **cut off 1** make it impossible to reach a place. **2** deprive of a supply. **3** break a telephone connection with someone. **cut out 1** exclude someone. **2** (of an engine) suddenly stop operating. **cut-throat** ruthless and fierce.

cutaneous /kyoo-**tay**-ni-uhss/ adjective having to do with the skin.

cutback noun a reduction.

cute adjective **1** charmingly pretty; sweet. **2** informal, chiefly N. Amer. clever; shrewd. ■ **cutely** adverb.

cuticle /**kyoo**-ti-k'l/ noun the dead skin at the base of a fingernail or toenail.

cutlass noun a short sword with a slightly curved blade, formerly used by sailors.

cutlery noun knives, forks, and spoons used for eating or serving food.

cutlet noun **1** a lamb or veal chop from just behind the neck. **2** a flat cake of minced meat, nuts, etc., covered in breadcrumbs and fried.

cutter noun **1** a person or thing that cuts. **2** a light, fast patrol boat or sailing boat. **3** a small boat carried by a ship.

cutting noun **1** an article cut from a newspaper. **2** a piece cut from a plant to grow a new one. **3** a way dug through higher ground for a railway, road, etc. adjective hurtful: *a cutting remark*. □ **the cutting edge** the most advanced or modern stage; the forefront.

cuttlefish noun a sea creature resembling a squid.

CV abbreviation curriculum vitae.

cwt. abbreviation hundredweight.

cyan /**sy**-uhn/ noun a greenish-blue colour.

cyanide noun a highly poisonous compound containing a metal combined with carbon and nitrogen atoms.

cybernetics noun the science of

communications and control in machines (e.g. computers) and living things (e.g. by the nervous system). ■ **cybernetic** adjective.

cyberspace noun the hypothetical environment in which communication over computer networks occurs.

cyclamen /sik-luh-muhn/ noun a plant having pink, red, or white flowers with backward-curving petals.

cycle noun **1** a series of events that are regularly repeated in the same order. **2** a complete sequence of changes associated with something recurring such as an alternating electric current. **3** a series of musical or literary works composed around a particular theme. **4** a bicycle. verb (**cycles**, **cycling**, **cycled**) ride a bicycle. ■ **cyclist** noun.

cyclic /syk-lik, sik-lik/ or **cyclical** adjective occurring in cycles.

cyclone noun **1** a system of winds rotating inwards to an area of low atmospheric pressure. **2** a violent tropical storm. ■ **cyclonic** adjective.

cygnet /sig-nit/ noun a young swan.

cylinder noun **1** a three-dimensional shape with straight parallel sides and circular or oval ends. **2** a chamber in which a piston moves in an engine. ■ **cylindrical** adjective.

cymbal noun a musical instrument consisting of a round brass plate which is either struck against another one or hit with a stick.

cynic noun **1** a person who believes that people always act from selfish motives. **2** a person who raises doubts about something. ■ **cynicism** noun.

cynical adjective **1** believing that people always act from selfish motives. **2** doubtful or sneering. **3** concerned only with your own interests. ■ **cynically** adverb.

cypher ⇒ CIPHER.

cypress noun an evergreen coniferous tree with small dark leaves.

Cypriot noun a person from Cyprus. adjective relating to Cyprus.

Cyrillic /si-ril-lik/ noun the alphabet used for Russian and related languages.

cyst /sist/ noun a sac or cavity in the body containing fluid.

cystic adjective **1** having to do with cysts. **2** relating to the bladder or the gall bladder. □ **cystic fibrosis** an inherited disease which causes too much mucus to be produced and often leads to blockage of tubes in the body.

cystitis /si-sty-tiss/ noun inflammation of the bladder.

cytoplasm noun the material of a living cell, excluding the nucleus.

czar etc. ⇒ TSAR etc.

Czech /chek/ noun **1** a person from the Czech Republic or (formerly) Czechoslovakia. **2** the language spoken in the Czech Republic.

Dd

D or **d** noun (plural **Ds** or **D's**) **1** the fourth letter of the alphabet. **2** the Roman numeral for 500. abbreviation (**d**) (before decimal currency was brought in) penny or pence.

'd short form had or would.

DA abbreviation (in the US) district attorney.

dab verb (**dabs**, **dabbing**, **dabbed**) **1** press lightly with something absorbent. **2** apply with light, quick strokes. noun a small amount of something applied lightly. □ **dab hand** Brit. informal a person who is very good at something.

dabble verb (**dabbles**, **dabbling**, **dab-**

bled) **1** gently move your hands or feet around in water. **2** take part in an activity in a casual way. ■ **dabbler** noun.

dace noun (plural **dace**) a small freshwater fish related to the carp.

dachshund noun a breed of dog with a long body and very short legs.

dad or **daddy** noun (plural **dads** or **daddies**) informal your father. □ **daddy-long-legs** Brit. informal a crane fly.

daffodil noun a plant that has bright yellow flowers with a long trumpet-shaped centre.

daffy adjective informal silly or mildly eccentric.

daft adjective informal silly; foolish.

dagger noun a short pointed knife, used as a weapon.

daguerreotype /duh-**ger**-ruh-typ/ noun an early kind of photograph produced using a silver-coated plate.

dahlia /**day**-li-uh/ noun a garden plant with brightly coloured flowers.

daily adjective & adverb every day or every weekday.

dainty adjective (**daintier**, **daintiest**) delicately small and pretty. noun (plural **dainties**) a small, tasty item of food. ■ **daintily** adverb.

dairy noun (plural **dairies**) a building where milk and milk products are produced. adjective **1** made from milk. **2** involved in milk production.

dais /**day**-iss/ noun a low platform that supports a throne, or that people stand on to make a speech.

daisy noun (plural **daisies**) a small plant that has flowers with a yellow centre and white petals.

dale noun (in northern England) a valley.

dally verb (**dallies**, **dallying**, **dallied**) **1** do something in a leisurely way. **2** (**dally with**) have a casual relationship with. ■ **dalliance** noun.

Dalmatian /dal-**may**-sh'n/ noun a breed of large dog with short white hair and dark spots.

dam¹ noun a barrier constructed across a river to hold back water. verb

(**dams**, **damming**, **dammed**) build a dam across.

dam² noun the female parent of an animal.

damage noun **1** physical harm that makes something less valuable or effective. **2** (**damages**) money paid to compensate for a loss or injury. verb (**damages**, **damaging**, **damaged**) cause damage to; harm.

damask noun a rich, heavy fabric with a pattern woven into it.

dame noun **1** (**Dame**) (in the UK) the title of a woman awarded a knighthood, equivalent to *Sir*. **2** N. Amer. informal a woman. **3** Brit. a comic female character in pantomime, played by a man.

damn verb **1** (**be damned**) (in Christian belief) be condemned by God to eternal punishment in hell. **2** harshly condemn. **3** curse.

damnable /**dam**-nuh-b'l/ adjective very bad or unpleasant.

damnation noun the fate of being condemned to eternal punishment in hell.

damned adjective said to emphasize anger or frustration.

damp adjective slightly wet. noun moisture in the air, on a surface, or in a solid. verb **1** make something damp. **2** (**damp down**) control a feeling or situation. □ **damp course** a layer of waterproof material in a wall near the ground, to prevent rising damp. **damp squib** Brit. something that turns out to be much less impressive than expected.

dampen verb **1** make damp. **2** make less strong or intense.

damper noun **1** a pad for silencing a piano string. **2** a movable metal plate for controlling the air flow in a chimney. □ **put a damper on** informal make something less enjoyable or lively.

damsel noun old use a young unmarried woman.

damson noun a small purple-black fruit resembling a plum.

dance verb (**dances**, **dancing**, **danced**) **1** move rhythmically to music. **2** move in a quick and lively way. **noun 1** a series of steps and movements performed to music. **2** a social gathering at which people dance. ■ **dancer** noun.

dandelion noun a weed with large bright yellow flowers.

dander noun (**get your dander up**) informal lose your temper.

dandle verb (**dandles, dandling, dandled**) gently bounce a young child on your knees or in your arms.

dandruff noun flakes of dead skin on a person's scalp and in the hair.

dandy noun (plural **dandies**) a man who is too concerned with looking stylish and fashionable. **adjective** (**dandier, dandiest**) N. Amer. informal excellent. ■ **dandified** adjective.

Dane noun a person from Denmark.

danger noun **1** the possibility of suffering harm or of experiencing something unpleasant. **2** a cause of harm.

dangerous adjective likely to cause harm. ■ **dangerously** adverb.

dangle verb (**dangles, dangling, dangled**) **1** hang or swing freely. **2** offer something as an incentive.

dank adjective damp and cold.

dapper adjective (of a man) neat in appearance; smart.

dapple verb (**dapples, dappling, dappled**) mark with patches of colour or of light and shadow. **noun** a patch of colour or light.

dare verb (**dares, daring, dared**) **1** have the courage to do something. **2** challenge someone to do something. **noun** a challenge to do something brave or risky.

daredevil noun a person who enjoys doing dangerous things.

daring adjective fearlessly bold. **noun** adventurous courage. ■ **daringly** adverb.

dark adjective **1** with little or no light. **2** of a deep colour. **3** mysterious: *a dark secret.* **4** depressing or cheerless. **5** evil; wicked. **noun 1** (**the dark**) the absence of light. **2** nightfall. □ **the Dark Ages** the period *c.*500–1100 in

Europe, thought of as being uncultured. **dark horse** a person who is secretive about themselves. **in the dark** in a state of ignorance. **a shot in the dark** a wild guess. ■ **darkly** adverb **darkness** noun.

darken verb **1** make or become darker. **2** become unhappy or angry.

darkroom noun a darkened room for developing photographs.

darling noun **1** an affectionate form of address. **2** a lovable person. **adjective 1** much loved. **2** charming.

darn[1] verb mend a hole in something knitted by weaving yarn across it.

darn[2] or **darned** adjective informal another way of saying **DAMNED**.

dart noun **1** a small pointed missile fired as a weapon or thrown in the game of darts. **2** (**darts**) an indoor game in which you throw darts at a circular board marked with numbers. **3** a sudden rapid movement. **4** a tapered tuck in a garment. **verb** move suddenly or rapidly.

dash verb **1** run or travel in a great hurry. **2** strike or throw with great force. **3** destroy: *his hopes were dashed.* **4** (**dash off**) write something hurriedly. **noun 1** an act of dashing. **2** N. Amer. a sprint. **3** a small amount added. **4** impressive style; flair. **5** a horizontal stroke in writing (-).

dashboard noun the panel of instruments and controls facing the driver of a vehicle.

dashing adjective excitingly attractive and stylish.

dastardly /dass-terd-li/ adjective old use wicked and cruel.

data noun **1** facts, statistics, or other information. **2** information stored by a computer.

> ℹ️ **data** is the plural of the Latin word **datum**. Scientists use it as a plural noun, taking a plural verb (for example, *the data were classified*). In everyday use, however, **data** is usually treated as a singular noun with a singular verb, as in *data was collected over a number of years.*

PUNCTUATION

Dash

A dash is used:

1 to mark the beginning and end of an interruption in the structure of a sentence:

My son—where has he gone?—would like to meet you.

2 to show faltering speech in conversation:

Yes—well—I would—only you see—it's not very easy.

3 to show other kinds of break in a sentence, where a comma, semicolon, or colon would traditionally be used, e.g.

The most important thing is this—don't rush the work.

Do not use a dash in this way when writing formally.

---

database noun a set of data held in a computer.

date¹ noun **1** the day of the month or year as specified by a number. **2** a day or year when a given event occurred or will occur. **3** informal a social or romantic appointment. **4** a musical or theatrical performance. verb (**dates, dating, dated**) **1** establish the date of. **2** mark something with a date. **3** (**date back to**) originate at a particular time in the past. **4** informal go on a date or regular dates with. □ **to date** until now. ■ **datable** (or **dateable**) adjective.

date² noun the sweet, dark brown, oval fruit of a palm tree.

dated adjective old-fashioned.

dative noun Grammar (in Latin, Greek, German, etc.) the case of nouns and pronouns that indicates an indirect object or the person or thing affected by a verb.

datum noun (plural **data**) a piece of information.

daub verb smear something with a thick substance. noun **1** plaster, clay, or a similar substance, used in building. **2** a smear of a thick substance.

daughter noun **1** a girl or woman in relation to her parents. **2** a female descendant. □ **daughter-in-law** (plural **daughters-in-law**) the wife of your son.

daunt verb (**be daunted**) feel intimidated or apprehensive. ■ **daunting** adjective.

dauntless adjective fearless and determined.

dawdle verb (**dawdles, dawdling, dawdled**) move slowly; take your time.

dawn noun **1** the first appearance of light in the sky in the morning. **2** the beginning of something new. verb **1** (of a day) begin. **2** come into existence. **3** (**dawn on**) (of a fact) become clear to. □ **dawn chorus** the early-morning singing of birds.

day noun **1** a period of twenty-four hours, reckoned from midnight to midnight. **2** the time between sunrise and sunset. **3** (usu. **days**) a particular period of the past. **4** (**the day**) the present time or the time in question. □ **call it a day** decide to stop doing something. **day in, day out** continuously over a long period.

daybreak noun dawn.

daydream noun a series of pleasant thoughts that distract your attention from the present. verb have a daydream.

daylight noun **1** the natural light of the day. **2** dawn. □ **daylight robbery** Brit. informal blatant overcharging.

daze noun a state of stunned confusion or bewilderment. ■ **dazed** adjective **dazedly** adverb.

dazzle verb (dazzles, dazzling, dazzled) **1** (of a bright light) blind someone temporarily. **2** amaze someone by being very impressive. noun blinding brightness. ■ **dazzling** adjective.

dB abbreviation decibels.

DC abbreviation **1** direct current. **2** District of Columbia.

deacon /dee-kuhn/ noun **1** a Christian minister just below the rank of priest. **2** (in some Protestant Churches) a person who assists a minister. ■ **deaconess** noun.

deactivate verb (deactivates, deactivating, deactivated) stop equipment from working by disconnecting or destroying it.

dead adjective **1** no longer alive. **2** (of a part of the body) numb. **3** displaying no emotion. **4** lacking activity or excitement. **5** complete; absolute: *dead silence.* adverb **1** absolutely, exactly, or directly: *you're dead right.* **2** Brit. informal very. □ **dead duck** informal an unsuccessful or useless person or thing. **dead end** a closed-off end of a road or passage. **dead heat** a race in which two or more competitors are exactly level. **dead loss** an unproductive or useless person or thing. **dead reckoning** a way of finding out your position by estimating the direction and distance travelled. **dead ringer** a person or thing very like another. **dead wood** useless or unproductive people or things.

deadbeat noun informal an idle or aimless person.

deaden verb **1** make a noise or sensation less strong or intense. **2** make something insensitive or inactive.

deadhead verb remove dead flower heads from a plant.

deadline noun the time or date by which you have to complete something.

deadlock noun **1** a situation in which no one can make any progress. **2** Brit. a lock operated by a key. verb (be deadlocked) be in a deadlock.

deadly adjective (deadlier deadliest) **1** causing or able to cause death. **2** (of

a voice, glance, etc.) filled with hate. **3** extremely accurate or effective. **4** informal extremely boring. adverb extremely: *she was deadly serious.*

deadpan adjective not showing any emotion; expressionless.

deadweight noun **1** the weight of a motionless person or thing. **2** the total weight which a ship can carry.

deaf adjective **1** wholly or partially unable to hear. **2** (deaf to) unwilling to listen to. □ **deaf mute** offensive a person who is deaf and unable to speak. ■ **deafness** noun.

deafen verb **1** make someone deaf. **2** (deafening) extremely loud. ■ **deafeningly** adverb.

deal[1] verb (deals, dealing, dealt) **1** give out cards to players of a card game. **2** (deal out) distribute. **3** trade in a commodity commercially. **4** informal buy and sell illegal drugs. noun **1** a formal agreement or pact. **2** a particular form of treatment received. □ **big deal** informal an important thing. **deal with 1** do business with. **2** do things to put a problem right. **3** cope with. **4** have a particular subject. **a good (or great) deal 1** a large amount. **2** to a great extent; a lot. **a square deal** a fair bargain or treatment. ■ **dealer** noun.

deal[2] noun fir or pine wood.

dealer noun **1** a person who buys and sells goods. **2** a person who buys and sells shares directly (rather than as a broker or agent). **3** a player who deals cards in a card game.

dean noun **1** the head of a cathedral's governing body. **2** the head of a university department or medical school.

dear adjective **1** much loved. **2** used in the polite introduction to a letter. **3** expensive. noun **1** an affectionate form of address. **2** a lovable person.

dearly adverb **1** very much. **2** at great cost.

dearth noun a lack of something.

death noun **1** the action of dying. **2** an instance of a person or an animal dying. **3** the state of being dead. **4** the end of something. □ **at death's door** so ill that you may die. **death knell 1** the tolling of a bell to mark someone's death. **2** an event that signals the end of something. **death penalty** punishment by being executed. **death row** a block of cells for prisoners who have been sentenced to death. **death-watch beetle** a beetle that makes a ticking sound which people used to think was an omen of death.

deathly adjective suggesting death: *a deathly hush.*

debacle /day-**bah**-k'l/ noun an utter failure or disaster.

debar verb (**debars, debarring, debarred**) officially prevent someone from doing something.

debase verb (**debases, debasing, debased**) make something worse in quality, value, or character. ■ **debasement** noun.

debatable adjective open to discussion or argument.

debate noun **1** a formal discussion in which people present opposing arguments. **2** an argument. verb (**debates, debating, debated**) **1** discuss or argue about. **2** consider a possible course of action.

debauch verb **1** corrupt morally. **2** (**debauched**) indulging in a lot of pleasures in a way considered immoral. ■ **debauchery** noun.

debilitate /di-**bil**-i-tayt/ verb (**debilitates, debilitating, debilitated**) severely weaken.

debility noun (plural **debilities**) physical weakness.

debit noun **1** an entry in an account recording a sum owed. **2** a payment that has been made or that is owed. verb (**debits, debiting, debited**) (of a bank) remove money from a customer's account. □ **debit card** a card that lets you buy something with money from your bank account.

debonair adjective (of a man) confident, stylish, and charming.

debrief verb question someone in detail about a mission they have completed.

debris /**deb**-ree/ noun **1** scattered items or pieces of rubbish. **2** loose broken pieces of rock.

debt noun **1** a sum of money owed. **2** a situation where you owe someone money. **3** gratitude for a favour or service.

debtor noun a person who owes money.

debug verb (**debugs, debugging, debugged**) remove errors from computer hardware or software.

debunk verb show that something believed in by many people is false or exaggerated.

debut /**day**-byoo/ noun a person's first appearance in a role. verb make a debut.

debutant /**deb**-yoo-ton(t)/ noun a person making a debut.

debutante /**deb**-yoo-tont/ noun a young upper-class woman making her first appearance in society.

decade noun a period of ten years.

decadent adjective **1** immoral and interested only in pleasure. **2** luxuriously self-indulgent. ■ **decadence** noun **decadently** adverb.

decaffeinated adjective (of tea or coffee) having had most or all of its caffeine removed.

decagon noun a figure with ten straight sides and angles.

decahedron /de-kuh-**hee**-druhn/ noun (plural **decahedra** or **decahedrons**) a solid figure with ten sides.

decamp verb depart suddenly or secretly.

decant /di-**kant**/ verb pour liquid from one container into another.

decanter noun a glass container with a stopper, for wine or spirits.

decapitate verb (**decapitates, decapitating, decapitated**) cut off the head of. ■ **decapitation** noun.

decathlon /di-**kath**-luhn/ noun an athletic event in which each competitor takes part in the same ten events. ■ **decathlete** noun.

decay verb **1** rot; decompose. **2** become weaker or less good. noun **1** the state or process of decaying. **2** rotten matter or tissue.

decease noun formal or Law death.

deceased formal or Law noun (**the deceased**) the recently dead person in question. adjective recently dead.

deceit noun **1** the practice of deceiving. **2** something done or said to deceive others.

deceitful adjective acting to deceive others. ■ **deceitfully** adverb.

deceive verb (**deceives**, **deceiving**, **deceived**) **1** deliberately cause someone to believe something false. **2** (of a thing) give a mistaken impression. ■ **deceiver** noun.

 i before *e* except after *c*: dece**i**ve.

decelerate verb (**decelerates**, **decelerating**, **decelerated**) slow down. ■ **deceleration** noun.

December noun the twelfth month of the year.

decency noun (plural **decencies**) **1** decent behaviour. **2** (**decencies**) standards of acceptable behaviour.

decennial /di-**sen**-i-uhl/ adjective lasting for or happening every ten years.

decent adjective **1** having good moral standards. **2** of an acceptable quality. **3** Brit. informal kind or generous. ■ **decently** adverb.

decentralize or **decentralise** verb (**decentralizes**, **decentralizing**, **decentralized**) transfer authority from central to local government. ■ **decentralization** noun.

deception noun **1** the action of deceiving. **2** a thing that deceives.

deceptive adjective giving a false impression.

deceptively adverb to a lesser or greater extent than appears the case.

ℹ beware of confusion when using **deceptively**, as it can mean both one thing and its complete opposite. A *deceptively smooth surface* is one that appears smooth but in fact is not smooth at all, while a *deceptively spacious room* is one that does not look spacious at first, but in fact is spacious.

decibel /**dess**-i-bel/ noun a unit for measuring the loudness of a sound or the power of an electrical signal.

decide verb (**decides**, **deciding**, **decided**) **1** consider and make a judgement or decision. **2** settle an issue or contest.

decided adjective definite; clear. ■ **decidedly** adverb.

decider noun a contest that settles the winner of a series of contests.

deciduous adjective (of a tree or shrub) shedding its leaves annually.

decimal adjective having to do with a system of numbers based on the number ten. noun a fractional number in the decimal system, written with figures either side of a full point. □ **decimal place** the position of a digit to the right of a decimal point. **decimal point** a full point placed after the figure representing units in a decimal fraction.

decimate verb (**decimates**, **decimating**, **decimated**) **1** kill or destroy a large proportion of. **2** drastically reduce in strength. ■ **decimation** noun.

decipher verb (**deciphers**, **deciphering**, **deciphered**) **1** convert something from code into normal language. **2** succeed in understanding something that is hard to interpret.

decision noun **1** a conclusion or resolution reached after consideration. **2** decisiveness.

decisive adjective **1** settling an issue quickly. **2** able to make decisions quickly. ■ **decisively** adverb **decisiveness** noun.

deck noun **1** a floor of a ship. **2** a floor or platform. **3** chiefly N. Amer. a pack of cards. **4** a player or recorder for discs or tapes. **verb** decorate something festively.

deckchair noun a folding chair with a wooden frame and a canvas seat.

decking noun material used in making a deck.

declaim verb speak or recite in a dramatic or passionate way.

declamation noun the action or art of declaiming. ■ **declamatory** adjective.

declaration noun **1** a formal statement or announcement. **2** the action of declaring.

declare verb (**declares, declaring, declared**) **1** announce solemnly or officially. **2** (**declare yourself**) reveal your intentions or identity. **3** acknowledge that you have income or goods on which tax or duty should be paid. **4** Cricket voluntarily close an innings with wickets remaining.

declassify verb (**declassifies, declassifying, declassified**) officially declare information or documents to be no longer secret.

declension noun Grammar the changes in the form of a noun, pronoun, or adjective that identify its case, number, and gender.

decline verb (**declines, declining, declined**) **1** become smaller, weaker, or worse. **2** politely refuse. **3** Grammar form a word according to its case, number, and gender. **noun** a gradual loss of strength, numbers, or value.

declivity /di-**kliv**-i-ti/ noun (plural **declivities**) formal a downward slope.

decode verb (**decodes, decoding, decoded**) convert a coded message into understandable language. ■ **decoder** noun.

décolletage /day-kol-**tah**zh/ noun a low neckline on a woman's garment.

décolleté /day-**kol**-tay/ adjective having a low neckline.

decommission verb take a nuclear reactor or weapon out of use and make it safe.

decompose verb (**decomposes, decomposing, decomposed**) decay; rot.

■ **decomposition** noun.

decompress verb **1** reduce the pressure on. **2** expand compressed computer data to its normal size.

decompression noun **1** reduction in air pressure. **2** the decompressing of computer data. □ **decompression sickness** a serious condition that results when a deep-sea diver surfaces too quickly.

decongestant adjective (of a medicine) used to relieve a blocked nose.

deconstruct verb take something apart to expose its workings. ■ **deconstruction** noun.

decontaminate verb (**decontaminates, decontaminating, decontaminated**) remove dangerous substances from. ■ **decontamination** noun.

decor /**day**-kor/ noun the furnishing and decoration of a room.

decorate verb (**decorates, decorating, decorated**) **1** make something more attractive by adding decoration. **2** apply paint or wallpaper to. **3** give an award or medal to. ■ **decorator** noun.

decoration noun **1** the process or art of decorating. **2** a decorative object or pattern. **3** the way in which something is decorated. **4** a medal or award given as an honour.

decorative /**dek**-uh-ruh-tiv/ adjective **1** serving to make something look more attractive. **2** having to do with decoration. **3** pretty or attractive. ■ **decoratively** adverb.

decorator noun a person who decorates, in particular (Brit.) a person whose job is to paint interior walls or hang wallpaper.

decorous adjective in good taste; polite and restrained. ■ **decorously** adverb.

decorum /di-**kor**-uhm/ noun polite and socially acceptable behaviour.

decoy noun **1** a real or imitation bird or mammal, used by hunters to lure game. **2** a person or thing used to mislead or lure someone into a trap. **verb** lure by means of a decoy.

decrease verb (**decreases, decreas-**

ing, decreased) make or become smaller or fewer. **noun** the process of decreasing, or the amount by which something decreases.

decree noun 1 an official order that has the force of law. **2** a judgement of certain law courts. **verb (decrees, decreeing, decreed)** order officially.

decrepit adjective 1 worn out or ruined because of age or neglect. **2** elderly and infirm. ■ **decrepitude** noun.

decriminalize or **decriminalise verb (decriminalizes, decriminalizing, decriminalized)** stop treating something as illegal.

decry verb (decries, decrying, decried) publicly declare something to be wrong or bad.

decrypt verb convert a coded or unclear message into understandable language.

dedicate verb (dedicates, dedicating, dedicated) 1 devote to a particular subject, task, or purpose. **2** address a book to someone as a sign of respect or affection.

dedicated adjective 1 devoting a lot of time and attention to a particular task or subject. **2** exclusively given over to a particular purpose.

dedication noun 1 devotion to a particular task or subject. **2** the action of dedicating. **3** the words with which a book is dedicated to someone.

deduce verb (deduces, deducing, deduced) reach a conclusion by thinking about the information or evidence that is available.

deduct verb take an amount away from a total. ■ **deductible** adjective.

deduction noun 1 the action of deducting. **2** an amount that is or may be deducted. **3** the action of deducing. ■ **deductive** adjective.

deed noun 1 something that is done deliberately. **2 (deeds)** legal documents. □ **deed poll** Law a legal deed made by one party only.

deem verb formal consider in a specified way.

deep adjective 1 extending far down or in from the top or surface. **2** extend-

ing a specified distance from the top or surface. **3** (of sound) not shrill. **4** (of colour) dark and intense. **5** very intense, profound, or extreme: *a deep sleep*. **6** difficult to understand. **7** (in ball games) far down or across the field. **noun (the deep)** literary the sea. □ **deep freeze** (or **deep freezer**) a freezer. **deep-fry** fry food in enough fat or oil to cover it completely. ■ **deeply** adverb.

deepen verb make or become deep or deeper.

deer noun (plural deer) a grazing mammal with hooves, the male of which usually has antlers.

deerstalker noun a soft cloth cap, with peaks in front and behind and ear flaps which can be tied together over the top.

deface verb (defaces, defacing, defaced) spoil the surface or appearance of.

de facto /day **fak**-toh/ **adjective & adverb** existing or happening in fact, whether it is supposed to or not.

defame verb (defames, defaming, defamed) damage the good reputation of. ■ **defamation** noun **defamatory** adjective.

default noun 1 failure to do what you are supposed to do. **2** an option adopted by a computer program or other mechanism when no alternative is specified. **verb 1** fail to do what you are supposed to do. **2 (default to)** go back automatically to a default option. □ **by default** because there is no opposition or positive action. ■ **defaulter** noun.

defeat verb 1 win a victory against; beat. **2** prevent someone from achieving an aim. **3** reject or block a proposal or motion. **noun** an instance of defeating or of being defeated.

defeatist noun a person who gives in to difficulty or failure too easily. ■ **defeatism** noun.

defecate /**def**-i-kayt, **dee**-fi-kayt/ **verb** discharge waste matter from the bowels. ■ **defecation** noun.

defect[1] noun /**dee**-fekt/ a fault or imperfection.

defect[2] /di-**fekt**/ verb abandon your country or cause in favour of an opposing one. ■ **defection** noun **defector** noun.

defective adjective imperfect or faulty.

defence (US spelling **defense**) noun **1** the action of defending something. **2** something that protects a building, country, etc. against attack. **3** attempted justification of something. **4** the case presented by the person being accused or sued in a lawsuit. **5 (the defence)** the lawyer or lawyers for the person being accused or sued in a lawsuit. **6** (in sport) the action of defending the goal or wicket, or the players who perform this role.

defenceless (US spelling **defenseless**) adjective completely vulnerable.

defend verb **1** protect from harm or danger. **2** argue in support of the person being accused or sued in a lawsuit. **3** attempt to justify. **4** compete to hold on to a title or seat in a contest or election. **5** (in sport) protect your goal or wicket rather than attempt to score against your opponents. ■ **defender** noun.

defendant noun a person sued or accused in a court of law.

defensible adjective **1** able to be justified by argument. **2** able to be protected.

defensive adjective **1** used or intended to defend or protect. **2** very anxious to defend yourself against criticism. ■ **defensively** adverb **defensiveness** noun.

defer[1] verb (**defers, deferring, deferred**) put something off to a later time. ■ **deferment** noun **deferral** noun.

defer[2] verb (**defers, deferring, deferred**) (**defer to**) humbly give in to.

deference noun humble respect.

deferential adjective humble and respectful. ■ **deferentially** adverb.

defiance noun bold disobedience.

defiant adjective boldly disobedient. ■ **defiantly** adverb.

deficiency noun (plural **deficiencies**) **1** a lack or shortage of something. **2** a failing or shortcoming.

deficient adjective **1** not having enough of a specified quality or ingredient. **2** insufficient.

deficit noun **1** the amount by which something falls short. **2** the amount by which money spent is greater than money earned in a particular period of time.

defile[1] verb (**defiles, defiling, defiled**) **1** make dirty. **2** treat something sacred with disrespect.

defile[2] noun a narrow, steep-sided gorge or passage.

define verb (**defines, defining, defined**) **1** describe the exact nature or scope of. **2** give the meaning of a word or phrase. **3** mark out the limits or outline of. ■ **definable** adjective.

definite adjective **1** clearly stated or decided. **2** (of a person) certain about something. **3** known to be true or real. **4** having exact and measurable physical limits. □ **the definite article** Grammar the word *the*. ■ **definitely** adverb.

 -ite, not *-ate*: defin*ite*.

definition noun **1** a statement of the exact meaning of a word or the nature or scope of something. **2** the degree of sharpness in outline of an object or image. □ **by definition** by its very nature.

definitive adjective **1** (of a conclusion or agreement) decisive and with authority. **2** (of a text) the most accurate of its kind. ■ **definitively** adverb.

deflate verb (**deflates, deflating, deflated**) **1** let air or gas out of a tyre, balloon, etc. **2** make someone suddenly depressed. **3** reduce price levels in an economy.

deflation noun **1** the action or process of deflating. **2** reduction of the general level of prices in an economy. ■ **deflationary** adjective.

deflect verb **1** turn something aside from a straight course. **2** make someone change their mind about doing something. ■ **deflection** noun.

deflower verb old use have sex with a woman who is a virgin.

defoliate verb (**defoliates, defoliating, defoliated**) remove the leaves from trees or plants. ■ **defoliant** noun **defoliation** noun.

deforest verb clear an area of trees. ■ **deforestation** noun.

deform verb distort the shape or form of. ■ **deformed** adjective.

deformity noun (plural **deformities**) **1** a deformed part. **2** the state of being deformed.

defraud verb illegally obtain money from someone by deception.

defray verb provide money to pay a cost.

defrock verb remove the official status of a Christian priest.

defrost verb **1** remove ice from something. **2** thaw frozen food.

deft adjective quick and neatly skilful. ■ **deftly** adverb **deftness** noun.

defunct adjective no longer existing or functioning.

defuse verb (**defuses, defusing, defused**) **1** remove the fuse from an explosive device to prevent it from exploding. **2** reduce the danger or tension in a difficult situation.

> ℹ️ do not confuse **defuse** with **diffuse**, which means 'spread over a wide area'.

defy verb (**defies, defying, defied**) **1** openly resist or refuse to obey. **2** challenge someone to do or prove something.

degenerate verb /di-**jenn**-uh-rayt/ (**degenerates, degenerating, degenerated**) deteriorate physically or morally; get worse. adjective /di-**jenn**-uh-ruht/ having very low moral standards. noun /di-**jenn**-uh-ruht/ a person with very low moral standards. ■ **degeneracy** noun **degeneration** noun.

degenerative adjective (of a disease) causing gradual deterioration.

degrade verb (**degrades, degrading, degraded**) **1** cause someone to lose dignity or self-respect. **2** make worse in character or quality. **3** make something break down or deteriorate chemically. ■ **degradable** adjective **degradation** noun.

degree noun **1** the amount, level, or extent to which something happens or is present. **2** a unit for measuring angles, equivalent to one ninetieth of a right angle. **3** a stage in a scale, e.g. of temperature or hardness. **4** a qualification awarded to someone who has successfully completed a course at a university.

dehumanize or **dehumanise** verb (**dehumanizes, dehumanizing, dehumanized**) remove the positive human qualities from.

dehumidify verb (**dehumidifies, dehumidifying, dehumidified**) remove moisture from the air or a gas. ■ **dehumidifier** noun.

dehydrate verb (**dehydrates, dehydrating, dehydrated**) **1** make someone lose a lot of water from their body. **2** remove water from food to preserve it. ■ **dehydration** noun.

de-ice verb (**de-ices, de-icing, de-iced**) remove ice from. ■ **de-icer** noun.

deify /**day**-i-fl/ verb (**deifies, deifying, deified**) treat or worship someone as a god. ■ **deification** noun.

deign verb (**deign** to do) do something that you think you are too important to do.

deity /**day**-i-ti/ noun (plural **deities**) a god or goddess.

déjà vu /day-zhah **voo**/ noun a feeling of having already experienced the present situation.

dejected adjective sad and dispirited. ■ **dejection** noun.

delay verb **1** make someone late or slow. **2** hesitate or be slow. **3** put off or postpone. noun the period or length of time that someone or something is delayed.

delectable adjective lovely, delightful, or delicious. ■ **delectably** adverb.

delectation /dee-lek-**tay**-sh'n/ noun formal pleasure and delight.

delegate noun /**del**-i-guht/ **1** a person sent to represent others. **2** a member of a committee. verb /**del**-i-gayt/ (delegates, delegating, delegated) **1** entrust a task or responsibility to someone else, especially someone more junior. **2** authorize someone to act as a representative.

delegation noun **1** a body of delegates. **2** the process of delegating.

delete verb (deletes, deleting, deleted) remove written or printed text. ■ **deletion** noun.

deleterious /de-li-**tee**-ri-uhss/ adjective formal causing harm or damage.

deli noun (plural **delis**) informal a delicatessen.

deliberate adjective /di-**lib**-uh-ruht/ **1** done on purpose; intentional. **2** careful and unhurried. verb /di-**lib**-uh-rayt/ (deliberates, deliberating, deliberated) think about something carefully and for a long time. ■ **deliberately** adverb.

deliberation noun **1** long and careful consideration. **2** slow and careful movement or thought.

deliberative adjective having to do with consideration or discussion.

delicacy noun (plural **delicacies**) **1** delicate texture or structure. **2** discretion and tact. **3** a tasty, expensive food.

delicate adjective **1** very fine in texture or structure. **2** easily broken or damaged. **3** tending to become ill easily. **4** requiring careful handling: *a delicate issue.* **5** skilful; deft. **6** (of food or drink) subtly and pleasantly flavoured. ■ **delicately** adverb.

delicatessen noun a shop selling unusual or foreign prepared foods.

delicious adjective **1** very pleasant to the taste. **2** delightful: *a delicious irony.* ■ **deliciously** adverb.

delight verb **1** greatly please. **2** (delight in) take great pleasure in. noun great pleasure, or something that causes it.

delighted adjective very pleased.

■ **delightedly** adverb.

delightful adjective causing delight; very pleasing. ■ **delightfully** adverb.

delineate /di-**lin**-i-ayt/ verb (delineates, delineating, delineated) describe or indicate something precisely. ■ **delineation** noun.

delinquency noun (plural **delinquencies**) minor crime.

delinquent adjective tending to commit crime. noun a delinquent person.

deliquesce /de-li-**kwess**/ verb (deliquesces, deliquescing, deliquesced) (of a solid) become liquid by absorbing moisture. ■ **deliquescence** noun **deliquescent** adjective.

delirious adjective **1** suffering from delirium. **2** extremely excited or happy. ■ **deliriously** adverb.

✓ note there's an *i*, not an *e*, in the middle: deli*r*ious.

delirium noun a disturbed state of mind in which a person becomes very restless, has illusions, and is unable to think clearly.

deliver verb **1** bring something and hand it over to the person who is supposed to receive it. **2** provide something promised or expected. **3** save or set free. **4** assist in the birth of. **5** give birth to. **6** launch or aim a blow or attack.

deliverance noun the process of being rescued or set free.

delivery noun (plural **deliveries**) **1** the action of delivering something. **2** the process of giving birth. **3** an act of throwing or bowling a ball.

dell noun literary a small valley.

delphinium /del-**fin**-i-uhm/ noun (plural **delphiniums**) a garden plant that has tall spikes of blue flowers.

delta[1] noun the fourth letter of the Greek alphabet (Δ, δ).

delta[2] noun an area of land where the mouth of a river has split into several channels.

delude verb (deludes, deluding, deluded) persuade someone to believe something that is not true.

deluge noun **1** a severe flood or very heavy fall of rain. **2** a great quantity of something arriving at the same time: *a deluge of complaints.* verb (deluges, deluging, deluged) **1** overwhelm someone with a great quantity of something. **2** flood.

delusion noun a belief or impression that is not real. ■ **delusional** adjective.

de luxe /di **luks**/ adjective of a superior kind; luxurious.

delve verb (delves, delving, delved) **1** reach inside a container and search for something. **2** research intensively into something. **3** literary dig.

demagnetize or **demagnetise** verb (demagnetizes, demagnetizing, demagnetized) stop something being magnetic.

demagogue /**dem**-uh-gog/ noun a political leader who appeals to people's desires and prejudices rather than using reasoned arguments.

demand noun **1** a very firm request for something. **2** (demands) pressing requirements. **3** the desire of consumers for a particular product or service. verb **1** ask very firmly. **2** insist on having. **3** require; need. ◻ **in demand** wanted by many people.

demanding adjective requiring a lot of skill or effort.

demarcate /**dee**-mar-kayt/ verb (demarcates, demarcating, demarcated) set the boundaries of. ■ **demarcation** noun.

dematerialize or **dematerialise** verb (dematerializes, dematerializing, dematerialized) stop being physically present.

demean verb make someone lose dignity or respect.

demeanour (US spelling **demeanor**) noun the way a person behaves or looks.

demented adjective **1** suffering from dementia. **2** informal wild and irrational.

dementia /di-**men**-shuh/ noun a disorder in which a person is unable to remember things or think clearly.

demerara sugar /dem-uh-**rair**-uh/ noun a type of light brown sugar.

demerit noun a fault or disadvantage.

demigod noun a being that is partly a god and partly a human.

demilitarize or **demilitarise** verb (demilitarizes, demilitarizing, demilitarized) remove all military forces from an area. ■ **demilitarization** noun.

demi-monde /de-mi-**mond**/ noun a group of people on the fringes of respectable society.

demise /di-**myz**/ noun **1** a person's death. **2** the end or failure of something.

demist verb Brit. clear condensation from. ■ **demister** noun.

demo noun (plural **demos**) informal **1** a political demonstration. **2** a demonstration recording or piece of software.

demob verb (demobs, demobbing, demobbed) Brit. informal demobilize.

demobilize or **demobilise** verb (demobilizes, demobilizing, demobilized) take troops out of active service. ■ **demobilization** noun.

democracy /di-**mok**-ruh-si/ noun (plural **democracies**) **1** a form of government in which the people have a say in who should hold power. **2** a state governed in such a way. **3** control of a group by the majority of its members.

democrat noun **1** a supporter of democracy. **2** (Democrat) (in the US) a member of the Democratic Party.

democratic adjective **1** relating to or supporting democracy. **2** open to anyone. **3** (Democratic) (in the US) relating to or supporting the Democratic Party. ■ **democratically** adverb.

democratize or **democratise** verb (democratizes, democratizing, democratized) introduce a democratic system or democratic ideas to. ■ **democratization** noun.

demography noun the study of human population. ■ **demographic** adjective.

demolish /di-**mol**-ish/ verb **1** knock down a building. **2** thoroughly prove a theory wrong. **3** humorous eat up food quickly. ■ **demolition** noun.

demon noun an evil spirit or devil. **adjective** very forceful or skilful: *a demon cook*.

demoniac /di-**moh**-ni-ak/ or **demoniacal** /dee-muh-**ny**-u-k'l/ adjective demonic.

demonic /di-**mon**-ik/ adjective having to do with demons or evil spirits. ■ **demonically** adverb.

demonize or **demonise** verb (demonizes, demonizing, demonized) portray someone as wicked and threatening.

demonstrable adjective clearly apparent or able to be proved. ■ **demonstrably** adverb.

demonstrate verb (demonstrates, demonstrating, demonstrated) **1** clearly show that something exists or is true. **2** show and explain how something works. **3** express a feeling or quality by your actions. **4** take part in a public demonstration. ■ **demonstrator** noun.

demonstration noun **1** the action of demonstrating. **2** a public meeting or march expressing an opinion on an issue.

demonstrative /di-**mon**-struh-tiv/ adjective **1** tending to show your feelings openly. **2** demonstrating something. ■ **demonstratively** adverb.

demoralize or **demoralise** verb (demoralizes, demoralizing, demoralized) make someone lose confidence or hope.

demote verb (demotes, demoting, demoted) move someone to a less senior position. ■ **demotion** noun.

demotivate verb make someone less eager to work or make an effort.

demur /di-**mer**/ verb (demurs, demurring, demurred) show reluctance. **noun** (also **demurral**) the showing of reluctance.

demure adjective (of a woman) reserved, modest, and shy. ■ **demurely** adverb.

demystify verb (demystifies, demystifying, demystified) make a subject less difficult to understand.

den noun **1** a wild animal's lair or home. **2** informal a person's private room. **3** a place where people meet to do something immoral or forbidden: *an opium den*.

denationalize or **denationalise** verb (denationalizes, denationalizing, denationalized) transfer a company from public to private ownership.

denial noun **1** the action of denying. **2** Psychology refusal to acknowledge an unacceptable truth or emotion.

denier /**den**-yer/ noun a unit of measurement for the fineness of textile fibre.

denigrate verb (denigrates, denigrating, denigrated) criticize someone unfairly. ■ **denigration** noun.

denim noun **1** a hard-wearing cotton fabric. **2** (denims) jeans or other clothes made of denim.

denizen /**den**-i-zuhn/ noun formal an inhabitant or occupant.

denominate verb (denominates, denominating, denominated) formal call; name.

denomination noun **1** a recognized branch of a Church or religion. **2** the face value of a banknote, coin, postage stamp, etc. **3** formal a name or designation. ■ **denominational** adjective.

denominator noun Mathematics the number below the line in a fraction, for example 4 in ¼.

denote verb (denotes, denoting, denoted) **1** be a sign of. **2** be a name or symbol for.

denouement /day-**noo**-mon/ noun the final part of a play, film, or narrative, in which matters are explained or resolved.

denounce verb (denounces, denouncing, denounced) publicly declare that someone is wrong or evil.

dense adjective **1** closely packed together. **2** containing parts crowded closely together. **3** informal stupid. ■ **densely** adverb.

density noun (plural **densities**) **1** the degree to which something is dense. **2** the quantity of people or things in a given area.

dent noun a slight hollow in a surface made by a blow or pressure. verb **1** mark with a dent. **2** have a bad effect on.

dental adjective relating to the teeth or to dentistry.

dentine /den-teen/ noun the hard, bony tissue that teeth are made of.

dentist noun a person who is qualified to treat the diseases and conditions that affect the teeth and gums. ■ dentistry noun.

denture /den-cher/ noun a removable plate or frame fitted with one or more false teeth.

denude verb (denudes, denuding, denuded) make something bare or empty.

denunciation noun the action of denouncing.

deny verb (denies, denying, denied) **1** refuse to admit that something is true. **2** refuse to give someone a thing that they want. **3** (deny yourself) go without something you want.

deodorant noun a substance which prevents unpleasant bodily odours.

deodorize or **deodorise** verb (deodorizes, deodorizing, deodorized) prevent an unpleasant smell in.

depart verb **1** leave; go away. **2** (depart from) do something different from the usual or accepted thing.

departed adjective deceased; dead.

department noun **1** a division of a large organization or building. **2** an administrative district in some countries, e.g. France. **3** informal a person's area of special knowledge or responsibility. □ **department store** a large shop that stocks many types of goods in different departments. ■ departmental adjective departmentally adverb.

departure noun the action of departing, or an instance when someone or something departs.

depend verb (depend on) **1** be deter-

mined by. **2** rely on.

dependable adjective trustworthy and reliable. ■ dependability noun dependably adverb.

dependant or **dependent** noun a person who relies on another for financial support.

☑ the correct spelling of the noun is either **dependant** or **dependent**. The adjective is always spelled **dependent**.

dependency noun (plural dependencies) **1** a country or province controlled by another. **2** the state of being dependent.

dependent adjective **1** (dependent on) determined by. **2** relying on someone or something for support. **3** (dependent on) unable to do without. noun ⇨ **DEPENDANT**. ■ dependence noun dependently adverb.

depict verb **1** represent something by a drawing, painting, or other art form. **2** portray in words. ■ depiction noun.

depilate /dep-i-layt/ verb (depilates, depilating, depilated) remove the hair from. ■ depilation noun depilatory adjective.

deplete verb (depletes, depleting, depleted) reduce the number or quantity of. ■ depletion noun.

deplorable adjective shockingly bad. ■ deplorably adverb.

deplore verb (deplores, deploring, deplored) strongly disapprove of.

deploy verb **1** bring or move forces into position for military action. **2** use a resource or quality effectively. ■ deployment noun.

depopulate verb (depopulates, depopulating, depopulated) greatly reduce the population of a place. ■ depopulation noun.

deport verb expel a foreigner or immigrant from a country. ■ deportation noun deportee noun.

deportment noun **1** the way a person stands and walks. **2** N. Amer. a person's behaviour or manners.

depose verb (deposes, deposing, deposed) remove someone from office suddenly and forcefully.

deposit noun **1** a sum of money placed in an account. **2** a payment made as a first instalment in buying something. **3** a returnable sum paid to cover possible loss or damage when renting something. **4** a layer or body of collected matter. verb (deposits, depositing, deposited) **1** put something down in a specific place. **2** store something with someone for safekeeping. **3** pay a sum as a deposit. **4** lay down matter as a layer or covering.

deposition noun **1** the action of deposing someone from office. **2** Law the giving of sworn evidence. **3** Law a sworn statement to be used as evidence. **4** the action of depositing.

depository noun (plural **depositories**) a place where things are stored.

depot /**dep**-oh/ noun **1** a place where large quantities of goods are stored. **2** a place where vehicles are housed and maintained. **3** N. Amer. /**dee**-poh/ a railway or bus station.

deprave verb (depraves, depraving, depraved) make someone morally bad; corrupt.

depravity /di-**prav**-i-ti/ noun immoral behaviour or character.

deprecate /**dep**-ri-kayt/ verb (deprecates, deprecating, deprecated) **1** express disapproval of. **2** dismiss something as being unimportant. ■ **deprecation** noun.

depreciate /di-**pree**-shi-ayt/ verb (depreciates, depreciating, depreciated) **1** decrease in value over a period of time. **2** dismiss something as being unimportant. ■ **depreciation** noun.

depredations plural noun acts that cause harm or damage.

depress verb **1** make someone feel utterly dejected. **2** make something less active. **3** push or pull down.

depressant adjective slowing down the natural processes of the body.

depressed adjective **1** feeling very sad, hopeless, and dejected. **2** suffer-

ing the damaging effects of an economic slump.

depression noun **1** a mental state in which a person has feelings of great sadness and hopelessness. **2** a long and severe slump in an economy or market. **3** the action of depressing. **4** a sunken place or hollow. **5** an area of low pressure which may bring rain.

depressive adjective tending to cause or feel depression.

deprivation /dep-ri-**vay**-sh'n/ noun **1** hardship resulting from not having enough of the things necessary for life. **2** the action of depriving.

deprive verb (deprives, depriving, deprived) prevent someone from having or using something.

deprived adjective not having enough of the things necessary for life.

Dept abbreviation Department.

depth noun **1** the distance from the top or surface down, or from front to back. **2** complex or meaningful thought. **3** extensive and detailed study. **4** strength of emotion. **5** (the depths) the deepest, lowest, or innermost part of something. □ **depth charge** a device designed to explode under water, used for attacking submarines.

deputation noun a group of people who are sent to do something on behalf of a larger group.

depute verb (deputes, deputing, deputed) instruct someone to do something that you are responsible for.

deputize or **deputise** verb (deputizes, deputizing, deputized) temporarily act on behalf of someone else.

deputy noun (plural **deputies**) a person appointed to do the work of a more senior person in that person's absence.

derail verb **1** make a train leave the tracks. **2** obstruct a process by diverting it from its intended course. ■ **derailment** noun.

derange verb (deranges, deranging, deranged) **1** make insane. **2** throw into disorder. ■ **derangement** noun.

deranged adjective mad; insane.

Derby /dar-bi/ noun (plural **Derbies**) **1** an annual flat race for three-year-old horses, founded by the Earl of Derby. **2** (**derby** or **local derby**) a sports match between two rival teams from the same area.

deregulate verb (**deregulates, deregulating, deregulated**) remove regulations or restrictions from. ■ **deregulation** noun.

derelict /der-i-likt/ adjective **1** in a very poor condition as a result of disuse and neglect. **2** chiefly N. Amer. shamefully negligent. noun a person without a home, job, or property.

dereliction noun **1** an abandoned and run-down state. **2** (usu. **dereliction of duty**) shameful failure to do something you are supposed to do.

deride verb (**derides, deriding, derided**) express contempt for; ridicule.

de rigueur /duh ri-ger/ adjective required by etiquette or current fashion.

derision noun scornful ridicule or mockery.

derisive /di-ry-siv/ adjective expressing contempt or ridicule. ■ **derisively** adverb.

derisory /di-ry-suh-ri/ adjective **1** ridiculously small or inadequate. **2** expressing contempt or ridicule; derisive.

derivation noun **1** the deriving of something from a source. **2** the formation of a word from another word.

derivative adjective imitating the work of another artist, writer, etc.; not original. noun something which is derived from another source.

derive verb (**derives, deriving, derived**) (**derive from**) **1** obtain something from a source. **2** arise or originate from.

dermatitis /der-muh-ty-tiss/ noun inflammation of the skin as a result of irritation or an allergic reaction.

dermatology noun the branch of medicine concerned with skin disorders. ■ **dermatological** adjective **dermatologist** noun.

derogatory /di-rog-uh-tri/ adjective critical or disrespectful.

derrick noun **1** a kind of crane with a movable pivoted arm. **2** the framework over an oil well for holding the drilling machinery.

derring-do noun old use heroic actions.

dervish noun a member of a Muslim religious group known for their wild rituals.

descant /dess-kant/ noun an independent melody sung or played above a basic melody.

descend verb **1** move down or downwards. **2** slope or lead downwards. **3** (**descend to**) do something very shameful. **4** (**descend on**) make a sudden attack on or unwelcome visit to. **5** (**be descended from**) have a particular person as an ancestor.

descendant noun a person that is descended from a particular ancestor.

> ☑ the correct spelling of the noun **descendant** is with -*ant*, not -*ent*, at the end; **descendent** is an adjective and means 'descending'.

descent noun **1** an act of descending. **2** a downward slope. **3** a person's origin or nationality.

describe verb (**describes, describing, described**) **1** give a detailed account of something in words. **2** mark out or draw a shape.

description noun **1** a spoken or written account. **2** the process of describing. **3** a sort, kind, or class: *people of any description*.

descriptive adjective describing something, especially in a vivid style. ■ **descriptively** adverb.

descry verb (**descries, descrying, descried**) literary catch sight of.

desecrate /dess-i-krayt/ verb (**desecrates, desecrating, desecrated**) treat something sacred with violent disrespect. ■ **desecration** noun.

desegregate verb (**desegregates, desegregating, desegregated**) end a policy by which people of different races are kept separate. ■ **desegregation** noun.

deselect verb Brit. (of a local branch of a political party) reject an existing MP as a candidate in a forthcoming election. ■ **deselection** noun.

desensitize or **desensitise** verb (**desensitizes, desensitizing, desensitized**) make less sensitive.

desert[1] /di-**zert**/ verb **1** leave someone without help or support. **2** leave a place, causing it to appear empty. **3** illegally run away from military service. ■ **deserter** noun **desertion** noun.

desert[2] /**dez**-ert/ noun an empty, waterless area of land with little or no vegetation.

> [i] don't confuse **desert** (a waterless area) with **dessert** (the sweet course)!

deserts /di-**zerts**/ plural noun (**get your just deserts**) get the reward or punishment that you deserve.

deserve verb (**deserves, deserving, deserved**) do something worthy of a particular reward or punishment. ■ **deservedly** adverb.

deserving adjective worthy of being treated well or helped.

déshabillé /day-za-bee-**yay**/ noun the state of being only partly clothed.

desiccate verb (**desiccates, desiccating, desiccated**) remove the moisture from.

design noun **1** a plan or drawing produced before something is made. **2** the production of such plans or drawings. **3** purpose or deliberate planning. **4** a decorative pattern. verb **1** produce a design for. **2** (**be designed**) be intended for a purpose. □ **have designs on** aim to obtain.

designate verb /**dez**-ig-nayt/ (**designates, designating, designated**) **1** officially give a particular status or name to. **2** appoint someone to a job or position. adjective /**dez**-ig-nuht/ appointed to a position but not yet having taken it up: *the Director designate*.

designation noun **1** the action of des-

ignating. **2** an official title or description.

designer noun a person who designs things. adjective made by a famous fashion designer: *designer jeans*.

desirable adjective **1** wished for as being attractive, useful, or necessary. **2** (of a person) attractive; good-looking. ■ **desirability** noun.

desire noun a strong feeling of wanting to have something or wishing for something to happen. verb (**desires, desiring, desired**) **1** strongly wish for or want. **2** find someone attractive.

desirous adjective (**desirous of** or **to do**) wanting a particular thing.

desist verb stop doing something.

desk noun **1** a piece of furniture with a flat or sloping surface for writing on. **2** a counter in a hotel, bank, etc.

desktop noun **1** the working surface of a desk. **2** a computer suitable to be used at an ordinary desk. **3** the area of a computer screen that you can work in.

desolate adjective **1** bleak and dismally empty. **2** very unhappy. verb (**be desolated**) be very unhappy. ■ **desolation** noun.

despair noun the complete loss or absence of hope. verb lose hope, or be without hope.

> [✓] des-, not dis-: despair.

despatch ⇒ **DISPATCH**.

desperado /dess-puh-**rah**-doh/ noun (plural **desperadoes** or **desperados**) dated a desperate or reckless criminal.

desperate adjective **1** feeling, showing, or involving despair. **2** extremely serious: *a desperate shortage*. **3** very violent or dangerous. ■ **desperately** adverb **desperation** noun.

> [✓] desperate, not -parate.

despicable adjective deserving hatred and contempt. ■ **despicably** adverb.

despise verb (**despise, despising, despised**) hate or feel disgusted by.

despite preposition in spite of.

despoil verb literary steal valuable possessions from.

despondent adjective very sad and without much hope. ■ **despondency** noun **despondently** adverb.

despot /**dess**-pot/ noun a ruler with unlimited power. ■ **despotic** adjective **despotism** noun.

dessert /di-**zert**/ noun the sweet course eaten at the end of a meal.

> 🛈 don't confuse **dessert** (the sweet course) with **desert** (a waterless area)!

dessertspoon noun a spoon smaller than a tablespoon and larger than a teaspoon.

destabilize or **destabilise** verb (**destabilizes, destabilizing, destabilized**) make a country or government less stable.

destination noun the place to which someone or something is going or being sent.

destine verb 1 (**be destined for** or **to do**) be intended for a particular purpose, or certain to do a specified thing. 2 (**be destined for**) be bound for a particular place.

destiny noun (plural **destinies**) 1 the things that will happen to a person. 2 the hidden power believed to control what will happen in the future.

destitute adjective extremely poor and without a home or other things necessary for life. ■ **destitution** noun.

destroy verb 1 make something stop existing by damaging or attacking it. 2 kill an animal by humane means.

destroyer noun 1 a person or thing that destroys. 2 a small, fast warship.

destruction noun the destroying of something.

destructive adjective 1 causing destruction. 2 negative and unhelpful. ■ **destructively** adverb.

desultory /**dez**-uhl-tuh-ri/ adjective 1 without much purpose or enthusiasm. 2 going constantly from one subject to another in a half-hearted way.

■ **desultorily** adverb.

detach verb 1 remove something that is attached to something larger. 2 (**be detached**) Military be sent on a mission. ■ **detachable** adjective.

> only one t: de*tach*, not *-tatch*.

detached adjective 1 separate or disconnected. 2 not involved or interested; aloof.

detachment noun 1 a feeling of being uninvolved or aloof. 2 a group of troops, ships, etc. sent away on a mission.

detail noun 1 a small individual item or fact. 2 small items or facts as a group: *attention to detail*. 3 a small part of a picture reproduced separately. 4 a small group of troops or police officers given a special duty. verb 1 describe something item by item. 2 instruct someone to undertake a particular task.

detailed adjective having many details.

detain verb 1 keep someone back. 2 keep someone in custody.

detainee noun a person who is kept in custody.

detect verb 1 discover or notice that something is present. 2 discover or investigate a crime or criminal. ■ **detectable** adjective **detection** noun.

detective noun a person whose job is investigating crimes.

detector noun a device designed to detect that something, e.g. smoke or gas, is present.

détente /day-**tahnt**/ noun the easing of hostility or strained relations between countries.

detention noun 1 the action of detaining someone. 2 the punishment of being kept in school after hours.

deter verb (**deters, deterring, deterred**) 1 make someone decide not to do something because they are afraid of the consequences. 2 prevent something occurring.

detergent noun a chemical substance used for cleaning.

deteriorate verb (deteriorates, deteriorating, deteriorated) become gradually worse. ■ **deterioration** noun.

determination noun **1** persistence in continuing to do something even when it is difficult. **2** the process of establishing something exactly.

determine verb **1** be the main factor in establishing something. **2** firmly decide. **3** ascertain or establish by research or calculation.

determined adjective persisting in doing something even when it is difficult; resolute. ■ **determinedly** adverb.

determiner noun **1** a person or thing that determines. **2** Grammar a word that comes before a noun to show how the noun is being used, e.g. *a, the, every*.

deterrent noun a thing that deters or is intended to deter. ■ **deterrence** noun.

detest verb dislike intensely.

detestable adjective deserving intense dislike.

detestation noun intense dislike.

dethrone verb (dethrones, dethroning, dethroned) remove a ruler from power.

detonate verb (detonates, detonating, detonated) explode, or make something explode. ■ **detonation** noun.

detonator noun a device used to detonate an explosive.

detour noun a long or roundabout route taken to avoid something or to visit something along the way. verb make a detour.

detoxify verb (detoxifies, detoxifying, detoxified) remove poisonous substances from.

detract verb (detract from) make something seem less valuable or impressive.

detractor noun a person who speaks critically about someone or something.

detriment noun harm or damage. ■ **detrimental** adjective.

detritus /di-**try**-tuhss/ noun debris or waste material.

deuce /dyooss/ noun **1** Tennis the score of 40 all in a game, at which two consecutive points are needed to win the game. **2** (**the deuce**) informal said instead of 'devil' when making an exclamation.

Deutschmark /**doych**-mark/ noun the chief unit of money in Germany.

devalue verb (devalues, devaluing, devalued) **1** make something seem less important than it is. **2** reduce the value of a currency in relation to other currencies. ■ **devaluation** noun.

devastate verb (devastates, devastating, devastated) **1** destroy or ruin. **2** (**be devastated**) be overwhelmed with shock or grief. ■ **devastation** noun.

devastating adjective **1** highly destructive. **2** extremely distressing. **3** informal very impressive or attractive. ■ **devastatingly** adverb.

develop verb (develops, developing, developed) **1** make or become larger or more advanced. **2** start to exist; come into being. **3** start to experience or possess something. **4** convert land to a new purpose. **5** treat a photographic film with chemicals to make a visible image. ■ **developer** noun.

 there is no *e* at the end: devel*op*.

development noun **1** the action of developing. **2** a new product or idea. **3** a new stage in a changing situation. **4** an area of land with new buildings on it. ■ **developmental** adjective.

deviant adjective different from what is considered normal. noun disapproving a deviant person. ■ **deviance** noun.

deviate verb (deviates, deviating, deviated) depart from an established course or from normal standards. ■ **deviation** noun.

device noun **1** a thing made for a particular purpose. **2** a plan, scheme, or trick. **3** an emblem or design. □ **leave someone to their own devices** leave someone to do as they wish.

devil noun **1** (**the Devil**) (in Christian

and Jewish belief) the supreme spirit of evil. **2** an evil spirit; a demon. **3** a very wicked or cruel person. **4** informal a person of a specified sort: *the poor devil*. □ **devil-may-care** cheerful and reckless. **devil's advocate** a person who expresses an unpopular opinion in order to provoke debate.

devilish adjective **1** like a devil in evil and cruelty. **2** mischievous. **3** very difficult to deal with. ■ **devilishly** adverb.

devilment noun reckless mischief.

devilry noun **1** wicked activity. **2** reckless mischief.

devious adjective **1** behaving in a cunning way to get what you want. **2** (of a route or journey) indirect. ■ **deviously** adverb **deviousness** noun.

devise verb (**devises**, **devising**, **devised**) plan or invent a complex procedure or device.

devoid adjective (**devoid of**) entirely without.

devolution noun the transferring of power by central government to local or regional governments.

devolve verb (**devolves**, **devolving**, **devolved**) **1** transfer power to a lower level. **2** (**devolve on** or **to**) (of responsibility) pass to.

devote verb (**devotes**, **devoting**, **devoted**) (**devote to**) give time or resources to.

devoted adjective very loving or loyal. ■ **devotedly** adverb.

devotee /dev-oh-**tee**/ noun **1** a person who is very enthusiastic about someone or something. **2** a follower of a particular religion or god.

devotion noun **1** great love or loyalty. **2** religious worship. **3** (**devotions**) prayers or other religious practices. ■ **devotional** adjective.

devour verb **1** eat something greedily. **2** (of a force) consume something destructively. **3** read something quickly and eagerly. **4** (**be devoured**) be totally absorbed by an emotion.

devout adjective **1** deeply religious. **2** earnestly sincere: *a devout hope*. ■ **devoutly** adverb.

dew noun tiny drops of moisture that form on cool surfaces at night, when water vapour in the air condenses. ■ **dewy** adjective.

dewlap noun a fold of loose skin hanging from the neck or throat of an animal or bird.

dewy adjective (**dewier**, **dewiest**) **1** wet with dew. **2** (of a person's skin) appearing soft and shining.

dexterity noun skill in performing tasks.

dexterous or **dextrous** adjective showing neat skill. ■ **dexterously** adverb.

diabetes /dy-uh-**bee**-teez/ noun an illness in which the body cannot absorb sugar and starch properly because it does not have enough of the hormone insulin.

diabetic adjective having to do with diabetes. noun a person with diabetes.

diabolical adjective **1** (also **diabolic**) of or like the Devil. **2** informal very bad. ■ **diabolically** adverb.

diadem noun a crown.

diagnose verb (**diagnoses**, **diagnosing**, **diagnosed**) identify which illness or problem a person is suffering from by examining the symptoms. ■ **diagnostic** adjective.

diagnosis noun (plural **diagnoses**) the identification of which illness or problem a person is suffering from by examining the symptoms.

diagonal adjective **1** (of a straight line) joining opposite corners of a rectangle, square, or other figure. **2** straight and at an angle; slanting. noun a diagonal line. ■ **diagonally** adverb.

diagram noun a simplified drawing showing the appearance or structure of something. ■ **diagrammatic** adjective.

dial noun **1** a disc marked to show the time or to indicate a measurement. **2** a disc with numbered holes on a telephone, turned to make a call. **3** a disc turned to select a setting on a radio, cooker, etc. verb (**dials**, **dialling**,

Dialect

Everyone speaks a particular dialect, i.e. a particular type of English distinguished by its vocabulary and its grammar. Different parts of the world and different groups of people speak different dialects: for example, Australians may say *arvo* while others say *afternoon*, and a London Cockney may say *I done it* while most other people say *I did it*. A dialect is not the same thing as an accent, which is the way a person pronounces words.

---

dialled; US spelling **dials, dialing, dialed**) call a telephone number by turning a dial or pressing numbered keys.

dialect noun a form of a language used in a particular region or by a particular social group. ■ **dialectal** adjective.

dialectic or **dialectics** noun a way of discovering whether ideas are true by discussion and logical argument. ■ **dialectical** adjective.

dialogue (US spelling **dialog**) noun **1** conversation between two or more people in a book, play, or film. **2** a discussion intended to explore a subject or solve a problem.

dialysis /dy-**al**-i-siss/ noun the use of a machine to purify the blood of a person whose kidneys do not work properly.

diamanté /dy-uh-**mon**-tay/ adjective decorated with artificial jewels.

diameter noun a straight line passing from side to side through the centre of a circle or sphere.

diametrical adjective **1** complete: *he's the diametrical opposite of Gabriel.* **2** having to do with a diameter. ■ **diametrically** adverb.

diamond noun **1** a clear precious stone, the hardest naturally occurring substance. **2** a figure with four straight sides of equal length forming two opposite acute angles and two opposite obtuse angles. □ **diamond jubilee** the sixtieth anniversary of a notable event. **diamond wedding** the sixtieth anniversary of a wedding.

diaper /dy-uh-per/ noun N. Amer. a baby's nappy.

diaphanous /dy-**af**-uh-nuhss/ adjective light, delicate, and semi-transparent.

diaphragm /dy-uh-fram/ noun **1** a layer of muscle between the lungs and the stomach. **2** a piece of flexible material in mechanical or sound systems. **3** a thin contraceptive cap fitting over the cervix.

diarist noun a person who writes a diary.

diarrhoea /dy-uh-**ree**-uh/ (US spelling **diarrhea**) noun a condition in which a person has frequent liquid bowel movements.

> ✓ two *r*s, and *-hoea* at the end:
>   **diarrhoea**.

diary noun (plural **diaries**) a book in which you keep a daily record of events and experiences, or note down future appointments.

diatonic /dy-uh-**ton**-ik/ adjective Music involving only the notes of the appropriate major or minor scale.

diatribe /**dy**-uh-tryb/ noun a speech or piece of writing forcefully attacking someone.

dice noun (plural **dice**) a small cube whose sides are marked with one to six dots, used in games of chance. verb (**dices, dicing, diced**) **1** cut food into small cubes. **2** (**dice with**) take great risks with: *dicing with death.*

dicey adjective (**dicier, diciest**) informal difficult or risky.

dichotomy /dy-**kot**-uh-mi/ noun (plural **dichotomies**) a separation or contrast between two things.

dicky adjective Brit. informal not strong, healthy, or working properly.

dictate verb /dik-**tayt**/ (dictates, dictating, dictated) **1** give orders with great authority. **2** speak words for someone else to type or write down. **3** control or determine. noun /**dik**tayt/ an order or principle that must be obeyed. ■ **dictation** noun.

dictator noun a ruler who has total power over a country. ■ **dictatorial** adjective.

dictatorship noun **1** government by a dictator. **2** a country governed by a dictator.

diction noun **1** the choice and use of words in speech or writing. **2** a person's way of pronouncing words.

dictionary noun (plural **dictionaries**) a book that lists the words of a language and gives their meaning, or their equivalent in a different language.

dictum noun (plural **dicta** or **dictums**) **1** a formal announcement made by someone in authority. **2** a short statement that expresses a general principle.

did past of **DO**.

didactic adjective intended to teach or give moral instruction.

diddle verb (diddles, diddling, diddled) informal cheat or swindle.

didgeridoo noun an Australian Aboriginal musical instrument in the form of a long wooden tube, which produces a deep sound when blown.

didn't short form did not.

die[1] verb (dies, dying, died) **1** stop living. **2** (**die out**) become extinct. **3** become less loud or strong. **4** (**be dying for** or **to do**) informal be very eager for. □ **never say die** do not give up hope.

die[2] noun **1** a dice. **2** (plural **dies**) a device for cutting or moulding metal or for stamping a design on to coins or medals. □ **die-cast** formed by pouring molten metal into a mould. **the die is cast** something has happened that cannot be changed.

diehard noun a person who obstinately continues to support something in spite of opposition or changing circumstances.

diesel /**dee**-zuhl/ noun **1** a type of engine in which heat produced by compressing air is used to ignite the fuel. **2** a form of petroleum used as fuel in diesel engines.

diet noun **1** the kinds of food that a person or animal usually eats. **2** a range of food which you restrict yourself to in order to lose weight or for medical reasons. verb (diets, dieting, dieted) go on a diet to lose weight.

dietary /dy-uh-tri/ adjective **1** having to do with diets or dieting. **2** provided by the food you eat.

dietitian or **dietician** noun an expert on diet and nutrition.

differ verb (differs, differing, differed) **1** be different. **2** disagree.

difference noun **1** a way in which people or things are unlike each other. **2** a disagreement or dispute. **3** what is left when one number or amount is subtracted from another.

different adjective **1** not the same as another or each other. **2** separate. **3** informal new and unusual. ■ **differently** adverb.

> **i** say **different from**, not **different to**; **different than** is American.

differential /dif-fuh-**ren**-sh'l/ adjective involving a difference. noun **1** Brit. a difference in wages between industries or between categories of worker. **2** Mathematics a minute difference between successive values of a variable. **3** a gear that allows a vehicle's wheels to revolve at different speeds when going around corners.

differentiate /dif-fuh-**ren**-shi-ayt/ verb (differentiates, differentiating, differentiated) **1** recognize things as being different from each other; distinguish. **2** make things appear different from each other. ■ **differentiation** noun.

difficult adjective **1** needing a lot of effort or skill to do or understand; hard. **2** causing or involving problems. **3** not easy to please or satisfy; awkward.

difficulty noun (plural **difficulties**) **1** being difficult. **2** a difficult or dangerous situation; a problem.

diffident adjective not having much self-confidence. ■ **diffidence** noun **diffidently** adverb.

diffract verb cause a beam of light to be spread out as a result of passing through a narrow opening or across an edge. ■ **diffraction** noun.

diffuse verb /dif-**fyooz**/ (**diffuses**, **diffusing**, **diffused**) **1** spread over a wide area. **2** (of a gas or liquid) become mingled with a substance. adjective /dif-**fyooss**/ **1** spread out over a large area; not concentrated. **2** not clearly or briefly expressed. ■ **diffusely** adverb **diffusion** noun.

> **i** do not confuse **diffuse** with **defuse**, which means 'remove the fuse from' or 'reduce the danger or tension in'.

dig verb (**digs**, **digging**, **dug**) **1** cut into earth in order to turn it over or move it. **2** remove or produce something by digging. **3** push or poke sharply. **4** (**dig into** or **through**) search or rummage in. **5** (**dig out** or **up**) discover facts. **6** (**dig in**) start eating heartily. **7** informal, dated like. noun **1** an act of digging. **2** an investigation of a site by archaeologists. **3** a sharp push or poke. **4** informal a critical remark. **5** (**digs**) informal lodgings. □ **dig in your heels** stubbornly refuse to do or agree to something. ■ **digger** noun.

digest verb /dy-**jest**/ **1** break down food in the stomach and intestines so that it can be absorbed by the body. **2** reflect on and absorb information. noun /**dy**-jest/ a summary or collection of material or information. ■ **digestible** adjective.

digestion noun **1** the process of digesting food. **2** a person's ability to digest food.

digestive adjective relating to the digestion of food. noun Brit. a semi-sweet biscuit made with wholemeal flour.

digit noun **1** any of the numerals from 0 to 9. **2** a finger or thumb.

digital adjective **1** having to do with information represented as a series of binary digits, as in a computer. **2** (of a clock or watch) showing the time by displaying numbers electronically, rather than having a clock face. **3** having to do with a finger or fingers. ■ **digitally** adverb.

digitize or **digitise** verb (**digitizes**, **digitizing**, **digitized**) convert pictures or sound into a digital form.

dignified adjective having or showing dignity.

dignify verb (**dignifies**, **dignifying**, **dignified**) make something impressive or worthy of respect.

dignitary /**dig**-ni-tuh-ri/ noun (plural **dignitaries**) a very important or high-ranking person.

dignity noun (plural **dignities**) **1** the quality of being worthy of respect. **2** a calm or serious manner. **3** pride in yourself.

digress verb temporarily leave the main subject in speech or writing. ■ **digression** noun.

dike ⇨ **DYKE**.

diktat /**dik**-tat/ noun an order given by someone in power.

dilapidated adjective old and in poor condition. ■ **dilapidation** noun.

> ✓ **dil**-, not **del**-: **dilapidated**.

dilate verb (**dilates**, **dilating**, **dilated**) become wider, larger, or more open. ■ **dilation** noun.

dilatory /**di**-luh-tri/ adjective **1** slow to act. **2** intended to cause delay.

dilemma /di-**lem**-muh, dy-**lem**-muh/ noun a difficult situation in which you have to make a choice between alternatives.

dilettante /di-li-**tan**-ti/ noun (plural **dilettanti** or **dilettantes**) a person who does something for enjoyment but does not take it very seriously.

diligent adjective showing care and effort in a task or duty. ■ **diligence** noun **diligently** adverb.

dill noun a herb used in cookery and medicine.

dilly-dally verb (dilly-dallies, dilly-dallying, dilly-dallied) informal be slow or indecisive.

dilute verb (dilutes, diluting, diluted) **1** make a liquid thinner or weaker by adding water or other liquid. **2** weaken something by modifying it or adding other elements. adjective (of a liquid) diluted; weak. ▪ **dilution** noun.

dim adjective (dimmer, dimmest) **1** not shining brightly or clearly. **2** not clearly seen or remembered. **3** not able to see clearly. **4** informal stupid. verb (dims, dimming, dimmed) make or become dim. □ **take a dim view of** regard with disapproval. ▪ **dimly** adverb **dimness** noun.

dime noun N. Amer. a ten-cent coin.

dimension noun **1** a measure of how long, broad, high, etc. something is. **2** an aspect or feature. ▪ **dimensional** adjective.

diminish verb make or become less.

diminution noun a reduction.

diminutive adjective extremely or unusually small. noun a shortened form of a name, used informally.

dimmer noun a device for varying the brightness of an electric light.

dimple noun a small depression formed in the cheeks when you smile. ▪ **dimpled** adjective.

dimwit noun informal a stupid person. ▪ **dim-witted** adjective.

din noun a prolonged loud and unpleasant noise. verb (dins, dinning, dinned) (din into) teach something to someone by constantly repeating it.

dine verb (dines, dining, dined) eat dinner.

diner noun **1** a person who dines. **2** a carriage providing meals on a train. **3** N. Amer. a small roadside restaurant.

dinghy /ding-gi, ding-i/ noun (plural dinghies) **1** a small open boat with a mast and sails. **2** a small inflatable rubber boat.

dingo /ding-goh/ noun (plural dingoes or dingos) a wild or semi-domesticated Australian dog.

dingy /din-ji/ adjective (dingier, dingiest) gloomy and drab.

dinky adjective (dinkier, dinkiest) Brit. informal attractively small and neat.

dinner noun **1** the main meal of the day, eaten either around midday or in the evening. **2** a formal evening meal. ▪ **dinner jacket** a black or white jacket worn by men for formal evening occasions.

dinosaur noun an extinct reptile that lived millions of years ago, some kinds of which were very large.

dint noun a dent. □ **by dint of** by means of.

diocese /dy-uh-siss/ noun (plural dioceses /dy-uh-seez, dy-uh-seez-iz/) a district under the control of a bishop in the Christian Church.

diode noun an electrical device that has two terminals and allows current to flow in one direction only.

dioxide noun an oxide with two atoms of oxygen to one of a metal or other element.

dip verb (dips, dipping, dipped) **1** (dip in or into) put or lower briefly in or into. **2** sink, drop, or slope downwards. **3** (of a level or amount) temporarily become lower or smaller. **4** lower something briefly. **5** (dip into) take something out of a bag or container. noun **1** an act of dipping. **2** a thick sauce in which pieces of food are dipped before eating. **3** a brief swim. **4** a brief downward slope followed by an upward one.

diphtheria /dip-theer-i-uh/ noun a serious illness that causes inflammation of the mucous membranes, especially in the throat.

diphthong /dif-thong/ noun a sound formed by the combination of two vowels in a single syllable (as in coin).

diploma noun a certificate awarded to someone who has successfully completed a course of study.

diplomacy noun **1** the management of relations between countries. **2** skill and tact in dealing with people.

diplomat noun an official who represents a country abroad.

diplomatic adjective **1** having to do with diplomacy. **2** tactful. ■ **diplomatically** adverb.

dipper noun **1** a bird that dives into fast-flowing streams to feed. **2** a ladle.

dippy adjective informal foolish or eccentric.

dipsomania /dip-suh-**may**-ni-uh/ noun alcoholism. ■ **dipsomaniac** noun.

dipstick noun a rod for measuring the depth of a liquid.

dire adjective **1** extremely serious or urgent. **2** informal of a very poor quality.

direct adjective **1** going from one place to another without changing direction or stopping. **2** with nothing or no one in between. **3** saying exactly what you mean; frank. **4** clear and explicit. adverb in a direct way or by a direct route. verb **1** aim something toward. **2** tell or show someone the way. **3** control the operations of. **4** supervise the production of a film, play, etc. **5** give an order to. □ **direct current** an electric current that flows in one direction only. **direct debit** Brit. an arrangement by which a bank transfers money from your account to pay a particular person or organization.

direction noun **1** a course along which someone or something moves, or which leads to a destination. **2** a point to or from which someone or something moves or faces. **3** the directing or managing of people. **4** (**directions**) instructions on how to reach a destination or how to do something.

■ **directional** adjective.

directive noun an official instruction.

directly adverb **1** in a direct manner. **2** exactly in a specified position. **3** immediately. conjunction Brit. as soon as.

director noun **1** a person who is in charge of an organization or activity. **2** a member of the board which manages a business. **3** a person responsible for directing a film, play, etc. □ **director-general** (plural **directors-general**) the chief executive of a large organization. ■ **directorial** adjective.

directory noun (plural **directories**) a book that lists individuals or organizations and gives their addresses, telephone numbers, etc.

dirge noun **1** a piece of music expressing sadness for someone's death. **2** a slow, boring song or piece of music.

dirigible /di-**rij**-i-b'l/ noun an airship.

dirk noun a kind of short dagger formerly carried by Scottish Highlanders.

dirt noun **1** a substance that causes something not to be clean. **2** soil or earth. **3** informal scandalous or sordid information.

dirty adjective (**dirtier, dirtiest**) **1** covered or marked with dirt; not clean. **2** obscene. **3** dishonest; dishonourable. **4** (of weather) rough and unpleasant. verb (**dirties, dirtying, dirtied**) make dirty. □ **dirty look** informal a look expressing disapproval, disgust, or anger.

disability noun (plural **disabilities**) **1** a physical or mental condition that restricts your movements, senses, or

WORD FORMATION

dis-

Words that begin with **dis-** have the meaning:

- not, or the reverse of, as in *disadvantage* and *discharge*
- separation or removal, e.g. *disperse*
- completeness or intensification of an action, as in *disgruntled*.

dis- comes originally from Latin. It is not the same as **dys-**, which comes from ancient Greek and is used, particularly in medical terms, to give the meaning 'bad' or 'difficult' (as in *dyslexia* or *dyspepsia*).

activities. **2** a disadvantage or handicap.

disable verb (disables, disabling, disabled) **1** cause someone to be disabled. **2** put something out of action. ■ **disablement** noun.

disabled adjective having a disability.

disabuse verb (disabuses, disabusing, disabused) (disabuse of) persuade someone that an idea or belief is mistaken.

disadvantage noun something that causes a problem or reduces the chances of success. verb (disadvantages, disadvantaging, disadvantaged) **1** put someone in an unfavourable position. **2** (disadvantaged) having less money and fewer opportunities than most people. ■ **disadvantageous** adjective.

disaffected adjective unhappy with the people in authority or with the organization you belong to, and no longer willing to support them. ■ **disaffection** noun.

disagree verb (disagrees, disagreeing, disagreed) **1** have a different opinion. **2** be inconsistent. **3** (disagree with) make someone slightly unwell. ■ **disagreement** noun.

disagreeable adjective **1** unpleasant. **2** bad-tempered.

disallow verb declare that something is not valid.

disappear verb **1** stop being visible. **2** cease to exist. ■ **disappearance** noun.

☑️ one s, two ps: dis**appear**.

disappoint verb **1** make someone sad or displeased through failing to fulfil their hopes or expectations. **2** prevent hopes or expectations being fulfilled. ■ **disappointed** adjective.

☑️ one s, two ps: dis**appoint**.

disappointment noun **1** sadness or displeasure felt when hopes or expectations are not fulfilled. **2** a person or thing that causes disappointment.

disapprobation noun strong disapproval.

disapprove verb (disapproves, disapproving, disapproved) feel that someone or something is bad or immoral. ■ **disapproval** noun.

disarm verb **1** take a weapon or weapons away from. **2** give up or reduce armed forces or weapons. **3** remove the fuse from a bomb. **4** win over a hostile or suspicious person, especially through being charming.

disarmament noun the reduction or withdrawal of military forces and weapons.

disarrange verb (disarranges, disarranging, disarranged) make something untidy or disordered.

disarray noun a state of disorder or confusion. verb throw into a state of disarray.

disassociate = **DISSOCIATE**.

disaster noun **1** a sudden accident or natural event that causes great damage or loss of life. **2** a sudden misfortune.

disastrous adjective **1** causing great damage. **2** informal highly unsuccessful. ■ **disastrously** adverb.

 no *e*: disas*trous*, not *-erous*.

disavow verb deny that you are responsible for or in favour of something. ■ **disavowal** noun.

disband verb (of an organized group) break up.

disbar verb (**disbars, disbarring, disbarred**) stop a barrister from working as a lawyer.

disbelief noun **1** inability or refusal to accept that something is true or real. **2** lack of faith.

disbelieve verb (**disbelieves, disbelieving, disbelieved**) be unable to believe.

disburse verb (**disburses, disbursing, disbursed**) pay out money from a fund. ■ **disbursement** noun.

disc (US spelling **disk**) noun **1** a flat, thin, round object. **2** (**disk**) a device on which computer data is stored. **3** a layer of cartilage that separates vertebrae in the spine. **4** dated a record. □ **disc jockey** a person who plays recorded popular music on radio or at a club.

discard verb /diss-**kard**/ get rid of something useless or unwanted. noun /**diss**-kard/ something that has been discarded.

discern verb /di-**sern**/ verb **1** recognize or be aware of. **2** see or hear something with difficulty. ■ **discernible** adjective.

discerning adjective having or showing good judgement. ■ **discernment** noun.

discharge verb (**discharges, discharging, discharged**) **1** dismiss or allow to leave. **2** send out a liquid, gas, or other substance. **3** fire a gun or missile. **4** fulfil a responsibility. noun **1** the action of discharging. **2** a substance that has been discharged.

disciple /di-**sy**-puhl/ noun **1** a person who followed Jesus during his life, es-

pecially one of the twelve Apostles. **2** a follower of a teacher, leader, or philosophy.

disciplinarian noun a person who enforces firm discipline.

disciplinary adjective having to do with discipline.

discipline noun **1** the training of people to obey rules or a code of behaviour. **2** controlled behaviour resulting from such training. **3** a branch of academic study. verb (**disciplines, disciplining, disciplined**) **1** train someone to be obedient or self-controlled. **2** formally punish someone for an offence. **3** (**disciplined**) behaving in a controlled way.

 there's a *c* in the middle: dis*c*ipline.

disclaim verb refuse to acknowledge that you are responsible for or interested in something.

disclaimer noun a statement disclaiming responsibility for something.

disclose verb (**discloses, disclosing, disclosed**) **1** make information known. **2** allow to be seen.

disclosure noun **1** the disclosing of information. **2** a secret that is disclosed.

disco noun (plural **discos**) informal a club or party at which people dance to pop music.

discolour (US spelling **discolor**) verb make something stained or changed in colour. ■ **discoloration** (or **discolouration**) noun.

discomfit /diss-**kum**-fit/ verb (**discomfits, discomfiting, discomfited**) make someone uneasy or embarrassed. ■ **discomfiture** noun.

discomfort noun **1** slight pain. **2** slight anxiety or embarrassment. verb cause someone discomfort.

discompose verb (**discomposes, discomposing, discomposed**) disturb or agitate.

disconcert verb unsettle or upset.

disconnect verb **1** break the connection between two things. **2** detach an electrical device from a power supply. ■ **disconnection** noun.

disconsolate adjective very unhappy and unable to be consoled.

discontent noun a feeling of unhappiness or dissatisfaction. ■ **discontented** adjective **discontentment** noun.

discontinue verb (**discontinues, discontinuing, discontinued**) stop doing, providing, or making. ■ **discontinuation** noun.

discontinuous adjective having intervals or gaps; not continuous. ■ **discontinuity** noun.

discord noun **1** lack of agreement or harmony. **2** lack of harmony between musical notes sounding together.

discordant adjective **1** not in harmony or agreement. **2** (of a sound or sounds) harsh and unpleasant.

discotheque /diss-kuh-tek/ = DISCO.

discount noun an amount by which the usual cost of something is reduced. verb **1** reduce the usual price of something. **2** decide not to believe something because you think it is improbable.

discourage verb (**discourages, discouraging, discouraged**) **1** cause someone to lose confidence or enthusiasm. **2** try to persuade someone not to do something. ■ **discouragement** noun.

discourse noun **1** written or spoken communication or debate. **2** a formal discussion of a topic. verb (**discourses, discoursing, discoursed**) speak or write about something with authority.

discourteous adjective rude and lacking consideration for others.

discourtesy noun (plural **discourtesies**) rude and inconsiderate behaviour.

discover verb (**discovers, discovering, discovered**) **1** find something unexpectedly or in the course of a search. **2** gain knowledge about, or become aware of. **3** be the first to find or observe something.

discovery noun (plural **discoveries**)

1 the action of discovering. **2** a person or thing discovered.

discredit verb (**discredits, discrediting, discredited**) **1** make someone seem less trustworthy or honourable. **2** make something seem false or unreliable. noun damage to someone's reputation.

discreditable adjective bringing discredit; shameful.

discreet adjective careful not to attract attention or give offence. ■ **discreetly** adverb.

> ⓘ don't confuse **discreet** with **discrete**, which means 'separate, distinct'.

discrepancy noun (plural **discrepancies**) a difference between things that should be the same.

discrete adjective individually separate and distinct. ■ **discretely** adverb.

discretion noun **1** the quality of being discreet. **2** the freedom to decide what should be done in a particular situation.

discretionary adjective done or used according to the judgement of a particular person.

discriminate verb (**discriminates, discriminating, discriminated**) **1** recognize a difference. **2** treat people unfairly on the grounds of race, sex, or age.

discriminating adjective having or showing good taste or judgement.

discrimination noun **1** the action of discriminating against people. **2** recognition of the difference between one thing and another. **3** good judgement or taste.

discriminatory adjective showing discrimination or prejudice.

discursive adjective (of writing) flowing and wide-ranging.

discus noun (plural **discuses**) a heavy disc thrown in athletic contests.

discuss verb **1** talk about something in order to reach a decision. **2** talk or write about a topic in detail.

discussion noun **1** conversation or debate about something. **2** a detailed treatment of a topic in writing.

disdain noun the feeling that someone or something does not deserve respect. verb treat with disdain. ■ **disdainful** adjective.

disease noun an illness in a human, animal, or plant. ■ **diseased** adjective.

disembark verb leave a ship, aircraft, or train. ■ **disembarkation** noun.

disembodied adjective 1 separated from the body, or existing without a body. 2 (of a sound) lacking any obvious physical source.

disembowel verb (disembowels, disembowelling, disembowelled; US spelling disembowels, disembowelling, disemboweled) cut open and remove the internal organs of.

disempower verb (disempowers, disempowering, disempowered) make someone less powerful or confident.

disenchant verb make someone disillusioned. ■ **disenchantment** noun.

disenfranchise verb (disenfranchises, disenfranchising, disenfranchised) 1 deprive someone of the right to vote. 2 deprive someone of a right or privilege.

disengage verb (disengages, disengaging, disengaged) 1 release or detach. 2 remove troops from an area of conflict. ■ **disengagement** noun.

disentangle verb (disentangles, disentangling, disentangled) stop something being tangled.

disestablish verb end the official status of a national Church.

disfavour (US spelling disfavor) noun disapproval or dislike.

disfigure verb (disfigures, disfiguring, disfigured) spoil the appearance of. ■ **disfigurement** noun.

disgorge verb (disgorges, disgorging, disgorged) 1 cause something to pour out. 2 bring up food from the stomach.

disgrace noun 1 the loss of other people's respect as the result of behaving badly. 2 a shamefully bad person or thing. verb (disgraces, disgracing, disgraced) bring disgrace to.

disgraceful adjective shockingly unacceptable. ■ **disgracefully** adverb.

disgruntled adjective angry or dissatisfied.

disguise verb (disguises, disguising, disguised) 1 change the appearance of someone or something so they cannot be recognized. 2 hide a feeling or situation. noun 1 a way of disguising yourself. 2 the state of being disguised.

disgust noun revulsion or strong disapproval. verb give someone a feeling of disgust.

disgusting adjective causing revulsion or strong disapproval.

dish noun 1 a shallow container for cooking or serving food. 2 (the dishes) all the crockery and utensils used for a meal. 3 a particular kind of food. 4 a shallow, concave object. 5 informal an attractive person. verb (dish out or up) put food on to plates before a meal.

disharmony noun lack of harmony.

dishearten verb cause someone to lose determination or confidence.

dishevelled (US spelling disheveled) adjective untidy in appearance.

dishonest adjective not honest, trustworthy, or sincere. ■ **dishonesty** noun.

dishonour (US spelling dishonor) noun shame or disgrace. verb 1 bring dishonour to. 2 fail to honour an agreement or cheque.

dishonourable (US spelling dishonorable) adjective bringing shame or disgrace.

dishwasher noun a machine for washing dishes automatically.

dishy adjective (dishier, dishiest) informal good-looking; attractive.

disillusion noun disappointment caused by discovering that your beliefs are mistaken or unrealistic. verb cause someone to experience disillusion. ■ **disillusionment** noun.

disincentive noun a factor that discourages someone from doing a particular thing.

disinclination noun a reluctance to do something.

disinclined adjective reluctant; unwilling.

disinfect verb make something free from infection with a disinfectant. ■ **disinfection** noun.

disinfectant noun a chemical liquid that destroys bacteria.

disinformation noun information which is intended to mislead people.

disingenuous adjective not sincere, especially in pretending ignorance about something.

disinherit verb (**disinherits**, **disinheriting**, **disinherited**) deprive someone of an inheritance.

disintegrate verb (**disintegrates**, **disintegrating**, **disintegrated**) break up into small parts as a result of impact or decay. ■ **disintegration** noun.

disinter /diss-in-**ter**/ verb (**disinters**, **disinterring**, **disinterred**) dig up something buried.

disinterest noun **1** impartiality. **2** lack of interest.

disinterested adjective not influenced by personal feelings; impartial.

> **i** don't confuse **disinterested** and **uninterested**. Disinterested means 'impartial', while **uninterested** means 'not interested'.

disjointed adjective lacking a logical sequence or clear connection; disconnected.

disjunction noun a difference or lack of agreement between things that you might expect to be the same.

disk ⇒ **DISC**. □ **disk drive** a device which allows a computer to read from and write on to computer disks.

diskette noun a floppy disk.

dislike verb (**dislike**, **disliking**, **disliked**) not like; feel distaste for. noun **1** a feeling of distaste or hostility. **2** a person or thing that you dislike.

dislocate verb (**dislocates**, **dislocating**, **dislocated**) **1** put a bone out of its proper position in a joint. **2** stop something from working properly; disrupt. ■ **dislocation** noun.

dislodge verb (**dislodges**, **dislodging**, **dislodged**) remove something from its position.

disloyal adjective not loyal or faithful. ■ **disloyalty** noun.

dismal adjective **1** causing or showing gloom or depression. **2** informal disgracefully bad. ■ **dismally** adverb.

dismantle verb (**dismantles**, **dismantling**, **dismantled**) take something to pieces.

dismay noun a feeling of unhappiness and discouragement. verb cause someone to feel dismay.

dismember verb (**dismembers**, **dismembering**, **dismembered**) **1** tear or cut the limbs from. **2** divide up a territory or organization. ■ **dismemberment** noun.

dismiss verb **1** order or allow someone to leave. **2** order an employee to leave a job. **3** treat something as not being worthy of serious consideration. **4** refuse to allow a legal case to continue. **5** Cricket end the innings of a batsman or side. ■ **dismissal** noun.

dismissive adjective showing that you feel something is not worthy of serious consideration. ■ **dismissively** adverb.

dismount verb get off or down from a horse or bicycle.

disobedient adjective failing or refusing to be obedient. ■ **disobedience** noun.

disobey verb fail or refuse to obey.

disorder noun **1** lack of order; confusion. **2** the disruption of peaceful and law-abiding behaviour. **3** an illness or disease. ■ **disordered** adjective.

disorderly adjective **1** untidy or disorganized. **2** involving a breakdown of peaceful behaviour.

disorganized or **disorganised** adjective **1** not well planned and controlled. **2** not able to plan your activities efficiently. ■ **disorganization** noun.

disorientate verb (**disorientates, disorienting, disorientated**) confuse someone so that they lose their bearings. ■ **disorientation** noun.

disown verb show or decide that you no longer want to have anything to do with someone.

disparage /diss-pa-rij/ verb (**disparages, disparaging, disparaged**) speak critically or negatively about.

disparate /**diss**-puh-ruht/ adjective **1** very different from one another. **2** containing elements that are very different from one another.

disparity noun (plural **disparities**) a great difference.

dispassionate adjective rational and impartial. ■ **dispassionately** adverb.

dispatch or **despatch** verb **1** send someone or something off to a destination or for a particular purpose. **2** deal with a task or problem quickly and efficiently. **3** kill. noun **1** the action of dispatching. **2** a report on the latest situation in state or military affairs. **3** promptness and efficiency.

dispel verb (**dispels, dispelling, dispelled**) make a doubt, feeling, or belief disappear.

dispensable adjective able to be replaced or done without.

dispensary noun (plural **dispensaries**) a room where medicines are prepared and provided.

dispensation noun **1** special permission not to obey a rule. **2** the religious system of a particular time. **3** the action of dispensing.

dispense verb (**dispenses, dispensing, dispensed**) **1** distribute something to a number of people. **2** (of a chemist) prepare and supply medicine according to a prescription. **3** (**dispense with**) get rid of or manage without. ■ **dispenser** noun.

disperse verb (**disperses, dispersing, dispersed**) **1** move apart and go in different directions. **2** (of gas, smoke, etc.) thin out and eventually disappear. ■ **dispersal** noun **disper-**

sion noun.

dispirited adjective discouraged or depressed. ■ **dispiriting** adjective.

displace verb (**displaces, displacing, displaced**) **1** move something from its proper or usual position. **2** take over the position or role of.

displacement noun **1** the action of displacing something, or the amount by which something is displaced. **2** the volume or weight of water displaced by a floating ship, used as a measure of the ship's size.

display verb **1** put something on show in a noticeable and attractive way. **2** show data or an image on a screen. **3** show a quality or feeling. noun **1** a performance, show, or event for public entertainment. **2** a collection of objects being displayed. **3** the displaying of a quality or feeling. **4** the data or image shown on a screen.

displease verb (**displeases, displeasing, displeased**) annoy or upset.

displeasure noun annoyance or dissatisfaction.

disport verb (**disport yourself**) old use enjoy yourself unrestrainedly.

disposable adjective **1** intended to be used once and then thrown away. **2** (of money) available to be used.

disposal noun the action of disposing. □ **at your disposal** available to be used whenever or however you wish.

dispose verb (**disposes, disposing, disposed**) **1** (**dispose of**) get rid of. **2** arrange something in a particular position. **3** (**be disposed to**) be inclined to do or think something. **4** (**disposed**) having a specified attitude: *they were favourably disposed towards him.*

disposition noun **1** a person's natural qualities of character. **2** an inclination or tendency. **3** the way in which something is arranged.

dispossess verb deprive someone of a possession. ■ **dispossession** noun.

disproportionate adjective too large or too small in comparison with something else. ■ **disproportionately** adverb.

disprove verb (**disproves, disproving, disproved**) prove something to be false.

disputation noun debate or argument.

disputatious adjective fond of arguing.

dispute verb (**disputes, disputing, disputed**) **1** argue about. **2** question whether something is true or valid. **3** compete for. noun an argument or disagreement. ■ **disputable** adjective.

disqualify verb (**disqualifies, disqualifying, disqualified**) prevent someone performing an activity or taking an office because they have broken a rule or are not suitable. ■ **disqualification** noun.

disquiet noun a feeling of anxiety. ■ **disquieting** adjective.

disquisition noun a long or complex discussion of a topic.

disregard verb pay no attention to. noun the action of disregarding something.

disrepair noun poor condition due to being neglected.

disreputable adjective not respectable in appearance or character.

disrepute noun the state of having a bad reputation.

disrespect noun lack of respect or courtesy. ■ **disrespectful** adjective.

disrobe verb (**disrobes, disrobing, disrobed**) take off your clothes.

disrupt verb interrupt or disturb an activity or process. ■ **disruption** noun.

disruptive adjective causing disruption.

dissatisfied adjective not content or happy. ■ **dissatisfaction** noun.

dissect verb **1** cut up the dead body of a person or animal to study its internal parts. **2** analyse in great detail. ■ **dissection** noun.

 dissect has a double s.

dissemble verb (**dissembles, dis-** sembling, dissembled) hide or disguise your motives or feelings.

disseminate verb (**disseminates, disseminating, disseminated**) spread information widely. ■ **dissemination** noun.

dissension noun disagreement that causes trouble within a group.

dissent verb **1** express disagreement with a widely held view. **2** disagree with the doctrine of an established Church. **3** (in sport) disagree with the referee's decision. noun disagreement with a widely held view. ■ **dissenter** noun.

dissertation noun a long essay, especially one written for a university degree.

disservice noun a harmful action.

dissident noun a person who opposes official policy. adjective opposing official policy. ■ **dissidence** noun.

dissimilar adjective not similar; different. ■ **dissimilarity** noun.

dissimulate verb (**dissimulates, dissimulating, dissimulated**) hide or disguise your thoughts or feelings. ■ **dissimulation** noun.

dissipate verb (**dissipates, dissipating, dissipated**) **1** dispel or disperse. **2** waste money, energy, or resources. **3** (**dissipated**) indulging too much in physical pleasures. ■ **dissipation** noun.

dissociate verb (**dissociates, dissociating, dissociated**) **1** disconnect or separate. **2** (**dissociate yourself from**) say publicly that you are not connected with. ■ **dissociation** noun.

dissolute adjective indulging too much in physical pleasures.

dissolution noun **1** the formal closing down or ending of an official body or agreement. **2** the action of dissolving or decomposing.

dissolve verb (**dissolves, dissolving, dissolved**) **1** (of a solid) mix with a liquid and form a solution. **2** close down or end an assembly or agreement. **3** (**dissolve into** or **in**) give way to strong emotion.

dissonant adjective without harmony; discordant. ■ **dissonance** noun.

dissuade verb (dissuades, dissuading, dissuaded) persuade or advise someone not to do something. ■ **dissuasion** noun.

distaff /diss-tahf/ noun a stick or spindle on to which wool or flax is wound for spinning. □ **distaff side** the female side of a family.

distance noun 1 the length of the space between two points. 2 the state of being distant. 3 a far-off point or place. 4 the full length or time of a race. verb (distances, distancing, distanced) (distance yourself) become less friendly or supportive.

distant adjective 1 far away in space or time. 2 at a specified distance. 3 far apart in terms of resemblance or relationship. 4 aloof or reserved. ■ **distantly** adverb.

distaste noun dislike.

distasteful adjective unpleasant or disliked. ■ **distastefully** adverb.

distemper noun 1 a kind of paint used on walls. 2 a disease of dogs, causing fever and coughing.

distend verb swell because of internal pressure. ■ **distension** noun.

distil (US spelling distill) verb (distils, distilling, distilled) 1 purify a liquid by heating it until it vaporizes, then condensing the vapour and collecting the resulting liquid. 2 make spirits in this way. 3 extract the most important aspects of. ■ **distiller** noun **distillation** noun.

distillery noun (plural distilleries) a factory that makes spirits.

distinct adjective 1 recognizably different. 2 able to be perceived clearly by the senses. ■ **distinctly** adverb.

distinction noun 1 a noticeable difference. 2 outstanding excellence. 3 a special honour or recognition.

distinctive adjective characteristic of a person or thing and distinguishing it from others. ■ **distinctively** adverb.

distinguish verb 1 recognize the difference between two people or things. 2 manage to see or hear. 3 be a char-

acteristic that makes two people or things different. 4 (distinguish yourself) do something very well. ■ **distinguishable** adjective.

distinguished adjective 1 dignified in appearance. 2 worthy of great respect.

distort verb 1 pull or twist out of shape. 2 give a misleading account of. ■ **distortion** noun.

distract verb 1 prevent someone from giving their full attention to something. 2 divert attention from something.

distracted adjective unable to concentrate on something.

distraction noun 1 a thing that distracts someone's attention. 2 something that provides entertainment. 3 preoccupation.

distraught adjective very worried and upset.

distress noun 1 extreme anxiety, pain, or exhaustion. 2 the state of a ship or aircraft when in danger or difficulty. verb cause distress to.

distribute verb (distributes, distributing, distributed) 1 hand or share out to a number of people. 2 (be distributed) be spread over an area. 3 supply goods to retailers.

distribution noun 1 the action of distributing. 2 the way in which something is distributed.

distributor noun 1 a company that supplies goods to retailers. 2 a device in a petrol engine for passing electric current to each spark plug in turn.

district noun a particular area of a town or region.

distrust noun lack of trust. verb have little trust in. ■ **distrustful** adjective.

disturb verb 1 interrupt the sleep, relaxation, or privacy of. 2 move something from its normal position. 3 make someone anxious. 4 (disturbed) having emotional or mental problems.

disturbance noun 1 the action of disturbing, or the state of being disturbed. 2 a riot or other breakdown of peaceful behaviour.

disunited adjective not united. ■ **disunity** noun.

disuse noun the state of not being used; neglect. ■ **disused** adjective.

ditch noun a narrow channel dug to hold or carry water. verb **1** (of an aircraft) come down in a forced landing on the sea. **2** informal get rid of.

dither verb (**dithers, dithering, dithered**) be indecisive.

ditto noun **1** the same thing again (used in lists). **2** a symbol consisting of two apostrophes (") placed under the item to be repeated.

ditty noun (plural **ditties**) a short, simple song.

diuretic /dy-uh-**ret**-ik/ adjective (of a drug) making you pass more urine.

diurnal /dy-**er**-n'l/ adjective **1** of or during the daytime. **2** daily.

diva /**dee**-vuh/ noun a celebrated female opera singer.

divan noun **1** a bed consisting of a base and mattress but no headboard. **2** a long, low sofa without a back or arms.

dive verb (**dives, diving, dived**; US past and past participle also **dove** /rhymes with rove/) **1** plunge head first into water. **2** (of a submarine or swimmer) go under water. **3** plunge steeply downwards through the air. **4** move quickly or suddenly in a downward direction or under cover. noun an act of diving. **2** informal a disreputable nightclub or bar. □ **dive-bomb** bomb a target while diving steeply in an aircraft.

diver noun **1** a person who dives under water. **2** a large diving waterbird.

diverge verb (**diverges, diverging, diverged**) **1** (of a route or line) separate from another route and go in a different direction. **2** (**diverge from**) be different from or disagree with. ■ **divergence** noun **divergent** adjective.

diverse adjective widely varied.

diversify verb (**diversifies, diversifying, diversified**) **1** make or become more varied. **2** (of a company) expand its range of products or area of operation. ■ **diversification** noun.

diversion noun **1** the action of diverting something from its course. **2** Brit. an alternative route used when a road is closed. **3** something intended to distract attention. **4** a recreation or pastime. ■ **diversionary** adjective.

diversity noun (plural **diversities**) **1** the state of being varied. **2** a range of different things.

divert verb **1** change the direction or course of. **2** distract a person or their attention. **3** amuse or entertain.

divest verb (**divest of**) **1** deprive of. **2** (**divest yourself of**) remove or get rid of.

divide verb (**divides, dividing, divided**) **1** separate into parts. **2** share out. **3** make people or groups disagree. **4** form a boundary between. **5** find how many times one number contains another. noun a difference or disagreement between two groups.

dividend noun **1** a sum of money that is divided among a number of people, such as the part of a company's profits paid to its shareholders. **2** (**dividends**) benefits.

divider noun **1** a screen that divides a room into separate parts. **2** (**dividers**) a measuring compass.

divination noun the use of supernatural means to find out about the future or the unknown.

divine[1] adjective **1** having to do with God or a god. **2** informal excellent. ■ **divinely** adverb.

divine[2] verb (**divines, divining, divined**) **1** discover by guesswork or intuition. **2** have supernatural insight into the future. ■ **diviner** noun.

divinity noun (plural **divinities**) **1** the state of being divine. **2** a god or goddess. **3** the study of religion; theology.

divisible adjective **1** capable of being divided. **2** (of a number) containing another number a number of times without a remainder.

division noun **1** the action of dividing, or the state of being divided. **2** each of the parts into which something is divided. **3** a major section of an organization. **4** a number of sports teams or competitors grouped to compete against each other. **5** a partition. □ **division sign** the sign ÷, placed between two numbers showing that the first is to be divided by the second, as in $6 ÷ 3 = 2$. ■ **divisional** adjective.

divisive adjective causing disagreement or hostility between people.

divorce noun the legal ending of a marriage. **verb (divorces, divorcing, divorced) 1** legally end your marriage with. **2 (divorce from)** separate or detach from.

divorcee noun a divorced person.

divot /di-vuht/ noun a piece of turf cut out of the ground.

divulge verb (**divulges, divulging, divulged**) reveal information.

DIY abbreviation Brit. do it yourself.

dizzy adjective (**dizzier, dizziest**) **1** having a sensation of spinning around and losing your balance. **2** informal (of a woman) silly. **verb (dizzies, dizzying, dizzied)** make unsteady or confused. ■ **dizzily** adverb **dizziness** noun.

DJ noun a disc jockey.

DNA noun a substance carrying genetic information that is found in the cells of nearly all animals and plants.

| ℹ️ | short for *deoxyribonucleic acid*. |

do verb (**does, doing, did**; past participle **done**) **1** carry out or complete an action, duty, or task. **2** have a specified amount of success. **3** make or provide. **4** have a particular result or effect on. **5** work at for a living or take as a subject of study. **6** be suitable or acceptable. **7** informal swindle; cheat. **auxiliary verb 1** used before a verb in questions and negative statements. **2** used to refer back to a verb already mentioned. **3** used in commands, or to give emphasis to a verb. **noun** (plural **dos** or **do's**) informal, chiefly Brit. a party or other social event. □ **be (or have) done with** stop being concerned about. **do away with** informal put an end to or kill. **do in** informal **1** kill. **2 (be done in)** be tired out. **do out of** unfairly deprive someone of something. **do up 1** fasten, wrap, or arrange. **2** informal renovate or redecorate.

docile adjective willing to accept control or instruction quietly; submissive. ■ **docilely** adverb **docility** noun.

dock[1] noun an enclosed area of water in a port for loading, unloading, and repairing ships. **verb 1** (of a ship) come into a dock. **2** (of a spacecraft) join with a space station or another spacecraft in space.

dock[2] noun the enclosure in a criminal court for a person on trial.

dock[3] noun a weed with broad leaves.

dock[4] verb **1** take away money from a person's wages before they are paid. **2** cut short an animal's tail.

docker noun a person employed in a port to load and unload ships.

docket noun Brit. a document accompanying a batch of goods that lists its contents, shows that duty has been paid, etc.

dockyard noun an area with docks and equipment for repairing and building ships.

doctor noun **1** a person who is qualified to practise medicine. **2** (**Doctor**) a person who holds the highest university degree. **verb 1** change something in order to deceive people. **2** add a harmful or strong ingredient to food or drink. **3** Brit. remove the sexual organs of an animal.

doctoral adjective relating to a doctorate.

doctorate noun the highest degree awarded by a university.

doctrinaire adjective very strict in applying beliefs or principles.

doctrine /dok-trin/ noun a set of beliefs or principles held by a religious or political group. ■ **doctrinal** /dok-try-n'l/ adjective.

document noun a piece of written, printed, or electronic material that provides information or evidence. **verb** record something in written or other form.

documentary adjective **1** consisting of documents and other material. **2** using film, photographs, and sound recordings of real events to provide a factual report. noun (plural **documentaries**) a documentary film or television or radio programme.

documentation noun documents providing official information, evidence, or instructions.

dodder verb be slow and unsteady. ■ **doddery** adjective.

doddle noun Brit. informal a very easy task.

dodecagon /doh-**dek**-uh-guhn/ noun a figure with twelve straight sides and angles.

dodecahedron /doh-de-kuh-hee-druhn/ noun (plural **dodecahedra** or **dodecahedrons**) a three-dimensional shape with twelve faces.

dodge verb (**dodges**, **dodging**, **dodged**) **1** avoid something by a sudden quick movement. **2** avoid something in a cunning or dishonest way. noun an act of avoiding something. ■ **dodger** noun.

dodgem noun a small electric car driven at a funfair with the aim of bumping other such cars.

dodgy adjective Brit. informal **1** dishonest. **2** risky. **3** not good or reliable.

dodo noun (plural **dodos** or **dodoes**) a large extinct flightless bird formerly found on Mauritius.

doe noun **1** a female deer or reindeer. **2** the female of some other animals, such as a rabbit or hare.

does 3rd person singular present of **DO**.

doesn't short form does not.

doff verb remove your hat when greeting someone.

dog noun **1** a four-legged meat-eating mammal, kept as a pet or used for work or hunting. **2** any member of the dog family, such as the wolf or fox. **3** the male of an animal of the dog family. verb (**dogs**, **dogging**, **dogged**) **1** follow someone closely and persistently. **2** cause continual trouble for. □ **a dog in the manger** a person who stops others having things that they do not need themselves. **dog collar** informal a white upright collar worn by Christian priests. **dog-eared** having worn or battered corners. **dog-end** informal a cigarette end. **dog-leg** a sharp bend. **dog-tooth** a small check pattern with notched corners. **go to the dogs** informal get much worse.

dogfight noun a close combat between military aircraft.

dogfish noun a small shark with a long tail.

dogged /dog-gid/ adjective very persistent. ■ **doggedly** adverb.

doggerel noun badly written verse.

doggo adverb (**lie doggo**) Brit. informal hide by keeping still and quiet.

doggy-paddle noun a simple swimming stroke like that of a dog.

doghouse noun N. Amer. a dog's kennel. □ **in the doghouse** informal in disgrace.

dogma noun a firm set of principles.

dogmatic adjective firmly putting forward your opinions and expecting that other people will accept them. ■ **dogmatically** adverb.

dogsbody noun (plural **dogsbodies**) Brit. informal a person who is given boring, menial tasks.

doily noun (plural **doilies**) a small ornamental mat made of lace or paper.

doings plural noun a person's actions or activities.

doldrums plural noun (**the doldrums**) a state of being inactive or feeling depressed.

dole noun Brit. informal benefit paid by the state to unemployed people. verb (**doles**, **doling**, **doled**) (**dole out**) distribute.

doleful adjective sad or depressing. ■ **dolefully** adverb.

doll noun a small model of a human figure, used as a child's toy. verb (**be dolled up**) informal be dressed in smart or fancy clothes.

dollar noun the chief unit of money in the US, Canada, Australia, and some other countries.

dollop informal **noun** a shapeless mass or lump. **verb** (**dollops, dolloping, dolloped**) casually add or serve out a mass of something.

dolour /**dol**-er/ (US spelling **dolor**) **noun** literary great sorrow or distress. ■ **dolorous** adjective.

dolphin **noun** a small whale with a beak-like snout and a curved fin on the back.

dolphinarium **noun** (plural **dolphinariums** or **dolphinaria**) an aquarium in which dolphins are kept and trained for public entertainment.

dolt **noun** a stupid person.

domain **noun 1** an area controlled by a ruler or government. **2** an area of activity or knowledge.

dome **noun 1** a rounded roof with a circular base. **2** a stadium or other building with a rounded roof. ■ **domed** adjective.

domestic **adjective 1** relating to a home or family. **2** for use in the home. **3** (of an animal) tame and kept by humans. **4** existing or occurring within a country; not foreign. ■ **domestically** adverb.

domesticate **verb** (**domesticates, domesticating, domesticated**) tame an animal and keep it as a pet or on a farm. ■ **domestication** noun.

domesticity **noun** home life.

domicile /**dom**-i-syl/ formal or Law **noun 1** the country in which a person lives permanently. **2** a person's home. **verb** (**be domiciled**) be living in a particular country or place.

dominant **adjective 1** most important, powerful, or influential. **2** (of a high place or object) overlooking others. ■ **dominance** noun **dominantly** adverb.

dominate **verb** (**dominates, dominating, dominated**) **1** have a very strong influence over. **2** be the most important or noticeable person or thing in. ■ **domination** noun.

domineering **adjective** arrogantly trying to control other people.

dominion **noun 1** supreme power or control. **2** the territory of a ruler or government.

domino **noun** (plural **dominoes**) any of twenty-eight small oblong pieces marked with 0–6 pips in each half, used in the game of **dominoes**.

don[1] **noun** a university teacher.

don[2] **verb** (**dons, donning, donned**) put on an item of clothing.

donate **verb** (**donates, donating, donated**) give to a good cause.

donation **noun** something given to a good cause.

done past participle of **DO**. **adjective 1** cooked thoroughly. **2** no longer happening or existing. **3** informal socially acceptable: *the done thing.* **exclamation** (in response to an offer) I accept!

doner kebab /**doh**-ner, **don**-er/ **noun** a Turkish dish of spiced lamb cooked on a spit and served in slices.

donkey **noun** (plural **donkeys**) a domesticated mammal of the horse family with long ears and a braying call. ◻ **donkey jacket** Brit. a heavy jacket with a patch of waterproof material across the shoulders. **donkey's years** informal a very long time.

donor **noun** a person who donates something.

don't **short form** do not.

donut US spelling of **DOUGHNUT**.

doodle **verb** (**doodles, doodling, doodled**) scribble absent-mindedly. **noun** a drawing made absent-mindedly.

doom **noun** death, destruction, or another terrible fate. **verb** (**be doomed**) be fated to fail or be destroyed.

doomsday **noun** the last day of the world's existence.

door **noun** a movable barrier at the entrance to a building, room, vehicle, etc. ◻ **out of doors** in or into the open air.

doorman **noun** a man who is on duty at the entrance to a large building.

doormat **noun 1** a mat placed in a doorway for wiping the shoes. **2** informal a person who lets others control them.

doorstep **noun** a step leading up to the outer door of a house.

doorstop **noun** an object that keeps a

door open or in place.

dope noun **1** informal an illegal drug, especially cannabis. **2** a drug used to improve the performance of an athlete, racehorse, or greyhound. **3** informal a stupid person. **verb** (**dopes, doping, doped**) give a drug to.

dopey or **dopy** adjective informal **1** in a semi-conscious state from sleepiness or a drug. **2** stupid.

doppelgänger /dop-puhl-geng-er, dop-puhl-gang-er/ noun a ghost or double of a living person.

Doppler effect noun an apparent change in the frequency of sound or light waves as the source and the observer move towards or away from each other.

dormant adjective **1** (of an animal) in a deep sleep. **2** (of a plant or bud) alive but not growing. **3** (of a volcano) temporarily inactive.

dormer window noun a window set vertically into a sloping roof.

dormitory noun (plural **dormitories**) a bedroom for a number of people in an institution. **adjective** (of a town) from which people travel to work in a nearby city.

dormouse noun (plural **dormice**) a small mouse-like rodent with a bushy tail.

dorsal adjective having to do with the upper side or back.

dose noun **1** a quantity of a medicine taken at one time. **2** an amount of radiation absorbed at one time. **verb** (**doses, dosing, dosed**) give a dose of medicine to. ■ **dosage** noun.

dosh noun Brit. informal money.

doss verb Brit. informal **1** sleep in rough or makeshift conditions. **2** spend time idly. ■ **dosser** noun.

dossier /**doss**-i-er, **doss**-i-ay/ noun a collection of documents about a person or subject.

dot noun a small round mark or spot. **verb** (**dots, dotting, dotted**) **1** mark with a dot or dots. **2** cover an area with a scattering of something. □ **dotcom** a company that conducts its business on the Internet. **on the dot**

informal exactly on time. **the year dot** Brit. informal a very long time ago.

dotage /**doh**-tij/ noun the period of life in which a person is old and weak.

dote verb (**dotes, doting, doted**) (**dote on**) be excessively fond of.

dotty adjective Brit. informal slightly mad or eccentric.

double adjective **1** consisting of two equal, identical, or similar parts or things. **2** having twice the usual size, quantity, or strength. **3** designed to be used by two people. **4** having two different roles or meanings. **adverb** twice the amount or quantity. **noun 1** a thing which is twice as large as usual or is made up of two parts. **2** a person who looks exactly like another. **3** (**doubles**) a game involving sides made up of two players. **verb** (**doubles, doubling, doubled**) **1** make or become double. **2** fold or bend over on itself. **3** (**double up**) curl up with pain or laughter. **4** (**double as**) be used in or play a different role. □ **at the double** very fast. **double agent** an agent who pretends to act as a spy for one country while in fact acting for its enemy. **double back** go back in the direction you have come from. **double-barrelled** Brit. (of a surname) having two parts joined by a hyphen. **double bass** the largest and lowest-pitched instrument of the violin family. **double-breasted** (of a jacket or coat) having a large overlap at the front and two rows of buttons. **double chin** a roll of flesh below a person's chin. **double cream** Brit. thick cream with a high fat content. **double-cross** betray a person that you are supposed to be helping. **double-dealing** deceitful behaviour. **double-decker** a bus with two levels. **double Dutch** Brit. informal language that is hard to understand. **double glazing** windows having two layers of glass with a space between them. **double-jointed** (of a person) having unusually flexible joints. **double standard** a rule or principle applied unfairly in different ways to different people. **double take**

a delayed reaction to something unexpected. ■ **doubly** adverb.

double entendre /doo-b'l on-**ton**-druh/ **noun** (plural **double entendres** /doo-b'l on-**ton**-druh/) a word or phrase with two meanings, one of which is usually rude.

doublet noun historical a man's short close-fitting padded jacket.

doubloon /dub-**loon**/ noun historical a Spanish gold coin.

doubt noun a feeling of uncertainty. verb **1** feel uncertain about. **2** question whether something is true. □ **no doubt** certainly; probably.

doubtful adjective **1** feeling uncertain. **2** causing uncertainty. **3** unlikely or improbable. ■ **doubtfully** adverb.

doubtless adverb very probably.

douche /doosh/ noun a jet of water applied to part of the body.

dough noun **1** a thick mixture of flour and liquid, for baking into bread or pastry. **2** informal money. ■ **doughy** adjective.

doughnut (US spelling **donut**) noun a small fried cake or ring of sweetened dough.

doughty /**dow**-ti/ adjective old use brave and determined.

dour adjective very severe, stern, or gloomy.

douse or **dowse** verb (**douses, dousing, doused**) **1** drench with liquid. **2** extinguish a fire.

dove[1] /duv/ noun **1** a bird with a cooing voice, very similar to a pigeon. **2** a person who favours a policy of peace and negotiation.

dove[2] US past and past participle of **DIVE**.

dovecote or **dovecot** /**duv**-kot/ noun a shelter with nest holes for domesticated pigeons.

dovetail noun a wedge-shaped joint formed by interlocking two pieces of wood. verb **1** join by means of a dovetail. **2** fit together neatly.

dowager /**dow**-uh-jer/ noun **1** a widow who has a title or property from her late husband. **2** informal a dignified elderly woman.

dowdy adjective unfashionable and dull in appearance.

dowel noun a peg used to hold together parts of a structure.

down[1] adverb **1** towards, in, or at a lower place, position, or level. **2** to a smaller amount or size. **3** in or into a weaker or worse position or condition. **4** away from a central place or the north. **5** from an earlier to a later point in time or order. **6** in or into writing. **7** (of a computer system) out of action. preposition **1** from a higher to a lower point of. **2** at or to a point further along the course of. **3** informal at or to. adjective **1** directed or moving downwards. **2** unhappy. verb informal **1** knock or bring to the ground. **2** consume a drink. □ **down and out** homeless and without money; destitute. **down at heel** shabby because of lack of money. **down payment** an initial payment made when buying something on credit. **down-to-earth** practical and realistic. **down under** informal Australia and New Zealand.

down[2] noun fine, soft feathers or hairs.

downbeat adjective **1** gloomy. **2** relaxed and low-key.

downcast adjective **1** (of eyes) looking downwards. **2** discouraged; dejected.

downer noun informal **1** a tranquillizing or depressant drug. **2** something depressing.

downfall noun a loss of power, prosperity, or status.

downgrade verb (**downgrades, downgrading, downgraded**) bring someone down to a lower rank or level of importance.

downhearted adjective discouraged; dejected.

downhill adverb & adjective **1** towards the bottom of a slope. **2** into a steadily worsening situation.

download verb copy data from one computer system to another.

downmarket adjective chiefly Brit. cheap and of low quality.

downplay verb make something appear less important than it really is.

downpour noun a heavy fall of rain.

downright adjective utter; complete. adverb extremely.

downs noun gently rolling hills.

downside noun the negative aspect of something.

Down's syndrome noun a congenital disorder causing mental and physical abnormalities.

downstairs adverb & adjective on or to a lower floor.

downstream or **downriver** adverb in the direction in which a stream or river flows.

downtown adjective & adverb chiefly N. Amer. in, to, or towards the central area of a city.

downtrodden adjective treated badly by those in power.

downward adjective & adverb towards a lower point or level. ∎ **downwards** adverb.

downwind adverb in the direction in which the wind is blowing.

downy adjective covered with fine soft hair or feathers.

dowry noun (plural **dowries**) property or money brought by a bride to her husband on their marriage.

dowse[1] verb (**dowses**, **dowsing**, **dowsed**) search for underground water or minerals with a pointer which is supposedly moved by unseen influences.

dowse[2] ⇒ **DOUSE**.

doyen /doy-yen/ noun (feminine **doyenne** /doy-yen/) the most respected or prominent person in a field.

doze verb (**dozes**, **dozing**, **dozed**) sleep lightly. noun a short, light sleep. ∎ **dozy** adjective.

dozen noun 1 (plural **dozen**) a group or set of twelve. 2 (**dozens**) a lot. ▢ **talk nineteen to the dozen** Brit. talk fast and continuously.

DPhil abbreviation Doctor of Philosophy.

Dr abbreviation Doctor.

drab adjective (**drabber**, **drabbest**) dull and uninteresting.

drachma /drak-muh/ noun (plural **drachmas** or **drachmae** /drak-mee/) the chief unit of money in Greece.

draconian /druh-koh-ni-uhn/ adjective (of laws) excessively harsh.

draft noun 1 a rough version of a piece of writing. 2 a written order requesting a bank to pay a specified sum. 3 (**the draft**) US compulsory recruitment for military service. 4 US spelling of **DRAUGHT**. verb 1 prepare a rough version of a text. 2 select someone for a particular purpose. 3 (**be drafted**) US be conscripted for military service.

drafty US spelling of **DRAUGHTY**.

drag verb (**drags**, **dragging**, **dragged**) 1 pull along forcefully, roughly, or with difficulty. 2 trail along the ground. 3 (of time) pass slowly. 4 (**drag out**) prolong unnecessarily. 5 search the bottom of a body of water with hooks or nets. 6 (**drag on**) informal inhale the smoke from a cigarette. noun 1 the action of dragging. 2 informal a boring or tiresome person or thing. 3 informal women's clothing worn by a man. 4 informal an act of inhaling smoke from a cigarette. 5 the force exerted by air or water to slow down a moving object. ▢ **drag race** a short race between two cars to see which can accelerate fastest from a standstill.

dragnet noun a net drawn through water or across ground to trap fish or game.

dragon noun a mythical monster that can breathe out fire.

dragonfly noun a long-bodied insect with two pairs of large transparent wings.

dragoon noun a member of any of several British cavalry regiments. verb force someone into doing something.

drain verb 1 cause the liquid in something to run out. 2 (of liquid) run off or out. 3 exhaust the strength or resources of. 4 drink the entire contents of. noun **1** a channel or pipe for carrying off surplus liquid. **2** a thing that uses up a resource or strength. □ **draining board** Brit. a surface next to a sink, on which crockery is left to drain.

drainage noun **1** the action of draining. **2** a system of drains.

drainpipe noun **1** a pipe for carrying off rainwater from a building. **2** (**drainpipes**) trousers with very narrow legs.

drake noun a male duck.

dram noun a small drink of spirits.

drama noun **1** a play. **2** plays as a literary form. **3** an exciting series of events.

dramatic adjective **1** relating to drama. **2** sudden and striking. **3** exciting or impressive. noun (**dramatics**) **1** the practice of presenting plays. **2** exaggerated or overemotional behaviour. ■ **dramatically** adverb.

dramatist noun a person who writes plays.

dramatize or **dramatise** verb (**dramatizes, dramatizing, dramatized**) **1** present a novel or story as a play. **2** make something seem more exciting or serious than it really is. ■ **dramatization** noun.

drank past of **DRINK**.

drape verb (**drapes, draping, draped**) **1** arrange cloth or clothing loosely on or round something. **2** rest part of your body on something in a relaxed way. noun (**drapes**) long curtains.

draper noun Brit. dated a person who sells fabrics.

drapery noun (plural **draperies**) curtains or fabric hanging in loose folds.

drastic adjective having a strong or far-reaching effect. ■ **drastically** adverb.

draught (US spelling **draft**) noun **1** a current of cool air indoors. **2** an act of drinking or breathing in. **3** old use a quantity of a medicinal liquid. **4** the depth of water needed to float a particular ship. **5** (**draughts**) Brit. a game played on a chequered board. verb =

DRAFT. adjective **1** (of beer) served from a cask. **2** (of an animal) used for pulling heavy loads.

draughtsman noun **1** a person who makes technical plans or drawings. **2** an artist skilled in drawing.

draughty (US spelling **drafty**) adjective uncomfortable because of draughts of cold air.

draw verb (**draws, drawing, drew**; past participle **drawn**) **1** produce a picture or diagram by making lines and marks on paper. **2** pull or drag a vehicle. **3** move in a specified direction. **4** pull curtains shut or open. **5** arrive at a point in time. **6** take from a container or source. **7** be the cause of a specified response. **8** attract people to a place or an event. **9** persuade someone to reveal something. **10** reach a conclusion. **11** finish a contest or game with an even score. **12** take in a breath. noun **1** a random selection of names for prizes, sporting fixtures, etc. **2** a contest that ends with the scores even. **3** a person or thing that is very attractive or interesting. **4** an act of inhaling smoke from a cigarette. □ **draw in** (of successive days) become shorter. **draw the line** at refuse to do or tolerate. **draw on 1** (of a period of time) pass by and approach its end. **2** suck smoke from a cigarette or pipe. **draw out 1** make something last longer. **2** persuade someone to be more talkative. **draw up 1** come to a halt. **2** prepare a plan or document.

ℹ️ do not confuse **draw** with **drawer** meaning 'sliding storage compartment'.

---

drawback noun a disadvantage or problem.

drawbridge noun a bridge which is hinged at one end so that it can be raised.

drawer noun **1** a storage compartment that slides horizontally in and out of a desk or chest. **2** (**drawers**) dated knickers or underpants. **3** a person who draws something.

drawing noun a picture or diagram made with a pencil, pen, or crayon.

□ **drawing pin** Brit. a short flat-headed pin for fastening paper to a surface.
drawing room a sitting room.

drawl verb speak in a slow, lazy way with prolonged vowel sounds. noun a drawling accent.

drawn past participle of **DRAW**. adjective looking strained from illness or exhaustion.

drawstring noun a string in the seam of a garment or bag, which can be pulled to tighten or close it.

dray noun a low truck or cart for delivering barrels or other loads.

dread verb think about something with great fear or anxiety. noun great fear or anxiety.

dreadful adjective **1** extremely bad or serious. **2** used for emphasis: *he's a dreadful flirt.* ■ **dreadfully** adverb.

dreadlocks plural noun a Rastafarian hairstyle in which the hair is twisted into tight braids or ringlets.

dream noun **1** a series of images and feelings that occur in your mind while you are asleep. **2** a long-held ambition or ideal. **3** informal a wonderful or perfect person or thing. verb (**dreams, dreaming, dreamed** or **dreamt** /dremt/) **1** experience dreams during sleep. **2** have daydreams or fantasies. **3** think of something as possible. **4** (**dream up**) imagine or invent. ■ **dreamer** noun.

dreamy adjective **1** resembling a dream. **2** tending to daydream. ■ **dreamily** adverb.

dreary adjective (**drearier, dreariest**) dull, bleak, and depressing. ■ **drearily** adverb **dreariness** noun.

dredge verb (**dredges, dredging, dredged**) **1** scoop out mud and objects from the bed of a harbour or river. **2** (**dredge up**) bring something unwelcome and forgotten to people's attention. noun an apparatus for dredging a river or seabed. ■ **dredger** noun.

dregs noun **1** the last remaining amount of a liquid left in a cup, together with any sediment. **2** the most worthless parts: *the dregs of society.*

drench verb **1** wet thoroughly. **2** cover with large amounts of something.

dress verb **1** (also **get dressed**) put on your clothes. **2** put clothes on someone. **3** wear clothes in a particular way or of a particular type. **4** decorate or arrange in an artistic or attractive way. **5** clean or apply a dressing to a wound. **6** prepare food for cooking or eating. noun **1** a woman's garment that covers the body and extends down over the legs. **2** clothing of a specified kind. □ **dress rehearsal** a final rehearsal in which costumes are worn and things are done as if it is a real performance. **dress up** dress in smart clothes or in a special costume.

dressage /dress-ah*zh*/ noun the training of a horse to perform a series of precise movements at the rider's command.

dresser noun a sideboard with shelves above it.

dressing noun **1** a sauce for salads, usually consisting of oil and vinegar with flavourings. **2** a piece of material placed on a wound to protect it. □ **dressing-down** informal a severe telling-off or reprimand. **dressing gown** a long robe worn after getting out of bed. **dressing room** a room in which performers change their clothes. **dressing table** a table used while dressing or putting on make-up.

dressy adjective (**dressier, dressiest**) (of clothes) smart or formal.

drew past of **DRAW**.

dribble verb (**dribbles, dribbling, dribbled**) **1** (of a liquid) fall slowly in drops or a thin stream. **2** let saliva run from the mouth. **3** (in sport) take the ball forward with slight touches. noun **1** a thin stream of liquid. **2** (in sport) an act of dribbling.

dribs and drabs plural noun informal scattered or irregular amounts.

dried past and past participle of **DRY**.

drier[1] ⇒ **DRYER**.

drier[2] comparative of **DRY**.

drift verb **1** be carried slowly by a current of air or water. **2** walk or move slowly or casually. **3** (of snow, leaves, etc.) be blown into heaps by the wind. noun **1** a continuous slow movement from one place to another. **2** the general meaning of someone's remarks. **3** a large mass of snow, leaves, etc. piled up by the wind.

drifter noun a person who moves from place to place, with no fixed home or job.

driftwood noun pieces of wood floating on the sea or washed ashore.

drill noun **1** a tool or machine used for boring holes. **2** training in military exercises. **3** (**the drill**) informal the correct procedure. **4** a machine for sowing seed in rows. verb **1** bore a hole with a drill. **2** give someone military training or other strict instruction.

drily or **dryly** adverb in a matter-of-fact or ironically humorous way.

drink verb (**drinks**, **drinking**, **drank**; past participle **drunk**) **1** take a liquid into the mouth and swallow it. **2** drink alcohol. noun **1** a liquid consumed for refreshment or nourishment. **2** a quantity of liquid swallowed at one time. □ **drink-driving** Brit. the crime of driving a vehicle after drinking too much alcohol. ■ **drinkable** adjective **drinker** noun.

drip verb (**drips**, **dripping**, **dripped**) fall in small drops of liquid. noun **1** a small drop of a liquid. **2** a device which slowly passes a substance into a patient's body through a vein. **3** informal a weak person. □ **drip-feed** put liquid into something drop by drop. ■ **drippy** adjective.

dripping noun Brit. fat that has dripped from roasting meat. adjective extremely wet.

drive verb (**drives**, **driving**, **drove**; past participle **driven**) **1** operate a motor vehicle. **2** carry in a motor vehicle. **3** carry or urge along. **4** make someone behave in a particular way. **5** provide energy to make an engine or machine work. **6** Golf hit the ball from the tee. noun **1** a journey in a car. **2** (also **driveway**) a short private road

leading to a house. **3** a natural urge. **4** an organized effort to achieve something. **5** determination and ambition. ■ **driver** noun.

drivel /driv-uhl/ noun nonsense.

drizzle noun light rain falling in fine drops. verb (**drizzles**, **drizzling**, **drizzled**) **1** (**it drizzles**, **it is drizzling**, etc.) rain lightly. **2** Cookery pour a thin stream of liquid over a dish.

droll /drohl/ adjective amusing in a strange or quaint way.

dromedary /drom-i-duh-ri/ noun (plural **dromedaries**) a kind of camel with one hump.

drone verb (**drones**, **droning**, **droned**) **1** make a low continuous humming sound. **2** speak tediously at length. noun **1** a low continuous humming sound. **2** a male bee which does no work but can fertilize a queen.

drool verb (**drools**, **drooling**, **drooled**) **1** drop saliva uncontrollably from the mouth. **2** (often **drool over**) informal show great pleasure or desire.

droop verb **1** bend or hang downwards limply. **2** sag down from weariness or dejection. noun an instance of drooping.

droopy adjective (**droopier**, **droopiest**) **1** hanging down limply. **2** not having much strength or spirit.

drop verb (**drops**, **dropping**, **dropped**) **1** fall, or let fall. **2** make or become lower or less. **3** abandon a course of action. **4** (often **drop off**) set down or unload a passenger or goods. **5** (in sport) lose a point or match. noun **1** a small round or pear-shaped particle of liquid. **2** a small drink. **3** an abrupt fall or slope. **4** a sweet or lozenge. □ **drop kick** a kick made by dropping a ball and kicking it as it bounces. **drop off** fall asleep. **drop out** stop participating. **2** start living an alternative lifestyle.

droplet noun a very small drop of a liquid.

dropout noun a person who has started living an alternative lifestyle, or abandoned a course of study.

droppings plural noun the excrement of animals.

dross noun rubbish.

drought /drowt/ noun a prolonged period of abnormally low rainfall.

drove[1] past of **DRIVE**.

drove[2] noun **1** a flock of animals being driven. **2** a large number of people doing the same thing.

drown verb **1** die through taking water into the lungs, or kill someone in this way. **2** flood an area. **3** (usu. **drown out**) make something impossible to hear by being much louder.

drowsy adjective (**drowsier, drowsiest**) sleepy. ■ **drowsily** adverb **drowsiness** noun.

drub verb (**drubs, drubbing, drubbed**) beat repeatedly. ■ **drubbing** noun.

drudge noun a person who is made to do hard or dull work.

drudgery noun hard or dull work.

drug noun **1** a substance used as a medicine. **2** an illegal substance taken for the effects it has on the body. verb (**drugs, drugging, drugged**) affect someone by giving them a drug. ■ **druggy** adjective.

drugstore noun N. Amer. a shop which sells medicines and also cosmetics and other articles.

Druid /droo-id/ noun a priest in the ancient Celtic religion.

drum noun **1** a percussion instrument which you play by hitting it with sticks or the hands. **2** a cylindrical object or part. **3** a sound resembling that made by a drum. verb (**drums, drumming, drummed**) **1** play on a drum. **2** make a continuous rhythmic noise. **3** (**drum into**) instruct someone in something by constantly repeating it. □ **drum and bass** a type of dance music consisting largely of electronic drums and bass. ■ **drummer** noun.

drumstick noun **1** a stick used for beating a drum. **2** the lower joint of the leg of a cooked chicken.

drunk past participle of **DRINK**. adjective having drunk so much alcohol that you cannot think or speak clearly. noun a person who is drunk or who often drinks too much.

drupe noun Botany a fruit with a central stone, e.g. a plum or olive.

dry adjective (**drier, driest**) **1** free from moisture. **2** dull and serious. **3** (of humour) subtle and expressed in a matter-of-fact way. **4** (of wine) not sweet. verb (**dries, drying, dried**) **1** make or become dry. **2** preserve something by evaporating the moisture. **3** (**dry up**) (of a supply) decrease and stop. □ **dry-clean** clean a garment with a chemical rather than by washing it. **dry ice** white mist produced as a theatrical effect. **dry rot** a fungus that causes wood to decay. **dry run** informal a rehearsal. ■ **dryness** noun.

dryer or **drier** noun a machine or device for drying something.

dryly ⇨ **DRILY**.

drystone adjective Brit. (of a stone wall) built without using mortar.

dual adjective consisting of two parts or aspects. □ **dual carriageway** Brit. a road with two or more lanes in each direction.

dualism noun **1** division into two contrasted aspects, such as good and evil. **2** duality. ■ **dualist** noun & adjective.

duality noun (plural **dualities**) the state of having two parts or aspects.

dub[1] verb (**dubs, dubbing, dubbed**) **1** give an unofficial name to. **2** knight someone by touching their shoulder with a sword.

dub[2] verb (**dubs, dubbing, dubbed**) **1** give a film a soundtrack in a different language from the original. **2** add sound effects or music to a film or recording.

dubbin noun Brit. a grease used for softening and waterproofing leather.

dubious adjective **1** hesitating or doubting. **2** not reliable or of certain quality. ■ **dubiously** adverb.

ducal /dyoo-k'l/ adjective relating to a duke or dukedom.

ducat /duk-uht/ noun a gold coin formerly used in Europe.

duchess noun **1** the wife or widow of a duke. **2** a woman holding a rank equivalent to duke.

duchy noun (plural **duchies**) the territory of a duke or duchess.

duck[1] noun (plural **duck** or **ducks**) **1** a waterbird with a broad blunt bill, short legs, and webbed feet. **2** a female duck. □ **duck-billed platypus** ⇒ **PLATYPUS**.

duck[2] verb **1** lower yourself quickly to avoid being hit or seen. **2** push someone under water. **3** informal avoid an unwelcome duty.

duck[3] noun Cricket a batsman's score of nought.

duckboards plural noun wooden slats joined together to form a path over muddy ground.

duckling noun a young duck.

duct noun **1** a tube or passageway for air, cables, etc. **2** a tube in the body through which fluid passes.

ductile adjective (of a metal) able to be drawn out into a thin wire.

dud informal noun a thing that fails to work properly. adjective failing to work properly.

dude noun N. Amer. informal a man.

dudgeon noun deep resentment.

due adjective **1** expected at a certain time. **2** owing; needing to be paid or given. **3** (of a person) owed or deserving something. **4** proper or adequate. noun **1** (someone's **due** or **dues**) what someone deserves or is owed. **2** (**dues**) fees. adverb directly: *head due south*. □ **due to 1** caused by. **2** because of.

duel noun **1** historical a contest with deadly weapons between two people to settle a point of honour. **2** a contest between two parties. verb (**duels**, **duelling**, **duelled**; US spelling **duels**, **dueling**, **dueled**) fight a duel.

duet noun **1** a performance by two singers or musicians. **2** a musical composition for two performers.

duff Brit. informal adjective worthless or false. verb (**duff up**) beat someone up.

duffel bag or **duffle bag** noun a cylinder-shaped canvas bag closed by a drawstring.

duffel coat or **duffle coat** noun a hooded coat made of a coarse woollen material.

duffer noun informal an incompetent or stupid person.

dug[1] past and past participle of **DIG**.

dug[2] noun the udder, teat, or nipple of a female animal.

dugout noun **1** a trench that is roofed over as a shelter for troops. **2** a low shelter at the side of a sports field for a team's coaches and substitutes.

duke noun **1** the highest rank of nobleman in Britain and certain other countries. **2** historical (in parts of Europe) a male ruler of a small independent state. ■ **dukedom** noun.

dulcet /dul-sit/ adjective (of a sound) sweet and soothing.

dulcimer /dul-si-mer/ noun a musical instrument which you play by hitting the strings with small hammers.

dull adjective **1** not very interesting. **2** not vivid or bright. **3** (of the weather) overcast. **4** slow to understand. verb make or become dull. ■ **dullness** noun **dully** adverb.

dullard noun a slow or stupid person.

duly adverb in accordance with what is required or expected.

dumb adjective **1** offensive unable to speak; lacking the power of speech. **2** temporarily unable or unwilling to speak. **3** N. Amer. informal stupid. verb (**dumb down**) informal make less intellectually challenging. □ **dumb-bell** a short bar with a weight at each end, used for exercise. **dumb waiter** a small lift for carrying food and crockery between floors.

dumbfounded adjective greatly astonished.

dumbstruck adjective so shocked or surprised that you cannot speak.

dumdum bullet noun a kind of soft-nosed bullet that expands on impact.

dummy noun (plural **dummies**) **1** a model or replica of a human being. **2** an object designed to resemble and take the place of another. **3** Brit. a rubber or plastic teat for a baby to suck on. **4** (in sport) a movement made to deceive an opponent into thinking that you are about to kick or pass the ball. **5** informal, chiefly N. Amer. a stupid person. □ **dummy run** a practice or trial.

dump noun **1** a place where rubbish or waste is left. **2** a temporary store of weapons or military provisions. **3** informal an unpleasant or dull place. verb **1** dispose of something unwanted. **2** put down something carelessly. **3** informal abandon someone.

dumpling noun a small savoury ball of dough boiled in water or in a stew.

dumps plural noun (**down in the dumps**) informal depressed or unhappy.

dumpy adjective short and stout.

dun noun a dull greyish-brown colour.

dunce noun a person who is slow at learning.

dune noun a mound or ridge of sand formed by the wind.

dung noun manure.

dungarees /dung-guh-**reez**/ noun a garment consisting of trousers held up by straps over the shoulders.

dungeon noun a strong underground prison cell.

dunk verb **1** dip food into a drink or soup before eating it. **2** put something in water.

dunnock noun a small bird with a grey head and a reddish-brown back.

duo noun (plural **duos**) **1** a pair of people or things, especially in music or entertainment. **2** Music a duet.

duodenum /dyoo-uh-**dee**-nuhm/ noun (plural **duodenums** or **duodena**) the first part of the small intestine immediately beyond the stomach.

dupe verb (**dupes**, **duping**, **duped**) deceive; trick. noun a person who is tricked or deceived.

duple /**dyoo**-p'l/ adjective Music (of rhythm) based on two main beats to the bar.

duplex /**dyoo**-pleks/ noun **1** N. Amer. a

building divided into two flats. **2** N. Amer. & Austral. a semi-detached house. adjective having two parts.

duplicate adjective /**dyoo**-pli-kuht/ **1** exactly like something else. **2** having two corresponding parts. noun /**dyoo**-pli-kuht/ each of two or more identical things. verb /**dyoo**-pli-kayt/ (**duplicates, duplicating, duplicated**) **1** make or be an exact copy of. **2** multiply by two. **3** do something again unnecessarily. ■ **duplication** noun **duplicator** noun.

duplicity /dyoo-**pli**-si-ti/ noun deceitful behaviour. ■ **duplicitous** adjective.

durable adjective **1** hard-wearing. **2** (of goods) not for immediate consumption and so able to be kept.

duration noun the time during which something continues.

duress noun threats or violence used to force a person to do something.

during preposition **1** throughout the course of. **2** at a particular point in the course of.

dusk noun the darker stage of twilight.

dusky adjective dark, or darkish in colour.

dust noun fine, dry powder, especially tiny particles of earth, sand, etc. verb **1** remove dust from the surface of. **2** cover lightly with a powdered substance. □ **dust-up** informal a fight. ■ **dusty** adjective.

dustbin noun Brit. a large container for household rubbish.

dustcart noun Brit. a vehicle used for collecting household rubbish.

duster noun Brit. a cloth for dusting furniture.

dustman noun Brit. a man employed to remove rubbish from dustbins.

dustpan noun a hand-held container into which you sweep dust and waste.

Dutch adjective relating to the Netherlands or its language. noun the language of the Netherlands. □ **Dutch courage** confidence gained from drinking alcohol. **go Dutch** share the cost of a meal equally.

dutiable adjective on which duty needs to be paid.

dutiful adjective carrying out all your obligations; doing your duty. ■ **dutifully** adverb.

duty noun (plural **duties**) **1** a moral or legal obligation. **2** a person's regular work, or a task required as part of their job. **3** a charge made when some goods are imported, exported, or sold. □ **duty-bound** morally or legally obliged. **duty-free** not requiring duty to be paid.

duvet /**dyoo**-vay, **doo**-vay/ noun chiefly Brit. a thick quilt used instead of an upper sheet and blankets.

DVD abbreviation digital versatile disc.

dwarf noun (plural **dwarfs** or **dwarves**) **1** a member of a mythical race of short human-like creatures. **2** an abnormally small person. verb make something seem small in comparison.

dwell verb (**dwells**, **dwelling**, past and past participle **dwelt** or **dwelled**) **1** formal live in or at a place. **2** (**dwell on**) think about something at length.

dwelling noun formal a house or home.

dwindle verb (**dwindles**, **dwindling**, **dwindled**) gradually lessen or fade.

dye noun a substance used to colour something. verb (**dyes**, **dyeing**, **dyed**) make something a particular colour with dye. □ **dyed in the wool** unchanging in a particular belief.

dying present participle of **DIE**¹.

dyke or **dike** noun **1** a barrier built to prevent flooding from the sea. **2** a ditch or water-filled channel. **3** informal a lesbian.

dynamic adjective **1** characterized by constant change or activity. **2** full of energy and new ideas. **3** Physics relating to forces that produce motion. ■ **dynamically** adverb.

dynamics plural noun **1** the study of the forces involved in movement. **2** forces which stimulate change. **3** the varying levels of sound in a musical performance.

dynamism noun the quality of being dynamic.

dynamite noun a kind of high explosive. verb (**dynamites**, **dynamiting**, **dynamited**) blow up something with dynamite.

dynamo noun (plural **dynamos**) a machine for converting mechanical energy into electrical energy.

dynasty /**di**-nuh-sti/ noun (plural **dynasties**) a series of related rulers or powerful people.

dysentery /**diss**-uhn-tri/ noun a disease of the intestines which results in severe diarrhoea.

dysfunctional adjective **1** not operating properly. **2** unable to deal with normal social relations.

dyslexia /diss-**lek**-si-uh/ noun a disorder involving difficulty in learning to read words and letters. ■ **dyslexic** adjective & noun.

dyspepsia noun indigestion.

dyspeptic adjective **1** suffering from indigestion. **2** irritable.

Ee

E or **e** noun (plural **Es** or **E's**) the fifth letter of the alphabet. **abbreviation 1** East or Eastern. **2** informal the drug Ecstasy. □ **E-number** Brit. a code number starting with the letter E, given to food additives according to European Union instructions.

each determiner & pronoun every one of two or more people or things, regarded separately. **adverb** to, for, or by every one of a group.

eager adjective very much wanting to do or have something. ■ **eagerly** adverb.

eagle noun a large bird of prey with long, broad wings. □ **eagle-eyed** very observant.

ear noun **1** the organ of hearing in humans and animals. **2** an ability to recognize and appreciate music or language. **3** the seed-bearing head of a cereal plant. □ **within** (or **out of**) **earshot** near enough (or too far away) to be heard.

earache noun pain inside the ear.

eardrum noun a membrane in the ear which vibrates in response to sound waves.

earl noun a British nobleman ranking above a viscount. ■ **earldom** noun.

early adjective (**earlier, earliest**) & adverb **1** before the expected time. **2** at the beginning of a particular time, period, or sequence.

earmark verb choose for a particular purpose.

earmuffs plural noun a pair of fabric coverings worn over the ears to protect them from cold or noise.

earn verb **1** be given money in return for labour or services. **2** gain a reward for hard work or good qualities. ■ **earner** noun.

earnest adjective extremely serious. □ **in earnest** with sincere and serious intention. ■ **earnestly** adjective.

earnings plural noun money or income earned.

earphones plural noun devices worn on the ears to listen to radio, recorded sound, etc.

earpiece noun the part of a telephone or other device that is applied to the ear during use.

earplug noun a piece of wax, cotton wool, etc., placed in the ear as protection against noise or water.

earring noun a piece of jewellery worn on the lobe or edge of the ear.

earth noun **1** (also **Earth**) the planet on which we live. **2** the ground. **3** soil. **4** Brit. a wire that connects an electrical circuit to the ground and makes it safe. **5** the underground lair of a badger or fox. **verb** Brit. connect an electrical device to earth.

earthen adjective made of clay or compressed earth.

earthenware noun pottery made of fired clay.

earthling noun (in science fiction) a person from the earth.

earthly adjective **1** having to do with the earth or human life. **2** remotely possible: *no earthly reason*.

earthquake noun a sudden violent shaking of the ground, caused by movements within the earth's crust.

earthwork noun a large man-made bank of soil.

earthworm noun a burrowing worm that lives in the soil.

earthy adjective (**earthier, earthiest**) **1** resembling soil. **2** direct and unembarrassed about sexual subjects or bodily functions.

earwig noun a small insect with a pair of pincers at its rear end. **verb** (**earwigs, earwigging, earwigged**) informal eavesdrop.

ease noun **1** absence of difficulty or effort. **2** freedom from problems. **verb**

WORD FORMATION

e-

Words that begin with **e-** refer to the electronic transfer of data by computers, especially through the Internet. **e-** is short for *electronic*, and was first used in the word *email*, or electronic mail. Some examples are:

e-cash	financial transactions conducted via computer networks
e-commerce	buying things via the Internet
e-tailer	a company that sells things over the Internet.

(eases, easing, eased) 1 make or become less serious. **2** move carefully or gradually. **3** (**ease off** or **up**) do something in a less intense way.

easel noun a wooden frame on legs used by artists for holding the picture they are working on.

east noun **1** the direction in which the sun rises. **2** the eastern part of a place. adjective & adverb **1** towards or facing the east. **2** (of a wind) blowing from the east. ■ **eastward** adjective & adverb **eastwards** adverb.

Easter noun the Christian festival celebrating the resurrection of Jesus. □ **Easter egg** a chocolate egg given as a gift at Easter.

easterly adjective & adverb **1** facing or moving towards the east. **2** (of a wind) blowing from the east.

eastern adjective **1** situated in or facing the east. **2** (**Eastern**) having to do with the part of the world to the east of Europe.

easterner noun a person from the east of a region.

easy adjective (**easier**, **easiest**) **1** able to be done without great effort. **2** free from worry or problems. **3** not anxious or awkward. □ **easy-going** relaxed and open-minded. **easy listening** popular music that is tuneful and undemanding. ■ **easily** adverb.

eat verb (**eats**, **eating**, **ate**; past participle **eaten**) **1** put food into the mouth and chew and swallow it. **2** (**eat away**) gradually wear away or destroy. **3** (**eat up**) use resources in very large quantities. □ **eat your words** admit that what you previously said was wrong. ■ **eatable** adjective.

eatery noun (plural **eateries**) informal a restaurant or cafe.

eau de cologne /oh duh kuh-**lohn**/ = **COLOGNE**.

eaves plural noun the part of a roof that meets or overhangs the walls of a building.

eavesdrop verb (**eavesdrops**, **eavesdropping**, **eavesdropped**) secretly listen to a conversation.

ebb noun the movement of the tide out to sea. verb **1** (of the tide) move away from the land. **2** (**ebb away**) gradually lessen or reduce. □ **at a low ebb** in a poor state.

ebony noun **1** heavy dark wood from a tree of tropical and warm regions. **2** a very dark brown or black colour.

ebullient /i-**bul**-yuhnt/ adjective cheerful and full of energy. ■ **ebullience** noun.

EC abbreviation European Community.

eccentric adjective unconventional and slightly strange. noun an eccentric person. ■ **eccentrically** adverb **eccentricity** noun.

ecclesiastical /i-klee-zi-**ass**-ti-k'l/ adjective relating to the Christian Church or its clergy.

echelon /**esh**-uh-lon/ noun a level or rank in an organization, profession, or society.

echo noun (plural **echoes**) **1** a sound caused by the reflection of sound waves from a surface back to the listener. **2** a reflected radio or radar beam. verb (**echoes**, **echoing**, **echoed**) **1** (of a sound) reverberate or be repeated after the original sound has stopped. **2** continue to have significance or influence. **3** repeat someone's words or opinions. □ **echo chamber** an enclosed space for producing echoes. ■ **echoey** adjective.

eclair /i-**klair**, ay-**klair**/ **noun** a cake of light pastry filled with cream and topped with chocolate icing.

éclat /ay-**klah**/ **noun** a notably brilliant or successful effect.

eclectic **adjective** taking ideas from a wide range of sources.

eclipse **noun 1** an occasion when one planet, the moon, etc. passes between another and the observer, or in front of a planet's source of light. **2** a sudden loss of significance or power. **verb** (**eclipses, eclipsing, eclipsed**) **1** (of a planet, the moon, etc.) obscure the light coming from or shining on another. **2** make less significant or powerful.

eco-friendly **adjective** not harmful to the environment.

ecology **noun** the study of how animals and plants relate to one another and to their surroundings. ■ **ecological** adjective **ecologist** noun.

economic **adjective 1** relating to economics or the economy. **2** profitable, or concerned with profitability.

economical **adjective 1** giving good value in relation to the resources used or money spent. **2** careful in the use of resources or money. ■ **economically** adverb.

economics **plural noun** the study of the production, consumption, and transfer of wealth.

economist **noun** an expert in economics.

economize or **economise** **verb** (**economizes, economizing, economized**) spend less; be economical.

economy **noun** (plural **economies**) **1** the state of a country or region in terms of the production and consumption of goods and services and the supply of money. **2** careful management of resources. **3** a financial saving.

ecosystem **noun** all the plants and animals of a particular area considered in terms of how they interact with their environment.

ecstasy **noun** (plural **ecstasies**) **1** an overwhelming feeling of great happiness or joyful excitement. **2** an emotional or religious frenzy. **3** (**Ecstasy**) an illegal drug that produces feelings of excitement and happiness.

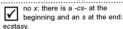

no *x*: there is a -*cs*- at the beginning and an *s* at the end: ecstatic.

ecstatic **adjective** feeling ecstasy. ■ **ecstatically** adverb.

ectoplasm **noun** a substance that is thought by some people to come out of the body of a medium during a seance.

ecumenical **adjective 1** representing a number of different Christian Churches. **2** wishing for the world's Christian Churches to be united.

eczema /**eks**-i-muh/ **noun** a condition in which patches of skin become rough and inflamed.

eddy **noun** (plural **eddies**) a circular movement of water causing a small whirlpool. **verb** (**eddies, eddying, eddied**) (of water, air, etc.) move in a circular way.

edelweiss /**ay**-duhl-vyss/ **noun** a mountain plant with small flowers.

edema US spelling of **OEDEMA**.

Eden **noun 1** (also **Garden of Eden**) the place where Adam and Eve lived in the biblical account of the Creation. **2** a place of unspoilt happiness or beauty.

edge **noun 1** the outside limit of an object, area, or surface. **2** the line along which two surfaces meet. **3** the sharpened side of a blade. **4** a slight advantage over close rivals. **verb** (**edges, edging, edged**) **1** provide with an edge. **2** move slowly and carefully. □ **on edge** tense or irritable.

edgeways or **edgewise** **adverb** with the edge uppermost or towards the viewer. □ **get a word in edgeways** manage to break into a conversation.

edgy **adjective** (**edgier, edgiest**) tense,

nervous, or irritable.

edible adjective fit to be eaten.

edict /ee-dikt/ noun an official order or proclamation.

edifice /ed-i-fiss/ noun a large, imposing building.

edify /ed-i-fÿ/ verb (edifies, edifying, edified) teach someone something that is educational or morally improving. ■ edification noun.

edit verb (edits, editing, edited) 1 prepare written material for publication by correcting or shortening it. 2 prepare material for a recording or broadcast. 3 be editor of a newspaper or magazine. noun a change made as a result of editing.

edition noun 1 a particular form of a published text. 2 the total number of copies of a book, newspaper, etc. that are issued. 3 a particular example of a regular programme or broadcast.

editor noun 1 a person who is in charge of a newspaper or magazine. 2 a person who prepares material for publication or broadcasting.

editorial adjective relating to the editing of material. noun a newspaper article giving the editor's opinion.

educate verb (educates, educating, educated) train or instruct someone to improve their mind or character. □ educated guess a guess based on knowledge and experience.

education noun 1 the process of educating or being educated. 2 the theory and practice of teaching. 3 training in a subject. ■ educational adjective.

Edwardian /ed-wor-di-uhn/ adjective relating to the reign of King Edward VII (1901–10).

EEC abbreviation European Economic Community.

eel noun a snake-like fish with a slender body.

eerie adjective (eerier, eeriest) strange and frightening. ■ eerily adverb.

efface verb (effaces, effacing, effaced) 1 rub off a mark from a surface. 2 (efface yourself) make

yourself appear unimportant.

effect noun 1 a change that something causes in something else; a result. 2 operation or effectiveness. 3 the extent to which something succeeds. 4 (effects) personal belongings. 5 (effects) the lighting, sound, or scenery used in a play or film. verb make something happen. □ in effect in practice, even if not formally acknowledged.

> **i** don't confuse **effect** and **affect**. Effect means 'a result' and means 'make something happen', as in *she effected a cost-cutting exercise*, while **affect** chiefly means 'make a difference to'.

effective adjective 1 producing a desired or intended result; successful. 2 (of a law or policy) in operation. 3 existing in fact, though not formally acknowledged as such. ■ effectively adverb effectiveness noun.

effectual adjective producing the intended result; effective.

effeminate adjective disapproving (of a man) looking, behaving, or sounding like a woman. ■ effeminacy noun.

effervesce verb (effervesces, effervescing, effervesced) (of a liquid) give off bubbles.

effervescent adjective 1 (of a liquid) giving off bubbles; fizzy. 2 lively and enthusiastic. ■ effervescence noun.

effete /i-feet/ adjective 1 weak; feeble. 2 (of a man) effeminate.

efficacious /ef-fi-kay-shuhss/ adjective formal effective.

efficacy /ef-fi-kuh-si/ noun formal effectiveness.

efficient adjective working well with no waste of money or effort. ■ efficiency noun efficiently adverb.

effigy /ef-fi-ji/ noun (plural effigies) a sculpture or statue of a person.

effluent noun liquid waste or sewage discharged into a river or the sea.

effluvium /i-floo-vi-uhm/ noun (plural effluvia /i-floo-vi-uh/) an unpleasant or harmful odour or discharge.

effort noun 1 a vigorous or determined attempt. 2 strenuous exertion.

effortless adjective done or achieved without effort; natural and easy. ∎ **effortlessly** adverb.

effrontery /i-**frun**-tuh-ri/ noun rude and disrespectful behaviour.

effusion noun **1** an instance of giving off a liquid, light, or smell. **2** unrestrained speech or writing.

effusive adjective expressing pleasure or approval in a warm and emotional way. ∎ **effusively** adverb.

e.g. abbreviation for example.

> ℹ️ short for Latin *exempli gratia*, meaning 'for the sake of example'.

egalitarian /i-gal-i-**tair**-i-uhn/ adjective believing that all people are equal and deserve equal rights and opportunities. noun an egalitarian person. ∎ **egalitarianism** noun.

egg[1] noun **1** a small oval or round object laid by a female bird, reptile, fish, etc., and containing a cell which can develop into a new creature. **2** the female reproductive cell of a human or animal. **3** informal, dated a person of a specified kind: *a good egg*.

egg[2] verb (**egg on**) urge someone to do something foolish.

egghead noun informal a very intelligent and hard-working person.

eggplant noun N. Amer. an aubergine.

ego /**ee**-goh/ noun (plural **egos**) **1** a person's sense of their own value and importance. **2** the part of the mind that is responsible for a person's sense of who they are.

egocentric adjective self-centred.

egomania noun obsessive egotism.

egotism or **egoism** noun the quality of being excessively conceited or self-absorbed. ∎ **egotist** (or **egoist**) noun **egotistical** (or **egoistical**) adjective.

egregious /i-**gree**-juhss/ adjective outstandingly bad.

egress /**ee**-gress/ noun formal **1** the action of going out of a place. **2** a way out.

egret /**ee**-grit/ noun a kind of heron with white plumage.

eider /**I**-der/ noun (plural same or **eiders**) a black and white duck that lives in northern countries.

eiderdown noun Brit. a quilt filled with down or some other soft material.

eight cardinal number **1** one more than seven; 8. (Roman numeral: **viii** or **VIII**.) **2** an eight-oared rowing boat.

eighteen cardinal number one more than seventeen; 18. (Roman numeral: **xviii** or **XVIII**.) ∎ **eighteenth** ordinal number.

eighth ordinal number **1** at number eight in a sequence; 8th. **2** (**an eighth** or **one eighth**) each of eight equal parts of something.

> ✓ there are two *h*'s: eig*hth*.

eighty cardinal number (plural **eighties**) ten less than ninety; 80. (Roman numeral: **lxxx** or **LXXX**.) ∎ **eightieth** ordinal number.

eisteddfod /I-**steth**-vod/ noun a Welsh festival with music and poetry competitions.

either conjunction & adverb **1** used before the first of two alternatives specified. **2** used to indicate a similarity or link with a statement just made. **3** for that matter; moreover. determiner & pronoun **1** one or the other of two people or things. **2** each of two.

ejaculate verb (**ejaculates, ejaculating, ejaculated**) **1** (of a man or male animal) eject semen from the penis at the moment of orgasm. **2** dated say something quickly and suddenly. ∎ **ejaculation** noun.

eject verb **1** force or throw out violently or suddenly. **2** (of a pilot) escape from an aircraft by means of an ejection seat. **3** make someone leave a place. ☐ **ejection seat** (or **ejector seat**) a seat that can throw the pilot out of the aircraft in an emergency. ∎ **ejection** noun.

eke verb (**ekes, eking, eked**) (**eke out**) **1** make a supply of something last a long time. **2** make a living with difficulty.

elaborate adjective /i-**lab**-uh-ruht/ involving many carefully arranged parts; complicated. **verb** /i-**lab**-uh-rayt/ (**elaborates, elaborating, elaborated**) develop something in more detail. ■ **elaborately** adverb **elaboration** noun.

elan /ay-**lan**, ay-**lon**/ noun energy and flair.

elapse verb (**elapses, elapsing, elapsed**) (of time) pass.

elastic adjective **1** able to go back to its normal shape after being stretched or squeezed. **2** flexible. **noun** cord or fabric which returns to its original length or shape after being stretched. □ **elastic band** a rubber band. ■ **elasticity** noun.

elasticated adjective Brit. (of a garment or material) made elastic with rubber thread or tape.

elated adjective extremely happy and excited.

elation noun great happiness and excitement.

elbow noun the joint between the forearm and the upper arm. **verb 1** strike with the elbow. **2** push someone away roughly. □ **elbow grease** informal hard work in cleaning something.

elder[1] adjective older. **noun 1** (**your elder**) a person who is older than you are. **2** a leader or senior figure in a tribe.

elder[2] noun a small tree or shrub with white flowers and bluish-black or red berries (**elderberries**).

elderly adjective old or ageing.

eldest adjective oldest.

elect verb **1** choose someone to hold a position by voting. **2** choose to do something. **adjective 1** chosen or singled out. **2** elected to a position but not yet in office: *the President Elect*.

election noun **1** a procedure by which a person is elected. **2** the action of electing.

electioneering noun the action of campaigning to be elected.

elective adjective **1** using or chosen by election. **2** (of study, treatment, etc.) chosen; not compulsory.

elector noun a person who has the right to vote in an election.

electoral adjective relating to elections or electors. □ **electoral roll** (or **electoral register**) an official list of the people in a district who are entitled to vote in an election.

electorate noun the people who are entitled to vote in an election.

electric adjective **1** of, worked by, or producing electricity. **2** thrillingly exciting. noun (**electrics**) Brit. the system of electric wiring and parts in a house or vehicle. □ **electric blue** a brilliant light blue. **electric chair** a chair in which convicted criminals are executed by electrocution. **electric shock** a sudden discharge of electricity through a part of the body. **electric storm** a thunderstorm.

electrical adjective concerned with, operating by, or producing electricity. ■ **electrically** adverb.

electrician noun a person who installs and maintains electrical equipment.

electricity noun **1** a form of energy resulting from charged particles. **2** the supply of electric current to a building for heating, lighting, etc. **3** thrilling excitement.

electrify verb (**electrifies, electrifying, electrified**) **1** charge something with electricity. **2** convert something to use electrical power. **3** (**electrifying**) thrillingly exciting.

electroconvulsive adjective (of therapy for mental illness) using electric shocks applied to the brain.

electrocute verb (**electrocutes, electrocuting, electrocuted**) injure or kill by electric shock. ■ **electrocution** noun.

electrode noun a conductor through which electricity enters or leaves something.

electrolysis /i-lek-**trol**-i-siss/ noun **1** the separation of a liquid into its chemical parts by passing an electric current through it. **2** the removal of hair roots or small blemishes on the skin by means of an electric current.

electrolyte noun a liquid or gel that an electric current can pass through, e.g. in a battery.

electromagnet noun a metal core made into a magnet by passing electric current through a surrounding coil.

electromagnetic adjective relating to electric currents and magnetic fields. ■ **electromagnetism** noun.

electromotive adjective tending to produce an electric current.

electron noun a subatomic particle with a negative charge found in all atoms. □ **electron microscope** a powerful microscope using electron beams instead of light.

electronic adjective **1** having parts such as microchips and transistors that control and direct electric currents. **2** relating to electrons or electronics. **3** carried out by means of a computer. □ **electronic mail** email. ■ **electronically** adverb.

electronics plural noun **1** the study of the behaviour and movement of electrons. **2** circuits or devices using transistors, microchips, etc.

electroplate verb (**electroplates**, **electroplating**, **electroplated**) coat a metal object with another metal using electrolysis.

elegant adjective **1** graceful and stylish. **2** pleasingly ingenious and simple. ■ **elegance** noun **elegantly** adverb.

elegiac /el-i-**jy**-uhk/ adjective **1** characteristic of an elegy. **2** wistfully mournful.

elegy /**el**-i-ji/ noun (plural **elegies**) a mournful poem, typically a lament for a dead person.

element noun **1** a basic part of something. **2** each of more than one hundred substances that cannot be changed or broken down. **3** any of the four substances (earth, water, air, and fire) which were formerly believed to make up all matter. **4** a trace. **5** a distinct group within a larger group. **6** (**the elements**) the weather. **7** a part in an electric device through which

an electric current is passed to provide heat.

elemental adjective **1** fundamental. **2** of or resembling the primitive forces of nature.

elementary adjective **1** relating to the most basic aspects of a subject. **2** straightforward and uncomplicated.

elephant noun (plural **elephant** or **elephants**) a very large mammal with a trunk, long curved tusks, and large ears, found in Africa and Asia.

elephantine /el-i-**fan**-tyn/ adjective resembling an elephant.

elevate verb (**elevates**, **elevating**, **elevated**) **1** lift to a higher position. **2** raise to a higher level or status.

elevated adjective of a high intellectual or moral level.

elevation noun **1** the action of elevating. **2** height above a given level, especially sea level. **3** the angle of something with the horizontal.

elevator noun **1** N. Amer. a lift in a building. **2** a machine for lifting grain to a storage space. **3** a hinged flap on the tailplane of an aircraft used to control its motion.

eleven cardinal number **1** one more than ten; 11. (Roman numeral: **xi** or **XI**.) **2** a sports team of eleven players. □ **eleven-plus** (in the UK) an examination that children used to take at the age of 11–12 to decide what type of secondary school they should go to. **the eleventh hour** the latest possible moment. ■ **eleventh** ordinal number.

elevenses plural noun Brit. informal light refreshments taken at about eleven o'clock in the morning.

elf noun (plural **elves**) (in folk tales) a creature resembling a small human figure with pointed ears.

elfin adjective (of a person) small and delicate.

elicit /i-**liss**-it/ verb (**elicits**, **eliciting**, **elicited**) produce or draw out a response or reaction.

elide /i-**lyd**/ verb (**elides**, **eliding**, **elided**) **1** omit a sound or syllable when speaking. **2** join together.

eligible adjective **1** satisfying the conditions to do or receive something. **2** desirable as a husband or wife.

eliminate verb (eliminates, eliminating, eliminated) **1** completely remove or get rid of. **2** exclude a competitor from a sporting competition by beating them. ■ **elimination** noun.

elision /i-li-zh'n/ noun the omission of a sound or syllable in speech.

elite /i-leet, ay-leet/ noun a group of people regarded as the best in a particular society or organization.

elitism noun **1** the belief that a society should be run by an elite. **2** the superior attitude associated with an elite. ■ **elitist** adjective & noun.

elixir /i-lik-ser, i-lik-seer/ noun a potion believed to make people live for ever or have other magical effects.

Elizabethan adjective relating to the reign of Queen Elizabeth I (1558–1603).

elk noun (plural **elk** or **elks**) a kind of large deer.

ellipse noun a regular oval shape.

ellipsis /i-lip-siss/ noun (plural **ellipses** /i-lip-seez/) **1** the omission of words from speech or writing. **2** a set of dots indicating such an omission.

elliptical adjective **1** (also **elliptic**) having the form of an ellipse. **2** (of speech or text) having a word or words deliberately left out.

elm noun a tall tree with rough leaves.

elocution noun the skill of clear and expressive speech.

elongate verb (elongates, elongating, elongated) make or become longer.

elope verb (elopes, eloping, eloped) run away secretly to get married.

eloquence noun fluent or persuasive speaking or writing.

eloquent adjective **1** fluent or persuasive in speech or writing. **2** clearly expressive. ■ **eloquently** adverb.

else adverb **1** in addition. **2** different; instead. □ **or else** if not; otherwise.

elsewhere adverb in, at, or to some other place or other places.

elucidate verb (elucidates, elucidating, elucidated) make clear; explain. ■ **elucidation** noun.

elude verb (eludes, eluding, eluded) **1** cleverly escape from or avoid. **2** fail to be understood or achieved by.

elusive adjective difficult to find, catch, or achieve.

elver noun a young eel.

elves plural of **ELF**.

emaciated /i-may-si-ay-tid/ adjective abnormally thin and weak. ■ **emaciation** noun.

email noun the sending of electronic messages from one computer user to another via a network. verb send a message using email.

emanate /em-uh-nayt/ verb (emanates, emanating, emanated) **1** (emanate from) come out from a place or source. **2** give out. ■ **emanation** noun.

emancipate verb (emancipates, emancipating, emancipated) **1** set free from restrictions. **2** free from slavery. ■ **emancipation** noun.

emasculate verb (emasculates, emasculating, emasculated) **1** make weaker or less effective. **2** deprive a man of his male role or identity. ■ **emasculation** noun.

embalm verb treat a dead body to preserve it from decay.

embankment noun **1** a wall or bank built to prevent flooding by a river. **2** a bank of earth or stone built to carry a road or railway over an area of low ground.

embargo /em-bar-goh/ noun (plural **embargoes**) an official ban, especially on trade with a particular country. verb (embargoes, embargoing, embargoed) impose an embargo on.

embark verb **1** go on board a ship or aircraft. **2** (embark on) begin a new project or course of action. ■ **embarkation** noun.

embarrass verb **1** make someone feel awkward or ashamed. **2** (be embarrassed) be in financial difficulties. ■ **embarrassment** noun.

 two *r*s, two *s*s: emba*rr*a*ss*.

embassy noun (plural **embassies**) the official residence or offices of an ambassador.

embattled adjective 1 surrounded by enemy forces. 2 having a lot of difficulties.

embed or **imbed** verb (**embeds**, **embedding**, **embedded**) fix something firmly in a surrounding mass.

embellish verb 1 make more attractive; decorate. 2 add extra details to a story.

ember noun a piece of burning wood or coal in a dying fire.

embezzle verb (**embezzles**, **embezzling**, **embezzled**) steal money that you have been given responsibility for. ■ **embezzler** noun.

embittered adjective bitter or resentful.

emblazon /im-**blay**-zuhn/ verb conspicuously display a design on something.

emblem noun a design or symbol as a badge of a nation, organization, or family.

emblematic adjective representing a particular quality or idea.

embody verb (**embodies**, **embodying**, **embodied**) 1 give a tangible or visible form to an idea or quality. 2 include or contain a part. ■ **embodiment** noun.

embolden verb make someone braver or more confident.

embolism /**em**-buh-li-z'm/ noun obstruction of an artery by a clot of blood or an air bubble.

emboss verb carve a raised design on.

embrace verb (**embraces**, **embracing**, **embraced**) 1 hold someone closely in your arms. 2 include or contain. 3 willingly accept or support a belief or change. noun an act of embracing.

embrocation noun a liquid medication rubbed on the body to relieve pain from strains.

embroider verb (**embroiders**, **embroidering**, **embroidered**) 1 sew decorative needlework patterns on. 2 add false or exaggerated details to.

embroidery noun (plural **embroideries**) 1 the art of embroidering. 2 embroidered cloth.

embroil verb (usu. **embroil in**) involve someone in a conflict or difficult situation.

embryo /**em**-bri-oh/ noun (plural **embryos**) an unborn or unhatched baby or animal in the early stages of development.

embryonic adjective 1 relating to an embryo. 2 at a rudimentary stage.

emend verb correct and revise a text.

emerald noun 1 a green precious stone. 2 a bright green colour.

emerge verb (**emerges**, **emerging**, **emerged**) 1 become gradually visible. 2 (of facts) become known. 3 recover from a difficult period. ■ **emergence** noun.

emergency noun (plural **emergencies**) a serious and unexpected situation requiring immediate action.

emergent adjective new and still developing.

emeritus /i-**me**-ri-tuhss/ adjective having retired but allowed to keep a title as an honour: *an emeritus professor.* ·

emery board noun a strip of thin wood or card coated with a rough material and used as a nail file.

emetic /i-**met**-ik/ adjective causing vomiting.

emigrant noun a person who emigrates.

emigrate verb (**emigrates**, **emigrating**, **emigrated**) leave your own country and settle permanently in another. ■ **emigration** noun.

émigré /**em**-i-gray/ noun a person who has emigrated.

eminence noun 1 the quality of being very accomplished and respected in a particular area. **2** an important or distinguished person.

eminent adjective **1** very accomplished and respected; distinguished. **2** outstanding or conspicuous. ■ **eminently** adverb.

emir /e-**meer**/ or **amir** /uh-**meer**/ noun a title of some Muslim rulers.

emissary /**em**-i-suh-ri/ noun (plural **emissaries**) a person sent as a diplomatic representative on a mission.

emission noun **1** the action of emitting. **2** a substance which is emitted.

emit verb (**emits, emitting, emitted**) **1** discharge; send out. **2** make a sound.

emollient /i-**mol**-li-uhnt/ adjective **1** softening or soothing the skin. **2** attempting to avoid confrontation; calming. ■ **emollience** noun.

emolument /i-**mol**-yuu-muhnt/ noun formal a salary or fee.

emotion noun **1** a strong feeling, such as joy or anger. **2** instinctive feeling as opposed to reasoning.

emotional adjective **1** relating to the emotions. **2** arousing or showing emotion. ■ **emotionally** adverb.

emotive adjective arousing intense feeling.

empathize or **empathise** verb (**empathizes, empathizing, empathized**) understand and share the feelings of someone else.

empathy noun the ability to understand and share the feelings of someone else.

> ℹ️ strictly, **empathy** does not mean the same thing as **sympathy**: if you have **empathy** for someone you understand and share their feelings, whereas if you have **sympathy** for them you feel sorry for them.

emperor noun the ruler of an empire.

emphasis /**em**-fuh-siss/ noun (plural **emphases** /**em**-fuh-seez/) **1** special importance or value given to something. **2** stress laid on a word or words in speaking.

emphasize or **emphasise** verb (**emphasizes, emphasizing, emphasized**) give special importance or prominence to.

emphatic adjective **1** showing or giving emphasis. **2** definite and clear. ■ **emphatically** adverb.

emphysema /em-fi-**see**-muh/ noun a condition that affects the lungs, causing breathlessness.

empire noun **1** a large group of countries under a single authority or ruler. **2** a large commercial organization under the control of one person or group.

empirical adjective based on observation or experience rather than theory or logic. ■ **empirically** adverb **empiricism** noun **empiricist** noun.

emplacement noun a structure or platform where a gun is placed for firing.

employ verb **1** give work to someone and pay them for it. **2** make use of. **3** keep someone occupied.

employee noun a person who is employed by a company or individual.

employer noun a company or individual that employs people.

employment noun **1** the action of employing. **2** a person's work or profession.

emporium /em-**por**-i-uhm/ noun (plural **emporia** or **emporiums**) a large store selling a wide variety of goods.

empower verb (**empowers, empowering, empowered**) **1** give authority or power to. **2** give strength and confidence to. ■ **empowerment** noun.

empress noun **1** a female emperor. **2** the wife or widow of an emperor.

empty adjective (**emptier, emptiest**) **1** containing nothing; not filled or occupied. **2** (of words or gestures) having no real meaning: *an empty threat.* verb (**empties, emptying, emptied**) **1** make or become empty. **2** remove everything that is in a container. **3** (of a river) flow into the sea or a lake. ■ **emptiness** noun.

emu noun a large flightless bird similar to an ostrich, found in Australia.

emulate verb (emulates, emulating, emulated) try to equal or surpass. ■ **emulation** noun.

emulsify verb (emulsifies, emulsifying, emulsified) combine two liquids into a smooth mixture. ■ **emulsifier** noun.

emulsion noun **1** a smooth liquid in which particles of oil or fat are evenly distributed. **2** a type of paint for walls and ceilings. **3** a light-sensitive coating for photographic film.

enable verb (enables, enabling, enabled) **1** provide with the ability or means to do something. **2** make something possible.

enact verb **1** pass a law. **2** act out a role or play. ■ **enactment** noun.

enamel noun **1** a coloured glassy substance applied to metal, glass, or pottery for decoration or protection. **2** the hard substance that covers the crown of a tooth. **3** a paint that dries to give a hard coat. verb (enamels, enamelling, enamelled; US spelling enamels, enameling, enameled) coat or decorate with enamel.

enamour (US spelling enamor) verb (be enamoured of, with, or by) be filled with love or admiration for.

en bloc /on blok/ adverb all together, or all at once.

encamp verb settle in or establish a camp.

encampment noun a place where a camp is set up.

encapsulate verb (encapsulates, encapsulating, encapsulated) **1** symbolize or sum up. **2** summarize clearly in few words.

encase verb (encases, encasing, encased) enclose or cover in a case.

encephalitis /en-sef-uh-ly-tiss/ noun inflammation of the brain.

enchant verb **1** delight; charm. **2** put under a spell. ■ **enchanter** noun **enchantment** noun **enchantress** noun.

enchanting adjective delightfully charming or attractive.

encircle verb (encircles, encircling, encircled) form a circle around.

enclave /en-klayv/ noun a small area of one country's territory surrounded by another country.

enclose verb (encloses, enclosing, enclosed) **1** surround or close off on all sides. **2** put a document or object in an envelope along with a letter.

enclosure noun **1** an enclosed area. **2** a document or object put in an envelope along with a letter.

encode verb (encodes, encoding, encoded) convert into a coded form.

encompass verb **1** surround and hold something. **2** include comprehensively.

encore /ong-kor/ noun a short extra performance given at the end of a concert in response to calls by the audience.

encounter verb (encounters, encountering, encountered) unexpectedly meet or be faced with. noun **1** an unexpected or casual meeting. **2** a confrontation.

encourage verb (encourages, encouraging, encouraged) **1** give support, confidence, or hope to. **2** help the development of. ■ **encouragement** noun **encouraging** adjective.

encroach verb **1** (encroach on) gradually intrude on a person's territory, rights, etc. **2** gradually advance beyond expected or acceptable limits. ■ **encroachment** noun.

encrust verb cover with a hard crust.

encrypt verb convert into code. ■ **encryption** noun.

encumber verb (encumbers, encumbering, encumbered) be a burden to.

encumbrance noun a burden or impediment.

encyclopedia or **encyclopaedia** noun a book or set of books giving information on many subjects. ■ **encyclopedic** adjective.

end noun **1** the final part of something. **2** the furthest or most extreme part. **3** the stopping of a state or situation. **4** a person's death or downfall. **5** a goal or desired result. verb **1** come or bring to an end. **2** (end in) have a specified result. **3 (end up)** eventually reach or come to a particular state or place. □ **make ends meet** earn just enough money to live on.

endanger verb (**endangers, endangering, endangered**) put in danger.

endangered adjective in danger of extinction.

endear verb (**endear to**) make someone loved or liked by.

endearing adjective inspiring love or affection. ■ **endearingly** adverb.

endearment noun **1** love or affection. **2** a word or phrase expressing affection.

endeavour (US spelling **endeavor**) verb try hard to achieve something. noun **1** an attempt to achieve something. **2** concentrated hard work and effort.

endemic /en-**dem**-ik/ adjective **1** (of a disease or condition) regularly found among particular people or in a certain area. **2** (of a plant or animal) native to a certain area.

ending noun an end or final part.

endive /**en**-dyv, **en**-div/ noun a plant with bitter leaves, eaten in salads.

endless adjective **1** having or seeming to have no end. **2** innumerable. ■ **endlessly** adverb.

endocrine /**en**-duh-kryn/ adjective (of a gland) secreting hormones or other products directly into the blood.

endorphin /en-**dor**-fin/ noun a pain-killing hormone within the brain and nervous system.

endorse verb (**endorses, endorsing, endorsed**) **1** publicly state that you approve of. **2** sign a cheque on the back so that it can be paid into an account. **3** Brit. mark details of a driving offence on a driving licence. ■ **endorsement** noun.

endow verb **1** give someone your property, or leave it to them in your will. **2** donate a large sum of money to an institution, from which they will be able to receive a regular income. **3** (**be endowed with**) have as a natural quality or characteristic.

endowment noun **1** property or a regular income that has been given or left to a person or an institution. **2** a quality or ability that you are born with. □ **endowment mortgage** Brit. a mortgage linked to an insurance policy, in which the sum received when the policy matures is used to pay back the money borrowed.

endpaper noun a leaf of paper at the beginning or end of a book, fixed to the inside of the cover.

endurance noun **1** the ability to do or cope with something painful or difficult for a long time. **2** the quality of lasting for a long time before wearing out.

endure verb (**endures, enduring, endured**) **1** experience and be able to cope with prolonged pain or difficulty. **2** tolerate. **3** last for a long time.

enema /**en**-i-muh/ noun a process in which liquid is injected into the rectum to clean it out.

enemy noun (plural **enemies**) **1** a person who is hostile to you. **2** (**the enemy**) a country that your own is fighting in a war.

energetic adjective having a lot of energy. ■ **energetically** adverb.

energize or **energise** verb (**energizes, energizing, energized**) give energy and enthusiasm to.

energy noun (plural **energies**) **1** the strength and vitality that you need in order to be active. **2** (**energies**) a person's physical and mental powers. **3** power obtained from physical or chemical resources to provide light and heat or to work machines.

enervate /**en**-er-vayt/ verb (**enervates, enervating, enervated**) cause someone to feel drained of energy.

enfant terrible /on-fon te-**ree**-bluh/ noun (plural **enfants terribles** /on-fon te-**ree**-bluh/) a person who is known for being unconventional or controversial.

enfeeble verb (**enfeebles, enfeebling, enfeebled**) make someone weak.

enfold verb envelop someone.

enforce verb (**enforces, enforcing, enforced**) **1** make sure a law or rule is obeyed. **2** force something to happen or someone to do something. ■ **enforceable** adjective **enforcement** noun **enforcer** noun.

enfranchise verb (**enfranchises, enfranchising, enfranchised**) **1** give a person or group the right to vote. **2** historical free a slave. ■ **enfranchisement** noun.

engage verb (**engages, engaging, engaged**) **1** attract or involve someone's interest or attention. **2** (**engage in** or **with**) become involved in. **3** chiefly Brit. employ or hire. **4** move a part of a machine or engine into position.

engaged adjective **1** occupied. **2** Brit. (of a telephone line) unavailable because already in use. **3** having formally agreed to get married.

engagement noun **1** a formal agreement to get married. **2** an appointment. **3** the state of being involved in something. **4** fighting between armed forces.

engaging adjective charming and attractive. ■ **engagingly** adverb.

engender verb (**engenders, engendering, engendered**) give rise to.

engine noun **1** a machine with moving parts that converts power into motion. **2** a railway locomotive.

engineer noun **1** a person who is qualified in engineering. **2** a person who maintains or controls an engine or machine. **3** a person who makes something happen. verb (**engineers, engineering, engineered**) **1** design and build. **2** arrange for something to happen.

engineering noun the study of the design, building, and use of engines, machines, and structures.

English noun the language of England, used in many varieties throughout the· world. adjective relating to England.

engorged adjective swollen.

engrained ⇒ **INGRAINED**.

engrave verb (**engraves, engraving, engraved**) **1** carve a text or design on a hard surface or object. **2** (**be engraved on** or **in**) be fixed in the mind. ■ **engraver** noun.

engraving noun **1** a print made from an engraved plate or block. **2** the process of engraving.

engross /in-**grohss**/ verb (often **be engrossed in**) absorb all of someone's attention.

engulf verb (of a natural force) sweep over someone or something and completely surround or cover them.

enhance verb (**enhances, enhancing, enhanced**) increase the quality, value, or extent of something. ■ **enhancement** noun.

enigma noun a mysterious or puzzling person or thing. ■ **enigmatic** adjective **enigmatically** adverb.

enjoin verb instruct or urge someone to do something.

enjoy verb **1** get pleasure from. **2** (**enjoy yourself**) have a good time. **3** have and benefit from. ■ **enjoyment** noun.

enjoyable adjective giving pleasure. ■ **enjoyably** adverb.

enlarge verb (**enlarges, enlarging, enlarged**) **1** make or become bigger. **2** (**enlarge on**) speak or write about something in greater detail.

enlargement noun **1** the state of being enlarged. **2** a photograph that is larger than the original negative or than an earlier print.

enlighten verb **1** give someone greater knowledge and understanding. **2** (**enlightened**) well informed and able to make good judgements. ■ **enlightenment** noun.

enlist verb **1** join the armed services. **2** ask for someone's help in doing something. ■ **enlistment** noun.

enliven verb **1** make something more interesting. **2** make someone more cheerful or animated.

en masse /on **mass**/ adverb all together.

enmesh verb (usu. **be enmeshed in**) entangle.

enmity noun (plural **enmities**) hostility.

ennoble verb (**ennobles, ennobling, ennobled**) give greater dignity to.

ennui /on-**wee**/ noun a feeling of listlessness, boredom, and dissatisfaction.

enormity noun (plural **enormities**) **1** (**the enormity of**) the extreme seriousness of something bad. **2** great size or scale. **3** a grave crime or sin.

enormous adjective very large. ■ **enormously** adverb.

enough determiner & pronoun as much or as many as is necessary or desirable. adverb **1** to the required degree. **2** to a moderate degree.

enquire verb (**enquires, enquiring, enquired**) **1** ask for information. **2** (**enquire after**) ask how someone is. **3** (**enquire into**) investigate.

enquiry noun (plural **enquiries**) **1** an act of asking for information. **2** an official investigation.

enrage verb (**enrages, enraging, enraged**) make someone very angry.

enrapture verb (**enraptures, enrapturing, enraptured**) give intense pleasure or joy to someone.

enrich verb **1** improve the quality or value of. **2** improve something by adding an extra item or ingredient. ■ **enrichment** noun.

enrol (US spelling **enroll**) verb (**enrols, enrolling, enrolled**) officially register or recruit someone as a member or student. ■ **enrolment** (US spelling **enrollment**) noun.

en route /on **root**/ adverb on the way.

ensconce verb (**ensconces, ensconcing, ensconced**) establish in a comfortable, safe, or secret place.

ensemble /on-**som**-buhl/ noun **1** a group of musicians, actors, or dancers who perform together. **2** a group of items viewed as a whole.

enshrine verb (**enshrines, enshrining, enshrined**) preserve a right, tradition, or idea in a form that gives it protection and respect.

enshroud verb completely envelop something and hide it from view.

ensign noun a flag.

enslave verb (**enslaves, enslaving, enslaved**) **1** make someone a slave. **2** make someone dependent on something. ■ **enslavement** noun.

ensnare verb (**ensnares, ensnaring, ensnared**) **1** catch an animal in a trap. **2** keep someone in a situation from which they cannot escape.

ensue verb (**ensues, ensuing, ensued**) happen afterwards or as a result.

en suite /on **sweet**/ adjective & adverb Brit. (of a bathroom) leading directly off a bedroom.

ensure verb (**ensures, ensuring, ensured**) **1** make certain that something will turn out in a particular way. **2** (**ensure against**) make sure that a problem does not occur.

entail verb involve something as an inevitable part or consequence.

entangle verb (**entangles, entangling, entangled**) **1** cause something to become tangled. **2** involve someone in complicated circumstances. ■ **entanglement** noun.

entente /on-**tont**/ or **entente cordiale** /on-tont kor-di-**ahl**/ noun a friendly understanding between people or countries.

enter verb (**enters, entering, entered**) **1** come or go into. **2** (often **enter into** or **on**) begin to be involved in or do. **3** join an institution or profession. **4** register as a participant in. **5** (**enter into**) undertake to be bound by a contract or agreement. **6** record information in a book, computer, etc.

enterprise noun **1** a project. **2** the ability to think of and set up new projects. **3** a business or company.

enterprising adjective having the ability to think of and set up new projects.

entertain verb **1** provide someone with interest or amusement. **2** receive someone as a guest and provide them with food and drink. **3** give consideration to. ■ **entertainer** noun.

entertaining adjective providing amusement or enjoyment. ■ **entertainingly** adverb.

entertainment noun **1** the action of entertaining. **2** an event or activity designed to entertain others.

enthral (US spelling **enthrall**) verb (**enthrals**, **enthralling**, **enthralled**) fascinate someone and hold their attention.

> ☑ one *l* in **enthral** and **enthrals**, two in **enthralled** and **enthralling**.

enthrone verb (**enthrones**, **enthroning**, **enthroned**) mark the new reign of a king or queen by a ceremony in which they sit on a throne. ■ **enthronement** noun.

enthuse verb (**enthuses**, **enthusing**, **enthused**) **1** (often **enthuse over**) express enthusiasm about something. **2** make someone enthusiastic.

enthusiasm noun excited interest in and enjoyment of something.

enthusiast noun a person who is very interested in and greatly enjoys a particular activity.

enthusiastic adjective feeling very interested in and happy about something. ■ **enthusiastically** adverb.

entice verb (**entices**, **enticing**, **enticed**) attract someone by offering them something desirable. ■ **enticingly** adverb.

entire adjective with no part left out; whole.

entirely adverb **1** wholly; completely. **2** solely.

entirety noun (**the entirety**) the whole. □ **in its entirety** as a whole.

entitle verb (**entitles**, **entitling**, **entitled**) **1** give someone a right to do or have something. **2** give a title to a book, play, etc. ■ **entitlement** noun.

entity noun (plural **entities**) a thing which exists independently.

entomb verb **1** place someone in a tomb. **2** bury or completely cover.

entomology noun the study of insects. ■ **entomological** adjective **entomologist** noun.

entourage /on-toor-ah*zh*/ noun a group of people attending an important person.

entrails plural noun a person's or animal's intestines or internal organs.

entrance[1] /en-truhnss/ noun **1** a door or passageway into a place. **2** an act of entering. **3** the right or opportunity to go into a place.

entrance[2] /in-**trahnss**/ verb (**entrances**, **entrancing**, **entranced**) **1** fill someone with wonder and delight. **2** cast a spell on.

entrant noun a person who joins or takes part in something.

entrap verb (**entraps**, **entrapping**, **entrapped**) **1** catch a person or animal in a trap. **2** trick someone into committing a crime in order to have them prosecuted. ■ **entrapment** noun.

entreat verb ask someone earnestly or anxiously to do something.

entreaty noun (plural **entreaties**) an earnest request.

entrée /**on**-tray/ noun **1** the main course of a meal. **2** Brit. a dish served between the first and main courses at a formal dinner. **3** the right to enter a place or social group.

entrench verb **1** establish a military force in fortified positions. **2** (**be entrenched**) be so firmly established that change is difficult. ■ **entrenchment** noun.

entrepreneur /on-truh-pruh-**ner**/ noun a person who is successful in setting up businesses. ■ **entrepreneurial** /on-truh-pruh-**ner**-i-uhl/ adjective.

entropy noun Physics a quantity expressing how much of a system's thermal energy is unavailable for conversion into mechanical work.

entrust verb make someone responsible for doing or looking after something.

entry noun (plural **entries**) **1** an act of entering. **2** a door or passageway into a place. **3** the right or opportunity to enter. **4** an item included in a list, reference book, etc.

entwine verb (**entwines**, **entwining**, **entwined**) wind or twist together.

enumerate verb (enumerates, enumerating, enumerated) mention a number of things one by one. ■ enumeration noun.

enunciate verb (enunciates, enunciating, enunciated) **1** say or pronounce clearly. **2** set something out clearly and precisely. ■ enunciation noun.

envelop /in-**vel**-uhp/ verb (envelops, enveloping, enveloped) wrap up, cover, or surround completely.

 unlike the noun *envelope*, the verb **envelop** has no *e* on the end.

envelope /en-vuh-lohp/ noun **1** a flat paper container with a sealable flap, used to enclose a letter or document. **2** a covering or enclosing structure or layer.

enviable adjective offering something desirable. ■ enviably adverb.

envious adjective feeling discontented because you want something that someone else has. ■ enviously adverb.

environment noun **1** the surroundings in which a person, animal, or plant lives or operates. **2** (the environment) the natural world. ■ environmental adjective environmentally adverb.

 remember the *n*: environment.

environmentalist noun a person who is concerned with the protection of the environment. ■ environmentalism noun.

environs plural noun the surrounding area or district.

envisage /in-**viz**-ij/ verb (envisages, envisaging, envisaged) **1** see something as a possibility. **2** form a mental picture of.

envoy noun a messenger or representative.

envy noun (plural envies) **1** a feeling of wanting something that belongs to someone else. **2** (the envy of) a thing that is much desired by. verb (envies, envying, envied) wish that you had the same possessions or opportunities as someone.

enzyme /en-zym/ noun a substance produced by an animal or plant which helps a chemical change happen without being changed itself.

eon US spelling of **AEON**.

epaulette /e-puh-**let**/ (US spelling **epaulet**) noun a flap attached to the shoulder of a coat or jacket.

ephemera /i-**fem**-uh-ruh, i-**feem**-uh-ruh/ plural noun things that people use or are interested in for only a short time.

ephemeral adjective lasting only for a short time.

epic noun **1** a long poem about the actions of great men or women or about a nation's history. **2** a long film or book dealing with a long period of time. adjective **1** having to do with an epic. **2** great and impressive in scale or character.

epicentre (US spelling **epicenter**) noun the point on the earth's surface where the effects of an earthquake are felt most strongly.

epicure noun a person who enjoys and is interested in good food and drink. ■ epicurean noun & adjective.

epidemic noun a situation in which a large number of people have caught the same infectious disease.

epidermis noun **1** the surface layer of an animal's skin, overlying the dermis. **2** the outer layer of tissue in a plant. ■ epidermal adjective.

epidural noun an anaesthetic injected into the space around the spinal cord, especially during childbirth.

epiglottis noun a flap of cartilage in the throat that descends during swallowing to cover the opening of the windpipe.

epigram noun **1** a concise and witty saying. **2** a short witty poem. ■ epigrammatic adjective.

epigraph noun **1** an inscription on a building, statue, or coin. **2** a short quotation introducing a book or chapter.

epilepsy noun a disorder of the nervous system that causes regular convulsions and loss of consciousness. ■ **epileptic** adjective & noun.

epilogue (US spelling **epilog**) noun a section at the end of a book or play which comments on what has happened.

epiphany noun (plural **epiphanies**) **1** (Epiphany) (in the Bible) the time when the Magi visited the baby Jesus in Bethlehem. **2** a sudden and inspiring revelation.

episcopacy /i-**piss**-kuh-puh-si/ noun (plural **episcopacies**) **1** government of a Church by bishops. **2** (the episcopacy) the bishops of a region or church as a group.

episcopal /i-**piss**-kuh-puhl/ adjective having to do with a bishop or bishops.

episcopalian /i-piss-kuh-**pay**-li-uhn/ adjective having to do with the government of a Church by bishops. noun a supporter of government of a Church by bishops.

episode noun **1** an event or group of events occurring as part of a sequence. **2** each of the separate parts into which a serialized story or programme is divided.

episodic adjective **1** made up of a series of separate events. **2** occurring at irregular intervals.

epistemology /i-piss-ti-**mol**-uh-ji/ noun the branch of philosophy that deals with knowledge.

epistle /i-**piss**-uhl/ noun **1** formal a letter. **2** (Epistle) a book of the New Testament in the form of a letter from an Apostle.

epistolary adjective **1** relating to the writing of letters. **2** (of a literary work) in the form of letters.

epitaph noun words written in memory of a person who has died.

epithet noun a word or phrase describing someone or something's character or most important quality.

epitome /i-**pit**-uh-mi/ noun (the epitome of) a perfect example of something.

epitomize or **epitomise** verb (epitomizes, epitomizing, epitomized) be a perfect example of.

epoch /**ee**-pok/ noun a long and distinct period of time.

eponym /**ep**-uh-nim/ noun **1** a person after whom something is named. **2** a word or phrase based on someone's name.

eponymous /i-**pon**-i-muhss/ adjective **1** (of a person) giving their name to something. **2** (of a thing) named after a particular person.

epsilon noun the fifth letter of the Greek alphabet (Ε, ε).

equable /**ek**-wuh-b'l/ adjective **1** calm and even-tempered. **2** (of a climate) not changing very much. ■ **equably** adverb.

equal adjective **1** the same in quantity, size, value, or status. **2** evenly balanced. **3** (equal to) able to face a challenge. noun a person or thing that is equal to another. verb (equals, equalling, equalled; US spelling equals, equaling, equaled) **1** be equal to. **2** be as good as. ■ **equally** adverb.

equality noun the state of having the same rights, opportunities, or advantages as others.

equalize or **equalise** verb (equalizes, equalizing, equalized) **1** make things equal. **2** level the score in a match by scoring a goal. ■ **equalization** noun **equalizer** noun.

equanimity /ek-wuh-**nim**-i-ti/ noun calmness; evenness of temper.

equate verb (equates, equating, equated) consider one thing as equal to another.

equation noun **1** the process of equating one thing with another. **2** Mathematics a statement that the values of two mathematical expressions are equal (indicated by the sign =). **3** Chemistry a formula representing the changes which occur in a chemical reaction.

equator noun an imaginary line around the earth at an equal distance from the two poles, dividing the earth into northern and southern hemispheres.

equatorial adjective having to do with the equator.

equerry /i-**kwe**-ri, ek-wuh-ri/ noun (plural **equerries**) an officer of the British royal household who assists members of the royal family.

equestrian /i-**kwess**-tri-uhn/ adjective relating to horse riding. noun a person on horseback.

equestrianism noun the skill or sport of horse riding.

equidistant adjective at equal distances.

equilateral adjective having all its sides of the same length.

equilibrium noun (plural **equilibria**) **1** a state in which opposing forces are balanced. **2** the state of being physically balanced. **3** a calm state of mind.

equine adjective **1** relating to horses. **2** resembling a horse.

equinoctial adjective **1** having to do with the equinox. **2** at or near the equator.

equinox noun the time or date (twice each year, about 22 September and 20 March) when day and night are of equal length.

equip verb (**equips**, **equipping**, **equipped**) **1** supply someone with the things they need for a particular activity. **2** prepare someone mentally for a situation or task.

equipment noun the items needed for a particular activity.

equitable adjective fair and impartial. ■ **equitably** adverb.

equity noun (plural **equities**) **1** the quality of being fair and impartial. **2** (in law) a system of natural justice to be used alongside existing laws. **3** the value of the shares issued by a company.

equivalent adjective (often **equivalent to**) **1** equal in value, amount, function, meaning, etc. **2** having the same effect. noun a person or thing that is equivalent to another. ■ **equivalence** noun **equivalently** adverb.

equivocal /i-**kwiv**-uh-k'l/ adjective (of words or intentions) unclear because they can be interpreted in more than one way. ■ **equivocally** adverb.

equivocate /i-**kwiv**-uh-kayt/ verb (**equivocates**, **equivocating**, **equivocated**) use language that can be interpreted in more than one way in order to conceal the truth or avoid committing yourself. ■ **equivocation** noun.

era noun a long and distinct period of history.

eradicate verb (**eradicates**, **eradicating**, **eradicated**) remove or destroy completely. ■ **eradication** noun.

erase verb (**erases**, **erasing**, **erased**) **1** rub out something written in pencil. **2** remove all traces of.

eraser noun a piece of rubber or plastic used to rub out something written in pencil.

ere /air/ preposition & conjunction old use before (in time).

erect adjective **1** rigidly upright. **2** (of the penis) enlarged and stiffened. verb **1** construct a building, wall, etc. **2** create or establish.

erectile adjective able to become erect.

erection noun **1** the action of erecting a structure or object. **2** a building or other upright structure. **3** an erect state of the penis.

ergo /**er**-goh/ adverb therefore.

ergonomics /er-guh-**nom**-iks/ noun the study of people's efficiency in their working environment. ■ **ergonomic** adjective.

ERM abbreviation Exchange Rate Mechanism.

ermine /**er**-min/ noun (plural **ermine** or **ermines**) **1** a stoat. **2** the white winter fur of the stoat.

erode verb (**erodes**, **eroding**, **eroded**) **1** gradually wear away. **2** gradually destroy.

erogenous /i-**roj**-i-nuhss/ adjective (of a part of the body) giving pleasure in a sexual way when it is touched.

erosion noun the process of eroding.

erotic adjective having to do with sexual desire or excitement. ■ **erotically** adverb.

erotica noun literature or art that is intended to make people feel sexually excited.

eroticism noun **1** the use of images that are intended to be sexually exciting. **2** sexual desire or excitement.

err verb **1** make a mistake. **2** do wrong.

errand noun a short journey made to deliver or collect something.

errant adjective **1** doing something wrong or unacceptable. **2** old use travelling in search of adventure.

erratic adjective moving or acting in an irregular or uneven way. ■ **erratically** adverb.

erratum /e-**rah**-tuhm/ noun (plural **errata**) **1** a mistake in a book or printed document. **2** (**errata**) a list of corrected errors added to a publication.

erroneous adjective incorrect. ■ **erroneously** adverb.

error noun **1** a mistake. **2** the state of being wrong.

ersatz adjective **1** (of a product) artificial and not as good as the real thing. **2** not genuine.

erstwhile adjective former.

erudite adjective having or showing knowledge gained from reading and study. ■ **erudition** noun.

erupt verb **1** (of a volcano) become active and eject lava, ash, and gases. **2** break out suddenly. **3** give vent to feelings in a sudden and noisy way. **4** (of a spot, rash, etc.) suddenly appear on the skin. ■ **eruption** noun.

escalate verb (**escalates**, **escalating**, **escalated**) **1** increase rapidly. **2** become more serious. ■ **escalation** noun.

escalator noun a moving staircase consisting of a circulating belt of steps driven by a motor.

escalope /i-**ska**-luhp/ noun a thin slice of meat coated in breadcrumbs and fried.

escapade noun an adventure.

escape verb (**escapes**, **escaping**, **es-**

caped) **1** break free from captivity or control. **2** succeed in avoiding something bad. **3** fail to be noticed or remembered by. noun **1** an act of escaping. **2** a means of escaping. ■ **escapee** noun **escaper** noun.

escapism noun the doing of enjoyable things that stop you thinking about unpleasant realities. ■ **escapist** noun & adjective.

escapologist /ess-kuh-**pol**-uh-jist/ noun an entertainer whose act consists of breaking free from ropes and chains. ■ **escapology** noun.

escarpment noun a long, steep slope at the edge of an area of high land.

eschew /is-**choo**/ verb deliberately avoid doing or having something.

escort noun **1** a person, vehicle, or group accompanying someone to protect or honour them. **2** a person who accompanies a member of the opposite sex to a social event. verb accompany someone as an escort.

escudo /ess-**kyoo**-doh/ noun (plural **escudos**) the basic unit of money of Portugal.

escutcheon /i-**sku**-chuhn/ noun a shield or emblem bearing a coat of arms.

Eskimo noun (plural **Eskimo** or **Eskimos**) a member of a people inhabiting northern Canada, Alaska, Greenland, and eastern Siberia.

> ⓘ many of the peoples traditionally called **Eskimos** now prefer to call themselves **Inuit**.

esophagus US spelling of OE-SOPHAGUS.

esoteric /e-suh-**te**-rik, ee-suh-te-rik/ adjective intended for or understood by only a small number of people with a specialized knowledge.

ESP abbreviation extrasensory perception.

espadrille /ess-puh-**dril**/ noun a light canvas shoe with a plaited fibre sole.

especial adjective **1** special. **2** for or belonging chiefly to one person or thing.

especially adverb **1** in particular.

WORD FORMATION

-ess

-ess is used at the end of a word to show that it refers to a female person or animal, as in

actress	*a female actor*
adulteress	*a woman who commits adultery*
tigress	*a female tiger.*

However, in modern English people tend to use the 'neutral' or male form of a word (e.g. **manager** or **poet**) rather than the female form (e.g. **manageress** or **poetess**) to refer to people of either sex.

2 to a great extent.

espionage /ess-pi-uh-nah*zh*/ **noun** the practice of spying.

esplanade /ess-pluh-**nayd**/ **noun** a long, open, level area used for leisurely walking.

espouse /i-**spowz**/ **verb** (**espouses, espousing, espoused**) support or adopt a particular belief or way of doing things. ■ **espousal** noun.

espresso /ess-**press**-oh/ **noun** (plural **espressos**) strong black coffee made by forcing steam through ground coffee beans.

> ☑ **espresso** is an Italian word (from *caffè espresso*, meaning 'pressed out coffee') and should be spelled the Italian way, with an *s*, not an *x*.

esprit de corps /e-spree duh **kor**/ **noun** a feeling of pride and loyalty that unites the members of a group.

espy verb (**espies, espying, espied**) literary catch sight of.

Esq. abbreviation Esquire.

Esquire /i-**skwyr**/ **noun** Brit. a polite title placed after a man's name when no other title is used.

essay noun 1 a piece of writing on a particular subject. **2** formal an attempt. **verb** formal attempt to do something. ■ **essayist** noun.

essence noun 1 the quality which is most important in making something what it is. **2** an extract obtained from a plant or other substance and used for flavouring or scent.

essential adjective 1 absolutely ne-

cessary. **2** relating to the most important part or basic nature of something. **noun** (**essentials**) **1** things that are absolutely necessary. **2** things that are part of the basic nature of something. □ **essential oil** a natural oil extracted from a plant. ■ **essentially** adverb.

establish verb 1 set something up on a firm or permanent basis. **2** start something. **3** (**be established**) be settled in a place or role. **4** show something to be true.

establishment noun 1 the action of establishing something. **2** a business organization, public institution, or household. **3** (**the Establishment**) the group in society who have control over policy and resist change.

estate noun 1 a property consisting of a large house with grounds. **2** Brit. a group of modern houses, or of buildings used by businesses. **3** a property where crops such as coffee or grapes are cultivated. **4** all the money and property owned by a person at the time of their death. □ **estate agent** a person who sells or rents out houses or flats for clients. **estate car** Brit. a car with a large storage area behind the seats and an extra door at the rear.

esteem noun respect and admiration. **verb** respect and admire someone.

ester noun Chemistry an organic compound formed by a reaction between an acid and an alcohol.

esthetic US spelling of **AESTHETIC**.

estimable adjective deserving respect and admiration.

estimate noun /ess-ti-muht/ **1** an approximate calculation. **2** a written statement indicating the likely price that will be charged for work. **3** a judgement. verb /ess-ti-mayt/ (**estimates, estimating, estimated**) form an estimate of. ∎ **estimation** noun.

estranged adjective **1** no longer involved with or familiar with something. **2** (of someone's husband or wife) no longer living with them.

estrogen US spelling of **OESTROGEN**.

estuary noun (plural **estuaries**) the mouth of a large river where it becomes shaped by tides.

eta /ee-tuh/ noun the seventh letter of the Greek alphabet (Η, η).

et al. abbreviation and others.

 Latin, short for *et alii*.

etc. abbreviation et cetera.

et cetera or **etcetera** /et set-uh-ruh/ adverb and other similar things; and so on.

etch verb **1** engrave metal, glass, or stone by applying a coating, drawing on it with a needle, and then covering the surface with acid to attack the exposed parts. **2** cut a text or design on a surface. **3** cause something to be clearly defined.

etching noun **1** the process of etching. **2** a print produced by etching.

eternal adjective lasting or existing forever. ∎ **eternally** adverb.

eternity noun (plural **eternities**) **1** unending time. **2** (**an eternity**) informal an undesirably long period of time.

ethane noun a flammable gas present in petroleum and natural gas.

ether /ee-ther/ noun **1** a highly flammable liquid used as an anaesthetic and a solvent. **2** literary the upper regions of the air.

ethereal /i-theer-i-uhl/ adjective **1** extremely delicate and light. **2** heavenly or spiritual.

ethic noun **1** (also **ethics**) a set of principles concerning right and wrong and how people should behave. **2** (**ethics**) the branch of philosophy concerned with moral principles.

ethical adjective **1** having to do with principles about right and wrong. **2** morally correct. ∎ **ethically** adverb.

ethnic adjective **1** having to do with people from the same national or cultural background. **2** referring to a person's origins rather than their present nationality. **3** belonging to a non-Western cultural tradition. □ **ethnic cleansing** the expulsion or killing of members of one ethnic or religious group in an area by those of another. **ethnic minority** a group which has a different ethnic origin from the main population. ∎ **ethnically** adverb **ethnicity** noun.

ethos /ee-thoss/ noun the characteristic spirit of a culture, period, etc.

ethyl /e-thil, ee-thyl/ noun Chemistry a radical derived from ethane, present in alcohol and ether.

etiquette noun the code of polite behaviour in a society.

etymology noun (plural **etymologies**) an account of the origins and the developments in meaning of a word. ∎ **etymological** adjective.

EU abbreviation European Union.

eucalyptus /yoo-kuh-**lip**-tuhss/ noun (plural **eucalyptuses** or **eucalypti** /yoo-kuh-**lip**-tI/) an evergreen Australasian tree.

Eucharist /yoo-kuh-krist/ noun **1** the Christian ceremony commemorating the Last Supper, in which consecrated bread and wine are consumed. **2** the consecrated bread and wine used in this ceremony.

eugenics /yoo-**jen**-iks/ noun the study of ways to increase the occurrence of desirable characteristics in a population by choosing which people become parents.

eulogize or **eulogise** /yoo-luh-jyz/ verb (**eulogizes, eulogizing, eulogized**) praise someone highly.

eulogy /yoo-luh-ji/ noun (plural **eulogies**) a speech or piece of writing that praises someone highly.

eunuch /**yoo**-nuhk/ noun a man who has had his testicles removed.

euphemism /**yoo**-fuh-mi-z'm/ noun a less direct word used instead of one that is harsh or blunt. ■ **euphemistic** adjective **euphemistically** adverb.

euphonious /yoo-**foh**-ni-uhss/ adjective sounding pleasant. ■ **euphoniously** adverb.

euphonium /yoo-**foh**-ni-uhm/ noun a brass musical instrument resembling a small tuba.

euphony /**yoo**-fuh-ni/ noun (plural euphonies) the quality of sounding pleasant.

euphoria /yoo-**for**-i-uh/ noun a feeling of intense happiness. ■ **euphoric** adjective.

Eurasian adjective **1** of mixed European and Asian parentage. **2** relating to Eurasia (the land mass of Europe and Asia together).

eureka /yuu-**ree**-kuh/ exclamation a cry of joy or satisfaction when you discover something.

euro noun the single European currency, introduced in the European Union in 1999.

European noun **1** a person from Europe. **2** a person who is white or of European parentage. adjective having to do with Europe or the European Union. □ **European Union** an economic and political association of certain European countries.

euthanasia /yoo-thuh-**nay**-zi-uh/ noun the painless killing of a patient suffering from an incurable disease.

evacuate verb (evacuates, evacuating, evacuated) **1** remove someone from a place of danger to a safer place. **2** leave a dangerous place. **3** empty the bowels. ■ **evacuation** noun.

evacuee noun a person who is evacuated from a place of danger.

evade verb (evades, evading, evaded) **1** escape or avoid. **2** avoid giving a direct answer to a question.

evaluate verb (evaluates, evaluat-

ing, evaluated) form an idea of the amount or value of. ■ **evaluation** noun.

evanescent /ev-uh-**ness**-uhnt/ adjective soon passing out of existence; fleeting. ■ **evanescence** noun.

evangelical adjective **1** having to do with the teaching of the gospel or Christianity. **2** having to do with a tradition within Protestant Christianity which emphasizes Biblical authority and personal conversion. **3** fervently showing support for something. noun a member of the evangelical tradition in the Christian Church. ■ **evangelicalism** noun.

evangelist noun **1** a person who sets out to convert others to Christianity. **2** the writer of one of the four Gospels. **3** a passionate supporter of something. ■ **evangelism** noun **evangelistic** adjective.

evangelize or **evangelise** verb (evangelizes, evangelizing, evangelized) **1** set out to convert people to Christianity. **2** preach the gospel.

evaporate verb (evaporates, evaporating, evaporated) **1** turn from liquid into vapour. **2** cease to exist. □ **evaporated milk** thick sweetened milk from which some of the liquid has been evaporated. ■ **evaporation** noun.

evasion noun the action of avoiding something.

evasive adjective **1** avoiding committing yourself or revealing things about yourself. **2** (of an action) intended to avoid or escape something. ■ **evasively** adverb.

eve noun **1** the day or period of time immediately before an event or occasion. **2** evening.

even[1] adjective **1** flat and smooth; level. **2** equal in number, amount, or value. **3** regular. **4** equally balanced. **5** placid; calm. **6** (of a number) able to be divided by two without a remainder. verb (evens, evening, evened) make or become even. adverb used for emphasis: *he knows even less than I do.* □ **even-handed** fair and impartial. **even though** despite the fact that. ■ **evenly** adverb **evenness** noun.

even² noun old use evening.

evening noun the period of time at the end of the day. □ **evening star** the planet Venus, seen shining in the western sky after sunset.

evensong noun a service of evening prayers, psalms, and canticles.

event noun **1** a thing that happens or takes place. **2** a public or social occasion. **3** each of several contests making up a sports competition.

eventful adjective marked by interesting or exciting events.

eventual adjective occurring at the end of or resulting from a process or period of time. ■ **eventually** adverb.

eventuality noun (plural **eventualities**) a possible event or outcome.

ever adverb **1** at any time. **2** used for emphasis in comparisons and questions: *better than ever.* **3** always. **4** increasingly.

evergreen adjective (of a plant) retaining green leaves throughout the year.

everlasting adjective lasting forever or a very long time. ■ **everlastingly** adverb.

evermore adverb always; forever.

every determiner **1** used to refer to all the individual members of a set without exception. **2** used to indicate something happening at specified intervals: *every thirty minutes.* **3** all possible: *every effort was made.*

everybody pronoun every person.

everyday adjective **1** daily. **2** commonly occurring.

everyone pronoun every person.

everything pronoun **1** all things, or all the things of a group. **2** the most important thing.

everywhere adverb **1** in or to all places. **2** in many places.

evict verb expel someone legally from a property. ■ **eviction** noun.

evidence noun **1** information indicating whether something is true or valid. **2** the information presented in a law court to establish facts. **verb** (**evidences, evidencing, evidenced**) be or show evidence of. □ **in evidence** noticeable.

evident adjective plain or obvious. ■ **evidently** adverb.

evil adjective **1** deeply immoral and wicked. **2** very unpleasant. **noun 1** extreme wickedness. **2** something harmful or undesirable. ■ **evilly** adverb.

evince verb (**evinces, evincing, evinced**) formal reveal the presence of.

eviscerate /i-**viss**-uh-rayt/ verb (**eviscerates, eviscerating, eviscerated**) formal remove the intestines of.

evocative adjective bringing strong images, memories, or feelings to mind.

evoke verb (**evokes, evoking, evoked**) **1** bring a feeling or memory into someone's mind. **2** obtain a response. ■ **evocation** noun.

evolution noun **1** the process by which different kinds of animals and plants develop from earlier forms. **2** gradual development. ■ **evolutionary** adjective.

evolve verb (**evolves, evolving, evolved**) **1** develop gradually. **2** (of an animal or plant) develop and change over many generations by evolution.

ewe noun a female sheep.

ewer /**yoo**-er/ noun a large jug with a wide mouth.

ex noun informal a former husband, wife, boyfriend, or girlfriend. **prefix** (**ex-**) **1** out. **2** upward. **3** thoroughly. **4** referring to removal or release. **5** former: *ex-husband.*

exacerbate verb (**exacerbates, exacerbating, exacerbated**) make something that is already bad worse. ■ **exacerbation** noun.

exact adjective **1** precise. **2** accurate in all details. **verb 1** demand and obtain something from someone. **2** inflict revenge. ■ **exactness** noun.

exacting adjective (of a task) making you concentrate or work very hard.

exactitude noun the quality of being exact.

exactly adverb **1** in an exact way. **2** used to agree with what has just been said.

exaggerate verb (**exaggerates, exaggerating, exaggerated**) make something seem greater, more important, etc. than it really is. ∎ **exaggeration** noun.

 two g's: exag**g**erate.

exalt verb **1** praise someone or something highly. **2** give someone or something a higher rank or status.

exaltation noun **1** extreme happiness. **2** the action of exalting.

exalted adjective **1** having high rank or status. **2** noble; high-flown.

exam noun an examination in a subject or skill.

examination noun **1** a detailed inspection. **2** a formal test of knowledge or ability in a subject or skill. **3** the action of examining.

examine verb (**examines, examining, examined**) **1** inspect something closely. **2** (of a doctor or dentist) look closely at a part of a person's body to detect any problems. **3** test someone's knowledge or ability. ∎ **examinee** noun **examiner** noun.

example noun **1** a thing that is typical of or represents a particular group. **2** something that shows or supports a general rule. **3** a person or thing seen in terms of how suitable they are to be copied.

exasperate verb (**exasperates, exasperating, exasperated**) irritate someone intensely. ∎ **exasperation** noun.

excavate verb (**excavates, excavating, excavated**) **1** make a hole by digging. **2** dig material out from the ground. **3** carefully remove earth from an area in order to find buried remains. ∎ **excavation** noun.

exceed verb **1** be greater in number or size than. **2** go beyond a set limit. **3** go beyond what is expected.

exceedingly adverb extremely.

excel verb (**excels, excelling, excelled**) **1** be exceptionally good at something. **2** (**excel yourself**) do something exceptionally well.

Excellency noun (plural **Excellencies**) (**His, Your,** etc. **Excellency**) a form of address for certain high officials of state or of the Roman Catholic Church.

excellent adjective extremely good; outstanding. ∎ **excellence** noun excellently adverb.

except preposition not including. **conjunction** used before a statement that forms an exception to one just made. **verb** exclude.

 don't forget the c in **except** and related words.

excepting preposition except for.

exception noun a person or thing that is excluded or that does not follow a rule. □ **take exception to** object strongly to.

exceptionable adjective formal causing disapproval or offence.

don't confuse **exceptionable** and **exceptional**.

exceptional adjective **1** unusual. **2** unusually good. ∎ **exceptionally** adverb.

excerpt noun a short extract from a film or piece of music or writing.

excess noun **1** an amount that is more than necessary, permitted, or desirable. **2** lack of moderation. **3** (**excesses**) outrageous behaviour. **4** Brit. a part of an insurance claim to be paid by the person insured. **adjective** exceeding a set or desirable amount.

excessive adjective more than is necessary, normal, or desirable. ∎ **excessively** adverb.

exchange verb (**exchanges, exchanging, exchanged**) give something else in return. **noun 1** an act of exchanging. **2** a short conversation or argument. **3** the giving of money for its equivalent in the currency of another country. **4** a building used for financial trading. **5** a set of equipment that connects telephone lines during a call. □ **exchange rate**

PUNCTUATION

Exclamation Mark !

An exclamation mark is used instead of a full stop at the end of a sentence to show that the speaker or writer is very angry, enthusiastic, disappointed, hurt, surprised, etc., e.g.:

I'm not pleased at all!   *I wish I could go!*
I just love sweets!   *Ouch!*
Go away!   *He didn't even say goodbye!*

---

the value at which one currency may be exchanged for another.

exchequer noun **1** a royal or national treasury. **2** (**Exchequer**) Brit. the account at the Bank of England into which public money is paid.

excise¹ /**ek**-syz/ noun a tax imposed on certain goods, materials, and licences.

excise² /ik-**syz**/ verb (**excises, excising, excised**) **1** cut something out surgically. **2** remove a section from a text or piece of music. ■ **excision** noun.

excitable adjective easily excited. ■ **excitability** noun **excitably** adverb.

excite verb (**excites, exciting, excited**) **1** cause strong feelings of enthusiasm and eagerness in someone. **2** make someone feel sexually aroused. **3** give rise to. **4** produce a state of increased energy or activity in a physical or biological system. ■ **excitation** noun **exciting** adjective **excitingly** adverb.

 don't forget the *c*: excite.

excitement noun **1** a feeling of great enthusiasm and eagerness. **2** something that arouses such a feeling. **3** sexual arousal.

exclaim verb cry out suddenly.

exclamation noun a sudden cry or remark. ■ **exclamatory** adjective.

exclude verb (**excludes, excluding, excluded**) **1** choose not to include something in what you are counting or considering. **2** prevent someone from being a part of something.

exclusion noun the process of excluding, or the state of being excluded.

exclusive adjective **1** excluding or not admitting other things. **2** restricted to the person, group, or area concerned. **3** catering for or available to a select group. **4** not published or broadcast elsewhere. noun a story or film that has not been published or broadcast elsewhere. ■ **exclusively** adverb **exclusivity** noun.

excommunicate verb (**excommunicates, excommunicating, excommunicated**) officially bar someone from membership of the Christian Church. ■ **excommunication** noun.

excoriate verb (**excoriates, excoriating, excoriated**) **1** Medicine damage or remove part of the surface of the skin. **2** formal criticize someone severely. ■ **excoriation** noun.

excrement noun waste material passed from the body through the bowels.

excrescence noun an abnormal growth protruding from a body or plant.

excreta noun waste material that is passed out of the body.

excrete verb (**excretes, excreting, excreted**) pass waste material from the body. ■ **excretion** noun **excretory** adjective.

excruciating adjective **1** intensely painful. **2** very embarrassing, awkward, or tedious. ■ **excruciatingly** adverb.

exculpate /**eks**-kul-payt/ verb (**exculpates, exculpating, exculpated**) formal say that someone is not guilty of doing something wrong.

excursion noun a short journey or trip taken for pleasure.

excuse verb /ik-**skyooz**/ (**excuses, excusing, excused**) **1** give reasons why something that someone has done wrong may be justified. **2** release someone from a duty. **3** forgive someone for something they have done wrong. **4** allow someone to leave a room or meeting. **5** (**excuse yourself**) say politely that you are leaving. noun /ik-**skyooss**/ **1** a reason put forward to justify a fault or offence. **2** something said to conceal the real reason for an action. **3** informal a very poor example of something. ■ **excusable** adjective.

ex-directory adjective Brit. not listed in a telephone directory at your own request.

execrable /**ek**-si-kruh-b'l/ adjective extremely bad or unpleasant.

execrate /**ek**-si-krayt/ verb (**execrates, execrating, execrated**) feel or express great hatred for. ■ **execration** noun.

execute verb (**executes, executing, executed**) **1** carry out a plan, order, etc. **2** kill a condemned person as a legal punishment. **3** carry out an activity or manoeuvre.

execution noun **1** the carrying out of something. **2** the killing of a condemned person.

executioner noun an official who executes condemned criminals.

executive adjective having the power to put plans, actions, or laws into effect. noun **1** a senior manager in a business organization. **2** a group of people who run an organization or business. **3** (**the executive**) the branch of a government responsible for putting plans, actions, or laws into effect.

executor /ig-**zek**-yuu-ter/ noun Law a person appointed by someone to carry out the terms of their will.

exegesis /ek-si-**jee**-siss/ noun (plural **exegeses** /ek-si-**jee**-seez/) an explanation or interpretation of a text.

exemplar /ig-**zem**-pler/ noun a person or thing serving as a typical example or a good model.

exemplary adjective **1** representing the best of its kind. **2** (of a punishment) serving as a warning.

exemplify verb (**exemplifies, exemplifying, exemplified**) be or give a typical example of. ■ **exemplification** noun.

exempt adjective not having to do or pay something that other people have to do or pay. verb make someone exempt. ■ **exemption** noun.

exercise noun **1** physical activity done to stay healthy or become stronger. **2** a set of movements, activities, or questions that test your ability or help you practise a skill. **3** an activity carried out for a specific purpose. **4** the putting into practice of a power, right, or process. verb (**exercises, exercising, exercised**) **1** use or apply a power, right, or process. **2** engage in exercise. **3** worry or perplex. □ **exercise book** Brit. a booklet with blank pages for students to write in.

exert verb **1** use a force, influence, or quality to make something happen. **2** (**exert yourself**) make a physical or mental effort. ■ **exertion** noun.

exeunt /**ek**-si-uhnt/ verb (in a play) a stage direction telling actors to leave the stage.

exfoliate verb (**exfoliates, exfoliating, exfoliated**) **1** shed from a surface in scales or layers. **2** rub the skin with a grainy substance to remove dead cells. ■ **exfoliation** noun.

exhale verb (**exhales, exhaling, exhaled**) **1** breathe out. **2** give off vapour or fumes. ■ **exhalation** noun.

exhaust verb **1** tire someone out. **2** use up all of something. **3** talk about a subject until there is nothing left to say. noun **1** waste gases that are expelled from the engine of a car or other machine. **2** the system through which such gases are expelled. ■ **exhaustible** adjective.

exhaustion noun the state of being exhausted.

exhaustive adjective thoroughly covering all aspects of something. ■ **exhaustively** adverb.

exhibit verb **1** display an item in an art gallery or museum. **2** show a particular quality. noun **1** an object or collection on display in an art gallery or museum. **2** an object produced in a court of law as evidence.

exhibition noun **1** a public display of items in an art gallery or museum. **2** a display or demonstration of a skill or quality.

exhibitionism noun behaviour that is intended to make people notice you. ■ **exhibitionist** noun.

exhilarate verb (**exhilarates, exhilarating, exhilarated**) make someone feel very happy and full of energy. ■ **exhilaration** noun.

 remember the h: ex**h**ilarate.

exhort verb strongly urge someone to do something.

exhortation noun an appeal to someone strongly urging them to do something.

exhume verb (**exhumes, exhuming, exhumed**) dig out from the ground something that has been buried.

exigency /**ek**-si-juhn-si/ noun (plural **exigencies**) formal urgent need.

exigent /**ek**-si-juhnt/ adjective formal pressing; urgent.

exiguous /eg-**zig**-yoo-uhss/ adjective formal very small.

exile noun **1** the state of being forbidden to live or spend time in your own country. **2** a person who lives in exile. verb (**exiles, exiling, exiled**) expel and bar someone from their own country.

exist verb **1** be present in a place or situation. **2** live.

existence noun **1** the fact or state of existing. **2** a way of living: *a rural existence*.

 -**ence**, not -ance: exist**ence**.

existential /eg-zi-**sten**-sh'l/ adjective **1** having to do with existence. **2** Philosophy concerned with existentialism.

existentialism noun a theory in philosophy which says that each human being exists as a free individual, with responsibility for their own actions, in a world that otherwise has no meaning. ■ **existentialist** noun & adjective.

exit noun **1** a way out of a place. **2** an act of leaving. verb (**exits, exiting, exited**) go out of or leave a place. □ **exit poll** a poll of people leaving a polling station, asking how they voted.

exodus noun a mass departure of people.

exonerate /ig-**zon**-uh-rayt/ verb (**exonerates, exonerating, exonerated**) **1** declare someone free from blame. **2** (**exonerate from**) release someone from a duty. ■ **exoneration** noun.

exorbitant adjective (of an amount charged) unreasonably high. ■ **exorbitantly** adverb.

✓ no h: ex**o**rbitant.

exorcize or **exorcise** verb (**exorcizes, exorcizing, exorcizes**) drive an evil spirit from a person or place. ■ **exorcism** noun **exorcist** noun.

exotic adjective **1** coming from or characteristic of a distant foreign country. **2** strikingly colourful or unusual. ■ **exotically** adverb **exoticism** noun.

expand verb **1** make or become larger or more extensive. **2** (**expand on**) give a fuller account of. ■ **expandable** adjective **expansion** noun.

expanse noun a wide continuous area of something.

expansive adjective **1** covering a wide area. **2** relaxed, friendly, and communicative. ■ **expansively** adverb.

expat = **EXPATRIATE**.

expatiate /ig-**spay**-shi-ayt/ verb (**expatiates, expatiating, expatiated**) (**expatiate on**) speak or write in detail about something.

expatriate noun /eks-**pat**-ri-uht/ a person who lives outside their own country.

expect verb **1** think something is likely to happen. **2** think someone is likely to do or be something. **3** believe that someone will arrive soon. **4** assume or demand that someone will do something because it is their duty or responsibility. **5 (be expecting)** informal be pregnant.

expectancy noun (plural **expectancies**) the belief or hope that something will happen.

expectant adjective **1** believing or hoping that something is about to happen. **2** (of a woman) pregnant. ■ **expectantly** adverb.

expectation noun **1** belief that something will happen or be the case. **2** a thing that is expected to happen.

expectorant noun a medicine which helps to bring up phlegm from the air passages, used to treat a cough.

expectorate verb (**expectorates, expectorating, expectorated**) cough or spit out phlegm from the throat or lungs.

expedient /ik-**spee**-di-uhnt/ adjective **1** useful or helpful for a particular purpose. **2** useful in achieving something, rather than morally correct. noun a means of achieving something. ■ **expediency** noun.

expedite /**eks**-pi-dyt/ verb (**expedites, expediting, expedited**) make something happen more quickly.

expedition noun a journey with a particular purpose, made by a group of people. ■ **expeditionary** adjective.

expeditious /eks-pi-**di**-shuhss/ adjective quick and efficient. ■ **expeditiously** adverb.

expel verb (**expels, expelling, expelled**) **1** force someone or something out. **2** force a pupil to leave a school.

expend verb spend or use up a resource.

expendable adjective **1** suitable to be used once only. **2** able to be dismissed because unimportant when compared to an overall purpose.

expenditure noun **1** the action of spending money. **2** the amount of money spent.

expense noun **1** the amount something costs. **2** something on which money must be spent. **3 (expenses)** money spent in doing a particular thing. **4 (expenses)** money paid for meals, fares, etc. by an employee in the course of their work, which they can claim back from their employer.

expensive adjective costing a lot of money. ■ **expensively** adverb.

experience noun **1** the fact of being present at or taking part in something. **2** knowledge or skill gained over time. **3** an event which affects you in some way. verb (**experiences, experiencing, experienced**) **1** be present at or take part in something. **2** feel an emotion.

experienced adjective having a lot of knowledge or skill in a field that has been gained over time.

experiment noun **1** a scientific procedure carried out to make a discovery, test a theory, or demonstrate a fact. **2** a new course of action that you try out without being sure of the outcome. verb **1** perform a scientific experiment. **2** try out new things. ■ **experimentation** noun.

experimental adjective **1** based on a new idea and not yet fully tested. **2** having to do with scientific experiments. **3** (of art, music, etc.) new and unconventional. ■ **experimentally** adverb.

expert noun a person who has great knowledge or skill in a particular field. adjective having or involving great knowledge or skill. ■ **expertly** adverb.

expertise noun great skill or knowledge in a particular field.

expiate /**ek**-spi-ayt/ verb (**expiates, expiating, expiated**) do something to make up for having done something wrong. ■ **expiation** noun.

expire verb (**expires, expiring, expired**) **1** (of a document or agreement) cease to be valid. **2** (of a period of time) come to an end. **3** (of a person) die. **4** breath out air from the lungs.

expiry noun the end of the period for which something is valid.

explain verb **1** describe something in a way that makes it easy to understand. **2** give a reason for something. **3** (explain yourself) say why you are doing something in order to justify or excuse it. ■ **explanation** noun.

explanatory adjective giving the reason for something, or making something clear.

expletive /ik-**splee**-tiv/ noun a swear word.

explicable adjective able to be explained.

explicit adjective **1** clear, detailed, and easy to understand. **2** showing or describing sexual activity openly and clearly. ■ **explicitly** adverb.

explode verb (explodes, exploding, exploded) **1** burst or shatter violently as a result of the release of internal energy. **2** show sudden violent emotion. **3** increase suddenly in number or extent. **4** show a belief to be false.

exploit verb /ik-**sployt**/ **1** make good use of a resource. **2** make use of someone unfairly. noun /**ek**-sployt/ a daring act. ■ **exploitation** noun **exploitative** adjective.

explore verb (explores, exploring, explored) **1** travel through an unfamiliar area in order to learn about it. **2** examine or discuss something in detail. **3** investigate. ■ **exploration** noun **exploratory** adjective **explorer** noun.

explosion noun an instance of exploding.

explosive adjective **1** able or likely to explode. **2** likely to cause anger or controversy. **3** (of an increase) sudden and dramatic. noun a substance which can be made to explode. ■ **explosively** adverb.

exponent /ik-**spoh**-nuhnt/ noun **1** a promoter of an idea or theory. **2** a person who does a particular thing skilfully. **3** Mathematics a raised figure beside a number indicating how many times that number is to be multiplied by itself (e.g. ^{3} in $2^3 = 2 \times 2 \times 2$).

exponential /eks-puh-**nen**-sh'l/ adjective **1** (of an increase) becoming more and more rapid. **2** Mathematics having to do with a mathematical exponent. ■ **exponentially** adverb.

export verb /ik-**sport**/ **1** send goods or services to another country for sale. **2** introduce an idea or custom to another country. noun /**ek**-sport/ **1** the exporting of goods or services. **2** an exported item. ■ **exportation** noun **exporter** noun.

expose verb (exposes, exposing, exposed) **1** uncover something and make it visible. **2** show someone or something's true nature. **3** (exposed) unprotected from the weather. **4** (expose to) make someone vulnerable to. **5** subject photographic film to light. **6** (expose yourself) show your sexual organs in public.

exposé /ik-**spoh**-zay/ noun a report in the news revealing shocking information about someone.

exposition noun **1** a careful setting out of the facts or ideas involved in something. **2** an exhibition. **3** Music the part of a movement in which the principal themes are first presented.

expostulate verb (expostulates, expostulating, expostulated) express strong disapproval or disagreement. ■ **expostulation** noun.

exposure noun **1** the state of being exposed to something harmful. **2** a physical condition resulting from being exposed to severe weather conditions. **3** the action of exposing a photographic film. **4** the quantity of light reaching a photographic film. **5** the revealing of something secret. **6** the publicizing of information.

expound verb set out and explain the facts or ideas involved in something.

express[1] verb **1** show by words or actions what you are thinking or feeling. **2** squeeze out liquid or air.

express[2] adjective operating or delivered at high speed. adverb by express train or delivery service. noun 1 a train that travels quickly and stops at few stations. 2 a special delivery service.

express[3] adjective 1 stated very clearly. 2 excluding anything else. ■ **expressly** adverb.

expression noun 1 the action of expressing. 2 the look on someone's face. 3 a word or phrase expressing an idea. 4 Mathematics a collection of symbols expressing a quantity. ■ **expressionless** adjective.

expressionism noun a style in art, music, or drama in which the artist or writer shows the inner world of emotion rather than external reality. ■ **expressionist** noun & adjective.

expressive adjective clearly showing thoughts or feelings. ■ **expressively** adverb **expressiveness** noun.

expropriate verb (**expropriates, expropriating, expropriated**) take property from its owner with official approval. ■ **expropriation** noun.

expulsion noun the action of expelling.

expunge /ik-**spunj**/ verb (**expunges, expunging, expunged**) remove something completely.

expurgate /**eks**-per-gayt/ verb (**expurgates, expurgating, expurgated**) remove unsuitable material from a text. ■ **expurgation** noun.

exquisite adjective 1 of great beauty and delicacy. 2 highly refined. 3 intensely felt. ■ **exquisitely** adverb.

extant adjective still in existence.

extemporary adjective spoken or done without preparation.

extempore /ik-**stem**-puh-ri/ adjective & adverb spoken or done without preparation.

extemporize or **extemporise** verb (**extemporizes, extemporizing, extemporized**) make something up as you go along.

extend verb 1 make something larger in area. 2 make something last longer. 3 occupy a specified area or continue for a specified distance. 4 hold out a part of your body towards someone. 5 offer something to someone. □ **extended family** a family group consisting of parents and children and close relatives living nearby. ■ **extendable** (or **extendible**) adjective **extensible** adjective.

extension noun 1 the action or process of extending. 2 a part added to a building to make it bigger. 3 an additional period of time. 4 a secondary or additional telephone. □ **extension lead** a length of electric cable which can be plugged into a socket and has another socket on the end.

extensive adjective 1 covering a large area. 2 large in amount or scale. ■ **extensively** adverb.

extent noun 1 the area covered by something. 2 size or scale. 3 the degree to which something is the case.

extenuating /ik-**sten**-yoo-ay-ting/ adjective serving to make an offence less serious by partially excusing it: *extenuating circumstances*.

exterior adjective having to do with the outside of something. noun the outer surface or structure of something.

exterminate verb (**exterminates, exterminating, exterminated**) destroy something completely. ■ **extermination** noun **exterminator** noun.

external adjective 1 having to do with the outside of something. 2 coming from outside an organization or situation. 3 having to do with another country or institution. noun (**externals**) the outward aspects of something. ■ **externally** adverb.

externalize or **externalise** verb (**externalizes, externalizing, externalized**) express a thought or feeling in words or actions.

extinct adjective 1 no longer in existence. 2 (of a volcano) not having erupted in recorded history. ■ **extinction** noun.

extinguish verb 1 put out a fire or light. 2 put an end to. ■ **extinguisher** noun.

extirpate /ek-ster-payt/ verb (extirpates, extirpating, extirpated) search out and destroy something completely. ■ extirpation noun.

extol verb (extols, extolling, extolled) praise enthusiastically.

extort verb obtain something by force, threats, or other unfair means. ■ extortion noun.

extortionate adjective (of a price) much too high. ■ extortionately adverb.

extra adjective added to an existing or usual amount or number. adverb 1 to a greater extent than usual. 2 in addition. noun 1 an item for which an extra charge is made. 2 an extra item. 3 a person employed to take part in a crowd scene in a film or play. prefix (extra-) 1 outside: extramarital. 2 beyond the scope of: extra-curricular.

extract verb /ik-strakt/ 1 remove something with care or effort. 2 obtain something from someone unwilling to give it. 3 separate out a substance by a special method. noun /ek-strakt/ 1 a short passage taken from a text, film, or piece of music. 2 an extracted substance. □ extractor fan a device that removes steam and smells from a room.

extraction noun 1 the action of extracting. 2 the ethnic origin of someone's family.

extradite /ek-struh-dyt/ verb (extradites, extraditing, extradited) hand over a person accused or convicted of committing a crime in a foreign state to the legal authority of that state. ■ extradition noun.

extramarital adjective occurring outside marriage.

extramural adjective Brit. (of a course of study) for people who are not full-time members of an educational establishment.

extraneous /ik-stray-ni-uhss/ adjective 1 unrelated to the subject being dealt with. 2 of external origin.

extraordinaire /ek-struh-or-di-nair/ adjective outstanding in a particular capacity: she was a gardener extraordinaire.

extraordinary adjective 1 very unusual or remarkable. 2 (of a meeting) held for a particular reason rather than being one of a regular series. ■ extraordinarily adverb.

✓ the beginning is extra-, not just extr-: extraordinary.

extrapolate /ik-strap-uh-layt/ verb (extrapolates, extrapolating, extrapolated) use a fact or conclusion that is valid for one situation and apply it to a larger or different one. ■ extrapolation noun.

extrasensory perception noun the supposed ability to perceive things by means other than the known senses, e.g. by telepathy.

extraterrestrial adjective having to do with things that come from beyond the earth or its atmosphere. noun a fictional being from outer space.

extravagant adjective 1 spending or using more than is necessary or more than you can afford. 2 costing a great deal. 3 exceeding what is reasonable. ■ extravagance noun extravagantly adverb.

extravaganza noun an elaborate and spectacular entertainment.

extreme adjective 1 to the highest degree. 2 highly unusual. 3 very severe or serious. 4 not moderate. 5 furthest from the centre or a given point. noun 1 either of two abstract things that are as different from each other as possible. 2 the most extreme degree. ■ extremely adverb.

extremist noun a person who holds extreme political or religious views. ■ extremism noun.

extremity noun (plural extremities) 1 the furthest point or limit. 2 (extremities) a person's hands and feet. 3 extreme hardship.

extricate verb (extricates, extricating, extricated) 1 free someone from a difficult situation. 2 free something that is trapped.

extrinsic adjective coming or operating from outside.

extrovert noun an outgoing, lively person. adjective outgoing and lively.

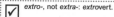

✓ extro-, not extra-: extrovert.

extrude verb (extrudes, extruding, extruded) thrust or force something out.

exuberant adjective 1 lively and cheerful. 2 growing thickly. ■ **exuberance** noun **exuberantly** adverb.

exude verb (exudes, exuding, exuded) 1 discharge or be discharged slowly and steadily. 2 display an emotion or quality strongly and openly.

exult verb show or feel triumphant joy. ■ **exultant** adjective **exultantly** adverb **exultation** noun.

eye noun 1 the organ of sight in humans and animals. 2 a dark spot on a potato from which a new shoot grows. 3 the small hole in a needle through which the thread is passed. 4 a small metal loop into which a hook is fitted as a fastener on a garment. 5 the calm region at the centre of a storm. 6 a person's opinion or feelings. verb (eyes, eyeing or eying, eyed) 1 look at something closely. 2 (eye up) informal look at someone in a way that reveals a sexual interest. □ **eye socket** a cavity in the skull which encloses the eye and its surrounding muscles. **make**

eyes at look at someone in a way that indicates sexual interest. **see eye to eye** be in full agreement.

eyeball noun the round part of the eye of a vertebrate, within the eyelids.

eyebrow noun the strip of hair growing on the ridge above a person's eye socket.

eyeful noun informal 1 a long, steady look. 2 an eye-catching person.

eyeglass noun a single lens for correcting eyesight.

eyelash noun each of the short hairs growing on the edges of the eyelids.

eyelet noun 1 a small round hole for threading a lace or cord through. 2 a metal ring strengthening an eyelet.

eyelid noun each of the upper and lower folds of skin which cover the eye when it is closed.

eyeliner noun a cosmetic applied as a line round the eyes.

eyeshadow noun a cosmetic applied to the skin around the eyes.

eyesight noun a person's ability to see.

eyesore noun a thing that is very ugly.

eyewitness noun a person who has seen something happen.

eyrie /eer-i, I-ri/ (US spelling **aerie**) noun a large nest of a bird of prey.

Ff

F or **f** noun (plural **Fs** or **F's**) the sixth letter of the alphabet. abbreviation Fahrenheit.

FA abbreviation Football Association.

fable noun 1 a short story which contains a message about doing right and wrong. 2 a supernatural story containing elements of myth and legend.

fabled adjective 1 famous. 2 mythical.

fabric noun 1 cloth. 2 the walls, floor,

and roof of a building. 3 the basic structure of a system or organization.

fabricate verb (fabricates, fabricating, fabricated) 1 make up facts that are not true. 2 make an industrial product. ■ **fabrication** noun.

fabulous adjective 1 great; extraordinary. 2 informal wonderful. 3 mythical. ■ **fabulously** adverb.

facade /fuh-**sahd**/ noun 1 the front of

a building. **2** a misleading outward appearance.

face noun **1** the front part of the head from the forehead to the chin. **2** an expression on someone's face. **3** the surface of a thing. **4** a vertical or sloping side of a mountain or cliff. **5** an aspect of something. **verb (faces, facing, faced) 1** be positioned with the face or front towards a specified direction. **2** confront and deal with. **3** have a difficulty ahead of you. **4** cover the surface of something with a layer of material. □ **face pack** a cream or gel spread over the face to clean and tone the skin. **face the music** be confronted with the unpleasant consequences of your actions. **face value 1** the value stated on a coin or postage stamp. **2** the value that something seems to have before you look at it closely. **lose (or save) face** suffer (or avoid) humiliation. **on the face of it** apparently.

facecloth noun a small towelling cloth for washing your face.

faceless adjective remote and impersonal; anonymous.

facelift noun an operation to remove wrinkles in the face by tightening the skin.

facet noun **1** one side of something that has many sides. **2** an aspect of something. ■ **faceted** adjective.

facetious /fuh-**see**-shuhss/ adjective trying to be funny or clever about something that should be treated seriously. ■ **facetiously** adverb.

facia ⇒ **FASCIA**.

facial adjective having to do with the face. noun a beauty treatment for the face. ■ **facially** adverb.

facile /fa-syl/ adjective **1** produced without careful thought. **2** too simple, or too easily achieved.

facilitate verb **(facilitates, facilitating, facilitated)** make something possible or easier. ■ **facilitation** noun **facilitator** noun.

facility noun (plural **facilities**) **1** a building, service, or piece of equipment provided for a particular pur-

pose. **2** a natural ability to do something well and easily.

facing noun **1** a reinforcing strip of material at the neck, armhole, etc. of a garment. **2** an outer layer covering the surface of a wall.

facsimile /fak-**sim**-i-li/ noun **1** an exact copy of written or printed material. **2** a fax.

fact noun **1** a thing that is definitely the case. **2** (**facts**) information used as evidence or as part of a report. □ **the facts of life** information about sexual matters.

faction noun a small group within a larger one. ■ **factional** adjective.

factious /**fak**-shuhss/ adjective having opposing views.

factitious /fak-**ti**-shuhss/ adjective made up; not genuine.

factor noun **1** a circumstance, fact, or influence that contributes to a result. **2** (in mathematics) a number or quantity that when multiplied with another produces a given number or expression. **3** any of a number of substances in the blood which are involved in clotting. **4** a business or land agent. verb (**factor in** or **out**) consider (or ignore) something when making a decision.

factory noun (plural **factories**) a building where goods are made or assembled in large numbers. □ **factory farming** the rearing of poultry, pigs, or cattle indoors under strictly controlled conditions.

factotum /fak-**toh**-tuhm/ noun (plural **factotums**) a person employed to do a wide variety of jobs.

factual adjective based on or concerned with facts. ■ **factually** adverb.

faculty noun (plural **faculties**) **1** a basic mental or physical power. **2** a talent. **3** a department or group of related departments in a university.

fad noun **1** a craze. **2** a fussy liking or disliking of something unimportant. ■ **faddish** adjective **faddy** adjective.

fade verb **(fades, fading, faded) 1** gradually grow faint and disappear. **2** lose colour. **3** (**fade in** or **out**) make a film or video image or sound more or less clear or loud. **noun** an instance of fading.

faeces /fee-seez/ (US spelling **feces**) **plural noun** waste matter discharged from the bowels. ■ **faecal** /fee-k'l/ adjective.

fag[1] Brit. informal **noun 1** a tiring or boring task. **2** a junior pupil at a public school who does minor chores for a senior pupil.

fag[2] **noun** Brit. informal a cigarette.

faggot noun 1 Brit. a ball of seasoned chopped liver which is baked or fried. **2** a bundle of sticks bound together as fuel. **3** N. Amer. informal, disapproving a homosexual man.

Fahrenheit /fa-ruhn-hyt/ **noun** a scale of temperature on which water freezes at 32° and boils at 212°.

fail verb 1 be unsuccessful in an undertaking. **2** be unable to meet the standards set by a test. **3** neglect to do. **4** stop working properly. **5** become weaker or less good. **6** desert or let someone down. **noun** a mark which is not high enough to pass an examination. □ **fail-safe 1** (of machinery) going back to a safe condition if it is faulty. **2** unlikely or unable to fail. **without fail** whatever happens.

failing noun a weakness in a person's character. **preposition** if not.

failure noun 1 lack of success. **2** an unsuccessful person or thing. **3** the ceasing of something to function. **4** an instance of not doing something that is expected.

faint adjective 1 not clearly seen, heard, or smelt. **2** slight. **3** close to losing consciousness. **verb** briefly lose consciousness. **noun** a sudden loss of consciousness. □ **faint-hearted** timid. ■ **faintly** adverb.

fair[1] **adjective 1** treating people equally. **2** just or appropriate. **3** quite large in size or amount. **4** moderately good. **5** (of hair or complexion) light; blonde. **6** (of weather) fine and dry. **7** old use beautiful. □ **fair copy** the final corrected copy of a document. **fair game** a person or thing that

people feel they can criticize or exploit. **fair-weather friend** a person who stops being a friend when you have problems.

fair[2] **noun 1** a gathering of stalls and amusements for public entertainment. **2** a periodic gathering for goods to be sold. **3** an exhibition to promote particular products.

fairground noun an outdoor area where a fair is held.

fairing noun a structure added to make a vehicle, boat, or aircraft more streamlined.

fairly adverb 1 with justice. **2** moderately. **3** actually; really.

fairway noun the part of a golf course between a tee and a green.

fairy noun (plural **fairies**) **1** a small imaginary being that has magical powers. □ **fairy godmother** a female character in fairy stories who brings good fortune to the hero or heroine. **fairy lights** small electric lights used to decorate a Christmas tree. **fairy story** (or **fairy tale**) **1** a children's story about magical beings and lands. **2** an untrue account.

fait accompli /fayt uh-**kom**-pli/ **noun** something that has been done and cannot be changed.

faith noun 1 complete trust or confidence. **2** belief in a religion. **3** a system of religious belief. □ **faith healing** healing achieved by religious faith, rather than by medical treatment.

faithful adjective 1 remaining loyal and committed. **2** accurate; true to the facts. **noun** (**the faithful**) the people who believe in a particular religion. ■ **faithfully** adverb.

faithless adjective disloyal; unable to be trusted.

fake adjective not genuine. **noun** a person or thing that is not genuine. **verb** (**fakes, faking, faked**) **1** make a copy or imitation of something in order to deceive. **2** pretend to have an emotion or illness.

fakir /**fay**-keer/ **noun** a Muslim or

Hindu holy man who lives by begging.

falcon noun a fast-flying bird of prey with long pointed wings.

falconry noun the keeping and training of birds of prey. ■ **falconer** noun.

fall verb (**falls, falling, fell**; past participle **fallen**) **1** move downwards quickly and without control. **2** collapse to the ground. **3** incline or slope down. **4** become less or lower. **5** become. **6** happen; come about. **7** (of someone's face) show dismay. **8** be captured or defeated. noun **1** an act of falling. **2** a thing which falls or has fallen. **3** (falls) a waterfall. **4** a drop in size or number. **5** a defeat or downfall. **6** N. Amer. autumn. □ **fall back** retreat. **fall back on** turn to something for help. **fall for** informal **1** fall in love with. **2** be tricked by. **fall foul of** come into conflict with. **fall guy** informal a person who is blamed for something that is not their fault. **fall in with** meet and become involved with. **fall on 1** attack fiercely or unexpectedly. **2** be the duty of. **fall out** have an argument. **fall short** fail to reach a required standard. **fall through** fail. **fall to** become the duty of.

fallacious /fuh-**lay**-shuhss/ adjective based on a mistaken belief.

fallacy /**fal**-luh-si/ noun (plural **fallacies**) **1** a mistaken belief. **2** a false or misleading argument.

fallback noun an alternative plan for use in an emergency.

fallible /**fal**-li-b'l/ adjective capable of making mistakes. ■ **fallibility** noun.

Fallopian tube /fuh-**loh**-pi-uhn/ noun either of a pair of tubes along which eggs travel from the ovaries to the uterus of a female mammal.

fallout noun **1** radioactive particles that are spread over a wide area after a nuclear explosion. **2** the negative effects of a situation.

fallow adjective (of farmland) ploughed but left for a period without being planted with crops.

false adjective **1** not in accordance with the truth or facts. **2** fake; artificial. **3** deceptive; not what it seems. **4** disloyal. □ **false alarm** a warning given about something that does not happen. **false pretences** behaviour that is intended to deceive. ■ **falsely** adverb **falsity** noun.

falsehood noun **1** the state of being untrue. **2** a lie.

falsetto /fawl-**set**-toh/ noun (plural **falsettos**) a high-pitched voice used by male singers.

falsify verb (**falsifies, falsifying, falsified**) alter something in order to mislead people. ■ **falsification** noun.

falter verb (**falters, faltering, faltered**) **1** lose strength or momentum. **2** move or speak hesitantly.

fame noun the state of being famous.

famed adjective famous; well known.

familial /fuh-**mil**-i-uhl/ adjective having to do with a family.

familiar adjective **1** well known. **2** frequently encountered; common. **3** (**familiar with**) having a good knowledge of. **4** friendly or informal. noun a spirit believed to accompany a witch. ■ **familiarity** noun **familiarly** adverb.

familiarize or **familiarise** verb (**familiarizes, familiarizing, familiarized**) (**familiarize with**) give someone knowledge of something. ■ **familiarization** noun.

family noun (plural **families**) **1** a group of parents and their children. **2** a group of people related by blood or marriage. **3** the children of a person or couple. **4** a group of things that are alike in some way. **5** a group of related plants or animals. adjective designed to be suitable for children as well as adults. □ **family planning** control of the number of children in a family by using contraceptives. **family tree** a diagram showing the relationship between people in a family.

famine noun a period when food is very scarce.

famished adjective informal extremely hungry.

famous adjective **1** known about by many people. **2** informal magnificent. ■ **famously** adverb.

fan[1] noun **1** a device which uses rotating blades to create a current of air. **2** a semicircular object that you wave to cool yourself. verb (**fans, fanning, fanned**) **1** make a current of air blow towards. **2** make a belief or emotion stronger. **3** (**fan out**) spread out from a central point. □ **fan belt** a belt driving the fan that cools the radiator of a motor vehicle.

fan[2] noun a person who is very interested in a sport, celebrity, etc.

fanatic noun a person who is too enthusiastic about something. ■ **fanatical** adjective **fanatically** adverb **fanaticism** noun.

fancier noun a person who keeps or breeds a particular type of animal: *a pigeon fancier.*

fanciful adjective **1** existing only in the imagination. **2** very unusual or creative. ■ **fancifully** adverb.

fancy verb (**fancies, fancying, fancied**) **1** Brit. informal feel a desire for. **2** Brit. informal find someone attractive. **3** imagine; think. adjective (**fancier, fanciest**) elaborate or highly decorated. noun (plural **fancies**) **1** a brief feeling of attraction. **2** the ability to imagine things. **3** a belief or idea that may not be true. □ **fancy dress** an unusual costume or disguise worn at a party. **fancy-free** not in a serious relationship.

fandango /fan-**dang**-goh/ noun (plural **fandangoes** or **fandangos**) a lively Spanish dance for two people.

fanfare noun a short tune played on brass instruments to announce someone or something.

fang noun **1** a canine tooth of a dog or wolf. **2** a tooth with which a snake injects poison.

fanlight noun a small semicircular window over a door or window.

fanny noun (plural **fannies**) **1** Brit. vulgar a woman's genitals. **2** N. Amer. informal a person's bottom.

fantasize or **fantasise** verb (**fantasizes, fantasizing, fantasized**) daydream about something that is desired.

fantastic adjective **1** hard to believe; fanciful. **2** strange or exotic. **3** informal very good or large. ■ **fantastical** adjective **fantastically** adverb.

fantasy noun (plural **fantasies**) **1** the imagining of things that do not exist in reality. **2** a daydream about something that is desired. **3** a type of fiction that involves magic and adventure.

fanzine noun a magazine for fans of a particular performer, team, etc.

far adverb (**further, furthest** or **farther, farthest**) **1** at, to, or by a great distance in space or time. **2** by a great deal. **3** extreme. adjective **1** distant in space or time. **2** extreme. □ **be a far cry from** be very different to. **far-fetched** exaggerated or unlikely. **far-flung** spread out; scattered. **far out 1** unconventional. **2** informal, dated excellent. **the Far East** China, Japan, and other countries of east Asia.

farad noun the basic unit of electrical capacitance.

faraway adjective **1** remote or distant. **2** lost in thought; dreamy.

farce noun **1** a comedy based on situations which are ridiculous and improbable. **2** an absurd event.

farcical adjective absurd or ridiculous. ■ **farcically** adverb.

fare noun **1** the money which a passenger pays to travel on public transport. **2** a range of food. verb (**fares, faring, fared**) get along; have a specified amount of success.

farewell exclamation old use goodbye. noun an act of leaving.

farm noun **1** an area of land and buildings used for growing crops and rearing animals. **2** a farmhouse. verb **1** make a living by growing crops or keeping animals. **2** (**farm out**) give work to other people to do.

farmer noun a person who owns or manages a farm.

farmhouse noun a house attached to a farm.

farrago /fuh-**rah**-goh/ noun (plural **farragos** or **farragoes**) a confused mixture.

farrier noun a person who shoes horses.

farrow noun a litter of pigs. verb (of a sow) give birth to piglets.

fart informal verb **1** discharge wind from the anus. **2** (**fart about** or **around**) waste time on silly or trivial things. noun **1** a discharge of wind from the anus. **2** a boring or unpleasant person.

farther ⇨ **FURTHER**.

farthest ⇨ **FURTHEST**.

farthing noun a former UK coin, worth a quarter of an old penny.

fascia or Brit. **facia** /**fay**-shuh/ noun **1** a board covering the ends of rafters or other fittings. **2** a signboard on a shopfront. **3** chiefly Brit. the dashboard of a motor vehicle.

fascinate verb (**fascinates, fascinating, fascinated**) interest or charm someone greatly. ■ **fascination** noun.

fascism /**fash**-i-z'm/ noun **1** a right-wing system of government characterized by extreme nationalistic beliefs. **2** an attitude which is extremely intolerant or right-wing. ■ **fascist** noun & adjective.

 there is an s before the c: fascism.

fashion noun **1** a popular style or trend. **2** a way of doing something. verb make or shape. □ **after a fashion** to a certain extent but not perfectly.

fashionable adjective in a style that is currently popular. ■ **fashionably** adverb.

fast¹ adjective **1** moving or capable of moving at high speed. **2** taking place quickly. **3** (of a clock or watch) ahead of the correct time. **4** firmly fixed or attached. **5** (of a dye) not fading. adverb **1** quickly. **2** firmly or securely.

fast² verb go without food or drink. noun a period of fasting.

fasten verb **1** close or do up securely. **2** fix or hold in place. **3** (**fasten on**) pick out and concentrate on.

fastener or **fastening** noun a device used to fasten something.

fastidious /fa-**stid**-i-uhss/ adjective

1 paying a lot of attention to detail. **2** very concerned about cleanliness. ■ **fastidiously** adverb.

fastness noun **1** a place that is secure and well protected. **2** the ability of a dye to keep its colour.

fat noun **1** an oily substance found in animals. **2** a substance used in cooking made from the fat of animals, or from plants. adjective (**fatter, fattest**) **1** having too much fat. **2** informal large; substantial. □ **fat cat** disapproving a wealthy and powerful businessman. **live off the fat of the land** have the best of everything. ■ **fatness** noun.

fatal adjective **1** causing death. **2** leading to disaster. ■ **fatally** adverb.

fatalism noun the belief that all events are decided in advance by a supernatural power. ■ **fatalist** noun **fatalistic** adjective.

fatality noun (plural **fatalities**) a death occurring in a war, or caused by an accident or disease.

fate noun **1** a supernatural power believed to control all events. **2** the things that will inevitably happen to someone. verb (**be fated**) be destined to happen in a particular way.

fateful adjective having important, often unpleasant, consequences.

father noun **1** a male parent. **2** an important figure in the early history of something. **3** literary a male ancestor. **4** a priest. **5** (**the Father**) God. verb (**fathers, fathering, fathered**) be the father of. □ **father-in-law** (plural **fathers-in-law**) the father of your husband or wife. ■ **fatherhood** noun.

fatherland noun a person's native country.

fatherly adjective protective and affectionate.

fathom noun a measure of the depth of water, equal to six feet (1.8 metres). verb understand after much thought.

fatigue noun **1** extreme tiredness. **2** weakness in metals caused by repeated stress. **3** (**fatigues**) loose-fitting clothing worn by soldiers. verb (**fatigues, fatiguing, fatigued**) make someone extremely tired.

fatten verb make or become fat or fatter.

fatty adjective (**fattier**, **fattiest**) containing a lot of fat. noun (plural **fatties**) informal a fat person.

fatuity /fuh-**tyoo**-i-ti/ noun **1** foolishness. **2** a foolish act.

fatuous adjective silly and pointless. ■ **fatuously** adverb.

fatwa /**fat**-wah/ noun an authoritative ruling on a point of Islamic law.

faucet /**faw**-sit/ noun N. Amer. a tap.

fault noun **1** a defect or mistake. **2** responsibility for an accident or misfortune. **3** (in tennis) a service that is against the rules. **4** a break in the layers of rock of the earth's crust. verb find a defect or mistake in someone or something. □ **to a fault** excessively. ■ **faultless** adjective.

faulty adjective (**faultier**, **faultiest**) having faults.

faun noun (in Roman mythology) a god of woods and fields, with a human body and a goat's horns, ears, legs, and tail.

fauna noun the animals of a particular region or period.

faux pas /foh **pah**/ noun (plural **faux pas**) a mistake which causes embarrassment in a social situation.

favour (US spelling **favor**) noun **1** approval or liking. **2** a kind or helpful act. **3** special treatment of one person or group. verb **1** regard or treat with favour. **2** work to the advantage of. **3** (favour with) give something desired to. □ **in favour of 1** to be replaced by. **2** in support of.

favourable (US spelling **favorable**) adjective **1** expressing approval or consent. **2** advantageous or helpful. ■ **favourably** adverb.

favourite (US spelling **favorite**) adjective preferred to all others of the same kind. noun **1** a favourite person or thing. **2** the competitor thought most likely to win.

favouritism (US spelling **favoritism**) noun the unfair favouring of one person or group.

fawn[1] noun **1** a young deer. **2** a light brown colour.

fawn[2] verb try to gain someone's approval by flattering them.

fax noun **1** a copy of a document which has been scanned and transmitted electronically. **2** a machine for transmitting and receiving faxes. verb send a document by fax.

faze verb (**fazes**, **fazing**, **fazed**) informal disturb or disconcert.

FBI abbreviation (in the US) Federal Bureau of Investigation.

FC abbreviation Football Club.

fear noun **1** an unpleasant emotion caused by the threat of danger. **2** the likelihood of something unwelcome happening. verb **1** be afraid of. **2** (fear for) be anxious about.

fearful adjective **1** feeling afraid. **2** causing fear. **3** informal very great. ■ **fearfully** adverb.

fearless adjective having no fear; brave. ■ **fearlessly** adverb.

fearsome adjective very impressive and frightening. ■ **fearsomely** adverb.

feasible adjective **1** able to be done easily. **2** informal likely. ■ **feasibility** noun **feasibly** adverb.

feast noun **1** a large meal marking a special occasion. **2** an annual religious celebration. verb **1** have a feast. **2** (feast on) eat large quantities of. □ **feast your eyes on** gaze at with pleasure.

feat noun an achievement requiring great courage, skill, or strength.

feather noun any of the structures growing from a bird's skin, consisting of a hollow shaft fringed with fine strands. verb (**feathers**, **feathering**, **feathered**) turn an oar so that the blade passes through the air edgeways. □ **a feather in your cap** an achievement to be proud of. **feather your nest** make money dishonestly. ■ **feathery** adjective.

feature noun **1** a distinctive element or aspect. **2** a part of the face. **3** a prominent article in a newspaper or magazine. **4** (also **feature film**) the main film showing at a cinema. verb (**features, featuring, featured**) **1** have as a feature. **2** have an important part in something. ■ **featureless** adjective.

febrile /**fee**-bryl/ **adjective 1** having the symptoms of a fever. **2** overactive and excitable.

February /**feb**-ruu-ri, **feb**-yuu-ri, **feb**-yuu-uh-ri/ **noun** (plural **Februaries**) the second month of the year.

 -ruary, not *-uary*: February.

feces US spelling of **FAECES**.

feckless adjective **1** having little determination or purpose. **2** irresponsible.

fecund adjective highly fertile. ■ **fecundity** noun.

fed past and past participle of **FEED**. ◻ **fed up** informal annoyed or bored.

federal adjective **1** having a system of government in which several states unite under a central authority. **2** having to do with the central government of a federation. **3** (**Federal**) US historical having to do with the Northern States in the Civil War. ■ **federalism** noun **federalist** noun & adjective **federally** adverb.

federate verb (**federates, federating, federated**) join as a federation.

federation noun **1** a group of states united under a central authority in which individual states keep control of their internal affairs. **2** a group organized like a federation.

fee noun **1** a payment given for professional advice or services. **2** a sum paid to be allowed to do something.

feeble adjective (**feebler, feeblest**) **1** weak. **2** lacking force; unconvincing. ■ **feebleness** noun **feebly** adverb.

feed verb (**feeds, feeding, fed**) **1** give food to. **2** provide enough food for. **3** (of an animal) eat. **4** supply with material or information. **5** pass something gradually through a confined space. noun **1** an act of feeding. **2** food for domestic animals.

feedback noun **1** comments made in response to something you have done. **2** the return of part of the output of an amplifier to its input, causing a whistling sound.

feeder noun **1** a thing that feeds or supplies something. **2** a minor route that links outlying areas with the main route.

feel verb (**feels, feeling, felt**) **1** be aware of, examine, or search by touch. **2** give a particular sensation when touched. **3** experience an emotion or sensation. **4** be affected by. **5** have a belief or opinion. noun **1** an act of feeling. **2** the sense of touch. **3** a sensation or impression. **4** (**a feel for**) a sensitive appreciation of.

feeler noun **1** an organ used by certain animals for testing things by touch. **2** a cautious proposal intended to find out someone's opinion.

feeling noun **1** an emotional state or reaction. **2** (**feelings**) the emotional side of a person's character. **3** strong emotion. **4** the ability to feel. **5** the sensation of touching or being touched. **6** a belief or opinion. **7** (**feeling for**) an understanding of.

feet plural of **FOOT**.

feign verb pretend to feel or have.

feint /faynt/ **noun** a movement made to deceive an opponent, especially in boxing or fencing. verb make a feint.

feisty /**fy**-sti/ adjective (**feistier, feistiest**) informal spirited and exuberant.

felicitations plural noun congratulations.

felicitous /fuh-**li**-si-tuhss/ adjective well chosen or appropriate.

felicity noun (plural **felicities**) **1** great happiness. **2** the ability to express yourself in an appropriate way. **3** a pleasing feature of an artistic work.

feline adjective having to do with a cat or cats. noun a cat or other animal of the cat family.

fell[1] past of **FALL**.

fell[2] verb **1** cut down a tree. **2** knock down.

fell[3] noun a hill or stretch of high moorland in northern England.

fellow noun **1** informal a man or boy. **2** a person in the same situation as you.

3 a thing of the same kind as another. **4** a member of a learned society. **5** Brit. a member of the governing body of certain colleges. **adjective** in the same situation: *a fellow sufferer.*

fellowship noun **1** friendship between people who share an interest. **2** a group of people who share an interest. **3** the position of a fellow of a college or society.

felon noun a person who has committed a felony.

felonious /fuh-**loh**-ni-uhss/ adjective having to do with crime.

felony noun (plural **felonies**) (in the US and formerly also in English Law) a serious crime.

felt[1] noun cloth made from wool that has been rolled and pressed. ◻ **felt-tip pen** a pen with a writing point made of felt or tightly packed fibres.

felt[2] past and past participle of **FEEL**.

female adjective **1** of the sex that can bear offspring or produce eggs. **2** having to do with women. **3** (of a plant or flower) having a pistil but no stamens. **4** (of a fitting) having a hollow so that a corresponding part can be inserted. **noun** a female person, animal, or plant.

feminine adjective **1** having qualities associated with women. **2** female. **3** Grammar (of nouns and adjectives in some languages) having a gender regarded as female. ■ **femininity** noun.

feminism noun a movement or theory that supports the rights of women. ■ **feminist** noun & adjective.

feminize or **feminise** verb (**feminizes**, **feminizing**, **feminized**) make more feminine or female.

femme fatale /fam fuh-**tahl**/ (plural **femmes fatales** /fam fuh-**tahl**/) an attractive and seductive woman.

femur /**fee**-mer/ noun (plural **femurs** or **femora** /**fem**-uh-ruh/) the bone of the thigh. ■ **femoral** adjective.

fen noun a low and marshy or frequently flooded area of land.

fence noun **1** a barrier made of wire or wood that encloses an area of land. **2** an obstacle for horses to jump over

in a competition. **3** informal a dealer in stolen goods. **verb** (**fences**, **fencing**, **fenced**) **1** surround or protect with a fence. **2** informal deal in stolen goods. **3** practise the sport of fencing. ◻ **sit on the fence** avoid making a decision or commitment. ■ **fencer** noun.

fencing noun **1** the sport of fighting with blunted swords. **2** fences or material for making fences.

fend verb **1** (**fend for yourself**) look after yourself without help from others. **2** (**fend off**) defend yourself from.

fender noun **1** a low frame around a fireplace to stop coals from falling out. **2** a soft object that is hung over the side of ship to protect it from collisions. **3** N. Amer. the mudguard or area around the wheel of a vehicle.

feng shui /feng **shoo**-i, fung **shway**/ noun an ancient Chinese system of designing buildings and arranging objects to ensure a favourable flow of energy.

fennel noun a plant, whose leaves and seeds are used as a herb, and whose base is eaten as a vegetable.

feral adjective **1** (of an animal) wild, especially after having been domesticated. **2** savage or fierce.

ferment verb /fer-**ment**/ **1** break down chemically through the action of yeast or bacteria. **2** stir up disorder. **noun** /**fer**-ment/ social unrest or disorder. ■ **fermentation** noun.

fern noun (plural **fern** or **ferns**) a plant which has feathery fronds and no flowers. ■ **ferny** adjective.

ferocious adjective very fierce or violent. ■ **ferociously** adverb.

ferocity noun the state of being ferocious.

ferret noun a small, fierce animal with a long thin body, used for catching rabbits. **verb** (**ferrets**, **ferreting**, **ferreted**) **1** (**ferreting**) hunting with ferrets. **2** search amongst a lot of things. **3** (**ferret out**) discover something by searching thoroughly.

Ferris wheel noun a fairground ride

consisting of a large upright revolving wheel.

ferrous adjective (of a metal) containing iron.

ferrule noun a metal cap which protects the end of a stick or umbrella.

ferry noun (plural **ferries**) a boat or ship that transports passengers and goods as a regular service. verb (**ferries, ferrying, ferried**) carry by ferry or other transport.

fertile adjective **1** (of soil or land) producing abundant vegetation or crops. **2** (of a person, animal, or plant) able to produce babies or seeds. **3** producing a lot of good results or ideas. ∎ **fertility** noun.

fertilize or **fertilise** verb (**fertilizes, fertilizing, fertilized**) **1** introduce sperm or pollen into an egg or plant so that a new individual develops. **2** add fertilizer to. ∎ **fertilization** noun.

fertilizer or **fertiliser** noun a chemical or natural substance added to soil to make it more fertile.

fervent adjective intensely passionate. ∎ **fervently** adverb.

fervid adjective fervent.

fervour (US spelling **fervor**) noun intense and passionate feeling.

festal adjective relating to a festival.

fester verb (**festers, festering, festered**) **1** (of a wound or sore) become septic. **2** become rotten. **3** become worse or more intense.

festival noun **1** a time when people celebrate a special occasion. **2** an organized series of concerts, films, etc.

festive adjective relating to a festival.

festivity noun (plural **festivities**) **1** joyful celebration. **2** (**festivities**) activities or events celebrating a special occasion.

festoon noun a decorative chain of flowers, leaves, or ribbons. verb decorate with festoons.

fetal or Brit. **foetal** adjective relating to a fetus.

fetch verb **1** go for something and bring it back. **2** sell for a particular price. **3** (**fetch up**) informal arrive or come to rest somewhere. **4** informal hit. **5** (**fetching**) attractive.

fête /fayt/ noun Brit. an outdoor event to raise funds for a special purpose. verb (**fêtes, fêting, fêted**) praise or entertain someone lavishly.

fetid or **foetid** adjective smelling very unpleasant.

fetish noun **1** an object worshipped for its supposed magical powers. **2** a form of sexual desire in which pleasure is gained from a particular object. ∎ **fetishism** noun **fetishist** noun.

fetlock noun a joint of a horse's leg between the knee and the hoof.

fetter noun **1** a chain placed around a prisoner's ankles. **2** (**fetters**) restraints or controls. verb (**fetters, fettering, fettered**) **1** restrain with fetters. **2** (**be fettered**) be restricted.

fettle noun condition.

fettuccine /fet-tuh-**chee**-ni/ plural noun pasta made in ribbons.

fetus or Brit. **foetus** noun (plural **fetuses**) an unborn baby of a mammal.

feud noun a long and bitter dispute. verb take part in a feud.

feudal adjective having to do with feudalism.

feudalism noun the social system in medieval Europe, in which people worked and fought for a nobleman in return for land.

fever noun **1** an abnormally high body temperature. **2** a state of nervous excitement. ∎ **feverish** adjective.

fevered adjective **1** affected with fever. **2** nervously excited.

few determiner, pronoun, & adjective **1** (a few) a small number of; some. **2** not many. noun (**the few**) a select minority.

> ℹ️ make sure you distinguish between **fewer** and **less**. Use **fewer** with plural nouns, as in *there are fewer people here today*; use **less** with nouns referring to things that can't be counted, as in *there is less blossom on this tree*.

fey adjective **1** unworldly and vague. **2** able to see into the future.

fez noun (plural **fezzes**) a conical red hat with a flat top, worn by men in some Muslim countries.

ff. abbreviation following pages.

fiancé /fi-on-say/ noun (feminine **fiancée** /fi-on-say/) a person to whom you are engaged to be married.

fiasco noun (plural **fiascos**) a ridiculous or humiliating failure.

fiat /fy-at/ noun an official order.

fib noun a trivial lie. verb (**fibs, fibbing, fibbed**) tell a fib. ■ **fibber** noun.

fibre (US spelling **fiber**) noun **1** each of the thin threads which form plant or animal tissue, cloth, or minerals. **2** a material made from fibres. **3** the part of some foods that is difficult to digest and which helps food to pass through the body. **4** strength of character. □ **fibre optics** the use of glass fibres to send information in the form of light. ■ **fibrous** adjective.

fibreboard (US spelling **fiberboard**) noun a building material made of compressed wood fibres.

fibreglass (US spelling **fiberglass**) noun **1** a strong material made from glass fibres and plastic. **2** a fabric made from woven glass fibres.

fibula /fib-yuu-luh/ noun (plural **fibulae** /fib-yuu-lee/ or **fibulas**) the outer of the two bones between the knee and the ankle.

fickle adjective changeable in your loyalties.

fiction noun **1** literature describing imaginary events and people. **2** something that is invented and not true. ■ **fictional** adjective.

fictionalize or **fictionalise** verb (**fictionalizes, fictionalizing, fictionalized**) make into a fictional story.

fictitious /fik-tish-uhss/ adjective imaginary or invented; not real.

fiddle informal noun **1** a violin. **2** an act of fraud. verb (**fiddles, fiddling, fiddled**) **1** (**fiddle with**) touch or move something in a nervous way. **2** (**fiddle**

about or around) pass time aimlessly without achieving anything. **3** change the details of something dishonestly. □ **play second fiddle to** take a less important role to. ■ **fiddler** noun.

fiddly adjective Brit. informal complicated and awkward to do or use.

fidelity noun **1** faithfulness to a person or belief. **2** the accuracy with which something is copied or reproduced.

fidget verb (**fidgets, fidgeting, fidgeted**) make small movements because you are nervous or impatient. noun **1** a person who fidgets. **2** (**fidgets**) restlessness. ■ **fidgety** adjective.

fief noun historical an estate held under the feudal system. ■ **fiefdom** noun.

field noun **1** an enclosed area of land for growing crops or keeping animals. **2** a piece of land used for a sport or game. **3** a subject of study or area of activity. **4** an area within which a force has an effect: *a magnetic field*. **5** (**the field**) all the people taking part in a contest or sport. verb **1** Cricket & Baseball attempt to catch or stop the ball after it has been hit. **2** select someone to play in a game or to stand in an election. **3** try to deal with. □ **field day** a good opportunity to do something without being stopped or hindered. **field events** athletic sports other than races. **field glasses** binoculars. **field marshal** the highest rank of officer in the British army. **field sports** hunting, shooting, and fishing. **play the field** informal have a series of casual sexual relationships. ■ **fielder** noun.

fiend noun **1** an evil spirit. **2** a very wicked or cruel person. **3** informal an enthusiast or fanatic: *an exercise fiend*.

fiendish adjective **1** extremely cruel or unpleasant. **2** extremely difficult. ■ **fiendishly** adverb.

fierce adjective **1** violent or aggressive. **2** intense or powerful. ■ **fiercely** adverb **fierceness** noun.

i before *e* except after *c*: **fierce**.

fiery adjective (**fierier, fieriest**) **1** consisting of or resembling fire. **2** quick-tempered or passionate.

fiesta noun (in Spanish-speaking countries) a religious festival.

fife noun a small, shrill flute used in military bands.

fifteen cardinal number one more than fourteen; 15. (Roman numeral: **xv** or **XV**.) ■ **fifteenth** ordinal number.

fifth ordinal number **1** being number five in a sequence; 5th. **2** (**a fifth** or **one fifth**) each of five equal parts of something. □ **fifth column** a group within a country at war who are working for its enemies.

fifty cardinal number (plural **fifties**) ten less than sixty; 50. (Roman numeral: **l** or **L**.) □ **fifty-fifty** with equal shares or chances. ■ **fiftieth** ordinal number.

fig noun a soft, sweet fruit with many small seeds.

fight verb (**fights, fighting, fought**) **1** take part in a violent struggle involving physical force. **2** (**fight off**) defend yourself against an attacker. **3** struggle to overcome, eliminate, or prevent. noun a period of fighting. □ **fighting chance** a possibility of succeeding if you make an effort. **fighting fit** in excellent health. **fight shy of** be unwilling to do or accept.

fighter noun **1** a person or animal that fights. **2** a fast military aircraft designed for attacking other aircraft.

figment noun a thing that exists only in the imagination.

figurative adjective **1** not using words literally; metaphorical. **2** (of art) representing things as they appear in real life. ■ **figuratively** adverb.

figure noun **1** a number or numerical symbol. **2** the body shape of a person, especially a woman. **3** an important or distinctive person. **4** a shape defined by one or more lines. **5** a diagram or drawing. verb (**figures, figuring, figured**) **1** play a significant part. **2** (**figure out**) calculate by arithmetic. **3** (**figure out**) informal understand. **4** N. Amer. informal think; consider. □ **figure of speech** a word or phrase used in a way different from its usual sense. **figure skating** the sport of skating in set patterns.

figurehead noun **1** a wooden statue of a person at the front of a sailing ship. **2** a leader without real power.

figurine noun a small statue of a human form.

filament noun **1** something slender like a thread. **2** a metal wire in a light bulb, which glows when an electric current is passed through it.

filbert noun a cultivated hazelnut.

filch verb informal steal.

file¹ noun **1** a folder or box for keeping loose papers together. **2** a collection of computer data stored under a single name. **3** a line of people or things one behind another. verb (**files, filing, filed**) **1** place in a file. **2** officially present a legal document, charge, etc. **3** walk one behind the other.

file² noun a tool with a roughened surface, used for smoothing or shaping. verb (**files, filing, filed**) smooth or shape with a file.

filial adjective having to do with a son or daughter.

filibuster noun a prolonged speech which obstructs progress in a law-making assembly.

filigree noun delicate ornamental work of fine wire.

filings plural noun small particles rubbed off by a file.

fill verb **1** make or become full. **2** block up a hole or gap. **3** appoint a person to a vacant post. **4** hold a particular position or role. noun (**your fill**) as much as you want or can bear. □ **fill in 1** make a hole completely full of material. **2** complete a form. **3** inform someone fully about a matter. **4** act as a substitute. **fill out** put on weight.

filler noun something used to fill a hole or gap, or to increase bulk.

fillet noun **1** a boneless piece of meat. **2** a side of a fish with the bones taken out. **3** a band or ribbon binding the hair. **verb** (**fillets, filleting, filleted**) make a fish into fillets.

filling noun a quantity or piece of material used to fill something. **adjective** (of food) giving you a pleasantly full feeling.

fillip noun a stimulus or boost.

filly noun (plural **fillies**) **1** a young female horse. **2** humorous a lively girl or young woman.

film noun 1 a thin flexible strip coated with light-sensitive material, used in a camera to make photographs or motion pictures. **2** a story or event recorded by a camera and shown in a cinema or on television. **3** material in the form of a very thin flexible sheet. **4** a thin layer covering a surface. **verb** make a film of; record on film.

filmy adjective (**filmier, filmiest**) thin and almost transparent.

filter noun 1 a device or substance that lets liquid or gas pass through but holds back solid particles. **2** a device that absorbs some of the light passing through it. **3** Brit. (at a junction) a set of lights that lets vehicles turn but stops traffic waiting to go straight ahead. **verb** (**filters, filtering, filtered**) **1** pass through a filter. **2** move gradually in or out of somewhere.

filth noun 1 disgusting dirt. **2** obscene and offensive language or material.

filthy adjective (**filthier, filthiest**) **1** disgustingly dirty. **2** obscene and offensive. **3** informal very unpleasant.

filtrate noun a liquid which has passed through a filter.

filtration noun the action of passing something through a filter.

fin noun 1 a flattened projection on the body of a fish or whale, used for swimming and balancing. **2** an underwater swimmer's flipper. **3** a projection on an aircraft, rocket, etc., for making it more stable.

final adjective 1 coming at the end; last. **2** allowing no further doubt or dispute. **noun 1** the last game in a tournament, which will decide the overall winner. **2** (**finals**) Brit. a series of examinations at the end of a degree course. ▪ **finally adverb**.

finale /fi-**nah**-li/ **noun** the last part of a piece of music or entertainment.

finalist noun a person or team competing in a final.

finality noun the fact or quality of being final.

finalize or **finalise verb** (**finalizes, finalizing, finalized**) decide on or conclude a plan or agreement.

finance noun 1 the management of large amounts of money by governments or large companies. **2** money to support an enterprise. **3** (**finances**) the money held by a state, organization, or person. **verb** (**finances, financing, financed**) provide funding for.

financial adjective relating to finance. □ **financial year** a year as reckoned for purposes of tax or accounting. ▪ **financially adverb**.

financier noun a person who manages money for large organizations.

finch noun a small bird with a short, stubby bill.

find verb (**finds, finding, found**) **1** discover by chance or by searching. **2** discover that something is the case. **3** work out or confirm by research or calculation. **4** (of a law court) officially declare. **noun** a valuable or interesting discovery. □ **find out 1** discover information. **2** discover that someone has lied or been dishonest. ▪ **finder noun**.

finding noun a conclusion reached as a result of an inquiry or trial.

fine¹ adjective 1 of very high quality. **2** satisfactory. **3** in good health and feeling well. **4** (of the weather) bright and clear. **5** (of a thread, strand, or hair) thin. **6** consisting of small particles. **7** delicate or complex. **8** difficult to distinguish because precise or subtle. **verb** (**fines, fining, fined**) (**fine down**) make or become thinner. □ **fine art** art such as painting or sculpture. **fine-tune** make small adjustments to. **with a fine-tooth comb** (or **fine-toothed comb**) with a very thorough search or examination. ▪ **finely adverb fineness noun**. **8**

fine² noun a sum of money that someone has to pay as a punishment. verb (fines, fining, fined) punish by a fine.

finery noun smart, colourful clothes or decoration.

finesse /fi-ness/ noun 1 elegant or delicate skill. 2 subtle skill in handling people or situations.

finger noun 1 each of the four long, thin parts attached to either hand (or five, if the thumb is included). 2 an object shaped like a finger. 3 an amount of alcohol in a glass equivalent to the width of a finger. verb (fingers, fingering, fingered) touch or feel with the fingers.

fingerboard noun a flat strip on the neck of a stringed instrument, against which you press the strings.

fingering noun a way of using the fingers to play a musical instrument.

fingernail noun the nail on the upper surface of the tip of each finger.

fingerprint noun a mark made on a surface by a person's fingertip, which can be used to identify the person. verb record the fingerprints of.

finial /fin-i-uhl/ noun an ornamental top or end of a roof or object.

finicky adjective 1 fussy. 2 excessively detailed or elaborate.

finish verb 1 bring or come to an end. 2 (finish with) have nothing more to do with. 3 reach the end of a race or other competition. 4 (finish off) kill or completely defeat. 5 give an article an attractive surface appearance. noun 1 an end or final stage. 2 the place at which a race or competition ends. 3 the way in which a manufactured article is finished. □ finishing school a college where girls are taught how to behave in fashionable society. ■ finisher noun.

finite /fy-nyt/ adjective limited in size or extent.

Finn noun a person from Finland.

fiord ⇒ FJORD.

fir noun an evergreen coniferous tree with needle-shaped leaves.

fire noun 1 the light, heat, and smoke produced when something burns. 2 an occasion in which a building is damaged or destroyed by a fire. 3 a bundle of wood or coal burnt for heating or cooking. 4 Brit. an appliance for heating a room that uses electricity or gas as fuel. 5 passionate emotion or enthusiasm. 6 the firing of guns. verb (fires, firing, fired) 1 send a bullet, shell, etc. from a gun or other weapon. 2 informal dismiss an employee from a job. 3 direct a rapid series of questions or statements towards someone. 4 supply a furnace or power station with fuel. 5 set fire to. 6 stimulate. 7 bake or dry pottery or bricks in a kiln. □ fire brigade Brit. a body of people employed to put out fires. fire door a strong door for preventing the spread of fire. fire drill a practice of the emergency procedures to be used in case of fire. fire engine a vehicle carrying firefighters and their equipment. fire escape a staircase or ladder for escaping from a building where there is a fire. fire extinguisher a device that discharges a jet of liquid, foam, or gas to put out a fire. fire-raiser Brit. a person who deliberately sets buildings on fire. fire station the headquarters of a fire brigade. the firing line 1 the front line of troops in a battle. 2 a position where you are likely to be criticized. firing squad a group of soldiers ordered to shoot a condemned person.

firearm noun a rifle, pistol, or other portable gun.

fireball noun 1 a ball of flame. 2 an energetic or hot-tempered person.

firebomb noun a bomb intended to cause a fire.

firebrand noun a person who passionately supports a particular cause and stirs up unrest.

firebreak noun a strip of open space cleared in a forest to stop a fire from spreading.

firecracker noun a firework that makes a loud bang.

firefighter noun a person whose job is to put out fires.

firefly noun a kind of beetle which glows in the dark.

fireguard noun a protective screen or grid placed in front of an open fire.

fireman noun a male firefighter.

fireplace noun a space at the base of a chimney for a lighting a fire.

firepower noun the destructive capacity of guns, missiles, or forces.

fireproof adjective able to withstand fire or great heat.

firestorm noun a very fierce fire fanned by strong currents of air.

firetrap noun a building that is difficult to escape from if there is a fire.

firewood noun wood that is burnt as fuel.

firework noun **1** a device that is ignited to produce spectacular effects and explosions. **2** (**fireworks**) an outburst of anger or a display of skill.

firm¹ adjective **1** not giving way under pressure. **2** solidly in place and stable. **3** having steady power or strength. **4** showing determination and strength of character. **5** fixed or definite. verb make firm. ∎ **firmly** adverb **firmness** noun.

firm² noun a business organization.

firmament noun literary the heavens; the sky.

first ordinal number **1** coming before all others in time, order, or importance. **2** before doing something else. **3** informal something never previously done or occurring. **4** Brit. a place in the top grade in an examination for a degree. ◻ **first aid** emergency medical help given to a sick or injured person. **first class 1** the best accommodation in a train, ship, etc. **2** excellent. **firstdegree** (of burns) causing only reddening of the skin. **first-footing** the practice of being the first person to cross someone's threshold in the New Year. **first-hand** from the original source or personal experience; direct. **first lady** the wife of the President of the United States. **first name** a name given to someone when they are born or baptized. **first-rate** excellent. ∎ **firstly** adverb.

firstborn noun the first child to be born to someone.

firth noun a narrow channel of the sea that runs inland.

fiscal adjective relating to the income received by a government, especially from taxes. ∎ **fiscally** adverb.

fish noun (plural **fish** or **fishes**) **1** a cold-blooded animal with a backbone, gills and fins, living in water. **2** the flesh of fish as food. **3** informal a person: *he's an odd fish.* verb **1** try to catch fish. **2** (**fish out**) pull or take out of water or a container. **3** (**fish for**) search or feel for something hidden. **4** (**fish for**) try to obtain something: *fishing for compliments.* ◻ **have other fish to fry** have more important things to do.

fisherman noun a person who catches fish for a living or for sport.

fishery noun (plural **fisheries**) a place where fish are reared for food, or caught in numbers.

fisheye lens noun a very wide-angle lens which gives a curved image.

fishmonger noun a person who sells fish for food.

fishnet noun an open mesh fabric resembling a fishing net.

fishwife noun a woman with a loud, coarse voice.

fishy adjective (**fishier, fishiest**) **1** resembling fish. **2** informal causing feelings of doubt or suspicion.

fissile adjective **1** able to undergo nuclear fission. **2** (of rock) easily split.

fission noun **1** the action of splitting into two or more parts. **2** a reaction in which an atomic nucleus splits in two, releasing a great deal of energy. **3** reproduction by means of a cell dividing into two or more new cells.

fissure noun a long, narrow crack.

fist noun a person's hand when the fingers are bent in towards the palm and held there tightly. ∎ **fistful** noun.

fisticuffs plural noun fighting with the fists.

fit¹ adjective (**fitter, fittest**) **1** of a suitable quality, standard, or type. **2** in good health. verb (**fits, fitting, fitted**)

1 be the right shape and size for. **2** be able to occupy a particular position or space. **3** fix into place. **4** provide with a part or attachment; equip. **5** be in harmony with; match. **6** (fit in) be well suited. ■ **fitness** noun **fitter** noun.

fit² **noun 1** a sudden attack when a person makes violent, uncontrolled movements. **2** a sudden attack of coughing, fainting, etc. **3** a sudden burst of intense feeling or activity. □ **in fits and starts** with irregular bursts of activity.

fitful adjective occurring or working irregularly. ■ **fitfully** adverb.

fitment noun Brit. a fixed item of furniture or piece of equipment.

fitted adjective made to fill a space or to cover something closely.

fitting noun 1 a part that is attached to something. **2** (fittings) items which are fixed in a building but can be removed when the owner moves. **3** a time when someone tries on a garment that is being made or altered. **adjective** appropriate. ■ **fittingly** adverb.

five cardinal number one more than four; 5. (Roman numeral: v or V.) □ (fives) a game in which a ball is hit with a gloved hand or a bat against a wall.

fiver noun Brit. informal a five-pound note.

fix verb 1 attach or position securely. **2** repair or restore. **3** decide or settle on. **4** make arrangements for. **5** make something unchanging or permanent. **6** informal dishonestly influence the outcome of. **noun** informal **1** an act of fixing. **2** a difficult or awkward situation. **3** a dose of an addictive drug. □ **fix up 1** arrange or organize. **2** informal provide with. ■ **fixer** noun.

fixate verb (fixates, fixating, fixated) (fixate on or be fixated on) be obsessed with.

fixation noun an excessive interest in someone or something; an obsession.

fixative noun a substance used to fix or protect something.

fixity noun the state of being unchanging or permanent.

fixture noun 1 a piece of equipment or furniture which is fixed in position. **2** (fixtures) articles attached to a house that normally remain in place when the owner moves. **3** Brit. a sporting event arranged to take place on a particular date.

fizz verb make a hissing sound, like gas escaping in bubbles from a liquid. **noun 1** the sound of fizzing. **2** liveliness.

fizzle verb (fizzles, fizzling, fizzled) **1** make a weak hissing sound. **2** (fizzle out) end or fail in a weak or disappointing way.

fizzy adjective (fizzier, fizziest) (of a drink) containing bubbles of gas.

fjord or **fiord** /fyord, fee-ord/ **noun** a long, narrow inlet of the sea between high cliffs, especially in Norway.

fl. abbreviation fluid.

flab noun informal excess fat on a person's body.

flabbergast verb (be flabbergasted) informal be greatly surprised.

flabby adjective (flabbier, flabbiest) (of a part of a person's body) fat and floppy. ■ **flabbiness** noun.

flaccid /flass-id/ **adjective** soft and limp. ■ **flaccidity** noun.

flack ⇒ **FLAK**.

flag¹ **noun** a piece of cloth that is attached to a pole or rope and used as a symbol of a country or organization or as a signal. **verb** (flags, flagging, flagged) **1** mark something as needing attention. **2** (flag down) signal to a driver to stop.

flag² or **flagstone noun** a flat stone slab used for paving.

flag³ **verb** (flags, flagging, flagged) become tired or less enthusiastic.

flagellate /fla-juh-layt/ **verb** whip someone as a form of religious punishment or for sexual pleasure. ■ **flagellation** noun.

flagon noun a large bottle or jug for wine, cider, or beer.

flagpole or **flagstaff noun** a pole

used for flying a flag.

flagrant /**flay**-gruhnt/ adjective very obvious and unashamed. ■ **flagrantly** adverb.

flagship noun **1** the ship in a fleet which carries the admiral in command. **2** the best or most important thing owned or produced by an organization.

flail noun a tool or machine that is swung to separate grains of wheat from the husks. verb **1** swing something wildly. **2** (**flail around** or **about**) move around in an uncontrolled way.

flair noun **1** a natural ability or talent. **2** stylishness.

flak or **flack** noun **1** anti-aircraft fire. **2** strong criticism.

flake noun a small, flat, very thin piece of something. verb (**flakes, flaking, flaked**) **1** come away from a surface in flakes. **2** separate into flakes. **3** (**flake out**) informal fall asleep or drop from exhaustion. ■ **flaky** adjective.

flambé /**flom**-bay/ verb (**flambés, flambéing, flambéed**) cover food with spirits and set it alight briefly.

flamboyant adjective **1** very confident and lively. **2** brightly coloured or highly decorated. ■ **flamboyance** noun **flamboyantly** adverb.

flame noun **1** a glowing stream of burning gas produced by something on fire. **2** a brilliant orange-red colour. verb (**flames, flaming, flamed**) **1** give off flames. **2** set alight. **3** (of a strong emotion) appear suddenly and fiercely. **4** informal send insulting or hostile email messages to. □ **flamethrower** a weapon that sprays out burning fuel. **old flame** informal a former lover.

flamenco noun a lively style of Spanish guitar music accompanied by singing and dancing.

flamingo noun (plural **flamingos** or **flamingoes**) a wading bird with mainly pink or scarlet plumage and a long neck and legs.

flammable adjective easily set on fire.

flan noun a baked dish consisting of an open pastry case with a savoury or sweet filling.

flange noun a projecting flat rim for strengthening an object or attaching it to something.

flank noun **1** the side of the body between the ribs and the hip. **2** the side of something such as a mountain. **3** the left or right side of a group of people. verb be on the side of.

flannel noun **1** a kind of soft woollen or cotton fabric. **2** (**flannels**) men's trousers made of woollen flannel. **3** Brit. a small piece of towelling for washing yourself. **4** Brit. informal empty or flattering talk. verb (**flannels, flannelling, flannelled**) Brit. informal talk in an empty or flattering way.

flannelette noun a cotton fabric resembling flannel.

flap verb (**flaps, flapping, flapped**) **1** move up and down or from side to side. **2** informal be agitated; panic. noun **1** a piece of something attached on one side only, that covers an opening. **2** a movable section of an aircraft wing, used to control upward movement. **3** a flapping movement. **4** informal a panic.

flapjack noun **1** Brit. a soft biscuit made from oats and butter. **2** N. Amer. a pancake.

flapper noun informal a fashionable young woman of the 1920s.

flare noun **1** a sudden brief burst of flame or light. **2** a device that produces a very bright flame as a signal or marker. **3** (**flares**) trousers whose legs widen from the knees down. verb (**flares, flaring, flared**) **1** burn or shine with a sudden intensity. **2** (usu. **flare up**) suddenly become intense or violent. **3** gradually become wider at one end.

flash verb **1** shine with a bright but brief or irregular light. **2** move swiftly. **3** display words or images briefly or repeatedly. **4** informal display something in an obvious way to impress people. **5** informal (of a man) show his genitals in public. noun **1** a sudden brief burst of bright light. **2** a camera attachment that produces a flash of light, for taking photographs in poor light. **3** a sudden or brief occurrence. **4** Brit. a coloured patch on a uniform, used to identify a regiment, country, etc. **adjective** informal stylish or expensive in a showy way. □ **flash flood** a sudden local flood resulting from very heavy rainfall. **flash in the pan** a sudden but brief success. ■ **flasher** noun.

flashback noun **1** a scene in a film or novel set in a time earlier than the main story. **2** a sudden vivid memory of a past event.

flashgun noun a device which gives a brief flash of intense light, used for taking photographs in poor light.

flashing noun a strip of metal used to seal the join of a roof with another surface.

flashlight noun **1** an electric torch with a strong beam. **2** a flashgun.

flashpoint noun a point or place at which anger or violence flares up.

flashy adjective (flashier, flashiest) attractive in a showy or cheap way.

flask noun **1** a bottle with a narrow neck. **2** Brit. a container that keeps a substance hot or cold by means of a double wall that encloses a vacuum.

flat¹ adjective (flatter, flattest) **1** having a level and even surface. **2** not sloping; horizontal. **3** with a level surface and little height or depth. **4** not lively or interesting. **5** (of a sparkling drink) no longer fizzy. **6** (of something inflated) having lost its air. **7** Brit. (of a battery) having used up its charge. **8** (of a charge or price) fixed. **9** definite and firm. **10** (of a musical sound) below the proper pitch. **11** (of a note or key) lower by a semitone than a specified note or key. **adverb** informal completely; absolutely. **noun 1** the flat part of something. **2** (flats) low level ground near water. **3** informal a flat tyre. **4** (the Flat) Brit. flat racing. **5** a musical note that is a semitone lower than the named note, shown by the sign ♭. □ **flat feet** feet with arches that are lower than usual. **flat out** as fast or as hard as possible. **flat race** a

horse race over a course with no jumps. ■ **flatly** adverb **flatness** noun.

flat² noun Brit. a set of rooms forming an individual home within a larger building.

flatfish noun a sea fish, such as a plaice, that has both eyes on the upper side of its flattened body.

flatmate noun Brit. a person that you share a flat with.

flatten verb make or become flat or flatter.

flatter verb (flatters, flattering, flattered) **1** compliment someone excessively or in an insincere way. **2** (be flattered) feel honoured and pleased. **3** make someone appear attractive.

flattery noun excessive or insincere praise.

flatulent adjective suffering from a build-up of gas in the intestines or stomach. ■ **flatulence** noun.

flatworm noun a type of worm with a simple flattened body.

flaunt verb display proudly or obviously.

> ⓘ don't confuse **flaunt** with **flout**, which means 'ignore a rule'.

flautist noun a flute player.

flavour (US spelling **flavor**) noun **1** the distinctive taste of a food or drink. **2** a particular quality. **verb** give flavour to. ■ **flavouring** noun **flavourless** adjective.

flaw noun **1** a mark or fault that spoils something. **2** a weakness or mistake. ■ **flawed** adjective **flawless** adjective.

flax noun a blue-flowered plant that is grown for its seed (linseed) and for its stalks, from which thread is made.

flaxen adjective literary (of hair) pale yellow.

flay verb **1** strip the skin from a body. **2** whip or beat very harshly.

flea noun a small wingless jumping insect which feeds on the blood of mammals and birds. □ **flea market** a street market selling second-hand goods.

fleapit noun Brit. informal a run-down cinema.

fleck noun **1** a very small patch of

colour or light. **2** a small particle. **verb** mark or dot with flecks.

fledged /flejd/ **adjective** (of a young bird) having developed wing feathers that are large enough for it to fly.

fledgling or **fledgeling** **noun** a young bird that has just learned to fly.

flee **verb** (**flees, fleeing, fled**) run away.

fleece **noun 1** the wool coat of a sheep. **2** a soft, warm fabric with a pile. **verb** (**fleeces, fleecing, fleeced**) informal swindle someone. ■ **fleecy** adjective.

fleet[1] **noun 1** a group of ships travelling together. **2** a group of vehicles or aircraft with the same owner.

fleet[2] **adjective** literary fast and nimble.

fleeting **adjective** lasting for a very short time. ■ **fleetingly** adverb.

flesh **noun 1** the soft substance in the body consisting of muscle and fat. **2** the edible part of a fruit or vegetable. **3** (**the flesh**) the physical aspects and needs of the body. **verb** (**flesh out**) make more detailed. □ **in the flesh** in person.

fleshly **adjective** relating to the body and its needs.

fleshpots **plural noun** humorous places with a lot of nightlife and lively entertainment.

fleshy **adjective** (**fleshier, fleshiest**) **1** plump. **2** soft and thick.

fleur-de-lis or **fleur-de-lys** /flerduh-lee/ **noun** (plural **fleurs-de-lis** /flerduh-lee/) a design showing a lily made up of three petals bound together at the bottom.

flew past of **FLY**[1].

flex **verb 1** bend a limb or joint. **2** tighten a muscle. **3** warp or bend and then return to shape. **noun** Brit. a cable for carrying electric current to an appliance.

flexible **adjective 1** able to bend easily without breaking. **2** able to adapt to different circumstances. ■ **flexibility** noun **flexibly** adverb.

flexitime **noun** a system that lets you vary your working hours.

flick **noun 1** a sudden sharp movement up and down or from side to side. **2** informal a cinema film. **verb 1** make a sudden sharp movement. **2** hit or remove with a quick, light movement. **3** (**flick through**) look quickly through a book, magazine, etc. □ **flick knife** Brit. a knife with a blade that springs out from the handle when you press a button.

flicker **verb** (**flickers, flickering, flickered**) **1** shine or burn unsteadily. **2** appear briefly. **3** make small, quick movements. **noun 1** a flickering movement or light. **2** a brief occurrence of a feeling.

flier ⇨ **FLYER**.

flight **noun 1** the action of flying. **2** a journey made in an aircraft or in space. **3** the path of something through the air. **4** the action of running away. **5** a group of birds or aircraft flying together. **6** a series of steps between floors or levels. **7** the tail of an arrow or dart. □ **flight deck 1** the cockpit of a large aircraft. **2** the deck of an aircraft carrier. **flight of fancy** a highly imaginative idea or story. ■ **flightless** adjective.

flighty **adjective** unreliable and uninterested in serious things.

flimsy **adjective** (**flimsier, flimsiest**) **1** weak and fragile. **2** (of clothing) light and thin. **3** unconvincing: *a flimsy excuse*.

flinch **verb 1** make a quick, nervous movement as a reaction to fear or pain. **2** (**flinch from**) avoid something because you are scared or anxious.

fling **verb** (**flings, flinging, flung**) **1** throw or move forcefully. **2** (**fling on** or **off**) put on or take off clothes carelessly and rapidly. **noun 1** a short period of enjoyment or wild behaviour. **2** a short sexual relationship.

flint **noun 1** a hard grey rock. **2** a piece of flint or a metal alloy, used to produce a spark in a cigarette lighter.

flintlock **noun** an old-fashioned type of gun fired by a spark from a flint.

flip **verb** (**flips, flipping, flipped**) **1** turn over with a quick, smooth movement.

2 move or throw with a sudden sharp movement. **3** (also **flip your lid**) informal suddenly become very angry or lose self-control. **noun** a flipping action or movement. **adjective** not serious or respectful; flippant. □ **flip side** informal **1** the less important side of a pop single. **2** the reverse or unwelcome aspect of a situation.

flip-flop **noun** a light sandal with a thong that passes between the big and second toes.

flippant **adjective** not properly serious or respectful. ■ **flippancy** noun **flippantly** adverb.

flipper **noun 1** a broad, flat limb used for swimming by sea creatures such as turtles. **2** a flat rubber attachment worn on each foot for swimming underwater.

flirt **verb 1** behave as if you are trying to attract someone sexually, but without serious intentions. **2** (**flirt with**) show a casual interest in. **3** (**flirt with**) deliberately risk danger or death. **noun** a person who likes to flirt. ■ **flirtation** noun **flirty** adjective.

flirtatious **adjective** liking to flirt.

flit **verb** (**flits**, **flitting**, **flitted**) move quickly and lightly.

flitter **verb** move quickly here and there.

float **verb 1** rest on the surface of a liquid without sinking. **2** move or be held up in a liquid or the air. **3** put forward a suggestion. **4** (**floating**) unsettled in your opinions, where you live, etc. **5** put shares in a company on sale for the first time. **noun 1** a lightweight object designed to float on water. **2** a vehicle that carries a display in a procession. **3** Brit. a sum of money available for minor expenses. ■ **floaty** adjective.

floatation ⇒ **FLOTATION**.

flock¹ **noun 1** a number of birds, sheep, or goats together. **2** (**a flock or flocks**) a large number or crowd. **3** a Christian congregation. **verb** gather or move in a flock.

flock² **noun 1** a soft material for stuffing cushions and quilts. **2** powdered wool or cloth, used to give a raised pattern on wallpaper.

floe **noun** a sheet of floating ice.

flog **verb** (**flogs**, **flogging**, **flogged**) **1** beat with a whip or stick as a punishment. **2** Brit. informal sell.

flood **noun 1** an overflow of a large amount of water over dry land. **2** an overwhelming quantity or outpouring. **3** the rising of the tide. **verb 1** cover with water in a flood. **2** (of a river) overflow its banks. **3** arrive in very large numbers. □ **flood plain** a low-lying area next to a river that is regularly flooded. **flood tide** an incoming tide.

floodgate **noun 1** a gate that can be opened or closed to control a flow of water. **2** (**floodgates**) controls that hold back something powerful.

floodlight **noun** a large, powerful lamp used to light up a sports ground. **verb** (**floodlights**, **floodlighting**, **floodlit**) light up with floodlights.

floor **noun 1** the lower surface of a room. **2** a storey of a building. **3** the bottom of the sea, a cave, etc. **4** (**the floor**) the part of a law-making body in which members sit. **verb 1** provide a room with a floor. **2** informal knock to the ground. **3** informal baffle completely. □ **floor show** an entertainment presented on the floor of a nightclub or restaurant.

floorboard **noun** a long plank making up part of a wooden floor.

floozy or **floozie** **noun** (plural **floozies**) informal an immoral or sexually provocative girl or woman.

flop **verb** (**flops**, **flopping**, **flopped**) **1** hang or swing loosely. **2** sit or lie down heavily. **3** informal fail totally. **noun 1** a heavy and clumsy fall. **2** informal a total failure.

floppy **adjective** not firm or rigid. □ **floppy disk** a flexible disk used for storing computer data.

flora **noun** the plants of a particular area or period.

floral **adjective** having to do with flowers.

floret **noun 1** each of the small flowers

making up a flower head. **2** each of the flowering stems making up a head of cauliflower or broccoli.

florid adjective **1** having a red or flushed complexion. **2** over-elaborate or ornate.

florin noun a former British coin worth two shillings.

florist noun a person who sells cut flowers.

floss noun **1** silk thread used in embroidery. **2** (also **dental floss**) soft thread used to clean between the teeth. **verb** clean between the teeth with dental floss.

flotation or **floatation** noun **1** the action of floating. **2** the offering of a company's shares for sale for the first time.

flotilla noun a small fleet of ships or boats.

flotsam noun wreckage found floating on the sea.

flounce verb (**flounces, flouncing, flounced**) move in an angry or impatient way. **noun 1** an exaggerated action expressing annoyance or impatience. **2** a wide strip of material sewn to a skirt or dress.

flounder[1] verb (**flounders, floundering, floundered**) **1** stagger clumsily in mud or water. **2** have trouble doing or understanding something.

flounder[2] noun a flatfish.

flour noun a powder produced by grinding grain, used to make bread, cakes, and pastry. ■ **floury** adjective.

flourish verb **1** grow or develop in a healthy or vigorous way. **2** be successful. **3** wave about in a noticeable way. **noun 1** a bold or unrestrained gesture. **2** an ornamental flowing curve in handwriting. **3** a fanfare played by brass instruments.

flout verb openly fail to follow a rule, law, or custom.

> ⓘ don't confuse **flout** with **flaunt**, which means 'display proudly or obviously'.

flow verb **1** move steadily and continuously in a current or stream. **2** hang loosely and elegantly. **noun** a steady, continuous stream. □ **flow chart** a diagram that shows the sequence of stages making up a complex process.

flower noun **1** the part of a plant from which the seed or fruit develops, usually having brightly coloured petals. **2** (**the flower of**) the best of a group. **verb** (**flowers, flowering, flowered**) **1** produce flowers. **2** develop fully and richly.

flowerpot noun a container for growing plants in.

flowery adjective **1** full of or decorated with flowers. **2** (of speech or writing) elaborate.

flown past participle of **FLY**[1].

flu noun influenza or any similar, milder infection.

fluctuate verb (**fluctuates, fluctuating, fluctuated**) rise and fall irregularly in number or amount. ■ **fluctuation** noun.

flue noun a pipe that takes smoke and gases away from a chimney, heater, etc.

fluent adjective **1** able to use a language in a clear and natural way. **2** smoothly graceful and easy. ■ **fluency** noun **fluently** adverb.

fluff noun **1** soft fibres gathered in small, light clumps. **2** the soft fur or feathers of a young mammal or bird. **3** trivial entertainment or writing. **verb 1** (usu. **fluff up**) make fuller and softer by shaking or patting. **2** informal fail to do something properly.

fluffy adjective (**fluffier, fluffiest**) **1** covered with fluff. **2** (of food) light in texture.

flugelhorn /floo-guhl-horn/ noun a brass musical instrument like a cornet but with a broader tone.

fluid noun a liquid or gas. adjective **1** able to flow easily. **2** not fixed or stable. **3** graceful. □ **fluid ounce** Brit. one twentieth of a pint. ■ **fluidity** noun **fluidly** adverb.

fluke noun something lucky that happens by chance. ■ **fluky** adjective.

flume noun **1** an artificial channel for carrying water. **2** a water slide at a swimming pool or amusement park.

flummery noun (plural **flummeries**) empty talk or compliments.

flummox verb informal baffle someone completely.

flung past and past participle of **FLING**.

flunk verb informal, chiefly N. Amer. fail an examination.

flunkey or **flunky** noun (plural **flunkeys** or **flunkies**) **1** a uniformed male servant. **2** a person who does menial tasks.

fluoresce verb (**fluoresces, fluorescing, fluoresced**) shine or glow brightly.

fluorescent adjective **1** giving off bright light when exposed to radiation such as ultraviolet light. **2** vividly colourful. ■ **fluorescence** noun.

☑ fluor-, not flour-: fluorescent.

fluoridate verb (**fluoridates, fluoridating, fluoridated**) add fluoride to a water supply. ■ **fluoridation** noun.

fluoride /floo-uh-ryd, flor-yd/ noun a compound of fluorine that is added to water supplies or toothpaste to reduce tooth decay.

fluorine /floo-uh-reen, flor-een/ noun a poisonous pale yellow gas.

fluorite noun a mineral found in the form of crystals.

fluorspar = **FLUORITE**.

flurry noun (plural **flurries**) **1** a small swirling mass of snow, leaves, etc. moved by a gust of wind. **2** a sudden short spell of commotion or excitement. **3** a number of things arriving suddenly and at the same time.

flush¹ verb **1** (of a person's skin or face) become red and hot. **2** glow with warm colour or light. **3** (**be flushed with**) be elated by. **4** clean something by passing large quantities of water through it. **5** drive a bird or animal from cover. noun **1** a reddening of the face or skin. **2** a sudden rush of intense emotion. **3** a period of freshness and vigour: *the first flush of youth.* **4** an act of flushing.

flush² adjective **1** completely level with another surface. **2** informal having plenty of money.

flush³ noun (in poker or brag) a hand of cards all of the same suit.

fluster noun an agitated and confused state.

flustered adjective agitated and confused.

flute noun **1** a high-pitched wind instrument that you hold sideways and play by blowing across a hole at one end. **2** a tall, narrow wine glass.

fluted adjective having ornamental vertical grooves.

flutter verb (**flutters, fluttering, fluttered**) **1** fly unsteadily by flapping the wings quickly and lightly. **2** move or fall with a light trembling motion. **3** (of a pulse or heartbeat) beat feebly or irregularly. noun **1** a state of nervous excitement. **2** Brit. informal a small bet. ■ **fluttery** adjective.

fluvial /floo-vi-uhl/ adjective technical having to do with a river.

flux noun **1** continuous change. **2** a flow.

fly¹ verb (**flies, flying, flew**; past participle **flown**) **1** (of a winged creature or aircraft) move through the air under control. **2** control the flight of an aircraft. **3** move quickly through the air. **4** go or move quickly. **5** (of a flag) be displayed on a flagpole. **6** (**fly into**) suddenly go into a rage or temper. **7** (**fly at**) attack. **8** old use run away. noun (plural **flies**) **1** (Brit. also **flies**) an opening at the crotch of a pair of trousers, closed with a zip or buttons. **2** a flap of material covering the opening of a tent. **3** (**the flies**) the space over the stage in a theatre. □ **fly-by-night** unreliable or untrustworthy. **flying picket** Brit. a person who travels to picket a workplace where there is a strike. **fly-post** Brit. put up advertising posters without permission. **flying saucer** a disc-shaped flying craft supposedly piloted by aliens. **flying squad** a division of a police force which is capable of reaching an incident quickly. **flying start** a good beginning that gives an advantage over competitors. **fly in the face of** do the opposite of what is usual or expected. **fly off the handle** informal lose your temper. **with flying colours** with distinction.

fly² noun (plural **flies**) **1** a flying insect with transparent wings. **2** an artificial flying insect used as a fishing bait. □ **a fly in the ointment** a minor irritation that spoils the enjoyment of something. **fly on the wall** an unnoticed observer.

fly³ adjective (**flyer, flyest**) Brit. informal knowing and clever.

flyaway adjective (of hair) fine and difficult to control.

flyblown adjective contaminated by contact with flies.

flycatcher noun a small bird that catches flying insects.

flyer or **flier** noun **1** a person or thing that flies. **2** informal a fast-moving person or thing. **3** a small printed advertisement. **4** a flying start.

flyleaf noun (plural **flyleaves**) a blank page at the beginning or end of a book.

flyover noun Brit. a bridge carrying one road or railway line over another.

flypaper noun strips of sticky paper that are hung up to catch and kill flies.

flysheet noun Brit. a fabric cover over a tent for keeping the rain out.

flywheel noun a heavy revolving wheel in a machine that helps it to work smoothly.

FM abbreviation frequency modulation.

foal noun a young horse or related animal. **verb** give birth to a foal.

foam noun **1** a mass of small bubbles formed on the surface of liquid. **2** a liquid substance containing many small bubbles. **3** a lightweight form of rubber or plastic that is full of small holes. **verb** form or produce foam. ■ **foamy** adjective.

fob¹ noun **1** a chain attached to a watch for carrying in a pocket. **2** a tab on a key ring.

fob² verb (**fobs, fobbing, fobbed**) **1** (**fob off**) try to deceive someone into accepting excuses or something inferior. **2** (**fob off on**) give something inferior to.

focal adjective relating to a focus. □ **focal point 1** the point at which rays or waves of light, sound, etc. meet, or from which they seem to come. **2** the centre of interest or activity.

fo'c'sle ⇒ **FORECASTLE**.

focus /foh-kuhss/ noun (plural **focuses** or **foci** /foh-sI/) **1** the centre of interest or activity. **2** the state of having or producing a clear and defined image: *his face is out of focus*. **3** the point at which an object must be situated for a lens or mirror to produce a clear image of it. **4** a focal point. **verb** (**focuses, focusing** or **focussing, focused** or **focussed**) **1** adapt to the amount of light available and become able to see clearly. **2** adjust the focus of a telescope, camera, etc. **3** (of rays or waves) meet at a single point. **4** (**focus on**) pay particular attention to. □ **focus group** a group of people assembled to assess a new product, political campaign, etc.

fodder noun **1** food for cattle and other livestock. **2** a person or thing regarded only as material to satisfy a need.

foe noun an enemy or opponent.

foetid ⇒ **FETID**.

foetus ⇒ **FETUS**.

fog noun a thick cloud of water droplets which is difficult to see through. **verb** (**fogs, fogging, fogged**) **1** become covered with steam. **2** confuse.

fogey noun (plural **fogeys** or **fogies**) a very old-fashioned or conservative person.

foggy adjective (**foggier, foggiest**) **1** full of fog. **2** confused.

foghorn noun a device that makes a loud, deep sound as a warning to ships in fog.

foible noun a minor weakness or eccentricity.

foil¹ verb prevent someone doing

something; thwart.

foil[2] noun **1** metal in the form of a thin flexible sheet. **2** a person or thing that goes well with another.

foil[3] noun a light, blunt-edged fencing sword.

foist verb (**foist on**) impose an unwelcome person or thing on.

fold[1] verb **1** bend something over on itself so that one part of it covers another. **2** be able to be folded into a flatter shape. **3** clasp someone in your arms. **4** informal (of a company) stop trading as a result of financial problems. **5** (**fold in** or **into**) mix one ingredient gently with another. noun **1** a folded part. **2** a line or crease produced by folding.

fold[2] noun **1** a pen or enclosure for livestock. **2** (**the fold**) a group or community.

folder noun a folding cover or wallet for storing loose papers.

foliage noun the leaves of plants.

folic acid noun a vitamin found especially in green vegetables, liver, and kidney.

folio /foh-li-oh/ noun (plural **folios**) **1** a sheet of paper folded once to form four pages of a book. **2** a large-sized book made up of such sheets.

folk plural noun **1** (also **folks**) informal people in general. **2** (**your folks**) informal your family. **3** (also **folk music**) traditional music that is passed on from person to person. □ **folk dance** a traditional dance of a particular place. **folk tale** a traditional story passed on by word of mouth.

folklore noun the traditional stories and customs of a community.

folksy adjective traditional and homely.

follicle noun one of the small holes in the skin that hair grows out of.

follow verb **1** move behind. **2** go after someone to observe them. **3** go along a route. **4** come after in time or order. **5** be a result or consequence. **6** act according to an instruction or example. **7** understand or pay attention to. **8** practise or undertake a career or

course of action. **9** (**follow through**) continue an action or task to its end. **10** (**follow up**) pursue something further. □ **follow suit** do the same as someone else.

follower noun **1** a person who follows. **2** a supporter, fan, or disciple.

following preposition coming after or as a result of. noun a body of supporters. adjective **1** next in time or order. **2** about to be mentioned.

folly noun (plural **follies**) **1** foolishness. **2** a foolish act. **3** an ornamental building with no practical purpose.

foment /foh-**ment**/ verb stir up revolution or conflict.

fond adjective **1** (**fond of**) having an affection for. **2** affectionate. **3** hoped for but unlikely to be fulfilled. ■ **fondly** adverb **fondness** noun.

fondant noun a thick paste made of sugar and water, used in making sweets and icing cakes.

fondle verb (**fondles, fondling, fondled**) stroke or caress lovingly or erotically.

fondue noun a dish in which you dip small pieces of food into melted cheese or a hot sauce.

font noun **1** a large stone bowl in a church for the water used in baptizing people. **2** (Brit. also **fount**) a set of type used in printing.

food noun any substance that people or animals eat to maintain life. □ **food chain** a series of creatures in which each depends on the next as a source of food. **food for thought** something that makes you think seriously. **food poisoning** illness caused by food contaminated by bacteria.

foodstuff noun a substance that can be eaten as food.

fool[1] noun **1** a person who acts unwisely. **2** historical a jester or clown. verb **1** trick or deceive. **2** (**fool about** or **around**) act in a joking or silly way. □ **fool's gold** a yellowish mineral that can be mistaken for gold. **fool's paradise** a happy state that is based on ignoring possible trouble.

fool[2] noun Brit. a cold dessert made of

puréed fruit and cream.

foolhardy adjective recklessly bold or rash.

foolish adjective lacking good sense; silly or unwise. ■ **foolishly** adverb **foolishness** noun.

foolproof adjective incapable of going wrong or being wrongly used.

foolscap noun Brit. a size of paper, about 330 × 200 (or 400) mm.

foot noun (plural **feet**) **1** the part of the leg below the ankle, on which a person walks. **2** the bottom of something vertical. **3** the end of a bed where the occupant's feet normally rest. **4** a unit of length equal to 12 inches (30.48 cm). **5** a group of syllables making up a basic unit of rhythm in poetry. verb informal pay a bill. □ **feet of clay** a flaw in a person who is greatly admired. **foot-and-mouth disease** a disease of cattle and sheep, causing ulcers on the hoofs and around the mouth.

footage noun a length of film made for cinema or television.

football noun **1** a team game involving kicking a ball, in particular (in the UK) soccer or (in the US) American football. **2** a large inflated ball used in football. ■ **footballer** noun.

footbridge noun a bridge for pedestrians.

footfall noun the sound of a footstep or footsteps.

foothill noun a low hill at the base of a mountain.

foothold noun **1** a place where you can put a foot down securely while climbing. **2** a secure position from which to make further progress.

footing noun **1** a secure grip with the feet. **2** the basis on which something is established or operates.

footlights plural noun a row of spotlights along the front of a stage at the level of the actors' feet.

footling adjective unimportant and irritating.

footloose adjective free to do as you please.

footman noun a servant who lets in visitors and waits at table.

footnote noun an additional piece of information printed at the bottom of a page.

footpad noun (in the past) a highwayman who operated on foot.

footpath noun a path for people to walk along.

footprint noun the mark left by a foot or shoe on the ground.

footsore adjective having sore feet from walking.

footstep noun a step taken in walking.

footstool noun a low stool for resting the feet on when sitting.

fop noun a man who is too concerned with his clothes and appearance. ■ **foppish** adjective.

for preposition **1** affecting or relating to. **2** in favour of. **3** on behalf of. **4** because of. **5** so as to get, have, or do. **6** in place of. **7** in exchange for. **8** in the direction of. **9** over a distance or during a period. **10** so as to happen at. conjunction literary because.

fora plural of **FORUM**.

forage verb (**forages, foraging, foraged**) search for food. noun food for horses and cattle. •

foray noun **1** a sudden attack or move into enemy territory. **2** a brief but spirited attempt to become involved in a new activity.

forbear[1] /for-**bair**/ verb (**forbears, forbearing, forbore**; past participle **forborne**) stop yourself from doing something.

forbear[2] /for-**bair**/ ⇒ **FOREBEAR**.

forbearance noun patient self-control.

forbearing adjective patient and self-controlled.

forbid verb (**forbids, forbidding, forbade** or **forbad**; past participle **forbidden**) **1** refuse to allow. **2** order someone not to do.

forbidding adjective appearing unfriendly or threatening. ■ **forbiddingly** adverb.

force noun **1** physical strength or energy that causes something to move. **2** violence used to obtain or achieve something. **3** effect or influence. **4** a person or thing that has influence. **5** an organized body of soldiers, police, or workers. **6 (the forces)** Brit. informal the army, navy, and air force. **verb (forces, forcing, forced) 1** make someone do something against their will. **2** use physical strength to move something. **3** achieve by effort. **4 (force on)** impose something on. □ **force-feed** force someone to eat food. **in force 1** in great strength or numbers. **2** (of a law or rule) in effect.

forceful adjective powerful and confident. ■ **forcefully** adverb.

forcemeat noun chopped meat or vegetables used as a stuffing.

forceps /for-seps/ plural noun a pair of pincers used in surgery.

forcible adjective done by force. ■ **forcibly** adverb.

ford noun a shallow place in a river or stream where it can be crossed. **verb** cross a river or stream at a ford.

fore adjective found or placed in front. **noun** the front part of something. **combining form (fore-) 1** in front. **2** in advance. **3** coming before: *forefather*. **exclamation** called out as a warning to people in the path of a golf ball.

forearm[1] **noun** the part of a person's arm from the elbow to the wrist or the fingertips.

forearm[2] **verb (be forearmed)** be prepared in advance for danger or attack.

forebear or **forbear** noun an ancestor.

foreboding noun a feeling that something bad will happen. **adjective** suggesting that something bad will happen.

forecast verb **(forecasts, forecasting, forecast** or **forecasted)** predict what will happen in the future. **noun** a prediction. ■ **forecaster** noun.

forecastle or **fo'c's'le** /fohk-suhl/ **noun** the front part of a ship below the deck.

foreclose verb **(forecloses, foreclosing, foreclosed)** take possession of a property because the occupant has failed to keep up their mortgage payments. ■ **foreclosure** noun.

forecourt noun **1** an open area in front of a large building or petrol station. **2** Tennis the part of the court between the service line and the net.

forefather noun an ancestor.

forefinger noun the finger next to the thumb.

forefoot noun **(plural forefeet)** each of the two front feet of a four-footed animal.

forefront noun the leading position.

forego[1] ⇨ **FORGO**.

forego[2] verb **(foregoes, foregoing, forewent;** past participle **foregone)** old use come before in place or time. □ **foregone conclusion** a result that can be easily predicted.

foregoing adjective previously mentioned.

foreground noun **1** the part of a view or image nearest to the observer. **2** the most important position.

forehand noun (in tennis and similar games) a stroke played with the palm of the hand facing in the direction of the stroke.

forehead noun the part of the face above the eyebrows.

foreign adjective **1** having to do with a country or language other than your own. **2** coming from outside. **3 (foreign to)** unfamiliar to or untypical of. □ **foreign body** a piece of unwanted matter that has entered something. **foreign exchange** the money of other countries.

> ☑ single *r*, silent *g*: for*eig*n is an exception to the *i* before *e* rule.

foreigner noun **1** a person from a foreign country. **2** informal a stranger.

foreknowledge noun awareness of something before it happens.

forelock noun a lock of hair growing just above the forehead.

foreman noun **1** a worker who supervises other workers. **2** (in a law court) a person who is head of a jury.

foremast noun the mast of a ship nearest the bow.

foremost adjective the highest in rank, importance, or position. adverb in the first place.

forename noun a person's first name.

forensic /fuh-**ren**-sik/ adjective **1** having to do with the use of scientific methods in investigating crime. **2** having to do with courts of law.

foreplay noun things such as kissing and touching that people do before having sex.

forerunner noun a person or thing which exists before another comes or is developed.

foresee verb (foresees, foreseeing, foresaw; past participle foreseen) be aware of something before it happens; predict. ■ foreseeable adjective.

foreshadow verb be a warning or indication of a future event.

foreshore noun the part of a shore between the highest and lowest levels reached by the sea.

foreshorten verb **1** portray something as being closer or shallower than it really is. **2** end something prematurely.

foresight noun the ability to predict future events and needs.

foreskin noun the roll of skin covering the end of the penis.

forest noun **1** a large area covered thickly with trees and plants. **2** a large number of tangled or upright objects. ■ forested adjective.

forestall verb prevent or delay something by taking action in advance.

forestry noun the science or practice of planting and taking care of forests. ■ forester noun.

foretaste noun a sample of something that lies ahead.

foretell verb (foretells, foretelling, foretold) predict.

forethought noun careful consideration of what will be necessary or

may happen in the future.

forever adverb **1** (also for ever) for all future time. **2** a very long time. **3** continually.

forewarn verb warn in advance.

forewent past of **FOREGO**[1], **FOREGO**[2].

foreword noun a short introduction to a book.

forfeit /**for**-fit/ verb (forfeits, forfeiting, forfeited) be deprived of something as a penalty for doing wrong. noun a penalty for doing wrong. adjective lost or given up as a forfeit.

forge[1] verb (forges, forging, forged) **1** shape a metal object by heating and hammering it. **2** create something through effort. **3** produce a copy of a banknote, signature, etc. to deceive people. noun **1** a blacksmith's workshop. **2** a furnace for melting or refining metal. ■ forger noun forgery noun.

forge[2] verb (forges, forging, forged) **1** move forward gradually or steadily. **2** (forge ahead) make progress.

forget verb (forgets, forgetting, forgot; past participle forgotten or chiefly US forgot) **1** be unable to remember. **2** fail to remember to do something. **3** stop thinking of something. **4** (forget yourself) behave inappropriately. □ forget-me-not a plant with light blue flowers. ■ forgettable adjective.

forgetful adjective tending to forget things. ■ forgetfully adverb.

forgive verb (forgives, forgiving, forgave; past participle forgiven) **1** stop feeling angry or resentful towards a person who has done something hurtful or wrong. **2** excuse an offence or mistake. ■ forgivable adjective.

forgiveness noun the action of forgiving, or the state of being forgiven.

forgo or **forego** verb (forgoes, forgoing, forwent; past participle forgone) go without something that you want.

fork noun **1** a small implement with two or more prongs used for lifting or holding food. **2** a similar-shaped farm or garden tool used for digging or lifting. **3** the point where a road, river, etc. divides into two parts. **4** either of two such parts. verb **1** divide into two parts. **2** take one route or the other at a fork. **3** dig or lift with a fork. **4 (fork out)** informal pay money.

forked adjective **1** having a divided or fork-shaped end. **2** in the shape of a zigzag.

forklift truck noun a vehicle with a device on the front for lifting and carrying heavy loads.

forlorn /fer-**lorn**/ adjective **1** pitifully sad and lonely. **2** unlikely to succeed. ◻ **forlorn hope** a hope that is unlikely to be fulfilled. ■ **forlornly** adverb.

form noun **1** the shape or arrangement of something. **2** a particular way in which a thing exists. **3** a type. **4** the way something is usually done. **5** a printed document with blank spaces for information to be filled in. **6** Brit. a class or year in a school. **7** the current standard of play of a sports player or team. **8** a person's mood and state of health. verb **1** create something by shaping material or bringing together parts. **2** go to make up. **3** establish or develop. ■ **formless** adjective.

formal adjective **1** suitable for official or important occasions. **2** officially recognized. **3** arranged in a precise or regular way. ■ **formally** adverb.

formaldehyde /for-**mal**-di-hyd/ noun a strong-smelling gas mixed with water and used as a preservative and disinfectant.

formalin /**for**-muh-lin/ noun a solution of formaldehyde in water.

formality noun (plural **formalities**) **1** the rigid following of rules or customs. **2** a thing done simply to follow customs or rules. **3 (a formality)** a thing done as a matter of course.

formalize or **formalise** verb (formalizes, formalizing, formalized) make an arrangement official.

format noun **1** the way in which something is arranged or presented. **2** the shape, size, and presentation of a book, document, etc. verb (formats, formatting, formatted) give some-

thing a particular format.

formation noun **1** the action of forming. **2** something that has been formed. **3** a particular structure or arrangement.

formative adjective having a strong influence in the way something is formed.

former[1] adjective **1** having previously been the specified thing. **2** in the past. **3 (the former)** referring to the first of two things mentioned.

former[2] noun **1** a person or thing that forms something. **2** Brit. a person in a particular school year.

formerly adverb in the past.

Formica noun trademark a hard plastic material used for worktops, cupboard doors, etc.

formic acid noun an acid present in the fluid discharged by some ants.

formidable adjective frightening or intimidating through being very large, powerful, or capable. ■ **formidably** adverb.

formula noun (plural **formulae** /for-myuu-lee/ or **formulas**) **1** a mathematical relationship or . rule expressed in symbols. **2** a set of chemical symbols showing what elements are present in a compound. **3** a fixed form of words used in particular situations. **4** a method for achieving something. **5** a list of ingredients with which something is made. **6** a powder-based milky drink for babies.

formulaic adjective **1** containing a set form of words. **2** made by closely following a rule or style.

formulate verb (formulates, formulating, formulated) **1** create or prepare something methodically. **2** express an idea clearly and briefly. ■ **formulation** noun.

fornicate verb (fornicates, fornicating, fornicated) formal have sex with someone you are not married to. ■ **fornication** noun **fornicator** noun.

forsake verb (forsakes, forsaking, forsook; past participle **forsaken**) literary **1** abandon. **2** give up.

forsooth adverb old use indeed.

forswear verb (forswears, forswearing, forswore; past participle forsworn) formal **1** agree to give up or do without. **2 (forswear yourself** or **be forsworn)** lie after swearing to tell the truth.

forsythia noun a shrub with bright yellow flowers.

fort noun a building constructed to defend a place against attack. □ hold the fort be responsible for something in someone's absence.

forte /for-tay/ noun a thing for which someone has a particular talent.

forth adverb old use **1** forwards or into view. **2** onwards in time.

forthcoming adjective **1** about to happen or appear. **2** made available when required. **3** willing to reveal information.

forthright adjective direct and outspoken.

forthwith adverb without delay.

fortify verb (fortifies, fortifying, fortified) **1** strengthen a place to protect it against attack. **2** give strength or energy to. **3** add alcohol or vitamins to food or drink. ■ fortification noun.

fortissimo /for-**tiss**-i-moh/ adverb & adjective Music very loud or loudly.

fortitude noun courage and strength when facing pain or trouble.

fortnight noun Brit. a period of two weeks.

fortnightly Brit. adjective & adverb happening or produced every two weeks.

fortress noun a building or town which has been strengthened against attack.

fortuitous /for-**tyoo**-i-tuhss/ adjective **1** happening by chance. **2** lucky. ■ fortuitously adverb.

fortunate adjective **1** involving good luck. **2** advantageous or favourable. ■ fortunately adverb.

fortune noun **1** chance or luck as it affects human affairs. **2 (fortunes)** the success or failure of a person or undertaking. **3** a large amount of money or property. □ tell someone's fortune make predictions about a person's future.

forty cardinal number (plural forties) ten less than fifty; 40. (Roman numeral: **xl** or **XL**.) □ forty winks informal a short daytime sleep. ■ fortieth ordinal number.

 for-, not four-: forty.

forum noun (plural forums) **1** a meeting or opportunity for exchanging views. **2** (plural fora) (in ancient Roman cities) a square or marketplace used for public business.

forward adverb & adjective **1** in the direction that you are facing or travelling. **2** towards a successful end. **3** ahead in time. **4** in or near the front of a ship or aircraft. adjective bold or over-familiar in manner. noun an attacking player in sport. verb send a letter, especially on to a further destination. ■ forwards adverb.

forwent past of FORGO.

fossil noun **1** the remains of a prehistoric plant or animal that have become hardened into rock. **2** humorous a very out-of-date person or thing. □ fossil fuel a fuel such as coal or gas that is formed from the remains of animals and plants.

fossilize or **fossilise** verb (fossilizes, fossilizing, fossilized) preserve an animal or plant so that it becomes a fossil. ■ fossilization noun.

foster verb (fosters, fostering, fostered) **1** encourage the development of. **2** bring up a child that is not your own by birth.

fought past and past participle of FIGHT.

foul adjective **1** having a disgusting smell or taste. **2** very unpleasant. **3** wicked or obscene. **4** polluted. noun (in sport) a piece of play that is not allowed by the rules. verb **1** make foul or dirty. **2** (in sport) commit a foul against. **3 (foul up)** make a mistake with. **4** entangle or jam a rope or cable. □ foul-mouthed using bad language. **foul play 1** unfair play in sport. **2** criminal or violent activity. ■ foully adverb.

found¹ past and past participle of FIND.

found² verb **1** establish an institution or organization. **2 (be founded on)** be based on a particular concept.

found³ verb melt and mould metal to make an object.

foundation noun **1** the lowest part of a building, that bears the weight. **2** an underlying basis or reason. **3** an institution or organization. **4** the action of founding. **5** a cream or powder applied to the face as a base for other make-up.

founder¹ noun a person who founds an institution or settlement.

founder² verb **(founders, foundering, foundered) 1** (of a ship) fill with water and sink. **2** (of a plan or undertaking) fail or break down.

foundling noun a child that has been abandoned by its parents and is discovered and cared for by others.

foundry noun (plural **foundries**) a workshop or factory for casting metal.

fount noun **1** a source of a desirable quality. **2** literary a spring or fountain. **3** ⇒ **FONT**.

fountain noun **1** a decorative structure in a pool or lake from which a jet of water is pumped into the air. **2** literary a natural spring of water. □ **fountain pen** a pen with a container from which ink flows to the nib.

fountainhead noun an original source of something.

four cardinal number **1** one more than three; 4. (Roman numeral: **iv** or **IV.**) **2** Cricket a hit that reaches the boundary after first striking the ground, scoring four runs. □ **four-letter word** a short coarse or offensive word. **four-poster bed** a bed with a post at each corner holding up a canopy. **four-square** having a square shape and solid appearance.

foursome noun a group of four people.

fourteen cardinal number one more than thirteen; 14. (Roman numeral: **xiv** or **XIV.**) ■ **fourteenth** ordinal number.

fourth ordinal number **1** number four in a sequence; 4th. **2 (a fourth or one fourth)** a quarter. □ **the fourth estate** the press. ■ **fourthly** adverb.

fowl noun (plural **fowl** or **fowls**) **1** a domesticated bird kept for its eggs or meat. **2** birds as a group.

fox noun **1** an animal with a pointed muzzle, bushy tail, and a reddish coat. **2** informal a sly or crafty person. verb informal baffle or deceive.

foxglove noun a tall plant with erect spikes of flowers shaped like the fingers of gloves.

foxhole noun a hole in the ground used by troops as a shelter against the enemy or as a place to fire from.

foxhound noun a breed of dog trained to hunt foxes in packs.

foxtrot noun a ballroom dance which involves switching between slow and quick steps. verb **(foxtrots, foxtrotting, foxtrotted)** dance the foxtrot.

foxy adjective **(foxier, foxiest) 1** like a fox. **2** informal crafty or sly.

foyer /**foy**-ay/ noun a large entrance hall in a hotel or theatre.

fracas /**fra**-kah/ noun (plural **fracas** /**fra**-kah or **fra**-kahz/) a noisy disturbance or quarrel.

fraction noun **1** a number that is not a whole number (e.g. ½, 0.5). **2** a very small part or amount.

fractional adjective **1** having to do with a fraction. **2** very small in amount. ■ **fractionally** adverb.

fractious adjective **1** bad-tempered. **2** difficult to control.

fracture noun **1** the cracking or breaking of a hard object or material. **2** a crack or break. verb **(fractures, fracturing, fractured) 1** break. **2** (of a group or organization) break up.

fragile adjective **1** easily broken or damaged. **2** (of a person) delicate and vulnerable. ■ **fragility** noun.

fragment noun /**frag**-muhnt/ a small part that has broken off or come from something larger. verb /frag-**ment**/ break into fragments. ■ **fragmentary** adjective **fragmentation** noun.

fragrance noun **1** a pleasant, sweet smell. **2** a perfume or aftershave.

fragrant adjective having a pleasant, sweet smell.

frail adjective **1** weak and delicate. **2** easily damaged or broken.

frailty noun (plural **frailties**) **1** the condition of being frail. **2** weakness in a person's character.

frame noun **1** a rigid structure surrounding a picture, door, etc. or giving support to a building or vehicle. **2** the structure of a person's body. **3** a single picture in a series forming a cinema or video film. **4** a single game of snooker. verb (**frames**, **framing**, **framed**) **1** put a picture in a frame. **2** create or develop a plan or system. **3** informal produce false evidence against someone to make them appear guilty of a crime. □ **frame of mind** a particular mood.

framework noun a supporting or underlying structure.

franc noun the basic unit of money of France, Belgium, and several other countries.

franchise noun **1** a licence allowing a person or company to use or sell certain products. **2** a business that has been given a franchise. **3** the right to vote in elections.

frank[1] adjective **1** honest and direct. **2** open or undisguised. ■ **frankly** adverb **frankness** noun.

frank[2] verb stamp a mark on a letter or parcel to indicate that postage has been paid or does not need to be paid.

frankfurter noun a seasoned smoked sausage made of beef and pork.

frankincense noun a kind of sweet-smelling gum that is burnt as incense.

frantic adjective **1** agitated because of fear, anxiety, etc. **2** done in a hurried and chaotic way. ■ **frantically** adverb.

fraternal adjective **1** brotherly. **2** having to do with a fraternity.

fraternity noun (plural **fraternities**) **1** a group of people sharing a common profession or interests. **2** N. Amer. a male students' society in a university or college. **3** friendship and support within a group.

fraternize or **fraternise** verb (**fraternizes**, **fraternizing**, **fraternized**) be on friendly terms. ■ **fraternization** noun.

fratricide noun **1** the killing by someone of their brother or sister. **2** the accidental killing of your own forces in war.

fraud noun **1** the crime of deceiving someone to gain money or goods. **2** a person who deceives others by claiming to be something they are not.

fraudster noun a person who commits fraud.

fraudulent adjective **1** involving fraud. **2** deceitful or dishonest. ■ **fraudulently** adverb.

fraught adjective **1** (**fraught with**) filled with something undesirable. **2** causing or feeling anxiety or stress.

fray[1] verb **1** (of a fabric or rope) unravel or become worn at the edge. **2** (of a person's nerves or temper) show the effects of strain.

fray[2] noun (**the fray**) **1** a battle or fight. **2** an intensely competitive situation.

frazzle noun (**a frazzle**) informal **1** an exhausted state. **2** a charred or burnt state. ■ **frazzled** adjective.

freak noun **1** a person, animal, or plant which is abnormal or deformed. **2** a very unusual and unexpected event. **3** informal a person who is obsessed with a particular interest: *a fitness freak.* verb (**freak out**) informal behave in a wild and irrational way. ■ **freakish** adjective **freaky** adjective.

freckle noun a small light brown spot on the skin. ■ **freckled** adjective **freckly** adjective.

free adjective (**freer**, **freest**) **1** not under the control of someone else. **2** not confined, obstructed, or fixed. **3** not being used. **4** (**free of** or **from**) not subject to or affected by. **5** given or available without charge. **6** (**free with**) using or giving something generously or lavishly. **7** unrestrained in speech or manner. **8** (of literature, music, etc.) not following the normal rules. **adverb** without cost or payment. **verb** (**frees, freeing, freed**) make free. □ **free enterprise** a system in which private businesses compete with each other. **free fall** unrestricted downward movement under the force of gravity. **free-for-all** a disorganized situation in which everyone may take part. **free-form** not in a regular or formal structure. **a free hand** freedom to do exactly what you want. **free house** Brit. a pub not controlled by a brewery. **free kick** (in soccer and rugby) an unopposed kick of the ball awarded when the opposition have broken the rules. **the free market** a system in which prices are determined by unrestricted competition between privately owned businesses. **free-range** referring to farming in which animals are kept in natural conditions where they can move around freely. **free-standing** not supported by another structure. **free trade** unrestricted international trade without taxes or regulations on imports and exports. **free will** the power to act according to your own wishes. ■ **freely** adverb.

freebie **noun** informal a thing given free of charge.

freedom **noun 1** the right to act or speak freely. **2** the state of not being a prisoner or slave. **3** (**freedom from**) not being subject to or affected by something undesirable. **4** unrestricted use of something. **5** a special honour given to someone by a city.

freehand **adjective & adverb** drawn by hand without a ruler or other aid.

freehold **noun** permanent possession of land or property with the freedom to sell it whenever you wish. ■ **freeholder** noun.

freelance **adjective** self-employed and working for different companies on particular assignments. **noun** (also **freelancer**) a freelance worker. **verb** (**freelances, freelancing, freelanced**) work as a freelance.

freeloader **noun** informal a person who takes advantage of other people's generosity.

freeman **noun 1** a person who has been given the freedom of a city. **2** historical a person who was not a slave or serf.

Freemason **noun** a member of an organization whose members help each other and hold secret ceremonies. ■ **Freemasonry** noun.

freesia /**free**-zi-uh/ **noun** a plant with fragrant, colourful flowers.

freestyle **adjective** (of a contest or sport) having few restrictions on the technique that competitors use.

freethinker **noun** a person who questions or rejects accepted opinions.

freeway **noun** N. Amer. a dual-carriageway main road.

freewheel **verb** ride a bicycle without using the pedals.

freeze **verb** (**freezes, freezing, froze**; past participle **frozen**) **1** (of a liquid) turn into a solid as a result of extreme cold. **2** become blocked or rigid with ice. **3** be very cold. **4** preserve something by storing it at a very low temperature. **5** suddenly become motionless with fear, shock, etc. **6** (of a computer screen) suddenly become locked. **7** keep or stop at a fixed level. **noun 1** an act of freezing. **2** informal a period of very cold weather. □ **freeze-dry** preserve something by rapidly freezing it and then drying it in a vacuum. **freeze-frame** the facility of stopping a film or videotape to obtain a single motionless image.

freezer **noun** a refrigerated cabinet or room for preserving food at very low temperatures.

freezing **adjective 1** having a temperature below 0°C. **2** informal very cold.

freight **noun** goods transported by truck, train, ship, or aircraft. **verb** transport goods by truck, train, etc.

freighter **noun** a large ship or aircraft designed to carry freight.

French **adjective** having to do with France or its language. **noun** the language of France, also used in parts of Belgium, Switzerland, Canada, etc. □ **French dressing** a salad dressing of vinegar, oil, and seasonings. **French**

fries chiefly N. Amer. chips. **French horn** a brass instrument with a coiled tube and a wide opening at the end. **French kiss** a kiss with contact between tongues. **French polish** a kind of polish used on wood to give it a very glossy finish. **French windows** glazed doors in an outside wall.

frenetic adjective fast and energetic in a rather wild and uncontrolled way. ■ **frenetically** adverb.

frenzy noun (plural **frenzies**) a state of uncontrolled excitement or wild behaviour. ■ **frenzied** adjective **frenziedly** adverb.

frequency noun (plural **frequencies**) **1** the rate at which something occurs. **2** the state of being frequent. **3** the number of cycles per second of a sound, light, or radio wave. **4** the particular waveband at which radio signals are transmitted.

frequent adjective /free-kwuhnt/ **1** occurring or done many times at short intervals. **2** doing something often. verb /fri-**kwent**/ visit a place often. ■ **frequently** adverb.

fresco noun (plural **frescoes** or **frescos**) a painting that is done on wet plaster on a wall or ceiling.

fresh adjective **1** new or different. **2** (of food) recently made or obtained. **3** recently created and not faded. **4** (of water) not salty. **5** (of the wind) cool and fairly strong. **6** pleasantly clean and cool. **7** full of energy and vigour. **8** informal over-confident or disrespectful. ■ **freshly** adverb **freshness** noun.

freshen verb **1** make or become fresh. **2** (**freshen up**) wash and tidy yourself.

fresher noun Brit. informal a first-year student at college or university.

freshman noun a first-year student at university or (in N. Amer.) at high school.

fret[1] verb (**frets**, **fretting**, **fretted**) be anxious and restless.

fret[2] noun each of the ridges on the neck of guitars and similar instruments.

fretful adjective anxious and restless. ■ **fretfully** adverb.

fretwork noun ornamental design in wood.

friable /fry-uh-b'l/ adjective easily crumbled.

friar noun a member of certain religious orders of men.

friary noun (plural **friaries**) a building or community occupied by friars.

fricassée /fri-kuh-say, fri-kuh-see/ noun a dish of stewed or fried pieces of meat served in a thick white sauce.

friction noun **1** the resistance that one surface or object encounters when moving over another. **2** the action of one surface or object rubbing against another. **3** conflict or disagreement.

Friday noun the day of the week before Saturday and following Thursday.

fridge noun a refrigerator.

fried past and past participle of **FRY**[1].

friend noun **1** a person that you know well and like. **2** a supporter of a cause or organization. **3** (**Friend**) a Quaker. ■ **friendless** adjective **friendship** noun.

> ✓ *-ie-*, not *-ei-*: fri**end**.

friendly adjective (**friendlier**, **friendliest**) **1** treating someone as a friend; on good terms. **2** kind and pleasant. **3** not harmful to a specified thing: *environment-friendly*. noun (plural **friendlies**) Brit. a game not forming part of a serious competition. ■ **friendliness** noun.

frieze noun a broad horizontal band of sculpted or painted decoration.

frigate noun a kind of fast warship.

fright noun **1** a sudden intense feeling of fear. **2** a shock.

frighten verb **1** make someone afraid. **2** (**frighten off**) drive someone away by frightening them. ■ **frightening** adjective **frighteningly** adverb.

frightful adjective **1** very unpleasant, serious, or shocking. **2** informal terrible; awful. ■ **frightfully** adverb.

frigid /frij-id/ adjective **1** literary very cold. **2** disapproving (of a woman) not interested in sex. ■ **frigidity** noun.

frill noun **1** a decorative strip of gathered or pleated cloth attached to the edge of clothing or material. **2 (frills)** unnecessary extra features. ■ **frilled** adjective **frilly** adjective.

fringe noun **1** a decorative border of threads or tassels attached to the edge of clothing or material. **2** Brit. a part of someone's hair that hangs over the forehead. **3** the outer part of an area, group, etc. verb **(fringes, fringing, fringed)** add a fringe to something. □ **fringe benefit** something extra given to someone as well as wages.

frippery noun (plural **fripperies**) **1** (**fripperies**) frivolous ornaments or details. **2** unnecessary ornamentation.

frisbee noun trademark a plastic disc that you skim through the air as an outdoor game.

frisk verb **1** pass your hands over someone in a search for hidden weapons or drugs. **2** skip or move playfully. noun a playful skip or leap.

frisky adjective (**friskier, friskiest**) playful and full of energy.

frisson /free-son/ noun a thrill.

fritillary /fri-til-luh-ri/ noun **1** a plant with hanging bell-like flowers. **2** a butterfly with orange-brown wings.

fritter[1] verb (**fritters, frittering, frittered**) (**fritter away**) waste time or money on unimportant matters.

fritter[2] noun a piece of food that is coated in batter and deep-fried.

frivolous adjective **1** not having any serious purpose or value. **2** (of a person) carefree and not serious. ■ **frivolity** noun **frivolously** adverb.

frizz verb (of hair) form into a mass of tight curls. noun a mass of tightly curled hair. ■ **frizzy** adjective.

frock noun **1** chiefly Brit. a woman's or girl's dress. **2** a loose outer garment, worn by priests. □ **frock coat** a man's formal, long-skirted jacket.

frog noun a tailless amphibian with a short body and very long hind legs for leaping. □ **have a frog in your throat** informal be hoarse.

frogman noun a diver equipped with a rubber suit, flippers, and breathing equipment.

frogmarch verb force someone to walk forward by holding their arms from behind.

frogspawn noun a mass of frogs' eggs surrounded by transparent jelly.

frolic verb (**frolics, frolicking, frolicked**) play or move about in a cheerful and lively way. noun a playful action or movement.

frolicsome adjective lively and playful.

from preposition **1** indicating the point at which a journey, process, or action starts. **2** indicating the source of something. **3** indicating separation, removal, or prevention. **4** indicating a cause. **5** indicating a difference.

fromage frais /from-ahzh fray/ noun a type of smooth, soft cheese.

frond noun the leaf of a palm, fern, or similar plant.

front noun **1** the part of an object that presents itself to view or that is normally seen first. **2** the position directly ahead. **3** the furthest position that an army has reached. **4** a particular situation or sphere. **5** (in weather forecasting) the forward edge of an advancing mass of air. **6** a false appearance or way of behaving. **7** a person or organization that is a cover for secret or illegal activities. **8** bold and confident manner. adjective having to do with the front. verb **1** have the front facing towards. **2** be at the front of. **3** (**be fronted with**) have the front covered with. **4** be the leader or presenter of. **5** act as a front for. □ **the front line** the part of an army that is closest to the enemy. **front-runner** the leader in a competition.

frontage noun **1** the front of a building. **2** a strip of land next to a street or waterway.

frontal adjective having to do with the front. ■ **frontally** adverb.

frontier noun **1** a border separating two countries. **2** the furthest part of land that has been settled. **3** the limit of what is known in a particular area.

frontispiece noun an illustration facing the title page of a book.

frontman noun a representative of a group or organization.

frost noun **1** white ice crystals that form on surfaces when the temperature falls below freezing. **2** a period of cold weather when frost forms.

frostbite noun injury to parts of the body caused by exposure to extreme cold. ■ **frostbitten** adjective.

frosted adjective **1** covered with frost. **2** (of glass) having a semi-transparent textured surface. **3** N. Amer. (of a cake) covered with icing.

frosting noun N. Amer. icing.

frosty adjective (**frostier**, **frostiest**) **1** (of the weather) very cold with frost forming on surfaces. **2** cold and unfriendly. ■ **frostily** adverb.

froth noun **1** a mass of small bubbles in liquid. **2** appealing but trivial ideas or activities. verb produce or contain froth. ■ **frothy** adjective.

frown verb **1** make an angry or worried expression by bringing your eyebrows together so that lines appear on your forehead. **2** (**frown on**) disapprove of. noun a frowning expression.

frowsty adjective Brit. warm and stuffy.

frowzy or **frowsy** adjective scruffy and neglected in appearance.

froze past of **FREEZE**.

frozen past participle of **FREEZE**.

fructose /fruk-tohz/ noun a kind of sugar found in honey and fruit.

frugal /froo-g'l/ adjective careful in the use of money or food. ■ **frugality** noun **frugally** adverb.

fruit noun **1** a fleshy part of a plant that contains seed and can be eaten as food. **2** Botany the seed-bearing part of a plant, e.g. an acorn. **3** the result of work or activity. verb produce fruit. □ **fruit machine** Brit. a coin-operated gambling machine.

fruiterer noun chiefly Brit. a person who sells fruit.

fruitful adjective **1** producing a lot of fruit. **2** producing good results.

■ **fruitfully** adverb **fruitfulness** noun.

fruition /fruu-i-sh'n/ noun the fulfilment of a plan or project.

fruitless adjective failing to achieve the desired results. ■ **fruitlessly** adverb.

fruity adjective (**fruitier**, **fruitiest**) **1** having to do with fruit. **2** (of someone's voice) mellow, deep, and rich. **3** Brit. informal sexually suggestive.

frump noun an unattractive woman who wears unfashionable clothes. ■ **frumpy** adjective.

frustrate verb (**frustrates**, **frustrating**, **frustrated**) **1** prevent a plan or action from succeeding. **2** prevent someone from doing or achieving something. **3** make someone feel dissatisfied or unfulfilled. ■ **frustrating** adjective **frustration** noun.

fry[1] verb (**fries**, **frying**, **fried**) cook in hot fat or oil. noun (**fries**) N. Amer. French fries; chips. □ **frying pan** a shallow pan used for frying food. **out of the frying pan into the fire** from a bad situation to one that is worse. ■ **fryer** (or **frier**) noun.

fry[2] plural noun young fish.

ft abbreviation foot or feet.

fuchsia /fyoo-shuh/ noun a shrub with drooping purplish-red flowers.

fuck vulgar verb **1** have sex with. **2** (also **fuck up**) damage or ruin. exclamation a strong expression of annoyance or contempt.

fuddled adjective confused or dazed.

fuddy-duddy noun (plural **fuddy-duddies**) informal a person who is very old-fashioned and pompous.

fudge noun **1** a soft sweet made from sugar, butter, and milk or cream. **2** an attempt to present an issue in a vague way. verb present something in a vague or deceptive way.

fuel noun **1** material such as coal, gas, or oil that is burned to produce heat or power. **2** something that inflames argument or intense emotion. verb (**fuels**, **fuelling**, **fuelled**; US spelling **fuels**, **fueling**, **fueled**) **1** supply or power with fuel. **2** inflame intense feeling. □ **fuel injection** the direct introduction of fuel into the cylinders of an engine.

fug noun Brit. informal a warm, stuffy atmosphere.

fugitive /fyoo-ji-tiv/ noun a person who has escaped from captivity or is in hiding.

fugue /fyoog/ noun a piece of music in which a short melody is introduced and then successively taken up by other instruments or voices.

führer or **fuehrer** /fyoo-ruh/ noun the title that Hitler held as leader of Germany.

fulcrum /fuul-kruhm/ noun the point on which a lever turns or is supported.

fulfil (US spelling fulfill) verb (fulfils, fulfilling, fulfilled) 1 do or achieve something that was desired, promised, or predicted. 2 meet a requirement. 3 (fulfil yourself) fully develop your abilities. ∎ fulfilment noun.

full adjective 1 holding as much or as many as possible. 2 (full of) having a large number or quantity of. 3 (also full up) filled to capacity. 4 complete: *full details.* 5 plump or rounded. 6 (of flavour, sound, or colour) strong or rich. adverb straight; directly. □ full-blooded whole-hearted and enthusiastic. full-blown fully developed. full board Brit. accommodation and all meals at a hotel. full-bodied rich and satisfying in flavour or sound. full-frontal fully exposing the front of the body. full house 1 a theatre that is filled to capacity. 2 a poker hand with three of a kind and a pair. 3 a winning card at bingo. full moon the moon when its whole disc is illuminated. full-scale 1 (of a model or plan) of the same size as the thing represented. 2 complete and thorough. full time the end of a sports match. full-time working for the whole of the available time. ∎ fullness (or fulness) noun.

fullback noun (in soccer and similar sports) a defender who plays at the side.

fuller noun a person who treats cloth to make it thicker.

fully adverb 1 completely. 2 no less or fewer than. □ fully fledged Brit. completely developed or established.

fulminate verb (fulminates, fulminating, fulminated) protest strongly. ∎ fulmination noun.

fulsome adjective 1 excessively flattering. 2 of large size or quantity. ∎ fulsomely adverb.

fumble verb (fumbles, fumbling, fumbled) 1 use the hands clumsily while doing something. 2 deal with something clumsily. 3 fail to catch a ball cleanly. noun an act of fumbling.

fume noun a gas or vapour that smells strongly or is dangerous to breathe in. verb (fumes, fuming, fumed) 1 send out fumes. 2 be very angry.

fumigate verb (fumigates, fumigating, fumigated) disinfect with chemical fumes. ∎ fumigation noun.

fun noun 1 light-hearted pleasure, or something that provides it. 2 playfulness. □ make fun of laugh at in a mocking way.

function noun 1 a purpose or natural activity of a person or thing. 2 a large social event. 3 a basic task of a computer. 4 Mathematics a quantity whose value depends on the varying values of others. verb 1 work or operate. 2 (function as) fulfil the purpose of.

functional adjective 1 having to do with a function. 2 designed to be practical and useful. 3 working or operating. ∎ functionality noun functionally adverb.

functionary noun (plural functionaries) an official.

fund noun 1 a sum of money saved or made available for a purpose. 2 (funds) financial resources. 3 a large stock. verb provide money for.

fundamental adjective of basic importance. noun a basic rule or principle. ∎ fundamentally adverb.

fundamentalism noun strict following of the basic teachings of a religion. ∎ fundamentalist noun & adjective.

funeral noun a ceremony in which a dead person is buried or cremated. □ funeral director an undertaker.

funerary | furbelow

PUNCTUATION

Full stop

A full stop is used:

1 at the end of a sentence, e.g.

> I'm going to the cinema tonight.
> The film begins at seven.

It is replaced by a question mark at the end of a question, and by an exclamation mark at the end of an exclamation.

2 after an abbreviation, e.g.

> H. G. Wells
> p. 19 (= page 19)
> Sun. (= Sunday).

Full stops are **not** used with:

- numerical abbreviations, e.g. *1st, 2nd, 15th, 23rd*
- acronyms (i.e. words formed from the first letters of other words), e.g. *NATO*
- abbreviations that are used as ordinary words, e.g. *con, demo, recap*
- chemical symbols, e.g. Fe, K, H_2O

Full stops are generally not used for:

- abbreviations consisting entirely of capitals, e.g. BBC, PLC
- C (= *Celsius*), F (= *Fahrenheit*)
- measures of length, weight, time, etc., except for *in.* (= *inch*)
- *Dr, Revd, Mr, Mrs, Ms, St* (= *Saint*), *p* (= *penny* or *pence*).

---

funerary /fyoo-nuh-ruh-ri/ adjective having to do with a funeral or the commemoration of the dead.

funereal /fyoo-neer-i-uhl/ adjective solemn, in a way appropriate to a funeral.

funfair noun Brit. a fair consisting of rides, sideshows, etc.

fungicide noun a chemical that destroys fungus.

fungus noun (plural fungi /fung-gI/) an organism, such as a mushroom, that has no leaves or flowers and grows on plants or decaying vegetable matter and reproduces by spores. ■ **fungal** adjective.

funicular railway /fyuu-nik-yuu-ler/ noun a railway on a steep slope which is operated by cable.

funk[1] noun informal a state of panic or depression.

funk[2] noun a style of popular dance music with a strong rhythm.

funky adjective (funkier, funkiest) informal **1** (of music) having a strong dance rhythm. **2** modern and stylish.

funnel noun **1** an object that is wide at the top and narrow at the bottom, used for guiding liquid or powder into a small opening. **2** a chimney on a ship or steam engine. verb (funnels, funnelling, funnelled; US spelling funnels, funneling, funneled) guide through a funnel or narrow space.

funny adjective (funnier, funniest) **1** causing laughter or amusement. **2** strange; odd. **3** suspicious; apparently dishonest. **4** informal slightly unwell. □ **funny bone** informal the part of the elbow over which a very sensitive nerve passes. ■ **funnily** adverb.

fur noun **1** the short, soft hair of certain animals. **2** the skin of an animal with fur on it. **3** Brit. a coating formed by hard water on the inside surface of a pipe, kettle, etc. ■ **furred** adjective.

furbelow noun **1** a flounce on a skirt

or petticoat. **2 (furbelows)** showy trimmings.

furious adjective **1** extremely angry. **2** very intense or energetic. ■ **furiously** adverb.

furl verb roll or fold up neatly.

furlong noun an eighth of a mile, 220 yards.

furlough /fer-loh/ noun leave of absence.

furnace noun **1** an enclosed space for heating material to very high temperatures. **2** a very hot place.

furnish verb **1** provide a room or building with furniture and fittings. **2** supply or provide.

furnishings noun furniture and fittings in a room or building.

furniture noun the movable articles that make a room or building suitable for living or working in.

furore /fyoo-ror-i/ (US spelling **furor** /fyoo-**ror**/) noun an outbreak of public anger or excitement.

furrier noun a person who deals in furs.

furrow noun **1** a long, narrow trench made in the ground by a plough. **2** a deep wrinkle on a person's face. verb make a furrow in.

furry adjective (**furrier**, **furriest**) covered with or like fur.

further adverb (also **farther**) **1** at, to, or by a greater distance. **2** at or to a more advanced stage. **3** in addition. adjective (also **farther**) more distant in space. **2** additional. verb (**furthers**, **furthering**, **furthered**) help the progress of. □ **further education** Brit. education below degree level for people older than school age.

furtherance noun the advancement of a plan or interest.

furthermore adverb in addition.

furthest or **farthest** adverb & adjective at or to the greatest distance.

furtive adjective secretively trying to avoid notice. ■ **furtively** adverb.

fury noun (plural **furies**) **1** extreme anger. **2** extreme strength or violence. **2 (the Furies)** Greek Mythology three goddesses who punished people for their crimes.

furze = **GORSE**.

fuse[1] verb (**fuses**, **fusing**, **fused**) **1** join or combine to form a whole. **2** melt something so it joins with something else. **3** Brit. (of an electrical appliance) stop working when a fuse melts. **4** fit a circuit or electrical appliance with a fuse. noun **1** a safety device consisting of a strip of wire that melts and breaks an electric circuit if the current goes beyond a safe level. **2** a length of material which is lit to explode a bomb or firework. **3** a device in a bomb that controls the timing of the explosion.

fuselage /fyoo-zuh-lah*z*h/ noun the main body of an aircraft.

fusible adjective able to be melted easily.

Fusilier /fyoo-zi-**leer**/ noun a member of a British regiment formerly armed with muskets called **fusils**.

fusillade /fyoo-zi-**layd**, fyoo-zi-**lahd**/ noun a series of shots fired at the same time or quickly one after the other.

fusion noun **1** the joining of two or more things together to form a whole. **2** a reaction in which the nuclei of atoms fuse to form a heavier nucleus, releasing a great deal of energy.

fuss noun **1** unnecessary excitement or activity. **2** a protest or complaint. verb (usu. **fuss over**) show unnecessary concern about something.

fussy adjective (**fussier**, **fussiest**) **1** hard to please. **2** full of unnecessary detail. ■ **fussily** adverb **fussiness** noun.

fusty adjective **1** smelling stale or damp. **2** old-fashioned.

futile adjective pointless. ■ **futilely** adverb **futility** noun.

futon /**foo**-ton/ noun a padded mattress that can be rolled up.

future noun **1** (the future) time that is still to come. **2** a prospect of success or happiness. adjective **1** existing or occurring in the future. **2** Grammar (of a verb) expressing an event yet to happen.

futuristic adjective **1** having very

modern technology or design. **2** (of a film or book) set in the future.

futurity noun the future time.

fuzz noun **1** a frizzy mass of hair or fibre. **2** (**the fuzz**) informal the police.

fuzzy adjective (**fuzzier, fuzziest**) **1** having a frizzy texture or appearance. **2** blurred; not clear.

Gg

G or **g** noun (plural **Gs** or **G's**) the seventh letter of the alphabet. abbreviation **1** grams. **2** gravity. □ **G-string** a pair of skimpy knickers consisting of a narrow strip of cloth attached to a waistband.

gab verb (**gabs, gabbing, gabbed**) informal talk at length. □ **the gift of the gab** the ability to speak fluently and persuasively.

gabble verb (**gabbles, gabbling, gabbled**) talk very quickly and indistinctly. noun fast, indistinct talk.

gaberdine or **gabardine** /ga-ber-deen/ noun a smooth, hard-wearing cloth used for making raincoats.

gable noun the triangular upper part of a wall at the end of a roof.

gad verb (**gads, gadding, gadded**) (**gad about**) informal go around in search of pleasure.

gadfly noun **1** a fly that bites cattle. **2** an annoying or provoking person.

gadget noun a small mechanical device. ■ **gadgetry** noun.

Gaelic /gay-lik, ga-lik/ noun a language spoken in parts of Ireland and western Scotland.

gaff¹ noun a stick with a hook for landing large fish.

gaff² noun Brit. informal a person's home. □ **blow the gaff** reveal a secret.

gaffe noun an embarrassing blunder.

gaffer noun Brit. informal **1** a boss. **2** an old man.

gag¹ noun a piece of cloth put over a person's mouth to stop them speaking. verb (**gags, gagging, gagged**) **1** put a gag on. **2** choke or retch.

gag² noun a joke or funny story.

gaga /gah-gah/ adjective informal rambling in speech or thought, especially as a result of old age.

gage US spelling of **GAUGE**.

gaggle noun **1** a flock of geese. **2** informal a disorderly group of people.

gaiety (US spelling gayety) noun (plural **gaieties**) light-hearted and cheerful mood or behaviour.

gaily adverb **1** in a light-hearted and cheerful manner. **2** without thinking of the effect of your actions. **3** with a bright appearance.

gain verb **1** obtain or secure. **2** reach a place. **3** (**gain on**) get closer to someone or something that you are pursuing. **4** increase in weight, speed, or value. **5** (**gain in**) improve or advance in some respect. **6** (of a clock or watch) become fast. noun **1** a thing that is gained. **2** an increase in wealth or resources.

gainful adjective serving to increase wealth or resources. ■ **gainfully** adverb.

gainsay verb (**gainsays, gainsaying, gainsaid**) formal deny or contradict.

gait noun a way of walking.

gaiter noun a covering of cloth or leather for the ankle and lower leg.

gala /gah-luh, gay-luh/ noun **1** a celebration or special entertainment. **2** Brit. a special sports event, especially a swimming competition.

galactic adjective relating to a galaxy.

galaxy noun (plural **galaxies**) **1** a large system of stars. **2** (**the Galaxy**) the system of stars that includes the sun and the earth; the Milky Way.

gale noun **1** a very strong wind. **2** an outburst of laughter.

gall¹ noun **1** bold and impudent behaviour. **2** bitterness or cruelty. ◻ **gall bladder** a small organ beneath the liver, in which bile is stored.

gall² noun **1** annoyance; irritation. **2** a sore on the skin made by rubbing. verb annoy; irritate. ■ **galling** adjective.

gallant /gal-luhnt/ adjective **1** brave; heroic. **2** /guh-**lant**/ (of a man) polite and charming to women. noun /guh-**lant**/ a man who is polite and charming to women. ■ **gallantly** adverb.

gallantry noun (plural **gallantries**) **1** courageous behaviour. **2** polite attention given by men to women.

galleon noun historical a large sailing ship with three or more decks and masts.

gallery noun (plural **galleries**) **1** a room or building for displaying or selling works of art. **2** a balcony at the back of a large hall. **3** the highest part of a theatre.

galley noun (plural **galleys**) **1** historical a low, flat ship with one or more sails and up to three banks of oars. **2** a narrow kitchen in a ship or aircraft.

Gallic /gal-lik/ adjective having to do with France or the French.

gallivant verb informal go around in search of fun.

gallon noun **1** a unit of volume for measuring liquids, equal to eight pints. **2** (**gallons**) informal large quantities.

gallop noun **1** the fastest speed a horse can run. **2** a ride on a horse at its fastest speed. verb (**gallops**, **galloping**, **galloped**) **1** go at the speed of a gallop. **2** proceed very quickly.

gallows plural noun **1** a structure used for hanging a person. **2** (**the gallows**) execution by hanging. ◻ **gallows humour** grim humour in a desperate or hopeless situation.

gallstone noun a hard mass of crystals formed in the gall bladder or bile ducts, causing pain and obstruction.

galore adjective in abundance.

galoshes plural noun rubber shoes worn over normal shoes in wet weather.

galumph verb informal move in a clumsy or noisy way.

galvanic /gal-**van**-ik/ adjective relating to electric currents produced by chemical action.

galvanize or **galvanise** /gal-vuh-nyz/ verb (**galvanizes**, **galvanizing**, **galvanized**) **1** shock or excite someone into doing something. **2** (**galvanized**) (of iron or steel) coated with a protective layer of zinc.

galvanometer /gal-vuh-**nom**-i-ter/ noun an instrument for measuring small electric currents.

gambit noun something that somebody says or does that is meant to give them an advantage.

gamble verb (**gambles**, **gambling**, **gambled**) **1** play games of chance for money. **2** bet a sum of money. **3** risk losing something in the hope that you will be successful. noun a risky action. ■ **gambler** noun.

gambol verb (**gambols**, **gambolling**, **gambolled**; US spelling **gambols**, **gamboling**, **gamboled**) run or jump about playfully.

game¹ noun **1** an activity that you take part in for amusement. **2** a competitive activity or sport played according to rules. **3** a period of play, ending in a final result. **4** a section of a tennis match, forming a unit in scoring. **5** (**games**) a meeting for sporting contests. **6** a type of activity or business regarded as a game. **7** wild animals or birds that people hunt for sport or food. adjective eager and willing to do something new or challenging. verb (**games**, **gaming**, **gamed**) play at games of chance for money. ■ **gamely** adverb.

game² adjective (of a person's leg) lame.

gamekeeper noun a person employed to breed and protect game for a large estate.

gamesmanship noun the ability to

win games by making your opponent feel less confident.

gamete /**gam**-eet/ noun Biology a cell which is able to unite with another of the opposite sex in sexual reproduction to form a zygote.

gamine /ga-**meen**/ adjective (of a girl) having a mischievous, boyish charm.

gamma /**gam**-muh/ noun the third letter of the Greek alphabet (Γ, γ). □ **gamma rays** (or **gamma radiation**) electromagnetic radiation of shorter wavelength than X-rays.

gammon noun **1** ham which has been cured like bacon. **2** the part of a side of bacon that includes the hind leg.

gammy adjective Brit. informal (of a leg) unable to function normally because of injury or pain.

gamut /**gam**-uht/ noun the complete range or scope of something. □ **run the gamut** experience or perform the complete range of something.

gander /**gan**-der/ noun **1** a male goose. **2** informal a look.

gang noun **1** an organized group of criminals or disorderly young people. **2** informal a group of people who regularly meet and do things together. **3** an organized group of people doing manual work. verb **1** (**gang together**) form a group or gang. **2** (**gang up**) join together against someone.

gangling or **gangly** adjective (of a person) tall, thin, and awkward.

ganglion noun (plural **ganglia** or **ganglions**) **1** a mass of nerve cells. **2** a swelling in a tendon.

gangplank noun a movable plank used as a bridge between a boat and the shore.

gangrene noun the death of body tissue, caused by an obstructed blood supply or by infection.

gangster noun a member of an organized gang of violent criminals.

gangway noun **1** Brit. a passage between rows of seats. **2** a bridge placed between a ship and the shore.

gannet noun **1** a large seabird with mainly white plumage. **2** Brit. informal a greedy person.

gantry noun (plural **gantries**) a bridge-like structure used as a support.

gaol ⇒ **JAIL**.

gap noun **1** a hole in an object or between two objects. **2** an empty space or period of time; a break in something. ■ **gappy** adjective.

gape verb (**gapes**, **gaping**, **gaped**) **1** be or become wide open. **2** stare with your mouth open wide in amazement. noun **1** a wide opening. **2** an open-mouthed stare.

garage /**ga**-rah*zh*, ga-rahj, ga-rij/ noun **1** a building in which a car or other vehicle is kept. **2** a business which sells fuel or which repairs and sells motor vehicles. **3** a type of music with elements of drum and bass, house, and soul. verb (**garages**, **garaging**, **garaged**) keep a motor vehicle in a garage.

garb noun unusual or distinctive clothes. verb (**be garbed**) be dressed in distinctive clothes.

garbage noun chiefly N. Amer. **1** domestic rubbish or waste. **2** something worthless or meaningless.

garble verb (**garbles**, **garbling**, **garbled**) confuse or distort a message or transmission.

garden noun **1** chiefly Brit. a piece of ground next to or around a house. **2** (**gardens**) a public park. verb work in a garden. ■ **gardener** noun.

gargantuan adjective enormous.

gargle verb (**gargles**, **gargling**, **gargled**) hold liquid in your mouth and throat while slowly breathing out through it. noun **1** an act of gargling. **2** a liquid used for gargling.

gargoyle noun a spout in the form of an ugly person or animal that carries water away from the roof of a building.

garish /**gair**-ish/ adjective unpleasantly bright and showy. ■ **garishly** adverb.

garland noun a wreath of flowers and leaves. verb crown or decorate with a garland.

garlic noun a plant of the onion family with a strong taste and smell, used to give flavour to food.

garment noun an item of clothing.

garner verb (garners, garnering, garnered) gather or collect.

garnet noun a red semi-precious stone.

garnish verb decorate a dish of food. noun a decoration for food.

garret noun a room in the roof of a house.

garrison noun a body of troops stationed in a fortress or town to defend it. verb provide a place with a garrison.

garrotte /guh-rot/ (US spelling **garrote**) verb (garrottes, garrotting, garrotted) strangle someone with a wire or cord. noun a wire or cord used for garrotting.

garrulous adjective extremely talkative. ■ garrulity noun.

garter noun a band worn around the leg to keep up a stocking or sock.

gas noun (plural gases or chiefly US gasses) **1** an air-like substance which expands to fill any available space. **2** a type of gas used as a fuel. **3** a type of gas that stops you feeling pain, used during a medical operation. **4** N. Amer. informal gasoline. verb (gases, gassing, gassed) **1** attack with, expose to, or kill with gas. **2** informal talk excessively; chatter. □ **gas chamber** an airtight room that can be filled with poisonous gas to kill people or animals. **gas mask** a mask used as protection against poisonous gas.

☑ in British English, the spelling of the plural is *gases*: no double *s*.

gaseous /gass-i-uhss/ adjective relating to or like a gas.

gash noun a long deep cut or wound. verb make a gash in.

gasket /gass-kit/ noun a rubber seal at the junction between two surfaces in an engine.

gaslight noun light from a gas lamp. ■ gaslit adjective.

gasoline or **gasolene** noun N. Amer. petrol.

gasometer /ga-som-i-ter/ noun a large tank for the storage of gas.

gasp verb **1** take a quick breath with your mouth open, because you are surprised or in pain. **2** (gasp for) struggle for air. **3** (be gasping for) informal be desperate to have. noun a sudden quick breath.

gassy adjective (gassier, gassiest) **1** full of gas. **2** informal talkative.

gastric adjective having to do with the stomach.

gastro-enteritis noun inflammation of the stomach and intestines.

gastronomy noun the practice or art of cooking and eating good food. ■ gastronomic adjective.

gasworks plural noun a place where gas is processed.

gate noun **1** a hinged barrier used to close an opening in a wall, fence, or hedge. **2** an exit from an airport building to an aircraft. **3** a barrier that controls the flow of water on a river or canal. **4** the number of people who pay to attend a sports event.

gateau /gat-oh/ noun (plural gateaus or gateaux /gat-ohz/) Brit. a cake.

gatecrash verb go to a party without an invitation or ticket. ■ gatecrasher noun.

gatefold noun an oversized page in a book or magazine, intended to be opened out for reading.

gatehouse noun a house standing by the gateway to a country estate.

gatekeeper noun an attendant at a gate.

gatepost noun a post on which a gate is hinged or against which it shuts.

gateway noun **1** an opening that can be closed by a gate. **2** (gateway to) a means of entering somewhere or achieving something.

gather verb (gathers, gathering, gathered) **1** come or bring together; assemble. **2** harvest a crop. **3** collect plants or fruits for food. **4** draw something towards yourself. **5** increase in force, speed, etc. **6** infer; understand.

7 pull fabric into folds by drawing thread through it. **noun (gathers)** a series of folds in fabric, formed by gathering.

gathering noun an assembly of people.

gauche /gohsh/ **adjective** socially awkward or unsophisticated.

gaucho /gow-choh/ **noun (plural gauchos)** a cowboy from the South American pampas.

gaudy adjective (gaudier, gaudiest) extravagantly or tastelessly bright and showy. ■ **gaudily** adverb.

gauge /gayj/ (US spelling **gage**) **noun 1** an instrument for measuring the amount or level of something. **2** the thickness or size of a wire, tube, bullet, etc. **3** the distance between the rails of a railway track. **verb (gauges, gauging, gauged) 1** estimate or measure something. **2** judge a situation or mood.

> ☑ unlike **guard**, **gauge** has *-au-* in the middle: *gauge*.

gaunt adjective 1 (of a person) looking thin and exhausted. **2** (of a place) grim or desolate.

gauntlet noun 1 a strong glove with a long loose wrist. **2** a glove worn as part of medieval armour. □ **run the gauntlet** go through an intimidating crowd or experience in order to reach a goal. **throw down the gauntlet** set a challenge.

gauze noun 1 a thin transparent fabric. **2** a fine wire mesh. ■ **gauzy** adjective.

gave past of **GIVE**.

gavel noun a small hammer used to hit a surface by a judge or auctioneer in order to get people's attention.

gavotte /guh-**vot**/ **noun** a French dance, popular in the 18th century.

gawk verb stare in a stupid or rude way.

gawky adjective awkward and clumsy.

gawp verb Brit. informal gawk.

gay adjective (gayer, gayest) 1 (especially of a man) homosexual. **2** relating to homosexuals. **3** dated light-hearted and carefree. **4** dated brightly coloured. **noun** a homosexual person, especially a man.

gayety US spelling of **GAIETY**.

gaze verb (gazes, gazing, gazed) look steadily. **noun** a steady look.

gazebo /guh-**zee**-boh/ **noun (plural gazebos** or **gazeboes)** a summer house offering a pleasant view.

gazelle noun a small antelope.

gazette noun a journal or newspaper.

gazetteer /ga-zuh-**teer**/ **noun** a list of place names.

gazump /guh-**zump**/ **verb** Brit. informal offer or accept a higher price for a house after a lower offer has already been accepted.

GB abbreviation 1 Great Britain. **2** (also **Gb**) Computing gigabytes.

GBH abbreviation Brit. grievous bodily harm.

GC abbreviation George Cross.

GCE abbreviation General Certificate of Education.

GCSE abbreviation (in the UK except Scotland) General Certificate of Secondary Education (the lower of the two main levels of the GCE examination).

gear noun 1 (gears) a set of toothed wheels that connect the engine to the wheels of a vehicle and work together to alter its speed. **2** a particular position of gears in a vehicle: *fifth gear*. **3** informal equipment or clothing. **verb 1 (gear to)** adjust or adapt something to. **2** adjust the gears in a vehicle to a particular level. **3 (gear up)** get prepared for something. □ **gear lever** Brit. a lever used to change gear in a motor vehicle.

gearbox noun a set of gears with its casing.

gecko noun (plural geckos or **geckoes)** a lizard with adhesive pads on the feet, active at night.

gee¹ or **gee whiz exclamation** informal, chiefly N. Amer. a mild expression of surprise, enthusiasm, or sympathy.

gee² exclamation (**gee up**) a command to a horse to go faster.

geek noun informal **1** an awkward or unfashionable person. **2** a person who is obsessed with something: *a computer geek.* ■ **geeky** adjective.

geese plural of **GOOSE**.

geezer noun informal a man.

Geiger counter noun a device for measuring radioactivity.

geisha /**gay**-shuh/ noun (plural **geisha** or **geishas**) a Japanese woman who is paid to accompany and entertain men.

gel¹ noun a jelly-like substance used on the hair or skin. verb (**gels, gelling, gelled**) smooth your hair with gel.

gel² ⇒ **JELL**.

gelatin /**jel**-uh-tin/ or **gelatine** /**jel-uh-teen**/ noun a clear substance obtained from animal bones and used to make jelly, glue, and photographic film. ■ **gelatinous** adjective.

geld verb castrate a male animal.

gelding noun a castrated male horse.

gelignite /**jel**-ig-nyt/ noun an explosive made from nitroglycerine.

gem noun **1** a precious stone. **2** an outstanding person or thing.

Gemini noun a sign of the zodiac (the Twins), 21 May–20 June.

gemstone noun a gem used in a piece of jewellery.

gen Brit. informal noun information. verb (**gens, genning, genned**) (**gen up**) provide with or obtain information.

gendarme /**zhon**-darm/ noun a member of the French police force.

gender noun **1** Grammar each of the classes into which nouns and pronouns are divided in some languages, usually referred to as masculine, feminine, and neuter. **2** the state of being male or female. **3** the members of one or other sex.

gene noun Biology a distinct sequence of DNA forming part of a chromosome, by which offspring inherit characteristics from a parent.

genealogy /jee-ni-**al**-uh-ji/ noun (plural **genealogies**) **1** a line of descent traced from an ancestor. **2** the study of lines of descent. ■ **genealogical** adjective **genealogist** noun.

genera plural of **GENUS**.

general adjective **1** affecting or concerning all or most people or things. **2** involving only the main features of something; not detailed. **3** chief or principal: *the general manager.* noun a commander of an army, or an army officer ranking above lieutenant general. □ **general anaesthetic** an anaesthetic that affects the whole body and causes a loss of consciousness. **general election** the election of representatives to a parliament by all the people of a country. **general practitioner** a doctor who treats patients in a local community rather than at a hospital.

generalist noun a person competent in several different fields.

generality noun (plural **generalities**) **1** a general statement rather than one that is specific or detailed. **2** the quality or state of being general.

generalize or **generalise** verb (**generalizes, generalizing, generalized**) **1** make a general or broad statement. **2** make something more common or more widely applicable. ■ **generalization** noun.

generally adverb **1** in most cases. **2** without regard to details. **3** widely.

generate verb (**generates, generating, generated**) create or produce something. ■ **generative** adjective.

generation noun **1** all the people born and living at about the same time. **2** the average period in which a person grows up and has children of their own. **3** a single stage in the history of a family. **4** the action of producing or generating.

generator noun a machine for producing electricity.

generic adjective **1** referring to a class or group of things. **2** (of goods) having no brand name. **3** Biology relating to a genus. ■ **generically** adverb.

generous adjective **1** freely giving more than is necessary or expected.

2 kind towards others. **3** larger or more plentiful than is usual. ■ **generosity** noun.

genesis /jen-i-siss/ noun **1** the origin or development of something. **2** (Genesis) the first book of the Bible.

genetic adjective **1** relating to genes. **2** relating to genetics. ■ **genetically** adverb. □ **genetically modified** (of an animal or plant) containing genetic material that has been altered in order to produce a desired characteristic. **genetic engineering** the changing of the characteristics of an animal or plant by altering its genetic material. **genetic fingerprinting** the analysis of genetic material in order to identify individuals.

genetics plural noun the study of the way characteristics are passed from one generation to another. ■ **geneticist** noun.

genial /jee-ni-uhl/ adjective friendly and cheerful. ■ **geniality** noun **genially** adverb.

genie /jee-ni/ noun (in Arabian folklore) a spirit.

genital adjective referring to the external reproductive organs of a person or animal. noun (genitals) the external reproductive organs.

genitalia /jen-i-tay-li-uh/ plural noun formal or technical the genitals.

genitive /jen-i-tiv/ adjective Grammar the form of a noun, pronoun, or adjective used to show possession.

genius noun (plural geniuses) **1** exceptional natural ability. **2** an exceptionally intelligent or able person.

genocide /jen-uh-syd/ noun the deliberate killing of a very large number of people from a particular ethnic group or nation. ■ **genocidal** adjective.

genre /zhon-ruh/ noun a type or style of art or literature.

gent noun informal **1** a gentleman. **2** (the Gents) Brit. a men's public toilet.

genteel adjective affectedly polite and refined. ■ **gentility** noun.

Gentile /jen-tyl/ adjective not Jewish. noun a person who is not Jewish.

gentle adjective (gentler, gentlest) **1** (of a person) mild and kind. **2** moderate; not harsh or severe. ■ **gentleness** noun **gently** adverb.

gentleman noun **1** a courteous or honourable man. **2** a man of good social position. **3** (in polite or formal use) a man. □ **gentleman's agreement** an arrangement based on trust rather than a legal contract.

gentry noun (the gentry) people of good social position.

genuflect /jen-yuu-flekt/ verb lower your body as a sign of respect by bending one knee. ■ **genuflection** noun.

genuine adjective **1** truly what it is said to be; authentic. **2** honest. ■ **genuinely** adverb.

genus /jee-nuhss/ noun (plural genera /jen-uh-ruh/) a category in the classification of animals and plants.

geodesic /jee-oh-dess-ik, jee-oh-dee-sik/ adjective relating to a method of construction based on straight lines between points on a curved surface.

geographical or **geographic** adjective relating to geography. ■ **geographically** adverb.

geography noun **1** the study of the physical features of the earth and how people relate to them. **2** the way in which places and physical features are arranged. ■ **geographer** noun.

geology noun **1** the scientific study of the physical structure and substance of the earth. **2** the geological features of a particular area. ■ **geological** adjective **geologist** noun.

geometric adjective **1** relating to geometry. **2** (of a design) incorporating regular lines and shapes. ■ **geometrical** adjective **geometrically** adverb.

geometry noun (plural geometries) **1** the branch of mathematics that deals with the properties and relationships of lines, angles, surfaces, and solids. **2** the shape and relationship of the parts of something.

Geordie noun Brit. informal a person from Tyneside.

Georgian adjective relating to the

reigns of the British Kings George I–IV (1714–1830).

geranium noun a plant cultivated for its red, pink, or white flowers.

gerbil noun a mouse-like rodent, often kept as a pet.

geriatric adjective relating to old people. noun an old person, especially one receiving special care.

germ noun 1 a micro-organism, especially one which causes disease. 2 a part of an organism that is able to develop into a new one. 3 an initial stage from which something may develop.

German noun 1 a person from Germany. 2 the language of Germany, Austria, and parts of Switzerland. adjective relating to Germany or German. □ German measles = RUBELLA. German shepherd a large breed of dog often used as guard dogs; an Alsatian.

germane adjective (germane to) relevant or appropriate to.

Germanic adjective 1 of the language family that includes English, German, Dutch, and the Scandinavian languages. 2 characteristic of Germans or Germany.

germicide noun a substance which destroys germs. ■ germicidal adjective.

germinal adjective 1 relating to a gamete or embryo. 2 in the earliest stage of development.

germinate verb (germinates, germinating, germinated) (of a seed) begin to grow. ■ germination noun.

gerontology noun the scientific study of old age and old people.

gerrymander verb (gerrymanders, gerrymandering, gerrymandered) change the boundaries of a constituency in order to favour one party in an election.

gerund /je-ruhnd/ noun Grammar a verb form which functions as a noun (e.g. asking in do you mind my asking?).

Gestapo /ge-stah-poh/ noun the German secret police under Nazi rule.

gestation noun 1 the growth of a baby inside its mother's body. 2 the development of a plan or idea over a period of time.

gesticulate verb (gesticulates, gesticulating, gesticulated) make gestures instead of speaking or in order to emphasize what you are saying. ■ gesticulation noun.

gesture noun 1 a movement of part of the body to express an idea or meaning. 2 an action performed to convey your feelings or intentions. verb (gestures, gesturing, gestured) make a gesture.

get verb (gets, getting, got; past participle got, N. Amer. or old use gotten) 1 come to have or hold; receive. 2 succeed in achieving or experiencing. 3 experience or suffer. 4 fetch. 5 reach a particular state or condition: it's getting late. 6 catch or thwart. 7 move to or from a particular place. 8 travel by or catch a form of transport. 9 begin to be or do something. □ get away with escape blame or punishment for. get by manage to live or do something with the things that you have. get down to begin to do or give serious attention to. get off informal escape a punishment. get on 1 make progress with a task. 2 chiefly Brit. have a friendly relationship. 3 (be getting on) informal be old. get over 1 recover from an illness or an unpleasant experience. 2 manage to communicate an idea. get your own back informal have your revenge. get round to chiefly Brit. deal with a task in due course. get-together an informal gathering. get through to 1 make contact with someone by telephone. 2 make someone understand what you are saying. get-up informal an unusual style of dress.

getaway noun an escape.

geyser /gee-zer/ noun a hot spring that sometimes sprays water and steam into the air.

ghastly adjective (ghastlier, ghastliest) 1 causing great horror or fear. 2 deathly white or pale. 3 informal very unpleasant. ■ ghastliness noun.

gherkin /ger-kin/ noun a small pickled cucumber.

ghetto /get-toh/ noun (plural **ghettos** or **ghettoes**) a part of a city lived in by a minority group. □ **ghetto blaster** informal a large portable radio and cassette or CD player.

ghost noun **1** a spirit of a dead person which is believed to appear to the living. **2 (a or the ghost of)** a faint trace of. verb act as ghost writer of. □ **ghost town** a town in which no one lives any more. **ghost writer** a person who writes something for someone else who is named as the author.

ghostly adjective of or like a ghost; eerie.

ghoul /gool/ noun **1** an evil spirit or phantom. **2** a person who is too interested in death or disaster. ■ **ghoulish** adjective.

GI noun (plural **GIs**) a private soldier in the US army.

giant noun **1** (in stories) a person of superhuman size and strength. **2** an unusually large person, animal, or plant. adjective unusually large.

gibber /jib-ber/ verb speak rapidly and unintelligibly. ■ **gibbering** adjective.

gibberish /jib-ber-ish/ noun speech or writing that is impossible to understand; nonsense.

gibbet /jib-bit/ historical noun a post and beam used for hanging people, or for displaying the bodies of those who had been executed.

gibbon noun a small ape with long, powerful arms, native to SE Asia.

gibe ⇨ **JIBE**.

giblets /jib-lits/ plural noun the liver, heart, gizzard, and neck of a chicken or other bird.

giddy adjective (**giddier**, **giddiest**) **1** having the feeling that everything is moving and that you are going to fall. **2** excitable and silly.

gift noun **1** a thing that you give to someone; a present. **2** a natural ability or talent. verb **1** give something as a gift. **2 (gifted)** having exceptional talent or ability.

gig[1] /gig, jig/ noun (in the past) a light two-wheeled carriage pulled by one horse.

gig[2] /gig/ informal noun a live performance by a musician.

gigabyte /gig-uh-byt, jig-uh-byt/ noun Computing a unit of information equal to one thousand million (10^9) bytes.

gigantic adjective of very great size or extent.

giggle verb (**giggles**, **giggling**, **giggled**) laugh lightly in a nervous or silly way. noun **1** a laugh of such a kind. **2** informal an amusing person or thing. ■ **giggly** adjective.

gigolo /jig-uh-loh/ noun (plural **gigolos**) a young man paid to be the companion or lover of an older woman.

gild verb **1** cover thinly with gold. **2 (gilded)** wealthy and privileged. ■ **gilding** noun.

gill[1] /gil/ noun **1** an organ of fishes and some amphibians, used for breathing. **2** the plates on the underside of mushrooms and many toadstools.

gill[2] /jil/ noun a unit for measuring liquids, equal to a quarter of a pint.

gillie /gil-li/ noun (in Scotland) a person who helps on a shooting or fishing trip.

gilt adjective covered thinly with gold. noun a thin layer of gold on a surface. □ **gilt-edged** (of investments) safe and reliable.

gimlet /gim-lit/ noun a T-shaped tool with a screw-tip for boring holes.

gimmick noun a trick or device intended to attract attention rather than fulfil a useful purpose. ■ **gimmicky** adjective.

gin[1] noun a strong, clear alcoholic drink flavoured with juniper berries.

gin[2] noun **1** a machine for separating cotton from its seeds. **2** a machine for raising and moving heavy weights. **3** a trap for catching small game.

ginger noun **1** a hot, fragrant spice obtained from the stem of an Asian plant. **2** a light reddish-yellow colour. □ **ginger ale** (or **ginger beer**) a fizzy drink flavoured with ginger.

gingerbread noun cake made with treacle and flavoured with ginger.

gingerly adverb in a careful or cautious way.

gingham /ging-uhm/ noun lightweight cotton cloth, typically checked.

gingivitis /jin-ji-vy-tiss/ noun inflammation of the gums.

ginormous adjective Brit. informal extremely large.

ginseng /jin-seng/ noun the root of an east Asian and North American plant, used in some medicines.

gipsy ⇒ GYPSY.

giraffe noun (plural giraffe or giraffes) a large mammal with a very long neck and forelegs.

gird verb (girds, girding, girded; past participle girded or girt) literary encircle with a belt or band. □ gird your loins get ready to do something.

girder noun a large metal beam.

girdle noun 1 a belt or cord worn round the waist. 2 a corset encircling the body from waist to thigh. verb (girdles, girdling, girdled) encircle with a girdle or belt.

girl noun 1 a female child. 2 a young woman. 3 a person's girlfriend. ■ girlish adjective.

girlfriend noun 1 a person's regular female romantic or sexual partner. 2 N. Amer. a woman's female friend.

giro noun (plural giros) 1 a system in which money is transferred electronically from one bank or post office account to another. 2 a cheque or payment by giro.

girt past participle of GIRD.

girth noun 1 the measurement around the middle of something. 2 a strap attached to a saddle and fastened around a horse's belly.

gist /jist/ noun the general meaning of a speech or text.

give verb (gives, giving, gave; past participle given) 1 make someone have, get, or experience something. 2 carry out an action or make a sound. 3 show: *he*

gave no sign of life. 4 state information. 5 (give off or out) send out a smell, heat, etc. 6 bend under pressure. noun the ability of something to bend under pressure. □ give away reveal something secret. give in to stop opposing something. give out stop operating. give rise to make happen. give up 1 stop making an effort and accept that you have failed. 2 stop doing, eating, or drinking something regularly. 3 hand over a wanted person.

given past participle of GIVE. adjective 1 specified or stated. 2 (given to) inclined to. preposition taking into account. □ given name a person's first name.

gizmo noun (plural gizmos) informal a gadget.

gizzard noun a muscular part of a bird's stomach for grinding food.

glacé /gla-say/ adjective (of fruit) preserved in sugar.

glacial /glay-sh'l, glay-si-uhl/ adjective 1 relating to ice and glaciers. 2 extremely cold.

glaciation noun the formation of glaciers.

glacier /glass-i-er, glay-si-er/ noun a slowly moving mass of ice formed by the accumulation of snow on mountains.

glad adjective (gladder, gladdest) 1 pleased; delighted. 2 (often glad of) grateful. 3 causing happiness. □ glad rags informal clothes for a party or special occasion.

gladden verb make glad.

glade noun an open space in a forest.

gladiator noun (in ancient Rome) a man trained to fight other men or animals in a public arena. ■ gladiatorial adjective.

gladiolus noun (plural gladioli or gladioluses) a plant with sword-shaped leaves and spikes of brightly coloured flowers.

glamorize or **glamorise** verb (glamorizes, glamorizing, glamorized) often disapproving make something seem glamorous or desirable.

glamorous adjective having glamour.
■ **glamorously** adverb.

✓ **glamorous** drops the *u* of **glamour**: glam*orous*.

glamour (US spelling **glamor**) noun an attractive and exciting quality.

glance verb (**glances**, **glancing**, **glanced**) **1** look briefly. **2** (**glance off**) hit something at an angle and bounce off obliquely. noun a brief or hurried look. ■ **glancing** adjective.

gland noun an organ of the body which produces a particular chemical substance.

glandular adjective relating to a gland or glands. □ **glandular fever** an infectious disease which causes swelling of the lymph glands and prolonged fatigue.

glare verb (**glares**, **glaring**, **glared**) **1** stare in an angry way. **2** shine with a dazzling light. **3** (**glaring**) extremely obvious. noun **1** a fierce or angry stare. **2** strong and dazzling light.

glasnost /glaz-nosst/ noun (in the former Soviet Union) the policy of more open government.

glass noun **1** a hard transparent substance made by fusing sand with soda and lime. **2** a drinking container made of glass. **3** chiefly Brit. a mirror. □ **glass-blowing** the craft of making glassware by blowing semi-liquid glass through a long tube. **glass fibre** chiefly Brit. a strong material containing glass filaments. ■ **glassy** adjective.

glasses plural noun a pair of lenses set in a frame that rests on the nose and ears, used to correct eyesight.

glasshouse noun Brit. a greenhouse.

glasspaper noun paper covered with powdered glass, used for smoothing and polishing.

glaucoma /glaw-**koh**-muh/ noun a condition of increased pressure within the eyeball, causing gradual loss of sight.

glaze verb (**glazes**, **glazing**, **glazed**) **1** fit panes of glass into a window frame or similar structure. **2** enclose or cover with glass. **3** cover with a glaze. **4** (**glaze over**) (of a person's eyes) lose brightness and animation. noun **1** a glass-like substance fused on to the surface of pottery to form a hard coating. **2** a liquid such as milk or beaten egg, used to form a shiny coating on food.

glazier /**glay**-zi-er/ noun a person who fits glass into windows and doors.

gleam verb shine brightly, especially with reflected light. noun **1** a faint or brief light. **2** a brief or faint show of a quality or emotion: *a gleam of hope*.

glean verb **1** collect information from various sources. **2** gather leftover grain after a harvest. ■ **gleanings** noun.

glee noun great delight.

gleeful adjective very happy or joyful.
■ **gleefully** adverb.

glen noun Scottish & Irish a narrow valley.

glib adjective using words easily but without much thought. ■ **glibly** adverb.

glide verb (**glides**, **gliding**, **glided**) **1** move with a smooth, quiet, continuous motion. **2** fly without power or in a glider. noun an instance of gliding.

glider noun a light aircraft designed to fly without using an engine.

glimmer verb (**glimmers**, **glimmering**, **glimmered**) shine faintly with a wavering light. noun **1** a faint or wavering light. **2** a faint sign of a feeling or quality.

glimpse noun a brief look at something. verb (**glimpses**, **glimpsing**, **glimpsed**) see something briefly or partially.

glint verb give off small flashes of light. noun a sudden flash of light.

glisten verb (of something wet) shine or sparkle.

glitch noun informal a sudden problem or fault.

glitter verb **1** shine with a shimmering reflected light. **2** (**glittering**) impressively successful or glamorous. noun **1** shimmering reflected light. **2** tiny pieces of sparkling material used for decoration. **3** an attractive but superficial quality. ■ **glittery** adjective.

glitz noun superficial glamour. ■ **glitzy** adjective.

gloaming noun (**the gloaming**) literary twilight; dusk.

gloat verb be smug or pleased about your own success or another person's failure. noun an act of gloating. ■ **gloating** adjective & noun.

glob noun informal a lump of a semi-liquid substance.

global adjective **1** relating to the whole world; worldwide. **2** relating to all the parts of something. ◻ **global warming** a gradual increase in the temperature of the earth's atmosphere due to the increase of gases such as carbon dioxide. ■ **globally** adverb.

globe noun **1** a spherical or rounded object. **2** (**the globe**) the earth. **3** a model of the earth with a map on its surface.

globetrotter noun informal a person who travels widely. ■ **globetrotting** noun & adjective.

globular adjective **1** shaped like a globe; spherical. **2** made of globules.

globule noun a small drop or ball of a substance.

glockenspiel /glok-uhn-speel, glok-uhn-shpeel/ noun a musical instrument made of metal bars that you hit with small hammers.

gloom noun **1** darkness. **2** a feeling of sadness and hopelessness.

gloomy adjective (**gloomier, gloomiest**) **1** dark or poorly lit. **2** sad or depressed.

glorify verb (**glorifies, glorifying, glorified**) **1** represent something as admirable. **2** (**glorified**) made to appear more important than in reality. **3** praise and worship God.

glorious adjective **1** having or bringing glory. **2** very beautiful or impressive. ■ **gloriously** adverb.

glory noun (plural **glories**) **1** fame and honour. **2** beauty or splendour. **3** a

very beautiful or impressive thing. **4** worship and praise of God. verb (**glories, glorying, gloried**) (**glory in**) take great pride or pleasure in.

gloss[1] noun **1** the shine on a smooth surface. **2** a type of paint which dries to a bright shiny surface. **3** an attractive appearance that hides something less attractive. verb **1** give a glossy appearance to. **2** (**gloss over**) try to conceal or pass over.

gloss[2] noun a translation or explanation of a word, phrase, or passage. verb provide a gloss for.

glossary noun (plural **glossaries**) a list of words and their meanings.

glossy adjective (**glossier, glossiest**) **1** shiny and smooth. **2** appearing attractive and stylish.

glottal adjective having to do with the glottis. ◻ **glottal stop** a speech sound made by opening and closing the glottis, sometimes used instead of a properly sounded *t*.

glottis noun the part of the larynx made up of the vocal cords and the narrow opening between them.

glove noun **1** a covering for the hand having separate parts for each finger. **2** a padded covering for the hand used in boxing and other sports. ◻ **glove compartment** a small storage recess in the dashboard of a car.

glow verb **1** give out a steady light. **2** have flushed skin after exercising. **3** look very happy. noun a steady light or heat. ◻ **glow-worm** a kind of beetle which gives out light.

glower /glow-er/ verb have an angry or sullen expression. noun an angry or sullen look.

glowing adjective expressing great praise: *a glowing report.*

glucose /gloo-kohz/ noun a type of sugar that is easily changed into energy by the body.

glue noun a sticky substance used for joining things together. verb (**glues, gluing** or **glueing, glued**) **1** join something with glue. **2** (**be glued to**) informal be paying very close attention to.

glum adjective sad and dejected. ■ **glumly** adverb.

glut noun an excessively large supply. verb (**gluts, glutting, glutted**) supply or fill to excess.

gluten noun a protein found in cereals.

glutinous adjective like glue in texture; sticky.

glutton noun **1** an extremely greedy eater. **2** a person who is very eager for something: *a glutton for adventure.*

gluttony noun the habit of eating too much.

glycerine (US spelling **glycerin**) noun a liquid made from fats and oils, used in medicines and cosmetics.

GM abbreviation **1** genetically modified. **2** George Medal.

gm abbreviation grams.

GMT abbreviation Greenwich Mean Time.

gnarled adjective knobbly or twisted.

gnash /nash/ verb grind your teeth together, especially as a sign of anger.

gnat /nat/ noun a small two-winged fly.

gnaw /naw/ verb **1** bite at or nibble something persistently. **2** cause persistent anxiety or pain.

gnocchi /nyo-ki/ plural noun (in Italian cooking) small dumplings.

gnome noun (in stories) a creature like a tiny man, who guards treasure.

gnomic /noh-mik/ adjective clever but hard to understand.

GNP abbreviation gross national product.

gnu /noo/ noun a large African antelope with a long head and a mane.

GNVQ abbreviation General National Vocational Qualification.

go verb (**goes, going, went**; past participle **gone**) **1** move to or from a place. **2** pass into or be in a particular state. **3** lie or extend in a certain direction. **4** come to an end. **5** disappear or be used up. **6** (of time) pass. **7** pass time in a particular way. **8** engage in a specified activity. **9** have a particular outcome. **10** (**be going to be** or **do**) used to express a future tense. **11** function or operate. **12** be harmonious or matching. **13** be acceptable or allowed. **14** fit into or be regularly kept in a particular place. **15** make a specified sound. noun (plural **goes**) informal **1** an attempt. **2** a turn to do or use something. **3** spirit or energy. □ **go about** begin or carry on work at something. **the go-ahead** informal permission to proceed. **go along with** agree to. **go back** on fail to keep a promise. **go-between** an intermediary or negotiator. **go-cart** (or **go-kart**) a small racing car with a lightweight body. **go down 1** be defeated in a contest. **2** obtain a specified reaction. **go for 1** decide on. **2** attempt to gain. **3** attack. **go in for 1** enter a contest as a competitor. **2** like or habitually take part in. **go into 1** investigate or enquire into. **2** (of a whole number) be capable of dividing another. **go off 1** (of a gun or bomb) explode or fire. **2** chiefly Brit. (of food) begin to decompose. **3** informal, chiefly Brit. begin to dislike. **go on 1** continue. **2** take place. **go out 1** be extinguished. **2** carry on a regular romantic relationship with someone. **go over** examine or check the details of. **go through 1** undergo a difficult experience. **2** examine carefully. **3** informal use up or spend. **go without** suffer lack or hardship. **have a go at** chiefly Brit. attack or criticize. ■ **goer** noun.

goad noun **1** a spiked stick used for driving cattle. **2** a thing that makes someone do something. verb **1** provoke someone do something. **2** urge on with a goad.

goal noun **1** (in soccer, rugby, etc.) a wooden frame into or over which the ball has to be sent to score. **2** an instance of sending the ball into or over a goal. **3** an aim or desired result. ■ **goalless** adjective.

goalkeeper noun (in soccer, hockey, etc.) a player whose role is to stop the ball from entering the goal.

goalpost noun either of the two upright posts of a goal.

goat noun an animal with horns and a hairy coat, often kept for milk.

goatee noun a small pointed beard like that of a goat.

goatherd noun a person who looks after goats.

gob informal noun 1 Brit. a person's mouth. 2 a lump of a slimy substance. verb (**gobs, gobbing, gobbed**) Brit. spit.

gobbet noun a piece of flesh, food, or other matter.

gobble verb (**gobbles, gobbling, gobbled**) (often **gobble up**) 1 eat hurriedly and noisily. 2 use a large amount of something very quickly. 3 (of a turkey) make a characteristic swallowing sound in the throat.

gobbledegook or **gobbledygook** noun informal pompous or unintelligible language.

goblet noun a drinking glass with a foot and a stem.

goblin noun (in stories) a mischievous, dwarf-like creature.

gobsmacked adjective Brit. informal utterly astonished.

gobstopper noun chiefly Brit. a hard round sweet.

goby /goh-bi/ noun (plural **gobies**) a small sea fish.

God noun 1 (in Christianity and some other religions) the creator and supreme ruler of the universe. 2 (god) a superhuman being or spirit. □ God-fearing earnestly religious.

godchild noun (plural **godchildren**) a person in relation to a godparent.

god-daughter noun a female godchild.

goddess noun a female deity.

godfather noun 1 a male godparent. 2 the male leader of an illegal organization.

godforsaken adjective lacking any merit or attraction.

godhead noun 1 (**the Godhead**) God. 2 divine nature.

godless adjective 1 not believing in God or a god. 2 wicked.

godly adjective very religious.

godmother noun a female godparent.

godparent noun a person who promises to be responsible for a child's religious education.

godsend noun something that is very helpful or welcome.

godson noun a male godchild.

goes 3rd person singular present of GO.

goggle verb (**goggles, goggling, goggled**) 1 look with wide open eyes. 2 (of the eyes) stick out or open wide. noun (**goggles**) close-fitting protective glasses.

going noun 1 the condition of the ground in terms of its suitability for horse racing or walking. 2 conditions for an activity: *the going gets tough*. adjective 1 chiefly Brit. existing or available. 2 (of a price) normal or current. □ going concern a thriving business. goings-on informal activities that are strange or dishonest.

goitre /goy-ter/ noun a swelling of the neck resulting from enlargement of the thyroid gland.

gold noun 1 a yellow precious metal. 2 a deep yellow or yellow-brown colour. 3 coins or articles made of gold. □ gold leaf gold beaten into a very thin sheet. gold medal a medal awarded for first place in a race or competition. gold rush a rapid movement of people to a place where gold has been discovered.

golden adjective 1 made of or resembling gold. 2 (of a period) very happy and prosperous. 3 excellent. □ golden age 1 an extremely happy time in the past. 2 the period when something is very successful. golden boy (or golden girl) informal a popular or successful young man or woman. golden eagle a large eagle with yellow-tipped head feathers. golden handshake informal a payment given to someone who is made redundant or retires early. golden jubilee the fiftieth anniversary of an important event.

golden rule a principle which should always be followed. **golden wedding** the fiftieth anniversary of a wedding.

goldfinch noun a brightly coloured finch with a yellow patch on each wing.

goldfish noun a small orange carp, often kept in ponds.

goldsmith noun a person who makes things out of gold.

golf noun a game played on an outdoor course, the aim of which is to strike a small ball with a club into a series of small holes. ∎ **golfer** noun.

golliwog noun a soft doll with a black face and fuzzy hair.

gonad /goh-nad/ noun an organ in the body that produces gametes; a testis or ovary.

gondola /gon-duh-luh/ noun a light flat-bottomed boat used on canals in Venice, worked by one oar at the stern.

gondolier /gon-duh-leer/ noun a person who propels a gondola.

gone past participle of **GO**. adjective no longer present or in existence. **preposition** Brit. **1** (of time) past. **2** (of age) older than.

goner /gon-er/ noun informal a person or thing that cannot be saved.

gong noun **1** a metal disc that makes a resonant sound when struck. **2** Brit. informal a medal or decoration.

gonorrhoea /gon-uh-ree-uh/ (US spelling **gonorrhea**) noun a sexually transmitted disease involving a discharge of pus from the urethra or vagina.

goo noun informal a sticky or slimy substance.

good adjective **1** having the right qualities; of a high standard. **2** behaving in a way that is morally right, polite, or obedient. **3** enjoyable or satisfying. **4** suitable or appropriate. **5** (**good for**) of benefit to. **6** thorough. noun (**goods**) **1** products or possessions. **2** Brit. freight. □ **as good as** very nearly. **for good** forever. **good faith** honesty or sincerity of intention.

good-for-nothing worthless. **Good Friday** the Friday before Easter Sunday, on which Christians commemorate the Crucifixion of Jesus. **make good 1** compensate for loss or damage. **2** fulfil a promise or claim. ∎ **goodness** noun.

goodbye exclamation used to express good wishes when parting or ending a conversation. noun (plural **goodbyes**) a parting.

goodly adjective (**goodlier**, **goodliest**) quite large in size or quantity.

goodwill noun friendly or helpful feelings towards other people.

goody or **goodie** noun (plural **goodies**) informal **1** Brit. a good person, especially a hero in a story or film. **2** (**goodies**) tasty things to eat. □ **goody-goody** informal a person who behaves well in order to impress others.

gooey adjective informal soft and sticky.

goof informal, chiefly N. Amer. noun **1** a mistake. **2** a foolish or stupid person. verb **1** fool around. **2** make a mistake.

goofy adjective informal **1** chiefly N. Amer. foolish; eccentric. **2** having front teeth that stick out.

goon noun informal **1** a foolish or eccentric person. **2** N. Amer. a thug.

goose noun (plural **geese**) **1** a large waterbird with a long neck and webbed feet. **2** the female of such a bird. **3** informal a foolish person. □ **goose pimples** little raised bumps on your skin, caused by feeling cold or frightened. **goose step** a way of marching in which the legs are kept straight.

gooseberry noun (plural **gooseberries**) **1** an edible yellowish-green berry with a hairy skin. **2** Brit. informal a third person in the company of two lovers.

gopher /goh-fer/ noun a burrowing rodent found in North America.

gore¹ noun blood that has been shed.

gore² verb (**gores**, **goring**, **gored**) (of an animal such as a bull) pierce with a horn or tusk.

gore³ noun a triangular piece of material used in making a garment, sail, or umbrella.

gorge noun a narrow valley or ravine. verb (**gorges**, **gorging**, **gorged**) eat a large amount greedily.

gorgeous adjective **1** beautiful. **2** informal very pleasant.

gorgon /**gor**-guhn/ noun Greek Mythology each of three sisters with snakes for hair, who had the power to turn anyone who looked at them to stone.

gorilla noun a powerfully built ape of central Africa.

gormless adjective Brit. informal stupid or slow-witted.

gorse noun a yellow-flowered shrub with spiny leaves.

gory adjective **1** involving violence and bloodshed. **2** covered in blood.

gosling noun a young goose.

gospel noun **1** the teachings of Jesus. **2** (the **Gospel**) the record of Jesus's life and teaching in the first four books of the New Testament. **3** (**Gospel**) each of these books. **4** (also **gospel truth**) something absolutely true. **5** (also **gospel music**) a style of black American religious singing.

gossamer noun a fine substance consisting of cobwebs spun by small spiders. adjective very fine and flimsy.

gossip noun **1** casual conversation about other people. **2** disapproving a person who likes talking about other people. verb (**gossips**, **gossiping**, **gossiped**) engage in gossip.

got past and past participle of GET.

Gothic adjective **1** of the style of architecture common in western Europe in the 12th to 16th centuries. **2** very gloomy or horrifying.

gotten N. Amer. or old use past participle of GET.

gouache /goo-**ash**/ noun **1** a method of painting using watercolours thickened with glue. **2** paint of this kind.

gouge verb (**gouges**, **gouging**, **gouged**) **1** make a rough hole in a surface. **2** (**gouge out**) cut out roughly. noun **1** a chisel with a concave blade. **2** a hole or groove made by gouging.

goulash /goo-lash/ noun a rich Hungarian stew of meat and vegetables.

gourd /goord/ noun a fruit with a hard skin, usually used as a container or for decoration rather than as food.

gourmand /goor-muhnd/ noun a person who enjoys eating.

gourmet /goor-may/ noun a person who knows a lot about good food. adjective suitable for a gourmet.

gout noun a disease causing the joints to swell and become painful.

govern verb **1** control the laws and affairs of a state, organization, or community. **2** control or influence.

governance noun the action or manner of governing.

governess noun a woman employed to teach the children of a family in their home.

government noun **1** the governing body of a state. **2** the system by which a state, organization, or community is governed. ■ **governmental** adjective.

governor noun **1** an official appointed to govern a town or region. **2** the head of a public institution. **3** a member of a governing body.

gown noun **1** a long dress worn for formal occasions. **2** a protective garment worn in hospital by surgeons or patients. **3** a loose cloak showing your profession or status, worn by a lawyer, academic, or university student.

GP abbreviation general practitioner.

gr. abbreviation **1** grains. **2** grams. **3** gross.

grab verb (**grabs**, **grabbing**, **grabbed**) **1** suddenly seize someone or something in a rough way. **2** informal take the opportunity to get something. **3** informal impress: *how does that grab you?* noun a sudden attempt to seize someone or something.

grace noun **1** elegance of movement. **2** polite respect. **3** (**graces**) attractive qualities or behaviour. **4** (in Christian belief) the unearned favour of God. **5** a person's favour. **6** a period officially allowed to do something: *three* *days' grace.* **7** a short prayer of thanks said at a meal. **8 (His, Her,** or **Your Grace)** used as a way of addressing a duke, duchess, or archbishop. **verb (graces, gracing, graced) 1** lend honour to someone or something by your presence. **2** make something more attractive. □ **grace note** Music an extra note which is not needed for the harmony or melody.

graceful adjective having or showing grace or elegance. ■ **gracefully** adverb.

graceless adjective lacking grace or charm.

gracious adjective **1** kind, pleasant, and polite. **2** showing the elegance associated with high social status or wealth. **3** (in Christian belief) showing divine grace. ■ **graciously** adverb.

gradation noun **1** a scale of gradual change from one thing to another. **2** a stage in a such a scale.

grade noun **1** a level of rank or ability. **2** a mark indicating the quality of a student's work. **verb (grades, grading, graded) 1** arrange people or things in grades. **2** pass gradually from one level to another. **3** N. Amer. give a grade to a student or their work. □ **make the grade** informal succeed.

gradient /**gray**-di-uhnt/ noun **1** a sloping part of a road or railway. **2** the degree to which something slopes.

gradual adjective **1** taking place in stages over a long period of time. **2** (of a slope) not steep. ■ **gradually** adverb.

graduate noun /**grad**-yuu-uht/ a person who has been awarded a university degree. **verb** /**grad**-yoo-ayt/ **(graduates, graduating, graduated) 1** successfully complete a degree or course. **2 (graduate to)** move up to something more advanced. **3** change something gradually. ■ **graduation** noun.

graffiti /gruh-**fee**-ti/ noun writing or drawings on a wall in a public place.

 in Italian the word **graffiti** is a plural noun but in English it is generally treated as a normal singular noun.

graft[1] noun **1** a shoot from one plant inserted into another to form a new growth. **2** a piece of bodily tissue that is transplanted from one part of the body to another part that has been damaged. **verb 1** insert or transplant as a graft. **2** add something to something else, especially in a way that seems inappropriate.

graft[2] Brit. informal noun hard work. **verb** work hard.

graft[3] informal noun bribery and other illegal methods used to gain advantage in politics or business.

Grail noun (in medieval legend) the cup or platter used by Jesus at the Last Supper.

grain noun **1** wheat or other cereal grown for food. **2** a single seed or fruit of a cereal. **3** a small, hard particle of a substance such as sand. **4** the smallest unit of weight in the troy and avoirdupois systems. **5** the smallest possible amount. **6** the arrangement of fibres in wood, fabric, etc. □ **against the grain** contrary to your nature. ■ **grainy** adjective.

gram or Brit. **gramme** noun a metric unit of mass equal to one thousandth of a kilogram.

grammar noun **1** the whole system and structure of a language. **2** knowledge and use of the rules of grammar. **3** a book on grammar. □ **grammar school** (in the UK, especially formerly) a state secondary school to which pupils are admitted on the basis of ability.

☑ *-ar,* not *-er:* grammar.

grammatical adjective **1** having to do with grammar. **2** in accordance with the rules of grammar. ■ **grammatically** adverb.

gramophone noun Brit. dated a record player. □ **gramophone record** a record for playing music.

grampus noun (plural **grampuses**) a killer whale or other dolphin-like sea creature.

gran noun Brit. informal your grandmother.

granary noun (plural **granaries**) a storehouse for grain. □ **granary bread** Brit. trademark a type of brown bread containing whole grains of wheat.

grand adjective 1 magnificent and imposing. 2 large, ambitious, or impressive in scope or scale. 3 of the highest importance or rank. 4 dignified, noble, or proud. 5 informal excellent. noun (plural **grand**) informal a thousand dollars or pounds. □ **grand piano** a large piano which has the body, strings, and soundboard arranged horizontally. **grand slam** the winning of each of a group of major sports championships or matches in the same year. **grand total** the final amount after everything is added up. ■ **grandly** adverb.

grandad or **granddad** noun informal your grandfather.

grandchild noun the child of a person's son or daughter.

granddaughter noun the daughter of a person's son or daughter.

grandee noun a person of high status and social rank.

grandeur /gran-dyer/ noun 1 an imposing quality; greatness. 2 high status and social rank.

grandfather noun the father of a person's father or mother. □ **grandfather clock** a large clock in a tall wooden case.

grandiloquent adjective pompous in style and using long and fancy words.

grandiose adjective (of a plan or building) very large and ambitious and intended to impress.

grandma noun informal your grandmother.

grandmother noun the mother of a person's father or mother.

grandpa noun informal your grandfather.

grandparent noun a grandmother or grandfather.

Grand Prix /gron pree/ noun (plural **Grands Prix** /gron pree/) a race forming part of a motor-racing or motorcycling world championship.

grandson noun the son of a person's son or daughter.

grandstand noun the main stand at a racecourse or sports ground.

grange noun Brit. a country house with farm buildings attached.

granite noun a hard grey rock.

granny or **grannie** noun (plural **grannies**) informal your grandmother. □ **granny flat** a small flat that is part of or attached to a house, in which an elderly relative can live. **granny knot** a reef knot with the ends crossed the wrong way and therefore liable to slip.

grant verb 1 agree to give something to someone or to allow them to do something. 2 give something formally or legally. 3 admit to someone that something is true. noun a sum of money given by a government or public body for a particular purpose.

granted adverb admittedly; it is true.

granulated adjective in the form of granules. ■ **granulation** noun.

granule noun a small compact particle of a substance. ■ **granular** adjective.

grape noun a green or purple-black berry growing in clusters on a vine, eaten as fruit and used in making wine.

grapefruit noun (plural **grapefruit**) a large yellow citrus fruit with an acid juicy pulp.

grapeshot noun (in the past) ammunition consisting of a number of small iron balls fired together from a cannon.

grapevine noun 1 a vine bearing grapes. 2 (**the grapevine**) the spreading of information through talk or rumour.

graph noun a diagram showing how two or more sets of numbers relate to each other. □ **graph paper** paper printed with small squares, used for graphs and scaled drawings.

WORD FORMATION ℹ️

-graphy, -graph

-graphy is used to form nouns that refer to:

1 writing about a particular subject or in a particular way, as in:

autobiography	an account of a person's own life
biography	an account of another person's life
calligraphy	decorative handwriting.

2 the production of images or diagrams, e.g.:

cartography	the drawing of maps
photography	the taking of photographs.

3 the science or study of something, e.g.:

geography	the study of the earth and its peoples
oceanography	the study of the sea.

-graph is used to refer to something written or drawn in a particular way, as in *autograph*, or to an instrument that records something, e.g. *seismograph* (an instrument that measures the force of earthquakes). Both **-graphy** and **-graph** come from the ancient Greek word *graphē*, which means 'writing'.

---

graphic adjective **1** relating to visual art, especially involving drawing and the design of printed material. **2** giving vivid detail. noun **1** a pictorial image or symbol on a computer screen. **2** (**graphics**) the use of designs or pictures to illustrate books, magazines, etc. □ **graphic design** the design of books, posters, and other printed material. ■ **graphically** adverb.

graphite noun a grey form of carbon used as a solid lubricant and as pencil lead.

graphology noun the study of handwriting as a guide to personality. ■ **graphologist** noun.

grapple verb (**grapples, grappling, grappled**) **1** struggle or fight physically with someone. **2** (**grapple with**) struggle to deal with or understand. noun an act of grappling. □ **grappling hook** a device with iron claws, used for dragging or grasping.

grasp verb **1** seize and hold something firmly. **2** understand something. noun **1** a firm grip. **2** a person's ability to understand something.

grasping adjective greedy.

grass noun **1** vegetation consisting of plants with long narrow leaves. **2** ground covered with grass. **3** informal cannabis. **4** Brit. informal a police informer. verb **1** cover an area with grass. **2** Brit. informal inform the police of someone's criminal activity. □ **grass roots** the ordinary people in an organization or society, rather than the leaders. ■ **grassy** adjective.

grasshopper noun an insect with long hind legs which it uses for jumping and for producing a chirping sound.

grate¹ verb (**grates, grating, grated**) **1** shred food by rubbing it on a grater. **2** make an unpleasant rasping sound. **3** have an irritating effect.

grate² noun a metal frame or basket in a fireplace in which the coals or wood are placed.

grateful adjective feeling thankful and appreciative. ■ **gratefully** adverb.

grater noun a device having a surface covered with sharp-edged holes, used for grating food.

gratify verb (**gratifies, gratifying, gratified**) **1** give someone pleasure or satisfaction. **2** indulge or satisfy a desire. ▪ **gratification** noun.

grating[1] adjective **1** sounding harsh and unpleasant. **2** irritating.

grating[2] noun a grid of metal bars used as a barrier.

gratis /grat-iss, grah-tiss/ adverb & adjective free of charge.

gratitude noun appreciation of kindness; thankfulness.

gratuitous /gruh-tyoo-i-tuhss/ adjective having no justifiable reason or purpose. ▪ **gratuitously** adverb.

gratuity noun (plural **gratuities**) a small financial reward; a tip.

grave[1] noun **1** a hole dug in the ground to receive a coffin or corpse. **2** (the grave) death.

grave[2] adjective **1** giving cause for alarm or concern. **2** solemn. ▪ **gravely** adverb.

grave accent /grahv/ noun a mark (`) placed over a vowel in some languages to indicate a change in its sound quality.

gravel noun a loose mixture of small stones used for paths and roads.

gravelly adjective **1** resembling or containing gravel. **2** (of a voice) deep and rough.

graven image noun a carved figure.

gravestone noun a stone slab marking a grave.

graveyard noun a burial ground.

gravitas /gra-vi-tahss/ noun a serious and dignified manner.

gravitate verb (**gravitates**, **gravitating**, **gravitated**) be drawn towards.

gravitation noun movement towards a centre of gravity.

gravity noun **1** the force that attracts a body towards the centre of the earth, or towards any other physical body having mass. **2** extreme importance or seriousness. **3** a solemn manner.

gravy noun (plural **gravies**) a sauce made from the fat and juices that come out of meat during cooking. □ **gravy boat** a long, narrow jug used for serving gravy.

gray US spelling of **GREY**.

graze[1] verb (**grazes**, **grazing**, **grazed**) (of cattle, sheep, etc.) eat grass.

graze[2] verb (**grazes**, **grazing**, **grazed**) **1** scrape the skin on a part of your body. **2** touch something lightly in passing. noun an area where the skin has been scraped.

grazing noun grassland suitable for use as pasture.

grease noun **1** a thick oily substance used as a lubricant. **2** animal fat used or produced in cooking. verb (**greases**, **greasing**, **greased**) smear or lubricate something with grease.

greasepaint noun a waxy substance used as make-up by actors.

greaseproof adjective not allowing grease to pass through it.

greasy adjective (**greasier**, **greasiest**) **1** covered with or resembling grease. **2** polite in an unpleasantly insincere way. □ **greasy spoon** informal a cheap cafe serving fried foods.

great adjective **1** considerably above average in extent, amount, or intensity. **2** considerably above average in ability or quality. **3** informal excellent. **4** used to emphasize something: *I was a great fan of Hank's*. □ **great-aunt** (or **great-uncle**) an aunt (or uncle) of your mother or father. ▪ **greatness** noun.

greatcoat noun a long heavy overcoat.

greatly adverb very much.

grebe noun a diving bird with a long neck.

Grecian /gree-sh'n/ adjective relating to ancient Greece.

greed noun **1** a strong and selfish desire for possessions, wealth, or power. **2** a desire to eat more food than you need.

greedy adjective (**greedier**, **greediest**) having or showing greed. ▪ **greedily** adverb.

Greek noun **1** a person from Greece. **2** the ancient or modern language of Greece. adjective relating to Greece.

green adjective **1** of a colour between

blue and yellow, as of grass. **2** covered with grass or other vegetation. **3** (**Green**) concerned with or supporting protection of the environment. **4** inexperienced or naive. *noun* **1** a green colour. **2** a piece of grassy land for public use. **3** an area of smooth grass used for cricket or bowls, or surrounding a hole on a golf course. **4** (**greens**) cabbage or other green vegetables. **5** (**Green**) a supporter of a Green political party. □ **green belt** an area of open land around a city, on which building is restricted. **green card** (in the US) a permit allowing a foreigner to live and work permanently in the US. **green-eyed monster** *humorous* jealousy. **green fingers** *Brit.* natural ability in growing plants. **green light 1** a green traffic light indicating that you can go. **2** permission to go ahead with a project. **green pepper** the unripe fruit of a sweet pepper.

greenery *noun* green foliage or vegetation.

greenfield *adjective* (of a site) previously undeveloped.

greenfinch *noun* a large finch with green and yellow plumage.

greenfly *noun* a green aphid.

greengage *noun* a sweet greenish fruit resembling a small plum.

greengrocer *noun* *Brit.* a person who has a shop selling fruit and vegetables.

greenhouse *noun* a glass structure in which plants are kept to protect them from cold weather. □ **greenhouse effect** the tendency of atmospheric temperature to rise because certain gases absorb infrared radiation from the earth. **greenhouse gas** a gas that contributes to the greenhouse effect by absorbing infrared radiation.

greet *verb* **1** express friendliness or welcome when meeting someone. **2** acknowledge or react to someone or something in a particular way.

greeting *noun* **1** an expression of friendliness or welcome. **2** (**greet-**

ings) a formal expression of good wishes.

gregarious *adjective* **1** enjoying being with people; sociable. **2** (of animals) living in flocks or colonies.

Gregorian chant *noun* medieval church music for voices.

gremlin *noun* a mischievous sprite regarded as responsible for unexplained mechanical or electrical faults.

grenade *noun* a small bomb that is thrown by hand.

grenadier /gre-nuh-**deer**/ *noun* **1** *historical* a soldier armed with grenades. **2** (**Grenadiers** or **Grenadier Guards**) a regiment of the royal household infantry.

grew past of **GROW**.

grey (US spelling **gray**) *adjective* **1** of a colour between black and white, as of ashes or lead. **2** (of hair) turning grey or white with age. **3** (of the weather) cloudy and dull. **4** dull and lacking distinctive character. *noun* a grey colour. *verb* (of hair) become grey with age. □ **grey area** a subject or area of activity that does not easily fit into existing categories. **grey matter** *informal* the brain.

greyhound *noun* a swift, slender breed of dog used in racing.

grid *noun* **1** a set of bars lying parallel to or crossing each other. **2** a network of lines that cross each other to form a series of squares or rectangles. **3** a network of cables or pipes for distributing power.

griddle *noun* an iron plate that is heated and used for cooking food.

gridiron /**grid**-luhn/ *noun* a frame of metal bars used for grilling food over an open fire.

gridlock *noun* a traffic jam affecting a whole network of intersecting streets. ■ **gridlocked** *adjective*.

grief *noun* **1** intense sorrow and sadness, especially caused by someone's death. **2** *informal* trouble or annoyance.

grievance *noun* a cause for complaint.

grieve verb (grieves, grieving, grieved) **1** feel intense sorrow and sadness. **2** cause someone distress.

grievous adjective formal (of something bad) very severe or serious. □ **grievous bodily harm** Law serious physical injury deliberately inflicted on someone. ■ **grievously** adverb.

griffin or **gryphon** noun a mythical creature with the head and wings of an eagle and the body of a lion.

griffon noun **1** a small terrier-like dog. **2** a large vulture with pale brown plumage.

grill noun Brit. **1** a device on a cooker that radiates heat downwards for cooking food. **2** a gridiron used for cooking food on an open fire. **3** a dish of food cooked using a grill. **4** ⇒ **GRILLE**. verb **1** cook food with a grill. **2** informal subject someone to intense questioning.

grille or **grill** noun a framework of metal bars or wires.

grim adjective (grimmer, grimmest) **1** very serious and forbidding. **2** horrifying or depressing. ■ **grimly** adverb.

grimace noun a twisted expression on a person's face, showing disgust, pain, or wry amusement. verb (grimaces, grimacing, grimaced) make a grimace.

grime noun dirt ingrained on a surface. ■ **grimy** adjective.

grin verb (grins, grinning, grinned) smile broadly. noun a broad smile.

grind verb (grinds, grinding, ground) **1** reduce something to small particles or powder by crushing it. **2** sharpen or smooth something with an abrasive disc or tool. **3** rub together or move gratingly. **4** (grind down) wear someone down with harsh treatment. **5** (grind out) produce something slowly and laboriously. **6** (grinding) oppressive and seemingly endless. noun **1** an act or process of grinding. **2** hard dull work.

grindstone noun **1** a revolving disc of abrasive material used for sharpening or polishing metal objects. **2** a millstone. □ **keep your nose to the grindstone** keep working hard.

grip verb (grips, gripping, gripped) **1** hold something tightly. **2** deeply affect someone. **3** hold someone's attention. noun **1** a firm hold on something. **2** understanding of something. **3** a part or attachment by which something is held in the hand. □ **come** (or **get**) **to grips with** begin to deal with or understand.

gripe verb (gripes, griping, griped) **1** informal grumble. **2** give someone a pain in the stomach or intestines. noun **1** informal a trivial complaint. **2** pain in the stomach or intestines.

gripping adjective very exciting and holding your attention.

grisly /griz-li/ adjective (grislier, grisliest) causing horror or revulsion.

> [i] don't confuse **grisly** with **grizzly**, as in *grizzly bear*.

grist noun corn that is ground to make flour. □ **grist to the mill** useful experience or knowledge.

gristle noun tough inedible cartilage in meat. ■ **gristly** adjective.

grit noun **1** small loose particles of stone or sand. **2** (also **gritstone**) a coarse sandstone. **3** courage and determination. verb (grits, gritting, gritted) **1** clench the teeth in determination. **2** spread grit on an icy road.

gritty adjective (grittier, grittiest) **1** containing or covered with grit. **2** brave and determined. **3** tough and uncompromising. ■ **grittily** adverb.

grizzle verb (grizzles, grizzling, grizzled) Brit. informal cry fretfully.

grizzled adjective having grey or grey-streaked hair.

grizzly bear noun a large brown bear, often with white-tipped fur.

groan verb make a deep sound of pain or despair. noun a groaning sound.

groat noun historical an English silver coin worth four old pence.

grocer noun a person who sells food and small household goods.

grocery noun (plural groceries) **1** a grocer's shop or business. **2** (grocer-

ies) items of food sold in a grocer's shop or supermarket.

grog noun spirits mixed with water.

groggy adjective (**groggier, groggiest**) dazed and unsteady.

groin noun **1** the area between the stomach and the thigh. **2** US spelling of **GROYNE**.

grommet noun **1** a protective metal ring or eyelet. **2** a tube fitted in the eardrum to drain fluid from the middle ear.

groom verb **1** brush and clean the coat of a horse or dog. **2** give a neat and tidy appearance to. **3** train someone for a particular activity. noun **1** a person employed to take care of horses. **2** a bridegroom.

groove noun **1** a long, narrow cut in a hard surface. **2** a spiral track cut in a music record. **3** a routine or habit. verb (**grooves, grooving, grooved**) **1** make a groove or grooves in. **2** informal listen or dance to jazz or pop music.

groovy adjective (**groovier, grooviest**) informal, dated fashionable and interesting.

grope verb (**gropes, groping, groped**) **1** feel about with your hands. **2** ease your way forward using your hands to guide you. **3** informal feel someone's body for sexual pleasure. noun informal an act of groping someone.

gross adjective **1** unattractively large. **2** vulgar; unrefined. **3** informal very unpleasant; repulsive. **4** complete and blatant. **5** (of income, profit, or interest) before tax has been deducted. **6** (of weight) including contents or other variable items; overall. adverb in total. verb earn a particular amount of money as gross profit or income. noun **1** (plural **gross**) twelve dozen; 144. **2** (plural **grosses**) a gross profit or income. ■ **grossly** adverb.

grotesque /groh-**tesk**/ adjective **1** ugly or distorted in a way that is funny or frightening. **2** shocking. noun a grotesque figure or image. ■ **grotesquely** adverb.

grotto noun (plural **grottoes** or **grottos**) a small cave, or a construction imitating one.

grotty adjective (**grottier, grottiest**) Brit. informal **1** unpleasant and of poor quality. **2** unwell.

grouch noun informal **1** a grumpy person. **2** a complaint. ■ **grouchy** adjective.

ground¹ noun **1** the solid surface of the earth. **2** land or soil of a particular kind. **3** an area of land or sea with a particular use. **4** (**grounds**) an area of enclosed land surrounding a large house. **5** (**grounds**) good reasons for doing or believing something. verb **1** ban or prevent a pilot or aircraft from flying. **2** run a ship aground. **3** (**be grounded in** or **on**) have as a foundation or basis. □ **groundbreaking** involving completely new methods or discoveries. **ground control** the people who direct the flight and landing of aircraft or spacecraft. **ground floor** Brit. the floor of a building at ground level. **ground rent** Brit. rent paid by the owner of a building to the owner of the land on which it is built. **ground rule** a basic principle governing how something is done.

ground² past and past participle of **GRIND**.

grounding noun basic training or instruction in a subject.

groundless adjective not based on any good reason.

groundnut noun = **PEANUT**.

groundsel noun a plant with small yellow flowers.

groundsheet noun a waterproof sheet spread on the ground inside a tent.

groundsman noun Brit. a person who maintains a sports ground or the grounds of a large building.

groundswell noun **1** a large swell in the sea. **2** a build-up of public opinion.

groundwork noun preliminary or basic work.

group noun **1** a number of people or things placed or classed together. **2** a band of pop musicians. **verb** put into a group.

groupie noun informal a fan who follows a pop group or celebrity around.

grouse[1] **noun** (plural **grouse**) a game bird with a plump body.

grouse[2] **verb** (**grouses, grousing, groused**) complain; grumble. **noun** a grumble or complaint.

grout noun a substance used for filling the gaps between tiles. **verb** fill between tiles with grout.

grove noun a small wood, orchard, or group of trees.

grovel verb (**grovels, grovelling, grovelled**; US spelling **grovels, groveling, groveled**) **1** crouch or crawl on the ground. **2** act very humbly towards someone to make them forgive you or treat you favourably.

grow verb (**grows, growing, grew**; past participle **grown**) **1** (of a living thing) develop and get bigger. **2** become larger or greater over a period of time. **3** become gradually or increasingly: *we grew braver*. **4** (**grow up**) become an adult. **5** (**grow on**) become gradually more appealing to. □ **grown-up 1** adult. **2** informal an adult. ■ **grower** noun.

growl verb 1 (of a dog) make a low hostile sound in the throat. **2** say something in a low grating voice. **3** make a low or harsh rumbling sound. **noun** a growling sound.

growth noun 1 the process of growing. **2** something that has grown or is growing. **3** a tumour.

groyne (US spelling **groin**) **noun** a low wall built out into the sea from a beach to prevent the beach from shifting or being eroded.

grub noun 1 the larva of an insect. **2** informal food. **verb** (**grubs, grubbing, grubbed**) **1** dig shallowly in soil. **2** (**grub up**) dig something up.

grubby adjective (**grubbier, grubbiest**) **1** dirty; grimy. **2** sordid.

grudge noun a persistent feeling of anger or dislike resulting from a past insult or injury. **verb** (**grudges, grudging, grudged**) **1** be unwilling to give or allow something. **2** feel resentful that someone has achieved something.

grudging adjective reluctantly given or allowed. ■ **grudgingly** adverb.

gruel noun a thin liquid food of oatmeal boiled in milk or water.

gruelling (US spelling **grueling**) **adjective** extremely tiring and demanding.

gruesome adjective causing repulsion or horror.

gruff adjective 1 (of a voice) rough and low. **2** abrupt in manner. ■ **gruffly** adverb.

grumble verb (**grumbles, grumbling, grumbled**) **1** complain in a quiet but bad-tempered way. **2** make a low rumbling sound. **noun** a complaint.

grumpy adjective bad-tempered and sulky. ■ **grumpily** adverb.

grunge noun a style of rock music characterized by a raucous guitar sound. ■ **grungy** adjective.

grunt verb 1 (of an animal) make a short, low sound. **2** (of a person) make a low sound of physical effort or to show agreement. **noun** a grunting sound.

gryphon ⇨ **GRIFFIN**.

guano /gwah-noh/ **noun** the excrement of seabirds, used as fertilizer.

guarantee noun 1 a promise that certain things will be done. **2** a promise that a product will remain in working order for a particular length of time. **3** something that makes a particular outcome certain. **4** (also **guaranty**) an undertaking to pay or do something on behalf of someone if they fail to do it. **verb** (**guarantees, guaranteeing, guaranteed**) **1** provide a guarantee for something. **2** promise something with certainty. **3** provide financial security for.

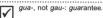 *gua-*, not *gau-*: *guarantee*.

guarantor /ga-ruhn-**tor**/ **noun** a person or organization that gives a guarantee.

guard verb 1 watch over in order to protect or control. **2** (**guard against**) take precautions against. **noun 1** a person who guards or keeps watch. **2** a body of soldiers guarding a place or person. **3** a state of vigilance: *she was on guard.* **4** a device worn or fitted to prevent injury or damage. **5** Brit. an official in charge of a train. **6** N. Amer. a prison warder.

 gua-, not *gau-*: gua**rd**.

guarded adjective cautious.

guardian noun **1** a person who defends and protects something. **2** a person who is legally responsible for someone who cannot manage their own affairs. □ **guardian angel** a spirit who is believed to watch over and protect you. ■ **guardianship** noun.

guava /**gwah**-vuh/ **noun** a tropical fruit with pink juicy flesh.

gudgeon noun a small freshwater fish.

guerrilla or **guerilla** /guh-**ril**-luh/ **noun** a member of a small independent group fighting against the government or regular forces.

guess verb **1** estimate or suppose something without having the information you need to be sure. **2** correctly estimate or suppose. **noun** an attempt to guess something.

guesswork noun the process or results of guessing.

guest noun **1** a person who is invited to someone's house or to a social occasion. **2** a performer invited to take part in an entertainment. **3** a person staying at a hotel or guest house. □ **guest house** a private house offering accommodation to paying guests.

guffaw noun a loud, deep laugh. verb give a loud deep laugh.

guidance noun advice and information given by an experienced or skilled person.

guide noun **1** a person who advises or shows the way to others. **2** a thing that helps you to form an opinion or make a decision. **3** a book providing information on a subject. **4** a structure or marking which directs the

movement or positioning of something. **5** (**Guide**) a member of the Guides Association, a girls' organization corresponding to the Scouts. **verb** (**guides**, **guiding**, **guided**) **1** show someone the way. **2** direct the movement or positioning of something. **3** (**guided**) directed by remote control or internal equipment. □ **guide dog** a dog trained to lead a blind person.

guidebook noun a book containing information about a place for visitors.

guideline noun a general rule, principle, or piece of advice.

guild noun **1** a medieval association of craftsmen or merchants. **2** an association of people who do the same work.

guilder /**gil**-der/ **noun** (plural **guilder** or **guilders**) the basic unit of money in the Netherlands.

guildhall noun **1** the meeting place of a guild or corporation. **2** Brit. a town hall.

guile noun cunning intelligence.

guileless adjective innocent and honest.

guillemot /**gil**-li-mot/ **noun** a seabird with a narrow pointed bill.

guillotine /**gil**-luh-teen/ **noun 1** a machine with a heavy blade, used for beheading people. **2** a device with a descending or sliding blade used for cutting paper or sheet metal. **verb** (**guillotines, guillotining, guillotined**) behead someone with a guillotine.

guilt noun **1** the fact of having committed an offence or crime. **2** a feeling of having done something wrong. ■ **guiltless** adjective.

guilty adjective (**guiltier, guiltiest**) **1** responsible for doing something wrong. **2** having or showing a feeling of guilt. ■ **guiltily** adverb.

guinea /**gi**-ni/ **noun** (in the past) a British gold coin worth 21 shillings (£1.05).

guineafowl noun (plural **guineafowl**) a large African game bird with grey, white-spotted feathers.

guinea pig noun **1** a tailless South

American rodent. **2** a person or thing used as a subject for experiment.

guise /gyz/ **noun** an external form, appearance, or manner.

guitar **noun** a stringed musical instrument which you play by plucking or strumming. ∎ **guitarist** noun.

gulch **noun** N. Amer. a narrow ravine.

gulf **noun 1** a deep inlet of the sea with a narrow mouth. **2** a deep ravine. **3** a large difference in opinion between two people or groups.

gull[1] **noun** a white seabird with long wings and a grey or black back.

gull[2] **verb** fool or deceive. **noun** a person who is deceived.

gullet **noun** the passage by which food passes from the mouth to the stomach.

gullible **adjective** easily believing what people tell you. ∎ **gullibility** noun.

gully or **gulley** **noun** (plural **gullies** or **gulleys**) **1** a ravine formed by the action of water. **2** a gutter or drain.

gulp **verb 1** swallow food or drink quickly or in large mouthfuls. **2** swallow with difficulty because you are upset or nervous. **noun 1** an act of gulping. **2** a large mouthful of liquid hastily drunk.

gum[1] **noun 1** a sticky substance produced by some trees. **2** glue used for sticking paper or other light materials together. **3** chewing gum or bubble gum.

gum[2] **noun** the firm area of flesh around the roots of the teeth.

gumboot **noun** Brit. dated a tall rubber boot; a wellington.

gumdrop **noun** a firm, jelly-like sweet.

gummy[1] **adjective** viscous; sticky.

gummy[2] **adjective** toothless.

gumption **noun** informal initiative and resourcefulness.

gun **noun 1** a weapon with a metal tube from which bullets or shells are fired by means of a small explosion. **2** a device for discharging something in a required direction. **verb** (guns,

gunning, gunned) (**gun down**) injure or kill with a gun. □ **gun dog** a dog trained to collect game that has been shot. **jump the gun** act before the proper or right time. **stick to your guns** refuse to compromise.

gunboat **noun** a small ship armed with guns.

gunge **noun** Brit. informal unpleasantly sticky or messy matter.

gung-ho **adjective** unthinkingly eager to take part in fighting.

gunk **noun** informal unpleasantly sticky or messy matter.

gunman **noun** a man who uses a gun to commit a crime.

gunmetal **noun 1** a grey form of bronze containing zinc. **2** a dull bluish-grey colour.

gunnel ⇒ **GUNWALE**.

gunner **noun 1** a person who operates a gun. **2** a British artillery soldier.

gunnery **noun** the design, manufacture, or firing of heavy guns.

gunpoint **noun** (**at gunpoint**) while threatening someone or being threatened with a gun.

gunpowder **noun** an explosive consisting of a powdered mixture of saltpetre, sulphur, and charcoal.

gunrunner **noun** a person involved in the illegal sale or importing of firearms. ∎ **gunrunning** noun.

gunship **noun** a heavily armed helicopter.

gunwale or **gunnel** /gun-uhl/ **noun** the upper edge or planking of the side of a boat.

guppy **noun** (plural **guppies**) a small freshwater fish native to tropical America.

gurgle **verb** (gurgles, gurgling, gurgled) make a hollow bubbling sound. **noun** a hollow bubbling sound.

Gurkha /ger-kuh/ **noun** a member of a Nepalese regiment in the British army.

gurn or **girn** **verb** Brit. pull a grotesque face.

guru **noun 1** a Hindu spiritual teacher. **2** a person who is an expert on a subject and has a lot of followers.

gush verb **1** flow in a strong, fast stream. **2** express approval in an unrestrained way. noun a rapid and strong stream. ▪ **gushing** adjective.

gushy adjective unrestrained in expressing approval.

gusset noun a piece of material sewn into a garment to strengthen or enlarge a part of it.

gust noun **1** a brief, strong rush of wind. **2** a burst of sound or emotion. verb blow in gusts. ▪ **gusty** adjective.

gusto noun enthusiastic energy.

gut noun **1** the stomach or intestine. **2** (guts) internal organs that have been removed or exposed. **3** (guts) the internal parts or essence of something. **4** (guts) informal courage and determination. verb (guts, gutting, gutted) **1** take out the internal organs of a fish before cooking. **2** remove or destroy the internal parts of something.

gutless adjective informal lacking courage or determination.

gutsy adjective (gutsier, gutsiest) informal brave and determined.

gutted adjective Brit. informal bitterly disappointed or upset.

gutter noun **1** a shallow trough beneath the edge of a roof, or a channel at the side of a street, for carrying off rainwater. **2** (the gutter) a very poor or squalid environment. verb (gutters, guttering, guttered) (of a flame) flicker and burn unsteadily.

guttering noun chiefly Brit. the gutters of a building.

guttersnipe noun disapproving a poor, badly behaved child.

guttural adjective (of a speech sound) produced in the throat.

guy[1] noun **1** informal a man. **2** (guys) N. Amer. informal people of either sex. **3** Brit. a stuffed figure that is traditionally burnt on a bonfire on 5 November. verb make fun of someone.

guy[2] noun a rope or line fixed to the ground to secure a tent.

guzzle verb (guzzles, guzzling, guzzled) eat or drink greedily.

gym noun informal **1** a gymnasium. **2** gymnastics.

gymkhana /jim-**kah**-nuh/ noun a horse-riding event consisting of a series of competitions.

gymnasium noun (plural gymnasiums or gymnasia) a hall or building equipped for gymnastics and other sports.

gymnast noun a person trained in gymnastics.

gymnastics plural noun exercises involving physical agility and coordination. ▪ **gymnastic** adjective.

gymslip noun Brit. dated a sleeveless tunic reaching from the shoulder to the knee, worn by schoolgirls.

gynaecology /gy-ni-**kol**-uh-ji/ (US spelling gynecology) noun the branch of medicine concerned with conditions and diseases experienced by women. ▪ **gynaecological** adjective **gynaecologist** noun.

gypsum /**jip**-suhm/ noun a soft white or grey mineral used to make plaster of Paris and in the building industry.

gypsy or **gipsy** noun (plural gypsies) a member of a travelling people.

gyrate /jy-**rayt**/ verb (gyrates, gyrating, gyrated) **1** move in a circle or spiral. **2** dance in a wild manner. ▪ **gyration** noun.

gyroscope noun a device, used to provide stability or maintain a fixed direction, consisting of a wheel or disc spinning rapidly about an axis which is itself free to alter in direction.

Hh

H or **h** noun (plural **Hs** or **H's**) the eighth letter of the alphabet. **abbreviation** (h) hours. □ **H-bomb** a hydrogen bomb.

ha abbreviation hectares.

habeas corpus /hay-bi-uhss **kor**-puhss/ **noun** Law a written order saying that a person must come before a judge or court.

haberdashery **noun** Brit. materials used in dressmaking and sewing.

habit **noun** **1** a thing you do regularly and repeatedly. **2** informal an addiction to a drug. **3** a long, loose garment worn by a monk or nun.

habitable **adjective** suitable to live in.

habitat **noun** the natural home or environment of a plant or animal.

habitation **noun** **1** the state of inhabiting. **2** formal a house or home.

habitual /huh-**bit**-yuu-uhl/ **adjective** **1** done constantly or as a habit. **2** regular; usual. ■ **habitually** adverb.

habituate **verb** (**habituates, habituating, habituated**) make or become accustomed to something.

habitué /huh-**bit**-yuu-ay/ **noun** a frequent visitor to a place.

hacienda /ha-si-**en**-duh/ **noun** (in Spanish-speaking countries) a large estate with a house.

hack¹ **verb** **1** cut or hit at something with rough or heavy blows. **2** use a computer to gain unauthorized access to data. **noun** a rough cut or blow. □ **hacking cough** a harsh, dry, frequent cough. ■ **hacker** noun.

hack² **noun** **1** a journalist producing dull, unoriginal work. **2** a horse for ordinary riding.

hackles **plural noun** hairs along an animal's back which rise when it is angry or alarmed.

hackney **noun** (plural **hackneys**) (in the past) a horse-drawn vehicle kept for hire. □ **hackney carriage** a taxi.

hackneyed **adjective** (of a phrase or idea) unoriginal and dull.

hacksaw **noun** a saw with a narrow blade set in a frame.

had past and past participle of **HAVE**.

haddock **noun** (plural **haddock**) a silvery-grey sea fish used for food.

hadn't **short form** had not.

haematology /hee-muh-**tol**-uh-ji/ (US spelling **hematology**) **noun** the study of the blood.

haemoglobin /hee-muh-**gloh**-bin/ (US spelling **hemoglobin**) **noun** a red protein in the blood that carries oxygen.

haemophilia /hee-muh-**fi**-li-uh/ (US spelling **hemophilia**) **noun** a condition in which the ability of the blood to clot is reduced, causing severe bleeding from even a slight injury. ■ **haemophiliac** noun.

haemorrhage /**hem**-uh-rij/ (US spelling **hemorrhage**) **noun** an escape of blood from a burst blood vessel. **verb** (**haemorrhages, haemorrhaging, haemorrhaged**) suffer a haemorrhage.

haemorrhoid /**hem**-uh-royd/ (US spelling **hemorrhoid**) **noun** a swollen vein in the region of the anus.

haft **noun** the handle of a knife, axe, or spear.

hag **noun** an ugly old woman.

haggard **adjective** looking exhausted and unwell.

haggis **noun** (plural **haggises**) a Scottish dish consisting of sheep's or calf's offal mixed with suet and oatmeal.

haggle **verb** (**haggles, haggling, haggled**) dispute or bargain persistently. **noun** a period of haggling.

hagiography /ha-gi-**og**-ruh-fi/ **noun** **1** writing about the lives of saints. **2** a biography that idealizes its subject.

ha-ha **noun** a trench which serves as a boundary to a park or garden without interrupting the view.

haiku /**hy**-koo/ noun (plural **haiku** or **haikus**) a Japanese poem of three lines and seventeen syllables.

hail[1] noun **1** pellets of frozen rain falling in showers. **2** a large number of things hurled forcefully through the air. verb (**it hails**, **it is hailing**, **it hailed**) hail falls.

hail[2] verb **1** call out to someone to attract their attention. **2** (**hail as**) enthusiastically describe as. **3** (**hail from**) have your home or origins in.

hailstone noun a pellet of hail.

hair noun **1** each of the thread-like strands growing from the skin of animals, or from plants. **2** strands of hair collectively. □ **hair-raising** extremely alarming or frightening. **hair shirt** (in the past) a prickly shirt made with horsehair, worn as a form of punishing yourself. **hair trigger** a firearm trigger set for release at the slightest pressure. **let your hair down** informal behave in an unrestrained way. **split hairs** make fussy distinctions.

hairband noun a band for holding back the hair.

haircut noun **1** the style in which someone's hair is cut. **2** an act of cutting someone's hair.

hairdo noun (plural **hairdos**) informal the style of a person's hair.

hairdresser noun a person who cuts and styles hair. ■ **hairdressing** noun.

hairdryer or **hairdrier** noun an electrical device for drying the hair with warm air.

hairgrip noun Brit. a hairpin.

hairline noun the edge of a person's hair. adjective very thin or fine.

hairnet noun a fine net for holding the hair in place.

hairpiece noun a piece of false hair worn with your own hair to make it look thicker.

hairpin noun a U-shaped pin for fastening the hair. □ **hairpin bend** Brit. a sharp U-shaped bend in a road.

hairspray noun a solution sprayed on to hair to keep it in place.

hairstyle noun a way in which a person's hair is cut or arranged. ■ **hairstylist** noun.

hairy adjective (**hairier**, **hairiest**) **1** covered with or resembling hair. **2** informal alarming and difficult.

hake noun a long-bodied sea fish used for food.

halal /huh-**lahl**/ adjective (of meat) prepared according to Muslim law.

halberd /**hal**-berd/ noun historical a combined spear and battleaxe.

halcyon /**hal**-si-uhn/ adjective (of a past time) extremely happy and peaceful.

hale adjective (of an old person) strong and healthy.

half noun (plural **halves**) **1** either of two equal parts into which something is or can be divided. **2** Brit. informal half a pint of beer. **3** informal a half-price fare. predeterminer & pronoun an amount equal to a half. adverb **1** to the extent of half. **2** partly. □ **at half mast** (of a flag) flown halfway down its mast, as a mark of respect for a person who has died. **half-and-half** in equal parts. **half-baked** poorly planned or considered. **half board** Brit. bed, breakfast, and one main meal at a hotel or guest house. **half-brother** (or **half-sister**) a brother (or sister) with whom you have one parent in common. **half-caste** offensive a person of mixed race. **half-crown** (or **half a crown**) (in the past) a British coin equal to two shillings and sixpence (12½p). **half-dozen** (or **half a dozen**) a group of six. **half-hearted** without enthusiasm or energy. **half-hour** (or **half an hour**) a period of thirty minutes. **half-life** the time taken for the radioactivity of a substance to fall to half its original value. **half measure** an inadequate action or policy. **half nelson** a hold in wrestling in which you pass one arm under your opponent's arm from behind while applying your other hand to their neck. **half-term** Brit. a short holiday halfway through a school term. **half-timbered** having walls with a timber frame and a brick or plaster filling. **half-time** (in sport) a short gap between two halves of a match. **not half 1** not nearly. **2** Brit. informal to an extreme degree.

halfback noun a player in a ball game whose position is between the forwards and fullbacks.

halfpenny or **ha'penny** /hayp-ni/ noun (plural **halfpennies** or **halfpence** /hay-p'nss/) (in the past) a British coin equal to half an old penny.

halfway adverb & adjective **1** at or to a point equal in distance between two others. **2** to some extent.

halfwit noun informal a stupid person. ■ **half-witted** adjective.

halibut noun (plural **halibut**) a large flat sea fish which is used for food.

halitosis /hali-**toh**sis/ noun bad-smelling breath.

hall noun **1** (also **hallway**) a room or space inside a front door, or between a number of rooms. **2** a large room for meetings, concerts, etc. **3** (also **hall of residence**) Brit. a university building in which students live. **4** Brit. a large country house.

hallelujah /hal-li-**loo**-yuh/ or **alleluia** /al-li-**loo**-yuh/ exclamation God be praised.

hallmark noun **1** an official mark stamped on articles of pure gold, silver, or platinum. **2** a distinctive feature. verb stamp with a hallmark.

hallo ⇒ HELLO.

hallowed /hal-lohd/ adjective **1** made holy. **2** greatly honoured and respected.

Halloween or **Hallowe'en** noun the night of 31 October, the evening before All Saints' Day.

hallucinate verb (**hallucinates**, **hallucinating**, **hallucinated**) see something which is not actually there. ■ **hallucination** noun **hallucinatory** adjective.

hallucinogen /huh-**loo**-si-nuh-juhn/ noun a drug causing hallucinations. ■ **hallucinogenic** adjective.

halo /hay-loh/ noun (plural **haloes** or **halos**) **1** (in a painting) a circle of light surrounding the head of a holy person. **2** a circle of light round the sun or moon.

halogen /hal-uh-juhn/ noun any of a group of elements including fluorine, chlorine, bromine, and iodine.

halt¹ verb come or bring to a sudden stop. noun **1** a stopping of movement or activity. **2** Brit. a minor stopping place on a railway line.

halt² adjective old use lame.

halter noun a rope or strap placed around the head of an animal and used to lead it. □ **halter neck** a style of neckline on a woman's garment that is held in place by a strap passing behind the neck.

halting adjective slow and hesitant.

halve verb (**halves**, **halving**, **halved**) **1** divide into two halves. **2** reduce or be reduced by half.

halves plural of HALF.

halyard /hal-yerd/ noun a rope used for raising and lowering a sail, yard, or flag on a ship.

ham¹ noun **1** meat from the upper part of a pig's leg which is salted and dried or smoked. **2** (**hams**) the back of the thighs. □ **ham-fisted** clumsy.

ham² noun **1** an actor who overacts. **2** (also **radio ham**) informal an amateur radio operator. verb (**hams**, **hamming**, **hammed**) informal overact. ■ **hammy** adjective.

hamburger noun a small cake of minced beef, fried or grilled and typically served in a bread roll.

hamlet noun a small village.

hammer noun **1** a tool with a heavy metal head and a wooden handle, for driving in nails. **2** an auctioneer's mallet, tapped to indicate a sale. **3** a part of a mechanism that hits another. **4** a heavy metal ball attached to a wire for throwing in an athletic contest. verb (**hammers**, **hammering**, **hammered**) **1** hit repeatedly with a hammer. **2** (**hammer away**) work hard and persistently. **3** (**hammer in** or **into**) make something stick in someone's mind by constantly repeating it. **4** (**hammer out**) laboriously work out the details of a plan or agreement.

hammerhead noun a shark with flattened extensions on either side of the head.

hammock noun a wide strip of canvas or rope mesh suspended at both ends, used as a bed.

hamper[1] noun a basket used for food and other items needed for a picnic.

hamper[2] verb (**hampers, hampering, hampered**) slow down or prevent the movement or progress of.

hamster noun a burrowing rodent with a short tail and large cheek pouches.

 no p: hamster, not hamp-.

hamstring noun any of five tendons at the back of a person's knee. verb (**hamstrings, hamstringing,** past and past participle **hamstrung**) **1** cripple by cutting the hamstrings. **2** severely restrict.

hand noun **1** the end part of the arm beyond the wrist, with four fingers and a thumb. **2** a pointer on a clock or watch indicating the passing of time. **3** (**hands**) a person's power or control. **4** an active role. **5** help in doing something. **6** a person who does physical work. **7** informal a round of applause. **8** the set of cards dealt to a player in a card game. **9** a unit of measurement of a horse's height, equal to 4 inches (10.16 cm). verb **1** give or pass something to. **2** (**hand over**) officially pass something to someone else. □ **at hand** (or **on** or **to hand**) near; easy to reach. **from hand to mouth** meeting only your immediate needs. **hand grenade** a grenade that is thrown by hand. **hand in glove** working very closely together. **hand-me-down** a garment that has been passed on from another person. **hand-pick** select carefully. **hands-on** involving direct participation rather than theory. **hand-to-hand** (of fighting) at close quarters. **in hand 1** in progress. **2** (of money) ready for use if needed. **out of hand 1** not under control. **2** without taking time to think.

handbag noun Brit. a small bag used by a woman to carry everyday personal items.

handball noun **1** a game in which the ball is hit with the hand in a walled court. **2** Soccer unlawful touching of the ball with the hand or arm.

handbill noun a small printed advertisement handed out in the street.

handbook noun a book giving basic information or instructions.

handbrake noun a brake operated by hand, used to hold an already stationary vehicle.

handcuff noun (**handcuffs**) a pair of lockable linked metal rings for securing a prisoner's wrists. verb put handcuffs on.

handful noun **1** a quantity that fills the hand. **2** a small number or amount. **3** informal a person who is difficult to deal with or control.

handgun noun a gun designed for use with one hand.

handhold noun something for a hand to grip on.

handicap noun **1** a thing that makes it difficult for someone to do something. **2** dated a permanent physical or mental disability. **3** a disadvantage given to a leading competitor in a sport in order to make the chances more equal. **4** the extra weight given as a handicap to a racehorse. **5** the number of strokes by which a golfer normally exceeds par for a course. verb (**handicaps, handicapping, handicapped**) make it difficult for someone to do something.

handicapped adjective having a handicap or disability.

ⓘ when used in reference to people with physical and mental disabilities, the word **handicapped** sounds dated and may cause offence; it is better to use **disabled**.

handicraft noun **1** the skilled making of decorative objects by hand. **2** an object made in this way.

handiwork noun **1** (**your handiwork**)

something that you have made or done. **2** the making of things by hand.

handkerchief noun (plural **handkerchiefs** or **handkerchieves**) a square of material for wiping or blowing the nose on.

handle verb (**handles**, **handling**, **handled**) **1** feel or move something with the hands. **2** control an animal, vehicle, or tool. **3** deal with a situation. **4** control, manage, or deal in something commercially. **5** (**handle yourself**) behave. noun **1** the part by which a thing is held, carried, or controlled. **2** a means of understanding or approaching a person or situation. ■ **handler** noun.

handlebar or **handlebars** noun the steering bar of a bicycle or motorbike.

handmade adjective made by hand rather than machine.

handmaid or **handmaiden** noun old use a female servant.

handout noun **1** a parcel of food, clothes, or money given to a needy person. **2** a piece of printed information provided free of charge.

handset noun **1** the part of a telephone that you speak into and listen to. **2** a hand-held control device for a piece of electronic equipment.

handshake noun an act of shaking a person's hand.

handsome adjective (**handsomer**, **handsomest**) **1** (of a man) good-looking. **2** (of a woman) striking and impressive rather than pretty. **3** (of a thing) impressive and of good quality. **4** (of an amount) large. ■ **handsomely** adverb.

handspring noun a jump through the air on to your hands followed by another on to your feet.

handstand noun an act of balancing on your hands with your legs in the air.

handwriting noun **1** writing with a pen or pencil rather than by typing or printing. **2** a person's particular style of writing. ■ **handwritten** adjective.

handy adjective (**handier**, **handiest**) **1** convenient to handle or use. **2** close by and ready for use. ■ **handily** adverb.

handyman noun a person employed to do general building repairs.

hang verb (**hangs**, **hanging**, past and past participle **hung** except in sense 2) **1** suspend or be suspended from above with the lower part dangling freely. **2** (past and past participle **hanged**) kill someone by suspending them from a rope tied around the neck. **3** (of a garment) fall or drape in a particular way. □ **get the hang of** informal learn how to do something. **hang-glider** an unpowered apparatus for flying, from which you are suspended in a harness. **hang out** informal spend time relaxing or enjoying yourself. **hang-up** informal an emotional problem.

> ℹ️ **hang** has two past tense and past participle forms, **hanged** and **hung**: use **hung** in general contexts, as in *they hung out the washing*, and **hanged** in reference to execution by hanging, as in *the prisoner was hanged*.

hangar /**hang**-er/ noun a large building for housing aircraft.

> ✓ *-ar*, not *-er*: hang**ar**.

hangdog adjective having a sad or guilty appearance.

hanger noun **1** a person who hangs something. **2** (also **coat hanger**) a curved frame with a hook at the top, for hanging clothes from a rail. □ **hanger-on** (plural **hangers-on**) a person who tries to be friendly with someone of higher status.

hanging noun a decorative piece of fabric hung on the wall of a room or around a bed.

hangman noun an executioner who hangs condemned people.

hangnail noun a piece of torn skin at the root of a fingernail.

hangover noun **1** a headache or other after-effects caused by drinking too much alcohol. **2** a thing that has survived from the past.

hank noun a coil or length of wool, hair, or other material.

hanker verb (hanker after or for or to do) feel a strong desire for or to do.

hanky or **hankie** noun (plural hankies) informal a handkerchief.

hanky-panky noun informal naughty behaviour.

hansom /han-suhm/ or **hansom cab** noun (in the past) a horse-drawn carriage with two wheels and a hood, for two passengers.

haphazard adjective lacking order or organization. ■ haphazardly adverb.

hapless adjective unlucky.

happen verb 1 take place without being planned or as the result of something. 2 (happen to do) do by chance. 3 (happen on) come across by chance. 4 (happen to) be experienced by. 5 (happen to) become of.

happening noun an event or occurrence. adjective informal fashionable.

happy adjective (happier, happiest) 1 feeling or showing pleasure. 2 willing to do something. 3 fortunate and convenient. □ happy-go-lucky cheerfully unconcerned about the future. **happy hour** a period of the day when drinks are sold at reduced prices in a bar. ■ happily adverb happiness noun.

hara-kiri /ha-ruh-ki-ri/ noun a Japanese method of ritual suicide in which a person cuts open their stomach with a sword.

harangue /huh-rang/ verb (harangues, haranguing, harangued) use loud and aggressive language in criticizing someone or trying to persuade them to do something. noun an act of haranguing.

harass /ha-ruhss, huh-rass/ verb 1 subject someone to constant interference or bullying. 2 make repeated small-scale attacks on an enemy in order to wear down resistance. ■ harassment noun.

☑ only one r: harass.

harbinger /har-bin-jer/ noun a person or thing that announces or signals the approach of something.

harbour (US spelling harbor) noun a sheltered area of coast, where ships can be moored. verb 1 keep a thought or feeling secretly in your mind. 2 give a refuge or shelter to. 3 carry the germs of a disease.

hard adjective 1 solid, firm, and rigid. 2 needing a lot of endurance or effort; difficult. 3 (of a person) not showing any signs of weakness; tough. 4 (of information) precise and definitely true. 5 harsh or unpleasant to the senses. 6 done with a great deal of force or strength. 7 (of drink) strongly alcoholic. 8 (of a drug) potent and addictive. adverb 1 with a great deal of effort or force. 2 so as to be solid or firm. □ hard-boiled 1 (of an egg) boiled until the yolk is firm. 2 (of a person) tough and cynical. **hard cash** coins and banknotes as opposed to other forms of payment. **hard copy** a printed version of data held in a computer. **hard core 1** the most committed or uncompromising members of a group. 2 pop music that is loud and aggressive in style. 3 pornography of a very explicit kind. **hard disk** (or hard drive) (in a computer) a rigid magnetic disk on which a large amount of data can be stored. **hard done by** Brit. harshly or unfairly treated. **hard feelings** feelings of resentment. **hard-headed** tough and realistic. **hard line** a strict policy or attitude. **hard-nosed** realistic and tough-minded. **hard shoulder** Brit. a strip of road alongside a motorway for use in an emergency. **hard up** informal short of money. ■ hardness noun.

hardback noun a book bound in stiff covers.

hardbitten adjective tough and cynical.

hardboard noun stiff board made of compressed wood pulp.

harden verb make or become hard or harder.

hardly adverb 1 scarcely; barely. 2 only with great difficulty.

ℹ️ don't use **hardly** in a negative construction, such as *I can't hardly wait;* say *I can hardly wait* instead.

hardship noun severe suffering.

hardware noun **1** tools and other items used in the home and in activities such as gardening. **2** the machines, wiring, and other parts of a computer. **3** heavy military equipment such as tanks and missiles.

hardwood noun the wood from a broadleaved tree as distinguished from that of conifers.

hardy adjective (**hardier, hardiest**) capable of surviving difficult conditions. ■ **hardiness** noun.

hare noun a fast-running mammal resembling a large rabbit, with long hind legs. verb (**hares, haring, hared**) run with great speed. □ **hare-brained** crazy and unlikely to succeed.

harebell noun a plant with pale blue bell-shaped flowers.

harelip noun a cleft lip.

ℹ️ the word **harelip** can cause offence; use **cleft lip** instead.

harem /hah-reem, hah-**reem**/ noun **1** the separate part of a Muslim household reserved for women. **2** the women living in a harem.

haricot /ha-ri-koh/ noun a round white bean.

hark verb **1** literary listen. **2** (**hark at**) informal said to draw attention to a foolish or arrogant remark. **3** (**hark back**) recall an earlier period.

harken ⇒ **HEARKEN.**

harlequin noun (**Harlequin**) (in traditional pantomime) a character who wears a mask and a diamond-patterned costume. adjective in varied colours.

harlot noun old use a prostitute.

harm noun **1** hurt or injury to a person. **2** damage done to a thing. **3** a bad effect on something. verb **1** hurt or injure someone. **2** damage or have a bad effect on something.

harmful adjective causing or likely to cause harm. ■ **harmfully** adverb.

harmless adjective not able or likely to cause harm. ■ **harmlessly** adverb.

harmonic adjective relating to or characterized by harmony.

harmonica noun a small rectangular wind instrument with a row of metal reeds capable of producing different notes.

harmonious adjective **1** tuneful. **2** arranged in a pleasing way so that each part goes well with the others. **3** free from conflict. ■ **harmoniously** adverb.

harmonium noun a keyboard instrument in which the notes are produced by air driven through metal reeds by foot-operated bellows.

harmonize or **harmonise** verb (**harmonizes, harmonizing, harmonized**) **1** add notes to a melody to produce harmony. **2** make or be harmonious.

harmony noun (plural **harmonies**) **1** the combination of musical notes sounded at the same time to produce chords with a pleasing effect. **2** a pleasing quality when things are arranged together well. **3** agreement.

harness noun **1** a set of straps by which a horse or other animal is fastened to a cart, plough, etc. **2** an arrangement of straps used for attaching a person's body to something. verb **1** fit a person or animal with a harness. **2** control and make use of resources.

harp noun a musical instrument consisting of a frame supporting a series of strings of different lengths, played by plucking with the fingers. verb (**harp on**) keep talking about something in a boring way. ■ **harpist** noun.

harpoon noun a barbed spear-like missile used for catching whales and other large sea creatures. verb spear with a harpoon.

harpsichord noun a keyboard instrument with horizontal strings plucked by points operated by pressing the keys.

harpy noun (plural **harpies**) **1** Greek and Roman Mythology a cruel creature with a woman's head and body and a bird's wings and claws. **2** a greedy or cruel woman.

harridan noun a bossy or aggressive old woman.

harrier noun **1** a hound used for hunting hares. **2** a bird of prey.

harrow noun an implement consisting of a heavy frame set with teeth which is dragged over ploughed land to break up or spread the soil. **verb** draw a harrow over.

harrowing adjective very distressing.

harry verb (**harries, harrying, harried**) **1** carry out repeated attacks on an enemy. **2** persistently harass.

harsh adjective **1** unpleasantly rough or jarring to the senses. **2** cruel or severe. **3** (of climate or conditions) difficult to survive in; hostile. ■ **harshly** adverb **harshness** noun.

hart noun an adult male deer.

harvest noun **1** the process or period of gathering in crops. **2** the season's yield or crop. **verb** gather in a crop. ■ **harvester** noun.

has 3rd person singular present of **HAVE**. □ **has-been** informal a person who is no longer important.

hash[1] noun **1** a dish of chopped cooked meat reheated with potatoes. **2** a jumble. □ **make a hash of** informal make a mess of.

hash[2] = **HASHISH**.

hash[3] noun the symbol #.

hashish /ha-sheesh/ noun cannabis.

hasn't short form has not.

hasp noun a hinged metal plate that is fitted over a metal loop and secured by a pin or padlock to fasten something.

hassle informal noun **1** annoying inconvenience. **2** deliberate harassment. **verb** (**hassles, hassling, hassled**) harass or pester someone.

hassock noun a cushion for kneeling on in church.

haste noun speed or urgency of action.

hasten verb **1** move or act quickly. **2** make something happen sooner than expected.

hasty adjective (**hastier, hastiest**) hurried; rushed. ■ **hastily** adverb.

hat noun a shaped covering for the head. □ **hat-trick** three successes of the same kind.

hatch[1] noun **1** a small opening in a floor, wall, or roof allowing access to an area. **2** a door in an aircraft, spacecraft, or submarine.

hatch[2] verb **1** (of a young bird, fish, or reptile) come out of its egg. **2** (of an egg) open and produce a young animal. **3** devise a plot or plan.

hatch[3] verb (in drawing) shade an area with closely drawn parallel lines. ■ **hatching** noun.

hatchback noun a car with a door across the full width and height at the back end for easy loading.

hatchet noun a small axe with a short handle. □ **bury the hatchet** end a quarrel.

hatchling noun a newly hatched young animal.

hate verb (**hates, hating, hated**) feel very strong dislike for. noun **1** very strong dislike. **2** informal a disliked person or thing.

hateful adjective very unkind or unpleasant.

hatred noun very strong dislike; hate.

haughty adjective (**haughtier, haughtiest**) arrogant and contemptuous of others. ■ **haughtily** adverb.

haul verb **1** pull or drag something with a lot of effort. **2** transport something in a lorry or cart. noun **1** a quantity of something obtained, especially illegally. **2** a number of fish caught at one time.

haulage noun the commercial transport of goods.

haulier noun Brit. a person or company employed in the commercial transport of goods by road.

haulm /hawm/ noun a plant stalk.

haunch noun **1** a person's or animal's buttock and thigh. **2** the leg and loin of an animal, as food.

haunt **verb 1** (of a ghost) appear regularly in a place. **2** (of a person) visit a place frequently. **3** keep coming into someone's mind in a disturbing way. **noun** a place where a particular type of person frequently goes.

haunted **adjective 1** visited by a ghost. **2** showing signs of mental suffering.

haunting **adjective** making someone feel sad or thoughtful. ■ **hauntingly** adverb.

haute couture /oht kuu-**tyoor**/ **noun** the designing and making of high-quality clothes by leading fashion houses.

haute cuisine /oht kwi-**zeen**/ **noun** high-quality cooking in the traditional French style.

have **verb** (**has, having, had**) **1** possess or own. **2** experience. **3** be able to make use of. **4** (**have to**) be obliged to; must. **5** perform an action. **6** show a personal characteristic. **7** suffer from an illness or disability. **8** cause something to be or be done. **9** place, hold, or keep something in a particular position. **10** take or be the host of. **11** eat or drink something. **auxiliary verb** used with a past participle to form the perfect, pluperfect, and future perfect tenses, and the conditional mood. □ **have on** Brit. informal try to make someone believe something untrue.

haven **noun 1** a place of safety. **2** a harbour or small port.

haven't short form have not.

haver /**hay**-ver/ **verb** (**havers, havering, havered**) **1** Scottish talk foolishly. **2** Brit. be indecisive.

haversack **noun** a small, sturdy bag carried on the back or over the shoulder.

havoc **noun 1** widespread destruction. **2** great confusion or disorder. □ **play havoc with** completely disrupt.

hawk[1] **noun 1** a fast-flying bird of prey with a long tail. **2** a person who favours aggressive policies in foreign affairs. **verb** (of a hawk or other flying creature) hunt prey on the wing. ■ **hawkish** adjective.

hawk[2] **verb** offer goods for sale in the street. ■ **hawker** noun.

hawk[3] **verb** clear the throat noisily.

hawser /**haw**-zer/ **noun** a thick rope for mooring or towing a ship.

hawthorn **noun** a thorny shrub or tree with small dark red fruits called **haws.**

hay **noun** grass that has been mown and dried for use as fodder. □ **hay fever** an allergy to pollen or dust, causing sneezing and watery eyes.

haystack or **hayrick** **noun** a large packed pile of hay.

haywire **adjective** informal out of control.

hazard **noun 1** a danger. **2** an obstacle, such as a bunker, on a golf course. **verb 1** dare to say. **2** put at risk.

hazardous **adjective** dangerous.

haze **noun 1** a thin mist caused by fine particles of dust, water, etc. **2** a state of mental confusion.

hazel **noun 1** a shrub or small tree bearing round nuts called **hazelnuts.** **2** a rich reddish-brown colour.

hazy **adjective** (**hazier, haziest**) **1** covered by a haze. **2** vague or unclear. ■ **hazily** adverb.

he **pronoun 1** used to refer to a man, boy, or male animal previously mentioned or easily identified. **2** used to refer to a person or animal of unspecified sex.

> **i** until recently, **he** was used to refer to any person, male or female (as in *every child needs to know that he is loved*), but many people now think that this is old-fashioned and sexist. **He or she** is clumsy; **they** is now often used instead, as in *everyone needs to feel that they matter.*

head **noun 1** the upper part of the body, containing the brain, mouth, and sense organs. **2** a person in charge. **3** the front, forward, or upper part of something. **4** a person considered as a unit: *fifty pounds per head.* **5** a specified number of cattle or sheep. **6** a compact mass of leaves or flowers at the top of a stem. **7** a part of a computer or a tape or video recorder which transfers information to and from a tape or disk. **8** the source of a river or stream. **9** the foam on top of a glass of beer. **10 (heads)** the side of a coin bearing the image of a head. **11** pressure of water or steam in an enclosed space. adjective chief. verb **1** be the head of. **2** give a heading to. **3** move in a specified direction. **4 (head off)** obstruct and turn aside. **5** Soccer hit the ball with the head. □ **come to a head** reach a crisis. **head of state** the official leader of a country. **head-on 1** with the front of a vehicle. **2** involving direct confrontation. **head start** an advantage gained at the beginning of something. ■ **headless** adjective **headship** noun.

headache noun **1** a continuous pain in the head. **2** informal something that causes worry.

headband noun a band of fabric worn around the head.

headboard noun an upright panel at the head of a bed.

headbutt verb attack someone by hitting them with the head. noun an act of headbutting.

headdress noun an ornamental covering for the head.

header noun **1** Soccer a shot or pass made with the head. **2** a line of text at the top of each page of a book or document.

headhunt verb find someone who is suitable for a vacant post.

heading noun **1** a title at the head of a page or section of a book. **2** a direction or bearing.

headland noun a narrow piece of land that sticks out into the sea.

headlight or **headlamp** noun a powerful light at the front of a motor vehicle.

headline noun **1** a heading at the top of a newspaper or magazine article. **2 (the headlines)** a summary of the most important items of news. verb **(headlines, headlining, headlined)** **1** give an article a headline. **2** appear

as the star performer at a concert.

headlock noun a method of restraining someone by holding an arm firmly around their head.

headlong adverb & adjective **1** with the head first. **2** in a rush.

headmaster or **headmistress** noun chiefly Brit. a teacher in charge of a school; a head teacher.

headphones plural noun a pair of earphones joined by a band placed over the head.

headquarters noun the place from which an organization or military operation is directed.

headset noun a set of headphones with a microphone attached.

headstone noun an stone slab set up at the head of a grave.

headstrong adjective very independent and determined to have your own way.

headway noun forward progress.

headwind noun a wind blowing from directly in front.

headword noun a word which begins a separate entry in a dictionary or encyclopedia.

heady adjective **(headier, headiest)** **1** (of alcohol) strong. **2** having a strong or exciting effect.

heal verb **1** make or become healthy again. **2** put right. ■ **healer** noun.

health noun **1** the state of being free from illness or injury. **2** a person's mental or physical condition. □ **health farm** a place where people try to become healthier through dieting, exercise, and treatment. **health food** natural food that is believed to be good for your health.

healthful adjective good for the health.

healthy adjective **(healthier, healthiest)** **1** in good health, or helping towards good health. **2** normal, sensible, or desirable. **3** of a very satisfactory size or amount. ■ **healthily** adverb.

heap noun **1** a pile of a substance or of a number of objects. **2** informal a large amount or number. **3** informal an old vehicle in bad condition. **verb 1** put in or form a heap. **2 (heap with)** load heavily with. **3 (heap on)** give large amounts of something to.

hear verb (**hears, hearing, heard**) **1** be aware of a sound with the ears. **2** be told of. **3 (have heard of)** be aware of the existence of. **4 (hear from)** receive a letter or phone call from. **5** listen to. **6** listen to and judge a case in a law court. ■ **hearer** noun.

hearing noun 1 the ability to hear sounds. **2** the range within which sounds can be heard. **3** an opportunity to state your case. **4** an act of listening to evidence. □ **hearing aid** a small device worn by a partially deaf person to make them hear better.

hearken or **harken** /har-k'n/ **verb** (usu. **hearken to**) old use listen.

hearsay noun information received from other people which is possibly unreliable.

hearse /herss/ **noun** a vehicle for carrying the coffin to a funeral.

heart noun 1 the organ in the chest that pumps the blood around the body. **2** the central or innermost part of something. **3** a person's capacity for feeling love or compassion. **4** mood or feeling. **5** courage or enthusiasm. □ **heart attack** a sudden failure of the heart to work properly. **heart-rending** very sad or distressing. **heart-searching** thorough examination of your feelings and motives. **heart-throb** a very good-looking famous man. **heart-to-heart** (of a conversation) very intimate. **heart-warming** emotionally rewarding or uplifting. **tug** (or **pull**) **at the heartstrings** arouse deep compassion or love. **wear your heart on your sleeve** show your feelings openly.

heartache noun emotional suffering or grief.

heartbeat noun 1 a pulsation of the heart. **2** a very brief moment of time. □ **a heartbeat away** very close.

heartbreak noun extreme distress. ■ **heartbreaking** adjective **heartbroken** adjective.

heartburn noun a form of indigestion felt as a burning sensation in the chest.

hearten verb make more cheerful or confident. ■ **heartening** adjective.

heartfelt adjective deeply and strongly felt.

hearth /harth/ **noun** the floor or surround of a fireplace.

hearthrug noun a rug laid in front of a fireplace.

heartily adverb 1 in a hearty manner. **2** very.

heartless adjective completely unfeeling or inconsiderate.

hearty adjective (**heartier, heartiest**) **1** enthusiastic and friendly. **2** strong and healthy. **3** heartfelt. **4** (of a meal) wholesome and filling.

heat noun 1 the quality of being hot. **2** hot weather or high temperature. **3** strength of feeling. **4** (**the heat**) informal pressure. **5** a preliminary round in a race or contest. **verb 1** make or become hot or warm. **2** (**heat up**) become more intense and exciting. **3** (**heated**) passionate. □ **on heat** ready for mating. ■ **heatedly** adverb.

heater noun a device for heating something.

heath noun an area of open uncultivated land covered with heather, gorse, etc.

heathen /hee-thuhn/ **noun** old use a person who does not belong to a widely held religion.

heather noun a shrub with small purple flowers, found on moors and heaths.

heating noun equipment used to provide heat.

heatstroke noun a feverish condition caused by being exposed to very high temperatures.

heatwave noun a period of abnormally hot weather.

heave verb (**heaves, heaving, heaved** or chiefly Nautical **hove**) **1** lift or drag with great effort. **2** produce a sigh noisily. **3** informal throw something heavy. **4** rise and fall. **5** try to vomit. **6 (heave to)** Nautical come to a stop. **7 (heaving)** Brit. informal extremely crowded. □ **heave in sight** (or **into view)** Nautical come into view.

heaven noun **1** (in Christianity and some other religions) the place where God or the gods live and where good people go when they die. **2 (the heavens)** literary the sky. **3** informal a place or state of extreme happiness. □ **in seventh heaven** very happy.

heavenly adjective **1** having to do with heaven. **2** having to do with the sky. **3** informal wonderful. □ **heavenly body** a planet, star, etc.

heavy adjective **(heavier, heaviest) 1** of great weight. **2** thick or dense. **3** of more than the usual size, amount, or force. **4** hard or forceful. **5** not delicate or graceful; clumsy: *heavy-handed.* **6** needing a lot of physical effort. **7** very important or serious. **8** (of music) having a strong bass part and a forceful rhythm. noun (plural **heavies**) informal **1** a large, strong man. **2** an important person. □ **heavy-duty** designed to withstand a lot of use or wear. **heavy industry** large-scale production of large, heavy articles and materials. **heavy metal** very loud, forceful rock music. ■ **heavily** adverb **heaviness** noun.

heavyweight noun **1** the heaviest weight in boxing. **2** informal an influential person.

Hebrew /hee-broo/ noun an ancient language still spoken in Israel.

heckle verb **(heckles, heckling, heckled)** interrupt a public speaker with comments or abuse. ■ **heckler** noun.

hectare /hek-tair/ noun a unit of area equal to 10,000 square metres (2.471 acres).

hectic adjective full of frantic activity. ■ **hectically** adverb.

hector verb talk to someone in a bullying way.

he'd short form he had or he would.

hedge noun a fence formed by closely growing bushes or shrubs. verb **(hedges, hedging, hedged) 1** surround with a hedge. **2** avoid making a definite statement or decision. □ **hedge your bets** avoid committing yourself.

hedgehog noun a small mammal with a spiny coat, which can roll itself into a ball for defence.

hedgerow noun a hedge of wild shrubs and trees bordering a field.

hedonism noun the pursuit of pleasure. ■ **hedonist** noun **hedonistic** adjective.

heebie-jeebies plural noun **(the heebie-jeebies)** informal a state of nervous fear or anxiety.

heed verb pay attention to. □ **pay** (or **take) heed** pay careful attention.

heedless adjective showing a reckless lack of care or attention.

heel[1] noun **1** the back part of the foot below the ankle. **2** the part of a shoe or boot supporting the heel. **3** the part of the palm of the hand next to the wrist. verb renew the heel on a shoe. □ **cool** (or Brit. **kick) your heels** be kept waiting.

heel[2] verb (of a ship) lean over to one side.

heft verb lift or carry something heavy.

hefty adjective **(heftier, heftiest) 1** large, heavy, and powerful. **2** (of a number or amount) considerable.

hegemony /hi-jem-uh-ni, hi-gem-uh-ni/ noun formal leadership or dominance.

heifer /hef-er/ noun a young cow.

height noun **1** measurement from head to foot or from base to top. **2** distance above sea level or the ground. **3** the quality of being tall or high. **4** a high place. **5** the most intense or extreme part.

heighten verb **1** make higher. **2** make or become more intense.

heinous /hay-nuhss, hee-nuhss/ adjective utterly wicked.

heir /air/ noun **1** a person who will inherit the property or rank of another when that person dies. **2** a person who continues the work of someone. □**heir apparent** (plural **heirs apparent**) **1** an heir whose rights cannot be taken away by the birth of another heir. **2** a person who is most likely to succeed to the place of another.

heiress noun a female heir.

heirloom noun a valuable object that has belonged to a family for several generations.

heist /hyst/ noun informal, chiefly N. Amer. a robbery.

held past and past participle of **HOLD**[1].

helical /he-li-k'l, hee-li-k'l/ adjective in the shape of a helix.

helicopter noun a type of aircraft which is powered and lifted by horizontally revolving blades.

helium /hee-li-uhm/ noun a light colourless gas that does not burn.

helix /hee-liks/ noun (plural **helices** /hee-li-seez/) an object in the shape of a spiral.

hell noun **1** (in Christianity and some other religions) a place of evil and suffering where wicked people are sent after death. **2** a state or place of great suffering. □**hell-bent** determined to achieve something.

he'll short form he shall or he will.

Hellenic /he-len-ik/ adjective Greek.

hellhole noun an unbearable place.

hellish adjective **1** relating to or like hell. **2** informal extremely difficult or unpleasant. ■ **hellishly** adverb.

hello, **hallo**, or **hullo** exclamation **1** used as a greeting. **2** Brit. used to express surprise or to attract someone's attention.

hellraiser noun a person who causes trouble by drunken or outrageous behaviour.

helm noun **1** a tiller or wheel for steering a ship or boat. **2** (**the helm**) the position of leader.

helmet noun a hard or padded protective hat.

helmsman noun a person who steers a boat.

help verb **1** make it easier for someone

to do something. **2** improve a situation or problem. **3** (**help to**) serve someone with food or drink. **4** (**help yourself**) take something without asking for it first. **5** (**cannot help**) be unable to stop yourself doing. noun a person or thing that helps someone. ■ **helper** noun.

helpful adjective **1** ready to give help. **2** useful. ■ **helpfully** adverb.

helping noun a portion of food served to one person at one time.

helpless adjective **1** unable to defend yourself or to act without help. **2** uncontrollable. ■ **helplessly** adverb.

helpmate or **helpmeet** noun a helpful companion.

helter-skelter adjective & adverb in disorderly haste or confusion. noun Brit. a tall slide winding around a tower at a fair.

hem noun the edge of a piece of cloth or clothing which has been turned under and sewn. verb (**hems, hemming, hemmed**) **1** give something a hem. **2** (**hem in**) surround and restrict the movement of.

hematology etc. US spelling of **HAEMATOLOGY** etc.

hemisphere noun **1** a half of a sphere. **2** a half of the earth. ■ **hemispherical** adjective.

hemline noun the level of the lower edge of a skirt or coat.

hemlock noun a poison obtained from a plant with small white flowers.

hemp noun **1** the cannabis plant, the fibre of which is used to make rope, fabrics, etc. **2** the drug cannabis.

hen noun **1** a female bird, especially of a domestic fowl. **2** (**hens**) domestic fowls of either sex. □**hen night** Brit. informal an all-female celebration for a woman who is about to get married.

hence adverb **1** for this reason. **2** from now.

henceforth or **henceforward** adverb from this time on.

henchman noun chiefly disapproving a faithful follower.

henna noun a reddish-brown dye made from the powdered leaves of a tropical shrub. ■ **hennaed** adjective.

henpeck verb (of a woman) continually criticize and order about her husband.

hepatitis /he-puh-**ty**-tiss/ noun a serious disease of the liver, mainly transmitted by viruses.

heptagon /**hep**-tuh-guhn/ noun a figure with seven straight sides and angles. ■ **heptagonal** adjective.

heptathlon noun an athletic contest for women that consists of seven separate events. ■ **heptathlete** noun.

her pronoun used as the object of a verb or preposition to refer to a female person or animal previously mentioned. **possessive determiner** belonging to or associated with a female person or animal previously mentioned.

herald noun **1** (in the past) a person who carried official messages and supervised tournaments. **2** a sign that something is about to happen or arrive. verb **1** be a sign that something is about to happen or arrive. **2** publicly describe or announce.

heraldic /he-**ral**-dik/ adjective having to do with heraldry.

heraldry noun the system by which coats of arms are organized and controlled.

herb noun **1** a plant used for flavouring food or in medicine. **2** Botany a plant which dies down to the ground after flowering. ■ **herbal** adjective.

herbaceous /her-**bay**-shuhss/ adjective relating to herbs (in the botanical sense). □ **herbaceous border** a garden border containing plants which flower every year.

herbage noun herbaceous plants.

herbalism noun the use of plants in medicine and cookery. ■ **herbalist** noun.

herbivore /**her**-bi-vor/ noun an animal that feeds on plants. ■ **herbivorous** /her-**biv**-uh-ruhss/ adjective.

Herculean /her-kyuu-**lee**-uhn/ adjective requiring great strength or effort: *a Herculean task.*

herd noun **1** a large group of animals that live or are kept together. **2** disapproving a large group of people. verb make animals or people move in a large group.

here adverb in, at, or to this place or position.

hereabouts or **hereabout** adverb near this place.

hereafter adverb formal **1** from now on or at some time in the future. **2** after death. noun (**the hereafter**) life after death.

hereby adverb formal as a result of this.

hereditary adjective **1** passed on by parents to their children or young. **2** having to do with inheritance.

heredity /hi-**red**-i-ti/ noun **1** the passing on of characteristics from one generation to another. **2** the inheriting of a title, office, etc.

herein adverb formal in this document, book, or matter.

hereof adverb formal of this document.

heresy noun (plural **heresies**) **1** belief which goes against traditional religious teachings. **2** opinion greatly at odds with what is generally accepted.

heretic noun a person who is guilty of heresy. ■ **heretical** adjective.

hereto adverb formal to this matter or document.

heretofore adverb formal before now.

herewith adverb formal with this.

heritable adjective able to be inherited.

heritage noun valued things such as historic buildings that have been passed down from previous generations.

hermaphrodite /her-**maf**-ruh-dyt/ noun a person, animal, or plant with both male and female sex organs or characteristics.

hermetic /her-**met**-ik/ adjective (of a seal or closure) complete and airtight. ■ **hermetically** adverb.

hermit noun a person who lives completely alone, especially for religious reasons.

hernia noun a condition in which part of an organ protrudes through the wall of the cavity containing it.

hero noun (plural **heroes**) **1** a person who is admired for their courage or outstanding achievements. **2** the chief male character in a book, play, or film. □ **hero worship** excessive admiration for someone.

heroic adjective **1** very brave. **2** very grand or ambitious in scale. noun (**heroics**) bold or dramatic behaviour or talk. ■ **heroically** adverb.

heroin noun a highly addictive pain-killing drug.

heroine noun **1** a woman admired for her courage or outstanding achievements. **2** the chief female character in a book, play, or film.

heroism noun great bravery.

heron noun a large fish-eating bird with long legs, a long neck, and a long pointed bill.

herpes /**her**-peez/ noun an infectious disease that causes blisters on the skin.

herring noun a silvery fish which is found in shoals and is used for food.

herringbone noun a zigzag pattern consisting of columns of short slanting parallel lines.

hers possessive pronoun used to refer to something belonging to or associated with a female person or animal previously mentioned.

 no apostrophe: her**s**.

herself pronoun **1** used as the object of a verb or preposition to refer to a female person or animal previously mentioned as the subject of the clause. **2** she or her personally.

hertz noun (plural **hertz**) the basic unit of frequency, equal to one cycle per second.

he's short form he is or he has.

hesitant adjective slow to act or speak through indecision or reluctance. ■ **hesitancy** noun **hesitantly** adverb.

hesitate verb (**hesitates, hesitating, hesitated**) **1** pause indecisively. **2** be reluctant to do something. ■ **hesitation** noun.

hessian noun a strong, coarse fabric.

heterogeneous /het-uh-ruh-**jee**-ni-uhss/ adjective varied. ■ **heterogeneity** /het-uh-ruh-juh-**nee**-i-ti/ noun.

heterosexual adjective sexually attracted to people of the opposite sex. noun a heterosexual person. ■ **heterosexuality** noun.

het up adjective informal angry and agitated.

hew verb (**hews, hewing, hewed,** past participle **hewn** or **hewed**) chop wood, coal, etc. with an axe or other tool.

hex chiefly N. Amer. verb cast a spell on. noun a magic spell.

hexagon /**hek**-suh-guhn/ noun a figure with six straight sides and angles. ■ **hexagonal** adjective.

hexameter /hek-**sam**-i-ter/ noun a line of verse made up of six groups of syllables.

heyday noun (**your heyday**) the period when you are most successful or active.

HGV abbreviation Brit. heavy goods vehicle.

hiatus /hy-**ay**-tuhss/ noun (plural **hiatuses**) a pause or gap in a series or sequence.

hibernate verb (**hibernates, hibernating, hibernated**) (of an animal) spend the winter in a state like deep sleep. ■ **hibernation** noun.

hibiscus /hi-**biss**-kuhss/ noun a plant with large brightly coloured flowers.

hiccup or **hiccough** /**hik**-up/ noun **1** a sudden gulping sound caused by an involuntary spasm of the diaphragm. **2** a minor setback. verb (**hiccups, hiccuping, hiccuped**) make the sound of a hiccup.

hick noun informal, chiefly N. Amer. an unsophisticated country person.

hickory noun a tree with edible nuts.

hide[1] verb (**hides, hiding, hid**; past participle **hidden**) **1** put or keep something out of sight. **2** conceal yourself.

3 keep secret. **noun** Brit. a concealed shelter used to observe wildlife at close quarters. □ **hide-and-seek** a game in which one player hides and the others have to look for them.

hide² **noun** the skin of an animal.

hideaway **noun** a hiding place.

hidebound **adjective** unwilling to change because of tradition.

hideous **adjective 1** extremely ugly. **2** extremely unpleasant. ■ **hideously** adverb.

hideout **noun** a hiding place.

hiding **noun 1** a physical beating. **2** informal a severe defeat. □ **be on a hiding to nothing** Brit. be unlikely to succeed.

hierarchy /hy-uh-rah-ki/ **noun** (plural **hierarchies**) **1** a system in which people are ranked one above the other according to status or authority. **2** a classification of things according to their relative importance. ■ **hierarchical** adjective.

✓ *-ie-*, not *-ei-*, and remember the second *r*: hierarchy.

hieroglyphic **noun** (**hieroglyphics**) writing in which a picture represents a word, syllable, or sound, as used in ancient Egypt. **adjective** having to do with hieroglyphics.

hi-fi informal **adjective** having to do with high-fidelity sound. **noun** (plural **hi-fis**) a set of equipment for reproducing high-fidelity sound.

higgledy-piggledy **adverb & adjective** in confusion or disorder.

high **adjective 1** extending far upwards. **2** of a specified height. **3** far above ground or sea level. **4** large in amount, size, or intensity. **5** (of a period or movement) at its peak. **6** great in status; important. **7** (of a sound or note) not deep or low. **8** informal under the influence of drugs or alcohol. **9** (of food) beginning to go bad. **noun 1** a high point, level, or figure. **2** an area of high atmospheric pressure. **3** informal a state of high spirits. **adverb** (of a sound) at a high pitch. □ **High Church** the section of the Church of England which emphasizes ritual and the authority of bishops and priests. **high commission** an embassy of one Commonwealth country in another. **high court** a supreme court of justice. **higher education** education to degree level or its equivalent, provided at universities and colleges. **high explosive** powerful chemical explosive used in shells and bombs. **high fidelity** the reproduction of sound with little distortion. **high-flown** grand-sounding. **high-flyer** (or **high-flier**) a very successful person. **high gear** a gear that causes a vehicle to move quickly. **high-handed** using authority without considering the feelings of other people. **high jinks** high-spirited fun. **the high jump** an athletic event in which competitors try to jump over a bar. **high-rise** (of a building) having many storeys. **high school** a secondary school. **the high seas** the open ocean. **high-spirited** lively and cheerful. **high tea** Brit. a meal eaten in the late afternoon or early evening. **high-tech** using advanced technology. **high technology** advanced technology. **high-tensile** (of metal) very strong under tension. **high tide** the time when the sea is closest to the land.

highbrow **adjective** very intellectual or refined in taste.

highfalutin /hy-fuh-**loo**-tin/ **adjective** informal grand or self-important in a pretentious way.

highland or **highlands** **noun 1** an area of high or mountainous land. **2** (**the Highlands**) the mountainous northern part of Scotland. ■ **highlander** noun.

highlight **noun 1** an outstanding part of an event or period of time. **2** a bright area in a picture. **3** (**highlights**) bright tints in the hair. **verb 1** draw attention to. **2** create highlights in hair. ■ **highlighter** noun.

highly **adverb 1** to a high degree or level. **2** favourably. □ **highly strung** Brit. very nervous and easily upset.

Highness **noun** (His, Your, etc. **High-**

ness) a title given to a person of royal rank.

highway noun **1** chiefly N. Amer. a main road. **2** a public road.

highwayman noun (in the past) a man who held up and robbed travellers.

hijack verb **1** illegally seize control of an aircraft while it is travelling somewhere. **2** take over something and use it for a different purpose. noun an instance of hijacking. ∎ **hijacker** noun.

hike noun **1** a long walk or walking tour. **2** a sharp increase. verb (**hikes, hiking, hiked**) **1** go on a hike. **2** pull or lift up clothing. **3** increase a price sharply. ∎ **hiker** noun.

hilarious adjective extremely amusing. ∎ **hilariously** adverb **hilarity** noun.

hill noun a naturally raised area of land, not as high as a mountain. ☐ **over the hill** informal old and past your best.

hillbilly noun (plural **hillbillies**) N. Amer. informal an unsophisticated country person.

hillock noun a small hill or mound.

hilly adjective (**hillier, hilliest**) having many hills.

hilt noun the handle of a sword, dagger, or knife. ☐ **to the hilt** completely.

him pronoun used as the object of a verb or preposition to refer to a male person or animal previously mentioned.

himself pronoun **1** used as the object of a verb or preposition to refer to a male person or animal previously mentioned as the subject of the clause. **2** he or him personally.

hind[1] adjective situated at the back.

hind[2] noun a female deer.

hinder verb (**hinders, hindering, hindered**) delay or obstruct.

Hindi noun a language of northern India.

hindmost adjective furthest back.

hindquarters plural noun the rear part and hind legs of a four-legged animal.

hindrance noun a thing that hinders

someone or something.

hindsight noun understanding of a situation or event after it has happened.

Hindu noun (plural **Hindus**) a follower of Hinduism.

Hinduism noun a religion of the Indian subcontinent, with a large number of gods and goddesses.

hinge noun a movable joint or mechanism by which a door, gate, or lid opens and closes. verb (**hinges, hinging** or **hinging, hinged**) **1** attach or join with a hinge. **2** (**hinge on**) depend entirely on.

hint noun **1** a slight or indirect suggestion. **2** a very small trace of something. **3** a small piece of practical information. verb **1** suggest indirectly. **2** (**hint at**) be a slight suggestion of.

hinterland noun **1** the areas of a country away from the coast. **2** the area around or beyond a major town.

hip[1] noun a projection formed by the pelvis and upper thigh bone on each side of the body.

hip[2] noun the fruit of a rose.

hip[3] adjective (**hipper, hippest**) informal fashionable. ∎ **hipness** noun.

hip hop noun a style of popular music featuring rap with an electronic backing.

hippo = HIPPOPOTAMUS.

hippopotamus noun (plural **hippopotamuses** or **hippopotami** /hip-puh-pot-uh-mI/) a large African mammal with massive jaws, living partly on land and partly in water.

hippy or **hippie** noun (plural **hippies**) a young person with long hair and unconventional clothes.

hipsters noun Brit. trousers with the waistline at the hips.

hire verb (**hires, hiring, hired**) **1** chiefly Brit. pay to be allowed to use something temporarily. **2** (**hire out**) allow something to be used temporarily in return for payment. **3** pay someone to work for you. noun the action of hiring. ☐ **hire purchase** Brit. a system by which you pay for a thing in regular instalments while having the use of it.

hireling noun a person who is hired to do menial or unpleasant work.

hirsute /her-syoot/ adjective hairy.

his possessive determiner & pronoun belonging to or associated with a male person or animal previously mentioned.

Hispanic adjective having to do with Spain or other Spanish-speaking countries.

hiss verb **1** make a sharp sound like that made when pronouncing the letter *s*. **2** whisper something in an urgent or angry way. noun a hissing sound.

histamine /hiss-tuh-meen/ noun a substance which is released by cells in response to an injury or allergy.

historian noun an expert in history.

historic adjective famous or important in history, or likely to be seen as such in the future.

historical adjective **1** having to do with history. **2** belonging to or set in the past. ■ **historically** adverb.

history noun (plural **histories**) **1** the study of past events. **2** the past considered as a whole. **3** the past events connected with someone or something. **4** a continuous record of past events or trends.

histrionic adjective excessively theatrical or dramatic. noun (**histrionics**) excessively dramatic behaviour intended to attract attention.

hit verb (**hits, hitting, hit**) **1** strike with the hand or a tool, weapon, bat, etc. **2** strike a target. **3** cause harm or distress to. **4** be suddenly realized by. **5** (**hit out**) criticize or attack strongly. **6** informal reach. **7** (**hit on**) suddenly discover or think of. noun **1** an instance of hitting or being hit. **2** a successful film, pop record, etc. **3** informal, chiefly N. Amer. a murder carried out by a criminal organization. **4** informal a dose of an addictive drug. □**hit-and-miss** (**or hit-or-miss**) not done in a careful, planned way; random. **hit-and-run** (of

a road accident) in which the driver responsible leaves rapidly without helping others involved. **hit it off** informal be naturally well suited.

hitch verb **1** move into a different position with a jerk. **2** fasten with a rope. **3** informal travel by hitch-hiking. noun **1** a temporary difficulty. **2** a temporary knot. □**get hitched** informal get married. **hitch-hike** travel by getting free rides in passing vehicles. ■ **hitcher** noun.

hither adverb old use to or towards this place.

hitherto adverb until this point in time.

HIV abbreviation human immunodeficiency virus (the virus causing Aids).

hive noun **1** a beehive. **2** a place full of people working hard. □**hive off** separate from a larger group.

hives plural noun a rash of red, itchy marks on the skin, caused by an allergy.

HM abbreviation Her (or His) Majesty or Majesty's.

HMS abbreviation Her or His Majesty's Ship.

HND abbreviation Higher National Diploma.

hoard noun a store of money, valued objects, or useful information. verb build up a store of something. ■ **hoarder** noun.

> ⓘ don't confuse **hoard** with **horde**: a **hoard** is a store of something valuable; a **horde** is a large group of people.

hoarding noun Brit. **1** a large board used to display advertisements. **2** a temporary board fence around a building site.

hoar frost noun a feathery greyish-white deposit of frost.

hoarse adjective (of a voice) rough and harsh. ■ **hoarsely** adverb.

hoary adjective (**hoarier, hoariest**) **1** greyish-white. **2** having grey hair. **3** old and unoriginal.

hoax noun a humorous or cruel trick.

verb deceive with a hoax. ■ **hoaxer** noun.

hob noun Brit. the flat top part of a cooker, with hotplates or burners.

hobble verb (**hobbles, hobbling, hobbled**) **1** walk awkwardly. **2** strap together the legs of a horse to stop it wandering away. noun **1** an awkward way of walking. **2** a rope or strap for hobbling a horse.

hobby noun (plural **hobbies**) an activity that you do regularly in your leisure time for pleasure. □ **hobby horse 1** a child's toy consisting of a stick with a model of a horse's head at one end. **2** something that a person talks about very often.

hobgoblin noun a mischievous imp.

hobnail noun a short nail used to strengthen the soles of boots. ■ **hobnailed** adjective.

hobnob verb (**hobnobs, hobnobbing, hobnobbed**) informal mix socially.

hobo noun (plural **hoboes** or **hobos**) N. Amer. a homeless person.

Hobson's choice noun a choice of taking what is offered or nothing at all.

hock¹ noun the middle joint in an animal's back leg.

hock² noun Brit. a dry white wine from Germany.

hock³ verb informal pawn. □ **in hock 1** having been pawned. **2** in debt.

hockey noun a team game played using hooked sticks to drive a small, hard ball towards a goal.

hocus-pocus noun **1** meaningless talk used to deceive people. **2** a form of words used by a magician.

hod noun **1** a builder's V-shaped open trough attached to a short pole, used for carrying bricks. **2** a metal container for storing coal.

hoe noun a long-handled gardening tool with a thin metal blade. verb (**hoes, hoeing, hoed**) break up soil or dig up weeds with a hoe.

hoedown noun N. Amer. a lively folk dance.

hog noun **1** a castrated male pig reared for its meat. **2** informal a greedy person. verb (**hogs, hogging, hogged**) informal take or hoard selfishly. □ **go the whole hog** informal do something fully.

Hogmanay /hog-muh-nay/ noun (in Scotland) New Year's Eve.

hogshead noun a large cask.

hogwash noun informal nonsense.

hoick verb Brit. informal lift or pull with a jerk.

hoi polloi /hoy puh-loy/ plural noun disapproving the common people.

hoist verb **1** raise with ropes and pulleys. **2** haul or lift up. noun an apparatus for hoisting something.

hoity-toity adjective informal snobbish.

hokey-cokey noun a group song and dance performed in a circle, involving the shaking of each limb in turn.

hokum /hoh-kuhm/ noun informal **1** nonsense. **2** unoriginal or sentimental material in a film, book, etc.

hold verb (**holds, holding, held**) **1** grasp, carry, or support. **2** keep or detain. **3** contain or be capable of containing. **4** have, possess, or occupy. **5** stay or keep at a certain level. **6** (**hold to**) make someone keep a promise. **7** (**hold in**) regard in a specified way. **8** N. Amer. informal refrain from adding or using. noun **1** a grip. **2** a place to grip while climbing. **3** a degree of control. **4** a storage space in the lower part of a ship or aircraft. □ **hold back** hesitate. **hold down** informal succeed in keeping a job. **hold fast 1** remain tightly secured. **2** stick to a principle. **hold forth** talk at length. **hold off 1** resist an attacker. **2** (of bad weather) fail to occur. **hold on 1** wait. **2** keep going in difficult circumstances. **hold out 1** resist difficult circumstances. **2** continue to be sufficient. **hold over** postpone. **hold up 1** delay. **2** rob someone using the threat of violence. **3** remain strong. **hold-up 1** a cause of delay. **2** a robbery carried out with the threat of violence. **no holds barred** without restrictions. **on hold 1** waiting to be connected by telephone. **2** temporarily not being dealt with. ■ **holder** noun.

holdall noun Brit. a large bag with handles and a shoulder strap.

holding noun **1** an area of land held by lease. **2 (holdings)** stocks and property owned by a person or organization.

hole noun **1** a hollow space or opening in a solid object or surface. **2** (in golf) a hollow in the ground which you try to hit the ball into. **3** informal an awkward or unpleasant place or situation. verb **(holes, holing, holed) 1** make a hole or holes in. **2** (in golf) hit the ball into a hole. **3 (hole up)** informal hide yourself. ■ **holey** adjective.

holiday noun **1** Brit. an extended period of leisure. **2** a day when most people do not have to work. verb spend a holiday.

holidaymaker noun Brit. a tourist.

holiness noun **1** the state of being holy. **2 (His or Your Holiness)** the title of the Pope and some other religious leaders.

holistic noun treating the whole person rather than just the symptoms of a disease. ■ **holism** noun.

holler informal verb **(hollers, hollering, hollered)** give a loud shout. noun a loud shout.

hollow adjective **1** having empty space inside. **2** curving inwards. **3** (of a sound) echoing. **4** insignificant or insincere. noun **1** a hole. **2** a small valley. verb (usu. **hollow out**) make hollow.

holly noun an evergreen shrub with prickly dark green leaves and red berries.

hollyhock noun a tall plant with large showy flowers.

holocaust /hol-uh-kawst/ noun **1** destruction or slaughter on a very large scale. **2 (the Holocaust)** the mass murder of Jews under the German Nazi regime in World War II.

hologram noun a picture that looks three-dimensional when it is lit up. ■ **holographic** adjective.

holster noun a holder for carrying a handgun.

holy adjective **(holier, holiest) 1** dedicated to God or a religious purpose. **2** morally and spiritually good. □ **the holy of holies** a very sacred place. **Holy Spirit** (or **Holy Ghost**) (in Christianity) God as a spirit that is active in the world. **Holy Week** the week before Easter.

homage noun honour shown to someone in public.

homburg noun a man's felt hat with a narrow curled brim.

home noun **1** the place where you live. **2** a place where people that need special care live. **3** a place where something flourishes or where it started. adjective **1** relating to your home. **2** relating to your own country. **3** (of a sports match) played at a team's own ground. adverb **1** to or at your home. **2** to the intended position. verb **(homes, homing, homed) 1** (of an animal) return by instinct to its territory. **2 (home in on)** move or be aimed towards. □ **home economics** the study of cookery and household management. **home help** Brit. a person employed to help with household work. **home page** the main page of an individual's or organization's Internet site. **home rule** the government of a place by its own citizens. **home run** Baseball a hit that allows the batter to make a run around all the bases. **home truth** an unpleasant fact about yourself that someone else tells you. ■ **homeless** adjective **homeward** adjective & adverb **homewards** adverb.

homeland noun a person's native land.

homely adjective **(homelier, homeliest) 1** Brit. simple but comfortable. **2** unsophisticated. **3** N. Amer. (of a person) unattractive.

homeopathy or **homoeopathy** /hoh-mi-op-uh-thi/ noun a system of treating diseases by tiny doses of substances that would normally produce symptoms of the disease. ■ **homeopath** noun **homeopathic** adjective.

homesick adjective feeling upset because you are missing your home.

homespun adjective simple and unsophisticated.

homestead noun a house with surrounding land and outbuildings.

homework noun **1** school work that you are expected to do at home. **2** preparation for an event.

homicide /**hom**-i-syd/ noun murder. ■ homicidal adjective.

homily /**hom**-i-li/ noun (plural **homilies**) **1** a talk on a religious subject. **2** a dull talk on a moral issue.

homoeopathy ⇒ **HOMOEOPATHY**.

homogeneous /hom-uh-**jee**-ni-uhss/ adjective **1** alike. **2** made up of parts all of the same kind. ■ homogeneity /hom-uh-ji-**nee**-i-ti/ noun.

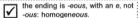 ☑ the ending is *-eous*, with an e, not *-ous*: homogen*eous*.

homogenize or **homogenise** verb (**homogenizes, homogenizing, homogenized**) **1** treat milk so that the cream is mixed in. **2** make alike.

homonym /**hom**-uh-nim/ noun a word that has the same spelling or pronunciation as another but a different meaning and origin.

homophobia noun extreme hatred or fear of homosexuality and homosexuals. ■ homophobic adjective.

Homo sapiens /hoh-moh **sap**-i-enz/ noun the species to which modern humans belong.

homosexual adjective sexually attracted to people of your own sex. noun a homosexual person. ■ homosexuality noun.

Hon abbreviation Honorary or Honourable.

hone verb (**hones, honing, honed**) **1** sharpen a tool with a stone. **2** make sharper or more efficient.

honest adjective **1** truthful and sincere. **2** fairly earned. **3** simple and straightforward. ■ honestly adverb.

honesty noun the quality of being honest.

honey noun (plural **honeys**) a sweet, sticky yellowish-brown fluid made by bees from flower nectar.

honeybee noun the common bee.

honeycomb noun a structure of six-sided wax compartments made by bees to store honey and eggs.

honeydew noun a sweet, sticky substance produced by small insects feeding on the sap of plants.

honeyed adjective **1** literary resembling honey. **2** (of words) soothing and soft.

honeymoon noun **1** a holiday taken by a newly married couple. **2** an initial period of enthusiasm or goodwill. verb spend a honeymoon.

honeypot noun a place that many people are attracted to.

honeysuckle noun a climbing shrub with sweet-smelling flowers.

honk noun **1** the cry of a goose. **2** the sound of a car horn. verb make a honk.

honky-tonk noun informal **1** N. Amer. a bar. **2** ragtime piano music.

honorary adjective **1** (of a title or position) given as an honour. **2** Brit. unpaid.

☑ honor-, not honour-: honorary.

honorific adjective given as a mark of respect.

honour (US spelling **honor**) noun **1** great respect. **2** a privilege. **3** a clear sense of what is right. **4** a person or thing that brings credit. **5** an award or title given as a reward for achievement. **6** (**honours**) a university course of a higher level than an ordinary one. **7** (**His, Your,** etc. **Honour**) a title for a judge. verb **1** regard or treat with great respect. **2** fulfil an obligation or keep an agreement.

honourable (US spelling **honorable**) adjective **1** deserving honour. **2** having high moral standards. **3** (**Honourable**) a title given to MPs, nobles, etc. ■ honourably adverb.

hooch noun informal alcoholic drink.

hood[1] noun **1** a covering for the head and neck with an opening for the face. **2** Brit. a folding waterproof cover of a vehicle. **3** N. Amer. the bonnet of a vehicle. **4** a protective canopy. ■ hooded adjective.

hood² noun N. Amer. informal a gangster or violent criminal.

hoodlum noun a gangster or violent criminal.

hoodoo noun **1** voodoo. **2** a run or cause of bad luck.

hoodwink verb deceive or trick.

hoof noun (plural **hoofs** or **hooves**) the horny part of the foot of a horse, cow, etc. **verb** informal **1** kick a ball powerfully. **2** (**hoof it**) go on foot. ■ **hoofed** adjective.

hook noun **1** a curved object for catching hold of things or hanging things on. **2** a curved cutting instrument. **3** a punch made with the elbow bent and rigid. **4** a catchy passage in a song. **verb 1** catch or fasten with a hook. **2** (**hook up**) link to electronic equipment. **3** (**be hooked**) informal be addicted. **4** (in sport) hit the ball in a curving path. □ **by hook or by crook** by any possible means. **hook, line, and sinker** completely; entirely. ■ **hooked** adjective.

hookah noun a kind of tobacco pipe in which the smoke is drawn through water to cool it.

hooker noun **1** Rugby the player in the middle of the front row of the scrum. **2** informal, chiefly N. Amer. a prostitute.

hookworm noun a worm which can infest the intestines.

hooligan noun a violent young troublemaker. ■ **hooliganism** noun.

hoop noun **1** a rigid circular band. **2** a large ring used as a toy or for circus performers to jump through. **3** a metal arch through which you hit the balls in croquet. **4** a contrasting horizontal band on a sports shirt. ■ **hooped** adjective.

hoopla noun **1** Brit. a game in which you try to throw rings over a prize. **2** informal unnecessary fuss.

hooray exclamation hurrah.

hoot noun **1** a low sound made by owls, or a similar sound made by a horn, siren, etc. **2** a shout of scorn or disapproval. **3** an outburst of laughter. **4** (**a hoot**) informal an amusing person or thing. **verb** make a hoot.

hooter noun **1** Brit. a siren, horn, etc. **2** informal a person's nose.

Hoover Brit. **noun** trademark a vacuum cleaner. **verb** (**hoover**) (**hoovers, hoovering, hoovered**) clean with a vacuum cleaner.

hooves plural of **HOOF**.

hop verb (**hops, hopping, hopped**) **1** move by jumping on one foot. **2** (of a bird or animal) move by jumping. **3** jump over or on to. **4** (**hop it**) Brit. informal go away. **noun 1** a hopping movement. **2** a short journey or distance. □ **on the hop** Brit. informal **1** unprepared. **2** busy.

hope noun **1** a feeling that something you want may happen. **2** a cause for hope. **3** something that you wish for. **verb** (**hopes, hoping, hoped**) **1** expect and want something to happen. **2** intend if possible to do something.

hopeful adjective feeling or inspiring hope. **noun** a person likely or hoping to succeed.

hopefully adverb **1** in a hopeful manner. **2** it is to be hoped that.

> ℹ️ some people feel that the meaning 'it is to be hoped that' is wrong, although it is now the more common one.

hopeless adjective **1** feeling or causing despair. **2** not at all skilful. ■ **hopelessly** adverb.

hopper noun a container that tapers downwards and empties its contents at the bottom.

hops noun the dried flowers of a climbing plant, used to give beer a bitter flavour.

hopscotch noun a children's game in which you hop over squares marked on the ground.

horde noun chiefly disapproving a large group of people.

> ℹ️ don't confuse **horde** with **hoard**: a **horde** is a large group of people, whereas a **hoard** is a store of something valuable.

horizon noun **1** the line at which the earth's surface and the sky appear to meet. **2** (**horizons**) the limits of a person's understanding, experience, or interest.

horizontal adjective parallel to the horizon. noun a horizontal line or surface. ■ **horizontally** adverb.

hormone noun a substance produced in the body that stimulates cells or tissues to action. ■ **hormonal** adjective.

horn noun **1** a hard bony growth on the heads of cattle, sheep, and other animals. **2** the substance that horns are made of. **3** a wind instrument shaped like a cone or wound into a spiral. **4** an instrument sounding a signal. ■ **horned** adjective.

hornblende /**horn**-blend/ noun a dark brown, black, or green mineral.

hornet noun a kind of large wasp.

hornpipe noun a lively solo dance traditionally performed by sailors.

horny adjective (**hornier, horniest**) **1** made of or resembling horn. **2** hard and rough. **3** informal sexually arousing or aroused.

horology /ho-**rol**-uh-ji/ noun **1** the study and measurement of time. **2** the art of making clocks and watches.

horoscope noun a forecast of a person's future based on the positions of the stars and planets at the time of their birth.

horrendous adjective extremely unpleasant or horrifying. ■ **horrendously** adverb.

horrible adjective **1** causing horror. **2** informal very unpleasant. ■ **horribly** adverb.

horrid adjective horrible.

horrific adjective causing horror. ■ **horrifically** adverb.

horrify verb (**horrifies, horrifying, horrified**) fill with horror.

horror noun **1** a strong feeling of fear, shock, or disgust. **2** a thing causing such a feeling. **3** very great dismay. **4** informal a badly behaved person.

hors d'oeuvre /or **derv**/ noun (plural **hors d'oeuvre** or **hors d'oeuvres** /or **derv**, or **dervz**/) a small savoury first course of a meal.

horse noun **1** a large four-legged mammal used for riding and for pulling loads. **2** cavalry. verb (**horses, horsing, horsed**) (**horse around**) informal fool about. □ **horse chestnut 1** a large tree that produces nuts (conkers) in a spiny case. **2** a conker. **horse sense** common sense. **on horseback** mounted on a horse. ■ **horsey** (or **horsy**) adjective.

horsebox noun Brit. a vehicle or trailer for transporting horses.

horsefly noun a large fly that bites horses and other large mammals.

horseman or **horsewoman** noun a rider on horseback.

horseplay noun rough, high-spirited play.

horsepower noun (plural **horsepower**) a unit measuring the power of an engine.

horseradish noun a plant with strong-tasting roots which are made into a sauce.

horseshoe noun a U-shaped iron shoe for a horse.

horsewhip noun a long whip for controlling horses. verb (**horsewhips, horsewhipping, horsewhipped**) beat with a horsewhip.

hortatory adjective formal strongly urging someone to do something.

horticulture noun the cultivation of gardens. ■ **horticultural** adjective.

hosanna noun an exclamation of praise or joy used in the Bible.

hose noun **1** (Brit. also **hosepipe**) a flexible tube that conveys water. **2** stockings, socks, and tights. verb (**hoses, hosing, hosed**) spray with a hose.

hosiery /**hoh**-zi-uh-ri/ noun stockings, socks, and tights.

hospice noun a home for people who are terminally ill.

hospitable adjective **1** friendly and welcoming to strangers or guests. **2** (of an environment) pleasant and favourable for living in. ■ **hospitably** adverb.

hospital noun a place where sick or injured people are looked after.

hospitality noun the friendly and generous treatment of guests or strangers.

hospitalize or **hospitalise** verb (**hospitalizes, hospitalizing, hospitalized**) admit someone to hospital for treatment. ∎ **hospitalization** noun.

host[1] noun **1** a person who receives or entertains guests. **2** the presenter of a television or radio programme. **3** the place that holds an event to which others are invited. **4** Biology an animal or plant on or in which a parasite lives. verb act as host at.

host[2] noun (**a host** or **hosts of**) a large number of.

host[3] noun (**the Host**) the bread used in the Christian ceremony of the Eucharist.

hostage noun a person who is captured and held in an attempt to pressure people into giving in to a demand.

hostel noun a place which provides cheap food and accommodation for a particular group of people.

hostelry noun (plural **hostelries**) old use or humorous a pub.

hostess noun **1** a female host. **2** a woman employed to welcome customers at a nightclub or bar.

hostile adjective **1** aggressively unfriendly. **2** having to do with a military enemy.

hostility noun (plural **hostilities**) **1** hostile behaviour. **2** (**hostilities**) acts of warfare.

hot adjective (**hotter, hottest**) **1** having a high temperature. **2** feeling or producing an uncomfortable sensation of heat. **3** very exciting. **4** currently popular or interesting. **5** informal (of goods) stolen. **6** (**hot on**) informal very knowledgeable about. **7** (**hot on**) informal strict about. verb (**hots, hotting, hotted**) (**hot up**) Brit. informal become more exciting. □ **hot air** informal empty or boastful talk. **hot-blooded** passionate. **hot cross bun** a bun marked with a cross, eaten on Good Friday. **hot dog** a hot sausage served in a long, soft roll. **hot rod** a car specially ad-

apted to be fast. **hot-water bottle** a container filled with hot water and used for warming a bed. **hot-wire** informal start a vehicle without using the ignition switch. ∎ **hotly** adverb.

hotbed noun a place where a lot of·a particular activity is happening.

hotchpotch noun a confused mixture.

hotel noun a place providing accommodation and meals for travellers and tourists.

hotelier noun a person who owns or manages a hotel.

hotfoot adverb in eager haste. □ **hotfoot it** hurry eagerly.

hothead noun an impetuous or quick-tempered person.

hothouse noun a heated greenhouse.

hotplate noun a flat heated surface on an electric cooker.

hotpot noun Brit. a casserole of meat and vegetables with a covering layer of sliced potato.

hotshot noun informal an important or very skilled person.

hound noun a hunting dog. verb harass someone.

hour noun **1** a twenty-fourth part of a day and night; 60 minutes. **2** (**hours**) a period set aside for a particular purpose. **3** a particular point in time. **4** (**hours**) informal a very long time.

hourglass noun a device with two connected glass bulbs containing sand that takes an hour to fall from the upper to the lower bulb.

hourly adverb & adjective **1** every hour. **2** by the hour.

house noun /howss/ **1** a building for people to live in. **2** a firm or institution. **3** chiefly Brit. a group of pupils living in the same building at a boarding school. **4** a long-established and powerful family. **5** (also **house music**) a style of popular dance music. verb /howz/ (**houses, housing, housed**) **1** provide with accommodation. **2** provide space for. **3** enclose something. □ **house arrest** the state of being kept as a prisoner in your own house. **House of Commons** the chamber of the UK Parliament whose members are elected. **House of Lords** the chamber of the UK Parliament whose members are peers and bishops. **house-proud** very concerned with the appearance of your home. **house-train** Brit. train a pet to urinate and defecate outside the house. **house-warming** a party held to celebrate moving into a new home. **on the house** at the management's expense.

houseboat noun a boat that people can live in.

housebound adjective unable to leave your house.

housebreaking noun the action of breaking into a building to commit a crime.

household noun a house and all the people living in it. □ **household name** a famous person or thing. ■ **householder** noun.

housekeeper noun a person employed to shop, cook, and clean the house. ■ **housekeeping** noun.

housemaid noun a female servant in a house.

housemaster or **housemistress** noun a teacher in charge of a house at a boarding school.

housewife noun (plural **housewives**) a woman whose main occupation is looking after her family and the home.

housework noun cleaning, cooking, etc. done in running a home.

housing noun **1** houses and flats as a whole. **2** a hard cover for a piece of equipment.

hove chiefly Nautical past tense of **HEAVE**.

hovel noun a small house that is dirty and run-down.

hover verb (**hovers**, **hovering**, **hovered**) **1** remain in one place in the air. **2** wait about uncertainly. **3** remain at or near a particular level.

hovercraft noun (plural **hovercraft**) a vehicle that travels over land or water on a cushion of air.

how adverb **1** in what way or by what means. **2** in what condition. **3** to what extent or degree. **4** the way in which.

howdah /how-duh/ noun a seat for riding on the back of an elephant.

however adverb **1** used to begin a statement that contrasts with something that has just been said. **2** in whatever way or to whatever extent.

howitzer /how-it-ser/ noun a short gun for firing shells at a high angle.

howl noun **1** a long wailing cry made by an animal. **2** a loud cry of pain, amusement, etc. verb make a howl.

howler noun informal a stupid mistake.

h.p. or **HP** abbreviation **1** Brit. hire purchase. **2** horsepower.

HQ abbreviation headquarters.

HRH abbreviation Brit. Her (or His) Royal Highness.

HTML noun Computing Hypertext Markup Language.

hub noun **1** the central part of a wheel. **2** the centre of an activity or region.

hubbub noun a loud confused noise caused by a crowd.

hubris /hyoo-briss/ noun excessive pride or self-confidence.

huckster noun **1** a person who sells things forcefully. **2** a person who sells small items in the street.

huddle verb (**huddles**, **huddling**, **huddled**) **1** crowd together. **2** curl your body into a small space. noun a number of people or things crowded together.

hue noun **1** a colour or shade. **2** a particular aspect of something.

hue and cry noun a strong public outcry.

huff verb (often **huff and puff**) breathe out noisily. noun a bad mood. ■ **huffy** adjective.

hug verb (**hugs**, **hugging**, **hugged**) **1** hold tightly in your arms. **2** keep close to. noun an act of hugging.

huge adjective (**huger**, **hugest**) very large. ■ **hugely** adverb **hugeness** noun.

hugger-mugger adjective confused or disorderly.

hula noun a dance performed by Hawaiian women, in which the dancers sway their hips. □ **hula hoop** a large hoop spun round the body by moving the hips in a circular way.

hulk noun **1** an old ship stripped of fittings and no longer used. **2** a large or clumsy person or thing.

hulking adjective informal very large or clumsy.

hull[1] noun the main body of a ship.

hull[2] noun **1** the outer covering of a fruit or seed. **2** the cluster of leaves and stalk on a strawberry or raspberry. verb remove the hulls from.

hullabaloo noun informal an uproar.

hullo ⇒ **HELLO**.

hum verb (**hums, humming, hummed**) **1** make a low continuous sound like that of a bee. **2** sing a tune with closed lips. **3** informal be in a state of great activity. noun a low continuous sound.

human adjective **1** having to do with men, women, or children. **2** showing the better qualities of people. noun (also **human being**) a man, woman, or child. □ **human rights** basic rights which belong to all people, such as freedom. ■ **humanly** adverb.

humane /hyuu-**mayn**/ adjective showing concern and kindness towards others. ■ **humanely** adverb.

humanism noun **1** a system of thought that sees people as able to live their lives without the need for religious beliefs. ■ **humanist** noun & adjective **humanistic** adjective.

humanitarian adjective concerned with the welfare of people. noun a humanitarian person.

humanity noun **1** people as a whole. **2** the condition of being human. **3** sympathy and kindness towards others. **4** (**humanities**) studies concerned with human culture, such as literature or history.

humanize or **humanise** verb (**humanizes, humanizing, humanized**) make more pleasant or suitable for people.

humankind noun people as a whole.

humanoid adjective like a human in appearance. noun a humanoid being.

humble adjective (**humbler, humblest**) **1** having a modest or low opinion of your own importance. **2** of low rank. **3** not large or important. verb (**humbles, humbling, humbled**) make someone seem less important. □ **eat humble pie** make a humble apology. ■ **humbly** adverb.

humbug noun **1** false or misleading talk or behaviour. **2** a person who is not sincere or honest. **3** Brit. a boiled peppermint sweet.

humdrum adjective ordinary; dull.

humerus /**hyoo**-muh-ruhss/ noun (plural **humeri** /**hyoo**-muh-rI/) the bone of the upper arm, between the shoulder and the elbow.

humid adjective (of the air or weather) damp and warm. ■ **humidity** noun.

humiliate verb (**humiliates, humiliating, humiliated**) make someone feel ashamed or stupid. ■ **humiliation** noun.

humility noun the quality of being humble.

hummingbird noun a small bird able to hover by beating its wings extremely fast.

hummock noun a small hill or mound.

hummus or **houmous** /**huu**-muhss/ noun a Middle Eastern dip made from chickpeas and sesame seeds.

humorist noun a writer or speaker who is known for being amusing.

humorous adjective **1** causing amusement. **2** showing a sense of humour. ■ **humorously** adverb.

 -or- not -our-: humorous.

humour (US spelling **humor**) noun **1** the quality of being amusing. **2** a state of mind. verb agree with the wishes of someone in order to keep them happy. ■ **humourless** adjective.

hump noun **1** a round part on the back of a camel or other animal. **2** a large lump on a person's back, caused by an unusual curve of the spine. **3** a round lump that sticks out of the ground. **verb** informal lift or carry with difficulty. ■ **humped** adjective.

humus /hyoo-muhss/ **noun** a substance found in soil, made from dead leaves and plants.

hunch verb raise your shoulders and bend the top part of your body forward. **noun** an idea based on a feeling rather than evidence.

hunchback noun offensive a person with an abnormal hump on their back.

hundred cardinal number 1 ten more than ninety; 100. (Roman numeral: c or C.) **2** (**hundreds**) informal a large number. ■ **hundredth** ordinal number.

hundredweight noun (plural **hundredweight** or **hundredweights**) **1** Brit. a unit of weight equal to 112 lb (about 50.8 kg). **2** US a unit of weight equal to 100 lb (about 45.4 kg).

hung past and past participle of **HANG**. **adjective 1** having no political party with an overall majority. **2** (of a jury) unable to agree on a verdict. **3** (**hung up**) informal emotionally confused or disturbed. □ **hung-over** suffering from a hangover.

hunger noun 1 a lack of food. **2** a feeling of discomfort caused by a lack of food. **3** a strong desire. **verb** (**hungers, hungering, hungered**) (**hunger after** or **for**) have a strong desire for. □ **hunger strike** the act of not eating as a protest about something.

hungry adjective (**hungrier, hungriest**) **1** feeling that you want to eat something. **2** having a strong desire for something. ■ **hungrily** adverb.

hunk noun 1 a large piece cut or broken from something larger. **2** informal a good-looking man. ■ **hunky** adjective.

hunky-dory adjective informal fine; satisfactory.

hunt verb 1 chase and kill a wild animal for sport or food. **2** search for something. **3** (**hunt down**) chase and capture someone. **4** (**hunted**) looking like you are being chased; harassed. **noun 1** an act of hunting. **2** a group of

people who meet regularly to hunt animals as a sport. ■ **hunter** noun.

huntsman noun a person who hunts.

hurdle noun 1 each of a series of upright frames that an athlete jumps over in a race. **2** a frame used as a temporary fence. **3** an obstacle or difficulty. **verb** (**hurdles, hurdling, hurdled**) jump over an obstacle while running. ■ **hurdler** noun.

hurdy-gurdy noun (plural **hurdy-gurdies**) a musical instrument played by turning a handle.

hurl verb 1 throw something with great force. **2** shout insults.

hurling or **hurley noun** an Irish game resembling hockey.

hurly-burly noun busy and noisy activity.

hurrah, hooray, or **hurray exclamation** used to express joy or approval.

hurricane noun a severe storm with a violent wind.

hurry verb (**hurries, hurrying, hurried**) **1** move or act quickly. **2** do something quickly or too quickly. **noun** great haste. ■ **hurriedly** adverb.

hurt verb (**hurts, hurting, hurt**) **1** make someone feel physical pain; injure. **2** feel pain. **3** upset someone. **noun** injury or pain.

hurtful adjective upsetting; unkind. ■ **hurtfully** adverb.

hurtle verb (**hurtles, hurtling, hurtled**) move at great speed.

husband noun the man that a woman is married to. **verb** use something carefully without wasting it.

husbandry noun 1 farming. **2** careful management of resources.

hush verb 1 make or become quiet. **2** (**hush up**) stop something from becoming known. **noun** a silence.

husk noun the dry outer covering of some fruits or seeds. **verb** remove the husk from.

husky[1] **adjective** (**huskier, huskiest**) **1** (of a voice) deep and rough. **2** big and strong. ■ **huskily** adverb.

husky[2] **noun** (plural **huskies**) a powerful dog used for pulling sledges.

hussar /huu-**zar**/ noun historical a soldier in a light cavalry regiment.

hussy noun (plural **hussies**) dated or humorous a girl or woman who behaves in an immoral or cheeky way.

hustings noun the political meetings and speeches that take place before an election.

hustle verb (**hustles, hustling, hustled**) **1** push or move roughly. **2** (**hustle into**) rush someone into doing something. **3** informal, chiefly N. Amer. obtain something dishonestly. noun busy movement and activity. ■ **hustler** noun.

hut noun a small, simple house or shelter.

hutch noun a box with a front made of wire, used for keeping rabbits.

hyacinth /**hy**-uh-sinth/ noun a plant with bell-shaped flowers.

hyaena ⇒ **HYENA**.

hybrid noun **1** the offspring of two plants or animals of different species or varieties. **2** something made by combining two different things.

hydrangea /hy-**drayn**-juh/ noun a shrub with white, blue, or pink clusters of flowers.

hydrant noun a water pipe with a nozzle for attaching a fire hose.

hydrate verb (**hydrates, hydrating, hydrated**) make something absorb or combine with water. ■ **hydration** noun.

hydraulic adjective operated by a liquid moving through pipes under pressure. noun (**hydraulics**) the branch of science concerned with the use of liquids moving under pressure to provide mechanical force. ■ **hydraulically** adverb.

hydrocarbon noun any of the compounds of hydrogen and carbon.

hydrocephalus /hy-druh-**sef**-uh-luhss/ noun a condition in which fluid collects in the brain.

hydrochloric acid noun an acid containing hydrogen and chlorine.

hydroelectric adjective having to do with the use of flowing water to generate electricity.

hydrofoil noun a boat designed to rise above the water when it is travelling fast.

hydrogen noun a highly flammable gas which is the lightest of the chemical elements. □ **hydrogen bomb** a very powerful nuclear bomb. **hydrogen sulphide** a poisonous gas with a smell of bad eggs.

hydrophobia noun **1** extreme fear of water, especially as a symptom of rabies. **2** rabies. ■ **hydrophobic** adjective.

hydroplane noun a light, fast motor boat designed to skim over the surface of water.

hydrous adjective containing water.

hydroxide noun a compound containing oxygen and hydrogen together with a metallic element.

hyena or **hyaena** noun a doglike African mammal.

hygiene noun the practice of keeping yourself and your surroundings clean in order to prevent illness and disease.

hygienic adjective clean and not likely to spread disease. ■ **hygienically** adverb.

☑ remember, *i* before *e* except after *c*: hygienic.

hygienist noun an expert in hygiene.

hymen /**hy**-muhn/ noun a membrane which partially closes the opening of the vagina and is usually broken when a woman or girl first has sex.

hymn noun a religious song of praise, especially a Christian one. verb praise or celebrate.

hymnal noun a book of hymns.

hype informal noun excessive or exaggerated publicity. verb (**hypes, hyping, hyped**) **1** publicize in an excessive or exaggerated way. **2** (**be hyped up**) be very excited or tense.

hyper adjective informal having a lot of nervous energy.

hyperactive adjective extremely active; unable to keep still.

hyperbola /hy-**per**-buh-luh/ noun

WORD FORMATION   ⓘ

hyper-, hypo-

hyper- and **hypo-** look very similar but actually have opposite meanings.

hyper- means:
- over, beyond, or above, as in *hypersonic*
- excessively or above normal, e.g. *hyperactive* or *hypercorrect*.

hypo- means:
- under, as in *hypodermic* (= under the skin)
- below normal, e.g. *hypothermia* (the condition of having an abnormally low body temperature).

(plural **hyperbolas** or **hyperbolae** /hy-**per**-buh-lee/) a symmetrical curve formed when a cone is cut by a plane nearly parallel to the cone's axis.

hyperbole /hy-**per**-buh-li/ noun a way of speaking or writing that exaggerates things and is not meant to be understood literally.

hyperbolic adjective **1** deliberately exaggerated. **2** relating to a hyperbola.

hyperlink noun Computing a link from a hypertext document to another location.

hypermarket noun Brit. a very large supermarket.

hypersensitive adjective excessively sensitive.

hypersonic adjective **1** relating to speeds of more than five times the speed of sound. **2** relating to sound frequencies above about a thousand million hertz.

hypertension noun abnormally high blood pressure.

hypertext noun Computing a system that lets you move quickly between documents or sections of text.

hyperventilate verb (**hyperventilates, hyperventilating, hyperventilated**) breathe at an abnormally rapid rate. ■ **hyperventilation** noun.

hyphen noun the sign (-) used to join words together or to divide a word into parts between one line and the next.

hyphenate verb join or divide words with a hyphen. ■ **hyphenation** noun.

hypnosis noun the practice of causing a person to enter a state in which they respond very readily to suggestions or commands.

hypnotherapy noun the use of hypnosis to treat physical or mental problems.

hypnotic adjective **1** having to do with hypnosis. **2** making you feel very relaxed or sleepy. ■ **hypnotically** adverb.

hypnotism noun the study or practice of hypnosis. ■ **hypnotist** noun.

hypnotize or **hypnotise** verb (**hypnotizes, hypnotizing, hypnotized**) put someone into a state of hypnosis.

hypoallergenic adjective unlikely to cause an allergic reaction.

hypochondria /hy-puh-**kon**-dri-uh/ noun excessive anxiety about your health.

hypochondriac noun a person who is excessively anxious about their health.

hypocrisy /hi-**pok**-ruh-si/ noun behaviour in which a person pretends to have higher standards than they really have.

hypocrite noun a person who pretends to have higher standards than they really have. ■ **hypocritical** adjective.

hypodermic adjective (of a needle or syringe) used to inject a drug or other substance beneath the skin. noun a hypodermic syringe or injection.

hypotension noun abnormally low blood pressure.

PUNCTUATION ⓘ

Hyphen

A hyphen is used:

1 to join two or more words so as to form a compound or single expression, e.g.

mother-in-law   *non-stick*   *dressing-table*

Today people are increasingly doing without such hyphens:

nonstick   *treelike*   *dressing table*

2 to join words in a compound expression that is put before a noun, e.g.

a well-known man (but *the man is well known*)
an out-of-date list (but *the list is out of date*)

3 to join a prefix to a proper name, e.g.

anti-Darwinian   *half-Italian*   *non-British*

4 to make a meaning clear by linking words, e.g.

twenty-odd people/twenty odd people

or by separating a prefix, e.g.

re-cover/recover   *re-present/represent*   *re-sign/resign*

5 to separate two identical letters in adjacent parts of word, e.g.

pre-exist   *Ross-shire*

6 to represent a second element that is shared by all the items of a list, e.g.

two-, three-, or fourfold

7 to divide a word if there is no room to complete it at the end of the line, e.g.

... diction-
ary ...

---

hypotenuse /hy-**pot**-uh-nyooz/ **noun** the longest side of a right-angled triangle, opposite the right angle.

hypothermia noun the condition of having an abnormally low body temperature.

hypothesis /hy-**po**-thi-siss/ **noun** (plural **hypotheses** /hy-**po**-thi-seez/) an idea that has not yet been proved to be true or correct.

hypothesize or **hypothesise verb** (**hypothesizes, hypothesizing, hypothesized**) put forward as a hypothesis.

hypothetical adjective based on a situation which is imagined rather than true. ■ **hypothetically** adverb.

hysterectomy noun (plural **hysterectomies**) a surgical operation to remove all or part of the womb.

hysteria noun 1 a medical condition in which a person loses control of their emotions. **2** extreme or uncontrollable emotion or excitement.

hysterical adjective 1 having to do with hysteria. **2** wildly uncontrolled. **3** informal very funny. ■ **hysterically** adverb.

hysterics plural noun 1 wildly emotional behaviour. **2** informal uncontrollable laughter.

Hz abbreviation hertz.

I i

I[1] or **i** noun (plural **Is** or **I's**) **1** the ninth letter of the alphabet. **2** the Roman numeral for one.

I[2] pronoun used by a speaker to refer to himself or herself.

iambic /I-**am**-bik/ adjective (of rhythm in poetry) having one unstressed syllable followed by one stressed syllable.

ibex /I-beks/ noun (plural **ibexes**) a wild mountain goat with long horns.

ibid. adverb in the same book as the one that has just been mentioned.

> **i** short for Latin *ibidem*, meaning 'in the same place'.

ibis /I-biss/ noun (plural **ibises**) a large wading bird with a long curved bill.

ice noun **1** water that has frozen and become solid. **2** chiefly Brit. an ice cream. verb (**ices**, **icing**, **iced**) **1** decorate with icing. **2** (**ice up** or **over**) become covered with ice. □ **ice age** a period of time when ice covered much of the earth's surface. **ice-breaker** a ship designed for breaking a channel through ice. **ice cap** a large area that is permanently covered with ice, especially at the North and South Poles. **ice cream** a frozen dessert made with sweetened milk fat. **ice hockey** a form of hockey played on an ice rink. **ice pack** a bag filled with ice and put on part of the body to reduce swelling or lower temperature. **ice skate** a boot with a blade attached to the sole, used for skating on ice. **on thin ice** in a risky situation.

iceberg noun a large mass of ice floating in the sea. □ **the tip of the iceberg** the small visible part of a much larger problem that remains hidden.

icebox noun **1** a chilled container for keeping food cold. **2** Brit. a compartment in a refrigerator for making and storing ice.

iced adjective **1** cooled or mixed with ice. **2** decorated with icing.

ichthyology /ik-thi-**ol**-uh-ji/ noun the branch of zoology concerned with fishes. ■ **ichthyologist** noun.

icicle noun a hanging piece of ice formed when dripping water freezes.

icing noun Brit. a mixture of sugar and water or fat, used to cover cakes. □ **the icing on the cake** an extra thing that makes something good even better. **icing sugar** finely powdered sugar used to make icing.

icon /I-kon/ noun **1** (also **ikon**) (in the Orthodox Church) a painting of a holy person that is also regarded as holy. **2** a person or thing that is seen as a symbol of something. **3** Computing a symbol on a computer screen that represents a program. ■ **iconic** adjective.

iconify /I-**kon**-i-fI/ verb (**iconifies**, **iconifying**, **iconified**) Computing reduce a window to an icon.

iconoclast /I-**kon**-uh-klast/ noun a person who attacks established customs and values. ■ **iconoclasm** noun **iconoclastic** adjective.

iconography /I-kuh-**nog**-ruh-fi/ noun **1** the use or study of pictures or symbols in visual arts. **2** the pictures or symbols associated with a person or movement. ■ **iconographic** adjective.

icy adjective (**icier**, **iciest**) **1** covered with ice. **2** very cold. **3** very unfriendly; hostile. ■ **icily** adverb.

ID abbreviation identification or identity.

I'd short form **1** I had. **2** I should or I would.

id noun the part of the mind that consists of a person's unconscious instincts and feelings.

idea noun **1** a thought or suggestion about a possible course of action. **2** a mental picture or impression. **3** a belief. **4** (**the idea**) the aim or purpose.

ideal adjective **1** most suitable; perfect.

2 existing only in the imagination. **noun 1** a person or thing regarded as perfect. **2** a principle or standard that is worth trying to achieve. ■ **ideally** adverb.

idealism noun 1 the belief that ideals can be achieved. **2** the representation of things as better than they really are. ■ **idealist** noun **idealistic** adjective.

idealize or **idealise** verb (**idealizes, idealizing, idealized**) represent something as better than it really is. ■ **idealization** noun.

identical adjective 1 exactly alike. **2** the same. **3** (of twins) very similar in appearance. ■ **identically** adverb.

identification noun 1 the action of identifying. **2** an official document or other proof of your identity.

identify verb (**identifies, identifying, identified**) **1** prove or recognize that someone or something is a specified person or thing. **2** recognize as being worthy of attention. **3** (**identify with**) feel that you understand or share the feelings of. **4** (**identify with**) consider something to be the same as. ■ **identifiable** adjective.

identity noun (plural **identities**) **1** the fact of being who or what a person or thing is. **2** a close similarity or feeling of understanding. □ **identity parade** Brit. a group of people assembled so that an eyewitness may identify a suspect for a crime from among them.

ideology /I-di-ol-uh-ji/ **noun** (plural **ideologies**) **1** a system of ideas that an economic or political theory is based on. **2** the set of beliefs held by a particular group. ■ **ideological** adjective.

idiocy noun (plural **idiocies**) extremely stupid behaviour.

idiom noun 1 a group of words whose overall meaning is different from the meanings of the individual words (e.g. *over the moon*). **2** a form of language used by a particular group of people. **3** a style of music or art.

idiomatic adjective using expressions that are natural to a native speaker of a language.

idiosyncrasy /id-i-oh-**sing**-kruh-si/ **noun** (plural **idiosyncrasies**) **1** a person's particular way of behaving or thinking. **2** a distinctive or peculiar feature. ■ **idiosyncratic** adjective.

idiot noun a stupid person.

idiotic adjective very stupid. ■ **idiotically** adverb.

idle adjective (**idler, idlest**) **1** avoiding work; lazy. **2** not working or in use. **3** having no purpose or effect. **verb** (**idles, idling, idled**) **1** spend time doing nothing. **2** (of an engine) run slowly while out of gear. ■ **idleness** noun **idler** noun **idly** adverb.

idol noun 1 a statue or picture of a god that is worshipped. **2** a person who is greatly admired.

idolatry /I-**dol**-uh-tri/ **noun** worship of idols.

idolize or **idolise** verb (**idolizes, idolizing, idolized**) admire or love someone greatly or excessively.

idyll /i-dil/ **noun 1** a very happy or peaceful time or situation. **2** a short piece of writing describing a peaceful scene of country life.

idyllic adjective very happy, peaceful, or beautiful. ■ **idyllically** adverb.

i.e. abbreviation that is to say.

> ℹ️ short for Latin *id est*, meaning 'that is'.

if conjunction 1 on the condition or in the event that. **2** despite the possibility that. **3** whether. **4** whenever.

igloo noun a dome-shaped Eskimo house built from blocks of solid snow.

igneous /**ig**-ni-uhss/ **adjective** (of rock) formed when molten rock has solidified.

ignite verb (**ignites, igniting, ignited**) **1** catch fire, or set on fire. **2** provoke or stir up.

ignition noun 1 the action of igniting. **2** the mechanism in a vehicle that ignites the fuel to start the engine.

ignoble adjective not good or honest; dishonourable.

ignominious /ig-nuh-**min**-i-uhss/ adjective deserving or causing disgrace or shame. ■ **ignominiously** adverb.

ignominy /**ig**-nuh-mi-ni/ noun public shame or disgrace.

ignoramus /ig-nuh-**ray**-muhss/ noun (plural **ignoramuses**) an ignorant or stupid person.

ignorance noun lack of knowledge or information.

ignorant adjective **1** lacking knowledge or awareness. **2** informal not polite; rude.

ignore verb (**ignores, ignoring, ignored**) **1** deliberately take no notice of. **2** fail to consider something important.

iguana /i-**gwah**-nuh/ noun a large tropical American lizard with a spiny crest along the back.

ikon ⇒ **ICON**.

ilk noun a type.

I'll short form I shall or I will.

ill adjective **1** not in good health; unwell. **2** poor in quality. **3** harmful, hostile, or unfavourable. adverb **1** badly or wrongly. **2** only with difficulty. noun **1** a problem or misfortune. **2** evil or harm. □ **ill-advised** unwise or badly thought out. **ill at ease** uncomfortable or embarrassed. **ill-fated** destined to fail or be unlucky. **ill-favoured** unattractive. **ill-gotten** obtained by illegal or unfair means. **ill-starred** unlucky. **ill-treat** treat cruelly. **ill will** hostility.

illegal adjective against the law. ■ **illegality** noun **illegally** adverb.

> ℹ️ **what is the difference between illegal** and **unlawful**? Both can mean 'against the law', but **unlawful** has a broader meaning 'not permitted by rules': thus handball in soccer is **unlawful**, but not **illegal**.

illegible adjective not clear enough to be read. ■ **illegibility** noun.

illegitimate adjective **1** not allowed by law or rules. **2** (of a child) born of parents not married to each other. ■ **illegitimacy** noun.

illiberal adjective not allowing freedom of thought or behaviour.

illicit adjective forbidden by law, rules, or standards. ■ **illicitly** adverb.

illiterate adjective **1** unable to read or write. **2** not knowing very much about a particular subject. ■ **illiteracy** noun.

illness noun a disease, or a period of being ill.

illogical adjective not sensible or based on sound reasoning. ■ **illogicality** noun **illogically** adverb.

illuminate verb (**illuminates, illuminating, illuminated**) **1** light up. **2** help to explain or make clear. **3** decorate a manuscript with coloured designs.

illumination noun **1** lighting or light. **2** (**illuminations**) lights used in decorating a building for a special occasion. **3** understanding.

illumine verb literary light up; illuminate.

illusion noun **1** a false idea or belief. **2** a thing that seems to be something that it is not.

illusionist noun a magician or conjuror.

illusory or **illusive** adjective not real, although seeming to be.

illustrate verb (**illustrates, illustrating, illustrated**) **1** provide a book or magazine with pictures. **2** make something clear by using examples, charts, etc. **3** act as an example of. ■ **illustrative** adjective **illustrator** noun.

illustration noun **1** a picture illustrating a book or magazine. **2** the action of illustrating. **3** an example that helps to explain something.

illustrious adjective famous and admired for what you have achieved.

I'm short form I am.

image noun **1** a picture or statue of someone or something. **2** a picture seen on a television or computer screen, through a lens, or reflected in a mirror. **3** a picture in the mind. **4** the impression that a person or group gives to the public. **5** (**the image of**) a person or thing that looks very similar to another. **6** a word or phrase describing something in an imaginative way; a simile or metaphor. **verb** (**images, imaging, imaged**) make or form an image of.

imagery noun 1 language that produces images in the mind. **2** pictures as a whole.

imaginary adjective existing only in the imagination.

imagination noun 1 the part of the mind that imagines things. **2** the ability to be creative or solve problems.

imaginative adjective using the imagination in a creative or inventive way. ■ **imaginatively** adverb.

imagine verb (**imagines, imagining, imagined**) **1** form a mental picture of. **2** think that something is probable. **3** believe that something unreal exists. ■ **imaginable** adjective.

imam /i-**mahm**/ **noun** the person who leads prayers in a mosque.

imbalance noun a lack of proportion or balance.

imbecile /**im**-bi-seel/ **noun** informal a stupid person. ■ **imbecilic** adjective **imbecility** noun.

imbed ⇒ **EMBED**.

imbibe verb (**imbibes, imbibing, imbibed**) **1** formal drink alcohol. **2** absorb ideas or knowledge.

imbroglio /im-**broh**-li-oh/ **noun** (plural **imbroglios**) a very confused or complicated situation.

imbue verb (**imbues, imbuing, imbued**) fill with a feeling or quality.

imitate verb (**imitates, imitating, imitated**) **1** follow as a model; copy. **2** copy the way that a person speaks or behaves in order to amuse people. ■ **imitator** noun.

imitation noun 1 a copy. **2** the action of imitating.

imitative /**im**-i-tuh-tiv/ **adjective** imitating or copying something.

immaculate adjective 1 completely clean or tidy. **2** free from mistakes; perfect. ■ **immaculately** adverb.

immanent adjective 1 present within something; inherent. **2** (of God) permanently present throughout the universe. ■ **immanence** noun.

immaterial adjective 1 unimportant under the circumstances. **2** spiritual rather than physical.

immature adjective 1 not fully developed. **2** behaving in a way that is typical of someone younger. ■ **immaturity** noun.

immeasurable adjective too large or extreme to measure. ■ **immeasurably** adverb.

immediate adjective 1 occurring or done at once. **2** nearest in time, space, or relationship. **3** most urgent; current. **4** without anything coming between; direct. ■ **immediacy** noun.

immediately adverb 1 at once. **2** very close in time, space, or relationship. **conjunction** chiefly Brit. as soon as.

 -*tely*, not -*tly*: immedia*tely*.

immemorial adjective existing for longer than people can remember.

immense adjective very large or great. ■ **immensely** adverb **immensity** noun.

immerse verb (**immerses, immersing, immersed**) **1** dip or cover completely in a liquid. **2** (**immerse in**) involve deeply in an activity.

immersion noun 1 the action of immersing. **2** deep involvement in an activity. □ **immersion heater** an electric device in a water tank which heats water for a house.

immigrant noun a person who comes to live permanently in a foreign country.

immigrate verb (**immigrates, immigrating, immigrated**) come to live permanently in a foreign country. ■ **immigration** noun.

imminent adjective about to happen. ■ **imminence** noun **imminently** adverb.

immiscible /i-**miss**-i-b'l/ **adjective** (of liquids) not able to be mixed together.

immobile adjective not moving or able to move. ■ **immobility** noun.

immobilize or **immobilise verb** (**immobilizes, immobilizing, immo-**

bilized) prevent from moving or operating normally. ■ **immobilization** noun.

immoderate adjective not sensible or controlled; excessive.

immodest adjective not humble or decent.

immolate verb kill or sacrifice by burning. ■ **immolation** noun.

immoral adjective not following accepted standards of morality. ■ **immorality** noun.

immortal adjective 1 living forever. 2 deserving to be remembered forever. noun 1 an immortal god. 2 a person who will be famous for a very long time. ■ **immortality** noun.

immortalize or **immortalise** verb (immortalizes, immortalizing, immortalized) make immortal.

immovable adjective 1 not able to be moved. 2 unable to be changed or persuaded. ■ **immovably** adverb.

immune adjective 1 having a natural ability to resist a particular infection. 2 not affected by something. 3 exempt or protected from something.

immunity noun (plural **immunities**) 1 the body's ability to resist a particular infection. 2 freedom from a duty or punishment.

immunize or **immunise** verb (immunizes, immunizing, immunized) make immune to infection. ■ **immunization** noun.

immunology noun the branch of medicine and biology concerned with immunity to infection. ■ **immunological** adjective **immunologist** noun.

immure verb (immures, immuring, immured) confine or imprison.

immutable /im-**myoo**-tuh-b'l/ adjective unchanging or unchangeable.

imp noun 1 a small, mischievous devil or sprite. 2 a mischievous child.

impact noun /im-pakt/ 1 an instance of one object hitting another. 2 a noticeable effect or influence. verb /im-**pakt**/ 1 hit another object with force. 2 (impact on) have a strong effect on. 3 press firmly. 4 (impacted) (of a

tooth) wedged between another tooth and the jaw.

impair verb weaken or damage. ■ **impairment** noun.

impale verb (impales, impaling, impaled) pierce with a sharp instrument.

impalpable adjective 1 unable to be felt by touch. 2 not easily understood.

impart verb 1 communicate information. 2 give a particular quality to.

impartial adjective not favouring one person or thing more than another. ■ **impartiality** noun **impartially** adverb.

impassable adjective impossible to travel along or over.

impasse /am-pahss/ noun a situation in which no progress is possible.

impassioned adjective filled with or showing great emotion.

impassive adjective not feeling or showing emotion. ■ **impassively** adverb.

impasto /im-**pass**-toh/ noun the technique of laying on paint thickly so that it stands out from the surface of a painting.

impatient adjective 1 not having much patience or tolerance. 2 restlessly eager. ■ **impatience** noun **impatiently** adverb.

impeach verb chiefly US charge the holder of a public office with a serious crime. ■ **impeachment** noun.

impeccable adjective without faults or mistakes. ■ **impeccably** adverb.

impecunious /im-pi-**kyoo**-ni-uhss/ adjective having little or no money.

impedance noun the total resistance of an electric circuit to the flow of alternating current.

impede verb (impedes, impeding, impeded) delay or block the progress of.

impediment noun 1 something that delays or blocks progress. 2 (also speech impediment) a defect in a person's speech, such as a stammer.

impel verb (impels, impelling, impelled) force to do something.

impending adjective be about to happen.

impenetrable adjective 1 impossible to get through or into. 2 impossible to understand.

impenitent adjective not feeling shame or regret.

imperative adjective 1 of vital importance. 2 giving a command. 3 Grammar (of a verb) expressing a command, as in *come here!* noun an essential or urgent thing.

imperceptible adjective too slight or gradual to be seen or felt. ■ **imperceptibly** adverb.

imperfect adjective 1 faulty or incomplete. 2 Grammar (of a verb) referring to a past action that is not yet completed. ■ **imperfection** noun **imperfectly** adverb.

imperial adjective 1 relating to an empire or an emperor. 2 (of weights and measures) in a non-metric system formerly used in the UK.

imperialism noun a system in which one country influences others, by defeating them in war, forming colonies, etc. ■ **imperialist** noun & adjective.

imperil verb (imperils, imperilling, imperilled; US spelling imperils, imperiling, imperiled) put into danger.

imperious /im-**peer**-i-uhss/ adjective expecting to be obeyed. ■ **imperiously** adverb.

impermanent adjective not permanent. ■ **impermanence** noun.

impermeable adjective not allowing a liquid or gas to pass through.

impersonal adjective 1 not influenced by or involving personal feelings. 2 lacking human feelings or atmosphere. 3 Grammar (of a verb) used only with *it* as a subject (as in *it is snowing*). ■ **impersonality** noun **impersonally** adverb.

impersonate verb (impersonates, impersonating, impersonated) pretend to be another person in order to entertain or deceive people. ■ **impersonation** noun **impersonator** noun.

impertinent adjective not showing proper respect. ■ **impertinence** noun.

imperturbable adjective unable to be upset or excited.

impervious adjective 1 not allowing a liquid or a gas to pass through. 2 (**impervious to**) unable to be affected by.

impetuous adjective acting quickly and without thinking or being careful. ■ **impetuously** adverb.

impetus noun 1 the force or energy with which something moves. 2 the force that makes something happen.

impinge verb (impinges, impinging, impinged) (**impinge on**) have an effect or impact on.

impious /**im**-pi-uhss/ adjective not showing respect or reverence.

implacable adjective 1 unwilling to stop being hostile towards someone or something. 2 unstoppable. ■ **implacably** adverb.

implant verb /im-**plahnt**/ 1 put tissue or an artificial object into someone's body, by means of a surgical operation. 2 fix an idea firmly in someone's mind. noun /**im**-plahnt/ a thing that is implanted. ■ **implantation** noun.

implausible adjective not seeming reasonable or probable. ■ **implausibility** noun **implausibly** adverb.

implement noun /**im**-pli-muhnt/ a tool that is used for a particular purpose. verb /**im**-pli-ment/ put into effect. ■ **implementation** noun.

implicate verb (implicates, implicating, implicated) 1 show that someone is involved in a crime. 2 (**be implicated in**) be partly responsible for.

implication noun 1 a conclusion that can be drawn from something. 2 a possible effect. 3 involvement in something.

implicit adjective 1 suggested without being directly expressed. 2 (**implicit in**) forming part of something. 3 not doubted or questioned. ■ **implicitly** adverb.

implode verb (implodes, imploding, imploded) collapse violently inwards. ■ **implosion** noun.

implore verb (implores, imploring,

implored) beg earnestly or desperately.

imply verb (**implies, implying, implied**) **1** suggest rather than state directly. **2** suggest as a possible effect.

> **i** don't confuse the words **imply** and **infer**. They can describe the same situation, but from different points of view. If you **imply** something, as in *he implied that the General was a traitor*, it means that you are suggesting something though not saying it directly. If you **infer** something from what has been said, as in *we inferred from his words that the General was a traitor*, you come to the conclusion that this is what the speaker really means, although they are not saying it directly.

impolite adjective not having good manners.

impolitic adjective unwise.

imponderable adjective difficult or impossible to assess. noun an imponderable part of something.

import verb /im-**port**/ **1** bring goods into a country from abroad. **2** transfer computer data into a file. noun /**im**-port/ **1** an imported article or service. **2** the action of importing. **3** the implied meaning of something. **4** importance. ■ **importation** noun **importer** noun.

important adjective **1** having a great effect or value. **2** (of a person) having great authority or influence. ■ **importance** noun **importantly** adverb.

importunate /im-**por**-tyuu-nuht/ adjective very persistent.

importune verb (**importunes, importuning, importuned**) ask someone persistently for something.

impose verb (**imposes, imposing, imposed**) **1** force something to be accepted. **2** (often **impose on**) take unfair advantage of someone.

imposing adjective grand and impressive.

imposition noun **1** the action of imposing something. **2** something that is imposed and felt to be unfair.

impossible adjective **1** not able to exist or be done. **2** very difficult to deal with. ■ **impossibility** noun **impossibly** adverb.

impostor or **imposter** noun a person who pretends to be someone else in order to deceive others.

imposture noun an act of pretending to be someone else in order to deceive.

impotent /**im**-puh-tuhnt/ adjective **1** helpless or powerless. **2** (of a man) unable to achieve an erection. ■ **impotence** noun.

impound verb **1** officially seize something. **2** shut up domestic animals in an enclosure.

impoverish verb **1** make poor. **2** make worse in quality. ■ **impoverishment** noun.

impracticable adjective not able to be done.

impractical adjective not sensible or realistic.

imprecation noun formal a spoken curse.

imprecise adjective not exact. ■ **imprecision** noun.

impregnable adjective **1** (of a building) unable to be captured or broken into. **2** unable to be defeated.

impregnate verb (**impregnates, impregnating, impregnated**) **1** soak with a substance. **2** fill with a feeling or quality. **3** make pregnant. ■ **impregnation** noun.

impresario /im-pri-**sah**-ri-oh/ noun (plural **impresarios**) a person who organizes plays, concerts, or operas.

impress verb **1** make someone feel admiration and respect. **2** make a mark or design using a stamp or seal. **3** (**impress on**) make someone aware of something important.

impression noun **1** an idea, feeling, or opinion. **2** the effect that something has on someone. **3** an imitation of the way that a person speaks or behaves done in order to entertain people. **4** a mark made by pressing on a surface.

impressionable adjective easily influenced.

Impressionism noun a style of painting concerned with showing the visual impression of a particular moment. ■ **Impressionist** noun & adjective.

impressionist noun an entertainer who impersonates famous people.

impressionistic adjective based on personal ideas or feelings.

impressive adjective arousing admiration through size, quality, or skill. ■ **impressively** adverb.

imprimatur /im-pri-**mah**-ter/ noun the authority or approval of someone.

imprint verb /im-**print**/ make a mark on an object by pressing something on to it. noun /**im**-print/ **1** a mark made by pressing something on an object. **2** a publisher's name and other details printed in a book.

imprison verb put or keep in prison. ■ **imprisonment** noun.

improbable adjective not likely to be true or to happen. ■ **improbability** noun **improbably** adverb.

impromptu /im-**promp**-tyoo/ adjective & adverb done without being planned or rehearsed.

improper adjective **1** not fitting in with accepted standards of behaviour. **2** not modest or decent.

impropriety /im-pruh-**pry**-uh-ti/ noun (plural **improprieties**) improper behaviour.

improve verb (**improves**, **improving**, **improved**) **1** make or become better. **2** (**improve on**) produce something better than. ■ **improvement** noun.

improvident adjective not thinking about or preparing for the future.

improvise verb (**improvises**, **improvising**, **improvised**) **1** invent and perform music or drama without planning it in advance. **2** make something from whatever is available. ■ **improvisation** noun.

imprudent adjective not sensible or careful.

impudent adjective not showing respect for another person. ■ **impudence** noun **impudently** adverb.

impugn /im-**pyoon**/ verb formal express doubts about whether something is true or honest.

impulse noun **1** a sudden urge to do something. **2** a force that makes something happen.

impulsive adjective acting without thinking ahead. ■ **impulsively** adverb.

impunity /im-**pyoo**-ni-ti/ noun freedom from being punished or hurt.

impure adjective **1** mixed with unwanted substances. **2** morally wrong.

impurity noun (plural **impurities**) **1** the state of being impure. **2** a thing which makes something less pure.

impute /im-**pyoot**/ verb (**imputes**, **imputing**, **imputed**) (**impute to**) believe that something has been done or caused by someone. ■ **imputation** noun.

in preposition **1** expressing the position of something that is enclosed or surrounded. **2** expressing movement which results in something being enclosed or surrounded. **3** expressing a period of time before or during which something happens. **4** expressing a state or quality. **5** indicating that something is included or involved. **6** indicating the language or material used by someone. **7** used to express a value as a proportion of a whole. adverb **1** expressing the state of being enclosed or surrounded. **2** expressing movement which results in being enclosed or surrounded. **3** present at your home or office. **4** having arrived at a destination. **5** (of the tide) rising or at its highest level. adjective informal fashionable. □ **in-depth** thorough and detailed. **in-house** within an organization. **in-joke** a joke shared only by a small group. **the ins and outs** informal all the details.

in. abbreviation inches.

inability noun the state of being unable to do something.

in absentia /in ab-**sen**-ti-uh/ adverb while not present.

inaccessible adjective **1** unable to be

reached or used. **2** difficult to understand.

inaccurate adjective not accurate. ■ **inaccurately** adverb.

inaction noun lack of action.

inactive adjective not active or working. ■ **inactivity** noun.

inadequate adjective **1** not enough or not good enough. **2** unable to deal with a situation. ■ **inadequacy** noun (plural **inadequacies**) **inadequately** adverb.

inadmissible adjective (of evidence in court) not accepted as valid.

inadvertent adjective not deliberate; unintentional. ■ **inadvertently** adverb.

 -*ent*, not -*ant*: inadvert*ent*.

inadvisable adjective likely to have unfortunate results.

inalienable adjective unable to be taken away or given away.

inane adjective lacking sense; silly. ■ **inanely** adverb **inanity** noun.

inanimate adjective **1** not alive. **2** showing no sign of life.

inapplicable adjective not relevant or appropriate.

inappropriate adjective not suitable or appropriate. ■ **inappropriately** adverb.

inarticulate adjective **1** unable to express your ideas clearly. **2** not expressed in words.

inasmuch adverb (**inasmuch as**) **1** to the extent that. **2** considering that; since.

inattentive adjective not paying attention. ■ **inattention** noun.

inaudible adjective unable to be heard. ■ **inaudibly** adverb.

inaugural adjective marking the start of something important.

inaugurate verb (**inaugurates**, **inaugurating**, **inaugurated**) **1** begin or introduce a system or project. **2** mark the beginning of an organization or the opening of a building with a ceremony. ■ **inauguration** noun.

inauspicious adjective not likely to

lead to success.

inauthentic noun not genuine or sincere.

inborn adjective existing from birth.

inbred adjective **1** produced by breeding from closely related people or animals. **2** existing from birth; inborn.

inbreeding noun breeding from closely related people or animals.

inbuilt adjective existing as an original or important part.

Inc. abbreviation N. Amer. Incorporated.

incalculable adjective too great to be calculated or estimated.

incandescent adjective glowing as a result of being heated. ■ **incandescence** noun.

incantation noun a magic spell or charm. ■ **incantatory** adjective.

incapable adjective **1** (**incapable of**) not able to do something. **2** not able to look after yourself.

incapacitate verb (**incapacitates**, **incapacitating**, **incapacitated**) prevent from working in a normal way. ■ **incapacitation** noun.

incapacity noun (plural **incapacities**) inability to do something.

incarcerate verb (**incarcerates**, **incarcerating**, **incarcerated**) imprison. ■ **incarceration** noun.

incarnate adjective in human form.

incarnation noun **1** a god, spirit, or quality in human form. **2** (**the Incarnation**) (in Christian belief) God taking human form as Jesus.

incautious adjective not concerned about possible problems.

incendiary adjective **1** (of a bomb) designed to cause fires. **2** tending to cause strong feelings. noun (plural **incendiaries**) an incendiary bomb.

incense[1] /in-senss/ noun a substance that produces a sweet smell when you burn it.

incense[2] /in-senss/ verb (**incenses**, **incensing**, **incensed**) make very angry.

incentive noun something that influences or encourages you to do something.

inception noun the beginning of an organization or activity.

incessant adjective never stopping. ■ **incessantly** adverb.

incest noun sex between people who are very closely related in a family.

incestuous adjective **1** involving incest. **2** involving a group of people who are very close and do not want to include others.

inch noun **1** a unit of length equal to one twelfth of a foot (2.54 cm). **2** a very small amount or distance. verb move along slowly and carefully.

incidence noun **1** the extent to which something happens. **2** Physics the meeting of a line or ray with a surface.

incident noun **1** something that happens. **2** a violent event.

incidental adjective **1** occurring in connection with something else. **2** relatively unimportant. □ **incidental music** background music in a film or play. ■ **incidentally** adverb.

incinerate verb (**incinerates**, **incinerating**, **incinerated**) destroy by burning. ■ **incineration** noun.

incinerator noun a device for incinerating rubbish.

incipient adjective beginning to happen or develop.

incise verb (**incises**, **incising**, **incised**) mark a surface by cutting into it.

incision noun **1** a cut made as part of a surgical operation. **2** the action of cutting into something.

incisive adjective **1** showing clear thought and good understanding. **2** quick and direct.

incisor noun a narrow-edged tooth at the front of the mouth.

incite verb (**incites**, **inciting**, **incited**) encourage someone to do something violent or unlawful. ■ **incitement** noun.

incivility noun rude speech or behaviour.

inclement /in-**klem**-uhnt/ adjective (of the weather) unpleasantly cold or wet. ■ **inclemency** noun.

inclination noun **1** a tendency to do things in a particular way. **2** (**inclination for** or **to do**) an interest in or liking for. **3** a slope or slant.

incline verb /in-**klyn**/ (**inclines**, **inclining**, **inclined**) **1** (**incline to** or **be inclined to**) tend to do or think in a particular way. **2** lean or bend. noun /**in**-klyn/ a slope.

include verb (**includes**, **including**, **included**) **1** have something as part of a whole. **2** make part of a whole.

including preposition having as part of a whole.

inclusion noun **1** the act of including. **2** a person or thing that is included.

inclusive adjective **1** including everything expected or required. **2** between the limits stated.

incognito /in-kog-**nee**-toh/ adjective & adverb having your true identity concealed.

incoherent adjective **1** hard to understand; unclear. **2** not logical or well organized. ■ **incoherence** noun **incoherently** adverb.

incombustible adjective (of a material) that does not burn.

income noun money received for work or from investments. □ **income tax** tax that must be paid on personal income.

incomer noun Brit. a person who has come to live in an area in which they have not grown up.

incoming adjective **1** coming in or arriving. **2** (of a public official) having just been chosen to replace someone.

incommensurable /in-kuh-**men**-shuh-ruh-b'l/ adjective not able to be compared.

incommensurate /in-kuh-**men**-shuh-ruht/ adjective (**incommensurate with**) out of proportion with.

incommode verb (**incommodes**, **incommoding**, **incommoded**) formal cause inconvenience to.

incommunicado /in-kuh-myoo-ni-**kah**-doh/ adjective & adverb not able to communicate with other people.

incomparable /in-**kom**-puh-ruh-b'l/ **adjective** so good that nothing can be compared to it. ■ **incomparably** adverb.

incompatible adjective 1 (of two things) not able to exist or be used together. **2** (of two people) unable to live or work together without disagreeing. ■ **incompatibility** noun.

incompetent adjective not having the skill to do something well. ■ **incompetence** noun **incompetently** adverb.

incomplete adjective not complete. ■ **incompletely** adverb.

incomprehensible adjective not able to be understood. ■ **incomprehension** noun.

inconceivable adjective not able to be imagined or believed. ■ **inconceivably** adverb.

inconclusive adjective not leading to a firm conclusion. ■ **inconclusively** adverb.

incongruous /in-kong-groo-uhss/ **adjective** out of place. ■ **incongruity** noun **incongruously** adverb.

inconsequential adjective not important. ■ **inconsequentially** adverb.

inconsiderable adjective small in size or amount.

inconsiderate adjective not thinking about other people's feelings.

inconsistent adjective 1 having parts that contradict each other. **2** (**inconsistent with**) not in keeping with. ■ **inconsistency** noun.

inconsolable adjective not able to be comforted.

inconspicuous adjective not noticeable. ■ **inconspicuously** adverb.

inconstant adjective 1 formal not faithful or dependable. **2** frequently changing.

incontestable adjective not able to be disputed.

incontinent adjective 1 unable to control your bladder or bowels. **2** lacking control. ■ **incontinence** noun.

incontrovertible adjective not able to be denied or disputed. ■ **incontro-**

vertibly adverb.

inconvenience noun slight trouble or difficulty. **verb** (**inconveniences, inconveniencing, inconvenienced**) cause someone inconvenience. ■ **inconvenient** adjective **inconveniently** adverb.

incorporate verb (**incorporates, incorporating, incorporated**) include something as part of a whole. ■ **incorporation** noun.

incorporated adjective (of a company) formed into a legal corporation.

incorporeal /in-kor-**por**-i-uhl/ **adjective** without a body or form.

incorrect adjective 1 not true or accurate. **2** not following accepted standards. ■ **incorrectly** adverb.

incorrigible adjective having bad habits that cannot be changed.

incorruptible adjective 1 too honest to be corrupted by taking bribes. **2** not prone to death or decay.

increase verb /in-**kreess**/ (**increases, increasing, increased**) make or become greater in size, amount, or intensity. **noun** /**in**-kreess/ a rise in amount, size, or intensity.

increasingly adverb more and more.

incredible adjective 1 impossible or hard to believe. **2** informal extremely good. ■ **incredibly** adverb.

incredulity /in-kre-**dyoo**-li-ti/ **noun** unwillingness or inability to believe something.

incredulous adjective unwilling or unable to believe something. ■ **incredulously** adverb.

increment /**ing**-kri-muhnt/ **noun** an increase in a number or amount. ■ **incremental** adjective.

incriminate verb (**incriminates, incriminating, incriminated**) make it look as though someone has done something wrong or illegal. ■ **incrimination** noun.

incubate verb (**incubates, incubating, incubated**) **1** (of a bird) sit on eggs to keep them warm so that they hatch. **2** keep bacteria and cells at a suitable temperature so that they develop. **3** (of an infectious disease) develop slowly without obvious signs. ■ **incubation** noun **incubator** noun.

inculcate /in-kul-kayt/ verb (**inculcates, inculcating, inculcated**) fix ideas in someone's mind by repeating them. ■ **inculcation** noun.

incumbency noun (plural **incumbencies**) the period during which an official position is held.

incumbent adjective **1** (**incumbent on**) necessary for someone as a duty. **2** currently holding an official position. noun the holder of an official position.

incur verb (**incurs, incurring, incurred**) make something unwelcome happen.

> ☑ one *r* in *incur* and *incurs*, two in *incurred* and *incurring*.

incurable adjective not able to be cured. ■ **incurably** adverb.

incurious adjective not curious.

incursion noun a sudden invasion or attack.

indebted adjective **1** feeling grateful to someone. **2** owing money.

indecent adjective **1** causing offence by showing too much of the body or involving sex. **2** not appropriate. ■ **indecency** noun **indecently** adverb.

indecipherable adjective not able to be read or understood.

indecisive adjective **1** not able to make decisions quickly. **2** not settling an issue. ■ **indecision** noun **indecisively** adverb **indecisiveness** noun.

indeed adverb **1** used to emphasize a statement or answer. **2** used to introduce a further and stronger point.

indefatigable adjective never tiring.

indefensible adjective not able to be justified or defended.

indefinable adjective not able to be defined or described exactly.

indefinite adjective **1** not clearly stated, seen, or heard; vague. **2** lasting for an unknown length of time. ▢ **indefinite article** Grammar the word *a*

or *an*. ■ **indefinitely** adverb.

indelible adjective **1** (of ink or a mark) unable to be removed. **2** unable to be forgotten. ■ **indelibly** adverb.

indelicate adjective **1** lacking sensitivity; tactless. **2** slightly indecent.

indemnify verb (**indemnifies, indemnifying, indemnified**) **1** pay money to someone to compensate for harm or loss. **2** insure someone against legal responsibility for their actions.

indemnity noun (plural **indemnities**) **1** insurance against legal responsibility for your actions. **2** a sum of money paid to compensate for damage or loss.

indent verb /in-dent/ **1** form hollows or notches in. **2** begin a line of writing further from the margin than the other lines. noun /in-dent/ **1** Brit. an official order for goods. **2** a hollow or notch. ■ **indentation** noun.

indenture noun a formal agreement or contract.

independent adjective **1** free from the control or influence of others. **2** (of a country) self-governing. **3** having or earning enough money to support yourself. **4** not connected with another; separate. noun an independent person or body. ■ **independence** noun **independently** adverb.

> ☑ *-ent*, not *-ant*: independ**ent**.

indescribable adjective too extreme or unusual to be described. ■ **indescribably** adverb.

indestructible adjective not able to be destroyed.

indeterminate adjective not certain; vague.

index noun (plural **indexes** or **indices** /in-di-seez/) **1** a list of names or subjects referred to in a book, arranged in alphabetical order. **2** an alphabetical list or catalogue of books or documents. **3** a sign or measure of something. verb record in or provide with an index. ▢ **index finger** the forefinger.

Indian noun **1** a person from India.

2 an American Indian. **adjective 1** relating to India. **2** relating to American Indians. ◻ **Indian ink** deep black ink used in drawing. **Indian summer** a period of dry, warm weather in late autumn.

indicate verb (**indicates, indicating, indicated**) **1** point something out. **2** be a sign of. **3** mention briefly. **4** (**be indicated**) formal be necessary or recommended. ■ **indication** noun.

indicative /in-**dik**-uh-tiv/ **adjective 1** acting as a sign. **2** Grammar (of a verb) expressing a simple statement of fact (e.g. *she left*).

indicator noun 1 a thing that shows the state or level of something. **2** a light on a vehicle that flashes to show that it is about to turn left or right.

indict /in-**dyt**/ **verb** formally accuse or charge someone with a serious crime. ■ **indictable** adjective.

indictment /in-**dyt**-muhnt/ **noun 1** a formal charge or accusation of a serious crime. **2** an indication that something is bad and deserves to be condemned.

indifferent adjective 1 having no interest or sympathy; unconcerned. **2** not very good; mediocre. ■ **indifference** noun **indifferently** adverb.

indigenous /in-**dij**-i-nuhss/ **adjective** belonging to a place; native.

indigent /**in**-di-juhnt/ **adjective** poor; needy.

indigestible adjective difficult or impossible to digest.

indigestion noun pain or discomfort caused by difficulty in digesting food.

indignant adjective feeling or showing indignation. ■ **indignantly** adverb.

indignation noun anger caused by something that you consider to be unfair.

indignity noun (plural **indignities**) a thing that causes you to feel ashamed or embarrassed.

indigo /**in**-di-goh/ **noun** a dark blue colour or dye.

indirect adjective 1 not going in a

straight line. **2** not saying something in a straightforward way. **3** happening as a secondary effect or consequence. ◻ **indirect question** a question in reported speech (e.g. *they asked who I was*). **indirect speech** reported speech. ■ **indirectly** adverb.

indiscipline noun lack of discipline.

indiscreet adjective too ready to reveal things that should remain secret or private. ■ **indiscreetly** adverb.

indiscretion noun 1 indiscreet behaviour. **2** an indiscreet act or remark.

indiscriminate adjective done or acting without careful judgement. ■ **indiscriminately** adverb.

indispensable adjective absolutely necessary.

 -able, not *-ible*: indispens*able*.

indisposed adjective 1 slightly unwell. **2** unwilling.

indisposition noun 1 a slight illness. **2** unwillingness.

indisputable adjective unable to be challenged or denied. ■ **indisputably** adverb.

indissoluble adjective unable to be destroyed; lasting.

indistinct adjective not clear or sharply defined. ■ **indistinctly** adverb.

indistinguishable adjective not able to be distinguished. ■ **indistinguishably** adverb.

individual adjective 1 considered separately; single. **2** having to do with one particular person. **3** striking or unusual; original. **noun 1** a single person or item as distinct from a group. **2** a distinctive or original person. ■ **individually** adverb.

individualism noun 1 the quality of doing things in your own way; independence. **2** the belief that individual people should have freedom of action. ■ **individualist** noun & adjective **individualistic** adjective.

individuality noun the quality or character of a person or thing that makes them different from others.

individualize or **individualise** verb (individualizes, individualizing, individualized) give something an individual character.

indivisible adjective unable to be divided or separated.

indoctrinate verb (indoctrinates, indoctrinating, indoctrinated) force someone to accept a set of beliefs. ■ **indoctrination** noun.

Indo-European noun the family of languages spoken over most of Europe and Asia as far as northern India. adjective relating to Indo-European.

indolent /in-duh-luhnt/ adjective lazy. ■ **indolence** noun.

indomitable /in-**dom**-i-tuh-b'l/ adjective impossible to defeat or subdue.

indoor adjective situated, done, or used inside a building. adverb (indoors) into or inside a building.

indubitable /in-**dyoo**-bi-tuh-b'l/ adjective impossible to doubt; unquestionable. ■ **indubitably** adverb.

induce verb (induces, inducing, induced) **1** persuade or influence someone to do something. **2** bring about or cause. **3** make a woman begin to give birth to her baby by means of special drugs.

inducement noun a thing that persuades someone to do something.

induct verb introduce someone formally to a post or organization.

inductance noun a process by which a change in the current of an electric circuit produces an electromotive force.

induction noun **1** introduction to a post or organization. **2** the action of inducing. **3** a method of reasoning in which a general rule or conclusion is drawn from particular facts or examples. **4** the passing of electricity or magnetism from one object to another without them touching. ■ **inductive** adjective.

indulge verb (indulges, indulging, indulged) **1** (indulge in) allow yourself to do something that you enjoy. **2** satisfy a desire or interest. **3** allow someone to do or have whatever they wish.

indulgence noun **1** the action of indulging in something. **2** a thing that is indulged in; a luxury. **3** willingness to tolerate someone's faults.

indulgent adjective allowing someone to do or have whatever they want or overlooking their faults. ■ **indulgently** adverb.

industrial adjective having to do with industry. □ **industrial action** Brit. a strike or other action taken by workers as a protest. **industrial estate** Brit. an area of land developed as a site for factories. ■ **industrially** adverb.

industrialist noun a person who owns or controls a large factory or manufacturing business.

industrialize or **industrialise** verb (industrializes, industrializing, industrialized) develop industries in a country or region on a wide scale. ■ **industrialization** noun.

industrious adjective hard-working. ■ **industriously** adverb.

industry noun (plural **industries**) **1** the manufacture of goods in factories. **2** a branch of economic or commercial activity. **3** hard work.

inebriate /i-**nee**-bri-ayt/ verb (inebriates, inebriating, inebriated) make someone drunk. ■ **inebriation** noun.

inedible adjective not fit for eating.

ineffable adjective too great or extreme to be expressed in words.

ineffective adjective not having any effect or achieving what you want. ■ **ineffectively** adverb.

ineffectual adjective **1** ineffective. **2** not forceful enough to do something well. ■ **ineffectually** adverb.

inefficient adjective failing to make the best use of time or resources. ■ **inefficiency** noun **inefficiently** adverb.

inelegant adjective not elegant or graceful. ■ **inelegance** noun.

ineligible adjective not qualified to have or do something.

ineluctable adjective rare unable to be resisted or avoided.

inept adjective lacking skill. ■ **inepti-**

tude noun **ineptly** adverb.

inequality noun (plural **inequalities**) lack of equality.

inequitable adjective unfair; unjust.

inequity noun (plural **inequities**) lack of fairness or justice.

ineradicable adjective unable to be rooted out or destroyed.

inert adjective **1** lacking the ability or strength to move or act. **2** without active chemical properties.

inertia /i-**ner**-shuh/ noun **1** a tendency to do nothing or to remain unchanged. **2** Physics a property by which matter remains still or continues moving unless acted on by an external force.

inescapable adjective unable to be avoided or denied.

inessential adjective not absolutely necessary.

inestimable adjective too great to be measured.

inevitable adjective certain to happen; unavoidable. ■ **inevitability** noun **inevitably** adverb.

inexact adjective not quite accurate.

inexcusable adjective too bad to be justified or tolerated.

inexhaustible adjective (of a supply) never ending because available in unlimited quantities.

inexorable /in-**ek**-suh-ruh-b'l/ adjective **1** impossible to stop or prevent. **2** unable to be persuaded. ■ **inexorably** adverb.

inexpensive adjective not costing a lot of money.

inexperience noun lack of experience. ■ **inexperienced** adjective.

inexpert adjective lacking skill or knowledge in a particular field.

inexplicable /in-ik-**splik**-uh-b'l/ adjective unable to be explained. ■ **inexplicably** adverb.

inexpressive adjective showing no feelings.

in extremis /in ek-**stree**-miss/ adverb **1** in an extremely difficult situation. **2** at the point of death.

inextricable adjective impossible to untangle or separate. ■ **inextricably** adverb.

infallible adjective incapable of making mistakes or being wrong. ■ **infallibly** adverb.

infamous /in-fuh-muhss/ adjective **1** well known for some bad quality or deed. **2** morally bad. ■ **infamously** adverb **infamy** noun.

infancy noun **1** the state or period of early childhood or babyhood. **2** an early stage of development.

infant noun **1** a very young child or baby. **2** Brit. a schoolchild between the ages of about five and seven.

infanticide /in-**fan**-ti-syd/ noun the killing of a child.

infantile adjective **1** relating to infants. **2** disapproving childish.

infantry noun soldiers who fight on foot.

infatuate verb (**be infatuated with**) have an intense but short-lived passion for. ■ **infatuation** noun.

infect verb **1** pass to a person, animal, or plant a germ that causes disease. **2** contaminate with something harmful. **3** make someone share a particular feeling.

infection noun **1** the process of infecting. **2** an infectious disease.

infectious adjective **1** (of a disease or germ) able to be passed on through the environment. **2** liable to spread infection. **3** likely to spread to or influence others. ■ **infectiously** adverb.

infer verb (**infers, inferring, inferred**) work something out from the information you have available.

> 🛈 on the difference between the words **imply** and **infer**, see the note at **IMPLY**.

inference noun **1** a conclusion drawn from the information available to you. **2** the process of inferring.

inferior adjective lower in quality or status. noun a person who is lower in status or less good at doing something. ■ **inferiority** noun.

infernal adjective **1** having to do with

hell or the underworld. **2** informal terrible.

inferno noun (plural **infernos**) a large uncontrollable fire.

infertile adjective **1** unable to have babies or other young. **2** (of land) unable to sustain crops or vegetation. ∎ **infertility** noun.

infest verb (especially of insects or rats) be present in large numbers so as to cause damage or disease. ∎ **infestation** noun.

infidel /**in**-fi-duhl/ noun old use a person who has no religion or whose religion is not that of the majority.

infidelity noun (plural **infidelities**) the action or state of not being faithful to your sexual partner.

infighting noun conflict within a group or organization.

infiltrate verb **1** enter or gain access to an organization or place secretly and gradually. **2** filter into a place. ∎ **infiltration** noun **infiltrator** noun.

infinite adjective **1** having no limits and impossible to measure. **2** very great in amount or degree. ∎ **infinitely** adverb.

infinitesimal /in-fi-ni-**tess**-i-muhl/ adjective extremely small. ∎ **infinitesimally** adverb.

infinitive /in-**fin**-i-tiv/ noun the basic uninflected form of a verb, normally occurring in English with the word *to* (as in *to see*, *to ask*).

infinity noun (plural **infinities**) **1** the state or quality of being infinite. **2** a very great number or amount.

infirm adjective physically weak.

infirmary noun (plural **infirmaries**) a place where sick people are cared for.

infirmity noun (plural **infirmities**) physical or mental weakness.

inflame verb (inflames, inflaming, inflamed) **1** make someone feel something passionately. **2** make a difficult situation worse. **3** cause inflammation in.

inflammable adjective easily set on fire.

> ℹ️ **inflammable** and **flammable** both mean 'easily set on fire'. It's safer to use **flammable**, however, as some people think that **inflammable** means 'non-flammable'.

---

inflammation noun a condition in which an area of the skin is red, swollen, and hot.

inflammatory adjective **1** making people feel angry. **2** relating to or causing inflammation.

inflatable adjective capable of being inflated. noun an inflatable plastic or rubber boat.

inflate verb (inflates, inflating, inflated) **1** expand something by filling it with air or gas. **2** increase something by a large amount. **3** bring about inflation of a currency. **4** (inflated) exaggerated.

inflation noun **1** the action of inflating. **2** a general increase in prices. ∎ **inflationary** adjective.

inflect verb **1** Grammar (of a word) be changed by inflection. **2** vary the tone or pitch of your voice.

inflection noun **1** Grammar a change in the form of a word to show its grammatical function, number, or gender. **2** a variation in the tone or pitch of a voice.

inflexible adjective **1** not able to be altered or adapted. **2** unwilling to change or compromise. **3** not able to be bent.

inflict verb (inflict on) impose something unpleasant or painful on someone. ∎ **infliction** noun.

influence noun **1** the power or ability to affect someone's beliefs or actions. **2** a person or thing with such ability or power. **3** the power arising out of status, contacts, or wealth. verb (influences, influencing, influenced) have an influence on.

influential adjective having great influence.

influenza noun a disease spread by a virus and causing fever, aching, and catarrh.

influx noun the arrival or entry of

large numbers of people or things.

inform verb **1** give facts or information to. **2** (inform on) give information about someone's involvement in a crime to the police.

informal adjective **1** relaxed and friendly, and not following strict rules of behaviour. **2** (of clothes) suitable for wearing when relaxing. **3** (of language) used in everyday speech and writing, rather than official contexts. ■ informality noun informally adverb.

informant noun a person who gives information to another.

information noun facts or details supplied to or learned by someone. □ information technology the use of computers and telecommunications for storing, retrieving, and sending information.

informative adjective providing useful information.

informed adjective **1** having or showing knowledge. **2** (of a judgement) based on a sound understanding of the facts.

informer noun a person who informs on another person to the police.

infraction noun a breaking of a law or agreement.

infra dig /in-fruh **dig**/ adjective informal beneath your dignity.

infrared adjective (of electromagnetic radiation) having a wavelength just greater than that of red light.

infrastructure noun the basic things (e.g. buildings, roads, power supplies) needed for the operation of a society or enterprise.

infrequent adjective not occurring often. ■ infrequency noun infrequently adverb.

infringe verb **1** break a law or agreement. **2** intrude on a right or privilege. ■ infringement noun.

infuriate verb (infuriates, infuriating, infuriated) make someone angry. ■ infuriating adjective.

infuse verb (infuses, infusing, infused) **1** spread throughout something. **2** soak tea, herbs, etc. to extract the flavour or healing properties.

infusion noun **1** a drink or extract prepared by infusing. **2** the action or process of infusing.

ingenious adjective clever, original, and inventive. ■ ingeniously adverb.

ingénue /an-*zh*uh-nyoo/ noun a naive young woman.

ingenuity noun the quality of being ingenious.

ingenuous /in-jen-nyoo-uhss/ adjective innocent and unsuspecting.

ingest verb take food or drink into the body by swallowing it.

inglenook noun a space on either side of a large fireplace.

inglorious adjective not making you feel proud; rather shameful.

ingoing adjective going towards or into.

ingot noun a rectangular block of steel, gold, or other metal.

ingrained or **engrained** adjective **1** (of a habit or belief) firmly established. **2** (of dirt) deeply embedded.

ingratiate /in-gray-shi-ayt/ verb (ingratiates, ingratiating, ingratiated) (ingratiate yourself) do things in order to make someone like you.

ingratitude noun a lack of appropriate gratitude.

ingredient noun **1** any of the substances that are combined to make a particular dish. **2** a component part or element.

ingress noun **1** the action of entering or coming in. **2** a place or means of access.

ingrown or **ingrowing** adjective (of a toenail) having grown into the flesh.

inhabit verb (inhabits, inhabiting, inhabited) live in or occupy. ■ inhabitable adjective.

inhabitant noun a person or animal that lives in or occupies a place.

inhale verb (inhales, inhaling, inhaled) breathe in air, smoke, etc. ■ inhalation noun.

inhaler noun a portable device used

for inhaling a drug.

inherent adjective existing in something as a permanent or essential quality. ■ **inherently** adverb.

inherit verb (**inherits**, **inheriting**, **inherited**) **1** receive money or property from someone when they die. **2** have a quality or characteristic passed on to you from your parents or ancestors. **3** be left with something previously belonging to someone else.

inheritance noun **1** a thing that is inherited. **2** the action of inheriting.

inhibit verb (**inhibits**, **inhibiting**, **inhibited**) **1** prevent or slow down a process. **2** make someone unable to act in a relaxed and natural way.

inhibition noun a feeling that makes you unable to act in a relaxed and natural way.

inhospitable adjective **1** (of an environment) harsh and difficult to live in. **2** unwelcoming.

inhuman adjective **1** lacking positive human qualities; cruel and barbaric. **2** not human in nature or character.

inhumane adjective without pity; cruel.

inhumanity noun (plural **inhumanities**) cruel and brutal behaviour.

inimical adjective tending to obstruct or harm; hostile.

inimitable adjective impossible to imitate; unique. ■ **inimitably** adverb.

iniquity noun (plural **iniquities**) great injustice or unfairness. ■ **iniquitous** adjective.

initial adjective existing or occurring at the beginning. noun the first letter of a name or word. verb (**initials**, **initialling**, **initialled**; N. Amer. **initials**, **initialing**, **initialed**) mark something with your initials as a sign of approval or agreement. ■ **initially** adverb.

initiate verb (**initiates**, **initiating**, **initiated**) **1** make a process or action start. **2** admit someone into a society or group with a formal ceremony. **3** (**initiate into**) introduce someone to a new activity. ■ **initiation** noun.

initiative noun **1** the ability to act independently and with a fresh approach. **2** the power or opportunity to act before others do. **3** a new development or approach to a problem.

inject verb **1** introduce a drug or other substance into the body with a syringe. **2** introduce a new or different element.

injection noun **1** an act of injecting someone with a drug or other substance. **2** an introduction of something fresh and new.

injudicious adjective unwise.

injunction noun **1** Law an order saying that someone must or must not carry out a certain action. **2** a strong warning.

injure verb (**injures**, **injuring**, **injured**) **1** do physical harm to; wound. **2** offend or hurt.

injurious /in-joor-i-uhss/ adjective causing or likely to cause injury.

injury noun (plural **injuries**) **1** harm done to the body. **2** hurt feelings.

injustice noun **1** lack of justice. **2** an unjust act.

ink noun **1** a coloured fluid used for writing, drawing, or printing. **2** a black liquid produced by a cuttlefish, octopus, or squid. verb cover with ink before printing. ■ **inky** adjective.

inkling noun a slight suspicion; a hint.

inland adjective & adverb in or into the interior of a country. □ **inland revenue** Brit. the government department responsible for collecting income tax.

in-law noun a relative by marriage.

inlay verb (**inlays**, **inlaying**, **inlaid**) fix pieces of a different material into a surface as a form of decoration. noun decoration of such a type.

inlet noun **1** a small arm of the sea, a lake, or a river. **2** a place or means of entry.

in loco parentis /in loh-koh puh-ren-tiss/ adverb & adjective having the same responsibility for a child or young person as a parent has.

inmate noun a person living in an institution such as a prison or hospital.

inn noun a pub, especially in the country.

innards plural noun informal **1** internal organs. **2** the internal workings of a device or machine.

innate adjective natural or inborn. ■ **innately** adverb.

inner adjective **1** situated inside or close to the centre. **2** remaining private and unsaid. **3** mental or spiritual. □ **inner city** an area in or near the centre of a large city. **inner tube** a separate inflatable tube inside a tyre.

innermost adjective **1** furthest in; closest to the centre. **2** (of thoughts) most private.

innings noun (plural **innings**) Cricket each of the divisions of a game during which one side has a turn at batting.

innkeeper noun old use a person who runs an inn.

innocent adjective **1** not guilty of a crime or offence. **2** having little experience of life. **3** not intended to cause offence. noun an innocent person. ■ **innocence** noun **innocently** adverb.

innocuous /in-**nok**-yoo-uhss/ adjective not harmful or offensive.

innovate verb (**innovates**, **innovating**, **innovated**) introduce new ideas or products. ■ **innovative** adjective **innovator** noun.

innovation noun **1** the introduction of new ideas or products. **2** a new idea or product.

innuendo /in-yuu-**en**-doh/ noun (plural **innuendoes** or **innuendos**) a remark which makes a vague and indirect reference to something.

innumerable adjective too many to be counted.

innumerate adjective without a basic knowledge of mathematics and arithmetic.

inoculate verb treat someone with a vaccine to stop them getting a disease. ■ **inoculation** noun.

 one *n*, one *c*: i**n**oc**u**late.

inoffensive adjective causing no offence or harm.

inoperable adjective **1** (of an illness) not able to be cured by an operation. **2** not able to be used or operated.

inoperative adjective not working or taking effect.

inopportune adjective occurring at an inconvenient time.

inordinate adjective unusually large; excessive. ■ **inordinately** adverb.

inorganic adjective **1** not arising from natural growth. **2** (of a chemical compound) not containing carbon.

inpatient noun a patient who is staying day and night in a hospital.

input noun **1** what is put or taken into a system or process. **2** the putting or feeding in of something. **3** a person's contribution. verb (**inputs**, **inputting**, **input** or **inputted**) put data into a computer.

inquest noun **1** a legal inquiry to gather the facts relating to an incident. **2** Brit. an inquiry by a coroner's court into the cause of a death.

inquire = ENQUIRE.

inquiry = ENQUIRY.

inquisition noun **1** a long period of questioning or investigation. **2** the verdict of a coroner's jury.

inquisitive adjective **1** eager to find things out. **2** prying. ■ **inquisitively** adverb.

inquisitor noun a person conducting an inquisition.

inroad noun a gradual entry into or effect on a place or situation.

inrush noun a sudden inward rush or flow.

insalubrious /in-suh-**loo**-bri-uhss/ adjective seedy; unwholesome.

insane adjective **1** seriously mentally ill. **2** extremely foolish. ■ **insanely** adverb **insanity** noun.

insanitary adjective so dirty as to be a danger to health.

insatiable /in-**say**-shuh-b'l/ adjective

always wanting more and not able to be satisfied. ■ **insatiably** adverb.

inscribe verb (**inscribes, inscribing, inscribed**) **1** write or carve something on a surface. **2** write a dedication to someone in a book.

inscription noun words or symbols written or carved on a surface or in a book.

inscrutable adjective impossible to understand or interpret. ■ **inscrutably** adverb.

insect noun a small animal with six legs and no backbone.

insecticide noun a substance used for killing insects.

insectivore noun an animal that eats insects. ■ **insectivorous** adjective.

insecure adjective **1** not confident or assured. **2** not firm or firmly fixed. ■ **insecurity** noun.

inseminate verb (**inseminates, inseminating, inseminated**) introduce semen into a woman or a female animal. ■ **insemination** noun.

insensate adjective **1** lacking physical sensation. **2** lacking sympathy; unfeeling. **3** lacking good sense.

insensible adjective **1** unconscious. **2** numb; without feeling.

insensitive adjective **1** showing or feeling no concern for the feelings of others. **2** not sensitive to physical sensation. **3** not appreciative of something. ■ **insensitively** adverb **insensitivity** noun.

inseparable adjective unable to be separated or treated separately. ■ **inseparably** adverb.

insert verb /in-sert/ place, fit, or incorporate something into something else. noun /in-sert/ a loose page or section in a magazine. ■ **insertion** noun.

inset noun /in-set/ a thing inserted. verb /in-set/ (**insets, insetting, inset** or **insetted**) insert.

inshore adjective & adverb **1** at sea but close to the shore. **2** towards the shore.

inside noun **1** the inner side or surface of a thing. **2** the inner part; the interior. **3** (**insides**) informal a person's stomach and bowels. adjective situated on or in the inside. preposition & adverb **1** situated or moving within. **2** informal in prison. **3** within a particular time. □ **inside out** with the inner surface turned outwards.

insider noun a person working within an organization.

insidious adjective proceeding in a gradual and harmful way. ■ **insidiously** adverb.

insight noun **1** the ability to understand the truth about people and situations. **2** understanding of this kind. ■ **insightful** adjective.

insignia /in-sig-ni-uh/ noun (plural **insignia**) a badge or symbol indicating someone's rank, office, or membership of an association.

insignificant adjective having very little importance or value. ■ **insignificance** noun **insignificantly** adverb.

insincere adjective saying or doing things that you do not mean. ■ **insincerely** adverb **insincerity** noun.

insinuate verb (**insinuates, insinuating, insinuated**) **1** suggest or hint at something bad in an indirect way. **2** (**insinuate yourself into**) move yourself gradually into a favourable position.

insinuation noun an unpleasant hint or suggestion.

insipid adjective **1** lacking flavour. **2** lacking liveliness or interest.

insist verb **1** demand forcefully that something is done. **2** firmly state that something is the case, without letting anyone disagree. **3** (**insist on**) persist in doing something.

insistent adjective **1** insisting that someone does something or that something is the case. **2** continuing for a long time and demanding attention. ■ **insistence** noun **insistently** adverb.

 -ent, not *-ant*: insistent.

in situ /in sit-yoo/ adverb & adjective in the natural or original place.

insole noun the inner sole of a boot or shoe.

insolent adjective rude and disrespectful. ■ **insolence** noun **insolently** adverb.

insoluble adjective 1 impossible to solve. 2 (of a substance) incapable of being dissolved.

insolvent adjective not having enough money to pay your debts. ■ **insolvency** noun.

insomnia noun inability to sleep. ■ **insomniac** noun & adjective.

insomuch adverb (insomuch that or as) to the extent that.

insouciant /in-**soo**-si-uhnt/ adjective carefree and unconcerned. ■ **insouciance** noun.

inspect verb 1 look at something closely. 2 make an official visit to a school, factory, etc. to check on standards. ■ **inspection** noun.

inspector noun 1 an official who makes sure that regulations are obeyed. 2 a police officer ranking below a chief inspector.

inspiration noun 1 the process of being inspired. 2 a person or thing that inspires. 3 a sudden clever idea. ■ **inspirational** adjective.

inspire verb (inspires, inspiring, inspired) 1 fill someone with the urge or ability to do something. 2 create a feeling in a person. 3 give rise to.

inspired adjective showing or characterized by inspiration.

instability noun (plural instabilities) lack of stability.

install verb (installs, installing, installed) 1 place or fix equipment in position ready for use. 2 establish someone in a new place or role.

> ✓ **install** is spelled with two *l*'s, while **instalment** is spelled with only one.

installation noun 1 the installing of something. 2 a large piece of equipment installed for use. 3 a military or industrial establishment. 4 a large piece of art constructed within a gallery.

instalment (US spelling **installment**) noun 1 each of several payments made over a period of time. 2 each of several parts of something published or broadcast at intervals.

instance noun a particular example or occurrence of something. verb (instances, instancing, instanced) mention something as an example. □ **for instance** as an example.

instant adjective 1 happening immediately. 2 (of food) processed so that it can be prepared very quickly. noun 1 a precise moment of time. 2 a very short time. ■ **instantly** adverb.

instantaneous adjective happening or done immediately or at the same time. ■ **instantaneously** adverb.

instead adverb 1 as an alternative. 2 (instead of) in place of.

instep noun the part of a person's foot between the ball and the ankle.

instigate verb (instigates, instigating, instigated) make something happen or come about. ■ **instigation** noun.

instil or **instill** verb (instils, instilling, instilled) gradually but firmly establish an idea or attitude in someone's mind.

instinct noun 1 an inborn tendency to behave in a certain way. 2 a natural ability or skill. ■ **instinctual** adjective.

instinctive adjective based on instinct rather than thought or training. ■ **instinctively** adverb.

institute noun an organization for the promotion of science, education, or a profession. verb (institutes, instituting, instituted) set up or establish.

institution noun 1 an important organization or public body. 2 an organization providing residential care for people with special needs. 3 an established law or custom. ■ **institutional** adjective.

institutionalize or **institutionalise** verb (institutionalizes, institutionalizing, institutionalized) 1 establish something as a feature of an organization or culture. 2 place someone in a residential institution. **3 (become institutionalized)** lose your individuality as a result of staying for a long time in a residential institution.

instruct verb **1** direct or command. **2** teach. **3** inform someone of a fact or situation.

instruction noun **1** a direction or order. **2** teaching or education. ■ **instructional** adjective.

instructive adjective useful and informative.

instructor noun a teacher.

instrument noun **1** a tool or implement for precise work. **2** a measuring device. **3** (also **musical instrument**) a device for producing musical sounds.

instrumental adjective **1** important in making something happen. **2** (of music) performed on instruments. noun a piece of music performed by instruments, with no vocals.

instrumentalist noun a player of a musical instrument.

instrumentation noun **1** the instruments used in a piece of music. **2** the arrangement of a piece of music for particular instruments.

insubordinate adjective disobedient. ■ **insubordination** noun.

insubstantial adjective lacking strength and solidity.

insufferable adjective **1** intolerable. **2** unbearably arrogant or conceited. ■ **insufferably** adverb.

insufficient adjective not enough. ■ **insufficiency** noun **insufficiently** adverb.

insular adjective **1** narrow-minded through being isolated from outside influences. **2** relating to an island. ■ **insularity** noun.

insulate verb (**insulates, insulating, insulated**) **1** place material between one thing and another to prevent loss of heat or intrusion of sound. **2** cover something with non-conducting material to prevent the passage of electricity. **3** protect from something unpleasant. ■ **insulator** noun.

insulation noun **1** the insulating of something. **2** material used to insulate something.

insulin noun a hormone which regulates glucose levels in the blood.

insult verb /in-sult/ say or do hurtful or disrespectful things to someone. noun /in-sult/ an insulting remark or action.

insuperable adjective impossible to overcome.

insupportable adjective **1** unable to be supported or justified. **2** intolerable.

insurance noun **1** the action of insuring. **2** the business of providing insurance. **3** money paid to insure someone or something. **4** a thing that provides protection in case anything bad happens.

insure verb (**insures, insuring, insured**) **1** pay money in order to receive financial compensation if something is lost or damaged or someone is hurt or killed. **2** (**insure against**) provide protection in case anything bad happens. **3** = **ENSURE**.

insurgent adjective fighting against a system or authority. noun a rebel or revolutionary. ■ **insurgency** noun.

insurmountable adjective too great to be overcome.

insurrection noun a violent uprising against authority.

intact adjective not damaged.

intake noun **1** an amount or quantity of something that is taken in. **2** a set of people entering a school or college at a particular time.

intangible adjective **1** not solid or real. **2** vague and abstract. noun an intangible thing. ■ **intangibly** adverb.

integer /in-ti-jer/ noun a whole number.

integral /in-ti-gruhl, in-teg-ruhl/ adjective **1** necessary to make a whole complete; fundamental. **2** included as part of a whole.

integrate verb (**integrates, integrating, integrated**) **1** combine with something to form a whole. **2** make

---

inter-, intra-, intro-

The prefixes **inter-**, **intra-**, and **intro-** can easily be confused.

inter- means:

- between or among, e.g. *interbreed*
- done or functioning in both directions, reciprocal, as in *interactive*.

intra- means 'on the inside, within', as in *intravenous*. So the **Internet** is an international computer network, while an **Intranet** is a network used only within an organization.

intro- means 'into or inwards', as in *introvert*, literally a person that is 'turned inwards'.

---

someone accepted within a social group. ■ **integration** noun.

integrity noun **1** the quality of being honest, fair, and good. **2** the state of being whole or unified. **3** soundness of construction.

intellect noun the power of using your mind to reason and understand.

intellectual adjective **1** relating or appealing to the intellect. **2** having a highly developed intellect. noun a person with a highly developed intellect. ■ **intellectually** adverb.

intellectualize or **intellectualise** verb (**intellectualizes**, **intellectualizing**, **intellectualized**) talk or write in an intellectual way.

intelligence noun **1** the ability to gain and apply knowledge and skills. **2** the secret gathering of information about an enemy or opponent. **3** information of this sort. □ **intelligence quotient** a number representing a person's reasoning ability, 100 being average.

intelligent adjective good at learning, understanding, and thinking. ■ **intelligently** adverb.

intelligentsia /in-tel-li-**jent**-si-uh/ noun intellectuals or highly educated people.

intelligible adjective able to be understood. ■ **intelligibly** adverb.

intemperate adjective lacking self-control. ■ **intemperance** noun.

intend verb **1** have something as your aim or plan. **2** plan that something should be, do, or mean something. **3** (**intend for** or **to do**) design or plan something for a particular purpose.

intended adjective planned or meant. noun informal the person you are engaged to be married to.

intense adjective (**intenser**, **intensest**) **1** of extreme force, degree, or strength. **2** extremely earnest or serious. ■ **intensely** adverb **intensity** noun (plural **intensities**).

intensify verb (**intensifies**, **intensifying**, **intensified**) make or become more intense.

intensive adjective **1** very thorough or vigorous. **2** (of agriculture) aiming to produce the highest possible yields. □ **intensive care** special medical treatment given to a dangerously ill patient. ■ **intensively** adverb.

intent noun intention or purpose. adjective **1** (**intent on**) determined to do. **2** (**intent on**) attentively occupied with. **3** showing earnest and eager attention. □ **to all intents and purposes** in all important respects. ■ **intently** adverb.

intention noun **1** an aim or plan. **2** the fact of intending something. **3** (**intentions**) a man's plans with regard to getting married.

intentional adjective deliberate. ■ **intentionally** adverb.

inter /in-**ter**/ verb (**inters**, **interring**, **interred**) place a dead body in a grave or tomb.

interact verb (of two people or things) do things which have an effect on each other. ■ **interaction** noun.

interactive adjective **1** influencing each other. **2** (of a computer or other electronic device) allowing a two-way flow of information between it and a user.

interbreed verb (interbreeds, interbreeding, interbred) breed with an animal of a different species.

intercede verb intervene on behalf of someone else.

intercept verb stop someone or something and prevent them from continuing to a destination. ■ **interceptor** noun **interception** noun.

intercession noun **1** the action of interceding. **2** the saying of a prayer on behalf of another person.

interchange verb /in-ter-**chaynj**/ (interchanges, interchanging, interchanged) **1** (of two people) exchange things with each other. **2** put each of two things in the place of the other. noun /**in**-ter-chaynj/ **1** the action of interchanging. **2** an exchange of words. **3** a road junction built on several levels. ■ **interchangeable** adjective **interchangeably** adverb.

intercity adjective existing or travelling between cities.

intercom noun a system of communication by telephone or radio inside a building or group of buildings.

interconnect verb (of two things) connect with each other.

intercontinental adjective relating to or travelling between continents.

intercourse noun **1** communication or dealings between people. **2** sexual intercourse.

intercut verb (intercuts, intercutting, intercut) alternate scenes with contrasting scenes in a film.

interdependent adjective (of two or more people or things) dependent on each other.

interest noun **1** the state of wanting to know about something or someone. **2** the quality of making someone curious or holding their attention. **3** a subject about which you are concerned or enthusiastic. **4** money that is paid for the use of money lent. **5** a person's advantage or benefit. **6** a share, right, or stake in property or a financial undertaking. verb **1** make someone curious or attentive. **2** (interest in) persuade someone to do or buy something. **3** (interested) not impartial. ■ **interesting** adjective **interestingly** adverb.

interface noun **1** a point where two things meet and interact. **2** a device or program enabling a user to communicate with a computer, or for connecting two items of hardware or software. verb (interfaces, interfacing, interfaced) (interface with) **1** interact with. **2** connect by an interface.

interfere verb (interferes, interfering, interfered) **1** (interfere with) prevent something from continuing or being carried out properly. **2** (interfere with) handle or adjust something without permission. **3** become involved in something without being asked. **4** (interfere with) Brit. sexually molest.

interference noun **1** the action of interfering. **2** disturbance to radio signals caused by unwanted signals from other sources.

interferon /in-ter-**feer**-on/ noun a protein released by animal cells which prevents a virus from reproducing itself.

intergalactic adjective relating to or situated between galaxies.

interim noun (the interim) the time between two events. adjective lasting for a short time, until a replacement is found.

interior adjective **1** situated within or inside; inner. **2** remote from the coast or frontier; inland. **3** relating to a country's internal affairs. **4** existing or occurring in the mind or soul. noun **1** the interior part. **2** the internal affairs of a country.

interject verb say something suddenly as an interruption. ■ **interjection** noun.

interlace verb (interlaces, interlacing, interlaced) **1** interweave. **2** (interlace with) mingle something with.

interleave verb **1** insert between the pages of a book. **2** place between the layers of something else.

interlock verb (of two parts, fibres, etc.) engage with each other by overlapping or fitting together.

interlocutor /in-ter-**lok**-yuu-ter/ noun formal a person who takes part in a conversation.

interloper noun a person who intrudes on someone else's affairs.

interlude noun **1** a period of time that contrasts with what goes before and after. **2** a pause between the acts of a play. **3** a piece of music played between other pieces.

intermarry verb (intermarries, intermarrying, intermarried) (of people of different races or religions) marry each other. ■ **intermarriage** noun.

intermediary noun (plural intermediaries) a person who tries to settle a dispute between others.

intermediate adjective **1** coming between two things in time, place, character, etc. **2** having more than basic knowledge or skills but not yet advanced. noun an intermediate person or thing.

interment /in-**ter**-muhnt/ noun the burial of a dead body.

intermezzo /in-ter-**met**-soh/ noun (plural intermezzi /in-ter-**met**-si/ or intermezzos) a short piece of music connecting parts of an opera or other work.

interminable adjective lasting a very long time and therefore boring. ■ **interminably** adverb.

intermingle verb (intermingles, intermingling, intermingled) mix or mingle together.

intermission noun **1** a pause or break. **2** an interval between parts of a play or film.

intermittent adjective stopping and starting at irregular intervals. ■ **intermittently** adverb.

intern noun /**in**-tern/ N. Amer. **1** a recent medical graduate receiving supervised training in a hospital. **2** a student or trainee doing a job to gain work experience. verb /in-**tern**/ confine someone as a prisoner. ■ **internment** noun.

internal adjective **1** of or situated on the inside. **2** inside the body. **3** relating to affairs and activities within a country. **4** existing or used within an organization. **5** within the mind. □ **internal-combustion engine** an engine in which power is generated by the expansion of hot gases from the burning of fuel with air inside the engine. ■ **internally** adverb.

internalize or **internalise** verb (internalizes, internalizing, internalized) make a feeling or belief part of the way you think.

international adjective **1** existing or occurring between nations. **2** agreed on or used by all or many nations. noun Brit. a game or contest between teams representing different countries. ■ **internationally** adverb.

internationalism noun belief in the value of cooperation between nations.

internationalize or **internationalise** verb (internationalizes, internationalizing, internationalized) make something international.

internecine /in-ter-**nee**-syn/ adjective (of fighting) taking place between members of the same country or group.

Internet noun an international information network linking computers.

interpersonal adjective relating to relationships or communication between people.

interplanetary adjective situated or travelling between planets.

interplay noun the way in which things interact.

interpolate /in-**ter**-puh-layt/ verb (interpolates, interpolating, interpolated) **1** add a remark to a conversation. **2** add something to a piece of writing. ■ **interpolation** noun.

interpose verb (interposes, interposing, interposed) **1** place something between two other things. **2** intervene between parties. **3** say something as an interruption.

interpret verb (interprets, interpreting, interpreted) **1** explain the meaning of. **2** translate aloud the words of a person speaking a different language. **3** understand something as having a particular meaning. ■ interpretation noun interpreter noun.

interracial adjective existing between or involving different races.

interregnum /in-ter-**reg**-nuhm/ noun (plural interregnums or interregna /in-ter-**reg**-nuh/) a period between regimes when normal government is suspended.

interrelate verb (interrelates, interrelating, interrelated) (of two people or things) relate or connect to one other. ■ interrelation noun.

interrogate verb (interrogates, interrogating, interrogated) ask someone questions in a thorough or aggressive manner. ■ interrogation noun interrogator noun.

interrogative /in-ter-**rog**-uh-tiv/ adjective in the form of or used in a question. noun a word used in questions, e.g. *how* or *what*.

interrupt verb **1** stop the continuous progress of. **2** stop a person who is speaking by saying or doing something. **3** break the continuity of a line, surface, or view. ■ interruption noun.

 two *r*s in the middle: inter**r**upt.

intersect verb **1** divide something by passing or lying across it. **2** (of lines, roads, etc.) cross or cut each other.

intersection noun **1** a point or line where lines or surfaces intersect. **2** a point where roads intersect.

intersperse verb (intersperses, interspersing, interspersed) place or scatter among or between other things.

interstate adjective existing or carried on between states.

interstellar adjective occurring or situated between stars.

interstice /in-**ter**-stiss/ noun a small crack or space in something.

intertwine verb (intertwines, intertwining, intertwined) twist or twine together.

interval noun **1** a period of time between two events. **2** a pause or break. **3** Brit. a pause between parts of a play, concert, etc. **4** the difference in pitch between two sounds.

intervene verb (intervenes, intervening, intervened) **1** become involved in a situation in order to improve or control it. **2** occur in the time or space between other things. ■ intervention noun.

interview noun **1** a meeting at which a journalist asks someone questions about their work or their opinions. **2** a spoken examination of an applicant for a job or college place. **3** a session of formal questioning of someone by the police. verb ask someone questions in an interview. ■ interviewee noun interviewer noun.

interweave verb (interweaves, interweaving, interwove; past participle interwoven) weave two or more fibres or strands together.

intestate /in-**tess**-tayt/ adjective (of someone who has died) not having made a will.

intestine or **intestines** noun the long tube leading from the stomach to the anus. ■ intestinal adjective.

intimacy noun (plural intimacies) **1** close familiarity or friendship. **2** an intimate act or remark.

intimate[1] /**in**-ti-muht/ adjective **1** familiar. **2** private and personal. **3** (of two people) having a sexual relationship. **4** involving a very close connection. **5** (of knowledge) detailed. **6** having a friendly, informal atmosphere. noun a very close friend. ■ intimately adverb.

intimate[2] /**in**-ti-mayt/ verb (intimates, intimating, intimated) say or suggest that something is the case. ■ intimation noun.

intimidate verb (intimidates, intimidating, intimidated) frighten or overawe someone, especially to force them to do something. ∎ **intimidation** noun.

into preposition **1** expressing motion or direction to a point on or within. **2** expressing a change of state or the result of an action. **3** indicating the direction towards which something is turned. **4** indicating an object of interest. **5** expressing division.

intolerable adjective unable to be endured. ∎ **intolerably** adverb.

intolerant adjective not willing to accept ideas or ways of behaving that are different to your own. ∎ **intolerance** noun.

intonation noun the rise and fall of the voice in speaking.

intone verb (intones, intoning, intoned) say or recite something with your voice hardly rising or falling.

intoxicate verb (intoxicates, intoxicating, intoxicated) **1** (of alcoholic drink or a drug) cause someone to lose control of themselves. **2** (be intoxicated) be excited or exhilarated by something. ∎ **intoxication** noun.

intractable adjective **1** hard to solve or deal with. **2** stubborn.

intranet noun a computer network for use within an organization.

intransigent /in-**tran**-si-juhnt/ adjective refusing to change your views or behaviour. ∎ **intransigence** noun.

intransitive adjective (of a verb) not taking a direct object, e.g. *look* in *look at the sky*.

intrauterine /in-truh-**yoo**-tuh-ryn/ adjective within the womb.

intravenous /in-truh-**vee**-nuhss/ adjective within or into a vein.

intrepid adjective not held back by fear. ∎ **intrepidly** adverb.

intricacy noun (plural intricacies) **1** the quality of being intricate. **2** (intricacies) details.

intricate adjective very complicated or detailed. ∎ **intricately** adverb.

intrigue verb /in-**treeg**/ (intrigues, intriguing, intrigued) **1** arouse great curiosity in someone. **2** plot something illegal or harmful. noun /in-treeg/ **1** the plotting of something illegal or harmful. **2** a secret plan or relationship. ∎ **intriguing** adjective **intriguingly** adverb.

intrinsic adjective part of the real and fundamental nature of something. ∎ **intrinsically** adverb.

introduce verb (introduces, introducing, introduced) **1** bring something into use or operation for the first time. **2** present someone by name. **3** (introduce to) bring a subject to someone's attention for the first time. **4** insert or bring something into. **5** occur at the start of. **6** provide an opening announcement for.

introduction noun **1** the action of introducing or being introduced. **2** a thing which introduces another, such as a section at the beginning of a book. **3** a thing newly brought in. **4** a book or course intended to introduce a newcomer to a subject of study. **5** a person's first experience of a subject or activity.

introductory adjective serving as an introduction; basic.

introspection noun concentration on your own thoughts or feelings. ∎ **introspective** adjective.

introvert noun a shy, quiet person who is focused on their own thoughts and feelings. adjective (also **introverted**) of or characteristic of an introvert.

intrude verb (intrudes, intruding, intruded) come into a place or situation where you are unwelcome or uninvited.

intruder noun **1** a person who intrudes. **2** a person who goes into a building or an area illegally.

intrusion noun **1** the action of intruding. **2** a person or thing that has intruded.

intrusive adjective having a disturbing and unwelcome effect.

intuit /in-**tyoo**-it/ verb understand or work something out by intuition.

intuition noun the ability to understand or know something without conscious reasoning.

intuitive adjective able to understand or know something without conscious reasoning. ∎ **intuitively** adverb.

Inuit /in-yuu-it, in-uu-it/ **noun** (plural **Inuit** or **Inuits**) a member of a people of northern Canada and parts of Greenland and Alaska; an Eskimo.

> ℹ️ **Inuit** is the official term in Canada, and many of the peoples traditionally called **Eskimos** prefer it.

inundate verb (**inundates, inundating, inundated**) **1** flood a place. **2** overwhelm someone with things to be dealt with. ∎ **inundation** noun.

inure /i-nyoor/ **verb** (**inures, inuring, inured**) (usu. **be inured to**) accustom someone to something unpleasant.

invade verb (**invades, invading, invaded**) **1** enter a country so as to conquer or occupy it. **2** enter a place in large numbers. **3** (of a parasite or disease) spread into. **4** intrude on.

invalid[1] /in-vuh-lid/ **noun** a person suffering from illness or injury. **verb** (**invalids, invaliding, invalided**) (**be invalided**) be removed from active military service because of injury or illness.

invalid[2] /in-val-id/ **adjective 1** not recognized in law. **2** not true because based on incorrect information or unsound reasoning.

invalidate verb (**invalidates, invalidating, invalidated**) make something invalid.

invalidity noun 1 Brit. the condition of being an invalid. **2** the fact of being invalid.

invaluable adjective extremely useful.

invariable adjective 1 never changing. **2** Mathematics (of a quantity) constant.

invariably adverb always.

invasion noun 1 an act of invading a country. **2** the arrival of a large number of unwelcome people or things.

invasive adjective 1 tending to invade or intrude. **2** (of medical procedures) involving the introduction of instruments or other objects into the body.

invective noun strongly abusive or critical language.

inveigh /in-vay/ **verb** (**inveigh against**) speak or write about someone or something with great hostility.

inveigle /in-vay-g'l, in-vee-g'l/ **verb** (**inveigles, inveigling, inveigled**) (**inveigle into**) cleverly persuade someone to do something. **2** (**inveigle yourself into**) gain entry into a place or situation by persuasion or trickery.

invent verb 1 create or design a new device or process. **2** make up a false story, name, etc. ∎ **inventor** noun.

invention noun 1 the action of inventing. **2** a thing that has been invented. **3** a false story. **4** creative ability.

inventive adjective having or showing creativity or original thought. ∎ **inventively** adverb.

inventory /in-vuhn-tuh-ri/ **noun** (plural **inventories**) **1** a complete list of items. **2** a quantity of goods in stock.

inverse adjective opposite in position, direction, order, or effect. **noun 1** a thing that is the opposite or reverse of another. **2** Mathematics a reciprocal quantity. ∎ **inversion** noun.

invert verb put something upside down or in the opposite position, order, or arrangement. ◻ **inverted comma** a quotation mark.

invertebrate /in-ver-ti-bruht/ **noun** an animal that has no backbone.

invest verb 1 put money into financial schemes, shares, or property in the hope of making a profit. **2** put time or energy into something in the hope of worthwhile results. **3** (**invest in**) informal buy something expensive. **4** (**invest with**) give something a particular quality. **5** give a rank or office to. ∎ **investor** noun.

investigate verb 1 carry out a systematic inquiry so as to establish the truth of something. **2** carry out research into a subject. ∎ **investigation** noun **investigative** adjective **investigator** noun.

investiture noun **1** the action of formally investing a person with honours or rank. **2** a ceremony at which this takes place.

investment noun **1** the process of investing in something. **2** a thing worth buying because it may be profitable or useful in the future.

inveterate adjective **1** having done a particular thing so often that you are now unlikely to stop doing it. **2** (of a feeling or habit) firmly established.

invidious adjective unfair and likely to arouse resentment or anger in others.

invigilate verb (invigilates, invigilating, invigilated) Brit. supervise candidates during an examination. ■ **invigilation** noun **invigilator** noun.

invigorate verb (invigorates, invigorating, invigorated) give strength or energy to.

invincible adjective too powerful to be defeated or overcome.

inviolable adjective unable to be attacked or dishonoured.

inviolate adjective free from injury or violation.

invisible adjective **1** unable to be seen, either by nature or because concealed. **2** ignored. ■ **invisibility** noun **invisibly** adverb.

invitation noun **1** a request that someone should join you in going somewhere or doing something. **2** the action of inviting. **3** a situation or action that is likely to provoke a particular outcome or response.

invite verb (invites, inviting, invited) **1** ask someone to join you in going somewhere or doing something. **2** ask formally or politely for a response to something. **3** tend to provoke a particular outcome or response. noun informal an invitation.

inviting adjective tempting or attractive. ■ **invitingly** adverb.

in vitro /in **vee**-troh/ adjective & adverb taking place in a test tube, culture dish, or elsewhere outside a living animal or plant.

invocation noun **1** the action of invoking. **2** an appeal to a god or supernatural being.

invoice noun a list of goods or services provided, with a statement of the payment that is due. verb (invoices, invoicing, invoiced) send an invoice to someone.

invoke verb (invokes, invoking, invoked) **1** appeal to someone or something as an authority or in support of an argument. **2** call on a god or supernatural being. **3** call earnestly for.

involuntary adjective **1** done without conscious control. **2** (especially of muscles or nerves) unable to be consciously controlled. **3** done against someone's will. ■ **involuntarily** adverb.

involve verb (involves, involving, involved) **1** (of a situation or event) include something as a necessary part or result. **2** encourage someone to experience or take part in something. ■ **involvement** noun.

involved adjective **1** connected with someone or something on an emotional or personal level. **2** complicated.

invulnerable adjective impossible to harm or damage.

inwards or **inward** adverb **1** towards the inside. **2** into or towards the mind, spirit, or soul.

iodine /**I**-uh-deen, **I**-uh-dyn/ noun **1** a black, non-metallic chemical element. **2** a solution of iodine in alcohol used as an antiseptic.

ion noun an atom or molecule with a net electric charge through loss or gain of electrons. ■ **ionic** adjective.

ionize or **ionise** verb convert an atom, molecule, or substance into an ion or ions. ■ **ionization** noun.

ionizer noun a device which produces ions, used to improve the quality of the air in a room.

ionosphere /**I**-on-uh-sfeer/ noun the layer of the atmosphere above the mesosphere.

iota /**I**-oh-tuh/ noun **1** the ninth letter of the Greek alphabet (I, ι). **2** an extremely small amount.

IOU noun a signed document acknowledging a debt.

ipso facto /ip-soh **fak**-toh/ adverb by that very fact or act.

IQ abbreviation intelligence quotient.

IRA abbreviation Irish Republican Army.

irascible /i-**rass**-i-b'l/ adjective hot-tempered; irritable.

irate adjective extremely angry.

ire /rhymes with fire/ noun literary anger.

iridescent adjective showing bright colours that seem to change when seen from different angles. ■ **iridescence** noun.

 just one *r*: iridescent.

iris noun **1** the round coloured part of the eye, with the pupil in the centre. **2** a plant with sword-shaped leaves and purple, yellow, or white flowers.

Irish noun (also **Irish Gaelic**) the language of Ireland. adjective relating to Ireland or Irish.

irk verb irritate; annoy.

irksome adjective irritating; annoying.

iron noun **1** a strong magnetic silvery-grey metal. **2** a tool or implement made of iron. **3** a hand-held implement with a heated steel base, used to smooth clothes and linen. **4** a golf club used for hitting the ball at a high angle. **5** (**irons**) fetters or handcuffs. verb **1** smooth clothes with an iron. **2** (**iron out**) settle a difficulty or problem. □ **Iron Age** an ancient period when weapons and tools were made of iron. **Iron Curtain** an imaginary barrier separating the former Soviet bloc and the West before communism in eastern Europe ended.

ironic /I-**ron**-ik/ adjective **1** using or characterized by irony. **2** happening in the opposite way to what is expected. ■ **ironically** adverb.

ironmonger noun Brit. a person who sells tools and other hardware. ■ **ironmongery** noun.

ironworks noun a place where iron is

smelted or iron goods are made.

irony noun (plural **ironies**) **1** the use of words that say the opposite of what you really mean in order to make a point. **2** aspects of a situation that are opposite to what are expected.

> ⓘ **irony** and **sarcasm** don't mean exactly the same thing. **Irony** is generally gentle or humorous, whereas **sarcasm** tends to be used to mock someone or convey contempt.

irradiate verb (**irradiates**, **irradiating**, **irradiated**) **1** expose to radiation. **2** shine light on. ■ **irradiation** noun.

irrational adjective not logical or reasonable. ■ **irrationality** noun **irrationally** adverb.

irreconcilable adjective **1** incompatible. **2** mutually and relentlessly hostile.

irrecoverable adjective not able to be recovered or remedied.

irredeemable adjective not able to be saved, improved, or corrected. ■ **irredeemably** adverb.

irreducible adjective not able to be reduced or simplified.

irrefutable adjective impossible to deny or disprove.

irregular adjective **1** not regular in shape, arrangement, or occurrence. **2** against a rule, standard, or convention. **3** not belonging to regular army units. **4** Grammar (of a word) having inflections that do not conform to the usual rules. ■ **irregularity** noun (plural **irregularities**).

irrelevant adjective not relevant. ■ **irrelevance** noun **irrelevantly** adverb.

> ✓ -ant, not -ent: irrelevant.

irreligious adjective indifferent or hostile to religion.

irremediable /ir-ri-**mee**-di-uh-b'l/ adjective impossible to remedy.

irreparable /ir-**rep**-uh-ruh-b'l/ adjective impossible to put right or repair. ■ **irreparably** adverb.

irreplaceable adjective impossible to replace if lost or damaged.

irrepressible adjective not able to be restrained.

irreproachable adjective blameless and impossible to criticize.

irresistible adjective too tempting or powerful to be resisted. ■ **irresistibly** adverb.

 -ible, not *-able*: irresis*tible*.

irresolute adjective uncertain.

irrespective adjective (**irrespective of**) regardless of.

irresponsible adjective not showing a proper sense of responsibility. ■ **responsibly** adverb.

irretrievable adjective not able to be brought back or made right. ■ **irretrievably** adverb.

irreverent adjective disrespectful. ■ **irreverence** noun **irreverently** adverb.

irreversible adjective impossible to be reversed or altered. ■ **irreversibly** adverb.

irrevocable /ir-**rev**-uh-kuh-b'l/ adjective not able to be changed or reversed. ■ **irrevocably** adverb.

irrigate verb (**irrigates, irrigating, irrigated**) supply water to land or crops through channels. ■ **irrigation** noun.

irritable adjective **1** easily annoyed or angered. **2** Medicine unusually sensitive. ■ **irritability** noun **irritably** adverb.

irritant noun **1** a substance that irritates the skin or a part of the body. **2** a source of continual annoyance.

irritate verb (**irritates, irritating, irritated**) **1** make someone annoyed or angry. **2** cause soreness, itching, or inflammation. ■ **irritating** adjective **irritatingly** adverb **irritation** noun.

is 3rd person singular present of BE.

ISA abbreviation individual savings account.

Islam noun **1** the religion of the Muslims, revealed through Muhammad as the Prophet of Allah. **2** the Muslim world. ■ **Islamic** adjective.

island noun **1** a piece of land surrounded by water. **2** a thing that is isolated, detached, or surrounded.

■ **islander** noun.

isle noun literary an island.

islet /**I**-lit/ noun a small island.

isn't short form is not.

isobar /**I**-soh-bar/ noun a line on a map connecting points having the same atmospheric pressure.

isolate verb (**isolates, isolating, isolated**) **1** place something or someone apart from others and alone. **2** extract a substance in a pure form. ■ **isolation** noun.

isolated adjective **1** (of a place) remote. **2** (of a person) cut off from others; lonely. **3** single; exceptional.

isolationism noun a policy of remaining apart from the political affairs of other countries.

isomer /**I**-suh-mer/ noun Chemistry each of two or more compounds with the same formula but a different arrangement of atoms.

isometric adjective having equal dimensions.

isosceles /**I**-**soss**-i-leez/ adjective (of a triangle) having two sides of equal length.

isotope /**I**-suh-tohp/ noun each of two or more forms of the same element that contain equal numbers of protons but different numbers of neutrons in their nuclei.

Israeli /iz-**ray**-li/ noun (plural **Israelis**) a person from Israel. **adjective** relating to the modern country of Israel.

Israelite /iz-ruh-lyt/ noun a member of the people of ancient Israel.

issue noun **1** an important topic to be resolved. **2** the action of supplying something. **3** each of a regular series of publications. **verb** (**issues, issuing, issued**) **1** supply or give out. **2** formally send out or make known. **3** (**issue from**) come, go, or flow out from. □ **take issue with** challenge someone.

isthmus /**isth**-muhss, **iss**-muhss/ noun (plural **isthmuses**) a narrow strip of land with sea on either side, linking two larger areas of land.

IT abbreviation information technology.

WORD FORMATION

-ize, -ise

-ize or **-ise** is used to form verbs that mean:
- make or become, as in *privatize*
- cause to resemble, e.g. *Americanize*.

What is the difference between **-ize** or **-ise**? In most cases either one is correct. Despite what some people think, **-ize** is not American, although **-ise** is more common in British English.

-ise is obligatory in certain words, often words that come from French or that are based on English nouns with **-s-** in the stem. Verbs that can't end with **-ize** include:

advertise	*compromise*	*revise*
advise	*despise*	*supervise*
chastise	*devise*	*surprise*
circumcise	*exercise*	*televise*
comprise	*improvise*	

it pronoun 1 used to refer to a thing previously mentioned or easily identified. **2** referring to an animal or child of unspecified sex. **3** used in the normal subject position in statements about time, distance, or weather. **4** the situation or circumstances.

Italian noun 1 a person from Italy. **2** the language of Italy. **adjective** relating to Italy or Italian.

italic adjective (of a typeface) sloping to the right, used especially for emphasis and for foreign words. **noun** (also **italics**) an italic typeface or letter. ■ **italicize** (or **italicise**) verb.

itch noun 1 an uncomfortable sensation that makes you want to scratch your skin. **2** informal an impatient desire. **verb 1** experience an itch. **2** informal feel an impatient desire to do something. ■ **itchy** adjective.

it'd short form 1 it had. **2** it would.

item noun an individual article or unit.

itemize or **itemise verb** (itemizes, itemizing, itemized) present a quantity as a list of individual items or parts.

itinerant /I-**tin**-uh-ruhnt/ **adjective** travelling from place to place. **noun** an itinerant person.

itinerary /I-**tin**-uh-ruh-ri/ **noun** (plural itineraries) a planned route or journey.

itinerary, not *-ery*.

it'll short form 1 it shall. **2** it will.

its possessive determiner 1 belonging to or associated with a thing previously mentioned or easily identified. **2** belonging to or associated with a child or animal of unspecified sex.

don't confuse the possessive **its** (as in *turn the camera on its side*) with the form **it's** (short for either **it is** or **it has**, as in *it's my fault* or *it's been a hot day*).

it's short form 1 it is. **2** it has.

itself pronoun 1 used to refer to something previously mentioned as the subject of the clause. **2** used to emphasize a particular thing mentioned.

ITV abbreviation Independent Television.

IUD abbreviation intrauterine device.

I've short form I have.

IVF abbreviation in vitro fertilization.

ivory noun (plural **ivories**) **1** the hard creamy-white substance which elephants' tusks are made of. **2** the creamy-white colour of ivory. **3** (the ivories) informal the keys of a piano. □ **ivory tower** a situation in which someone leads a privileged life and does not have to face normal difficulties.

ivy noun an evergreen climbing plant.

Jj

J or **j** noun (plural **Js** or **J's**) the tenth letter of the alphabet. **abbreviation** joules.

jab verb (**jabs, jabbing, jabbed**) poke someone with something sharp or pointed. noun **1** a quick, sharp poke or blow. **2** Brit. informal a vaccination.

jabber verb (**jabbers, jabbering, jabbered**) talk quickly and excitedly but with little sense.

jack noun **1** a device for lifting a motor vehicle off the ground so that a wheel can be changed or the underside inspected. **2** a playing card ranking next below a queen. **3** a connection between two pieces of electrical equipment. **4** (in bowls) a small white ball at which players aim the bowls. verb (**jack up**) **1** raise something with a jack. **2** informal increase something by a large amount. □ **jack-in-the-box** a toy consisting of a box containing a figure on a spring, which pops up when the lid is opened.

jackal noun a wild dog that often hunts or scavenges in packs.

jackass noun **1** a stupid person. **2** a male ass or donkey.

jackdaw noun a small grey-headed crow.

jacket noun **1** an outer garment extending to the waist or hips, with sleeves. **2** a covering placed around something for protection or insulation. **3** the skin of a potato. □ **jacket potato** Brit. a potato that is baked and served with the skin on.

jackknife noun (plural **jackknives**) **1** a large knife with a folding blade. **2** a dive in which the body is bent at the waist and then straightened. verb (**jackknifes, jackknifing, jackknifed**) **1** move your body into a bent or doubled-up position. **2** (of an articulated vehicle) bend into a V-shape in an uncontrolled skidding movement.

jackpot noun a large cash prize in a game or lottery.

Jacobean /jak-uh-bee-uhn/ adjective having to do with the reign of James I of England (1603–1625). noun a person who lived in the Jacobean period.

Jacobite /jak-uh-byt/ noun a supporter of the deposed James II and his descendants in their claim to the British throne.

jacquard /ja-kard/ noun **1** a loom used for weaving patterned and brocaded fabrics. **2** a fabric made on a jacquard loom.

jacuzzi /juh-koo-zi/ noun (plural **jacuzzis**) trademark a large, wide bath having jets of water to massage the body.

jade noun a hard bluish-green precious stone.

jaded adjective tired out or lacking enthusiasm after having had too much of something.

jagged /jag-gid/ adjective with rough, sharp points or edges sticking out.

jaguar /jag-yuu-er/ noun a large cat with a spotted coat, found in Central and South America.

jail or Brit. **gaol** noun a place for holding people who are accused or convicted of a crime. verb put someone in jail. ■ **jailer** (or Brit. **gaoler**) noun.

jalopy /juh-lop-i/ noun (plural **jalopies**) informal an old car.

jam[1] verb (**jams, jamming, jammed**) **1** squeeze or pack tightly into a space. **2** push roughly and forcibly into a position. **3** block something through crowding. **4** make or become unable to function because a part is stuck. **5** (**jam on**) apply a brake or switch forcibly. **6** interrupt a radio transmission by causing interference. **7** informal improvise with other musicians. noun **1** an instance of something being jammed. **2** informal a difficult situation. **3** informal an improvised performance by a group of musicians.

jam² noun chiefly Brit. a spread made from fruit and sugar.

jamb /jam/ noun a side post of a doorway, window, or fireplace.

jamboree noun a lavish or noisy celebration or party.

jammy adjective (**jammier, jammiest**) **1** covered or filled with jam. **2** Brit. informal lucky.

jangle verb (**jangles, jangling, jangled**) **1** make a ringing metallic sound. **2** (of your nerves) be set on edge. noun a ringing metallic sound. ■ **jangly** adjective.

janitor noun a caretaker of a building.

January noun (plural **Januaries**) the first month of the year.

Japanese noun (plural same) **1** a person from Japan. **2** the language of Japan. adjective relating to Japan.

jape noun a practical joke.

jar¹ noun a cylindrical container made of glass or pottery.

jar² verb (**jars, jarring, jarred**) **1** send a painful shock through a part of the body. **2** strike against something with an unpleasant vibration or jolt. **3** have an unpleasant or strange effect. noun an instance of jarring.

jargon noun words or phrases used by a particular group that are difficult for others to understand.

jasmine noun a shrub or climbing plant with fragrant flowers.

jasper noun a reddish-brown variety of quartz.

jaundice /**jawn-diss**/ noun **1** a condition in which the skin takes on a yellow colour. **2** bitterness or

resentment. ■ **jaundiced** adjective.

jaunt noun a short trip or excursion taken for pleasure.

jaunty adjective (**jauntier, jauntiest**) having a lively and self-confident manner. ■ **jauntily** adverb.

javelin noun a long spear thrown in a competitive sport or as a weapon.

jaw noun each of the upper and lower bony structures forming the framework of the mouth and containing the teeth. verb informal talk at length.

jawbone noun the lower jaw, or the lower part of the face.

jay noun a noisy bird of the crow family with boldly patterned plumage.

jaywalk verb chiefly N. Amer. walk in or across a road without regard for approaching traffic. ■ **jaywalker** noun.

jazz noun a type of mainly instrumental music characterized by improvisation. verb (**jazz up**) make something more lively.

jazzy adjective (**jazzier, jazziest**) **1** of or in the style of jazz. **2** bright, colourful, and showy.

jealous adjective **1** envious of someone else's achievements or advantages. **2** resentful of someone who you think is a sexual rival. **3** fiercely protective of your rights or possessions. ■ **jealously** adverb **jealousy** noun.

jeans noun hard-wearing trousers made of denim or other cotton fabric.

jeep noun trademark a sturdy motor vehicle with four-wheel drive.

jeer verb (**jeers, jeering, jeered**) make rude and mocking remarks at someone. noun a rude and mocking remark.

Jehovah /ji-**hoh**-vuh/ noun a form of the Hebrew name of God used in some translations of the Bible.

jejune /ji-**joon**/ adjective **1** naive and simplistic. **2** dull.

jell or **gel** verb (**jells, jelling, jelled**) **1** (of jelly or a similar substance) set or become firmer. **2** take definite form or begin to work well.

jelly noun (plural **jellies**) **1** Brit. a dessert

set with gelatin to form a semi-solid mass. **2** a substance of a similar consistency. **3** a small sweet made with gelatin. ▫**jelly baby** Brit. a jelly sweet in the shape of a baby. ■ **jellied** adjective.

jellyfish noun a sea creature with a soft jelly-like body that has stinging tentacles around the edge.

jemmy noun (plural **jemmies**) a short crowbar. verb (**jemmies, jemmying, jemmied**) informal force something open with a jemmy.

je ne sais quoi /zhuh nuh say kwah/ noun a quality that cannot be easily identified.

jenny noun (plural **jennies**) a female donkey or ass.

jeopardize or **jeopardise** verb (**jeopardizes, jeopardizing, jeopardized**) risk harming or destroying something.

jeopardy noun danger of loss, harm, or failure.

jerboa /jer-boh-uh/ noun a desert rodent with very long hind legs.

jerk noun **1** a quick, sharp, sudden movement. **2** informal, chiefly N. Amer. an annoyingly stupid person. verb move or raise with a jerk.

jerkin noun a sleeveless jacket.

jerky adjective (**jerkier, jerkiest**) characterized by abrupt stops and starts.

jerry-built adjective badly or hastily built.

jerrycan or **jerrican** noun a large flat-sided metal container for liquids.

jersey noun (plural **jerseys**) **1** a knitted garment with long sleeves. **2** a distinctive shirt worn by people who play certain sports. **3** a soft knitted fabric. **4** (**Jersey**) a breed of light brown dairy cattle.

Jerusalem artichoke noun a knobbly root vegetable with white flesh.

jest noun a joke. verb speak or behave in a joking manner.

jester noun a man who entertained people in a medieval court.

Jesuit /jez-yuu-it/ noun a member of the Society of Jesus, a Roman Cath-

olic order. ■ **Jesuitical** adjective.

Jesus or **Jesus Christ** noun the central figure of the Christian religion, considered by Christians to be the son of God.

jet[1] noun **1** a rapid stream of liquid or gas forced out of a small opening. **2** an aircraft powered by jet engines. verb (**jets, jetting, jetted**) **1** spurt out in a jet. **2** travel by jet aircraft. ▫**jet engine** an aircraft engine which gives propulsion by sending out a high-speed jet of gas obtained by burning fuel. **jet lag** extreme tiredness felt after a long flight across different time zones. **the jet set** informal wealthy people who frequently travel abroad for pleasure. **jet ski** trademark a small vehicle which skims across the surface of water.

jet[2] noun **1** a hard black semi-precious mineral. **2** (also **jet black**) a glossy black colour.

jetsam noun unwanted material thrown overboard from a ship and washed ashore.

jettison verb **1** throw or drop something from an aircraft or ship. **2** abandon or discard something.

jetty noun (plural **jetties**) a landing stage or small pier where boats can be moored.

Jew noun a member of the people whose religion is Judaism and who trace their origins to the Hebrew people of ancient Israel. ▫**Jew's harp** a small musical instrument like a U-shaped harp, held between the teeth and struck with a finger.

jewel noun **1** a precious stone. **2** (**jewels**) pieces of jewellery. **3** a highly valued person or thing. ■ **jewelled** (US spelling **jeweled**) adjective.

jeweller (US spelling **jeweler**) noun a person who makes or sells jewellery.

jewellery (US spelling **jewelry**) noun personal ornaments such as necklaces, rings, or bracelets.

Jewish adjective having to do with Jews or Judaism. ■ **Jewishness** noun.

Jewry noun Jews as a group.

Jezebel noun an immoral woman.

jib¹ **noun 1** Sailing a triangular sail in front of the mast. **2** the projecting arm of a crane.

jib² **verb** (jibs, jibbing, jibbed) (usu. jib at) **1** be unwilling to do or accept something. **2** (of a horse) stop and refuse to go on.

jibe or **gibe noun** an insulting remark. **verb** (jibes, jibing, jibed) make jibes.

jiffy or **jiff noun** informal a moment.

jig noun 1 a lively leaping dance. **2** a device that holds something firm and guides the tools working on it. **verb** (jigs, jigging, jigged) **1** dance a jig. **2** move up and down with a quick jerky motion.

jiggle verb (jiggles, jiggling, jiggled) move lightly and quickly from side to side or up and down. **noun** a quick, light shake. ■ **jiggly** adjective.

jigsaw noun 1 a picture printed on cardboard or wood and cut into numerous interlocking shapes that have to be fitted together. **2** a machine saw with a fine blade allowing it to cut curved lines in a sheet of wood, metal, etc.

jihad or **jehad** /ji-**hahd**, ji-**had**/ **noun** a holy war waged by Muslims against unbelievers.

jilt verb abruptly break off a relationship with a lover.

jingle noun 1 a light ringing sound. **2** a short easily remembered slogan, verse, or tune. **verb** (jingles, jingling, jingled) make a jingle. ■ **jingly** adjective.

jingoism noun excessive pride in your country. ■ **jingoistic** adjective.

jink verb change direction suddenly and nimbly. **noun** a sudden quick change of direction.

jinx noun a person or thing that brings bad luck. **verb** bring bad luck to.

jitterbug noun a fast dance performed to swing music, popular in the 1940s.

jitters noun informal a feeling of extreme nervousness. ■ **jittery** adjective.

jive noun a style of lively dance popular in the 1940s and 1950s, performed to swing music or rock and roll. **verb** (jives, jiving, jived) dance the jive.

job noun 1 a paid position of regular employment. **2** a task. **3** informal a crime. **4** informal a procedure to improve the appearance of something. **verb** (jobs, jobbing, jobbed) do casual or occasional work. □ **job lot** a batch of articles sold or bought at one time.

job-share (of two part-time employees) share a single full-time job. ■ **jobless** adjective.

jobcentre noun (in the UK) a government office which gives out information about available jobs to unemployed people.

jockey noun (plural jockeys) a professional rider in horse races. **verb** (jockeys, jockeying, jockeyed) struggle to gain or achieve something.

jockstrap noun a support or protection for the male genitals.

jocose /juh-**kohss**/ **adjective** formal playful or humorous.

jocular /**jok**-yuu-ler/ **adjective** humorous. ■ **jocularity noun jocularly** adverb.

jocund /**jo**-kuhnd/ **adjective** formal cheerful and light-hearted.

jodhpurs /**jod**-perz/ **plural noun** trousers worn for horse riding that are close-fitting below the knee.

jog verb (jogs, jogging, jogged) **1** run at a steady, gentle pace. **2** (of a horse) move at a slow trot. **3** (jog along) continue in a steady, uneventful way. **4** knock or nudge slightly. **5** trigger your memory. **noun 1** a spell of jogging. **2** a gentle running pace. **3** a slight knock or nudge. ■ **jogger** noun.

joggle verb (joggles, joggling, joggled) move with repeated small bobs or jerks.

joie de vivre /zhwah duh **vee**-vruh/ **noun** lively and cheerful enjoyment of life.

join verb 1 connect things together, or become connected. **2** come together to form a whole. **3** become a member or employee of. **4** (join up) become a member of the armed forces. **5** take part in an activity. **6** come into the company of. **noun** a place where two or more things are joined.

joiner noun a person who puts together the wooden parts of a building.

joinery noun **1** the wooden parts of a building. **2** the work of a joiner.

joint noun **1** a point at which parts are joined. **2** a structure in a body which joins two bones. **3** the part of a plant stem from which a leaf or branch grows. **4** Brit. a large piece of meat. **5** informal a particular kind of place: *a burger joint.* **6** informal a cannabis cigarette. **adjective 1** shared, held, or made by two or more people. **2** sharing in an achievement or activity. **verb** cut the body of an animal into joints. ■ **jointed** adjective **jointly** adverb.

joist noun a length of timber or steel supporting part of the structure of a building.

jojoba /huh-**hoh**-buh/ noun an oil extracted from the seeds of a North American shrub.

joke noun **1** a thing that someone says to cause amusement or laughter. **2** a trick played for fun. **3** informal a person or thing that is ridiculously inadequate. **verb** (**jokes**, **joking**, **joked**) make jokes. ■ **jokey** (or **joky**) adjective.

joker noun **1** a person who is fond of joking. **2** informal a foolish or incompetent person. **3** a playing card with the figure of a jester, used as a wild card.

jollification noun time spent having fun.

jollity noun **1** lively and cheerful activity. **2** the quality of being jolly.

jolly adjective (**jollier**, **jolliest**) **1** happy and cheerful. **2** lively and entertaining. **verb** (**jollies**, **jollying**, **jollied**) informal encourage someone in a friendly way. **adverb** Brit. informal very.

jolt verb **1** push or shake abruptly and roughly. **2** shock someone into taking action. **noun 1** an act of jolting. **2** a shock.

josh verb informal tease playfully.

joss stick noun a thin stick of a sweet-smelling substance, burnt as incense.

jostle verb (**jostles**, **jostling**, **jostled**) **1** push or bump against someone roughly. **2** (**jostle for**) struggle for.

jot verb (**jots**, **jotting**, **jotted**) write something quickly. **noun** a very small amount.

jotter noun Brit. a small notebook.

joule /jool/ noun a unit of work or energy.

journal noun **1** a newspaper or magazine dealing with a particular subject. **2** a diary or daily record.

journalese noun informal a style of writing characteristic of journalism.

journalism noun the activity or profession of being a journalist.

journalist noun a person who writes for newspapers or magazines or prepares news to be broadcast. ■ **journalistic** adjective.

journey noun (plural **journeys**) an act of travelling from one place to another. **verb** (**journeys**, **journeying**, **journeyed**) travel.

journeyman noun a worker who is reliable but not outstanding.

joust verb **1** (of medieval knights) fight each other with lances while on horseback. **2** compete for superiority. **noun** a jousting contest.

jovial adjective cheerful and friendly. ■ **joviality** noun **jovially** adverb.

jowl noun the lower part of a person's or animal's cheek. ■ **jowly** adjective.

joy noun **1** great pleasure and happiness. **2** something that brings joy. **3** Brit. informal success or satisfaction. ■ **joyless** adjective.

joyful adjective feeling or causing joy. ■ **joyfully** adverb.

joyous adjective full of happiness and joy. ■ **joyously** adverb.

joyride noun informal **1** a fast ride in a stolen vehicle. **2** a ride for enjoyment. ■ **joyrider** noun **joyriding** noun.

joystick noun informal **1** the rod used for controlling an aircraft. **2** a lever for controlling the movement of an image on a computer screen.

JP abbreviation Justice of the Peace.

jubilant adjective happy and triumphant. ■ **jubilantly** adverb.

jubilation noun a feeling of great happiness and triumph.

jubilee noun a special anniversary.

Judaism /joo-day-i-z'm/ noun **1** the religion of the Jews, based on the Old Testament and the Talmud. **2** Jews as a group. ■ **Judaic** adjective.

Judas noun a person who betrays a friend.

judder verb (**judders**, **juddering**, **juddered**) shake rapidly and forcefully. noun an instance of juddering. ■ **juddery** adjective.

judge noun **1** a public officer who decides cases in a law court. **2** a person who decides the results of a competition. **3** a person who is qualified to give an opinion. verb (**judges**, **judging**, **judged**) **1** form an opinion about something. **2** give a verdict on a case or person in a law court. **3** decide the results of a competition.

judgement or **judgment** noun **1** the ability to make considered decisions or form sensible opinions. **2** an opinion or conclusion. **3** a decision of a law court or judge. □ **Judgement Day** the time of the Last Judgement.

judgemental or **judgmental** adjective **1** having to do with the use of judgement. **2** being too critical of others.

judicature noun **1** the organization and putting into practice of justice. **2** (**the judicature**) judges as a group.

judicial adjective having to do with a law court or judge. ■ **judicially** adverb.

judiciary noun (plural **judiciaries**) (**the judiciary**) judges as a group.

judicious /joo-**di**-shuhss/ adjective having or done with good judgement. ■ **judiciously** adverb.

judo noun a kind of unarmed combat performed as a sport.

jug noun a cylindrical container with a handle and a lip, for holding and pouring liquids. verb (**jugs**, **jugging**, **jugged**) stew a hare or rabbit in a covered container.

juggernaut noun Brit. a large, heavy lorry.

juggle verb (**juggles**, **juggling**, **juggled**) **1** continuously toss and catch a number of objects so as to keep at least one in the air at any time. **2** do several things at the same time. **3** presents facts or figures in a way that makes them seem good. noun an act of juggling. ■ **juggler** noun.

jugular or **jugular vein** noun any of several large veins in the neck, carrying blood from the head.

juice noun **1** the liquid present in fruit and vegetables. **2** a drink made from this liquid. **3** (**juices**) fluid produced by the stomach. **4** (**juices**) liquid coming from food during cooking. **5** informal electrical energy. **6** informal petrol. **7** (**juices**) informal creative abilities. verb (**juices**, **juicing**, **juiced**) extract the juice from.

juicy adjective (**juicier**, **juiciest**) **1** full of juice. **2** informal interestingly scandalous. **3** informal profitable.

ju-jitsu /joo jit-soo/ noun a Japanese system of unarmed combat.

jukebox noun a machine that plays a selected musical recording when a coin is inserted.

julep /**joo**-lep/ noun a sweet drink made from sugar syrup.

July noun (plural **Julys**) the seventh month of the year.

jumble noun **1** an untidy collection of things. **2** Brit. articles collected for a jumble sale. verb (**jumbles**, **jumbling**, **jumbled**) mix things up in a confused way. □ **jumble sale** Brit. a sale of second-hand items.

jumbo informal noun (plural **jumbos**) **1** a very large person or thing. **2** (also **jumbo jet**) a very large airliner. adjective very large.

jump verb **1** push yourself off the ground using the muscles in your legs and feet. **2** move over something by jumping. **3** make a sudden involuntary movement in surprise. **4** (**jump at** or **on**) accept something eagerly. **5** (often **jump on**) informal attack someone suddenly. **6** pass abruptly from one subject or state to another. **7** (**be jumping**) informal (of a place) be very lively. noun **1** an act of jumping. **2** a large or sudden change or increase. **3** an obstacle to be jumped by a horse. □ **jumped-up** informal considering yourself to be more important than you really are. **jump jet** a jet aircraft that can take off and land without a runway. **jump leads** Brit. a pair of cables used to recharge a battery in a motor vehicle by connecting it to the battery of a vehicle whose engine is running. **jump the queue** move ahead of your proper place in a queue. **jump ship** (of a sailor) leave a ship without permission. **jump-start** start a car with jump leads or by a sudden release of the clutch while it is being pushed.

jumper¹ noun **1** Brit. a pullover or sweater. **2** N. Amer. a pinafore dress.

jumper² noun a person or animal that jumps.

jumpsuit noun a one-piece garment incorporating trousers and a sleeved top.

jumpy adjective (**jumpier, jumpiest**) informal **1** anxious and uneasy. **2** stopping and starting abruptly.

junction noun **1** a point where things meet or are joined. **2** a place where roads or railway lines meet.

juncture noun **1** a particular point in time. **2** a place where things join.

June noun the sixth month of the year.

jungle noun **1** an area of land with thick forest and tangled vegetation. **2** a style of dance music with very fast electronic drum tracks.

junior adjective **1** having to do with young or younger people. **2** Brit. having to do with schoolchildren aged 7–11. **3** (after a name) referring to the younger of two with the same name in a family. **4** low or lower in status. noun **1** a person who is a specified number of years younger than someone else: *he's five years her junior.* **2** Brit. a child at a junior school. **3** a person with low status.

juniper noun an evergreen shrub with

sweet-smelling berry-like cones.

junk¹ informal noun useless or worthless articles. verb get rid of something unwanted. □ **junk food** unhealthy food. **junk mail** unwanted advertising material sent to you in the post.

junk² noun a flat-bottomed sailing boat used in China and the East Indies.

junket noun **1** a dish of sweetened curds of milk. **2** informal an extravagant trip or party.

junkie or **junky** noun informal a drug addict.

junta noun a group ruling a country after taking power by force.

jurisdiction noun **1** the official power to make legal decisions. **2** the area over which the legal authority of a court or other institution extends.

jurisprudence noun the study of law.

jurist noun an expert in law.

juror noun a member of a jury.

jury noun (plural **juries**) **1** a group of people who are required to attend a legal case and come to a verdict based on the evidence presented. **2** a group of people judging a competition.

just adjective **1** right and fair. **2** deserved. **3** (of an opinion) well founded. adverb **1** exactly. **2** exactly or nearly at that moment. **3** very recently. **4** barely. **5** only. ■ **justly** adverb.

justice noun **1** just behaviour or treatment. **2** the quality of being fair and reasonable. **3** a judge or magistrate. □ **Justice of the Peace** (in the UK) a non-professional magistrate appointed to hear minor cases.

justifiable adjective able to be shown to be right or reasonable. ■ **justifiably** adverb.

justify verb (**justifies, justifying, justified**) **1** prove something to be right or reasonable. **2** be a good reason for. **3** Printing adjust text so that the lines of type form straight edges at both sides. ■ **justification** noun.

jut verb (**juts, jutting, jutted**) extend out beyond the main body or line of something.

jute noun rough fibre made from the stems of a tropical plant, used for making rope or woven into sacking.

juvenile adjective **1** having to do with young people, birds, or animals. **2** childish. noun **1** a young person, bird, or animal. **2** Law a person below the age at which they have adult status in law (18 in most countries). □ **juvenile delinquent** a young person who regularly commits crimes.

juxtapose verb (**juxtaposes, juxtaposing, juxtaposed**) place two things close together. ■ **juxtaposition** noun.

Kk

K or **k** noun (plural **Ks** or **K's**) the eleventh letter of the alphabet. **abbreviation** informal a thousand.

kaftan or **caftan** noun **1** a man's long tunic, worn in the East. **2** a woman's long, loose dress or top.

kaiser /**ky**-zer/ noun historical the German or Austrian Emperor.

kale noun a type of cabbage with large curly leaves.

kaleidoscope /kuh-**ly**-duh-skohp/ noun **1** a tube containing mirrors and pieces of coloured glass or paper, whose reflections produce changing patterns when the tube is turned. **2** a constantly changing pattern. ■ **kaleidoscopic** adjective.

kamikaze /ka-mi-**kah**-zi/ noun (in the Second World War) a Japanese aircraft loaded with explosives and deliberately crashed on to an enemy target in a suicide mission. adjective potentially causing death or harm to yourself.

kangaroo noun a large Australian animal with a long powerful tail and strong hind legs that enable it to travel by leaping. □ **kangaroo court** a court set up unofficially with the aim of finding someone guilty.

kaolin /**kay**-uh-lin/ noun a fine soft white clay, used for making china and in medicine.

kapok /**kay**-pok/ noun a substance resembling cotton wool which grows around the seeds of a tropical tree, used as padding.

kaput /kuh-**puut**/ adjective informal broken and useless.

karaoke /ka-ri-**oh**-ki/ noun a form of entertainment in which people sing popular songs over pre-recorded backing tracks.

karate /kuh-**rah**-ti/ noun an oriental system of unarmed combat using the hands and feet.

karma noun (in Hinduism and Buddhism) the sum of a person's actions in this and previous lives, seen as affecting their future fate.

karst noun a limestone region with underground streams and many cavities.

kart noun a small unsprung racing-car with the engine at the back.

kasbah or **casbah** noun **1** a North African citadel. **2** the area of old, narrow streets surrounding such a citadel.

kayak /**ky**-ak/ noun a canoe made of a light frame with a watertight covering. verb (**kayaks, kayaking, kayaked**) travel in a kayak.

kazoo noun a simple musical instrument consisting of a pipe that produces a buzzing sound when you hum into it.

kebab noun a dish of pieces of meat, fish, or vegetables roasted or grilled on a skewer or spit.

kedgeree /**kej**-uh-ree/ noun a dish of smoked fish, rice, and hard-boiled eggs.

keel noun a structure running along

the length of the base of a ship. **verb** (**keel over**) **1** (of a boat or ship) turn over on its side. **2** informal fall over.

keelhaul verb (in the past) punish someone by dragging them through the water from one side of a boat to the other.

keen¹ adjective **1** eager and enthusiastic. **2** (of a blade) sharp. **3** mentally sharp. **4** Brit. (of prices) very low. ■ **keenly** adverb **keenness** noun.

keen² verb **1** wail in grief for a dead person. **2** make an eerie wailing sound.

keep verb (**keeps, keeping, kept**) **1** have or retain possession of. **2** retain something for use in the future. **3** store in a regular place. **4** (of food) remain in good condition. **5** continue in a particular situation, position, or activity. **6** honour or fulfil a commitment or undertaking. **7** record a note about something. **8** provide accommodation and food for. **9** (**kept**) supported financially in return for sexual favours. noun **1** food, clothes, and other essentials for living. **2** the strongest or central tower of a castle. □ **keep-fit** regular exercises done to improve fitness. **keep up 1** move at the same time as someone or something else. **2** continue a course of action. **keep up with 1** be aware of current events or developments. **2** continue to be in contact with someone.

keeper noun **1** a person who manages or looks after something or someone. **2** a goalkeeper or wicketkeeper.

keeping noun the action of owning, maintaining, or protecting something. □ **in** (or **out of**) **keeping with** in (or out of) harmony with.

keepsake noun a small item kept in memory of the person who gave it or originally owned it.

keg noun a small barrel.

kelim ⇒ **KILIM**.

kelp noun a very large brown seaweed.

kelvin noun a unit of temperature, equal to one degree Celsius.

ken noun (**your ken**) the range of your knowledge and experience. **verb** (**kens, kenning, kenned** or **kent**) Scottish & N. English know or recognize.

kennel noun **1** a small shelter for a dog. **2** (**kennels**) a place where dogs are looked after or bred.

kept past and past participle of **KEEP**.

keratin /ke-ruh-tin/ noun a protein forming the basis of hair, feathers, hoofs, claws, and horns.

kerb (US spelling **curb**) noun a stone edging to a pavement. □ **kerb-crawling** Brit. driving slowly along the edge of the road in search of a prostitute.

kerbstone noun a long, narrow stone or concrete block, laid end to end with others to form a kerb.

kerchief /ker-chif/ noun **1** a piece of fabric used to cover the head. **2** a handkerchief.

kerfuffle noun Brit. informal a commotion or fuss.

kernel noun **1** the softer part inside the shell of a nut, seed, or fruit stone. **2** the seed and hard husk of a cereal. **3** the central part of something.

 -el, not *-al*: kernel.

kerosene noun a light fuel oil distilled from petroleum; paraffin oil.

kestrel noun a small falcon that hovers with rapidly beating wings.

ketch noun a small sailing boat with two masts.

ketchup noun a spicy sauce made from tomatoes and vinegar.

kettle noun a container with a spout and handle, used for boiling water.

kettledrum noun a large drum shaped like a bowl.

key noun (plural **keys**) **1** a small piece of shaped metal which is inserted into a lock and turned to open or close it. **2** an instrument for turning a screw, peg, or nut. **3** a lever pressed down by the finger in playing an instrument such as the organ, piano, or flute. **4** each of several buttons on a panel for operating a computer or typewriter. **5** a list explaining the symbols used in a map or table. **6** a word or system for solving a code. **7** Music a group of notes making up a scale. **adjective** of central importance. **verb (keys, keying, keyed) 1** enter data using a computer keyboard. **2 (be keyed up)** be nervous, tense, or excited. **3 (key into** or **in with)** be connected or in harmony with.

keyboard noun 1 a panel of keys for use with a computer or typewriter. **2** a set of keys on a musical instrument. **3** an electronic musical instrument with keys arranged as on a piano. **verb** enter data by means of a keyboard. ∎ **keyboarder** noun.

keyhole noun a hole in a lock into which the key is inserted. ▢ **keyhole surgery** surgery carried out through a very small surface cut.

keynote noun 1 a central theme. **2** Music the note on which a key is based. **adjective** (of a speech) setting out the theme of a conference.

keypad noun a small keyboard or set of buttons for operating a portable electronic device or telephone.

keystone noun 1 a central stone at the top of an arch. **2** the central part of a policy or system.

keystroke noun a single depression of a key on a keyboard.

keyword noun 1 a significant word mentioned in an index. **2** a word used in a computer system to indicate the content of a document.

kg abbreviation kilograms.

khaki /**kah**-ki/ **noun** (plural **khakis**) **1** a dull greenish- or yellowish-brown colour. **2** a cotton or wool fabric of this colour.

khan noun a title given to rulers and officials in central Asia, Afghanistan, and certain other Muslim countries.

kHz abbreviation kilohertz.

kibbled adjective (of beans, grain, etc.) coarsely ground or chopped.

kibbutz /kib-**buuts**/ **noun** a farming settlement in Israel in which work is shared between all of its members.

kibosh /**ky**-bosh/ **noun (put the kibosh on)** informal firmly put an end to.

kick verb 1 strike or propel something forcibly with the foot. **2** strike out with the foot or feet. **3** informal succeed in giving up a habit. **4 (kick against)** disagree or be frustrated with. **5 (kick off)** (of a football match) start or resume with a kick of the ball from the centre. **6 (kick out)** informal force someone to leave. **7** (of a gun) spring back when fired. **noun 1** an instance of kicking. **2** informal a sharply stimulating effect. **3** informal a thrill of excitement. ▢ **kick-boxing** a form of martial art which combines boxing with kicking with bare feet. **kick-off** the start of a football match. **kick-start 1** start a motorcycle engine with a downward thrust of a lever. **2** stimulate something to start afresh. **kick the bucket** informal die. ∎ **kicker** noun.

kickback noun 1 a sudden forceful springing back. **2** informal an underhand payment to someone who has helped in a business deal.

kid¹ noun 1 informal a child or young person. **2** a young goat. ▢ **treat (or handle) with kid gloves** deal with very carefully.

kid² verb (kids, kidding, kidded) informal fool someone into believing something.

kidnap verb (kidnaps, kidnapping, kidnapped; US spelling **kidnaps, kidnaping, kidnaped)** take someone by force and hold them captive. **noun** an instance of kidnapping. ∎ **kidnapper** noun.

kidney noun (plural **kidneys**) **1** each of a pair of organs that remove waste products from the blood and secrete urine. **2** the kidney of a sheep, ox, or pig as food. ▢ **kidney bean** an edible dark red bean shaped like a kidney. **kidney machine** an apparatus that performs the functions of a kidney, used if a person has a damaged kidney. **kidney stone** a hard mass formed in the kidneys.

kilim or **kelim** /ki-**leem**, kee-lim/ **noun** a carpet or rug of a kind made in

Turkey, Kurdistan, and neighbouring areas.

kill verb **1** cause the death of. **2** put an end to. **3** informal overwhelm someone with an emotion. **4** informal cause pain to. **5** pass time. noun **1** an act of killing. **2** an animal or animals killed by a hunter or another animal.

killer noun **1** a person or thing that kills. **2** informal something that is very difficult or challenging. □ **killer whale** = ORCA.

killing noun an act of causing death. adjective informal exhausting. □ **make a killing** make a great deal of money out of something.

killjoy noun a person who spoils the enjoyment of others.

kiln noun an oven for baking or drying things.

kilo noun (plural **kilos**) a kilogram.

kilobyte noun Computing a unit of memory or data equal to 1,024 bytes.

kilogram or **kilogramme** noun a unit of mass, equal to 1,000 grams (approximately 2.205 lb).

kilometre /**kil**-uh-mee-ter, ki-**lom**-i-ter/ (US spelling **kilometer**) noun a metric unit of measurement equal to 1,000 metres (0.62 miles).

kiloton or **kilotonne** noun a unit of explosive power equivalent to 1,000 tons of TNT.

kilovolt noun 1,000 volts.

kilowatt noun 1,000 watts. □ **kilowatt-hour** a measure of electrical energy equivalent to one kilowatt operating for one hour.

kilt noun a skirt of pleated tartan cloth, traditionally worn by men as part of Scottish Highland dress.

kilter noun (**out of kilter**) out of balance.

kimono /ki-**moh**-noh/ noun (plural **kimonos**) a long, loose Japanese robe with wide sleeves, tied with a sash.

kin plural noun your family and relations.

kind[1] noun a class or type of similar people or things. □ **in kind 1** in the same way. **2** (of payment) in goods or services instead of money.

> **i** avoid the ungrammatical construction *these kind*: say *these kinds of questions are not relevant* rather than *these kind of questions are not relevant*.

kind[2] adjective considerate and generous.

kindergarten noun a nursery school.

kindle verb (**kindles**, **kindling**, **kindled**) **1** light a flame. **2** arouse an emotion.

kindling noun small sticks used for lighting fires.

kindly adverb **1** in a kind manner. **2** please (used in a polite request). adjective (**kindlier**, **kindliest**) kind. □ **take kindly to** be pleased by. ■ **kindliness** noun.

kindness noun **1** the quality of being kind. **2** a kind act.

kindred plural noun your family and relations. adjective similar in kind. □ **kindred spirit** a person whose interests or attitudes are similar to your own.

kinetic adjective relating to or resulting from motion. ■ **kinetically** adverb.

king noun **1** the male ruler of an independent state. **2** the best or most important person or thing in a sphere or group. **3** a playing card ranking next below an ace. **4** the most important chess piece, which the opponent has to checkmate in order to win. □ **king-sized** (or **king-size**) of a larger than normal size. ■ **kingly** adjective **kingship** noun.

kingdom noun **1** a country, state, or territory ruled by a king or queen. **2** each of the three divisions (animal, vegetable, and mineral) in which natural objects are classified.

kingfisher noun a colourful bird with a long sharp beak which dives to catch fish in streams and ponds.

kingpin noun **1** a large bolt in a central position. **2** a vertical bolt used as a pivot. **3** a person or thing that is essential to the success of an organization or operation.

kink noun **1** a sharp twist in something long and narrow. **2** a flaw or difficulty. **3** a peculiar habit or characteristic. **verb** form a kink.

kinky adjective (**kinkier**, **kinkiest**) **1** having kinks or twists. **2** informal having to do with unusual sexual behaviour.

kinsfolk or **kinfolk** plural noun your family and relations.

kinship noun **1** the relationship between members of the same family. **2** the sharing of characteristics or origins.

kinsman or **kinswoman** noun one of your relations.

kiosk noun **1** a small open-fronted hut from which newspapers, refreshments, tickets, etc. are sold. **2** Brit. a public telephone booth.

kip Brit. informal noun a sleep. **verb** (**kips**, **kipping**, **kipped**) sleep.

kipper noun a herring that has been split open, salted, and dried or smoked. □ **kipper tie** a very wide tie.

kirk noun Scottish & N. English a church.

kismet /**kiz**-mit/ noun fate.

kiss verb touch someone or something with the lips as a sign of love, affection, or greeting. noun an act of kissing. □ **kiss curl** a small curl of hair on the forehead or in front of the ear. **the kiss of life** mouth-to-mouth resuscitation.

kit noun **1** a set of equipment or clothes for a specific purpose. **2** a set of drums, cymbals, and other percussion instruments. **verb** (**kits**, **kitting**, **kitted**) (**kit out**) provide with appropriate clothing or equipment.

kitbag noun a long canvas bag for carrying a soldier's possessions.

kitchen noun **1** a room where food is prepared and cooked. **2** a set of fittings and units installed in a kitchen. □ **kitchen garden** a part of a garden where vegetables, fruit, and herbs are grown.

kitchenette noun a small kitchen or cooking area.

kite noun **1** a toy consisting of a light frame with thin material stretched over it, flown in the wind at the end of a long string. **2** a long-winged bird of prey with a forked tail. **3** Geometry a four-sided figure having two pairs of equal sides next to each other.

kith noun (**kith and kin**) your family and relations.

kitsch /kich/ noun art, objects, or design that are unpleasantly bright or too sentimental. ■ **kitschy** adjective.

kitten noun **1** a young cat. **2** the young of certain other animals, such as the rabbit and beaver. □ **have kittens** Brit. informal be very nervous or upset.

kittenish adjective playful, lively, or flirtatious.

kitty[1] noun (plural **kitties**) **1** a fund of money for use by a number of people. **2** a pool of money in some card games.

kitty[2] noun (plural **kitties**) informal a cat.

kiwi noun (plural **kiwis**) **1** a flightless and tailless bird from New Zealand. **2** (**Kiwi**) informal a person from New Zealand. □ **kiwi fruit** the fruit of an Asian climbing plant, with green flesh and black seeds.

klaxon /**klak**-suhn/ noun trademark a vehicle horn or warning hooter.

kleptomania noun a recurring urge to steal. ■ **kleptomaniac** noun & adjective.

km abbreviation kilometres.

knack noun **1** a skill at performing a task. **2** a tendency to do something.

knacker Brit. noun a person who disposes of dead or unwanted animals. **verb** (**knackers**, **knackering**, **knackered**) informal **1** wear out. **2** (**knackered**) extremely tired. □ **knacker's yard** a place where old or injured animals are slaughtered.

knapsack noun a bag with shoulder straps, carried on the back.

knave noun **1** old use a dishonest man. **2** (in cards) a jack. ■ **knavish** adjective.

knead verb **1** work dough or clay with

the hands. **2** massage something as if kneading it.

knee noun **1** the joint between the thigh and the lower leg. **2** the upper surface of a sitting person's thigh. verb (**knees, kneeing, kneed**) hit someone with your knee. □ **knee-jerk** automatic and unthinking. **knees-up** Brit. informal a lively party.

kneecap noun the bone in front of the knee joint. verb (**kneecaps, kneecapping, kneecapped**) shoot someone in the knee as a punishment.

kneel verb (**kneels, kneeling, knelt** or **kneeled**) be in a position in which you rest your weight on your knees.

knell literary verb (of a bell) ring solemnly. noun the sound of a bell rung solemnly.

knew past of **KNOW**.

knickerbockers plural noun loose-fitting trousers or knickers gathered at the knee or calf.

knickers plural noun Brit. women's or girl's underpants.

knick-knack noun a small worthless object.

knife noun (plural **knives**) a cutting instrument consisting of a blade fixed into a handle. verb (**knifes, knifing, knifed**) **1** stab someone with a knife. **2** cut through or into something like a knife. □ **at knifepoint** under threat of injury from a knife. **knife-edge** a very tense or dangerous situation.

knight noun **1** (in the Middle Ages) a man of noble rank with a duty to fight for his king. **2** (in the UK) a man awarded a title by the king or queen and entitled to use 'Sir' in front of his name. **3** a chess piece that moves by jumping to the opposite corner of a rectangle two squares by three. verb give a man the title of knight. ■ **knighthood** noun.

knit verb (**knits, knitting, knitted** or **knit**) **1** make a garment by looping yarn together with knitting needles or on a machine. **2** make a plain stitch in knitting. **3** join together. **4** tighten your eyebrows in a frown. noun (**knits**) knitted garments.

knitwear noun knitted garments.

knob noun **1** a rounded lump at the end or on the surface of something. **2** a ball-shaped handle. **3** a round button on a machine. **4** a small lump of something.

knobble noun Brit. a small lump on something. ■ **knobbly** adjective.

knock verb **1** strike a surface noisily to attract attention. **2** collide forcefully with. **3** strike someone or something so that they move or fall. **4** make a hole, dent, etc. in something by striking it. **5** informal criticize. **6** (of a motor) make a thumping or rattling noise. noun **1** a sound of knocking. **2** a blow or collision. **3** a setback. □ **knock-kneed** having legs that curve inward at the knee. **knock off** informal **1** stop work. **2** produce a piece of work quickly and easily. **knock-on effect** an effect or consequence that spreads to other things. **knock out 1** make someone unconscious. **2** informal astonish or greatly impress. **3** eliminate from a knockout competition.

knockabout adjective (of comedy) rough and using slapstick.

knocker noun a hinged object fixed to a door and rapped by visitors to attract attention.

knockout noun **1** an act of knocking someone out. **2** Brit. a tournament in which the loser in each round is eliminated. **3** informal an extremely impressive person or thing.

knoll noun a small hill or mound.

knot noun **1** a loop of string or rope that is fastened on itself and tightened. **2** a tangled mass in hair, wool, etc. **3** a hard mass in wood at the point where the trunk and a branch join. **4** a hard lump of muscle tissue. **5** a small group of people. **6** a unit of speed of a ship, aircraft, or the wind equivalent to one nautical mile per hour. verb (**knots, knotting, knotted**) **1** fasten with a knot. **2** tangle. **3** cause a muscle to become tense and hard. □ **tie the knot** informal get married.

knotty adjective (**knottier, knottiest**)

1 full of knots. **2** extremely complex.

know verb (**knows**, **knowing**, **knew**; past participle **known**) **1** be aware of something as a result of observing, asking, or being told. **2** be absolutely sure of something. **3** be familiar with. **4** have a good command of a subject or language. **5** have personal experience of. **6** (**be known as**) be regarded as having a particular characteristic or title. □ **be in the know** be aware of something known only to a few people. **know-all** informal a person who behaves as if they know everything. **know-how** practical knowledge or skill. **know the ropes** have experience of the correct way of doing something. ■ **knowable** adjective.

knowing adjective **1** suggesting that you have secret knowledge. **2** experienced or cunning. ■ **knowingly** adverb.

knowledge noun **1** information and awareness acquired through experience or education. **2** the sum of what is known.

> ☑ remember the *d*: knowle*d*ge.

knowledgeable or **knowledgable** adjective intelligent and well informed. ■ **knowledgeably** adverb.

known past participle of **KNOW**. adjective **1** recognized, familiar, or within the scope of knowledge. **2** publicly acknowledged to be. **3** Mathematics (of a quantity or variable) having a value that can be stated.

knuckle noun **1** each of the joints of a finger. **2** a knee joint of a four-legged animal, or the part joining the leg to the foot. verb (**knuckles**, **knuckling**, **knuckled**) **1** (**knuckle down**) apply yourself seriously to a task. **2** (**knuckle under**) accept someone's authority.

knuckleduster noun a metal fitting worn over the knuckles in fighting to increase the effect of blows.

koala /koh-**ah**-luh/ noun a bear-like Australian animal that lives in trees.

kohl noun a black powder used as eye make-up.

kohlrabi noun (plural **kohlrabies**) a variety of cabbage with an edible turnip-like stem.

kookaburra /kuu-kuh-bur-ruh/ noun a very large, noisy kingfisher living in Australia and New Zealand.

Koran /ko-**rahn**/ noun the sacred book of Islam, believed to be the word of God as told to Muhammad and written down in Arabic.

kosher /**koh**-sher/ adjective **1** (of food) prepared according to the requirements of Jewish law. **2** informal genuine and legitimate.

kowtow /kow-**tow**/ verb **1** (in the past, as part of Chinese custom) kneel and touch the ground with the forehead, in worship or as a sign of respect. **2** be too meek and obedient towards someone.

kraal /krahl/ noun S. African **1** a traditional African village of huts. **2** an enclosure for sheep and cattle.

krill plural noun small shrimp-like crustaceans which are the main food of baleen whales.

krona noun **1** (plural **kronor**) the basic unit of money of Sweden. **2** (plural **kronur**) the unit of money of Iceland.

krone /**kroh**-nuh/ noun (plural **kroner**) the basic unit of money of Denmark and Norway.

krypton /**krip**-ton/ noun a gaseous chemical element used in some kinds of electric light.

kudos noun praise and honour.

> ℹ **kudos** is a singular noun and does not take a plural verb.

kumquat /**kum**-kwot/ noun a small orange-like fruit.

kung fu /kung **foo**/ noun a Chinese martial art resembling karate.

Kurd noun a member of an Islamic people living in Kurdistan, a region in the Middle East.

kV abbreviation kilovolts.

kW abbreviation kilowatts.

LI

L or **l** noun (plural **Ls** or **L's**) **1** the twelfth letter of the alphabet. **2** the Roman numeral for 50. **abbreviation 1** Brit. learner driver: *L-plates*. **2** (**l**) litres. **3** (**l**.) old use pounds.

£ abbreviation pounds.

lab noun informal a laboratory.

label noun **1** a small piece of paper, fabric, etc. attached to an object and giving information about it. **2** the name or trademark of a fashion company. **3** a company that produces recorded music. **4** a classifying name given to a person or thing. verb (**labels, labelling, labelled**; US spelling **labels, labeling, labeled**) **1** attach a label to. **2** put something in a category.

 -el, not -le: **label**.

labia /**lay**-bi-uh/ plural noun (singular **labium**) the inner and outer folds of the vulva. ■ **labial** adjective.

labor etc. US spelling of **LABOUR** etc.

laboratory noun (plural **laboratories**) a room or building for scientific research or teaching, or for the making of drugs or chemicals.

laborious adjective **1** requiring much time and effort. **2** showing obvious signs of effort. ■ **laboriously** adverb.

labour (US spelling **labor**) noun **1** work. **2** workers as a group. **3** (**Labour** or **the Labour Party**) a left-wing political party formed to represent ordinary working people. **4** the process of childbirth. verb **1** work hard. **2** work at an unskilled manual job. **3** have difficulty despite working hard. **4** move with difficulty. **5** (**labour under**) be misled by a mistaken belief. □ **labour camp** a prison camp where prisoners have to do hard labour. **labour force** the members of a population who are able to work. **labour-intensive** needing a large amount of work. **labour the point** talk about something at excessive length.

laboured (US spelling **labored**) adjective **1** done with great difficulty. **2** not spontaneous or natural.

labourer (US spelling **laborer**) noun a person who does unskilled manual work.

Labrador noun a breed of dog with a black or yellow coat, used as a retriever and as a guide dog.

laburnum noun a small tree with hanging clusters of yellow flowers.

labyrinth noun a complicated irregular network of passages. ■ **labyrinthine** /lab-uh-**rin**-thyn/ adjective.

lace noun **1** a delicate open fabric made by looping, twisting, or knitting thread in patterns. **2** a cord used to fasten a shoe or garment. verb (**laces, lacing, laced**) **1** fasten something with a lace or laces. **2** add an ingredient to a drink or dish to make it stronger or improve the flavour.

lacerate verb (**lacerates, lacerating, lacerated**) tear or deeply cut the flesh or skin. ■ **laceration** noun.

lachrymal or **lacrimal** /**lak**-ri-muhl/ adjective connected with weeping or tears.

lachrymose /**lak**-ri-mohss/ adjective literary tearful.

lack noun the state of being without or not having enough of something. verb (also **lack for**) be without or without enough of.

lackadaisical adjective lacking enthusiasm and thoroughness.

lackey noun (plural **lackeys**) **1** a servant. **2** a person who is too willing to serve or obey others.

lacklustre (US spelling **lackluster**) adjective **1** lacking in energy, force, or inspiration. **2** (of the hair or eyes) not shining.

laconic /luh-**kon**-ik/ adjective using

very few words. ■ **laconically** adverb.

lacquer /lak-ker/ noun **1** a varnish made from the resin of an Asian tree, or a similar synthetic substance. **2** decorative wooden goods coated with lacquer. **3** Brit. a chemical substance sprayed on hair to keep it in place. verb (**lacquers, lacquering, lacquered**) coat something with lacquer.

lacrimal ⇒ **LACHRYMAL**.

lacrosse /luh-**kross**/ noun a team game in which a ball is thrown, caught, and carried with a long-handled stick bearing a net at one end.

lactate /lak-**tayt**/ verb (**lactates, lactating, lactated**) (of a woman or female animal) produce milk in the breasts or mammary glands, for feeding babies or young. ■ **lactation** noun.

lactic adjective relating to or obtained from milk. □ **lactic acid** an acid present in sour milk, and produced in the muscles during strenuous exercise.

lactose noun a sugar present in milk.

lacuna /luh-**kyoo**-nuh/ noun (plural **lacunae** /luh-**kyoo**-nee/ or **lacunas**) a gap or missing portion.

lacy adjective (**lacier, laciest**) made of, resembling, or trimmed with lace.

lad noun informal a boy or young man.

ladder noun **1** a structure consisting of a series of bars or steps between two uprights, used for climbing up or down. **2** a series of stages by which progress can be made: *the career ladder.* **3** Brit. a strip of unravelled fabric in tights or stockings. verb (**ladders, laddering, laddered**) Brit. cause a ladder to develop in a pair of tights or a stocking.

laddish adjective behaving in a boisterously macho way.

laden adjective heavily loaded or weighed down.

la-di-da or **lah-di-dah** adjective informal affected or snobbish.

ladle noun a large spoon with a cup-shaped bowl and a long handle, for serving soup, stew, etc. verb (**ladles,**

ladling, ladled) **1** serve or transfer soup, stew, etc. with a ladle. **2** (**ladle out**) give out in large amounts.

lady noun (plural **ladies**) **1** (in polite or formal use) a woman. **2** a well-mannered or refined woman, or a woman of high social position. **3** (**Lady**) a title used by peeresses, female relatives of peers, and the wives and widows of knights. **4** (**the Ladies**) Brit. a women's public toilet. □ **lady-in-waiting** (plural **ladies-in-waiting**) a woman who accompanies and looks after a queen or princess.

ladybird noun a small beetle that has a red back with black spots.

ladykiller noun informal a man who is successful in seducing women.

ladylike adjective typical of a well-mannered woman or girl.

lag[1] verb (**lags, lagging, lagged**) fall behind. noun (also **time lag**) a period of time between two events.

lag[2] verb (**lags, lagging, lagged**) cover a water tank or pipes with insulating material.

lager noun a light fizzy beer.

laggard noun a person who falls behind others.

lagging noun material wrapped round a water tank and pipes to prevent heat loss.

lagoon noun a stretch of salt water separated from the sea by a low sandbank or coral reef.

lah-di-dah ⇒ **LA-DI-DA**.

laid past and past participle of **LAY**[1]. □ **laid-back** informal relaxed and easy-going.

lain past participle of **LIE**[1].

lair noun **1** a wild animal's resting place. **2** a person's secret den.

laird noun (in Scotland) a person who owns a large estate.

laissez-faire /less-ay-**fair**/ noun a policy of leaving things to take their own course, without interfering.

laity /**lay**-i-ti/ noun (**the laity**) people who are not priests or ministers of the Church; ordinary people.

lake noun a large area of water surrounded by land.

lam verb (lams, lamming, lammed) informal hit something hard.

lama /lah-muh/ noun 1 a title given to a spiritual leader in Tibetan Buddhism. 2 a Tibetan or Mongolian Buddhist monk.

lamb noun 1 a young sheep. 2 a gentle or innocent person. verb 1 (of a ewe) give birth to lambs. 2 look after ewes at lambing time. ■ **lambing** noun.

lambada /lam-bah-duh/ noun a fast Brazilian dance.

lambaste /lam-baysst/ or **lambast** /lam-bast/ verb (lambastes or lambasts, lambasting, lambasted) criticize someone harshly.

lambent /lam-buhnt/ adjective literary lit up or flickering with a soft glow.

lame adjective 1 walking with difficulty because of an injury or illness affecting the leg or foot. 2 (of an explanation or excuse) unconvincing and feeble. 3 (of something meant to be entertaining) dull and uninspiring. verb (lames, laming, lamed) make a particular person or animal lame. □ **lame duck** an unsuccessful person or thing. ■ **lamely** adverb **lameness** noun.

lamé /lah-may/ noun fabric with interwoven gold or silver threads.

lament /luh-ment/ noun 1 a passionate expression of grief. 2 a song or poem expressing grief or regret. verb 1 mourn a person's death. 2 express regret or disappointment about. ■ **lamentation** noun.

lamentable /la-muhn-tuh-b'l/ adjective very bad or regrettable. ■ **lamentably** adverb.

laminate verb /lam-i-nayt/ (laminates, laminating, laminated) 1 cover a flat surface with a layer of protective material. 2 make something by placing layer on layer. 3 split into layers or leaves. 4 beat or roll metal into thin plates. noun /lam-i-nuht/ a laminated structure or material. ■ **lamination** noun.

lamp noun a device using electricity, oil, or gas to give light.

lampoon verb mock or ridicule. noun a mocking attack.

lamprey /lam-pri/ noun (plural lampreys) an eel-like jawless fish that has a sucker mouth with horny teeth.

lance noun (in the past) a weapon with a long shaft and a pointed steel head, used by people on horseback. verb (lances, lancing, lanced) Medicine prick or cut open a boil or wound with a sharp instrument. □ **lance corporal** a rank of non-commissioned officer in the army, below corporal.

lancer noun (in the past) a soldier armed with a lance.

lancet /lahn-sit/ noun a small two-edged knife with a sharp point, used in surgery.

land noun 1 the part of the earth's surface that is not covered by water. 2 an area of ground. 3 (the land) ground or soil used as a basis for cultivation. 4 a country or state. verb 1 put or go ashore. 2 come or bring down to the ground. 3 bring a fish out of the water with a net or rod. 4 informal succeed in obtaining or achieving. 5 (land up) reach a particular place or destination. 6 (land up with) end up with an unwelcome situation. 7 (land in) informal put someone in a difficult situation. 8 (land with) inflict something unwelcome on someone. 9 informal inflict a blow on someone.

landau /lan-dor/ noun an enclosed horse-drawn carriage.

landed adjective owning a lot of land.

landfall noun arrival on land after a sea journey.

landfill noun 1 the disposal of rubbish by burying it. 2 buried rubbish.

landing noun 1 a level area at the top of a staircase. 2 a place where people and goods can be landed from a boat. □ **landing craft** a boat for putting troops and equipment ashore on a beach. **landing gear** the undercarriage of an aircraft.

landless adjective owning no land.

landlocked adjective (of a place) surrounded by land.

landlord or **landlady** noun **1** a person who rents out property or land. **2** Brit. a person who runs a pub.

landlubber noun informal a person unfamiliar with the sea or sailing.

landmark noun **1** an object or feature that is easily seen from a distance. **2** an important stage or turning point.

landmine noun an explosive mine laid on or just under the surface of the ground.

landscape noun **1** all the visible features of an area of land. **2** a picture of an area of countryside. verb (**landscapes, landscaping, landscaped**) improve the appearance of land by changing its contours, planting trees and shrubs, etc.

landslide noun **1** (Brit. also **landslip**) a mass of earth or rock that slides down a mountain or cliff. **2** an overwhelming majority of votes for one party in an election.

lane noun **1** a narrow road. **2** a division of a road for a single line of traffic. **3** a strip of track or water for each of the competitors in a race. **4** a course followed by ships or aircraft.

language noun **1** human communication through the use of spoken or written words. **2** a particular system or style of spoken or written communication. **3** a system of symbols and rules for writing computer programs.

 -guage, not *-gauge*: lan**guage**.

languid /lang-gwid/ adjective **1** reluctant to exert yourself physically. **2** weak or faint. ∎ **languidly** adverb.

languish verb **1** become weak or faint. **2** be kept in an unpleasant place or situation.

languor /lang-ger/ noun pleasurable tiredness or inactivity. ∎ **languorous** adjective.

lank adjective (of hair) long, limp, and straight.

lanky adjective (**lankier, lankiest**) awkwardly thin and tall.

lanolin noun a fatty substance from sheep's wool, used in skin cream.

lantern noun a lamp enclosed in a metal frame with glass panels.

lanthanum /lan-thuh-nuhm/ noun a silvery-white metallic element.

lanyard /lan-yerd/ noun **1** a rope used on a ship. **2** a cord around the neck or shoulder for holding a whistle or similar object.

lap[1] noun the flat area between the waist and knees of a seated person.

lap[2] noun **1** one circuit of a track or racetrack. **2** an overlapping part. verb (**laps, lapping, lapped**) overtake a competitor in a race to become a lap ahead.

lap[3] verb (**laps, lapping, lapped**) **1** (of an animal) take up liquid with the tongue. **2** (**lap up**) accept something with obvious pleasure. **3** (of water) wash against something with a gentle rippling sound.

lapdog noun **1** a small pampered pet dog. **2** a person who is completely under the influence of another.

lapel noun the part which is folded back at the front opening of a jacket or coat.

lapidary /la-pi-duh-ri/ adjective **1** relating to the engraving, cutting, or polishing of stone or gems. **2** (of language) elegant and concise.

lapis lazuli /lap-iss laz-yuu-li/ noun a bright blue stone used in jewellery.

Lapp noun a member of a people of the extreme north of Scandinavia.

🛈 the people themselves prefer to be called **Sami**.

lapse noun **1** a brief failure of concentration, memory, or judgement. **2** a decline from previously high standards. **3** an interval of time. verb (**lapses, lapsing, lapsed**) **1** (of a right, agreement, etc.) become invalid because it is not used or renewed. **2** stop following a religion or doctrine. **3** (**lapse into**) pass gradually into a different state.

laptop noun a portable microcomputer.

lapwing noun a black and white bird with a crest on the head.

larboard = PORT³.

larceny /**lar**-suh-ni/ noun (plural **larcenies**) theft of personal property.

larch noun a coniferous tree with needles that fall in winter.

lard noun fat from a pig, used in cooking. verb **1** insert strips of fat or bacon in meat before cooking. **2** add technical or obscure expressions to talk or writing.

larder noun a room or large cupboard for storing food.

large adjective **1** of relatively great size, extent, or capacity. **2** of wide range or scope. □ **at large 1** escaped or not yet captured. **2** as a whole.

largely adverb on the whole; mostly.

largesse /lar-**zhess**/ noun **1** generosity. **2** money or gifts given generously.

largo /**lar**-goh/ adverb & adjective Music in a slow tempo and dignified style.

lariat /**la**-ri-uht/ noun a rope used as a lasso or for tethering animals.

lark¹ noun a brown bird that sings while flying.

lark² informal noun **1** an amusing adventure or escapade. **2** Brit. a foolish or trivial activity. verb (**lark about** or **around**) behave in a playful and mischievous way.

larva noun (plural **larvae** /**lar**-vee/) an immature form of an insect that looks very different from the adult creature, e.g. a caterpillar.

laryngitis /la-rin-**jy**-tiss/ noun inflammation of the larynx.

larynx /**la**-rinks/ noun (plural **larynges** /luh-**rin**-jeez/) the area at the top of the throat forming an air passage to the lungs and containing the vocal cords.

lasagne /luh-**zan**-yuh/ noun pasta in the form of sheets, baked in layers with meat or vegetables and a cheese sauce.

lascivious /luh-**siv**-i-uhss/ adjective feeling or showing an open or offensive sexual desire. ■ **lasciviously** adverb **lasciviousness** noun.

laser noun a device that produces an intense narrow beam of light.

laserdisc noun a disc resembling a large compact disc, used for high-quality video and multimedia.

lash verb **1** beat with a whip or stick. **2** beat strongly against. **3** (**lash out**) attack verbally or physically. **4** (of an animal) move the tail quickly and violently. **5** fasten securely with a cord or rope. noun **1** a sharp blow with a whip or stick. **2** the flexible part of a whip. **3** an eyelash.

lashings plural noun Brit. informal a large amount of something.

lass or **lassie** noun Scottish & N. English a girl or young woman.

lassitude noun lack of energy.

lasso /luh-**soo**/ noun (plural **lassos** or **lassoes**) a rope with a noose at one end, used for catching cattle. verb (**lassoes**, **lassoing**, **lassoed**) catch with a lasso.

last¹ adjective **1** coming after all others in time or order. **2** most recent in time. **3** lowest in importance or rank. **4** (**the last**) the least likely or suitable. **5** only remaining. adverb on the last occasion before the present. noun (plural **last**) **1** the last person or thing. **2** (**the last of**) the only remaining part of. □ **Last Judgement** (in some religions) the judgement of humankind expected to take place at the end of the world. **last rites** Christian rites given to a person who is about to die. ■ **lastly** adverb.

last² verb **1** continue for a specified period of time. **2** remain operating for a considerable or specified length of time. **3** be enough for someone to use for a specified length of time.

last³ noun a block used by a shoemaker for shaping or repairing shoes.

latch noun **1** a bar with a catch and lever used for fastening a door or gate. **2** a type of door lock which can be opened from the outside only with a key. verb **1** fasten with a latch. **2** (**latch on to**) associate yourself enthusiastically with.

latchkey noun (plural **latchkeys**) a key to an outer door of a house.

late adjective **1** acting, arriving, or happening after the proper or usual time. **2** far on in a period. **3** far on in the day or night. **4** (of a person) recently dead. **5** (**latest**) of most recent date or origin. adverb **1** after the proper or usual time. **2** towards the end of a period. **3** far on in the day or night. **4** (**later**) afterwards or in the near future. □ **of late** recently. ■ **lateness** noun.

lately adverb recently; not long ago.

latent adjective existing but not yet developed, showing, or active. ■ **latency** noun.

lateral adjective of, at, towards, or from the side or sides. □ **lateral thinking** chiefly Brit. the solving of a problem by thinking of new ways to approach it. ■ **laterally** adverb.

latex noun **1** a milky fluid in some plants which thickens when exposed to the air. **2** a synthetic product resembling this, used to make paints, coatings, etc.

lath /lahth, lath/ noun (plural **laths**) a thin, flat strip of wood.

lathe noun a machine that shapes pieces of wood or metal by turning them against a cutting tool.

lather noun **1** a frothy mass of bubbles produced by soap when mixed with water. **2** heavy sweat visible on a horse's coat as a white foam. verb (**lathers**, **lathering**, **lathered**) **1** cover with or form a lather. **2** cover or spread generously with a substance.

Latin noun the language of ancient Rome and its empire. adjective relating to the Latin language. □ **Latin America** the parts of the American continent where Spanish or Portuguese is spoken.

Latino /luh-tee-noh/ noun (plural **Latinos**) N. Amer. a Latin American inhabitant of the United States.

latitude noun **1** the distance of a place north or south of the equator. **2** (**latitudes**) regions at a particular distance from the equator. **3** scope for freedom of action or thought.

latrine noun a communal toilet, especially a temporary one in a camp.

latter adjective **1** nearer to the end than to the beginning. **2** recent. **3** (**the latter**) referring to the second-mentioned of two people or things. □ **latter-day** modern or contemporary. ■ **latterly** adverb.

lattice noun a structure or pattern of strips crossing each other with square or diamond-shaped spaces left between.

laud /lawd/ verb formal praise highly.

laudable adjective deserving praise and commendation.

laudanum /law-duh-nuhm/ noun a liquid containing opium, formerly used as a sedative.

laudatory /law-duh-tuh-ri/ adjective formal expressing praise.

laugh verb **1** make sounds and movements that express amusement. **2** (**laugh at**) make fun of; ridicule. **3** (**laugh off**) dismiss something by treating it light-heartedly. noun **1** an act of laughing. **2** (**a laugh**) informal a cause of laughter. □ **laughing gas** nitrous oxide, used as an anaesthetic. **laughing stock** a person who is ridiculed.

laughable adjective so ludicrous as to be amusing. ■ **laughably** adverb.

laughter noun the action or sound of laughing.

launch[1] verb **1** move a boat or ship from land into the water. **2** send out a missile into the air. **3** begin an enterprise or introduce a new product. **4** (**launch into**) begin something energetically and enthusiastically. noun an act of launching. ■ **launcher** noun.

launch[2] noun a large motor boat.

launder verb (**launders**, **laundering**, **laundered**) **1** wash and iron clothes or linen. **2** informal pass illegally obtained money through a bank or business to conceal its origins.

launderette or **laundrette** noun a place with coin-operated washing machines and dryers for public use.

laundry noun (plural **laundries**) **1** clothes and linen that need to be washed or that have been newly washed. **2** a room or building where clothes and linen are washed.

laurel noun **1** an evergreen shrub or small tree with dark green glossy leaves. **2** (**laurels**) a crown of bay leaves awarded as a mark of honour in classical times. **3** (**laurels**) honour or praise. □ **rest on your laurels** be so satisfied with what you have achieved that you make no more effort.

lava noun hot molten rock that erupts from a volcano, or solid rock formed when this cools.

lavatorial adjective **1** relating to lavatories. **2** (of humour) characterized by reference to bodily functions.

lavatory noun (plural **lavatories**) a toilet.

lavender noun **1** a strong-smelling shrub with bluish-purple flowers. **2** a pale bluish-purple colour.

lavish adjective **1** very rich, elaborate, or luxurious. **2** giving or given in great amounts. **verb** give something in abundant or extravagant quantities. ■ **lavishly** adverb.

law noun **1** a rule or system of rules that governs the actions of the people in a country or community. **2** a rule laying down the correct procedure or behaviour in a sport. **3** a statement of fact to the effect that a particular phenomenon always occurs if certain conditions are present. □ **be a law unto yourself** behave in an unconventional or unpredictable manner.

lawful adjective allowed by or obeying law or rules. ■ **lawfully** adverb.

lawless adjective not governed by or obedient to laws. ■ **lawlessness** noun.

lawn noun **1** an area of mown grass in a garden or park. **2** a fine linen or cotton fabric.

lawnmower noun a machine for cutting the grass on a lawn.

lawsuit noun a claim brought to a law court to be decided.

lawyer noun a person who practises or studies law.

lax adjective **1** not sufficiently strict, severe, or careful. **2** (of limbs or muscles) relaxed. ■ **laxity** noun.

laxative adjective tending to make someone empty their bowels. **noun** a laxative drug or medicine.

lay¹ verb (**lays**, **laying**, past and past participle **laid**) **1** put something down gently or carefully. **2** put something down in position for use. **3** assign or place. **4** (of a female bird, reptile, etc.) produce an egg from inside the body. **5** stake an amount of money in a bet. **6** vulgar have sex with. □ **lay-by** (plural **lay-bys**) Brit. an area at the side of a road where vehicles may stop. **lay off 1** discharge a worker because of a shortage of work. **2** informal give up. **lay-off** a temporary break from an activity. **lay out** arrange according to a plan. **lay up** put out of action through illness or injury.

> **ℹ** don't confuse **lay** and **lie**. You *lay* something, as in *they are going to lay the carpet*, but you *lie* down on a bed or other flat surface. The past tense and past participle of *lay* is **laid**, as in *they laid the groundwork* or *she had laid careful plans*; the past tense of **lie** is **lay** (*he lay on the floor*) and the past participle is **lain** (*she had lain on the bed for hours*).

lay² adjective **1** not having an official position in the Church. **2** not having professional qualifications or expert knowledge.

lay³ noun a short poem intended to be sung.

lay⁴ past of **LIE¹**.

layabout noun disapproving a person who does little or no work.

layer noun a sheet or thickness of material covering a surface. **verb** arrange or cut in a layer or layers.

layman noun **1** a member of a Church who is not a priest or minister. **2** a person without professional or specialized knowledge.

layout noun the way in which something is laid out.

laze verb (**lazes**, **lazing**, **lazed**) spend

time relaxing or doing very little.

lazy adjective (**lazier, laziest**) **1** unwilling to work or use energy. **2** showing a lack of effort or care. ■ **lazily** adverb **laziness** noun.

lazybones noun informal a lazy person.

lb abbreviation pounds (in weight).

> ℹ️ short for Latin *libra* 'pound, balance'.

lbw abbreviation Cricket leg before wicket.

lea noun literary an area of grassy land.

leach verb be removed from soil by the action of water.

lead¹ verb (**leads, leading, led**) **1** cause a person or animal to go with you. **2** be a route or means of access. **3** (**lead to**) result in. **4** cause someone to do or believe something. **5** be in charge of. **6** have the advantage in a race or game. **7** have a particular way of life. **8** (**lead up to**) come before or result in. **9** (**lead on**) deceive someone into believing that you are attracted to them. noun **1** an example for others to copy. **2** a position of advantage in a contest. **3** the chief part in a play or film. **4** a clue to follow in trying to solve a problem. **5** Brit. a strap or cord for restraining and guiding a dog. **6** a wire conveying electric current.

lead² noun **1** a heavy bluish-grey metal. **2** the part of a pencil that makes a mark.

leaded adjective **1** framed or covered with lead. **2** (of petrol) containing lead.

leaden adjective **1** dull, heavy, or slow. **2** dull grey in colour.

leader noun **1** a person or thing that leads. **2** the most successful or advanced person or thing in a particular area. **3** the principal player in a music group. **4** a leading article in a newspaper. ■ **leadership** noun.

leading adjective most important, or in first place. ◻ **leading article** Brit. a newspaper article giving the editor's opinion. **leading light** a prominent or influential person. **leading question**

a question that encourages someone to give the answer that you want.

leaf noun (plural **leaves**) **1** a flat green part of a plant that is attached to a stem. **2** the state of having leaves. **3** a single sheet of paper in a book. **4** gold or silver in the form of very thin foil. **5** a hinged or detachable part of a table. verb (**leaf through**) turn over pages or papers, reading them quickly or casually. ◻ **turn over a new leaf** start to behave in a better way. ■ **leafy** adjective.

leaflet noun **1** a printed sheet of paper containing information or advertising. **2** a small leaf. verb (**leaflets, leafleting, leafleted**) distribute leaflets to.

league¹ noun **1** a collection of people, countries, or groups that combine for a particular purpose. **2** a group of sports clubs which play each other over a period for a championship. **3** a class of quality or excellence. ◻ **in league** (of two or more people) making secret plans.

league² noun a former measure of distance, of about three miles.

leak verb **1** accidentally allow contents to escape or enter through a hole or crack. **2** (of liquid, gas, etc.) escape or enter accidentally through a hole or crack. **3** intentionally give out secret information. noun **1** a hole or crack through which contents leak. **2** an instance of leaking. ■ **leakage** noun **leaky** adjective.

lean¹ verb (**leans, leaning,** past and past participle **leaned** or Brit. **leant**) **1** be in a sloping position. **2** (**lean against** or **on**) rest against. **3** (**lean on**) rely on for support. **4** (**lean to** or **towards**) favour a view or position. ◻ **lean-to** (plural **lean-tos**) a small building sharing a wall with a larger building.

lean² adjective **1** (of a person) having little fat; thin. **2** (of meat) containing little fat. **3** unproductive.

leaning noun a tendency or preference.

leap verb (**leaps, leaping,** past or past

participle **leaped** or **leapt**) **1** jump or spring a long way. **2** jump across. **3** move quickly and suddenly. **4** (**leap at**) accept eagerly. **5** increase dramatically. **noun** an instance of leaping. □ **leap year** a year with 366 days, occurring every four years.

leapfrog **noun** a game in which players in turn vault over others who are bending down. **verb** (**leapfrogs, leapfrogging, leapfrogged**) **1** vault over someone in leapfrog. **2** overtake others to move into a leading position.

learn **verb** (**learns, learning,** past and past participle **learned** or **learnt**) **1** gain knowledge or skill through study or experience. **2** become aware of something through observing or hearing about it. **3** memorize.

learned /**ler**-nid/ **adjective** having gained a great deal of knowledge by studying.

learning **noun** knowledge or skills gained through study.

lease **noun** an agreement by which one person uses the land, property, etc. of another for a specified time in return for payment. **verb** (**leases, leasing, leased**) let out or rent by a lease.

leasehold **noun** the holding of property by a lease.

leash **noun** a dog's lead.

least **determiner & pronoun** (usu. **the least**) smallest in amount, extent, or significance. **adverb** to the smallest extent or degree. □ **at least 1** not less than. **2** if nothing else. **3** anyway.

leather **noun** a material made from the skin of an animal by tanning or a similar process.

leathery **adjective** tough and hard like leather.

leave[1] **verb** (**leaves, leaving, left**) **1** go away from. **2** stop living at or working for. **3** allow something to remain. **4** (**be left**) remain to be used or dealt with. **5** let someone do something without interfering. **6** deposit something to be collected or attended to. **7** (**leave out**) fail to include.

leave[2] **noun 1** (also **leave of absence**) time when you have permission to be absent from work or duty. **2** formal permission. □ **take your leave** formal say goodbye.

leaven /**lev**-uhn/ **noun** a substance added to dough to make it ferment and rise. **verb** modify or improve by adding something.

leaves plural of **LEAF**.

lecher **noun** a lecherous man. ■ **lechery** **noun**.

lecherous **adjective** (of a man) showing sexual desire in an offensive way.

lectern **noun** a tall stand with a sloping top from which a speaker can read while standing up.

lecture **noun 1** an educational talk to an audience. **2** a long telling-off or critical talk. **verb** (**lectures, lecturing, lectured**) **1** give a lecture. **2** give someone a critical lecture. ■ **lecturer** **noun**.

led past and past participle of **LEAD**[1].

ledge **noun** a narrow horizontal surface sticking out from a wall, cliff, etc.

ledger **noun** a book in which financial accounts are kept.

lee **noun** the side of something that provides shelter from wind or weather.

leech **noun 1** a worm that sucks the blood of animals or people. **2** a person who lives off others.

leek **noun** a plant with a long cylindrical bulb which is eaten as a vegetable.

leer **verb** look in a lustful or unpleasant way. **noun** a lustful or unpleasant look.

leery **adjective** informal wary.

lees /leez/ **plural noun** dregs left in the bottom of a barrel of wine.

leeward /lee-werd, **loo**-erd/ **adjective & adverb** on or towards the side that is sheltered from the wind.

leeway **noun** the amount of freedom to move or act that is available.

left[1] **adjective 1** on or towards the side of a person or thing which is to the west when the person or thing is facing north. **2** left-wing. **adverb** on or to the left side. **noun 1 (the left)** the left-hand part, side, or direction. **2** a left turn. **3 (often the Left)** a left-wing group or party. □ **left-field** unconventional or experimental. **left wing** radical, reforming, or socialist.

left[2] past and past participle of **LEAVE**[1].

leftover noun something remaining after the rest has been used. **adjective** remaining; surplus.

lefty noun (plural **lefties**) informal a left-wing person.

leg noun 1 each of the limbs on which a person or animal moves and stands. **2** a long, thin support or prop. **3** a section of a journey, race, etc. **4** (in sport) each of two or more games making up a round of a competition. **verb (legs, legging, legged) (leg it)** informal **1** travel by foot; walk. **2** run away.

legacy noun (plural **legacies**) **1** an amount of money or property left to someone in a will. **2** something handed down by a predecessor.

legal adjective 1 having to do with the law. **2** permitted by law. □ **legal aid** money given to people who cannot afford to pay for a lawyer. **legal tender** accepted methods of payment such as coins or banknotes. ■ **legality** noun **legally** adverb.

legalize or **legalise verb (legalizes, legalizing, legalized)** make something legal. ■ **legalization** noun.

legate /le-**guht**/ **noun** a representative of the Pope.

legation /li-**gay**-sh'n/ **noun 1** a diplomat below the rank of ambassador, and their staff. **2** the official residence of a diplomat.

legato /li-**gah**-toh/ **adverb & adjective** Music in a smooth, flowing manner.

legend noun 1 a traditional story from long ago which is not definitely true. **2** an extremely famous person. **3** an inscription, caption, or key.

legendary adjective 1 described in legends. **2** remarkable enough to be famous.

leggings plural noun 1 women's tight-fitting stretchy trousers. **2** strong protective outer coverings for the legs.

leggy adjective (leggier, leggiest) long-legged.

legible adjective (of handwriting or print) clear enough to read. ■ **legibility** noun **legibly** adverb.

legion noun 1 a division of 3,000 to 6,000 men in the army of ancient Rome. **2 (a legion** or **legions of)** a vast number of. **adjective** literary great in number.

legionnaire /lee-juh-**nair**/ **noun** a member of a legion. □ **legionnaires' disease** a form of pneumonia.

legislate verb (legislates, legislating, legislated) 1 make laws. **2 (legislate for** or **against)** prepare for a situation or occurrence. ■ **legislator** noun.

legislation noun laws.

legislative adjective 1 having the power to make laws. **2** relating to laws.

legislature noun the group of people who make a country's laws.

legitimate adjective /li-**jit**-i-muht/ **1** allowed by the law or rules. **2** able to be defended; reasonable. **3** (of a child) born of parents who are married to each other. **verb** /li-**jit**-i-mayt/ **(legitimates, legitimating, legitimated)** make something legitimate. ■ **legitimacy** noun.

 leg-, not *lig-*: *legitimate.*

legitimize or **legitimise verb (legitimizes, legitimizing, legitimized)** make something legitimate.

legume /**leg**-yoom/ **noun** a plant with seeds in pods, such as the pea. ■ **leguminous** adjective.

leisure noun time spent not working; free time. □ **at leisure 1** not occupied; free. **2** in an unhurried manner.

leisurely adjective relaxed and unhurried. **adverb** without hurry.

lemming noun 1 a short-tailed Arctic rodent which periodically migrates in large numbers in search of food.

2 a person who unthinkingly joins a mass movement.

lemon noun **1** a pale yellow citrus fruit with thick skin and acidic juice. **2** a pale yellow colour. □ **lemon curd** a sweet spread made with lemons.

lemonade noun a sweet drink made with lemon juice or flavouring.

lemur /lee-mer/ noun an animal resembling a monkey, found only in Madagascar.

lend verb (**lends**, **lending**, **lent**) **1** allow someone to use something on the understanding that they will return it. **2** give someone money on condition that they will pay it back later. **3** add or contribute a particular quality. **4** (**lend itself to**) be suitable for. ■ **lender** noun.

length noun **1** the measurement or extent of something from end to end. **2** the amount of time that something lasts. **3** the quality of being long. **4** a stretch or piece of something. **5** the extent to which someone does something: *going to great lengths*.

lengthen verb make or become longer.

lengthways or **lengthwise** adverb in a direction parallel with a thing's length.

lengthy adjective (**lengthier**, **lengthiest**) lasting a long time. ■ **lengthily** adverb.

lenient /lee-ni-uhnt/ adjective not strict; merciful or tolerant. ■ **leniency** noun **leniently** adverb.

lens noun **1** a piece of transparent curved material that concentrates or spreads out light rays, used in cameras, spectacles, etc. **2** the transparent part of the eye that focuses light on to the retina.

Lent noun (in the Christian Church) the period immediately before Easter.

lent past and past participle of **LEND**.

lentil noun an edible seed with one flat and one curved side.

lento adverb & adjective Music slow or slowly.

Leo noun a sign of the zodiac (the Lion), 23 July–22 August.

leonine /lee-uh-nyn/ adjective of or resembling a lion or lions.

leopard noun (feminine **leopardess**) a large cat with a spotted coat, found in Africa and southern Asia.

leotard /lee-uh-tard/ noun a close-fitting, stretchy one-piece garment covering the body to the top of the thighs, worn for dance, exercise, etc.

leper noun **1** a person suffering from leprosy. **2** a person who is shunned by others.

leprechaun /lep-ruh-kawn/ noun (in Irish folklore) a mischievous sprite.

leprosy noun a contagious disease that affects the skin and can cause disfigurement and deformities. ■ **leprous** adjective.

lesbian noun a woman who is sexually attracted to other women. adjective relating to lesbians. ■ **lesbianism** noun.

lesion /lee-zhuhn/ noun an area of skin or part of the body which has suffered damage.

less determiner & pronoun **1** a smaller amount of; not as much. **2** fewer in number. adverb to a smaller extent; not so much. preposition minus.

> **i** make sure you distinguish between **less** and **fewer**. Use **fewer** with plural nouns, as in *there are fewer people here today*; use **less** with nouns referring to things that cannot be counted, as in *there is less blossom on this tree*. **Less** with a plural noun (*less people*) is wrong.

lessee noun a person who holds the lease of a property.

lessen verb make or become less.

lesser adjective not so great, large, or important as the other or the rest.

lesson noun **1** a period of learning or teaching. **2** a thing that has been learned. **3** a thing that serves as a warning or encouragement. **4** a passage from the Bible read aloud during a church service.

lessor noun a person who lets a property to another.

lest conjunction formal **1** with the intention of preventing; to avoid the risk of. **2** because of the possibility of.

let verb (**lets**, **letting**, **let**) **1** allow. **2** used to express an intention, suggestion, or order: *let's have a drink.* **3** allow someone to use a room or property in return for payment. noun **1** Brit. a period during which a room or property is rented. **2** (in racket sports) a situation in which a point is not counted and is played for again. □ **let alone** not to mention. **let down** fail to support or help. **let go** allow to go free. **let yourself go 1** act in a relaxed way. **2** become careless in your habits or appearance. **let off 1** cause a gun, firework, etc. to fire or explode. **2** choose not to punish someone. **let up** informal become less intense.

lethal adjective **1** able to cause death. **2** very harmful or destructive. ■ **lethally** adverb.

lethargic adjective affected by lethargy; sluggish and apathetic. ■ **lethargically** /leth-er-ji/ adverb.

lethargy /**leth**-er-ji/ noun a lack of energy and enthusiasm.

let's short form let us.

letter noun **1** any of the symbols of an alphabet. **2** a written communication sent by post or messenger. **3** (**letters**) old use knowledge of literature. verb (**letters**, **lettering**, **lettered**) **1** write something with letters. **2** (**lettered**) old use able to read and write. □ **letter bomb** an explosive device hidden in a small package, which explodes when the package is opened. **letter box** a slot in a door through which mail is delivered. **the letter of the law** the precise terms of a law or rule.

letterhead noun a printed heading on stationery.

lettuce noun a plant whose leaves are eaten in salads.

leucocyte or **leukocyte** /loo-koh-syt/ noun a white blood cell.

leukaemia /loo-**kee**-mi-uh/ (US spelling **leukemia**) noun a serious disease in which too many white blood cells are produced.

levee /**lev**-i/ noun an embankment built to stop a river overflowing.

level noun **1** a horizontal line or surface. **2** the amount of something that is present. **3** a position on a scale. **4** height in relation to the ground. **5** a particular floor in a building. adjective **1** having a flat, horizontal surface. **2** having the same relative height or position as someone or something else. verb (**levels**, **levelling**, **levelled**; US spelling **levels**, **leveling**, **leveled**) **1** make or become level. **2** aim or direct a weapon, criticism, or accusation. **3** (**level with**) informal be honest with. □ **level crossing** Brit. a place where a road crosses a railway at the same level. **level-headed** calm and sensible. ■ **levelly** adverb.

lever noun **1** a bar used to move a load with one end where pressure is applied to the other. **2** an arm or handle that is moved to operate a mechanism. verb (**levers**, **levering**, **levered**) lift or move with a lever.

leverage noun **1** the application of force with a lever. **2** the power to influence.

leveret noun a young hare.

leviathan /li-**vy**-uh-**thuhn**/ noun **1** (in the Bible) a sea monster. **2** a very large or powerful thing.

levitate verb (**levitates**, **levitating**, **levitated**) rise and hover in the air. ■ **levitation** noun.

levity noun the treatment of a serious matter with humour or lack of respect.

levy noun (plural **levies**) **1** the imposing of a tax, fine, etc. **2** a sum of money raised by a levy. **3** old use a body of enlisted troops. verb (**levies**, **levying**, **levied**) **1** impose a levy. **2** old use enlist someone for military service.

lewd adjective crude and offensive in a sexual way.

lexical adjective **1** relating to the words or vocabulary of a language. **2** relating to a lexicon or dictionary.

lexicography noun the writing of dictionaries. ■ **lexicographer** noun.

lexicon noun **1** the vocabulary of a person, language, or branch of knowledge. **2** a dictionary.

ley line noun a line of energy believed by some people to connect some ancient sites.

liability noun (plural **liabilities**) **1** the state of being liable. **2** an amount of money that a person or company owes. **3** a person or thing likely to cause you embarrassment or trouble.

liable adjective **1** responsible by law. **2** (**liable to**) able to be punished by law for something. **3** (**liable to do**) likely to do or to be affected by.

liaise /li-ayz/ verb (**liaises, liaising, liaised**) **1** cooperate on a matter of shared interest. **2** (**liaise between**) act as a link between two or more people or groups.

liaison noun **1** communication or cooperation between people or organizations. **2** a sexual relationship.

 remember the second *i*: *liaison*.

liana noun a tropical climbing plant that hangs from trees.

liar noun a person who tells lies.

libation noun (in the past) a drink poured as an offering to a god.

libel noun the crime of publishing something false that is damaging to a person's reputation. verb (**libels, libelling, libelled**; US spelling **libels, libeling, libeled**) publish something false about. ■ **libellous** (US spelling **libelous**) adjective.

liberal adjective **1** willing to respect and accept behaviour or opinions different from your own. **2** (in politics) supporting the freedom of individuals and favouring moderate political reform. **3** (**Liberal**) relating to the Liberal or Liberal Democrat Party. **4** not strictly literal or exact. **5** generous in applying or adding something. noun a person with liberal views. ■ **liberalism** noun **liberality** noun **liberally** adverb.

liberalize or **liberalise** verb (**liber-** alizes, liberalizing, liberalized) remove or loosen restrictions on. ■ **liberalization** noun.

liberate verb (**liberates, liberating, liberated**) **1** set free. **2** (**liberated**) free from social conventions. ■ **liberation** noun **liberator** noun.

libertine noun a man who is unprincipled in sexual matters.

liberty noun (plural **liberties**) **1** the state of being free. **2** a right or privilege. **3** the ability to act as you please. **4** informal a rude remark or action. □ **take liberties** behave in a disrespectful or over-familiar way.

libidinous /li-**bid**-i-nuhss/ adjective having a strong sexual drive.

libido /li-**bee**-doh/ noun (plural **libidos**) sexual desire.

Libra /**lee**-bruh/ noun a sign of the zodiac (the Scales or Balance), 23 September–22 October.

librarian noun a person who works in a library.

library noun (plural **libraries**) **1** a building or room containing a collection of books which people can read or borrow. **2** a private collection of books.

libretto noun (plural **libretti** /li-**bret**-ti/ or **librettos**) the words of an opera or musical. ■ **librettist** noun.

lice plural of **LOUSE**.

licence (US spelling **license**) noun **1** an official permit to own, use, or do something. **2** freedom to behave in an unrestrained way. □ **license plate** N. Amer. a number plate.

 lic*ence* is the spelling for the noun, and lic*ense* for the verb; in American English the -*ense* spelling is used for both.

license verb (**licenses, licensing, licensed**) **1** grant a licence to. **2** authorize.

licensee noun a person who holds a licence to sell alcoholic drinks.

licentious /ly-**sen**-shuhss/ adjective unprincipled in sexual matters.

lichen /**ly**-kuhn, **li**-chuhn/ noun a plant resembling moss which grows on rocks, walls, and trees.

lick verb **1** pass the tongue over something. **2** move lightly and quickly. **3** informal totally defeat. noun **1** an act of licking. **2** informal a small amount or quick application of something.

licorice US spelling of **LIQUORICE**.

lid noun **1** a removable or hinged cover for the top of a container. **2** an eyelid.

lido /lee-doh, ly-doh/ noun (plural **lidos**) a public open-air swimming pool.

lie[1] verb (**lies, lying, lay**; past participle **lain**) **1** be in a horizontal position on a supporting surface. **2** be in a particular state. **3** be situated or found. □ **the lie of the land 1** the features or characteristics of an area. **2** the current situation or state of affairs.

> ℹ️ don't confuse lay and lie: see the note at LAY[1].

lie[2] noun a false statement made deliberately by someone who knows it is not true. verb (**lies, lying, lied**) tell a lie or lies.

liege /leej/ noun historical **1** (also **liege lord**) a lord under the feudal system. **2** a subject or inferior.

lieu /lyoo/ noun (**in lieu of**) instead of.

lieutenant /lef-ten-uhnt/ noun **1** a deputy or substitute acting for a superior. **2** a rank of officer in the army and navy.

life noun (plural **lives**) **1** the condition of being alive. **2** the existence of an individual human being or animal. **3** a particular type or aspect of existence. **4** living things and their activity. **5** vitality or energy. **6** informal a sentence of imprisonment for life. □ **life insurance** (or **life assurance**) insurance that pays out money either when the insured person dies or after a set period. **life jacket** a jacket for keeping a person afloat in water. **life peer** (in the UK) a peer whose title cannot be inherited. **life raft** an inflatable raft used in an emergency at sea.

lifebelt noun a ring used to help a person who has fallen into water to stay afloat.

lifeblood noun a vital factor or force.

lifeboat noun a boat which is launched from land to rescue people at sea, or which is kept on a ship for use in an emergency.

lifeguard noun a person employed to rescue people who get into difficulty at a beach or swimming pool.

lifeless adjective **1** dead or apparently dead. **2** not containing living things. **3** lacking vigour or excitement.

lifelike adjective accurate in its representation of a living person or thing.

lifeline noun **1** a rope thrown to rescue someone in difficulties in water. **2** a thing which is essential for existence or communication.

lifelong adjective lasting or remaining throughout a person's life.

lifespan noun the length of time that a person or animal is likely to live.

lifestyle noun the way in which a person lives.

lifetime noun the length of time that a person lives or a thing functions.

lift verb **1** raise to a higher position. **2** pick up and move to a different position. **3** formally end a restriction. **4** (**lift off**) (of an aircraft, spacecraft, etc.) take off. noun **1** Brit. a device for moving people or things between different levels of a building, mine, etc. **2** a free ride in another person's vehicle. **3** a device for carrying people up or down a mountain. **4** a feeling of increased cheerfulness. **5** upward force exerted by the air on an aircraft wing or similar.

ligament /lig-uh-muhnt/ noun a band of tissue which connects two bones or cartilages or holds together a joint.

ligature /lig-uh-cher/ noun a thing used for tying something tightly, especially to tie up a bleeding artery.

light[1] noun **1** the natural energy that makes things visible. **2** a source of light. **3** a device that produces a flame or spark. **4** an expression in someone's eyes. **5** understanding; enlightenment. verb (**lights, lighting, lit**; past participle **lit** or **lighted**) **1** provide with light; illuminate. **2** ignite or be ignited. **3 (light up)** make or become animated or happy. **4 (light on)** discover by chance. **adjective 1** having a lot of light. **2** pale in colour. □ **in the light of** taking something into consideration. **light-fingered** tending to steal things. **light-headed** dizzy and slightly faint. **light-hearted** amusing and entertaining. **light year** the distance that light travels in one year, nearly 6 million million miles.

light² **adjective 1** of little weight; not heavy. **2** not heavy enough. **3** not strongly or heavily built. **4** relatively low in density, amount, or intensity. **5** gentle or delicate. **6** not profound or serious. ∎ **lightly** adverb **lightness** noun.

lighten **verb 1** make or become lighter in weight. **2** make or become brighter.

lighter¹ **noun** a device producing a small flame, used to light cigarettes.

lighter² **noun** a barge used to transfer goods to and from ships in harbour.

lighthouse **noun** a tower containing a powerful light to guide ships at sea.

lighting **noun 1** equipment for producing light. **2** the arrangement or effect of lights.

lightning **noun** the discharge of high-voltage electricity between a cloud and the ground or within a cloud, accompanied by a bright flash. **adjective** very quick. □ **lightning conductor** (or N. Amer. **lightning rod**) a rod or wire fixed to a high place to divert lightning into the ground.

| ✓ | the spelling is **lightning**, not -tening. |

lights **plural noun** the lungs of sheep, pigs, or bullocks as food.

lightweight **noun 1** a weight in boxing between featherweight and welterweight. **2** informal a person of little importance.

ligneous /lig-ni-uhss/ **adjective** consisting of, or resembling, wood.

like¹ **preposition 1** similar to. **2** in the manner of. **3** in a way appropriate to.

4 such as. **conjunction** informal **1** in the same way that. **2** as though. **noun (the like)** things of the same kind. **adjective** having similar characteristics to another.

| ⓘ | don't use **like** to mean 'as if', as in *he's behaving like he owns the place*. Use **as if** or **as though** instead. |

like² **verb (likes, liking, liked) 1** find agreeable or satisfactory. **2** wish for; want. **noun (likes)** the things that you like.

likeable or **likable** **adjective** pleasant; easy to like.

likelihood **noun** the state of being likely; probability.

likely **adjective (likelier, likeliest) 1** probable. **2** promising. **adverb** probably.

liken **verb (liken to)** point out the resemblance of someone or something to.

likeness **noun 1** resemblance. **2** outward appearance. **3** a portrait or representation.

likewise **adverb 1** also; moreover. **2** similarly.

liking **noun 1** a regard or fondness for something. **2 (your liking)** your taste.

lilac **noun 1** a shrub or small tree with fragrant violet, pink, or white blossom. **2** a pale pinkish-violet colour.

lilo **noun (plural lilos)** an inflatable mattress used for floating on water.

lilt **noun 1** a rising and falling of the voice when speaking. **2** a gentle rhythm in a tune. ∎ **lilting** adjective.

lily **noun** a plant with large trumpet-shaped flowers on a tall, slender stem. □ **lily-livered** cowardly. **lily of the valley** a plant with broad leaves and white bell-shaped flowers.

limb **noun 1** an arm, leg, or wing. **2** a large branch of a tree. □ **out on a limb** isolated.

limber **adjective** supple; flexible. **verb (limbers, limbering, limbered) (limber up)** warm up in preparation for exercise or activity.

limbo¹ **noun** an uncertain period of waiting.

limbo² noun (plural **limbos**) a West Indian dance in which you bend backwards to pass under a horizontal bar.

lime¹ noun a white alkaline substance used as a building material or fertilizer.

lime² noun **1** a green citrus fruit similar to a lemon. **2** a bright light green colour.

lime³ noun a deciduous tree with heart-shaped leaves and yellowish blossom.

limelight noun (**the limelight**) the focus of public attention.

limerick noun a humorous five-line poem with a rhyme scheme *aabba*.

limestone noun a hard rock composed mainly of calcium carbonate.

limit noun **1** a point beyond which something does not or may not pass. **2** a restriction on the size or amount of something. verb (**limits, limiting, limited**) impose a limit on. ◻ **off limits** out of bounds. ■ **limitless** adjective.

limitation noun **1** a restriction. **2** a fault or failing.

limited adjective **1** restricted in size, amount, or extent. **2** not great in ability. **3** (**Limited**) Brit. (of a company) whose owners have only a limited responsibility for its debts.

limo noun (plural **limos**) informal a limousine.

limousine noun a large, luxurious car.

limp¹ verb **1** walk with difficulty because of an injured leg or foot. **2** (of a damaged ship or aircraft) proceed with difficulty. noun a limping walk.

limp² adjective **1** not stiff or firm. **2** without energy or will. ■ **limply** adverb.

limpet noun a shellfish with a muscular foot for clinging tightly to rocks.

limpid adjective (of a liquid or the eyes) clear.

linchpin or **lynchpin** noun **1** a pin through the end of an axle keeping a wheel in position. **2** an extremely important person or thing.

linctus noun Brit. thick liquid medicine, especially cough mixture.

line¹ noun **1** a long, narrow mark or band. **2** a length of cord, wire, etc. **3** a row or series of people or things. **4** a row of written or printed words. **5** a direction, course, or channel. **6** a telephone connection. **7** a railway track or route. **8** a series of military defences facing an enemy force. **9** a wrinkle in the skin. **10** a range of commercial goods. **11** a sphere of activity: *their line of work.* **12** (**lines**) a way of doing something. **13** (**lines**) the words of an actor's part. **14** (**lines**) a school punishment in which you have to write out a sentence a number of times. verb (**lines, lining, lined**) **1** be positioned at intervals along a route. **2** (**line up**) arrange in a row. **3** (**line up**) have something prepared. **4** (**lined**) marked or covered with lines. ◻ **in line** under control. **in line for** likely to receive. **line dancing** country and western dancing in which a line of dancers follow a set pattern of steps. **line-up 1** a group of people or things assembled for a particular purpose. **2** an identity parade. **on the line** at serious risk. **out of line** informal behaving badly or wrongly.

line² verb (**lines, lining, lined**) cover the inner surface of something with different material.

lineage /lin-i-ij/ noun ancestry or pedigree.

lineal /lin-i-uhl/ adjective **1** in a direct line of descent or ancestry. **2** linear.

lineament /lin-i-uh-muhnt/ noun literary a distinctive feature, especially of the face.

linear /lin-i-er/ adjective **1** arranged in or extending along a straight line. **2** consisting of lines or outlines. **3** involving one dimension only. **4** progressing from one stage to another in a series of steps. ■ **linearity** noun.

linen noun **1** cloth woven from flax. **2** articles such as sheets or clothes made, or traditionally made, of linen.

liner[1] noun **1** a large passenger ship. **2** a cosmetic for outlining or emphasizing a facial feature.

liner[2] noun a lining of a garment, container, etc.

linesman noun (in sport) an official who assists the referee or umpire in deciding whether the ball is out of play.

ling[1] noun a long-bodied sea fish.

ling[2] noun the common heather.

linger verb **1** be slow or reluctant to leave. **2** (**linger over**) spend a long time over. **3** be slow to fade, disappear, or die.

lingerie /**lan**-zh uh-ri/ noun women's underwear and nightclothes.

lingo noun (plural **lingos** or **lingoes**) informal **1** a foreign language. **2** the jargon of a particular subject or group.

lingua franca /ling-gwuh **frang**-kuh/ noun (plural **lingua francas**) a language used as a common language between speakers whose native languages are different.

linguine /ling-**gwee**-nay, ling-**gwee**-ni/ plural noun small ribbons of pasta.

linguist noun **1** a person who is good at foreign languages. **2** a person who studies linguistics.

linguistic adjective relating to language or linguistics.

linguistics plural noun the scientific study of language.

liniment noun an ointment rubbed on the body to relieve pain or bruising.

lining noun a layer of material covering or attached to the inside of something.

link noun **1** a relationship or connection between people or things. **2** something that lets people communicate. **3** a means of contact or transport between two places. **4** a loop in a chain. verb connect or join.

linkage noun **1** the action of linking or the state of being linked. **2** a system of links.

links plural noun a golf course, especially on grassland near the sea.

linnet noun a finch with a reddish breast and forehead.

lino noun Brit. informal linoleum.

linoleum /li-**noh**-li-uhm/ noun a floor covering made from a mixture of linseed oil and powdered cork.

linseed noun the seeds of the flax plant, which are crushed to make oil that is used in paint, varnish, etc.

lint noun **1** short, fine fibres which separate from cloth when it is being made. **2** Brit. a fabric used for dressing wounds.

lintel noun a horizontal support across the top of a door or window.

lion noun (feminine **lioness**) **1** a large cat of Africa and NW India, the male of which has a shaggy mane. **2** a brave, strong, or fierce person. □ **the lion's share** the largest part of something.

lionize or **lionise** verb (**lionizes**, **lionizing**, **lionized**) treat as a celebrity.

lip noun **1** either of the two fleshy parts forming the edges of the mouth opening. **2** the edge of a hollow container or an opening. **3** informal cheeky talk. □ **lip-read** understand speech from watching a speaker's lip movements. **lip-sync** (**lip-syncs**, **lip-syncing**, **lip-synced**) move your lips in time with pre-recorded music or speech.

liposuction noun a technique in cosmetic surgery for sucking out excess fat from under the skin.

lippy adjective informal not showing proper respect; cheeky.

lipstick noun coloured cosmetic applied to the lips from a small solid stick.

liquefy /**lik**-wi-fI/ verb (**liquefies**, **liquefying**, **liquefied**) make or become liquid. ■ **liquefaction** noun.

 liquefy, not -ify.

liqueur /li-**kyoor**/ noun a strong, sweet flavoured alcoholic drink.

liquid noun a substance such as water or oil that flows freely. adjective **1** in the form of a liquid. **2** clear, like water. **3** (of a sound) pure and flowing. **4** (of assets) held in cash, or easily converted into cash.

liquidate verb (liquidates, liquidating, liquidated) **1** wind up the affairs of a company. **2** convert assets into cash. **3** pay off a debt. **4** informal kill.

liquidity /li-kwid-i-ti/ noun Finance **1** the availability of liquid assets. **2** liquid assets.

liquidize or **liquidise** verb (liquidizes, liquidizing, liquidized) Brit. convert solid food into a liquid or purée. ■ **liquidizer** noun.

liquor /lik-er/ noun **1** alcoholic drink, especially spirits. **2** liquid that has been produced in cooking.

liquorice /lik-uh-riss, lik-uh-rish/ (US spelling **licorice**) noun a black substance made from the juice of a root and used as a sweet and in medicine.

lira /leer-uh/ noun (plural **lire** /leer-uh/) the basic unit of money of Italy and Turkey.

lisp noun a speech defect in which the sound s is pronounced like th. verb speak with a lisp.

lissom or **lissome** adjective slim, supple, and graceful.

list[1] noun a number of connected items or names written one after the other. verb **1** make a list of. **2** include in a list. □ **list price** the price of an article as stated by the manufacturer.

list[2] verb (of a ship) lean over to one side.

listed adjective (of a building in the UK) officially protected because of its historical importance.

listen verb **1** give your attention to a sound. **2** make an effort to hear something. **3** pay attention to advice or a request. noun an act of listening. ■ **listener** noun.

listeria noun a type of bacterium which infects humans and animals through contaminated food.

listing noun **1** a list or catalogue. **2** an entry in a list.

listless adjective lacking energy or enthusiasm. ■ **listlessly** adverb.

lit past and past participle of **LIGHT**[1].

litany noun (plural **litanies**) **1** a series of

appeals to God used in church services. **2** a tedious recital.

liter US spelling of **LITRE**.

literacy noun the ability to read and write.

literal adjective **1** using or interpreting words in their usual or most basic sense. **2** (of a translation) representing the exact words of the original text. **3** not exaggerated or distorted.

literally adverb **1** in a literal way. **2** informal used to emphasize what you are saying: *we were literally killing ourselves laughing.*

literary adjective **1** having to do with literature. **2** (of language) characteristic of literature or formal writing.

literate adjective **1** able to read and write. **2** knowledgeable in a particular field: *computer-literate.*

literati /li-tuh-rah-ti/ plural noun educated people who are interested in literature.

literature noun **1** written works that are regarded as having artistic merit. **2** books and printed information on a particular subject.

lithe /lyth/ adjective slim, supple, and graceful.

lithium /li-thi-uhm/ noun a silver-white metallic element.

lithograph /li-thuh-grahf/ noun a print made by lithography.

lithography /li-thog-ruh-fi/ noun printing from a flat metal surface which has been prepared so that ink sticks only where it is required.

litigation noun the process of taking a dispute to a law court.

litigious /li-ti-juhss/ adjective frequently choosing to go to a law court to settle a dispute.

litmus noun a dye that is red under acid conditions and blue under alkaline conditions. □ **litmus paper** paper stained with litmus, used as a test for acids or alkalis. **litmus test** a reliable test of the quality or truth of something.

litre (US spelling **liter**) noun a metric

unit of capacity equal to 1,000 cubic centimetres (about 1.75 pints).

litter noun **1** rubbish left in an open or public place. **2** an untidy collection of things. **3** a number of young born to an animal at one time. **4** (also **cat litter**) absorbent material that is put into a tray for a cat to use as a toilet indoors. **5** straw or other material used as bedding for animals. **6** (also **leaf litter**) decomposing leaves forming a layer on top of soil. **7** (in the past) an enclosed chair or bed carried by men or animals. verb (**litters, littering, littered**) make a place untidy by dropping litter.

little adjective **1** small in size, amount, or degree. **2** (of a person) young or younger. **3** (of distance or time) short. determiner & pronoun not much. adverb hardly, or not at all. □ **a little 1** a small amount of. **2** a short time or distance. **3** to a limited extent.

liturgy /li-ter-ji/ noun (plural **liturgies**) a set form of public worship used in the Christian Church. ■ **liturgical** adjective.

live[1] verb (**lives, living, lived**) **1** remain alive. **2** be alive at a specified time. **3** spend your life in a particular way. **4** have your home in a particular place. **5** obtain the things necessary for staying alive. □ **live down** manage to make others forget something embarrassing. **live rough** live outdoors with no home. ■ **liveable** (or **livable**) adjective.

live[2] adjective **1** living. **2** (of music) played in front of an audience; not recorded. **3** (of a broadcast) transmitted at the time it happens, rather than recorded. **4** (of a wire or device) connected to a source of electric current. **5** containing explosive that can be detonated. adverb as a live performance. □ **live wire** informal an energetic and lively person.

livelihood noun a way of obtaining the things necessary for life.

lively adjective (**livelier, liveliest**) **1** full of life and energy. **2** (of a place) full of activity. ■ **liveliness** noun.

liven verb (**liven up**) make or become more lively or interesting.

liver noun **1** a large organ in the abdomen that produces bile. **2** the liver of some animals used as food.

livery noun (plural **liveries**) **1** a special uniform worn by a servant or official. **2** a distinctive design and colour scheme used on the vehicles or products of a company. ■ **liveried** adjective.

lives plural of **LIFE**.

livestock noun farm animals.

livid adjective **1** furiously angry. **2** having a dark, inflamed appearance.

living noun **1** being alive. **2** an income which is enough to live on. adjective alive. □ **living room** a room in a house used for relaxing in.

lizard noun a small four-legged reptile with a long body and tail.

llama /lah-muh/ noun a domesticated South American animal related to the camel.

lo exclamation old use used to draw attention to something.

loach noun a small freshwater fish.

load noun **1** a heavy or bulky thing that is being carried. **2** a source or source of pressure. **3** the total number or amount carried in a vehicle or container. **4** (**a load** or **loads of**) informal a lot of. verb **1** put a load on or in. **2** put ammunition into a gun. **3** put something into a device so that it will operate.

loaded adjective **1** carrying or bearing a load. **2** biased towards a particular outcome. **3** having an underlying meaning: *a loaded question*. **4** informal wealthy.

loaf[1] noun (plural **loaves**) a quantity of bread that is shaped and baked in one piece.

loaf[2] verb spend your time idly.

loafer noun **1** a person who spends their time idly. **2** trademark a casual leather shoe with a flat heel.

loam noun a fertile soil of clay and sand containing hummus.

loan noun **1** a sum of money that is lent to someone. **2** the action of lending something. verb give something as a loan. □ **loan shark** informal a money-lender who charges very high rates of interest.

loath or **loth** adjective (loath to do) reluctant or unwilling to do.

> ℹ don't confuse **loath** with **loathe**, which means 'dislike greatly'.

loathe verb (loathes, loathing, loathed) feel hatred or disgust for.

loathsome adjective causing hatred or disgust.

loaves plural of LOAF[1].

lob verb (lobs, lobbing, lobbed) throw or hit something in a high arc. noun (in soccer or tennis) a ball lobbed over an opponent.

lobby noun (plural lobbies) **1** an open area inside the entrance of a public building. **2** any of several large halls in the Houses of Parliament in which MPs meet members of the public. **3** each of two corridors in the Houses of Parliament where MPs vote. **4** a group of people who try to influence politicians on a particular issue. verb (lobbies, lobbying, lobbied) try to influence a politician on an issue. ■ **lobbyist** noun.

lobe noun **1** a roundish and flattish part that hangs down or projects from something. **2** each of the sections of the main part of the brain.

lobelia /luh-**bee**-li-uh/ noun a garden plant with blue or scarlet flowers.

lobotomy /luh-**bot**-uh-mi/ noun (plural lobotomies) an operation that involves cutting into part of the brain, formerly used to treat mental illness.

lobster noun a large edible shellfish with large pincers. □ **lobster pot** a basket-like trap in which lobsters are caught.

local adjective **1** having to do with a particular area, or with the place where you live. **2** affecting a particular part: *a local anaesthetic*. noun **1** a person who lives in a particular place. **2** Brit. informal a pub near where you live. ■ **locally** adverb.

locale /loh-**kahl**/ noun a place where something happens.

locality noun (plural localities) **1** an area or neighbourhood. **2** the position or site of something.

localize or **localise** verb (localizes, localizing, localized) restrict to a particular place. ■ **localization** noun.

locate verb (locates, locating, located) **1** discover the exact place or position of. **2** (be located) be situated in a particular place.

location noun **1** a place where something is located. **2** the action of locating. **3** an actual place in which a film or broadcast is made, as distinct from a studio.

loch /lok, lokh/ noun Scottish a lake, or a narrow strip of sea almost surrounded by land.

loci plural of LOCUS.

lock[1] noun **1** a mechanism for keeping a door or container fastened, operated by a key. **2** a similar device used to prevent a vehicle or other machine from operating. **3** a short section of a canal or river with gates at each end which can be opened or closed to change the water level, used for raising and lowering boats. **4** a hold in wrestling that prevents an opponent from moving a limb. **5** the turning of the front wheels of a car. verb **1** fasten with a lock. **2** shut in or imprison by locking a door. **3** become rigidly fixed or immovable. □ **lock, stock, and barrel** including everything. **lock-up 1** a makeshift jail. **2** Brit. a garage or small shop separate from living quarters, that can be locked up. ■ **lockable** adjective.

lock[2] noun **1** a coil or hanging piece of a person's hair. **2** (locks) literary a person's hair.

locker noun a small cupboard or compartment that can be locked.

locket noun a small ornamental case worn round a person's neck, used to hold a tiny photograph, a lock of hair, etc.

lockjaw noun a form of the disease tetanus in which the jaws become stiff and tightly closed.

lockout noun a situation in which an

employer refuses to allow employees to enter their place of work until they agree to certain conditions.

locksmith noun a person who makes and repairs locks.

locomotion noun movement from one place to another.

locomotive noun a powered railway vehicle used for pulling trains. adjective relating to locomotion.

locum /loh-kuhm/ noun a doctor or priest standing in for another who is temporarily away.

locus /loh-kuhss/ noun (plural loci /loh-sI/) technical a particular position, point, or place.

locust noun a large tropical grasshopper which migrates in vast swarms.

locution noun 1 a word or phrase. 2 a person's particular way of speaking.

lode noun a vein of metal ore in the earth.

lodestone noun a piece of magnetic iron ore used as a magnet.

lodge noun 1 a small house at the gates of a large house with grounds. 2 a room for a porter at the entrance of a large building. 3 a small country house where people stay while hunting and shooting. 4 a branch of an organization such as the Freemasons. 5 a beaver's den. verb (lodges, lodging, lodged) 1 formally present a complaint, appeal, etc. 2 firmly fix something in a place. 3 rent accommodation in another person's house. 4 leave something valuable in a safe place or with someone reliable.

lodger noun a person who pays rent to live in a house or flat with the owner.

lodging noun 1 temporary accommodation. 2 (usu. lodgings) a rented room or rooms, usually in the same house as the owner.

loft noun 1 a room or storage space directly under the roof of a house. 2 a large, open flat in a converted warehouse or factory. 3 a gallery in a church or hall. verb kick, hit, or throw a ball high into the air.

lofty adjective (loftier, loftiest) 1 tall and impressive. 2 morally good; noble. 3 proud and superior. ■ **loftily** adverb.

log¹ noun 1 a part of the trunk or a large branch of a tree that has fallen or been cut off. 2 an official record of the voyage of a ship or aircraft. 3 a device for measuring the speed of a ship. verb (logs, logging, logged) 1 enter facts in a log. 2 achieve a certain distance, speed, or time. 3 (log in/on or out/off) begin or finish using a computer system. 4 cut down an area of forest to use the wood commercially. ■ **logger** noun.

log² noun a logarithm.

loganberry noun an edible red soft fruit, similar to a large raspberry.

logarithm noun each of a series of numbers which allow you to do calculations by adding and subtracting rather than multiplying and dividing. ■ **logarithmic** adjective.

logbook noun 1 a log of a ship or aircraft. 2 Brit. a document recording details about a vehicle and its owner.

loggerheads plural noun (at loggerheads) in strong disagreement.

loggia /loh-ji-uh, lo-ji-uh, loh-juh, loh-ji-uh/ noun an open-sided gallery facing a garden.

logic noun 1 the science of reasoning. 2 clear, sound reasoning. 3 a set of principles used in preparing a computer or electronic device to perform a task. ■ **logician** noun.

logical adjective 1 following the rules of logic. 2 using clear, sound reasoning. 3 expected or reasonable under the circumstances. ■ **logically** adverb.

logistic adjective relating to logistics. noun (logistics) the detailed organization of a large and complex exercise. ■ **logistical** adjective.

logjam noun a situation that seems unable to be settled; deadlock.

logo /lo-goh, loh-goh/ noun (plural logos) a design or symbol used by an organization to identify its products.

loin noun 1 the part of the body between the ribs and the hip bones. 2 a joint of meat from this part of an

WORD FORMATION

-logy

-logy is used to form nouns that mean:

1 a subject of study or interest, as in:

anthropology	the study of humankind
biology	the study of living organisms
geology	the study of the physical structure of the earth
sociology	the study of human society.

2 a type of writing or speech, e.g.:

anthology	a collection of written works
mythology	the myths of a particular country or tradition
trilogy	a set of three works.

-logy comes from the ancient Greek word *logos*, meaning 'word or account'.

---

animal. **3 (loins)** literary a person's sexual organs.

loincloth noun a piece of cloth wrapped round the hips, worn by men in some hot countries.

loiter verb **(loiters, loitering, loitered)** stand around without any obvious purpose.

loll verb **1** sit, lie, or stand in a lazy, relaxed way. **2** hang loosely.

lollipop noun a large, flat, rounded boiled sweet on the end of a stick.

lollop verb **(lollops, lolloping, lolloped)** move in a series of clumsy bounding steps.

lolly noun (plural **lollies**) Brit. informal **1** a lollipop. **2** (also **ice lolly**) a piece of flavoured ice or ice cream on a stick. **3** money.

lone adjective **1** having no companions; solitary. **2** not having the support of others. □ **lone wolf** a person who prefers to be alone.

lonely adjective '(**lonelier, loneliest**) **1** sad because of having no friends or company. **2** (of time) spent alone. **3** (of a place) remote. ■ **loneliness** noun.

loner noun a person who prefers to be alone.

lonesome adjective N. Amer. lonely.

long[1] adjective **(longer, longest**) **1** of great or substantial length. **2** having or lasting a particular length, dis-

tance, or time. **3** (of a drink) large and refreshing. **4** (of odds in betting) reflecting a low level of probability. **5 (long on)** informal well supplied with. adverb **(longer, longest) 1** for a long time. **2** at a distant time. **3** throughout a specified period of time. □ **long-haul** involving transport over a long distance. **long in the tooth** rather old. **long johns** informal underpants with close-fitting legs extending to the ankles. **long jump** an athletic event in which competitors jump as far as possible. **long shot** a scheme or guess that has only the slightest chance of succeeding. **long-sighted** unable to see things clearly if they are close to the eyes. **long-suffering** patiently putting up with problems or annoying behaviour. **long-winded** long and boring.

long[2] verb **(long for** or **to do)** have a strong wish to do or have something.

longboat noun **1** historical the largest boat carried by a sailing ship. **2** = **LONGSHIP**.

longbow noun a large bow formerly used for shooting arrows.

longevity /lon-jev-i-ti/ noun long life.

longhand noun ordinary handwriting (as opposed to shorthand, typing, or printing).

longing noun a strong wish to do or have something. **adjective** strongly wishing for something. ■ **longingly** adverb.

longitude /long-i-tyood/ noun the distance of a place east or west of the Greenwich meridian, measured in degrees.

longitudinal /long-i-**tyoo**-di-n'l/ adjective **1** extending lengthwise. **2** relating to longitude. ■ **longitudinally** adverb.

longship noun a long, narrow warship with oars and a sail, used by the Vikings.

longways adverb lengthways.

loo noun Brit. informal a toilet.

loofah /**loo**-fuh/ noun a long, rough object used to wash yourself with in the bath, consisting of the dried inner parts of a tropical fruit.

look verb **1** direct your gaze in a particular direction. **2** have the appearance of being; seem. **3** face in a particular direction. noun **1** an act of looking. **2** appearance. **3** (looks) a person's facial appearance. **4** a style or fashion. □ **look after** take care of. **look down on** think that you are better than. **look for** try to find. **looking glass** a mirror. **look into** investigate. **look on** watch without getting involved. **look out** be alert for possible trouble. **look up 1** improve. **2** search for information in a reference work. **3** informal visit or contact a friend. **look up to** have a lot of respect for.

lookalike noun a person who looks very similar to another.

lookout noun **1** a place from which you can keep watch or view landscape. **2** a person who keeps watch for danger or trouble.

loom¹ noun a machine for weaving cloth.

loom² verb **1** appear as a vague and threatening shape. **2** (of something bad) seem about to happen.

loony informal noun (plural **loonies**) a mad or silly person. adjective mad or silly.

loop noun **1** a shape produced by a curve that bends round and crosses itself. **2** a strip of tape or film with the ends joined, allowing sounds or images to be continuously repeated. **3** a complete circuit for an electric current. verb form into or have the shape of a loop. □ **loop the loop** (of an aircraft) fly in a vertical circle.

loophole noun a mistake or piece of vague wording that lets someone avoid obeying a law or keeping to a contract.

loopy adjective informal mad or silly.

loose adjective **1** not firmly or tightly fixed in place. **2** not fastened or packaged together. **3** not tied up or shut in. **4** (of a garment) not fitting tightly or closely. **5** not dense or compact in structure. **6** not strict; inexact. **7** careless and indiscreet. **8** dated immoral. verb (looses, loosing, loosed) **1** unfasten or set free. **2** (loose off) fire a shot, bullet, etc. □ **be at a loose end** have nothing definite to do. **loose cannon** a person who behaves in an unpredictable and potentially harmful way. **loose-leaf** (of a folder) having sheets of paper that can be added or removed. ■ **loosely** adverb **looseness** noun.

┌─────────────────────────────┐
│ ℹ️ don't confuse **loose**, meaning │
│ 'unfasten or set free', with **lose**, │
│ which means 'cease to have' or │
│ 'become unable to find'. │
└─────────────────────────────┘

loosen verb **1** make or become loose. **2** (loosen up) warm up in preparation for an activity.

loot noun **1** property taken from an enemy in war or stolen by thieves. **2** informal money. verb steal goods from a building during a war or riot. ■ **looter** noun.

lop verb (lops, lopping, lopped) **1** cut off a branch or limb from a tree or body. **2** informal reduce by a particular amount. □ **lop-eared** (of an animal) having drooping ears.

lope verb (lopes, loping, loped) run with a long bounding stride. noun a long bounding stride.

lopsided adjective with one side lower or smaller than the other.

loquacious /lo-**kway**-shuhss/ adjective formal talkative. ■ **loquacity** noun.

lord noun **1** a nobleman. **2** (**Lord**) a title given to certain British peers or high officials. **3** (**the Lords**) the House of Lords. **4** a master or ruler. **5** (**Lord**) a name for God or Jesus. □ **lord it over** act in an arrogant and bullying way towards. **Lord Mayor** the title of the mayor in London and some other large cities.

lordly adjective proud or superior.

Lordship noun (**His, Your,** etc. **Lordship**) a form of address to a judge, bishop, or nobleman.

lore noun a body of traditions and knowledge on a subject.

lorgnette or **lorgnettes** /lor-nyet/ noun a pair of glasses held by a long handle at one side.

lorry noun (plural **lorries**) Brit. a large motor vehicle for transporting goods.

lose verb (**loses, losing, lost**) **1** have something or someone taken away from you; cease to have or keep. **2** become unable to find. **3** fail to win a game or contest. **4** earn less money than you are spending. **5** waste an opportunity. **6** (**be lost**) be destroyed or killed. **7** escape from. **8** (**lose yourself in** or **be lost in**) be or become deeply involved in. □ **lose heart** become discouraged. **lose out** not get a fair chance or share.

loser noun **1** the person who loses a contest. **2** informal a person who is generally unsuccessful in life.

loss noun **1** the losing of something or someone. **2** a person, object, or amount that you have lost. **3** the feeling of sadness after losing a valued person or thing. **4** a person or thing that is badly missed when lost. □ **at a loss** uncertain or puzzled. **2** losing more money than is being made. **loss-leader** a product sold at a loss to attract customers.

lost past and past participle of **LOSE**. □ **be lost for words** be so surprised or upset that you cannot think what to say. **be lost on** not be noticed or understood by. **lost cause** something that has no chance of success.

lot pronoun & adverb (**a lot** or informal **lots**) a large number or amount; a great deal. noun **1** an item or set of items for sale at an auction. **2** informal a particular group of people. **3** (**the lot**) informal the whole number or quantity. **4** a method of deciding something by chance in which one piece is chosen from a number of marked pieces of paper. **5** a person's luck or situation in life. **6** chiefly N. Amer. a plot of land.

> ✓ **a lot** is a two-word phrase, not one word.

loth ⇒ **LOATH**.

Lothario /luh-**thah**-ri-oh/ noun (plural **Lotharios**) a man who behaves selfishly in his sexual relationships.

lotion noun a creamy liquid put on the skin as a medicine or cosmetic.

lottery noun (plural **lotteries**) **1** a way of raising money by selling numbered tickets and giving prizes to the holders of numbers drawn at random. **2** something whose success is controlled by luck.

lotus noun a kind of large water lily. □ **lotus position** a cross-legged position with the feet resting on the thighs, used in meditation.

louche /loosh/ adjective having a bad reputation but still attractive.

loud adjective **1** producing a lot of noise. **2** expressed forcefully. **3** very brightly coloured and in bad taste. ▪ **loudly** adverb **loudness** noun.

loudhailer noun an electronic device for making the voice louder.

loudspeaker noun a device that converts electrical impulses into sound.

lough /lok, lokh/ noun Irish a loch.

lounge verb (**lounges, lounging, lounged**) lie, sit, or stand in a relaxed way. noun **1** Brit. a sitting room. **2** a room in a hotel, airport, etc. in which people can relax or wait. □ **lounge bar** Brit. a bar in a pub or hotel that is more comfortable than the public bar. **lounge suit** Brit. a man's ordinary suit.

lounger noun an outdoor chair that you can lie back in.

lour or **lower** /rhymes with flour/ **verb 1** scowl. **2** (of the sky) look dark and threatening.

louse noun **1** (plural **lice**) a small insect which lives as a parasite on animals or plants. **2** (plural **louses**) informal an unpleasant person. **verb** (**louses, lousing, loused**) (**louse up**) informal spoil something.

lousy adjective (**lousier, lousiest**) informal very poor or bad.

lout noun a rude or aggressive man or boy. ■ **loutish** adjective.

louvre /loo-ver/ (US spelling **louver**) noun each of a set of slanting slats fixed at intervals in a door, shutter, etc. to allow air or light through.

lovable or **loveable** adjective causing people to feel love or affection.

lovage noun a herb used in cookery.

love noun **1** a very strong feeling of affection. **2** a strong feeling of affection linked with sexual attraction. **3** a great interest and pleasure in something. **4** a person or thing that you love. **5** (in tennis, squash, etc.) a score of zero. **verb** (**loves, loving, loved**) **1** feel love for. **2** like very much. □ **love affair** a romantic or sexual relationship between two people who are not married to each other. **love child** a child born to parents who are not married to each other. **make love** have sex. ■ **loveless** adjective **lover** noun.

lovebird noun **1** a kind of small parrot that shows affection for its mate. **2** (**lovebirds**) informal an affectionate couple.

lovelorn adjective unhappy because you love someone who does not feel the same way about you.

lovely adjective (**lovelier, loveliest**) **1** very beautiful. **2** informal very pleasant. ■ **loveliness** noun.

lovesick adjective feeling weak or unhappy due to being in love.

low¹ adjective **1** not high or tall or far above the ground. **2** below average in amount, extent, or strength. **3** not good or important; inferior. **4** (of a sound) deep or quiet. **5** depressed or lacking energy. **6** unfavourable. **7** not honest or moral. **noun 1** a low point or level. **2** an area of low atmospheric pressure. **adverb** (of a sound) at a low pitch. □ **Low Church** the part of the Church of England that places little emphasis on ritual and the authority of bishops and priests. **the low-down** informal the important facts about something. **lowest common denominator** the lowest number that the bottom number of a group of fractions can be divided into exactly. **low gear** a gear that causes a vehicle to move slowly. **low-key** not elaborate or showy. **low life** dishonest or immoral people or activities. **low tide** the time when the sea is furthest out.

low² verb (of a cow) moo.

lowbrow adjective not intellectual or interested in culture.

lower¹ adjective **1** less high. **2** (in place names) situated to the south. **verb** (**lowers, lowering, lowered**) **1** make or become lower. **2** move downwards. **3** (**lower yourself**) behave in a humiliating way. □ **lower case** small letters as opposed to capitals.

lower² ⇨ **LOUR**.

lowland or **lowlands** noun **1** lowlying country. **2** (**the Lowlands**) the part of Scotland lying south and east of the Highlands. ■ **lowlander** noun.

lowly adjective (**lowlier, lowliest**) low in status or importance.

loyal adjective firm and faithful in your support for a person, organization, etc. ■ **loyally** adverb.

loyalist noun **1** a person who remains loyal to the established ruler or government. **2** (**Loyalist**) a person who believes that Northern Ireland should remain part of Great Britain. ■ **loyalism** noun.

loyalty noun (plural **loyalties**) **1** the state of being loyal. **2** a strong feeling of support.

lozenge noun **1** a diamond-shaped figure. **2** a tablet of medicine that is sucked to soothe a sore throat.

LP abbreviation long-playing (record).

LSD noun lysergic acid diethylamide, a

drug that causes hallucinations.

Ltd abbreviation Brit. Limited.

lubricant noun a substance, e.g. oil, for lubricating part of a machine.

lubricate /loo-bri-kayt/ verb (**lubricates**, **lubricating**, **lubricated**) apply oil or grease to machinery so that it moves easily. ■ **lubrication** noun.

lubricious /loo-**bri**-shuhss/ adjective formal referring to sexual matters in a rude or offensive way; lewd.

lucid /loo-sid/ adjective **1** easy to understand; clear. **2** able to think clearly. ■ **lucidity** noun **lucidly** adverb.

Lucifer /loo-si-fer/ noun the Devil.

luck noun **1** good or bad things that apparently happen by chance. **2** good fortune.

luckily adverb it is fortunate that.

luckless adjective unlucky.

lucky adjective (**luckier**, **luckiest**) having, bringing, or resulting from good luck. □ **lucky dip** Brit. a game in which prizes are concealed in a container for people to pick out at random.

lucrative adjective making a large profit.

lucre /loo-ker/ noun money.

Luddite /lud-dyt/ noun a person who is opposed to new technology.

ludicrous /loo-di-kruhss/ adjective absurd; ridiculous. ■ **ludicrously** adverb.

ludo noun Brit. a board game in which players move counters according to throws of a dice.

lug[1] verb (**lugs**, **lugging**, **lugged**) carry or drag with great effort.

lug[2] noun **1** informal an ear. **2** a projection on an object for carrying it or fixing it in place.

luggage noun suitcases or other bags for a traveller's belongings.

lugubrious /luu-goo-bri-uhss/ adjective sad and gloomy.

lukewarm adjective **1** only slightly warm. **2** unenthusiastic.

lull verb **1** make someone relaxed or calm. **2** make someone feel safe or confident, even if they are at risk of

something bad. noun a quiet period between times of activity.

lullaby noun (plural **lullabies**) a soothing song sung to send a child to sleep.

lumbago /lum-**bay**-goh/ noun pain in the lower back.

lumbar adjective relating to the lower back.

lumber noun **1** chiefly Brit. disused furniture. **2** chiefly N. Amer. timber sawn into rough planks. verb (**lumbers**, **lumbering**, **lumbered**) **1** Brit. informal give someone an unwanted responsibility. **2** move in a heavy, awkward way.

lumberjack noun a person who cuts down trees and saws them into logs.

luminary /loo-mi-nuh-ri/ noun (plural **luminaries**) an important or influential person.

luminescence noun light given off by a substance that has not been heated, e.g. fluorescent light. ■ **luminescent** adjective.

luminous adjective bright or shining, especially in the dark. ■ **luminosity** noun **luminously** adverb.

lump noun **1** an irregularly shaped piece of something hard or solid. **2** a swelling under the skin. verb (**lump together**) casually group together. □ **lump it** informal put up with something whether you like it or not. **lump sum** a single payment as opposed to a number of smaller payments. ■ **lumpy** adjective.

lumpen adjective **1** lumpy and misshapen. **2** stupid or loutish.

lumpish adjective **1** roughly or clumsily shaped. **2** stupid and lethargic.

lunacy noun **1** insanity; mental illness. **2** great stupidity.

lunar adjective having to do with the moon. □ **lunar eclipse** an eclipse in which the moon is obscured by the earth's shadow.

lunatic noun **1** a person who is mentally ill. **2** a very foolish person.

lunch noun a meal eaten in the middle of the day. verb eat lunch.

luncheon noun formal lunch.

lung noun each of a pair of organs in the chest into which humans and animals draw air when breathing.

lunge noun a sudden forward movement of the body. verb (**lunges, lunging** or **lungeing, lunged**) make a sudden forward movement.

lupin noun a plant with spikes of tall flowers.

lupine /loo-pyn/ adjective resembling a wolf.

lurch noun a sudden unsteady movement. verb make a sudden unsteady movement. □ **leave in the lurch** leave someone in a difficult situation without help or support.

lurcher noun Brit. a dog that is a cross between a greyhound and a retriever, collie, or sheepdog.

lure verb (**lures, luring, lured**) tempt someone to do something by offering a reward. noun **1** a type of bait used in fishing or hunting. **2** the attractive qualities of something.

lurex noun trademark yarn or fabric containing a glittering metallic thread.

lurid adjective **1** unpleasantly bright in colour. **2** (of a description) deliberately containing many shocking details. ■ **luridly** adverb.

lurk verb wait in hiding to attack someone.

luscious adjective **1** having a pleasingly rich, sweet taste. **2** (of a woman) very attractive.

lush adjective **1** (of plants) growing thickly and strongly. **2** rich or luxurious. noun N. Amer. informal a drunkard. ■ **lushly** adverb **lushness** noun.

lust noun **1** strong sexual desire. **2** a passionate desire for something. verb feel lust. ■ **lustful** adjective.

lustre (US spelling **luster**) noun **1** a soft glow or shine. **2** prestige or honour. ■ **lustrous** adjective.

lusty adjective (**lustier, lustiest**) healthy and strong; vigorous. ■ **lustily** adverb.

lute noun a stringed instrument with a long neck and a rounded body, which you play by plucking.

luxuriant /lug-*zh*ooriuhnt/ adjective growing thickly and strongly. ■ **luxuriance** noun **luxuriantly** adverb.

luxuriate /luk-*zhoor*-i-ayt/ verb (**luxuriates, luxuriating, luxuriated**) (**luxuriate in**) relax and enjoy something very pleasant.

luxurious adjective very comfortable or elegant and expensive. ■ **luxuriously** adverb.

luxury noun (plural **luxuries**) **1** comfortable and expensive living or surroundings. **2** something that is expensive and enjoyable but not essential.

lychee /ly-chee/ noun a small, sweet fruit with thin, rough skin.

lychgate noun a roofed gateway to a churchyard.

Lycra noun trademark an elastic fabric used for close-fitting clothing.

lye noun an alkaline solution used for washing or cleansing.

lying present participle of LIE¹, LIE².

lymph noun a colourless fluid in the body that contains white blood cells. □ **lymph node** (or **lymph gland**) each of a number of small swellings where lymph is filtered. ■ **lymphatic** adjective.

lynch verb (of a group) kill someone for an alleged crime without a legal trial.

lynchpin ⇒ LINCHPIN.

lynx noun a wild cat with a short tail and tufted ears.

lyre noun a stringed instrument like a small harp, used in ancient Greece.

lyric noun **1** (also **lyrics**) the words of a song. **2** a lyric poem. adjective (of poetry) expressing the writer's thoughts and emotions.

lyrical adjective **1** (of writing or music) expressing the writer's emotions in an imaginative and beautiful way. **2** relating to the words of a popular song. □ **wax lyrical** talk in a very enthusiastic and unrestrained way. ■ **lyrically** adverb.

lyricism noun expression of emotion

in writing or music in an imaginative and beautiful way.

lyricist noun a person who writes the words to popular songs.

Mm

M or **m** noun (plural **Ms** or **M's**) **1** the thirteenth letter of the alphabet. **2** the Roman numeral for 1,000. **abbreviation 1** Monsieur. **2** motorway. **3** (m) metres. **4** (m) miles. **5** (m) millions.

MA abbreviation Master of Arts.

ma'am noun madam.

mac noun Brit. informal a mackintosh.

macabre /muh-**kah**-bruh/ adjective disturbing and horrifying because concerned with death and injury.

macadam noun broken stone used for surfacing roads and paths.

macadamia noun the round edible nut of an Australian tree.

macaroni noun pasta in the form of narrow tubes.

macaroon noun a light biscuit made with ground almonds or coconut.

macaw /muh-**kaw**/ noun a brightly coloured parrot found in Central and South America.

mace¹ noun **1** (in the past) a heavy club with a spiked metal head. **2** a decorated stick carried by an official such as a mayor.

mace² noun a spice made from the dried outer covering of nutmeg.

macerate /**mass**-uh-rayt/ verb (**macerates, macerating, macerated**) soften food by soaking it in a liquid. ■ **maceration** noun.

Mach /mak/ noun (**Mach 1, Mach 2,** etc.)' the speed of sound, twice the speed of sound, etc.

machete /muh-**shet**-i/ noun a broad, heavy knife used as a tool or weapon.

Machiavellian /ma-ki-uh-**vel**-i-uhn/ adjective cunning and underhand.

machinations /ma-shi-**nay**-shuhnz/ plural noun plots and scheming.

machine noun **1** a mechanical device for performing a particular task. **2** a controlling system or group of people. verb (**machines, machining, machined**) make or work on something with a machine. ▢ **machine gun** a gun that fires many bullets in rapid succession. **machine-readable** in a form that a computer can process.

machinery noun **1** machines as a whole, or the parts of a machine. **2** an organized system or structure.

machinist noun a person who operates a machine or makes machinery.

machismo /muh-**kiz**-moh/ noun strong or aggressive male pride.

macho /**ma**-choh/ adjective male in an aggressive way.

mackerel noun an edible sea fish.

mackintosh or **macintosh** noun Brit. a full-length waterproof coat.

macramé /muh-**krah**-mi/ noun the craft of knotting cord to make decorative articles.

macrobiotic adjective (of diet) consisting of organic unprocessed foods.

macrocosm noun the whole of a complex structure.

mad adjective (**madder, maddest**) **1** insane. **2** very foolish; not sensible. **3** done without thought or control. **4** informal very enthusiastic about something. **5** informal very angry. ▢ **mad cow disease** BSE. ■ **madly** adverb **madness** noun.

madam noun **1** a polite form of address for a woman. **2** Brit. informal an arrogant or cheeky girl. **3** a woman who runs a brothel.

Madame /muh-**dam**/ noun (plural **Mesdames** /may-**dam**/) a form of address for a French woman.

madcap adjective acting without thought; reckless.

madden verb make someone mad or very annoyed.

madder noun a red dye obtained from the roots of a plant.

made past and past participle of **MAKE**.

Madeira noun a strong sweet white wine from the island of Madeira. □ **Madeira cake** Brit. a rich kind of sponge cake.

Mademoiselle /ma-duh-mwah-**zel**/ **noun** (plural **Mesdemoiselles** /may-duh-mwa-**zel**/) a form of address for an unmarried French woman.

Madonna noun (**the Madonna**) the Virgin Mary.

madrigal noun a 16th- or 17th-century song for several voices without instrumental accompaniment.

maelstrom /**mayl**-struhm/ **noun 1** a powerful whirlpool. **2** a situation of confusion or upheaval.

maestro /**my**-stroh/ **noun** (plural **maestros**) a famous and talented man, especially a classical musician.

Mafia noun 1 (**the Mafia**) an international criminal organization originating in Sicily. **2** (**mafia**) a powerful group who secretly influence matters.

Mafioso /ma-fi-**oh**-soh/ **noun** (plural **Mafiosi** /ma-fi-**oh**-si/) a member of the Mafia.

magazine noun 1 a periodical publication that contains articles and pictures. **2** the part of a gun that holds bullets before they are fired. **3** a store for weapons, ammunition, and explosives.

magenta noun a light crimson.

maggot noun the soft-bodied larva of a fly or other insect.

Magi /**may**-jI/ **plural noun** the three wise men from the East who brought gifts to the infant Jesus.

magic noun 1 the use of mysterious or supernatural forces to influence events. **2** conjuring tricks performed to entertain people. **3** a mysterious or wonderful quality. **adjective 1** having supernatural powers. **2** informal very exciting or good. **verb** (**magics**, **magicking**, **magicked**) affect something by magic.

magical adjective 1 relating to or using magic. **2** exceptionally beautiful or delightful. ■ **magically** adverb.

magician noun 1 a person with magic powers. **2** a conjuror.

magisterial /ma-ji-**steer**-i-uhl/ **adjective 1** having or showing great authority. **2** relating to a magistrate.

magistracy /**ma**-jiss-truh-si/ **noun** (plural **magistracies**) **1** the post of magistrate. **2** magistrates as a group.

magistrate noun an official who judges minor cases and holds preliminary hearings. ■ **magistracy** noun (plural **magistracies**).

magma /**mag**-muh/ **noun** very hot fluid or semi-fluid rock under the earth's crust.

magnanimous adjective generous or forgiving towards a rival or enemy. ■ **magnanimity** noun.

magnate noun a wealthy and influential person, especially in business.

magnesium /mag-**nee**-zi-uhm/ **noun** a silvery-white substance which burns with a brilliant white flame.

magnet noun 1 a piece of iron that attracts objects containing iron and that points north and south when suspended. **2** a person or thing that has a powerful attraction.

magnetic adjective 1 having the property of magnetism. **2** very attractive. □ **magnetic pole** each of the points near the geographical North and South Poles, which the needle of a compass points to. **magnetic tape** tape used in recording sound, pictures, or computer data. ■ **magnetically** adverb.

magnetism noun 1 the property displayed by magnets of attracting or pushing away metal objects. **2** the ability to attract and charm people.

magnetize or **magnetise verb** (**magnetizes**, **magnetizing**, **magnet-**

ized) make magnetic.

magneto /mag-**nee**-toh/ noun (plural **magnetos**) a small generator that uses a magnet to produce pulses of electricity.

magnification noun **1** the action of magnifying something. **2** the degree to which something is magnified.

magnificent adjective **1** very attractive and impressive; splendid. **2** very good. ■ **magnificence** noun **magnificently** adverb.

magnify verb (**magnifies**, **magnifying**, **magnified**) **1** make something appear larger than it is with a lens or microscope. **2** make larger or stronger. **3** old use praise. □ **magnifying glass** a lens used to help you see something very small by magnifying it.

magnitude noun **1** great size or importance. **2** size.

magnolia noun a tree or shrub with large white or pale pink flowers.

magnum noun (plural **magnums**) a wine bottle of twice the standard size, normally 1½ litres.

magpie noun **1** a black and white bird with a long tail. **2** a person who collects things of little use or value.

maharaja or **maharajah** noun (in the past) an Indian prince.

mah-jong or **mah-jongg** /mah-**jong**/ noun a Chinese game played with small rectangular tiles.

mahogany noun **1** hard reddish-brown wood from a tropical tree. **2** a rich reddish-brown colour.

mahout /muh-**howt**/ noun a person who works with elephants.

maid noun **1** a female servant. **2** old use a girl or young unmarried woman.

maiden noun **1** old use a girl or young unmarried woman. **2** (also **maiden over**) Cricket an over in which no runs are scored. adjective first of its kind: *a maiden voyage.* □ **maiden name** the surname of a married woman before her marriage.

maidenhead noun old use a girl's or woman's virginity.

mail[1] noun **1** letters and parcels sent by post. **2** the postal system. **3** email. verb **1** send by post. **2** send post or email to. □ **mail order** the buying or selling of goods by post.

mail[2] noun (in the past) armour made of metal rings or plates.

maim verb inflict a permanent injury on.

main adjective greatest or most important. noun **1** a chief water or gas pipe or electricity cable. **2** (**the mains**) Brit. the network of pipes and cables supplying water, gas, and electricity. □ **in the main** on the whole.

mainframe noun a large high-speed computer supporting a network of workstations.

mainland noun the main area of land of a country, not including islands and separate territories.

mainly adverb for the most part; chiefly.

mainspring noun the most important or influential part of something.

mainstay noun a thing on which something depends or is based.

mainstream noun the ideas, attitudes, or activities that are shared by most people.

maintain verb **1** keep something in the same state or at the same level. **2** regularly check and repair a building, machine, etc. **3** provide someone with financial support. **4** strongly state that something is the case.

maintenance noun **1** the action of maintaining. **2** financial support that someone gives to their former husband or wife after divorce.

☑ -ten-, not -tain-: maintenance.

maisonette noun a flat on two storeys of a larger building.

maize noun chiefly Brit. a cereal plant with grains set in rows on a cob.

majestic adjective impressively grand or beautiful. ■ **majestically** adverb.

majesty noun (plural **majesties**) **1** impressive beauty or grandeur. **2** (**His**,

Your, etc. **Majesty**) a title given to a king or queen or their wife or widow.

major adjective **1** important or serious. **2** greater or more important; main. **3** Music (of a scale) having intervals of a semitone between the third and fourth, and seventh and eighth notes. noun **1** the rank of army officer above captain. **2** N. Amer. a student specializing in a specified subject. verb (**major in**) N. Amer. & Austral./NZ specialize in a particular subject at college or university. □ **major general** the rank of army officer above brigadier.

major-domo noun (plural **major-domos**) the chief steward of a large household.

majority noun (plural **majorities**) **1** the greater number. **2** Brit. the number of votes by which one party or candidate in an election defeats the opposition. **3** the age when a person becomes an adult in law, usually 18 or 21.

make verb (**makes, making, made**) **1** form something by putting parts together or mixing substances. **2** cause something to happen or come into existence. **3** force someone to do something. **4** add up to. **5** be suitable as. **6** estimate as or decide on. **7** earn money or profit. **8** arrive at or achieve. **9** (**make it**) become successful. **10** prepare to go in a particular direction or to do something. noun the manufacturer or trade name of a product. □ **make-believe** fantasy or pretence. **make do** manage with something that is not satisfactory. **make for 1** move towards. **2** tend to result in. **3** (**be made for**) be very suitable for. **make of 1** give attention or importance to. **2** understand the meaning of. **make off** leave hurriedly. **make off with** steal. **make out 1** manage with difficulty to see, hear, or understand. **2** claim or pretend to be. **3** draw up a list or document. **4** informal make progress. **make up 1** put together from parts or ingredients. **2** invent a story. **3** be friendly again after a quarrel. **4** apply cosmetics to.

make-up cosmetics applied to the face. **make up for** compensate for. **make up your mind** make a decision. **on the make** informal trying to make money or gain an advantage. ■ **maker** noun.

makeover noun a transformation of someone's appearance with cosmetics, hairstyling, and clothes.

makeshift adjective temporary and improvised.

makeweight noun something added to make up a required weight.

malachite /**ma**-luh-kyt/ noun a bright green mineral.

maladjusted adjective not able to cope well with normal life.

maladroit /mal-uh-**droyt**/ adjective clumsy.

malady noun (plural **maladies**) formal a disease or illness.

malaise /ma-**layz**/ noun **1** a general feeling of illness or low spirits. **2** a long-standing problem that is difficult to identify.

malapropism /**mal**-uh-prop-i-z'm/ noun the mistaken use of a word in place of a similar-sounding one.

malaria noun a disease that causes fever and is transmitted by the bite of some mosquitoes. ■ **malarial** adjective.

malarkey noun informal nonsense.

malcontent noun a person who is dissatisfied and rebellious.

male adjective **1** of the sex that can fertilize or inseminate the female. **2** having to do with men. **3** (of a plant or flower) having stamens but not a pistil. **4** (of a fitting) made to fit inside a corresponding part. noun a male person, animal, or plant.

malediction /mal-i-**dik**-sh'n/ noun formal a curse.

malefactor /**mal**-i-fak-ter/ noun formal a criminal or wrongdoer.

malevolent /muh-**lev**-uh-luhnt/ adjective wishing to harm other people. ■ **malevolence** noun.

malformation noun the state of being abnormally shaped or formed. ■ **malformed** adjective.

malfunction verb (of equipment or machinery) fail to function normally. noun a failure to function normally.

malice noun the desire to harm someone.

malicious adjective meaning to harm other people. ■ **maliciously** adverb.

malign /muh-**lyn**/ adjective harmful or evil. verb say unpleasant things about. ■ **malignity** /muh-**lig**-ni-ti/ noun.

malignancy noun (plural **malignancies**) **1** a cancerous growth. **2** the quality of being harmful or evil.

malignant adjective **1** harmful; malevolent. **2** (of a tumour) cancerous.

malinger verb (**malingers**, **malingering**, **malingered**) pretend to be ill in order to avoid work. ■ **malingerer** noun.

mall /mawl/ noun **1** a large enclosed shopping area. **2** a sheltered walk or promenade.

mallard noun a kind of duck with a dark green head.

malleable /**mal**-li-uh-b'l/ adjective **1** able to be hammered or pressed into shape. **2** easily influenced.

mallet noun **1** a hammer with a large wooden head. **2** a wooden stick with a head like a hammer, for hitting a croquet or polo ball.

mallow noun a plant with pink or purple flowers.

malnourished adjective suffering from malnutrition.

malnutrition noun poor health caused by not having enough food, or not enough of the right food.

malodorous adjective smelling very unpleasant.

malpractice noun illegal, corrupt, or careless behaviour by a professional person.

malt noun barley or other grain that has been soaked in water and then dried. ■ **malted** adjective.

maltreat verb treat badly or cruelly. ■ **maltreatment** noun.

mama or **mamma** noun dated or N. Amer. your mother.

mamba noun a large, highly poisonous African snake.

mammal noun a warm-blooded animal that has hair or fur, produces milk, and bears live young. ■ **mammalian** adjective.

mammary adjective relating to the breasts or the milk-producing organs of other mammals.

Mammon noun money thought of as being worshipped like a god.

mammoth noun a large extinct form of elephant with a hairy coat and long curved tusks. adjective huge.

man noun (plural **men**) **1** an adult human male. **2** a person. **3** human beings in general. **4** a figure or token used in a board game. verb (**mans**, **manning**, **manned**) provide a place or machine with people to operate or defend it. □ **man-made** made or caused by human beings. **man of the cloth** a clergyman. **man of letters** a male scholar or author. **man-of-war** historical an armed sailing ship. ■ **manhood** noun.

manacle noun a metal band fastened around a person's hands or ankles to restrict their movement. verb (**manacles**, **manacling**, **manacled**) restrict someone with manacles.

manage verb (**manages**, **managing**, **managed**) **1** be in charge of people or an organization. **2** succeed in doing. **3** be able to cope despite difficulties. **4** control the use of money or other resources. ■ **manageable** adjective.

management noun **1** the action of managing. **2** the managers of an organization.

manager noun **1** a person who manages staff, an organization, or a sports team. **2** a person in charge of the business affairs of a sports player or performer. ■ **managerial** adjective.

manageress noun a woman who manages a business.

manatee /**man**-uh-tee/ noun a large plant-eating mammal that lives in tropical seas.

mandarin noun **1** (Mandarin) the official form of the Chinese language.

2 (in the past) a high-ranking Chinese official. **3** a powerful official. **4** a small citrus fruit with a loose yellow-orange skin.

mandate noun /man-dayt/ **1** an official order or permission to do something. **2** the authority to carry out a policy that is given by voters to the winner of an election. verb /man-dayt/ (mandates, mandating, mandated) give someone authority to do something.

mandatory /man-duh-tuh-ri/ adjective required by law or rules; compulsory.

mandible noun **1** the lower jawbone in mammals or fishes. **2** either of the upper and lower parts of a bird's beak. **3** either of the parts of an insect's mouth that crush its food.

mandolin noun a musical instrument with a rounded back and metal strings.

mandrake noun a plant whose root is used in herbal medicine and magic.

mandrill noun a large baboon with a red and blue face.

mane noun **1** a growth of long hair on the neck of a horse, lion, etc. **2** a person's long hair.

maneuver US spelling of **MANOEUVRE**.

manful adjective brave and determined. ■ manfully adverb.

manganese noun a hard grey metallic element.

mange noun a skin disease of some animals that causes itching and hair loss.

mangel-wurzel noun a variety of beet grown as feed for farm animals.

manger noun a long trough from which horses or cattle eat.

mangetout /monzh-too/ (plural mangetout or mangetouts /monzh-too/) chiefly Brit. a variety of pea with an edible pod.

mangle verb (mangles, mangling, mangled) destroy or severely damage by crushing or twisting. noun a machine with rollers for squeezing wet laundry to remove the water.

mango noun (plural mangoes or mangos) a tropical fruit with yellow flesh.

mangrove noun a tropical tree or shrub found in coastal swamps.

mangy /mayn-ji/ adjective **1** (of an animal) having mange. **2** in poor condition; shabby.

manhandle verb (manhandles, manhandling, manhandled) **1** move a heavy object with effort. **2** push or drag someone roughly.

manhole noun a covered opening giving access to a sewer or other underground structure.

mania /may-ni-uh/ noun **1** mental illness in which a person imagines things and has periods of wild excitement. **2** an extreme enthusiasm.

maniac /may-ni-ak/ noun **1** a person who behaves in an extremely wild or violent way. **2** informal a person with an extreme enthusiasm for something. ■ maniacal /muh-ny-uh-k'l/ adjective.

manic adjective **1** having to do with mania. **2** showing wild excitement and energy. □ manic depression a mental disorder with alternating periods of excitement and depression. ■ manically adverb.

manicure noun treatment to improve the appearance of the hands and nails. ■ manicured adjective manicurist noun.

manifest adjective clear and obvious. verb **1** show or display. **2** appear; become apparent. noun a document listing the cargo, crew, and passengers of a ship or aircraft. ■ manifestly adverb.

manifestation noun **1** a sign or evidence of something. **2** an appearance of a ghost or spirit.

manifesto noun (plural manifestos) a public declaration of the policy and aims of a political party.

manifold adjective many and various. noun a pipe with several openings, especially in a car engine.

manikin noun a very small person.

manioc /man-i-ok/ = **CASSAVA**.

manipulate verb (manipulates, manipulating, manipulated) **1** handle skilfully. **2** control or influence in a clever or underhand way. ■ **manipulation** noun **manipulator** noun.

manipulative adjective manipulating others in a clever or underhand way.

mankind noun human beings as a whole.

manky adjective Brit. informal **1** of poor quality. **2** dirty.

manly adjective (manlier, manliest) **1** having good qualities associated with men, such as courage and strength. **2** suitable for a man. ■ **manliness** noun.

manna noun **1** (in the Bible) the substance supplied by God as food to the Israelites in the wilderness. **2** something unexpected and beneficial.

mannequin /man-ni-kin/ noun a dummy used to display clothes in a shop window.

manner noun **1** a way in which something is done or happens. **2** a person's outward behaviour. **3** (manners) polite social behaviour. **4** literary a kind or sort.

mannered adjective **1** behaving in a specified way: *well-mannered.* **2** artificial and affected.

mannerism noun a distinctive gesture or way of speaking.

mannerly adjective well-mannered; polite.

mannish adjective (of a woman) like a man in appearance or manner.

manoeuvre /muh-**noo**-ver/ (US spelling **maneuver**) noun **1** a movement or series of moves requiring skill and care. **2** a carefully planned scheme. **3** (manoeuvres) a large-scale military exercise. verb (manoeuvres, manoeuvring, manoeuvred) **1** make a movement or series of moves skilfully and carefully. **2** guide skilfully or craftily. ■ **manoeuvrable** adjective.

☑ the British spelling has -oeu- in the middle and -re at the end: man*oeu*vre.

manometer noun an instrument for measuring the pressure of fluids.

manor noun a large country house with lands. ■ **manorial** adjective.

manpower noun the number of people working or available for work.

manse noun the house of a Christian minister in Scotland.

mansion noun a large, impressive house.

manslaughter noun the crime of killing a person without meaning to do so.

mantel noun a mantelpiece or mantelshelf.

mantelpiece noun **1** a structure surrounding a fireplace. **2** (also **mantelshelf**) a shelf forming the top of a mantelpiece.

mantilla /man-**til**-luh/ noun a lace or silk scarf worn by Spanish women over the hair and shoulders.

mantis or **praying mantis** noun (plural **mantis** or **mantises**) a large insect that waits motionless for its prey with its forelegs folded like hands in prayer.

mantle noun **1** a woman's loose sleeveless cloak. **2** a close covering, e.g. of snow. **3** a cover around a gas jet that produces a glowing light when heated. **4** a role or responsibility that passes from one person to another. **5** the region of very hot, dense rocks between the earth's crust and its core.

mantra noun a word or sound repeated to aid concentration when meditating.

manual adjective **1** having to do with the hands. **2** operated by or using the hands. noun a book giving instructions or information. ■ **manually** adverb.

manufacture verb (manufactures, manufacturing, manufactured) **1** make something on a large scale using machinery. **2** invent evidence or a story. noun the manufacturing of things. ■ **manufacturer** noun.

manure noun animal dung used for fertilizing land.

manuscript noun **1** a handwritten book, document, etc. **2** an author's text before printing and publication.

Manx adjective relating to the Isle of Man. □ **Manx cat** a breed of cat that has no tail.

many determiner, pronoun, & adjective a large number of. noun **(the many)** the majority of people.

Maori /mow-ri/ noun (plural **Maori** or **Maoris**) a member of the aboriginal people of New Zealand.

map noun a flat diagram of an area showing physical features, cities, roads, etc. verb (**maps, mapping, mapped**) **1** show on a map. **2** (**map out**) plan in detail.

maple noun a tree with five-pointed leaves.

mar verb (**mars, marring, marred**) spoil the appearance or quality of.

maraca /muh-**rak**-uh/ noun a container filled with small beans or stones, shaken as a musical instrument.

marathon noun **1** a long-distance running race, strictly one of 26 miles 385 yards (42.195 km). **2** a long-lasting and difficult task.

maraud verb make a raid in search of things to steal. ■ **marauder** noun.

marble noun **1** a hard stone, usually white with coloured streaks, which can be polished and used in sculpture and building. **2** a small ball of coloured glass used as a toy. **3** (**your marbles**) informal your mental powers.

marbled adjective patterned with coloured streaks.

March noun the third month of the year.

march verb **1** walk in time and with regular paces, like a soldier. **2** walk quickly and with determination. **3** force someone to walk quickly. **4** take part in an organized procession to make a protest. noun **1** an act of marching. **2** a procession organized as a protest. **3** (**Marches**) land on the border between two territories. ■ **marcher** noun.

marchioness /mar-shuh-**ness**/ noun

1 the wife or widow of a marquess. **2** a woman who holds the rank of marquess.

Mardi Gras /mar-di **grah**/ noun a carnival held in some countries on Shrove Tuesday.

mare noun the female of a horse or related animal.

margarine noun a butter substitute made from vegetable oils or animal fats.

margin noun **1** an edge or border. **2** the blank border on each side of the print on a page. **3** an amount above or below a given level. □ **margin of error** a small amount allowed for in case of miscalculation.

marginal adjective **1** in a margin. **2** slight, or of minor importance. **3** Brit. (of a parliamentary seat) held by only a small majority. ■ **marginality** noun **marginally** adverb.

marginalize or **marginalise** verb (**marginalizes, marginalizing, marginalized**) reduce the power or importance of. ■ **marginalization** noun.

marigold noun a plant of the daisy family with yellow or orange flowers.

marijuana /ma-ri-**hwah**-nuh/ noun cannabis.

marina noun a purpose-built harbour with moorings for yachts and small boats.

marinade noun /ma-ri-**nayd**/ a mixture of ingredients in which food is soaked before cooking to flavour or soften it. verb /**ma**-ri-nayd/ (**marinades, marinading, marinaded**) = **MARINATE**.

marinate verb (**marinates, marinating, marinated**) soak food in a marinade.

marine adjective **1** relating to the sea. **2** relating to shipping or matters concerning a navy. noun a member of a body of troops trained to serve on land or sea.

mariner noun literary a sailor.

marionette noun a puppet worked by strings.

marital adjective relating to marriage or the relations between a husband and wife.

maritime adjective 1 relating to shipping or other activity taking place at sea. **2** living or found in or near the sea. **3** (of a climate) moist and having a mild temperature due to the influence of the sea.

marjoram noun 1 a sweet-smelling plant of the mint family, used as a herb in cooking. **2** = **OREGANO**.

mark¹ noun 1 a small area on a surface having a different colour from its surroundings. **2** something that indicates position or acts as a pointer. **3** a line, figure, or symbol made to identify or record something. **4** a sign of a quality or feeling. **5** a characteristic feature of something. **6** a point awarded for a correct answer or for a piece of work. **7** a particular model of a vehicle or machine. **verb 1** make a mark on. **2** write a word or symbol on an object in order to identify it. **3** indicate the position of. **4** (**mark out**) distinguish or indicate something precisely. **5** indicate or acknowledge a significant event. **6** (**mark up** or **down**) increase or reduce the price of an item. **7** assess and give a mark to a piece of work. **8** pay careful attention to. **9** Brit. (in team games) stay close to an opponent in order to prevent them getting or passing the ball. □ **mark time 1** (of troops) march on the spot without moving forward. **2** fill in time with routine activities. **mark-up** the difference between the basic cost of producing something and the amount it is sold for. **on your marks** be ready to start (used to instruct competitors in a race). **up to the mark** up to the required standard.

mark² noun the basic unit of money of Germany, equal to 100 pfennig.

marked adjective 1 having an identifying mark. **2** clearly noticeable. **3** singled out as a target for attack. ■ **markedly adverb**.

marker noun 1 an object used to indicate a position, place, or route. **2** a felt-tip pen with a broad tip. **3** (in

team games) a player who marks an opponent.

market noun 1 a regular gathering for the buying and selling of food, livestock, or other goods. **2** an outdoor space or large hall where traders offer their goods for sale. **3** a particular area of trade or competitive activity. **4** demand for a particular product or service. **verb** (**markets, marketing, marketed**) advertise or promote. □ **market garden** a place where vegetables and fruit are grown to be sold. **market research** gathering of information about what people choose to buy. **market town** a medium-sized town where a regular market is held. **market value** the amount for which something can be sold in a competitive market. **on the market** available for sale. ■ **marketable adjective**.

marketing noun the promoting and selling of products or services.

marketplace noun 1 an open space where a market is held. **2** the world of trade.

marking noun 1 an identification mark. **2** (also **markings**) a pattern of marks on an animal's fur, feathers, or skin.

marksman noun a person skilled in shooting. ■ **marksmanship noun**.

marl¹ noun a rock or soil consisting of clay and lime.

marl² noun a mottled yarn or fabric of differently coloured threads.

marmalade noun a preserve made from oranges.

marmoreal /mar-mor-i-uhl/ **adjective** literary made of or resembling marble.

marmoset noun a small tropical American monkey with a long tail.

marmot noun a heavily built burrowing rodent.

maroon¹ noun a dark brownish-red colour.

maroon² verb (**be marooned**) be abandoned or isolated in a place which cannot be reached.

marque noun a make of car, as distinct from a specific model.

marquee noun **1** chiefly Brit. a large tent used for special events. **2** N. Amer. a roof-like canopy over the entrance to a building.

marquess noun a British nobleman ranking above an earl and below a duke.

marquetry /mar-ki-tri/ noun inlaid work made from small pieces of variously coloured wood, used for the decoration of furniture.

marquis /mar-kwiss/ noun (in some European countries) a nobleman ranking above a count and below a duke.

marquise /mar-keez/ noun the wife or widow of a marquis, or a woman holding the rank of marquis in her own right.

marriage noun **1** the formal union of a man and woman, by which they become husband and wife. **2** the relationship between a husband and wife. ■ **marriageable** adjective.

married adjective joined in marriage. noun (**marrieds**) married people.

marrow noun **1** Brit. a long gourd with a green skin and white flesh, eaten as a vegetable. **2** (also **bone marrow**) a soft fatty substance inside bones, in which blood cells are produced.

marrowbone noun a bone containing edible marrow.

marry verb (**marries, marrying, married**) **1** become the husband or wife of. **2** join two people in marriage. **3** (**marry into**) become a member of a family by marriage. **4** (**marry up**) join two parts together.

marsh noun an area of low-lying land which usually remains waterlogged. ■ **marshy** adjective.

marshal noun **1** an officer of the highest rank in the armed forces of some countries. **2** (in the US) a type of law enforcement officer. **3** an official responsible for supervising public events. verb (**marshals, marshalling, marshalled**; US spelling **marshals, marshaling, marshaled**) **1** assemble a group of people in order. **2** bring facts together in an organized way.

marshmallow noun a spongy sweet made from sugar, egg white, and gelatin.

marsupial /mar-soo-pi-uhl/ noun a mammal whose young are carried and suckled in a pouch on the mother's belly.

mart noun a trade centre or market.

marten noun a weasel-like forest animal, sometimes hunted for fur.

martial adjective having to do with war. □ **martial arts** sports which started as forms of self-defence or attack, such as judo and karate. **martial law** government by the military forces of a country.

Martian adjective relating to the planet Mars. noun a supposed inhabitant of Mars.

martin noun a small short-tailed swallow.

martinet noun a person who is very strict and insists on being obeyed.

martyr noun **1** a person who is killed because of their beliefs. **2** a person who exaggerates their difficulties in order to obtain sympathy or admiration. verb make a martyr of. ■ **martyrdom** noun.

marvel verb (**marvels, marvelling, marvelled**; US spelling **marvels, marveling, marveled**) be filled with wonder. noun a person or thing that causes a feeling of wonder.

marvellous (US spelling **marvelous**) adjective **1** extremely good. **2** causing great wonder. ■ **marvellously** adverb.

Marxism noun the political and economic theories of Karl Marx (1818–83) and Friedrich Engels (1820–95), which formed the basis for communism. ■ **Marxist** noun & adjective.

marzipan noun a sweet paste of ground almonds, sugar, and egg whites.

mascara noun a cosmetic for darkening and thickening the eyelashes.

mascot noun a person, animal, or object that is supposed to bring good luck.

masculine adjective **1** relating to

men. **2** having the qualities or appearance traditionally associated with men. **3** Grammar referring to a gender of nouns and adjectives seen as male. ■ **masculinity** noun.

mash noun **1** a soft mass made by crushing a substance into a pulp. **2** Brit. informal boiled and mashed potatoes. **verb** reduce or beat to a mash.

mask noun **1** a covering for all or part of the face, worn for protection, as a disguise, or for theatrical effect. **2** a likeness of a person's face moulded in clay or wax. **verb 1** cover with a mask. **2** conceal or disguise. **3** cover an area to protect it during a process such as painting.

masochism /**mass**-uh-ki-z'm/ noun enjoyment felt in being hurt or humiliated by someone. ■ **masochist** noun **masochistic** adjective.

mason noun **1** a person who works with stone. **2** (**Mason**) a Freemason.

Masonic adjective relating to Freemasons.

masonry noun stonework.

masque /mahsk/ noun (in the past) a form of entertainment consisting of dancing and acting performed by masked players.

masquerade /mass-kuh-**rayd**/ noun **1** a pretence. **2** a ball at which people wear masks. **verb** (**masquerades**, **masquerading**, **masqueraded**) pretend to be someone or something else.

Mass noun **1** the Christian service of the Eucharist or Holy Communion. **2** a musical setting of parts of this service.

mass noun **1** a body of matter with no definite shape. **2** a large number of people or objects gathered together. **3** (**the masses**) the ordinary people. **4** (**a mass of**) a large amount of. **5** Physics the quantity of matter which a body contains. **verb** assemble into a single body or mass. □ **mass market** commercial activity in which goods are produced for the broad population. **mass-produced** produced in large quantities in a factory.

massacre noun a brutal slaughter of a large number of people. **verb** (**massacres**, **massacring**, **massacred**) brutally kill a large number of people.

massage noun the rubbing and kneading of parts of the body with the hands to relieve tension or pain. **verb** (**massages**, **massaging**, **massaged**) **1** give a massage to. **2** manipulate figures to give a more acceptable result. □ **massage parlour 1** a place where massage is provided. **2** a brothel.

masseur /ma-**ser**/ noun (feminine **masseuse** /ma-**serz**/) a person who provides massage professionally.

massif /ma-**seef**/ noun a compact group of mountains.

massive adjective **1** large and heavy or solid. **2** exceptionally large, powerful, or severe. ■ **massively** adverb.

mast¹ noun **1** a tall upright post on a boat carrying a sail or sails. **2** any tall upright post or structure.

mast² noun nuts and other fruit that has fallen from trees.

mastectomy noun (plural **mastectomies**) an operation to remove a breast.

master noun **1** a man in a position of authority, control, or ownership. **2** a person skilled in a particular art or activity. **3** the head of a college or school. **4** chiefly Brit. a male schoolteacher. **5** a person who holds a second or further degree. **6** an original film, recording, or document from which copies can be made. **verb** (**masters, mastering, mastered**) **1** acquire complete knowledge or skill in. **2** gain control of. □ **master key** a key that opens several locks, each of which has its own key. **master of ceremonies** a person in charge of proceedings at a special event.

masterclass noun a class given to students by a leading musician.

masterful adjective **1** powerful and able to control others. **2** performed or performing very skilfully. ■ **masterfully** adverb.

masterly adjective performed or performing very skilfully.

mastermind noun a person who plans and directs a complex scheme or project. verb plan and direct a complex scheme or project.

masterpiece noun a work of outstanding skill.

mastery noun **1** complete knowledge or command of a subject or skill. **2** control or superiority.

masthead noun **1** the highest part of a ship's mast. **2** the name of a newspaper or magazine printed at the top of the first page.

mastic noun **1** a gum from the bark of a Mediterranean tree, used in making varnish and chewing gum. **2** a putty-like waterproof substance used in building.

masticate verb (**masticates, masticating, masticated**) chew food. ■ **mastication** noun.

mastiff noun a dog of a large, strong breed with drooping ears and lips.

mastodon noun a large extinct elephant-like mammal.

mastoid noun a part of the bone behind the ear, which has air spaces linked to the middle ear.

masturbate verb (**masturbates, masturbating, masturbated**) stimulate your genitals with your hand for sexual pleasure. ■ **masturbation** noun **masturbator** noun **masturbatory** adjective.

mat noun **1** a thick piece of material placed on the floor, used for decoration or to protect the floor. **2** a piece of springy material for landing on in gymnastics or similar sports. **3** a small piece of material placed on a surface to protect it. **4** a thick layer of hairy or woolly material.

matador noun a bullfighter.

match¹ noun **1** an event at which two people or teams compete against each other. **2** a person or thing that can compete with another as an equal in quality or strength. **3** an exact equivalent. **4** a pair of things which correspond or are very similar. **5** a potential husband or wife. verb **1** cor-

respond or fit with something. **2** be equal to. **3** place a person or team in competition with another. □ **match point** (in tennis) a point which if won by one of the players will also win them the match.

match² noun a short, thin stick tipped with a substance that ignites when rubbed against a rough surface.

matchbox noun a small box in which matches are sold.

matchless adjective unequalled.

matchmaker noun a person who tries to bring about marriages or relationships between other people.

matchstick noun the stem of a match.

mate¹ noun **1** Brit. informal a friend. **2** the sexual partner of an animal. **3** an assistant to a skilled worker. verb (**mates, mating, mated**) (of animals or birds) come together for breeding.

matelot /mat-loh/ noun Brit. informal a sailor.

material noun **1** the matter from which something is or can be made. **2** items needed for doing or creating something. **3** cloth. adjective **1** having to do with physical things rather than the mind or spirit. **2** essential or relevant. ■ **materially** adverb.

materialism noun a strong interest in material possessions and physical comfort rather than spiritual values. ■ **materialist** adjective & noun **materialistic** adjective.

materialize or **materialise** verb (**materialize, materializing, materialized**) **1** become fact; happen. **2** appear in bodily form.

maternal adjective **1** having to do with a mother. **2** related through the mother's side of the family. ■ **maternally** adverb.

maternity noun motherhood.

matey adjective (**matier, matiest**) Brit. informal familiar and friendly.

mathematics noun the branch of science concerned with numbers, quantities, and space. ■ **mathematical** adjective **mathematically** adverb **mathematician** noun.

maths or N. Amer. **math noun** mathematics.

matinee /ma-ti-nay/ **noun** an afternoon performance in a theatre or cinema.

matins noun a service of morning prayer.

matriarch /may-tri-ark/ **noun** a woman who is the head of a family or tribe.

matriarchy noun a society led or controlled by women. ■ **matriarchal** adjective.

matricide /ma-tri-syd, may-tri-syd/ **noun 1** the killing by someone of their own mother. **2** a person who kills their mother.

matriculate verb (**matriculates, matriculating, matriculated**) enrol or be enrolled at a college or university. ■ **matriculation** noun.

matrimony noun the state of being married. ■ **matrimonial** adjective.

matrix /may-triks/ **noun** (plural **matrices** /may-tri-seez/ or **matrixes**) **1** an environment or material in which something develops. **2** a mould in which something is cast or shaped. **3** a grid-like arrangement of elements.

matron noun 1 a woman in charge of medical and living arrangements at a boarding school. **2** a dignified or sedate married woman. **3** Brit., dated a woman in charge of nursing in a hospital. □ **matron of honour** a married woman attending the bride at a wedding. ■ **matronly** adjective.

matt or **matte adjective** not shiny.

matted adjective (of hair or fur) tangled into a thick mass.

matter noun 1 physical substance or material. **2** a subject or situation to be considered or dealt with. **3** (**the matter**) the reason for a problem. **verb** (**matters, mattering, mattered**) be important or significant. □ **matter-of-fact** unemotional and practical. **no matter 1** regardless of. **2** it is of no importance.

mattock noun a farming tool similar to a pickaxe.

mattress noun a fabric case filled with soft or firm material and sometimes incorporating springs, used for sleeping on.

mature adjective 1 fully grown. **2** like a sensible adult. **3** (of thought or planning) wise and thorough. **4** (of certain foodstuffs or drinks) developed over a long period in order to achieve a full flavour. **verb** (**matures, maturing, matured**) **1** become mature. **2** (of an insurance policy) reach the end of its term and so become payable. ■ **maturation** noun **maturely** adverb.

maturity noun 1 the state or period of being mature. **2** the time when an insurance policy matures.

maudlin /mawd-lin/ **adjective** sentimental in a self-pitying way.

maul verb 1 wound by scratching and tearing. **2** treat roughly.

maunder verb (**maunders, maundering, maundered**) move, talk, or act in a rambling way.

mausoleum /maw-suh-lee-uhm/ **noun** (plural **mausolea** /maw-suh-lee-uh/ or **mausoleums**) a building housing a tomb or tombs.

mauve noun a pale or reddish purple colour.

maverick noun an unconventional and independent-minded person.

maw noun the jaws or throat.

mawkish adjective sentimental in a feeble way.

max abbreviation maximum.

maxim noun a short statement expressing a general truth or rule of behaviour.

maximize or **maximise verb** (**maximizes, maximizing, maximized**) **1** make something as large or great as possible. **2** make the best use of.

maximum noun (plural **maxima** or **maximums**) the greatest amount, size, or strength that is possible or that has been gained. **adjective** greatest in amount, size, or strength. ■ **maximal** adjective.

May noun 1 the fifth month of the year.

2 (may) the hawthorn or its blossom.

may modal verb (3rd singular present **may**; past **might**) **1** expressing possibility. **2** expressing permission. **3** expressing a wish or hope.

maybe adverb perhaps.

Mayday noun an international distress signal used by ships and aircraft.

mayhem noun violent disorder.

mayn't short form may not.

mayonnaise /may-uh-**nayz**/ noun a creamy dressing made from egg yolks, oil, and vinegar.

mayor noun the elected head of a city or borough council. ■ **mayoral** adjective.

mayoralty /**mair**-uhl-ti/ noun (plural **mayoralties**) the period of office of a mayor.

mayoress noun **1** the wife of a mayor. **2** a woman elected as mayor.

maypole noun a decorated pole with long ribbons attached to the top, traditionally used for dancing round on the first day of May.

maze noun an intricate network of paths and walls or hedges, providing a challenge to find a way through.

mazurka noun a lively Polish dance.

MBA abbreviation Master of Business Administration.

MBE abbreviation Member of the Order of the British Empire.

MC abbreviation **1** Master of Ceremonies. **2** Military Cross.

MD abbreviation **1** Doctor of Medicine. **2** Brit. Managing Director.

ME abbreviation myalgic encephalomyelitis, a medical condition causing aching and prolonged tiredness.

me pronoun used as the object of a verb or preposition or after 'than', 'as', or the verb 'to be', to refer to the speaker himself or herself.

> 🛈 it is wrong to use *me* as the subject of a verb, as in *John and me went to the shops*; in this case use *I* instead.

mead noun an alcoholic drink made from fermented honey and water.

meadow noun an area of grassland.

meagre (US spelling **meager**) adjective small in quantity and poor in quality. ■ **meagreness** noun.

meal[1] noun **1** any of the regular daily occasions when food is eaten. **2** the food eaten on such an occasion.

meal[2] noun the edible part of any grain or pulse ground to powder.

mealy adjective having to do with meal. □ **mealy-mouthed** not wanting to speak frankly.

mean[1] verb (**means**, **meaning**, **meant**) **1** intend to say or show something. **2** (of a word) have as its explanation in the same language or its equivalent in another language. **3** intend something to occur or be the case. **4** have something as a result. **5** intend something for a particular purpose. **6** be of specified importance.

mean[2] adjective **1** unwilling to give or share. **2** unkind or unfair. **3** vicious or aggressive. **4** poor in quality and appearance. ■ **meanly** adverb **meanness** noun.

mean[3] noun **1** the average value of a set of quantities. **2** something in the middle of two extremes. adjective **1** calculated as a mean. **2** equally far from two extremes.

meander /mi-**an**-der/ verb (**meanders**, **meandering**, **meandered**) **1** follow a winding course. **2** wander in a leisurely way. noun a winding bend of a river or road.

meaning noun **1** the thing or idea that a word, signal, or action represents. **2** a sense of purpose.

meaningful adjective **1** having meaning. **2** worthwhile. **3** expressive. ■ **meaningfully** adverb **meaningfulness** noun.

meaningless adjective having no meaning or significance. ■ **meaninglessly** adverb **meaninglessness** noun.

means noun **1** a thing or method used to achieve a result. **2** money. **3** wealth.

□ **by all means** of course. **by no means** certainly not. **means test** an official investigation of a person's finances to find out whether they qualify for welfare benefits.

meant past and past participle of **MEAN**[1].

meantime adverb **(in the meantime)** meanwhile.

meanwhile adverb **1** in the period of time between two events. **2** at the same time.

measles noun an infectious disease causing fever and a red rash.

measly adjective informal ridiculously small or few.

measure verb **(measures, measuring, measured) 1** find out what the size, amount, or degree of something is in standard units. **2** be of a particular size, amount, or degree. **3 (measure out)** take an exact quantity of. **4 (measure up)** reach the required standard. noun **1** a course of action taken to achieve a purpose. **2** a law-making proposal. **3** a standard unit used to express size, amount, or degree. **4** a measuring device marked with such units. **5 (a measure of)** a certain amount of. **6 (a measure of)** an indication of the extent or quality of. □ **for good measure** as an amount or item that is additional to what is strictly required. **have the measure of** understand the character of. ■ **measurable** adjective **measurably** adverb.

measured adjective **1** slow and regular in rhythm. **2** carefully considered.

measurement noun **1** the action of measuring. **2** an amount, size, or extent found by measuring.

meat noun the flesh of an animal used as food.

meatball noun a ball of minced or chopped meat.

meaty adjective **(meatier, meatiest) 1** full of meat. **2** fleshy or muscular. **3** substantial or challenging.

Mecca noun a place which attracts many people.

mechanic noun a skilled worker who repairs and maintains machinery.

mechanical adjective **1** relating to or operated by a machine or machinery. **2** done without thought. **3** relating to physical forces or movement. ■ **mechanically** adverb.

mechanics noun **1** the branch of study concerned with the forces producing movement. **2** machinery or working parts. **3** the practical aspects of something.

mechanism noun **1** a piece of machinery. **2** the way in which something works or is made to happen.

mechanize or **mechanise** verb **(mechanizes, mechanizing, mechanized)** equip with machines or automatic devices. ■ **mechanization** noun.

medal noun a metal disc with an inscription or design on it, awarded to someone for a special achievement.

medallion noun **1** a piece of jewellery in the shape of a medal, worn as a pendant. **2** a decorative oval or circular painting, panel, or design.

medallist (US spelling **medalist**) noun a person who has been awarded a medal.

meddle verb **(meddles, meddling, meddled)** interfere in something that is not your concern. ■ **meddler** noun.

meddlesome adjective fond of interfering in other people's affairs.

media noun **1** television, radio, and newspapers as providers of information. **2** plural of **MEDIUM**.

> [i] the word **media** comes from the Latin plural of **medium**. In its normal sense, 'television, radio, and newspapers', it can be used with either a singular or a plural verb.

mediaeval ⇨ **MEDIEVAL**.

median adjective technical situated in the middle. noun **1** a median value. **2** Geometry a straight line drawn from one of the angles of a triangle to the middle of the opposite side.

mediate verb **(mediates, mediating, mediated)** try to settle a dispute between others. ■ **mediation** noun **mediator** noun.

medic noun informal a doctor or medical student.

medical adjective relating to the science or practice of medicine. noun an examination to see how healthy someone is. ■ **medically** adverb.

medicament noun a medicine.

medicate verb (medicates, medicating, medicated) **1** give medicine or a drug to. **2** (medicated) containing a medicinal substance.

medication noun **1** a medicine or drug. **2** treatment with medicines.

medicinal adjective **1** having healing properties. **2** relating to medicines. ■ **medicinally** adverb.

medicine noun **1** the science or practice of the treatment and prevention of disease. **2** a substance taken by mouth in order to treat or prevent disease. □ **medicine man** a person believed to have supernatural healing powers.

medieval or **mediaeval** /me-di-ee-v'l, mee-di-ee-v'l/ adjective relating to the Middle Ages, the period between about 1000 and 1450.

medievalist or **mediaevalist** noun a person who studies medieval history or literature.

mediocre /mee-di-oh-ker/ adjective of only average or fairly low quality. ■ **mediocrity** noun.

meditate verb (meditates, meditating, meditated) **1** focus your mind and free it of uncontrolled thoughts, as a spiritual exercise or for relaxation. **2** (meditate on or about) think carefully about. ■ **meditation** noun **meditative** adjective **meditatively** adverb.

Mediterranean adjective relating to the Mediterranean Sea or the countries around it.

 one d, one t, double r: Mediterranean.

medium noun (plural **media** or **mediums**) **1** a means by which something is communicated or achieved. **2** a substance that something lives or exists in, or through which it travels. **3** the type of material used by an artist. **4** (plural **mediums**) a person who claims to be able to communicate with the spirits of dead people. **5** the middle state between two extremes. adjective between two extremes.

medlar noun a fruit resembling a small brown apple.

medley noun (plural **medleys**) a varied mixture.

meek adjective quiet, gentle, and obedient. ■ **meekly** adverb.

meerkat noun a small southern African mongoose.

meet verb (meets, meeting, met) **1** come together with someone at the same place and time. **2** be introduced to or come across someone for the first time. **3** touch or join. **4** come across a situation. **5** (meet with) receive a particular reaction. **6** fulfil or satisfy a requirement. noun a gathering or meeting.

meeting noun **1** an occasion when people meet to discuss or decide something. **2** a situation in which people come together.

mega adjective informal **1** very large. **2** excellent.

megabyte noun Computing a unit of information equal to one million bytes.

megalith noun a large stone that forms a prehistoric monument or part of one. ■ **megalithic** adjective.

megalomania noun the belief that you are very powerful and important. ■ **megalomaniac** noun & adjective.

megaphone noun a cone-shaped device for amplifying the voice.

megaton noun a unit for measuring the power of an explosive, equivalent to one million tons of TNT.

megawatt noun a unit of power equal to one million watts.

melamine /mel-uh-meen/ noun a hard plastic used to coat the surfaces of tables or worktops.

melancholia /me-luhn-koh-li-uh/ noun great sadness or depression.

melancholy noun deep and long-lasting sadness. **adjective** sad or depressed. ∎ **melancholic** adjective.

melanin noun a dark pigment in the hair and skin, responsible for the tanning of skin exposed to sunlight.

melanoma noun a form of skin cancer.

meld verb blend.

melee /mel-ay/ noun **1** a confused fight or scuffle. **2** a disorderly mass of people.

mellifluous adjective pleasingly smooth and musical to hear.

mellow adjective **1** pleasantly smooth or soft in sound, taste, or colour. **2** relaxed and good-humoured. verb make or become mellow.

melodic adjective **1** relating to melody. **2** sounding pleasant. ∎ **melodically** adverb.

melodious adjective tuneful.

melodrama noun **1** a sensational play with exaggerated characters and exciting events. **2** behaviour or events that are very dramatic.

melodramatic adjective too dramatic and exaggerated. ∎ **melodramatically** adverb.

melody noun (plural **melodies**) **1** a piece of music with a clear or simple tune. **2** the main tune in a piece of music.

melon noun a large round fruit with sweet pulpy flesh.

melt verb **1** make or become liquid by heating. **2 (melt away)** gradually disappear. **3** become more tender or loving. ▫ **melting pot** a place where different peoples, ideas, or styles are mixed together.

meltdown noun an accident in a nuclear reactor in which the fuel overheats and melts the reactor core.

member noun **1** a person or organization belonging to a group or society. **2** old use a part of the body. ∎ **membership** noun.

membrane noun **1** a skin-like tissue that connects, covers, or lines cells or parts of the body. **2** a layer of thin, skin-like material. ∎ **membranous** adjective.

memento noun (plural **mementos** or **mementoes**) an object kept as a reminder.

memo noun (plural **memos**) a written note sent from one person to another within an organization.

memoir /mem-war/ noun **1** a historical account or biography written from personal knowledge. **2 (memoirs)** an account written by a public figure of their life and experiences.

memorabilia plural noun objects kept or collected because of their associations with people or events.

memorable adjective worth remembering or easily remembered. ∎ **memorably** adverb.

memorandum noun (plural **memoranda** or **memorandums**) **1** formal a memo. **2** a note recording something for future use.

memorial noun a column or other structure made or built in memory of a person or event. adjective created or done in memory of someone.

memorize or **memorise** verb **(memorizes, memorizing, memorized)** learn and remember exactly.

memory noun (plural **memories**) **1** the power that the mind has to store and remember information. **2** a thing remembered. **3** the length of time over which you can remember things. **4** a computer's equipment or capacity for storing data.

men plural of **MAN**.

menace noun **1** a dangerous or troublesome person or thing. **2** a threatening quality. verb **(menaces, menacing, menaced)** threaten.

ménage à trois /may-nahzh ah trwah/ noun an arrangement in which a married couple and the lover of one of them live together.

menagerie /muh-naj-uh-ri/ noun a small zoo.

mend verb **1** restore something so that it is no longer broken, torn, or out of action. **2** improve an unpleasant situation. noun a repair.

mendacious /men-**day**-shuss/ **adjective** untruthful; lying. ■ **mendacity** noun.

mendicant /**men**-di-kuhnt/ **adjective** **1** depending on charitable donations. **2** engaged in begging. noun **1** a member of a mendicant religious order. **2** a beggar.

menhir /**men**-heer/ **noun** a tall upright prehistoric stone erected as a monument.

menial /**mee**-ni-uhl/ **adjective** (of work) requiring little skill and lacking status. noun a person with a menial job.

meningitis /men-in-**jy**-tiss/ **noun** an infectious disease in which the membranes enclosing the brain and spinal cord become inflamed.

meniscus /mi-**niss**-kuhss/ **noun** (plural **menisci** /mi-**niss**-I/) **1** the curved upper surface of a liquid in a tube. **2** a thin lens curving outwards on one side and inwards on the other.

menopause /**men**-uh-pawz/ **noun** the time when a woman gradually stops having menstrual periods, on average around the age of 50. ■ **menopausal** adjective.

menorah /mi-**nor**-uh/ **noun** a large branched candlestick used in Jewish worship.

menstrual **adjective** having to do with menstruation.

menstruate **verb** (**menstruates, menstruating, menstruated**) (of a woman) discharge blood from the lining of the womb each month. ■ **menstruation** noun.

mental **adjective** **1** having to do with the mind. **2** relating to disorders of the mind. **3** informal mad. ■ **mentally** adverb.

mentality **noun** (plural **mentalities**) a characteristic way of thinking.

menthol **noun** a substance found in peppermint oil, used as a flavouring and in decongestant medicines. ■ **mentholated** adjective.

mention **verb** **1** refer to something briefly. **2** refer to someone by name. noun **1** a reference to someone or something. **2** a formal acknowledgement that someone has done something well.

mentor **noun** an experienced person who advises you over a period of time.

menu **noun** **1** a list of dishes available in a restaurant. **2** the food to be served in a restaurant or at a meal. **3** Computing a list of commands or facilities displayed on screen.

meow ⇒ **MIAOW**.

MEP **abbreviation** Member of the European Parliament.

mercantile /**mer**-kuhn-tyl/ **adjective** relating to trade or commerce.

mercenary **adjective** wanting to do only things that make you money. noun (plural **mercenaries**) a professional soldier who is hired to serve in a foreign army.

merchandise **noun** goods for sale.

merchant **noun** a trader who sells goods in large quantities. **adjective** (of ships, sailors, or shipping activity) involved with commerce. ◻ **merchant bank** a bank whose customers are large businesses. **merchant navy** a country's commercial shipping.

merchantable **adjective** suitable for sale.

merciful **adjective** **1** showing mercy. **2** giving relief from suffering. ■ **mercifully** adverb.

merciless **adjective** showing no mercy. ■ **mercilessly** adverb.

mercurial /mer-**kyoor**-i-uhl/ **adjective** **1** tending to change mood suddenly. **2** having to do with the element mercury.

mercury **noun** a heavy silvery-white liquid metallic element used in some thermometers and barometers.

mercy **noun** (plural **mercies**) **1** compassion or forgiveness shown towards someone who is in your power. **2** something to be grateful for. ◻ **at the mercy of** in the power of.

mere **adjective** **1** being no more than what is stated or described. **2** (**the merest**) the smallest or slightest.

merely **adverb** only.

meretricious /me-ri-**tri**-shuhss/ **adjective** superficially attractive but having no real value.

merge verb (**merges**, **merging**, **merged**) **1** combine or be combined into a whole. **2** blend gradually into something else.

merger noun a merging of two organizations into one.

meridian noun a circle passing at the same longitude through a given place on the earth's surface and the two poles.

meringue /muh-**rang**/ noun beaten egg whites and sugar baked until crisp.

merino noun (plural **merinos**) a soft wool obtained from a breed of sheep with a long fleece.

merit noun **1** the quality of being good and deserving praise. **2** a good point or feature. verb (**merits**, **meriting**, **merited**) deserve.

meritocracy noun (plural **meritocracies**) a society in which power is held by those people who have the greatest ability. ■ **meritocratic** adjective.

meritorious adjective deserving reward or praise.

mermaid noun a mythical sea creature with a woman's head and body and a fish's tail instead of legs.

merriment noun fun.

merry adjective (**merrier**, **merriest**) **1** cheerful and lively. **2** Brit. informal slightly drunk. □ **merry-go-round** a revolving platform fitted with model horses or cars, on which people ride for amusement. ■ **merrily** adjective.

merrymaking noun partying and having fun.

Mesdames plural of **MADAME**.

Mesdemoiselles plural of **MADEMOISELLE**.

mesh noun **1** material made of a network of wire or thread. **2** the spacing of the strands of a net. **3** a complex or constricting situation. verb **1** (**mesh with**) be in harmony with. **2** become entangled or entwined. **3** (of a gearwheel) lock together with another.

mesmeric adjective hypnotic.

mesmerism noun hypnotism.

mesmerize or **mesmerise** verb (**mesmerizes**, **mesmerizing**, **mesmerized**) capture someone's attention so that they are completely engrossed.

mess noun **1** a dirty or untidy state. **2** a state of confusion or difficulty. **3** a portion of semi-solid food. **4** a dog or cat's excrement. **5** a place where members of the armed forces eat and relax. verb **1** make something untidy or dirty. **2** (**mess about** or **around**) behave in a silly or playful way. **3** (**mess with**) informal meddle with.

message noun **1** a spoken or written communication. **2** a significant point or central theme.

messenger noun a person who carries a message.

messiah noun a great leader or saviour.

messianic /mess-i-**an**-ik/ adjective relating to a messiah.

Messieurs plural of **MONSIEUR**.

Messrs plural of **MR**.

messy adjective (**messier**, **messiest**) **1** untidy or dirty. **2** confused and difficult to deal with. ■ **messily** adverb **messiness** noun.

met past and past participle of **MEET**[1].

metabolism /mi-**tab**-uh-li-z'm/ noun the process by which food is used for the growth of tissue or the production of energy. ■ **metabolic** adjective.

metabolize or **metabolise** verb (**metabolizes**, **metabolizing**, **metabolized**) process by metabolism.

metal noun **1** a hard, solid, shiny material which conducts electricity and heat. **2** (also **road metal**) broken stone used in making road surfaces.

metalled adjective Brit. (of a road) having a hard surface.

metallic adjective **1** having to do with metal. **2** (of sound) sharp and ringing.

metallurgy /mi-**tal**-ler-ji, met-uh-**ler**-ji/ noun the scientific study of metals. ■ **metallurgical** adjective **metallurgist** noun.

metamorphic adjective (of rock) having been changed by heat and pressure.

metamorphosis /met-uh-**mor**-fuh-siss/ noun (plural **metamorphoses** /met-uh-**mor**-fuh-seez/) **1** the transformation of an insect or amphibian from an immature form or larva to an adult form. **2** a change in form or nature. ■ **metamorphose** verb.

metaphor /**met**-uh-fer/ noun a word or phrase used in an imaginative way to represent or stand for something else (e.g. *the long arm of the law*).

metaphorical /met-uh-**fo**-ri-k'l/ or **metaphoric** adjective having to do with metaphor. ■ **metaphorically** adverb.

metaphysical adjective **1** relating to metaphysics. **2** beyond physical matter. ■ **metaphysically** adverb.

metaphysics noun the branch of philosophy dealing with the nature of existence, truth, and knowledge.

mete verb (**metes, meting, meted**) (**mete out**) deal out justice, punishment, etc.

meteor noun a small body of matter from space that glows as a result of friction with the earth's atmosphere, and appears as a shooting star.

meteoric adjective **1** relating to meteors or meteorites. **2** rapid in achieving success or promotion.

meteorite noun a piece of rock or metal that has fallen to the earth from space.

meteorology noun the study of conditions in the atmosphere, especially for weather forecasting. ■ **meteorological** adjective **meteorologist** noun.

meter[1] noun a device that measures and records the quantity, degree, or rate of something. verb (**meters, metering, metered**) measure something with a meter.

meter[2] US spelling of **METRE**[1], **METRE**[2].

methadone noun a powerful painkiller, used as a substitute for morphine and heroin in treating people addicted to these drugs.

methane noun a flammable gas which is the main constituent of natural gas.

methanol noun a poisonous flammable alcohol, used to make methylated spirit.

methinks verb (past **methought**) old use it seems to me.

method noun **1** a way of doing something. **2** the quality of being well planned and organized.

methodical or **methodic** adjective done or doing something in a well organized and systematic way. ■ **methodically** adverb.

Methodist noun a member of a Christian Protestant group which separated from the Church of England in the 18th century. adjective relating to Methodists or their beliefs. ■ **Methodism** noun.

methodology noun (plural **methodologies**) a particular system of methods. ■ **methodological** adjective.

meths noun Brit. informal methylated spirit.

methylated spirit or **methylated spirits** noun alcohol for use as a solvent or fuel, made unfit for drinking by the addition of methanol and a violet dye.

meticulous adjective very careful and precise. ■ **meticulously** adverb.

métier /**may**-ti-ay/ noun a person's trade, profession, or special ability.

metre[1] (US spelling **meter**) noun the basic unit of length in the metric system, equal to 100 centimetres (approximately 39.37 inches).

metre[2] (US spelling **meter**) noun the rhythm of a piece of poetry.

metric adjective relating to or using the metric system. □ **metric system** the decimal measuring system based on the metre, litre, and gram. **metric ton** (or **metric tonne**) a unit of weight equal to 1,000 kilograms (2,205 lb).

metrical adjective having to do with poetic metre. ■ **metrically** adverb.

metricate verb (metricates, metricating, metricated) convert a system of measurement to the metric system. ■ metrication noun.

metro noun (plural metros) an underground railway system in a city.

metronome noun a device that marks time at a selected rate by giving a regular tick, used by musicians. ■ metronomic adjective.

metropolis noun the main city of a country or region.

metropolitan adjective relating to large and densely populated areas.

mettle noun spirit and strength of character.

mew verb (of a cat or gull) make a soft, high-pitched sound like a cry.

mewl verb 1 cry feebly. 2 mew.

mews noun (plural mews) Brit. a row of houses or flats converted from stables in a small street or square.

mezzanine /mets-uh-neen/ noun a floor extending over only part of the full area of a building, built between two full floors.

mezzo /met-zoh/ or **mezzo-soprano** noun (plural mezzos) a female singer with a voice pitched between soprano and contralto.

mg abbreviation milligrams.

MHz abbreviation megahertz.

miaow or **meow** noun the characteristic cry of a cat. verb make a miaow.

miasma /mi-az-muh/ noun an unpleasant or unhealthy atmosphere.

mica /my-kuh/ noun a mineral found as tiny shiny scales in rocks.

mice plural of MOUSE.

mickey noun (take the mickey) Brit. informal tease or ridicule someone.

microbe noun a bacterium; a germ. ■ microbial adjective.

microbiology noun the scientific study of living creatures that are so tiny that they can only be seen using a microscope.

microchip noun a miniature electronic circuit made from a tiny wafer of silicon.

microclimate noun the climate of a very small or restricted area.

microcosm noun a thing that has the features and qualities of something much larger.

microfiche /my-kroh-feesh/ or **microfilm** noun a piece of film containing greatly reduced photographs of the pages of a newspaper, book, etc.

microlight noun Brit. a very small, light, one- or two-seater aircraft.

micrometer /my-krom-i-ter/ noun an instrument which measures small distances or thicknesses.

micro-organism noun an organism that is so small that it can only be seen using a microscope.

microphone noun an instrument for changing sound waves into electrical energy which is then amplified and transmitted or recorded.

microprocessor noun an integrated circuit which can function as the main part of a computer.

microscope noun an instrument for magnifying very small objects.

microscopic adjective so small as to be visible only with a microscope. ■ microscopically adverb.

microscopy /my-kross-kuh-pi/ noun the use of a microscope.

microsurgery noun surgery performed using very small instruments and a microscope.

microwave noun 1 an electromagnetic wave with a wavelength in the range 0.001–0.3 m. 2 (also microwave oven) an oven that uses microwaves to cook or heat food. verb (microwaves, microwaving, microwaved) cook food in a microwave oven.

mid adjective having to do with the middle position of a range. preposition literary amid; in the middle of.

Midas touch noun the ability to make a lot of money out of anything you do.

midday noun twelve o'clock in the day; noon.

midden noun a heap of dung.

middle adjective **1** positioned at an equal distance from the edges or ends of something. **2** medium in rank, quality, or ability. noun **1** a middle point or position. **2** informal a person's waist and stomach. □ **middle age** the period when a person is between about 45 and 60 in age. **Middle Ages** the period of European history between about 1000 and 1450. **middle class** the social group between the aristocracy and the working class. **middle ear** the air-filled central cavity of the ear, behind the eardrum. **Middle East** an area of SW Asia and northern Africa, stretching from the Mediterranean to Pakistan.

middleman noun **1** a person who buys goods from the company who makes them and sells them on to shops or consumers. **2** a person who arranges business or political deals between other people.

middling adjective average in size, amount, or rank.

midfield noun the central part of a sports field. ■ **midfielder** noun.

midge noun a small fly that breeds near water.

midget noun an extremely small person. adjective extremely small.

midland noun **1** the middle part of a country. **2** (**the Midlands**) the inland counties of central England.

midnight noun twelve o'clock at night.

midriff noun the front of the body between the chest and the waist.

midship noun the middle part of a ship or boat.

midshipman noun a low-ranking officer in the Royal Navy.

midships = **AMIDSHIPS**.

midst old use preposition in the middle of. noun the middle point or part.

midstream noun the middle of a stream or river.

midsummer noun **1** the middle part of summer. **2** the summer solstice. □ **Midsummer Day** (or **Midsummer's Day**) 24 June.

midterm noun the middle of a period of office, an academic term, or a pregnancy.

midway adverb & adjective in or towards the middle.

midweek noun the middle of the week. adjective & adverb in the middle of the week.

midwife noun a nurse who is trained to help women give birth. ■ **midwifery** /mid-**wif**-uh-ri/ noun.

midwinter noun **1** the middle part of winter. **2** the winter solstice.

mien /meen/ noun a person's look or manner.

miffed adjective informal slightly angry or upset.

might¹ modal verb (3rd singular present **might**) past of **MAY¹**. **1** used to express possibility or make a suggestion. **2** used politely in questions and requests.

might² noun great power or strength.

mightn't short form might not.

mighty adjective (**mightier**, **mightiest**) very strong or powerful. adverb informal extremely. ■ **mightily** adverb.

migraine /**mee**-grayn, **my**-grayn/ noun a severe headache which is accompanied by symptoms such as nausea and disturbed vision.

migrant noun **1** an animal that migrates. **2** a worker who moves from one place to another to find work. adjective tending to migrate or having migrated.

migrate verb (**migrates**, **migrating**, **migrated**) **1** (of an animal) move to warmer regions in the winter and back to colder regions in the summer. **2** move to settle in a new area in order to find work. ■ **migration** noun **migratory** adjective.

mike noun informal a microphone.

milch adjective (of an animal) giving or kept for milk.

mild adjective **1** calm and gentle. **2** not severe or harsh. **3** not sharp or strong in flavour. **4** (of weather) not very cold; pleasant. noun Brit. a kind of dark beer not strongly flavoured with hops. ■ **mildly** adverb **mildness** noun.

mildew noun a coating of tiny fungi on plants or damp material such as paper or leather. ■ **mildewed** adjective.

mile noun **1** a unit of length equal to 1,760 yards (approximately 1.609 kilometres). **2 (miles)** informal a very long way. adverb **(miles)** informal by a great amount or a long way.

mileage noun **1** a number of miles covered. **2** informal advantage.

mileometer ⇨ **MILOMETER**.

milestone noun **1** a stone set up beside a road, marking the distance in miles to a place further along the road. **2** an event marking a significant new development or stage.

milieu /mi-lyer/ noun (plural **milieux** /mi-**lyer**/ or **milieus** /mi-**lyerz**/) the social environment that you live or work in.

militant adjective supporting a cause in a forceful and confrontational way. noun a militant person. ■ **militancy** noun **militantly** adverb.

militarism noun a belief in the value of military strength. ■ **militarist** noun & adjective **militaristic** adjective.

militarize or **militarise** verb (**militarizes, militarizing, militarized**) supply a place with soldiers and military equipment.

military adjective having to do with soldiers or armed forces. noun **(the military)** the armed forces of a country. ■ **militarily** adverb.

militate verb (**militates, militating, militated**) (**militate against**) be a powerful factor in preventing.

> [i] don't confuse **militate** with **mitigate**, which means 'make something bad less severe'.

militia /mi-li-shuh/ noun **1** a group of people who are not professional soldiers but who act as an army. **2** a rebel force opposing a regular army.

milk noun **1** a white fluid produced by female mammals to feed their young. **2** the milk of cows as a food and drink for humans. **3** the milk-like juice of certain plants. verb **1** draw milk from

an animal. **2** take money from someone dishonestly and over a period of time. **3** take full advantage of a situation. □ **milk chocolate** solid chocolate made with milk. **milk float** Brit. an electrically powered van with open sides, used for delivering milk to houses. **milk round** Brit. a fixed route along which a milkman delivers milk to houses. **milk tooth** a temporary tooth in a child or young mammal.

milkmaid noun old use a girl or woman who worked in a dairy.

milkman noun a man who delivers milk to houses.

milkshake noun a cold drink made from milk whisked with ice cream.

milksop noun a timid person.

milky adjective **1** containing milk. **2** having a soft white colour or clouded appearance. □ **Milky Way** the galaxy of which our solar system is a part, visible at night as a faint band of light crossing the sky. ■ **milkily** adverb **milkiness** noun.

mill noun **1** a building equipped with machinery for grinding grain into flour. **2** a device for grinding coffee beans, peppercorns, etc. **3** a building fitted with machinery for a manufacturing process. verb **1** grind in a mill. **2** cut or shape metal with a rotating tool. **3** produce regular ribbed markings on the edge of a coin. **4** (**mill about** or **around**) move around in a confused mass. □ **mill wheel** a wheel used to drive a watermill.

millenary /mi-len-uh-ri/ noun (plural **millenaries**) **1** a period of a thousand years. **2** a thousandth anniversary. adjective consisting of a thousand.

millennium /mi-len-i-uhm/ noun (plural **millennia** or **millenniums**) **1** a period of a thousand years. **2** (**the millennium**) the point at which one period of a thousand years ends and another begins. **3** an anniversary of a thousand years. ■ **millennial** adjective.

> [✓] double *l*, double *n*: mil**lennium**.

miller noun a person who owns or

works in a grain mill.

millet noun a cereal used to make flour or alcoholic drinks.

millibar noun a unit for measuring the pressure of the atmosphere.

milligram or **milligramme** noun one thousandth of a gram.

millilitre (US spelling **milliliter**) noun one thousandth of a litre.

millimetre (US spelling **millimeter**) noun one thousandth of a metre.

milliner noun a person who makes or sells women's hats. ■ **millinery** noun.

million cardinal number (plural **millions** or (with another word or number) **million**) **1** a thousand times a thousand; 1,000,000. **2** (also **millions**) informal a very large number or amount. ■ **millionth** ordinal number.

millionaire noun a person whose money and property are worth one million pounds or dollars or more.

millipede noun an insect-like creature with a long body and a lot of legs.

millisecond noun one thousandth of a second.

millpond noun **1** the pool created by a mill dam, providing the head of water that powers a watermill. **2** a very still and calm stretch of water.

millstone noun **1** each of a pair of circular stones used for grinding grain. **2** a burden of responsibility.

milometer or **mileometer** /my-lom-i-ter/ noun Brit. an instrument on a vehicle for recording the number of miles travelled.

mime noun the use of silent gestures and facial expressions to tell a story or show feelings. verb (**mimes**, **miming**, **mimed**) **1** use mime to tell a story or show feelings. **2** pretend to sing or play an instrument as a recording is being played.

mimic verb (**mimics**, **mimicking**, **mimicked**) **1** imitate the voice or actions of someone else. **2** (of an animal or plant) take on the appearance of another in order to hide or for protection. noun **1** a person skilled in

mimicking. **2** an animal or plant that mimics. ■ **mimicry** noun.

mimosa noun an acacia tree with delicate fern-like leaves and yellow flowers.

minaret /min-uh-ret/ noun a slender tower of a mosque, with a balcony from which Muslims are called to prayer.

minatory /min-uh-tuh-ri/ adjective formal threatening.

mince verb **1** cut or grind meat into very small pieces. **2** walk with short, quick steps and swinging hips. noun Brit. minced meat. □ **mince your words** be tactful.

mincemeat noun a mixture of dried fruit, candied peel, sugar, spices, and suet.

mind noun **1** the faculty of consciousness and thought. **2** a person's intellect or memory. **3** a person's attention or will. verb **1** be distressed or annoyed by. **2** remember or take care to do. **3** watch out for. **4** temporarily take care of. **5** (**be minded**) be inclined to do. □ **out of your mind** not thinking sensibly; crazy.

minded adjective inclined to think in a particular way.

minder noun **1** a person who is employed to look after someone or something. **2** informal a bodyguard.

mindful adjective **1** (**mindful of** or **that**) aware of or recognizing that. **2** formal inclined to do something.

mindless adjective **1** acting or done without good reason and with no concern for the consequences. **2** (**mindless of**) not thinking of or concerned about. **3** (of an activity) simple and repetitive. ■ **mindlessly** adverb.

mindset noun a person's particular way of thinking and set of beliefs.

mine[1] possessive pronoun referring to a thing or things belonging to or associated with the person speaking. possessive determiner old use my.

mine[2] noun **1** a hole or channel dug in the earth for extracting coal or other minerals. **2** an abundant source. **3** a type of bomb placed on or in the ground or water, which explodes on contact. **verb** (**mines, mining, mined**) **1** obtain coal or other minerals from a mine. **2** lay explosive mines on or in.

minefield noun **1** an area planted with explosive mines. **2** a subject or situation presenting unseen dangers.

miner noun a person who works in a mine.

mineral noun **1** a solid substance occurring naturally, such as copper and silicon. **2** an inorganic substance needed by the human body for good health, such as calcium and iron. □ **mineral water** water containing dissolved salts.

mineralogy noun the scientific study of minerals. ■ **mineralogical** adjective **mineralogist** noun.

mineshaft noun a deep, narrow shaft that gives access to a mine.

minestrone /mi-ni-**stroh**-ni/ noun an Italian soup containing vegetables and pasta.

minesweeper noun a warship equipped for detecting and removing or destroying explosive mines.

mingle verb (**mingles, mingling, mingled**) mix together.

mingy /**min**-ji/ adjective informal not generous.

mini adjective very small of its kind. **noun** (plural **minis**) a very short skirt.

miniature adjective of a much smaller size than normal. **noun 1** a thing that is much smaller than normal. **2** a tiny, detailed portrait or picture.

☑ *-ia-* in the middle: min*ia*ture.

miniaturist noun an artist who paints miniatures.

miniaturize or **miniaturise** verb (**miniaturizes, miniaturizing, miniaturized**) make a smaller version of.

minibar noun a small refrigerator in a hotel room containing a selection of drinks.

minibus noun a small bus for about ten to fifteen passengers.

minicab noun Brit. a taxi that you order by telephone but cannot hail in the street.

minidisc noun a disc similar to a small CD but able to record sound or data as well as play it back.

minim noun a musical note that lasts as long as two crotchets.

minimal adjective **1** of a minimum amount, quantity, or degree. **2** using simple forms or structures. ■ **minimally** adverb.

minimalism noun the use of simple, economical forms and structures. ■ **minimalist** adjective & noun.

minimize or **minimise** verb (**minimizes, minimizing, minimized**) **1** make something as small as possible. **2** represent something as less important or significant than it really is.

minimum noun (plural **minima** or **minimums**) the smallest amount, extent, or strength possible. **adjective** smallest in amount, extent, or strength.

minion noun a lowly worker or unimportant person.

miniskirt noun a very short skirt.

minister noun **1** a head of a government department. **2** a person who represents their government in a foreign country. **3** a person who carries out religious duties in the Christian Church. **verb** (**ministers, ministering, ministered**) (**minister to**) attend to the needs of. ■ **ministerial** adjective.

ministrations plural noun the providing of help or care.

ministry noun (plural **ministries**) **1** a government department headed by a minister. **2** a period of government under one Prime Minister. **3** the work of a minister in the Church.

mink noun a small stoat-like animal that is farmed for its fur.

minnow noun a small freshwater fish.

minor adjective **1** not important or serious. **2** Music (of a scale) having intervals of a semitone between the second and third, fifth and sixth, and seventh and eighth notes. **noun** a person under the age of full legal responsibility.

minority noun (plural **minorities**) **1** the smaller number or part. **2** a relatively small group of people differing from the majority in race, religion, etc.

minster noun a large or important church.

minstrel noun a medieval singer or musician.

mint[1] noun **1** a sweet-smelling plant, used as a herb in cookery. **2** the flavour of mint. **3** a peppermint sweet. ■ **minty** adjective.

mint[2] noun **1** a place where money is made. **2** (**a mint**) informal a large sum of money. verb make a coin by stamping metal. ◻ **in mint condition** new, or as good as new.

minuet noun a ballroom dance popular in the 18th century.

minus preposition **1** with the subtraction of. **2** (of temperature) falling below zero by. **3** informal lacking. adjective **1** (before a number) below zero. **2** (after a grade) slightly below. **3** having a negative electric charge. noun **1** (also **minus sign**) the symbol −, indicating subtraction or a negative value. **2** informal a disadvantage.

minuscule /**min**-uhss-kyool/ adjective extremely tiny.

 -*u*-, not -*i*-, in the middle: min*u*scule.

minute[1] /**mi**-nit/ noun **1** a period of time equal to sixty seconds or a sixtieth of an hour. **2** (**a minute**) informal a very short time. **3** a measurement of an angle equal to one sixtieth of a degree.

minute[2] /my-**nyoot**/ adjective (**minutest**) **1** extremely small. **2** precise and careful. ■ **minutely** adverb.

minute[3] /**mi**-nit/ noun **1** (**minutes**) a written summary of the points discussed at a meeting. **2** an official written message. verb (**minutes, minuting, minuted**) **1** record the points discussed at a meeting. **2** send a minute to.

minutiae /mi-**nyoo**-shi-ee/ plural noun small or precise details.

minx noun a cheeky or cunning girl or young woman.

miracle noun **1** a welcome event that is so extraordinary that it is thought to be the work of God or a saint. **2** an outstanding example or achievement. ◻ **miracle play** a medieval play based on stories from the Bible.

miraculous adjective **1** having the nature of a miracle. **2** very surprising and welcome. ■ **miraculously** adverb.

mirage /mi-**rahzh**/ noun **1** an effect caused by hot air, in which a sheet of water seems to appear in a desert or on a hot road. **2** something that appears real or possible but is not in fact so.

mire noun **1** a stretch of swampy or boggy ground. **2** a difficult situation from which it is hard to escape. verb (**mires, miring, mired**) (**be mired**) **1** become stuck in or covered with mud. **2** be in difficulties.

mirror noun **1** a surface which reflects a clear image. **2** something that accurately represents something else. verb reflect. ◻ **mirror image** an image which is identical in form to another but is reversed, as if seen in a mirror.

mirth noun amusement. ■ **mirthful** adjective.

miry adjective very muddy or boggy.

misadventure noun **1** (also **death by misadventure**) Law death caused accidentally and not involving negligence or crime. **2** a mishap.

misalliance noun an unsuitable or unhappy relationship or marriage.

misanthrope /**mi**-zuhn-throhp/ or **misanthropist** /mi-**zan**-thruhp-ist/ noun a person who dislikes and avoids other people. ■ **misanthropic** adjective **misanthropy** noun.

misapprehension noun a mistaken belief.

misappropriate verb (**misappropriates, misappropriating, misappropriated**) dishonestly take something for your own use. ■ **misappropriation** noun.

misbegotten adjective badly thought about or planned.

misbehave verb (misbehaves, misbehaving, misbehaved) behave badly. ■ **misbehaviour** noun.

miscalculate verb (miscalculates, miscalculating, miscalculated) calculate or assess wrongly. ■ **miscalculation** noun.

miscarriage noun the birth of a baby or fetus before it is able to survive independently. □ **miscarriage of justice** a situation in which a court of law fails to achieve justice.

miscarry verb (miscarries, miscarrying, miscarried) **1** (of a pregnant woman) have a miscarriage. **2** (of a plan) fail.

miscast verb (miscasts, miscasting, miscast) (be miscast) (of an actor) be given an unsuitable role.

miscellaneous adjective consisting of many different kinds.

miscellany /mi-**sel**-luh-ni/ noun (plural **miscellanies**) a collection of different things.

mischance noun bad luck.

mischief noun **1** playful misbehaviour. **2** harm caused by someone or something.

mischievous /**miss**-chi-vuhss/ adjective **1** causing mischief. **2** intended to cause trouble. ■ **mischievously** adverb.

> ☑ the ending is *-ous*, not *-ious*: mischievous.

miscible /**miss**-i-b'l/ adjective (of liquids) able to be mixed together.

misconceive verb (misconceives, misconceiving, misconceived) **1** fail to understand something correctly. **2** (be misconceived) be badly judged or planned.

misconception noun a failure to understand something correctly.

misconduct noun /miss-**kon**-dukt/ bad behaviour.

misconstruction noun a failure to interpret something correctly.

misconstrue verb (misconstrues, misconstruing, misconstrued) interpret something wrongly.

miscreant /**miss**-kri-uhnt/ noun a person who behaves badly or unlawfully.

misdeed noun a wrongful act.

misdemeanour (US spelling **misdemeanor**) noun an action that is bad or unacceptable, but does not amount to a serious crime.

misdiagnose verb (misdiagnoses, misdiagnosing, misdiagnosed) diagnose something incorrectly. ■ **misdiagnosis** noun.

misdirect verb direct or instruct wrongly. ■ **misdirection** noun.

miser noun a person who hoards wealth and spends as little as possible.

miserable adjective **1** very unhappy or depressed. **2** causing unhappiness or discomfort. **3** (of a person) gloomy and humourless. **4** very small or inadequate. ■ **miserably** adverb.

misericord /mi-**zerr**-i-kord/ noun a ledge projecting from the underside of a hinged seat in the choir of a church, giving support to someone standing when the seat is folded up.

miserly adjective **1** unwilling to spend money; ungenerous. **2** (of a quantity) too small. ■ **miserliness** noun.

misery noun (plural **miseries**) **1** great unhappiness. **2** a cause of this. **3** Brit. informal a person who is constantly miserable.

misfire verb (misfires, misfiring, misfired) **1** (of a gun) fail to fire properly. **2** (of an internal-combustion engine) fail to ignite the fuel correctly. **3** fail to produce the intended result.

misfit noun **1** a person whose attitudes and actions set them apart from other people. **2** something that does not fit.

misfortune noun **1** bad luck. **2** an unfortunate event.

misgivings plural noun feelings of doubt or worry.

misguided adjective badly judged.

mishandle verb (mishandles, mis-

mishap | mist

handling, mishandled) handle unwisely or wrongly.

mishap noun an unlucky accident.

mishear verb (mishears, mishearing, misheard) hear incorrectly.

mishit verb (mishits, mishitting, mishit) hit or kick a ball badly.

mishmash noun a confused mixture.

misinform verb give someone false or inaccurate information. ■ misinformation noun.

misinterpret verb (misinterprets, misinterpreting, misinterpreted) interpret something wrongly. ■ misinterpretation noun.

misjudge verb (misjudges, misjudging, misjudged) **1** form a wrong opinion about. **2** estimate wrongly. ■ misjudgement (or misjudgment) noun.

mislay verb (mislays, mislaying, mislaid) lose something because you have forgotten where you put it.

mislead verb (misleads, misleading, misled) give someone a wrong impression or wrong information.

mismanage verb (mismanages, mismanaging, mismanaged) manage something badly or wrongly. ■ mismanagement noun.

mismatch noun a combination of things or people that do not go together well. verb match people or things unsuitably or incorrectly.

misnomer /miss-**noh**-mer/ noun **1** a name that doesn't fit or suit. **2** the wrong use of a name or term.

misogynist /mi-**soj**-uh-nist/ noun a man who hates women. ■ misogynistic adjective misogyny noun.

misplace verb (misplaces, misplacing, misplaced) put in the wrong place.

misplaced adjective **1** incorrectly placed. **2** unwise or inappropriate.

misprint noun a mistake in printed text. verb print wrongly.

mispronounce verb (mispronounces, mispronouncing, mispronounced) pronounce wrongly.

misquote verb (misquotes, misquoting, misquoted) quote inaccurately.

misread verb (misreads, misreading, misread) read or interpret wrongly.

misrepresent verb give a false or misleading account of. ■ misrepresentation noun.

misrule noun **1** bad government. **2** disorder.

miss[1] verb **1** fail to hit, reach, or come into contact with. **2** be too late for. **3** fail to notice, hear, or understand. **4** fail to be present. **5** avoid. **6** (miss out) omit. **7** feel sad because of the absence of. noun a failure to hit, catch, or reach something.

miss[2] noun **1** (Miss) a title coming before the name of an unmarried woman or girl. **2** (Miss) used as a form of address to a teacher. **3** dated a girl or young woman.

missal noun a book of the texts used in the Catholic Mass.

misshapen adjective not having the normal or natural shape.

missile noun an object or weapon that is thrown or fired at a target.

missing adjective **1** absent and unable to be found. **2** not present when expected to be.

mission noun **1** an important assignment, typically involving travel abroad. **2** an organization involved in a long-term assignment abroad. **3** a military or scientific expedition. **4** the work of teaching people about Christianity. **5** a strongly felt aim or calling.

missionary noun (plural missionaries) a person sent on a religious mission. adjective having to do with a religious mission.

missive noun formal a letter.

misspell verb (misspells, misspelling, past and past participle misspelt or misspelled) spell wrongly.

misspend verb (misspends, misspending, misspent) spend foolishly.

missus or **missis** noun informal a person's wife.

mist noun a thin cloud of tiny water droplets that makes it difficult to see.

verb cover or become covered with mist.

mistake noun **1** a thing that is incorrect. **2** an error of judgement. **verb** (mistakes, mistaking, mistook; past participle **mistaken**) **1** be wrong about. **2** (mistake for) confuse with.

mistaken adjective **1** wrong in your opinion or judgement. **2** based on a misunderstanding. ∎ **mistakenly** adverb.

mister noun **1** (Mister) = MR. **2** informal a form of address to a man.

mistime verb (mistimes, mistiming, mistimed) choose an inappropriate moment to do or say.

mistletoe noun a plant which grows as a parasite on trees, and bears white berries in winter.

mistreat verb treat badly or unfairly. ∎ **mistreatment** noun.

mistress noun **1** a woman in a position of authority. **2** a woman who is highly skilled in something. **3** a woman having a sexual relationship with a man who is married to someone else. **4** Brit. a female schoolteacher. **5** (Mistress) old use Mrs.

mistrial noun a trial that is not considered valid because of a mistake in proceedings.

mistrust verb have no trust in. noun lack of trust.

misty adjective (mistier, mistiest) **1** covered with mist. **2** having an unclear outline.

misunderstand verb (misunderstands, misunderstanding, misunderstood) fail to understand correctly. ∎ **misunderstanding** noun.

misuse verb (misuses, misusing, misused) **1** use wrongly. **2** treat badly or unfairly. noun the action of misusing.

mite noun **1** a tiny insect-like creature. **2** a small child or animal. **3** a very small amount. adverb (a mite) informal slightly.

mitigate verb (mitigates, mitigating, mitigated) make less severe or serious. ∎ **mitigation** noun.

ⓘ don't confuse **mitigate** with **militate**: militate against means 'be a powerful factor in preventing'.

---

mitre (US spelling **miter**) noun **1** a tall headdress that tapers to a point at the front and back, worn by bishops. **2** a joint made between two pieces of wood cut at an angle in order to form a corner of 90°.

mitt noun **1** a mitten. **2** a glove leaving the fingers and thumb uncovered. **3** informal a person's hand.

mitten noun a glove having a single section for all four fingers, with a separate section for the thumb.

mix verb **1** combine or be combined to form a whole. **2** make by mixing ingredients. **3** combine different recordings to form one piece of music. **4** (mix up) spoil the arrangement of. **5** (mix up) confuse a person or thing with another. **6** meet different people socially. noun **1** a mixture. **2** the proportion of different people or things making up a mixture. **3** a version of a piece of music mixed in a different way from the original. □ **mix-up** informal a confusion or misunderstanding.

mixed adjective **1** made up of different qualities or things. **2** having to do with males and females. □ **mixed bag** a varied assortment.

mixer noun **1** a machine or device for mixing things. **2** a soft drink that can be mixed with alcohol.

mixture noun **1** a substance made by mixing other substances together. **2** (a mixture of) a combination of different things in which each component is distinct.

mizzen or **mizzenmast** noun the mast behind a ship's mainmast.

ml abbreviation **1** miles. **2** millilitres.

mm abbreviation millimetres.

mnemonic /ni-**mon**-ik/ noun a pattern of letters or words used to help remember something. adjective designed to help remember something.

moan noun **1** a low mournful sound, usually expressing suffering. **2** informal a trivial complaint. verb **1** make a moan. **2** informal complain; grumble.

moat noun a wide defensive ditch surrounding a castle or town.

mob noun **1** a disorderly crowd of people. **2** Brit. informal a group of people. **3 (the Mob)** N. Amer. the Mafia. **4 (the mob)** disapproving the ordinary people. **verb (mobs, mobbing, mobbed)** crowd round someone in an unruly way.

mobile adjective **1** able to move or be moved freely or easily. **2** (of a shop, library, etc.) set up inside a vehicle and able to travel around. **3** able to change your occupation, social class, or where you live. **4** (of a person's face) easily changing expression. noun **1** a decoration that is hung so as to turn freely in the air. **2** (also **mobile phone**) a portable telephone.

mobility noun the quality of being mobile.

mobilize or **mobilise** verb (**mobilizes, mobilizing, mobilized**) **1** organize troops for active service. **2** organize people or resources for a particular task. ■ **mobilization** noun.

mobster noun informal a gangster.

moccasin noun a soft leather shoe with the sole turned up and sewn to the upper, originally worn by North American Indians.

mocha /mok-uh/ noun **1** a fine-quality coffee. **2** a drink made with coffee and chocolate.

mock verb **1** tease scornfully; ridicule. **2** imitate in an unkind way. adjective **1** not genuine or real. **2** (of an examination, battle, etc.) arranged for training or practice. noun (**mocks**) Brit. informal examinations taken in school as training for public examinations. ▫ **mock-up** a model of a machine or structure that is used for teaching or testing.

mockery noun (plural **mockeries**) **1** ridicule. **2** (**a mockery of**) an absurd representation of something. ▫ **make a mockery of** make something appear foolish or absurd.

mockingbird noun a long-tailed American songbird, noted for copying the calls of other birds.

modal adjective relating to mode or form as opposed to substance. ▫ **modal verb** Grammar an auxiliary verb expressing necessity or possibility, e.g. *must, shall, will.*

mode noun **1** a way in which something occurs or is done. **2** a style in clothes, art, etc.

model noun **1** a three-dimensional representation of something. **2** something used as an example. **3** a simplified mathematical description of a system or process. **4** a person or thing seen as an excellent example of a quality. **5** a person employed to display clothes by wearing them. **6** a person employed to pose for an artist. **7** a particular design or version of a product. verb (**models, modelling, modelled**; US spelling **models, modeling, modeled**) **1** fashion or shape a figure in clay, wax, etc. **2** devise a mathematical model of. **3** (**model on**) use as an example for something else. **4** work as a model.

modem /moh-dem/ noun a device that connects a computer to a telephone line.

moderate adjective **1** average in amount, intensity, or degree. **2** (of a political position) not radical or extreme. noun a person with moderate views. verb (**moderates, moderating, moderated**) **1** make or become less extreme or intense. **2** check examination papers to ensure that they have been marked consistently. ■ **moderately** adverb.

moderation noun **1** the avoidance of extremes in your actions or opinions. **2** the process of moderating.

moderator noun **1** a person who helps others to solve a dispute. **2** a chairman of a debate. **3** a person who moderates examination papers.

modern adjective **1** relating to the present or to recent times. **2** using the most up-to-date techniques or equipment. **3** (in art, architecture, etc.) marked by a departure from traditional values. ■ **modernity** noun.

modernism noun **1** modern ideas, methods, or styles. **2** a movement in the arts or religion that aims to break with traditional forms or ideas. ■ **modernist** noun & adjective.

modernize or **modernise** verb (**modernizes**, **modernizing**, **modernized**) make modern.

modest adjective **1** humble in the way you view your abilities or achievements. **2** relatively moderate, limited, or small. **3** decent. ■ **modestly** adverb **modesty** noun.

modicum /mod-i-kuhm/ noun a small quantity of something.

modification noun **1** the action of modifying. **2** a change made.

modifier noun **1** a person or thing that modifies. **2** Grammar a word that qualifies the sense of a noun (e.g. *family* in *a family house*).

modify verb (**modifies**, **modifying**, **modified**) make partial changes to.

modish adjective fashionable.

modular adjective made up of separate units.

modulate verb (**modulates**, **modulating**, **modulated**) **1** adjust, change or control something. **2** vary the strength, tone, or pitch of your voice. **3** Music change from one key to another.

module noun **1** each of a set of parts or units that can be used to create a more complex structure. **2** a unit forming part of a course. **3** an independent unit of a spacecraft.

moggie or **moggy** noun (plural **moggies**) Brit. informal a cat.

mogul /moh-guhl/ noun informal an important or powerful person.

mohair noun a yarn or fabric made from the hair of the angora goat.

Mohican /moh-hee-kuhn/ noun a hair style in which the sides of the head are shaved and a central strip of hair is made to stand up.

moiety /moy-i-ti/ noun (plural **moieties**) formal a half.

moist adjective slightly wet; damp. ■ **moisten** verb.

moisture noun tiny droplets of water making something damp.

moisturize or **moisturise** verb (**moisturizes**, **moisturizing**, **moisturized**) make something less dry.

moisturizer or **moisturiser** noun a cream for moisturizing the skin.

molar noun a grinding tooth at the back of the mouth.

molasses /muh-lass-iz/ noun a thick brown liquid obtained from raw sugar.

mold US spelling of **MOULD**[1], **MOULD**[2].

mole[1] noun **1** a small burrowing mammal with dark fur, a long muzzle, and very small eyes. **2** someone within an organization who secretly passes confidential information to another organization or country.

mole[2] noun a dark blemish on the skin.

mole[3] noun **1** a solid structure serving as a pier, breakwater, or causeway. **2** a harbour formed by a mole.

mole[4] noun Chemistry the amount of a particular substance which contains as many atoms or molecules as there are atoms in a standard amount of carbon.

molecule /mol-i-kyool/ noun a group of atoms forming the smallest unit into which a substance can be divided. ■ **molecular** adjective.

molehill noun a small mound of earth thrown up by a burrowing mole.

moleskin noun **1** the skin of a mole used as fur. **2** a thick cotton fabric with a soft surface.

molest verb **1** pester in a hostile way. **2** sexually assault. ■ **molestation** noun **molester** noun.

moll noun informal a gangster's female companion.

mollify verb (**mollifies**, **mollifying**, **mollified**) **1** make someone feel less angry. **2** reduce the severity of.

mollusc (US spelling **mollusk**) noun an animal of a group with a soft unsegmented body and often an external shell, such as slugs and snails.

mollycoddle verb (**mollycoddles, mollycoddling, mollycoddled**) treat someone too indulgently or protectively.

molt US spelling of **MOULT**.

molten adjective (especially of metal and glass) made liquid by heat.

molto /**mol**-toh/ adverb Music very.

molybdenum /muh-**lib**-duh-nuhm/ noun a brittle silver-grey metallic element.

mom N. Amer. = **MUM**[1].

moment noun 1 a brief period of time. 2 an exact point in time. 3 formal importance.

momentarily adverb 1 for a very short time. 2 N. Amer. very soon.

momentary adjective very brief or short-lived.

momentous adjective of great importance or significance.

momentum noun (plural **momenta**) the force gained by a moving object.

mommy N. Amer. = **MUMMY**[1].

monarch noun a king, queen, or emperor. ■ **monarchical** adjective.

monarchist noun someone who supports the monarchy. ■ **monarchism** noun.

monarchy noun (plural **monarchies**) 1 government by a monarch. 2 a state with a monarch.

monastery noun (plural **monasteries**) a community of monks living under religious vows.

monastic adjective 1 relating to monks or nuns. 2 resembling monks or their way of life.

Monday noun the day of the week before Tuesday and following Sunday.

monetarism noun the theory that inflation is best controlled by limiting the supply of money. ■ **monetarist** noun & adjective.

monetary adjective having to do with money.

money noun 1 a means of paying for things in the form of coins and bank-

notes. 2 wealth. 3 payment or financial gain. 4 (**moneys** or **monies**) formal sums of money. □ **money order** a postal order. **money spider** a very small black spider.

moneyed adjective having a lot of money.

Mongol noun 1 a person from Mongolia. 2 (**mongol**) offensive a person with Down's syndrome.

mongoose noun (plural **mongooses**) a small meat-eating mammal with a long body and tail, native to Africa and Asia.

mongrel noun a dog of no definite breed.

moniker noun informal a name.

monitor noun 1 a person or device that monitors something. 2 a television used to view a picture from a particular camera or a display from a computer. 3 a school pupil with special duties. 4 (also **monitor lizard**) a large tropical lizard. verb keep under observation.

monk noun a man belonging to a religious community typically living under vows of poverty, chastity, and obedience.

monkey noun (plural **monkeys**) a primate typically having a long tail and living in trees in tropical countries. verb (**monkeys, monkeying, monkeyed**) 1 (**monkey about** or **around**) behave in a silly or playful way. 2 (**monkey with**) tamper with. □ **monkey nut** Brit. a peanut. **monkey puzzle** a coniferous tree with branches covered in spirals of tough spiny leaves. **monkey wrench** a spanner with large adjustable jaws.

mono noun monophonic sound.

monochrome adjective (of a photograph or picture) produced in black and white or in varying tones of one colour. ■ **monochromatic** adjective.

monocle noun a single lens worn at one eye.

monogamy /muh-**nog**-uh-mi/ noun the practice of having only one wife or husband at any one time. ■ **monogamous** adjective.

monogram noun a motif of two or more interwoven letters, typically a person's initials. ■ **monogrammed** adjective.

monograph noun a short text written on a single subject.

monolingual adjective speaking or expressed in only one language.

monolith noun a large single upright block of stone.

monolithic adjective **1** formed of a single large block of stone. **2** very large and impersonal.

monologue noun **1** a long speech by one actor in a play or film. **2** a long, boring speech by one person.

monomania noun an obsession with one thing. ■ **monomaniac** noun.

monomer /mon-uh-mer/ noun Chemistry a molecule that can be linked to other identical molecules to form a polymer.

monophonic adjective (of sound reproduction) using only one channel.

monoplane noun an aircraft with one pair of wings.

monopolize or **monopolise** verb (**monopolizes, monopolizing, monopolized**) dominate or take control of.

monopoly noun (plural **monopolies**) **1** the complete control, possession, or use of something by one person or organization. **2** complete control of trade in particular goods or the supply of a service.

monorail noun a railway in which the track consists of a single rail.

monosyllabic adjective **1** (of a word) having one syllable. **2** (of a person) saying very little.

monosyllable noun a word of one syllable.

monotheism /mon-oh-thee-i-z'm/ noun the belief that there is only one god. ■ **monotheistic** adjective.

monotone noun a continuing sound that does not change pitch.

monotonous adjective boring and unchanging. ■ **monotonously** adverb **monotony** noun.

monoxide noun Chemistry an oxide containing one atom of oxygen.

Monsieur /muh-syer/ noun (plural **Messieurs** /mess-yer/) a title for a French man, corresponding to *Mr* or *sir*.

Monsignor /mon-seen-yer/ noun (plural **Monsignori** /mon-seen-yor-i/) the title of a senior Roman Catholic priest.

monsoon noun **1** a seasonal wind in the Indian subcontinent and SE Asia. **2** the rainy season accompanying the monsoon.

monster noun **1** a frightening imaginary creature. **2** a cruel or wicked person. **3** something that is excessively large: *a monster of a book*.

monstrosity noun (plural **monstrosities**) something that is very large and unattractive.

monstrous adjective **1** very large, ugly, or frightening. **2** shocking and morally wrong. ■ **monstrously** adverb.

montage /mon-tahzh/ noun a picture or film made by putting together pieces from other pictures or films.

month noun **1** each of the twelve periods of time into which a year is divided. **2** a period of time between a date in one month and the same date in the next month. **3** a period of 28 days or four weeks.

monthly adjective & adverb happening or produced once a month.

monty noun (**the full monty**) Brit. informal the full amount or extent.

monument noun **1** a statue or structure built in memory of a person or event. **2** a site of historical importance. **3** a lasting example of something: *a monument to good taste*.

monumental adjective **1** very large or impressive. **2** serving as a monument. ■ **monumentally** adverb.

moo verb (**moos, mooing, mooed**) (of a cow) make a long, deep sound.

mooch verb Brit. informal stand or walk around in a bored way.

mood noun **1** the way you feel at a particular time. **2** a period of being bad tempered. **3** the atmosphere of a work of art. **4** Grammar a form of a verb expressing fact, command, question, wish, or a condition.

moody adjective (**moodier**, **moodiest**) **1** having moods that change quickly. **2** gloomy or bad-tempered.

moon noun **1** (also **Moon**) the natural satellite of the earth. **2** a natural satellite of any planet. **3** literary a month. verb **1** (**moon about** or **around**) behave or walk about in a dreamy way. **2** informal expose your buttocks to someone as an insult or joke. □ **over the moon** Brit. informal delighted.

moonlight noun the light of the moon. verb (**moonlights**, **moonlighting**, **moonlighted**) informal do a second job without declaring it for tax purposes. ■ **moonlit** adjective.

moonscape noun a landscape that is rocky and barren like the moon.

moonshine noun informal **1** foolish talk or ideas. **2** N. Amer. liquor that is made and sold illegally.

moonstone noun a white semi-precious mineral.

moony adjective **1** like the moon. **2** dreamy because in love.

Moor noun a member of a NW African Muslim people. ■ **Moorish** adjective.

moor[1] noun a high open area of land that is not cultivated.

moor[2] verb fasten a boat to the shore or to an anchor.

moorhen noun a waterbird with black feathers.

mooring or **moorings** noun a place where a boat is moored, or the ropes used to moor it.

moose = ELK.

moot adjective uncertain or undecided: *a moot point*. verb put forward a topic for discussion.

mop noun **1** a bundle of thick strings or a sponge attached to a handle, used for wiping floors. **2** a thick mass of hair. verb (**mops**, **mopping**, **mopped**) **1** clean or soak up by wiping. **2** (**mop up**) clear up or put an end to.

mope verb (**mopes**, **moping**, **moped**) be listless and in low spirits.

moped /mow-ped/ noun a motorcycle with a small engine.

moraine noun rocks and stones deposited by a glacier.

moral adjective **1** concerned with the principles of right and wrong behaviour. **2** conforming to accepted standards of behaviour. noun **1** a lesson about right or wrong that you learn from a story or experience. **2** (**morals**) standards of good behaviour. ■ **morally** adverb.

morale noun a feeling of confidence and satisfaction.

moralist noun a person with strict views about morals. ■ **moralistic** adjective.

morality noun (plural **moralities**) **1** principles concerning the difference between right and wrong or good and bad behaviour. **2** moral behaviour. **3** the extent to which an action is right or wrong.

moralize or **moralise** verb (**moralizes**, **moralizing**, **moralized**) comment on moral issues, usually in a disapproving way.

morass /muh-rass/ noun **1** an area of muddy or boggy ground. **2** a complicated or confused situation.

moratorium noun (plural **moratoriums** or **moratoria**) a temporary ban on an activity.

morbid adjective **1** having a strong interest in unpleasant subjects, especially death and disease. **2** Medicine having to do with disease. ■ **morbidity** noun **morbidly** adverb.

mordant adjective (of humour) sharply sarcastic.

more determiner & pronoun a greater or additional amount or degree. adverb **1** forming the comparative of adjectives and adverbs. **2** to a greater extent. **3** again. **4** (**more than**) extremely.

morello noun (plural **morellos**) a kind of sour dark cherry.

moreover adverb as a further matter; besides.

mores /mor-ayz/ plural noun the customs of a community.

morgue noun a mortuary.

moribund adjective **1** at the point of death. **2** about to come to an end.

Mormon noun a member of the Church of Jesus Christ of Latter-Day Saints. ■ **Mormonism** noun.

morn noun literary morning.

morning noun **1** the period of time between midnight and noon, especially from sunrise to noon. **2** sunrise. **adverb (mornings)** informal every morning. □ **morning sickness** nausea felt by a woman when she is pregnant.

moron noun informal a stupid person. ■ **moronic** adjective.

morose adjective unhappy and bad-tempered. ■ **morosely** adverb.

morph verb (in computer animation) change smoothly and gradually from one image to another.

morphine noun a drug made from opium and used to relieve pain.

morris dancing noun traditional English folk dancing.

morrow noun (the morrow) old use the next day.

Morse or **Morse code** noun a code in which letters are represented by combinations of long and short sounds or flashes of light.

morsel noun a small piece of food.

mortal adjective **1** having to die at some time. **2** causing death. **3** (of a battle or enemy) lasting until death. **noun** a human being. □ **mortal sin** (in Christian belief) a sin so serious as to result in damnation. ■ **mortally** adverb.

mortality noun **1** the state of being mortal. **2** death. **3** (also **mortality rate**) the number of deaths in a particular area or period of time.

mortar noun **1** a mixture of lime with cement, sand, and water, used to stick bricks or stones together. **2** a cup-shaped container in which substances are crushed with a pestle. **3** a short cannon for firing bombs at high angles. □ **mortar board 1** an academic cap with a flat square top and a tassel. **2** a small square board used for holding mortar.

mortgage noun **1** a legal agreement by which a bank or building society lends you money, using your house as security. **2** an amount of money borrowed or lent under such an agreement. **verb (mortgages, mortgaging, mortgaged)** give a bank or building society the right to hold your house as security for the money they agree to lend you.

mortician noun N. Amer. an undertaker.

mortify verb (mortifies, mortifying, mortified) cause someone to feel embarrassed or ashamed. ■ **mortification** noun.

mortise or **mortice** noun a slot cut in a piece of wood in order to hold the end of another piece of wood. **verb (mortises, mortising, mortised) 1** join things in this way. **2** cut a mortise in. □ **mortise lock** a lock fitted into a hole in a door.

mortuary noun (plural mortuaries) a room or building in which dead bodies are kept until they are buried or cremated.

mosaic noun a picture or pattern made by fitting together small coloured pieces of stone, tile, or glass.

mosey verb (moseys, moseying, moseyed) informal walk in a leisurely way.

Moslem ⇒ **MUSLIM**.

mosque noun a Muslim place of worship.

mosquito noun (plural mosquitoes) a small long-legged fly, some kinds of which transmit diseases through their bite.

moss noun a very small green spreading plant which grows in damp places. ■ **mossy** adjective.

most determiner & pronoun **1** greatest in amount or degree. **2** the majority of. **adverb 1** to the greatest extent. **2** forming the superlative of adjectives and adverbs. **3** very.

mostly adverb **1** on the whole; mainly. **2** usually.

mote noun a speck.

motel noun a roadside hotel designed for motorists.

motet /moh-tet/ noun a short piece of choral music.

moth noun an insect like a butterfly which is active at night. □ **moth-eaten 1** eaten by the larvae of moths. **2** shabby and worn.

mothball noun a small ball of camphor, placed among stored clothes to deter moths.

mother noun **1** a female parent. **2** (Mother) (especially as a title or form of address) the head of a convent. verb look after somebody protectively. □ **mother-in-law** (plural **mothers-in-law**) the mother of a person's husband or wife. **mother-of-pearl** a smooth pearly substance lining the shells of oysters. **mother tongue** a person's native language. ■ **motherhood** noun **motherly** adjective.

motherland noun your native country.

motif /moh-teef/ noun **1** a pattern or design. **2** a theme that is repeated in a work of literature or piece of music.

motion noun **1** the action of moving. **2** a movement or gesture. **3** a formal proposal that is discussed at a meeting. **4** Brit. an emptying of the bowels. verb direct someone with a gesture. □ **motion picture** N. Amer. a cinema film. ■ **motionless** adjective.

motivate verb (**motivates, motivating, motivated**) **1** provide someone with a motive for doing something. **2** make someone want to do something. ■ **motivator** noun.

motivation noun **1** the reason for your actions or behaviour. **2** enthusiasm. ■ **motivational** adjective.

motive noun something that makes someone act in a particular way. adjective causing motion.

motley adjective made up of a variety of different things.

motocross noun cross-country racing on motorcycles.

motor noun **1** a device that produces power and movement for a vehicle or machine. **2** Brit. informal a car. adjective giving or producing motion. verb Brit. informal travel in a car. □ **motor vehicle** a road vehicle powered by an engine.

motorbike noun a motorcycle.

motorboat noun a boat powered by a motor.

motorcade noun a procession of motor vehicles.

motorcycle noun a heavy bicycle powered by a motor. ■ **motorcycling** noun **motorcyclist** noun.

motorist noun the driver of a car.

motorway noun Brit. a road designed for fast traffic, typically with three lanes in each direction.

mottled adjective marked with patches of a different colour.

motto noun (plural **mottoes** or **mottos**) a short sentence or phrase that expresses a belief or aim.

mould¹ (US spelling **mold**) noun **1** a container into which you pour hot liquid in order to produce a solid object of a desired shape when it cools. **2** a distinctive style or character. verb **1** form an object of a particular shape out of a soft substance. **2** influence the development of something.

mould² (US spelling **mold**) noun a furry growth of tiny fungi that occurs in moist warm conditions. ■ **mouldy** adjective.

moulder (US spelling **molder**) verb (**moulders, mouldering, mouldered**) slowly decay.

moulding (US spelling **molding**) noun a carved or moulded strip of wood, stone, or plaster as a decorative feature on a building.

moult (US spelling **molt**) verb shed old feathers, hair, or skin. noun a period of moulting.

mound noun **1** a raised mass of earth or other material. **2** a small hill. **3** a heap or pile. verb heap up into a mound.

mount¹ verb **1** climb up or on to. **2** get up on an animal or bicycle to ride it.

3 increase in size, number, or intensity. **4** organize a campaign, bid, etc. **5** put or fix something in place. **noun 1** (also **mounting**) something on which an object is mounted for support or display. **2** a horse used for riding.

mount² **noun** old use a mountain or hill.

mountain **noun 1** a very high and steep hill. **2** a large pile or quantity.

mountaineering **noun** the sport or activity of climbing mountains. ■ **mountaineer** noun.

mountainous **adjective 1** having many mountains. **2** huge.

mountebank **noun** a swindler.

mourn **verb** feel deep sorrow following the death or loss of.

mourner **noun** a person who attends a funeral.

mournful **adjective** very sad or depressing. ■ **mournfully** adverb.

mourning **noun 1** the expression of deep sorrow for someone who has died. **2** black clothes worn in a period of mourning.

mouse **noun** (plural **mice**) **1** a small rodent with a pointed snout and a long thin tail. **2** a timid and quiet person. **3** (plural also **mouses**) Computing a small hand-held device which controls the cursor on a computer screen.

moussaka /moo-**sah**-kuh/ **noun** a Greek dish of minced lamb layered with aubergines and tomatoes and topped with a cheese sauce.

mousse **noun 1** a dish made from whipped cream and egg whites. **2** a light preparation for the skin or hair.

moustache (US spelling **mustache**) **noun** a strip of hair above a man's upper lip.

mousy or **mousey** **adjective 1** (of hair) of a light brown colour. **2** timid.

mouth **noun 1** the opening in the body through which food is taken and sounds are made. **2** an opening or entrance to something. **3** the place

where a river enters the sea. **verb 1** move your lips as if you were saying something. **2** say something in a pompous way. □ **mouth organ** a harmonica. **mouth-watering** smelling or looking delicious.

mouthful **noun 1** an amount of food or drink that fills your mouth. **2** a long or complicated word or phrase.

mouthpiece **noun** a part of a musical instrument, telephone, etc. that is put in or against the mouth.

mouthwash **noun** an antiseptic liquid for rinsing the mouth or gargling.

mouthy **adjective** informal inclined to talk a lot.

move **verb** (**moves**, **moving**, **moved**) **1** go or make something go in a specified direction or manner. **2** change or make something change position. **3** change the place where you live. **4** change from one state or activity to another. **5** take action. **6** make progress. **7** provoke a strong feeling in someone. **noun 1** an instance of moving. **2** an action taken towards achieving a purpose. **3** a player's turn during a board game. ■ **movable** (or **moveable**) adjective.

movement **noun 1** an act of moving. **2** the process of moving. **3** a group of people who share the same aims. **4** a trend or development. **5** (**movements**) a person's activities during a particular period of time. **6** Music a main division of a musical work.

movie **noun** N. Amer. a cinema film.

moving **adjective 1** in motion. **2** arousing strong emotion. ■ **movingly** adverb.

mow **verb** (**mows**, **mowing**, **mowed**; past participle **mowed** or **mown**) **1** cut down or trim grass, hay, etc. **2** (**mow down**) kill by gunfire or by knocking down with a motor vehicle. ■ **mower** noun.

mozzarella /mot-suh-**rel**-luh/ **noun** a firm white Italian cheese made from buffalo's or cow's milk.

MP **abbreviation** Member of Parliament.

Mr noun a title used before a man's surname or full name.

Mrs noun a title used before a married woman's surname or full name.

MS abbreviation **1** manuscript. **2** multiple sclerosis.

Ms noun a title used before a married or unmarried woman's surname or full name.

MSc abbreviation Master of Science.

Mt abbreviation Mount.

mu /myoo/ noun the twelfth letter of the Greek alphabet (**M**, **μ**).

much determiner & pronoun a large amount. adverb **1** to a great extent. **2** often.

muck noun **1** dirt or rubbish. **2** manure. verb **1** (**muck up**) informal spoil. **2** (**muck about or around**) Brit. informal behave in a silly way. **3** (**muck about with or around with**) Brit. informal interfere with. **4** (**muck in**) Brit. informal share a task. **5** (**muck out**) Brit. remove manure and dirt from a stable.

mucky adjective (**muckier, muckiest**) **1** covered with muck; dirty. **2** indecent.

mucous /myoo-kuhss/ adjective having to do with mucus. □**mucous membrane** a tissue that secretes mucus, lining the nose, mouth, and other organs.

mucus /myoo-kuhss/ noun a slimy substance secreted by the mucous membranes.

mud noun wet earth that is soft and sticky. □**mud-slinging** informal the casting of insults and accusations.

muddle verb (**muddles, muddling, muddled**) **1** bring into a disordered or confusing state. **2** confuse someone. **3** (**muddle up**) confuse two or more things with each other. noun a muddled state. □**muddle along** (or **through**) cope more or less satisfactorily. ■ **muddled** adjective.

muddy adjective (**muddier, muddiest**) **1** covered in mud. **2** not bright or clear. verb (**muddies, muddying, muddied**) make something muddy.

mudflap noun a flap hung behind the wheel of a vehicle to protect against mud and stones thrown up from the road.

mudflat noun a stretch of muddy land left uncovered at low tide.

mudguard noun a curved strip fitted over a wheel of a bicycle or motorcycle to protect against water and dirt thrown up from the road.

muesli /myooz-li/ noun (plural **mueslis**) a mixture of oats, dried fruit, and nuts, eaten with milk.

muezzin /moo-ez-zin/ noun a man who calls Muslims to prayer.

muff[1] noun a short tube made of fur or other warm material into which the hands are placed for warmth.

muff[2] verb informal handle something clumsily or badly.

muffin noun **1** a type of flat bread roll, usually eaten toasted with butter. **2** N. Amer. a small domed cake.

muffle verb (**muffles, muffling, muffled**) **1** wrap or cover for warmth. **2** make a sound quieter.

muffler noun a scarf.

mufti /muf-ti/ noun (plural **muftis**) **1** a Muslim legal expert allowed to give rulings on religious matters. **2** civilian clothes when worn by military or police staff.

mug[1] noun **1** a large cylindrical cup with a handle. **2** informal a person's face. **3** Brit. informal a stupid or gullible person. verb (**mugs, mugging, mugged**) attack and rob someone in a public place.

mug[2] verb (**mugs, mugging, mugged**) (**mug up**) Brit. informal learn a subject quickly and intensively.

mugger noun a person who attacks and robs someone in a public place.

muggins noun (plural **muggins** or **mugginses**) Brit. informal a foolish person.

muggy adjective (of the weather) unpleasantly warm and humid.

mugshot noun informal a photograph of a person's face made for an official purpose.

mulatto noun (plural **mulattoes** or mulattos) a person with one white and one black parent.

mulberry noun **1** a dark red or white fruit resembling the loganberry. **2** a dark red or purple colour.

mulch noun a mass of leaves or compost, used to protect the base of a plant or to enrich the soil. verb cover with mulch.

mule noun the offspring of a male donkey and a female horse.

mulish adjective stubborn.

mull[1] verb (mull over) think about something at length.

mull[2] verb warm wine or beer and add sugar and spices to it.

mullah /muul-luh/ noun a Muslim who is an expert in Islamic theology and sacred law.

mullet noun a sea fish that is caught for food.

mulligatawny noun a spicy meat soup originally made in India.

mullion noun a vertical bar between the panes of glass in a window. ■ mullioned adjective.

multicoloured or **multicolour** (US spelling multicolored or multicolor) adjective having many colours.

multicultural adjective relating to or made up of several cultural or ethnic groups. ■ multiculturalism noun.

multifaceted adjective having many sides or aspects.

multifarious adjective having great variety and diversity.

multilateral adjective involving three or more participants.

multilingual adjective in or using several languages.

multimedia noun the use of sound and pictures as well as text on a computer screen.

multinational adjective involving several countries. noun a company operating in several countries.

multiple adjective **1** involving several parts or elements. **2** numerous and varied. **3** (of a disease or injury) complex in its nature or effect; affecting several parts of the body. noun a number that may be divided by another number without a remainder. □ multiple-choice (of a question in an examination) giving several possible answers, from which you must choose one. multiple sclerosis ⇒ **SCLEROSIS**.

multiplex noun a cinema with several separate screens.

multiplication noun the process of multiplying. □ multiplication sign the symbol ×, indicating that one number is to be multiplied by another.

multiplicity noun (plural multiplicities) a large number or variety of something.

multiply verb (multiplies multiplying multiplied) **1** add a number to itself a specified number of times. **2** increase in number or quantity. **3** increase in number by reproducing. ■ multiplier noun.

multiracial adjective having to do with people of many races.

multi-storey adjective (of a building) having several storeys. noun Brit. informal a multi-storey car park.

multitude noun **1** a large number of people or things. **2** (the multitude) the mass of ordinary people.

multitudinous adjective very numerous.

mum[1] noun Brit. informal your mother.

mum[2] adjective (keep mum) informal stay silent so as not to reveal a secret. □ mum's the word it is a secret.

mumble verb (mumbles mumbling mumbled) say something quietly and unclearly. noun quiet and unclear speech.

mumbo-jumbo noun informal language that sounds mysterious but has no real meaning.

mummify verb (mummifies mummifying mummified) preserve a body as a mummy. ■ mummification noun.

mummy[1] noun (plural mummies) Brit. informal your mother.

mummy[2] noun (plural mummies) (especially in ancient Egypt) a body that has been embalmed and wrapped in bandages in order to preserve it.

mumps **plural noun** a disease causing swelling of the glands at the sides of the face.

munch **verb** eat something steadily and often noisily.

mundane **adjective** lacking interest or excitement.

municipal **adjective** relating to a municipality.

municipality **noun** (plural **municipalities**) a town or district with its own local government.

munificent **adjective** very generous. ■ **munificence** noun.

munitions **plural noun** military weapons, ammunition, and equipment.

mural **noun** a painting done directly on a wall. **adjective** relating to walls.

murder **noun** the unlawful planned killing of one person by another. **verb** (**murders, murdering, murdered**) kill someone unlawfully, having planned to in advance. ■ **murderer** noun **murderess** noun.

murderous **adjective** capable of murdering someone or being extremely violent.

murk **noun** darkness or fog.

murky **adjective** (**murkier, murkiest**) **1** dark and gloomy. **2** (of water) dirty or cloudy. **3** suspicious and kept hidden.

murmur **noun** **1** the sound made by a person speaking quietly. **2** a low continuous background noise. **verb** **1** say something in a murmur. **2** make a low continuous sound.

muscle **noun** **1** a band of body tissue that can be tightened or relaxed in order to move a part of the body. **2** power or strength. **verb** (**muscle in**) informal involve yourself in something that does not concern you. ■ **muscly** adjective.

muscular **adjective** **1** having to do with the muscles. **2** having well-developed muscles. □ **muscular dystrophy** an inherited condition in which the muscles gradually become weaker.

musculature **noun** the arrangement of muscles in a body.

muse[1] **noun** **1** (**Muse**) (in Greek and Roman mythology) each of nine goddesses who preside over the arts and sciences. **2** a woman who is the inspiration for a creative artist.

muse[2] **verb** (**muses, musing, mused**) **1** be absorbed in thought. **2** say something to yourself in a thoughtful manner.

museum **noun** a building in which objects of interest are kept and shown to the public.

mush **noun** **1** a soft, wet, pulpy mass. **2** something that is excessively sentimental. ■ **mushy** adjective.

mushroom **noun** a fungus in the form of a domed cap on a short stalk, often edible. **verb** increase or develop quickly. □ **mushroom cloud** a mushroom-shaped cloud of dust formed after a nuclear explosion.

music **noun** **1** the sounds of voices or instruments arranged in a pleasing way. **2** the art of writing or playing music. **3** the written or printed signs representing a piece of music. □ **music hall 1** (in the past) a popular form of entertainment involving singing, dancing, and comedy. **2** a theatre where such entertainment took place.

musical **adjective** **1** relating to or accompanied by music. **2** fond of or skilled in music. **3** having a pleasant sound. **noun** a play or film which involves singing or dancing. ■ **musically** adverb.

musician **noun** a person who plays a musical instrument or writes music. ■ **musicianship** noun.

musicology **noun** the study of the history and theory of music.

musk **noun** a strong-smelling substance secreted by the male musk deer, used as an ingredient in making perfume. □ **musk deer** a small East Asian deer. ■ **musky** adjective.

musket noun (in the past) a light gun with a long barrel.

musketeer noun (in the past) a soldier armed with a musket.

muskrat noun a large North American rodent with a musky smell.

Muslim or **Moslem** noun a follower of Islam. adjective relating to Muslims or Islam.

muslin noun lightweight cotton cloth in a plain weave.

musquash noun Brit. the fur of the muskrat.

mussel noun a small shellfish with a dark brown or purplish-black shell.

must[1] modal verb (past **had to** or in reported speech **must**) **1** be obliged to; should. **2** used to insist on something. **3** used to say that something is very likely: *you must be tired.* noun informal something that should not be missed.

must[2] noun grape juice before it is fermented.

mustache US spelling of **MOUSTACHE**.

mustang noun a small wild horse of the south-western US.

mustard noun **1** a hot-tasting yellow or brown paste made from the crushed seeds of a plant. **2** a brownish yellow colour. ■ **mustard gas** is a liquid whose vapour causes severe irritation and blistering, used in chemical weapons.

muster verb (musters, mustering, mustered) **1** bring troops together in preparation for battle. **2** (of people) gather together. **3** summon up a feeling or attitude. noun an instance of mustering troops. □ **pass muster** be accepted as satisfactory.

mustn't short form must not.

musty adjective having a stale or mouldy smell. ■ **mustiness** noun.

mutable adjective able or tending to change. ■ **mutability** noun.

mutant adjective resulting from or showing the effect of mutation. noun a mutant form.

mutate verb (mutates, mutating, mutated) undergo mutation.

mutation noun **1** the process of changing. **2** a change in genetic structure which may be passed on to subsequent generations. **3** a distinct form resulting from such a change.

mute adjective **1** not speaking. **2** dated unable to speak. **3** (of a letter) not pronounced. noun **1** dated a person who is unable to speak. **2** a device used to make the sound of a musical instrument quieter or softer. verb (mutes, muting, muted) **1** make the sound of something quieter or softer. **2** reduce the strength or intensity of. ■ **mutely** adverb.

mutilate verb (mutilates, mutilating, mutilated) severely injure or damage. ■ **mutilation** noun.

mutineer noun a person who mutinies.

mutinous adjective rebellious.

mutiny noun (plural **mutinies**) an open rebellion against authority, especially by soldiers or sailors against their officers. verb (mutinies, mutinying, mutinied) engage in mutiny; rebel.

mutt noun informal **1** a mongrel dog. **2** a stupid person.

mutter verb (mutters, muttering, muttered) **1** say in a voice which can barely be heard. **2** talk or grumble in private. noun speech that can barely be heard.

mutton noun the flesh of mature sheep used as food.

mutual adjective **1** experienced by two or more people equally. **2** (of two or more people) having the same specified relationship to each other. **3** shared by two or more people: *a mutual friend.* ■ **mutuality** noun **mutually** adverb.

muzzle noun **1** the nose and mouth of an animal. **2** a guard fitted over an animal's muzzle to stop it biting. **3** the open end of the barrel of a gun. verb (muzzles, muzzling, muzzled) **1** put a muzzle on an animal. **2** prevent someone speaking freely.

muzzy adjective **1** dazed or confused. **2** blurred or indistinct.

my possessive determiner belonging to or associated with the speaker.

myalgia /my-**al**-juh/ noun pain in a muscle.

mycology noun the scientific study of fungi.

mynah bird noun an Asian or Australasian bird, some kinds of which can mimic human speech.

myopia /my-**oh**-pi-uh/ noun short-sightedness. ■ **myopic** adjective.

myriad /**mi**-ri-uhd/ literary noun (also **myriads**) a countless or very great number. adjective countless.

myrrh /mer/ noun a sweet-smelling substance obtained from certain trees, used in perfumes and incense.

myrtle noun an evergreen shrub with white flowers and purple-black berries.

myself pronoun **1** used by a speaker to refer to himself or herself as the object of a verb or preposition when he or she is the subject of the clause. **2** I or me personally.

mysterious adjective difficult or impossible to understand or explain. ■ **mysteriously** adverb.

mystery noun (plural **mysteries**) **1** something that is difficult or impossible to understand or explain. **2** secrecy. **3** a novel, film, etc. dealing with a puzzling crime. □ **mystery play** a medieval play based on biblical stories or the lives of the saints.

mystic noun a person who seeks to know God through prayer and contemplation. adjective mystical.

mystical adjective **1** relating to mystics or mysticism. **2** having a spiritual significance that goes beyond human understanding. **3** inspiring a sense of spiritual mystery and awe.

mysticism noun **1** the belief that knowledge of God can be found through prayer and contemplation. **2** vague or ill-defined religious or spiritual belief.

mystify verb (**mystifies**, **mystifying**, **mystified**) **1** confuse or bewilder. **2** make something uncertain or mysterious. ■ **mystifying** adjective.

mystique noun an atmosphere of mystery or secrecy that makes something seem impressive or attractive.

myth noun **1** a traditional story that describes the early history of a people or explains a natural event. **2** a widely held but false belief. **3** an imaginary person or thing.

mythical adjective **1** occurring in or characteristic of myths or folk tales. **2** imaginary or not real.

mythology noun (plural **mythologies**) **1** a collection of myths. **2** a set of widely held but exaggerated or false beliefs. ■ **mythological** adjective.

myxomatosis /mik-suh-muh-**toh**-siss/ noun a highly infectious and usually fatal disease of rabbits.

Nn

N or **n** noun (plural **Ns** or **N's**) the fourteenth letter of the alphabet. abbreviation North or Northern.

n/a abbreviation not applicable.

naan ⇨ **NAN²**.

nab verb (**nabs**, **nabbing**, **nabbed**) informal **1** catch a wrong-doer. **2** take or grab suddenly.

nacho /**na**-choh/ noun (plural **nachos**) a small piece of tortilla topped with melted cheese, peppers, etc.

nadir /**nay**-deer/ noun **1** the point in space directly opposite the zenith and below an observer. **2** the lowest or most unsuccessful point.

naff adjective Brit. informal lacking taste or style.

nag¹ verb (**nags**, **nagging**, **nagged**)

1 constantly tell someone they should be doing something. **2** be constantly worrying or painful. **noun 1** a person who nags. **2** a persistent feeling of anxiety.

nag² noun informal an old horse.

naiad /ny-ad/ noun (plural **naiads** or **naiades** /ny-uh-deez/) (in classical mythology) a water nymph.

nail noun **1** a small metal spike with a flat head, used for joining pieces of wood together. **2** a thin hard layer covering the upper part of the tip of the finger and toe. **verb 1** fasten with a nail or nails. **2** informal detect or catch a criminal. □**nail-biting** making you feel great anxiety or tension.

naive or **naïve** /ny-eev/ adjective lacking experience or judgement. ■ **naively** adverb

naivety /ny-eev-ti/ or **naïveté** /ny-eev-tay/ noun **1** lack of experience, wisdom, or judgement. **2** innocence.

naked adjective **1** without clothes. **2** (of an object) without the usual covering or protection. **3** (of feelings) not concealed; undisguised. **4** vulnerable. □**the naked eye** the ability to see things without using a telescope, microscope, etc. ■ **nakedly** adverb **nakedness** noun.

namby-pamby adjective lacking strength or courage; feeble.

name noun **1** a word or words by which someone or something is known. **2** a famous person. **3** a reputation: *he made a name for himself.* verb (**names, naming, named**) **1** give a name to. **2** identify or mention by name. **3** specify a sum, time, or place. **4** appoint. □**in someone's name 1** belonging to or reserved for someone. **2** on behalf of someone. **in the name of** for the sake of. **name-dropping** mentioning the names of famous people as if you know them, in order to impress other people.

nameless adjective **1** having no name. **2** having a name that is kept secret.

namely adverb that is to say.

namesake noun a person or thing with the same name as another.

nan¹ noun Brit. informal your grandmother.

nan² or **naan** /nahn/ noun a type of soft flat Indian bread.

nanny noun (plural **nannies**) **1** a woman employed to look after a child in its own home. **2** (also **nanny goat**) a female goat.

nanosecond noun one thousand millionth of a second.

nap¹ noun a short sleep. verb (**naps, napping, napped**) have a nap.

nap² noun short raised fibres on the surface of certain fabrics.

napalm /nay-pahm/ noun a highly flammable form of petrol, used in fire-bombs and flame-throwers.

nape noun the back of the neck.

naphtha /naf-thuh/ noun a flammable oil extracted from coal, shale, or petroleum.

napkin noun a piece of cloth or paper used at a meal to wipe the fingers or lips and to protect clothes.

nappy noun (plural **nappies**) Brit. a piece of material wrapped round a baby's bottom and between its legs to absorb urine and faeces.

narcissism /nar-si-si-z'm/ noun excessive interest in yourself and your appearance. ■ **narcissist** noun **narcissistic** adjective.

narcissus /nar-si-suhss/ noun (plural **narcissi** or **narcissuses**) a daffodil with a flower that has pale outer petals and an orange or yellow centre.

narcotic noun **1** an addictive drug which affects mood or behaviour. **2** a drug which causes drowsiness or unconsciousness, or relieves pain. adjective relating to narcotics.

nark Brit. informal noun a police informer. verb annoy.

narrate verb (**narrates, narrating, narrated**) **1** give an account of something. **2** provide a commentary for a film, television programme, etc. ■ **narration** noun **narrator** noun.

narrative noun an account of connected events; a story. **adjective** having to do with narration.

narrow adjective (**narrower, narrowest**) **1** of small width in comparison to length. **2** limited in extent, amount, or scope. **3** barely achieved: *a narrow escape*. **verb 1** become or make narrower. **2** (**narrow down**) reduce the number of possibilities of something. **noun** (**narrows**) a narrow channel connecting two larger areas of water. □ **narrow-minded** unwilling to listen to or accept the views of others. ■ **narrowly** adverb.

narrowboat noun Brit. a canal boat less than 7 ft (2.1 metres) wide.

NASA abbreviation (in the US) National Aeronautics and Space Administration.

nasal adjective relating to the nose. ■ **nasally** adverb.

nascent /**na**-suhnt, **nay**-suhnt/ **adjective** just coming into existence and beginning to develop.

nasturtium /nuh-**ster**-shuhm/ **noun** a garden plant with bright orange, yellow, or red flowers.

nasty adjective (**nastier, nastiest**) **1** unpleasant or disgusting. **2** spiteful, violent, or bad-tempered. **3** painful or harmful: *a nasty bang on the head*. ■ **nastily** adverb **nastiness** noun.

natal /**nay**-t'l/ **adjective** relating to the place or time of your birth.

nation noun a large group of people sharing the same language, culture, or history and inhabiting a particular territory.

national adjective 1 having to do with a nation. **2** owned, controlled, or financially supported by the state. **noun** a citizen of a particular country. □ **national curriculum** a curriculum of study laid down to be taught in state schools. **national debt** the total amount of money which a country's government has borrowed. **national grid** Brit. **1** the network of power lines between major power stations. **2** the system of geographical coordinates used in maps of the British Isles. **National Insurance** (in the UK) a system

of payments made by employees and employers to provide help for people who are sick, unemployed, or retired. **national park** an area of countryside that is protected by the state. **national service** a period of compulsory service in the armed forces during peacetime. ■ **nationally** adverb.

nationalism noun 1 excessive patriotic feeling. **2** belief in independence for a particular country. ■ **nationalist** noun & adjective **nationalistic** adjective.

nationality noun (plural **nationalities**) **1** the status of belonging to a particular nation. **2** an ethnic group.

nationalize or **nationalise verb** (**nationalizes, nationalizing, nationalized**) put an industry or business under the control of the government. ■ **nationalization** noun.

nationwide adjective & adverb throughout the whole nation.

native noun 1 a person born in a specified place. **2** a local inhabitant. **3** an animal or plant that lives or grows naturally in a particular area. **adjective 1** associated with the place where you were born. **2** (of a plant or animal) living or growing naturally in a place. **3** having to do with the original inhabitants of a place. **4** in a person's character: *his native wit*. □ **native speaker** a person who has spoken a particular language from earliest childhood. **Native American** a member of any of the original peoples of North and South America.

> ⓘ avoid using the noun **native** in reference to non-white people in remote places, as in *this dance is a favourite with the natives*; phrases such as *a native of Boston* are quite acceptable, however.

nativity noun (plural **nativities**) **1** a person's birth. **2** (**the Nativity**) the birth of Jesus.

NATO or **Nato abbreviation** North Atlantic Treaty Organization.

natter informal **verb** (**natters, nattering, nattered**) chat. **noun** a lengthy chat.

natty adjective (**nattier, nattiest**) informal smart and fashionable.

natural adjective **1** existing in or obtained from nature; not made or caused by people. **2** in accordance with nature; normal. **3** born with a particular skill or quality: *a natural leader.* **4** relaxed and unaffected. **5** (of a parent or child) related by blood. **6** Music (of a note) not sharp or flat. noun **1** a person with a particular gift or talent. **2** an off-white colour. **3** Music a natural note or a sign (♮) denoting one. □ **natural gas** gas that is found underground and used as fuel. **natural history** the scientific study of animals or plants. **natural selection** the evolutionary process by which organisms better adapted to their environment tend to survive and produce more offspring. ■ **naturally** adverb.

naturalism noun a style in art or literature that shows things how they are in everyday life.

naturalist noun a person who studies animals or plants.

naturalistic adjective **1** having to do with real life or nature. **2** based on the theory of naturalism.

naturalize or **naturalise** verb (**naturalizes, naturalizing, naturalized**) **1** make a foreigner a citizen of a country. **2** introduce a plant or animal into a region where it is not native.

nature noun **1** the physical world, including plants, animals, and all things that are not made by people. **2** the typical qualities or character of a person, animal, or thing. **3** a type or kind of something.

naturism noun nudism. ■ **naturist** noun & adjective.

naught pronoun old use nothing.

naughty adjective (**naughtier, naughtiest**) **1** (of a child) disobedient; badly behaved. **2** informal mildly rude or indecent. ■ **naughtiness** noun.

nausea /naw-zi-uh/ noun **1** a feeling of sickness and wanting to vomit. **2** disgust or revulsion.

nauseate verb (**nauseates, nauseating, nauseated**) make someone feel sick or disgusted.

nauseous adjective **1** affected with nausea. **2** causing nausea.

nautical adjective having to do with sailors or navigation. □ **nautical mile** a unit used to measure distances at sea, equal to 1,852 metres (approximately 2,025 yards).

naval adjective having to do with a navy or navies.

nave noun the central part of a church.

navel noun the small hollow in the centre of a person's belly where the umbilical cord was cut at birth.

navigable adjective able to be used by boats and ships.

navigate verb (**navigates, navigating, navigated**) **1** plan and direct the route of a ship, aircraft, etc. **2** guide a boat or vehicle over a particular route. ■ **navigator** noun.

navigation noun **1** the activity of navigating. **2** the movement of ships. ■ **navigational** adjective.

navvy noun (plural **navvies**) Brit. dated a labourer employed in building a road, railway, or canal.

navy noun (plural **navies**) **1** the branch of a country's armed forces which fights at sea. **2** (also **navy blue**) a dark blue colour.

nay adverb old use or dialect no.

Nazi /naht-si/ noun (plural **Nazis**) historical a member of the far-right National Socialist German Workers' Party. ■ **Nazism** noun.

NB abbreviation note well.

ℹ️ short for Latin *nota bene*.

NE abbreviation north-east or north-eastern.

Neanderthal /ni-an-der-tahl/ noun an extinct human living in Europe between about 120,000 and 35,000 years ago.

neap tide noun the tide when there is least difference between high and low water.

near adverb **1** at or to a short distance in space or time. **2** almost. preposition (also **near to**) **1** at or to a short distance in space or time from. **2** close to. **adjective 1** at a short distance away. **2** close to being. **3** closely related. **near** approach. □ **Near East** the countries of SW Asia between the Mediterranean and India (including the Middle East). **near-sighted** short-sighted. ■ **nearness** noun.

nearby adjective & adverb not far away.

nearly adverb very close to; almost.

nearside noun the side of a vehicle nearest the kerb.

neat adjective 1 tidy or carefully arranged. **2** clever but simple. **3** (of a drink of spirits) not diluted. **4** N. Amer. informal excellent. ■ **neatly** adverb.

neaten verb make something neat.

nebula /neb-yuu-luh/ **noun** (plural **nebulae** /neb-yuu-lee/ or **nebulas**) a cloud of gas or dust in outer space.

nebulous adjective not clearly defined; vague.

necessarily adverb as a necessary result; unavoidably.

necessary adjective 1 needing to be present, or to be done or achieved. **2** unavoidable.

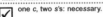 one *c*, two *s*'s: necessary.

necessitate verb (**necessitates**, **necessitating**, **necessitated**) make something necessary.

necessity noun (plural **necessities**) **1** the fact of being necessary. **2** a thing that is essential to have.

neck noun 1 the part connecting the head to the rest of the body. **2** the part of a bottle near the mouth. **3** the part of a violin, guitar, etc. bearing the fingerboard. **verb** informal kiss and caress. □ **neck and neck** level in a race or other competition.

neckerchief noun a square of cloth worn round the neck.

necklace noun a piece of jewellery consisting of a chain, string of beads, etc., worn round the neck.

necklet noun a close-fitting, rigid ornament worn around the neck.

neckline noun the edge of a woman's garment at or below the neck.

necromancy /nek-ruh-man-si/ **noun 1** attempted communication with dead people in order to predict the future. **2** witchcraft or black magic. ■ **necromancer** noun.

necrophilia /nek-ruh-**fil**-i-uh/ **noun** sexual activity with or interest in dead bodies. ■ **necrophiliac** noun.

necropolis /ne-**krop**-uh-liss/ **noun** a cemetery.

necrosis /ne-**kroh**-siss/ **noun** the death of cells in an organ or tissue.

nectar noun 1 a fluid produced by flowers and made into honey by bees. **2** (in Greek and Roman mythology) the drink of the gods.

nectarine noun a variety of peach with smooth skin.

née /nay/ **adjective** born (used in giving a married woman's maiden name).

need verb 1 require something because it is essential or very important. **2** used to express what should or must be done. **noun 1** a situation in which something is necessary or must be done. **2** a thing that is needed. **3** the state of being very poor.

needful adjective necessary.

needle noun 1 a very thin pointed piece of metal with a hole or eye for thread at the blunter end, used in sewing. **2** a long, thin rod used in knitting. **3** the pointed hollow end of a hypodermic syringe. **4** a stylus used to play records. **5** a thin pointer on a dial, compass, etc. **6** the thin, stiff leaf of a fir or pine tree. **verb** (**needles**, **needling**, **needled**) informal annoy.

needlecord noun Brit. a lightweight corduroy fabric with narrow ridges.

needlepoint noun closely stitched embroidery worked over canvas.

needless adjective unnecessary; avoidable. ■ **needlessly** adverb.

needlework noun sewing or embroidery.

needn't short form need not.

needy adjective (needier, neediest) very poor.

ne'er /nair/ short form old use or dialect never. □ **ne'er-do-well** a useless or lazy person.

nefarious /ni-**fair**-i-uhss/ adjective bad or illegal.

negate verb (negates, negating, negated) **1** stop or undo the effect of. **2** say that something does not exist. ■ negation noun.

negative adjective **1** showing the absence rather than the presence of something. **2** expressing denial, disagreement, or refusal. **3** not hopeful or favourable. **4** (of a quantity) less than zero. **5** having to do with the kind of electric charge carried by electrons. **6** (of a photograph) showing light and shade or colours reversed from those of the original. noun **1** a negative word or statement. **2** a negative photograph, from which positive prints may be made. ■ negatively adverb negativity noun.

neglect verb **1** fail to give enough care or attention to. **2** fail to do. noun the action of neglecting.

neglectful adjective failing to give enough care or attention.

negligee /**neg**-li-zhay/ noun a woman's dressing gown made of a very light, thin fabric.

negligence noun a failure to give someone or something enough care or attention. ■ negligent adjective.

negligible adjective so small or unimportant as to be not worth considering.

negotiate verb (negotiates, negotiating, negotiated) **1** reach an agreement by discussion. **2** bring something about by discussion. **3** find a way through a difficult path or route. **4** transfer a cheque, bill, etc. to the legal ownership of someone else. ■ negotiable adjective negotiation noun negotiator noun.

> ☑ *-tiate*, not *-ciate*: nego*tiate*.

Negro noun (plural Negroes) a black person.

> ℹ️ the term **Negro** is now regarded as old-fashioned or even offensive; it is better to use black.

neigh noun a high-pitched cry made by a horse. verb make this cry.

neighbour (US spelling neighbor) noun a person who lives next door to you, or very close by. verb be next or very close to. ■ neighbourly adjective.

neighbourhood (US spelling neighborhood) noun **1** a district within a town or city. **2** the area surrounding a place, person, or object.

neither determiner & pronoun not either. adverb used to show that a negative statement is true of two things, or also true of something else.

> ☑ *neither* is an exception to the rule '*i* before *e* except after *c*'.

nemesis noun (plural nemeses /**nem**-i-seez/) something that brings about someone's deserved and unavoidable downfall.

neoclassical adjective relating to the revival of a classical style in the arts. ■ neoclassicism noun.

Neolithic adjective relating to the later part of the Stone Age.

neologism /ni-**ol**-uh-ji-z'm/ noun a new word or expression.

neon noun a gas that glows when electricity is passed through it, used in fluorescent lighting.

neonatal adjective relating to birth and newborn children.

neophyte /**nee**-oh-fyt/ noun **1** a person who is new to a subject, skill, or belief. **2** a novice in a religious order, or a newly ordained priest.

nephew noun a son of your brother or sister.

nephritis /ni-**fry**-tiss/ noun inflammation of the kidneys.

nepotism /**nep**-uh-ti-z'm/ noun favouritism shown to relatives or friends.

nerd noun informal an unfashionable person who is obsessed with a particular interest.

nerve noun **1** a fibre or bundle of fibres in the body along which impulses of sensation pass. **2** steady courage in a difficult situation. **3** (nerves) nervousness. **4** informal cheeky boldness. verb (nerves, nerving, nerved) (nerve yourself) brace yourself for a difficult situation. □ get on someone's nerves informal irritate someone. nerve cell a neuron. nerve gas a poisonous gas which affects the nervous system. nerveracking (or nerve-wracking) causing nervousness or fear.

nerveless adjective · **1** lacking strength or feeling. **2** confident.

nervous adjective **1** easily frightened or worried. **2** anxious. **3** having to do with the nerves. □ nervous breakdown a period of mental illness resulting from severe depression or stress. nervous system the network of nerves which transmits nerve impulses between parts of the body. ■ nervously adverb nervousness noun.

nervy adjective (nervier, nerviest) Brit. nervous or tense.

nest noun **1** a structure made by a bird in which it lays eggs and shelters its young. **2** a place where an animal or insect breeds or shelters. **3** a set of similar objects that are designed to fit inside each other. verb **1** use or build a nest. **2** fit an object inside a larger one. □ nest egg a sum of money saved for the future.

nestle verb (nestles, nestling, nestled) **1** settle comfortably within or against something. **2** (of a place) lie in a sheltered position.

nestling noun a bird that is too young to leave the nest.

net¹ noun **1** a material made of strands of twine or cord that are knotted together to form small open squares. **2** a piece or structure of net for catching fish or insects, surrounding a goal, etc. **3** a thin fabric with a very open weave. **4** (the Net) the Internet. verb (nets, netting, netted) **1** catch something in a net. **2** score a goal.

net² or Brit. **nett** adjective **1** (of a sum of money) remaining after tax or ex-

penses have been deducted. **2** (of a weight) not including the packaging. **3** (of an effect or result) overall. verb (nets, netting, netted) acquire a sum of money as clear profit.

netball noun a team game in which goals are scored by throwing a ball through a net hanging from a hoop.

nether adjective lower in position.

nettle noun a plant with leaves that are covered with stinging hairs. verb (nettles, nettling, nettled) annoy.

network noun **1** an arrangement of intersecting horizontal and vertical lines. **2** a complex system of railways, roads, etc., that cross or connect with each other. **3** a group of broadcasting stations that connect to broadcast a programme at the same time. **4** a number of interconnected computers, operations, etc. **5** a group of people who keep in contact with each other to exchange information. verb keep in contact with others to exchange information. ■ networker noun.

neural /nyoor-uhl/ adjective relating to a nerve or the nervous system.

neuralgia /nyoo-ral-juh/ noun intense pain along a nerve in the head or face. ■ neuralgic adjective.

neurology noun the branch of medicine concerned with the nervous system. ■ neurological adjective neurologist noun.

neuron or **neurone** noun a cell that transmits nerve impulses.

neurosis /nyoo-roh-siss/ noun (plural neuroses /nyoo-roh-seez/) a mild mental illness in which a person feels depressed or anxious, or behaves in an obsessive way.

neurotic adjective **1** having to do with neurosis. **2** informal obsessive, or too sensitive or anxious.

neuter adjective **1** (of a noun) neither masculine or feminine. **2** having no sexual or reproductive organs. verb (neuters, neutering, neutered) operate on an animal so that it cannot produce young; castrate or spay.

neutral adjective **1** not supporting either side in a dispute or war. **2** lack-

ing noticeable or strong qualities.
3 Chemistry neither acid nor alkaline;
having a pH of about 7. **noun** a position
of a gear mechanism in which the engine is disconnected from the driven
parts. ■ **neutrality** noun **neutrally** adverb.

neutralize or **neutralise** verb (neutralizes, neutralizing, neutralized)
1 stop something from having an effect. **2** make neutral. ■ **neutralization**
noun.

neutrino /nyoo-**tree**-noh/ **noun** (plural
neutrinos) a subatomic particle with
a mass close to zero and no electric
charge.

neutron noun a subatomic particle of
about the same mass as a proton but
without an electric charge.

never adverb **1** not ever. **2** not at all.
□ **the never-never** Brit. informal hire
purchase.

nevermore adverb never again.

nevertheless adverb in spite of
that.

new adjective **1** made, introduced, discovered, or experienced recently.
2 not previously used or owned.
3 (new to) not experienced in. **4** different from a recent previous one.
5 better than before; renewed or re-
formed. adverb newly. □ **New Age** an
alternative movement concerned
with spirituality, care for the environment, etc. **new moon** the phase of the
moon when it first appears as a thin
crescent. **New Testament** the second
part of the Christian Bible, recording
the life and teachings of Jesus. **New
World** North and South America.
new year the calendar year that has
just begun or is about to begin, following 31 December.

newborn adjective recently born.

newcomer noun **1** a person who has
recently arrived. **2** a person who is
new to an activity or situation.

newel /**nyoo**-uhl/ noun the post at the
top or bottom of a stair rail.

newfangled adjective disapproving
newly developed and unfamiliar.

newly adverb **1** recently. **2** again;

afresh. □ **newly-wed** a person who
has recently married.

news noun **1** new information about
recent events. **2** (**the news**) a broadcast or published news report.

newsagent noun Brit. a shopkeeper
who sells newspapers and magazines.

newscast noun a broadcast news report. ■ **newscaster** noun.

newsflash noun a brief item of important news, interrupting other
radio or television programmes.

newsgroup noun a group of Internet
users who exchange email on a topic
of shared interest.

newsletter noun a bulletin issued on
a regular basis to the members of a
society or organization.

newspaper noun a daily or weekly
publication containing news and articles on current affairs.

newsprint noun cheap, low-quality
paper used for newspapers.

newsreader noun Brit. a person who
reads the news on radio or television.

newsreel noun a short cinema film
showing news and current affairs.

newsroom noun the area in a newspaper or broadcasting office where
news is processed.

newsworthy adjective important
enough to be mentioned as news.

newt noun a small animal with a slender body and a long tail, that can live
in water or on land.

newton noun Physics a unit of force.

next adjective **1** coming immediately
after the present one in time, space,
or order. **2** (of a day of the week) nearest (or the nearest but one) after the
present. adverb immediately afterwards. noun the next person or thing.
□ **next door** in or to the next house or
room. **next of kin** a person's closest
living relative or relatives.

nexus noun (plural **nexus** or **nexuses**) a
connection or series of connections.

NHS abbreviation National Health Service.

nib noun the pointed end part of a pen.

nibble verb (nibbles, nibbling, nibbled) **1** take small bites out of. **2** bite gently. noun **1** an instance of nibbling. **2** a small piece of food bitten off. **3** (nibbles) informal small savoury snacks.

nice adjective **1** enjoyable or attractive; pleasant. **2** good-natured; kind. **3** involving a very small detail or difference. ■ **nicely** adverb **niceness** noun.

nicety noun (plural niceties) **1** a very small detail or difference. **2** accuracy.

niche /neesh, nich/ noun **1** a small hollow in a wall. **2** (your niche) a role or job that suits you.

nick noun **1** a small cut. **2** (the nick) Brit. informal prison or a police station. **3** Brit. informal condition. verb **1** make a nick or nicks in. **2** Brit. informal steal. **3** Brit. informal arrest. □ **in the nick of time** only just in time.

nickel noun **1** a silvery-white metallic element. **2** N. Amer. informal a five-cent coin.

nickname noun another name by which someone is known. verb (nicknames, nicknaming, nicknamed) give a nickname to.

nicotine noun a poisonous oily liquid found in tobacco.

niece noun a daughter of your brother or sister.

i before *e*: n*ie*ce.

niff Brit. informal noun an unpleasant smell. verb smell unpleasant.

nifty adjective (niftier, niftiest) informal skilful, neat, or speedy.

niggardly adjective not generous; mean.

nigger noun offensive a black person.

niggle verb (niggles, niggling, niggled) slightly worry or annoy. noun a minor worry or criticism.

nigh adverb, preposition, & adjective old use near.

night noun **1** the time from sunset to sunrise. **2** an evening.

nightcap noun **1** (in the past) a soft hat or bonnet worn in bed. **2** a hot or alcoholic drink taken at bedtime.

nightclub noun a club that is open at night, with a bar and music.

nightdress or **nightgown** noun a light, loose garment worn by a woman or girl in bed.

nightfall noun dusk.

nightie noun informal a nightdress.

nightingale noun a small bird with a tuneful song, often heard at night.

nightlife noun social activities or entertainment available at night.

nightly adjective & adverb happening or done every night.

nightmare noun **1** a frightening or unpleasant dream. **2** a very unpleasant experience. ■ **nightmarish** adjective.

nightshade noun (deadly nightshade) a plant with purple flowers and poisonous black berries.

nightshirt noun a long shirt worn in bed.

nightspot noun informal a nightclub.

nihilism /ny-hi-li-z'm/ noun the belief that nothing has any value. ■ **nihilist** noun **nihilistic** adjective.

nil noun nothing; zero.

nimble adjective (nimbler, nimblest) quick and agile in movement or thought. ■ **nimbly** adverb.

nimbus noun (plural nimbi /nim-bI/ or nimbuses) a large grey rain cloud.

nincompoop noun a stupid person.

nine cardinal number one less than ten; 9. (Roman numeral: ix or IX.)

nineteen cardinal number one more than eighteen; 19. (Roman numeral: xix or XIX.) ■ **nineteenth** ordinal number.

ninety cardinal number (plural nineties) ten less than one hundred; 90. (Roman numeral: xc or XC.) ■ **ninetieth** ordinal number.

ninny noun (plural ninnies) informal a foolish or weak person.

ninth ordinal number **1** at number nine

in a sequence; 9th. **2 (a ninth** or **one ninth)** each of nine equal parts into which something is divided.

nip[1] verb **(nips, nipping, nipped) 1** pinch, squeeze, or bite sharply. **2** Brit. informal go quickly. noun **1** an act of nipping. **2** a sharp feeling of coldness.

nip[2] noun a small quantity or sip of spirits.

nipper noun **1** informal a child. **2 (nippers)** pliers or pincers.

nipple noun a small projection in the centre of each breast, from which (in a woman who has recently had a baby) a baby is able to suck milk.

nippy adjective **(nippier, nippiest)** informal **1** quick; nimble. **2** chilly.

nirvana /neer-vah-nuh/ noun (in Buddhism) a state of perfect happiness.

nit noun informal **1** the egg of a human head louse. **2** Brit. a stupid person. □ **nit-picking** petty criticism.

nitrate noun a salt or ester of nitric acid.

nitric acid noun a very corrosive acid.

nitrite noun a salt or ester of nitrous acid.

nitrogen noun a gas forming about 78 per cent of the earth's atmosphere.

nitroglycerine or **nitroglycerin** noun an explosive liquid used in dynamite.

nitrous oxide noun a colourless gas used as an anaesthetic.

nitty-gritty noun informal the most important details.

nitwit noun informal a foolish person.

no determiner not any. exclamation used to refuse or disagree with something. adverb not at all. noun (plural **noes**) a decision or vote against something. □ **no-claims bonus** Brit. a reduction in an insurance premium when no claim has been made over an agreed period. **no-ball** a ball in cricket that is unlawfully bowled, counting as an extra run to the batting side.

no. abbreviation number.

nob noun Brit. informal an upper-class person.

nobble verb **(nobbles, nobbling, nobbled)** Brit. informal **1** try to influence or thwart. **2** stop and talk to.

nobility noun **1** the quality of being noble. **2** the aristocracy.

noble adjective **(nobler, noblest) 1** belonging to the aristocracy. **2** having personal qualities that people admire, such as courage and honesty. **3** magnificent; impressive. noun a nobleman or noblewoman. ■ **nobly** adverb.

nobleman or **noblewoman** noun a member of the aristocracy.

nobody pronoun no person. noun (plural **nobodies**) a person who is not considered important.

nocturnal adjective done or active at night. ■ **nocturnally** adverb.

nocturne noun a short piece of music of a dreamy, romantic nature.

nod verb **(nods, nodding, nodded) 1** lower and raise your head briefly to show agreement or as a greeting or signal. **2** let your head fall forward when you are drowsy or asleep. **3 (nod off)** informal fall asleep. noun an act of nodding.

node noun technical **1** a point in a network at which lines cross or branch. **2** the part of a plant stem from which one or more leaves grows. **3** a small mass of tissue in the body.

nodule noun a small swelling or lump. ■ **nodular** adjective.

Noel noun Christmas.

noggin noun a small quantity of alcoholic drink.

Noh noun a type of traditional Japanese theatre with dance and song.

noise noun **1** a sound or series of sounds, especially an unpleasant one. **2** disturbances that accompany and interfere with an electrical signal. ■ **noiseless** adjective.

noisome /noy-suhm/ adjective literary having a very unpleasant smell.

noisy adjective **(noisier, noisiest)** full of or making a lot of noise. ■ **noisily** adverb.

nomad noun a member of a people that travels from place to place to find fresh pasture for its animals.

nomadic adjective having the life of a nomad; wandering.

nom de plume /nom duh **ploom**/ noun (plural **noms de plume** /nom duh **ploom**/) a name used by a writer instead of their real name; a pen name.

nomenclature /noh-**men**-kluh-cher/ noun a system of names used in a particular subject.

nominal adjective **1** in name but not in reality. **2** (of a sum of money) very small. ■ **nominally** adverb.

nominate verb (nominates, nominating, nominated) **1** put someone forward as a candidate for a job or award. **2** arrange a time, date, or place. ■ **nomination** noun **nominee** noun.

nominative noun Grammar the case used for the subject of a verb.

non- prefix not: non-existent.

> **i** for the difference between the prefixes **non-** and **un-** see the box at **UN-**.

nonagenarian /noh-nuh-juh-**nair**-i-uhn/ noun a person between 90 and 99 years old.

nonchalant /non-shuh-luhnt/ adjective relaxed and unconcerned. ■ **nonchalance** noun **nonchalantly** adverb.

non-commissioned adjective (of a military officer) appointed from the lower ranks.

non-committal adjective not showing what you think or which side you are on. ■ **non-committally** adverb.

non compos mentis /non kom-poss **men**-tiss/ adjective not in your right mind; distracted or mad.

nonconformist noun **1** a person who does not follow accepted ideas or behaviour. **2** (**Nonconformist**) a member of a Protestant Church which does not follow the beliefs of the established Church of England. ■ **nonconformity** noun.

nondescript adjective having no interesting or special features.

none pronoun **1** not any. **2** no one. adverb (**none the**) not at all.

nonentity noun (plural **nonentities**) an unimportant person or thing.

nonetheless or **none the less** adverb in spite of that; nevertheless.

non-event noun a very disappointing or uninteresting event.

non-existent adjective not real or present.

no-nonsense adjective simple and straightforward; sensible.

nonplussed adjective surprised and confused.

non-proliferation noun the prevention of an increase in the number of nuclear weapons that are produced.

nonsense noun **1** words or statements that make no sense. **2** silly behaviour.

nonsensical adjective making no sense.

non sequitur /non **sek**-wi-ter/ noun a statement that does not follow on logically from what has just been said.

non-starter noun informal something that has no chance of succeeding.

non-stick adjective (of a pan) covered with a substance that prevents food sticking to it during cooking.

non-stop adjective & adverb **1** continuing without stopping. **2** having no stops on the way to a destination.

noodles plural noun thin, long strips of pasta.

nook noun a place that is sheltered or hidden.

noon noun twelve o'clock in the day; midday.

noonday adjective taking place or appearing in the middle of the day.

no one pronoun no person.

noose noun a loop with a knot which tightens as the rope or wire is pulled, used to hang people or trap animals.

nor conjunction & adverb and not; and not either.

Nordic adjective relating to Scandinavia, Finland, and Iceland.

norm noun **1** (**the norm**) the usual or standard thing. **2** a standard that is required or acceptable.

normal adjective usual and typical; what you would expect. noun the normal state or condition. ■ **normality** noun **normally** adverb.

normalize or **normalise** verb (**normalizes, normalizing, normalized**) make or become normal. ■ **normalization** noun.

Norman noun a member of a people from Normandy in northern France who conquered England in 1066. adjective relating to the Normans or Normandy.

normative adjective relating to or setting a standard or norm.

Norse noun ancient or medieval Norwegian or another Scandinavian language. adjective relating to ancient or medieval Norway or Scandinavia.

north noun 1 the direction which is on your left-hand side when you are facing east. 2 the northern part of a place. adjective 1 lying towards or facing the north. 2 (of a wind) blowing from the north. adverb to or towards the north. ■ **northward** adjective & adverb **northwards** adverb.

north-east noun the direction or region halfway between north and east. adjective & adverb 1 towards or facing the north-east. 2 (of a wind) blowing from the north-east. ■ **north-eastern** adjective.

north-easterly adjective & adverb 1 facing or moving towards the north-east. 2 (of a wind) blowing from the north-east.

northerly adjective & adverb 1 facing or moving towards the north. 2 (of a wind) blowing from the north.

northern adjective 1 situated in or facing the north. 2 coming from or characteristic of the north. □ **northern lights** the aurora borealis.

northerner noun a person from the north of a region.

north-west noun the direction or region halfway between north and west. adjective & adverb 1 towards or facing the north-west. 2 (of a wind) blowing from the north-west. ■ **north-western** adjective.

north-westerly adjective & adverb 1 facing or moving towards the north-west. 2 (of a wind) blowing from the north-west.

nose noun 1 the part of the face containing the nostrils and used in breathing and smelling. 2 the front end of an aircraft, car, or other vehicle. 3 a talent for finding something. 4 the characteristic smell of a wine. verb (**noses, nosing, nosed**) 1 thrust the nose against or into. 2 look around or pry into something. 3 make your way slowly forward.

nosebag noun a bag containing fodder, hung from a horse's head.

nosebleed noun an instance of bleeding from the nose.

nosedive noun a steep downward plunge by an aircraft. verb (**nosedives, nosediving, nosedived**) make a nosedive.

nosegay noun a small bunch of flowers.

nosh informal noun food. verb eat enthusiastically.

nostalgia noun longing for the happy times of the past. ■ **nostalgic** adjective.

nostril noun either of the two openings of the nose through which air passes to the lungs.

nostrum noun 1 a favourite method for improving something. 2 an ineffective medicine.

nosy or **nosey** adjective (**nosier, nosiest**) informal too inquisitive about other people's affairs.

not adverb 1 used to express a negative. 2 less than.

notable adjective deserving to be noticed or given attention. noun a famous or important person. ■ **notably** adverb.

notary noun (plural **notaries**) a lawyer who is authorized to be a witness when people sign documents.

notation noun a system of symbols used in music, mathematics, etc.

notch noun 1 a V-shaped cut on an edge or surface. 2 a point or level on a scale. **verb 1** make notches in. **2** (**notch up**) score or achieve.

note noun **1** a brief written record of something. **2** a short written message. **3** Brit. a banknote. **4** a single sound of a particular pitch and length made by a musical instrument or voice, or a symbol representing this. **verb** (**notes, noting, noted**) **1** pay attention to. **2** record something in writing. ◻ **of note** important. **take note** pay attention.

notebook noun **1** a small book for writing notes in. **2** a portable computer smaller than a laptop.

noted adjective well known.

notepaper noun paper for writing letters on.

noteworthy adjective interesting or important.

nothing pronoun **1** not anything. **2** something that is not important or interesting. **3** nought. adverb not at all. ◻ **sweet nothings** words of affection between lovers.

nothingness noun a state of not existing, or in which nothing exists.

notice noun **1** the fact of being aware of or paying attention to something. **2** warning that something is going to happen. **3** a formal statement that you are going to leave a job or end an agreement. **4** a sheet of paper displaying information. **5** a small published announcement or advertisement in a newspaper. **6** a short published review of a new film, play, or book. **verb** (**notices, noticing, noticed**) become aware of.

noticeable adjective easily seen or noticed. ∎ **noticeably** adverb.

 remember the *e* in the middle: noticeable.

notifiable adjective (of an infectious disease) that must be reported to the health authorities.

notify verb (**notifies, notifying, notified**) formally tell someone about something. ∎ **notification** noun.

notion noun **1** an idea or belief. **2** an understanding.

notional adjective based on an idea rather than reality. ∎ **notionally** adverb.

notoriety /noh-tuh-**ry**-i-ti/ noun the state of being notorious.

notorious adjective famous for something bad. ∎ **notoriously** adverb.

notwithstanding preposition in spite of. adverb nevertheless.

nougat /**noo**-gah, **nug**-uht/ noun a sweet made from sugar or honey, nuts, and egg white.

nought noun the figure 0. pronoun nothing.

noun noun a word (other than a pronoun) that refers to a person, place, or thing.

nourish verb **1** give a person, animal, or plant the food and other substances they need in order to grow and be healthy. **2** keep a feeling or belief in your mind for a long time.

nourishment noun the food and other substances necessary for life, growth, and good health.

nous /nowss/ noun Brit. informal common sense.

nouveau riche /noo-voh **reesh**/ noun people who have recently become rich and who display their wealth in an obvious or tasteless way.

nova noun (plural **novae** /**noh**-vee/ or **novas**) a star that suddenly becomes very bright for a short period.

novel[1] noun a story of book length about imaginary people and events.

novel[2] adjective new in an interesting or unusual way.

novelist noun a person who writes novels.

novella /nuh-**vel**-luh/ noun a short novel or long short story.

novelty noun (plural **novelties**) **1** the quality of being new and unusual. **2** a new or unfamiliar thing. **3** a small toy or ornament.

November noun the eleventh month of the year.

novice noun **1** a person who is new to and lacks experience in a job or situation. **2** a person who has entered a

PARTS OF SPEECH ℹ️

Noun

A noun is the name of a person or thing. There are four kinds:

1 common nouns (the words for articles and creatures), e.g.

shoe	in	*the red shoe was left on the shelf*
box	in	*the large box stood in the corner*
plant	in	*the plant grew to two metres*
horse	in	*a horse and rider galloped by*

2 proper nouns (the names of people, places, ships, institutions, and animals, which always begin with a capital letter), e.g.

Jane   *Grand Hotel*
London   *Bambi*
USS Enterprise

3 abstract nouns (the words for qualities, things we cannot see or touch, and things which have no physical reality), e.g.

truth   *absence*
explanation   *warmth*

4 collective nouns (the words for groups of things), e.g.

committee	*squad*	*the Cabinet*
herd	*swarm*	*the public*
majority	*team*	

religious order but has not yet taken their vows.

novitiate or **noviciate noun 1** a period of being a novice in a religious order. **2** a place where novitiates live.

now adverb 1 at the present time. **2** immediately. **conjunction** as a result of the fact.

nowadays adverb at the present time, in contrast with the past.

nowhere adverb not anywhere. **pronoun** no place.

noxious adjective harmful or very unpleasant.

nozzle noun a spout used to control a stream of liquid or gas.

nuance /**nyoo**-ahnss/ **noun** a very slight difference in meaning, expression, sound, etc.

nub noun 1 (**the nub**) the central point of a matter. **2** a small lump.

nubile adjective (of a girl or young woman) sexually mature and attractive.

nuclear adjective 1 relating to the nucleus of an atom or cell. **2** using energy released in the fission or fusion of atomic nuclei. **3** possessing or involving nuclear weapons. □ **nuclear family** a couple and their children. **nuclear physics** the science of atomic nuclei and the way they interact.

nucleic acid /nyoo-**klay**-ik/ **noun** either of two substances, DNA and RNA, that are present in all living cells.

nucleus /**nyoo**-kli-uhss/ **noun** (plural **nuclei** /**nyoo**-kli-I/) **1** the central and most important part of an object or group. **2** Physics the positively charged central core of an atom. **3** Biology a structure present in most cells, containing the genetic material.

nude adjective wearing no clothes. **noun** a painting or sculpture of a naked human figure. ■ **nudity** noun.

nudge verb (**nudges, nudging,**

nudged) 1 prod someone with your elbow to attract their attention. **2** touch or push something gently. **noun** a light prod or push.

nudist noun a person who prefers to wear no clothes. ■ **nudism noun**.

nugatory /**noo**-guh-tuh-ri/ **adjective** formal having no purpose or value.

nugget noun a small lump of precious metal found in the earth.

nuisance noun a person or thing that causes annoyance or difficulty.

nuke informal **noun** a nuclear weapon. **verb** (**nukes, nuking, nuked**) attack with nuclear weapons.

null adjective (**null and void**) having no legal force; invalid.

nullify verb (**nullifies, nullifying, nullified**) **1** make something legally invalid. **2** cancel out the effect of. ■ **nullification noun**.

nullity noun (plural **nullities**) **1** the state of being legally invalid. **2** a thing of no value or importance.

numb adjective 1 (of a part of the body) having no sensation. **2** lacking the power to feel, think, or react. **verb** make something numb. ■ **numbly** adverb **numbness noun**.

number noun 1 a quantity or value expressed by a word or symbol. **2** a quantity or amount. **3** (**a number of**) several. **4** a single issue of a magazine. **5** a song, dance, or piece of music. **verb** (**numbers, numbering, numbered**) **1** amount to. **2** give a number to each thing in a series. **3** count. **4** include as a member of a group. □ **number plate** Brit. a sign on the front and rear of a vehicle showing its registration number. ■ **numberless adjective**.

numbskull or **numskull noun** informal a stupid person.

numeral noun a symbol or word representing a number.

numerate /**nyoo**-muh-ruht/ **adjective** having a good basic knowledge of arithmetic. ■ **numeracy noun**.

numeration noun the action of numbering or calculating.

numerator noun Mathematics the number above the line in a fraction.

numerical adjective having to do with numbers. ■ **numerically adverb**.

numerous adjective 1 many. **2** consisting of many members.

numinous adjective having a strong religious or spiritual quality.

numismatic adjective having to do with coins or medals. **noun** (**numismatics**) the study or collection of coins, banknotes, and medals. ■ **numismatist noun**.

numskull ⇒ **NUMBSKULL**.

nun noun a member of a female religious community who has taken vows of chastity and obedience.

nuncio /**nun**-si-oh/ **noun** (plural **nuncios**) a person who represents the pope in a foreign country.

nunnery noun (plural **nunneries**) a convent.

nuptial /**nup**-sh'l/ **adjective** having to do with marriage or weddings. **noun** (**nuptials**) a wedding.

nurse noun 1 a person who is trained to care for sick or injured people. **2** dated a person employed to look after young children. **verb** (**nurses, nursing, nursed**) **1** look after a sick person. **2** treat or hold carefully or protectively. **3** feed a baby from the breast. **4** hold on to a belief or feeling for a long time. □ **nursing home** a place providing accommodation and health care for old people.

nursemaid noun dated a woman or girl employed to look after a young child.

nursery noun (plural **nurseries**) **1** a room in a house where young children sleep or play. **2** a nursery school. **3** a place where young plants and trees are grown for sale or for planting elsewhere. □ **nursery rhyme** a simple traditional song or poem for children. **nursery school** a school for young children between the ages of three and five.

nurture verb (**nurtures, nurturing, nurtured**) **1** care for and protect a child or young plant so that it will grow and develop. **2** maintain a feeling or belief for a long time. **noun** the state of being nurtured.

nut noun 1 a fruit consisting of a hard shell around an edible kernel. **2** the kernel of such a fruit. **3** a small flat piece of metal with a hole through the centre, for screwing on to a bolt. **4** informal a crazy person. **5** (**nuts**) informal mad. **6** informal a person's head. □ **in a nutshell** in the fewest possible words. **nuts and bolts** informal basic facts or practical details. ■ **nutty** adjective.

nutcase noun informal a mad or foolish person.

nutcrackers plural noun a device for cracking nuts.

nutmeg noun a spice made from the seed of a tropical tree.

nutrient noun a substance that provides nourishment.

nutriment noun nourishment.

nutrition noun the process of eating or taking nourishment. ■ **nutritional** adjective **nutritionist noun**.

nutritious adjective full of nourishing things; good for you.

nutritive adjective 1 having to do with nutrition. **2** nutritious.

nutter noun Brit. informal a mad person.

nuzzle verb (**nuzzles, nuzzling, nuzzled**) gently rub or push against someone or something with the nose.

NVQ abbreviation National Vocational Qualification.

NW abbreviation north-west or north-western.

nylon noun 1 a strong, lightweight synthetic material. **2** (**nylons**) nylon stockings or tights.

nymph noun 1 (in Greek and Roman mythology) a spirit in the form of a beautiful young woman. **2** an immature form of an insect such as a dragonfly.

nymphet noun an attractive and sexually mature young girl.

nymphomania noun excessive sexual desire in a woman. ■ **nymphomaniac noun**.

Oo

O or **o noun** (plural **Os** or **O's**) **1** the fifteenth letter of the alphabet. **2** zero. □ **O level** (in the past) the lower of the two main levels of the GCE examination.

oaf noun a stupid, rude, or clumsy man. ■ **oafish** adjective.

oak noun a large tree which produces acorns and a hard wood used in building and for furniture.

oaken adjective literary made of oak.

OAP abbreviation Brit. old-age pensioner.

oar noun a pole with a flat blade, used for rowing a boat.

oarsman or **oarswoman noun** a rower.

oasis noun (plural **oases**) a fertile place in a desert where water rises to ground level.

oast house noun a building containing a kiln for drying hops.

oat noun 1 a cereal plant grown in cool climates. **2** (**oats**) the grain of this cereal.

oatcake noun an oatmeal biscuit.

oath noun (plural **oaths**) **1** a solemn promise to do something or that something is true. **2** a swear word.

oatmeal noun meal made from ground oats, used in making porridge and oatcakes.

obdurate /**ob**-dyuu-ruht/ **adjective** refusing to change your mind; stubborn. ■ **obduracy noun**.

OBE abbreviation Officer of the Order

of the British Empire.

obedient adjective willingly doing what you are told. ■ **obedience** noun **obediently** adverb.

obeisance /oh-**bay**-suhnss/ noun **1** respect for someone and willingness to obey them. **2** a gesture expressing this, such as a bow.

obelisk noun a stone pillar that tapers to a point, set up as a monument.

obese adjective very fat. ■ **obesity** noun.

obey verb do what a person or a rule tells you to do.

obfuscate /**ob**-fuss-kayt/ verb (obfuscates, obfuscating, obfuscated) make something unclear or hard to understand. ■ **obfuscation** noun.

obituary /oh-**bi**-tyuu-ri/ noun (plural obituaries) a short piece of writing about a person and their life which is published in a newspaper when they die.

object noun /**ob**-jikt/ **1** a thing that you can see and touch. **2** a person or thing to which an action or feeling is directed. **3** a purpose. **4** Grammar a noun acted on by a transitive verb or by a preposition. verb /uhb-**jekt**/ say that you disagree with or disapprove of something. ■ **objector** noun.

objectify verb (objectifies, objectifying, objectified) **1** refer to something abstract as if it has a physical form. **2** treat someone as an object rather than a person. ■ **objectification** noun.

objection noun a statement of disagreement or disapproval.

objectionable adjective unpleasant or offensive.

objective adjective **1** considering the facts about something without being influenced by personal feelings or opinions. **2** having actual existence outside the mind. noun a goal or aim. ■ **objectively** adverb **objectivity** noun.

objet d'art /ob-zhay dar/ noun (plural objets d'art /ob-zhay dar/) a small decorative object or piece of art.

oblate /**ob**-layt/ adjective (of a sphere) flattened at each pole.

oblation noun a thing presented or offered to a god.

obligate verb (obligates, obligating, obligated) (be obligated) be obliged to do something.

obligation noun **1** something you must do in order to keep to an agreement or fulfil a duty. **2** the state of having to do something of this kind.

obligatory adjective required by a law, rule, or custom; compulsory.

oblige verb (obliges, obliging, obliged) **1** make someone do something because it is a law, a necessity, or their duty. **2** do something to help someone. **3** (be obliged) be grateful.

obliging adjective willing to help. ■ **obligingly** adverb.

oblique /uh-**bleek**/ adjective **1** at an angle; slanting. **2** not done in a direct way. ■ **obliquely** adverb.

obliterate /uh-**bli**-tuh-rayt/ verb (obliterates, obliterating, obliterated) destroy or remove all signs of something. ■ **obliteration** noun.

oblivion noun **1** the state of being unaware of what is happening around you. **2** the state of being forgotten or destroyed.

oblivious adjective not aware of what is happening around you.

oblong adjective rectangular in shape. noun an oblong shape.

obloquy /**ob**-luh-kwi/ noun **1** strong public criticism. **2** disgrace.

obnoxious /uhb-**nok**-shuhss/ adjective very unpleasant and offensive.

oboe noun a woodwind instrument of treble pitch, that you play by blowing through a reed. ■ **oboist** noun.

obscene adjective **1** dealing with sexual matters in an offensive way. **2** (of a payment, pay rise, etc.) unacceptably large. ■ **obscenely** adverb.

obscenity noun (plural obscenities) obscene language or behaviour, or an obscene action or word.

obscure adjective **1** not discovered or known about. **2** hard to understand or see. verb (obscures, obscuring, obscured) make something difficult to

GRAMMAR

Object

There are two types of object:

1 The direct object of a sentence or phrase is the person or thing directly affected by the verb or by a preposition, e.g.

The electors chose Mr Smith

Charles wrote a letter.

2 An indirect object is usually a person or thing that receives something from the subject of the verb, e.g.

He gave me *the pen* (me *is the indirect object, and* the pen *is the direct object*)

I sent my bank a letter (my bank *is the indirect object, and* a letter *is the direct object*).

Sentences containing an indirect object usually contain a direct object as well, but not always, e.g. *pay me.*

see, hear, or understand. ■ **obscurely** adverb.

obscurity noun (plural **obscurities**) **1** the state of being unknown or forgotten. **2** the quality of being hard to understand.

obsequies /ob-si-kwiz/ plural noun things that are done ceremonially at a funeral.

obsequious /uhb-**see**-kwi-uhss/ adjective too attentive and respectful towards someone. ■ **obsequiously** adverb **obsequiousness** noun.

observance noun **1** the obeying of a rule or following of a custom. **2** (**observances**) acts performed for religious or ceremonial reasons.

observant adjective quick to notice things.

observation noun **1** the close watching of someone or something. **2** the ability to notice important details. **3** a comment. ■ **observational** adjective.

observatory noun (plural **observatories**) a building housing a telescope for looking at the stars and planets.

observe verb (**observes**, **observing**, **observed**) **1** notice. **2** watch something carefully. **3** make a remark. **4** obey a rule. **5** celebrate or take part in a particular festival. ■ **observable** adjective **observer** noun.

obsess verb preoccupy someone to a disturbing extent.

obsession noun **1** the state of being obsessed. **2** something that you can't stop thinking about. ■ **obsessional** adjective.

obsessive adjective unable to stop thinking about someone or something. ■ **obsessively** adverb **obsessiveness** noun.

obsidian /uhb-**sid**-i-uhn/ noun a dark glass-like volcanic rock.

obsolescent /ob-suh-**less**-uhnt/ adjective becoming obsolete. ■ **obsolescence** noun.

obsolete adjective no longer produced or used; out of date.

obstacle noun a thing that blocks the way or prevents progress.

obstetrician /ob-stuh-**tri**-sh'n/ noun a doctor who is trained in obstetrics.

obstetrics noun the branch of medicine concerned with childbirth. ■ **obstetric** adjective.

obstinate adjective **1** refusing to change your mind or stop what you are doing. **2** hard to deal with. ■ **obstinacy** noun **obstinately** adverb.

obstreperous adjective noisy and difficult to control.

obstruct verb be in the way or stop the progress of.

obstruction noun **1** a thing that is in the way; an obstacle or blockage. **2** the obstructing of someone or something.

obstructive adjective deliberately causing a delay or difficulty.

obtain verb **1** get possession of. **2** formal be established or usual. ■ **obtainable** adjective.

obtrude verb (**obtrudes, obtruding, obtruded**) become noticeable in an unwelcome way.

obtrusive adjective noticeable in an unwelcome way.

obtuse /uhb-**tyooss**/ adjective **1** annoyingly slow to understand. **2** (of an angle) more than 90° and less than 180°. **3** not sharp or pointed; blunt.

obverse noun **1** the side of a coin or medal bearing the head or main design. **2** the opposite of something.

obviate /**ob**-vi-ayt/ verb (**obviates, obviating, obviated**) remove or prevent a need or difficulty.

obvious adjective easily seen or understood; clear. ■ **obviously** adverb.

ocarina /o-kuh-**ree**-nuh/ noun a small egg-shaped wind instrument with holes for the fingers.

occasion noun **1** a particular event, or the time at which it happens. **2** a special event or celebration. **3** a suitable time for something. **4** formal reason or cause. verb formal cause.

> ☑ two c's and one s: occasion.

occasional adjective happening or done from time to time. ■ **occasionally** adverb.

occidental /ok-si-**den**-tuhl/ adjective relating to the countries of the West.

occlude verb (**occludes, occluding, occluded**) technical close up; block.

occult /o-**kult**, **o**-kult/ noun (**the occult**) the world of magic and supernatural beliefs and practices. adjective relating to the occult. ■ **occultism** noun **occultist** noun.

occupancy noun **1** the action of occupying a place. **2** the proportion of accommodation that is occupied.

occupant noun a person who occupies a place.

occupation noun **1** a job or profession. **2** a way of spending time. **3** the occupying of a place.

occupational adjective having to do with a job or profession. □ **occupational therapy** the use of certain activities and crafts to help someone recover from an illness.

occupy verb (**occupies, occupying, occupied**) **1** live or work in a building. **2** enter and take control of a place. **3** fill or take up a space, time, or position. **4** keep someone busy. ■ **occupier** noun.

occur verb (**occurs, occurring, occurred**) **1** happen. **2** be found or present. **3** (**occur to**) come into someone's mind.

> ☑ double c, and there is a double r in **occurred, occurring,** and **occurrence**.

occurrence /uh-**kur**-ruhnss/ noun **1** a thing that happens or exists. **2** the fact of something happening or existing.

ocean noun a very large expanse of sea.

oceanic /oh-si-**an**-ik/ adjective relating to the ocean.

oceanography noun the study of the sea. ■ **oceanographer** noun.

ocelot /**oss**-i-lot/ noun a medium-sized striped and spotted wild cat, found in South and Central America.

ochre /**oh**-ker/ (US spelling **ocher**) noun a type of light yellow or reddish earth, used as a pigment.

o'clock adverb used to say which hour it is when telling the time.

octagon noun a figure with eight straight sides and eight angles. ■ **octagonal** adjective.

octahedron /ok-tuh-**hee**-druhn/ noun (plural **octahedra** or **octahedrons**) a three-dimensional shape with eight flat faces.

octane noun a liquid hydrocarbon present in petroleum spirit.

octave noun **1** a series of eight musical notes occupying the interval between (and including) two notes. **2** the interval between two such notes.

octavo /ok-**tah**-voh/ **noun** (plural **octavos**) a size of book page that results from folding each printed sheet into eight leaves (sixteen pages).

octet noun 1 a group of eight musicians. **2** a composition for an octet.

October noun the tenth month of the year.

octogenarian /ok-tuh-ji-**nair**-i-uhn/ **noun** a person who is between 80 and 89 years old.

octopus noun (plural **octopuses**) a sea creature with a soft body and eight long tentacles.

ocular adjective having to do with the eyes.

oculist noun a doctor who examines and treats people's eyes.

OD verb (**OD's**, **OD'ing**, **OD'd**) informal take an overdose of a drug.

odd adjective 1 unusual or unexpected; strange. **2** (of whole numbers such as 3 and 5) having one left over as a remainder when divided by two. **3** occasional. **4** spare; available. **5** separated from a pair or set. **6** in the region of.
■ **oddly** adverb **oddness** noun.

oddball noun informal a strange or eccentric person.

oddity noun (plural **oddities**) **1** the quality of being strange. **2** a strange person or thing.

oddment noun an item or piece left over from a larger piece or set.

odds plural noun 1 the ratio between the amount placed as a bet and the money which would be received if the bet was won. **2** (**the odds**) the chances of something happening. **3** (**the odds**) the balance of advantage on one side rather than the other. □ **at odds** in conflict or disagreement. **odds-on 1** (of a horse) with betting odds in favour of winning. **2** very likely to happen or succeed.

ode noun a poem addressed to a person or thing or celebrating an event.

odious adjective very unpleasant; hateful.

odium noun widespread hatred or disgust.

odoriferous adjective smelly.

odour (US spelling **odor**) **noun** a smell.
■ **odorous** adjective **odourless** adjective.

odyssey /**od**-i-si/ **noun** (plural **odysseys**) a long, eventful journey.

oedema /i-**dee**-muh/ (US spelling **edema**) **noun** a build-up of watery fluid in the tissues of the body.

oesophagus /ee-**so**-fuh-guhss/ (US spelling **esophagus**) **noun** (plural **oesophagi** /ee-**so**-fuh-jI/ or **oesophaguses** /ee-**so**-fuh-guh-siz/) the muscular tube which connects the throat to the stomach.

oestrogen /**ee**-struh-juhn/ (US spelling **estrogen**) **noun** a hormone which produces female physical and sexual characteristics.

oeuvre /**er**-vruh/ **noun** the body of work of an artist, composer, or author.

of preposition 1 expressing the relationship between a part and a whole. **2** belonging to; coming from. **3** used in expressions of measurement, value, or age. **4** made from. **5** used to show position. **6** used to show that something belongs to a category.

> ⓘ don't write **of** instead of **have** in constructions such as *I could have told you* (not *I could of told you*).

off adverb 1 away from a place. **2** so as to be removed or separated. **3** starting a journey or race. **4** so as to finish or be discontinued. **5** (of an electrical appliance or power supply) not working or connected. **6** having a particular level of wealth. **preposition 1** away from. **2** situated or leading in a direction away from. **3** so as to be removed or separated from. **4** informal having a temporary dislike of. **adjective 1** (of food) no longer fresh. **2** Brit. informal annoying or unfair. **noun** Brit. informal the start of a race or journey. □ **off-colour** Brit. slightly unwell. **off-licence** Brit. a shop selling alcoholic drink to be drunk elsewhere. **off-**

peak at a time when demand is less.

off-putting unpleasant or unsettling.

off white a white colour with a grey or yellowish tinge.

> ℹ️ use **off**, not **off of**, in a sentence like *it fell off the table*.

offal noun the internal organs of an animal used as food.

offbeat adjective informal unconventional; unusual.

offcut noun a piece of wood, fabric, etc. left behind after a larger piece has been cut off.

offence (US spelling **offense**) noun **1** an act that breaks a law or rule. **2** a feeling of hurt or annoyance.

offend verb **1** make someone feel upset, insulted, or annoyed. **2** be displeasing to. **3** do something illegal. ■ **offender** noun.

offensive adjective **1** causing someone to feel upset, insulted, or annoyed. **2** used in attack. noun a campaign to attack or achieve something. ■ **offensively** adverb.

offer verb (**offers, offering, offered**) **1** make something available to someone. **2** say you are willing to do something for someone. **3** provide. noun **1** an expression of readiness to do or give something. **2** an amount of money that someone is willing to pay for something. **3** a specially reduced price. □ **on offer 1** available. **2** for sale at a reduced price.

offering noun something that is offered; a gift or contribution.

offertory /off-er-tuh-ri/ noun (plural **offertories**) **1** the offering of the bread and wine at Christian Holy Communion. **2** a collection of money made at a Christian church service.

offhand adjective rudely casual or cool in manner. adverb without previous thought.

office noun **1** a room, set of rooms, or building where people work at desks. **2** a position of authority. **3** (**offices**) things done for other people.

officer noun **1** a person holding a position of authority, especially in the

armed forces. **2** a policeman or policewoman.

official adjective **1** relating to an authority or public organization. **2** agreed or done by a person or group in a position of authority. noun a person holding public office or having official duties. ■ **officialdom** noun **officially** adverb.

officiate /uh-fi-shi-ayt/ verb (**officiates, officiating, officiated**) **1** act as an official in charge of something. **2** perform a religious service or ceremony.

officious adjective using your authority or interfering in a bossy way.

offing noun (**in the offing**) likely to happen or appear soon.

offload verb **1** unload a cargo. **2** get rid of.

offset verb (**offsets, offsetting, offset**) cancel out something with an equal and opposite force or effect.

offshoot noun a thing that develops from something else.

offshore adjective & adverb **1** at sea some distance from the shore. **2** (of the wind) blowing towards the sea from the land. **3** situated or registered abroad.

offside adjective & adverb (in games such as football) occupying a position on the field where playing the ball is not allowed.

offspring noun (plural **offspring**) a person's child or children.

offstage adjective & adverb (in a theatre) not on the stage.

often adverb **1** frequently. **2** in many instances.

ogle verb (**ogles, ogling, ogled**) stare at someone in a lecherous way.

ogre noun **1** (in stories) a man-eating giant. **2** a cruel or terrifying person.

ohm noun the basic unit of electrical resistance.

oik noun informal a rude person.

oil noun **1** a thick, sticky liquid obtained from petroleum. **2** a thick liquid which cannot be dissolved in water and is obtained from plants.

3 (also **oils**) oil paint. **verb** treat or coat with oil. □ **oil paint** artist's paint made from ground pigment mixed with linseed or other oil.

oilfield noun an area where oil is found beneath the ground or seabed.

oilskin noun **1** heavy cotton cloth waterproofed with oil. **2** (**oilskins**) a set of garments made of oilskin.

oily adjective (**oilier**, **oiliest**) **1** containing or covered with oil. **2** resembling oil. **3** (of a person) insincerely smooth and flattering. ■ **oiliness** noun.

oink noun the grunting sound made by a pig. **verb** make such a sound.

ointment noun a smooth substance that is rubbed on the skin for medicinal purposes.

OK or **okay** informal **exclamation** said to express agreement or acceptance. **adjective 1** satisfactory, but not especially good. **2** permissible; allowed. **adverb** in a satisfactory way. **noun** an authorization. **verb** (**OK's**, **OK'ing**, **OK'd**) give approval to.

okapi /oh-**kah**-pi/ noun (plural same or **okapis**) a large plant-eating African mammal with stripes on the hindquarters and upper legs.

okra /**ok**-ruh/ noun the long seed pods of a tropical plant, eaten as a vegetable.

old adjective (**older**, **oldest**) **1** having lived for a long time. **2** made, built, or originating long ago. **3** possessed or used for a long time. **4** former. **5** of a specified age. □ **old age** the later part of normal life. **old boy** (or **old girl**) a former pupil of a school. **Old English** the language of the Anglo-Saxons. **old-fashioned** no longer current; dated. **the old guard** the longstanding, conservative members of a group. **old hand** a very experienced person. **old hat** informal boringly familiar or out of date. **old maid** disapproving a single woman thought of as too old for marriage. **old master** a great painter of former times. **Old Nick** the Devil. **Old Testament** the first part of the Christian Bible. **old wives' tale** a widely held traditional belief that is incorrect. **Old World** Europe, Asia, and Africa.

olden adjective of a former age.

oleaginous /oh-li-**aj**-i-nuhss/ adjective **1** oily. **2** excessively flattering.

olfactory /ol-**fak**-tuh-ri/ adjective relating to the sense of smell.

oligarch /**ol**-i-gark/ noun a ruler in an oligarchy.

oligarchy noun (plural **oligarchies**) **1** a small group of people having control of a state. **2** a state governed by a small group of people. ■ **oligarchic** adjective.

olive noun **1** a small oval fruit with a hard stone and bitter flesh. **2** (also **olive green**) a greyish-green colour like that of an unripe olive. **adjective** (of a person's complexion) yellowish brown. □ **olive branch** an offer to restore friendly relations. **olive oil** oil obtained from olives, used in cookery and salad dressing.

Olympiad noun a staging of the Olympic Games.

Olympian adjective **1** having to do with Mount Olympus, traditional home of the Greek gods. **2** relating to the Olympic Games. **noun 1** any of the twelve main Greek gods. **2** a competitor in the Olympic Games.

Olympic adjective relating to the Olympic Games. **noun** (**the Olympics** or **the Olympic Games**) a sports competition held every four years, or the ancient Greek festival of sport and arts that it was based on.

ombudsman /**om**-buudz-muhn/ noun an official who investigates people's complaints against companies or the government.

omega /**oh**-mi-guh/ noun the last letter of the Greek alphabet (Ω, ω).

omelette (US spelling **omelet**) noun a dish of beaten eggs cooked in a frying pan, usually with a savoury filling.

omen noun an event seen as a sign of future good or bad luck.

ominous adjective giving the worrying impression that something bad is going to happen. ■ **ominously** adverb.

omission noun **1** the action of leaving something out. **2** a failure to do something. **3** something that has been left out or not done.

omit verb (**omits**, **omitting**, **omitted**) **1** leave out or exclude. **2** fail to do.

> ☑ just one *m*: omit.

omni- combining form **1** of all things: *omniscient*. **2** in all ways or places: *omnipresent*.

omnibus noun **1** a volume containing several works previously published separately. **2** a single edition of two or more programmes previously broadcast separately. **3** dated a bus.

omnipotent /om-**ni**-puh-tuhnt/ adjective having unlimited or very great power. ■ **omnipotence** noun.

omnipresent adjective **1** (of God) present everywhere at the same time. **2** widespread. ■ **omnipresence** noun.

omniscient /om-**ni**-si-uhnt/ adjective knowing everything. ■ **omniscience** noun.

omnivore /**om**-ni-vor/ noun an animal that eats both plants and meat.

omnivorous /om-**ni**-vuh-ruhss/ adjective eating both plants and meat.

on preposition & adverb in contact with and supported by a surface. preposition **1** (also **on to**) into contact with a surface, or aboard a vehicle. **2** about; concerning. **3** as a member of. **4** stored in or broadcast by. **5** in the course of. **6** indicating the day or time when something takes place. **7** engaged in. **8** regularly taking a drug or medicine. **9** informal paid for by. adverb **1** with continued movement or action. **2** (of clothing) being worn. **3** taking place or being presented. **4** (of an electrical appliance or power supply) functioning.

onanism /**oh**-nuh-ni-z'm/ noun formal masturbation.

once adverb **1** on one occasion or for one time only. **2** formerly. **3** multiplied by one. conjunction as soon as. □ **at once 1** immediately. **2** at the same time. **once-over** informal a rapid inspec-

tion, search, or piece of work.

oncoming adjective moving towards you.

one cardinal number **1** the lowest cardinal number; 1. (Roman numeral: **i** or **I**.) **2** single, or a single person or thing. **3** (before a person's name) a certain. **4** the same. pronoun **1** used to refer to a person or thing previously mentioned or easily identified. **2** used to refer to the speaker, or to represent people in general. □ **one-armed bandit** informal a fruit machine operated by pulling a long handle at the side. **one-liner** informal a short joke or witty remark. **one-off** Brit. informal done, made, or happening only once. **one-upmanship** informal the technique of gaining an advantage over someone else.

oneness noun the state of being whole or in agreement.

onerous /**oh**-nuh-ruhss/ adjective involving a lot of effort and difficulty.

oneself pronoun **1** used as the object of a verb or preposition when this is the same as the subject of the clause and the subject is 'one'. **2** used to emphasize that one is doing something individually or unaided. **3** in one's normal state of body or mind.

ongoing adjective still in progress.

onion noun a bulb with a strong taste and smell, used as a vegetable.

online adjective & adverb controlled by or connected to a computer.

onlooker noun a spectator.

only adverb **1** and no one or nothing more besides. **2** no longer ago than. **3** not until. **4** with the negative result that. adjective **1** single or solitary. **2** alone deserving consideration. conjunction informal except that.

onomatopoeia /on-uh-mat-uh-**pee**-uh/ noun the use of words that sound like the thing they refer to (e.g. *sizzle*). ■ **onomatopoeic** adjective.

onrush noun a surging rush forward. ■ **onrushing** adjective.

onset noun the beginning of something.

onshore adjective & adverb **1** situated

on land. **2** (of the wind) blowing from the sea towards the land.

onside adjective & adverb (in sport) not offside.

onslaught noun **1** a fierce or destructive attack. **2** an overwhelmingly large quantity of people or things.

onstage adjective & adverb (in a theatre) on the stage.

onto ⇒ *on to* (see **ON**).

ontology noun philosophy concerned with the nature of being. ■ **ontological** adjective.

onus noun a duty or responsibility.

onward adjective & adverb in a forward direction. ■ **onwards** adverb.

onyx /on-iks/ noun a semi-precious stone with layers of different colours.

oodles plural noun informal a very great number or amount.

oomph noun informal excitement or energy.

ooze verb (oozes, oozing, oozed) slowly seep out. noun the sluggish flow of a fluid. ■ **oozy** adjective.

op noun informal an operation.

opacity /oh-**pa**-si-ti/ noun the condition of being opaque.

opal noun a semi-transparent gemstone in which small points of shifting colour can be seen.

opalescent adjective having small points of shifting colour.

opaque /oh-**payk**/ adjective **1** not able to be seen through. **2** difficult or impossible to understand.

op. cit. adverb in the work already cited.

> ℹ️ short for Latin *opere citato*.

open adjective **1** not closed, fastened, or restricted. **2** not covered or protected. **3** (open to) likely to suffer from or be affected by. **4** spread out, expanded, or unfolded. **5** accessible or available. **6** not concealing thoughts and feelings. **7** undisguised. **8** not finally settled. verb **1** make or become open. **2** formally begin or es-

tablish. **3** (open on to or into) give access to. **4** (open out or up) begin to talk freely. noun (the open) fresh air or open countryside. ◻ **the open air** a free or unenclosed space outdoors. **open-and-shut** straightforward. **open-heart surgery** surgery in which the heart is exposed. **open house** a place or situation in which all visitors are welcome. **open letter** a letter addressed to a particular person but intended to be published. **open market** a situation in which competitors can trade without restrictions. **open-minded** willing to consider new ideas. **open-plan** having large rooms with few or no dividing walls. **open verdict** Law a verdict that a person's death is suspicious but that the cause is not known. ■ **opener** noun **openly** adverb **openness** noun.

opencast adjective Brit. (of mining) in which coal or ore is extracted from a level near the earth's surface, rather than from shafts.

opening noun **1** a gap. **2** the beginning of something. **3** a ceremony at which a building, show, etc. is declared to be open. **4** an opportunity to achieve something. **5** an available job or position. adjective coming at the beginning.

opera[1] noun a dramatic work that is set to music for singers and musicians. ◻ **opera glasses** small binoculars used at the opera or theatre.

opera[2] plural of **OPUS**.

operable adjective **1** able to be used. **2** able to be treated by a surgical operation.

operate verb (operates, operating, operated) **1** function or work. **2** use or control a machine. **3** (of an organization or armed force) carry out activities. **4** be in effect. **5** perform a surgical operation.

operatic adjective having to do with opera.

operation noun **1** the action of operating. **2** an act of cutting into a patient's body to remove or repair a damaged part. **3** an organized action involving a number of people. **4** a business organization.

operational adjective **1** ready for use, or being used. **2** relating to the functioning of an organization. ■ **operationally** adverb.

operative adjective **1** functioning. **2** (of a word) having the most significance in a phrase. **3** relating to surgery. noun a worker.

operator noun **1** a person who operates equipment or a machine. **2** a person who works at the switchboard of a telephone exchange. **3** a person or company that runs a business or enterprise. **4** informal a person who acts in a specified way: *a smooth operator.*

operetta noun a short opera on a light or humorous theme.

ophthalmic adjective relating to the eye and its diseases.

ophthalmology /off-thal-**mol**-uh-ji/ noun the study and treatment of disorders and diseases of the eye. ■ **ophthalmologist** noun.

opiate /**oh**-pi-uht/ noun a drug containing opium.

opine /oh-**pyn**/ (opines, opining, opined) formal say something as your opinion.

opinion noun **1** a personal view not necessarily based on fact or knowledge. **2** the views of people in general. **3** a formal statement of advice by an expert. ◻ **opinion poll** the questioning of a small number of people in order to assess the views of people in general.

opinionated adjective tending to put forward your views forcefully.

opium noun an addictive drug made from the juice of a poppy.

opossum /uh-**poss**-uhm/ noun **1** an American mammal with a tail which it can use for grasping. **2** Austral./NZ a possum.

opponent noun **1** a person who competes with another in a contest or argument. **2** a person who disagrees with a proposal or practice.

opportune /**op**-per-tyoon/ adjective happening at a good or convenient time.

opportunist noun a person who takes advantage of opportunities without worrying about whether or not they are right to do so. adjective (also **opportunistic**) taking advantage of opportunities when they come up. ■ **opportunism** noun.

opportunity noun (plural **opportunities**) **1** a good time or set of circumstances for doing something. **2** a chance for employment or promotion.

 two *p*'s: *opportunity.*

oppose verb (opposes, opposing, opposed) **1** (also **be opposed to**) disapprove of, resist, or be hostile to. **2** compete with or fight. **3** (opposed) (of two or more things) contrasting or conflicting. **4** (opposing) opposite.

opposite adjective **1** facing. **2** completely different. **3** being the other of a contrasted pair: *the opposite sex.* noun an opposite person or thing. adverb in an opposite position. preposition **1** in a position opposite to. **2** costarring with.

opposition noun **1** resistance or disagreement. **2** a group of opponents. **3** (**the Opposition**) Brit. the main party in parliament that is opposed to the one in government. **4** a contrast or direct opposite. ■ **oppositional** adjective.

oppress verb **1** treat in a harsh and unfair way. **2** make someone feel distressed or anxious. ■ **oppression** noun **oppressor** noun.

 double *p*, double *s*: *oppress.*

oppressive adjective **1** harsh and unfair. **2** causing depression or anxiety. **3** (of weather) close and sultry. ■ **oppressively** adverb.

opprobrious /uh-**proh**-bri-uhss/ adjective formal highly scornful.

opprobrium /uh-**proh**-bri-uhm/ noun formal **1** harsh criticism or scorn. **2** public disgrace as a result of bad behaviour.

opt verb make a choice. ◻ **opt out**

choose not to participate.

optic adjective relating to the eye or vision. noun Brit. trademark a device fastened to the neck of an upside-down bottle for measuring out spirits.

optical adjective relating to vision, light, or optics. □ **optical fibre** a thin glass fibre through which light can be transmitted. **optical illusion** something that deceives the eye by appearing to be different from what it is. ■ **optically** adverb.

optician noun a person qualified to examine people's eyes and to prescribe glasses and contact lenses.

optics noun the study of vision and the behaviour of light.

optimal adjective best or most favourable. ■ **optimally** adverb.

optimism noun hopefulness and confidence about the future or success of something. ■ **optimist** noun.

optimistic adjective hopeful and confident about the future. ■ **optimistically** adverb.

optimize or **optimise** verb (optimizes, optimizing, optimized) make the best use of.

optimum adjective most likely to lead to a favourable outcome. noun (plural **optima** or **optimums**) the most favourable conditions for growth or success.

option noun **1** a thing that you may choose. **2** the freedom or right to choose. **3** a right to buy or sell something at a specified price within a set time.

optional adjective available to be chosen, but not compulsory. ■ **optionally** adverb.

optometry noun the occupation of measuring people's eyesight, prescribing lenses, and detecting eye disease. ■ **optometrist** noun.

opulent adjective showily rich and luxurious. ■ **opulence** noun **opulently** adverb.

opus /oh-puhss/ noun (plural **opuses** or **opera** /op-uh-ruh/) **1** a musical composition or set of compositions. **2** an artistic work.

or conjunction **1** used to link alternatives. **2** introducing a word that means the same as a preceding word or phrase, or that explains it. **3** otherwise.

oracle noun (in ancient Greece or Rome) a priest or priestess through whom the gods were believed to give prophecies about the future.

oracular /o-rak-yuu-ler/ adjective having to do with an oracle.

oral adjective **1** spoken rather than written. **2** relating to the mouth. **3** done or taken by the mouth. noun a spoken examination. ■ **orally** adverb.

orange noun **1** a large round citrus fruit with a tough reddish-yellow rind. **2** a bright reddish-yellow colour.

orangeade noun Brit. a fizzy soft drink flavoured with orange.

orang-utan or **orang-utang** noun a large ape with reddish hair.

oration noun a formal speech.

orator noun a person who is good at public speaking.

oratorio noun (plural **oratorios**) a large-scale musical work on a religious theme for orchestra and voices.

oratory[1] noun (plural **oratories**) a small chapel.

oratory[2] noun **1** formal public speaking. **2** exciting and inspiring speech. ■ **oratorical** adjective.

orb noun **1** a spherical object or shape. **2** a golden globe with a cross on top, carried by a king or queen.

orbit noun **1** the regularly repeated course of a moon, spacecraft, etc. around a star or planet. **2** a particular area of activity or influence. verb (**orbits**, **orbiting**, **orbited**) move in orbit round a star or planet.

orbital adjective **1** relating to an orbit or orbits. **2** Brit. (of a road) passing round the outside of a town.

orca noun a large whale with teeth and black and white markings.

orchard noun a piece of enclosed land planted with fruit trees.

orchestra noun **1** a large group of

musicians with string, woodwind, brass, and percussion sections. **2** (also **orchestra pit**) the part of a theatre where the orchestra plays. ■ **orchestral** adjective.

orchestrate verb (**orchestrates, orchestrating, orchestrated**) **1** arrange music to be performed by an orchestra. **2** direct a situation to produce a desired effect. ■ **orchestration** noun.

orchid noun a plant with bright, unusually shaped flowers.

ordain verb **1** make someone a priest or minister. **2** order officially.

ordeal noun a prolonged painful or horrific experience.

order noun **1** the arrangement of people or things according to a particular sequence or method. **2** a situation in which everything is in its correct place. **3** a situation in which the law is being obeyed and no one is behaving badly. **4** a command. **5** a request for something to be made, supplied, or served. **6** the procedure followed in a meeting, court, or religious service. **7** quality or class. **8** a social class or system. **9** a classifying category of plants and animals. **10** (**orders** or **holy orders**) the rank of an ordained Christian minister. **11** a group of people living in a religious community. **12** an institution founded by a ruler to honour people: *the Order of the Garter.* verb (**orders, ordering, ordered**) **1** give a command. **2** request that something be made, supplied, or served. **3** arrange methodically. □ **(of (or in) the order of** approximately. **out of order 1** not functioning. **2** Brit. informal unacceptable.

orderly adjective **1** neatly and methodically arranged. **2** well behaved. noun (plural **orderlies**) **1** a hospital attendant responsible for various non-medical tasks. **2** a soldier who carries orders or performs minor tasks. ■ **orderliness** noun.

ordinal adjective relating to order in a series. □ **ordinal number** a number defining a thing's position in a series, such as 'first' or 'second'.

ordinance noun formal **1** an official order. **2** a religious rite.

ordinary adjective normal or usual. □ **ordinary level** an O level. **out of the ordinary** unusual. ■ **ordinarily** adverb **ordinariness** noun.

ordination noun the ordaining of someone as a priest or minister.

ordnance noun **1** mounted guns. **2** US military equipment and stores.

ordure noun formal dung; excrement.

ore noun a naturally occurring material from which a metal or mineral can be extracted.

oregano /o-ri-**gah**-noh/ noun a sweet-smelling plant used in cooking.

organ noun **1** a part of the body that has a particular function, e.g. the heart or kidneys. **2** a musical keyboard instrument with rows of pipes supplied with air from bellows, or one that produces similar sounds electronically. **3** a newspaper which puts forward particular views. ■ **organist** noun.

organic adjective **1** having to do with living matter. **2** produced without the aid of artificial chemicals such as fertilizers. **3** (of chemical compounds) containing carbon. **4** having to do with an organ of the body. **5** (of development or change) continuous or natural. ■ **organically** adverb.

organism noun **1** an individual animal, plant, or life form. **2** a whole made up of parts which are dependent on each other.

organization or **organisation** noun **1** the action of organizing. **2** a systematic arrangement or approach. **3** an organized group of people, e.g. a business. ■ **organizational** adjective.

organize or **organise** verb (**organizes, organizing, organized**) **1** arrange in an orderly way. **2** Brit. make arrangements for. ■ **organizer** noun.

orgasm noun an intensely pleasurable sensation that is felt as the climax of sexual activity. verb have an orgasm. ■ **orgasmic** adjective.

orgiastic /or-ji-**ass**-tik/ adjective like an orgy.

orgy noun (plural **orgies**) **1** a wild party with a lot of drinking and sexual activity. **2** an excessive amount of a specified activity.

oriel noun a projecting part of an upper storey with a window.

orient noun (**the Orient**) literary the countries of the East. **verb** (also **orientate**) **1** position something in relation to the points of a compass or other points. **2** (**orient yourself**) find your position in relation to your surroundings. **3** tailor something to meet particular needs.

oriental adjective having to do with the Far East. **noun** dated or offensive a person of Far Eastern descent.

orientation noun **1** the action of orienting. **2** a position in relation to something else. **3** a person's attitude or natural tendency.

orienteering noun the sport of finding your way across country with the aid of a map and compass.

orifice noun an opening.

origami /o-ri-**gah**-mi/ noun the Japanese art of folding paper into decorative shapes.

origin noun **1** the point where something begins. **2** a person's background or ancestry.

original adjective **1** existing from the beginning. **2** not a copy. **3** inventive or novel. **noun** the earliest form of something, from which copies can be made. ◻ **original sin** (in Christian belief) the tendency to commit sin that is thought to be present in all human beings. ■ **originality** noun **originally** adverb.

originate verb (**originates, originating, originated**) **1** begin in a particular place or situation. **2** create. ■ **origination** noun **originator** noun.

ormolu noun a gold-coloured alloy of copper, zinc, and tin.

ornament noun **1** an object used as a decoration. **2** decorative items considered together. ■ **ornamental** adjective **ornamentation** noun.

ornate adjective elaborately decorated. ■ **ornately** adverb.

ornithology noun the scientific study of birds. ■ **ornithological** adjective **ornithologist** noun.

orphan noun a child whose parents are dead. **verb** (**be orphaned**) (of a child) be made an orphan.

orphanage noun a place where orphans are looked after.

orthodontist /or-thuh-**don**-tist/ noun a dentist who treats irregularities in the position of the teeth and jaws.

orthodox adjective **1** in keeping with generally accepted beliefs. **2** normal. **3** (**Orthodox**) relating to the Orthodox Church. ◻ **Orthodox Church** the branch of the Christian Church in Greece and eastern Europe.

orthodoxy noun (plural **orthodoxies**) **1** the traditional beliefs or practices of a religion. **2** a generally accepted idea. **3** (**Orthodoxy**) the Orthodox Church or its members.

orthography noun (plural **orthographies**) the spelling system of a language. ■ **orthographic** adjective.

orthopaedics /or-thuh-**pee**-diks/ (US spelling **orthopedics**) noun the branch of medicine concerned with bones and muscles. ■ **orthopaedic** adjective.

Oscar noun a gold statuette given annually for achievement in various categories of film-making; an Academy award.

oscillate /**oss**-i-layt/ verb (**oscillates, oscillating, oscillated**) **1** move back and forth at a regular rate. **2** waver in your opinions or emotions. ■ **oscillation** noun **oscillator** noun.

osier /**oh**-zi-er/ noun a type of willow with long, flexible shoots that are used for making baskets.

osmium noun a hard, dense silvery-white metallic element.

osmosis /oz-**moh**-siss/ noun **1** a process by which molecules pass through a membrane from a less concentrated solution into a more concentrated one. **2** the gradual absorbing of ideas. ■ **osmotic** adjective.

osprey noun (plural **ospreys**) a large fish-eating bird of prey.

osseous /oss-i-uhss/ **adjective** consisting of bone.

ossify /oss-i-fI/ **verb** (**ossifies, ossifying, ossified**) **1** turn into bone or bony tissue. **2** stop developing or progressing. ■ **ossification** noun.

ostensible **adjective** apparently true, but not necessarily so. ■ **ostensibly** adverb.

ostentation noun flamboyant display which is intended to impress.

ostentatious **adjective** flamboyant or pretentious in a way that is designed to impress. ■ **ostentatiously** adverb.

osteoarthritis noun a disease that causes pain and stiffness in the joints of the body.

osteopathy /oss-ti-**op**-uh-thi/ noun a system of complementary medicine involving manipulation of the bones and muscles. ■ **osteopath** noun.

osteoporosis /oss-ti-oh-puh-**roh**-siss/ **noun** a medical condition in which the bones become brittle.

ostinato /oss-ti-**nah**-toh/ noun (plural **ostinatos** or **ostinati** /oss-ti-**nah**-ti/) a continually repeated musical phrase or rhythm.

ostler /**oss**-ler/ noun (in the past) a man employed at an inn to look after customers' horses.

ostracize or **ostracise** verb (**ostracizes, ostracizing, ostracized**) exclude someone from a society or group. ■ **ostracism** noun.

ostrich noun a large flightless African bird with a long neck and long legs.

other **adjective & pronoun 1** used to refer to a person or thing that is different from one already mentioned or known. **2** additional. **3** the alternative of two. **4** those not already mentioned. □ **other-worldly 1** relating to an imaginary or spiritual world. **2** unaware of the realities of life.

otherness noun the quality of being different or unusual.

otherwise adverb **1** in different circumstances. **2** in other respects. **3** in a different way. **4** alternatively.

otiose /**oh**-ti-ohss/ **adjective** serving no practical purpose.

otter noun a fish-eating mammal with a long body, living partly in water and partly on land.

ottoman noun (plural **ottomans**) a low upholstered seat without a back or arms.

oubliette /oo-bli-**et**/ noun a secret dungeon with access only through a trapdoor in its ceiling.

ought modal verb (3rd singular present and past **ought**) **1** used to indicate duty or correctness. **2** used to indicate something that is probable. **3** used to indicate a desirable or expected state. **4** used to give or ask advice.

> [i] when using **ought** in a negative construction, say *he ought not to have gone* rather than *he didn't/hadn't ought to have gone*.

oughtn't short form ought not.

Ouija board /**wee**-juh/ noun trademark a board marked with letters, used at a seance supposedly to receive messages from dead people.

ounce noun **1** a unit of weight of one sixteenth of a pound (approximately 28 grams). **2** a very small amount.

our possessive determiner **1** belonging to or associated with the speaker and one or more others. **2** belonging to or associated with people in general.

ours possessive pronoun used to refer to something belonging to or associated with the speaker and one or more others.

ourselves pronoun **1** used as the object of a verb or preposition when this is the same as the subject of the clause and the subject is the speaker and one or more other people. **2** we or us personally.

oust verb force someone out from a job or position.

out adverb **1** away from a place. **2** away from your home or office. **3** outdoors. **4** so as to be revealed, heard, or known. **5** to an end. **6** not possible or worth considering. **7** (of the tide) falling or at its lowest level. **8** (of the ball in tennis, squash, etc.) not in the playing area. **9** (in cricket, baseball, etc.) no longer batting. **verb** informal reveal that someone is homosexual. □ **out of 1** from. **2** not having a supply of something. **out of date 1** old-fashioned. **2** no longer valid.

ⓘ you should say **out of** rather than simply **out** in sentences such as *he threw it out of the window.*

outback noun (**the outback**) a remote or sparsely populated inland area.

outbid verb (**outbids, outbidding, outbid**) bid more than.

outboard adjective & adverb on, towards, or near the outside of a ship or aircraft. □ **outboard motor** a motor attached to the outside of a boat.

outbreak noun a sudden occurrence of war, disease, etc.

outbuilding noun a smaller building in the grounds of a main building.

outburst noun a sudden violent occurrence or release of something.

outcast noun a person who is rejected by their social group.

outclass verb be far better than.

outcome noun a consequence.

outcrop noun a part of a rock formation that is visible on the surface.

outcry noun (plural **outcries**) a strong expression of public disapproval.

outdated adjective no longer used or fashionable.

outdistance verb (**outdistances, outdistancing, outdistanced**) leave a competitor or pursuer far behind.

outdo verb (**outdoes, outdoing, outdid**; past participle **outdone**) do better than someone else.

outdoor adjective **1** done, situated, or used outdoors. **2** fond of being outdoors.

outdoors adverb in or into the open air. **noun** any area outside buildings or shelter.

outer adjective **1** outside. **2** further from the centre or the inside.

outermost adjective furthest from the centre.

outface verb (**outfaces, outfacing,**

outfaced) unsettle or defeat someone by confronting them boldly.

outfall noun the place where a river or drain empties into the sea, a river, or a lake.

outfit noun **1** a set of clothes worn together. **2** informal a group of people doing a particular thing together. **verb** (**outfits, outfitting, outfitted**) provide someone with an outfit of clothes. ■ **outfitter** noun.

outflank verb **1** surround in order to attack. **2** defeat.

outfox verb informal defeat someone by being more cunning than them.

outgoing adjective **1** friendly and confident. **2** leaving an office or position. **3** going out or away from a place. **noun** (**outgoings**) Brit. money that you spend regularly.

outgrow verb (**outgrows, outgrowing, outgrew**; past participle **outgrown**) **1** grow too big for. **2** stop doing something as you mature.

outhouse noun a smaller building attached or close to a house.

outing noun a brief journey, adventure, or new experience.

outlandish adjective bizarre or unfamiliar.

outlast verb last longer than.

outlaw noun a person who has broken the law and remains at large. **verb** make something illegal.

outlay noun an amount of money spent.

outlet noun **1** a pipe or hole through which water or gas may escape. **2** a point from which goods are sold or distributed. **3** a way of expressing your talents, energy, or emotions.

outline noun **1** a sketch or diagram showing the shape of an object. **2** the outer edges of an object. **3** a general description of something, with no detail. **verb** (**outlines, outlining, outlined**) **1** draw the outer edge or shape of. **2** give a summary of.

outlive verb live or last longer than.

outlook noun **1** a person's attitude to

life. **2** a view. **3** what is likely to happen in the future.

outlying adjective situated far from a centre.

outmanoeuvre verb (**outmanoeuvres, outmanoeuvring, outmanoeuvred**) gain an advantage over an opponent by using skill and cunning.

outmoded adjective old-fashioned.

outnumber verb (**outnumbers, outnumbering, outnumbered**) be more numerous than.

outpace verb (**outpaces, outpacing, outpaced**) go faster than.

outpatient noun a patient attending a hospital for treatment without staying overnight.

outperform verb perform better than.

outplay verb play better than.

outpost noun **1** a small military camp at a distance from the main army. **2** a remote part of a country or empire.

outpouring noun **1** something that streams out rapidly. **2** an outburst of strong emotion.

output noun **1** the amount of something produced. **2** the process of producing something. **3** the power, energy, etc. supplied by a device or system. **4** a place where power, information, etc. leaves a system.

outrage noun **1** an extremely strong reaction of anger or annoyance. **2** an extremely immoral or shocking act. verb (**outrages, outraging, outraged**) make someone feel outrage.

outrageous adjective **1** shockingly bad or excessive. **2** very bold and unusual. ■ **outrageously** adverb.

outran past of **OUTRUN**.

outrank verb have a higher rank than.

outré /oo-tray/ adjective unusual and rather shocking.

outreach noun an organization's involvement with the community.

outrider noun a person in a vehicle or on horseback who escorts another vehicle.

outrigger noun a structure projecting

from a boat's side to help keep it stable.

outright adverb **1** altogether. **2** openly. **3** immediately. adjective **1** open and direct. **2** complete.

outrun verb (**outruns, outrunning, outran;** past participle **outrun**) run or travel faster or further than.

outsell verb (**outsells, outselling, outsold**) be sold in greater quantities than.

outset noun the beginning.

outshine verb (**outshines, outshining, outshone**) **1** shine more brightly than. **2** be much better than.

outside noun **1** the external side or surface of something. **2** the external appearance of someone or something. **3** the side of a curve where the edge is longer. adjective **1** situated on or near the outside. **2** not belonging to a particular group. preposition & adverb **1** situated or moving beyond the boundaries of. **2** beyond the limits of. **3** not being a member of.

outsider noun **1** a person who does not belong to a particular group. **2** a competitor thought to have little chance of success.

outsize or **outsized** adjective exceptionally large.

outskirts plural noun the outer parts of a town or city.

outsmart verb defeat someone by being cleverer than them.

outsold past and past participle of **OUTSELL**.

outspoken adjective stating your opinions in an open and direct way.

outstanding adjective **1** exceptionally good. **2** clearly noticeable. **3** not yet dealt with or paid. ■ **outstandingly** adverb.

outstay verb stay for longer than the expected or permitted time.

outstrip verb (**outstrips, outstripping, outstripped**) **1** move faster than. **2** surpass.

outvote verb (**outvotes, outvoting, outvoted**) defeat by gaining more votes.

outward adjective & adverb **1** on or from the outside. **2** out or away from a place. ■ **outwardly** adverb **outwards** adverb.

outweigh verb be more significant than.

outwit verb (**outwits, outwitting, outwitted**) deceive someone through being cleverer than them.

ouzo /oo-zoh/ noun an aniseed-flavoured Greek spirit.

ova plural of **OVUM**.

oval adjective having a rounded and slightly elongated outline. noun an oval object, design, or course.

ovary noun (plural **ovaries**) **1** a female reproductive organ in which eggs are produced. **2** the base of the reproductive organ of a flower. ■ **ovarian** adjective.

ovation noun a long, enthusiastic round of applause.

oven noun **1** an enclosed compartment in which food is cooked or heated. **2** a small furnace or kiln.

ovenproof adjective suitable for use in an oven.

over preposition & adverb **1** expressing movement across an area. **2** beyond and falling or hanging from a point. preposition **1** extending upwards from or above. **2** above so as to cover or protect. **3** expressing length of time. **4** higher or more than. **5** expressing authority or control. adverb **1** in or to the place indicated. **2** expressing action and result. **3** finished. **4** expressing repetition of a process. noun Cricket a sequence of six balls bowled by a bowler from one end of the pitch.

overact verb act a role in an exaggerated way.

overactive adjective excessively active.

overall adjective & adverb including everything; taken as a whole. noun (also **overalls**) Brit. a loose-fitting garment worn over ordinary clothes to protect them.

overarching adjective covering or dealing with everything.

overarm adjective & adverb done with the hand brought forward and down from above shoulder level.

overawe verb (**overawes, overawing, overawed**) impress someone so much that they are nervous or silent.

overbalance verb (**overbalances, overbalancing, overbalanced**) fall due to loss of balance.

overbearing adjective unpleasantly overpowering.

overblown adjective exaggerated or pretentious.

overboard adverb from a ship into the water. □ **go overboard 1** be very enthusiastic. **2** go too far.

overcast adjective cloudy.

overcharge verb (**overcharges, overcharging, overcharged**) charge too high a price.

overcoat noun **1** a long, warm coat. **2** a top layer of paint or varnish.

overcome verb (**overcomes, overcoming, overcame**; past participle **overcome**) **1** succeed in dealing with a problem. **2** defeat; overpower.

overcommit verb (**overcommits, overcommitting, overcommitted**) (**overcommit yourself**) undertake to do more than you are capable of.

overcompensate verb (**overcompensates, overcompensating, overcompensated**) do too much when trying to correct a problem.

overcrowded adjective filled beyond what is usual or comfortable.

overdo verb (**overdoes, overdoing, overdid**; past participle **overdone**) **1** do excessively or in an exaggerated way. **2** (**overdone**) cooked too much.

overdose noun an excessive and dangerous dose of a drug. verb (**overdoses, overdosing, overdosed**) take an overdose.

overdraft noun an arrangement with a bank that lets you take out more money than your account holds.

overdrawn adjective having taken out more money than there is in your bank account.

overdressed adjective dressed too

elaborately or formally.

overdrive noun **1** a mechanism in a motor vehicle providing an extra gear above the usual top gear. **2** a state of high activity.

overdue adjective not having arrived, happened, or been done at the expected or required time.

overestimate verb (overestimates, overestimating, overestimated) estimate that something is larger or better than it really is. noun an estimate which is too high.

overexpose verb (overexposes, overexposing, overexposed) **1** subject photographic film to too much light. **2** (overexposed) seen too much on television, in the newspapers, etc.

overflow verb **1** flow over the brim of a container. **2** be too full or crowded. **3** (overflow with) be very full of an emotion. noun **1** the excess not able to be accommodated by a space. **2** an outlet for excess water.

overground adverb & adjective on or above the ground.

overgrown adjective **1** covered with plants that have grown wild. **2** having grown too large.

overhang verb (overhangs, overhanging, overhung) project outwards over. noun an overhanging part.

overhaul verb **1** examine and repair something. **2** Brit. overtake. noun an act of overhauling something.

overhead adverb & adjective above your head. noun (overheads) expenses incurred in running a business or organization.

overhear verb (overhears, overhearing, overheard) hear something accidentally.

overheat verb make or become too hot.

overindulge verb (overindulges, overindulging, overindulged) **1** have too much of something enjoyable. **2** give in to the wishes of someone too easily. ■ **overindulgence** noun.

overjoyed adjective extremely happy.

overkill noun an excessive amount of something.

overland adjective & adverb by land.

overlap verb (overlaps, overlapping, overlapped) **1** extend over something so as to cover it partially. **2** (of two events) occur at the same time for part of their duration. noun an overlapping part or amount.

overlay verb (overlays, overlaying, overlaid) **1** coat the surface of. **2** add a quality, feeling, etc. to. noun a covering.

overleaf adverb on the other side of the page.

overload verb **1** load too heavily. **2** put too great a demand on. noun an excessive amount.

overlook verb **1** fail to notice. **2** ignore or disregard. **3** have a view of something from above.

overlord noun a ruler.

overly adverb excessively.

overmuch adverb & pronoun too much.

overnight adverb & adjective **1** during or for a night. **2** happening suddenly or very quickly.

overpass noun a bridge by which a road or railway line passes over another.

overplay verb give too much importance to.

overpower verb (overpowers, overpowering, overpowered) **1** defeat through having greater strength. **2** overwhelm.

overpriced adjective too expensive.

overqualified adjective too highly qualified.

overrated adjective rated more highly than is deserved.

overreach verb (overreach yourself) fail through being too ambitious or trying too hard.

overreact verb react more strongly than is justified. ■ **overreaction** noun.

override verb (overrides, overriding, overrode; past participle overridden) **1** use your authority to reject someone else's decision or order. **2** interrupt the action of an automatic device. **3** be more important than. **noun** a device on a machine for overriding an automatic process.

overrule verb (overrules, overruling, overruled) use your authority to reject someone else's decision or order.

overrun verb (overruns, overrunning, overran; past participle overrun) **1** occupy a place in large numbers. **2** use more time or money than expected.

overseas adverb & adjective in or to a foreign country.

oversee verb (oversees, overseeing, oversaw; past participle overseen) supervise. ■ **overseer** noun.

oversexed adjective having unusually strong sexual desires.

overshadow verb **1** tower above and cast a shadow over. **2** make something sad or less enjoyable. **3** appear more important or successful than.

overshoot verb (overshoots, overshooting, overshot) go past the place you intended to stop at.

oversight noun an unintentional failure to notice or do something.

oversimplify verb (oversimplifies, oversimplifying, oversimplified) simplify something so much that an inaccurate impression of it is given.

oversized or **oversize** adjective bigger than the usual size.

oversleep verb (oversleeps, oversleeping, overslept) sleep later than you intended to.

overspend verb (overspends, overspending, overspent) spend too much.

overspill noun Brit. people who move from an overcrowded area to live elsewhere.

overstate verb (overstates, overstating, overstated) state too strongly; exaggerate. ■ **overstatement** noun.

overstay verb stay longer than is allowed by.

overstep verb (oversteps, overstepping, overstepped) go beyond a limit.

overstretch verb make excessive demands on a resource.

oversubscribed adjective offering too few places to satisfy demand.

overt adjective done or shown openly. ■ **overtly** adverb.

overtake verb (overtakes, overtaking, overtook; past participle overtaken) **1** pass while travelling in the same direction. **2** suddenly affect.

overthrow verb (overthrows, overthrowing, overthrew; past participle overthrown) remove from power by force. **noun** a removal from power.

overtime noun time worked in addition to normal working hours.

overtone noun a subtle or secondary quality or implication.

overture noun **1** an orchestral piece at the beginning of a musical work. **2** an orchestral composition in one movement. **3** (overtures) approaches made with the aim of opening negotiations or establishing a relationship.

overturn verb **1** turn over and come to rest upside down. **2** abolish or reverse a decision, system, etc.

overuse verb (overuses, overusing, overused) use too much. **noun** excessive use.

overview noun a general review or summary.

overweening adjective showing too much confidence or pride.

overweight adjective heavier or fatter than is usual or desirable.

overwhelm verb **1** bury or drown beneath a huge mass. **2** overpower. **3** have a strong emotional effect on.

overwork verb **1** work too hard. **2** use a word or idea too much. **noun** excessive work.

overwrite verb (overwrites, overwriting, overwrote; past participle overwritten) **1** write on top of other writing. **2** destroy computer data by entering new data in its place.

overwrought adjective **1** in a state of nervous excitement or anxiety. **2** too elaborate or complicated.

ovulate /ov-yuu-layt/ **verb** (**ovulates, ovulating, ovulated**) (of a woman or female animal) discharge ova (reproductive cells) from the ovary. ■ **ovulation** noun.

ovum /oh-vuhm/ **noun** (plural **ova**) a female reproductive cell, which can develop into an embryo if fertilized by a male cell.

owe **verb** (**owes, owing, owed**) **1** be required to give money or goods to someone in return for something received. **2** be obliged to show someone gratitude, respect, etc. **3** (**owe to**) have something because of.

owing **adjective** yet to be paid or supplied. □ **owing to** because of.

owl **noun** a bird of prey with large eyes, which is active at night.

owlish **adjective** resembling an owl.

own **adjective & pronoun** belonging to or done by the person specified. **verb 1** possess. **2** formal admit that something is the case. **3** (**own up**) admit that you have done something wrong or embarrassing. □ **come into your own** become fully effective. **hold your own** remain in a strong position.

owner **noun** a person who owns something. ■ **ownership** noun.

ox **noun** (plural **oxen**) **1** a cow or bull. **2** a castrated bull.

Oxbridge **noun** Oxford and Cambridge universities classed together.

oxidation **noun** the process of oxidizing, or the result of being oxidized.

oxide **noun** a compound of oxygen with another substance.

oxidize or **oxidise** **verb** (**oxidizes, oxidizing, oxidized**) cause to combine with oxygen. ■ **oxidization** noun.

oxtail **noun** the tail of an ox, used in making soup.

oxygen **noun** a colourless, odourless gas that forms about 20 per cent of the earth's atmosphere.

oxygenate **verb** (**oxygenates, oxygenating, oxygenated**) supply or treat with oxygen.

oxymoron /ok-si-**mor**-on/ **noun** a figure of speech in which apparently contradictory terms appear together (e.g. *bittersweet*).

oyster **noun** **1** a shellfish with two hinged shells, some kinds of which are edible. **2** a shade of greyish white. □ **the world is your oyster** you have a wide range of opportunities.

oz **abbreviation** ounces.

ozone **noun** **1** a strong-smelling, poisonous form of oxygen. **2** informal fresh, invigorating air. □ **ozone layer** a layer in the stratosphere containing a lot of ozone, which protects the earth from the sun's ultraviolet radiation.

Pp

P or **p** **noun** (plural **Ps** or **P's**) the sixteenth letter of the alphabet. **abbreviation 1** page. **2** Brit. penny or pence.

PA **abbreviation 1** Brit. personal assistant. **2** public address.

p.a. **abbreviation** per year.

> [i] short for Latin *per annum*.

pace **noun 1** a single step taken when walking or running. **2** rate of motion or development. **verb** (**paces, pacing, paced**) **1** walk at a steady speed. **2** measure a distance by counting the number of steps taken to cover it. **3** (**pace yourself**) do something at a controlled and steady rate. □ **keep pace with** progress at the same speed as. **put someone through their paces** make someone demonstrate their abilities.

pacemaker noun a device for stimulating and regulating the heart muscle.

pachyderm /pak-i-derm/ noun an elephant or other very large mammal with thick skin.

pacific adjective **1** formal peaceful. **2 (Pacific)** having to do with the Pacific Ocean.

pacifism noun the belief that disputes should be settled by peaceful means and that violence should never be used. ■ **pacifist** noun & adjective.

pacify verb (**pacifies, pacifying, pacified**) **1** make someone less angry or agitated. **2** make a country peaceful. ■ **pacification** noun.

pack noun **1** a cardboard or paper container and the items inside it. **2** Brit. a set of playing cards. **3** a group of animals that live and hunt together. **4** chiefly disapproving a group of similar things or people. **5 (the pack)** the main body of competitors following the leader in a race. **6** Rugby a team's forwards. **7 (Pack)** an organized group of Cub Scouts or Brownies. **8** a rucksack. **9** an absorbent pad used for treating an injury. verb **1** fill a bag with items needed for travel. **2** put something in a container for transport or storage. **3** cram a large number of things into. **4** (**packed**) crowded. **5** cover, surround, or fill. □ **pack ice** a mass of ice floating in the sea. **pack in** informal give up an activity or job. **pack off** informal send somewhere without much notice. **pack up** Brit. informal (of a machine) break down. **send packing** informal dismiss abruptly.

package noun **1** an object or group of objects wrapped in paper or packed in a box. **2** N. Amer. a packet. **3** a set of proposals or terms as a whole. verb (**packages, packaging, packaged**) **1** put into a box or wrapping. **2** present something in an attractive way.

packet noun **1** a paper or cardboard container or parcel. **2 (a packet)** informal a lot of money.

packhorse noun a horse that is used to carry loads.

pact noun a formal agreement between individuals or parties.

pacy adjective fast-moving.

pad noun **1** a thick piece of soft or absorbent material. **2** the fleshy underpart of an animal's foot or of a human finger. **3** a protective guard worn by a sports player. **4** a number of sheets of blank paper fastened together at one edge. **5** a structure or area used for helicopter take-off and landing or for launching rockets. **6** informal a person's home. verb (**pads, padding, padded**) **1** fill or cover with padding. **2** (**pad out**) lengthen a speech or piece of writing with unnecessary material. **3** walk with quiet, steady steps.

padding noun **1** soft material used to pad or stuff something. **2** unnecessary material added to lengthen a book, speech, etc.

paddle noun **1** a short pole with a broad end, used to propel a small boat. **2** a paddle-shaped implement for stirring or mixing. **3** a short-handled bat used e.g. in table tennis. verb (**paddles, paddling, paddled**) **1** walk with bare feet in shallow water. **2** propel a boat with a paddle or paddles. **3** (of a bird or other animal) swim with short fast strokes. □ **paddle steamer** a boat powered by steam and propelled by large wheels which move the water as they turn.

paddock noun **1** a small field or enclosure for horses. **2** an enclosure where horses or cars are displayed before a race.

paddy[1] noun (plural **paddies**) a field where rice is grown.

paddy[2] noun Brit. informal a fit of temper.

padlock noun a detachable lock which is attached by a hinged hook. verb secure with a padlock.

paean /pee-uhn/ noun formal a song of praise or triumph.

paediatrics /pee-di-at-riks/ (US spelling **pediatrics**) noun the branch of medicine concerned with children and their diseases. ■ **paediatric** adjective **paediatrician** noun.

paedophile /**pee**-duh-fyl/ (US spelling **pedophile**) **noun** a person who is sexually attracted to children. ■ **paedophilia** noun.

paella /py-**el**-luh/ **noun** a Spanish dish of rice, chicken, seafood, etc.

pagan noun a person who holds religious beliefs other than those of the main world religions. **adjective** relating to pagans or their beliefs. ■ **paganism** noun.

page¹ **noun 1** one side of a leaf of a book, magazine, etc. **2** both sides of such a leaf considered as a single unit. **3** a section of data displayed on a computer screen. **verb (pages, paging, paged) (page through)** leaf through.

page² **noun 1** a boy or young man employed in a hotel to run errands, open doors, etc. **2** a young boy who attends a bride at a wedding. **3** historical a boy in training for knighthood. **verb (pages, paging, paged)** summon someone over a public address system or with a pager.

pageant /**pa**-juhnt/ **noun** an entertainment performed by people in elaborate or historical costumes.

pageantry noun elaborate display or ceremony.

pager noun a small device which bleeps or vibrates to inform you that it has received a message.

paginate noun (paginates, paginating, paginated) give numbers to the pages of a book, magazine, etc. ■ **pagination** noun.

pagoda noun a Hindu or Buddhist temple or other sacred building.

paid past and past participle of **PAY**. □ **put paid to** informal stop something abruptly.

pail noun a bucket.

pain noun 1 a strongly unpleasant bodily sensation caused e.g. by illness or injury. **2** mental suffering. **3** informal an annoying or boring person or thing. **4 (pains)** great care or trouble. **verb 1** cause pain to. **2 (pained)** showing or suffering pain. □ **on** (or **under**) **pain of** with the threat of being punished by.

painful adjective 1 suffering or causing pain. **2** informal very bad. ■ **painfully** adverb.

painkiller noun a medicine for relieving pain.

painless adjective 1 not causing pain. **2** involving little effort or stress. ■ **painlessly** adverb.

painstaking adjective very careful and thorough. ■ **painstakingly** adverb.

paint noun a coloured substance which is spread over a surface to give a thin decorative or protective coating. **verb 1** apply paint to. **2** apply a liquid to a surface with a brush. **3** produce a picture with paint. **4** give a description of.

painter¹ **noun 1** an artist who paints pictures. **2** a person who paints buildings.

painter² **noun** a rope attached to the bow of a boat for tying it to a quay.

painting noun 1 the action of painting. **2** a painted picture.

paintwork noun painted surfaces in a building or on a vehicle.

pair noun 1 a set of two things used together or seen as a unit. **2** an article consisting of two joined or corresponding parts. **3** two people or animals related in some way or considered together. **verb 1** join or connect to form a pair. **2 (pair off** or **up)** form a couple.

paisley noun an intricate pattern of curved feather-shaped figures.

pajamas US spelling of **PYJAMAS**.

pal informal **noun** a friend. **verb (pals, palling, palled) (pal up)** form a friendship.

palace noun a large building where a king, queen, president, etc. lives.

palaeontology /pa-li-on-**tol**-uh-ji/ (US spelling **paleontology**) **noun** the study of fossil animals and plants. ■ **palaeontologist** noun.

palatable adjective 1 pleasant to taste. **2** acceptable.

palate noun 1 the roof of the mouth. **2** a person's ability to distinguish between different flavours.

palatial /puh-**lay**-sh'l/ adjective impressively spacious.

palaver /puh-**lah**-ver/ noun informal a lot of fuss about something.

pale[1] adjective **1** of a light shade or colour. **2** (of a person's face) having little colour, especially as a result of illness or shock. verb (**pales**, **paling**, **paled**) **1** become pale in your face. **2** seem or become less important.

pale[2] noun **1** a wooden stake used with others to form a fence. **2** a boundary. □ **beyond the pale** outside the boundaries of acceptable behaviour.

palette /**pa**-lit/ noun **1** a thin board on which an artist lays and mixes paints. **2** the range of colours used by an artist. □ **palette knife** a blunt knife with a flexible blade, for applying or removing paint.

palimpsest noun a parchment on which writing has been applied over earlier writing.

palindrome noun a word or phrase that reads the same backwards as forwards, e.g. *madam*.

paling noun **1** a fence made from stakes. **2** a stake used in such a fence.

palisade noun a fence of stakes or iron railings.

pall[1] /pawl/ noun **1** a cloth spread over a coffin, hearse, or tomb. **2** a dark cloud of smoke or dust. **3** a general atmosphere of gloom or fear. □ **pall-bearer** a person helping to carry a coffin at a funeral.

pall[2] /pawl/ verb become less appealing through being too familiar.

palladium noun a rare silvery-white metallic element.

pallet[1] noun a straw mattress.

pallet[2] noun a portable platform on which goods can be moved, stacked, and stored.

palliate verb (**palliates**, **palliating**, **palliated**) **1** reduce the pain or bad effects of a disease, though not curing it. **2** make something bad easier to cope with. ■ **palliative** adjective.

pallid adjective **1** pale, especially because of poor health. **2** feeble.

pallor noun an unhealthy pale appearance.

pally adjective informal having a close, friendly relationship.

palm[1] noun an evergreen tree of warm regions, with a crown of large feathered or fan-shaped leaves.

palm[2] noun the inner surface of the hand between the wrist and fingers. verb (**palm off**) informal **1** sell or dispose of something in a way that is dishonest or unfair. **2** persuade someone to accept something that has little value.

palmistry noun the activity of interpreting a person's character or predicting their future by examining their palm. ■ **palmist** noun.

palmtop noun a computer small and light enough to be held in one hand.

palmy adjective comfortable and prosperous.

palomino /pa-luh-**mee**-noh/ noun (plural **palominos**) a tan-coloured horse with a white mane and tail.

palpable adjective **1** able to be touched or felt. **2** (of a feeling or quality) very strong or obvious. ■ **palpably** adverb.

palpate verb (**palpates**, **palpating**, **palpated**) (of a doctor or nurse) examine a part of the body by touching it.

palpitate verb (**palpitates**, **palpitating**, **palpitated**) **1** (of the heart) beat rapidly or irregularly. **2** shake; tremble.

palpitation noun **1** throbbing or trembling. **2** (**palpitations**) a noticeably rapid, strong, or irregular heartbeat.

palsy /**pawl**-zi/ noun (plural **palsies**) dated paralysis. ■ **palsied** adjective.

paltry adjective (**paltrier**, **paltriest**) **1** (of an amount) very small. **2** petty; trivial.

pampas noun large treeless plains in South America.

pamper verb (**pampers**, **pampering**,

pampered) give someone too much care and attention.

pamphlet noun a small booklet or leaflet. verb (**pamphlets, pamphleting, pamphleted**) distribute pamphlets.

pan[1] noun **1** a metal container for cooking food in. **2** a bowl fitted at either end of a pair of scales. **3** Brit. the bowl of a toilet. **4** a hollow in the ground in which water collects. verb (**pans, panning, panned**) **1** informal severely criticize. **2** (**pan out**) informal end up or conclude. **3** wash gravel in a pan to separate out gold.

pan[2] verb (**pans, panning, panned**) swing a video or film camera to give a panoramic effect or follow a subject.

pan- combining form including everything or everyone: *pan-African.*

panacea /pan-uh-**see**-uh/ noun something that will cure all diseases or solve all difficulties.

panache /puh-**nash**/ noun impressive skill and confidence.

panama noun a man's wide-brimmed hat made of straw-like material.

panatella noun a long, thin cigar.

pancake noun a thin, flat cake of batter, cooked in a frying pan.

pancreas /**pang**-kri-uhss/ noun (plural **pancreases**) a large gland behind the stomach which produces insulin and a liquid used in digestion. ■ **pancreatic** adjective.

panda noun **1** (also **giant panda**) a large black and white bear-like mammal native to bamboo forests in China. **2** (also **red panda**) a raccoon-like Himalayan mammal with thick reddish-brown fur and a bushy tail.

pandemic /pan-**dem**-ik/ adjective (of a disease) widespread over a whole country or large part of the world. noun an outbreak of such a disease.

pandemonium noun a state of uproar and confusion.

pander verb (**panders, pandering, pandered**) (**pander to**) indulge someone in an unreasonable desire or bad habit.

pane noun a single sheet of glass in a window or door.

panegyric /pa-ni-**ji**-rik/ noun a speech or text in praise of someone or something.

panel noun **1** a section in a door, vehicle, garment, etc. **2** a flat board on which instruments or controls are fixed. **3** a small group of people brought together to investigate a matter, or to take part in a broadcast quiz or game. ■ **panelled** (US spelling **paneled**) adjective **panellist** (US spelling **panelist**) noun.

pang noun a sudden sharp pain or painful emotion.

panic noun **1** sudden uncontrollable fear or anxiety. **2** frenzied hurry to do something. verb (**panics, panicking, panicked**) feel sudden uncontrollable fear or anxiety. ■ **panicky** adjective.

pannier noun each of a pair of bags, boxes, or baskets fitted on either side of a bicycle or motorcycle, or carried by a horse or donkey.

panoply /**pan**-uh-pli/ noun a large and impressive collection or number of things.

panorama noun **1** a broad view of a surrounding region. **2** a complete survey of a subject or sequence of events. ■ **panoramic** adjective.

pan pipes plural noun a musical instrument made from a row of short pipes fixed together.

pansy noun **1** a plant with flowers in rich colours. **2** informal an effeminate or homosexual man.

pant verb breathe with short, quick breaths. noun short, quick breath.

pantaloons plural noun **1** women's baggy trousers gathered at the ankles. **2** (in the past) men's close-fitting trousers fastened below the calf or at the foot.

pantechnicon noun Brit. dated a large van for transporting furniture.

pantheism /**pan**-thee-i-z'm/ noun the belief that God is all around us and is present in all things. ■ **pantheist** noun **pantheistic** adjective.

pantheon /**pan**-thi-uhn/ noun **1** all

the gods of a people or religion. **2** an ancient temple dedicated to all the gods. **3** a group of particularly famous or important people.

panther noun **1** a black leopard. **2** N. Amer. a puma or a jaguar.

panties plural noun informal brief underpants worn by women and girls.

pantile /pan-tyl/ noun a curved roof tile, fitted to overlap its neighbour.

panto noun (plural **pantos**) Brit. informal a pantomime.

pantomime noun Brit. an entertainment in the theatre involving music and slapstick comedy.

pantry noun (plural **pantries**) a small room or cupboard for storing food.

pants plural noun **1** Brit. underpants or knickers. **2** chiefly N. Amer. trousers.

pantyhose plural noun N. Amer. women's thin nylon tights.

pap noun **1** bland soft or semi-liquid food suitable for babies or invalids. **2** trivial books, television programmes, etc.

papa noun N. Amer. or dated your father.

papacy noun (plural **papacies**) the position or role of the pope.

papal adjective relating to the pope or the papacy.

paparazzo /pa-puh-**rat**-zoh/ noun (plural **paparazzi** /pa-puh-**rat**-zi/) a photographer who pursues celebrities to get photographs of them.

papaya /puh-**py**-uh/ noun a tropical fruit like a long melon, with orange flesh and small black seeds.

paper noun **1** material manufactured in thin sheets from the pulp of wood, used for writing or printing on or as wrapping material. **2** (**papers**) sheets of paper covered with writing or printing. **3** a newspaper. **4** a government report or policy document. **5** an essay or dissertation read at a conference or published in a journal. **6** a set of examination questions. verb (**papers, papering, papered**) **1** cover a wall with wallpaper. **2** (**paper over**) conceal or disguise an awkward problem instead of resolving it. □ **on**

paper 1 in writing. **2** in theory rather than in reality. **paper clip** a piece of bent wire or plastic used for holding sheets of paper together. **paper round** a regular delivery of newspapers to people's homes. **paper tiger** a person or thing that appears threatening but is actually weak.

paperback noun a book bound in stiff paper or flexible card.

paperknife noun a blunt knife used for opening envelopes.

paperweight noun a small, heavy object for weighting down loose papers.

paperwork noun routine work involving written documents.

papier mâché /pa-pi-ay **mash**-ay/ noun a mixture of paper and glue that becomes hard when dry.

papist /**pay**-pist/ noun disapproving a Roman Catholic.

paprika /**pap**-ri-kuh, puh-**pree**-kuh/ noun a powdered spice made from sweet red peppers.

papyrus /puh-**py**-ruhss/ noun (plural **papyri** /puh-**py**-rl/ or **papyruses**) a material made in ancient Egypt from the stem of a water plant, used for writing or painting on.

par noun Golf the number of strokes a first-class player normally requires for a particular hole or course. □ **above** (or **below** or **under**) **par** above (or below) the usual or expected level or amount. **on a par with** equal to.

parable noun a simple story that teaches a moral or spiritual lesson.

parabola /puh-**rab**-uh-luh/ noun (plural **parabolas** or **parabolae** /puh-**rab**-uh-lee/) a curve of the kind formed by the intersection of a cone with a plane parallel to its side. ■ **parabolic** adjective.

paracetamol noun (plural same or **paracetamols**) Brit. a drug used to relieve pain and reduce fever.

parachute noun a cloth canopy which allows a person or heavy object attached to it to descend slowly when dropped from a high position. verb (**parachutes, parachuting, para-**

chuted) drop by parachute. ■ **parachutist** noun.

parade noun **1** a public procession. **2** a formal occasion when soldiers march or stand in line in order to be inspected or for display. **3** a series or succession. **4** a boastful or showy display. **5** Brit. a public square, promenade, or row of shops. verb (**parades, parading, paraded**) **1** walk, march, or display in a parade. **2** display something publicly in order to impress people or attract attention.

paradigm /**pa**-ruh-dym/ noun **1** a typical example, pattern, or model of something. **2** a model underlying the theories and practice of a scientific subject. ■ **paradigmatic** adjective.

paradise noun **1** (in some religions) heaven. **2** the Garden of Eden. **3** an ideal place or state.

paradox noun **1** a statement that sounds absurd or seems to contradict itself, but is in fact true. **2** a person or thing that combines two contradictory features or qualities. ■ **paradoxical** adjective **paradoxically** adverb.

paraffin noun **1** a waxy substance obtained from petroleum, used for sealing and waterproofing and in candles. **2** Brit. an oily liquid obtained from petroleum, used as a fuel.

paragliding noun a sport in which a person glides with a wide parachute after jumping from or being hauled to a height.

paragon noun a model of excellence or of a particular quality.

paragraph noun a distinct section of a piece of writing, beginning on a new line.

parakeet or **parrakeet** noun a small parrot with green feathers and a long tail.

parallax noun the apparent difference in the position of an object when viewed from different positions.

parallel adjective **1** (of lines or surfaces) side by side and having the same distance continuously between them. **2** occurring or existing at the same time or in a similar way; corresponding. noun **1** a person or thing that is similar to or can be compared to to another. **2** a similarity or comparison. **3** each of the imaginary parallel circles of latitude on the earth's surface. verb (**parallels, paralleling, paralleled**) **1** run or lie parallel to. **2** be similar or corresponding to.

☑ two *l*'s in the middle: paral*l*el.

parallelogram noun a figure with four straight sides and opposite sides parallel.

paralyse (US spelling **paralyze**) verb (**paralyses, paralysing, paralysed**) **1** make someone unable to move a part of their body. **2** prevent something from functioning normally.

paralysis /puh-**ral**-i-siss/ noun (plural **paralyses** /puh-**ral**-i-seez/) **1** the loss of the ability to move part of the body. **2** inability to do things or function.

paralytic adjective **1** relating to paralysis. **2** informal extremely drunk.

paramedic noun a person who is trained to do medical work but is not a fully qualified doctor.

parameter /puh-**ram**-i-ter/ noun a thing which decides or limits the way in which something can be done.

paramilitary adjective organized on similar lines to a military force. noun (plural **paramilitaries**) a member of a paramilitary organization.

paramount adjective **1** more important than anything else. **2** having supreme power.

paramour noun old use a lover.

paranoia noun a mental condition in which people wrongly believe that others are wanting to harm them, or that they are very important.

paranoid adjective **1** wrongly believing that other people want to harm you. **2** having to do with paranoia.

paranormal adjective beyond the scope of scientific knowledge.

parapet noun a low wall along the edge of a roof, bridge, or balcony.

paraphernalia noun the objects needed for a particular activity.

paraphrase verb (paraphrases, paraphrasing, paraphrased) express the meaning of something using different words. noun a rewording of a passage.

paraplegia /pa-ruh-**plee**-juh/ noun paralysis of the legs and lower body. ■ **paraplegic** adjective & noun.

paraquat noun a powerful weed-killer.

parasite noun 1 an animal or plant which lives on or inside another, and gets its food from it. 2 a person who relies on or benefits from someone else but gives nothing in return. ■ **parasitic** adjective **parasitism** noun.

parasol noun a light umbrella used to give shade from the sun.

paratroops plural noun troops equipped to be dropped by parachute from aircraft. ■ **paratrooper** noun.

parboil verb boil something until it is partly cooked.

parcel noun 1 an object or collection of objects wrapped in paper in order to be carried or sent by post. 2 a quantity or amount of something. verb (parcels, parcelling, parcelled; US spelling parcels, parceling, parceled) 1 (parcel up) make something into a parcel. 2 (parcel out) divide something between several people.

parch verb 1 make something dry through strong heat. 2 (parched) informal extremely thirsty.

parchment noun 1 (in the past) a stiff material made from the skin of a sheep or goat and used for writing on. 2 thick paper resembling parchment.

pardon noun 1 forgiveness for an error or offence. 2 a cancellation of the punishment for an offence. verb 1 forgive or excuse a person, mistake, or offence. 2 give an offender a pardon. exclamation used to ask a speaker to repeat something because you did not hear or understand it. ■ **pardonable** adjective.

pare verb (pares, paring, pared) 1 trim something by cutting away the outer edges. 2 (pare away or down) gradually reduce the amount of.

parent noun 1 a father or mother. 2 an animal or plant from which young or new ones are produced. 3 an organization or company which owns or controls a number of smaller organizations or companies. verb be or act as a parent to. ■ **parental** adjective **parenthood** noun.

parentage noun the identity and origins of your parents.

parenthesis /puh-**ren**-thi-siss/ noun (plural parentheses /puh-**ren**-thi-seez/) 1 a word or phrase giving extra information as an aside, indicated in writing by brackets, dashes, or commas. 2 (parentheses) a pair of round brackets () surrounding a word or phrase. ■ **parenthetic** (or **parenthetical**) adjective.

par excellence /par ek-suh-**lonss**/ adjective better or more than all others of the same kind: *a designer par excellence.*

pariah /puh-**ry**-uh/ noun a person who is rejected by others; an outcast.

parings plural noun thin strips pared off from something.

parish noun 1 (in the Christian Church) a district with its own church and church ministers. 2 Brit. the smallest unit of local government in rural areas.

parishioner noun a person who lives in a particular Church parish.

parity noun the quality of being equal with or equivalent to something.

park noun 1 a large public garden in a town. 2 a large area of land attached to a country house. 3 an area devoted to a particular purpose. 4 an area in which vehicles are parked. verb temporarily leave a vehicle somewhere.

parka noun a windproof hooded jacket.

Parkinson's disease noun a disease of the brain and nervous system marked by trembling, stiffness in the muscles, and slow, imprecise movement.

parky adjective Brit. informal chilly.

parlance noun a way of speaking.

parley noun (plural parleys) a meeting

between enemies to discuss terms for a truce. **verb** (**parleys, parleying, parleyed**) hold a parley.

parliament noun **1** (**Parliament**) (in the UK) the highest law-making body, consisting of the king or queen, the House of Lords, and the House of Commons. **2** a similar body in other countries. ■ **parliamentary** adjective.

☑ -*lia*- in the middle, not -*la*-: parl**ia**ment.

parliamentarian noun a member of a parliament. **adjective** relating to a parliament.

parlour (US spelling **parlor**) noun **1** dated a sitting room. **2** a shop providing particular goods or services.

parlous /par-luhss/ **adjective** old use dangerously uncertain; precarious.

Parmesan /par-mi-zan/ noun a hard, dry Italian cheese.

parochial /puh-roh-ki-uhl/ **adjective** **1** relating to a parish. **2** having a narrow outlook. ■ **parochialism** noun.

parody noun (plural **parodies**) a piece of writing, art, or music that deliberately copies the style of someone or something, in order to be funny. **verb** (**parodies, parodying, parodied**) produce a parody of.

parole noun the temporary or permanent release of a prisoner before the end of their sentence, on the condition that they behave well. **verb** (**paroles, paroling, paroled**) release a prisoner on parole.

paroxysm /pa-ruhk-si-z'm/ noun a sudden attack of pain, coughing, etc., or a sudden feeling of overwhelming emotion. ■ **paroxysmal** adjective.

parquet /par-kay/ noun flooring composed of wooden blocks arranged in a geometric pattern.

parrakeet ⇒ **PARAKEET**.

parricide noun the killing by someone of their own parent or other close relative.

parrot noun a tropical bird with brightly coloured feathers and a hooked bill, some kinds of which can copy human speech. **verb** (**parrots,**

parroting, parroted) repeat something unthinkingly. □ **parrot-fashion** repeated in an unthinking way.

parry verb (**parries, parrying, parried**) **1** ward off a weapon or attack. **2** say something in order to avoid answering a question directly. noun (plural **parries**) an act of parrying.

parse /parz/ verb analyse a sentence in terms of grammar.

parsimony /par-si-muh-ni/ noun extreme unwillingness to spend money. ■ **parsimonious** adjective.

parsley noun a herb with crinkly or flat leaves, used in cooking.

parsnip noun a long tapering cream-coloured root, eaten as a vegetable.

parson noun (in the Church of England) a parish priest. □ **parson's nose** a piece of fatty flesh at the tail end of a cooked turkey, goose, etc.

parsonage noun a house provided by the Church for a parson.

part noun **1** a piece or segment which is combined with others to make up a whole. **2** some but not all of something. **3** a role played by an actor or actress. **4** a person's contribution to an action or situation. **5** (**parts**) informal a region. **verb 1** move apart or divide to leave a central space. **2** (of two or more people) leave each other. **3** (**part with**) give up possession of; hand over. **adverb** partly. □ **part company** go in different directions. **part of speech** a category in which a word is placed according to its function in grammar, e.g. noun, adjective, and verb. **part song** a song with three or more voice parts and no musical accompaniment. **part-time** for only part of the usual working day or week. **take the part of** give support to.

partake verb (**partakes, partaking, partook**; past participle **partaken**) formal **1** (**partake in**) participate in. **2** (**partake of**) be characterized by. **3** (**partake of**) eat or drink.

partial adjective **1** not complete or whole. **2** favouring one side in a dispute. **3** (**partial to**) liking something. ■ **partiality** noun **partially** adverb.

participate verb (participates, participating, participated) join in something; take part. ■ **participant** noun **participation** noun **participatory** adjective.

participle noun Grammar a word formed from a verb (e.g. *going, gone, being, been*) and used as an adjective or noun (as in *burnt toast*).

particle noun 1 a tiny portion of matter. 2 a minute piece of matter smaller than an atom, e.g. an electron.

particular adjective 1 relating to an individual member of a group or class. 2 more than is usual. 3 very careful or concerned about something. noun a detail. □ **in particular** especially.

particularly adverb 1 more than is usual. 2 in particular; especially.

☑ particularly, not -culy.

parting noun 1 an act of leaving someone and going away. 2 Brit. a line of scalp which is visible when the hair is combed in different directions.

partisan /par-ti-zan/ noun 1 a committed supporter of a cause, group, or person. 2 a member of an armed group fighting secretly against an occupying force. adjective prejudiced.

partition noun 1 a structure that divides a space into separate areas. 2 division into parts. verb 1 divide into parts. 2 divide a room with a partition.

partly adverb not completely but to some extent.

partner noun 1 each of two people doing something as a pair. 2 the person you are having a sexual relationship with. 3 each of two or more people who are involved in a project or undertaking or who own a business. verb (partners, partnering, partnered) be the partner of. ■ **partnership** noun.

partook past of **PARTAKE**.

partridge noun (plural **partridge** or **partridges**) a game bird with brown feathers and a short tail.

parturition noun formal or technical the action of giving birth.

party noun (plural **parties**) 1 a social event with food and drink and sometimes dancing. 2 an organized political group that puts forward candidates for election to government. 3 a group of people taking part in an activity or trip. 4 a person or group forming one side in an agreement or dispute. verb (parties, partying, partied) informal enjoy yourself at a party. □ **be party to** be involved in. **party line** a policy officially adopted by a political party. **party wall** a wall between two adjoining houses or rooms.

parvenu /par-vuh-nyoo/ noun disapproving a person from a poor background who has recently joined a group of wealthy or famous people.

pascal noun a unit of pressure.

pass¹ verb 1 move or go onward, past, through, or across. 2 change from one state or condition to another. 3 transfer something to someone. 4 kick, hit, or throw the ball to a teammate. 5 (of time) go by. 6 spend time. 7 be done or said. 8 come to an end. 9 be successful in an examination or test. 10 declare something to be satisfactory. 11 approve a proposal or law by voting. 12 express an opinion or judgement. noun 1 an act of passing. 2 a success in an examination. 3 an official document which allows you to go somewhere or use something. 4 informal a sexual advance. 5 a particular state of affairs. □ **pass away** die. **pass off** happen in a particular way. **pass off as** pretend that something is something else. **pass out** become unconscious. **pass up** choose not to take up an opportunity.

pass² noun a route over or through mountains.

passable adjective 1 acceptable, but not outstanding. 2 able to be travelled along or on. ■ **passably** adverb.

passage noun 1 the passing of someone or something. 2 a way through or across something. 3 a journey by sea or air. **4** the right to pass through a place. **5** a short section from a text or musical composition.

passageway noun a corridor or other narrow passage between buildings or rooms.

passé /**pass**-ay/ adjective no longer fashionable.

passenger noun a person travelling in a car, bus, train, ship, or aircraft, other than the driver, pilot, or crew.

passer-by noun (plural **passers-by**) a person who happens to be walking past something or someone.

passim adverb occurring at various places throughout the text.

passing adjective **1** done quickly and casually. **2** (of a similarity) slight. noun **1** the ending of something. **2** a person's death.

passion noun **1** very strong emotion. **2** intense sexual love. **3** an intense enthusiasm for something. **4** (the Passion) Jesus's suffering and death on the cross. □ **passion flower** a climbing plant with distinctive flowers. **passion fruit** the edible fruit of some species of passion flower. **passion play** a play about Jesus's crucifixion.

passionate adjective showing or caused by passion. ■ **passionately** adverb.

passive adjective **1** accepting what happens without resistance. **2** Grammar (of a verb) having the form used when the subject is affected by the action of the verb (e.g. *they were killed* as opposed to the active form *he killed them*). □ **passive smoking** the inhaling of smoke from other people's cigarettes. ■ **passively** adverb **passivity** noun.

Passover noun the major Jewish spring festival, commemorating the liberation of the Israelites from slavery in Egypt.

passport noun an official document that identifies you as a citizen of a particular country and is required in order to enter and leave other countries.

password noun a secret word or

phrase used to gain admission.

past adjective **1** gone by in time and no longer existing. **2** (of time) that has gone by. **3** Grammar (of a tense of a verb) expressing a past action or state. noun **1** a past period or the events in it. **2** a person's or thing's history or earlier life. preposition **1** beyond in time or space. **2** in front of or from one side to the other of. **3** beyond the scope or power of. adverb **1** so as to pass from one side to the other. **2** used to indicate the passage of time. □ **past master** an expert in a particular activity. **past participle** Grammar the form of a verb which is used in perfect and passive tenses and sometimes as an adjective, e.g. *looked* in *have you looked?*

pasta noun dough formed into various shapes and cooked in boiling water.

paste noun **1** a soft, moist substance. **2** an adhesive made from water and starch. **3** a hard substance used in making imitation gems. verb (**pastes, pasting, pasted**) **1** coat or stick with paste. **2** (in computing) insert a section of text into a document.

pastel noun **1** a crayon made of powdered pigments bound with gum or resin. **2** a pale shade of a colour. adjective (of a colour) pale.

pasteurize or **pasteurise** verb (**pasteurizes, pasteurizing, pasteurized**) destroy the germs in milk by a process of heating and cooling. ■ **pasteurization** noun.

pastiche /pa-**steesh**/ noun a piece of writing or work of art produced in a style that imitates that of another work, artist, or period.

pastille /**pass**-tuhl/ noun a small sweet or lozenge.

pastime noun an activity done regularly for enjoyment.

pastor noun a minister in charge of a Christian Church or group.

pastoral adjective **1** relating to the farming or grazing of sheep or cattle. **2** (of a creative work) showing country life. **3** relating to the work of a

Christian minister in giving personal and spiritual guidance. **4** relating to a teacher's responsibility for the well-being of students. **noun** a pastoral poem, picture, or piece of music.

pastrami /pass-**trah**-mi/ **noun** highly seasoned smoked beef.

pastry **noun** (plural **pastries**) **1** a dough of flour, fat, and water, used in baked dishes such as pies. **2** a cake consisting of sweet pastry with a filling.

pasture **noun** land covered with grass, suitable for grazing cattle or sheep. **verb** (**pastures, pasturing, pastured**) put animals to graze in a pasture. ◼ **pasturage noun**.

pasty[1] or **pastie** /**pass**-ti/ **noun** (plural **pasties**) Brit. a folded pastry case filled with seasoned meat and vegetables.

pasty[2] /**pay**-sti/ **adjective** (**pastier, pastiest**) **1** of or like paste. **2** (of a person's skin) unhealthily pale.

pat[1] **verb** (**pats, patting, patted**) tap quickly and gently with the flat of your hand. **noun** **1** an act of patting. **2** a compact mass of a soft substance.

pat[2] **adjective** (of something said) too quick or easy; not convincing. ◻ **have off pat** know facts or words perfectly so that you can repeat them without hesitation.

patch **noun** **1** a piece of material used to mend a hole or strengthen a weak point. **2** a small area differing in colour or texture from its surroundings. **3** a cover worn over an injured eye. **4** a small plot of land. **5** Brit. informal a period of time. **6** Brit. informal an area for which someone is responsible or in which they operate. **verb** **1** mend, strengthen, or protect with a patch. **2** (**patch up**) informal treat injuries or repair damage quickly or temporarily. ◻ **not a patch on** Brit. informal much less good than.

patchwork **noun** needlework in which small pieces of cloth of different colours are sewn edge to edge.

patchy **adjective** (**patchier, patchiest**) **1** existing or happening in small, isolated areas. **2** uneven in quality;

inconsistent.

pate /rhymes with gate/ **noun** old use a person's head.

pâté /**pa**-tay/ **noun** a rich savoury paste made from meat, fish, etc.

patella /puh-**tel**-luh/ **noun** (plural **patellae** /puh-**tel**-lee/) the kneecap.

patent /**pay**-t'nt, **pa**-t'nt/ **noun** a government licence giving someone the sole right to make, use, or sell their invention for a set period. **verb** obtain a patent for. **adjective** /**pay**-t'nt/ **1** easily recognizable; obvious. **2** made and marketed under a patent. ◻ **patent leather** glossy varnished leather.

paterfamilias /pay-ter-fuh-**mi**-li-ass/ **noun** the man who is the head of a family or household.

paternal **adjective** **1** of or like a father. **2** related through the father. ◼ **paternally adverb**.

paternalism **noun** the policy of protecting the people you have control over but also of restricting their freedom. ◼ **paternalist** noun & adjective **paternalistic** adjective.

paternity **noun** **1** the state of being a father. **2** descent from a father.

paternoster **noun** (in the Roman Catholic Church) the Lord's Prayer.

path **noun** **1** a way or track laid down for walking or made by repeated treading. **2** the direction in which a person or thing moves. **3** a course of action.

pathetic **adjective** **1** arousing pity or sadness. **2** informal weak or inadequate. ◼ **pathetically adverb**.

pathological **adjective** **1** of or caused by a disease. **2** informal extreme or compulsive. ◼ **pathologically adverb**.

pathology **noun** **1** the study of the causes and effects of diseases. **2** the typical behaviour of a disease. ◼ **pathologist** noun.

pathos /**pay**-thoss/ **noun** a quality that arouses pity or sadness.

pathway **noun** a path or route.

patience **noun** **1** the ability to accept delay, trouble, or suffering without becoming angry or upset. **2** Brit. a card game for one player.

WORD FORMATION ⓘ

-pathy

1 Some words ending in *-pathy* relate to the sense 'feeling', e.g.:

antipathy	strong dislike
apathy	lack of interest or enthusiasm
empathy	understanding and sharing the feelings of someone else
sympathy	the feeling of being sorry for someone else
telepathy	communication of thoughts by means other than the known senses.

2 Other *-pathy* words are connected to medical disorders and treatments, such as:

homeopathy	the treatment of diseases by tiny doses of substances that would normally produce symptoms of the disease
osteopathy	a system of complementary medicine involving manipulation of the bones and muscles.

-pathy comes from the ancient Greek word *patheia*, 'suffering, feeling'.

---

patient **adjective** having or showing patience. **noun** a person receiving or registered to receive medical treatment. ■ **patiently** adverb.

patina /pa-ti-nuh/ **noun 1** a green or brown film on the surface of old bronze. **2** a soft glow on wooden furniture produced by age and polishing.

patio **noun** (plural **patios**) a paved area outside a house.

patisserie /puh-**tiss**-uh-ri/ **noun** a shop where pastries and cakes are sold.

patois /**pat**-wah/ **noun** (plural **patois** /**pat**-wahz/) the dialect of a region.

patriarch /**pay**-tri-ark/ **noun 1** a man who is the head of a family or tribe. **2** a biblical figure regarded as a father of the human race. **3** a respected older man.

patriarchy **noun** (plural **patriarchies**) a society led or controlled by men. ■ **patriarchal** adjective.

patrician /puh-**tri**-sh'n/ **noun** an aristocrat. **adjective** relating to or characteristic of aristocrats.

patricide **noun 1** the killing by someone of their own father. **2** a person who kills their father.

patrimony /**pa**-tri-muh-ni/ **noun** (plural **patrimonies**) property inherited from your father or male ancestor.

patriot **noun** a person who strongly supports their country and is prepared to defend it. ■ **patriotic** adjective **patriotism** noun.

patrol **noun 1** a person or group sent to keep watch over an area. **2** the action of patrolling an area. **verb** (**patrols, patrolling, patrolled**) keep watch over an area by regularly walking or travelling around it.

patron **noun 1** a person who gives financial support to a person or organization. **2** a regular customer of a restaurant, hotel, etc. ▫ **patron saint** a saint who is believed to protect a particular place or group of people.

patronage **noun 1** support given by a patron. **2** custom attracted by a restaurant, hotel, etc.

patronize or **patronise** **verb** (**patronizes, patronizing, patronized**) **1** treat someone as if they lack experience or are not very intelligent. **2** go regularly to a restaurant, hotel, etc.

patter¹ **verb** (**patters, pattering, pattered**) make a repeated light tapping sound. **noun** a repeated light tapping sound.

patter² **noun** fast continuous talk.

pattern **noun 1** a repeated decorative

design. 2 a regular form or order in which a series of things occur. **3** a model, design, or set of instructions for making something. **4** an example for others to follow. verb **1** decorate something with a pattern. **2** give a regular form to.

patty noun (plural **patties**) a small pie or pasty.

paucity /paw-si-ti/ noun smallness or scarcity of something.

paunch noun an abdomen or stomach that is large and sticks out. ■ **paunchy** adjective.

pauper noun a very poor person.

pause verb (**pauses, pausing, paused**) stop talking or doing something for a short time before continuing again. noun a temporary stop.

pave verb (**paves, paving, paved**) cover a piece of ground with flat stones. ■ **paving** noun.

pavement noun **1** Brit. a raised path for pedestrians at the side of a road. **2** a horizontal expanse of bare rock.

pavilion noun **1** Brit. a building at a sports ground used for changing and taking refreshments. **2** a summer house in a park or large garden. **3** a temporary display stand at a trade exhibition.

pavlova noun a dessert consisting of a meringue base covered with whipped cream and fruit.

paw noun an animal's foot that has claws and pads. verb **1** feel or scrape something with a paw or hoof. **2** informal touch someone in a way that is clumsy or unwanted.

pawn[1] noun **1** a chess piece of the smallest size and value. **2** a person used by others for their own purposes.

pawn[2] verb leave an object with a pawnbroker in exchange for money. □ **in pawn** held by a pawnbroker.

pawnbroker noun a person who is licensed to lend money in exchange for an object that is left with them, and which they can sell if the borrower fails to pay the money back.

pawnshop noun a pawnbroker's

shop.

pawpaw noun Brit. a papaya.

pay verb (**pays, paying, paid**) **1** give someone money for work or goods. **2** give a sum of money that is owed. **3** be profitable, or result in an advantage. **4** suffer something as a consequence of an action. **5** give someone attention, respect, or a compliment. **6** make a visit or a call to. noun money that you get for work you have done. □ **pay back** take revenge on someone. **pay-off** informal a payment made to someone as a bribe or so that they will not cause trouble. ■ **payable** adjective.

PAYE abbreviation pay as you earn.

payee noun a person to whom money is paid.

paymaster noun an official who pays troops or workers.

payment noun **1** the process of paying someone or of being paid. **2** an amount that is paid.

payola /pay-oh-luh/ noun N. Amer. the illegal payment of money to someone in return for their promoting a product in the media.

payroll noun a list of a company's employees and the amount of money they are to be paid.

PC abbreviation **1** personal computer. **2** police constable. **3** politically correct, or political correctness.

PE abbreviation physical education.

pea noun an edible round green seed growing in pods on a climbing plant. □ **pea-souper** Brit. a very thick fog.

peace noun **1** freedom from disturbance, noise, or anxiety. **2** freedom from war, or the ending of war.

peaceable adjective **1** wanting to avoid war. **2** free from conflict; peaceful. ■ **peaceably** adverb.

peaceful adjective **1** free from disturbance or noise. **2** not involving war or violence. **3** wanting to avoid conflict. ■ **peacefully** adverb.

peach noun **1** a round fruit with yellow skin flushed with red and juicy yellow flesh, with a rough stone inside. **2** a pinkish-orange colour.

peacock noun a large, colourful bird with very long tail feathers that can be fanned out in display.

peahen noun the female of the peacock.

peak noun **1** the pointed top of a mountain, or a mountain with a pointed top. **2** a stiff brim at the front of a cap. **3** the point of highest intensity, activity, or achievement. verb reach a maximum or the highest point. adjective **1** greatest; maximum. **2** involving the greatest number of people; busiest.

peaked¹ adjective (of a cap) having a peak.

peaked² or informal **peaky** adjective pale from illness or tiredness.

peal noun **1** the loud ringing sound of a bell or bells. **2** a loud sound of thunder or laughter. **3** a set of bells. verb ring or sound loudly.

peanut noun **1** an oval edible seed that develops in a pod underground. **2** (**peanuts**) informal a very small sum of money. □ **peanut butter** a spread made from ground roasted peanuts.

pear noun a green edible fruit which has a narrow top and rounded base.

pearl noun **1** a small hard, shiny white ball that sometimes forms inside the shell of an oyster and has great value as a gem. **2** a thing that is highly valued. □ **pearl barley** barley that is reduced to small round grains by grinding. ■ **pearly** adjective.

pearlescent adjective having a soft iridescent sheen resembling that of mother-of-pearl.

peasant noun (in the past, or in poor countries) a poor smallholder or agricultural labourer. ■ **peasantry** noun.

pease plural noun old use peas. □ **pease pudding** a dish of dried peas boiled and mashed to a pulp.

peat noun a soft brown or black substance formed in damp areas from decayed plants. ■ **peaty** adjective.

pebble noun a small, smooth round stone. □ **pebble-dash** mortar mixed with small pebbles, used to coat the outside of houses. ■ **pebbly** adjective.

pecan /pee-k'n/ noun a smooth nut obtained from a hickory tree of the southern US.

peccadillo /pek-kuh-**dil**-loh/ noun (plural **peccadilloes** or **peccadillos**) a small sin or fault.

peck¹ verb **1** (of a bird) strike or bite with its beak. **2** kiss someone lightly or casually. noun **1** an act of pecking. **2** a light or casual kiss. □ **pecking order** the order of importance that people or animals give each other within a group.

peck² noun a measure of dry goods, equal to a quarter of a bushel.

pecker noun (**keep your pecker up**) Brit. informal remain cheerful.

peckish adjective informal hungry.

pectin noun a substance present in ripe fruits, used as a setting agent in jams and jellies.

pectoral adjective relating to the breast or chest. noun each of four large paired muscles which cover the front of the ribcage.

peculiar adjective **1** strange or odd. **2** (**peculiar to**) belonging only to. ■ **peculiarly** adverb.

☑ -ar, not -er: peculiar.

peculiarity noun (plural **peculiarities**) **1** a feature or habit that is strange or unusual, or that belongs only to a particular person, thing, or place. **2** the state of being peculiar.

pecuniary /pi-**kyoo**-ni-uh-ri/ adjective formal relating to money.

pedagogue /**ped**-uh-gog/ noun formal a teacher. ■ **pedagogy** noun.

pedal noun **1** each of a pair of levers that you press with your foot to power a bicycle. **2** a lever that you press with your foot to operate a throttle, brake, or clutch in a motor vehicle. **3** a similar lever on a piano or organ used to sustain or soften the tone. verb (**pedals**, **pedalling**, **pedalled**; US spelling **pedals**, **pedaling**, **pedaled**) work the pedals of a bicycle to move along.

i don't confuse **pedal** with **peddle**, which means 'sell goods'.

pedalo /ped-uh-loh/ **noun** (plural **pedalos** or **pedaloes**) Brit. a small pedal-operated pleasure boat.

pedant **noun** a person who cares too much about small details or rules. ■ **pedantic** adjective **pedantry** noun.

peddle **verb** (**peddles**, **peddling**, **peddled**) **1** sell goods by going from house to house. **2** sell an illegal drug or stolen item. **3** disapproving spread or promote an idea or view.

i don't confuse **peddle** with **pedal**.

peddler ⇒ **PEDLAR**.

pederasty /ped-uh-rass-ti/ **noun** sexual intercourse between a man and a boy. ■ **pederast** noun.

pedestal **noun 1** the base or support on which a statue, obelisk, or column is mounted. **2** the supporting column of a washbasin or toilet.

pedestrian **noun** a person who is walking rather than travelling in a vehicle. **adjective** dull.

pediatrics US spelling of **PAEDIATRICS**.

pedicure **noun** treatment to improve the appearance of the feet and toenails.

pedigree **noun 1** the record of an animal's origins, showing that all the animals from which it is descended are of the same breed. **2** a person's family history and background.

pediment **noun** the triangular upper part of the front of a classical building, above the columns.

pedlar or **peddler** **noun 1** a trader who peddles goods. **2** a person who sells illegal drugs or stolen goods. **3** disapproving a person who spreads or promotes an idea or view.

pedometer /pi-dom-i-ter/ **noun** an instrument for estimating how far you are walking by recording the number of steps you take.

pee informal **verb** (**pees**, **peeing**, **peed**) urinate. **noun 1** an act of urinating.

2 urine.

peek **verb 1** look quickly or secretly. **2** be just visible. **noun** a quick look.

peel **verb 1** remove the skin or rind from a fruit or vegetable. **2** remove a thin covering or layer from. **3** (of a surface) come off in small pieces. **noun** the outer covering or rind of a fruit or vegetable.

peep[1] **verb 1** look quickly and secretly. **2** (**peep out**) be just visible. **noun 1** a quick or secret look. **2** a momentary or partial view of something. □ **peeping Tom** a person who likes to spy on people undressing or having sex. **peep show** a series of pictures in a box which you look at through a small opening.

peep[2] **noun** a short high-pitched sound. **verb** make a short high-pitched sound.

peephole **noun** a small hole in a door or wall which you can look through.

peer[1] **verb** (**peers**, **peering**, **peered**) **1** look at something with difficulty or concentration. **2** be just visible.

peer[2] **noun 1** a member of the nobility in Britain or Ireland. **2** a person who is the same age or has the same social status as you. □ **peer group** a group of people of approximately the same age, status, and interests.

peerage **noun 1** the title and rank of peer or peeress. **2** (**the peerage**) all the peers in Britain or Ireland.

peeress **noun 1** a woman holding the rank of a peer in her own right. **2** the wife or widow of a peer.

peerless **adjective** better than all others.

peeve informal **verb** (**peeves**, **peeving**, **peeved**) annoy; irritate. **noun** a cause of annoyance.

peevish **adjective** irritable.

peewit **noun** Brit. a lapwing.

peg **noun 1** a pin or bolt used for hanging things on, securing something in place, or marking a position. **2** a clip for holding things together or hanging up clothes. **verb** (**pegs**, **pegging**, **pegged**) **1** fix, attach, or mark something with a peg or pegs. **2** fix a price, rate, etc. at a particular level. **3 (peg out)** *informal* die. □ **off the peg** (of clothes) not made to order; readymade.

peignoir /pay-nwar/ **noun** a woman's light dressing gown or negligee.

pejorative /pi-jorr-uh-tiv/ **adjective** expressing contempt or disapproval. ■ **pejoratively** adverb.

☑ *pej-*, not *perj-*: *pejorative.*

Pekinese **noun** (plural **Pekinese**) a small dog with long hair and a snub nose.

pelican **noun** a large waterbird with a bag of skin hanging from a long bill. □ **pelican crossing** (in the UK) a pedestrian crossing with traffic lights that are operated by the pedestrians.

pellagra /pi-**lag**-ruh/ **noun** a disease caused by an inadequate diet, of which the symptoms are inflamed skin, diarrhoea, etc.

pellet **noun 1** a small compressed mass of a substance. **2** a lightweight bullet or piece of small shot.

pell-mell **adjective & adverb** in a confused or rushed way.

pellucid /pel-**loo**-sid/ **adjective** translucent or transparent; clear.

pelmet **noun** a structure or strip of fabric fitted across the top of a window to conceal the curtain fittings.

pelt[1] **verb 1** hurl missiles at. **2 (pelt down)** fall very heavily. □ **(at) full pelt** as fast as possible.

pelt[2] **noun** the skin of an animal with the fur, wool, or hair still on it.

pelvis /**pel**-viss/ **noun** the large bony frame at the base of the spine to which the legs are attached. ■ **pelvic** adjective.

pen[1] **noun** an instrument for writing or drawing with ink. **verb** (**pens**, **penning**, **penned**) write or compose. □ **pen name** a name used by a writer that is not their real name.

pen[2] **noun** a small enclosure for farm animals. **verb** (**pens**, **penning**, **penned**) **1** put or keep animals in a pen. **2 (pen up** or **in)** confine someone in a restricted space.

penal **adjective 1** relating to the use of punishment as part of the legal system. **2** extremely severe.

penalize or **penalise** **verb** (**penalizes, penalizing, penalized**) **1** give someone a penalty or punishment. **2** put in an unfavourable position.

penalty **noun** (plural **penalties**) **1** a punishment given to someone for breaking a law, rule, or contract. **2** something unpleasant suffered as a result of an action or circumstance. **3** (also **penalty kick**) Soccer a free shot at the goal awarded to the attacking team after a foul within the area around the goal (the **penalty area**).

penance **noun 1** punishment given by a priest for having done wrong. **2** a religious act in which a member of the Church confesses sins to a priest and is given penance or formal forgiveness.

pence plural of **PENNY.**

ℹ it is wrong to use **pence** in the singular to mean 'penny', as in *the chancellor will put one pence on income tax.*

penchant /**pon**-shon/ **noun** a strong liking for something.

pencil **noun** an instrument for writing or drawing, consisting of a stick of wood with a core of graphite. **verb** (**pencils, pencilling, pencilled**; US spelling **pencils, penciling, penciled**) **1** write or draw something with a pencil. **2 (pencil in)** provisionally enter a time or date in your diary.

pendant **noun 1** a piece of jewellery worn hanging from a chain around the neck. **2** a light designed to hang from the ceiling. **adjective** (also **pendent**) hanging downwards.

pending **adjective 1** waiting to be decided or settled. **2** about to happen. **preposition** awaiting the outcome of.

pendulous **adjective** hanging down; drooping.

pendulum **noun** a weight hung from a fixed point so that it can swing freely, used in regulating the mechanism of a clock.

penetrate verb (penetrates, penetrating, penetrated) **1** force a way into or through. **2** gain access to an enemy organization or a competitor's market. **3** understand or gain insight into something. **4 (penetrating)** (of a sound) clearly heard through or above other sounds. **5** (of a man) insert the penis into the vagina or anus of a sexual partner. ■ **penetration** noun **penetrative** adjective.

penfriend noun a person with whom you form a friendship through exchanging letters.

penguin noun a flightless black and white seabird living in the Antarctic.

penicillin noun an antibiotic originally obtained from certain sorts of mould.

peninsula noun a long, narrow piece of land projecting out into the sea. ■ **peninsular** adjective.

penis noun the male organ used for urinating and having sex.

penitent adjective feeling sorrow and regret for having done wrong. noun a person who is doing penance. ■ **penitence** noun **penitential** adjective.

penitentiary /pen-i-ten-shuh-ri/ noun (plural penitentiaries) N. Amer. a prison for people convicted of serious crimes.

penknife noun a small knife with a blade which folds into the handle.

pennant noun a tapering, triangular, or swallow-tailed flag.

penne /pen-nay/ plural noun pasta in the form of short wide tubes.

penniless adjective having no money.

penny noun (plural pennies (for separate coins); pence (for a sum of money)) **1** a British bronze coin worth one hundredth of a pound. **2** (in the past) a British coin worth one twelfth of a shilling and 240th of a pound. □ **penny-farthing** an early type of bicycle with a very large front wheel and a small rear wheel. **penny-pinching** unwilling to spend money.

penny whistle a tin whistle.

pension¹ /pen-sh'n/ noun a regular payment made to retired people, widows, etc., either by the state or from an investment fund. verb (**pension off**) dismiss someone from employment and pay them a pension. ■ **pensionable** adjective **pensioner** noun.

pension² /pon-syon/ noun a small hotel or boarding house in France and other European countries.

pensive adjective thinking deeply about something. ■ **pensively** adverb.

pentacle noun a pentagram.

pentagon noun **1** a figure with five straight sides and five angles. **2 (the Pentagon)** the headquarters of the US Department of Defense.

pentagram noun a five-pointed star used as a magical symbol.

pentameter /pen-tam-i-ter/ noun a line of poetry with five stressed syllables.

pentathlon noun an athletic event consisting of five different activities. ■ **pentathlete** noun.

Pentecost noun the Christian festival celebrating the coming of the Holy Spirit to the disciples of Jesus after his Ascension.

Pentecostal adjective **1** relating to Pentecost. **2** having to do with a Christian movement which emphasizes the gifts of the Holy Spirit, e.g. the supposed healing of the sick.

penthouse noun a flat on the top floor of a tall building.

penultimate adjective last but one.

penumbra /pi-num-bruh/ noun the partially shaded outer part of a shadow.

penurious /pi-nyoor-i-uhss/ adjective formal extremely poor.

penury /pen-yuu-ri/ noun extreme poverty.

peony /pee-uh-ni/ noun a plant cultivated for its showy flowers.

people plural noun **1** human beings in general. **2 (the people)** all those living in a country or society. **3** (plural

peoples) the members of a particular nation, community, or ethnic group. **verb (peoples, peopling, peopled)** live in a place or fill it with people.

pep informal **noun** liveliness. **verb (peps, pepping, pepped) (pep up)** make more lively. □ **pep talk** a talk given to someone to make them feel braver or more enthusiastic.

pepper noun 1 a pungent, hot-tasting powder made from peppercorns, used to flavour food. **2** the fruit of a tropical American plant, of which sweet peppers and chilli peppers are varieties. **verb (peppers, peppering, peppered) 1** season food with pepper. **2 (pepper with)** scatter large amounts of something over an area. **3** hit a place repeatedly with small missiles or gunshot. ■ **pepperiness** noun **peppery** adjective.

peppercorn noun the dried berry of a climbing vine, used whole as a spice or crushed to make pepper. □ **peppercorn rent** a very low rent.

peppermint noun 1 a plant of the mint family which produces aromatic leaves and oil, used as a flavouring in food. **2** a sweet flavoured with peppermint oil.

pepperoni /pep-puh-**roh**-ni/ **noun** a dried sausage made from beef and pork and seasoned with pepper.

peptic adjective relating to digestion. □ **peptic ulcer** an ulcer in the lining of the stomach or small intestine.

per preposition 1 for each. **2** by means of. **3 (as per)** in accordance with.

perambulate verb (perambulates, perambulating, perambulated) formal walk or travel from place to place. ■ **perambulation** noun.

perambulator noun formal a pram.

per annum adverb for each year.

per capita adverb & adjective for each person.

perceive verb (perceives, perceiving, perceived) 1 become aware of something through starting to see, smell, or hear it. **2 (perceive as)** understand or interpret something in a particular way. ■ **perceivable** adjective.

 remember, *i* before *e* except after *c*: perceive.

per cent adverb by a specified amount in or for every hundred. **noun** one part in every hundred.

percentage noun 1 a rate, number, or amount in each hundred. **2** a proportion or share of a whole.

percentile /per-**sen**-tyl/ **noun** Statistics each of 100 equal groups into which a population can be divided.

perceptible adjective able to be noticed or felt. ■ **perceptibly** adverb.

perception noun 1 the ability to see, hear, or become aware of something. **2** a particular understanding of something. **3** the process of perceiving.

perceptive adjective having good understanding of people and situations. ■ **perceptively** adverb.

perceptual adjective relating to the ability to perceive.

perch[1] **noun 1** a branch, bar, or ledge on which a bird rests or roosts. **2** a high or narrow seat or resting place. **verb 1** sit or rest somewhere. **2** place or balance something somewhere.

perch[2] **noun** (plural **perch** or **perches**) a freshwater fish with a spiny fin on its back.

perchance adverb old use by some chance; perhaps.

percipient adjective having good insight or understanding.

percolate verb (percolates, percolating, percolated) 1 filter through a porous surface or substance. **2** (of information or ideas) spread gradually through a group of people. **3** prepare coffee in a percolator. ■ **percolation** noun.

percolator noun a machine for making coffee, consisting of a pot in which boiling water is circulated through a small chamber that holds the ground beans.

percussion noun musical instruments that you play by striking or shaking them. ■ **percussionist** noun.

perdition noun (in Christian thinking) a state of eternal damnation into which people who have sinned and not repented pass when they die.

peregrinations plural noun old use journeys or wanderings from place to place.

peregrine noun a powerful falcon with a bluish-grey back and wings.

peremptory adjective insisting on immediate attention or obedience. ■ **peremptorily** adverb.

perennial adjective 1 lasting or doing something for a long time or for ever. **2** (of a plant) living for several years. **noun** a perennial plant. ■ **perennially** adverb.

perestroika /pe-ri-**stroy**-kuh/ **noun** (in the former Soviet Union) the economic and political reforms introduced during the 1980s.

perfect adjective /**per**-fikt/ **1** having all the parts and qualities that are needed or wanted, and no flaws or weaknesses. **2** total; complete: *it made perfect sense.* **3** Grammar (of a verb) referring to a completed action or to a state in the past. **verb** /per-**fekt**/ make something perfect. ■ **perfectly** adverb.

perfection noun 1 the process of perfecting, or the state of being perfect. **2** a perfect person or thing.

perfectionism noun the refusal to be satisfied with something unless it is done perfectly. ■ **perfectionist** noun & adjective.

perfidious /per-**fid**-i-uhss/ **adjective** deceitful and disloyal.

perfidy /**per**-fi-di/ **noun** literary deceit; disloyalty.

perforate verb (**perforates, perforating, perforated**) pierce and make a hole or holes in. ■ **perforation** noun.

perforce adverb formal necessarily; inevitably.

perform verb 1 carry out an action, task, or function. **2** work, function, or do something to a particular standard. **3** entertain an audience by playing a piece of music, acting in a play, etc. ■ **performer** noun.

performance noun 1 an act of performing a play, piece of music, etc. **2** the process of performing. **3** informal a display of exaggerated behaviour; a fuss. **4** the capabilities of a machine or product. ▫ **performance art** an art form that combines visual art with drama.

perfume /per-**fyoom**/ **noun 1** a fragrant liquid used to give a pleasant smell to your body. **2** a pleasant smell. **verb** /per-**fyoom**/ (**perfumes, perfuming, perfumed**) **1** give a pleasant smell to. **2** apply perfume to. ■ **perfumery** noun.

perfunctory adjective carried out without much care or effort. ■ **perfunctorily** adverb.

pergola /**per**-guh-luh/ **noun** an arched structure forming a framework for climbing plants.

perhaps adverb possibly; maybe.

peril noun a situation of serious and immediate danger.

perilous adjective full of danger or risk. ■ **perilously** adverb.

perimeter noun the boundary or outside edge of something.

period noun 1 a length or portion of time. **2** a lesson in a school. **3** (also **menstrual period**) a flow of blood each month from the lining of a woman's womb. **4** chiefly N. Amer. a full stop. **adjective** belonging to or characteristic of a past historical time. ▫ **period piece** an object made or a book or play set in an earlier period.

periodic adjective appearing or occurring at intervals. ▫ **periodic table** a table of all the chemical elements.

periodical adjective 1 occurring or appearing at intervals. **2** (of a magazine or newspaper) published at regular intervals. **noun** a periodical magazine or newspaper. ■ **periodically** adverb.

peripatetic /pe-ri-puh-**tet**-ik/ **adjective** travelling from place to place.

peripheral /puh-**rif**-uh-ruhl/ **adjective 1** relating to or situated on an edge or boundary. **2** outside the core or most important part of something; marginal. ■ **peripherally** adverb.

periphery /puh-**rif**-uh-ri/ **noun** (plural **peripheries**) **1** the outside edge or boundary of something. **2** an area of activity that is outside the core or most important part of something.

periscope noun a device consisting of a tube attached to a set of mirrors, through which you can see things that are above or behind something else.

perish verb **1** die. **2** be completely ruined or destroyed. **3** (of rubber or a similar material) become weak or rot. **4** (**be perished**) Brit. informal feel very cold. **5** (**perishing**) Brit. informal very cold. □ **perish the thought** informal let that not happen or be true.

perishable adjective (of food) not able to be kept beyond a certain time because it will rot or decay.

peristalsis noun the contraction and relaxation of muscles in the digestive system and intestines, creating wave-like movements which push food through the body.

peritoneum /pe-ri-tuh-**nee**-uhm/ noun (plural **peritoneums** or **peritonea** /pe-ri-tuh-**nee**-uh/) a membrane lining the inside of the abdomen. ■ **peritoneal** adjective.

peritonitis noun inflammation of the peritoneum.

periwinkle noun **1** a plant with purple five-petalled flowers and glossy leaves. **2** = **WINKLE**.

perjure verb (**perjures, perjuring, perjured**) (**perjure yourself**) tell a lie in court after swearing to tell the truth; commit perjury.

perjury /**per**-juh-ri/ noun the offence of deliberately telling a lie in court after swearing to tell the truth.

perk[1] verb (**perk up**) make or become more cheerful or lively.

perk[2] noun informal an extra benefit given to an employee in addition to wages.

perky adjective (**perkier, perkiest**) cheerful and lively.

perm noun (also **permanent wave**) a method of setting the hair in waves or curls and treating it with chemicals so that the style lasts for several months. verb treat hair in such a way.

permafrost noun a layer of soil beneath the surface that remains below freezing point throughout the year.

permanent adjective lasting for a long time or forever. ■ **permanence** noun **permanently** adverb.

> ✓ permanent, not -ant.

permeable adjective allowing liquids or gases to pass through.

permeate verb (**permeates, permeating, permeated**) spread throughout.

permissible adjective allowable.

permission noun the act of allowing someone to do something.

permissive adjective allowing a lot of freedom. ■ **permissiveness** noun.

permit verb /per-**mit**/ (**permits, permitting, permitted**) **1** say that someone is allowed to do something. **2** make something possible. noun /**per**-mit/ an official document saying that someone is allowed to do something or go somewhere.

permutation noun each of several possible ways in which a number of things can be ordered or arranged.

pernicious adjective having a harmful effect.

pernickety adjective **1** fussy. **2** needing a careful approach.

peroration noun the concluding part of a speech.

peroxide noun (also **hydrogen peroxide**) a chemical that is used as a bleach or disinfectant. verb (**peroxides, peroxiding, peroxided**) bleach hair with peroxide.

perpendicular adjective at an angle of $90°$ to the ground, or to another line or surface. noun a perpendicular line.

perpetrate verb (**perpetrates, perpetrating, perpetrated**) carry out a bad or illegal action. ■ **perpetration** noun **perpetrator** noun.

perpetual adjective **1** never ending or changing. **2** so frequent as to seem continual. ■ **perpetually** adverb.

perpetuate verb (**perpetuates, per-**

petuating, perpetuated) cause something to continue indefinitely. ■ **perpetuation** noun.

perpetuity noun (plural **perpetuities**) the state of lasting forever.

perplex verb puzzle someone greatly.

perplexity noun (plural **perplexities**) **1** the state of being puzzled. **2** a puzzling situation or thing.

perquisite /per-kwi-zit/ noun formal a special right or privilege.

per se /per say/ adverb in itself.

persecute verb (**persecutes, persecuting, persecuted**) **1** treat badly over a long period. **2** harass. ■ **persecution** noun **persecutor** noun.

persevere verb continue doing something in spite of difficulty or lack of success. ■ **perseverance** noun.

Persian noun **1** a person from Persia (now Iran). **2** the language of ancient Persia or modern Iran. **3** a breed of cat with long hair. adjective relating to Persia or Iran.

persimmon /per-sim-muhn/ noun a fruit that looks like a large tomato but is very sweet.

persist verb **1** continue doing something in spite of difficulty or opposition. **2** continue to exist.

persistent adjective **1** continuing to do something in spite of difficulty or opposition. **2** continuing or recurring over a long period. ■ **persistence** noun **persistently** adverb.

 persist**ent**, not -*ant*.

person noun (plural **people** or **persons**) **1** an individual human being. **2** a person's body. **3** Grammar a category used in classifying pronouns and verb forms according to whether they indicate the speaker (**first person**), the person spoken to (**second person**), or a third party (**third person**). □ **in person** physically present.

persona /per-**soh**-nuh/ noun (plural **personas** or **personae** /per-**soh**-nee/) the part of a person's character that is revealed to other people.

personable adjective having a pleasant appearance and manner.

personage noun a person of importance or high status.

personal adjective **1** having to do with or belonging to a particular person. **2** done by a particular person themselves, rather than someone acting for them. **3** concerning a person's private rather than professional or public life. **4** referring to someone's character or appearance in a way that is offensive. **5** relating to a person's body. □ **personal column** a section of a newspaper listing private advertisements or messages. **personal pronoun** Grammar each of the pronouns that show person, gender, number, and case (such as *I, you, he, she,* etc.). **personal stereo** a small portable cassette or compact disc player, used with headphones. ■ **personally** adverb.

personality noun (plural **personalities**) **1** the qualities that form a person's character. **2** outgoing qualities that make someone interesting or popular. **3** a celebrity.

personalize or **personalise** verb (**personalizes, personalizing, personalized**) **1** design or produce something to meet someone's individual requirements. **2** cause an issue or argument to become concerned with personalities or feelings.

persona non grata /per-soh-nuh nohn **grah**-tuh/ noun a person who is not welcome in a place.

personify verb (**personifies, personifying, personified**) **1** give human characteristics to something that is not human. **2** be an example of a quality or characteristic. ■ **personification** noun.

personnel plural noun people employed in an organization.

perspective noun **1** the art of representing things in a picture so that they seem to have height, width, depth, and relative distance. **2** a view. **3** a way of seeing something. **4** understanding of how important things are in relation to others.

perspex noun trademark a tough transparent plastic.

perspicacious adjective quickly gaining insight into things. ■ **perspicacity** noun.

perspicuous adjective **1** clearly expressed and easily understood. **2** (of a person) expressing things clearly.

perspiration noun **1** sweat. **2** the process of sweating.

perspire verb (**perspires, perspiring, perspired**) produce sweat through the pores of your skin.

persuade verb (**persuades, persuading, persuaded**) use reasoning or argument to make someone do or believe something.

persuasion noun **1** the process of persuading or of being persuaded. **2** a belief or set of beliefs.

persuasive adjective **1** good at persuading someone to do or believe something. **2** providing evidence or reasoning that makes you believe something. ■ **persuasively** adverb.

pert adjective **1** attractively lively or cheeky. **2** (of a bodily feature) attractively small and firm.

pertain verb (**pertain to**) be appropriate, related, or relevant to.

pertinacious adjective formal persistent. ■ **pertinacity** noun.

pertinent adjective relevant or appropriate. ■ **pertinence** noun **pertinently** adverb.

perturb verb make anxious or unsettled. ■ **perturbation** noun.

peruse verb (**peruses, perusing, perused**) formal read or examine thoroughly or carefully. ■ **perusal** noun.

pervade verb (**pervades, pervading, pervaded**) spread or be present throughout.

pervasive adjective spreading widely through something. ■ **pervasively** adverb **pervasiveness** noun.

perverse adjective **1** deliberately choosing to behave in a way that other people find unacceptable. **2** contrary to what is accepted or expected. ■ **perversely** adverb **perversity** noun.

perversion noun **1** the action of perverting. **2** abnormal or unacceptable sexual behaviour.

pervert verb **1** change the form or meaning of something in a way that distorts it. **2** make someone perverted. noun a person whose sexual behaviour is abnormal and unacceptable.

perverted adjective sexually abnormal and unacceptable.

pervious /per-vi-uhss/ adjective allowing water to pass through.

peseta /puh-**say**-tuh/ noun the basic unit of money of Spain.

pesky adjective informal annoying.

pessary noun (plural **pessaries**) a small soluble block inserted into the vagina to treat infection or as a contraceptive.

pessimism noun a tendency to expect the worst to happen. ■ **pessimist** noun **pessimistic** adjective **pessimistically** adverb.

pest noun **1** a destructive insect or other animal that attacks plants, crops, or livestock. **2** informal an annoying person or thing.

pester verb (**pesters, pestering, pestered**) trouble someone with persistent requests or interruptions.

pesticide noun a substance for destroying insects or other pests.

pestilence noun old use a disease that spreads widely and causes deaths. ■ **pestilent** adjective.

pestilential adjective **1** old use relating to or causing a serious disease that spreads widely. **2** having the nature of a pest. **3** informal annoying.

pestle /**pess**-uhl/ noun a heavy implement with a rounded end, used for grinding substances in a mortar.

pesto noun a sauce of crushed basil leaves, pine nuts, garlic, Parmesan cheese, and olive oil, served with pasta.

pet noun **1** an animal or bird that you keep for pleasure. **2** a person treated with special favour. adjective favourite. verb (**pets, petting, petted**) **1** stroke or pat an animal. **2** caress someone sexually. □ **pet name** a name used to express fondness or familiarity.

petal noun each of the segments forming the outer part of a flower.

peter verb (**peters, petering, petered**) (**peter out**) gradually come to an end.

petite adjective (of a woman) small and dainty.

petit four /puh-ti **for**/ noun (plural **petits fours** /puh-ti **forz**/) a very small fancy cake, biscuit, or sweet.

petition noun an appeal or request, especially a written one signed by a large number of people and presented formally to someone in authority. verb make or present a petition to.

petit point noun embroidery on canvas, using small diagonal stitches.

petrel noun a seabird that flies far from land.

Petri dish noun a shallow transparent dish with a flat lid, used in laboratories.

petrify verb (**petrifies, petrifying, petrified**) **1** change organic matter into stone. **2** paralyse with fear.

petrochemical adjective relating to petroleum and natural gas. noun a chemical obtained from petroleum and natural gas.

petrol noun Brit. refined petroleum used as fuel in motor vehicles. □ **petrol bomb** a simple firebomb consisting of a bottle containing petrol and a cloth wick.

petroleum noun an oil that is refined to produce fuels including petrol, paraffin, and diesel oil.

petticoat noun a woman's light undergarment in the form of a skirt or dress.

pettifogging adjective petty; trivial.

pettish adjective childishly sulky. ■ **pettishly** adverb.

petty adjective (**pettier, pettiest**) **1** of little importance. **2** (of a person's behaviour) small-minded. **3** minor. □ **petty cash** a store of money that is available for spending on small items.

petty officer a rank of naval officer. ■ **pettiness** noun.

petulant adjective childishly sulky or bad-tempered. ■ **petulance** noun **petulantly** adverb.

petunia noun a plant with white, purple, or red funnel-shaped flowers.

pew noun **1** a long wooden bench with a back, arranged with others in rows to provide seating in a church. **2** Brit. informal a seat.

pewter noun a metal made by mixing tin with copper and antimony.

pfennig /**pfen**-nig/ noun a unit of money of Germany, equal to one hundredth of a mark.

PG abbreviation Brit. (in film classification) parental guidance.

pH noun a figure expressing how acid or alkaline a substance is.

phalanx noun (plural **phalanxes**) a body of people standing or moving forward closely together.

phallic adjective relating to or resembling a penis.

phallus noun (plural **phalli** /**fal**-lee/ or **phalluses**) a penis.

phantasm noun literary an illusion or figment of the imagination.

phantasmagoria noun a sequence of real or imaginary images like that seen in a dream.

phantom noun **1** a ghost. **2** a figment of the imagination. adjective not really existing.

pharaoh /**fair**-oh/ noun a ruler in ancient Egypt.

 remember, -*aoh*, not -*oah*: pharaoh.

Pharisee noun a member of an ancient Jewish sect who followed religious laws very strictly.

pharmaceutical adjective relating to medicinal drugs. noun a medicinal drug.

pharmacist noun a person who is qualified to prepare and dispense medicinal drugs.

pharmacology noun the branch of medicine concerned with drugs.

■ **pharmacological** adjective **pharmacologist** noun.

pharmacy noun (plural **pharmacies**) **1** a place where medicinal drugs are prepared or sold. **2** the science or practice of preparing and dispensing medicinal drugs.

pharynx noun (plural **pharynges** /fa-**rin**-jeez/) the cavity connecting the nose and mouth to the throat.

phase noun a distinct period or stage in a process of change or development. verb (**phases, phasing, phased**) **1** carry something out in gradual stages. **2** (**phase in** or **out**) gradually introduce or withdraw something.

PhD abbreviation Doctor of Philosophy.

pheasant noun a large long-tailed game bird.

phenomenal adjective extraordinary. ■ **phenomenally** adverb.

phenomenon noun (plural **phenomena**) **1** a fact or situation that is known to exist or happen. **2** a remarkable person or thing.

> i the word **phenomenon** comes from Greek, and its plural form is **phenomena**. Don't use **phenomena** as a singular form: say *this is a strange phenomenon*, not *this is a strange phenomena*.

pheromone /**ferr**-uh-mohn/ noun a chemical substance released by an animal and causing a response in others of its species.

phial /**fy**-uhl/ noun a small cylindrical glass bottle.

philander verb (**philanders, philandering, philandered**) (of a man) have numerous sexual relationships with women. ■ **philanderer** noun.

philanthropy noun the practice of helping people in need. ■ **philanthropic** adjective **philanthropist** noun.

philately /fi-**lat**-uh-li/ noun the hobby of collecting postage stamps. ■ **philatelist** noun.

philharmonic adjective devoted to music (used in the names of orchestras).

philippic noun a verbal attack.

Philistine noun **1** a member of a people of ancient Palestine who fought with the Israelites. **2** (**philistine**) a person who is not interested in culture and the arts. ■ **philistinism** noun.

philology noun the study of the structure and development of language and the relationships between languages. ■ **philological** adjective **philologist** noun.

philosopher noun **1** a person who is engaged in philosophy. **2** a person who thinks deeply about things.

philosophical adjective **1** relating to the study of philosophy. **2** having a calm attitude when things are difficult. ■ **philosophically** adverb.

philosophize or **philosophise** verb (**philosophizes, philosophizing, philosophized**) think carefully about serious issues.

philosophy noun (plural **philosophies**) **1** the study of the fundamental nature of knowledge, reality, and existence. **2** a set or system of beliefs.

phlegm /flem/ noun mucus in the nose and throat.

phlegmatic /fleg-**mat**-ik/ adjective calm and reasonable, and tending not to get upset.

phobia noun a strong irrational fear of something. ■ **phobic** adjective & noun.

phoenix /**fee**-niks/ noun (in classical mythology) a bird that burned itself on a funeral pyre and was born again from the ashes.

> ✓ -oe-, not -eo-: phoenix.

phone noun a telephone. verb (**phones, phoning, phoned**) make a telephone call to someone. □ **phone-in** a radio or television programme in which listeners or viewers participate over the telephone.

phonecard noun a card which you can use instead of cash to make calls on a public telephone.

phonetic adjective **1** having to do with speech sounds. **2** (of a system of writing) using symbols that represent

---

WORD FORMATION

-phile, -philia

Words ending in **-phile** mean 'a person or thing that is fond of or tends towards a particular thing'. Some examples are:

bibliophile	a person who loves books
Francophile	a person who likes France
halophile	an animal or plant that prefers salty conditions
oenophile	a wine connoisseur.

-philia forms related nouns, such as:

necrophilia	sexual interest in dead bodies
technophilia	enthusiasm for new technology.

-phile and **-philia** come from the ancient Greek word *philos*, 'loving'.

---

sounds. **noun** (phonetics) the study of speech sounds. ■ **phonetically** adverb.

phoney or **phony** informal **adjective** (**phonier, phoniest**) not genuine. **noun** (plural **phoneys** or **phonies**) a person or thing that is not genuine.

phonic adjective relating to speech sounds.

phonograph noun 1 Brit. an early form of gramophone that could record as well as reproduce sound. **2** N. Amer. a record player.

phosphate noun a salt or ester of phosphoric acid.

phosphorescence noun a faint light that is given out by a substance with little or no heat. ■ **phosphorescent** adjective.

phosphorus noun a yellowish waxy solid which can ignite spontaneously and which glows in the dark. ■ **phosphorous** adjective.

photo noun (plural **photos**) a photograph. □ **photo finish** a close finish of a race in which the winner can be identified only from a photograph of competitors crossing the line.

photocall noun Brit. a prearranged occasion when people pose for photographers.

photocopy noun (plural **photocopies**) a photographic copy of something produced by a process involving the action of light on a specially prepared surface. **verb** (**photocopies, photo-** copying, photocopied) make a photocopy of. ■ **photocopier** noun.

photoelectric adjective involving the production of electrons as a result of the action of light on a surface.

photofit noun Brit. a picture of a person made up from photographs of parts of other people's faces.

photogenic adjective looking attractive in photographs.

photograph noun a picture made with a camera. **verb** take a photograph of. ■ **photographer** noun **photographic** adjective.

photography noun the taking and processing of photographs.

photogravure noun an image produced from a photographic negative transferred to a metal plate and etched in.

photometer /foh-**tom**-i-ter/ **noun** an instrument measuring the strength of light.

photon /**foh**-ton/ **noun** a particle representing a quantum of light or other electromagnetic radiation.

photosensitive adjective responding to light.

photostat noun trademark **1** a type of machine for making photocopies on special paper. **2** a copy made by a photostat. **verb** (**photostats, photostatting, photostatted**) copy something with a photostat.

photosynthesis noun the process by

WORD FORMATION

-phobia

Words ending in **-phobia** mean 'extreme or irrational fear or dislike of something'. This is just a selection from the huge number of *-phobia* words:

agoraphobia	fear of open or public places
ailurophobia	fear of cats
arachnophobia	fear of spiders
claustrophobia	fear of confined places
xenophobia	dislike of foreigners.

Related words are **-phobe**, which forms nouns such as **technophobe**, 'a person who is afraid of technology', and **-phobic**, as in **xenophobic**, 'disliking foreigners'. **-phobia**, **-phobe**, and **-phobic** come from the ancient Greek word *phobos*, 'fear'.

which green plants use sunlight to form nutrients from carbon dioxide and water. ■ **photosynthetic** adjective.

phrase noun **1** a group of words forming a unit within a sentence. **2** Music a group of notes forming a unit within a longer passage. **verb** (**phrases, phrasing, phrased**) put an idea into a particular form of words. □ **phrase book** a book listing and translating useful phrases in a foreign language. ■ **phrasal** adjective.

phraseology /fray-zi-**ol**-uh-ji/ noun (plural **phraseologies**) a form of words used to express an idea.

phrenology noun (mainly in the past) the study of the shape and size of the skull in the belief that this can indicate someone's character.

phylum /**fy**-luhm/ noun (plural **phyla** /**fy**-luh/) a category used in the classification of animals.

physical adjective **1** relating to the body rather than the mind. **2** relating to things that you can see, hear, or feel. **3** involving bodily contact or activity. **4** relating to physics and natural forces such as heat, light, sound, etc. **noun** a medical examination to find out the state of someone's health. □ **physical education** instruction in physical exercise, sports, and games. ■ **physicality** noun **physically** adverb.

physician noun a person qualified to practise medicine.

physics noun the branch of science concerned with the nature and properties of matter and energy. ■ **physicist** noun.

physiognomy /fi-zi-**on**-uh-mi/ noun (plural **physiognomies**) a person's face or facial expression.

physiology noun the scientific study of the way in which living things function. ■ **physiological** adjective **physiologist** noun.

physiotherapy noun Brit. the treatment of disease and injury by massage and exercise. ■ **physiotherapist** noun.

physique noun the shape and size of a person's body.

pi /pI/ noun the sixteenth letter of the Greek alphabet (Π, π).

pianissimo /pi-uh-**niss**-i-moh/ adverb & adjective Music very soft or softly.

piano¹ /pi-**an**-oh/ noun (plural **pianos**) a musical instrument which you play by pressing black or white keys on a large keyboard, the sound being produced by small hammers hitting metal strings. ■ **pianist** noun.

piano² /pi-**ah**-noh/ adverb & adjective Music soft or softly.

pianoforte /pi-an-oh-**for**-tay/ formal a piano.

piazza /pi-**at**-zuh/ noun a public square or marketplace.

picador noun (in bullfighting) a

GRAMMAR

Phrase

A phrase is a group of words that has meaning but does not have a subject, verb, or object (unlike a clause or sentence). It can be:

1 a noun phrase, functioning as a noun, e.g.

> *I went to see* my friend Tom
> The only ones they have *are too small*.

2 an adjective phrase, functioning as an adjective, e.g.

> *I was* very pleased indeed
> *This one is* better than mine.

3 an adverb phrase, functioning as an adverb, e.g.

> *They drove off* in their car
> *I was there* ten days ago.

---

person on horseback who goads the bull with a lance.

picaresque adjective (of fiction) dealing with the adventures of a dishonest but appealing hero.

piccalilli noun a pickle of chopped vegetables, mustard, and hot spices.

piccaninny noun (plural **piccaninnies**) offensive a small black child.

piccolo noun (plural **piccolos**) a small flute sounding an octave higher than the ordinary flute.

pick¹ verb **1** choose from a number of alternatives. **2** remove a flower or fruit from where it is growing. **3 (pick up)** take hold of and lift something. **4** remove unwanted matter with a finger or pointed instrument. noun **1** an act of selecting something. **2 (the pick of)** informal the best person or thing in a particular group. □ **pick at 1** repeatedly pull at something with your fingers. **2** eat food in small amounts. **pick a fight** provoke an argument or fight. **pick holes in** find fault with. **pick a lock** open a lock with an instrument other than the proper key. **pick off** shoot one of a group from a distance. **pick on** single someone out for unfair treatment. **pick over (or through)** carefully sort through a number of items. **pick someone's pockets** steal something from a person's pocket. **pick up 1** go

to collect. **2** improve or increase. **3** informal flirtatiously start talking to a stranger. **4** obtain or learn. **5** detect or receive a signal or sound. ■ **picker** noun.

pick² or **pickaxe** noun **1** a tool consisting of a curved iron bar with pointed ends and a wooden handle, used for breaking up hard ground or rock. **2** a plectrum.

picket noun **1** a person or group of people standing outside a workplace and trying to persuade others not to work during a strike. **2** a pointed wooden stake driven into the ground. verb (**pickets**, **picketing**, **picketed**) act as a picket outside a workplace.

pickings plural noun **1** profits or gains. **2** scraps or leftovers.

pickle noun **1** Brit. a thick, spicy, cold sauce made from chopped vegetables and fruit. **2** a preserve of vegetables or fruit in vinegar or salt water. **3 (a pickle)** informal a difficult situation. verb (**pickles**, **pickling**, **pickled**) preserve food in vinegar or brine.

pickpocket noun a person who steals from people's pockets.

pickup noun **1** a small truck with low sides. **2** an act of picking up a person or goods. **3** the part of a record player that holds the stylus. **4** a device on an electric guitar which converts sound vibration into electrical signals for amplification.

picky adjective informal fussy.

picnic noun a meal that is eaten outdoors and away from home. verb (**picnics, picnicking, picnicked**) have a picnic. ∎ **picnicker** noun.

Pict noun a member of an ancient people inhabiting northern Scotland in Roman times.

pictograph or **pictogram** noun a small image or picture representing a word or phrase.

pictorial adjective having to do with or expressed in pictures.

picture noun 1 a painting, drawing, or photograph. 2 an image on a television screen. 3 a cinema film. 4 (**the pictures**) the cinema. 5 an image formed in the mind. verb (**pictures, picturing, pictured**) 1 represent in a picture. 2 form an image of something in your mind. ▫ **be (or look) a picture 1** be beautiful. 2 look amusingly startled. **picture window** a large window consisting of a single pane of glass.

picturesque adjective attractive in a quaint or charming way.

piddle verb (**piddles, piddling, piddled**) informal 1 urinate. 2 (**piddling**) very unimportant or trivial.

pidgin noun a simple form of a language with elements taken from local languages.

pie noun a baked dish of ingredients encased in or topped with pastry. ▫ **pie chart** a diagram in which a circle is divided into segments to show the size of particular amounts in relation to the whole. **pie-eyed** informal drunk. **pie in the sky** informal a plan that is attractive but not realistic.

piebald adjective (of a horse) having irregular patches of two colours.

piece noun 1 a portion that is separated or seen separately from the whole. 2 an item used in building something or forming part of a set. 3 a musical or written work. 4 a token used to make moves in a board game. 5 a coin of a particular value. verb (**pieces, piecing, pieced**) (**piece together**) assemble something from individual parts.

pièce de résistance /pyess duh ray-**ziss**-tonss/ noun the most important or impressive part of something.

piecemeal adjective & adverb done in stages over a period of time.

piecework noun work that is paid for by the amount done and not the hours worked.

pied /rhymes with ride/ adjective having two or more different colours.

pied-à-terre /pyay-dah-**tair**/ noun (plural **pieds-à-terre** /pyay-dah-**tair**/) a small flat or house kept for occasional use.

pier noun 1 a structure leading out to sea or into a lake, used as a landing stage for boats. 2 a pillar supporting an arch or bridge.

pierce verb (**pierces, piercing, pierced**) 1 make a hole in something with a sharp object. 2 force or cut a way through. 3 (**piercing**) very sharp, cold, or high-pitched.

piety /**py**-uh-ti/ noun (plural **pieties**) the quality of being religious in a respectful and serious way.

piffle noun informal nonsense.

piffling adjective informal trivial and unimportant.

pig noun 1 an animal with a short, curly tail and a flat snout. 2 informal a greedy, dirty, or unpleasant person. 3 an oblong mass of iron or lead from a smelting furnace. verb (**pigs, pigging, pigged**) informal gorge yourself with food. ▫ **pig-headed** stupidly stubborn. **pig iron** iron when it is first taken out of a smelting furnace. ∎ **piggish** adjective **piglet** noun.

pigeon noun a plump grey and white bird with a cooing voice. ▫ **pigeon-chested** having a projecting breastbone. **pigeon-toed** having the toes and feet turned inwards.

 note that there is no d: pigeon.

pigeonhole noun 1 a small hole in a

wall leading into a place where pigeons nest. **2** each of a set of small compartments in a workplace, college, etc. where letters or messages may be left for individuals. **3** a category in which someone or something is put. **verb** (**pigeonholes, pigeonholing, pigeonholed**) put into a particular category.

piggery noun (plural **piggeries**) a place where pigs are kept.

piggy noun (plural **piggies**) a child's word for a pig or piglet. **adjective** like a pig. □ **piggy bank** a money box shaped like a pig.

piggyback noun a ride on someone's back and shoulders. **adverb** on the back and shoulders of another person.

pigment noun **1** the substance that gives natural colouring to animal or plant tissue. **2** a coloured powder mixed with a liquid to make paints, crayons, etc. ■ **pigmentation** noun **pigmented** adjective.

pigmy ⇒ **PYGMY**.

pigskin noun leather made from the hide of a pig.

pigsty noun (plural **pigsties**) **1** an enclosure for a pig or pigs. **2** a very dirty or untidy place.

pigswill noun kitchen refuse and scraps fed to pigs.

pigtail noun a length of hair worn in a plait at the back or on each side of the head.

pike¹ noun (plural **pike**) a freshwater fish with a long body and sharp teeth.

pike² noun (in the past) a weapon with a pointed metal head on a long wooden shaft.

pikestaff noun (in the past) the wooden shaft of a pike. □ **(as) plain as a pikestaff** very obvious.

pilaster /pi-**lass**-ter/ noun a column that projects from a wall.

pilchard noun a small fish of the herring family.

pile¹ noun **1** a heap of things lying one on top of another. **2** informal a large

amount. **3** a large imposing building. **verb** (**piles, piling, piled**) **1** place things one on top of the other. **2** (**pile up**) form a pile or very large quantity. **3** (**pile into** or **out of**) get into or out of a vehicle in a disorganized way. □ **pile-up** informal a crash involving a lot of vehicles.

pile² noun a heavy post driven into the ground to support foundations.

pile³ noun the soft surface of a carpet or a fabric, consisting of many projecting small threads.

piledriver noun a machine for driving piles into the ground.

piles plural noun haemorrhoids.

pilfer verb (**pilfers, pilfering, pilfered**) steal small items of little value.

pilgrim noun a person who travels to a sacred place for religious reasons.

pilgrimage noun a pilgrim's journey.

pill noun **1** a small round mass of solid medicine for swallowing whole. **2** (**the Pill**) a contraceptive pill.

pillage verb (**pillages, pillaging, pillaged**) steal from a place in a rough and violent way. **noun** the action of pillaging.

pillar noun **1** a tall upright structure used as a support for a building. **2** a source of help and support. □ **from pillar to post** from one place to another in an unsatisfactory way. **pillar box** (in the UK) a red cylindrical public postbox.

pillbox noun **1** a small box for holding pills. **2** a hat of a similar shape. **3** a small concrete fort.

pillion noun a seat for a passenger behind a motorcyclist.

pillory noun (plural **pillories**) (in the past) a wooden framework with holes for the head and hands, in which people were locked and left on display as a punishment. **verb** (**pillories, pillorying, pilloried**) **1** put someone in a pillory. **2** attack or ridicule publicly.

pillow noun a soft pad used to support the head when you lie down in bed. □ **pillow talk** intimate conversation between a couple in bed.

pillowcase noun a removable cloth cover for a pillow.

pilot noun **1** a person who flies an aircraft. **2** a person qualified to take charge of a ship entering or leaving a harbour. **3** something done or produced as a test before being introduced more widely. verb (**pilots, piloting, piloted**) **1** act as a pilot of an aircraft or ship. **2** test a scheme, project, etc. before introducing it more widely. □ **pilot light** a small gas burner that is kept alight permanently, used to fire a boiler.

pimento or **pimiento** noun (plural pimentos) a sweet red pepper.

pimp noun a man who controls prostitutes and takes part of their earnings. verb act as a pimp.

pimple noun a small, hard inflamed spot on the skin. ■ **pimply** adjective.

PIN or **PIN number** abbreviation personal identification number.

pin noun **1** a very thin pointed piece of metal with a round head, used to hold pieces of fabric together or as a fastener. **2** a metal projection from a electric plug. **3** a small brooch. **4** a steel rod used to join the ends of broken bones while they heal. **5** a metal peg in a hand grenade that prevents it exploding. **6** a skittle in bowling. **7** (**pins**) informal legs. verb (**pins, pinning, pinned**) **1** attach or fasten with a pin or pins. **2** hold someone firmly so they are unable to move. **3** (**pin down**) force someone to describe their plans in detail. **4** (**pin down**) trap an enemy by firing at them. **5** (**pin on**) fix blame or responsibility on. □ **pin money** a small sum of money for spending on everyday items. **pins and needles** a tingling sensation in a part of the body that is recovering from numbness. **pin-tuck** a very narrow tuck or pleat in a garment. **pin-up** a poster of an attractive person.

pinafore noun a collarless, sleeveless dress worn over a blouse or jumper.

pinball noun a game in which balls are shot across a sloping board and score points by striking targets.

pince-nez /panss-**nay**/ noun a pair of glasses with a nose clip instead of earpieces.

pincer noun **1** (**pincers**) a metal tool with blunt inward-curving jaws for gripping and pulling things. **2** a front claw of a lobster or similar shellfish.

pinch verb **1** grip flesh tightly between your finger and thumb. **2** (of a shoe) hurt a foot by being too tight. **3** Brit. informal steal. noun **1** an act of pinching. **2** an amount of an ingredient that can be held between your fingers and thumb. □ **feel the pinch** experience financial hardship.

pinched adjective (of a person's face) tight with cold or suffering.

pincushion noun a small pad into which you stick pins to store them.

pine¹ noun an evergreen tree that bears cones and has clusters of long needle-shaped leaves. □ **pine nut** the edible seed of various pines.

pine² verb (**pines, pining, pined**) **1** become weak. **2** (**pine for**) miss someone and long for their return.

pineapple noun a large juicy tropical fruit consisting of yellow flesh surrounded by a tough skin.

ping noun a short high-pitched ringing sound. verb make such a sound. □ **ping-pong** informal table tennis.

pinion¹ noun the outer part of a bird's wing. verb **1** tie or hold someone's arms or legs. **2** cut off the pinion of a bird so that it cannot fly.

pinion² noun a small cogwheel or spindle that engages with a large cogwheel.

pink¹ adjective of a colour midway between red and white. noun **1** a pink colour. **2** (**the pink**) informal the best condition.

pink² noun a plant with sweet-smelling pink or white flowers.

pink³ verb cut a scalloped or zigzag edge on fabric. □ **pinking shears** scissors with a thick serrated blade, used for pinking fabric.

pinkie noun informal the little finger.

pinnacle noun **1** a high pointed piece

of rock. **2** a small pointed turret on a roof. **3** the most successful point.

pinpoint noun a tiny dot. adjective absolutely precise. verb locate something exactly.

pinprick noun **1** a prick caused by a pin. **2** a very small dot or amount.

pinstripe noun a very narrow white stripe woven into dark material. ■ **pinstriped** adjective.

pint noun **1** a unit of liquid or dry capacity equal to one eighth of a gallon, in Britain equal to 0.568 litre. **2** Brit. informal a pint of beer. □ **pint-sized** informal very small.

pinwheel noun a small cogwheel in which the teeth are formed by pins set into the rim.

pioneer noun **1** a person who explores or settles in a new region. **2** a developer of new ideas or techniques. verb (**pioneers, pioneering, pioneered**) be a pioneer of a new idea or technique.

pious adjective **1** religious in a very respectful and serious way. **2** pretending to be moral and good in order to impress other people. **3** (of a hope) very much wanted, but unlikely to be achieved. ■ **piously** adverb.

pip[1] noun a small hard seed in a fruit.

pip[2] noun Brit. a short high-pitched sound used as a signal on the radio or in a telephone.

pip[3] verb (**pips, pipping, pipped**) Brit. informal (**be pipped**) defeat by a very small amount or at the last moment.

pipe noun **1** a tube through which water, gas, oil, etc. can flow. **2** a device for smoking tobacco, consisting of a narrow tube that opens into a small bowl in which the tobacco is burned. **3** a wind instrument consisting of a single tube with holes along its length that you cover with your fingers to produce different notes. **4** each of the tubes by which notes are produced in an organ. **5** (**pipes**) bagpipes. verb (**pipes, piping, piped**) **1** send a liquid through a pipe. **2** transmit music, a programme, a signal, etc. by wire or cable. **3** play a tune on a pipe. **4** sing or say something in a high voice.

5 decorate something with piping. □ **pipe cleaner** a piece of wire covered with fibre, used to clean a tobacco pipe. **piped music** pre-recorded background music played through loudspeakers. **pipe dream** a hope or plan that is impossible to achieve. **pipe down** informal be less noisy. **pipe up** informal say something suddenly.

pipeline noun a long pipe for carrying oil, gas, etc. over a distance. □ **in the pipeline** in the process of being developed.

piper noun a person who plays a pipe or bagpipes.

pipette noun a thin tube used in a laboratory for transferring small quantities of liquid.

piping noun **1** lengths of pipe. **2** lines of icing or cream used to decorate cakes and desserts. **3** thin cord covered in fabric and used for decorating a garment or piece of furniture. □ **piping hot** (of food or water) very hot.

pipistrelle noun a small insect-eating bat.

pipit noun a bird that lives on the ground in open country.

pippin noun a sweet red and yellow apple.

pipsqueak noun informal an unimportant person.

piquant adjective having a pleasantly strong and sharp taste. ■ **piquancy** noun **piquantly** adverb.

pique /peek/ noun a feeling of irritation mixed with hurt pride. verb (**piques, piquing, piqued**) **1** (**be piqued**) feel both irritated and hurt. **2** stimulate someone's interest.

piracy noun **1** the attacking and robbing of ships at sea. **2** the reproduction of a film or recording for profit without permission.

piranha /pi-rah-nuh/ noun a freshwater fish with very sharp teeth.

pirate noun a person who attacks and robs ships at sea. adjective **1** (of a film or recording) having been reproduced and used for profit without permission. **2** (of an organization) broadcasting without permission. **verb** (**pirates**, **pirating**, **pirated**) reproduce a film or recording for profit without permission.

pirouette noun a movement in ballet involving spinning on one foot. **verb** (**pirouettes**, **pirouetting**, **pirouetted**) perform a pirouette.

piscatorial /piss-kuh-**tor**-i-uhl/ **adjective** having to do with fish.

Pisces /**py**-seez/ **noun** a sign of the zodiac (the Fish or Fishes), 21 February–19 March.

piss vulgar **verb** urinate. **noun 1** urine. **2** an act of urinating. □ **piss about** (or **around**) Brit. mess around. **piss off 1** go away. **2** annoy someone.

pissed adjective vulgar **1** Brit. drunk. **2** N. Amer. very annoyed.

pistachio /pi-**stah**-shi-oh/ noun (plural **pistachios**) a small pale green nut.

piste /peest/ noun a course or run for skiing.

pistil noun Botany the female organs of a flower, comprising the stigma, style, and ovary.

pistol noun a small gun designed to be held in one hand.

piston noun a sliding disc or cylinder fitting closely inside a tube in which it moves up and down as part of an engine or pump.

pit[1] **noun 1** a large hole in the ground. **2** a mine for coal, chalk, etc. **3** a hollow in a surface. **4** a sunken area in a workshop floor where people can work on the underside of vehicles. **5** an area at the side of a track where racing cars are serviced and refuelled. **6** a part of a theatre where the orchestra plays. **7** (**the pits**) informal a very bad place or situation. **verb** (**pits**, **pitting**, **pitted**) **1** (**pit against**) set someone or something to compete with. **2** make a hollow in the surface of something. □ **pit bull terrier** a fierce breed of bull terrier. **the pit of the stomach** an area low down in the stomach.

pit[2] chiefly N. Amer. **noun** the stone of a fruit. **verb** (**pits**, **pitting**, **pitted**) remove the stone from a fruit.

pit-a-pat noun a sound like quick light taps.

pitch[1] **noun 1** Brit. an area of ground used for outdoor team games. **2** the degree of highness or lowness in a sound or tone. **3** the steepness of a roof. **4** a particular level of intensity. **5** a form of words used when trying to sell something: *a sales pitch.* **6** Brit. a place on a street where someone performing or selling something has settled. **verb 1** throw heavily or roughly. **2** set your voice, a sound, or a piece of music at a particular pitch. **3** aim something at a particular level, target, or audience. **4** set up a tent or camp. **5** (**pitch in**) informal join in enthusiastically with an activity. **6** (**pitch up**) informal arrive. **7** (of a moving ship, aircraft, or vehicle) rock from side to side or from front to back. **8** (**pitched**) (of a roof) sloping. □ **pitched battle** a battle in which the time and place are decided beforehand.

pitch[2] **noun** a sticky black substance made from tar or turpentine and used for waterproofing. □ **pitch-black** (or **pitch-dark**) completely dark.

pitcher noun a large jug.

pitchfork noun a farm tool with a long handle and two sharp metal prongs, used for lifting hay.

piteous adjective deserving or arousing pity. ■ **piteously** adverb.

pitfall noun a hidden danger or difficulty.

pith noun **1** spongy white tissue lining the rind of citrus fruits. **2** spongy tissue in the stems of many plants. **3** the true nature of something. □ **pith helmet** a lightweight hat made from the dried pith of a plant, used for protection from the sun.

pithead noun the top of a mineshaft and the area around it.

pithy adjective (**pithier**, **pithiest**) **1** (of a fruit or plant) containing a lot of pith. **2** (of language) concise and clear.

pitiable adjective **1** deserving or arousing pity. **2** deserving contempt.

pitiful adjective **1** deserving or

arousing pity. **2** very small or poor. ∎ **pitifully** adverb.

pitiless adjective showing no pity.

piton noun (in rock climbing) a peg or spike driven into a crack to support a climber or hold a rope.

pitta noun a type of flat bread which can be split open to hold a filling.

pittance noun a very small or inadequate amount of money.

pitter-patter noun the sound of quick light steps or taps.

pituitary gland noun a gland at the base of the brain which controls growth and development.

pity noun (plural **pities**) **1** a feeling of sympathy and sadness caused by the suffering of other people. **2** a cause for regret or disappointment. verb (**pities, pitying, pitied**) feel pity for.

pivot noun the central point, pin, or shaft on which a mechanism turns or is balanced. verb (**pivots, pivoting, pivoted**) **1** turn on or as if on a pivot. **2** (**pivot on**) depend on.

pivotal adjective of central importance.

pixel noun any of the tiny areas of light on a computer screen which make up an image.

pixie or **pixy** noun (plural **pixies**) an imaginary being portrayed as a tiny man with pointed ears.

pizza noun a flat, round base of dough baked with a topping of tomatoes, cheese, and other ingredients.

pizzeria /peet-zuh-**ree**-uh/ noun a pizza restaurant.

pizzicato /pit-zi-**kah**-toh/ adverb & adjective plucking the strings of a stringed instrument such as a violin with your finger.

placard noun a large written sign fixed to a wall or carried during a demonstration.

placate verb (**placates, placating, placated**) make someone less angry or upset. ∎ **placatory** adjective.

place noun **1** a particular position or location. **2** an opportunity to study on a course or be a member of a team.

3 a position in a sequence. **4** (in place names) a square or short street. verb (**places, placing, placed**) **1** put something in a particular position or situation. **2** find an appropriate place or role for. **3** remember where you have seen someone before. **4** make a reservation or order. □ **take place** occur.

placebo /pluh-**see**-boh/ noun (plural **placebos**) a medicine given to a patient to make them feel happier or more confident rather than for any physical effect.

placement noun **1** the action of placing. **2** a temporary position given to someone in a workplace.

placenta /pluh-**sen**-tuh/ noun (plural **placentae** /pluh-**sen**-tee/ or **placentas**) an organ that is formed in the womb during pregnancy and which supplies blood and nourishment to the fetus through the umbilical cord.

placid adjective not easily upset or excited. ∎ **placidity** noun **placidly** adverb.

placket noun an opening in a garment, covering fastenings or giving access to a pocket.

plagiarize or **plagiarise** /**play**-juh-ryz/ verb (**plagiarizes, plagiarizing, plagiarized**) copy another person's words or ideas and pretend that they are your own. ∎ **plagiarism** noun **plagiarist** noun.

plague noun **1** an infectious disease causing fever and delirium. **2** an unusually and unpleasantly large number of insects or animals. verb (**plagues, plaguing, plagued**) **1** cause continual trouble to. **2** pester someone continually.

plaice noun (plural **plaice**) a flat brown fish with orange spots, used for food.

plaid /plad/ noun fabric woven in a chequered or tartan design.

plain adjective **1** simple or ordinary. **2** without a pattern. **3** unmarked. **4** easy to understand; clear. **5** (of a woman or girl) not attractive. **6** sheer; simple. noun a large area of flat land with few trees. □ **plain chocolate** Brit. dark, slightly bitter chocolate made without added milk. **plain clothes** ordinary clothes rather than uniform. **plain sailing** smooth and easy progress. ■ **plainly** adverb **plainness** noun.

plainsong or **plainchant** noun a kind of medieval church music that was sung by a number of voices without any accompanying instruments.

plaintiff noun a person who brings a case against someone in a court of law.

plaintive adjective sounding sad and mournful. ■ **plaintively** adverb.

plait noun Brit. a length of hair or rope made up of strands woven together. **verb** form into a plait or plaits.

plan noun **1** a detailed proposal for doing or achieving something. **2** an intention. **3** a scheme for making regular payments towards a pension, insurance policy, etc. **4** a map or diagram. **verb** (**plans, planning, planned**) **1** decide on and arrange something in advance. **2** intend to do something. **3** (**plan for**) make preparations for. **4** make a plan of a building, town, garden, etc. ■ **planner** noun.

plane¹ noun **1** a completely flat surface. **2** a level of existence or thought. **adjective 1** completely flat. **2** relating to two-dimensional surfaces or sizes. **verb** (**planes, planing, planed**) **1** (of a bird) soar without moving the wings. **2** skim over the surface of water.

plane² noun an aeroplane.

plane³ or **planer** noun a tool used to smooth a wooden surface by cutting thin shavings from it. **verb** (**planes, planing, planed**) smooth a surface with a plane.

plane⁴ noun a tall tree with broad leaves and peeling bark.

planet noun a large round mass in space that orbits round a star. ■ **planetary** adjective.

planetarium noun (plural **planetariums** or **planetaria** /plan-i-**tair**-i-uh/) a building in which images of stars, planets, and constellations are projected on to a domed ceiling.

plangent /plan-juhnt/ adjective (of a sound) loud and melancholy.

plank noun a long, flat piece of timber.

□ **walk the plank** (in the past) be forced to walk blindfold along a plank over the side of a ship to your death in the sea.

plankton noun tiny creatures living in the sea or fresh water.

plant noun **1** a living thing that absorbs substances through its roots and makes nutrients in its leaves by photosynthesis. **2** a place where a manufacturing process takes place. **3** machinery used in a manufacturing process. **4** a person placed in a group as a spy. **verb 1** place a seed, bulb, or plant in the ground so that it can grow. **2** place in a specified position. **3** secretly place a bomb. **4** hide something among someone's belongings to make them appear guilty of something. **5** send someone to join a group to act as a spy. **6** fix an idea in someone's mind. ■ **planter** noun.

Plantagenet /plan-**taj**-uh-nuht/ noun a member of the English royal house which ruled 1154–1485.

plantain noun **1** a low-growing plant with a rosette of leaves and a green flower spike. **2** a type of banana.

plantation noun **1** a large estate on which crops such as coffee, sugar, and tobacco are grown. **2** an area in which trees have been planted.

plaque noun **1** an ornamental tablet fixed to a wall in memory of a person or event. **2** a sticky deposit that forms on teeth and in which bacteria grow quickly.

plasma /plaz-muh/ noun **1** the colourless fluid part of blood, lymph, or milk, in which cells or fat globules are suspended. **2** a gas of positive ions and free electrons with little or no overall electric charge.

plaster noun **1** a soft mixture of lime with sand or cement and water for spreading on walls and ceilings to form a smooth hard surface when dried. **2** (also **plaster of Paris**) a hard white substance made by adding water to powdered gypsum, used for setting broken bones and making sculptures and casts. **3** a sticky strip of material for covering cuts and wounds. **verb** (**plasters, plastering, plastered**) **1** apply plaster to. **2** coat thickly. **3** make hair lie flat by applying liquid to it. **4** (**plastered**) informal drunk. ■ **plasterer** noun.

plasterboard **noun** board made of plaster set between two sheets of paper, used to line interior walls and ceilings.

plastic **noun** a chemically produced material that can be moulded into shape while soft and then set into a hard or slightly flexible form. **adjective 1** made of plastic. **2** easily shaped. **3** artificial. □ **plastic surgery** surgery performed to repair or reconstruct parts of the body. ■ **plasticity** noun **plasticky** adjective.

plasticine **noun** trademark a soft modelling material.

plate **noun 1** a flat dish for holding food. **2** bowls, cups, and other utensils made of gold or silver. **3** a thin, flat piece of metal, plastic, etc. **4** a small, flat piece of metal with writing on it fixed to a wall or door. **5** a printed photograph or illustration in a book. **6** each of the several rigid pieces which together make up the earth's surface. **verb** (**plates, plating, plated**) cover a metal object with a thin coating of a different metal. □ **plate glass** thick glass used for shop windows and doors.

plateau /**plat**-oh/ **noun** (plural **plateaux** /**plat**-ohz/ or **plateaus**) **1** an area of fairly level high ground. **2** a state of little or no change after a period of activity or progress. **verb** (**plateaus, plateauing, plateaued**) reach a plateau.

platelet **noun** a disc-shaped cell fragment found in large numbers in blood and involved in clotting.

platen /**plat**-uhn/ **noun 1** a plate in a small printing press which presses the paper against the type. **2** a cylindrical roller in a typewriter against which the paper is held.

platform **noun 1** a raised level surface on which people or things can stand. **2** a raised structure along the side of a railway track where passengers get on and off trains. **3** a raised structure standing in the sea from which oil or gas wells can be drilled. **4** the stated policy of a political party or group. **5** an opportunity for the expression or exchange of views. **6** a very thick sole on a shoe.

platinum **noun** a precious silvery-white metallic element.

platitude **noun** a remark that has been used too often to be interesting. ■ **platitudinous** adjective.

Platonic /pluh-**ton**-ik/ **adjective 1** having to do with the ideas of Plato, a philosopher of ancient Greece. **2** (**platonic**) (of love or friendship) intimate and affectionate but not sexual.

platoon **noun** a subdivision of a company of soldiers.

platter **noun** a large flat serving dish.

platypus or **duck-billed platypus** **noun** (plural **platypuses**) a mammal with a duck-like bill and webbed feet, which lays eggs.

plaudits **plural noun** praise.

plausible **adjective 1** seeming reasonable or probable. **2** skilled at making people believe something. ■ **plausibility** noun **plausibly** adverb.

play **verb 1** take part in games for enjoyment. **2** take part in a sport or contest. **3** compete against another player or team. **4** act the role of a character in a play or film. **5** perform on a musical instrument. **6** perform a piece of music. **7** move a piece or display a playing card when it is your turn in a game. **8** make a tape, CD, or record produce sounds. **9** move or flicker over a surface. **noun 1** games that people take part in for enjoyment. **2** the performing of a sporting match. **3** a move in a sport or game. **4** a piece of writing performed by actors. **5** freedom of movement. **6** constantly changing movement. □ **make great play of** draw attention to something in an exaggerated way. **make a play for** informal attempt to attract or gain. **play about** (or **around**) behave in a casual or irresponsible way. **play-act** pretend something in an attention-seeking way. **play along** pretend to cooperate. **play by ear** **1** perform music without having to read from a score. **2** (play it by ear) informal proceed without having formed a plan. **play down** disguise the importance of. **playing card** each of a set of rectangular pieces of card with numbers and symbols on one side, used in various games. **play-off** an extra match played to decide the outcome of a contest. **play on** exploit someone's weak point. **play up** **1** emphasize the extent or importance of. **2** (play up to) humour or flatter. **3** Brit. informal cause problems.

playboy noun a wealthy man who spends his time seeking pleasure.

player noun **1** a person taking part in a sport or game. **2** a person who has influence in a particular area. **3** a person who plays a musical instrument. **4** a device for playing compact discs, cassettes, etc. **5** an actor.

playful adjective **1** fond of games and amusement. **2** light-hearted. ■ **playfully** adverb.

playground noun an outdoor area provided for children to play in.

playgroup or **playschool** noun Brit. a regular supervised play session for pre-school children.

playhouse noun **1** a theatre. **2** a toy house for children to play in.

playmate noun a friend with whom a child plays.

playpen noun a small portable enclosure in which a baby or small child can play safely.

plaything noun **1** a toy. **2** a person who is treated as amusing but unimportant.

playwright noun a person who writes plays.

plaza noun **1** an open public space in a built-up area. **2** N. Amer. a shopping centre.

plc or **PLC** abbreviation Brit. public limited company.

plea noun **1** a request made in an urgent and emotional way. **2** a formal statement made by or on behalf of a person charged with an offence in a law court.

plead verb (**pleads**, **pleading**, **pleaded** or N. Amer., Scottish, or dialect **pled**) **1** make an emotional appeal. **2** argue in support of something. **3** state formally in court whether you are guilty or not guilty of the offence with which you are charged. **4** present something as an excuse for doing or not doing something. ■ **pleadingly** adverb.

pleasant adjective **1** satisfactory and enjoyable. **2** friendly and likeable. ■ **pleasantly** adverb.

pleasantry noun (plural **pleasantries**) **1** an unimportant remark made as part of a polite conversation. **2** a mildly amusing joke.

please verb (**pleases**, **pleasing**, **pleased**) **1** make someone feel happy and satisfied. **2** wish or desire to do something. **3** (please yourself) consider only your own wishes. adverb used in polite requests or questions, or to accept an offer.

pleased adjective feeling or showing pleasure and satisfaction.

pleasurable adjective enjoyable. ■ **pleasurably** adverb.

pleasure noun **1** a feeling of happy satisfaction and enjoyment. **2** an event or activity which you enjoy. verb (**pleasures**, **pleasuring**, **pleasured**) give pleasure to.

pleat noun a fold in fabric, held by stitching at the top or side. verb fold or form into pleats.

pleb noun informal, disapproving a member of the lower social classes.

plebeian /pli-bee-uhn/ noun a member of the ordinary people or the lower classes. adjective ordinary or unsophisticated.

plebiscite /pleb-i-syt/ noun a vote made by everyone entitled to do so on an important public question.

plectrum noun (plural **plectrums** or **plectra**) a thin flat piece of plastic or tortoiseshell used to pluck the strings of a guitar.

pled North American, Scottish, or

dialect past participle of **PLEAD**.

pledge noun **1** a solemn promise or undertaking. **2** something valuable promised as a guarantee that a debt will be paid or a promise kept, and forfeited if this does not happen. **3** a thing given as a token of love or loyalty. verb (**pledges**, **pledging**, **pledged**) **1** solemnly undertake to do or give something. **2** promise something as a pledge.

plenary /**plee**-nuh-ri/ adjective **1** full; complete. **2** (of a meeting at a conference or assembly) to be attended by all participants.

plenipotentiary /plen-i-puh-**ten**-shuh-ri/ noun (plural **plenipotentiaries**) a person given full power by a government to act on its behalf. adjective having full power to take independent action.

plenitude noun formal the condition of being full, complete, or abundant.

plenteous adjective literary plentiful.

plentiful adjective existing in or producing great quantities. ■ **plentifully** adverb.

plenty pronoun a large or sufficient amount or quantity. noun a situation in which food and other necessities are available in sufficiently large quantities.

plenum /**plee**-nuhm/ noun an assembly of all the members of a group or committee.

plethora /**pleth**-uh-ruh/ noun an excessive amount or number.

pleurisy /**ploor**-i-si/ noun inflammation of the membranes that line the chest and envelop the lungs, causing pain during breathing.

plexus noun (plural same or **plexuses**) a complex network or web-like structure.

pliable /**ply**-uh-b'l/ adjective **1** easily bent. **2** easily influenced or persuaded. ■ **pliability** noun.

pliant adjective pliable.

pliers plural noun pincers having jaws with flat surfaces, used for gripping small objects and bending or cutting wire.

plight[1] noun a dangerous or difficult situation.

plight[2] verb old use **1** solemnly promise faith or loyalty. **2** (**be plighted to**) be engaged to be married to.

plimsoll noun Brit. a light rubber-soled canvas sports shoe.

plink verb make a short, metallic ringing sound. noun a plinking sound.

plinth noun a heavy block or slab supporting a statue or forming the base of a column.

PLO abbreviation Palestine Liberation Organization.

plod verb (**plods**, **plodding**, **plodded**) **1** walk slowly with heavy steps. **2** work slowly and steadily at a dull task. noun a slow, heavy walk.

plonk[1] verb informal put something down heavily or carelessly.

plonk[2] noun Brit. informal cheap wine.

plonker noun Brit. informal a foolish or incompetent person.

plop noun a sound like that of a small, solid object dropping into water without a splash. verb (**plops**, **plopping**, **plopped**) fall or drop with a plop.

plot noun **1** a secret plan to do something illegal or harmful. **2** the main sequence of events in a play, novel, or film. **3** a small piece of ground marked out for building, gardening, etc. verb (**plots**, **plotting**, **plotted**) **1** secretly make plans to carry out something illegal or harmful. **2** mark a route or position on a chart or graph. ■ **plotter** noun.

plough (US spelling **plow**) noun **1** a large farming implement with one or more blades fixed in a frame, used to turn over soil. **2** (**the Plough**) a formation of seven stars shaped like a simple plough, in the constellation Ursa Major (the Great Bear). verb **1** turn earth with a plough. **2** move forward with difficulty or force. **3** (of a ship or boat) travel through an area of water. **4** (**plough in**) invest money in a business.

ploughman's lunch noun Brit. a meal of bread, cheese, and pickle.

plover /rhymes with lover/ noun a

short-billed wading bird.

ploy noun a cunning act performed to gain an advantage.

pluck verb **1** take hold of something and quickly remove it from its place. **2** pull out a hair or feather. **3** pull the feathers from a bird's carcass to prepare it for cooking. **4** pull at. **5** sound a stringed instrument with your fingers or a plectrum. **6** (**pluck up**) summon up enough courage to do something frightening. noun courage.

plucky adjective (**pluckier, pluckiest**) having a lot of courage and determination. ■ **pluckily** adverb.

plug noun **1** a piece of solid material that tightly blocks a hole. **2** a device with metal pins that fit into holes in a socket to make an electrical connection. **3** an electrical socket. **4** informal a piece of publicity promoting a product or event. verb (**plugs, plugging, plugged**) **1** block a hole. **2** (**plug in**) connect an appliance to an electric circuit. **3** informal promote a product or event by mentioning it publicly. **4** (**plug away**) informal proceed steadily with a task.

plughole noun Brit. a hole at the bottom or end of a sink or bath, through which the water drains away.

plum noun **1** an oval fruit which is purple, reddish, or yellow when ripe. **2** a reddish-purple colour. adjective informal highly desirable: *a plum job*.

plumage noun a bird's feathers.

plumb[1] verb **1** measure the depth of water. **2** explore or experience something fully. **3** test an upright surface to find out if it is vertical. noun a heavy object attached to a plumb line. adverb informal exactly. adjective vertical. □ **plumb line** a line with a heavy object attached to it, used for measuring the depth of water or checking that a wall, post, etc. is vertical.

plumb[2] verb (**plumb in**) install a bath, washing machine, etc. and connect it to water and drainage pipes.

plumber noun a person who fits and repairs the pipes and fittings used in the supply of water and heating in a building.

plumbing noun the system of pipes and fittings required for the water supply and heating in a building.

plume noun **1** a long, soft feather or group of feathers. **2** a long spreading cloud of smoke or vapour. ■ **plumed** adjective **plumy** adjective.

plummet verb (**plummets, plummeting, plummeted**) **1** fall straight down at high speed. **2** decrease rapidly in value or amount. noun a steep and rapid fall or drop.

plummy adjective (**plummier, plummiest**) Brit. informal (of a person's voice) typical of the English upper classes.

plump[1] adjective **1** full and rounded in shape. **2** rather fat. verb (**plump up**) make something more full and rounded.

plump[2] verb **1** set or sit down heavily. **2** (**plump for**) decide in favour of one of two or more possibilities.

plunder verb (**plunders, plundering, plundered**) force your way into a place and steal everything of value. noun **1** the action of plundering. **2** goods obtained by plundering.

plunge verb (**plunges, plunging, plunged**) **1** fall or move suddenly and uncontrollably. **2** jump or dive quickly. **3** (**plunge in**) begin a course of action without thought or care. **4** (**be plunged into**) be suddenly brought into a particular state. **5** push or thrust quickly. noun an act or instance of plunging. □ **take the plunge** informal commit yourself to a bold course of action.

plunger noun **1** a part of a device that works with a plunging or thrusting movement. **2** a rubber cup on a long handle, used to clear blocked pipes by means of suction.

plunk verb informal play a keyboard or pluck a stringed instrument in a heavy-handed way.

pluperfect adjective Grammar (of a tense) referring to an action completed earlier than some past point of time, formed by *had* and the past participle (as in *he had gone by then*).

plural adjective **1** more than one in number. **2** Grammar (of a word or form) referring to more than one. noun Grammar a plural word or form.

pluralism noun **1** a system in which power is shared among a number of political parties. **2** the acceptance within a society of a number of groups with different beliefs or ethnic backgrounds. ■ **pluralist** noun & adjective.

plurality noun (plural **pluralities**) **1** the fact or state of being plural. **2** a large number of people or things.

plus preposition **1** with the addition of. **2** informal together with. adjective **1** (after a number or amount) at least. **2** (after a grade) rather better than. **3** (before a number) above zero. **4** having a positive electric charge. noun **1** (also **plus sign**) the symbol +, indicating addition or a positive value. **2** informal an advantage. conjunction informal also. □ **plus fours** men's trousers that are cut wide over the thigh and are gathered in at mid-calf length.

plush noun a fabric with a long, soft nap. adjective informal luxurious.

plutocracy /ploo-tok-ruh-si/ noun (plural **plutocracies**) **1** government by the wealthy. **2** a society governed by the wealthy.

plutocrat noun a person who is powerful because of their wealth.

plutonium /ploo-toh-ni-uhm/ noun a radioactive metallic element used as a fuel in nuclear reactors and as an explosive in atomic weapons.

ply[1] noun (plural **plies**) a thickness or layer of a material.

ply[2] verb (**plies**, **plying**, **plied**) **1** work steadily using a tool. **2** work steadily at your job. **3** (of a ship or vehicle) travel regularly over a route. **4** (**ply with**) keep presenting someone with food, drink, or questions.

plywood noun board consisting of layers of wood glued together.

p.m. abbreviation after noon.

ⓘ short for Latin *post meridiem*.

pneumatic /nyoo-mat-ik/ adjective containing or operated by air or gas under pressure.

pneumonia /nyoo-moh-ni-uh/ noun an infection causing inflammation in the lungs.

poach[1] verb cook something by simmering it in a small amount of liquid.

poach[2] verb **1** hunt game or catch fish illegally from private or protected areas. **2** unfairly entice customers, workers, etc. away from someone else. ■ **poacher** noun.

pock noun a pockmark. ■ **pocked** adjective.

pocket noun **1** a small bag sewn into or on clothing, used for carrying small articles. **2** a small area or group that is different from its surroundings. **3** informal the money that you have available: *gifts to suit every pocket*. **4** an opening at the corner or on the side of a billiard table into which balls are struck. verb (**pockets**, **pocketing**, **pocketed**) **1** put something into your pocket. **2** take something that is not yours. □ **pocket money 1** a small amount of money given to children regularly by their parents. **2** a small amount of money for minor expenses.

pockmark noun **1** a hollow scar or mark on the skin left by a spot. **2** a mark or hollow area disfiguring a surface. ■ **pockmarked** adjective.

pod[1] noun a long seed case of a pea, bean, etc. verb (**pods**, **podding**, **podded**) remove peas or beans from their pods before cooking.

pod[2] noun a small herd of whales or similar sea mammals.

podgy adjective Brit. informal rather fat; chubby.

podium noun (plural **podiums** or **podia**) a small platform on which a person stands to conduct an orchestra or give a speech.

poem noun a piece of imaginative writing in verse.

poesy /poh-i-zi/ noun old use poetry.

poet noun a person who writes poems.

□ **Poet Laureate** (plural **Poets Laureate**) a poet officially appointed to write poems for important occasions.

poetic or **poetical** adjective **1** having to do with poetry. **2** expressed in a sensitive and imaginative way. □ **poetic justice** deserved punishment or reward. **poetic licence** freedom to change facts or the normal rules of language to achieve a special effect in writing. ■ **poetically** adverb.

poetry noun **1** poems as a whole or as a form of literature. **2** a quality of beauty and sensitivity.

po-faced adjective Brit. informal serious and disapproving.

pogo stick noun a toy for bouncing around on, consisting of a pole on a spring, with a bar to stand on and a handle at the top.

pogrom noun an organized massacre of an ethnic group, originally that of Jews in Russia or eastern Europe.

poignant /poy-nyuhnt/ adjective making you feel sadness or regret. ■ **poignancy** noun **poignantly** adverb.

point noun **1** the tapered, sharp end of a tool, weapon, or other object. **2** a particular place or moment. **3** an item, detail, or idea. **4** (**the point**) the most important part of what is being discussed. **5** the advantage or purpose of something. **6** a unit of scoring, value, or measurement. **7** a small dot used as punctuation or in decimal numbers. **8** each of thirty-two directions marked at equal distances round a compass. **9** a narrow piece of land jutting out into the sea. **10** (**points**) Brit. a junction of two railway lines. **11** (also **power point**) Brit. an electrical socket. **12** (**points**) a set of electrical contacts in the distributor of a motor vehicle. verb **1** direct someone's attention by extending your finger. **2** aim, indicate, or face in a particular direction. **3** (**point out**) make someone aware of. **4** (**point to**) indicate that something is likely to happen. **5** fill in the joints of brickwork or tiling with mortar or cement. □ **point of view** a particular attitude or opinion. **point-to-point** (plural **point-to-points**) a cross-country race for horses used in hunting.

pointed adjective **1** having a sharpened or tapered tip or end. **2** (of a remark or look) directed towards a particular person and expressing a clear message.

pointer noun **1** a long, thin piece of metal on a scale or dial which moves to give a reading. **2** a hint or tip. **3** a breed of dog that, when it scents game, stands rigid and looks towards it.

pointless adjective having little or no sense or purpose. ■ **pointlessly** adverb.

poise noun **1** a graceful way of holding your body. **2** a calm and confident manner. verb **1** cause to be balanced or suspended. **2** (**poised**) calm and confident. **3** (**be poised to do**) be ready to do.

poison noun **1** a substance that causes death or injury to a person or animal that swallows or absorbs it. **2** a harmful influence. verb **1** harm or kill a person or animal with poison. **2** put poison on or in. **3** have a harmful effect on. ■ **poisoner** noun.

poisonous adjective **1** producing or having the effect of poison. **2** extremely unpleasant or spiteful.

poke verb (**pokes**, **poking**, **poked**) **1** prod with a finger or a sharp object. **2** (**poke about** or **around**) look or search around. **3** push or stick out in a particular direction. noun an act of poking.

poker[1] noun a metal rod used for prodding an open fire.

poker[2] noun a card game in which the players bet on the value of the hands dealt to them. □ **poker face** a blank expression that hides your true feelings.

poky or **pokey** adjective (**pokier**, **pokiest**) (of a room or building) uncomfortably small and cramped.

polar adjective **1** relating to the North or South Poles or the regions around them. **2** having an electrical or magnetic field. **3** completely opposite. □ **polar bear** a large white bear from the Arctic.

polarity noun (plural **polarities**) **1** the state of having poles or opposites. **2** the direction of a magnetic or electric field.

polarize or **polarise** verb (**polarizes, polarizing, polarized**) **1** divide people into two sharply contrasting groups with different opinions. **2** Physics restrict the vibrations of a wave of light to one direction. **3** give magnetic or electric polarity to. ■ **polarization** noun.

Polaroid noun trademark **1** a material that polarizes the light passing through it, used in sunglasses. **2** a camera that produces a finished print rapidly after each exposure.

Pole noun a person from Poland.

pole[1] noun a long, thin rounded piece of wood or metal, used as a support. □ **pole vault** an athletic event in which competitors vault over a high bar with the aid of a long pole.

pole[2] noun **1** either of the two points (**North Pole** or **South Pole**) at opposite ends of the earth's axis. **2** each of the two opposite points of a magnet at which magnetic forces are strongest. **3** the positive or negative terminal of an electric cell or battery. □ **be poles apart** have nothing in common.

poleaxe (US spelling **poleax**) noun a large axe. verb (**poleaxes, poleaxing, poleaxed**) kill or knock down with a heavy blow.

polecat noun **1** a dark brown weasel-like animal with an unpleasant smell. **2** N. Amer. a skunk.

polemic /puh-**lem**-ik/ noun **1** a speech or piece of writing that argues strongly for or against something. **2** (also **polemics**) the practice of using fierce argument or discussion. adjective (also **polemical**) having to do with fierce argument or discussion. ■ **polemicist** noun.

police noun an official body of people employed by a state to prevent and solve crime and maintain public order. verb (**polices, policing, policed**) **1** maintain law and order in an area. **2** make sure that a set of rules is obeyed. □ **police state** a state in which people are employed by the government to watch people secretly and control their activities. **police station** the premises of a local police force.

policeman or **policewoman** noun a member of a police force.

policy[1] noun (plural **policies**) a course of action adopted or proposed by an organization or person.

policy[2] noun (plural **policies**) a contract of insurance.

polio or **poliomyelitis** /poh-li-oh-my-uh-**ly**-tiss/ noun a disease that can cause temporary or permanent paralysis.

Polish noun the language of Poland. adjective relating to Poland.

polish verb **1** make something smooth and shiny by rubbing. **2** (**polish up**) improve a skill. **3** (**polish off**) finish eating or doing something quickly. noun **1** a substance used to polish something. **2** an act of polishing. **3** smoothness or glossiness produced by polishing. **4** refinement or elegance. ■ **polisher** noun.

polite adjective (**politer, politest**) **1** respectful and considerate towards others; courteous. **2** civilized or well bred. ■ **politely** adverb **politeness** noun.

politic adjective (of an action) sensible and wise in the circumstances.

political adjective **1** relating to the government or public affairs of a country. **2** related to or interested in politics. □ **political correctness** the avoidance of language or behaviour that could offend certain groups of people. **political prisoner** a person who is imprisoned for their beliefs rather than because they have committed a crime. ■ **politically** adverb.

politician noun a person who holds an elected position within the government.

politicize or **politicise** verb (**politicizes, politicizing, politicized**)

1 make someone interested in politics. **2** make something a political issue. ∎ **politicization** noun.

politics noun **1** the activities concerned with governing a country or area. **2** a particular set of political beliefs. **3** activities concerned with gaining or using power within an organization or group: *office politics.*

polity noun (plural **polities**) **1** a form of government. **2** a society as a politically organized state.

polka noun a lively dance for couples. □ **polka dot** each of a number of dots that are evenly spaced to form a pattern.

poll /rhymes with pole or doll/ noun **1** the process of voting in an election. **2** a record of the number of votes cast. verb **1** record the opinion or vote of. **2** (of a candidate in an election) receive a particular number of votes. □ **poll tax** a tax paid at the same rate by every adult.

pollard verb cut off the top and side branches of a tree to encourage new growth.

pollen noun a powder produced by the male part of a flower, which is carried by bees, the wind, etc. and can fertilize other flowers. □ **pollen count** a measure of the amount of pollen in the air.

pollinate verb (**pollinates, pollinating, pollinated**) carry pollen to and fertilize a flower or plant. ∎ **pollination** noun.

pollster noun a person who carries out opinion polls.

pollutant noun a substance that causes pollution.

pollute verb (**pollutes, polluting, polluted**) make something dirty or poisonous with unwanted or harmful substances. ∎ **polluter** noun.

pollution noun the presence in the air, soil, or water of a substance with unpleasant or harmful effects.

polo noun a game similar to hockey, played on horseback with a long-handled mallet. □ **polo neck** Brit. a high, tight, turned-over collar on a

sweater. **polo shirt** a casual short-sleeved shirt with a collar and two or three buttons at the neck.

poltergeist /**pol**-ter-gyst/ noun a kind of ghost that is said to make loud noises and throw objects around.

polychrome adjective consisting of several colours. ∎ **polychromatic** adjective.

polyester noun a synthetic fibre or resin used to make fabric for clothes.

polygamy /puh-**lig**-uh-mi/ noun the practice of having more than one wife or husband at the same time. ∎ **polygamist** noun **polygamous** adjective.

polyglot adjective knowing or using several languages.

polygon noun a figure with three or more straight sides and angles.

polygraph noun a lie detector.

polyhedron /po-li-**hee**-druhn/ noun (plural **polyhedra** or **polyhedrons**) a solid figure with many sides.

polymath noun a person with a wide knowledge of many subjects.

polymer noun a substance with a molecular structure formed from many identical small molecules bonded together.

polymorphic or **polymorphous** adjective having several different forms.

polyp noun **1** a simple sea creature which remains fixed in the same place, such as coral. **2** Medicine a small lump sticking out from a mucous membrane.

polyphony /puh-**li**-fuh-ni/ noun the combination of a number of musical parts, each forming an individual melody and harmonizing with each other. ∎ **polyphonic** adjective.

polystyrene noun a light synthetic material.

polysyllabic adjective having more than one syllable.

polytechnic noun (in the past in the UK) a college offering courses at degree level (now called a 'university').

polytheism /**po**-li-thee-i-z'm/ noun the worship of more than one god.

■ **polytheistic** adjective.

polythene noun Brit. a tough, light, flexible plastic.

polyunsaturated adjective (of a fat) having a chemical structure that is thought not to lead to the formation of cholesterol in the blood.

polyurethane noun a synthetic resin used in paints and varnishes.

pomade noun a scented oil or cream for making the hair glossy and smooth.

pomander noun a ball or container of sweet-smelling substances used to perfume a room or cupboard.

pomegranate noun a round tropical fruit with a tough orange outer skin and red flesh containing many seeds.

pommel noun **1** the curving or projecting front part of a saddle. **2** a rounded knob on the handle of a sword.

Pommy or **Pom** noun (plural **Pommies** or **Poms**) Austral./NZ informal a British person.

pomp noun the special clothes, music, and customs that are part of a grand public ceremony.

pompom noun a small woollen ball attached to a garment for decoration.

pompous adjective showing in a rather solemn or arrogant way that you have a high opinion of yourself and your own views. ■ **pomposity** noun **pompously** adverb.

ponce Brit. informal noun **1** a man who lives off a prostitute's earnings. **2** disapproving an effeminate man. **verb** (**ponces, poncing, ponced**) (**ponce about** or **around**) behave in a way that wastes time or looks silly. ■ **poncey** (or **poncy**) adjective.

poncho noun (plural **ponchos**) a garment made of a thick piece of cloth with a slit in the middle for the head.

pond noun a small area of still water.

ponder verb (**ponders, pondering, pondered**) consider something carefully.

ponderous adjective **1** moving slowly and heavily. **2** boringly solemn or long-winded. ■ **ponderously** adverb.

pondweed noun a plant that grows in still or running water.

pong Brit. informal noun a strong, unpleasant smell. **verb** smell strongly and unpleasantly. ■ **pongy** adjective.

pontiff noun the Pope.

pontifical adjective having to do with a pope; papal.

pontificate verb /pon-ti-fi-kayt/ (**pontificates, pontificating, pontificated**) express your opinions in a pompous and overbearing way. **noun** (**the Pontificate**) /pon-ti-fi-kuht/ the office of pope or bishop.

pontoon[1] noun Brit. a card game in which players try to obtain cards with a value totalling twenty-one.

pontoon[2] noun **1** a flat-bottomed boat or hollow cylinder used with others to support a temporary bridge or floating landing stage. **2** a bridge or landing stage supported by pontoons.

pony noun (plural **ponies**) a small breed of horse, especially one below 15 hands. □ **pony-trekking** Brit. the riding of ponies across country as a leisure activity.

ponytail noun a hairstyle in which the hair is drawn back and tied at the back of the head.

pooch noun informal a dog.

poodle noun **1** a breed of dog with a curly coat that is usually clipped. **2** Brit. a person who is excessively willing to do as they are told.

poof or **pouf** noun Brit. informal an effeminate or homosexual man.

pooh or **poo** informal exclamation expressing disgust at an unpleasant smell. **noun** waste material from the bowels. **verb** pass waste material from the bowels. □ **pooh-pooh** dismiss an idea as being not worth considering.

pool[1] noun **1** a small area of still water. **2** (also **swimming pool**) an artificial pool for swimming in. **3** a small, shallow patch of liquid on a surface.

pool[2] noun **1** a supply of vehicles, goods, money, etc. that is shared between a number of people and available for use when needed. **2** (**the pools** or **football pools**) a form of gambling on the results of football matches. **3** a game played on a billiard table using sixteen balls. verb put something into a common fund to be used by a number of people.

poop or **poop deck** noun a raised deck at the back of a ship.

poor adjective **1** having very little money. **2** of a low standard or quality. **3** (**poor in**) lacking in. **4** deserving pity or sympathy.

poorhouse noun Brit. a workhouse.

poorly adverb in a poor way. adjective chiefly Brit. unwell.

pootle verb (**pootles, pootling, pootled**) Brit. informal move or travel in a leisurely manner.

pop[1] verb (**pops, popping, popped**) **1** make a sudden short explosive sound. **2** go or come quickly or unexpectedly. **3** put something somewhere quickly or for a short time. **4** (of a person's eyes) open wide and appear to bulge. noun **1** a sudden short explosive sound. **2** informal, dated a sweet fizzy drink. □ **pop-eyed** informal having bulging or staring eyes.

pop[2] noun (also **pop music**) modern popular music, usually with a strong melody and beat. adjective **1** relating to pop music. **2** often disapproving made easy for the general public to understand; popularized: *pop psychology*. □ **pop art** a style of art that uses images taken from popular culture, such as advertisements or films.

pop[3] noun informal, chiefly US father.

popcorn noun a snack consisting of maize kernels which are heated until they burst open.

pope noun the Bishop of Rome as head of the Roman Catholic Church.

popery noun disapproving Roman Catholicism. ■ **popish** adjective.

popinjay noun old use a person who is vain and dresses in a showy way.

poplar noun a tall, slender tree with soft wood.

poplin noun a cotton fabric with a finely ribbed surface.

poppadom noun (in Indian cookery) a thin circular piece of spiced bread that is fried until crisp.

popper noun Brit. informal a press stud.

poppet noun Brit. informal a pretty or charming child.

poppy noun a plant with bright flowers and small black seeds.

poppycock noun informal nonsense.

populace noun the general public.

popular adjective **1** liked or admired by many people. **2** suited to the tastes of the general public. **3** connected with or carried out by ordinary people. ■ **popularly** adverb.

popularity noun the state of being liked or supported by many people.

popularize or **popularise** verb (**popularizes, popularizing, popularized**) **1** make something popular. **2** make something understandable or interesting to the general public. ■ **popularization** noun.

populate verb (**populates, populating, populated**) **1** live in an area and form its population. **2** cause people to settle in an area.

population noun **1** all the people living in an area. **2** the number of people living in an area.

populist adjective aiming to appeal to ordinary people, especially in politics. noun a populist person. ■ **populism** noun.

populous adjective having a large population.

porcelain /por-suh-lin/ noun a type of delicate translucent china.

porch noun a covered shelter at the entrance to a building.

porcine /por-syn/ adjective relating to pigs, or like a pig.

porcupine noun an animal with long protective spines on the body and tail.

pore[1] noun each of many tiny openings in the skin or another surface.

pore[2] verb (**pores, poring, pored**)

(**pore over** or **through**) study or read something with close attention.

> ℹ️ don't confuse **pore** and **pour**: you **pore over** a book, not **pour over** it.

pork noun the flesh of a pig used as food.

porker noun a young pig raised and fattened for food.

porn noun informal pornography.

pornography noun pictures, writing, or films that are intended to arouse sexual excitement. ■ **pornographer** noun **pornographic** adjective.

porous adjective having tiny spaces through which liquid or air can pass. ■ **porosity** noun.

porpoise noun a type of small whale with a rounded snout.

porridge noun a dish consisting of oats or oatmeal boiled with water or milk.

port¹ noun **1** a town or city with a harbour. **2** a harbour. □ **port of call** a place where a ship or person stops on a journey.

port² noun a strong, sweet dark red wine from Portugal.

port³ noun the side of a ship or aircraft that is on the left when you are facing forward.

port⁴ noun **1** an opening in the side of a ship for boarding or loading. **2** an opening in an aircraft or vehicle through which a gun can be fired. **3** a socket in a computer network into which a device can be plugged.

portable adjective able to be carried or moved easily. noun a portable object. ■ **portability** noun.

portal noun a large and impressive doorway or gate.

portcullis noun a strong, heavy grating that can be lowered to block a gateway to a castle.

portend verb be a sign or warning that something important or unpleasant is likely to happen.

portent noun a sign or warning that something important or unpleasant

is likely to happen.

portentous adjective **1** warning or showing that something important is likely to happen. **2** excessively solemn. ■ **portentously** adverb.

porter¹ noun **1** a person employed to carry luggage and other loads. **2** a hospital employee who moves equipment or patients. **3** dark brown bitter beer.

porter² noun Brit. an employee in charge of the entrance of a large building.

portfolio noun (plural **portfolios**) **1** a thin, flat case for carrying drawings, maps, etc. **2** a set of pieces of creative work collected together to show someone's ability. **3** a range of investments held by a person or organization. **4** the position and duties of a government minister.

porthole noun a small window in the side of a ship or aircraft.

portico noun (plural **porticoes** or **porticos**) a roof supported by columns, built over the entrance to a building.

portion noun **1** a part or share of something. **2** an amount of food for one person. verb share something out in portions.

portly adjective rather fat.

portmanteau /port-**man**-toh/ noun (plural **portmanteaus** or **portmanteaux** /port-**man**-tohz/) a large travelling bag that opens into two parts.

portrait noun **1** a painting, drawing, or photograph of a particular person. **2** a piece of writing or film about a particular person.

portraiture noun the art of making portraits.

portray verb **1** show or describe in a work of art or literature. **2** describe in a particular way. ■ **portrayal** noun.

Portuguese noun (plural **Portuguese**) **1** a person from Portugal. **2** the language of Portugal and Brazil. adjective relating to Portugal.

> ✓ -*guese*, not -*gese*: Portu*guese*.

pose verb (**poses**, **posing**, **posed**)

1 present a problem, question, etc. **2** sit or stand in a particular position in order to be photographed, painted, or drawn. **3** (**pose as**) pretend to be. **4** behave in a way that is intended to impress people. **noun 1** a position adopted in order to be painted, drawn, or photographed. **2** a way of behaving that is intended to impress people.

poser noun **1** a person who behaves in a way intended to impress others. **2** a puzzling question or problem.

poseur /poh-**zer**/ noun a person who poses in order to impress; a poser.

posh adjective informal **1** very elegant or luxurious. **2** chiefly Brit. upper-class.

posit verb (**posits**, **positing**, **posited**) present something as a fact or as a basis for argument.

position noun **1** a place where something is situated. **2** a way in which someone or something is placed or arranged. **3** a situation or set of circumstances. **4** a job. **5** a person's place or importance in relation to others. **6** a point of view. verb put or arrange in a particular position. ■ **positional** adjective.

positive adjective **1** indicating agreement with or support for something. **2** hopeful, favourable, or confident. **3** with no possibility of doubt; certain. **4** (of the results of a test or experiment) showing the presence of something. **5** (of a quantity) greater than zero. **6** having to do with the kind of electric charge opposite to that carried by electrons. **7** (of an adjective or adverb) expressing the basic degree of a quality (e.g. *brave*). noun a positive quality. □ **positive discrimination** Brit. the policy of providing jobs or other opportunities to people who belong to groups which suffer discrimination. ■ **positively** adverb **positivity** noun.

positivism noun a system of philosophy that recognizes only things that can be scientifically or logically proved. ■ **positivist** noun & adjective.

positron noun a subatomic particle with the same mass as an electron and an equal but positive charge.

posse /**poss**-i/ noun **1** N. Amer. (in the past) a body of men summoned by a sheriff to enforce the law. **2** informal a group of people.

possess verb **1** have or own something. **2** (also **be possessed of**) have a particular ability or quality. **3** dominate or have complete power over someone. ■ **possessor** noun.

 two *s*'s in the middle: **possess**.

possession noun **1** the state of having or owning something. **2** a thing owned.

possessive adjective **1** demanding someone's total attention and love. **2** unwilling to share your possessions. **3** Grammar (of a pronoun, determiner, etc.) showing possession. ■ **possessively** adverb.

possibility noun (plural **possibilities**) **1** a thing that is possible. **2** the state of being possible. **3** (**possibilities**) qualities suggesting that something might be good or could be improved.

possible adjective **1** capable of existing, happening, or being done. **2** that may be so. noun a person or thing that may be chosen.

possibly adverb **1** perhaps. **2** in accordance with what is possible.

possum noun **1** a Australasian marsupial that lives in trees. **2** N. Amer. informal an opossum.

post[1] noun **1** a strong, upright piece of timber or metal used as a support or a marker. **2** (**the post**) a post marking the start or finish of a race. verb display a notice in a public place.

post[2] chiefly Brit. noun **1** the official service or system that delivers letters and parcels. **2** letters and parcels delivered. **3** a single collection or delivery of post. verb send something via the postal system. □ **keep posted** keep someone up to date with the latest news about something. **post office 1** the organization responsible for postal services. **2** a building where postal business is carried on.

post[3] noun **1** a place where someone is

on duty or where an activity is carried out. **2** a job. **verb 1** put a soldier, police officer, etc. in a particular place. **2** send someone to a place to take up a job.

post- prefix after: *postgraduate*.

postage noun **1** the sending of letters and parcels by post. **2** the charge for sending something by post.

postal adjective relating to or carried out by post. □ **postal order** Brit. a document that can be bought from a post office and sent to someone who exchanges it for money.

postbox noun a large public box into which letters are posted for collection by the post office.

postcard noun a card for sending a message by post without an envelope.

postcode noun Brit. a group of letters and numbers added to a postal address to help in the sorting of mail.

post-date verb (**post-dates, post-dating, post-dated**) **1** put a date later than the actual one on a cheque or document. **2** occur later than.

poster noun a large picture or notice used for decoration or advertisement.

poste restante /pohst ress-tuhnt/ noun Brit. a department in a post office that keeps people's letters until they are collected.

posterior adjective at or near the rear. noun humorous a person's bottom.

posterity noun all future generations of people.

postgraduate adjective relating to study done after completing a first degree. noun a person taking a course of postgraduate study.

post-haste adverb with great speed.

posthumous /poss-tyuu-muhss/ adjective happening or appearing after the person involved has died. ■ **posthumously** adverb.

posting noun chiefly Brit. an appointment to a job abroad.

postman noun Brit. a man employed to deliver or collect post.

postmark noun an official mark stamped on a letter or parcel, giving the date of posting and cancelling the postage stamp. **verb** stamp a letter or parcel with a postmark.

postmaster or **postmistress** noun a person in charge of a post office.

postmodernism noun a movement in the arts that features a deliberate mixing of different styles. ■ **postmodern** adjective **postmodernist** noun & adjective.

post-mortem noun an examination of a dead body to find out the cause of death.

post-natal adjective having to do with the period after childbirth.

postpone verb (**postpones, postponing, postponed**) arrange for something to take place at a time later than that first planned. ■ **postponement** noun.

postscript noun a remark added at the end of a letter.

postulant noun a person who has recently entered a religious order.

postulate verb (**postulates, postulating, postulated**) assume that something is true, as a basis for a theory or discussion. ■ **postulation** noun.

posture noun **1** a particular position of the body. **2** the usual way in which a person holds their body. **3** an approach or attitude towards something. **verb** (**postures, posturing, postured**) behave in a way that is meant to impress or mislead others. ■ **postural** adjective.

posy noun (plural **posies**) a small bunch of flowers.

pot[1] noun a rounded container used for storage or cooking. **verb** (**pots, potting, potted**) **1** plant a young plant in a pot. **2** preserve food in a sealed pot or jar. **3** informal hit or kill by shooting. **4** Billiards & Snooker strike a ball into a pocket. □ **go to pot** informal be ruined through neglect. **pot belly** a large stomach that sticks out. **pot luck** a situation in which you take a chance that whatever is available will be acceptable. **potting shed** a shed used for potting plants and storing garden tools.

pot² noun informal cannabis.

potable /poh-tuh-b'l/ adjective formal (of water) safe to drink.

potash noun a substance obtained from potassium, used in making soap and fertilizers.

potassium noun a soft silvery-white metallic element.

potato noun (plural **potatoes**) an oval vegetable with starchy white or yellow flesh and a brown skin, that grows underground as a tuber.

> ✓ the singular has no e on the end: potato.

potent adjective 1 very powerful. 2 (of a man) able to achieve an erection.
■ **potency** noun.

potentate noun a monarch or ruler.

potential adjective capable of becoming or developing into something. noun 1 qualities or abilities that may be developed and lead to future success. 2 the possibility of something happening. ■ **potentiality** noun **potentially** adverb.

pothole noun 1 a deep underground cave. 2 a hole in the surface of a road.
■ **potholed** adjective.

potholing noun exploring potholes as a pastime.

potion noun a drink with healing, magical, or poisonous powers.

pot-pourri /poh-puh-ree/ noun (plural **pot-pourris**) a mixture of dried petals and spices used to perfume a room.

potshot noun a shot aimed unexpectedly or at random.

pottage noun old use soup or stew.

potted adjective 1 preserved in a sealed pot. 2 put into a short, easily understandable form.

potter¹ verb (**potters, pottering, pottered**) 1 do minor tasks in a relaxed way. 2 move in an unhurried way.

potter² noun a person who makes pottery.

pottery noun (plural **potteries**) 1 articles made of fired clay. 2 the craft of making such articles. 3 a place where pottery is made.

potty¹ adjective Brit. informal 1 mad; crazy. 2 extremely enthusiastic about someone or something.

potty² noun (plural **potties**) informal a bowl for a child to sit on and use as a toilet.

pouch noun 1 a small flexible bag. 2 a pocket of skin in which animals such as kangaroos carry their young.

pouf ➪ POOF OR POUFFE.

pouffe or **pouf** /poof/ noun a large, firm cushion used as a seat or for resting your feet on.

poulterer noun Brit. a person who sells poultry.

poultice /pohl-tiss/ noun a soft, moist mass of flour or plant material that is put on the skin to reduce inflammation.

poultry noun chickens, turkeys, ducks, and geese.

pounce verb (**pounces, pouncing, pounced**) 1 suddenly spring to seize or attack something. 2 (**pounce on**) quickly notice and criticize something that someone has said or done. noun an act of pouncing.

pound¹ noun 1 a unit of weight equal to 16 oz avoirdupois (0.4536 kg), or 12 oz troy (0.3732 kg). 2 (also **pound sterling**) the basic unit of money of the UK, equal to 100 pence.

pound² verb 1 hit something heavily again and again. 2 walk or run with heavy steps. 3 beat or throb with a strong regular rhythm. 4 crush or grind something into a powder or paste.

pound³ noun a place where stray dogs or illegally parked vehicles are officially taken and kept until claimed.

pour verb 1 flow or cause to flow in a steady stream. 2 (of rain) fall heavily. 3 prepare and serve a drink. 4 come or go in large numbers. 5 (**pour out**) express your feelings freely.

ℹ️ don't confuse **pour** and **pore**: you **pore over** a book, not **pour over** it.

pout verb push your lips forward as a sign of sulking or to make yourself look sexually attractive. noun a pouting expression. ■ **pouty** adjective.

poverty noun **1** the state of being very poor. **2** the state of lacking in a particular quality.

powder noun **1** a mass of fine dry particles. **2** a cosmetic in this form applied to a person's face. verb (**powders, powdering, powdered**) **1** sprinkle powder over. **2** make something into a powder. □ **powder blue** a soft pale blue. ■ **powdery** adjective.

power noun **1** the ability to do something. **2** the ability to influence people or events. **3** the right or authority to do something. **4** political authority or control. **5** a country seen as having international influence and military strength. **6** strength, force, or energy. **7** capacity or performance of an engine or other device. **8** energy that is produced by mechanical, electrical, or other means. **9** Physics the rate of doing work, measured in watts or horse power. **10** Mathematics the product obtained when a number is multiplied by itself a certain number of times. verb (**powers, powering, powered**) **1** supply with power. **2** move with speed or force. □ **power cut** a temporary interruption in an electricity supply. **power station** a building where electrical power is generated. **power steering** steering aided by power from a vehicle's engine.

powerboat noun a fast motor boat.

powerful adjective having power. ■ **powerfully** adverb.

powerhouse noun a person or thing having great energy or power.

powerless adjective without the power to take action.

powwow noun **1** a North American Indian ceremony involving feasting and dancing. **2** informal a meeting for discussion.

pox noun **1** any disease that produces a rash of pus-filled pimples that leave pockmarks on healing. **2** (the pox) informal syphilis.

poxy adjective Brit. informal of poor quality.

pp or **p.p.** abbreviation used when signing a letter on someone else's behalf.

ℹ️ short for Latin *per procurationem*, literally 'through the agency of'.

PPS abbreviation **1** post postscript (additional postscript). **2** Brit. Parliamentary Private Secretary.

PR abbreviation **1** proportional representation. **2** public relations.

practicable adjective able to be done successfully. ■ **practicability** noun.

practical adjective **1** having to do with the actual doing or use of something rather than theory. **2** likely to be successful or useful. **3** skilled at making or doing things. noun Brit. an examination or lesson in which students have to do or make things. □ **practical joke** a trick played on someone to make them look silly.

practicality noun (plural **practicalities**) **1** the state of being practical. **2** (**practicalities**) the real facts or aspects of a situation.

practically adverb **1** almost; virtually. **2** in a practical manner.

practice noun **1** the actual doing of something rather than the theories about it. **2** the usual way of doing something. **3** the work, business, or place of work of a doctor, dentist, or lawyer. **4** the doing of something repeatedly to improve your skill. verb US spelling of **PRACTISE**.

ℹ️ do you mean **practice** or **practise**? **Practice** is the spelling for the noun, and in America for the verb as well; **practise** is the British spelling of the verb.

practise (US spelling practice) verb (**practises, practising, practised**) **1** do something repeatedly to improve your skill. **2** do something regularly as part of your normal behaviour. **3** be working in a particular profession. **4 (practised)** skilful as a result of experience. **5** follow the teaching and rules of a religion.

practitioner noun a person who practises a profession or activity.

pragmatic adjective dealing with things in a sensible and realistic way rather than being influenced by fixed theories. ■ **pragmatically** adverb.

pragmatism noun a pragmatic attitude or way of dealing with things. ■ **pragmatist** noun.

prairie noun (in North America) a large open area of grassland.

praise verb (**praises, praising, praised**) **1** show approval of or admiration for. **2** express thanks to or respect for God. noun words that show approval or admiration.

praiseworthy adjective deserving praise.

praline /prah-leen, pray-leen/ noun a sweet substance made from nuts boiled in sugar.

pram noun Brit. a four-wheeled vehicle for a baby, pushed by a person on foot.

prance verb (**prances, prancing, pranced**) walk with exaggerated movements.

prang verb Brit. informal crash a motor vehicle or aircraft.

prank noun a practical joke or mischievous act.

prankster noun a person who is fond of playing pranks.

prat noun Brit. informal a stupid person.

prate verb (**prates, prating, prated**) talk too much in a foolish or boring way.

prattle verb (**prattles, prattling, prattled**) talk in a foolish or trivial way. noun foolish or trivial talk.

prawn noun an edible shellfish like a large shrimp.

pray verb **1** say a prayer. **2** hope strongly for something. adverb formal or old use please. □ **praying mantis** ⇒ **MANTIS**.

prayer noun **1** a request for help or expression of thanks made to God or a god. **2 (prayers)** a religious service at which people gather to pray together. **3** an earnest hope or wish.

pre- prefix before: *pre-arrange*.

preach verb **1** give a religious talk to a group of people. **2** recommend a particular way of thinking or behaving. **3 (preach at)** tell someone how they should think or behave in an annoying way. ■ **preacher** noun.

preamble /pree-am-b'l/ noun an opening statement; an introduction.

pre-arrange verb (**pre-arranges, pre-arranging, pre-arranged**) arrange something in advance.

precarious adjective **1** likely to tip over or fall. **2** (of a situation) not safe or certain. ■ **precariously** adverb.

precaution noun something done to avoid problems or danger. ■ **precautionary** adjective.

precede verb (**precedes, preceding, preceded**) **1** happen before something in time or order. **2** go somewhere in front of someone.

precedence noun the state of coming before others in order or importance.

precedent noun an earlier event, action, or legal case that is taken as an example to be followed in similar situations.

precept noun a general rule about how to behave.

precinct noun **1** Brit. an area in a town that is closed to traffic. **2** an enclosed area around a place or building. **3** N. Amer. each of the districts into which a city or town is divided for elections or policing.

precious adjective **1** rare and worth a lot of money. **2** of great value or importance. **3** greatly loved. **4** ironic considerable: *a precious lot you know!* **5** sophisticated in a way that is artificial and exaggerated. □ **precious metal** a valuable metal such as gold, silver, or platinum. **precious stone** an attractive and valuable piece of mineral, used in jewellery.

precipice noun a tall and very steep rock face or cliff.

precipitate verb /pri-**sip**-i-tayt/ (pre-**cipitates**, **precipitating**, **precipitated**) **1** make something bad happen suddenly or sooner than it should. **2** make something move or happen suddenly and with force. **3** Chemistry cause a substance to be deposited in solid form from a solution. **4** cause moisture in the air to condense and fall as rain, snow, etc. adjective /pri-**sip**-i-tuht/ done or occurring suddenly or without careful thought. noun /pri-**sip**-i-tayt/ Chemistry a substance precipitated from a solution.

precipitation noun **1** rain, snow, sleet, or hail. **2** Chemistry the action of precipitating a substance from a solution.

precipitous adjective **1** dangerously high or steep. **2** sudden and considerable.

precis /**pray**-si/ noun (plural **precis** /**pray**-si, **pray**-seez/) a short summary. verb (**precises** /**pray**-seez/, **precising** /**pray**-see-ing/, **precised** /**pray**-seed/) make a precis of.

precise adjective **1** presented in a detailed and accurate way. **2** taking care to be exact and accurate. **3** particular.
■ **precisely** adverb.

precision noun the quality of being exact, accurate, and careful.

preclude verb (**precludes**, **precluding**, **precluded**) prevent something from happening.

precocious adjective having developed certain abilities or tendencies at an earlier age than usual.
■ **precocity** noun.

precognition noun knowledge of an event before it happens.

preconceived adjective (of an idea or opinion) formed before full knowledge or evidence is available.

preconception noun a preconceived idea or opinion.

precondition noun something that must exist or happen before other things can happen or be done.

precursor noun a person or thing that comes before another of the same kind.

pre-date verb (**pre-dates**, **pre-dating**, **pre-dated**) occur earlier than.

predator noun an animal that hunts and kills others for food.

predatory adjective **1** (of an animal) killing other animals for food. **2** taking advantage of weaker people.

predecease verb (**predeceases**, **predeceasing**, **predeceased**) formal die before another person.

predecessor noun **1** a person who held a job or office before the current holder. **2** a thing that has been followed or replaced by another.

predestination noun the belief that everything that happens has been decided in advance by God or fate.

predestined adjective already decided by God or fate.

predetermine verb (**predetermines**, **predetermining**, **predetermined**) establish or decide in advance.

predeterminer noun Grammar a word or phrase that occurs before a determiner, e.g. *both*.

predicament noun a difficult situation.

predicate noun /**pred**-i-kuht/ Grammar the part of a sentence or clause containing a verb and stating something about the subject (e.g. *went home* in *John went home*). verb /**pred**-i-kayt/ (**predicates**, **predicating**, **predicated**) (**predicate on**) found or base something on.

predicative /pri-**dik**-uh-tiv/ adjective Grammar (of an adjective or noun) forming part or the whole of the predicate, as *old* in *the dog is old*.

predict verb state that an event will happen in the future. ■ **predictive** adjective **predictor** noun.

predictable adjective **1** able to be predicted. **2** always behaving or occurring in the way that you would expect. ■ **predictability** noun **predictably** adverb.

prediction noun **1** a statement saying that something will happen; a forecast. **2** the action of predicting.

predilection noun /pree-di-**lek**-sh'n/ noun

a preference or special liking for something.

predispose verb (predisposes, predisposing, predisposed) make someone likely to be, do, or think something. ■ **predisposition** noun.

predominant adjective **1** present as the main part of something. **2** having the greatest power. ■ **predominance** noun **predominantly** adverb.

predominate verb (predominates, predominating, predominated) **1** be the main part of something. **2** have control or power.

pre-eminent adjective better than all others. ■ **pre-eminence** noun.

pre-empt verb **1** take action so as to prevent something happening. **2** stop someone from saying something by speaking first. ■ **pre-emption** noun **pre-emptive** adjective.

preen verb **1** (of a bird) tidy and clean its feathers with its beak. **2** attend to and admire your appearance. **3** (**preen yourself**) feel very pleased with yourself.

pre-existing adjective existing from an earlier time.

prefab noun informal a prefabricated building.

prefabricated adjective (of a building) made in previously constructed sections that can be easily put together on site.

preface /**pref**-uhss/ noun an introduction to a book. verb (prefaces, prefacing, prefaced) (**preface with** or **by**) say or do something to introduce a book, speech, or event.

prefect noun **1** Brit. a senior pupil in a school who has some authority over younger pupils. **2** a chief officer or regional governor in certain countries.

prefecture noun a district administered by a prefect.

prefer verb (prefers, preferring, preferred) like one person or thing better than another.

> ☑ double the *r* when forming the past tense: prefer**r**ed.

preferable adjective more desirable

or suitable. ■ **preferably** adverb.

preference noun **1** a greater liking for one person or thing than another. **2** a thing preferred. **3** favour shown to one person over another.

preferential adjective favouring a particular person or group. ■ **preferentially** adverb.

preferment noun formal promotion to a job or position.

prefigure verb (prefigures, prefiguring, prefigured) be an early sign or version of.

prefix noun **1** a word, letter, or number placed before another. **2** a letter or group of letters placed at the beginning of a word to alter its meaning (e.g. *non-*). verb add a prefix to.

pregnancy noun (plural pregnancies) the state or period of being pregnant.

pregnant adjective **1** (of a woman) having a baby developing inside her womb. **2** full of meaning.

prehensile /pri-**hen**-syl/ adjective (of an animal's limb or tail) capable of grasping things.

prehistoric adjective relating to the period before written records.

prehistory noun **1** the period of time before written records. **2** the early stages in the development of something.

pre-industrial adjective before the development of industries.

prejudge verb (prejudges, prejudging, prejudged) make a judgement before you have all the necessary information.

prejudice noun **1** an opinion that is not based on reason or experience. **2** unfair reactions or behaviour based on such opinions. verb (prejudices, prejudicing, prejudiced) **1** influence someone so that they form an opinion that is not based on reason or experience. **2** cause harm to.

prejudicial adjective harmful to someone or something.

prelate /**prel**-uht/ noun a bishop or

other high-ranking minister in the Christian Church.

preliminary adjective taking place before a main action or event. noun (plural **preliminaries**) a preliminary action or event.

prelude noun 1 an action or event acting as an introduction to something more important. 2 a piece of music introducing a longer piece.

premarital adjective occurring before marriage.

premature adjective 1 occurring or done before the proper time. 2 (of a baby) born before the normal length of pregnancy is completed. ■ **prematurely** adverb.

premeditated adjective (of a bad action or crime) planned in advance.

premenstrual adjective occurring or experienced in the time of the month before menstruation.

premier adjective first in importance, order, or position. noun a Prime Minister or other head of government. ■ **premiership** noun.

premiere /prem-i-air/ noun the first performance or showing of a play, film, ballet, etc. verb (**premieres, premiering, premiered**) present the premiere of.

premise or Brit. **premiss** /prem-iss/ noun a statement or idea that forms the basis for a theory or argument.

premises plural noun the building and land occupied by a business.

premium noun (plural **premiums**) 1 an amount paid for an insurance policy. 2 an extra sum added to a basic price. adjective of high quality and more expensive. □ **at a premium 1** scarce and in demand. 2 above the usual price. **put** (or **place**) **a premium on** treat something as particularly valuable.

premonition noun a strong feeling that something is going to happen. ■ **premonitory** adjective.

prenatal adjective before birth.

preoccupation noun 1 the state of being preoccupied. 2 a matter that preoccupies someone.

preoccupy verb (**preoccupies, preoccupying, preoccupied**) completely fill someone's mind.

preordained adjective decided or determined beforehand.

prep noun Brit. informal, dated school work done outside lessons. □ **prep school** a preparatory school.

prepaid adjective paid for in advance.

preparation noun 1 the process of getting ready for something. 2 something that is done to get ready for something. 3 a medicine, cosmetic, etc.

preparatory adjective done in order to prepare for something. □ **preparatory school** Brit. a private school for pupils aged seven to thirteen.

prepare verb (**prepares, preparing, prepared**) 1 make something ready for use. 2 get ready to do or deal with something. 3 (**be prepared to do**) be willing to do.

preparedness noun readiness.

preponderance noun a greater number or incidence of something.

preponderant adjective greater in number or happening more often.

preposition /prep-uh-zi-sh'n/ noun Grammar a word used with a noun or pronoun to show place, time, or method. ■ **prepositional** adjective.

prepossessing adjective attractive or appealing in appearance.

preposterous adjective completely ridiculous or outrageous. ■ **preposterously** adverb.

pre-pubescent adjective having to do with the period before puberty.

prerequisite /pree-rek-wi-zit/ noun a thing that must exist or happen before something else can exist or happen.

prerogative /pri-rog-uh-tiv/ noun a right or privilege belonging to a particular person or group.

presage verb /press-ij, pri-sayj/ (**presages, presaging, presaged**) be a sign or warning of. noun /press-ij/ an omen.

Presbyterian /prez-bi-teer-i-uhn/

PARTS OF SPEECH

Preposition

A preposition is used in front of a noun or pronoun to form a phrase. It describes the position of something, e.g. *under the chair*, the time at which something happens, e.g. *in the evening*, or the way in which something is done, e.g. *by train*.

Prepositions in common use are:

about	*behind*	*into*	*through*
above	*beside*	*like*	*till*
across	*between*	*near*	*to*
after	*by*	*of*	*towards*
against	*down*	*off*	*under*
along	*during*	*on*	*underneath*
among	*except*	*outside*	*until*
around	*for*	*over*	*up*
as	*from*	*past*	*upon*
at	*in*	*round*	*with*
before	*inside*	*since*	*without*

Some people believe that a preposition should never come at the end of a sentence, as in *where do you come from?*, and that you should say *from where do you come?* instead. However, this can result in English that sounds very awkward and unnatural, and is not a rule that has to be followed as long as the meaning of what you are saying is clear.

---

adjective relating to a Protestant Church governed by elders who are all of equal rank. **noun** a member of a Presbyterian Church. ■ **Presbyterianism** noun.

presbytery /prez-bi-tuh-ri/ **noun** (plural **presbyteries**) **1** an administrative body in a Presbyterian Church. **2** the house of a Roman Catholic parish priest. **3** the eastern part of a church near the altar.

prescient /press-i-uhnt/ **adjective** knowing about things before they happen. ■ **prescience** noun.

prescribe **verb** (**prescribes**, **prescribing**, **prescribed**) **1** recommend and permit the use of a medicine or treatment. **2** state officially that something should be done.

prescription noun **1** a piece of paper on which a doctor states that a patient may be supplied with a medicine or treatment. **2** the action of prescribing a medicine or treatment.

prescriptive **adjective** stating what should be done.

presence noun **1** the state of being in a particular place. **2** a person's impressive manner or appearance. **3** a person or thing that seems to be present but is not seen. **4** a group of soldiers or police stationed in a particular place. □ **presence of mind** the ability to remain calm and act sensibly in a difficult situation.

present¹ /pre-z'nt/ **adjective 1** being or occurring in a particular place. **2** existing or occurring now. **3** Grammar (of a tense of a verb) expressing an action or state happening or existing now. **noun** the period of time occurring now. □ **present participle** Grammar the form of a verb, ending in *-ing*, which is used in forming tenses describing continuous action (e.g. *I'm thinking*), as a noun (e.g. *good thinking*), and as an adjective (e.g. *running water*).

present² **verb** /pri-zent/ **1** formally give someone something. **2** offer something for consideration or payment. **3** formally introduce someone to someone else. **4** put a show or exhibition before the public. **5** introduce and take part in a television or radio show. **6** be the cause of a problem. **7** give a particular impression to others. **8** (**present yourself**) appear or attend on a formal or official occasion. noun /**pre**-z'nt/ a thing given to someone as a gift. ■ **presenter** noun.

presentable adjective looking smart enough to be seen in public.

presentation noun the action of presenting something, or the way in which it is presented. ■ **presentational** adjective.

presentiment /pri-**zen**-ti-muhnt/ noun a feeling that something unpleasant is going to happen.

presently adverb **1** soon. **2** now.

preservative noun a substance used to prevent food or wood from decaying.

preserve verb (**preserves, preserving, preserved**) **1** keep something in its original state or in good condition. **2** keep someone safe from harm. **3** treat food to prevent it from decaying. noun **1** a food preserved in sugar, salt, vinegar, or alcohol, such as jam or pickle. **2** something reserved for a particular person or group. **3** a place where game is protected and kept for private hunting. ■ **preservation** noun **preserver** noun.

preset verb (**presets, presetting, preset**) set the controls of an electrical device before it is used.

preside verb (**presides, presiding, presided**) lead or be in charge of a meeting or event.

presidency noun (plural **presidencies**) the job of president, or the period of time it is held.

president noun **1** the elected head of a republic. **2** the head of an organization. ■ **presidential** adjective.

presidium /pri-**si**-di-uhm/ noun a permanent decision-making committee within a political organization, especially a communist one.

press[1] verb **1** (**press against** or **to**) move into contact with something by using steady force. **2** push something that operates a device. **3** apply pressure to something to flatten or shape it. **4** move by pushing. **5** (**press on** or **ahead**) continue in what you are doing. **6** express or repeat an opinion or claim in a forceful way. **7** make strong efforts to persuade someone to do something. **8** (of time) be short. **9** (**be pressed to do**) have difficulty doing. noun **1** a device for crushing, flattening, or shaping something. **2** a printing press. **3** (**the press**) newspapers or journalists as a whole. **4** a closely packed mass of people. □ **press conference** a meeting with journalists in order to make an announcement or answer questions. **press release** a statement or piece of publicity issued to journalists. **press stud** Brit. a small fastener with two parts that fit together when pressed. **press-up** Brit. an exercise in which you lie face down on the floor and push your body up by pressing down with your hands and arms.

press[2] verb (in the past) force someone to serve in the army or navy. □ **press gang** a body of men employed to force men to serve in the army or navy. **press-gang** force someone into doing something. **press into service** put something to a particular use as a makeshift measure.

pressing adjective 1 needing urgent action. **2** strongly expressed and difficult to refuse or ignore. noun an object made by pressing.

pressure noun **1** steady force applied to an object by something that is in contact with it. **2** the use of persuasion or threats to make someone do something. **3** a feeling of stress caused by the need to do something. **4** the force per unit area applied by a fluid against a surface. verb (**pressures, pressuring, pressured**) persuade or force someone into doing something. □ **pressure cooker** a large airtight saucepan in which food is cooked quickly in steam held under pressure. **pressure group** a group that tries to influence public opinion and government to help a cause.

pressurize or **pressurise** verb (**pressurizes, pressurizing, pressurized**) **1** persuade or force someone into doing something. **2** keep the air pressure in an aircraft cabin the same as it is at ground level.

prestige noun respect and admiration resulting from achievements or high quality.

prestigious /press-ti-juhss/ adjective having or bringing prestige.

presto adverb & adjective Music in a quick tempo.

prestressed adjective (of concrete) strengthened by means of rods inserted under tension before setting.

presumably adverb as may be supposed.

presume verb (**presumes, presuming, presumed**) **1** suppose that something is probably true. **2** be bold enough to do something that you do not have authority or permission to do. **3** (**presume on**) take advantage of someone's kindness, friendship, etc.

presumption noun **1** something that is thought to be true or probable. **2** an act of presuming. **3** behaviour that is too confident.

presumptuous adjective behaving too confidently. ■ **presumptuously** adverb.

☑ -uous, not -ious: presumptu**ous**.

presuppose verb (**presupposes, presupposing, presupposed**) **1** need something to have happened in order to exist or be true. **2** assume, without knowing for sure, that something exists or is true and act on that basis. ■ **presupposition** noun.

pretence (US spelling **pretense**) noun **1** an act of pretending. **2** a claim to have or be something.

pretend verb **1** make it seem that something is the case when in fact it is not. **2** give the appearance of feeling or having an emotion or quality. **3** (**pretend to**) claim to have a skill, quality, or title.

pretender noun a person who claims a right to a title or position.

pretension noun **1** the act of trying to appear more important or better than you actually are. **2** (also **pretensions**) a claim to have or be something.

pretentious adjective trying to appear more important or better than you actually are so as to impress other people. ■ **pretentiousness** noun.

preternatural adjective beyond what is normal or natural. ■ **preternaturally** adverb.

pretext noun a false reason used to justify an action.

prettify verb (**prettifies, prettifying, prettified**) try to make something look pretty.

pretty adjective (**prettier, prettiest**) **1** (of a woman or girl) having an attractive face. **2** pleasant to look at. adverb informal to a certain extent; fairly. □ **be sitting pretty** informal be in a favourable position. ■ **prettily** adverb **prettiness** noun.

pretzel noun a crisp salty biscuit in the shape of a knot or stick.

prevail verb **1** (**prevail against** or **over**) be more powerful than. **2** (**prevail on**) persuade someone to do something. **3** be widespread or current.

prevalent adjective widespread; common. ■ **prevalence** noun.

prevaricate verb (**prevaricates, prevaricating, prevaricated**) avoid giving a direct answer to a question. ■ **prevarication** noun.

prevent verb **1** keep something from happening. **2** stop someone from doing something. ■ **preventable** adjective **prevention** noun.

preventive or **preventative** adjective designed to prevent something from happening.

preview noun **1** a viewing or showing of something before it becomes generally available. **2** a review of a forth-

coming film, book, or performance.
verb 1 present something for a preview. **2** write a preview of.

previous adjective 1 coming before something else in time or order. **2 (previous to)** before. ■ **previously** adverb.

prey noun 1 an animal that is hunted and killed by another for food. **2** a person who is harmed or deceived by someone or something. **verb (prey on) 1** hunt and kill for food. **2** take advantage of or cause distress to.

price noun 1 the amount of money for which something is bought or sold. **2** something unwelcome that must be done in order to achieve something. **3** the odds in betting. **verb (prices, pricing, priced)** decide the price of.

priceless adjective 1 very valuable. **2** informal very amusing.

pricey adjective (pricier, priciest) informal expensive.

prick verb 1 make a small hole in something with a sharp point. **2** cause someone to feel a small, sharp pain. **noun 1** a mark, hole, or pain caused by pricking. **2** vulgar a man's penis. **3** vulgar a stupid or unpleasant man. ▫ **prick up your ears 1** (of a horse or dog) raise the ears when alert. **2** suddenly begin to pay attention.

prickle noun 1 a small thorn on a plant or a pointed spine on an animal. **2** a tingling feeling on the skin. **verb (prickles, prickling, prickled)** have a tingling feeling on the skin.

prickly adjective 1 having prickles. **2** causing a prickling feeling. **3** easily offended or annoyed. ▫ **prickly pear** a cactus which produces prickly, pear-shaped fruits.

pride noun 1 deep pleasure or satisfaction felt if you or people close to you have done something well. **2** a cause or source of pride. **3** self-respect. **4** an excessively high opinion of yourself. **5** a group of lions. **verb (prides, priding, prided) (pride yourself on)** be especially proud of a quality or skill. ▫ **pride of place** the most noticeable

or important position.

priest noun 1 a person who is qualified to perform religious ceremonies in the Christian Church. **2** (also **priestess**) a person who performs ceremonies in a non-Christian religion. ■ **priesthood** noun **priestly** adjective.

prig noun a person who behaves as if they are superior to others. ■ **priggish** adjective.

prim adjective very formal and correct and disapproving of anything rude. ■ **primly** adverb.

prima ballerina /pree-muh bal-luh-ree-nuh/ **noun** the chief female dancer in a ballet company.

primacy noun the fact of being most important.

prima donna noun 1 the chief female singer in an opera. **2** a very temperamental and self-important person.

primaeval ⇒ **PRIMEVAL**.

prima facie /pry-muh fay-shi-ee/ **adjective & adverb** Law accepted as correct until proved otherwise.

primal adjective 1 having to do with early human life; primeval. **2** basic; fundamental.

primarily adverb for the most part; mainly.

primary adjective 1 of chief importance. **2** earliest in time or order. **3** (of education) for children between the ages of about five and eleven. **noun** (plural **primaries**) (in the US) a preliminary election to appoint delegates to a party conference or to select candidates for an election. ▫ **primary colour** each of the colours blue, red, and yellow, from which all other colours can be obtained by mixing. ■ **primarily** adverb.

primate noun 1 an animal belonging to the group that includes monkeys, apes, and humans. **2** (in the Christian Church) an archbishop.

prime¹ adjective 1 of chief importance. **2** of the highest quality; excellent. **3** (of a number) that can be divided only by itself and one (e.g. 2, 3, 5). **noun** the time in a person's life when they are the strongest and most successful. □ **prime minister** the head of a government. **prime time** the time at which a radio or television audience is greatest.

prime² verb (**primes, priming, primed**) **1** make something ready for use or action. **2** prepare someone for a situation by giving them information. **3** cover a surface with primer.

primer noun **1** a substance painted on a surface as a base coat. **2** a book for teaching children to read or giving a basic introduction to a subject.

primeval or **primaeval** /pry-**mee**-v'l/ adjective relating to the earliest times in history.

primitive adjective **1** relating to the earliest times in history or stages in development. **2** offering a very basic level of comfort. **3** (of behaviour or emotion) not based on reason; instinctive. ■ **primitively** adverb.

primordial /pry-**mor**-di-uhl/ adjective existing at the beginning of time.

primp verb make small adjustments to your appearance.

primrose noun a plant of woods and hedges with pale yellow flowers.

primula noun a plant of a group that includes primroses and cowslips.

Primus noun trademark a portable cooking stove that burns oil.

prince noun a son or other close male relative of a king or queen. □ **prince consort** the husband of a reigning queen who is himself a prince.

princeling noun **1** the ruler of a small country. **2** a young prince.

princely adjective **1** relating to or suitable for a prince. **2** (of a sum of money) generous.

princess noun **1** a daughter or other close female relative of a king or queen. **2** the wife or widow of a prince. □ **Princess Royal** a title given to the eldest daughter of a British king or queen.

principal adjective most important; main. noun **1** the most important person in an organization or group. **2** the head of a school or college. **3** a sum of

money lent or invested, on which interest is paid. □ **principal boy** Brit. a woman who takes the leading male role in a pantomime. ■ **principally** adverb.

⚠ don't confuse the words **principal** and **principle**. **Principal** is usually an adjective meaning 'main or most important', whereas **principle** is normally a noun meaning 'a rule or general law'.

---

principality noun (plural **principalities**) **1** a state ruled by a prince. **2** (**the Principality**) Brit. Wales.

principle noun **1** a law, rule, or theory that something is based on. **2** (**principles**) rules or beliefs that govern your actions and personal behaviour. **3** a scientific theorem or natural law that explains why something happens or how it works. □ **in principle** in theory. **on principle** because of your moral principles.

principled adjective acting according to strong moral principles.

print verb **1** produce a book, newspaper, etc. by a process involving the transfer of words or pictures to paper. **2** produce a photographic print from a negative. **3** write words clearly without joining the letters. **4** mark fabric with a coloured design. noun **1** printed words in a book, newspaper, etc. **2** a mark where something has pressed or touched a surface. **3** a printed picture or design. □ **in** (or **out of**) **print** (of a book) available (or no longer available) from the publisher. ■ **printable** adjective **printer** noun.

printing noun **1** the transfer of words or pictures to paper in the production of books, newspapers, etc. **2** handwriting in which the letters are written separately. □ **printing press** a machine for printing from type or plates.

printout noun a page of printed material from a computer's printer.

prion /**pree**-on/ noun a protein particle believed to be the cause of brain diseases such as BSE and CJD.

prior¹ adjective **1** coming before in

time, order, or importance. **2 (prior to)** before.

prior² noun (feminine **prioress**) **1** (in an abbey) the person next in rank below an abbot or abbess. **2** the head of a house of friars or nuns.

prioritize or **prioritise** verb (prioritizes, prioritizing, prioritized) **1** treat something as being more important than other things. **2** decide the order of importance of a number of tasks.

priority noun (plural **priorities**) **1** the condition of being more important than others. **2** a thing seen as more important than others. **3** the right to go before other traffic.

priory noun (plural **priories**) a monastery or nunnery governed by a prior or prioress.

prise (US spelling **prize**) verb (prises, prising, prised) force something open or apart.

prism noun **1** a piece of glass or other transparent material with facets, used to separate white light into a spectrum of colours. **2** a solid geometric figure whose two ends are parallel and of the same size and shape, and whose sides are parallelograms. ■ **prismatic** adjective.

prison noun a building where criminals are kept as a punishment.

prisoner noun **1** a person who has been found guilty of a crime and sent to prison. **2** a person who has been captured by someone and kept confined. □ **prisoner of conscience** a person imprisoned for their political or religious views. **prisoner of war** a person captured and imprisoned by the enemy in war.

prissy adjective too concerned with behaving in a correct and respectable way.

pristine adjective **1** in its original condition. **2** clean and fresh as if new.

privacy noun a state in which you are not watched or disturbed by others.

private adjective **1** intended for or involving a particular person or group. **2** (of thoughts, feelings, etc.) that you do not tell other people about. **3** not

sharing thoughts and feelings with others. **4** where you will not be disturbed; secluded. **5** (of a service or industry) provided by an individual or commercial company rather than the state. **6** not connected with a person's work or official role. noun (also **private soldier**) a soldier of the lowest rank in the army. □ **private company** Brit. a company whose shares may not be offered to the public for sale. **private detective** a detective who is not a police officer and who carries out investigations for clients. **private enterprise** business or industry managed by independent companies rather than the state. **private eye** informal a private detective. **private means** Brit. income from investments, property, etc., rather than from employment. **private member** a member of parliament who does not hold a government office. **private parts** a person's genitals. **private practice** the work of a doctor, lawyer, etc. who is self-employed. **private school** Brit. an independent school financed mainly by the fees paid by pupils. **private secretary 1** a secretary who deals with the personal matters of their employer. **2** a civil servant acting as an assistant to a senior government official. **private sector** the part of the national economy not under direct state control. ■ **privately** adverb.

privateer noun (in the past) an armed but privately owned ship, authorized by a government for use in war.

privation noun a state in which you do not have the basic things you need, such as food and warmth.

privatize or **privatise** verb (privatizes, privatizing, privatized) transfer a business or industry from ownership by the state to private ownership. ■ **privatization** noun.

privet noun a shrub with small white flowers.

privilege noun **1** a special right or advantage for a particular person or group. **2** an opportunity to do something regarded as a special honour. **3** the advantages available to people who are rich and powerful.

 -il-, not *-el-*, and no *d*: privi**l**ege.

privileged adjective **1** having a privilege or privileges. **2** (of information) protected from being made public.

privy adjective (privy to) sharing in the knowledge of something secret. noun (plural **privies**) a toilet in a small shed outside a house. □ **Privy Council** a group of politicians appointed to advise a king or queen.

prize[1] noun **1** a thing given to someone who wins a competition or race or to mark an outstanding achievement. **2** something that is worth struggling to achieve. adjective **1** having been awarded a prize. **2** outstanding. verb (**prizes, prizing, prized**) value highly.

prize[2] US spelling of **PRISE**.

pro[1] informal noun (plural **pros**) a professional. adjective professional.

pro[2] noun (plural **pros**) (usu. in **pros and cons**) an advantage or argument for something.

proactive adjective creating or controlling a situation rather than just responding to it. ■ **proactively** adverb.

probability noun (plural **probabilities**) **1** the extent to which something is probable. **2** an event that is likely to happen.

probable adjective likely to happen or be the case.

probably adverb almost certainly.

probate noun the official process of proving that a will is valid.

probation noun **1** a system in which a person who has committed a crime does not have to go to prison if they behave well and report regularly to an official. **2** a period of training and testing when you start a new job. ■ **probationary** adjective **probationer** noun.

probe noun **1** a surgical instrument used to examine the body. **2** a small device for measuring or testing something. **3** an investigation. **4** (also **space probe**) an unmanned exploratory spacecraft. verb (**probes, prob-**

ing, **probed**) **1** physically explore or examine something. **2** enquire into something closely. ■ **probing** adjective.

probity noun formal honesty and decency.

problem noun a thing that is difficult to deal with or understand.

problematic or **problematical** adjective causing a problem.

proboscis /pruh-**boss**-iss/ noun (plural **proboscis** /pruh-**boss**-eez/ or **proboscises**) **1** a mammal's long, flexible snout, e.g. an elephant's trunk. **2** the long, thin mouth of some insects.

procedure noun **1** an established or official way of doing something. **2** a series of actions conducted in a certain manner. ■ **procedural** adjective.

proceed verb **1** begin a course of action. **2** go on to do something. **3** carry on or continue.

proceedings plural noun **1** an event or a series of actions. **2** action taken in a law court to settle a dispute.

proceeds plural noun money obtained from an event or activity.

process[1] /**proh**-sess/ noun **1** a series of actions that are done to achieve a particular end. **2** a natural series of changes: *the ageing process.* verb **1** perform a series of actions on something to change or preserve it. **2** deal with someone using an established procedure. ■ **processor** noun.

process[2] /pruh-**sess**/ verb walk in procession.

procession noun **1** a number of people or vehicles moving forward in an orderly way. **2** a large number of people or things that come one after another.

proclaim verb **1** announce officially or publicly. **2** show something clearly. ■ **proclamation** noun.

proclivity noun (plural **proclivities**) a tendency to do something regularly.

procrastinate verb (**procrastinates, procrastinating, procrastinated**) delay or postpone action. ■ **procrastination** noun.

WORD FORMATION

pro-

Words starting with **pro-** mean:
- supporting or in favour of, as in *pro-choice*
- moving forwards, out, or away, e.g *propel*
- before: *proactive*.

pro- is sometimes used on its own, e.g. *my mother was pro the idea*.

---

procreate verb (procreates, procreating, procreated) produce a baby or young animal. ■ procreation noun.

proctor noun Brit. an officer in charge of discipline at some universities.

procurator noun an official who represents others in a court of law. ▢ procurator fiscal (in Scotland) a local coroner and public prosecutor.

procure verb (procures, procuring, procured) obtain. ■ procurement noun.

prod verb (prods, prodding, prodded) **1** poke with a finger or pointed object. **2** prompt or remind to do something. noun **1** a poke. **2** a prompt or reminder. **3** a pointed object like a stick.

prodigal adjective **1** wasting time, money, or materials; extravagant. **2** lavish. noun **1** a wasteful or extravagant person. **2** a person who leads a wasteful life but is later sorry.

prodigious adjective impressively large. ■ prodigiously adverb.

prodigy noun (plural prodigies) a young person with exceptional abilities.

produce verb /pruh-**dyooss**/ (produces, producing, produced) **1** make, manufacture, or create. **2** make something happen or exist. **3** show or provide something for consideration. **4** be in charge of the financial aspects of a film or the staging of a play. **5** supervise the making of a musical recording. noun /**prod**-yooss/ things that have been produced or grown. ■ producer noun.

product noun **1** an article or substance manufactured for sale. **2** a result of an action or process. **3** a substance produced during a natural, chemical, or manufacturing process. **4** Mathematics a quantity obtained by multiplying one number by another.

production noun **1** the action of producing something. **2** the amount of something produced. ▢ production line an assembly line.

productive adjective **1** producing large amounts of goods or crops. **2** doing or achieving a lot. ■ productively adverb.

productivity noun **1** the quality of being productive. **2** the efficiency with which things are produced.

profane adjective **1** not religious; secular. **2** not having respect for God or holy things. verb (profanes, profaning, profaned) treat something with a lack of respect.

profanity noun (plural profanities) **1** profane language or behaviour. **2** a swear word.

profess verb **1** claim that something is true. **2** declare your faith in a religion.

profession noun **1** a job that needs special training and a formal qualification. **2** a body of people engaged in a profession. **3** a claim. **4** a declaration of belief in a religion.

professional adjective **1** relating to or belonging to a profession. **2** doing something as a job rather than as a hobby. **3** having the skills or qualities of a professional person. noun **1** a professional person. **2** a person who is highly skilled at doing something. ■ professionally adverb.

> ☑ only one f: professional.

professionalism noun the ability or

skill that you expect from a professional person.

professor noun **1** a university academic of the highest rank. **2** N. Amer. a university teacher. ■ **professorial** adjective **professorship** noun.

proffer verb (**proffers, proffering, proffered**) offer something for someone to accept.

proficient adjective competent; skilled. ■ **proficiency** noun.

profile noun **1** an outline of someone's face, seen from the side. **2** a short article that describes someone or something. **3** the extent to which someone attracts attention: *her high profile.* verb (**profiles, profiling, profiled**) **1** describe in a short article. **2** (**be profiled**) appear in outline. □ **keep a low profile** try not to attract attention.

profit noun **1** a financial gain. **2** advantage; benefit. verb (**profits, profiting, profited**) benefit someone. □ **profit margin** the difference between the cost of producing something and the price at which it is sold.

☑ note that the forms **profited** and **profiting** have a single rather than a double t.

profitable adjective **1** (of a business or activity) making a profit. **2** useful. ■ **profitability** noun **profitably** adverb.

profiteering noun the making of a large profit in an unfair way.

profiterole noun a small ball of choux pastry filled with cream and covered with chocolate.

profligate adjective **1** wasting time, money, or materials; extravagant. **2** indulging too much in physical pleasures. noun a profligate person. ■ **profligacy** noun.

profound adjective (**profounder, profoundest**) **1** very great. **2** showing great knowledge or understanding. **3** requiring a lot of study or thought. ■ **profoundly** adverb **profundity** noun.

profuse adjective plentiful. ■ **profusely** adverb.

profusion noun an abundance or large quantity of something.

progenitor /proh-**jen**-i-ter/ noun **1** an ancestor or parent. **2** the originator of a movement.

progeny /**proj**-uh-ni/ noun offspring.

progesterone /pruh-**jess**-tuh-rohn/ noun a hormone that stimulates the uterus to prepare for pregnancy.

prognosis /prog-**noh**-siss/ noun (plural **prognoses** /prog-**noh**-seez/) **1** an opinion about how an illness is likely to develop. **2** the likely course of a situation. ■ **prognostic** adjective.

programmatic adjective having to do with or following a programme.

programme (US spelling **program**) noun **1** a plan of future events or things to be done. **2** a radio or television broadcast. **3** a sheet or booklet giving details about a play, concert, etc. **4** (**program**) a series of software instructions to control the operation of a computer. verb (**programmes, programming, programmed**) (**program**) **1** provide a computer with a program. **2** make something behave in a particular way. **3** arrange something according to a plan. ■ **programmable** adjective **programmer** noun.

progress noun **1** forward movement towards a place. **2** the process of improving or developing. verb **1** move forwards. **2** improve or develop.

progression noun **1** a gradual movement from one place or state to another. **2** a number of things coming one after another.

progressive adjective **1** proceeding gradually or in stages. **2** favouring new ideas or social reform. noun a person who is in favour of social reform. ■ **progressively** adverb.

prohibit verb (**prohibits, prohibiting, prohibited**) **1** formally forbid something by law. **2** prevent something from happening.

prohibition noun **1** the action of prohibiting. **2** an order that forbids something.

prohibitive adjective **1** forbidding or restricting something. **2** (of a price) too high. ■ **prohibitively** adverb.

project noun /**pro**-jekt/ **1** a piece of

work that is carefully planned to achieve a particular aim. **2** a piece of work by a school or college student in which they carry out their own research. **verb** /pruh-**jekt**/ **1** predict something based on what is happening now. **2** (**be projected**) be planned. **3** stick out beyond something else. **4** make light or an image fall on a surface or screen. **5** present yourself to other people in a particular way.

projectile noun an object that is fired or thrown at a target.

projection noun 1 a prediction about something based on what is happening now. **2** the projecting of an image, sound, etc. **3** a mental image viewed as reality. **4** a thing that sticks out from something else. ■ **projectionist** noun.

projector noun a device for projecting slides or film on to a screen.

prolapse noun a condition in which an organ of the body has slipped forward or down from its normal position.

proletarian /proh-li-**tair**-i-uhn/ **adjective** relating to the proletariat. **noun** a member of the proletariat.

proletariat noun workers or working-class people.

proliferate verb (**proliferates, proliferating, proliferated**) reproduce rapidly; increase rapidly in number. ■ **proliferation** noun.

prolific adjective 1 (of a plant or animal) producing a lot of fruit, leaves, or young. **2** producing many works. ■ **prolifically** adverb.

prolix /**proh**-liks/ **adjective** (of speech or writing) long and tedious. ■ **prolixity** noun.

prologue (US spelling **prolog**) **noun 1** a separate introductory part of a play, book, or piece of music. **2** an event that leads to another.

prolong verb make something last longer. ■ **prolongation** noun.

prolonged adjective continuing for a long time.

prom noun informal **1** Brit. a promenade by the sea. **2** Brit. a promenade con-

cert. **3** N. Amer. a formal dance at a high school or college.

promenade noun 1 a public place for walking, especially a paved path by the sea. **2** a leisurely walk, ride, or drive. **verb** (**promenades, promenading, promenaded**) take a promenade. ❑ **promenade concert** Brit. a concert of classical music at which part of the audience stands.

prominence noun the state of being prominent.

prominent adjective 1 important; famous. **2** sticking out. **3** particularly noticeable. ■ **prominently** adverb.

promiscuous /pruh-**miss**-kyuu-uhss/ **adjective** having many sexual relationships. ■ **promiscuity** noun.

promise noun 1 an assurance that you will do something or that something will happen. **2** potential excellence. **verb** (**promises, promising, promised**) **1** make a promise. **2** give good grounds for expecting something.

promising adjective showing signs of future success. ■ **promisingly** adverb.

promissory note noun a signed document containing a written promise to pay a stated amount of money.

promo noun (plural **promos**) informal a promotional film, video, etc.

promontory /**prom**-uhn-tuh-ri/ **noun** (plural **promontories**) a point of high land jutting out into the sea.

promote verb (**promotes, promoting, promoted**) **1** help something to happen. **2** publicize a product or celebrity. **3** raise someone to a higher position or rank. ■ **promoter** noun.

promotion noun 1 activity that supports or encourages a cause or aim. **2** the publicizing of a product or celebrity. **3** movement to a higher position or rank. ■ **promotional** adjective.

prompt verb 1 make something happen. **2** (**prompt to**) make someone take a course of action. **3** encourage someone to speak. **4** tell an actor a word that they have forgotten. **noun 1** an act of prompting. **2** a symbol on a computer screen to show that more input is needed. **3** a word or phrase used to prompt an actor. **adjective** done without delay. **adverb** Brit. exactly or punctually. ■ **prompter** noun **promptly** adverb.

promulgate verb (**promulgates, promulgating, promulgated**) **1** make an idea widely known. **2** announce the official beginning of a new law. ■ **promulgation** noun.

prone adjective **1** (**prone to** or **to do**) likely to suffer from, do, or experience something unfortunate. **2** lying flat, especially face downwards.

prong noun **1** each of two or more long pointed parts on a fork. **2** each of the separate parts of an attack.

pronominal /proh-**nom**-i-n'l/ **adjective** Grammar having to do with a pronoun.

pronoun noun a word used instead of a noun to indicate someone or something already mentioned or known, e.g. *I, this*.

pronounce verb (**pronounces, pronouncing, pronounced**) **1** make the sound of a word or part of a word. **2** declare or announce. **3** (**pronounce on**) pass judgement or make a decision on. ■ **pronouncement** noun.

pronounced adjective very noticeable.

pronto adverb informal promptly.

pronunciation noun the way in which a word is pronounced.

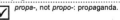 **pronunciation** has no *o* in the middle.

proof noun **1** evidence that shows that something is true. **2** the process of finding out whether something is true. **3** a series of stages in the solving of a mathematical problem. **4** a copy of printed material used for making corrections before final printing. **5** a standard used to measure the strength of alcoholic liquor. **adjective** resistant to: *draught-proof.* □ **proofread** read a text and mark any errors.

prop¹ noun **1** a pole or beam used as a temporary support. **2** a source of sup-

port or assistance. **3** (also **prop forward**) Rugby a forward at either end of the front row of a scrum. **verb** (**props, propping, propped**) **1** support with a prop. **2** lean something against something else. **3** (**prop up**) provide support for someone.

prop² noun a portable object used by actors during a play or film.

propaganda noun false or exaggerated information, used to win support for a political cause or point of view. ■ **propagandist** noun.

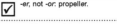 **propa-**, not **propo-**: propaganda.

propagate verb (**propagates, propagating, propagated**) **1** grow a new plant from a parent plant. **2** spread an idea or information widely. ■ **propagation** noun.

propane noun a flammable gas present in natural gas and used as fuel.

propel verb (**propels, propelling, propelled**) drive or push forwards.

propellant noun a gas which forces out the contents of an aerosol.

propeller noun a device which has two or more angled blades to propel a ship or aircraft.

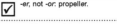 *-er*, not *-or*: propeller.

propensity noun (plural **propensities**) a tendency to behave in a particular way.

proper adjective **1** real or genuine. **2** in its true form: *the World Cup proper.* **3** appropriate or correct. **4** (**proper to**) belonging exclusively to. □ **proper fraction** a fraction that is less than one. **proper noun** (or **proper name**) a name of a person, place, or organization, written with a capital letter. ■ **properly** adverb.

property noun (plural **properties**) **1** a thing or things belonging to someone. **2** a building and the land belonging to it. **3** a characteristic or quality.

prophecy /**prof**-i-si/ noun (plural **prophecies**) **1** a prediction about what will happen in the future. **2** the

PARTS OF SPEECH   i

Pronoun

A pronoun is used as a substitute for a noun or a noun phrase, e.g.

> He *was upstairs*
> Anything *can happen now*
> *Did you see* that?
> It*'s lovely weather*

Using a pronoun often avoids repetition, e.g.

> *I found Jim*—he *was upstairs*
> (instead of *I found Jim—Jim was upstairs*)
> *Where are your keys?—I've got* them
> (instead of *Where are your keys?—I've got my keys*).

ability to predict the future.

prophesy /**prof**-i-sI/ **verb** (**prophesies, prophesying, prophesied**) predict that a particular thing will happen in the future.

prophet noun **1** a person regarded as being sent by God to teach people. **2** a person who predicts the future.

prophetic adjective **1** accurately predicting the future. **2** having to do with a prophet or prophecy.

prophylactic /prof-i-**lak**-tik/ adjective intended to prevent disease. noun a medicine intended to prevent disease.

propinquity /pruh-**ping**-kwi-ti/ noun nearness in time or space.

propitiate verb (**propitiates, propitiating, propitiated**) win or regain the favour of. ■ **propitiation** noun **propitiatory** adjective.

propitious adjective favourable.

proponent noun a person who proposes a theory or plan.

proportion noun **1** a part or share of a whole. **2** the relationship of one thing to another in terms of quantity or size. **3** the correct relationship between one thing and another. **4** (**proportions**) the size and shape of something.

proportional or **proportionate** adjective corresponding in size or amount to something else. ◻ **proportional representation** an electoral

system in which parties gain seats in proportion to the number of votes cast for them. ■ **proportionally** adverb.

proposal noun **1** a plan or suggestion. **2** the action of proposing something. **3** an offer of marriage.

propose verb (**proposes, proposing, proposed**) **1** put forward an idea or plan for consideration by others. **2** nominate someone for an official position. **3** plan or intend to do something. **4** make an offer of marriage to someone.

proposition noun **1** a statement that expresses an opinion. **2** a plan of action. **3** a problem to be dealt with. verb informal offer to have sex with someone.

propound verb put forward an idea or theory for consideration.

proprietary adjective **1** having to do with an owner or ownership. **2** (of a product) marketed under a registered trade name. ◻ **proprietary name** a name of a product or service registered as a trademark.

proprietor noun the owner of a business.

proprietorial adjective **1** relating to an owner. **2** possessive.

propriety noun (plural **proprieties**) **1** correctness of behaviour or morals. **2** the condition of being right or appropriate.

propulsion noun the action of propelling or driving forward. ■ **propulsive** adjective.

pro rata /proh **rah**-tuh/ **adjective** proportional. ■ **pro rata** adverb proportionally.

prosaic /proh-**zay**-ik/ **adjective 1** having the style of prose. **2** ordinary; unromantic. ■ **prosaically** adverb.

proscenium /pruh-**see**-ni-uhm/ **noun** (plural **prosceniums** or **proscenia** /pruh-**see**-ni-uh/) **1** the part of a stage in front of the curtain. **2** (also **proscenium arch**) an arch framing the opening between the stage and the part of the theatre in which the audience sits.

proscribe **verb** (proscribes, proscribing, proscribed) **1** forbid. **2** criticize or condemn. **3** (in the past) outlaw someone.

prose **noun** ordinary written or spoken language.

prosecute **verb** (prosecutes, prosecuting, prosecuted) **1** take legal proceedings against someone. **2** continue a course of action with a view to its completion. ■ **prosecutor** noun.

prosecution **noun 1** the action of prosecuting. **2** (**the prosecution**) the party prosecuting someone in a lawsuit.

proselyte /**pross**-i-lyt/ **noun** a person who has converted from one religion or belief to another.

proselytize or **proselytise** /**pross**-i-li-tyz/ **verb** (proselytizes, proselytizing, proselytized) convert from one religion or belief to another.

prosody /**pross**-uh-di/ **noun 1** the patterns of rhythm and sound used in poetry. **2** the study of these patterns.

prospect **noun 1** a possibility of something happening. **2** an idea about what will happen in the future. **3** (prospects) chances of being successful. **4** a person who is likely to be successful. **verb** search for mineral deposits. ■ **prospector** noun.

prospective **adjective** expected or likely to happen in the future. ■ **prospectively** adverb.

prospectus **noun** (plural **prospec-**

tuses) a printed booklet advertising a school, university, or business.

prosper **verb** (prospers, prospering, prospered) succeed or flourish.

prosperous **adjective** successful or flourishing. ■ **prosperity** noun.

prostate **noun** a gland in men and male mammals that produces a fluid part of semen.

prostitute **noun** a person who has sex for money. **verb** (prostitutes, prostituting, prostituted) (prostitute yourself) **1** work as a prostitute. **2** put your talents to an unworthy use in order to earn money. ■ **prostitution** noun.

prostrate **adjective** /**pross**-trayt/ **1** lying stretched out on the ground with the face downwards. **2** completely overcome or helpless. **verb** /pross-**trayt**/ (prostrates, prostrating, prostrated) **1** (prostrate yourself) throw yourself flat on the ground. **2** (be prostrated) be completely overcome with stress or exhaustion. ■ **prostration** noun.

protagonist **noun 1** the leading character in a drama, film, or novel. **2** an important person in a real event.

protean /proh-**tee**-uhn/ **adjective** tending or able to change or adapt.

protect **verb** keep something safe from harm or injury. ■ **protector** noun.

protection **noun 1** the action of protecting. **2** a person or thing that protects. **3** the payment of money to criminals so that they will not attack your property.

protectionism **noun** the theory of shielding a country's industries from foreign competition by taxing imports. ■ **protectionist** noun & adjective.

protective **adjective** serving, intended, or wishing to protect. ■ **protectively** adverb.

protectorate **noun** a state that is controlled and protected by another.

protégé /**prot**-i-zhay/ **noun** (feminine **protégée**) a person who is guided and supported by an older and more experienced person.

protein noun a substance which forms part of body tissues and is an important part of the human diet.

 protein is an exception to the usual rule of *i* before *e* except after *c*.

protest noun a statement or action expressing disapproval or objection to something. verb 1 express an objection to what someone has said or done. 2 take part in a public protest. 3 state strongly in response to an accusation: *she protested her innocence.* ■ **protester** (or **protestor**) noun.

Protestant /pro-tiss-tuhnt/ noun a member or follower of any of the Western Christian Churches that are separate from the Roman Catholic Church. adjective relating to or belonging to any of the Protestant Churches. ■ **Protestantism** noun.

protestation noun 1 a firm declaration that something is or is not the case. 2 an objection or protest.

proto- combining form original, primitive, or first: *prototype | protozoan.*

protocol noun 1 the system of rules governing formal occasions. 2 the accepted way to behave in a particular situation.

proton noun a subatomic particle with a positive electric charge.

prototype noun a first form of something from which other forms are copied or developed.

protozoan /proh-tuh-**zoh**-uhn/ noun a microscopic animal that is made up of a single cell.

protracted adjective lasting for a long time.

protractor noun an instrument for measuring angles, in the form of a flat semicircle marked with degrees.

protrude verb (protrudes, protruding, protruded) stick out from a surface. ■ **protrusion** noun.

protuberance noun a thing that protrudes from something else. ■ **protuberant** adjective.

☑ there is no *r* immediately after the *t*: pro**t**uberance.

proud adjective 1 feeling pleased or satisfied by your own or another's achievements. 2 having too high an opinion of yourself. 3 having respect for yourself. 4 slightly sticking out from a surface. □ **do someone proud** informal 1 cause someone to feel pleased or satisfied. 2 treat someone very well. ■ **proudly** adverb.

prove verb (proves, proving, proved; past participle **proved** or **proven** /**proo**-v'n or **proh**-v'n/) 1 use evidence to show that something is true or exists. 2 be found to be. 3 (**prove yourself**) show your abilities or courage. 4 (**proven**) found through experience to be effective or true. ■ **provable** adjective.

provenance noun the place where something originally comes from.

provender noun old use food or animal fodder.

proverb noun a short saying that gives advice or states something that is generally true.

proverbial adjective 1 referred to in a proverb. 2 well known. ■ **proverbially** adverb.

provide verb (provides, providing, provided) 1 make something available for someone to use. 2 (**provide with**) supply someone with. 3 (**provide for**) make enough preparation for a possible event.

provided or **providing** conjunction on the condition that.

providence noun 1 the protective care of God or of nature. 2 careful preparation for the future.

provident adjective careful in preparing for the future.

providential adjective happening at a favourable time.

province noun 1 a main administrative division of a country or empire. 2 (**the provinces**) the whole of a country outside the capital city.

provincial adjective 1 relating to a province or the provinces. 2 unsophisticated or narrow-minded. **noun** a person who lives in a province. ■ **provincialism** noun.

provision noun **1** the action of providing. **2** something supplied or provided. **3** (**provision for** or **against**) arrangements for possible future events or needs. **4** (**provisions**) supplies of food, drink, or equipment. **5** a condition or requirement in a legal document. **verb** supply with provisions.

provisional adjective arranged for the present time only, possibly to be changed later. ■ **provisionally** adverb.

proviso /pruh-vy-zoh/ noun (plural provisos) a condition attached to an agreement.

provocation noun **1** the action of provoking. **2** action or speech that provokes.

provocative adjective **1** intended to make someone annoyed or angry. **2** intended to make someone sexually interested. ■ **provocatively** adverb.

provoke verb (**provokes, provoking, provoked**) **1** cause a strong reaction. **2** deliberately make someone feel annoyed or angry. **3** stir someone up to do something.

provost noun **1** Brit. the head of certain university colleges and public schools. **2** N. Amer. a senior administrative officer in certain universities. **3** Scottish a mayor.

prow noun the pointed front part of a ship.

prowess noun skill or expertise.

prowl verb move about stealthily or restlessly. **noun** an act of prowling. ■ **prowler** noun.

proximity noun nearness or closeness. ■ **proximate** adjective.

proxy noun (plural **proxies**) **1** the authority to represent someone else. **2** a person authorized to act on behalf of another.

prude noun a person who is easily shocked by matters relating to sex. ■ **prudish** adjective.

prudent adjective acting in a cautious and sensible way. ■ **prudence** noun

prudently adverb.

prudential adjective prudent.

prune[1] noun a dried plum.

prune[2] verb (**prunes, pruning, pruned**) **1** trim a tree or bush by cutting away dead or overgrown branches. **2** remove unwanted parts from. **noun** an instance of pruning.

prurient adjective having too much interest in sexual matters. ■ **prurience** noun.

pry[1] verb (**pries, prying, pried**) enquire too eagerly about a person's private life.

pry[2] = **PRISE**.

PS abbreviation postscript.

psalm /sahm/ noun a song or poem that praises God.

psalter /sawl-ter/ noun a copy of the Book of Psalms in the Bible.

pseudo adjective not genuine; false.

pseudonym noun a false name, especially one used by an author.

psi /psI, sI/ noun the twenty-third letter of the Greek alphabet (Ψ, ψ).

psoriasis /suh-ry-uh-siss/ noun a condition in which patches of skin become red and itchy.

psych /syk/ verb **1** (**psych up**) informal prepare someone mentally for a difficult task. **2** (**psych out**) intimidate an opponent by appearing very confident or aggressive.

psyche /sy-ki/ noun the human soul, mind, or spirit.

psychedelia /sy-kuh-dee-li-uh/ noun music or art based on the experiences produced by psychedelic drugs.

psychedelic /sy-kuh-del-ik/ adjective **1** (of drugs) producing hallucinations. **2** having a strong, vivid colour or a swirling abstract pattern.

psychiatrist noun a doctor specializing in the treatment of mental illness.

psychiatry noun the branch of medicine concerned with mental illness. ■ **psychiatric** adjective.

psychic adjective **1** relating to or possessing abilities that cannot be explained by science, e.g. telepathy or clairvoyance. **2** relating to the mind. **noun** a person considered or claiming to have psychic powers. ▪ **psychically** adverb.

psycho noun (plural **psychos**) informal a psychopath.

psychoanalyse (US spelling **psychoanalyze**) **verb** (**psychoanalyses**, **psychoanalysing**, **psychoanalysed**) treat someone using psychoanalysis.

psychoanalysis noun a method of treating mental disorders by investigating the unconscious elements of the mind. ▪ **psychoanalyst** noun **psychoanalytic** adjective.

psychological adjective **1** having to do with the mind. **2** relating to psychology. ▪ **psychologically** adverb.

psychology noun **1** the scientific study of the human mind. **2** the way in which someone thinks or behaves. ▪ **psychologist** noun.

psychopath noun a person suffering from a serious mental illness which makes them behave violently. ▪ **psychopathic** adjective.

psychosis /sy-**koh**-siss/ noun (plural **psychoses** /sy-**koh**-seez/) a serious mental illness in which a person loses contact with external reality.

psychosomatic adjective (of a physical illness) caused or made worse by a mental factor such as stress.

psychotherapy noun the treatment of mental disorders by psychological rather than medical means. ▪ **psychotherapist** noun.

psychotic /sy-**kot**-ik/ adjective relating to or suffering from a psychosis.

PT abbreviation physical training.

Pt abbreviation **1** Part. **2** (**pt**) pint. **3** (in scoring) point.

PTA abbreviation parent–teacher association.

Pte abbreviation Private (in the army).

pterodactyl /te-ruh-**dak**-til/ noun a fossil flying reptile with a long, slender head and neck.

PTO abbreviation please turn over.

pub noun Brit. a building in which beer and other drinks are served.

puberty noun the period during which adolescents reach sexual maturity.

pubes /**pyoo**-beez/ noun the lower front part of the abdomen.

pubescence noun the time when puberty begins. ▪ **pubescent** adjective & noun.

pubic adjective relating to the pubes or pubis.

pubis /**pyoo**-biss/ noun (plural **pubes** /**pyoo**-beez/) either of a pair of bones forming the two sides of the pelvis.

public adjective **1** having to do with the people as a whole. **2** involved in the affairs of the community: *a public figure*. **3** done in open view. **4** provided by the government rather than an independent company. **noun 1** (**the public**) ordinary people in general. **2** a group of people with a particular interest: *the reading public*. □ **in public** when other people are present. **public address system** a system of microphones and loudspeakers used to amplify speech or music. **public company** (or **public limited company**) a company whose shares are traded freely on a stock exchange. **public house** a pub. **public relations** the business of keeping a good public image by an organization or famous person. **public school** (in the UK) a private fee-paying secondary school. **public sector** the part of an economy that is controlled by the state. **public transport** buses, trains, and other forms of transport that are available to the public and run on fixed routes. ▪ **publicly** adverb.

publican noun Brit. a person who owns or manages a pub.

publication noun **1** the action of publishing something. **2** a book or journal that is published.

publicist noun a person responsible for publicizing a product or celebrity.

publicity noun **1** attention given to someone or something by television, newspapers, etc. **2** information used for advertising a product.

publicize or **publicise** verb (**publicizes, publicizing, publicized**) **1** make something widely known. **2** advertise a product, event, etc.

publish verb **1** produce a book, newspaper, etc., for public sale. **2** print something in a book or newspaper. ■ **publisher** noun.

puce /pyooss/ noun a dark red or purple-brown colour.

puck noun a black disc made of hard rubber, used in ice hockey.

pucker verb (**puckers, puckering, puckered**) tightly gather into wrinkles or small folds. noun a wrinkle or small fold.

pudding noun chiefly Brit. **1** a cooked sweet dish eaten at the end of a meal. **2** the dessert course of a meal. **3** a savoury dish made with suet and flour.

puddle noun a small pool of liquid, especially of rain on the ground.

pudgy adjective (**pudgier, pudgiest**) informal fat or flabby.

puerile /pyoor-yl/ adjective childishly silly.

puff noun **1** a small amount of air or smoke that is blown out from somewhere. **2** an act of breathing in smoke from a pipe, cigarette, or cigar. **3** a hollow piece of light pastry that is filled with cream or jam. **4** informal breath: out of puff. verb **1** breathe in repeated short gasps. **2** move with short, noisy puffs of air or steam. **3** smoke a pipe, cigarette, or cigar. **4** (be puffed or puffed out) informal be out of breath. **5** (puff out or up) swell. □ **puff pastry** light flaky pastry.

puffball noun a fungus with a round head that bursts to release its seeds.

puffin noun a seabird with a large brightly coloured triangular bill.

puffy adjective (**puffier, puffiest**) **1** softly rounded: puffy clouds. **2** (of a part of the body) swollen and soft.

pug noun a very small breed of dog with a broad flat nose and deeply wrinkled face.

pugilist /pyoo-ji-list/ noun dated or humorous a boxer. ■ **pugilistic** adjective.

pugnacious adjective eager or quick to argue or fight. ■ **pugnaciously** adverb **pugnacity** noun.

puke informal verb (**pukes, puking, puked**) vomit. noun vomit.

pukka adjective **1** genuine. **2** socially acceptable. **3** informal excellent.

pulchritude /pul-kri-tyood/ noun literary beauty.

pull verb **1** apply force to something so as to move it towards yourself. **2** remove from a place by pulling. **3** move steadily: the bus pulled away. **4** strain a muscle. **5** attract someone's interest. **6** informal attract a potential sexual partner. **7** informal bring out a weapon for use. noun **1** an act of pulling. **2** a force, influence, or attraction. **3** a deep drink of something or a deep breath of smoke from a cigarette, pipe, etc. □ **pull back** retreat. **pull someone's leg** deceive someone for a joke. **pull off** informal succeed in doing something difficult. **pull out** withdraw. **pull strings** make use of your influence to gain an advantage. **pull yourself together** regain your self-control. **pull your weight** do your fair share of work.

pullet noun a young hen.

pulley noun (plural **pulleys**) a wheel around which a rope or chain passes, used to raise heavy weights.

pullover noun a knitted garment for the upper body.

pulmonary /pul-muh-nuh-ri/ adjective relating to the lungs.

pulp noun **1** a soft, wet mass of crushed material. **2** the soft fleshy part of a fruit. verb crush into a pulp. adjective (of writing) popular and badly written: pulp fiction. ■ **pulpy** adjective.

pulpit noun a raised platform in a church from which the preacher gives a sermon.

pulsar noun a star that gives off regular rapid pulses of radio waves.

pulsate verb (**pulsates, pulsating, pulsated**) **1** expand and contract with strong regular movements. **2** produce a regular throbbing sensation or sound. **3** (**pulsating**) very exciting. ■ **pulsation** noun.

pulse¹ noun **1** the regular beat of the blood as it is pumped around the body. **2** a single vibration or short burst of sound, electric current, light, etc. **3** a regular musical rhythm. verb (**pulses, pulsing, pulsed**) pulsate.

pulse² noun the edible seeds of various plants, such as lentils or beans.

pulverize or **pulverise** verb (**pulverizes, pulverizing, pulverized**) **1** crush into fine particles. **2** informal completely defeat.

puma noun a large American wild cat with a yellowish-brown or grey coat.

pumice /pum-iss/ noun a very light rock formed from lava.

pummel verb (**pummels, pummelling, pummelled**; US spelling **pummels, pummeling, pummeled**) strike repeatedly with the fists.

pump¹ noun a device, used to move liquids and gases or to force air into inflatable objects. verb **1** move with a pump. **2** fill something with liquid, gas, etc. **3** move something vigorously up and down. □ **pump iron** informal exercise with weights.

pump² noun **1** chiefly N. English a plimsoll. **2** a light shoe for dancing.

pumpkin noun **1** a large round fruit with a thick orange skin and edible flesh. **2** Brit. = SQUASH².

pun noun a joke that uses a word or words with more than one meaning. verb (**puns, punning, punned**) make a pun.

punch¹ verb **1** strike with the fist. **2** press a button or key on a machine. noun **1** a blow with the fist. **2** informal the power to impress someone. □ **punch-drunk** dazed by a series of punches. **2** very confused or shocked. **punch-up** informal a fight.

punch² noun a device for making holes in paper, metal, etc., or for impressing a design on a material. verb pierce a hole in something.

punch³ noun a drink made from wine or spirits mixed with water, fruit juices, and spices.

punchbag noun Brit. a heavy bag hung on a rope, used for punching as exercise or training.

punchbowl noun **1** a deep bowl for mixing and serving punch. **2** a deep round hollow in a hilly area.

punchline noun the final part of a joke, providing the humour.

punchy adjective (**punchier, punchiest**) effective; forceful.

punctilious adjective showing great attention to detail or correct behaviour.

punctual adjective happening or doing something at the appointed time. ■ **punctuality** noun **punctually** adverb.

punctuate verb (**punctuates, punctuating, punctuated**) **1** interrupt something at intervals. **2** add punctuation marks to a piece of writing.

punctuation noun **1** the marks, such as full stop, comma, and brackets, used in writing to separate sentences and make meaning clear. **2** the use of such marks.

puncture noun a small hole caused by a sharp object. verb (**punctures, puncturing, punctured**) make a puncture in.

pundit noun a person who frequently gives opinions about a subject in public.

pungent adjective **1** having a sharply strong taste or smell. **2** (of remarks or humour) having a strong effect. ■ **pungency** noun.

punish verb **1** impose a penalty on someone for an offence. **2** treat harshly or unfairly. ■ **punishable** adjective.

punishment noun **1** the action of punishing. **2** the penalty imposed for an offence. **3** harsh or rough treatment.

punitive /pyoo-ni-tiv/ adjective inflicting or intended as punishment.

punk noun **1** (also **punk rock**) a loud and aggressive form of rock music. **2** (also **punk rocker**) a person who likes or plays punk music. **3** N. Amer. informal a worthless person.

punnet noun Brit. a small container for fruit or vegetables.

punt[1] noun a long, narrow boat with a flat bottom, moved forward with a long pole. **verb** travel in a punt.

punt[2] verb kick a ball after it has dropped from the hands and before it reaches the ground. **noun** a kick of this kind.

punt[3] Brit. informal **verb** bet or make a risky investment. **noun** a bet.

punt[4] /puunt/ **noun** the basic unit of money of the Republic of Ireland.

punter noun Brit. informal **1** a person who gambles. **2** a customer or client.

puny adjective (**punier**, **puniest**) **1** small and weak. **2** not very impressive. ■ **punily** adverb.

pup noun **1** a young dog. **2** a young wolf, seal, rat, or other mammal. **verb** (**pups**, **pupping**, **pupped**) give birth to a pup or pups.

pupa /**pyoo**-puh/ noun (plural **pupae** /**pyoo**-pee/) an insect in the form between larva and adult. ■ **pupal** adjective.

pupate verb (**pupates**, **pupating**, **pupated**) become a pupa.

pupil[1] noun a person who is taught by another.

pupil[2] noun the dark circular opening in the centre of the iris of the eye.

puppet noun **1** a model of a person or animal which can be moved either by strings or by a hand inside it. **2** a person under the control of another. ■ **puppeteer** noun **puppetry** noun.

puppy noun (plural **puppies**) a young dog. □ **puppy fat** fat on a child's body that disappears with age. **puppy love** strong but short-lived love.

purblind adjective **1** partially sighted. **2** lacking awareness or understanding.

purchase verb (**purchases**, **purchasing**, **purchased**) buy. **noun 1** the action of buying. **2** a thing bought. **3** firm contact or grip. ■ **purchaser** noun.

purdah noun the practice in certain Muslim and Hindu societies of screening women from men or strangers.

pure adjective **1** not mixed with any other substance or material. **2** free of impurities. **3** innocent or morally good. **4** sheer; nothing but: *a shout of pure anger*. **5** theoretical rather than practical: *pure mathematics*. **6** (of a sound) perfectly in tune with and with a clear tone. ■ **purely** adverb.

purée /**pyoor**-ay/ **noun** a mass of crushed fruit or vegetables. **verb** (**purées**, **puréeing**, **puréed**) make a purée of.

purgative adjective strongly laxative in effect. **noun** a laxative.

purgatory noun (plural **purgatories**) (in Roman Catholic belief) a place inhabited by the souls of sinners who are making up for their sins before going to heaven.

purge verb (**purges**, **purging**, **purged**) **1** rid someone or something of undesirable or harmful people or things. **2** empty the bowels, especially as a result of taking a laxative. **noun 1** an act of purging. **2** dated a laxative.

purify verb (**purifies**, **purifying**, **purified**) make pure. ■ **purification** noun.

✓ *i not e*: purify.

purist noun a person who insists on following traditional rules, especially in language or style. ■ **purism** noun.

,**puritan** noun **1** (**Puritan**) a member of a group of English Protestants in the 16th and 17th centuries who tried to simplify forms of worship. **2** a person with strong moral beliefs who is critical of the behaviour of others. **adjective 1** (**Puritan**) relating to the Puritans. **2** characteristic of a puritan. ■ **puritanical** adjective.

purity noun the state of being pure.

purl adjective (of a knitting stitch) made by putting the needle through the front of the stitch from right to left. **verb** knit with a purl stitch.

purlieus /**per**-lyooz/ **plural noun** literary the area around or near a place.

purloin verb formal steal.

purple adjective of a colour between

red and blue. **noun** a purple colour. □ **purple patch** informal a run of success or good luck. **purple prose** prose that is too elaborate.

purport verb /per-**port**/ appear or claim to be or do. **noun** /**per**-port/ the meaning or purpose of something.

purpose noun 1 the reason for which something is done or for which something exists. **2** strong determination. **verb** (**purposes, purposing, purposed**) formal have as an aim. □ **on purpose** intentionally. ■ **purposeless** adjective.

purposeful adjective 1 having or showing determination. **2** having a purpose. ■ **purposefully** adverb.

purposely adverb on purpose.

purposive adjective having or done with a purpose.

purr verb 1 (of a cat) make a low continuous sound expressing contentment. **2** (of an engine) run smoothly while making a similar sound. **noun** a purring sound.

purse noun 1 a small pouch for carrying money. **2** N. Amer. a handbag. **3** money for spending. **4** a sum of money given as a prize. **verb** (**purses, pursing, pursed**) pucker or contract the lips.

purser noun a ship's officer who keeps the accounts.

pursuance noun formal the carrying out of a plan or action.

pursuant adverb (**pursuant to**) formal in accordance with.

pursue verb (**pursues, pursuing, pursued**) **1** follow someone or something in order to catch or attack them. **2** try to achieve a goal. **3** engage in an activity. **4** continue to investigate or discuss a topic.

 pur-, not per-: pursue.

pursuit noun 1 the action of pursuing. **2** a leisure or sporting activity.

purulent /**pyoor**-uu-luhnt/ **adjective** made up of or giving out pus.

purvey verb provide or supply food or drink as a business. ■ **purveyor** noun.

purview noun the scope or range of influence or interest.

pus noun a thick yellowish or greenish liquid produced in infected body tissue.

push verb 1 apply force to something so as to move it away from yourself. **2** move part of your body into a specified position. **3** move by using force. **4** encourage someone to work hard. **5** (**push for**) demand persistently. **6** informal promote the use, sale, or acceptance of. **7** informal sell an illegal drug. **noun 1** an act of pushing. **2** a great effort: *one last push.* □ **when push comes to shove** informal when you must commit yourself to doing something. ■ **pusher** noun.

pushbike noun Brit. informal a bicycle.

pushchair noun Brit. a folding chair on wheels, in which a young child can be pushed along.

pushover noun informal **1** a person who is easy to influence or defeat. **2** a thing that is easily done.

pushy adjective (**pushier, pushiest**) excessively self-assertive or ambitious.

pusillanimous adjective lacking courage. ■ **pusillanimity** noun.

pussy or **puss noun** (plural **pussies** or **pusses**) (also **pussy cat**) informal a cat. □ **pussy willow** a willow with soft, fluffy catkins that appear before the leaves.

pussyfoot verb (**pussyfoots, pussyfooting, pussyfooted**) act very cautiously.

pustule noun a small blister on the skin containing pus. ■ **pustular** adjective.

put verb (**puts, putting, put**) **1** move something into a particular position. **2** bring into a particular state or condition: *she tried to put me at ease.* **3** (**put on** or **on to**) make subject to. **4** give a value, figure, or limit to. **5** express in a particular way. **6** (of a ship) go in a particular direction: *the boat put out to sea.* **7** throw a shot or weight as a sport. □ **put down 1** suppress a riot by force. **2** kill a sick, old, or injured animal. **3** pay a sum as a deposit. **4** informal criticize someone in public. **put off 1** cancel or postpone. **2** make someone feel dislike or lose enthusiasm. **3** distract. **put on 1** organize an event. **2** gain weight. **3** adopt an expression, accent, etc. **put out** cause someone trouble or inconvenience. **put up 1** present, provide, or offer. **2** accommodate someone for a short time. **put up to** informal encourage someone to do something wrong. **put up with** tolerate.

putative /pyoo-tuh-tiv/ adjective formal generally considered to be.

putrefy verb (**putrefies, putrefying, putrefied**) decay or rot and produce a very unpleasant smell. ■ **putrefaction** noun.

 e, not *i*: putrefy.

putrid adjective **1** decaying or rotting and producing a very unpleasant smell. **2** informal very unpleasant.

putsch /puuch/ noun a violent attempt to overthrow a government.

putt verb (**putts, putting, putted**) strike a golf ball gently so that it rolls into or near a hole. noun a stroke of this kind. □ **putting green** a smooth area of short grass surrounding a hole on a golf course.

putter[1] noun a golf club designed for putting.

putter[2] noun the rapid irregular sound of a small petrol engine. verb (**putters, puttering, puttered**) make such a sound.

putty noun a soft paste that hardens as it sets, used for sealing glass in window frames.

puzzle verb (**puzzles, puzzling, puzzled**) **1** make someone feel confused because they cannot understand something. **2** think hard about something difficult to understand. noun **1** a game, toy, or problem designed to test mental skills or knowledge. **2** a person or thing that is difficult to understand. ■ **puzzlement** noun **puzzler** noun.

PVC abbreviation polyvinyl chloride, a sort of plastic.

pygmy or **pigmy** noun (plural **pygmies**) **1** a member of a race of very short people living in parts of Africa. **2** a very small person or thing. adjective very small.

pyjamas (US spelling **pajamas**) plural noun a loose jacket and trousers for sleeping in.

pylon noun a tall tower-like structure for carrying electricity cables.

pyramid noun a very large stone structure with a square or triangular base and sloping sides that meet in a point at the top. ■ **pyramidal** adjective.

pyre noun a large pile of wood for the ritual burning of a dead body.

pyrites /py-ry-teez/ or **pyrite** noun a shiny yellow mineral that is a compound of iron and sulphur.

pyromania noun a strong urge to set fire to things. ■ **pyromaniac** noun.

pyrotechnics plural noun **1** a firework display. **2** the art of making fireworks or staging firework displays. ■ **pyrotechnic** adjective.

pyrrhic /pir-rik/ adjective (of a victory) won at too great a cost to have been worthwhile.

python noun a large snake which crushes its prey.

Qq

Q or **q** noun (plural **Qs** or **Q's**) the seventeenth letter of the alphabet. **abbreviation** question.

QC abbreviation Law Queen's Counsel.

QED abbreviation used to say that something proves the truth of your claim.

> ℹ short for Latin *quod erat demonstrandum* 'which was to be demonstrated'.

qt abbreviation quarts.

qua /kway, kwah/ conjunction formal in the capacity of.

quack¹ noun the characteristic harsh sound made by a duck. **verb** make this sound.

quack² noun **1** a person who falsely claims to have medical knowledge. **2** Brit. informal a doctor. ■ **quackery** noun.

quad noun **1** a quadrangle. **2** a quadruplet.

quadrangle noun **1** a four-sided geometrical figure. **2** a square or rectangular courtyard enclosed by buildings. ■ **quadrangular** adjective.

quadrant noun **1** a quarter of a circle or a circle's circumference. **2** historical an instrument for measuring angles in astronomy and navigation.

quadraphonic or **quadrophonic** /kwod-ruh-**fon**-ik/ adjective (of sound reproduction) using four channels.

quadrate /kwod-ruht/ adjective roughly square or rectangular.

quadratic /kwod-**rat**-ik/ adjective Mathematics involving the second and no higher power of an unknown quantity.

quadriceps /**kwod**-ri-seps/ noun (plural **quadriceps**) a large muscle at the front of the thigh.

quadrilateral noun a four-sided figure. **adjective** having four straight sides.

quadrille /kwod-**ril**/ noun a square dance performed by four couples.

quadriplegia /kwod-ri-**plee**-juh/ noun Medicine paralysis of all four limbs. ■ **quadriplegic** adjective & noun.

quadruped /**kwod**-ruu-ped/ noun an animal which has four feet.

quadruple adjective **1** consisting of four parts. **2** four times as much or as many. **verb** (**quadruples**, **quadrupling**, **quadrupled**) multiply by four. noun a quadruple number or amount.

quadruplet noun each of four children born at one birth.

quaff /kwoff/ verb drink heartily.

quagmire /**kwog**-myr/ noun a soft boggy area of land.

quail¹ noun (plural **quail** or **quails**) a small short-tailed game bird.

quail² verb feel or show fear.

quaint adjective attractively unusual or old-fashioned. ■ **quaintly** adverb.

quake verb (**quakes**, **quaking**, **quaked**) **1** (especially of the earth) shake or tremble. **2** shudder with fear. noun informal an earthquake.

Quaker noun a member of the Religious Society of Friends, a Christian movement devoted to peaceful principles and rejecting set forms of worship. ■ **Quakerism** noun.

qualification noun **1** the action of qualifying. **2** a pass of an examination or an official completion of a course. **3** a quality that makes someone suitable for a job or activity. **4** a statement that limits the meaning of another statement.

qualifier noun **1** a person or team that qualifies for a competition. **2** a match or contest to decide which individuals or teams qualify for a competition. **3** Grammar a word or phrase used to qualify another word.

qualify verb (**qualifies**, **qualifying**, **qualified**) **1** (often **qualify for**) meet the necessary standard or conditions to be entitled to something. **2** become officially recognized as able to do a particular job. **3** make someone able to do something. **4** add something to a statement to limit its meaning. **5** Grammar (of a word or phrase) give a quality to another word.

qualitative /kwol-i-tuh-tiv/ **adjective** relating to or measured by quality. ■ **qualitatively** adverb.

quality noun (plural **qualities**) **1** the degree of excellence of something as measured against other similar things. **2** general excellence. **3** a distinctive characteristic.

qualm /kwahm/ **noun** a feeling of doubt about what you are doing.

quandary /kwon-duh-ri/ noun (plural **quandaries**) a state of uncertainty.

quango /kwang-goh/ **noun** (plural **quangos**) an organization that works independently but with support from the government.

quantify **verb** (**quantifies**, **quantifying**, **quantified**) express or measure the quantity of. ■ **quantifiable** adjective.

quantitative /kwon-ti-tuh-tiv/ **adjective** relating to or measured by quantity. ■ **quantitatively** adverb.

quantity noun (plural **quantities**) **1** a certain amount or number. **2** the property of something that can be measured in number, amount, size, or weight. **3** a considerable number or amount. □ **quantity surveyor** Brit. a person who calculates the amount and cost of materials needed for building work.

quantum /kwon-tuhm/ **noun** (plural **quanta**) Physics a distinct quantity of energy corresponding to that involved in the absorption or emission of energy by an atom. □ **quantum leap** a sudden large increase or advance. **quantum mechanics** the branch of physics concerned with describing the behaviour of subatomic particles in terms of quanta.

quarantine **noun** a period of time when an animal or person that may have a disease is kept in isolation.

verb (**quarantines**, **quarantining**, **quarantined**) put in quarantine.

quark /kwark/ **noun** any of a group of subatomic particles which carry a very small electric charge and are believed to form protons, neutrons, and other particles.

quarrel noun **1** an angry argument or disagreement. **2** a reason for disagreement. **verb** (**quarrels**, **quarrelling**, **quarrelled**; US spelling **quarrels**, **quarreling**, **quarreled**) **1** have a quarrel. **2** (**quarrel with**) disagree with.

quarrelsome **adjective** tending to quarrel with people.

quarry[1] **noun** (plural **quarries**) a place where stone or other materials are dug out of the earth. **verb** (**quarries**, **quarrying**, **quarried**) dig out stone or other materials from a quarry.

quarry[2] **noun** (plural **quarries**) an animal or person that is being hunted or chased.

quart **noun** a unit of liquid capacity equal to a quarter of a gallon or two pints, in Britain equal to 1.13 litres and in the US to 0.94 litre.

quarter **noun** **1** each of four equal parts of something. **2** a period of three months. **3** a quarter-hour. **4** one fourth of a pound weight, equal to 4 oz avoirdupois. **5** a part of a town. **6** a US or Canadian coin worth 25 cents. **7** one fourth of a hundredweight, in Britain equal to 28 lb and in the US equal to 25 lb. **8** (**quarters**) rooms or lodgings. **9** a person or area regarded as the source of something: *help from an unexpected quarter.* **10** mercy shown to an opponent. **verb** (**quarters**, **quartering**, **quartered**) **1** divide into quarters. **2** (**be quartered**) be stationed or lodged. **3** historical cut the body of an executed person into four parts. □ **quarter-final** a match of a competition coming before the semifinal. **quarter tone** Music half a semitone.

quarterdeck **noun** the part of a ship's upper deck near the stern.

quarterly **adjective & adverb** produced or occurring once every quarter of a

---

PUNCTUATION ℹ️

Question mark ?

This is used instead of a full stop at the end of a sentence to show that it is a question, e.g.

Have you seen the film yet?

It is **not** used at the end of a reported question, e.g.

I asked you whether you'd seen the film yet.

---

year. **noun** (plural **quarterlies**) a publication produced four times a year.

quartermaster noun a regimental officer in charge of accommodation and supplies.

quartet noun 1 a group of four people playing music or singing together. **2** a composition for a quartet. **3** a set of four.

quarto /**kwor**-toh/ **noun** (plural **quartos**) a size of page for a book, resulting from folding a sheet into four leaves.

quartz noun a hard mineral consisting of silica.

quasar /**kway**-zar/ **noun** (in astronomy) a kind of galaxy which gives off enormous amounts of energy.

quash verb 1 officially reject a decision as invalid. **2** put an end to.

quasi- /**kway**-zy/ **combining form** seemingly; as if: *quasi-scientific.*

quatrain /**kwot**-rayn/ **noun** a poem or verse of four lines.

quaver verb 1 (**quavers**, **quavering**, **quavered**) (of a voice) tremble. **noun 1** a tremble in a voice. **2** chiefly Brit. a musical note that lasts as long as half a crotchet. ■ **quavery** adjective.

quay /**kee**/ **noun** a platform in a harbour for loading and unloading ships.

quayside noun a quay and the area around it.

queasy adjective (**queasier**, **queasiest**) feeling sick. ■ **queasiness** noun.

queen noun 1 the female ruler of an independent state. **2** (also **queen consort**) a king's wife. **3** the best or most important woman or thing in a par-

ticular group. **4** a playing card ranking next below a king. **5** the most powerful chess piece, able to move in any direction. **6** a female that lays eggs for a colony of ants, bees, wasps, or termites. **7** informal a very feminine homosexual man. □ **queen mother** the widow of a king who is also mother of the current king or queen. ■ **queenly** adjective.

Queensberry Rules plural noun the standard rules of boxing.

queer adjective 1 strange; odd. **2** disapproving (of a man) homosexual. **noun** disapproving a homosexual man.

quell verb 1 put an end to a rebellion by force. **2** suppress a feeling.

quench verb 1 satisfy thirst by drinking. **2** satisfy a desire. **3** put out a fire. **4** suppress a feeling.

querulous /**kwe**-ruu-luhss/ **adjective** complaining in a bad-tempered manner. ■ **querulously** adverb.

query noun (plural **queries**) a question, especially one expressing a doubt about something. **verb** (**queries**, **querying**, **queried**) raise a query.

quest noun a long or difficult search. **verb** search for something.

question noun 1 a sentence worded so as to obtain information. **2** a doubt. **3** the raising of a doubt about something. **4** a problem needing to be solved. **5** a matter depending on conditions: *it's only a question of time.* **verb 1** ask questions of. **2** express doubt about. □ **out of the question** not possible. ■ **questioner** noun.

questionable adjective likely to be wrong.

questionnaire noun a set of questions written for a survey.

> ☑ there are two *n*s: questio**nn**aire.

queue noun a line of people or vehicles waiting their turn for something. verb (**queues**, **queuing** or **queueing**, **queued**) wait in a queue. □ **queue-jump** Brit. move forward out of turn in a queue.

quibble noun a minor objection. verb (**quibbles**, **quibbling**, **quibbled**) raise a minor objection.

quiche /keesh/ noun a baked flan with a savoury filling thickened with eggs.

quick adjective 1 moving fast. 2 lasting or taking a short time. 3 with little or no delay. 4 intelligent. 5 (of temper) easily roused. noun (the **quick**) 1 the tender flesh below the growing part of a fingernail or toenail. 2 your most sensitive feelings. □ **quick-tempered** easily angered. **quick-witted** able to think or respond quickly. ■ **quickly** adverb.

quicken verb 1 make or become quicker. 2 make or become active or alive.

quicklime noun a white caustic alkaline substance consisting of calcium oxide, obtained by heating limestone.

quicksand or **quicksands** noun loose wet sand that sucks in anything resting on it.

quicksilver noun liquid mercury. adjective moving or changing rapidly.

quickstep noun a fast foxtrot.

quid noun (plural **quid**) Brit. informal one pound sterling.

quid pro quo /kwid proh **kwoh**/ noun (plural **quid pro quos**) a favour given in return for something.

quiescent /kwi-**ess**-uhnt/ adjective not active. ■ **quiescence** noun.

quiet adjective (**quieter**, **quietest**) 1 making little or no noise. 2 free from activity or excitement. 3 without being disturbed: *a quiet drink.* 4 discreet: *a quiet word.* 5 (of a person) tranquil and reserved. noun absence of noise or disturbance. verb N.

Amer. make or become quiet. ■ **quietly** adverb.

quieten verb Brit. make or become quiet and calm.

quietude noun a state of calmness and quiet.

quiff noun Brit. a tuft of hair, brushed upwards and backwards from the forehead.

quill noun 1 a main wing or tail feather of a bird. 2 the hollow shaft of a feather. 3 a pen made from a quill. 4 a spine of a porcupine or hedgehog.

quilt noun a warm bed covering made of padding enclosed between layers of fabric. ■ **quilting** noun.

quilted adjective made of two layers of cloth filled with padding.

quin noun Brit. informal a quintuplet.

quince noun a hard yellow fruit resembling a pear.

quinine /kwi-**neen**/ noun a bitter drug made from the bark of a South American tree.

quintessence noun 1 a perfect example. 2 a refined extract of a substance.

quintessential adjective representing the most perfect example. ■ **quintessentially** adverb.

quintet noun 1 a group of five people playing music or singing together. 2 a composition for a quintet. 3 a set of five.

quintuple adjective 1 consisting of five parts or elements. 2 five times as much or as many. verb (**quintuples**, **quintupling**, **quintupled**) increase or be increased fivefold.

quintuplet noun each of five children born at one birth.

quip noun a witty remark. verb (**quips**, **quipping**, **quipped**) make a quip.

quire noun 1 four sheets of paper folded to form eight leaves. 2 25 sheets of paper; one twentieth of a ream.

quirk noun 1 a peculiar habit. 2 a strange thing that happens by chance. ■ **quirky** adjective.

quisling noun a traitor who

PUNCTUATION   ℹ️

Quotation marks

Also called inverted commas, quotation marks (' ' or " ") are used:

1 round a direct quotation; closing quotation marks come after any punctuation which is part of the quotation, e.g.

> *He said, 'That is nonsense.'*
> *'That,' he said, 'is nonsense.'*
> *'That, however,' he said, 'is nonsense.'*
> *Did he say, 'That is nonsense'?*
> *He asked, 'Is that nonsense?'*

2 round a quoted word or phrase, e.g.

> *What does 'integrated circuit' mean?*

3 round a word or phrase that is not being used in its central sense, e.g.

> *the 'king' of jazz*
> *He said he had enough 'dough' to buy a car.*

4 round the title of a book, song, poem, television programme, etc. (but not a book of the Bible), e.g.

> *'Hard Times' by Charles Dickens.*

5 as double quotation marks round a quotation within a quotation, e.g.

> *He asked, 'Do you know what "integrated circuit" means?'*

---

collaborates with an occupying enemy force.

quit verb (**quits, quitting, quitted** or **quit**) **1** leave a place. **2** resign from a job. **3** informal, chiefly N. Amer. stop doing something. ■ **quitter** noun.

quite adverb **1** to the greatest extent or degree; completely. **2** to a certain extent; moderately. **exclamation** expressing agreement.

quits adjective on equal terms because a debt or score has been settled.

quiver[1] verb (**quivers, quivering, quivered**) slightly shake or vibrate. **noun** a quivering movement or sound.

quiver[2] noun a case for carrying arrows.

quixotic /kwik-**sot**-ik/ adjective very eccentric and idealistic.

quiz noun (plural **quizzes**) a competition in which people answer questions that test their knowledge. **verb** (**quizzes, quizzing, quizzed**) question someone.

quizzical adjective showing mild or amused puzzlement. ■ **quizzically** adverb.

quoin /koyn, kwoyn/ noun **1** an external angle of a wall or building. **2** a cornerstone.

quoit /koyt, kwoyt/ noun a ring that you throw over an upright peg in the game of **quoits**.

quorate /**kwor**-uht/ adjective Brit. (of a meeting) having a quorum.

quorum noun (plural **quorums**) the minimum number of people that must be present at a meeting to make its business valid.

quota noun **1** a quantity allowed. **2** a share of something that must be done.

quotation noun **1** a passage or remark repeated by someone other than the person who originally said or wrote it. **2** a formal statement of the estimated cost of a job or service.

quote verb (**quotes, quoting, quoted**)

1 repeat a passage or remark by another person. **2 (quote as)** describe as. **3** give someone an estimated price. **4** give a company a listing on a stock exchange. **noun 1** a quotation. **2 (quotes)** quotation marks. ■ **quotable** adjective.

quoth /rhymes with oath/ **verb** old use said.

quotidian /kwuh-**tid**-i-uhn/ **adjective** formal **1** daily. **2** ordinary or everyday.

quotient /**kwoh**-shuhnt/ **noun** Mathematics a result obtained by dividing one quantity by another.

q.v. **abbreviation** used to direct a reader to another part of a book for further information.

 short for Latin *quod vide*, literally 'which see'.

Rr

R or **r** **noun** (plural **Rs** or **R's**) the eighteenth letter of the alphabet. ■ **abbreviation 1** Regina or Rex. **2** (R.) River.

rabbi /**rab**-by/ **noun** (plural **rabbis**) a Jewish religious leader or teacher of Jewish law. ■ **rabbinic** (or **rabbinical**) adjective.

rabbit **noun** a burrowing mammal with long ears and a short tail. **verb** (**rabbits, rabbiting, rabbited**) Brit. informal chatter. □ **rabbit punch** a sharp chop with the edge of the hand to the back of the neck.

rabble **noun 1** a disorderly crowd. **2 (the rabble)** ordinary people seen as common or uncouth. □ **rabble-rouser** a person who stirs up popular opinion for political reasons.

rabid /**rab**-id, **ray**-bid/ **adjective 1** affected with rabies. **2** extreme; fanatical. ■ **rabidly** adverb.

rabies /**ray**-beez/ **noun** a disease of dogs and other mammals, that can be transmitted through saliva to humans and cause madness and convulsions.

raccoon or **racoon** **noun** a greyish-brown American mammal with a black face and striped tail.

race¹ **noun 1** a competition to see who or which is fastest over a set course. **2** a strong current flowing through a narrow channel. **verb** (**races, racing, raced**) **1** compete in a race. **2** have a race with. **3** move or progress rapidly. **4** (of an engine) operate at excessive speed. ■ **racer** noun.

race² **noun 1** each of the major divisions of humankind. **2** a group of people or things with a common feature. **3** a subdivision of a species. □ **race relations** relations between members of different races within a country.

racecourse **noun** a ground or track for horse or dog racing.

racehorse **noun** a horse bred and trained for racing.

raceme /ra-**seem**/ **noun** a flower cluster with separate flowers along a central stem.

racetrack **noun 1** a racecourse. **2** a track for motor racing.

racial **adjective 1** having to do with race. **2** relating to relations or differences between races. ■ **racially** adverb.

racialism **noun** racism. ■ **racialist** noun & adjective.

racism **noun 1** the belief that certain races are better than others. **2** discrimination against, or hostility towards, other races. ■ **racist** noun & adjective.

rack **noun 1** a framework for holding or storing things. **2 (the rack)** a frame on which people were tortured by being stretched. **3** a joint of meat that includes the front ribs. **verb**

1 (also **wrack**) cause great pain to. **2** (**rack up**) achieve a score or amount. □ **go to rack and ruin** fall into a bad condition. **rack** (or **wrack**) **your brains** think very hard.

racket[1] or **racquet** noun **1** a bat with a round or oval frame, used in tennis, badminton, and squash. **2** (**rackets**) a ball game played with rackets in a four-walled court.

racket[2] noun **1** a loud, unpleasant noise. **2** informal a dishonest scheme for making money. ■ **rackety** adjective.

racketeer noun a person who makes money through dishonest activities. ■ **racketeering** noun.

raconteur /ra-kon-ter/ noun a person who tells stories in an interesting and amusing way.

racoon ⇒ **RACCOON**.

racy adjective lively and exciting.

radar noun a system for detecting aircraft, ships, etc., by sending out radio waves which are reflected back off the object.

raddled adjective showing signs of age and weariness.

radial adjective **1** arranged in lines coming out from a central point to the edge of a circle. **2** (of a tyre) in which the layers of fabric run at right angles to the circumference of the tyre. ■ **radially** adverb.

radian /ray-di-uhn/ noun an angle of 57.3 degrees, equal to the angle at the centre of a circle formed by an arc equal in length to the radius.

radiant adjective **1** shining or glowing brightly. **2** glowing with joy, love, or health. **3** transmitted by radiation. ■ **radiance** noun **radiantly** adverb.

radiate verb (**radiates**, **radiating**, **radiated**) **1** (of light, heat, or other energy) be sent out in rays or waves. **2** show a strong feeling or quality. **3** spread out from a central point.

radiation noun energy sent out as electromagnetic waves or subatomic particles.

radiator noun **1** a metal device for heating a room, usually filled with hot water pumped in through pipes.

2 a cooling device in a vehicle or aircraft engine.

radical adjective **1** having to do with the basic nature of something; fundamental. **2** supporting complete political or social reform. **3** departing from tradition; new. **4** Mathematics relating to the root of a number or quantity. noun **1** a supporter of radical reform. **2** Chemistry a group of atoms behaving as a unit in a compound. ■ **radicalism** noun **radically** adverb.

radii plural of **RADIUS**.

radio noun (plural **radios**) **1** the sending and receiving of electromagnetic waves carrying sound messages. **2** the activity or medium of broadcasting in sound. **3** an apparatus for receiving radio programmes, or for sending and receiving radio messages. verb (**radioes**, **radioing**, **radioed**) send a message to someone by radio.

radioactive adjective giving out harmful radiation or particles.

radioactivity noun harmful radiation or particles sent out when atomic nuclei break up.

radiocarbon noun a radioactive isotope of carbon used in carbon dating.

radiogram noun Brit. dated a combined radio and record player.

radiography noun the production of images by X-rays or other radiation. ■ **radiographer** noun.

radioisotope noun a radioactive isotope.

radiology noun the science of X-rays and similar radiation, especially as used in medicine. ■ **radiologist** noun.

radiotherapy noun the treatment of disease using X-rays or similar radiation.

radish noun the crisp, hot-tasting root of a plant, eaten as a salad vegetable.

radium noun a radioactive metallic element.

radius noun (plural **radii** /ray-di-I/ or **radiuses**) **1** a straight line from the centre to the edge of a circle or sphere. **2** a specified distance from a centre in all directions. **3** the thicker and shorter of the two bones in the human forearm.

radon noun a rare radioactive gas.

RAF abbreviation Royal Air Force.

raffia noun fibre from the leaves of a tropical palm tree.

raffish adjective slightly disreputable, but in an attractive way.

raffle noun a lottery with goods as prizes. **verb (raffles, raffling, raffled)** offer something as a prize in a raffle.

raft noun **1** a flat structure used as a boat or floating platform. **2** a small inflatable boat. **3** a large amount.

rafter noun a beam forming part of the internal framework of a roof.

rag noun **1** a piece of old cloth. **2 (rags)** old or tattered clothes. **3** informal a low-quality newspaper. **4** Brit. a programme of entertainments organized by students to raise money for charity. **5** a piece of ragtime music. □ **lose your rag** informal lose your temper. **the rag trade** informal the clothing or fashion industry.

ragamuffin noun a person in ragged, dirty clothes.

ragbag noun a collection of widely different things.

rage noun violent uncontrollable anger. **verb (rages, raging, raged) 1** feel or express rage. **2** continue with great force. □ **all the rage** temporarily very popular or fashionable.

ragged adjective **1** (of cloth or clothes) old and torn. **2** rough or irregular. **3** not smooth or steady. ■ **raggedly** adverb.

ragout /ra-goo/ noun a spicy stew of meat and vegetables.

ragtag adjective disorganized and very varied.

ragtime noun an early form of jazz played especially on the piano.

ragwort noun a plant with yellow flowers and ragged leaves.

raid noun **1** a sudden attack on an enemy, or on a building to commit a crime. **2** a surprise visit by police to arrest suspects or seize illegal goods.

verb make a raid on. ■ **raider** noun.

rail noun **1** a fixed bar forming part of a fence or barrier or used to hang things on. **2** each of the two metal bars laid on the ground to form a railway track. **3** railways as a means of transport. verb **1** enclose with a rail or rails. **2 (rail against** or **at)** complain strongly about. □ **go off the rails** informal behave in an uncontrolled way.

railhead noun a point at which a railway ends.

railing noun a fence or barrier made of rails.

raillery noun good-humoured teasing.

railroad noun N. Amer. a railway. verb informal rush or force someone into doing something.

railway noun Brit. **1** a track made of rails along which trains run. **2** a system of tracks and trains.

raiment /ray-muhnt/ noun old use or literary clothing.

rain noun **1** condensed moisture from the atmosphere falling in separate drops. **2 (rains)** falls of rain. **3** a large quantity of things falling together. verb **1 (it rains, it is raining, it rained)** rain falls. **2 (be rained off)** (of an event) be prevented by rain from continuing or taking place. **3** fall in large quantities.

rainbow noun an arch of colours in the sky, caused by the sun shining through water droplets in the atmosphere.

raincoat noun a coat made from water-resistant fabric.

rainfall noun the amount of rain falling.

rainforest noun a dense forest found in tropical areas with consistently heavy rainfall.

rainy adjective (**rainier, rainiest**) having a lot of rain. □ **a rainy day** a time in the future when money may be needed.

raise verb (**raises, raising, raised**) **1** lift or move upwards or into an upright position. **2** increase the amount, level, or strength of. **3** express doubts, objections, etc. **4** collect money. **5** bring up a child. **6** breed or grow animals or plants. **7** Brit. informal establish contact with someone by telephone or radio. **8 (raise to)** Mathematics multiply a quantity to a specified power. **noun** N. Amer. an increase in salary. □ **raise the roof** cheer very loudly.

raisin noun a partially dried grape.

raison d'être /ray-zon det-ruh/ noun (plural **raisons d'être** /ray-zon det-ruh/) the most important reason for someone or something's existence.

Raj /rahj/ noun **(the Raj)** the period of British rule in India.

raja or **rajah** /rah-juh/ noun historical an Indian king or prince.

rake¹ noun a pole with metal prongs at the end, used for drawing together leaves, smoothing soil, etc. **verb** (**rakes**, **raking**, **raked**) **1** draw together or smooth with a rake. **2** scratch or sweep with a long broad movement. **3** search through. □ **rake it in** informal make a lot of money. **rake up** bring up something that is best forgotten.

rake² noun a fashionable, wealthy, but immoral man.

rake³ verb (**rakes**, **raking**, **raked**) set at a sloping angle. **noun** the angle at which something slopes.

rakish adjective having a dashing, jaunty, or slightly disreputable appearance.

rally verb (**rallies**, **rallying**, **rallied**) **1** (of troops) come together again to continue fighting. **2** come together to give support. **3** recover health or strength. **4** (of shares or currency) increase in value after a fall. **5** (**rallying**) participation in a motor rally. **noun** (plural **rallies**) **1** a mass meeting held as a protest or in support of a cause. **2** a long-distance competition for motor vehicles over roads or rough terrain. **3** a strong recovery. **4** (in tennis and similar games) a long exchange of strokes between players.

ram noun **1** an adult male sheep. **2** a long, heavy object swung against a door to break it down. **3** a striking or plunging device in a machine. **verb** (**rams**, **ramming**, **rammed**) **1** roughly force into place. **2** hit with force. □ **ram raid** a robbery in which people ram a shop window with a vehicle to steal goods.

Ramadan /ram-uh-dan/ noun the ninth month of the Muslim year, during which Muslims do not eat from sunrise to sunset.

ramble verb (**rambles**, **rambling**, **rambled**) **1** walk for pleasure in the countryside. **2** talk or write in a confused way. **noun** a country walk taken for pleasure. ■ **rambler** noun.

ramekin /ra-mi-kin/ noun a small dish for baking and serving an individual portion of food.

ramifications plural noun complex results of an action or event.

ramp noun **1** a sloping surface joining two different levels. **2** a set of steps for entering or leaving an aircraft.

rampage verb /ram-payj/ (**rampages**, **rampaging**, **rampaged**) rush around in a wild and violent way. **noun** /ram-payj/ a period of wild and violent behaviour.

rampant adjective **1** flourishing or spreading in an uncontrolled way. **2** Heraldry (of an animal) shown standing on its left hind foot with its forefeet in the air.

rampart noun a wall defending a castle or town, having a broad top with a walkway.

ramrod noun a rod formerly used to ram down the charge of a firearm.

ramshackle adjective in a very bad condition.

ran past of **RUN**.

ranch noun a large farm in America where cattle or other animals are bred. ■ **rancher** noun.

rancid adjective (of food) stale and smelling or tasting unpleasant.

rancour (US spelling **rancor**) noun bitter feeling or resentment.■ **rancorous** adjective.

rand noun the basic unit of money of South Africa.

R & B abbreviation 1 rhythm and blues. 2 a kind of pop music with soulful vocals.

random adjective done or happening without order, purpose, or planning.
■ **randomly** adverb **randomness** noun.

randy adjective (**randier**, **randiest**) Brit. informal sexually excited.

rang past of **RING**².

range noun 1 the limits between which something varies. 2 a set of different things of the same general type. 3 the distance over which a sound, missile, etc. can travel. 4 a line of mountains or hills. 5 a large area of open land for grazing or hunting. 6 an area for testing military equipment or practising shooting. 7 a large stove with several burners or hotplates. verb (**ranges**, **ranging**, **ranged**) 1 vary between particular limits. 2 arrange things in a particular way. 3 (**range against**) be in opposition to. 4 travel over a wide area.

ranger noun a keeper of a park, forest, or area of countryside.

rangy /rayn-ji/ adjective (of a person) tall and slim with long limbs.

rank¹ noun 1 a position within the armed forces or an organization. 2 a row of people or things. 3 high social position. 4 (**the ranks**) (in the armed forces) those who are not commissioned officers. verb 1 give a rank to. 2 hold a specified rank. 3 arrange in a row or rows. □ **close ranks** unite to defend shared interests. **pull rank** use your higher rank to take advantage of someone. **rank and file** the ordinary members of an organization.

rank² adjective 1 having a very unpleasant smell. 2 (of vegetation) growing too thickly. 3 complete: *a rank amateur.*

rankle verb (**rankles**, **rankling**, **rankled**) cause continuing annoyance or resentment.

ransack verb go hurriedly through a place stealing or searching for things.

ransom noun a sum of money demanded for the release of someone who is held captive. verb cause someone to be released by paying a ransom. □ **hold to ransom 1** hold someone captive and demand payment for their release. 2 force someone to do something by threatening them. **a king's ransom** a huge amount of money.

rant verb speak in a loud, angry, and forceful way.

rap verb (**raps**, **rapping**, **rapped**) 1 hit a hard surface with a series of rapid blows. 2 strike sharply. 3 informal criticize sharply. 4 say sharply or suddenly. noun 1 a quick, sharp knock or blow. 2 informal a criticism. 3 a type of popular music in which words are spoken rhythmically over an instrumental backing. ■ **rapper** noun.

rapacious adjective very greedy.

rapacity /ruh-**pa**-si-ti/ noun greed.

rape¹ verb (**rapes**, **raping**, **raped**) 1 (of a man) force someone to have sex with him against their will. 2 spoil or destroy a place. noun an act of raping.

rape² noun a plant with bright yellow flowers, grown for its oil-rich seed.

rapid adjective very quick. noun (**rapids**) a part of a river where the water flows very fast. ■ **rapidity** noun **rapidly** adverb.

rapier noun a thin, light sword.

rapine /ra-pyn/ noun literary the violent seizure of property.

rapist noun a man who commits rape.

rapport /rap-**por**/ noun a close relationship in which people understand each other and communicate well.

rapprochement /ra-**prosh**-mon/ noun a renewal of friendly relations between two countries or groups.

rapscallion noun old use a rascal.

rapt adjective completely interested or absorbed in someone or something.

rapture noun 1 great pleasure or joy. 2 (**raptures**) the expression of great pleasure or enthusiasm.

rapturous adjective very pleased or enthusiastic. ■ **rapturously** adverb.

rare adjective (**rarer, rarest**) **1** not occurring or found very often. **2** unusually good. **3** (of red meat) lightly cooked, so that the inside is still red. □ **rare earth** any of a group of chemically similar metallic elements including cerium and lanthanum. ■ **rarely** adverb.

rarebit = **Welsh rarebit**.

rarefied adjective **1** (of air) of lower pressure than usual; thin. **2** understood by only a limited group of people.

 -ref-, not -rif-: rarefied.

raring adjective (**raring to do**) informal very eager to do something.

rarity noun (plural **rarities**) **1** the state of being rare. **2** a rare thing.

rascal noun **1** a mischievous or cheeky person. **2** dated a dishonest man. ■ **rascally** adjective.

rash[1] adjective acting or done without careful consideration of the possible results. ■ **rashly** adverb.

rash[2] noun **1** an area of red spots or patches on a person's skin. **2** a series of unpleasant things happening within a short time.

rasher noun a thin slice of bacon.

rasp noun **1** a coarse file. **2** a harsh, grating noise. verb **1** file with a rasp. **2** scrape roughly. **3** make a harsh, grating noise.

raspberry noun **1** a reddish-pink soft fruit. **2** informal a rude sound made with the tongue and lips.

Rasta noun a Rastafarian.

Rastafarian /rass-tuh-**fair**-i-uhn/ noun a member of a Jamaican religious movement which worships Haile Selassie, the former Emperor of Ethiopia. ■ **Rastafarianism** noun.

rat noun **1** a rodent resembling a large mouse. **2** informal an unpleasant or disliked person. verb (**rats, ratting, ratted**) **1** (**ratting**) hunting and killing rats. **2** (**rat on**) informal inform on. **3** (**rat on**) informal break an agreement

or promise. □ **the rat race** informal a way of life which is a fiercely competitive struggle for wealth or power.

ratatouille /ra-tuh-**too**-i/ noun a vegetable dish of stewed onions, courgettes, tomatoes, etc.

ratchet noun a device with a set of angled teeth in which a cog, tooth, or bar fits, allowing movement in one direction only.

rate[1] noun **1** a measure, quantity, or frequency measured against another. **2** the speed of something. **3** a fixed price paid or charged for something. **4** (**rates**) (in the UK) a tax on land and buildings paid to a local authority by a business. verb (**rates, rating, rated**) **1** give something a standard or value according to a particular scale. **2** regard in a certain way. **3** be worthy of; deserve. **4** informal have a high opinion of. ■ **rateable** (or **ratable**) adjective.

rate[2] verb old use scold angrily.

rather adverb **1** (**would rather**) would prefer. **2** to some extent; fairly. **3** used to correct something you have said or to be more precise. **4** instead of; as opposed to.

ratify verb (**ratifies, ratifying, ratified**) make a treaty, contract, etc. valid by signing or agreeing to it. ■ **ratification** noun.

rating noun **1** a classification based on quality, standard, or performance. **2** (**ratings**) the estimated audience size of a television or radio programme. **3** Brit. a sailor in the navy who does not hold a commission.

ratio noun (plural **ratios**) an indication of the relationship between two amounts, showing the number of times one contains the other.

ratiocination /ra-ti-oss-i-**nay**-sh'n/ noun formal the process of thinking in a logical way; reasoning.

ration noun **1** a fixed amount of food, fuel, etc., officially allowed to each person. **2** (**rations**) a regular allowance of food supplied to members of the armed forces. verb limit the supply of food, fuel, etc.

rational adjective **1** based on reason

rationale /ra-shuh-**nahl**/ noun the reasons for a course of action or a belief.

rationalism noun the belief that opinions and actions should be based on reason rather than on religious belief or emotions. ■ **rationalist** noun.

rationalize or **rationalise** verb (**rationalizes, rationalizing, rationalized**) **1** try to find a logical reason for. **2** make more efficient. ■ **rationalization** noun.

rattan /ruh-**tan**/ noun the thin, pliable stems of a tropical palm, used to make furniture.

rattle verb (**rattles, rattling, rattled**) **1** make a rapid series of short, sharp sounds. **2** informal make someone nervous or irritated. **3** (**rattle off**) say or do quickly and easily. **4** (**rattle on**) talk rapidly and at length. noun **1** a rattling sound. **2** a toy that makes a rattling sound.

rattlesnake noun an American viper with horny rings on the tail that produce a rattling sound.

ratty adjective Brit. informal irritable.

raucous adjective sounding loud and harsh. ■ **raucously** adverb.

raunchy adjective (**raunchier, raunchiest**) informal sexually direct.

ravage verb (**ravages, ravaging, ravaged**) cause great damage to. noun (**ravages**) the destruction caused by something.

rave verb (**raves, raving, raved**) **1** talk angrily or without making sense. **2** speak or write about someone or something with great enthusiasm. noun Brit. a large event with dancing to loud, fast electronic music. □ **rave-up** Brit. informal a lively, noisy party.

raven noun a large black crow. adjective (of hair) of a glossy black colour.

ravening adjective literary very fierce and hungry.

ravenous adjective very hungry. ■ **ravenously** adverb.

raver noun informal a person who has an exciting or wild social life.

ravine noun a deep, narrow gorge.

raving noun (**ravings**) wild senseless talk. adjective & adverb informal used for emphasis: *raving mad.*

ravioli /rav-i-**oh**-li/ plural noun small pasta cases containing minced meat, cheese, or vegetables.

ravish verb **1** old use seize and carry off by force. **2** dated rape. **3** (**ravishing**) very beautiful.

raw adjective **1** (of food) not cooked. **2** (of a material) in its natural state. **3** new to an activity and lacking experience. **4** (of the skin) red and painful from being rubbed or scraped. **5** (of an emotion or quality) strong and undisguised. **6** (of the weather) cold and damp. □ **raw-boned** bony or gaunt. ■ **rawness** noun.

ray[1] noun **1** a narrow line or beam of light or radiation. **2** a trace of something good: *a ray of hope.*

ray[2] noun a broad flat fish with a long, thin tail.

rayon noun a synthetic fabric made from viscose.

raze verb (**razes, razing, razed**) completely destroy a building, town, etc.

razor noun an instrument used to shave hair.

razzle noun (**on the razzle**) informal out celebrating or enjoying yourself.

razzmatazz or **razzamatazz** noun informal noisy and exciting activity designed to attract attention.

RC abbreviation Roman Catholic.

re /ree, ray/ preposition with regard to.

reach verb **1** stretch out an arm to touch or grasp something. **2** be able to touch something with an outstretched arm or leg. **3** arrive at; get as far as. **4** come to a particular level or point. **5** make contact with. noun **1** the distance to which someone can stretch out their arm or arms to touch something. **2** a continuous stretch of river between two bends.

react verb **1** respond to something in a particular way. **2** interact and

WORD FORMATION

re-

Words beginning with **re-** mean:

■ once more; again: *reactivate*.
■ so as to return to a previous state: *restore*.

re- words are usually spelled without a hyphen, e.g. *react*. However, if the original word begins with **e**, then a hyphen is used to make the new word clearer (*re-examine, re-enter*). You should also use a hyphen when a word formed with **re-** would be exactly the same as a word that already exists; so **re-cover** means 'cover again', whereas **recover** means 'get well again'.

undergo a chemical or physical change. ■ **reactive** adjective.

reaction noun **1** something done or experienced as a result of an event. **2** (**reactions**) a person's ability to respond to an event. **3** a bad response by the body to a drug or substance. **4** a process in which substances interact causing chemical or physical change. **5** a force exerted in opposition to an applied force.

reactionary adjective opposing political or social progress or reform. noun (plural **reactionaries**) a person holding reactionary views.

reactivate verb (**reactivates, reactivating, reactivated**) bring something back into action. ■ **reactivation** noun.

reactor noun an apparatus in which material is made to undergo a controlled nuclear reaction that releases energy.

read verb (**reads, reading, read**) **1** understand the meaning of written or printed words or symbols. **2** speak written or printed words aloud. **3** have a particular wording. **4** understand the nature or meaning of. **5** (**read into**) think that something has a meaning that it may not possess. **6** Brit. study a subject at a university. **7** (of an instrument) show a measurement or figure. noun informal a book that is interesting to read. □ **take as read** accept without the need for discussion. **well read** having read widely. ■ **reader** noun.

readership noun the readers of a publication regarded as a group.

readily adverb **1** willingly. **2** easily.

reading noun **1** the action of reading. **2** something that is read. **3** a figure recorded on a measuring instrument.

readjust verb **1** adjust again. **2** adapt to a changed situation. ■ **readjustment** noun.

ready adjective (**readier, readiest**) **1** prepared for an activity or situation. **2** made suitable and available for immediate use. **3** easily available or obtained. **4** (**ready to do**) willing or eager to do. **5** immediate or quick. noun (**readies** or **the ready**) Brit. informal available money; cash. verb (**readies, readying, readied**) prepare. ■ **readiness** noun.

reagent /ri-ay-juhnt/ noun a substance that produces a chemical reaction, used to detect the presence of another substance.

real adjective **1** actually existing or occurring. **2** not artificial; genuine. **3** worthy of the description; proper. adverb informal, N. Amer. really; very. □ **real estate** N. Amer. land or housing. **real tennis** the original form of tennis, played with a solid ball on an enclosed court.

realign verb change something to a different position or state. ■ **realignment** noun.

realism noun **1** the acceptance of a situation as it is. **2** the presentation of things in a way that is accurate and true to life. ■ **realist** noun.

realistic adjective **1** having a sensible and practical idea of what can be achieved. **2** showing things in a way that is accurate and true to life. ■ **realistically** adverb.

reality noun (plural **realities**) **1** the state of things as they actually exist. **2** a thing that is real. **3** the state of being real.

realize or **realise** verb (**realizes, realizing, realized**) **1** become fully aware of a fact. **2** achieve or fulfil a wish or plan. **3** be sold for a particular amount. **4** convert property, shares, etc. into money by selling them. ■ **realization** noun.

really adverb **1** in actual fact. **2** very; thoroughly. **exclamation** expressing interest, surprise, doubt, etc.

realm noun **1** chiefly literary a kingdom. **2** a field of activity or interest.

ream noun **1** 500 sheets of paper. **2** (**reams**) a large quantity.

reap verb **1** gather in a crop or harvest. **2** receive a reward or benefit as a result of your actions.

reaper noun a person or machine that harvests a crop. □ **the Grim Reaper** death, shown as a cloaked skeleton holding a scythe.

rear[1] noun the back part of something. **adjective** at the back. □ **rear admiral** the naval rank above commodore. ■ **rearmost** adjective **rearward** adjective & adverb **rearwards** adverb.

rear[2] verb **1** bring up offspring. **2** breed animals. **3** (of an animal) raise itself upright on its hind legs. **4** extend to a great height.

rearguard noun a body of troops protecting the rear of the main force.

rearm verb provide with or obtain a new supply of weapons. ■ **rearmament** noun.

rearrange verb (**rearranges, rearranging, rearranged**) arrange again in a different way. ■ **rearrangement** noun.

reason noun **1** a cause or explanation. **2** good or obvious cause to do something. **3** the power to think and draw conclusions logically. **4** (**your reason**) your sanity. **5** what is right, practical, or possible. **verb 1** think and draw con-

clusions logically. **2** (**reason with**) persuade by logical argument. □ **stand to reason** be logical.

reasonable adjective **1** fair and sensible. **2** appropriate in a particular situation. **3** fairly good. **4** not too expensive. ■ **reasonably** adverb.

reassure verb (**reassures, reassuring, reassured**) make someone feel less worried or afraid. ■ **reassurance** noun.

rebarbative adjective unpleasant.

rebate /ree-bayt/ noun **1** a partial refund to someone who has paid too much for tax, rent, etc. **2** a discount on a sum that is due.

rebel verb /ri-bel/ (**rebels, rebelling, rebelled**) **1** refuse to obey the government or ruler. **2** oppose authority, or refuse to behave conventionally. noun /reb-uhl/ a person who rebels.

rebellion noun **1** an act of rebelling. **2** opposition to authority or control.

rebellious adjective choosing to rebel. ■ **rebelliously** adverb.

rebirth noun a return to life or activity.

reborn adjective brought back to life or activity.

rebound verb /ri-bownd/ **1** bounce back after hitting a hard surface. **2** increase again. **3** (**rebound on**) have an unexpected and unpleasant effect on. noun /ree-bownd/ a ball or shot that rebounds. □ **on the rebound** while still upset after the ending of a romantic relationship.

rebuff verb reject in an abrupt or unkind way. noun an abrupt or unkind rejection.

rebuke verb (**rebukes, rebuking, rebuked**) sharply criticize or tell off. noun a sharp criticism.

rebus noun (plural **rebuses**) a puzzle in which words are represented by combinations of pictures and letters.

rebut verb (**rebuts, rebutting, rebutted**) claim or prove that something is false. ■ **rebuttal** noun.

recalcitrant /ri-kal-si-truhnt/ adjective unwilling to cooperate; disobedient. ■ **recalcitrance** noun.

recall verb **1** remember. **2** make someone think of; bring to mind. **3** officially order someone to return. **4** (of a manufacturer) ask for faulty products to be returned. noun **1** the action of remembering. **2** an official order for someone to return.

recant verb withdraw a former opinion or belief.

recap verb (**recaps, recapping, recapped**) informal recapitulate.

recapitulate verb (**recapitulates, recapitulating, recapitulated**) give a summary of. ■ **recapitulation** noun.

recapture verb (**recaptures, recapturing, recaptured**) **1** capture a person or animal that has escaped. **2** recover something taken or lost. **3** bring back or experience again a past time or feeling. noun an act of recapturing.

recast verb (**recasts, recasting, recast**) present something in a different form.

recce /rek-ki/ noun Brit. informal reconnaissance.

recede verb (**recedes, receding, receded**) **1** move back or further away. **2** gradually become weaker or smaller. **3** (**receding**) (of part of the face) sloping backwards.

receipt noun **1** the action of receiving something. **2** a written statement confirming that something has been paid for or received. **3** (**receipts**) the amount of money received over a period by a business.

receive verb (**receives, receiving, received**) **1** be given or paid. **2** accept something sent or offered. **3** form an idea or impression from an experience. **4** experience or meet with. **5** entertain or admit a guest or member. **6** detect or pick up broadcast signals. **7** (**received**) widely accepted as true. □ **received pronunciation** the standard form of British English pronunciation, based on educated speech in southern England.

✓	remember, the rule is *i* before *e* except after *c*: rece*i*ve.

receiver noun **1** a person or thing that receives something. **2** a radio or television apparatus that converts broadcast signals into sound or images. **3** the part of a telephone that converts electrical signals into sounds. **4** (also **official receiver**) a person appointed to manage the financial affairs of a bankrupt business. ■ **receivership** noun.

recent adjective having happened or been done shortly before the present. ■ **recently** adverb.

receptacle noun an object used to contain something.

reception noun **1** the action of receiving. **2** the way in which people react to something. **3** a formal social occasion held to welcome someone or celebrate an event. **4** the area in a hotel, office, etc. where visitors are greeted. **5** the quality with which broadcast signals are received.

receptionist noun a person who greets and deals with visitors to an office, hotel, etc.

receptive adjective **1** able or willing to receive something. **2** willing to consider new ideas. ■ **receptivity** noun.

receptor noun a nerve ending in the body that responds to a stimulus such as light.

recess noun **1** a small space set back in a wall or in a surface. **2** (**recesses**) remote or hidden places. **3** a break between sessions of a parliament, law court, etc. verb fit something so that it is set back into a surface.

recession noun a period during which trade and industrial activity in a country are reduced.

recessive adjective (of a gene) appearing in offspring only if a contrary gene is not also inherited.

recharge verb (**recharges, recharging, recharged**) charge a battery or device again. ■ **rechargeable** adjective.

recherché /ruh-**shair**-shay/ adjective unusual and not easily understood.

recidivist /ri-**sid**-i-vist/ noun a person who constantly commits crimes. ■ **recidivism** noun.

recipe noun **1** a list of ingredients and instructions for preparing a dish. **2** something likely to lead to a particular outcome: *a recipe for disaster.*

recipient /ri-**sip**-i-uhnt/ noun a person who receives something.

reciprocal /ri-**sip**-ruh-k'l/ adjective **1** given or done in return. **2** affecting two parties equally. ■ **reciprocally** adverb.

reciprocate verb (reciprocates, reciprocating, reciprocated) respond to an action or emotion with a similar one.

reciprocity /re-si-**pross**-i-ti/ noun a situation in which two parties provide the same help to each other.

recital noun **1** the performance of a programme of music by a soloist or small group. **2** a long account of a series of facts or events.

recite verb (recites, reciting, recited) **1** repeat a passage aloud from memory. **2** state facts, events, etc. in order. ■ **recitation** noun.

reckless adjective without thought or care for the results of an action. ■ **recklessly** adverb **recklessness** noun.

reckon verb **1** calculate. **2** have an opinion about; think. **3** (reckon on) rely on or expect. **4** (reckon with or without) take (or fail to take) into account. □ **to be reckoned with** to be treated as important.

reckoning noun **1** the action of calculating. **2** a person's opinion. **3** punishment for past actions. □ **into** (or **out of**) **the reckoning** among (or not among) those who are likely to be successful.

reclaim verb **1** get possession of something again. **2** make land usable. ■ **reclamation** noun.

recline verb (reclines, reclining, reclined) lie back in a relaxed position.

recluse /ri-**klooss**/ noun a person who avoids others and lives alone. ■ **reclusive** adjective.

recognition noun **1** the action of recognizing. **2** appreciation or acknowledgement.

recognize or **recognise** verb (recognizes, recognizing, recognized) **1** know someone or something from having come across them before. **2** accept something as genuine, legal, or valid. **3** show official appreciation of. ■ **recognizable** adjective.

recoil verb **1** suddenly move back in fear, horror, or disgust. **2** (of a gun) suddenly move backwards as a reaction on being fired. **3** (recoil on) have an unpleasant effect on. noun the action of recoiling.

recollect verb remember. ■ **recollection** noun.

recommend verb **1** say that someone or something is suitable for a particular purpose or role. **2** make something seem appealing or desirable. ■ **recommendation** noun.

recompense /**rek**-uhm-penss/ verb (recompenses, recompensing, recompensed) **1** compensate someone for loss or harm suffered. **2** pay or reward someone for effort or work. noun compensation or reward.

reconcile verb (reconciles, reconciling, reconciled) **1** make two people or groups friendly again. **2** find a satisfactory way of dealing with opposing facts, ideas, etc. **3** (reconcile to) make someone accept something unwelcome.

reconciliation noun **1** the end of a disagreement and the return to friendly relations. **2** the action of reconciling opposing ideas, facts, etc.

recondite /**rek**-uhn-dyt/ adjective obscure and little known.

recondition verb Brit. bring back to a good condition; renovate.

reconnaissance /ri-**kon**-ni-suhnss/ noun military observation of an area to gain information.

reconnoitre /rek-uh-**noy**-ter/ (US spelling **reconnoiter**) verb (reconnoitres, reconnoitring, reconnoitred) make a military observation of an area.

reconsider verb (reconsiders, reconsidering, reconsidered) consider again, with the possibility of changing a decision. ■ **reconsideration** noun.

reconstitute verb (**reconstitutes**, **reconstituting**, **reconstituted**) **1** change the form of an organization. **2** restore dried food to its original state by adding water. ■ **reconstitution** noun.

reconstruct verb **1** construct again. **2** show how a past event happened by interpreting evidence. ■ **reconstruction** noun.

record noun /rek-ord/ **1** a permanent account of something, kept for evidence or information. **2** the previous behaviour or performance of a person or thing. **3** (also **criminal record**) a list of a person's previous criminal convictions. **4** the best performance of its kind that has been officially recognized. **5** a thin plastic disc carrying recorded sound in grooves on each surface. verb /ri-kord/ **1** make a record of. **2** convert sound or vision into permanent form so that it can be reproduced later. □ **off the record** not made as an official statement. **record player** a device for playing records.

recorder noun **1** a device for recording sound, pictures, etc. **2** a person who keeps records. **3** a musical instrument which you play by blowing through a mouthpiece and putting fingers over holes.

recording noun **1** a piece of music, film, etc. that has been recorded. **2** the process of recording.

recount[1] verb describe something to someone.

recount[2] verb count again. noun an act of counting something again.

recoup verb recover a loss.

recourse noun **1** a source of help in a difficult situation. **2** (**recourse to**) the use of a particular source of help.

recover verb (**recovers**, **recovering**, **recovered**) **1** return to a normal state of health or strength. **2** regain possession or control of. **3** regain an amount of money that has been spent or lent. ■ **recoverable** adjective.

recovery noun (plural **recoveries**) the action or an act of recovering.

recreate verb (**recreates**, **recreating**, **recreated**) make or do again.

recreation[1] /rek-ri-ay-sh'n/ noun enjoyable leisure activity. ■ **recreational** adjective.

recreation[2] /ree-kri-ay-sh'n/ noun the action of recreating something.

recrimination noun an accusation made in response to one from someone else.

recrudescence /ree-kroo-dess-'nss/ noun formal a recurrence.

recruit verb take on someone to serve in the armed forces or work for an organization. noun a newly recruited person. ■ **recruitment** noun.

rectal adjective relating to or affecting the rectum.

rectangle noun a flat shape with four right angles and four straight sides, two of which are longer than the others. ■ **rectangular** adjective.

rectify verb (**rectifies**, **rectifying**, **rectified**) **1** put right; correct. **2** convert alternating current to direct current. ■ **rectification** noun.

rectilinear adjective having or moving in a straight line or lines.

rectitude noun morally correct behaviour.

recto noun (plural **rectos**) a right-hand page of an open book, or the front of a loose document.

rector noun **1** a Christian priest in charge of a parish. **2** the head of certain universities, colleges, and schools.

rectory noun (plural **rectories**) the house of a rector.

rectum noun the final section of the large intestine, ending at the anus.

recumbent adjective lying down.

recuperate verb (**recuperates**, **recuperating**, **recuperated**) **1** recover from illness or tiredness. **2** get back something that has been lost or spent. ■ **recuperation** noun.

recur verb (**recurs**, **recurring**, **re-**

curred) happen again or repeatedly. ■ **recurrence** noun.

recurrent adjective happening often or repeatedly.

recycle verb (**recycles, recycling, recycled**) **1** convert waste into a form in which it can be reused. **2** use something again. ■ **recyclable** adjective.

red adjective (**redder, reddest**) **1** of the colour of blood or fire. **2** (of hair or fur) of a reddish-brown colour. **3** informal, chiefly disapproving communist or socialist. noun **1** red colour or material. **2** informal, chiefly disapproving a communist or socialist. □ in the red having spent more than is in your bank account. **red-blooded** (of a man) energetic and healthy. **red card** (in soccer) a red card shown by the referee to a player being sent off the field. **red-handed** in the act of doing something wrong. **red herring** a thing that takes people's attention away from something important. **red-hot 1** so hot that it glows red. **2** very exciting. **Red Indian** dated, often offensive an American Indian. **red-letter day** an important or memorable day. **red-light district** an area with many brothels, strip clubs, etc. **red tape** complicated official rules which get in the way of progress. **see red** informal suddenly become very angry. ■ **reddish** adjective.

redcurrant noun a small edible red berry.

redden verb make or become red.

redeem verb **1** make up for the faults of. **2** save someone from sin or evil. **3** fulfil a promise. **4** regain possession of something in exchange for payment. **5** exchange a coupon for goods or money. **6** pay a debt.

redeemer noun **1** a person who redeems. **2** (the Redeemer) Jesus.

redemption noun the action of redeeming.

redeploy verb move troops, resources, etc. to a new place or task. ■ **redeployment** noun.

redhead noun a person with red hair.

redneck noun US informal a conservative working-class white person.

redolent /red-uh-luhnt/ adjective (**redolent of** or **with**) **1** strongly calling something to mind. **2** literary smelling of. ■ **redolence** noun.

redouble verb (**redoubles, redoubling, redoubled**) make or become greater or more intense.

redoubt noun a temporary or additional fortification.

redoubtable adjective worthy of respect or fear; formidable.

redound verb (**redound to**) formal be to someone's credit.

redress verb /ree-dress/ put right something unfair or wrong. noun /ri-dress/ payment or action to make amends for a wrong.

redskin noun dated or offensive an American Indian.

reduce verb (**reduces, reducing, reduced**) **1** make or become less. **2** (**reduce to**) change something to a simpler form. **3** (**reduce to**) bring someone to a particular state or condition. **4** boil a liquid so that it becomes thicker. □ **reduced circumstances** being poor after being relatively prosperous. ■ **reducible** adjective.

reduction noun **1** the action of reducing. **2** the amount by which something is reduced.

reductive adjective presenting something in an oversimplified form.

redundant adjective **1** no longer needed or useful. **2** Brit. unemployed because your job is no longer needed. ■ **redundancy** noun (plural **redundancies**).

redwood noun a giant coniferous tree with reddish wood.

reed noun **1** a tall, slender plant that grows in water or on marshy ground. **2** a piece of thin cane or metal in musical instruments such as the clarinet, which vibrates when air is blown over it and produces sound.

reedy adjective **1** (of a sound or voice) high and thin in tone. **2** full of reeds.

reef noun **1** a ridge of jagged rock or

coral just above or below the surface of the sea. **2** each of several strips across a sail that can be taken in when the wind is strong. **verb** make a sail smaller by taking in a reef. □ **reef knot** a type of secure knot.

reefer noun informal a cannabis cigarette.

reefer jacket noun a thick close-fitting double-breasted jacket.

reek verb have a very unpleasant smell. **noun** a very unpleasant smell.

reel noun **1** a cylinder on which film, thread, etc. can be wound. **2** a lively Scottish or Irish folk dance. **verb 1** (**reel in**) bring something towards you by turning a reel. **2** (**reel off**) recite something rapidly and with ease. **3** stagger. **4** feel giddy or bewildered.

re-entry noun (plural **re-entries**) **1** the action of entering again. **2** the return of a spacecraft or missile into the earth's atmosphere.

refectory noun (plural **refectories**) a room used for meals in an educational or religious institution.

refer verb (**refers**, **referring**, **referred**) (**refer to**) **1** write or say something about; mention. **2** (of a word or phrase) describe. **3** consult a person, book, etc. for information. **4** pass a person or matter on to someone else for help or a decision.

referee noun **1** an official who supervises a game to ensure that players keep to the rules. **2** a person who is willing to provide a reference for a person applying for a job. **3** a person who reads academic work before it is published. **verb** (**referees**, **refereeing**, **refereed**) be a referee of.

reference noun **1** the action of referring to something. **2** a mention of a source of information in a book or article. **3** a letter giving information about how suitable someone is for a new job.

> ✓ one *r* in the middle, not two: reference.

referendum noun (plural **referendums** or **referenda**) a vote by the people of a country on a single political issue.

referral noun the action of referring someone or something to a specialist or higher authority.

refine verb (**refines**, **refining**, **refined**) **1** make something pure by removing unwanted substances. **2** improve something by minor changes. **3** (**refined**) well educated, elegant, and having good taste.

refinement noun **1** the process of refining. **2** an improvement. **3** the quality of being well educated, elegant, and having good taste.

refinery noun (plural **refineries**) a factory where a substance is refined.

refit verb (**refits**, **refitting**, **refitted**) replace or repair equipment and fittings in a ship, building, etc. **noun** an act of refitting.

reflect verb **1** throw back heat, light, or sound from a surface. **2** (of a mirror) show an image of. **3** show in a realistic or appropriate way. **4** (**reflect well** or **badly on**) give a good or bad impression about. **5** (**reflect on**) think seriously about.

reflection noun **1** the process of reflecting. **2** a reflected image. **3** a sign of something's true nature. **4** something that brings discredit. **5** serious thought.

reflective adjective **1** providing a reflection. **2** thoughtful. ■ **reflectively** adverb.

reflector noun a piece of glass or plastic on the back of a vehicle for reflecting light.

reflex noun an action done without conscious thought as a response to something. **adjective 1** done as a reflex. **2** (of an angle) more than 180°.

reflexive adjective Grammar referring back to the subject of a clause or verb, e.g. *myself* in *I hurt myself*.

reflexology noun a system of massage used to relieve tension and treat illness. ■ **reflexologist** noun.

refocus verb (**refocuses**, **refocusing** or **refocussing**, **refocused** or **refocussed**) **1** adjust the focus of a lens or your eyes. **2** focus attention on something new or different.

reform verb **1** change something to improve it. **2** make someone improve their behaviour. **noun** an act of reforming. ■ **reformer** noun.

reformation noun **1** the action of reforming. **2** (**the Reformation**) a 16th-century movement for reforming the Roman Catholic Church, leading to the establishment of the Protestant Churches.

reformist adjective supporting political or social reform. **noun** a supporter of such reform. ■ **reformism** noun.

refract verb (of water, air, or glass) make a ray of light change direction when it enters at an angle. ■ **refraction** noun **refractive** adjective.

refractory adjective **1** stubborn or difficult to control. **2** (of an illness) not responding to treatment.

refrain¹ verb (**refrain from**) stop yourself from doing something.

refrain² noun a part of a song that is repeated at the end of each verse.

refresh verb give new energy to.

refresher noun a course intended to refresh your skills or knowledge.

refreshing adjective **1** making you feel less tired or hot. **2** pleasingly new or different. ■ **refreshingly** adverb.

refreshment noun **1** a snack or drink. **2** the giving of fresh energy.

refrigerant noun a substance used for keeping things cold.

refrigerate verb (**refrigerates**, **refrigerating**, **refrigerated**) make food or drink cold to keep it fresh. ■ **refrigeration** noun.

refrigerator noun an appliance in which food and drink are stored at a low temperature.

 no *d* in the middle: refri*g*erator, not -*ridg*-.

refuel verb (**refuels**, **refuelling**, **refuelled**; US spelling **refuels**, **refueling**, **refueled**) supply with more fuel.

refuge noun **1** shelter from danger or trouble. **2** a safe place.

refugee noun a person who has been

forced to leave their country because of a war or because they are being persecuted.

refund verb pay back money to. **noun** a repayment of a sum of money.

refurbish verb redecorate and improve a building or room. ■ **refurbishment** noun.

refuse¹ /ri-**fyooz**/ verb (**refuses**, **refusing**, **refused**) say that you are unwilling to do or accept something. ■ **refusal** noun.

refuse² /**ref**-yooss/ noun things thrown away; rubbish.

refute verb (**refutes**, **refuting**, **refuted**) prove a statement or person to be wrong. ■ **refutation** noun.

> **i** **refute** means 'prove wrong'; it does not mean simply 'deny'.

regain verb **1** get something back after losing possession of it. **2** get back to a place.

regal adjective having to do with a king or queen, especially in being magnificent or dignified. ■ **regally** adverb.

regale verb (**regales**, **regaling**, **regaled**) **1** entertain with conversation. **2** supply generously with food or drink.

regalia /ri-**gay**-li-uh/ noun **1** objects such as the crown and sceptre used at coronations or other state occasions. **2** the distinctive clothing and objects of an order, rank, or office.

regard verb **1** think of in a particular way. **2** look steadily at. **noun 1** concern or care. **2** high opinion; respect. **3** a steady look. **4** (**regards**) best wishes. □ **as regards** (or **with** or **in regard to**) concerning.

regarding preposition about; concerning.

regardless adverb **1** (**regardless of**) without regard for. **2** despite what is happening.

regatta noun a sporting event consisting of a series of boat or yacht races.

regency /**ree**-juhn-si/ noun (plural **regencies**) **1** a period of government by a regent. **2** (**the Regency**) the period when George, Prince of Wales, acted as regent in Britain (1811–20).

regenerate verb (**regenerates, regenerating, regenerated**) **1** bring new life or strength to. **2** grow new tissue. ■ **regeneration** noun.

regent noun a person appointed to rule a state because the king or queen is too young or unfit to rule, or is absent.

reggae /reg-gay/ noun a style of popular music originating in Jamaica.

regicide noun **1** the killing of a king. **2** a person who kills a king.

regime /ray-zheem/ noun **1** a government, especially one that strictly controls a state. **2** an ordered way of doing something; a system.

regimen /rej-i-muhn/ noun a course of medical treatment, diet, or exercise.

regiment noun **1** a permanent unit of an army. **2** a large number of people. ■ **regimental** adjective.

regimented adjective organized according to a strict system.

Regina noun the reigning queen (used in referring to lawsuits).

region noun **1** an area of a country or the world. **2** an administrative district of a city or country. **3** (**the regions**) the parts of a country outside the capital. **4** a part of the body. □ **in the region of** approximately. ■ **regional** adjective **regionally** adverb.

register noun **1** an official list or record. **2** a particular part of the range of a musical instrument or voice. **3** the level and style of a piece of writing or speech (e.g. informal, formal). verb (**registers, registering, registered**) **1** enter in a register. **2** put your name on a register. **3** express an opinion or emotion. **4** become aware of. **5** (of a measuring instrument) show a reading. □ **register office** (in the UK) a government building where marriages are performed and births, marriages, and deaths are recorded.

registrar noun **1** an official responsible for keeping official records. **2** Brit. a hospital doctor who is train-

ing to be a specialist.

registration noun **1** the action of registering. **2** (also **registration number**) Brit. the series of letters and figures shown on a vehicle's number plate.

registry noun (plural **registries**) **1** a place where registers are kept. **2** registration. □ **registry office** a register office.

regress /ri-gress/ verb return to an earlier or less advanced state. ■ **regression** noun.

regressive adjective **1** returning to a less advanced state. **2** (of a tax) taking a proportionally greater amount from those on lower incomes.

regret verb (**regrets, regretting, regretted**) feel sorry or disappointed about something you have done or should have done. noun a feeling of regretting something.

regretful adjective feeling or showing regret. ■ **regretfully** adverb.

regrettable adjective giving rise to regret. ■ **regrettably** adverb.

regular adjective **1** following or arranged in an evenly spaced pattern or sequence. **2** done or happening frequently. **3** doing the same thing often. **4** following an accepted standard. **5** usual. **6** Grammar (of a word) following the normal pattern of inflection. **7** belonging to the permanent professional armed forces of a country. **8** (of a geometrical figure) having all sides and angles equal. noun a regular customer, member of a team, etc. ■ **regularity** noun **regularly** adverb.

regularize or **regularise** verb (**regularizes, regularizing, regularized**) **1** make regular. **2** make a temporary situation legal or official.

regulate verb (**regulates, regulating, regulated**) **1** control the rate or speed of a machine or process. **2** control or supervise by means of rules. ■ **regulator** noun **regulatory** adjective.

regulation noun **1** a rule made by an authority. **2** the action of regulating. adjective informal of a familiar or expected type.

regurgitate /ri-**ger**-ji-tayt/ **verb** (re-gurgitates, regurgitating, regurgitated) **1** bring swallowed food up again to the mouth. **2** repeat information without understanding it. ■ **regurgitation** noun.

rehabilitate verb (rehabilitates, rehabilitating, rehabilitated) **1** help back to normal life after imprisonment or illness. **2** restore the reputation of someone previously out of favour. ■ **rehabilitation** noun.

rehash verb reuse old ideas or material. noun a reuse of old ideas or material.

rehearsal noun a trial performance of a play or other work for later public performance.

rehearse verb (rehearses, rehearsing, rehearsed) **1** practise a play, piece of music, etc. for later public performance. **2** state points that have been made many times before.

rehydrate verb (rehydrates, rehydrating, rehydrated) add moisture to something dehydrated. ■ **rehydration** noun.

Reich /ryk, rykh/ noun the former German state, in particular the **Third Reich** (the Nazi regime, 1933–45).

reign verb **1** rule as king or queen. **2** be the dominant quality or aspect. **3** (reigning) currently holding a particular title in sport. noun the period of rule of a king or queen.

reimburse verb (reimburses, reimbursing, reimbursed) repay money to. ■ **reimbursement** noun.

rein noun (reins) **1** long, narrow straps used to control a horse. **2** the power to direct and control something. verb **1** control a horse by pulling on its reins. **2** (rein in or back) restrain. □ **free rein** freedom of action.

reincarnate verb (be reincarnated) born again in another body. ■ **reincarnation** noun.

reindeer noun (plural reindeer or reindeers) a deer with large antlers, found in cold northern regions.

reinforce verb (reinforces, reinforcing, reinforced) **1** make stronger.

2 strengthen a military force with additional personnel.

reinforcement noun **1** the action of reinforcing. **2** (reinforcements) extra personnel sent to strengthen a military force.

reinstate verb (reinstates, reinstating, reinstated) restore to a former position. ■ **reinstatement** noun.

reiterate verb (reiterates, reiterating, reiterated) say something again or repeatedly. ■ **reiteration** noun.

reject verb /ri-**jekt**/ **1** refuse to accept or agree to. **2** fail to show proper affection or concern for. **3** (of the body) react against a transplanted organ or tissue. noun /**ree**-jekt/ a rejected person or thing. ■ **rejection** noun.

rejig verb (rejigs, rejigging, rejigged) Brit. rearrange.

rejoice verb (rejoices, rejoicing, rejoiced) feel or show great joy.

rejoin[1] verb join again.

rejoin[2] verb formal say in reply; retort.

rejoinder noun a quick reply.

rejuvenate verb (rejuvenates, rejuvenating, rejuvenated) make more lively or youthful. ■ **rejuvenation** noun.

rekindle verb (rekindles, rekindling, rekindled) **1** relight a fire. **2** revive something.

relapse /ri-**laps**/ verb (relapses, relapsing, relapsed) **1** become ill again after a period of improvement. **2** (relapse into) return to a worse state. noun /**ree**-laps/ a return to ill health after a temporary improvement.

relate verb (relates, relating, related) **1** give an account of. **2** (be related) be connected by blood or marriage. **3** (be related) have a link or connection. **4** (relate to) have to do with; concern. **5** (relate to) feel sympathy with.

relation noun **1** the way in which people or things are connected or related. **2** (relations) the way in which people or groups behave towards each other. **3** a relative.

relationship noun **1** the way in which people or things are related.

2 the way in which people or groups behave towards each other. **3** an emotional and sexual association between two people.

relative adjective **1** considered in relation or in proportion to something else. **2** existing or possessing a quality only in comparison to something else. **3** Grammar referring to an earlier noun, sentence, or clause. **noun** a person connected to another by blood or marriage.

relatively adverb **1** in comparison or proportion to something else. **2** quite.

relativism noun the idea that truth, morality, etc. exist only in relation to other things and are not absolute. ■ **relativist** noun.

relativity noun **1** the state of being relative; ability to be judged only in comparison with something else. **2** Physics a description of matter, energy, space, and time according to Albert Einstein's theories.

relax verb **1** become less tense, anxious, or rigid. **2** rest from work; do something recreational. **3** make a rule or restriction less strict. ■ **relaxation** noun.

relay noun **1** a group of people or animals engaged in a task for a time and then replaced by a similar group. **2** a race between teams of runners, each team member in turn covering part of the total distance. **3** an electrical device which opens or closes a circuit in response to a current in another circuit. **4** a device which receives, strengthens, and transmits a signal again. verb **1** receive and pass on information. **2** broadcast something by means of a relay.

release verb (**releases, releasing, released**) **1** set free from confinement. **2** free from a duty. **3** allow to move freely. **4** allow information to be made available. **5** make a film or recording available to the public. **noun 1** the action of releasing. **2** a film or recording made available to the public.

relegate verb **1** place in a lower rank or position. **2** Brit. transfer a sports team to a lower division of a league. ■ **relegation** noun.

relent verb **1** stop behaving in a harsh or cruel way. **2** become less severe.

relentless adjective **1** never ending; oppressively constant. **2** harsh or inflexible. ■ **relentlessly** adverb.

relevant adjective closely connected or appropriate to the current subject. ■ **relevance** noun.

reliable adjective able to be relied on. ■ **reliability** noun **reliably** adverb.

reliance noun dependence on or trust in someone or something. ■ **reliant** adjective.

relic noun **1** an object or custom that survives from an earlier time. **2** a part of a holy person's body or belongings kept after their death.

relief noun **1** a feeling of reassurance and relaxation after anxiety or stress. **2** a cause of relief. **3** the action of relieving. **4** (also **light relief**) a temporary break in a tense or boring situation. **5** help given to people in need or difficulty. **6** a person or group replacing others who have been on duty. **7** a way of carving in which the design stands out from the surface. □ **relief map** a map that indicates hills and valleys by shading.

relieve verb (**relieves, relieving, relieved**) **1** lessen or remove pain, difficulty, etc. **2** (**be relieved**) stop feeling anxious or stressed. **3** replace someone who is on duty. **4** (**relieve of**) take a burden or responsibility from. **5** bring military support for a place which is surrounded by the enemy. **6** make something less boring. **7** (**relieve yourself**) go to the toilet.

✓ remember, *i* before *e* except after *c*: rec*ei*ve.

religion noun **1** belief in and worship of a God or gods. **2** a particular system of faith and worship.

religious adjective **1** concerned with or believing in a religion. **2** very careful and regular. ■ **religiously** adverb.

 reli*gious*, not *-gous*.

relinquish verb give up something, especially unwillingly.

reliquary /rel-i-kwuh-ri/ noun (plural **reliquaries**) a container for holy relics.

relish noun **1** great enjoyment or anticipation. **2** a highly flavoured sauce or pickle. verb enjoy or look forward to.

relive verb (**relives, reliving, relived**) live through an experience or feeling again in your mind.

reload verb load something, especially a gun, again.

relocate verb (**relocates, relocating, relocated**) move your home or business to a new place. ■ **relocation** noun.

reluctant adjective unwilling and hesitant. ■ **reluctance** noun **reluctantly** adverb.

rely verb (**relies, relying, relied**) (**rely on**) **1** depend on; trust. **2** need or be dependent on.

remain verb **1** still be in the same place or condition. **2** continue to be. **3** be left over.

remainder noun **1** a part, number, or amount that is left over. **2** a part that is still to come. **3** the number which is left over when one quantity does not exactly divide another.

remains plural noun **1** things that remain or are left. **2** historical or archaeological relics. **3** a person's body after death.

remand verb send a defendant to wait for their trial, either on bail or in jail. □ **on remand** in jail before being tried.

remark verb **1** say as a comment. **2** notice. noun a comment.

remarkable adjective extraordinary or striking. ■ **remarkably** adverb.

rematch noun a second match between two sports teams or players.

remedial adjective **1** intended as a remedy. **2** provided for children with learning difficulties.

remedy noun (plural **remedies**) **1** a medicine or treatment for a disease

or injury. **2** a means of dealing with something undesirable. verb (**remedies, remedying, remedied**) put right an undesirable situation.

remember verb (**remembers, remembering, remembered**) **1** have in your mind someone or something from the past. **2** not fail to do something necessary. **3** (**remember to**) convey greetings from one person to another.

remembrance noun **1** the action of remembering. **2** a memory. **3** a thing serving as a reminder of someone.

remind verb **1** help someone to remember something. **2** (**remind of**) cause someone to think of something because of a resemblance.

reminder noun a thing that causes someone to remember something.

reminisce /re-mi-niss/ verb (**reminisces, reminiscing, reminisced**) think or talk about the past.

reminiscence noun **1** an account of something that you remember. **2** the enjoyable remembering of past events.

reminiscent adjective **1** (**reminiscent of**) tending to remind you of something. **2** absorbed in memories.

remiss /ri-miss/ adjective not paying proper attention to duty.

remission noun **1** the cancellation of a debt, penalty, etc. **2** Brit. the reduction of a prison sentence. **3** a temporary lessening of the severity of disease. **4** formal forgiveness of sins.

remit verb /ri-mit/ (**remits, remitting, remitted**) **1** cancel a debt or punishment. **2** send money in payment. **3** refer a matter to an authority. noun /ree-mit/ the task officially given to someone.

remittance noun **1** a sum of money sent as payment. **2** the action of remitting money.

remix verb produce a different version of a musical recording by altering the balance of the separate tracks. noun a remixed recording.

remnant noun a small remaining quantity of something.

remonstrate /**rem**-uhn-strayt/ **verb** (**remonstrates, remonstrating, remonstrated**) make a strongly critical protest. ■ **remonstration** noun.

remorse **noun** deep regret or guilt for something wrong you have done. ■ **remorseful** adjective.

remorseless **adjective** 1 without remorse. 2 (of something unpleasant) relentless. ■ **remorselessly** adverb.

remote **adjective** (**remoter, remotest**) 1 far away in space or time. 2 situated far from the main centres of population. 3 having very little connection. 4 (of a chance or possibility) unlikely to occur. 5 unfriendly and distant in manner. 6 operating or operated by means of radio or infrared signals. □ **remote control** 1 control of a machine from a distance by means of signals transmitted from a radio or electronic device. 2 a device that controls a machine in this way. ■ **remotely** adverb **remoteness** noun.

removal **noun** 1 the action of removing. 2 Brit. the transfer of furniture and other items when moving house.

remove **verb** (**removes, removing, removed**) 1 take something away from the position it occupies. 2 abolish or get rid of. 3 dismiss from a post. 4 (**be removed**) be very different from. 5 (**removed**) separated by a particular number of steps of descent: *a second cousin once removed.* **noun** the amount by which things are separated. ■ **removable** adjective.

remunerate /ri-**myoo**-nuh-rayt/ **verb** (**remunerates, remunerating, remunerated**) formal pay someone for work they have done. ■ **remuneration** noun.

remunerative **adjective** formal paying a lot of money.

Renaissance /ri-**nay**-sonss/ **noun** 1 the revival of classical styles in art and literature in the 14th–16th centuries. 2 (**renaissance**) a period of renewed interest in something.

renal /**ree**-n'l/ **adjective** technical having to do with the kidneys.

rename **verb** (**renames, renaming, renamed**) give a new name to.

renascence /ri-**nass**-uhnss/ **noun** formal a revival or rebirth. ■ **renascent** adjective.

rend **verb** (**rends, rending, rent**) literary 1 tear to pieces. 2 cause great emotional pain to.

render **verb** (**renders, rendering, rendered**) 1 provide or give a service, help, etc. 2 hand over for inspection, consideration, or payment. 3 cause to be or become. 4 interpret or perform artistically. 5 melt down fat to separate out its impurities. 6 cover a wall with a coat of plaster.

rendezvous /**ron**-day-voo/ **noun** (plural **rendezvous** /**ron**-day-voo/ or /**ron**-day-vooz/) 1 a meeting at an agreed time and place. 2 a meeting place. **verb** (**rendezvouses** /**ron**-day-vooz/, **rendezvousing** /**ron**-day-voo-ing/, **rendezvoused** /**ron**-day-vood/) meet at an agreed time and place.

rendition **noun** a performance or version of a piece of music or drama.

renegade /**ren**-i-gayd/ **noun** a person who deserts and betrays an organization, country, or set of principles.

renege /ri-**nayg**, ri-**neeg**/ **verb** (**reneges, reneging, reneged**) go back on an agreement or promise.

renew **verb** 1 start doing something again after an interruption. 2 give fresh life or strength to. 3 make a licence, subscription, etc. valid for a further period. 4 replace something broken or worn out. ■ **renewable** adjective **renewal** noun.

rennet **noun** curdled milk from the stomach of a calf, used in making cheese.

renounce **verb** (**renounces, renouncing, renounced**) 1 formally give up a title or possession. 2 state that you no longer have a particular belief or allegiance. 3 abandon a cause, habit, etc.

renovate **verb** (**renovates, renovating, renovated**) restore something old to a good state; repair. ■ **renovation** noun.

renown **noun** the state of being famous. ■ **renowned** adjective.

rent[1] noun a regular payment made for the use of property or land. verb **1** pay someone for the use of. **2** let someone use something in return for payment. □ rent boy Brit. informal a young male prostitute.

rent[2] noun a large tear in a piece of fabric.

rent[3] past and past participle of REND.

rental noun **1** an amount paid as rent. **2** the action of renting.

renunciation noun the action of renouncing or giving up something.

reorganize or **reorganise** verb (reorganizes, reorganizing, reorganized) change the organization of. ■ reorganization noun.

rep noun informal **1** a representative. **2** repertory.

repaid past and past participle of REPAY.

repair[1] verb restore something damaged or worn to a good condition. noun **1** an act of repairing something. **2** the condition of an object: in good repair. ■ repairer noun.

repair[2] verb (repair to) go to a place.

reparable adjective able to be repaired.

reparation noun **1** something done to make up for a wrong. **2** (reparations) compensation for war damage paid by a defeated country.

repartee /rep-ar-**tee**/ noun quick, witty comments or conversation.

repast /ri-**pahst**/ noun formal a meal.

repatriate /ree-**pat**-ri-ayt/ verb (repatriates, repatriating, repatriated) send someone back to their own country. ■ repatriation noun.

repay verb (repays, repaying, repaid) **1** pay back money owed to someone. **2** do something as a reward for a favour or kindness. **3** be worthy of investigation, attention, etc. ■ repayment noun.

repeal verb make a law no longer valid. noun the action of repealing.

repeat verb **1** say or do again. **2** (repeat yourself) say the same thing again. **3** (repeat itself) occur again in the same way or form. noun **1** an instance of repeating. **2** a repeated broadcast of a television or radio programme.

repel verb (repels, repelling, repelled) **1** drive back or away. **2** be repulsive or distasteful to. **3** force away something with a similar magnetic charge.

repellent adjective **1** able to repel a particular thing: water-repellent nylon. **2** causing disgust or distaste. noun **1** a substance that deters insects. **2** a substance used to treat something to make it repel water.

repent verb feel sorry for something bad that you have done. ■ repentance noun repentant adjective.

repercussions plural noun the consequences of an event or action.

repertoire /**rep**-er-twar/ noun the material known or regularly performed by a performer or company.

repertory /**rep**-er-tuh-ri/ noun (plural repertories) **1** the performance by a company of various plays, operas, etc. at regular intervals. **2** a repertoire.

repetition noun **1** the action of repeating. **2** a repeat of something.

repetitious adjective having too much repetition; repetitive. ■ repetitiously adverb.

repetitive adjective involving repetition; repeated many times. ■ repetitively adverb.

rephrase verb (rephrases, rephrasing, rephrased) express something in an alternative way.

repine verb (repines, repining, repined) literary be unhappy; fret.

replace verb (replaces, replacing, replaced) **1** take the place of. **2** provide a substitute for. **3** put something back in its previous position. ■ replaceable adjective.

replacement noun **1** the action of replacing. **2** a person or thing that takes the place of another.

replay verb **1** play back a recording. **2** play a match again. noun **1** an instance of replaying. **2** a replayed match.

replenish verb fill up a supply again after using some of it. ∎ **replenishment** noun.

replete adjective **1** (**replete with**) filled or well supplied with. **2** very full with food. ∎ **repletion** noun.

replica noun an exact copy or model of something.

replicate verb (**replicates, replicating, replicated**) make an exact copy of. ∎ **replication** noun.

reply verb (**replies, replying, replied**) **1** say or write a response to something said or written. **2** respond with a similar action. noun (plural **replies**) a spoken or written response.

report verb **1** give a spoken or written account of something. **2** (**be reported**) be said or rumoured. **3** make a formal complaint about. **4** tell someone in authority that you have arrived or are ready to do something. **5** (**report to**) be responsible to a manager. noun **1** a spoken or written account of something. **2** Brit. a teacher's written assessment of a pupil's progress. **3** the sound of an explosion or a gun being fired.

reportage /rep-or-**tah**zh/ noun the reporting of news by the press and the broadcasting media.

reporter noun a person who reports news for a newspaper or broadcasting company.

repose noun a state of restfulness, peace, or calm. verb (**reposes, reposing, reposed**) **1** rest. **2** have confidence or trust in.

repository noun (plural **repositories**) **1** a place or container for storage. **2** a place where a lot of something is found.

repossess verb take possession of something when a buyer fails to make the required payments. ∎ **repossession** noun.

reprehensible adjective deserving condemnation; bad.

represent verb **1** act and speak on behalf of. **2** amount to. **3** be a specimen or example of. **4** show or describe in a particular way. **5** depict in a work of art. **6** signify or symbolize.

representation noun **1** the action of representing. **2** an image, model, etc. of something. **3** (**representations**) statements made to an authority.

representational adjective **1** relating to representation. **2** (of art) not abstract.

representative adjective **1** typical of a class or group. **2** consisting of people chosen to act and speak on behalf of a wider group. **3** portraying or symbolizing something. noun **1** a person chosen to act and speak for another or others. **2** a person who travels around trying to sell their company's products. **3** an example of a class or group.

repress verb **1** bring under control by force. **2** restrain, prevent, or inhibit. **3** (**repressed**) tending to suppress feelings or desires. ∎ **repression** noun.

repressive adjective obstructing or restraining personal freedom.

reprieve verb (**reprieves, reprieving, reprieved**) cancel the punishment of. noun **1** the cancellation of a punishment. **2** a short rest from difficulty.

reprimand verb formally express disapproval of; tell off. noun a formal expression of disapproval.

reprint verb print again. noun **1** an act of reprinting. **2** a copy of a book that has been reprinted.

reprisal noun an act of retaliation.

reprise /ri-**preez**/ noun **1** a repeated passage in music. **2** a further performance of something. verb (**reprises, reprising, reprised**) repeat a piece of music or a performance.

reproach verb **1** express disapproval of or disappointment with. **2** (**reproach with**) accuse of. noun an expression of disapproval or disappointment. ∎ **reproachful** adjective **reproachfully** adverb.

reprobate /**rep**-ruh-bayt/ noun a person without moral principles. adjective unprincipled.

reproduce verb (reproduces, reproducing, reproduced) **1** produce a copy or representation of. **2** recreate in a different medium or context. **3** produce young or offspring.

reproduction noun **1** the process of reproducing. **2** a copy of a work of art. ■ **reproductive** adjective.

reproof noun a reprimand.

reprove verb (reproves, reproving, reproved) reprimand; tell off.

reptile noun a cold-blooded animal of a class that includes snakes, lizards, crocodiles, and tortoises. ■ **reptilian** adjective.

republic noun a state in which power is held by the people and their representatives, and which has a president rather than a king or queen.

republican adjective **1** belonging to or characteristic of a republic. **2** in favour of republican government. **3** (Republican) (in the US) relating to or supporting the Republican Party. noun **1** a person in favour of republican government. **2** (Republican) (in the US) a member or supporter of the Republican Party. **3** (Republican) a person who wants Ireland to be one country. ■ **republicanism** noun.

repudiate verb (repudiates, repudiating, repudiated) **1** refuse to accept or support. **2** deny that something is true or valid. ■ **repudiation** noun.

repugnance noun great disgust.

repugnant adjective extremely distasteful or unpleasant.

repulse verb (repulses, repulsing, repulsed) **1** drive back by force. **2** reject or refuse to accept. **3** make someone feel intense distaste or disgust. noun the action of repulsing.

repulsion noun **1** a feeling of intense distaste or disgust. **2** a force by which objects tend to push each other away.

repulsive adjective arousing strong distaste or disgust. ■ **repulsively** adverb.

reputable /rep-yuu-tuh-b'l/ adjective having a good reputation.

reputation noun the beliefs or opinions that people generally hold about someone or something.

repute noun **1** the opinion that people have of someone or something. **2** good reputation. verb (reputes, reputing, reputed) **1** (be reputed) have a particular reputation. **2** (reputed) believed to exist. ■ **reputedly** adverb.

request noun **1** an act of asking politely or formally for something. **2** something that is asked for in this way. verb **1** politely or formally ask for. **2** ask someone to do something.

requiem /rek-wi-em/ noun **1** a Christian Mass for the souls of dead people. **2** a musical composition based on such a Mass.

require verb (requires, requiring, required) **1** need or want something for a purpose. **2** instruct or expect someone to do something. **3** regard a particular thing as necessary or compulsory.

requirement noun **1** something that you need or want. **2** something specified as compulsory.

requisite /rek-wi-zit/ adjective necessary on account of circumstances or regulations. noun a thing that is needed for a particular purpose.

requisition noun **1** an official order allowing property or materials to be taken or used. **2** the taking of goods for military or public use. verb officially take possession of something, especially during a war.

rerun verb (reruns, rerunning, reran; past participle rerun) show, stage, or perform again. noun a rerun event, competition, or programme.

resat past and past participle of **RESIT**.

reschedule verb (reschedules, rescheduling, rescheduled) change the timing of.

rescind /ri-sind/ verb cancel or repeal a law, order, etc.

rescue verb (rescues, rescuing, rescued) save from danger or distress. noun an act of rescuing or being rescued. ■ **rescuer** noun.

research noun the study of materials

and sources in order to establish facts and reach new conclusions. **verb** carry out research into a subject, or for a book, programme, etc. ■ **researcher** noun.

resemblance noun **1** the state of resembling. **2** a way in which things resemble each other.

resemble verb (**resembles, resembling, resembled**) look or be like.

resent verb feel bitter towards.

resentful adjective bitter about something you think is unfair. ■ **resentfully** adverb.

resentment noun a feeling of bitterness about something unfair.

reservation noun **1** the action of reserving. **2** an arrangement for something to be reserved. **3** an area of land set aside for a native people. **4** an expression of doubt about a statement.

reserve verb (**reserves, reserving, reserved**) **1** keep something to be used in the future. **2** arrange for a seat, ticket, etc. to be kept for a particular person. **3** have or keep a right or power. noun **1** a supply of something available for use if required. **2** money kept available by a bank, company, etc. **3** a military force kept to reinforce others or for use in an emergency. **4** an extra player in a team, serving as a possible substitute. **5** (**the reserves**) the second-choice team. **6** an area of land set aside for wildlife or for a native people. **7** a lack of warmth or openness.

reserved adjective slow to reveal emotion or opinions.

reservist noun a member of a military reserve force.

reservoir noun **1** a large lake used as a source of water supply. **2** a place where fluid collects. **3** a supply or source of something.

reshuffle verb (**reshuffles, reshuffling, reshuffled**) **1** change the roles or positions of government ministers. **2** rearrange. noun an act of reshuffling.

reside verb (**resides, residing, resided**) formal **1** live in a particular place.

2 (**reside in** or **with**) (of a right or power) belong to a person or body. **3** (**reside in**) be naturally present in.

residence noun **1** the fact of living somewhere. **2** the place where a person lives.

residency noun (plural **residencies**) **1** the fact of living in a place. **2** a period spent by an artist, musician, etc. working at a particular place.

resident noun **1** a person who lives somewhere on a long-term basis. **2** Brit. a guest in a hotel. adjective living somewhere on a long-term basis.

residential adjective **1** involving residence. **2** providing accommodation. **3** occupied by private houses.

residual adjective remaining after the greater part has gone or been taken away.

residue noun a small amount of something that remains after the main part has gone or been taken.

resign verb **1** voluntarily leave a job or position of office. **2** (**be resigned**) accept that something bad cannot be avoided.

resignation noun **1** an act of resigning. **2** a document stating that you intend to resign. **3** acceptance of something bad but inevitable.

resilient adjective **1** able to spring back into shape after bending, stretching, or being compressed. **2** able to withstand or recover quickly from difficult conditions. ■ **resilience** noun.

resin noun **1** a sticky substance produced by some trees. **2** a synthetic substance used as the basis of plastics, adhesives, etc.

resist verb **1** withstand the action or effect of. **2** try to prevent or fight against. **3** stop yourself having or doing something tempting.

resistance noun **1** the action of resisting. **2** a secret organization that fights against an occupying enemy. **3** the ability not to be affected by something. **4** the degree to which a material or device resists the passage of an electric current. ∎ **resistant** adjective.

resistor noun a device that resists the passage of an electric current.

resit verb (**resits, resitting, resat**) Brit. take an examination again after failing.

resolute /rez-uh-loot/ adjective determined. ∎ **resolutely** adverb.

resolution noun **1** a firm decision. **2** a formal statement of opinion by a law-making body. **3** determination. **4** the resolving of a problem or dispute. **5** the degree to which detail is visible in an image.

resolve verb (**resolves, resolving, resolved**) **1** find a solution to. **2** decide firmly on a course of action. **3** take a decision by a formal vote. **4** (**resolve into**) separate into different parts. noun determination.

resonant adjective **1** (of sound) deep, clear, and ringing. **2** (**resonant with**) filled or resounding with. **3** suggesting images, memories, or emotions. ∎ **resonance** noun.

resonate verb (**resonates, resonating, resonated**) make a deep, clear, ringing sound.

resort verb (**resort to**) turn to a strategy or course of action so as to resolve a difficult situation. noun **1** a place visited for holidays or recreation. **2** a strategy or course of action.

resound verb **1** make a ringing, booming, or echoing sound. **2** (**resounding**) definite; unmistakable.

resource noun **1** (**resources**) a stock or supply of materials or assets. **2** something that can be used to help achieve an aim. **3** (**resources**) personal qualities that help you to cope with difficult circumstances. verb (**resources, resourcing, resourced**) provide with resources.

resourceful adjective able to find quick and clever ways to overcome difficulties. ∎ **resourcefully** adverb **resourcefulness** noun.

respect noun **1** a feeling of admiration for someone because of their qualities or achievements. **2** consideration for the feelings or rights of others. **3** (**respects**) polite greetings. **4** a particular aspect, point, or detail. verb **1** have respect for. **2** avoid harming or interfering with. **3** agree to observe a law, principle, etc.

respectable adjective **1** regarded by society as being correct or proper. **2** adequate or acceptable. ∎ **respectability** noun **respectably** adverb.

respectful adjective feeling or showing respect. ∎ **respectfully** adverb.

respecting preposition with reference to.

respective adjective belonging or relating separately to each of two or more people or things.

respectively adverb individually and in the order already mentioned.

respiration noun **1** the action of breathing. **2** a single breath.

respirator noun **1** an apparatus worn over the face to prevent you breathing in dust, smoke, etc. **2** an apparatus used to provide artificial respiration.

respiratory /ri-**spi**-ruh-tuh-ri/ adjective relating to breathing.

respire verb (**respires, respiring, respired**) technical breathe.

respite /ress-pyt/ noun a short period of rest or relief from something difficult or unpleasant.

resplendent adjective attractive and impressive.

respond verb say or do something in reply or as a reaction.

respondent noun **1** a defendant in a lawsuit. **2** a person who responds to a questionnaire or advertisement.

response noun an answer or reaction.

responsibility noun (plural **responsibilities**) **1** the state of being responsible. **2** the opportunity to act independently. **3** a thing which you are required to do as part of a job, role, or obligation.

responsible adjective **1** obliged to do something or look after someone. **2** being the cause of something and so able to be blamed or credited for it.

3 able to be trusted. **4** (of a job) involving important duties or decisions. **5** (**responsible to**) having to report to a senior person. ∎ **responsibly** adverb.

☑ respons*ible*, not *-able*.

responsive adjective responding readily and positively.

rest[1] verb **1** stop working or moving in order to relax or recover your strength. **2** place something so that it stays in a specified position. **3** remain or be left in a specified condition: *rest assured*. **4** (**rest on**) depend or be based on. **5** (**rest with**) (of power, responsibility, etc.) belong to. noun **1** a period of resting. **2** a motionless state. **3** an object that is used to hold or support something. **4** a brief interval of silence in a piece of music.

rest[2] noun the remaining part, people, or things.

restaurant /**ress**-tuh-ront/ noun a place where people pay to sit and eat meals that are cooked on the premises.

restaurateur /ress-tuh-ruh-**ter**/ noun a person who owns and manages a restaurant.

☑ note that there is no *n*: restaura*teur*.

restful adjective having a quiet and soothing quality.

restitution noun **1** the restoration of something lost or stolen to its proper owner. **2** payment for injury or loss that has been suffered.

restive adjective unable to keep still or silent; restless.

restless adjective unable to rest or relax. ∎ **restlessly** adverb.

restorative adjective able to restore health or strength.

restore verb (**restores**, **restoring**, **restored**) **1** bring back to a previous condition, place, or owner. **2** repair or renovate a building, work of art, etc. **3** bring back a previous practice, situation, etc. ∎ **restoration** noun **restorer** noun.

restrain verb **1** keep under control or within limits. **2** stop someone moving or acting freely.

restrained adjective **1** reserved or unemotional. **2** not richly decorated or brightly coloured; subtle.

restraint noun **1** the action of restraining. **2** a device which limits or prevents freedom of movement. **3** moderate behaviour; self-control.

restrict verb **1** put a limit on. **2** stop someone moving or acting freely.

restricted adjective **1** limited in extent, number, or scope. **2** not open to the public; secret.

restriction noun **1** a rule, law, etc. that prevents free movement or action. **2** the action of restricting.

restrictive adjective imposing restrictions.

restroom noun N. Amer. a toilet in a public building.

result noun **1** a consequence or effect. **2** a quantity, formula, etc. obtained by experiment or calculation. **3** a final score or mark in a sporting event or examination. **4** a satisfactory or favourable outcome. verb **1** occur or follow as a result. **2** (**result in**) have a specified outcome.

resultant adjective occurring or produced as a result.

resume verb (**resumes**, **resuming**, **resumed**) begin again or continue after a pause. ∎ **resumption** noun.

résumé /**rez**-yuu-may/ noun **1** a summary. **2** N. Amer. a curriculum vitae.

resurgent adjective becoming stronger or more popular again. ∎ **resurgence** noun.

resurrect verb **1** restore to life. **2** start using or doing again.

resurrection noun **1** the action of resurrecting. **2** (**the Resurrection**) (in Christian belief) the time when Jesus rose from the dead.

resuscitate /ri-**suss**-i-tayt/ verb (**resuscitates**, **resuscitating**, **resuscitated**) make someone conscious again. ∎ **resuscitation** noun.

☑ note that it is -*susc*-, not -*suss*-: re*susc*itate.

retail noun the sale of goods to the public. verb **1** sell goods to the public. **2** (**retail at** or **for**) be sold for a specified price. ■ **retailer** noun.

retain verb **1** continue to have; keep possession of. **2** absorb and continue to hold a substance. **3** keep in place.

retainer noun **1** a fee paid in advance to a barrister to secure their services. **2** (in the past) a servant.

retake verb (**retakes**, **retaking**, **retook**; past participle **retaken**) **1** take a test or examination again. **2** regain possession of. noun a test or examination that is retaken.

retaliate verb (**retaliates**, **retaliating**, **retaliated**) make an attack in return for a similar attack. ■ **retaliation** noun **retaliatory** adjective.

retard verb /ri-**tard**/ stop from developing or progressing. noun /ree-taard/ offensive a mentally disabled person. ■ **retardation** noun.

retarded adjective offensive less developed mentally than is usual at a particular age.

retch verb make the sound and movements of vomiting.

retention noun the action of retaining, or the state of being retained.

retentive adjective (of a person's memory) effective in retaining facts and impressions.

rethink verb (**rethinks**, **rethinking**, **rethought**) consider a policy or course of action again. noun an instance of rethinking.

reticent /ret-i-suhnt/ adjective not revealing your thoughts or feelings readily. ■ **reticence** noun.

retina noun (plural **retinas** or **retinae** /ret-i-nee/) a layer at the back of the eyeball that is sensitive to light and sends impulses to the brain.

retinue noun a group of assistants accompanying an important person.

retire verb **1** leave your job and stop working, because you have reached a particular age. **2** (of a sports player)

stop playing competitively. **3** withdraw from a race or match because of accident or injury. **4** formal leave a place. **5** (of a jury) leave the courtroom to decide the verdict of a trial. **6** formal go to bed. ■ **retired** adjective.

retirement noun **1** the action of retiring. **2** the period of life after retiring from work. **3** formal seclusion.

retiring adjective tending to avoid company; shy.

retook past of **RETAKE**.

retort[1] verb say something sharp or witty in answer to a remark or accusation. noun a sharp or witty reply.

retort[2] noun a glass container with a long neck, used for distilling liquids and heating chemicals.

retouch verb make slight enhancements to a painting, photograph, etc.

retrace verb (**retraces**, **retracing**, **retraced**) **1** go back over the route that you have just taken. **2** follow a route taken by someone else. **3** trace something back to its source.

retract verb **1** draw something back. **2** withdraw a statement or accusation. **3** go back on an undertaking. ■ **retractable** adjective **retraction** noun.

retreat verb **1** (of an army) withdraw from confrontation with enemy forces. **2** move back from a difficult situation. **3** withdraw to a quiet or secluded place. noun **1** an act of retreating. **2** a quiet or secluded place. **3** a quiet place where people go for a time to pray and meditate.

retrench verb reduce costs or spending in times of economic difficulty. ■ **retrenchment** noun.

retrial noun a second or further trial.

retribution noun severe punishment inflicted as revenge.

retrieve verb (**retrieves**, **retrieves**, **retrieving**) **1** get or bring back. **2** find or extract information stored in a computer. **3** improve a bad situation. ■ **retrieval** noun.

retriever noun a breed of dog used for finding and bringing back game that has been shot.

retrograde adjective directed or moving backwards or to a worse state.

retrogressive adjective going back to an earlier, inferior state. ∎ **retrogression** noun.

retrorocket noun a small rocket on a spacecraft or missile, fired in the direction of travel to slow it down.

retrospect noun (**in retrospect**) when looking back on a past event.

retrospective adjective **1** looking back on or dealing with past events or situations. **2** showing the development of an artist's work over a period of time. **3** taking effect from a date in the past. noun a retrospective exhibition. ∎ **retrospectively** adverb.

retroussé /ruh-**troo**-say/ adjective (of a person's nose) turned up at the tip.

retsina /ret-**see**-nuh/ noun a Greek white wine flavoured with resin.

return verb **1** come or go back to a place. **2** (**return to**) go back to a particular state or activity. **3** give, send, or put back. **4** feel, say, or do the same thing in response. **5** (in tennis) hit the ball back to an opponent. **6** (of a judge or jury) give a verdict. **7** yield a profit. **8** elect someone to office. noun **1** an act of returning. **2** a profit from an investment. **3** Brit. a ticket that lets you travel to a place and back again.

reunify verb (**reunifies, reunifying, reunified**) make a place a united country again. ∎ **reunification** noun.

reunion noun **1** the process of reuniting. **2** a gathering of people who have not seen each other for some time.

reunite verb (**reunites, reuniting, reunited**) bring two or more people or things together again.

reuse verb (**reuses, reusing, reused**) use something again. ∎ **reusable** adjective.

Rev. or **Revd** abbreviation Reverend.

rev informal noun (**revs**) the number of revolutions of an engine per minute. verb (**revs, revving, revved**) make an engine run quickly by pressing the accelerator.

revamp verb alter something so as to improve it. noun a new and improved

version of something.

reveal verb **1** make previously unknown or secret information known. **2** allow something hidden to be seen.

revealing adjective **1** giving out interesting or significant information. **2** (of a garment) allowing a lot of your body to be seen.

reveille /ri-**val**-li/ noun a signal sounded on a bugle, drum, etc. to wake up soldiers in the morning.

revel verb (**revels, revelling, revelled**; US spelling **revels, reveling, reveled**) **1** spend time enjoying yourself in a lively, noisy way. **2** (**revel in**) get great pleasure from. noun (**revels**) lively, noisy celebrations. ∎ **reveller** noun **revelry** noun (plural **revelries**).

revelation noun **1** the revealing of something previously unknown. **2** a surprising or remarkable thing.

revelatory adjective revealing something previously unknown.

revenge noun **1** retaliation for an injury or wrong. **2** the desire to inflict retaliation for an injury or wrong. verb (**revenges, revenging, revenged**) (**revenge yourself** or **be revenged**) harm someone in return for something bad that they did to you.

revenue noun the income received by an organization, or by a government from taxes.

reverberate verb (**reverberates, reverberating, reverberated**) **1** (of a loud noise) be repeated as an echo. **2** have continuing serious effects. ∎ **reverberation** noun.

revere verb (**reveres, revering, revered**) respect or admire deeply.

reverence noun deep respect.

reverend adjective a title given to Christian ministers. noun informal a Christian minister.

reverent adjective showing reverence; deeply respectful. ∎ **reverential** adjective **reverently** adverb.

reverie /**rev**-uh-ri/ noun a daydream.

reversal noun **1** a change to an opposite direction, position, or course of action. **2** a harmful change of fortune.

reverse verb (reverses, reversing, reversed) **1** move backwards. **2** make something the opposite of what it was. **3** turn something the other way round. **4** cancel a judgement by a lower court. adjective **1** going in or turned towards the opposite direction. **2** opposite to the usual way. noun **1** a complete change of direction or action. **2** (the reverse) the opposite or contrary. **3** a setback or defeat. **4** the opposite side of something to the observer. ■ **reversible** adjective.

reversion noun a return to a previous state, practice, etc.

revert verb (revert to) return to a previous state, practice, etc.

review noun **1** an examination of something to decide whether changes are necessary. **2** a critical assessment of a book, play, etc. **3** a report of an event that has already happened. **4** a ceremonial display of military forces. verb **1** carry out or write a review of. **2** view or inspect again. ■ **reviewer** noun.

revile verb (reviles, reviling, reviled) criticize in a rude or scornful way.

revise verb (revises, revising, revised) **1** examine and alter text. **2** reconsider and change an opinion. **3** Brit. reread work in order to prepare for an examination. ■ **revision** noun.

revisionism noun disapproving the changing of accepted theories or principles. ■ **revisionist** noun & adjective.

revitalize or **revitalise** verb (revitalizes, revitalizing, revitalized) give new life and vitality to. ■ **revitalization** noun.

revival noun **1** an improvement in the condition, strength, or popularity of something. **2** a new production of an old play.

revivalism noun the promotion of a return to religious faith. ■ **revivalist** noun & adjective.

revive verb (revives, reviving, revived) **1** make conscious, healthy, or strong again. **2** start doing, using, or performing something again.

revivify /ri-viv-i-fI/ verb (revivifies, revivifying, revivified) formal revive.

revoke verb (revokes, revoking, revoked) make a decree, law, etc. no longer valid. ■ **revocation** noun.

revolt verb **1** rebel against an authority. **2** make someone feel disgust. noun an act of rebellion or defiance.

revolting adjective extremely unpleasant; disgusting.

revolution noun **1** the overthrow of a government by force, in favour of a new system. **2** a dramatic and far-reaching change. **3** a single circular movement around a central point.

revolutionary adjective **1** involving or causing dramatic change. **2** engaged in, or relating to, political revolution. noun (plural **revolutionaries**) a person who starts or supports a political revolution.

revolutionize or **revolutionise** verb (revolutionizes, revolutionizing, revolutionized) change something completely or fundamentally.

revolve verb (revolves, revolving, revolved) **1** move in a circle around a central point. **2** (revolve around) treat as the most important element.

revolver noun a pistol with revolving chambers that allow several shots to be fired without reloading.

revue noun a theatrical show with short sketches, songs, and dances.

revulsion noun a sense of disgust and loathing.

reward noun something given in recognition of service, effort, or achievement. verb **1** give a reward to. **2** show appreciation of an action or quality by giving a reward.

rewarding adjective providing satisfaction.

rewind verb (rewinds, rewinding, rewound) wind a film or tape back to the beginning.

rewire verb (rewires, rewiring, rewired) provide with new wiring.

rework verb alter, revise, or reshape.

rhapsodize or **rhapsodise** verb (rhapsodizes, rhapsodizing, rhapsodized) express great enthusiasm about someone or something.

rhapsody noun (plural **rhapsodies**) **1** an expression of great enthusiasm. **2** a piece of music in one extended movement. ■ **rhapsodic** adjective.

rheostat /ree-uh-stat/ noun a device for varying the amount of resistance in an electrical circuit.

rhesus factor /ree-suhss/ noun a substance in red blood cells which can cause disease in a newborn baby.

rhesus monkey noun a small monkey found in southern Asia.

rhetoric /ret-uh-rik/ noun **1** effective or persuasive public speaking. **2** persuasive but insincere language.

rhetorical /ri-**torr**-i-k'l/ adjective **1** relating to rhetoric. **2** intended to persuade or impress. **3** (of a question) asked for effect or to make a statement rather than to obtain an answer. ■ **rhetorically** adverb.

rheumatic adjective relating to, or suffering from, rheumatism.

rheumatism /**roo**-muh-ti-z'm/ noun a disease with inflammation and pain in the joints and muscles.

rheumy /**roo**-mi/ adjective (of a person's eyes) watery.

rhinestone noun an imitation diamond.

rhino noun (plural **rhino** or **rhinos**) informal a rhinoceros.

rhinoceros /ry-**noss**-uh-ruhss/ noun (plural **rhinoceros** or **rhinoceroses**) a large plant-eating mammal with one or two horns on the nose and thick skin, found in Africa and Asia.

rhizome /**ry**-zohm/ noun a horizontal underground plant stem bearing both roots and shoots.

rho /roh/ noun the seventeenth letter of the Greek alphabet (P, ρ).

rhododendron noun a shrub with large clusters of bright flowers.

rhombus noun (plural **rhombuses** or **rhombi** /**rom**-bI/) a flat shape with four straight equal sides that form two opposite acute angles and two opposite obtuse angles.

rhubarb noun the thick leaf stalks of a

plant, cooked and eaten as fruit.

rhumba ⇒ **RUMBA**.

rhyme noun **1** a word that has the same sound or ends with the same sound as another. **2** a short poem with rhyming lines. **3** rhyming poetry or verse. verb (**rhymes**, **rhyming**, **rhymed**) **1** have or end with the same sound as another word or line. **2** (**rhyme with**) put a word together with another word that rhymes. □ **rhyming slang** slang in which you use words that rhyme with the word you mean (e.g. *butcher's*, short for *butcher's hook*, meaning 'look').

✓ remember the first *h*, following the *r*, in *rhyme* and *rhythm*.

rhythm noun **1** a strong, regular repeated pattern of sound or movement. **2** a regularly recurring sequence of events or actions. □ **rhythm and blues** a type of music that is a combination of blues and jazz.

rhythmic adjective **1** having or relating to rhythm. **2** happening regularly. ■ **rhythmically** adverb.

rib noun **1** each of a series of bones that are attached to the spine and curve around the chest. **2** a curved structure supporting an arched roof or forming part of a boat's framework. verb (**ribs**, **ribbing**, **ribbed**) informal tease someone good-naturedly.

ribald adjective humorous in a coarse or irreverent way. ■ **ribaldry** noun.

riband noun old use a ribbon.

ribbed adjective having a pattern of raised bands.

ribbon noun **1** a long, narrow strip of fabric, used for tying something or for decoration. **2** a long, narrow strip. **3** a narrow band of inked material used to produce the characters in some typewriters.

ribcage noun the bony frame formed by the ribs.

riboflavin /ry-boh-**flay**-vin/ noun vitamin B_2.

rice noun grains of a cereal plant which is grown for food on wet land in warm countries.

ricepaper noun thin edible paper made from the pith of a shrub, used in oriental painting and in baking biscuits and cakes.

rich adjective **1** having a great deal of money, assets, or resources. **2** of expensive materials or workmanship. **3** plentiful. **4** having or producing something in large amounts. **5** (of food) containing much fat, sugar, etc. **6** (of a colour, sound, or smell) pleasantly deep and strong. **7** (of soil or land) fertile.

riches plural noun **1** material wealth. **2** valuable natural resources.

richly adverb **1** in a rich way. **2** fully; thoroughly.

Richter scale /rik-ter/ noun a scale for measuring the severity of an earthquake.

rick¹ noun a stack of hay, corn, or straw.

rick² noun a slight sprain or strain. verb strain part of your body slightly.

rickets /ri-kits/ noun a disease of children in which the bones are softened and distorted.

rickety adjective poorly made and likely to collapse.

rickshaw noun a light two-wheeled vehicle pulled by a person walking or riding a bicycle.

ricochet /ri-kuh-shay/ verb (ricochets, ricocheting, ricocheted) (of a bullet or other fast-moving object) rebound off a surface. noun **1** a shot or hit that ricochets. **2** the action of ricocheting.

rictus noun a fixed grimace or grin.

rid verb (rids, ridding, rid) **1** (rid of) free a person or place of something unwanted. **2** (be or get rid of) be freed or relieved of.

riddance noun (good riddance) said when expressing relief at being rid of someone or something.

riddle¹ noun **1** a cleverly worded question that is asked as a game. **2** a puzzling person or thing.

riddle² verb (usu. be riddled with) **1** make a lot of holes in. **2** fill with something undesirable. noun a large coarse sieve.

ride verb (rides, riding, rode; past participle ridden) **1** sit on and control the movement of a horse, bicycle, or motorcycle. **2** travel in a vehicle. **3** be carried or supported by. **4** (ride up) (of clothing) gradually move upwards out of its proper position. **5** (ride on) depend on. **6** (ridden) full of or dominated by: *guilt-ridden.* noun **1** an act of riding. **2** a roller coaster, roundabout, etc. ridden at a fair or amusement park. **3** a path for horse riding. □ **take for a ride** informal deceive.

rider noun **1** a person who rides a horse, bicycle, etc. **2** an added condition on an official document.

ridge noun **1** a long, narrow hilltop or mountain range. **2** a narrow raised band on a surface. **3** the edge formed where the two sloping sides of a roof meet at the top. ■ **ridged** adjective.

ridicule noun contemptuous mockery. verb (ridicules, ridiculing, ridiculed) make fun of.

ridiculous adjective inviting mockery; absurd. ■ **ridiculously** adverb.

riding noun each of three former administrative divisions of Yorkshire.

rife adjective **1** (of something undesirable) widespread. **2** (rife with) full of.

riff noun a short repeated phrase in popular music or jazz.

riffle verb (riffles, riffling, riffled) **1** turn over pages quickly and casually. **2** (riffle through) search quickly through.

riff-raff noun people who are considered socially undesirable.

rifle¹ noun a gun with a long barrel. verb (rifles, rifling, rifled) **1** make spiral grooves in a gun barrel in order to make the bullet spin. **2** hit or kick a ball hard and straight.

rifle² verb (rifles, rifling, rifled) search through something hurriedly to find or steal something.

rift noun **1** a crack, split, or break. **2** a serious break in friendly relations.

rig verb (rigs, rigging, rigged) **1** fit sails and rigging on a boat. **2** (often rig up) set up a device or structure. **3** (**rig out**) provide with clothes of a particular type. **4** secretly arrange something in order to gain an advantage. noun **1** an apparatus for a particular purpose: *a lighting rig.* **2** a large piece of equipment for extracting oil or gas from the ground.

rigging noun the system of ropes or chains supporting a ship's masts.

right adjective **1** on or towards the side of a person or thing which is to the east when the person or thing is facing north. **2** justified or morally good. **3** factually correct. **4** most appropriate. **5** satisfactory, sound, or normal. **6** right-wing. adverb **1** on or to the right side. **2** completely; totally. **3** exactly; directly. **4** correctly or satisfactorily. noun **1** what is morally right. **2** an entitlement to have or do something. **3** (**rights**) the authority to perform, publish, or film a work or event. **4** (**the right**) the right-hand part, side, or direction. **5** a right turn. **6** (often **the Right**) a right-wing group or party. verb **1** put back in a normal or upright position. **2** correct or make up for a wrong. □ **by rights** if things were fair or correct. **in your own right** as a result of your own qualifications or efforts. **right angle** an angle of 90°, as in a corner of a square. **right of way 1** the legal right to go through someone's property along a specific route. **2** a public path across someone's property. **3** the right to proceed before another vehicle. **right wing** conservative or reactionary. ■ **rightly** adverb.

righteous /ry-chuhss/ adjective morally right. ■ **righteously** adverb.

rightful adjective **1** having a clear right to something. **2** proper; fitting. ■ **rightfully** adverb.

rigid adjective **1** unable to bend or be put out of shape. **2** (of a person) stiff and unmoving. **3** not able to be changed or adapted. ■ **rigidity** noun **rigidly** adverb.

rigmarole /rig-muh-rohl/ noun a lengthy and complicated procedure.

rigor mortis /ri-ger **mor**-tiss/ noun stiffening of the joints and muscles a few hours after death.

rigorous adjective **1** extremely thorough or accurate. **2** (of a rule, system, etc.) strictly applied or adhered to. **3** harsh or severe. ■ **rigorously** adverb.

rigour (US spelling **rigor**) noun **1** the quality of being rigorous. **2** (**rigours**) difficult or extreme conditions.

rile verb (**riles**, **riling**, **riled**) informal annoy or irritate.

rill noun literary a small stream.

rim noun **1** the upper or outer edge of something circular. **2** a limit or boundary. verb (**rims**, **rimming**, **rimmed**) provide with a rim.

rime noun literary hoar frost.

rind noun a tough outer layer or covering of fruit, cheese, bacon, etc.

ring[1] noun **1** a small circular metal band worn on a finger. **2** a circular band, object, or mark. **3** an enclosed space in which a sport, performance, or show takes place. **4** each of the flat plates on a cooker that are used for cooking on. **5** a group of people with a shared interest or goal. verb **1** surround. **2** draw a circle round. □ **ring binder** a binder with ring-shaped clasps. **ring pull** a ring on a can that you pull to open it. **ring road** a road encircling a town.

ring[2] verb (**rings**, **ringing**, **rang**; past participle **rung**) **1** make a clear, resonant sound. **2** (**ring with**) echo with a sound. **3** chiefly Brit. call someone by telephone. **4** (**ring off**) Brit. end a telephone call by replacing the receiver. **5** call for attention by sounding a bell. **6** (of the ears) be filled with a buzzing or humming sound. **7** (**ring up**) record an amount on a cash register. noun **1** an act of ringing. **2** a loud, clear sound or tone. **3** Brit. informal a telephone call. **4** a quality or feeling conveyed by words: *a ring of truth.* ■ **ringer** noun.

ringing adjective **1** having a clear, resonant sound. **2** forceful and clear.

ringleader noun a person who leads a forbidden activity.

ringlet noun a corkscrew-shaped curl of hair.

ringmaster noun the person who directs a circus performance.

ringworm noun a skin disease that causes small, itchy circular patches.

rink noun 1 (also **ice rink**) an enclosed area of ice for skating, ice hockey, or curling. 2 the strip of a bowling green used for a match.

rinse verb (**rinses**, **rinsing**, **rinsed**) 1 wash with clean water to remove soap or dirt. 2 remove soap or dirt by rinsing. noun 1 an act of rinsing. 2 an antiseptic solution for cleaning the mouth. 3 a liquid for conditioning or colouring the hair.

riot noun 1 a violent disturbance by a crowd. 2 a confused combination or display. 3 (**a riot**) informal a highly entertaining person or thing. verb take part in a riot. □ **run riot** behave in an unrestrained way. ■ **rioter** noun.

riotous adjective 1 involving public disorder. 2 wild and uncontrolled.

RIP abbreviation rest in peace.

rip verb (**rips**, **ripping**, **ripped**) 1 suddenly tear or become torn. 2 pull forcibly away. noun a long tear. □ **let rip** informal move or act without restraint. **rip off** informal 1 cheat someone. 2 steal. **rip-roaring** very energetic and forceful. **rip tide** a stretch of fast-flowing rough water caused by currents meeting.

riparian /ri-**pair**-i-uhn/ adjective technical of or on the banks of a river.

ripcord noun a cord that you pull to open a parachute.

ripe adjective 1 ready for harvesting and eating. 2 (of a cheese or wine) fully matured. 3 (**ripe for**) having reached the right time for. 4 (of a person's age) advanced. ■ **ripely** adverb **ripeness** adjective.

ripen verb become or make ripe.

riposte /ri-**posst**/ noun a quick reply.

ripple noun 1 a small wave or series of waves. 2 a feeling, effect, or sound that spreads through someone or something. 3 ice cream with wavy lines of syrup running through it.

verb (**ripples**, **rippling**, **rippled**) 1 form ripples. 2 (of a sound, feeling, etc.) spread through a person or place.

rise verb (**rises**, **rising**, **rose**; past participle **risen**) 1 come up or go up. 2 get up after lying, sitting, or kneeling. 3 increase in number, size, intensity, etc. 4 (of land) slope upwards. 5 (of the sun, moon, or stars) appear above the horizon. 6 (**rise above**) manage not to be restricted by. 7 (**rise to**) respond well to a difficult situation. 8 (**rise up**) rebel. 9 (of a river) have its source. noun 1 an instance of rising. 2 an upward slope or hill. 3 Brit. a pay increase.

riser noun 1 a person who gets up at a particular time. 2 a vertical section between the treads of a staircase.

risible /**ri**-zi-b'l/ adjective causing laughter. ■ **risibly** adverb.

rising adjective approaching a specified age. noun a revolt. □ **rising damp** Brit. moisture absorbed from the ground into a wall.

risk noun 1 a situation that involves being exposed to danger. 2 the possibility that something bad will happen. 3 a person or thing that causes a risk. verb 1 expose to danger or loss. 2 act in such a way that there is a chance of something bad happening.

risky adjective (**riskier**, **riskiest**) involving risk; dangerous. ■ **riskily** adverb **riskiness** noun.

risotto noun (plural **risottos**) a dish of rice with meat, seafood, etc.

 only one s: risotto.

risqué /**riss**-kay/ adjective slightly indecent or rude.

rissole noun a small flat mass of chopped meat that is coated in breadcrumbs and fried.

rite noun a religious ceremony, or other solemn procedure. □ **rite of passage** a ceremony or event that marks an important stage in someone's life.

ritual noun 1 a ceremony that involves a series of actions performed in a set order. **2** something that is habitually done in the same way. **adjective** done as a ritual. ■ **ritually** adverb.

ritzy adjective (**ritzier, ritziest**) informal expensively stylish.

rival noun **1** a person or thing competing with another for the same thing. **2** a person or thing equal to another in quality. **verb** (**rivals, rivalling, rivalled**; US spelling **rivals, rivaling, rivaled**) be comparable to. ■ **rivalry** noun (plural **rivalries**).

rive verb (**be riven**) be torn apart.

river noun **1** a large natural flow of water moving in a channel to the sea or another river. **2** a large quantity of a flowing substance.

rivet noun a short metal pin or bolt for holding together two metal plates. **verb** (**rivets, riveting, riveted**) **1** fasten with a rivet or rivets. **2** (**be riveted**) be completely intent or absorbed.

riviera /ri-vi-**air**-uh/ noun a coastal area of a warm country, especially in southern France and northern Italy.

rivulet noun a small stream.

RN abbreviation Royal Navy.

RNA noun a substance in living cells which carries instructions from DNA.

> ℹ️ short for *ribonucleic acid*.

roach¹ noun (plural **roach**) a common freshwater fish of the carp family.

roach² noun N. Amer. informal a cockroach.

road noun **1** a wide track with a hard surface for vehicles to travel on. **2** a way to achieving a particular outcome. □ **road rage** informal violent anger caused by conflict with the driver of another vehicle. **road test** a test of the performance of a vehicle or of other equipment.

roadblock noun a barrier put across a road by the police or army to stop and examine traffic.

roadholding noun the ability of a moving vehicle to remain stable.

roadie noun informal a person who sets up equipment for a rock group.

roadshow noun **1** a show broadcast from a different place each day. **2** a touring political or promotional campaign.

roadster noun an open-top sports car.

roadway noun **1** a road. **2** the part of a road intended for vehicles.

roadworks plural noun Brit. repairs to roads or to pipes under roads.

roadworthy adjective (of a vehicle) fit to be used on the road.

roam verb travel aimlessly over a wide area.

roan adjective (of a horse) having a bay, chestnut, or black coat with hairs of another colour.

roar noun a loud, deep sound made by a lion, engine, etc., or by a person who is angry, amused, or in pain. **verb** **1** make a roar. **2** laugh loudly. **3** move, act, or happen very fast. □ **a roaring trade** informal very good business.

roast verb **1** cook food in an oven or over a fire. **2** make or become very warm. **adjective** (of food) having been roasted. **noun** a joint of meat that has been roasted.

roasting informal **adjective** very hot and dry. **noun** a severe telling-off.

rob verb (**robs, robbing, robbed**) **1** unlawfully take property from a person or place by using force or threatening violence. **2** deprive someone of something. ■ **robber** noun.

robbery noun (plural **robberies**) the action of robbing a person or place.

robe noun **1** a loose garment reaching to the ankles, worn on formal or ceremonial occasions. **2** a dressing gown. **verb** (**robes, robing, robed**) clothe someone in a robe.

robin noun a small bird with a red breast and brown back and wings.

robot noun a machine capable of carrying out a complex series of actions automatically.

robotic adjective **1** relating to robots. **2** mechanical, stiff, or unemotional.

robotics plural noun the science of constructing and using robots.

robust adjective **1** sturdy or able to withstand difficult conditions. **2** strong and healthy. **3** uncompromising and forceful. ■ **robustly** adverb.

rock[1] noun **1** the hard material that makes up the earth's crust. **2** a projecting mass of rock. **3** a boulder. **4** Brit. a hard sweet in the form of a cylindrical stick. **5** informal a diamond or other precious stone. □ **on the rocks** informal **1** in difficulties and likely to fail. **2** (of a drink) served undiluted and with ice cubes. **rock bottom** the lowest possible level. **rock salt** salt occurring naturally as a mineral.

rock[2] verb **1** move gently to and fro or from side to side. **2** shake violently. **3** shock or distress greatly. **4** informal dance to or play rock music. noun **1** (also **rock music**) a type of loud popular music with a heavy beat. **2** a rocking movement. □ **rock and roll** a type of popular music with simple melodies, originating in the 1950s. **rocking chair** a chair mounted on a curved bar. **rocking horse** a model horse mounted on curved bars for a child to ride on.

rockabilly noun music that combines rock and roll and country music.

rocker noun **1** a person who performs or likes rock music. **2** a curved piece of wood on the bottom of a rocking chair. □ **off your rocker** informal mad.

rockery noun (plural **rockeries**) an arrangement of rocks in a garden with plants growing between them.

rocket noun **1** a tube-shaped missile or spacecraft propelled by a stream of burning gases. **2** a firework that shoots high in the air and explodes. **3** Brit. informal a severe telling-off. **4** a plant similar to lettuce, eaten in salads. verb (**rockets**, **rocketing**, **rocketed**) move or increase very rapidly and suddenly.

rocky adjective (**rockier**, **rockiest**) **1** consisting or formed of rock. **2** full of rocks. **3** unsteady or unstable.

rococo /ruh-**koh**-koh/ adjective in a highly decorated style of furniture or architecture of the 18th century.

rod noun **1** a thin straight bar of wood, metal, etc. **2** (also **fishing rod**) a long stick with a line and hook attached, for catching fish.

rode past of **RIDE**.

rodent noun a mammal of a large group including rats, mice, and squirrels, with large front teeth.

rodeo /**roh**-di-oh/ noun (plural **rodeos**) a contest or entertainment in which cowboys show their horseriding and lassoing skills.

roe noun the eggs or sperm of a fish, used as food.

roebuck noun a male roe deer.

roe deer noun a small deer with a coat that is reddish in summer.

roentgen /**runt**-yuhn/ noun a unit of ionizing radiation.

roger exclamation said in radio communication to show that a message has been received and understood.

rogue noun **1** a dishonest or unprincipled man. **2** a mischievous but likeable person. **3** an elephant that is living apart from the herd.

roguish adjective mischievous.

roister verb (**roisters**, **roistering**, **roistered**) old use enjoy yourself in a lively, noisy way.

role noun **1** an actor's part in a play, film, etc. **2** a person's or thing's function in a particular situation. □ **role model** a person that others look up to as an example to be imitated. **role play** the acting out of a role or situation.

roll verb **1** move by turning over and over. **2** move forward on wheels or with a smooth motion. **3** (of a moving ship, aircraft, etc) sway from side to side. **4** (of a machine or device) begin operating. **5** (often **roll up**) turn something flexible over and over on itself. **6** (**roll up**) curl up tightly. **7** flatten with a roller. **8** (of a loud, deep sound) reverberate. **9** (**roll up**) informal arrive. noun **1** a cylinder formed by rolling flexible material. **2** a rolling movement. **3** a gymnastic exercise in which you curl up and roll forwards or backwards. **4** a long, deep, reverberating sound. **5** a very small loaf of bread. **6** an official list or register of names. □ **roll-call** an occasion when a list of names is read out to discover who is present. **rolling pin** a cylinder for rolling out dough. **rolling stock** locomotives, carriages, and other vehicles used on a railway. **roll neck** a high turned-over collar. **roll-on** applied by means of a rotating ball.

roller noun **1** a rotating cylinder used to move, flatten, or spread something. **2** a small cylinder on which you roll your hair to make it curly. **3** a long wave moving towards the shore. □ **roller coaster** a fairground attraction in which you ride in an open carriage on a steep, twisting track. **roller skate** a boot with wheels on which you can glide across a hard surface.

Rollerblade noun trademark a roller skate with wheels in a single line along the sole. ■ **rollerblader** noun.

rollicking adjective cheerfully lively and amusing. noun Brit. informal a severe telling-off.

rollmop noun a rolled pickled herring fillet.

roly-poly noun Brit. a hot pudding made of suet pastry covered with jam and rolled up. adjective informal round and plump.

Roman adjective **1** relating to Rome or its ancient empire. **2** referring to the alphabet used for writing Latin, English, and most European languages. **3** (**roman**) (of a typeface) plain and upright, used in ordinary print. noun **1** an inhabitant of Rome. **2** (**roman**) roman type. □ **Roman Catholic 1** of the Christian Church which has the pope as its head. **2** a member of the Roman Catholic Church. **Roman numeral** each of the letters, I, V, X, L, C, and D, used in ancient Rome to represent numbers.

romance /roh-**manss**/ noun **1** a pleasurable feeling of excitement associated with love. **2** a love affair. **3** a book or film that deals with love in a sentimental or idealized way. **4** a feeling of mystery, excitement, and remoteness from everyday life.

5 (**Romance**) French, Spanish, Italian, and other languages descended from Latin. verb (**romances**, **romancing**, **romanced**) try to win the love of someone.

Romanesque /roh-muh-**nesk**/ adjective relating to a style of architecture common in Europe c.900–1200, with massive vaulting and round arches.

romantic adjective **1** having to do with love or romance. **2** thinking about or showing life in an idealized rather than realistic way. **3** (**Romantic**) relating to the artistic and literary movement of Romanticism. noun **1** a person with romantic beliefs or attitudes. **2** (**Romantic**) an artist or writer of the Romantic movement. ■ **romantically** adverb.

Romanticism noun a literary and artistic movement which emphasized creative inspiration and individual feeling.

romanticize or **romanticise** verb (**romanticizes**, **romanticizing**, **romanticized**) make something seem more attractive and inspiring than it really is.

Romany /roh-muh-ni/ noun (plural **Romanies**) **1** the language of the gypsies. **2** a gypsy.

Romeo noun (plural **Romeos**) an attractive, passionate male lover.

romp verb **1** play about roughly and energetically. **2** (**romp through**) informal do or achieve something easily. **3** (**romp ahead** or **home**) easily lead or win a race.

rompers or **romper suit** plural noun a young child's one-piece garment.

rondo noun (plural **rondos**) a piece of music with a recurring leading theme.

röntgen = **ROENTGEN**.

rood screen noun a screen of wood or stone separating the nave from the chancel of a church.

roof noun (plural **roofs**) **1** the upper covering of a building or vehicle. **2** the top inner surface of a covered space. verb construct a roof over. □ **roof rack** a framework for carrying luggage on the roof of a vehicle.

roofer noun a person who builds or repairs roofs.

rook¹ noun a crow that nests in colonies in treetops.

rook² noun a chess piece that can move in any direction.

rookery noun (plural **rookeries**) **1** a collection of rooks' nests high in a clump of trees. **2** a breeding place of seabirds.

rookie noun informal a new recruit.

room noun **1** a part of a building enclosed by walls, a floor, and a ceiling. **2** (**rooms**) a set of rooms rented out to a lodger. **3** empty space in which you can do or put things. verb N. Amer. share lodgings.

roomy adjective (**roomier**, **roomiest**) having plenty of space.

roost noun a place where birds regularly settle to rest. verb (of a bird) settle or gather for rest.

rooster noun a male domestic fowl.

root¹ noun **1** the part of a plant that is normally below ground, which acts as a support and collects water and nourishment. **2** the part of a structure such as a hair that is embedded in tissue. **3** the basic cause or origin of something. **4** (**roots**) your family or origins. **5** Mathematics a number that when multiplied by itself one or more times gives a specified number. verb **1** cause a plant or cutting to establish roots. **2** (**be rooted**) be firmly established. **3** (**be rooted in**) have something as an origin or cause. **4** (**root out**) find and get rid of.

root² verb **1** (of an animal) turn up the ground with its snout in search of food. **2** rummage. **3** (**root for**) informal support someone enthusiastically.

rootless adjective having nowhere where you feel settled and at home.

rootstock noun **1** a rhizome. **2** a plant on to which another variety is grafted.

rope noun **1** a length of thick cord made by twisting together strands of hemp, sisal, nylon, etc. **2** a number of objects strung together. **3** (**the ropes**) the ropes enclosing a boxing or wrestling ring. **4** (**the ropes**) informal the established way of doing something. verb (**ropes, roping, roped**) **1** secure something with rope. **2** (**rope in** or **into**) informal persuade someone to take part in something.

ropy or **ropey** adjective Brit. informal poor in quality or health.

rosary noun (plural **rosaries**) a string of beads used by some Roman Catholics for keeping count of how many prayers they have said.

rose¹ noun **1** a sweet-smelling flower that grows on a prickly bush. **2** a cap with holes in it attached to a spout, hose, shower, etc. to produce a spray. **3** a soft pink colour. □ **rose hip** the fruit of a rose.

rose² past of RISE.

rosé /roh-zay/ noun light pink wine made from red grapes, coloured by only brief contact with the skins.

rosemary noun an evergreen shrub with sweet-smelling leaves which are used as a herb in cooking.

rosette noun **1** a rose-shaped decoration made of ribbon, worn by supporters of a sports team or political party or awarded as a prize. **2** a piece of decoration in the shape of a rose.

rosewood noun the wood of a tropical tree, used for making furniture and musical instruments.

rosin /ro-zin/ noun a kind of resin that is rubbed on the bows of stringed instruments.

roster noun **1** a list of people's names and the jobs they have to do at a particular time. **2** a list of sports players available for team selection. verb (**rosters, rostering, rostered**) put a person's name on a roster.

rostrum noun (plural **rostra** or **rostrums**) a platform on which a person stands to make a speech, receive a prize, or conduct an orchestra.

rosy adjective (**rosier, rosiest**) **1** of a soft pink colour. **2** promising: *a rosy future.*

rot verb (**rots, rotting, rotted**) gradually decay. noun **1** the process of decaying. **2** informal rubbish.

rota noun a list of names and days or times, given to people who are to share a task or tasks.

rotary adjective **1** revolving around a centre or axis. **2** having a rotating part or parts.

rotate verb (**rotates, rotating, rotated**) **1** move in a circle round an axis. **2** (of a job) pass on a regular basis to each member of a group in turn. **3** grow different crops one after the other on a piece of land. ■ **rotation** noun **rotator** noun **rotatory** adjective.

rote noun regular repetition of something to be learned.

rotisserie /roh-**tiss**-uh-ri/ noun a rotating spit for roasting meat.

rotor noun **1** the rotating part of a turbine, electric motor, or other device. **2** a hub with a number of blades spreading out from it that is rotated to provide the lift for a helicopter.

rotten adjective **1** decayed. **2** corrupt. **3** informal very bad.

rotter noun informal, dated an unkind or unpleasant person.

Rottweiler /**rot**-vy-ler/ noun a large, powerful breed of dog.

rotund adjective rounded and plump.

rotunda noun a round building or room.

rouble or **ruble** /**roo**-b'l/ noun the basic unit of money in Russia.

roué /**roo**-ay/ noun a man who leads an immoral life.

rouge /roozh/ noun a red powder or cream used for colouring the cheeks.

rough adjective **1** not smooth or level. **2** not gentle. **3** (of weather or the sea) wild and stormy. **4** unsophisticated. **5** plain and basic. **6** harsh in sound or taste. **7** not worked out in every detail. **8** informal difficult and unpleasant. noun **1** a basic draft. **2** (on a golf course) the area of longer grass around the fairway and the green. verb **1** make a basic version of. **2** make a surface uneven. **3** (**rough it**) informal live with only very basic necessities. **4** (**rough up**) informal beat someone up.

□ **rough diamond 1** an uncut diamond. **2** a person who lacks good manners and education but has a good character. **rough justice** treatment that is not fair or in accordance with the law. **sleep rough** Brit. sleep outside or without a bed. ■ **roughness** noun.

roughage noun material in cereals, fruit, and vegetables that cannot be digested.

roughen verb make or become rough.

roughly adverb **1** in a rough way. **2** approximately.

roughneck noun **1** informal a rough, impolite person. **2** a person who works on an oil rig.

roughshod adjective (**ride roughshod over**) fail to consider someone's needs or wishes.

roulette noun a gambling game in which a ball is dropped on to a revolving wheel.

round adjective **1** shaped like a circle, sphere, or cylinder. **2** having a curved surface with no sharp projections. **3** (of a person's shoulders) bent forward. **4** (of a sound) rich and smooth. **5** (of a number) expressed in convenient units rather than exactly. noun **1** a circular shape or piece. **2** a route by which you visit a number of people or places in turn. **3** a sequence of things that you do regularly. **4** each of a sequence of stages in a process. **5** a single division of a boxing or wrestling match. **6** a song for three or more voices or parts, each singing the same theme but starting one after another. **7** the amount of ammunition needed to fire one shot. **8** a set of drinks bought for all the members of a group. **9** Brit. the quantity of sandwiches made from two slices of bread. adverb Brit. **1** so as to rotate or cause rotation. **2** so as to cover the whole area surrounding a particular centre. **3** so as to turn and face in the opposite direction. **4** used in describing the position of something: *the wrong way round.* **5** so as to surround someone or something. **6** so as to reach a new place or position. **preposition** chiefly Brit. **1** on every side of. **2** so as to encircle. **3** from or on the other side of. **4** so as to cover the whole area of. **verb 1** pass and go round. **2** (**round up** or **down**) make a figure less exact but easier to use in calculations. **3** make or become round in shape. □ **round off 1** smooth the edges of. **2** complete in a suitable or satisfying way. **round on** make a sudden attack on. **round robin 1** a tournament in which every player or team plays against every other player or team. **2** a petition. **round trip** a journey to a place and back again. **round up** collect a number of people or animals together.

roundabout noun Brit. **1** a road junction at which traffic moves in one direction round a central island to reach one of the roads leading off it. **2** a large revolving device in a playground, for children to ride on. **3** a merry-go-round. **adjective** not following a direct route.

rounded adjective 1 round or curved. **2** complete and balanced.

roundel noun a small disc or circular design.

rounders noun a ball game in which players run round a circuit after hitting the ball with a cylindrical wooden bat.

Roundhead noun a supporter of the Parliamentary party in the English Civil War.

roundly adverb 1 in a firm or thorough way. **2** in a circular shape.

roundworm noun a parasitic worm found in the intestines of animals.

rouse verb (**rouses, rousing, roused**) **1** wake someone up. **2** stir someone to action or excitement.

rousing adjective stirring.

rout /rowt/ **noun 1** a disorderly retreat of defeated troops. **2** a decisive defeat. **verb** defeat troops decisively and force them to retreat.

route /root/ **noun** a way taken in getting from a starting point to a destination. **verb** (**routes, routeing** or **routing, routed**) send along a particular route.

routine noun 1 the order and way in which you regularly do things. **2** a set sequence in a stage performance. **adjective 1** performed as part of a regular procedure. **2** without variety. ■ **routinely** adverb.

roux /roo/ **noun** (plural **roux**) a mixture of butter and flour used in making sauces.

rove verb (**roves, roving, roved**) **1** travel constantly without a fixed destination. **2** (of eyes) look around in all directions. ■ **rover** noun.

row[1] /roh/ **noun** a number of people or things in a more or less straight line.

row[2] /roh/ **verb** move a boat through water with oars.

row[3] /row/ Brit. informal **noun 1** an angry quarrel. **2** a loud noise or uproar. **verb** have an angry quarrel.

rowan /roh-uhn/ **noun** a small tree with white flowers and red berries.

rowdy adjective (**rowdier, rowdiest**) noisy and disorderly. **noun** (plural **rowdies**) a rowdy person. ■ **rowdily** adverb **rowdiness** noun.

rowlock /rol-luhk/ **noun** a fitting on the side of a boat for holding an oar.

royal adjective 1 having the status of a king or queen or a member of their family. **2** having to do with a king or queen. **3** of a quality or size suitable for a king or queen. **noun** informal a member of a royal family. □ **royal blue** a deep, vivid blue. **royal jelly** a substance produced by worker bees and fed by them to larvae raised to be queen bees. ■ **royally** adverb.

royalist noun 1 a person who supports the principle of having a king or queen. **2** a supporter of the King in the English Civil War.

royalty noun (plural **royalties**) **1** the members of a royal family. **2** the status or power of a king or queen. **3** a sum paid for the use of a patent, to an author for each copy of a book sold, or to a composer for each performance of a work.

RSPCA abbreviation Royal Society for

the Prevention of Cruelty to Animals.

RSVP abbreviation please reply.

> ℹ️ short for French *répondez s'il vous plaît*.

Rt Hon. abbreviation Brit. Right Honourable.

rub verb (rubs, rubbing, rubbed) **1** move your hand, a cloth, etc. over a surface while pressing down firmly. **2** press and move to and fro against a surface. **3** apply an ointment or polish with a rubbing action. **4** (rub off) come off a surface through being rubbed. **5** (rub out) erase marks with a rubber. **6** (rub down) dry, smooth, or clean by rubbing. noun **1** an act of rubbing. **2** an ointment for rubbing on the skin. **3** (the rub) the central difficulty.

rubber[1] noun **1** a tough stretchy waterproof substance obtained from a tropical plant or from chemicals. **2** Brit. a piece of this or a similar substance used for erasing pencil marks. **3** N. Amer. informal a condom. □ **rubber band** a stretchy loop of rubber for holding things together. **rubber plant** an evergreen plant with large shiny leaves. **rubber stamp** approval given for something. ■ **rubbery** adjective.

rubber[2] noun a unit of play in the card game bridge.

rubberneck verb informal turn to look at something as you pass it.

rubbing noun **1** the action of rubbing. **2** an impression of a design on brass or stone, made by placing paper over it and rubbing it with chalk or pencil.

rubbish Brit. noun **1** waste material and discarded items. **2** something that has no value or makes no sense. verb informal say that something is bad. ■ **rubbishy** adjective.

rubble noun rough fragments of stone, brick, or concrete.

rubella /roo-**bel**-luh/ noun a disease with symptoms like mild measles.

rubicund /**roo**-bi-kuhnd/ adjective having a red complexion.

ruble ⇒ **ROUBLE**.

rubric /**roo**-brik/ noun **1** a heading on a document. **2** a set of instructions.

ruby noun (plural **rubies**) **1** a deep red precious stone. **2** a deep red colour. □ **ruby wedding** the fortieth anniversary of a wedding.

RUC abbreviation Royal Ulster Constabulary.

ruche /roosh/ noun a frill or pleat of fabric. ■ **ruched** adjective.

ruck[1] noun **1** Rugby a loose scrum formed around a player with the ball on the ground. **2** a crowd of people. **3** Brit. informal a noisy fight. verb Rugby take part in a ruck.

ruck[2] verb (often **ruck up**) form creases or folds. noun a crease.

rucksack /**ruk**-sak/ noun a bag with two shoulder straps, that you carry on your back.

ruckus noun a row or commotion.

ruction noun informal **1** a disturbance or quarrel. **2** (ructions) trouble.

rudder noun a flat piece hinged in an upright position at the back of a boat, used for steering.

ruddy adjective (ruddier, ruddiest) **1** reddish. **2** (of a person's face) having a healthy red colour.

rude adjective **1** saying impolite things that offend and hurt someone. **2** referring to sex or the body in a way that people find offensive or embarrassing. **3** very abrupt. **4** Brit. hearty: *rude health*. ■ **rudely** adverb **rudeness** noun.

rudiment /**roo**-di-muhnt/ noun **1** (rudiments) the essential matters or facts relating to a subject. **2** (rudiments) a basic form of something.

rudimentary /roo-di-**men**-tuh-ri/ adjective **1** involving only basic matters or facts. **2** undeveloped.

rue verb (rues, rueing or ruing, rued) bitterly regret a past event or action.

rueful adjective expressing regret. ■ **ruefully** adverb.

ruff noun **1** a frill worn round the neck. **2** a ring of feathers or hair round the neck of a bird or mammal.

ruffian noun a rough person.

ruffle verb (**ruffles, ruffling, ruffled**) **1** disturb the smooth surface of. **2** upset or worry. **3** (**ruffled**) gathered into a frill. noun a gathered frill on a garment.

rug noun **1** a small carpet. **2** a thick woollen blanket.

rugby or **rugby football** noun a team game played with an oval ball that may be kicked, carried, and passed by hand.

rugged /**rug**-gid/ adjective **1** having a rocky surface. **2** tough and determined. **3** (of a man) having attractively masculine features. ■ **ruggedly** adverb **ruggedness** noun.

rugger noun Brit. informal rugby.

ruin verb **1** completely spoil or destroy. **2** make someone bankrupt or very poor. noun **1** the destruction or collapse of something. **2** (also **ruins**) a building that has been badly damaged. **3** the complete loss of a person's money and property.

ruination noun the process of ruining something.

ruinous adjective **1** disastrous or destructive. **2** in ruins.

rule noun **1** a statement saying what you must or must not do. **2** authority and control over a people or country. **3** (**the rule**) the normal state of things. **4** a ruler (for measuring or drawing). verb (**rules, ruling, ruled**) **1** have authority and control over a people or country. **2** control or influence. **3** state with legal authority that something is the case. **4** (**rule out**) say that something is not possible. **5** (**ruled**) (of paper) marked with thin horizontal lines. □ **rule of thumb** a rough guide.

ruler noun **1** a person who has authority and control over a people or country. **2** a strip of rigid material marked with centimeters or inches, used to measure short distances or draw straight lines.

ruling noun a decision or statement made by an authority.

rum[1] noun a strong alcoholic drink made from sugar cane.

rum[2] adjective (**rummer, rummest**) Brit. informal, dated peculiar.

rumba or **rhumba** noun a rhythmic dance with Spanish and African elements.

rumble verb (**rumbles, rumbling, rumbled**) **1** make a continuous deep sound, like distant thunder. **2** (**rumble on**) (of a dispute) continue in a low-key way. **3** Brit. informal discover that someone is doing something wrong. noun a continuous deep sound like that of distant thunder.

rumbustious /rum-**buss**-chuhss/ adjective Brit. informal high-spirited or difficult to control.

ruminant noun an animal that chews the cud, such as a cow or sheep.

ruminate verb (**ruminates, ruminating, ruminated**) **1** think deeply about something. **2** (of an animal) chew the cud.

rummage verb (**rummages, rummaging, rummaged**) search for something in a disorderly way. noun an act of rummaging.

rummy noun a card game in which the players try to form sets and sequences of cards.

rumour (US spelling **rumor**) noun a piece of information spread among a number of people which is unconfirmed and may be false. verb (**be rumoured**) be spread as a rumour.

rump noun **1** the hind part of the body of a mammal. **2** a piece left over from something larger.

rumple verb (**rumples, rumpling, rumpled**) make something less smooth and neat.

rumpus noun (plural **rumpuses**) a noisy disturbance.

run verb (**runs, running, ran**; past participle **run**) **1** move at a speed faster than a walk, never having both feet on the ground at the same time. **2** move about in a hurried way. **3** pass quickly in a particular direction. **4** (of a bus or train) make a regular journey on a particular route. **5** be in charge of. **6** continue, operate, or proceed. **7** function or cause to function.

8 pass into or reach a particular state or level. **9** (**run in**) (of a quality) be common or lasting in. **10** (of a liquid) flow. **11** (of dye or colour) dissolve and spread when wet. **12** stand as a candidate in an election. **13** compete in a race. **14** publish a story in a newspaper. **15** take someone somewhere in a car. **16** smuggle drugs. noun **1** an act or spell of running. **2** a journey or route. **3** a course that is regularly used: *a ski run*. **4** a continuous period or sequence. **5** an enclosed area in which chickens or animals can run around. **6** (**the run of**) unrestricted use of or access to a place. **7** a point scored in cricket or baseball. **8** a ladder in stockings or tights. □ **run across** meet or find by chance. **run something by** (or **past**) tell someone about something to find out their opinion. **run down 1** knock down with a vehicle. **2** criticize unfairly or unkindly. **3** reduce something in size or resources. **4** lose power. **5** gradually deteriorate. **run-down 1** in a poor or neglected state. **2** tired and rather unwell. **run-of-the-mill** ordinary. **run into 1** collide with. **2** meet someone by chance. **run out 1** be used up. **2** be no longer valid. **3** Cricket dismiss a batsman by hitting the bails with the ball while the batsman is still running. **run over 1** knock someone down with a vehicle. **2** exceed a limit. **run through** (or **over**) go over something as a quick rehearsal or reminder. **run up 1** allow a bill, score, etc. to build up. **2** make something quickly. **run-up** the period before an important event.

runaway noun a person who has run away from their home or an institution. adjective **1** (of an animal or vehicle) running out of control. **2** happening or done quickly or uncontrollably.

rundown noun a brief summary.

rune noun **1** a letter of an ancient Germanic alphabet. **2** a symbol with mysterious or magical significance. ■ **runic** adjective.

rung¹ noun **1** a horizontal support on a ladder for the foot. **2** a level or rank.

rung² past participle of **RING**².

runnel noun **1** a gutter. **2** a stream.

runner noun **1** a person who runs in a race or for exercise. **2** a messenger. **3** a rod, groove, or blade on which something slides. **4** a shoot which grows along the ground and can take root at points along its length. **5** a long, narrow rug. □ **runner bean** a climbing bean plant with long edible pods. **runner-up** (plural **runners-up**) a competitor who comes second.

running noun **1** the activity or movement of a runner. **2** the action of managing or operating something. adjective **1** (of water) flowing naturally or supplied through pipes and taps. **2** producing liquid or pus. **3** continuous or recurring. **4** done while running. **5** in succession: *the third week running*. □ **in** (or **out of**) **the running** in (or no longer in) with a chance of success. **running board** a footboard extending along the side of a vehicle. **running commentary** a description of events given as they happen.

runny adjective (**runnier**, **runniest**) **1** more liquid than is usual. **2** (of a person's nose) producing mucus.

runt noun the smallest animal in a litter.

runway noun a strip of hard ground where aircraft take off and land.

rupee /roo-pee/ noun the basic unit of money of India and Pakistan.

rupture verb (**ruptures**, **rupturing**, **ruptured**) **1** break or burst suddenly. **2** (**be ruptured** or **rupture yourself**) develop a hernia in the abdomen. noun **1** an instance of rupturing. **2** a hernia in the abdomen.

rural adjective having to do with the countryside. ■ **rurally** adverb.

ruse noun something done to deceive or trick someone.

rush¹ verb **1** move or act with urgent haste. **2** produce, deal with, or transport with urgent haste. **3** (of air or a liquid) flow strongly. **4** dash towards a person or place as a form of attack.

noun 1 a sudden quick movement towards something. **2** a sudden spell of hasty activity. **3** a sudden strong demand for a product. **4** a sudden strong feeling. **5** a sudden thrill experienced after taking certain drugs. **6** (**rushes**) the first prints made of a film after a period of shooting. □ **rush hour** a time at the start and end of the working day when traffic is at its heaviest.

rush² **noun** a water plant used in making mats, baskets, etc.

rusk **noun** a dry biscuit or piece of baked bread.

russet **adjective** reddish brown. **noun 1** a reddish-brown colour. **2** a kind of apple with a greenish-brown skin.

Russian roulette **noun** a dangerous game of chance in which a revolver loaded with a single bullet is passed to each participant in turn, who fires it at their own head.

rust **noun** a brown flaky coating which forms on iron or steel when it is wet. **verb** be affected with rust.

rustic **adjective 1** having to do with life in the country. **2** simple and charming in a way seen as typical of the countryside. **noun** an unsophisticated country person. ■ **rusticity** noun.

rustle **verb 1** make a soft crackling sound. **2** round up and steal cattle, horses, or sheep. **3** (**rustle up**) informal produce food or a drink quickly. **noun** a rustling sound. ■ **rustler** noun.

rusty **adjective 1** affected by rust. **2** of the colour of rust; reddish-brown. **3** (of knowledge or a skill) weakened by lack of recent practice.

rut¹ **noun 1** a long deep track made by the wheels of vehicles. **2** a way of living or working that has become routine and dull but is hard to change.

rut² **noun** an annual period of sexual activity in deer and some other animals, during which the males fight each other for access to the females. **verb** (**ruts, rutting, rutted**) engage in such activity.

ruthless **adjective** hard, determined, and showing no sympathy. ■ **ruthlessly** adverb **ruthlessness** noun.

rye **noun 1** a cereal plant which grows in poor soils and low temperatures. **2** whisky made from rye.

ryegrass **noun** a grass used for fodder and lawns.

Ss

S or **s** **noun** (plural **Ss** or **S's**) the nineteenth letter of the alphabet. **abbreviation** South or Southern.

sabbath **noun** (often **the Sabbath**) a day for rest and religious worship.

sabbatical **noun** a period of paid leave for study or travel.

sable **noun** a marten native to Japan and Siberia, hunted for its dark brown fur.

sabotage /sab-uh-tahzh/ **verb** (**sabotages, sabotaging, sabotaged**) deliberately damage or destroy. **noun** the action of sabotaging.

saboteur /sab-uh-**ter**/ **noun** a person who sabotages something.

sabre /**say**-ber/ (US spelling **saber**) **noun 1** a heavy sword with a curved blade. **2** a light fencing sword with a tapering blade.

sabretooth tiger or **sabre-toothed tiger** **noun** a large extinct member of the cat family with massive curved upper canine teeth.

sac **noun** a hollow, flexible structure resembling a bag or pouch.

saccharin /**sak**-kuh-rin/ **noun** a sweet-tasting substance used as a low-calorie substitute for sugar.

saccharine /sak-kuh-rin/ **adjective** too sweet or sentimental.

sacerdotal /sak-er-**doh**-t'l/ **adjective** relating to priests.

sachet /**sa**-shay/ **noun** Brit. a small sealed bag or packet.

sack[1] **noun 1** a large bag made of a material such as hessian or thick paper, used for storing and carrying goods. **2 (the sack)** informal dismissal from employment. **3 (the sack)** informal bed. **verb** informal dismiss someone from employment. ◻ **hit the sack** informal go to bed. ◼ **sackable** adjective.

sack[2] **verb** violently attack, steal from, and destroy a town or city (used when talking about the past). **noun** the sacking of a town or city.

sackcloth **noun** a coarse fabric woven from flax or hemp.

sacra plural of **SACRUM**.

sacrament /**sak**-ruh-muhnt/ **noun 1** (in the Christian Church) an important religious ceremony in which the people taking part are believed to receive the grace of God. **2** (also **the Blessed Sacrament** or **the Holy Sacrament**) (in Catholic use) the bread and wine used in the Eucharist. ◼ **sacramental** adjective.

sacred /**say**-krid/ **adjective 1** connected with a god or goddess and greatly respected. **2** (of a text) having to do with the teachings of a religion. **3** religious. ◻ **sacred cow** a thing that people believe must not be criticized.

sacrifice **noun 1** the killing of an animal or person or giving up of a possession as an offering to a god or goddess. **2** an animal, person, or object offered in this way. **3** an act of giving up something you value for the sake of something that is more important. **verb** (**sacrifices, sacrificing, sacrificed**) offer as a sacrifice. ◼ **sacrificial** adjective.

sacrilege /**sak**-ri-lij/ **noun** an act of treating a sacred or highly valued thing without respect. ◼ **sacrilegious** adjective.

    sacrilege, not *-relige* or *-rilige*.

sacristan **noun** a person in charge of a sacristy.

sacristy **noun** (plural **sacristies**) a room in a church where a priest prepares for a service.

sacrosanct **adjective** too important or valuable to be changed.

sacrum /**say**-kruhm/ **noun** (plural **sacra** or **sacrums**) a triangular bone in the lower back between the two hip bones.

sad **adjective** (**sadder, saddest**) **1** unhappy. **2** causing sorrow. **3** informal very inadequate or unfashionable. ◼ **sadly** adverb **sadness** noun.

sadden **verb** make someone unhappy.

saddle **noun 1** a seat with a raised ridge at the front and back, fastened on the back of a horse for riding. **2** a seat on a bicycle or motorcycle. **3** a piece of meat from the back of an animal. **verb** (**saddles, saddling, saddled**) **1** put a saddle on a horse. **2** (**saddle with**) burden someone with a responsibility or task.

saddlebag **noun** a bag attached to a saddle.

saddler **noun** a person who makes, sells, and repairs saddles and other equipment for horses.

saddlery **noun** (plural **saddleries**) **1** saddles and other equipment for horses. **2** a saddler's premises.

sadism /**say**-di-z'm/ **noun** enjoyment felt in hurting or humiliating other people. ◼ **sadist** noun **sadistic** adjective.

sadomasochism /say-doh-**mass**-uh-ki-z'm/ **noun** enjoyment felt in hurting or being hurt by someone else, especially during sex. ◼ **sadomasochist** noun **sadomasochistic** adjective.

safari **noun** (plural **safaris**) an expedition to observe or hunt animals in their natural environment. ◻ **safari park** an area of parkland where wild animals are kept in the open and may be observed by visitors.

safe **adjective 1** protected from danger

or risk. **2** not leading to harm or injury. **3** (of a place) giving security or protection. **4** unadventurous. **5** based on good reasons and not likely to be proved wrong. **noun** a strong fireproof cabinet with a complex lock, used for storing valuables. □**safe house** a house in a secret location, used by people in hiding. ■ **safely** adverb.

safeguard **noun** a thing done in order to protect or prevent something. **verb** protect with a safeguard.

safekeeping **noun** the keeping of something in a safe place.

safety **noun** (plural **safeties**) the condition of being safe. □**safety belt** a belt that secures a person to their seat in a vehicle or aircraft. **safety net** 1 a net to catch an acrobat should they fall. **2** something arranged as a safeguard. **safety pin** a pin with a point that is bent back to the head and held in a guard when closed.

saffron **noun** a yellow spice made from the dried stigmas of a crocus.

sag **verb** (**sags**, **sagging**, **sagged**) **1** sink downwards gradually under weight or pressure or through weakness. **2** hang down loosely or unevenly. **noun** an instance of sagging. ■ **saggy** adjective.

saga **noun** 1 a long traditional story describing brave acts. **2** a story covering a long period of time. **3** a long, complicated series of incidents.

sagacious **adjective** having good judgement; wise. ■ **sagacity** noun.

sage¹ **noun** a sweet-smelling Mediterranean plant with greyish-green leaves, used as a herb in cookery. •

sage² **noun** a very wise man. **adjective** wise. ■ **sagely** adverb.

Sagittarius /saj-i-**tair**-i-uhss/ **noun** a sign of the zodiac (the Archer), 22 November–20 December.

sago **noun** a pudding made with starchy granules obtained from a palm, cooked with milk.

sahib /sahb/ **noun** Indian a polite form of address for a man.

said past and past participle of **SAY**. **adjective** referring to someone or something already mentioned.

sail **noun** 1 a piece of material spread on a mast to catch the wind and propel a boat or ship. **2** a trip in a sailing boat or ship. **3** a flat board attached to the arm of a windmill. **verb** 1 travel in a sailing boat as a sport or pastime. **2** travel in a ship or boat using sails or engine power. **3** begin a voyage. **4** travel by ship on or across a particular route or sea. **5** direct or control a boat or ship. **6** move smoothly or confidently. **7** (**sail through**) informal succeed easily at. □**sail close to the wind** take risks. **sailing boat** (N. Amer. **sailboat**) a boat propelled by sails.

sailboard **noun** a board with a mast and a sail, used in windsurfing.

sailcloth **noun** 1 strong fabric used for making sails. **2** a similar fabric used for clothes.

sailor **noun** 1 a member of the crew of a ship or boat. **2** a person who sails as a sport or pastime. **3** (**a good** or **bad sailor**) a person who rarely (or often) becomes seasick.

saint **noun** 1 a good person who Christians believe will go to heaven when they die. **2** a person of great goodness who after their death is formally declared by the Church to be a saint, and to whom people offer prayers. **3** informal a very good or kind person. **verb** 1 formally declare someone to be a saint. **2** (**sainted**) very good and virtuous. □**saint's day** (in the Christian Church) a day each year when a particular saint is honoured. ■ **sainthood** noun.

St George's cross **noun** a red cross on a white background.

saintly **adjective** very holy or good. ■ **saintliness** noun.

sake¹ **noun** 1 (**for the sake of**) in the interest of. **2** (**for the sake of**) out of consideration for. **3** (**for old times' sake**) in memory of former times.

sake² /**sah**-ki/ **noun** a Japanese alcoholic drink made from rice.

salaam /suh-**lahm**/ **noun** a low bow with the hand touching the forehead, used by Muslims as a gesture of respect. **verb** make a salaam.

salacious /suh-**lay**-shuhss/ **adjective** containing too much sexual detail.

salad **noun** a cold dish of raw vegetables. □**your salad days** the time when you are young and inexperienced.

salamander **noun 1** a newt-like animal with a long tail, that can live in water or on land. **2** a mythical lizard-like creature said to be able to stay alive in fire.

salami **noun** (plural **salami** or **salamis**) a type of spicy preserved sausage.

salary **noun** (plural **salaries**) a fixed payment made every month to an employee. ■ **salaried** adjective.

sale **noun 1** the exchange of something for money. **2** (**sales**) the activity or profession of selling. **3** a period in which goods in a shop are sold at reduced prices. **4** a public event at which goods are sold or auctioned. ■ **saleable** (or **salable**) adjective.

saleroom or **salesroom** **noun** a room in which auctions are held or cars are sold.

salesman or **saleswoman** **noun** a person whose job involves selling goods. ■ **salesmanship** noun.

salient /**say**-li-uhnt/ **adjective** most noticeable or important. ■ **salience** noun.

saline /**say**-lyn/ **adjective** containing salt. ■ **salinity** noun.

saliva **noun** a watery liquid in the mouth produced by glands, that helps chewing, swallowing, and digestion. ■ **salivary** adjective.

salivate **verb** (**salivates**, **salivating**, **salivated**) have a lot of saliva in the mouth. ■ **salivation** noun.

sallow **adjective** (of a person's skin) yellowish or pale brown in colour.

sally **noun** (plural **sallies**) **1** a sudden charge or sortie out of a place surrounded by an enemy. **2** a witty or lively reply. **verb** (**sallies**, **sallying**, **sallied**) set out on sortie.

salmon /rhymes with gammon/ **noun** (plural **salmon** or **salmons**) a large fish with pink flesh, that matures in the sea and moves to freshwater streams to release eggs.

salmonella /sal-muh-**nel**-luh/ **noun** a germ that can cause food poisoning.

salon **noun 1** a place where a hairdresser, beautician, or clothes designer works. **2** a reception room in a large house. **3** (in the past) a regular gathering of writers and artists held in someone's house.

saloon **noun 1** Brit. a lounge bar. **2** N. Amer. old use a bar. **3** a large room for use as a lounge on a ship. **4** Brit. a car with a separate boot. **5** (also **saloon car**) Brit. a luxurious railway carriage used as a lounge or restaurant.

salopettes /sal-uh-**pets**/ **plural noun** padded trousers with a high waist and shoulder straps, worn for skiing.

salsa **noun 1** a Latin American dance performed to music that combines jazz and rock. **2** a spicy sauce.

salt **noun 1** sodium chloride, a white substance in the form of crystals, used for flavouring or preserving food. **2** Chemistry any compound formed by the reaction of an acid with a base. **verb 1** season or preserve food with salt. **2** sprinkle a road or path with salt in order to melt snow or ice. □**salt cellar** a container for salt. **the salt of the earth** a person of great goodness and strength of character. **take something with a pinch** (or **grain**) **of salt** recognize that something is being exaggerated or is untrue.

saltings **noun** Brit. an area of coastal land regularly covered by the tide.

saltpetre /sawlt-**pee**-ter/ (US spelling **saltpeter**) **noun** a white powder (potassium nitrate) used to make gunpowder and preserve meat.

salty **adjective** (**saltier**, **saltiest**) **1** containing or tasting of salt. **2** (of language or humour) rather rude. ■ **saltiness** noun.

salubrious **adjective 1** good for your health. **2** (of a place) well maintained and pleasant to be in.

salutary /**sal**-yuu-tuh-ri/ **adjective**

(with reference to something unpleasant) producing a good effect because it teaches you something.

salutation noun a greeting.

salute noun **1** a raising of a hand to the head, made as a formal gesture of respect by a member of a military force. **2** a gesture of admiration or respect. **3** the shooting of a gun or guns as a formal sign of respect or celebration. verb (**salutes, saluting, saluted**) **1** make a formal salute to. **2** greet. **3** express admiration and respect for.

salvage verb (**salvages, salvaging, salvaged**) **1** rescue something that is in danger of being lost or destroyed. **2** rescue a ship or its contents from being lost at sea. **3** break up disused vehicles and machinery in order to retrieve usable parts. noun **1** the action of salvaging. **2** contents rescued from a ship.

salvation noun **1** the saving of a person from sin and its consequences, believed by Christians to be brought about by faith in Jesus. **2** the protecting or saving of someone or something from harm or loss.

salve noun **1** an ointment that soothes the skin. **2** something that makes you feel less guilty. verb (**salves, salving, salved**) reduce feelings of guilt.

salver noun a tray.

salvo noun (plural **salvos** or **salvoes**) **1** a shooting of a number of guns at the same time. **2** a sudden series of aggressive statements or acts.

Samaritan noun **1** a member of a people living in Samaria, an ancient city and region of Palestine. **2** (**good Samaritan**) a helpful person.

samba /sam-buh/ noun a Brazilian dance of African origin. verb (**sambas, sambaing** /sam-buh-(r)ing/, **sambaed** /sam-buhd/) dance the samba.

same adjective **1** (**the same**) exactly alike. **2** (**this** or **that same**) referring to a person or thing just mentioned. pronoun **1** (**the same**) the same thing as previously mentioned. **2** (**the same**) identical people or things. ad-

verb in the same way. ■ **sameness** noun.

samey adjective Brit. informal lacking in variety.

samovar /sam-uh-var/ noun a highly decorated Russian tea urn.

sample noun **1** a small part or quantity of something intended to show what the whole is like. **2** a specimen taken for scientific testing. verb (**samples, sampling, sampled**) **1** take a sample of. **2** try out. **3** (**sampling**) the taking of a short extract from one musical recording and reusing it as part of another recording.

sampler noun **1** a piece of fabric decorated with a number of different embroidery stitches. **2** a device for sampling music.

samurai /sam-yuu-rI/ noun (plural **samurai**) (in the past) a member of a powerful Japanese military class.

sanatorium noun (plural **sanatoriums** or **sanatoria**) **1** a place like a hospital where people who have long-term illness or who are recovering from an illness are treated. **2** Brit. a place in a boarding school for children who are unwell.

sanctify verb (**sanctifies, sanctifying, sanctified**) **1** make something holy. **2** make something legal or right. ■ **sanctification** noun.

sanctimonious adjective disapproving making a show of being morally superior to other people.

sanction noun **1** a penalty for disobeying a law or rule. **2** (**sanctions**) measures taken by a state to try to force another to behave well. **3** official permission or approval. verb **1** give official permission for. **2** impose a penalty on.

sanctity noun (plural **sanctities**) **1** the state of being holy. **2** the state of being very important.

sanctuary noun (plural **sanctuaries**) **1** a place of safety. **2** a nature reserve. **3** a place where injured or unwanted animals are cared for. **4** a holy place. **5** the part of the chancel of a church containing the high altar.

sanctum noun **1** a sacred place. **2** a private place.

sand noun **1** a substance consisting of very fine particles resulting from the wearing down of rocks, found in beaches and deserts and on the sea-bed. **2** (**sands**) a wide area of sand. **verb** smooth a surface with sandpaper or a sander.

sandal noun a shoe with a partly open upper part or straps attaching the sole to the foot.

sandalwood noun the sweet-smelling wood of an Asian tree.

sandbag noun a bag of sand, used to protect or strengthen a structure or as a weight. **verb** (**sandbags, sandbagging, sandbagged**) protect or strengthen with sandbags.

sandbank noun a deposit of sand forming a shallow area in the sea or a river.

sandbar noun a long, narrow sandbank.

sandblast verb roughen or clean a surface with a jet of sand.

sandcastle noun a model of a castle built out of sand.

sander noun a power tool used for smoothing a surface.

sandpaper noun paper coated with sand or another rough substance, used for smoothing surfaces. **verb** smooth with sandpaper.

sandpit noun Brit. a shallow box or hollow containing sand, for children to play in.

sandstone noun rock formed from compressed sand.

sandstorm noun a strong wind in a desert carrying clouds of sand.

sandwich noun two pieces of bread with a filling between them. **verb** **1** (**sandwich between**) insert between two people or things. **2** (**sandwich together**) press or stick two things together. □ **sandwich board** a pair of boards hung in front of and behind a person's body as they walk around, used to advertise or proclaim something. **sandwich course** Brit. a course of study which includes periods working in business or industry.

sandy adjective (**sandier, sandiest**) **1** covered in or consisting of sand. **2** light yellowish brown.

sane adjective **1** not mad. **2** sensible.

sang past of **SING**.

sangfroid /song-frwah/ noun cool courage in difficult circumstances.

sanguinary /sang-gwi-nuh-ri/ adjective old use involving much bloodshed.

sanguine /sang-gwin/ adjective cheerful and confident about things that are going to happen.

sanitarium US = **SANATORIUM**.

sanitary adjective **1** relating to sanitation. **2** hygienic. □ **sanitary towel** a pad worn by women to absorb menstrual blood.

sanitation noun arrangements to protect public health, such as the provision of clean drinking water and the disposal of sewage.

sanitize or **sanitise** verb (**sanitizes, sanitizing, sanitized**) **1** make something hygienic. **2** make something unpleasant seem more acceptable. ■ **sanitization** noun.

sanity noun **1** the condition of being sane. **2** reasonable behaviour.

sank past of **SINK**.

Sanskrit /san-skrit/ noun an ancient language of India.

Santa Claus noun Father Christmas.

sap noun the liquid that circulates in plants, carrying food to all parts. **verb** (**saps, sapping, sapped**) gradually weaken a person's strength.

sapling noun a young tree.

sapphic /saf-fik/ adjective literary relating to lesbians or lesbianism.

sapphire /saf-fyr/ noun **1** a transparent blue precious stone. **2** a bright blue colour.

saprophyte /sap-ruh-fyt/ noun a plant or fungus that lives on decaying matter. ■ **saprophytic** adjective.

Saracen noun an Arab or Muslim at the time of the Crusades.

sarcasm noun the use of words which say the opposite of what you mean, as a way of hurting or mocking someone.

sarcastic adjective using sarcasm. ■ sarcastically adverb.

sarcophagus /sar-**kof**-fuh-guhss/ noun (plural **sarcophagi** /sar-**kof**-fuh-gy/) a stone coffin.

sardine noun a small herring-like fish.

sardonic adjective mocking. ■ sardonically adverb.

sari or **saree** noun (plural **saris** or **sarees**) a length of fabric draped around the body, worn by women from the Indian subcontinent.

sarky adjective Brit. informal sarcastic. ■ sarkily adverb.

sarnie noun Brit. informal a sandwich.

sarong noun a long piece of cloth wrapped round the body and tucked at the waist or under the armpits.

sartorial adjective having to do with the way a person dresses. ■ sartorially adverb.

sash[1] noun a strip of fabric worn over one shoulder or round the waist.

sash[2] noun a frame holding the glass in a window. □ **sash window** a window with two sashes which can be slid up and down to open it.

sashay verb informal swing the hips from side to side when walking.

Sassenach /**sass**-uh-nak/ Scottish & Irish disapproving noun an English person. adjective English.

sassy adjective (**sassier**, **sassiest**) informal confident, spirited, and cheeky.

SAT abbreviation standard assessment task.

sat past and past participle of **SIT**.

Satan noun the Devil.

satanic adjective having to do with Satan or the worship of Satan.

satanism noun the worship of Satan. ■ satanist noun & adjective.

satchel noun a bag with a long strap worn over one shoulder.

sated adjective having had as much or more of something than you want.

satellite noun **1** an artificial body placed in orbit round the earth or another planet to collect information or for communication. **2** Astronomy a celestial body orbiting a planet. **3** a thing that is separate from but controlled by something else. □ **satellite television** television in which the signals are broadcast via satellite.

satiate /**say**-shi-ayt/ verb give someone as much or more of something than they want. ■ satiation noun.

satiety /suh-**ty**-i-ti/ noun the state of being fully satisfied or of having had too much of something.

satin noun a smooth, glossy fabric. ■ satiny adjective.

satire /**sat**-yr/ noun **1** the use of humour, irony, exaggeration, or ridicule to reveal and criticize people's bad points. **2** a play or other piece of writing that uses satire. ■ satirist noun.

satirical or **satiric** adjective using satire. ■ satirically adverb.

satirize or **satirise** /**sat**-i-ryz/ verb (**satirizes**, **satirizing**, **satirized**) mock or criticize using satire.

satisfaction noun the feeling of pleasure that arises when you have the things you need or want or when the things you want to happen have happened.

satisfactory adjective acceptable. ■ satisfactorily adverb.

satisfy verb (**satisfies**, **satisfying**, **satisfied**) **1** give someone the things they need or want or bring about the things they want to happen. **2** meet a particular demand, desire, or need.

satsuma /sat-**soo**-muh/ noun a kind of tangerine with a loose skin.

saturate verb (**saturates**, **saturating**, **saturated**) **1** soak thoroughly with a liquid. **2** make a substance combine with, dissolve, or hold the greatest possible quantity of another substance. **3** fully magnetize or charge. **4** put more than is needed of a particular product into the market. ■ saturation noun.

saturated adjective Chemistry **1** (of a solution) containing the largest possible amount of a substance dissolved in it. **2** (of organic molecules) having only single bonds between carbon atoms.

Saturday noun the day of the week before Sunday and following Friday.

saturnine /sat-er-nyn/ **adjective 1** (of a person or their manner) gloomy. **2** (of looks) dark and brooding.

satyr /sat-er/ **noun** (in Greek mythology) a lecherous god of the woods, with a man's face and body and a horse's or goat's ears, tail, and legs.

sauce noun **1** thick liquid served with food to add moistness and flavour. **2** informal cheeky talk or behaviour. □ **sauce boat** a boat-shaped jug for serving sauce.

saucepan noun a deep cooking pan, with one long handle and a lid.

saucer noun a small shallow dish on which a cup stands.

saucy adjective (**saucier, sauciest**) informal **1** cheeky. **2** sexually suggestive in a light-hearted way. ■ **saucily** adverb.

sauerkraut /sow-er-krowt/ noun a German dish of pickled cabbage.

sauna /saw-nuh/ noun **1** a small room used as a hot-air or steam bath for cleaning and refreshing the body. **2** a session in a sauna.

saunter verb (**saunters, sauntering, sauntered**) walk in a slow, relaxed way. **noun** a leisurely stroll.

sausage noun **1** a short tube of raw minced meat encased in a skin and grilled or fried before eating. **2** a tube of seasoned minced meat that is cooked or preserved and eaten cold in slices. □ **sausage dog** Brit. informal a dachshund. **sausage meat** minced meat used in sausages or as a stuffing. **sausage roll** a portion of sausage meat baked in a roll of pastry.

sauté /soh-tay/ **adjective** fried quickly in shallow fat or oil. **verb** (**sautés, sautéing, sautéed or sautéd**) cook in such a way.

savage adjective 1 fierce and violent. **2** cruel and vicious. **3** primitive and uncivilized. **noun 1** a member of a people seen as primitive and uncivilized. **2** a brutal person. **verb** (**savages, savaging, savaged**) **1** ferociously attack and maul. **2** brutally criticize. ■ **savagely** adverb **savagery** noun.

savannah or **savanna** noun a grassy plain in hot regions.

savant or **savante** /sav-uhnt/ **noun** a wise and knowledgeable person.

save¹ verb (**saves, saving, saved**) **1** rescue or protect someone or something from harm or danger. **2** prevent someone from dying. **3** (in Christian use) prevent a soul from being damned. **4** store up for future use. **5** (in computing) store data. **6** avoid, lessen, or guard against. **7** prevent an opponent from scoring a goal. **noun** an act of preventing an opponent's goal. ■ **saver** noun.

save² preposition & conjunction formal except.

saveloy /sav-uh-loy/ **noun** Brit. a smoked pork sausage.

saving noun 1 a reduction in money, time, or some other resource. **2** (**savings**) money saved. **preposition** except. □ **saving grace** a good quality that makes up for something's faults.

saviour (US spelling **savior**) **noun 1** a person who saves someone or something from danger or harm. **2** (**Saviour**) (in Christianity) God or Jesus.

savoir faire /sav-war **fair**/ **noun** the ability to act appropriately in social situations.

savour (US spelling **savor**) **verb 1** eat or drink something slowly while enjoying its full flavour. **2** enjoy a feeling or experience thoroughly. **noun** a characteristic flavour or smell.

savoury (US spelling **savory**) **adjective 1** (of food) salty or spicy rather than sweet. **2** morally acceptable or respectable. **noun** (plural **savouries**) Brit. a savoury snack.

savvy informal **noun** sharp awareness and good judgement. **adjective** having sharp awareness and good judgement.

saw¹ noun a tool with a long, thin

WORD FORMATION ℹ

-saur, -saurus

-saur and **-saurus** are used in the names of fossil reptiles, in particular dinosaurs. They come from the ancient Greek word *sauros*, 'lizard'; *dinosaur* literally means 'terrible lizard'.

Some of the best-known **-saur** and **-saurus** words are:

apatosaurus or *brontosaurus*	a huge plant-eating dinosaur with a long neck and tail
plesiosaur	a fossil sea reptile with paddle-like limbs and a long flexible neck
stegosaurus	a plant-eating dinosaur with large bony plates along the back
tyrannosaurus rex	a meat-eating dinosaur that walked on its strong hind legs.

jagged blade, used with a backwards and forwards movement to cut wood and other hard materials. **verb** (**saws, sawing, sawed**; past participle Brit. **sawn** or N. Amer. **sawed**) cut through or cut off with a saw.

saw² past of **SEE¹**.

saw³ noun a proverb or wise saying.

sawdust noun powdery particles of wood produced by sawing.

sawmill noun a place where logs are sawn by machine.

sawtooth or **sawtoothed** adjective shaped like the jagged teeth of a saw.

sawyer noun a person who saws timber.

sax noun informal a saxophone.

Saxon noun a member of a people from Germany that settled in southern England in the 5th and 6th centuries.

saxophone noun a metal wind instrument with a reed like a clarinet. ∎ **saxophonist** noun.

say verb (**says, saying, said**) **1** utter words to communicate something. **2** (of a text or symbol) convey information or instructions. **3** (of a clock or watch) indicate a time. **4** (**be said**) be reported. **5** assume something in order to work out what its consequences would be. **noun** an opportunity to state your opinion.

saying noun a well-known statement expressing a general truth.

scab noun **1** a crust that forms over a wound as it heals. **2** disapproving a person who refuses to take part in a strike. **verb** (**scabs, scabbing, scabbed**) form a scab. ∎ **scabby** adjective.

scabbard noun a cover for the blade of a sword or dagger.

scabies noun a skin disease that causes itching and small red spots.

scabrous adjective **1** covered with scabs. **2** indecent or sordid.

scaffold noun **1** (in the past) a raised wooden platform on which people stood when they were to be executed. **2** a structure made using scaffolding.

scaffolding noun **1** a structure made of wooden planks and metal poles, for people to stand on when building or repairing a building. **2** the planks and poles used in such a structure.

scald verb **1** burn with very hot liquid or steam. **2** heat a liquid to near boiling point. **3** dip something briefly in boiling water. **noun** an injury caused by hot liquid or steam.

scale¹ noun **1** each of the small overlapping plates protecting the skin of fish and reptiles. **2** a dry flake of skin. **3** a white deposit which is left in a kettle, water pipe, etc, when water containing lime is heated. **4** a hard deposit that forms on teeth. **verb (scales, scaling, scaled) 1** remove the scales from. **2** form or flake off in scales.

scale² noun **1** (usu. **scales**) an instrument for weighing. **2** either of the dishes on a simple set of scales.

scale³ noun **1** a range of values forming a system for measuring or grading something. **2** a measuring instrument based on such a system. **3** relative size or extent. **4** a ratio of size in a map, model, drawing, or plan. **5** Music an arrangement of notes in order of pitch. **verb (scales, scaling, scaled) 1** climb up or over something high and steep. **2** represent something in a size that is larger or smaller than the original but exactly in proportion to it. **3** (**scale down** or **up**) reduce (or increase) in size, number, or extent. □ **to scale** reduced or enlarged uniformly.

scallion noun N. Amer an onion with a long neck and small bulb, like a spring onion or shallot.

scallop /skol-luhp, skal-luhp/ noun **1** an edible shellfish with two hinged fan-shaped shells. **2** each of a series of small curves like the edge of a scallop shell, forming a decorative edging. **verb (scallops, scalloping, scalloped)** decorate something with scallops.

scallywag noun informal a mischievous person.

scalp noun **1** the skin covering the top and back of the head. **2** (in the past, among American Indians) the scalp and hair cut away from an enemy's head as a battle trophy. **verb** take the scalp of an enemy.

scalpel noun a knife with a small sharp blade, used by a surgeon.

scaly adjective (**scalier, scaliest**) **1** covered in scales. **2** (of skin) dry and flaking.

scam noun informal a dishonest scheme for making money.

scamp noun informal a mischievous person.

scamper verb (**scampers, scampering, scampered**) run with quick light steps. noun an act of scampering.

scampi plural noun small lobster-like creatures prepared for eating.

scan verb (**scans, scanning, scanned**) **1** look at something quickly in order to find the parts that are most relevant or important. **2** move a detector or beam across. **3** convert a document or picture into digital form for storing or processing on a computer. **4** analyse the metre of a line of verse. **5** (of verse) follow metrical rules. noun **1** an act of scanning. **2** a medical examination using a scanner. **3** an image obtained by scanning.

scandal noun **1** an action or event that causes public outrage. **2** outrage or gossip arising from such an action or event. **3** an action or situation that you find shocking and unacceptable.

scandalize or **scandalise** verb (**scandalizes, scandalizing, scandalized**) shock others by acting in an improper or immoral way.

scandalous adjective **1** causing public outrage. **2** shocking and unacceptable. ■ **scandalously** adverb.

scanner noun **1** a machine that uses X-rays or ultrasound to record images, used by doctors to examine the inside of someone's body. **2** a device that scans documents or pictures and converts them into digital data.

scansion noun **1** the action of scanning a line of verse to find out its rhythm. **2** the rhythm of a line of verse.

scant adjective barely reaching the amount specified or needed.

scanty adjective (**scantier, scantiest**) too little in size or amount for what is needed. ■ **scantily** adverb.

scapegoat noun a person who is blamed for the things other people do wrong. **verb** make a scapegoat of.

scapula noun the shoulder blade.

scar¹ noun **1** a mark left on the skin or in body tissue after the healing of a wound. **2** a mark left at the point where a leaf or other part separates from a plant. **3** a lasting effect left after an unpleasant experience. **verb** (**scars, scarring, scarred**) mark or be marked with a scar.

scar² **noun** a steep high cliff or outcrop of rock.

scarab /ska-ruhb/ **noun** **1** a large dung beetle, seen as sacred in ancient Egypt. **2** an ancient Egyptian gem in the form of a scarab beetle.

scarce **adjective** **1** (of a resource) only available in small quantities that do not meet a demand. **2** rarely found. ■ **scarcity** noun.

scarcely **adverb** **1** only just. **2** just moments before. **3** definitely or very probably not.

scare **verb** (**scares, scaring, scared**) **1** frighten or become frightened. **2** (**scare away or off**) drive or keep someone away by frightening them. **noun** **1** a sudden attack of fright. **2** a period of general alarm.

scarecrow **noun** an object made to look like a person, set up to scare birds away from crops.

scarf **noun** (plural **scarves** or **scarfs**) a length or square of fabric worn around the neck or head.

scarify¹ **verb** (**scarifies, scarifying, scarified**) **1** rake out unwanted material from a lawn. **2** break up the surface of soil. **3** make shallow cuts in the skin. **4** criticize hurtfully.

scarify² **verb** (**scarifies, scarifying, scarified**) informal frighten.

scarlatina or **scarletina** **noun** scarlet fever.

scarlet **noun** a bright red colour. □ **scarlet fever** an infectious disease among children, causing fever and a scarlet rash.

scarp **noun** a very steep slope.

scarper **verb** (**scarpers, scarpering, scarpered**) Brit. informal run away.

scarves plural of **SCARF**.

scary **adjective** (**scarier, scariest**) informal frightening. ■ **scarily** adverb.

scat **verb** (**scats, scatting, scatted**) informal go away.

scathing **adjective** severely critical. ■ **scathingly** adverb.

scatological **adjective** obsessed with excrement and excretion. ■ **scatology** noun.

scatter **verb** (**scatters, scattering, scattered**) **1** throw in various random directions. **2** separate and move off in different directions. **3** (be **scattered**) be found at various places.

scatty or **scatterbrained** **adjective** informal disorganized and rather silly.

scavenge **verb** (**scavenges, scavenging, scavenged**) **1** search for and collect anything usable from waste. **2** (of an animal) search for and eat dead animals. ■ **scavenger** noun.

scenario **noun** (plural **scenarios**) **1** a possible sequence of events in the future. **2** a written outline of a film, play, or novel.

scene **noun** **1** the place where an incident occurs. **2** a view or landscape as seen by a spectator. **3** an incident: *scenes of violence*. **4** a sequence of continuous action in a play, film, etc. **5** an area of activity or interest: *the literary scene*. **6** a public display of emotion or anger. □ **behind the scenes** out of public view.

scenery **noun** **1** a landscape considered in terms of its appearance. **2** the background used to represent a place on a stage or film set.

scenic **adjective** having beautiful natural scenery. ■ **scenically** adverb.

scent **noun** **1** a distinctive smell, especially a pleasant one. **2** pleasant-smelling liquid worn on the skin; perfume. **3** a trail left by an animal, indicated by its smell. **verb** **1** give a pleasant scent to. **2** find or recognize something by using the sense of smell. **3** sense that something is about to happen. ■ **scented** adjective.

sceptic /skep-tik/ (US spelling **skeptic**) **noun** a person who questions accepted opinions. ■ **scepticism** noun.

sceptical (US spelling **skeptical**) **adjective** not easily convinced; having doubts. ■ **sceptically** adverb.

sceptre /sep-ter/ (US spelling **scepter**) **noun** a decorated rod carried by a king or queen on ceremonial occasions.

schedule /shed-yool, sked-yool/ **noun 1** a plan for doing something, with a list of intended events and times. **2** a timetable. **verb (schedules, scheduling, scheduled) 1** plan for something to happen at a particular time. **2 (scheduled)** (of a flight) forming part of a regular service rather than specially chartered.

schema /skee-muh/ **noun** (plural **schemata** /skee-muh-tuh/ or **schemas**) technical an outline of a plan or theory.

schematic adjective 1 (of a diagram) simplified and using symbols. **2** presented according to a plan. ■ **schematically** adverb.

scheme noun 1 a careful plan for achieving something. **2** a secret or devious plan; a plot. **3** a system or pattern. **verb (schemes, scheming, schemed)** make plans in a devious way; plot.

scherzo /skair-tsoh/ **noun** (plural **scherzos** or **scherzi** /skair-tsi/) a short, lively piece of music.

schism /si-z'm, ski-z'm/ **noun** a disagreement or division between two groups or within an organization. ■ **schismatic** adjective.

schist /shist/ **noun** a metamorphic rock which consists of layers of different minerals.

schizoid /skit-soyd/ **adjective 1** (of a person) detached and solitary. **2** schizophrenic.

schizophrenia noun a mental disorder whose symptoms include a withdrawal from reality into fantasy.

schizophrenic adjective 1 suffering from schizophrenia. **2** having contradictory elements. **noun** a schizophrenic person.

schmaltz noun informal excessive sentimentality. ■ **schmaltzy** adjective.

schnapps noun a strong alcoholic drink resembling gin.

scholar noun 1 a person who is studying at an advanced level. **2** a student holding a scholarship.

scholarly adjective 1 relating to serious academic study. **2** very knowledgeable and keen on studying.

scholarship noun 1 academic work. **2** an amount of money given to a student to help pay for their education.

scholastic adjective. having to do with schools and education.

school noun 1 a place where children are educated. **2** a place where instruction is given in a particular subject. **3** a group of artists, philosophers, etc. sharing similar ideas. **4** a large group of fish or sea mammals. **verb 1** formal or N. Amer. educate. **2** train in a particular skill or activity. □ **school of thought** a particular way of thinking.

schooling noun education received at school.

schooner /skoo-ner/ **noun 1** a sailing ship with two or more masts. **2** Brit. a large glass for sherry.

sciatic /sy-at-ik/ **adjective** having to do with the hip or with the nerve which goes down the back of the thigh (the sciatic nerve).

sciatica noun pain affecting the back, hip, and leg, caused by compression of the sciatic nerve.

science noun 1 study or knowledge of the physical and natural world, based on observation and experiment. **2** a particular branch of science. **3** a body of knowledge on any subject. □ **science fiction** fiction set in the future and dealing with imagined scientific advances. **science park** an area where a number of science-based companies are located.

scientific adjective 1 relating to or based on science. **2** systematic; methodical. ■ **scientifically** adverb.

scientist noun a person who studies or is an expert in science.

sci-fi noun science fiction.

scimitar /sim-i-ter/ **noun** a short sword with a curved blade.

scintillating adjective 1 sparkling or shining brightly. **2** very skilful and exciting.

scion /sy-uhn/ **noun 1** a young shoot or twig of a plant. **2** literary a descendant of a notable family.

scissors plural noun a device for cutting cloth and paper, consisting of two crossing blades pivoted in the middle.

sclerosis noun **1** abnormal hardening of body tissue. **2** (also **multiple sclerosis**) a serious disease of the nervous system that can cause partial paralysis.

scoff[1] verb speak about something in a scornful way.

scoff[2] verb Brit. informal eat quickly and greedily.

scold verb angrily criticize or tell off.

sconce noun a candle holder attached to a wall.

scone /skon, skohn/ noun a small unsweetened or lightly sweetened cake, usually eaten with butter.

scoop noun **1** an implement like a spoon, with a short handle and a deep bowl. **2** the bowl-shaped part of a digging machine. **3** informal a piece of news printed by one newspaper before its rivals. verb **1** pick up with a scoop. **2** create a hollow. **3** pick up in a quick, smooth movement. **4** informal be quicker than other newspapers to print a piece of news.

scoot verb informal move or go quickly.

scooter noun **1** (also **motor scooter**) a light motorcycle. **2** a child's vehicle with two wheels and a long steering handle, which you move by pushing one foot against the ground.

scope noun **1** the extent of the area or subject matter that something deals with or to which it is relevant. **2** the opportunity or possibility for doing something.

scorch verb **1** burn on the surface or edges. **2** (**scorched**) dried out and withered as a result of extreme heat.

scorcher noun informal a very hot day.

score noun **1** the number of points, goals, etc. achieved by a person or team in a game. **2** (plural **score**) a group or set of twenty. **3** (**scores of**) a lot of. **4** the written music for a composition. verb (**scores, scoring, scored**) **1** gain a point, goal, etc. in a game. **2** record the score during a game. **3** cut or scratch a mark on a surface. **4** (**score out**) cross out text. **5** arrange a piece of music.

scoreline noun the final score in a game.

scorn noun open contempt or disdain. verb **1** express scorn for. **2** reject in a contemptuous way.

scornful adjective showing or feeling scorn. ∎ **scornfully** adverb.

Scorpio noun a sign of the zodiac (the Scorpion), 23 October–21 November.

scorpion noun a small creature with six legs, pincers, and a poisonous sting at the end of its tail.

Scot noun a person from Scotland.

Scotch adjective (of a thing) Scottish. noun (also **Scotch whisky**) whisky distilled in Scotland. □ **Scotch egg** a hard-boiled egg enclosed in sausage meat.

| i | use **Scotch** only in reference to things: people are **Scots** or **Scottish**. |

scotch verb **1** decisively put an end to. **2** old use injure and make harmless.

scot-free adverb without suffering any punishment or injury.

Scots adjective Scottish. noun the form of English used in Scotland.

Scottish adjective relating to Scotland or its people.

scoundrel noun old use a dishonest or immoral person.

scour verb **1** clean by rubbing with rough material. **2** search a place thoroughly.

scourge noun **1** a whip. **2** a cause of great suffering. verb (**scourges, scourging, scourged**) **1** whip someone. **2** cause great suffering to.

Scouse Brit. informal noun **1** the dialect or accent of people from Liverpool. **2** (also **Scouser**) a person from Liverpool. adjective relating to Liverpool.

scout noun **1** a person who is sent ahead to gather information about the enemy. **2** a member of the Scout

Association, a boys' organization. **3** (also **talent scout**) a person whose job is searching for talented performers. **verb 1** search a place to find something or gather information. **2** act as a scout.

scowl noun a bad-tempered expression. **verb** frown in an angry or bad-tempered way.

scrabble verb (**scrabbles, scrabbling, scrabbled**) **1** grope around with your fingers to find or hold on to something. **2** move quickly and awkwardly; scramble.

scraggy adjective thin and bony.

scram verb (**scrams, scramming, scrammed**) informal leave quickly.

scramble verb (**scrambles, scrambling, scrambled**) **1** move quickly and awkwardly, using hands as well as feet. **2** muddle. **3** put a transmission into a form that can only be understood by using a decoding device. **4** cook beaten eggs in a pan. **5** (of fighter aircraft) take off immediately in an emergency. **noun 1** an act of scrambling. **2** Brit. a motorcycle race over rough and hilly ground.

scrap[1] noun **1** a small piece or amount of something. **2** (**scraps**) bits of uneaten food left after a meal. **3** unwanted metal that can be used again. **verb** (**scraps, scrapping, scrapped**) **1** remove from use. **2** abolish or cancel a plan, policy, etc.

scrap[2] noun a short fight or quarrel. **verb** (**scraps, scrapping, scrapped**) engage in a scrap.

scrapbook noun a book for sticking cuttings or pictures in.

scrape verb (**scrapes, scraping, scraped**) **1** drag something hard or sharp across a surface. **2** use a sharp or hard implement to remove unwanted matter. **3** rub against a rough or hard surface. **4** just manage to achieve, succeed, or pass. **noun 1** an act or sound of scraping. **2** an injury or mark caused by scraping. **3** informal an awkward or difficult situation.

scrappy adjective disorganized, untidy, or incomplete.

scrapyard noun Brit. a place where scrap metal is collected.

scratch verb **1** make a long mark or wound on a surface with something sharp or pointed. **2** rub part of the body with your fingernails to relieve itching. **3** (**scratch out**) cross out writing. **4** withdraw from a competition. **5** cancel or abandon. **noun 1** a mark or wound made by scratching. **2** informal a slight injury. **adjective** assembled from whatever is available: *a scratch squad.* □ **from scratch** from the very beginning. **up to scratch** to the required standard. **scratch card** a card with a section which you scrape to reveal whether a prize has been won. ■ **scratchy** adjective.

scrawl verb write in a hurried, careless way. **noun** scrawled handwriting.

scrawny adjective (**scrawnier, scrawniest**) thin and bony.

scream verb **1** make a loud, piercing cry or sound. **2** move very fast. **noun 1** a loud, piercing cry or sound. **2** (**a scream**) informal an extremely funny person or thing. ■ **screamer** noun.

scree noun a mass of small loose stones on a mountain slope.

screech noun a loud, harsh cry or sound. **verb** make a screech.

screed noun **1** a long speech or piece of writing. **2** a layer of material applied to make a floor level.

screen noun **1** an upright partition used to divide a room or conceal something. **2** the front part of a television or computer monitor, on which images and data are displayed. **3** a blank surface on which films are projected. **4** (**the screen**) films or television. **verb 1** conceal or protect with a screen. **2** show or broadcast a film or television programme. **3** protect from something unpleasant. **4** test a group of people for the presence of a disease. □ **screen printing** a process in which ink is forced through a screen of fine material to create a picture or pattern. **screen test** a filmed audition for a film part.

screenplay noun the script of a film,

including acting instructions.

screenwriter noun a person who writes a screenplay.

screw noun **1** a metal pin with a spiral thread running around it, which is turned and pressed into a surface to join things together. **2** a ship's or aircraft's propeller. **3** vulgar an act of sexual intercourse. **4** informal a prison warder. verb **1** fasten or tighten with a screw or screws. **2** rotate something to attach or remove it. **3** informal swindle. **4** vulgar have sexual intercourse with. □ **screw up 1** crush into a tight mass. **2** informal make something fail or go wrong. **3** informal make someone emotionally disturbed.

screwdriver noun a tool with a tip that fits into the head of a screw to turn it.

screwy adjective informal rather odd or eccentric.

scribble verb (**scribbles**, **scribbling**, **scribbled**) write or draw carelessly or hurriedly. noun a scribbled picture or piece of writing.

scribe noun (in the past) a person who copied out documents.

scrimmage noun a confused struggle or fight.

scrimp verb be very careful with money; economize.

script noun **1** the written text of a play, film, or broadcast. **2** handwriting as distinct from print. verb write a script for.

scripture or **scriptures** noun **1** the sacred writings of Christianity contained in the Bible. **2** the sacred writings of another religion. ■ **scriptural** adjective.

scrofula noun the name in the past for a form of tuberculosis. ■ **scrofulous** adjective.

scroll noun a roll of parchment or paper for writing or painting on. verb move text on a computer screen in order to view different parts of it.

Scrooge noun a person who is mean with money.

scrotum noun (plural **scrota** or **scrotums**) the pouch of skin containing the testicles.

scrounge verb (**scrounges**, **scrounging**, **scrounged**) informal try to get something from others without having to pay or work for it. ■ **scrounger** noun.

scrub¹ verb (**scrubs**, **scrubbing**, **scrubbed**) rub something hard to clean it. noun an act of scrubbing.

scrub² noun **1** vegetation consisting mainly of bushes and small trees. **2** land covered with such vegetation. ■ **scrubby** adjective.

scruff¹ noun the back of a person's or animal's neck.

scruff² noun Brit. informal a scruffy person.

scruffy adjective (**scruffier**, **scruffiest**) shabby and untidy or dirty.

scrum noun **1** (also **scrummage**) Rugby a formation in which players push against each other with heads down and the ball is thrown in. **2** Brit. informal a disorderly crowd.

scrummy adjective informal delicious.

scrump verb Brit. informal steal fruit from an orchard or garden.

scrumptious adjective informal extremely delicious.

scrumpy noun strong cider made in the west of England.

scrunch verb crush or squeeze into a tight mass.

scruple noun a feeling of doubt as to whether an action is morally right. verb (**scruples**, **scrupling**, **scrupled**) (**not scruple to do**) formal not hesitate to do something, even if it may be wrong.

scrupulous adjective **1** very careful and thorough. **2** very concerned to avoid doing wrong. ■ **scrupulously** adverb.

scrutinize or **scrutinise** verb (**scrutinizes**, **scrutinizing**, **scrutinized**) examine thoroughly.

scrutiny noun (plural **scrutinies**) close and critical examination.

scuba diving noun swimming underwater using an aqualung.

scud verb (**scuds**, **scudding**, **scud-**

ded) move quickly, driven by the wind.

scuff verb **1** scrape a shoe or other object against something. **2** mark by scuffing. **3** drag your feet when walking. noun a mark made by scuffing.

scuffle noun a short, confused fight or struggle. verb **(scuffles, scuffling, scuffled)** engage in a scuffle.

scull noun **1** each of a pair of small oars used by a single rower. **2** a light, narrow boat propelled by a single rower. verb propel a boat with sculls.

scullery noun (plural **sculleries**) a small room in an old house, used for washing dishes and laundry.

sculpt verb carve or shape.

sculptor noun (feminine **sculptress**) an artist who makes sculptures.

sculpture noun **1** the art of making three-dimensional figures and shapes by carving or shaping wood, stone, metal, etc. **2** a work of such a kind. verb **(sculptures, sculpturing, sculptured) 1** make or represent by sculpture. **2 (sculptured)** pleasingly shaped, with strong lines. ■ **sculptural** adjective.

scum noun **1** a layer of dirt or froth on the surface of a liquid. **2** informal a worthless person or group of people. ■ **scummy** adjective.

scupper verb **(scuppers, scuppering, scuppered)** Brit. **1** sink your own ship deliberately. **2** informal stop something working or succeeding.

scurf noun flakes of skin.

scurrilous adjective rude and insulting; slanderous.

scurry verb **(scurries, scurrying, scurried)** move hurriedly with short, quick steps.

scurvy noun a disease caused by a lack of vitamin C.

scut noun the short tail of a hare, rabbit, or deer.

scuttle[1] noun a metal container used to store coal for a domestic fire.

scuttle[2] verb **(scuttles, scuttling, scuttled)** run hurriedly or secretively with short, quick steps.

scuttle[3] verb **(scuttles, scuttling, scuttled) 1** sink your own ship deliberately. **2** cause a scheme to fail.

scythe noun a tool with a long curved blade for cutting grass or corn. verb **(scythes, scything, scythed)** cut with a scythe.

SE abbreviation south-east or south-eastern.

sea noun **1** the salt water that surrounds the land masses of the earth. **2** a particular area of sea. **3** a vast expanse or quantity. □ **all at sea** very confused and uncertain. **sea anemone** a sea creature with stinging tentacles that make it resemble a flower. **sea change** a great or remarkable transformation. **sea cow** a manatee or other large plant-eating sea mammal. **sea horse** a small sea fish that swims upright and has a head rather like a horse's. **sea level** the average level of the sea's surface, used in calculating the height of land. **sea lion** a large seal with a mane on the neck and shoulders. **sea mile** a nautical mile. **sea urchin** a small sea creature with a shell covered in spines.

seabird noun a bird that lives near the sea.

seaboard noun a region bordering the sea; the coastline.

seafaring adjective & noun travelling by sea. ■ **seafarer** noun.

seafood noun shellfish and sea fish as food.

seafront noun the part of a coastal town facing the sea.

seagoing adjective & noun travelling on the sea.

seagull noun a gull.

seal[1] noun **1** a device or substance used to join two things together or to stop fluid getting in. **2** a piece of wax with a design stamped into it, attached to letters and documents to guarantee they are genuine. **3** a confirmation or guarantee: *a seal of approval.* verb **1** fasten or close securely. **2 (seal off)** stop people entering and leaving an area. **3** coat a surface to stop fluid passing through it. **4** conclude; make definite. □ **sealing wax** a type of wax used to make seals for letters and documents. ■ **sealer** noun.

seal[2] noun a sea mammal with flippers and a streamlined body.

sealant noun material used to make something airtight or watertight.

seam noun **1** a line where two pieces of fabric are sewn together. **2** an underground layer of a mineral. verb join with a seam.

seaman noun a sailor, especially one below the rank of officer.

seamless adjective smooth and without seams or obvious joins. ■ **seamlessly** adverb.

seamstress noun a woman who sews, especially as a job.

seamy adjective (**seamier, seamiest**) sordid.

seance /say-onss/ noun a meeting at which people attempt to make contact with the dead.

seaplane noun an aircraft designed to land on and take off from water.

sear verb **1** scorch with a sudden intense heat. **2** (of pain) be experienced as a burning sensation.

search verb **1** try to find something by looking carefully and thoroughly. **2** examine something thoroughly in order to find something or someone. **3** (**searching**) investigating very deeply. noun an act of searching. □ **search warrant** a document authorizing a police officer to enter and search a place. ■ **searcher** noun **searchingly** adverb.

searchlight noun a powerful electric light with a concentrated beam that can be turned in any direction.

seascape noun a view or picture of an expanse of sea.

seashell noun the shell of a marine shellfish.

seashore noun an area of sandy, stony, or rocky land next to the sea.

seasick adjective suffering from nausea caused by the motion of a ship at sea. ■ **seasickness** noun.

seaside noun a place by the sea, especially a beach area or holiday resort.

season noun **1** each of the four divisions of the year (spring, summer, autumn, and winter). **2** a part of the year with particular weather, or when a sport is played. verb **1** add salt or spices to food. **2** make something more lively or interesting. **3** dry wood for use as timber. **4** (**seasoned**) experienced. □ **in season 1** ripe or ready to eat. **2** (of a female mammal) ready to mate. **season ticket** a ticket that lets you travel within a particular period or gain admission to a series of events.

seasonable adjective usual or appropriate for a particular season of the year.

seasonal adjective **1** relating to or characteristic of a particular season of the year. **2** changing according to the season. ■ **seasonally** adverb.

seasoning noun salt or spices added to food to improve the flavour.

seat noun **1** a thing made or used for sitting on. **2** the part of a chair designed for sitting on. **3** a place for a person to sit in a vehicle, theatre, etc. **4** a person's buttocks. **5** Brit. a place in an elected parliament or council. **6** Brit. a parliamentary constituency. **7** a site or location. **8** a large country house belonging to an aristocratic family. verb **1** arrange for someone to sit somewhere. **2** (**seat yourself** or **be seated**) formal sit down. **3** (of a place) have sufficient seats for. □ **seat belt** a belt used to secure someone in the seat of a motor vehicle or aircraft.

seaweed noun plants growing in the sea or on rocks by the sea.

seaworthy adjective (of a boat) in a good enough condition to sail on the sea.

sebaceous /si-bay-shuhss/ adjective technical producing oil or fat.

secateurs /sek-uh-terz/ plural noun Brit. a pair of pruning clippers for use with one hand.

secede verb (**secedes, seceding, seceded**) withdraw formally from an alliance or federation of states.

secession noun the action of seceding.

secluded adjective (of a place) sheltered and private.

seclusion noun the state of being private and away from other people.

second¹ ordinal number **1** that is number two in a sequence; 2nd. **2** lower in position, rank, or importance. **3** (**seconds**) goods of inferior quality. **4** a person who helps someone fighting in a duel or boxing match. **5** Brit. a place in the second highest grade in an examination for a degree. verb **1** formally support a nomination or resolution before voting or discussion. **2** express agreement with. □ **second best** not quite as good as the best. **second class 1** the second-best accommodation in a train, ship, etc. **2** inferior. **second-degree** (of burns) causing blistering but not permanent scars.   **second-guess** predict someone's actions or thoughts by guesswork. **second-hand 1** having had a previous owner. **2** heard from another person. **second nature** a habit that has become instinctive. **second-rate** of poor quality. **second sight** the supposed ability to foretell the future. **second thoughts** a change of opinion after reconsidering something. **second wind** fresh energy gained during exercise after having been out of breath. ■ **secondly** adverb.

second² noun **1** a unit of time equal to one-sixtieth of a minute. **2** (**a second**) informal a very short time. **3** a measurement of an angle equal to one sixtieth of a minute.

second³ /si-kond/ verb Brit. temporarily move a worker to another position or role. ■ **secondment** noun.

secondary adjective **1** coming after, or less important than, something else. **2** (of education) for children from the age of eleven to sixteen or eighteen. ■ **secondarily** adverb.

secret adjective **1** hidden from, or not known by, other people. **2** secretive. noun **1** something secret. **2** a method of achieving something that is not

generally known. □ **secret agent** a spy. **secret police** a police force working in secret against a government's opponents. **secret service** a government office or department concerned with spying. ■ **secrecy** noun **secretly** adverb.

secretariat /sek-ri-**tair**-i-uht/ noun a government office or department.

secretary noun (plural **secretaries**) **1** a person employed to type letters, keep records, etc. **2** an official of a society or other organization. □ **Secretary of State 1** (in the UK) the head of a major government department. **2** (in the US) the government official responsible for foreign affairs. ■ **secretarial** adjective.

secrete verb (**secretes**, **secreting**, **secreted**) **1** (of a cell, gland, or organ) produce and discharge a substance. **2** hide an object. ■ **secretion** noun.

secretive adjective inclined to hide your feelings or not to give out information. ■ **secretively** adverb.

sect noun a small religious or political group with different beliefs from those of the larger group that they belong to.

sectarian adjective having to do with a sect or group. ■ **sectarianism** noun.

section noun **1** any of the parts into which something is divided. **2** a distinct group within a larger body of people or things. **3** the shape that results from cutting through something. verb divide into sections.

sector noun **1** a distinct area or part. **2** a part of a circle between two lines drawn from its centre to its circumference.

secular adjective not religious or spiritual. ■ **secularism** noun.

secure adjective **1** certain to remain safe. **2** fixed or fastened so as not to give way or become loose. **3** free from fear or anxiety. verb (**secures**, **securing**, **secured**) **1** protect against danger or threat. **2** firmly fix or fasten. **3** succeed in obtaining. ■ **securely** adverb.

security noun (plural **securities**) **1** the

state of being or feeling secure. **2** the safety of a state or organization. **3** a valuable item offered as a guarantee that you will repay a loan.

sedan noun **1** an enclosed chair carried between two horizontal poles. **2** N. Amer. a car for four or more people.

sedate adjective **1** calm and unhurried. **2** respectable and rather dull. **verb** (sedates, sedating, sedated) give someone a sedative drug. ■ **sedately** adverb.

sedation noun the action of sedating someone.

sedative adjective having the effect of making someone calm or sleepy. **noun** a sedative drug.

sedentary /sed-uhn-tri/ adjective **1** sitting; seated. **2** sitting down a lot; taking little exercise. **3** staying in the same place for much of the time.

sedge noun a grass-like plant that grows in wet ground.

sediment noun **1** matter that settles to the bottom of a liquid. **2** material carried by water or wind and deposited on land. ■ **sedimentary** adjective.

sedition noun things done or said to stir up rebellion against a ruler or government. ■ **seditious** adjective.

seduce verb (seduces, seducing, seduced) **1** persuade to do something unwise. **2** persuade someone to have sex with you. ■ **seduction** noun.

seductive adjective tempting and attractive. ■ **seductively** adverb.

sedulous adjective dedicated and careful.

see¹ verb (sees, seeing, saw, past participle seen) **1** become aware of with the eyes. **2** experience or witness. **3** realize something after thinking or getting information. **4** think of in a particular way. **5** meet someone socially or by chance. **6** meet regularly as a boyfriend or girlfriend. **7** consult a specialist or professional. **8** guide or lead to a place. □ **see off** go with a person who is leaving to their point of departure. **see through 1** carry on with a project until it is completed.

2 not be deceived by. **see-through** transparent or semi-transparent. **see to 1** deal with. **2** make sure that.

see² noun the district or position of a bishop or archbishop.

seed noun **1** a small, hard object produced by a plant, from which a new plant may grow. **2** the beginning of a feeling, process, etc. **3** old use a man's semen. **4** any of the stronger competitors in a sports tournament who are kept apart from playing each other in the early rounds. **verb 1** sow land with seeds. **2** remove the seeds from. **3** (**be seeded**) make a sports competitor a seed in a tournament.

seedling noun a young plant raised from seed.

seedy adjective (seedier, seediest) unpleasant because dirty or immoral. ■ **seediness** noun.

seeing conjunction because; since.

seek verb (seeks, seeking, sought) **1** try to find or obtain. **2** (**seek out**) search for and find. **3** (**seek to do**) try or want to do. **4** ask for. ■ **seeker** noun.

seem verb **1** give the impression of being. **2** (**cannot seem to do**) be unable to do, despite having tried.

seeming adjective appearing to be real or true. ■ **seemingly** adverb.

seemly adjective respectable or in good taste.

seen past participle of SEE¹.

seep verb (of a liquid) flow or leak slowly through a substance. ■ **seepage** noun.

seer noun a person who is supposedly able to see visions of the future.

seersucker noun a fabric with a crinkled surface.

see-saw noun a long plank supported in the middle, on each end of which children sit and move up and down by pushing the ground with their feet. **verb** repeatedly change between two states or positions.

seethe verb (seethes, seething, seethed) **1** (of a liquid) boil or churn. **2** be very angry but try not to show it.

3 be filled with a crowd that is moving about.

segment noun /seg-muhnt/ each of the parts into which something is divided. **verb** /seg-**ment**/ divide into segments. ■ **segmental** adjective.

segregate verb (segregates, segregating, segregated) **1** keep separate from the rest or from each other. **2** keep people of different races, sexes, or religions separate. ■ segregation noun.

segue /seg-way/ verb (segues, seguing, segued) move without interruption from one song or film scene to another.

seine /rhymes with rain/ noun a fishing net which hangs vertically in the water, with floats at the top.

seismic /syz-mik/ adjective **1** having to do with earthquakes. **2** enormous in size or effect.

seismology noun the study of earthquakes. ■ **seismologist** noun.

seize verb (seized, seizing, seized) **1** take hold of suddenly and forcibly. **2** (of the police) officially take possession of. **3** take an opportunity eagerly and decisively. **4** (seize on) take advantage of eagerly. **5** (often seize up) (of a machine) become jammed.

> ☑ **seize** is an exception to the usual rule of *i* before *e* except after *c*.

seizure noun **1** the action of seizing. **2** a sudden attack of illness, especially a stroke or an epileptic fit.

seldom adverb not often.

select verb carefully choose from a group. **adjective 1** carefully chosen as being among the best. **2** used by, or made up of, wealthy people. □ **select committee** a small parliamentary committee appointed for a special purpose. ■ **selector** noun.

selection noun **1** the action of selecting. **2** a number of selected things. **3** a range of things from which you can choose.

selective adjective **1** involving selection. **2** choosing carefully. **3** affecting some things and not others. ■ select-

ively adverb **selectivity** noun.

selenium /si-lee-ni-uhm/ noun a grey crystalline chemical element.

self noun (plural selves) **1** a person's essential being that distinguishes them from others. **2** a person's particular nature or personality.

self-absorbed adjective obsessed with your own emotions or interests.

self-abuse noun masturbation.

self-addressed adjective (of an envelope) addressed to yourself.

self-adhesive adjective sticking without needing to be moistened.

self-appointed adjective having taken up a position or role without the approval of others.

self-assessment noun **1** assessment of your own performance. **2** a system in which you calculate yourself how much tax you owe.

self-assurance noun confidence in your own abilities or character. ■ **self-assured** adjective.

self-aware adjective knowledgeable about your own character, feelings, motives, etc. ■ **self-awareness** noun.

self-catering adjective Brit. (of a holiday or accommodation) offering facilities for you to cook your own meals.

self-centred adjective obsessed with yourself and your affairs.

self-confessed adjective admitting to having certain characteristics.

self-confidence noun a feeling of trust in your abilities and judgement. ■ **self-confident** adjective.

self-congratulation noun excessive pride in your achievements or qualities. ■ **self-congratulatory** adjective.

self-conscious adjective nervous or awkward through being worried about what other people think of you. ■ **self-consciously** adverb.

self-contained adjective **1** complete in itself. **2** not depending on or influenced by others.

self-control noun the ability to control your emotions or behaviour. ■ **self-controlled** adjective.

self-defeating adjective making

things worse rather than achieving the desired aim.

self-defence noun defence of yourself.

self-denial noun not allowing yourself to have things that you want.

self-deprecating adjective modest about yourself. ∎ **self-deprecation** noun.

self-destruct verb explode or disintegrate automatically.

self-destructive adjective causing harm to yourself.

self-determination noun the right or ability of a country or person to manage their own affairs.

self-discipline noun the ability to control your feelings and actions. ∎ **self-disciplined** adjective.

self-doubt noun lack of confidence in yourself and your abilities.

self-effacing adjective not wanting to attract attention.

self-employed adjective working for yourself rather than for an employer. ∎ **self-employment** noun.

self-esteem noun confidence in your own worth or abilities.

self-evident adjective obvious. ∎ **self-evidently** adverb.

self-explanatory adjective not needing explanation; clearly understood.

self-expression noun the expression of your feelings or thoughts.

self-fulfilling adjective (of a prediction) bound to come true because people behave in a way that makes it happen.

self-help noun reliance on your own efforts and resources to achieve things.

self-importance noun an exaggerated sense of your own value or importance. ∎ **self-important** adjective.

self-indulgent adjective indulging your desires excessively. ∎ **self-indulgence** noun.

self-interest noun your personal interest or advantage.

selfish adjective concerned mainly with your own needs and wishes. ∎ **selfishly** adverb **selfishness** noun.

selfless adjective concerned more with the needs and wishes of others than with your own.

self-made adjective having become successful by your own efforts.

self-pity noun excessive concern with and unhappiness over your own troubles. ∎ **self-pitying** adjective.

self-portrait noun a portrait by an artist of himself or herself.

self-possessed adjective calm, confident, and in control of your feelings. ∎ **self-possession** noun.

self-raising flour noun Brit. flour that has baking powder already added.

self-regard noun **1** consideration for yourself. **2** vanity. ∎ **self-regarding** adjective.

self-reliance noun reliance on your own powers and resources. ∎ **self-reliant** adjective.

self-respect noun pride and confidence in yourself.

self-righteous adjective certain that you are right or morally superior.

self-sacrifice noun the giving up of your own needs or wishes to help others. ∎ **self-sacrificing** adjective.

selfsame adjective (the selfsame) the very same.

self-satisfied adjective smugly pleased with yourself. ∎ **self-satisfaction** noun.

self-seeking or **self-serving** adjective concerned only with your own welfare and interests.

self-service adjective (of a shop or restaurant) where customers select goods for themselves and pay at a checkout.

self-styled adjective using a description or title that you have given yourself: *self-styled experts.*

self-sufficient adjective able to satisfy your basic needs without outside help. ∎ **self-sufficiency** noun.

self-worth noun self-esteem.

sell verb (**sells**, **selling**, **sold**) **1** hand over something in exchange for

WORD FORMATION

semi-

The prefix **semi-** means:
- half, as in *semicircular*
- partially, e.g. *semi-conscious*, *semi-precious*.

semi- comes from Latin. The prefixes **demi-** and **hemi-** (as in *demigod* and *hemisphere*) also mean 'half'.

---

money. **2** (of goods) achieve sales. **3** (**sell up**) sell all your property or assets. **4** persuade someone that something is good. □ **sell out 1** sell all your stock of something. **2** abandon your principles for reasons of convenience. **3** (of tickets for an event) be all sold. ■ **seller** noun.

Sellotape noun Brit. trademark transparent adhesive tape.

selvedge /sel-vij/ noun an edge on woven fabric that prevents it from unravelling.

selves plural of SELF.

semantic adjective having to do with meaning. ■ **semantically** adverb.

semantics plural noun **1** the study of the meaning of words and phrases. **2** the meaning of words, phrases, etc.

semaphore noun a system of sending messages by holding the arms or two flags in positions that represent letters of the alphabet.

semblance noun the way that something looks or seems.

semen /see-muhn/ noun a fluid containing sperm that is produced by men and male animals.

semester noun a half-year term in a school or university.

semi noun (plural **semis**) informal **1** Brit. a semi-detached house. **2** a semi-final.

semi-automatic adjective (of a gun) able to load bullets automatically but not fire continuously.

semibreve noun Brit. a musical note that lasts as long as two minims or four crotchets.

semicircle noun a half of a circle. ■ **semicircular** adjective.

semicolon noun a punctuation mark

(;) indicating a bigger pause than that indicated by a comma.

semiconductor noun a solid which conducts electricity, but to a smaller extent than a metal.

semi-detached adjective (of a house) joined to another house on one side by a common wall.

semi-final noun (in sport) a match or round coming immediately before the final. ■ **semi-finalist** noun.

seminal adjective **1** strongly influencing later developments. **2** referring to semen.

seminar noun **1** a meeting for discussion or training. **2** a university class for discussion of topics with a teacher.

seminary noun (plural **seminaries**) a training college for priests or rabbis.

semiotics plural noun the study of signs and symbols. ■ **semiotic** adjective.

semi-precious adjective (of minerals) used as gems but less valuable than precious stones.

semiquaver noun Brit. a musical note lasting half as long as a quaver.

semi-skimmed adjective Brit. (of milk) having had some of the cream removed.

semitone noun a musical interval equal to half a tone.

semolina noun the hard grains left after flour has been milled, used to make puddings and pasta.

senate noun **1** the smaller but higher law-making body in the US, France, etc. **2** the governing body of a university or college. **3** the state council of ancient Rome.

PUNCTUATION   🛈

Semicolon

A semicolon (;) is used:

1 between clauses that are too short or too closely related to be made into separate sentences, e.g.

To err is human; to forgive, divine
You could wait for him here; this would save you valuable time.

2 between items in a list which themselves contain commas, if it is necessary to avoid confusion, e.g.

The party consisted of three teachers, who had already climbed with the leader; seven pupils; and two parents.

---

senator noun a member of a senate.

send verb (sends, sending, sent) **1** cause to go or be taken to a destination. **2** cause to move sharply or quickly. **3** put someone into a specified state. □ **send down** Brit. **1** expel a student from a university. **2** informal sentence someone to imprisonment. **send for 1** order someone to come. **2** order by post. **send-off** a gathering to say goodbye to someone who is leaving. **send up** informal ridicule by imitating.

senile adjective suffering a loss of mental faculties because of old age. ∎ **senility** noun.

senior adjective **1** having to do with older people. **2** Brit. having to do with schoolchildren above the age of about eleven. **3** US of the final year at a university or high school. **4** (after a name) referring to the elder of two with the same name in a family. **5** high or higher in status. noun **1** a person who is a specified number of years older than someone else: *she was two years his senior.* **2** a student at a senior school. **3** (in sport) a competitor of above a certain age or of the highest status. □ **senior citizen** an old-age pensioner. ∎ **seniority** noun.

senna noun a laxative prepared from the dried pods of a tree.

sensation noun **1** a feeling resulting from something that happens to or comes into contact with the body. **2** the ability to have such feelings. **3** a vague awareness or impression. **4** a widespread reaction of interest and excitement, or a person or thing that causes it.

sensational adjective **1** causing or trying to cause great public interest and excitement. **2** informal very impressive or attractive. ∎ **sensationalism** noun **sensationalist** noun & adjective **sensationally** adverb.

sensationalize or **sensationalise** verb (sensationalizes, sensationalizing, sensationalized) present in a sensational way.

sense noun **1** any of the powers of sight, smell, hearing, taste, and touch, which allow the body to perceive things. **2** a feeling that something is the case. **3** (**sense of**) awareness of or sensitivity to. **4** a sensible and practical attitude or behaviour. **5** a meaning of a word or expression. verb (senses, sensing, sensed) **1** perceive by a sense or senses. **2** be vaguely aware of. □ **make sense** be understandable or sensible.

senseless adjective **1** unconscious or unable to feel. **2** lacking meaning, purpose, or common sense.

sensibility noun (plural **sensibilities**) **1** the ability to experience and understand emotion or art; sensitivity. **2** (**sensibilities**) the degree to which a person can be offended or shocked.

sensible adjective **1** having or showing common sense. **2** practical rather

GRAMMAR

Sentence

A sentence is the basic unit of language and expresses a complete thought. There are three types of sentence, each starting with a capital letter, and each ending with a full stop, a question mark, or an exclamation mark:

- Statement: *You're happy.*
- Question: *Is it raining?*
- Exclamation: *I wouldn't have believed it!*

A sentence normally contains a subject and a verb, but may not, e.g.

What a mess!
Where?
In the sink.

---

than decorative. ■ **sensibly** adverb.

sensitive adjective **1** quick to detect or be affected by slight changes. **2** appreciating the feelings of others. **3** easily offended or upset. **4** secret or controversial. ■ **sensitively** adverb.

sensitivity noun (plural **sensitivities**) **1** the quality of being sensitive. **2** (**sensitivities**) a person's feelings which might be offended or hurt.

sensitize or **sensitise** verb (**sensitizes, sensitizing, sensitized**) make sensitive or aware.

sensor noun a device which detects or measures a physical property.

sensory adjective relating to sensation or the senses.

sensual adjective relating to the physical senses as a source of pleasure. ■ **sensuality** noun **sensually** adverb.

sensuous adjective **1** relating to or affecting the senses rather than the intellect. **2** attractive or pleasing physically. ■ **sensuously** adverb.

sent past and past participle of **SEND**.

sentence noun **1** a set of words that is complete in itself, conveying a statement, question, exclamation, or command. **2** the punishment given to someone found guilty by a court. verb (**sentences, sentencing, sentenced**) say officially in a law court that an offender is to receive a particular punishment.

sententious /sen-**ten**-shuhss/ adjective given to making pompous comments on moral issues.

sentient adjective able to perceive or feel things.

sentiment noun **1** an opinion or feeling. **2** exaggerated and self-indulgent feelings of tenderness, sadness, or nostalgia.

sentimental adjective showing or having exaggerated and self-indulgent feelings of tenderness, sadness, or nostalgia. ■ **sentimentality** noun **sentimentally** adverb.

sentinel noun a guard whose job is to stand and keep watch.

sentry noun (plural **sentries**) a soldier whose job is to guard or control access to a place.

sepal /**sep**-uhl/ noun each of the leaf-like parts of a flower that surround the petals.

separable adjective able to be separated or treated separately.

separate adjective /**sep**-uh-ruht/ **1** forming a unit by itself. **2** different; distinct. verb /**sep**-uh-rayt/ (**separates, separating, separated**) **1** move or come apart. **2** stop living together as a couple. **3** divide into distinct parts. **4** form a distinction or boundary between. ■ **separately** adverb.

 the middle is *-par-*, not *-per-*: se**par**ate.

separation noun **1** the action of separating. **2** the state in which a husband and wife remain married but live apart.

separatism noun separation of a group of people from a larger group. ■ **separatist** noun & adjective.

sepia noun a reddish-brown colour.

sepoy /**see**-poy/ noun historical an Indian soldier who served the British.

sepsis noun the infection of body tissues with harmful bacteria.

September noun the ninth month of the year.

septet noun a group of seven people playing music or singing together.

septic adjective (of a wound or a part of the body) infected with bacteria. □ **septic tank** an underground tank in which sewage is allowed to decompose before draining slowly into the soil.

septicaemia /sep-ti-**see**-mi-uh/ (US spelling **septicemia**) noun blood poisoning caused by bacteria.

septuagenarian noun a person who is between 70 and 79 years old.

septum noun (plural **septa**) a wall between two parts of the body, especially the nostrils.

septuple adjective consisting of seven parts or elements.

septuplet noun each of seven children born at one birth.

sepulchral adjective **1** having to do with a tomb or burial. **2** gloomy.

sepulchre /**sep**-uhl-ker/ (US spelling **sepulcher**) noun a stone tomb for a dead person.

sequel noun **1** a book, film, or programme that continues the story of an earlier one. **2** something that takes place after or as a result of an earlier event.

sequence noun **1** a particular order in which things follow each other. **2** a set of things that follow each other in a particular order. verb (**sequences, sequencing, sequenced**) arrange in a sequence.

sequential adjective following in a logical order or sequence. ■ **sequen-**

tially adverb.

sequester verb (**sequesters, sequestering, sequestered**) **1** isolate or hide away. **2** sequestrate.

sequestrate verb (**sequestrates, sequestrating, sequestrated**) take legal possession of assets until a debt has been paid. ■ **sequestration** noun.

sequin noun a small, shiny disc sewn on to clothing for decoration. ■ **sequinned** (or **sequined**) adjective.

sequoia noun a redwood tree.

seraglio /si-**rah**-li-oh/ noun (plural **seraglios**) **1** the women's apartments in a Muslim palace. **2** a harem.

seraph noun (plural **seraphim** or **seraphs**) an angelic being associated with light and purity. ■ **seraphic** adjective.

serenade noun a piece of music sung or played by a man for a woman he loves, outdoors and at night. verb (**serenades, serenading, serenaded**) perform a serenade for.

serendipity noun the occurrence of something by chance in a fortunate way. ■ **serendipitous** adjective.

serene adjective calm and peaceful. ■ **serenely** adverb **serenity** noun.

serf noun (in the feudal system) an agricultural labourer who was tied to working on a particular estate. ■ **serfdom** noun.

serge noun a hard-wearing woollen fabric.

sergeant noun **1** the rank of officer in the army or air force above corporal. **2** Brit. a police officer just below the rank of inspector. □ **sergeant major** an officer in the British army who assists with administrative duties.

serial adjective **1** arranged in a series. **2** repeatedly committing the same offence or doing the same thing: *a serial killer.* noun a story published or broadcast in regular instalments. □ **serial number** an identification number given to a manufactured item.

serialize or **serialise** verb (**serializes, serializing, serialized**) **1** publish or broadcast a story in regular

instalments. **2** arrange in a series.
■ **serialization** noun.

series noun (plural **series**) **1** a number of related things coming one after another. **2** a sequence of related television or radio programmes.

serious adjective **1** demanding careful consideration or action. **2** solemn or thoughtful. **3** sincere and in earnest. **4** dangerous or severe: *serious injury.* ■ **seriously** adverb **seriousness** noun.

sermon noun a talk on a religious or moral subject, especially one given during a church service.

serpent noun literary a large snake.

serpentine adjective winding or twisting like a snake.

serrated adjective having a jagged edge like the teeth of a saw.

serration noun a tooth or point of a serrated edge.

serried adjective (of rows of people or things) standing close together.

serum noun (plural **sera** or **serums**) a thin liquid which separates out when blood solidifies.

servant noun a person employed to perform domestic duties in a household or for a person.

serve verb (**serves**, **serving**, **served**) **1** perform duties or services for. **2** be employed as a member of the armed forces. **3** spend a period in a job or in prison. **4** present food or drink to. **5** (of food or drink) be enough for. **6** attend to a customer in a shop. **7** fulfil a purpose. **8** treat in a specified way. **9** (in tennis, badminton, etc.) hit the ball or shuttlecock to begin play for each point of a game. noun an act of serving in tennis, badminton, etc. □ **serve someone right** be someone's deserved punishment.

server noun **1** a person or thing that serves. **2** a computer or program which controls or supplies information to a network of computers.

service noun **1** the action of serving. **2** a period of employment with an organization. **3** an act of assistance. **4** a ceremony of religious worship. **5** a system supplying a public need such as water or electricity. **6** a department or organization run by the state. **7** (**the services**) the armed forces. **8** a set of matching crockery. **9** (in tennis, badminton, etc.) a serve. **10** a routine inspection and maintenance of a vehicle or machine. **11** (**services** or **service area**) a roadside area with toilets, shop, cafe, etc. for motorists. verb (**services**, **servicing**, **serviced**) **1** perform routine maintenance or repair work on. **2** provide a service or services for. **3** pay interest on a debt. □ **in service** employed as a servant. **service industry** a business that provides a service rather than manufacturing things. **service station** a garage selling petrol, oil, etc.

serviceable adjective **1** in working order. **2** useful and hard-wearing.

serviceman or **servicewoman** noun a member of the armed forces.

serviette noun Brit. a table napkin.

servile adjective **1** excessively willing to serve or please others. **2** of a slave or slaves. ■ **servility** noun.

serving noun a quantity of food for one person.

servitude noun the state of being a slave, or of being completely subject to someone more powerful.

servo noun a device in a vehicle which converts a force into a larger force.

sesame /sess-uh-mi/ noun a tropical plant grown for its oil-rich seeds.

session noun **1** a period devoted to a particular activity. **2** a meeting of a council, court, etc., or the period when such meetings are held.

set verb (**sets**, **setting**, **set**) **1** put in a specified place or position. **2** bring into a specified state. **3** give someone a task. **4** decide on or fix a time or limit. **5** establish as an example or record. **6** adjust a device as required. **7** prepare a table for a meal. **8** harden into a solid, semi-solid, or fixed state. **9** arrange damp hair into the required style. **10** put a broken or dislocated bone into the right position for healing. **11** (of the sun, moon, etc.)

appear to move towards and below the earth's horizon. **noun 1** a number of things or people grouped together. **2** the way in which something is set. **3** a radio or television receiver. **4** (in tennis and similar games) a group of games counting as a unit towards a match. **5** a collection of scenery, furniture, etc., used for a scene in a play or film. **adjective 1** fixed or arranged in advance. **2** firmly fixed and unchanging. **3** having a conventional or fixed wording. **4** ready, prepared, or likely to do something. □ **set about** start doing. **set aside 1** temporarily stop using land for growing crops. **2** annul a legal decision. **set off 1** begin a journey. **2** make a bomb or alarm go off. **set on** attack violently. **set out 1** begin a journey. **2** aim or intend to do something. **3** arrange or display. **set piece 1** a formal or elaborate arrangement in a novel, film, etc. **2** a carefully organized move in a team game. **set square** a triangular plate with a right angle, for drawing lines and angles. **set up 1** place or erect in position. **2** establish a business, institution, etc. **3** informal make an innocent person appear guilty of something.

setback noun a difficulty or problem that holds back progress.

sett noun the earth of a badger.

settee noun a long upholstered seat for more than one person.

setter noun a breed of dog trained to stand rigid when it scents game.

setting noun 1 the way or place in which something is set. **2** the metal in which a precious stone or gem is fixed to form a piece of jewellery. **3** a piece of music composed for particular words. **4** (also **place setting**) a complete set of crockery and cutlery for one person at a meal.

settle¹ verb (**settles, settling, settled**) **1** resolve a dispute or difficulty. **2** make or become calmer. **3** (often **settle down**) start to live in a more steady or secure way. **4** make your home in a new place. **5** sit or rest comfortably or securely. **6** (often **settle in**) begin to feel comfortable in a

new situation. **7** pay a debt. **8** (**settle for**) accept after negotiation. ■ **settler** noun.

settle² noun a wooden bench with a high back and arms.

settlement noun 1 the process of settling. **2** an agreement that is intended to settle a dispute. **3** a place where people establish a community.

seven cardinal number one more than six; 7. (Roman numeral: **vii** or **VII**.)

seventeen cardinal number one more than sixteen; 17. (Roman numeral: **xvii** or **XVII**.) ■ **seventeenth** adjective & noun.

seventh ordinal number 1 at number seven in a sequence; 7th. **2** (**a seventh** or **one seventh**) each of seven equal parts of something.

seventy cardinal number (plural **seventies**) ten less than eighty; 70. (Roman numeral: **lxx** or **LXX**.) ■ **seventieth** ordinal number.

sever verb (**severs, severing, severed**) **1** cut off, or cut into two pieces. **2** put an end to a connection or relationship.

several determiner & pronoun more than two but not many. **adjective** separate or respective. ■ **severally** adverb.

severance noun 1 the ending of a connection, relationship, or period of employment. **2** the state of being separated or cut off.

severe adjective 1 (of something bad or difficult) very great. **2** strict or harsh. **3** very plain in style or appearance. ■ **severely** adverb **severity** noun.

sew verb (**sews, sewing, sewed**; past participle **sewn** or **sewed**) join or repair by making stitches with a needle and thread or a sewing machine. □ **sewing machine** a machine with a mechanically driven needle for sewing.

sewage /soo-ij/ **noun** human waste and water from drains that are carried away in sewers.

sewer /soo-er/ **noun** an underground channel for human waste and water from drains. ■ **sewerage** noun.

sex noun 1 either of the two main categories (male and female) into which humans and most other living things are divided. **2** the fact of being male or female. **3** the group of all members of either sex. **4** sexual intercourse. □ **sex appeal** the quality of being attractive in a sexual way. **sex symbol** a celebrity famous for being sexually attractive.

sexagenarian noun a person between 60 and 69 years old.

sexism noun prejudice or discrimination on the basis of sex. ■ **sexist** adjective & noun.

sexless adjective **1** not sexually attractive or active. **2** neither male nor female.

sextant noun an instrument for measuring angles and distances, used in navigation and surveying.

sextet noun **1** a group of six musicians. **2** a composition for a sextet.

sexton noun a person who looks after a church and churchyard.

sextuple adjective **1** made up of six parts or elements. **2** six times as much or as many.

sextuplet noun each of six children born at one birth.

sexual adjective **1** relating to sex, or to physical attraction or contact between individuals. **2** connected with the state of being male or female. **3** (of reproduction) involving the fusion of male and female cells. □ **sexual harassment** the making of unwanted sexual advances or remarks to someone, especially at work. **sexual intercourse** sexual contact in which the man inserts his erect penis into the woman's vagina. ■ **sexually** adverb.

sexuality noun (plural **sexualities**) **1** capacity for sexual feelings. **2** a person's sexual preference.

sexy adjective (**sexier**, **sexiest**) **1** sexually attractive or exciting. **2** sexually aroused. **3** informal exciting and interesting. ■ **sexily** adverb **sexiness** noun.

shabby adjective (**shabbier**, **shabbiest**) **1** worn out or scruffy. **2** mean and unfair. ■ **shabbily** adverb.

shack noun a roughly built hut or cabin. verb (**shack up with**) informal live

with someone as a lover.

shackle noun (**shackles**) **1** rings connected by a chain, used to fasten a prisoner's wrists or ankles together. **2** restraints or obstructions. verb (**shackles, shackling, shackled**) **1** chain with shackles. **2** restrain; limit.

shade noun **1** relative darkness and coolness caused by shelter from direct sunlight. **2** a colour, especially with regard to how light or dark it is. **3** a variety. **4** a slight amount. **5** (**shades**) informal sunglasses. **6** literary a ghost. verb (**shades, shading, shaded**) **1** screen from direct light. **2** cover or lessen the light of. **3** represent a darker area with pencil or a block of colour. **4** change gradually into something else.

shadow noun **1** a dark area or shape produced by an object coming between light rays and a surface. **2** partial or complete darkness. **3** sadness or gloom. **4** the slightest trace. **5** a weak or less good version. **6** a person who constantly accompanies or secretly follows another. verb **1** cast a shadow over. **2** follow and observe secretly. □ **shadow-boxing** boxing against an imaginary opponent as a form of training. ■ **shadowy** adjective.

shady adjective (**shadier**, **shadiest**) **1** giving, or situated in, shade. **2** informal of doubtful honesty or legality.

shaft noun **1** the long, narrow handle of a tool or club, body of a spear or arrow, etc. **2** a ray of light or bolt of lightning. **3** a narrow vertical passage giving access to a mine, accommodating a lift, etc. **4** each of the pair of poles between which a horse is harnessed to a vehicle. **5** a rotating rod for transmitting mechanical power in a machine. verb informal treat harshly or unfairly.

shag[1] noun coarse tobacco. adjective (of pile on a carpet) long and rough.

shag[2] noun a cormorant (seabird) with greenish-black plumage.

shag[3] Brit. vulgar verb (**shags, shagging, shagged**) have sexual intercourse with. **noun** an act of sexual intercourse.

shaggy adjective (**shaggier, shaggiest**) **1** (of hair or fur) long, thick, and untidy. **2** having shaggy hair or fur.

shah noun (in the past) the title of the king of Iran.

shake verb (**shakes, shaking, shook**; past participle **shaken**) **1** move quickly and jerkily up and down or to and fro. **2** tremble. **3** shock or disturb. **4** put an end to. **noun 1** an act of shaking. **2** informal a milkshake. □ **shake hands (with someone)** clasp someone's right hand in your own when meeting or leaving them, or as a sign of agreement. **shake on it** informal confirm an agreement by shaking hands. **shake up 1** stir someone into action. **2** make major changes to an institution or system. ■ **shaker** noun.

Shakespearean or **Shakespearian** adjective having to do with the English dramatist William Shakespeare or his works.

shaky adjective (**shakier, shakiest**) **1** shaking; unsteady. **2** not safe or certain. ■ **shakily** adverb.

shale noun soft rock formed from compressed mud or clay.

shall modal verb (3rd singular present **shall**) **1** used with *I* and *we* to express the future tense. **2** expressing a strong statement, intention, or order. **3** Brit. used in questions to make offers or suggestions: *shall we go?*

> ℹ️ the traditional rule is that you should use **shall** when forming the future tense with I and we (*I shall be late*) and **will** with you, he, she, it, and they (*he will not be there*).

shallot /shuh-lot/ noun a vegetable resembling a small onion.

shallow adjective **1** having a short distance between the top and the bottom; not deep. **2** not thinking or thought out seriously. **noun** (**shallows**) a shallow area of water. ■ **shallowly** adverb.

sham noun **1** a thing that is not what it appears to be or is not as good as it

seems. **2** a person who pretends to be something they are not. **adjective** not genuine; false. **verb** (**shams, shamming, shammed**) pretend.

shaman /shay-muhn/ noun (plural **shamans**) (in some societies) a person believed to be able to contact good and evil spirits. ■ **shamanic** adjective **shamanism** noun.

shamble verb (**shambles, shambling, shambled**) walk in a slow, shuffling, awkward way.

shambles noun informal a state of complete disorder.

shambolic adjective Brit. informal very disorganized.

shame noun **1** the feeling you have of embarrassment or distress when you know you have done something wrong or foolish. **2** loss of respect; dishonour. **3** a cause of shame. **4** a cause for regret or disappointment. **verb** (**shames, shaming, shamed**) make someone feel shame. □ **put to shame** be much better than.

shamefaced adjective showing shame.

shameful adjective causing a feeling of shame. ■ **shamefully** adverb.

shameless adjective showing no shame. ■ **shamelessly** adverb.

shammy noun (plural **shammies**) informal chamois leather.

shampoo noun **1** a liquid soap for washing the hair. **2** a similar substance for cleaning a carpet, car, etc. **3** an act of washing with shampoo. **verb** (**shampoos, shampooing, shampooed**) wash or clean with shampoo.

shamrock noun a clover-like plant with three leaves on each stem, the national emblem of Ireland.

shandy noun (plural **shandies**) beer mixed with lemonade or ginger beer.

shanghai /shang-hy/ verb (**shanghais, shanghaiing, shanghaied**) informal force or trick into doing something.

shank noun **1** the lower part of the leg. **2** the shaft of a tool. □ **Shanks's pony** your own legs as a means of transport.

shan't short form shall not.

shantung noun a type of silk fabric with a coarse surface.

shanty[1] noun (plural **shanties**) a small roughly built hut. □ **shanty town** a settlement in or near a town where poor people live in shanties.

shanty[2] noun (plural **shanties**) a song with alternating solo and chorus, sung by sailors when working.

shape noun **1** the form of something produced by its outline. **2** a piece of material, paper, etc. cut in a particular form. **3** a particular condition or state. **4** well defined structure or arrangement. verb (**shapes**, **shaping**, **shaped**) **1** give a shape to. **2** have a big influence on. □ **shape up 1** develop in a particular way. **2** improve your fitness, behaviour, etc. ■ **shaper** noun.

shapeless adjective lacking a definite or attractive shape.

shapely adjective having an attractive shape.

shard noun a sharp piece of broken pottery, glass, etc.

share noun **1** a part of a larger amount which is divided among or contributed to by a number of people. **2** any of the equal parts into which a company's wealth is divided, which can be bought by people in return for a proportion of the profits. **3** an amount thought to be normal or acceptable. verb (**shares**, **sharing**, **shared**) **1** have or give a share of. **2** have or use jointly with others. **3** (**share in**) participate in. **4** tell someone about. ■ **sharer** noun.

shareholder noun an owner of shares in a company.

shark[1] noun a large and sometimes aggressive sea fish with a triangular fin on its back.

shark[2] noun informal a person who dishonestly obtains money from others.

sharp adjective **1** having a cutting or piercing edge or point. **2** tapering to a point or edge. **3** sudden and noticeable. **4** clear and definite. **5** producing a sudden, piercing feeling. **6** quick to understand, notice, or respond. **7** quick to take advantage. **8** (of a taste or smell) intense and piercing. **9** (of musical sound) above true or normal pitch. **10** (of a note or key) higher by a semitone than a specified note or key. adverb **1** precisely. **2** suddenly or abruptly. noun a musical note raised a semitone above natural pitch, shown by the sign ♯. □ **sharp practice** dishonest business dealings. ■ **sharply** adverb **sharpness** noun.

sharpen verb make or become sharp. ■ **sharpener** noun.

sharpish informal adjective fairly sharp. adverb Brit. quickly.

sharpshooter noun a person skilled in shooting.

shat past and past participle of SHIT.

shatter verb (**shatters**, **shattering**, **shattered**) **1** break suddenly and violently into pieces. **2** damage or destroy. **3** upset greatly. **4** (**shattered**) informal completely exhausted.

shave verb (**shaves**, **shaving**, **shaved**) **1** remove hair by cutting it off close to the skin with a razor. **2** cut a thin slice or slices from something. **3** reduce something by a small amount. noun an act of shaving.

shaven adjective shaved.

shaver noun an electric razor.

shaving noun a thin strip cut off a surface.

shawl noun a large piece of fabric worn by women over the shoulders or head or wrapped round a baby.

she pronoun **1** used to refer to a female person or animal previously mentioned or easily identified. **2** used to refer to a ship, country, or other thing thought of as female.

sheaf noun (plural **sheaves**) **1** a bundle of grain stalks tied together after reaping. **2** a bundle of papers.

shear verb (**shears**, **shearing**, **sheared**; past participle **shorn** or **sheared**) **1** cut the wool off a sheep. **2** cut off something such as wool or grass with shears. **3** (**be shorn of**) have something taken away from you.

4 (**shear off**) tear or break off under pressure. ■ **shearer** noun.

shears plural noun a cutting implement like very large scissors.

sheath noun (plural **sheaths**) **1** a cover for the blade of a knife or sword. **2** a condom. **3** a close-fitting covering. **4** a close-fitting dress.

sheathe verb (**sheathes**, **sheathing**, **sheathed**) **1** put a knife or sword into a sheath. **2** encase something in a close-fitting or protective covering.

shebang /shi-**bang**/ noun (**the whole shebang**) informal the whole thing.

shed¹ noun a simple building used for storage.

shed² verb (**sheds**, **shedding**, **shed**) **1** allow leaves, hair, skin, etc. to fall off naturally. **2** get rid of. **3** take off clothes. **4** give off light. **5** accidentally drop or spill. **6** allow something to spill out. □ **shed tears** cry.

she'd short form she had or she would.

sheen noun a soft shine on a surface.

sheep noun (plural **sheep**) an animal with a thick woolly coat, kept in flocks for its wool or meat. □ **sheep dip** a liquid in which sheep are dipped to clean and disinfect their wool.

sheepdog noun a breed of dog trained to guard and herd sheep.

sheepish adjective feeling embarrassed from shame or shyness. ■ **sheepishly** adverb.

sheepskin noun a sheep's skin with the wool on.

sheer¹ adjective **1** nothing but; absolute. **2** (of a cliff or wall) vertical or almost vertical. **3** (of fabric) very thin. adverb vertically.

sheer² verb (**sheers**, **sheering**, **sheered**) **1** (especially of a boat) change course quickly. **2** move away from an unpleasant topic.

sheet¹ noun **1** a large rectangular piece of cotton or other fabric, used on a bed to lie on or under. **2** a broad flat piece of metal or glass. **3** a rectangular piece of paper. **4** a wide expanse or moving mass of water, flames, etc. □ **sheet music** music printed on loose sheets of paper.

sheet² noun a rope attached to the lower corner of a sail.

sheikh or **sheik** /shayk/ noun a Muslim or Arab leader.

sheila noun Austral./NZ informal a girl or woman.

shekel noun the basic unit of money of modern Israel.

shelf noun (plural **shelves**) **1** a flat length of wood or other rigid material, fixed horizontally and used to display or store things. **2** a ledge of rock. □ **off the shelf** taken from existing supplies, not made to order. **on the shelf** (of a woman) past an age when she might expect to be married. **shelf life** the length of time for which an item to be sold can be stored.

shell noun **1** the hard protective outer case of an animal such as a shellfish or turtle. **2** the outer covering of an egg, nut kernel, or seed. **3** a metal case filled with explosive, to be fired from a large gun. **4** a hollow case. **5** an outer structure or framework. verb **1** fire explosive shells at. **2** remove the shell or pod from. **3** (**shell out**) informal pay an amount of money. □ **shell shock** a mental condition resembling a state of shock, that can affect soldiers who have been in battle for a long time. **shell suit** an outfit consisting of a top and trousers with a soft lining and shiny outer layer.

she'll short form she shall or she will.

shellfish noun a water animal that has a shell and that can be eaten, such as a crab or oyster.

shelter noun **1** a place giving protection from bad weather or danger. **2** a place providing food and accommodation for the homeless. **3** protection from danger or bad weather. verb (**shelters**, **sheltering**, **sheltered**) **1** provide with shelter. **2** find protection or take cover. **3** (**sheltered**) protected from the more unpleasant aspects of life. **4** (**sheltered**) Brit. (of accommodation) designed for elderly or disabled people, and staffed by a warden.

shelve **verb** (**shelves**, **shelving**, **shelved**) **1** place something on a shelf. **2** decide not to continue with a plan for the time being. **3** (of ground) slope downwards.

shelves plural of **SHELF**.

shenanigans **plural noun** informal mischievous behaviour.

shepherd **noun** a person who looks after sheep. **verb 1** look after sheep. **2** guide or direct. □ **shepherd's pie** a dish of minced meat under a layer of mashed potato. ▪ **shepherdess** noun.

sherbet **noun 1** Brit. a sweet fizzing powder eaten alone or made into a drink. **2** (in Arab countries) a drink of sweet diluted fruit juices.

sheriff **noun 1** (also **high sheriff**) (in England and Wales) the chief executive officer in a county, working on behalf of a king or queen. **2** (in Scotland) a judge. **3** (in the US) an elected officer in a county, responsible for keeping the peace.

Sherpa **noun** (plural **Sherpa** or **Sherpas**) a member of a Himalayan people living on the borders of Nepal and Tibet.

sherry **noun** (plural **sherries**) a strong wine from southern Spain.

she's **short form** she is or she has.

Shetland pony **noun** a small breed of pony with a rough coat.

shiatsu /shi-at-soo/ **noun** a medical treatment from Japan in which pressure is applied with the hands to points on the body.

shibboleth /**shib**-buh-leth/ **noun** a long-standing belief or principle held by a group of people.

shied past and past participle of **SHY**[2].

shield **noun 1** a broad piece of armour held for protection against blows or missiles. **2** a sporting trophy consisting of an engraved metal plate mounted on a piece of wood. **3** a drawing or model of a shield used for displaying a coat of arms. **4** a person or thing that acts as a protective barrier or screen. **verb** protect or hide.

shift **verb 1** move or change from one position to another. **2** transfer blame or responsibility to someone else. **3** Brit. informal move quickly. **noun 1** a slight change in position or direction. **2** a period of time worked by someone who starts work as another finishes. **3** a straight dress without a fitted waist. **4** a key used to switch between two sets of characters or functions on a keyboard.

shiftless **adjective** lazy and lacking ambition.

shifty **adjective** informal seeming dishonest or untrustworthy.

shilling **noun 1** a former British coin worth one twentieth of a pound or twelve pence. **2** the basic unit of money of Kenya, Tanzania, and Uganda.

shilly-shally **verb** (**shilly-shallies**, **shilly-shallying**, **shilly-shallied**) be unable to make up your mind.

shimmer **verb** (**shimmers**, **shimmering**, **shimmered**) shine with a soft wavering light. **noun** a soft wavering light or shine. ▪ **shimmery** adjective.

shimmy **verb** (**shimmies**, **shimmying**, **shimmied**) move swiftly and smoothly.

shin **noun** the front of the leg below the knee. **verb** (**shins**, **shinning**, **shinned**) (**shin up** or **down**) climb quickly up or down by gripping with your arms and legs.

shindig **noun** informal a lively party.

shine **verb** (**shines**, **shining**, past and past participle **shone** or **shined**) **1** give out or reflect light. **2** direct a torch or other light somewhere. **3** (of a person's eyes) be bright with an emotion. **4** be very good at something. **5** (past and past participle **shined**) polish. **noun** a quality of brightness. □ **take a shine to** informal develop a liking for.

shiner **noun** informal a black eye.

shingle[1] **noun** a mass of small rounded pebbles on a seashore.

shingle[2] **noun** a wooden tile used on walls or roofs. ▪ **shingled** adjective.

shingles **noun** a disease with painful

blisters forming along the path of a nerve or nerves.

shiny adjective (**shinier**, **shiniest**) reflecting light.

ship noun a large boat for transporting people or goods by sea. verb (**ships**, **shipping**, **shipped**) **1** transport goods on a ship or by other means. **2** (of a boat) take in water over the side.

shipbuilder noun a person or company that designs and builds ships. ∎ **shipbuilding** noun.

shipment noun **1** the action of transporting goods. **2** an amount of goods shipped.

shipping noun **1** ships as a whole. **2** the transport of goods.

shipshape adjective orderly and neat.

shipwreck noun **1** the sinking or breaking up of a ship at sea. **2** a ship that has been lost or destroyed at sea. verb (**be shipwrecked**) suffer a shipwreck.

shipyard noun a place where ships are built and repaired.

shire noun **1** Brit. a county in England. **2** (the Shires) rural areas of England regarded as strongholds of traditional country life. □ **shire horse** a heavy, powerful breed of horse.

shirk verb avoid work or a duty. ∎ **shirker** noun.

shirred adjective gathered by means of threads in parallel rows.

shirt noun a garment for the upper body, with a collar and sleeves and buttons down the front.

shirtsleeves plural noun (**in your shirtsleeves**) wearing a shirt without a jacket.

shirty adjective Brit. informal tetchy.

shish kebab noun a dish of pieces of meat and vegetables cooked and served on skewers.

shit vulgar verb (**shits**, **shitting**, **shitted** or **shit** or **shat**) pass faeces from the body. noun **1** faeces. **2** rubbish; nonsense. **3** an unpleasant person. ∎ **shitty** adjective.

shiver verb (**shivers**, **shivering**, **shivered**) shake slightly from fear, cold, or excitement. noun a trembling movement. ∎ **shivery** adjective.

shoal[1] noun a large number of fish swimming together.

shoal[2] noun **1** an area of shallow water. **2** a submerged sandbank that can be seen at low tide.

shock[1] noun **1** a sudden upsetting or surprising event or experience. **2** an unpleasant feeling of sudden surprise and distress. **3** a serious medical condition associated with a fall in blood pressure, caused by loss of blood, severe burns, etc. **4** a violent shaking movement caused by an impact, explosion, or earthquake. **5** an electric shock. verb **1** greatly surprise and upset. **2** make someone feel outraged or disgusted. □ **shock absorber** a device for absorbing jolts and vibrations on a vehicle. **shocking pink** a very bright shade of pink. **shock troops** troops trained to carry out sudden attacks. **shock wave** a moving wave of very high pressure caused by an explosion or by something travelling faster than sound.

shock[2] noun an untidy or thick mass of hair.

shocking adjective **1** causing shock or disgust. **2** Brit. informal very bad. ∎ **shocker** noun **shockingly** adverb.

shoddy adjective **1** badly made or done. **2** dishonest or immoral.

shoe noun **1** a covering for the foot with a stiff sole. **2** a horseshoe. verb (**shoes**, **shoeing**, **shod**) **1** fit a horse with a shoe or shoes. **2** (**be shod**) be wearing shoes of a particular kind. □ **shoe tree** a shaped block put into a shoe when it is not being worn, to keep it in shape.

shoehorn noun a curved piece of metal or plastic, used for easing your heel into a shoe. verb force into a tight space.

shoelace noun a cord passed through holes or hooks on opposite sides of the opening in a shoe to fasten it.

shoestring noun informal (**on a shoe-**

string) with only a very small amount of money.

shogun noun (in the past, in Japan) a hereditary leader of the army.

shone past and past participle of **SHINE**.

shook past of **SHAKE**.

shoot verb (**shoots, shooting, shot**) **1** kill or wound someone with a bullet, arrow, etc. **2** fire a gun. **3** move suddenly and rapidly. **4** direct a glance, question, or remark at someone. **5** (in sport) kick, hit, or throw the ball in an attempt to score a goal. **6** photograph or film a scene or film. **7** (**shooting**) (of a pain) sudden and piercing. **8** (of a boat) sweep swiftly down rapids. **9** move a bolt to fasten a door. **10** send out buds or shoots. **11** (**shoot up**) informal inject yourself with a narcotic drug. noun **1** a new part growing from a plant. **2** an occasion of taking photographs or making a film. **3** an occasion when game is shot for sport. □ **shooting star** a small rapidly moving meteor that burns up on entering the earth's atmosphere. **shooting stick** a walking stick with a handle that unfolds to form a seat.

shooter noun **1** a person who uses a gun. **2** informal a gun.

shop noun **1** a building or part of a building where goods are sold. **2** a place where things are manufactured or repaired; a workshop. verb (**shops, shopping, shopped**) **1** go to a shop or shops to buy goods. **2** (**shop around**) look for the best available price or rate for something. **3** Brit. informal inform on. □ **shop floor** Brit. the area in a factory where things are made or put together by the workers. **shop-soiled** Brit. (of an article) dirty or damaged from being displayed or handled in a shop. **shop steward** Brit. a person elected by workers in a factory to represent them in dealings with the management. **talk shop** discuss work matters with a colleague when you are not at work. ■ **shopper** noun.

shopkeeper noun the owner and manager of a shop.

shoplifting noun the stealing of goods from a shop. ■ **shoplifter** noun.

shopping noun **1** the buying of goods from shops. **2** goods bought from shops. □ **shopping centre** a group of shops situated together.

shore¹ noun **1** the land along the edge of a sea or other stretch of water. **2** (**shores**) literary a foreign country or region. □ **on shore** on land.

shore² verb (**shores, shoring, shored**) (**shore up**) **1** hold up with a prop or beam. **2** support or strengthen.

shoreline noun the line along which a sea or other stretch of water meets the land.

shorn past participle of **SHEAR**.

short adjective **1** of a small length in space or time. **2** small in height. **3** smaller than is usual or expected. **4** (**short of** or **on**) not having enough of. **5** in scarce supply. **6** rude and abrupt. **7** (of odds in betting) reflecting a high level of probability. **8** (of pastry) containing a high proportion of fat to flour and therefore crumbly. adverb not as far as expected or required. noun Brit. informal a small drink of spirits. verb have a short circuit. □ **be caught short 1** be put at a disadvantage. **2** Brit. informal urgently need to go to the lavatory. **bring** (or **pull**) **up short** make someone stop abruptly. **short-change** cheat someone by giving them less than the correct change. **short circuit** a faulty connection in an electrical circuit in which the current flows along a shorter route than it should do. **short-circuit** cause a short circuit in. **short cut** a way of going somewhere or doing something that is quicker than usual. **short-handed** (or **short-staffed**) having fewer staff than you need or than is usual. **short-lived** lasting only a short time. **short shrift** abrupt and unsympathetic treatment. **short-sighted 1** unable to see things clearly unless they are close to your eyes. **2** not thinking carefully about the consequences of something. **short-tempered** losing your temper quickly.

stop short suddenly stop. ■ **shortness** noun.

shortage noun a lack of something needed.

shortbread or **shortcake** noun a rich, crumbly type of biscuit made with butter, flour, and sugar.

shortcoming noun a fault in someone's character or in a system.

shortcrust pastry noun Brit. crumbly pastry made with flour, fat, and a little water.

shorten verb make or become shorter.

shortening noun fat used for making pastry.

shortfall noun a situation in which something amounts to less than is required.

shorthand noun a way of writing very quickly when recording what someone is saying, by using abbreviations and symbols.

shortlist noun a list of selected candidates from which a final choice is made. verb put on a shortlist.

shortly adverb **1** in a short time; soon. **2** abruptly or sharply.

shorts plural noun short trousers that reach to the thighs or knees.

shot[1] noun **1** the firing of a gun, arrow, etc. **2** (in sport) a hit, stroke, or kick of the ball as an attempt to score. **3** informal an attempt. **4** a photograph. **5** a film sequence photographed continuously by one camera. **6** a person with a particular level of ability in shooting. **7** (also **lead shot**) tiny lead pellets used in a shotgun. **8** a heavy ball thrown in the sport of shot put. **9** the launch of a rocket. **10** informal a small drink of spirits. **11** informal an injection of a drug or vaccine. □ **like a shot** informal without hesitation. **a shot in the arm** informal a source of encouragement. **shot put** an athletic contest in which a very heavy round ball is thrown as far as possible.

shot[2] past and past participle of **SHOOT**. adjective woven with a warp and weft of different colours, giving a contrasting effect. □ **get** (or **be**) **shot of** Brit. informal get (or be) rid of. **shot through with** filled with a quality.

shotgun noun a gun for firing small bullets at short range. □ **shotgun wedding** informal a wedding arranged quickly because the bride is pregnant.

should modal verb (3rd singular **should**) **1** used to indicate what is right or ought to be done. **2** used to indicate what is probable. **3** formal used to state what would happen if something else was the case: *if you should change your mind, I'll be at the hotel.* **4** used with *I* and *we* to express a polite request, opinion, or hope.

shoulder noun the joint between the upper arm and the main part of the body. verb (**shoulders**, **shouldering**, **shouldered**) **1** carry on your shoulder. **2** take on a responsibility. **3** push aside with your shoulder. □ **shoulder blade** either of the triangular bones at the top of the back.

shouldn't short form should not.

shout verb **1** speak or call out very loudly. **2** (**shout down**) prevent someone from being heard by shouting. noun **1** a loud cry or call. **2** (**your shout**) Brit. informal your turn to buy a round of drinks.

shove verb (**shoves**, **shoving**, **shoved**) **1** push roughly. **2** place carelessly or roughly. **3** (**shove off**) informal go away. noun a strong push.

shovel noun a tool resembling a spade with a broad blade and upturned sides, used for moving earth, snow, etc. verb (**shovels**, **shovelling**, **shovelled**; US spelling **shovels**, **shoveling**, **shoveled**) **1** move earth, snow, etc. with a shovel. **2** (**shovel down** or **in**) informal eat food quickly and in large quantities.

show verb (**shows**, **showing**, **showed**; past participle **shown** or **showed**) **1** be or make visible. **2** offer for inspection or viewing. **3** present an image of. **4** lead or guide. **5** behave in a particular way towards someone. **6** be evidence of; prove. **7** make someone understand something by explaining it or doing it yourself. **8** (also **show up**) informal arrive for an appointment. **noun 1** a stage performance involving singing and dancing. **2** a light entertainment programme on television or radio. **3** an event or competition involving the public display of animals, plants, or products. **4** an impressive or pleasing sight. **5** a display of a quality or feeling. **6** a display intended to give a false impression. □ **show business** the world of theatre, films, television, and pop music as a profession or industry. **show off 1** try to impress other people by displaying your abilities or possessions. **2** display something that is a source of pride. **show-off** a person who tries to impress others by showing off. **show trial** a public trial held to influence or please people, rather than to ensure that justice is done. **show up 1** reveal as bad or faulty. **2** informal humiliate.

showbiz noun informal show business.

showcase noun 1 a glass case used for displaying articles. **2** an occasion for presenting something favourably.

showdown noun a final argument, fight, or test, to settle a dispute.

shower noun 1 a short period of rain or snow. **2** a large number of things that fall or arrive together. **3** a piece of equipment that creates a spray of water under which you stand to wash yourself. **4** an act of washing yourself in a shower. **verb** (**showers, showering, showered**) **1** fall or make things fall in a shower. **2** (**shower with**) give someone something in large quantities. **3** wash yourself in a shower. ■ **showery** adjective.

showgirl noun an actress who sings and dances in a musical or variety show.

showjumping noun the competitive sport of riding horses over a course of obstacles in an arena.

shown past participle of **SHOW**.

showpiece noun an outstanding example of its type.

showroom noun a room used to display cars, furniture, or other goods for sale.

showy adjective very bright or colourful and attracting a lot of attention.

shrank past of **SHRINK**.

shrapnel noun small metal fragments from an exploding shell or bomb.

shred noun 1 a strip of material that has been torn, cut, or scraped from something. **2** a very small amount. **verb** (**shreds, shredding, shredded**) tear or cut into shreds. ■ **shredder** noun.

shrew noun 1 a small mouse-like mammal with a long pointed snout. **2** a bad-tempered woman.

shrewd adjective having or showing good judgement. ■ **shrewdly** adverb **shrewdness** noun.

shrewish adjective (of a woman) bad-tempered or nagging.

shriek verb make a piercing cry. **noun** a piercing cry.

shrike noun a bird with a hooked bill, that impales its prey on thorns.

shrill adjective high-pitched and piercing. **verb** make a shrill noise. ■ **shrilly** adverb.

shrimp noun (plural **shrimp** or **shrimps**) a small edible shellfish.

shrine noun 1 a place connected with a holy person or event, where people go to pray. **2** a place containing a religious statue or object.

shrink verb (**shrinks, shrinking, shrank**; past participle **shrunk** or (especially as adjective) **shrunken**) **1** become or make smaller. **2** move back or away in fear or disgust. **3** (**shrink from**) be unwilling to do. **noun** informal a psychiatrist. □ **shrinking violet** informal a very shy person. **shrink-wrap** wrap in clinging plastic film. ■ **shrinkage** noun.

shrivel verb (**shrivels, shrivelling, shrivelled**; US spelling **shrivels, shriveling, shriveled**) wrinkle and shrink through loss of moisture.

shroud noun 1 a length of cloth in which a dead person is wrapped for burial. **2** a thing that closely surrounds or hides something. **3** (**shrouds**) a set of ropes supporting the mast of a sailing boat. **verb 1** wrap in a shroud. **2** cover or hide.

shrub noun a woody plant which is smaller than a tree and divided into separate stems from near the ground. ■ **shrubby** adjective.

shrubbery noun (plural **shrubberies**) an area planted with shrubs.

shrug verb (**shrugs**, **shrugging**, **shrugged**) **1** raise your shoulders slightly and briefly as a sign that you do not know or care about something. **2** (**shrug off**) treat as unimportant. noun an act of shrugging your shoulders.

shudder verb (**shudders**, **shuddering**, **shuddered**) tremble or shake violently. noun an act of shuddering.

shuffle verb (**shuffles**, **shuffling**, **shuffled**) **1** walk without lifting your feet completely from the ground. **2** move about restlessly while sitting or standing. **3** rearrange a pack of cards by sliding them over and under each other quickly. **4** rearrange people or things. noun an act of shuffling.

shun verb (**shuns**, **shunning**, **shunned**) avoid or reject.

shunt verb **1** push or pull a railway vehicle from one set of tracks to another. **2** move something around or along. **3** move someone to a less important position. ■ **shunter** noun.

shut verb (**shuts**, **shutting**, **shut**) **1** move something into position to block an opening. **2** (**shut in** or **out**) keep in or out by closing a door, gate, etc. **3** prevent access to a place or along a route. **4** Brit. (with reference to a shop or other business) stop operating for business. **5** close a book, curtains, etc. □ **shut down** stop opening for business, or stop working. **shut off** stop something from flowing or working. **shut up** informal stop talking.

shutter noun **1** each of a pair of hinged panels inside or outside a window that can be closed for security or to keep out the light. **2** a device that opens and closes to expose the film in a camera. verb (**shutters**, **shuttering**, **shuttered**) close the shutters of a window or building.

shuttle noun **1** a form of transport that travels regularly between two places. **2** (in weaving) a bobbin for carrying the weft thread across the warp. verb (**shuttles**, **shuttling**, **shuttled**) **1** travel regularly between places. **2** transport in a shuttle.

shuttlecock noun a light cone-shaped object that is struck with rackets in the game of badminton.

shy[1] adjective (**shyer**, **shyest**) **1** timid in the company of other people. **2** (**shy of**) informal short of. verb (**shies**, **shying**, **shied**) **1** (of a horse) turn aside in fright. **2** (**shy from**) avoid through lack of confidence. ■ **shyly** adverb.

shy[2] verb (**shies**, **shying**, **shied**) throw something at a target.

shyster noun informal a dishonest person, especially a lawyer.

SI abbreviation Système International, the international system of units of measurement.

Siamese adjective relating to Siam (the old name for Thailand). □ **Siamese cat** a breed of cat that has short pale fur with darker face, ears, feet, and tail. **Siamese twins** twins whose bodies are joined at birth.

sibilant adjective making a hissing sound. ■ **sibilance** noun.

sibling noun a brother or sister.

sibyl noun (in ancient Greece and Rome) a woman supposedly able to pass on messages from a god. ■ **sibylline** adjective.

sic adverb written exactly as it stands in the original.

sick adjective **1** physically or mentally ill. **2** wanting to vomit. **3** (**sick of**) bored by or annoyed about. **4** informal behaving in an abnormal or cruel way. **5** informal (of humour) dealing with unpleasant subjects in a way that is offensive. noun Brit. informal vomit. □ **be sick 1** be ill. **2** Brit. vomit. **sick leave** permission to be away from work because of illness.

sickbay noun a room set aside for sick people.

sickbed noun the bed of a person who is ill.

sicken verb **1** start to become ill. **2** disgust or shock.

sickle noun a tool for cutting corn, with a semicircular blade and a short handle.

sickly adjective (**sicklier, sickliest**) **1** often ill. **2** looking or seeming unhealthy. **3** (of flavour, colour, etc.) so bright or sweet as to cause sickness. **4** excessively sentimental.

sickness noun **1** the state of being ill. **2** a particular type of illness or disease. **3** nausea or vomiting.

side noun **1** a position to the left or right of an object, place, or central point. **2** either of the two halves into which something can be divided. **3** an upright or sloping surface of something that is not the top, bottom, front, or back. **4** each of the flat surfaces of a solid object, or either of the two surfaces of something flat and thin, e.g. paper. **5** each of the lines forming the boundary of a plane figure. **6** either of the two surfaces of a record or cassette tape. **7** a part near the edge of something. **8** a person or group against another in a dispute or contest. **9** a sports team. **10** a particular aspect. adjective additional or less important. verb (**sides, siding, sided**) (**side with** or **against**) support or oppose in a conflict or dispute. □ **side effect** a secondary effect of a drug. **side road** (or **street**) a minor road. **side-saddle** (of a rider) sitting with both feet on the same side of the horse. **take sides** support one person or cause against another.

sideboard noun **1** a piece of furniture with cupboards and drawers, used for storing crockery, glasses, etc. **2** (**sideboards**) Brit. sideburns.

sideburns plural noun a strip of hair growing down each side of a man's face in front of his ears.

sidecar noun a small, low vehicle attached to the side of a motorcycle for carrying passengers.

sidekick noun informal a person's assistant.

sidelight noun Brit. a small additional light on either side of a motor vehicle's headlights.

sideline noun **1** something you do in addition to your main job. **2** either of the two lines along the longer sides of a sports field or court. **3** (**the sidelines**) a position of watching a situation rather than being directly involved in it. verb (**sidelines, sidelining, sidelined**) remove from a team, game, or influential position.

sidelong adjective & adverb to or from one side; sideways.

sidereal /sy-**deer**-i-uhl/ adjective relating to the distant stars or their apparent positions in the sky.

sideshow noun a small show or stall at an exhibition, fair, or circus.

sidestep verb (**sidesteps, sidestepping, sidestepped**) **1** avoid by stepping sideways. **2** avoid dealing with a difficult issue.

sideswipe noun a critical or harsh remark made while discussing another matter.

sidetrack verb distract someone from the main issues of what they are discussing or doing.

sidewalk noun N. Amer. a pavement.

sideways adverb & adjective to, towards, or from the side.

siding noun a short track beside a main railway line, where trains are left.

sidle verb (**sidles, sidling, sidled**) walk in a secretive or timid way.

siege noun **1** a military operation in which forces surround a town and cut off its supplies. **2** a similar operation by a police team to force an armed person to surrender.

> ☑ remember, *i* before *e* in **siege** and **sieve**.

sienna noun a kind of earth used as a brown pigment in painting.

siesta noun an afternoon rest or nap.

sieve /siv/ noun a piece of mesh held in a frame, used for straining solids from liquids or separating coarser from finer particles. **verb** (**sieves, sieving, sieved**) put a substance through a sieve.

sift **verb 1** put through a sieve. **2** examine something thoroughly to sort out what is important or useful.

sigh **verb** let out a long, deep breath expressing sadness, relief, etc. **noun** such a breath.

sight **noun 1** the ability to see. **2** the act of seeing something. **3** the area or distance within which you can see something. **4** a thing that you see. **5** (**sights**) places of interest to tourists. **6** (**a sight**) informal a person or thing that looks ridiculous or unattractive. **7** (also **sights**) a device that you look through to aim a gun or see with a telescope. **verb** manage to see or glimpse. □ **raise** (or **lower**) **your sights** increase (or lower) your expectations. **set your sights on** hope strongly to obtain or achieve. **a sight for sore eyes** informal a person or thing that you are very pleased to see. **sight-read** read a score and perform the music without preparation.

sighted **adjective 1** having the ability to see; not blind. **2** having a particular kind of sight.

sightless **adjective** blind.

sightseeing **noun** the activity of visiting places of interest. ∎ **sightseer** noun.

sign **noun 1** an indication that something exists, is happening, or may happen. **2** a signal, gesture, or notice giving information or an instruction. **3** a symbol used to represent something in algebra, music, or other subjects. **4** each of the twelve divisions of the zodiac. **verb 1** write your name on something to authorize it. **2** recruit a sports player, musician, etc. by signing a contract. **3** use gestures to give information or instructions. □ **sign language** a system of signs made by the hands and face, used among deaf people. **sign off** end a letter, broadcast, or other message. **sign on 1** commit yourself to a job. **2** Brit. register as unemployed. **3** employ someone. **sign out** sign to show that you have borrowed or hired something. **sign up** commit yourself to a course, job, etc. ∎ **signer** noun.

signal[1] **noun 1** a gesture, action, or sound giving information or an instruction. **2** a sign indicating a particular situation. **3** a device that uses lights or a movable arm to tell drivers to stop or beware on a road or railway. **4** an electrical impulse or radio wave that is sent or received. **verb** (**signals, signalling, signalled**; US spelling **signals, signaling, signaled**) **1** give a signal. **2** indicate by means of a signal. □ **signal box** Brit. a building beside a railway track from which signals and points are controlled.

signal[2] **adjective** noteworthy.

signatory **noun** (plural **signatories**) a person who has signed an agreement.

signature **noun 1** a person's name written in a distinctive way, used in signing something. **2** the action of signing a document. **3** a distinctive product or quality by which someone or something can be recognized. □ **signature tune** a tune announcing a particular television or radio programme.

signet **noun** (in the past) a small seal used to authorize an official document. □ **signet ring** a ring with letters or a design set into it.

significance **noun 1** importance. **2** the meaning of something.

significant **adjective 1** important or large enough to have an effect or be noticed. **2** having a particular or secret meaning. ∎ **significantly** adverb.

signify **verb** (**signifies, signifying, signified**) **1** be a sign of; mean. **2** make known. ∎ **signification** noun.

signing **noun 1** Brit. a person who has recently been recruited to a sports team, record company, etc. **2** an event at which an author signs copies of their book. **3** the use of sign language.

signpost **noun** a sign on a post, giving information such as the direction and distance to a nearby place.

Sikh /seek/ **noun** a follower of a religion that developed from Hinduism. ■ **Sikhism** noun.

silage /**sy**-lij/ **noun** grass or other green crops that are stored in a silo without being dried, used as animal feed in the winter.

silence **noun** 1 complete lack of sound. 2 a situation in which someone is unwilling to speak or discuss something. **verb** (silences, silencing, silenced) 1 make something silent. 2 stop someone from speaking.

silencer **noun** a device for reducing the noise made by a gun or exhaust system.

silent **adjective** 1 where there is no sound. 2 not speaking or not spoken aloud. 3 (of a film) without a soundtrack. ■ **silently** adverb.

silhouette **noun** a dark shape and outline seen against a lighter background. **verb** (silhouettes, silhouetting, silhouetted) show as a silhouette.

silica **noun** a hard substance formed from silicon and oxygen that occurs as quartz and is found in sandstone and other rocks.

silicon **noun** a chemical element that is a semiconductor and is used to make electronic circuits. □ **silicon chip** a microchip.

| ✓ | **silicon** is an element used in electronic circuits and microchips, while **silicone** with an *e* at the end is the material used in cosmetic implants. |

silicone **noun** a synthetic substance made from silicon.

silk **noun** 1 a fine, soft shiny fibre produced by silkworms, made into thread or fabric. 2 Brit. informal a Queen's (or King's) Counsel. □ **take silk** Brit. become a Queen's (or King's) Counsel.

silken **adjective** 1 smooth and shiny like silk. 2 made of silk.

silkworm **noun** a caterpillar that spins a silk cocoon from which silk fibre is obtained.

silky **adjective** (silkier, silkiest) smooth and shiny like silk.

sill **noun** a shelf or slab at the foot of a window or doorway.

silly **adjective** (sillier, silliest) showing a lack of good judgement or common sense. ■ **silliness** noun.

silo **noun** (plural silos) 1 a tower used to store grain. 2 a pit or airtight structure for storing silage. 3 an underground chamber in which a guided missile is kept ready for firing.

silt **noun** fine sand or clay carried by running water and deposited as a sediment. **verb** (silt up) fill or block with silt. ■ **silty** adjective.

silver **noun** 1 a shiny greyish-white precious metal. 2 a shiny grey-white colour. 3 coins made from silver or from a metal that resembles silver. 4 silver dishes, containers, or cutlery. **verb** (silvers, silvering, silvered) cover or plate with silver. □ **silver birch** a birch tree with silver-grey bark. **silver jubilee** the twenty-fifth anniversary of an important event. **silver medal** a medal awarded for second place in a race or competition. **silver plate** 1 a thin layer of silver applied as a coating to another metal. 2 plates, dishes, etc. made of or plated with silver. **silver wedding** the twenty-fifth anniversary of a wedding. ■ **silvery** adjective.

silverfish **noun** a small silvery wingless insect that lives in buildings.

silverside **noun** the upper side of a cut of beef from the outside of the leg.

silversmith **noun** a person who makes silver articles.

simian **adjective** relating to or like apes or monkeys. **noun** an ape or monkey.

similar **adjective** like something but not exactly the same. ■ **similarity** noun **similarly** adverb.

simile /**sim**-i-li/ **noun** a word or phrase that compares one thing to another of a different kind (e.g. *the family was as solid as a rock*).

simmer **verb** (simmers, simmering,

simmered) 1 stay or cause to stay just below boiling point. **2** be in a state of anger or excitement which you only just keep under control. **3 (simmer down)** become calmer and quieter. **noun** a state or temperature just below boiling point.

simper verb (**simpers, simpering, simpered**) smile in a coy and silly way. **noun** a coy and silly smile.

simple adjective (**simpler, simplest**) **1** easily understood or done. **2** plain and basic. **3** composed of a single element; not compound. **4** of very low intelligence. □ **simple fracture** a fracture of a bone without any breaking of the skin.

simpleton noun a person with poor judgement or low intelligence.

simplicity noun the quality of being simple.

simplify verb (**simplifies, simplifying, simplified**) make easier to do or understand. ■ **simplification** noun.

simplistic adjective treating complex issues as more simple than they really are. ■ **simplistically** adverb.

simply adverb **1** in a simple way. **2** just; merely. **3** absolutely.

simulacrum /sim-yuu-**lay**-kruhm/ noun (plural **simulacra** or **simulacrums**) something that is similar to something else.

simulate verb (**simulates, simulating, simulated**) **1** imitate the appearance or nature of. **2** use a computer to create a model of something or conditions that are like those in real life. **3** pretend to have or feel a particular emotion. ■ **simulation** noun **simulator** noun.

simultaneous adjective occurring or done at the same time. ■ **simultaneity** noun **simultaneously** adverb.

✓ | the ending is *-eous*, not *-ious*: simultan*eous*.

sin noun **1** an act that breaks a religious or moral law. **2** an act that causes strong disapproval. **verb** (**sins, sinning, sinned**) commit a sin.

since preposition in the period be-

tween a time in the past and the present. **conjunction 1** during or in the time after. **2** because. **adverb 1** from the time mentioned until the present. **2** ago.

sincere adjective (**sincerer, sincerest**) not pretending anything or deceiving anyone; genuine and honest. ■ **sincerely** adverb **sincerity** noun.

sine /*rhymes with* line/ noun Mathematics (in a right-angled triangle) the ratio of the side opposite a particular acute angle to the hypotenuse.

sinecure /**sin**-i-kyoor/ noun a job for which you are paid but which requires little or no work.

sine qua non /see-nay kwah **nohn**/ noun a thing that is absolutely necessary.

sinew /**sin**-yoo/ noun a band of strong tissue that joins a muscle to a bone. ■ **sinewy** adjective.

sinful adjective **1** wicked. **2** disgraceful. ■ **sinfully** adverb **sinfulness** noun.

sing verb (**sings, singing, sang;** past participle **sung**) **1** make musical sounds with your voice. **2** perform a song in this way. **3** make a whistling sound. □ **sing-song 1** (in someone's voice) having a rising and falling sound. **2** informal an informal gathering for singing. ■ **singer** noun.

singalong noun an informal occasion when people sing together.

singe verb (**singes, singeing, singed**) burn the surface of something slightly. **noun** a slight burn.

single adjective **1** one only. **2** designed for one person. **3** consisting of one part. **4** taken separately from others. **5** not involved in a romantic or sexual relationship. **6** Brit. (of a ticket) valid for an outward journey only. **noun 1** a single person or thing. **2** a short record or CD. **3** (**singles**) a game or competition for individual players. **verb** (**singles, singling, singled**) (**single out**) select for special treatment. □ **single-breasted** (of a jacket or coat) fastened by one row of buttons at the centre of the front. **single file** a line of people arranged one behind another. **single-handed** done without help from others. **single-minded** determined to pursue a goal without being distracted. **single parent** a person bringing up a child or children without a partner. ■ **singly** adverb.

singlet noun Brit. a vest or similar sleeveless garment.

singleton noun a single person or thing.

singular adjective **1** exceptionally good or interesting; remarkable. **2** Grammar (of a word or form) referring to just one person or thing. noun Grammar the singular form of a word. ■ **singularity** noun **singularly** adverb.

sinister adjective seeming evil or dangerous.

sink verb (**sinks, sinking, sank**; past participle **sunk**) **1** go down below the surface of liquid. **2** go or cause to go to the bottom of the sea. **3** move slowly downwards. **4** gradually decrease in amount or strength. **5** (**sink into**) cause something sharp to go through a surface. **6** (**sink in**) become fully understood. **7** pass into a particular state. **8** (**sink into**) put money or resources into. noun a fixed basin with a water supply and outflow pipe.

sinker noun a weight used to keep a fishing line beneath the water.

sinner noun a person who sins.

sinuous adjective **1** having many curves and turns. **2** moving in a graceful, swaying way. ■ **sinuously** adverb.

sinus /sy-nuhss/ noun a hollow space within the bones of the face that connects with the nostrils.

sinusitis noun inflammation of a sinus.

sip verb (**sips, sipping, sipped**) drink something in small mouthfuls. noun a small mouthful of liquid.

siphon or **syphon** noun a tube used to move liquid from one container to another, using air pressure to maintain the flow. verb **1** draw off or move liquid by means of a siphon. **2** (**siphon off**) take small amounts of

money over a period of time.

sir noun **1** a polite form of address to a man. **2** used as a title for a knight or baronet.

sire noun **1** the male parent of an animal. **2** literary a father. **3** old use a respectful form of address to a king. verb (**sires, siring, sired**) be the male parent of.

siren noun **1** a device that makes a loud prolonged warning sound. **2** Greek Mythology each of a group of creatures who were part woman, part bird, whose singing lured sailors on to rocks. **3** a woman who is attractive but considered dangerous.

sirloin noun the best part of a loin of beef.

sirup US spelling of **SYRUP**.

sisal /sy-z'l/ noun fibre made from the leaves of a tropical Mexican plant, used for ropes or matting.

sissy noun (plural **sissies**) informal an effeminate or weak person.

sister noun **1** a woman or girl in relation to other children of her parents. **2** a female friend or colleague. **3** a member of a religious order of women. **4** Brit. a senior female nurse. ◻ **sister-in-law** (plural **sisters-in-law**) **1** the sister of your wife or husband. **2** the wife of your brother or brother-in-law. ■ **sisterly** adjective.

sisterhood noun **1** the relationship between sisters. **2** a bond of friendship and understanding between women. **3** a group of women linked by a shared interest.

sit verb (**sits, sitting, sat**) **1** rest your weight on your bottom with your back upright. **2** be in a particular position or state. **3** serve as a member of a council, jury, or other official body. **4** (of a parliament, committee, or court of law) be carrying on its business. **5** Brit. take an examination. ◻ **sit-in** the occupation of a college or workplace as a form of protest.

> 🛈 use **sitting** rather than **sat** with the verb 'to be': say *we were sitting there for hours* rather than *we were sat there for hours.*

sitar noun a long-necked Indian lute.

sitcom noun informal a situation comedy.

site noun a place where something is located or happens. verb (**sites**, **siting**, **sited**) build or establish something in a particular place.

> ⓘ don't confuse **site** with **sight**, which means 'the ability to see'.

sitter noun **1** a person who sits for a portrait. **2** a person who looks after children, pets, or a house while the parents or owners are away.

sitting noun **1** a period of posing for a portrait. **2** a period of time when a group of people are served a meal. **3** a period of time during which a court of law, committee, or parliament is carrying on its business. □ **sitting duck** informal a person or thing that is easy to attack. **sitting room** a room for sitting and relaxing in. **sitting tenant** Brit. a tenant who has the legal right to remain living in a property.

situate verb (**situates**, **situating**, **situated**) **1** put in a particular place. **2** (**be situated**) be in a particular set of circumstances.

situation noun **1** a set of circumstances. **2** the location and surroundings of a place. **3** a job. □ **situation comedy** a comedy series in which the characters are involved in amusing situations. ■ **situational** adjective.

six cardinal number **1** one more than five; 6. (Roman numeral: **vi** or **VI**.) **2** Cricket a hit that reaches the boundary without first striking the ground, scoring six runs. □ **at sixes and sevens** in a state of confusion. **knock for six** Brit. informal take completely by surprise.

sixpence noun Brit. (in the past) a coin worth six old pence (2½ p).

sixteen cardinal number one more than fifteen; 16. (Roman numeral: **xvi** or **XVI**.) ■ **sixteenth** ordinal number.

sixth ordinal number **1** being number six in a sequence; 6th. **2** (**a sixth** or **one sixth**) each of six equal parts of something. □ **sixth-form college** Brit.

a college for pupils aged 16 to 18. **sixth sense** a supposed ability to know things by intuition rather than using your sight, hearing, etc.

sixty cardinal number (plural **sixties**) ten more than fifty; 60. (Roman numeral: **lx** or **LX**.) ■ **sixtieth** ordinal number.

size¹ noun **1** the overall measurements or extent of something. **2** each of the series of standard measurements in which clothes, shoes, and other goods are made. verb (**sizes**, **sizing**, **sized**) **1** group things according to size. **2** (**size up**) informal form a judgement of. **3** alter the size of.

size² noun a sticky solution used in glazing paper, stiffening textiles, and preparing plastered walls for decoration. verb (**sizes**, **sizing**, **sized**) treat with size.

sizeable or **sizable** adjective fairly large.

sizzle verb (**sizzles**, **sizzling**, **sizzled**) **1** (of food) make a hissing sound when being fried. **2** (**sizzling**) informal very hot or exciting.

skate¹ noun an ice skate or roller skate. verb (**skates**, **skating**, **skated**) **1** move on skates. **2** (**skate over** or **round**) pass over or refer only briefly to. ■ **skater** noun.

skate² noun (plural **skate** or **skates**) an edible sea fish with a diamond-shaped body.

skateboard noun a short narrow board fitted with two small wheels at either end, on which a person can ride. verb ride on a skateboard. ■ **skateboarder** noun.

skedaddle verb (**skedaddles**, **skedaddling**, **skedaddled**) informal leave quickly.

skein noun a length of yarn held in a loose coil or knot.

skeletal adjective **1** having to do with or resembling a skeleton. **2** (of a plan) existing only in outline.

skeleton noun **1** a framework of bone or cartilage supporting or containing the body of an animal. **2** a supporting framework or structure. **3** a basic outline of a plan. adjective referring to an essential or minimum number of people: *a skeleton staff.* □ **skeleton in the cupboard** a shocking or embarrassing fact that someone wishes to keep secret. **skeleton key** a key designed to fit a number of locks.

skeptic US spelling of **SCEPTIC**.

skeptical US spelling of **SCEPTICAL**.

sketch noun 1 a rough drawing or painting. **2** a short humorous scene in a comedy show. **3** a brief written or spoken account. **verb 1** make a sketch of. **2** give a brief account of.

sketchbook noun a pad of drawing paper for sketching on.

sketchy adjective (**sketchier, sketchiest**) not thorough or detailed; rough. ■ **sketchily** adverb.

skew a bias towards one particular group or subject. **verb 1** suddenly change direction or move at an angle. **2** make biased or distorted.

skewbald adjective (of a horse) having patches of white and brown.

skewer noun a long piece of metal or wood used for holding pieces of food together during cooking. **verb** (**skewers, skewering, skewered**) hold or pierce with a pin or skewer.

ski noun (plural **skis**) each of a pair of long, narrow pieces of wood, metal, or plastic, attached to boots for travelling over snow. **verb** (**skis, skiing, skied**) travel on skis. □ **ski jump** a steep slope levelling off before a sharp drop to allow a skier to leap through the air. **ski lift** a system of moving seats attached to an overhead cable, used for taking skiers to the top of a run. ■ **skier** noun.

> ☑ the plural of the noun is **skis**, without an e.

skid verb (**skids, skidding, skidded**) **1** (of a vehicle) slide sideways in an uncontrolled way. **2** slip; slide. **noun 1** an act of skidding. **2** a runner attached to the underside of a helicopter and some other aircraft. □ **skid row** N. Amer. informal a run-down part of a town or city where homeless people and alcoholics live.

skiff noun a light rowing boat.

skilful (US spelling **skillful**) **adjective** having or showing skill. ■ **skilfully** adverb.

> ☑ there is only one *l* in the middle: ski*l*ful. The spelling with two *l*'s is American.

skill noun 1 the ability to do something well. **2** a particular ability.

skilled adjective 1 having or showing skill. **2** (of work) requiring special abilities or training.

skillet noun a frying pan.

skim verb (**skims, skimming, skimmed**) **1** remove a substance from the surface of a liquid. **2** move quickly and lightly over a surface or through the air. **3** read through quickly. **4** (**skim over**) deal with briefly. □ **skimmed milk** milk from which the cream has been removed.

skimp verb spend less money or use less of something than is really needed in an attempt to economize.

skimpy adjective (**skimpier, skimpiest**) **1** less than is necessary; meagre. **2** (of clothes) short and revealing.

skin noun 1 the thin layer of tissue forming the outer covering of the body. **2** the skin of a dead animal used for clothing or other items. **3** the peel or outer layer of a fruit or vegetable. **verb** (**skins, skinning, skinned**) **1** remove the skin from. **2** graze a part of your body. □ **by the skin of your teeth** only just. **get under someone's skin** informal annoy someone greatly. **have a thick skin** be unaffected by criticism or insults. **skin-deep** not deep or lasting; superficial. **skin-diving** swimming under water without a diving suit, using an aqualung and flippers.

skinflint noun informal a very mean person.

skinhead noun a young person of a group with very short shaved hair.

skinny adjective (**skinnier, skinniest**) **1** (of a person) very thin. **2** (of a garment) tight-fitting.

skint adjective Brit. informal having little or no money.

skintight adjective (of a garment) very tight-fitting.

skip[1] verb (**skips, skipping, skipped**) **1** move along lightly, stepping from one foot to the other with a little jump. **2** jump repeatedly over a rope turned over the head and under the feet. **3** omit or move quickly over. **4** fail to attend or deal with. noun a skipping movement.

skip[2] noun Brit. a large open-topped container for holding and carrying away bulky refuse.

skipper informal noun **1** the captain of a ship, boat, or aircraft. **2** the captain of a sports team. verb (**skippers, skippering, skippered**) be captain of.

skirl noun a shrill sound made by bagpipes. verb make such a sound.

skirmish noun a short spell of fighting. verb take part in a skirmish.

skirt noun a woman's garment that hangs from the waist and surrounds the lower body and legs. verb **1** go round or past the edge of. **2** (also **skirt around**) avoid dealing with.

skirting or **skirting board** noun Brit. a wooden board running along the base of the walls of a room.

skit noun a short comedy sketch that makes fun of something by imitating it.

skitter verb (**skitters, skittering, skittered**) move lightly and quickly.

skittish adjective **1** (of a horse) nervous and tending to shy. **2** lively or changeable. ■ **skittishly** adverb.

skittle noun **1** (**skittles**) a game played with wooden pins set up to be bowled down with a ball. **2** a pin used in the game of skittles.

skive verb (**skives, skiving, skived**) Brit. informal avoid work or a duty by staying away or leaving early. ■ **skiver** noun.

skivvy noun (plural **skivvies**) Brit. informal a female domestic servant.

skua noun a large seabird like a gull.

skulduggery or **skullduggery**

noun underhand behaviour.

skulk verb hide or move around in a secretive way.

skull noun the bony framework that surrounds and protects the brain. □ **skull and crossbones** a picture of a skull with two thigh bones crossed below it, used in the past by pirates and now as a sign of danger.

skullcap noun a small close-fitting cap without a peak.

skunk noun an animal with black and white stripes that can spray foul-smelling liquid at attackers.

sky noun (plural **skies**) the region of the upper atmosphere seen from the earth. □ **sky blue** a bright clear blue.

skydiving noun the sport of jumping from an aircraft and performing movements in the air before landing by parachute. ■ **skydiver** noun.

skylark noun a lark that sings while flying. verb behave in a playful and mischievous way.

skylight noun a window set in a roof.

skyline noun an outline of land and buildings seen against the sky.

skyrocket noun a rocket designed to explode high in the air as a signal or firework. verb (**skyrockets, skyrocketing, skyrocketed**) informal (of a price or amount) increase rapidly.

skyscraper noun a very tall building of many storeys.

slab noun **1** a large, thick, flat piece of stone or concrete. **2** a thick slice of cake, bread, etc.

slack adjective **1** not taut or held tightly. **2** (of business or trade) quiet. **3** careless or lazy. **4** (of a tide) between the ebb and the flow. noun **1** the part of a rope or line which is not held taut. **2** (**slacks**) casual trousers. verb **1** (**slack off** or **up**) decrease in intensity or speed. **2** Brit. informal work slowly or lazily. ■ **slacker** noun **slackly** adverb **slackness** noun.

slacken verb **1** make or become less active or intense. **2** make or become less tight.

slag noun **1** stony waste matter left when metal has been separated from ore by smelting or refining. **2** Brit. informal, disapproving a woman who has many sexual partners. verb (**slags, slagging, slagged**) (**slag off**) Brit. informal criticize rudely. □ **slag heap** a mound of waste material from a mine.

slain past participle of **SLAY**.

slake verb (**slakes, slaking, slaked**) satisfy a desire, thirst, etc.

slalom /slah-luhm/ noun a skiing or canoeing race following a winding course marked out by poles.

slam verb (**slams, slamming, slammed**) **1** shut forcefully and loudly. **2** put down with great force. **3** hit a ball with great force. **4** informal criticize severely. noun a loud bang caused when a door is slammed.

slander noun the crime of saying something untrue that harms a person's reputation. verb (**slanders, slandering, slandered**) say something untrue and damaging about. ■ **slanderous** adjective.

slang noun very informal words and phrases that are more common in speech than in writing and are used by a particular group of people. □ **slanging match** Brit. an angry argument in which people insult each other. ■ **slangy** adjective.

slant verb **1** slope or lean. **2** present information from a particular point of view. noun **1** a sloping position. **2** a point of view.

slap verb (**slaps, slapping, slapped**) **1** hit with the palm of your hand or a flat object. **2** hit against with a slapping sound. **3** (**slap down**) informal tell off forcefully. **4** (**slap on**) put on a surface quickly or carelessly. noun an act or sound of slapping. adverb (also **slap bang**) informal suddenly and with great force. □ **slap-up** Brit. informal (of a meal) large and extravagant.

slapdash adjective done too hurriedly and carelessly.

slapstick noun comedy consisting of deliberately clumsy actions and embarrassing situations.

slash verb **1** cut with a violent sweeping movement. **2** informal greatly reduce a price or quantity. noun **1** a cut made with a wide, sweeping stroke. **2** a slanting stroke (/) used between alternatives and in fractions and ratios.

slat noun each of a series of thin, narrow pieces of wood or other material, arranged so as to overlap or fit into each other. ■ **slatted** adjective.

slate noun a dark grey rock that is easily split into smooth, flat plates, used in building and in the past for writing on. verb (**slates, slating, slated**) Brit. informal severely criticize.

slather verb (**slathers, slathering, slathered**) informal spread or smear thickly over.

slattern noun old use a dirty, untidy woman. ■ **slatternly** adjective.

slaughter noun **1** the killing of farm animals for food. **2** the killing of a large number of people in a cruel or violent way. verb (**slaughters, slaughtering, slaughtered**) **1** kill animals for food. **2** kill a number of people in a cruel or violent way.

slaughterhouse noun a place where animals are killed for food.

Slav /slahv/ noun a member of a group of peoples in central and eastern Europe. ■ **Slavic** adjective.

slave noun **1** (in the past) a person who was the legal property of another and was forced to obey them. **2** a person who is strongly influenced or controlled by something. verb (**slaves, slaving, slaved**) work very hard. □ **slave-driver** informal a person who makes other people work very hard. **slave labour** very demanding work that is very poorly paid.

slaver /sla-ver, slay-ver/ verb (**slavers, slavering, slavered**) let saliva run from your mouth. noun saliva running from the mouth.

slavery noun **1** the state of being a slave. **2** the practice or system of owning slaves.

slavish adjective **1** showing no originality. **2** excessively obedient. ■ **slavishly** adverb.

slay verb (slays, slaying, slew; past participle slain) old use or N. Amer. violently kill.

sleaze noun informal immoral or dishonest behaviour.

sleazy adjective (sleazier, sleaziest) **1** immoral or dishonest. **2** (of a place) dirty and seedy.

sled noun & verb (sleds, sledding, sledded) N. Amer. = **SLEDGE**.

sledge noun **1** a vehicle on runners for travelling over snow or ice, sometimes pulled by dogs. **2** Brit. a toboggan. verb (sledges, sledging, sledged) ride or carry on a sledge.

sledgehammer noun a large, heavy hammer.

sleek adjective **1** smooth and glossy. **2** having a wealthy and smart appearance. **3** elegant and streamlined. ■ **sleekly** adverb.

sleep noun a condition of rest in which the eyes are closed, the muscles are relaxed, and the mind is unconscious. verb (sleeps, sleeping, slept) **1** be asleep. **2** (sleep in) remain asleep or in bed later than usual in the morning. **3** provide a particular number of people with beds. **4** (sleep with) have sex or be involved in a sexual relationship with. **5** (sleep around) have many sexual partners. □ **put to sleep** kill an animal painlessly. **sleeping bag** a warm padded bag for sleeping in when camping or travelling. **sleeping car** a railway carriage fitted with beds or berths. **sleeping partner** Brit. a partner who does not share in the actual work of a firm. **sleeping pill** a tablet taken to help you fall asleep. **sleeping policeman** Brit. a hump in the road for slowing down traffic. ■ **sleepless** adjective.

sleeper noun **1** Brit. each of the wooden supports on which a railway track rests. **2** Brit. a ring or bar worn in a pierced ear to keep the hole from closing. **3** a train carrying sleeping cars.

sleepwalk verb walk around while

asleep. ■ **sleepwalker** noun.

sleepy adjective (sleepier, sleepiest) **1** ready for, or needing, sleep. **2** (of a place) without much activity. ■ **sleepily** adverb **sleepiness** noun.

sleet noun rain containing some ice, or snow melting as it falls. verb (it sleets, it is sleeting, it sleeted) sleet falls.

sleeve noun **1** the part of a garment covering a person's arm. **2** a protective cover for a record. **3** a tube fitting over a rod or smaller tube. □ **up your sleeve** kept secret and ready for use when needed. ■ **sleeveless** adjective.

sleigh noun a sledge pulled by horses or reindeer.

sleight /rhymes with slight/ noun literary the use of skill or cunning. □ **sleight of hand 1** skilful use of the hands. **2** skilful deception.

slender adjective (slenderer, slenderest) **1** gracefully thin. **2** barely sufficient.

slept past and past participle of **SLEEP**.

sleuth /rhymes with truth/ noun informal a detective. ■ **sleuthing** noun.

slew[1] verb turn or slide violently or uncontrollably.

slew[2] past of **SLAY**.

slice noun **1** a thin, broad piece of food cut from a larger portion. **2** a portion or share. **3** an implement with a broad, flat blade for lifting cake, fish, etc. **4** (in sports) a sliced stroke or shot. verb (slices, slicing, sliced) **1** cut into slices. **2** cut with a sharp implement. **3** (often slice through) move easily and quickly. **4** (in sport) hit the ball so that it travels forward spinning or curves away to the side.

slick adjective **1** impressively smooth and efficient. **2** self-confident but insincere. **3** (of a surface) smooth, glossy, or slippery. noun a smooth patch of oil. verb make hair smooth and glossy with water, oil, or cream. ■ **slickly** adverb.

slide verb (slides, sliding, slid) **1** move along a smooth surface while remaining in contact with it. **2** move smoothly, quickly, or without being noticed. **3** become gradually lower or worse. **noun 1** a structure with a smooth sloping surface for children to slide down. **2** an act of sliding. **3** a piece of glass which you place an object on to look at it through a microscope. **4** a small piece of photographic film which you view using a projector. □ **slide rule** a ruler with a sliding central strip, used for making calculations quickly. **sliding scale** a scale of fees, wages, etc. that varies according to some other factor.

slight adjective **1** small in degree. **2** lacking depth; trivial. **3** not sturdy and strongly built. **verb** insult someone by treating them without proper respect or attention. **noun** an insult. ■ **slightly** adverb.

slim adjective (**slimmer, slimmest**) **1** gracefully thin. **2** small in width and long and narrow in shape. **3** very small: *a slim chance.* **verb** (**slims, slimming, slimmed**) make or become thinner. ■ **slimmer** noun.

slime noun an unpleasantly moist, soft, and slippery substance.

slimy adjective (**slimier, slimiest**) **1** like or covered by slime. **2** informal insincerely obedient or flattering.

sling noun **1** a loop of fabric used to support or raise a hanging weight. **2** a strap or loop used to hurl small missiles. **verb** (**slings, slinging, slung**) **1** hang or carry with a sling or strap. **2** hurl with a sling. **3** informal throw.

slingback noun a shoe held in place by a strap around the ankle.

slingshot noun a hand-held catapult.

slink verb (**slinks, slinking, slunk**) move quietly in a secretive way.

slinky adjective (**slinkier, slinkiest**) informal graceful and curvy.

slip[1] **verb** (**slips, slipping, slipped**) **1** lose your balance and slide for a short distance. **2** accidentally slide out of position or from someone's grasp. **3** fail to grip a surface. **4** get gradually worse. **5** (usu. **slip up**) make a careless error. **6** move or place quietly, quickly, or secretly.

7 get free from. **8** release the clutch of a motor vehicle. **noun 1** an instance of slipping. **2** a minor or careless mistake. **3** a loose-fitting short petticoat. **4** Cricket a fielding position close behind the batsman to one side. □ **slip knot** a knot that can be undone by a pull, or that can slide along the rope on which it is tied. **slip-on** (of shoes or clothes) having no fastenings. **slipped disc** a displaced disc in the spine that presses on nearby nerves and causes pain. **slip road** Brit. a road entering or leaving a motorway or dual carriageway. ■ **slippage** noun.

slip[2] noun **1** a small piece of paper. **2** a cutting from a plant.

slipper noun a comfortable slip-on shoe worn indoors.

slippery adjective **1** difficult to hold firmly or stand on through being smooth, wet, or slimy. **2** (of a person) difficult to pin down.

slippy adjective (**slippier, slippiest**) informal slippery.

slipshod adjective careless, thoughtless, or disorganized.

slipstream noun **1** a current of air or water driven back by a propeller or jet engine. **2** the partial vacuum created in the wake of a moving vehicle.

slipway noun a slope leading into water, used for launching and landing boats and ships.

slit noun a long, narrow cut or opening. **verb** (**slits, slitting, slit**) make a slit in.

slither verb (**slithers, slithering, slithered**) **1** move smoothly over a surface with a twisting motion. **2** slide unsteadily on a loose or slippery surface. **noun** a slithering movement. ■ **slithery** adjective.

sliver noun a small, narrow, sharp piece cut or split off a larger piece.

slob informal noun a lazy, untidy person. **verb** (**slobs, slobbing, slobbed**) behave in a lazy, untidy way.

slobber verb (**slobbers, slobbering, slobbered**) **1** have saliva dripping from the mouth. **2** (**slobber over**) be excessively enthusiastic about. **noun** saliva dripping from the mouth. ■ **slobbery** adjective.

sloe /rhymes with slow/ **noun** the small bluish-black fruit of the blackthorn.

slog **verb** (**slogs, slogging, slogged**) **1** work hard over a period of time. **2** move with difficulty or effort. **3** strike forcefully. **4** (**slog it out**) fight or compete fiercely. **noun** a spell of difficult, tiring work or travelling.

slogan **noun** a short, memorable phrase used in advertising or associated with a political group.

sloop **noun** a type of sailing boat with one mast.

slop **verb** (**slops, slopping, slopped**) **1** (of a liquid) spill over the edge of a container. **2** apply something casually or carelessly. **3** (**slop out**) empty the contents of a chamber pot. **4** (**slop about** or **around**) Brit. informal spend time relaxing in scruffy clothes. **noun** (**slops**) **1** waste liquid that has to be emptied by hand. **2** unappetizing semi-liquid food.

slope **noun 1** a surface with one end at a higher level than another. **2** a part of the side of a hill or mountain. **verb** (**slopes, sloping, sloped**) **1** slant up or down. **2** (**slope off**) informal leave without attracting attention.

sloppy **adjective** (**sloppier, sloppiest**) **1** containing too much liquid. **2** careless and disorganized. **3** too sentimental. ■ **sloppily** adverb **sloppiness** noun.

slosh **verb 1** (of liquid in a container) move around with a splashing sound. **2** move through liquid with a splashing sound. **3** pour liquid clumsily.

sloshed **adjective** informal drunk.

slot **noun 1** a long, narrow opening into which something may be inserted. **2** a place in an arrangement or scheme. **verb** (**slots, slotting, slotted**) **1** place into a slot. **2** (**slot in** or **into**) fit easily into a new role or situation. □ **slot machine** a fruit machine or (Brit.) vending machine.

sloth /slohth/ **noun 1** laziness. **2** a

slow-moving mammal that hangs upside down. ■ **slothful** adjective.

slouch **verb** stand, move, or sit in a lazy, drooping way. **noun** a lazy, drooping posture. □ **be no slouch** informal be fast or good at something.

slough¹ /rhymes with plough/ **noun 1** a swamp. **2** a situation without progress or activity.

slough² /rhymes with rough/ **verb** (of an animal) cast off an old skin.

slovenly **adjective 1** untidy and dirty. **2** careless. ■ **slovenliness** noun.

slow **adjective 1** moving or capable of moving only at a low speed. **2** taking a long time. **3** (of a clock or watch) showing a time earlier than the correct time. **4** not quick to understand, think, or learn. **verb** (often **slow down** or **up**) **1** reduce speed. **2** be less busy or active. □ **slow motion** the showing of film or video more slowly than it was made or recorded. **slow-worm** a small snake-like lizard. ■ **slowly** noun **slowness** noun.

slowcoach **noun** Brit. informal a person who acts or moves slowly.

sludge **noun** thick, soft, wet mud or a similar mixture. ■ **sludgy** adjective.

slug¹ **noun 1** a small creature like a snail without a shell. **2** informal a small amount of an alcoholic drink. **3** informal a bullet. **verb** (**slugs, slugging, slugged**) informal gulp a drink.

slug² informal **verb** (**slugs, slugging, slugged**) **1** strike with a hard blow. **2** (**slug it out**) settle a dispute by fighting or competing fiercely.

sluggard **noun** a lazy, inactive person.

sluggish **adjective 1** slow-moving or inactive. **2** not energetic or alert. ■ **sluggishly** adverb.

sluice /slooss/ **noun 1** (also **sluice gate**) a sliding device for controlling the flow of water. **2** a channel for carrying off surplus water. **verb** (**sluices, sluicing, sluiced**) wash or rinse with water.

slum **noun 1** a rundown area of a city or town inhabited by very poor people. **2** a house or building unfit to be lived in. **verb** (**slums, slumming, slummed**) (**slum it**) informal choose to spend time in uncomfortable conditions or at a low social level.

slumber **verb** (**slumbers, slumbering, slumbered**) sleep. **noun** a sleep.

slump **verb 1** sit, lean, or fall heavily and limply. **2** decline greatly. **noun** an instance of slumping.

slung past and past participle of **SLING**.

slunk past and past participle of **SLINK**.

slur **verb** (**slurs, slurring, slurred**) **1** speak in an unclear way. **2** perform a group of musical notes in a smooth, flowing way. **noun 1** an insult or accusation intended to damage someone's reputation. **2** a curved line indicating that notes are to be slurred.

slurp **verb** eat or drink with a loud sucking sound. **noun** a slurping sound.

slurry **noun** (plural **slurries**) a semi-liquid mixture of manure, cement, or coal and water.

slush **noun 1** partially melted snow or ice. **2** informal excessively sentimental talk or writing. □ **slush fund** a reserve of money used for something illegal. ■ **slushy** adjective.

slut **noun** disapproving a woman who has many sexual partners, or who is untidy and lazy. ■ **sluttish** adjective.

sly **adjective** (**slyer, slyest**) **1** cunning and deceitful. **2** (of a remark, glance, or expression) suggesting secret knowledge. ■ **slyly** adverb.

smack¹ **noun 1** a sharp blow with the palm of the hand. **2** a loud, sharp sound. **3** a loud kiss. **verb 1** give someone a smack. **2** smash or drive into. **3** part your lips noisily. **adverb** informal exactly or directly.

smack² **verb** (**smack of**) **1** smell or taste of. **2** seem to contain or involve something wrong or unpleasant.

smack³ **noun** a sailing boat with one mast.

smack⁴ **noun** informal heroin.

smacker **noun** informal **1** a loud kiss.

2 Brit. one pound sterling.

small **adjective 1** of less than normal size. **2** not great in amount, number, strength, or power. **3** young. □ **small arms** guns that can be carried in the hands. **small beer** Brit. something unimportant. **small change 1** coins of low value. **2** something unimportant. **small fry 1** young or small fish. **2** young or unimportant people or things. **the small hours** the early hours of the morning after midnight. **the small of the back** the lower part of a person's back where the spine curves in. **small print** details printed so that they are not easily noticed in an agreement or contract. **small talk** polite conversation about unimportant matters. ■ **smallness** noun.

smallholding **noun** Brit. a piece of agricultural land that is smaller than a farm. ■ **smallholder** noun.

smallpox **noun** a serious disease which causes blisters that usually leave permanent scars.

smarmy **adjective** Brit. informal excessively polite and friendly in an insincere way.

smart **adjective 1** clean, tidy, and stylish. **2** bright and fresh in appearance. **3** (of a place) fashionable and upmarket. **4** informal quick-witted. **5** chiefly N. Amer. cheekily clever. **6** quick. **verb 1** give a sharp, stinging pain. **2** feel upset and annoyed. □ **look smart** chiefly Brit. be quick. **smart card** a plastic card on which information is stored in electronic form. ■ **smartish** adjective **smartly** adverb **smartness** noun.

smarten **verb** (usu. **smarten up**) make or become smarter.

smash **verb 1** break violently into pieces. **2** hit or collide forcefully. **3** (in sport) strike the ball hard. **4** completely defeat, destroy, or foil. **noun 1** an act or sound of smashing. **2** (also **smash hit**) informal a very successful song, film, or show.

smashing **adjective** Brit. informal excellent. ■ **smasher** noun.

smattering **noun 1** a small amount. **2** a slight knowledge of a language.

smear verb **1** coat or mark with a greasy or sticky substance. **2** blur or smudge. **3** damage the reputation of someone by false accusations. noun **1** a greasy or sticky mark. **2** a false accusation. □ **smear test** a test to detect signs of cervical cancer.

smell noun **1** the ability to sense different things by means of the organs in the nose. **2** something sensed by the organs in the nose; an odour. **3** an act of breathing in to sense an odour. verb (**smells**, **smelling**, **smelt** or **smelled**) **1** sense by means of the organs in the nose. **2** sniff at something to find out its smell. **3** send out an smell. **4** have a strong or unpleasant smell. **5** sense or detect. **6** suggest or give an impression of. □ **smell a rat** informal suspect a trick. **smelling salts** a strong-smelling liquid formerly sniffed by people who felt faint.

smelly adjective (**smellier**, **smelliest**) having a strong or unpleasant smell.

smelt[1] verb extract metal from its ore by heating and melting it.

smelt[2] past and past participle of **SMELL**.

smidgen or **smidgeon** noun informal a tiny amount.

smile verb (**smiles**, **smiling**, **smiled**) form your features into a pleased, friendly, or amused expression, with the corners of the mouth turned up. noun an act of smiling.

smirk verb smile in a smug or silly way. noun a smug or silly smile.

smite verb (**smites**, **smiting**, **smote**; past participle **smitten**) **1** old use strike with a hard blow. **2** old use defeat or conquer. **3** (**be smitten**) be affected severely by a disease. **4** (**be smitten**) be strongly attracted to someone.

smith noun **1** a person who works in metal. **2** a blacksmith.

smithereens plural noun informal small pieces.

smithy noun (plural **smithies**) a blacksmith's workshop.

smock noun **1** a loose dress or blouse with the upper part gathered into decorative stitched pleats. **2** a loose overall worn to protect your clothes.

smog noun fog or haze made worse by pollution in the atmosphere.

smoke noun **1** a visible vapour in the air produced by a burning substance. **2** an act of smoking tobacco. **3** informal a cigarette or cigar. **4** (**the Smoke** or **the Big Smoke**) Brit. a big city. verb (**smokes**, **smoking**, **smoked**) **1** give out smoke. **2** breathe smoke from a cigarette, pipe, etc. in and out again. **3** preserve meat or fish by exposing it to smoke. **4** (**smoked**) (of glass) darkened. **5** (**smoke out**) drive out of a place by using smoke. □ **smoking jacket** a man's jacket formerly worn while smoking after dinner. ■ **smokeless** adjective **smoker** noun.

smokescreen noun **1** a cloud of smoke created to conceal military operations. **2** something designed to disguise intentions or activities.

smokestack noun a chimney or funnel that discharges smoke from a locomotive, ship, factory, etc.

smoky adjective (**smokier**, **smokiest**) producing, filled with, or like smoke.

smolder US spelling of **SMOULDER**.

smooch verb informal kiss and cuddle.

smooth adjective **1** having an even and regular surface. **2** (of a liquid) without lumps. **3** (of movement) without jerks. **4** without difficulties. **5** charming in a very confident or flattering way. **6** (of a flavour) not harsh or bitter. verb (also **smoothe**) (**smooths** or **smoothes**, **smoothing**, **smoothed**) **1** make something smooth. **2** (**smooth over**) deal successfully with a problem. □ **smooth-talk** informal talk to someone in a persuasively charming or flattering way. ■ **smoothly** adverb **smoothness** noun.

smorgasbord noun a meal at which you choose from a range of open sandwiches and savoury items.

smote past of **SMITE**.

smother verb (**smothers**, **smothering**, **smothered**) **1** suffocate someone by covering the nose and mouth. **2** (**smother in** or **with**) cover entirely with. **3** overwhelm someone by being too protective of them.

smoulder (US spelling **smolder**) verb (**smoulders**, **smouldering**, **smouldered**) **1** burn slowly with smoke but no flame. **2** feel strong and barely hidden anger, hatred, lust, etc.

smudge verb (**smudges**, **smudging**, **smudged**) make or become blurred or smeared. noun a smudged mark or image. ■ **smudgy** adjective.

smug adjective (**smugger**, **smuggest**) irritatingly pleased with yourself. ■ **smugly** adverb **smugness** noun.

smuggle verb (**smuggles**, **smuggling**, **smuggled**) **1** move goods illegally into or out of a country. **2** secretly convey. ■ **smuggler** noun.

smut noun **1** a small flake of soot or dirt. **2** indecent talk, writing, or pictures. **3** a disease of cereals. ■ **smutty** adjective.

snack noun a small quantity of food eaten between meals or in place of a meal. verb eat a snack.

snaffle noun a bit on a horse's bridle. verb (**snaffles**, **snaffling**, **snaffled**) informal secretly take.

snag noun **1** an unexpected difficulty. **2** a sharp or jagged projection. **3** a small tear. verb (**snags**, **snagging**, **snagged**) catch or tear on a snag.

snaggle-toothed adjective having irregular or projecting teeth.

snail noun a small, slow-moving creature with a spiral shell into which it can withdraw its whole body.

snake noun a reptile with no legs and a long slender body. verb (**snakes**, **snaking**, **snaked**) move with the twisting motion of a snake. □ **snake in the grass** a person who pretends to be someone's friend but is secretly working against them. ■ **snaky** adjective.

snap verb (**snaps**, **snapping**, **snapped**) **1** break with a sharp cracking sound. **2** (of an animal) make a sudden bite. **3** open or close with a brisk movement or sharp sound. **4** (**snap up**) quickly buy something that is in short supply. **5** suddenly

lose self-control. **6** say something quickly and irritably. **7** (**snap out of**) informal get out of a bad mood by a sudden effort. **8** take a snapshot of. noun **1** an act or sound of snapping. **2** a snapshot. **3** Brit. a card game in which players compete to call 'snap' as soon as two cards of the same type are exposed. adjective done on the spur of the moment: *a snap decision*. □ **cold snap** a brief spell of cold weather.

snapdragon noun a plant with brightly coloured flowers which have a mouth-like opening.

snapper noun a sea fish noted for snapping its jaws.

snappy adjective (**snappier**, **snappiest**) informal **1** irritable and sharp. **2** neat and stylish. □ **make it snappy** do it quickly.

snapshot noun an informal photograph, taken quickly.

snare noun **1** a trap for catching animals, consisting of a loop of wire that pulls tight. **2** a thing likely to lure someone into trouble. **3** (also **snare drum**) a drum with a length of wire stretched across the head to produce a rattling sound. verb (**snares**, **snaring**, **snared**) catch in a snare or trap.

snarl verb **1** growl with bared teeth. **2** say something aggressively. **3** (**snarl up**) entangle. noun an act of snarling. □ **snarl-up** informal a traffic jam

snatch verb **1** seize quickly in a rude or eager way. **2** informal steal or kidnap. **3** quickly take the chance to have. noun **1** an act of snatching. **2** a fragment of music or talk.

snazzy adjective (**snazzier**, **snazziest**) informal smart and stylish.

sneak verb (**sneaks**, **sneaking**, **sneaked** or N. Amer. informal **snuck**) **1** move or convey in a secretive way. **2** secretly acquire or obtain. **3** Brit. informal tell someone in authority of a person's wrongdoings. **4** (**sneaking**) (of a feeling) remaining persistently in the mind. noun Brit. informal a telltale. adjective secret or unofficial: *a sneak preview*.

sneaker noun chiefly N. Amer. a soft shoe

worn for sports or casual occasions.

sneaky adjective guiltily secretive or sly. ∎ **sneakily** adverb.

sneer noun a scornful or mocking smile, remark, or tone. verb (**sneers, sneering, sneered**) smile or speak in a scornful or mocking way.

sneeze verb (**sneezes, sneezing, sneezed**) suddenly expel air from the nose and mouth due to irritation of the nostrils. noun an act of sneezing. ◻ **not to be sneezed at** informal not to be rejected without consideration.

snick verb cut a small notch in. noun a small notch or cut.

snicker verb (**snickers, snickering, snickered**) 1 snigger. 2 (of a horse) make a gentle high-pitched neigh. noun a sound of snickering.

snide adjective disrespectful or mocking in an indirect way.

sniff verb 1 draw in air audibly through the nose. 2 (**sniff at**) show contempt or dislike for. 3 (**sniff around** or **round**) informal investigate secretly. 4 (**sniff out**) informal discover by investigation. noun 1 an act of sniffing. 2 informal a hint or sign. ∎ **sniffer** noun **sniffy** adjective.

sniffle verb (**sniffles, sniffling, sniffled**) sniff slightly or repeatedly. noun 1 an act of sniffling. 2 a slight cold. ∎ **sniffly** adjective.

snifter noun informal a small quantity of an alcoholic drink.

snigger noun a smothered or half-suppressed laugh. verb (**sniggers, sniggering, sniggered**) give a snigger.

snip verb (**snips, snipping, snipped**) cut with small, quick strokes. noun 1 an act of snipping. 2 a small piece cut off. 3 Brit. informal a bargain.

snipe noun (plural snipe or snipes) a wading bird with brown plumage and a long straight bill. verb (**snipes, sniping, sniped**) 1 shoot at someone from a hiding place at long range. 2 criticize someone in a sly or petty way. ∎ **sniper** noun.

snippet noun a small piece or brief extract.

snitch informal verb 1 steal. 2 inform on someone. noun an informer.

snivel verb (**snivels, snivelling, snivelled**; US spelling **snivels, sniveling, sniveled**) 1 cry and sniffle. 2 complain in a whining or tearful way.

snob noun 1 a person who greatly respects people with social status or wealth and looks down on lower-class people. 2 a person who believes that they have superior taste in a particular area: a wine snob. ∎ **snobbery** noun **snobbish** adjective **snobby** adjective.

snog Brit. informal verb (**snogs, snogging, snogged**) kiss and caress. noun a spell of kissing and caressing.

snood noun a hairnet worn at the back of a woman's head.

snook noun (**cock a snook at**) Brit. informal openly show contempt or disrespect for.

snooker noun 1 a game played with cues on a billiard table. 2 a position in a game of snooker or pool in which a player cannot make a direct shot at any permitted ball. verb (**snookers, snookering, snookered**) 1 subject your opponent to a snooker. 2 (**be snookered**) informal be placed in an impossible position.

snoop informal verb investigate secretly in order to find out something. noun an act of snooping. ∎ **snooper** noun.

snooty adjective (**snootier, snootiest**) informal superior or contemptuous towards others. ∎ **snootily** adverb.

snooze informal noun a short, light sleep. verb (**snoozes, snoozing, snoozed**) have a snooze.

snore noun a snorting sound in a person's breathing while they are asleep. verb (**snores, snoring, snored**) make a snorting sound while asleep.

snorkel noun a tube for a swimmer to breathe through while under water. ∎ **snorkelling** (US spelling **snorkeling**) noun.

snort noun 1 an explosive sound made by the sudden forcing of breath through the nose. 2 informal an small amount of a powdered drug that is breathed in through the nose. 3 informal a small alcoholic drink. **verb 1** make a snort. **2** informal inhale a drug.

snot noun informal mucus in the nose.

snotty adjective informal **1** full of, or covered with, mucus from the nose. **2** superior or arrogant.

snout noun **1** the projecting nose and mouth of an animal. **2** the projecting front or end of something such as a pistol. **3** Brit. informal a cigarette.

snow noun **1** frozen water vapour in the atmosphere that falls in light white flakes. **2** (snows) falls of snow. **verb 1** (it snows, it is snowing it snowed) snow falls. **2** (be snowed in or up) be unable to leave a place because of heavy snow. **3** (be snowed under) be overwhelmed with a large quantity of something.

snowball noun a ball of packed snow. **verb** increase rapidly in size, strength, or importance.

snowboard noun a board resembling a short, broad ski, used for sliding downhill on snow. ■ **snowboarder** noun **snowboarding** noun.

snowbound adjective **1** unable to travel or go out because of snow. **2** (of a place) cut off by snow.

snowdrift noun a bank of deep snow heaped up by the wind.

snowdrop noun a plant which bears drooping white flowers during the late winter.

snowfall noun **1** a fall of snow. **2** the quantity of snow falling within a certain area in a given time.

snowflake noun each of the many ice crystals that fall as snow.

snowline noun the altitude above which some snow remains on the ground throughout the year.

snowman noun a model of a human figure made with compressed snow.

snowplough (US spelling **snowplow**) noun a device or vehicle for clearing roads of snow.

snowshoe noun a flat device attached to the sole of a boot and used for walking on snow.

snowy adjective (**snowier**, **snowiest**)

1 having a lot of snow. **2** pure white.

snub verb (**snubs**, **snubbing**, **snubbed**) ignore or reject someone scornfully. noun an act of snubbing. adjective short and turned up at the end. □ **snub nose** a nose that is short and turned up at the end.

snuck N. Amer. informal past and past participle of **SNEAK**.

snuff¹ **verb 1** put out a candle. **2** (snuff out) abruptly put an end to. **3** (snuff it) Brit. informal die.

snuff² noun powdered tobacco that is sniffed up the nostril. **verb** sniff at.

snuffle verb (**snuffles**, **snuffling**, **snuffled**) **1** breathe noisily through a partially blocked nose. **2** (of an animal) make repeated sniffing sounds. noun **1** a snuffling sound. **2** (the snuffles) informal a cold.

snug adjective (**snugger**, **snuggest**) **1** warm and cosy. **2** close-fitting. noun Brit. a small, cosy bar in a pub or hotel. ■ **snugly** adverb.

snuggle verb (**snuggles**, **snuggling**, **snuggled**) settle into a warm, comfortable position.

so adverb **1** to such a great extent. **2** extremely; very much. **3** to the same extent; as. **4** that is the case. **5** similarly. **6** thus. conjunction **1** therefore. **2** (so that) with the result or aim that. **3** and then. **4** introducing a question or concluding statement. **5** in the same way. □ **or so** approximately.

so-and-so (plural **so-and-sos**) informal **1** a person whose name you do not know. **2** a disliked or unpleasant person. **so-called** wrongly called the specified thing; alleged. **so long!** informal goodbye. **so-so** neither very good nor very bad.

soak verb **1** make something thoroughly wet by leaving it in liquid. **2** (of a liquid) spread completely throughout. **3** (soak up) absorb a liquid. **4** (soak up) expose yourself to. noun **1** a period of soaking. **2** informal a heavy drinker.

soap noun **1** a substance used with water for washing and cleaning. **2** informal a soap opera. **verb** wash with soap. □ **soap opera** a television or radio serial that deals with the daily lives of a group of characters. ■ **soapy** adjective.

soapbox noun a box that someone stands on to speak in public.

soapstone noun a soft rock used for making ornaments.

soar verb **1** fly or rise high into the air. **2** increase rapidly.

sob verb (sobs, sobbing, sobbed) **1** cry with loud gasps. **2** say while sobbing. noun a sound of sobbing.

sober adjective (soberer, soberest) **1** not drunk. **2** serious. **3** (of a colour) not bright or likely to attract attention. verb (sobers, sobering, sobered) **1** (sober up) make or become sober after being drunk. **2** make or become serious. ■ **soberly** adverb.

sobriety /suh-**bry**-uh-ti/ noun the state of being sober.

sobriquet /**soh**-bri-kay/ or **soubriquet** /**soo**-bri-kay/ noun a person's nickname.

soccer noun a form of football played with a round ball which may not be handled during play except by the goalkeepers.

sociable adjective **1** keen to talk and do things with others. **2** friendly and welcoming. ■ **sociability** noun **sociably** adverb.

social adjective **1** having to do with society and its organization. **2** needing the company of others. **3** (of an activity) in which people meet each other for pleasure. **4** (of animals) breeding or living in organized communities. noun an informal social gathering. □ **social science 1** the study of human society and social relationships. **2** a subject within this field, such as economics. **social security** (in the UK) money provided by the state for poor or unemployed people. **social services** services provided by the state such as education and medical care. **social worker** a person whose job is to help improve the conditions of the poor, the old, etc. ■ **socially** adverb.

socialism noun the theory that a country's land, transport, industries, etc. should be owned or controlled by the community as a whole. ■ **socialist** noun & adjective.

socialite noun a person who mixes in fashionable society.

socialize or **socialise** verb (socializes, socializing, socialized) **1** mix socially with others. **2** make someone behave in a socially acceptable way.

society noun (plural societies) **1** people living together in an ordered community. **2** a community of people. **3** (also high society) people who are fashionable, wealthy, and influential. **4** an organization formed for a particular purpose. **5** the situation of being in the company of other people. ■ **societal** adjective.

sociology noun the study of human society. ■ **sociological** adjective **sociologist** noun.

sock noun **1** a knitted garment for the foot and lower part of the leg. **2** informal a hard blow. verb informal hit forcefully. □ **pull your socks up** informal make an effort to improve. **sock it to** informal make a forceful impression on.

socket noun **1** a hollow in which something fits or revolves. **2** an electrical device which a plug or light bulb fits into.

sod[1] noun **1** grass-covered ground. **2** a piece of turf.

sod[2] Brit. vulgar noun **1** an unpleasant person. **2** a person of a specified kind: *a lucky sod*. verb (sod off) go away!

soda noun **1** (also soda water) carbonated water. **2** N. Amer. a sweet fizzy drink. **3** a compound of sodium.

sodden adjective **1** soaked through. **2** having drunk an excessive amount of alcohol: *whisky-sodden*.

sodium noun a soft silver-white metallic element. □ **sodium bicarbonate** a white powder used in fizzy drinks and as a raising agent in baking. **sodium chloride** the chemical name for salt. **sodium hydroxide** a strongly alkaline white compound; caustic soda.

sodomite noun a person who engages in sodomy.

sodomy noun anal intercourse.

sofa noun a long upholstered seat with a back and arms.

soft adjective **1** easy to mould, cut, compress, or fold. **2** not rough in texture. **3** quiet and gentle. **4** (of light or colour) not harsh. **5** not strict enough. **6** informal requiring little effort. **7** informal foolish. **8** (soft on) informal having romantic feelings for. **9** (of a drink) not alcoholic. **10** (of a drug) not likely to cause addiction. **11** (of water) free from mineral salts. □ **have a soft spot for** be fond of. **soft focus** deliberate slight blurring in a photograph or film. **soft-hearted** kind and compassionate. **softly-softly** cautious and patient. **soft sell** the selling of something in a gently persuasive way. **soft-soap** informal use flattery to persuade someone. **soft-top** a car with a roof that can be folded back. **soft touch** informal a person who is easily persuaded or imposed on. ■ **softly** adverb **softness** noun.

softball noun a form of baseball played with a larger, softer ball.

soften verb **1** make or become soft or softer. **2** (soften up) make someone more easily persuaded or defeated.

software noun programs and other operating information used by a computer.

softwood noun the wood from a conifer as opposed to that of a broadleaved tree.

soggy adjective (soggier, soggiest) very wet and soft.

soil noun **1** the upper layer of earth, in which plants grow. **2** the territory of a particular nation. verb **1** make dirty. **2** bring discredit to.

soirée /swah-ray/ noun an evening social gathering.

sojourn /so-juhn/ literary noun a temporary stay. verb stay temporarily.

solace /sol-iss/ noun comfort in a difficult time. verb (solaces, solacing, solaced) give comfort to.

solar adjective having to do with the sun or its rays. □ **solar eclipse** an eclipse in which the sun is hidden by the moon. **solar plexus** a network of nerves at the pit of the stomach. **solar system** the sun together with the planets, asteroids, comets, etc. in orbit around it.

solarium noun a room equipped with sunlamps or sunbeds.

sold past and past participle of **SELL**.

solder noun a soft alloy used for joining metals. verb (solders, soldering, soldered) join with solder. □ **soldering iron** an electrical tool for melting and applying solder.

soldier noun **1** a person who serves in an army. **2** a private in an army. **3** Brit. informal a strip of bread or toast for dipping into a boiled egg. verb (soldiers, soldiering, soldiered) **1** serve as a soldier. **2** (soldier on) informal keep trying or working. □ **soldier of fortune** a mercenary. ■ **soldierly** adjective.

soldiery noun soldiers as a group.

sole[1] noun **1** the underside of the foot. **2** the underside of a piece of footwear. verb (soles, soling, soled) put a new sole on a shoe.

sole[2] noun a kind of edible flatfish.

sole[3] adjective **1** one and only. **2** belonging or restricted to one person or group. ■ **solely** adverb.

solecism /sol-i-si-z'm/ noun **1** a grammatical mistake. **2** an example of bad manners or incorrect behaviour.

solemn adjective **1** formal and dignified. **2** serious. **3** deeply sincere. ■ **solemnly** adverb.

solemnity noun (plural solemnities) **1** the quality of being solemn. **2** (solemnities) solemn rites or ceremonies.

solemnize or **solemnise** verb (solemnizes, solemnizing, solemnized) **1** perform a ceremony. **2** mark an occasion with a ceremony.

solenoid noun a coil of wire which becomes magnetic when an electric current is passed through it.

solicit verb (solicits, soliciting, solicited) **1** try to obtain something from someone. **2** (of a prostitute) approach someone. ■ **solicitation** noun.

solicitor noun Brit. a lawyer qualified to advise on property, wills, etc., instruct barristers, and represent clients in lower courts.

solicitous adjective showing interest or concern about a person's well-being. ■ **solicitously** adverb.

solicitude noun care or concern.

solid adjective (**solider**, **solidest**) **1** firm and stable in shape. **2** strongly built or made. **3** not hollow or having spaces or gaps. **4** consisting of the same substance throughout. **5** (of time) uninterrupted. **6** three-dimensional. noun **1** a solid substance or object. **2** (**solids**) food that is not liquid. □ **solid-state** (of an electronic device) using solid semiconductors, e.g. transistors, as opposed to valves. ■ **solidity** noun **solidly** adverb.

solidarity noun agreement and support resulting from shared interests, feelings, or opinions.

solidify verb (**solidifies**, **solidifying**, **solidified**) make or become hard or solid. ■ **solidification** noun.

soliloquy /suh-lil-uh-kwi/ noun (plural **soliloquies**) a speech in which a character speaks their thoughts aloud when alone on stage.

solipsism noun the view that the self is all that can be known to exist. ■ **solipsist** noun **solipsistic** adjective.

solitaire noun **1** a game for one player played by removing pegs from a board by jumping others over them. **2** the card game patience. **3** a single gem in a piece of jewellery.

solitary adjective **1** done or existing alone. **2** (of a place) secluded or isolated. **3** single. □ **solitary confinement** the isolating of a prisoner in a separate cell as a punishment.

solitude noun the state of being alone.

solo noun (plural **solos**) **1** a piece of music or dance for one performer. **2** a flight undertaken by a single pilot. adjective & adverb for or done by one person. verb (**soloes**, **soloing**, **soloed**) perform a solo. ■ **soloist** noun.

solstice noun each of the two times in the year when the sun reaches its highest or lowest point in the sky at noon, marked by the longest and shortest days.

soluble adjective **1** (of a substance) able to be dissolved. **2** (of a problem) able to be solved. ■ **solubility** noun.

solution noun **1** a way of solving a problem. **2** the correct answer to a puzzle. **3** a mixture formed when a substance is dissolved in a liquid. **4** the process of dissolving.

solve verb (**solves**, **solving**, **solved**) find an answer to, or way of dealing with, a problem or mystery.

solvency noun the state of having more money than you owe.

solvent adjective **1** having more money than you owe. **2** able to dissolve other substances. noun the liquid in which another substance is dissolved to form a solution.

sombre (US spelling somber) adjective **1** dark or dull. **2** very solemn or serious. ■ **sombrely** adverb.

sombrero noun (plural **sombreros**) a broad-brimmed felt or straw hat.

some determiner **1** an unspecified amount or number of. **2** unknown or unspecified. **3** approximately. **4** a considerable amount or number of. **5** a certain small amount or number of. **6** used to express admiration. pronoun a certain amount or number of people or things.

somebody pronoun someone.

some day or **someday** adverb at some time in the future.

somehow adverb **1** by one means or another. **2** for an unknown or unspecified reason.

someone pronoun **1** an unknown or unspecified person. **2** an important or famous person.

someplace adverb & pronoun N. Amer. somewhere.

somersault noun a movement in which a person turns head over heels and finishes on their feet. **verb** perform a somersault.

something pronoun an unspecified or unknown thing or amount.

sometime adverb at some unspecified or unknown time. **adjective** former.

sometimes adverb occasionally.

somewhat adverb to some extent.

somewhere adverb in or to an unspecified or unknown place. **pronoun** some unspecified place.

somnambulism noun formal sleepwalking. ■ **somnambulist** noun.

somnolent adjective 1 sleepy. 2 causing sleepiness. ■ **somnolence** noun.

son noun 1 a boy or man in relation to his parents. 2 a male descendant. 3 (**the Son**) Jesus Christ. □ **son-in-law** (plural **sons-in-law**) the husband of your daughter.

sonar noun a system for detecting objects under water by giving out sound pulses.

sonata /suh-nah-tuh/ noun a piece of music for a solo instrument, sometimes with piano accompaniment.

song noun 1 a set of words set to music. 2 singing. 3 the musical phrases uttered by some birds, whales, and insects. 4 literary a poem. □ **for a song** informal very cheaply. **on song** Brit. informal performing well.

songbird noun a bird with a musical song.

songster noun (feminine **songstress**) a person who sings.

sonic adjective relating to or using sound waves. □ **sonic boom** an explosive noise caused by the shock wave from an object travelling faster than the speed of sound. ■ **sonically** adverb.

sonnet noun a poem of fourteen lines using a fixed rhyme scheme.

sonorous adjective 1 (of a sound) deep and full. 2 (of speech) using powerful language. ■ **sonority** noun **sonorously** adverb.

soon adverb 1 in or after a short time. 2 early. 3 (**sooner**) rather.

soot noun a black powdery substance produced when wood, coal, etc. is burned. ■ **sooty** adjective.

soothe verb (**soothes**, **soothing**, **soothed**) 1 gently calm. 2 relieve pain or discomfort.

soothsayer noun a person supposed to be able to foresee the future.

sop noun a thing given or done to calm or please someone who is angry or disappointed. **verb** (**sops**, **sopping**, **sopped**) (**sop up**) soak up liquid.

sophism noun a false argument.

sophist noun a person who uses clever but false arguments. ■ **sophistry** noun.

sophisticate noun a sophisticated person.

sophisticated adjective 1 highly developed and complex. 2 having experience and taste in matters of culture or fashion. ■ **sophistication** noun.

sophomore noun N. Amer. a second-year university or high-school student.

soporific adjective causing drowsiness or sleep.

sopping adjective wet through.

soppy adjective (**soppier**, **soppiest**) Brit. informal 1 too sentimental. 2 feeble. ■ **soppily** adverb.

soprano noun (plural **sopranos**) the highest singing voice.

sorbet /sor-bay/ noun a water ice.

sorcerer noun (feminine **sorceress**) a person who practises magic. ■ **sorcery** noun.

sordid adjective 1 dishonest or immoral. 2 extremely dirty and unpleasant. ■ **sordidly** adverb.

sore adjective 1 painful or aching. 2 urgent: in sore need. 3 N. Amer. informal upset and angry. **noun** a raw or painful place on the body. **adverb** old use extremely: sore afraid. □ **sore point** an issue about which someone feels distressed or annoyed. ■ **soreness** noun.

sorely adverb seriously; badly.

sorghum /sor-guhm/ noun a cereal found in warm regions, grown for grain and animal feed.

sorority noun (plural **sororities**) N. Amer. a society for female students in a university or college.

sorrel noun **1** an edible plant with a bitter flavour. **2** a light reddish-brown colour.

sorrow noun **1** deep distress caused by loss or disappointment. **2** a cause of sorrow.

sorrowful adjective feeling or showing sorrow. ■ **sorrowfully** adverb.

sorry adjective (**sorrier, sorriest**) **1** feeling sympathy for someone else's misfortune. **2** feeling or expressing regret. **3** in a poor or pitiful state. **4** unpleasant and regrettable.

sort noun **1** a category of people or things with a common feature or features. **2** informal a person: *a friendly sort.* verb **1** arrange systematically in groups. **2** (often **sort out**) separate from a mixed group. **3** (**sort out**) deal with a problem or difficulty. □ **out of sorts** slightly unwell or unhappy.

sorted adjective Brit. informal **1** organized; arranged. **2** emotionally stable.

sortie noun **1** an attack made by troops from a position of defence. **2** a flight by an aircraft on a military operation. **3** a short trip.

SOS noun **1** an international signal sent when in great trouble. **2** an urgent appeal for help.

ⓘ letters chosen to be easily transmitted and recognized in Morse code, but often thought to be short for *save our souls.*

sot noun old use a person who is regularly drunk. ■ **sottish** adjective.

sotto voce /sot-toh **voh**-chay/ adverb & adjective in a quiet voice.

soubriquet ⇨ **SOBRIQUET**.

soufflé noun a light, spongy baked dish made by mixing egg yolks with beaten egg whites.

sought past and past participle of **SEEK**. □ **sought after** much in demand.

souk /sook/ noun an Arab market.

soul noun **1** the spiritual element of a person, believed by some to be im-

mortal. **2** a person's inner nature. **3** emotional energy or power. **4** (**the soul of**) a perfect example of a particular quality. **5** an individual: *poor soul!* **6** a kind of music that expresses strong emotions, made popular by American blacks. □ **soul-destroying** unbearably dull and repetitive. **soul-searching** close examination of your emotions and motives.

soulful adjective expressing deep feeling. ■ **soulfully** adverb.

soulless adjective **1** lacking character or interest. **2** lacking human feelings.

soulmate noun a person ideally suited to another.

sound¹ noun **1** vibrations which travel through the air and are sensed by the ear. **2** a thing that can be heard. **3** an impression given by words. verb **1** make sound. **2** say something; utter. **3** give a specified impression. **4** (**sound off**) express your opinions loudly or forcefully. □ **sound barrier** the point at which an aircraft approaches the speed of sound. **sound bite** a short, memorable extract from a speech or interview. **sound effect** a sound other than speech or music that is used in a play, film, etc. **sound wave** a wave by which sound travels through water, air, etc. ■ **soundless** adjective.

sound² adjective **1** in good condition. **2** based on solid judgement. **3** financially secure. **4** competent or reliable. **5** (of sleep) deep and unbroken. **6** severe or thorough. ■ **soundly** adverb.

sound³ verb **1** find out the depth of water using a line, pole, or sound echoes. **2** (**sound out**) question someone about their opinions or feelings.

sound⁴ noun a narrow stretch of water connecting two larger bodies of water.

sounding noun **1** a measurement taken by sounding. **2** (**soundings**) information found out before taking action. □ **sounding board** a person or group that you talk to in order to test out new ideas.

soundproof **adjective** preventing sound getting in or out. **verb** make soundproof.

soundtrack **noun** the sound accompaniment to a film.

soup **noun** a savoury liquid dish made by boiling meat, fish, or vegetables. **verb** (**soup up**) informal make a car more powerful. □ **soup kitchen** a place where free food is served to homeless or very poor people.

soupçon /soop-son/ **noun** a very small quantity of something.

sour **adjective** **1** having a sharp taste like lemon or vinegar. **2** unpleasantly stale. **3** resentful or angry. **verb** make or become sour. □ **sour cream** cream that has been made sour by adding bacteria. **sour grapes** an attitude of pretending to despise something because you cannot have it yourself. ■ **sourly** adverb **sourness** noun.

source **noun** **1** a place, person, or thing from which something originates. **2** a place where a river or stream starts. **3** a person, book, or document that provides information. **verb** (**sources**, **sourcing**, **sourced**) obtain from a particular source.

sourpuss **noun** informal a bad-tempered or sulky person.

souse /sowss/ **verb** (**souses**, **sousing**, **soused**) **1** soak in liquid. **2** (**soused**) pickled or marinaded.

south **noun** **1** the direction which is on your right-hand side when you are facing east. **2** the southern part of a place. **adjective** **1** lying towards or facing the south. **2** (of a wind) blowing from the south. **adverb** to or towards the south. ■ **southward** adjective & adverb **southwards** adverb.

south-east **noun** the direction or region halfway between south and east. **adjective & adverb** **1** towards or facing the south-east. **2** (of a wind) blowing from the south-east. ■ **south-eastern** adjective.

south-easterly **adjective & adverb** **1** in or towards the south-east. **2** (of a wind) blowing from the south-east.

southerly **adjective & adverb** **1** facing or moving towards the south. **2** (of a wind) blowing from the south.

southern **adjective** **1** situated in or facing the south. **2** coming from or characteristic of the south.

southerner **noun** a person from the south of a region.

south-west **noun** the direction or region halfway between south and west. **adjective & adverb** **1** towards or facing the south-west. **2** (of a wind) blowing from the south-west. ■ **south-western** adjective.

south-westerly **adjective & adverb** **1** in or towards the south-west. **2** (of a wind) blowing from the south-west.

souvenir **noun** a thing that is kept as a reminder of a person, place, or event.

sou'wester /sow-**wess**-ter/ **noun** a waterproof hat with a brim that covers the back of the neck.

sovereign **noun** **1** a king or queen who is the supreme ruler of a country. **2** a former British gold coin worth one pound sterling. **adjective 1** possessing supreme power. **2** (of a country) independent.

sovereignty **noun** (plural **sovereignties**) **1** supreme power or authority. **2** a self-governing state.

soviet **noun** **1** (**Soviet**) a citizen of the former Soviet Union. **2** an elected council in the former Soviet Union. **adjective** (**Soviet**) having to do with the former Soviet Union.

sow[1] /soh/ **verb** (past **sowed**; past participle **sown** or **sowed**) **1** plant seed by scattering it on or in the earth. **2** plant an area with seed. **3** spread or introduce something unwelcome.

sow[2] /sow/ **noun** an adult female pig.

soya bean **noun** an edible bean that is high in protein.

soy sauce **noun** a sauce made with fermented soya beans, used in Chinese and Japanese cooking.

sozzled **adjective** informal very drunk.

spa **noun** **1** a mineral spring considered to have health-giving properties. **2** a place with a mineral spring.

space noun **1** unoccupied ground or area. **2** an expanse of unoccupied ground. **3** a blank between typed or written words or characters. **4** the dimensions of height, depth, and width within which all things exist and move. **5** (also **outer space**) the universe beyond the earth's atmosphere. **6** an interval of time. **7** freedom to live and develop as you wish. verb (**spaces**, **spacing**, **spaced**) **1** position items at a distance from one another. **2** (**be spaced out**) informal be confused or not completely conscious. □ **space shuttle** a spacecraft used for journeys between earth and craft orbiting the earth. **space station** a large spacecraft used as a base for manned operations in space.

spacecraft noun (plural **spacecraft** or **spacecrafts**) a vehicle used for travelling in space.

spaceman noun a male astronaut.

spaceship noun a manned spacecraft.

spacesuit noun a pressurized suit covering the whole body that allows an astronaut to survive in space.

spacial ⇒ **SPATIAL**.

spacious adjective (of a room or building) having plenty of space.

spade noun a tool with a rectangular metal blade and a long handle, used for digging. □ **call a spade a spade** speak plainly and frankly.

spades noun one of the four suits in a pack of playing cards, represented by a black heart-shaped figure with a small stalk. □ **in spades** informal in large amounts or to a high degree.

spadework noun hard or routine work done to prepare for something.

spaghetti /spuh-get-ti/ plural noun pasta made in long, thin strands.

spake old-fashioned past of **SPEAK**.

spam noun trademark a canned meat product made mainly from ham.

span noun **1** width or extent from side to side. **2** the length of time for which something lasts. **3** a part of a bridge between the uprights supporting it. **4** the maximum distance between the

tips of the thumb and little finger. verb (**spans**, **spanning**, **spanned**) extend across or over.

spangle noun **1** a small piece of decorative glittering material. **2** a spot of bright colour or light. ■ **spangled** adjective **spangly** adjective.

Spaniard noun a person from Spain.

spaniel noun a breed of dog with a long silky coat and drooping ears.

Spanish noun the main language of Spain and of much of Central and South America. adjective relating to Spain or Spanish.

spank verb slap someone on the buttocks with your hand or a flat object. noun a slap on the buttocks.

spanking adjective **1** brisk. **2** informal impressive or pleasing. noun a series of spanks.

spanner noun Brit. a tool for gripping and turning a nut or bolt. □ **spanner in the works** something that prevents a plan being carried out successfully.

spar[1] noun **1** a thick, strong pole used to support the sails on a ship. **2** the main supporting structure of an aircraft's wing.

spar[2] verb (**spars**, **sparring**, **sparred**) **1** make the motions of boxing without landing heavy blows, as a form of training. **2** argue in a friendly way.

spare adjective **1** additional to what is required for ordinary use. **2** not being used or occupied. **3** thin. **4** elegantly simple. noun an item kept in case another is lost, broken, or worn out. verb (**spares**, **sparing**, **spared**) **1** let someone have something that you have enough of. **2** refrain from killing or harming. **3** protect from something unpleasant. □ **go spare** Brit. informal become extremely angry. **spare no expense** be prepared to pay any amount. **spare ribs** trimmed ribs of pork. **spare tyre** informal a roll of fat around a person's waist.

sparing adjective not wasteful; economical. ■ **sparingly** adverb.

spark noun **1** a small fiery particle produced by burning or caused by friction. **2** a flash of light produced by an electrical discharge. **3** a small but concentrated amount. **4** a sense of liveliness and excitement. **verb 1** give out or produce sparks. **2** ignite. **3** (usu. **spark off**) cause; trigger. □ **spark plug** a device that produces a spark to ignite the fuel in a vehicle engine. ■ **sparky** adjective.

sparkle **verb** (**sparkles, sparkling, sparkled**) **1** shine brightly with flashes of light. **2** be attractively lively and witty. **3** (**sparkling**) (of a drink) fizzy. **noun 1** a glittering flash of light. **2** attractive liveliness and wit. ■ **sparkly** adjective.

sparkler **noun** a hand-held firework that gives out sparks.

sparrow **noun** a small bird with brown and grey plumage.

sparrowhawk **noun** a small hawk that preys on small birds.

sparse **adjective** thinly scattered. ■ **sparsely** adverb **sparsity** noun.

spartan **adjective** not comfortable or luxurious.

spasm **noun 1** a sudden involuntary contraction of a muscle. **2** a sudden spell of an activity or sensation.

spasmodic **adjective** occurring or done in brief, irregular bursts. ■ **spasmodically** adverb.

spastic **adjective 1** relating to or affected by muscle spasm. **2** offensive having to do with cerebral palsy. **noun** offensive a person with cerebral palsy. ■ **spasticity** noun.

> **i** say *person with cerebral palsy* rather than **spastic**, which many people find offensive.

spat[1] past and past participle of **SPIT**[1].

spat[2] **noun** a cloth covering formerly worn by men over their ankles and shoes.

spat[3] **noun** informal a petty quarrel.

spate **noun 1** a large number of similar things coming quickly one after another. **2** a sudden flood in a river.

spathe /spayth/ **noun** a large sheath enclosing the flower cluster of certain plants.

spatial or **spacial** **adjective** having to do with space. ■ **spatially** adverb.

spatter **verb** (**spatters, spattering, spattered**) **1** cover with drops or spots. **2** splash over a surface. **noun** a spray or splash.

spatula **noun** an implement with a broad, flat, blunt blade, used for mixing or spreading.

spawn **verb 1** (of a fish, frog, etc.) release or deposit eggs. **2** give rise to. **noun** the eggs of fish, frogs, etc.

spay **verb** sterilize a female animal by removing the ovaries.

speak **verb** (**speaks, speaking, spoke**; past participle **spoken**) **1** say something. **2** communicate, or be able to communicate, in a specified language. **3** (**speak up**) speak more loudly. **4** (**speak out** or **up**) express your opinions frankly and publicly. □ **speak in tongues** speak in an unknown language during religious worship. **speak volumes** convey a great deal without using words.

speakeasy **noun** (plural **speakeasies**) (in the US during Prohibition) a secret illegal drinking club.

speaker **noun 1** a person who speaks. **2** (**Speaker**) the person who is in charge of proceedings in a law-making assembly. **3** a loudspeaker.

spear **noun 1** a weapon with a pointed metal tip and a long shaft. **2** a pointed stem of asparagus or broccoli. **verb** pierce or strike with a spear or other pointed object.

spearhead **noun** an individual or group that leads an attack or movement. **verb** lead an attack or movement.

spearmint **noun** common garden mint, used in cooking.

spec **noun** informal **1** (**on spec**) without any specific preparation or plan. **2** a detailed working description.

special **adjective 1** better or different from what is usual. **2** designed for or belonging to a particular person, place, or event. **3** exceptionally good. **noun 1** something designed or organized for a particular occasion or purpose. **2** a dish not on the regular menu but served on a particular day. □ **special constable** a person trained to act as a police officer on particular occasions. **special effects** illusions created for films and television by camerawork, computer graphics, etc. **special pleading** argument in which aspects unfavourable to your point of view are ignored.

specialist noun a person who is highly skilled or knowledgeable in a particular field. adjective involving detailed knowledge within a field. ■ **specialism** noun.

speciality (US spelling **specialty**) noun (plural **specialities**) **1** a skill or area of study in which someone is an expert. **2** a product for which a person or region is famous. **3** (usu. specialty) a branch of medicine or surgery.

specialize or **specialise** verb (specializes, specializing, specialized) **1** concentrate on and become expert in a particular skill or area. **2** (be specialized) be adapted or designed to serve a special function. ■ **specialization** noun.

specially adverb **1** for a special purpose. **2** particularly.

species noun (plural **species**) **1** a group of animals or plants that are capable of breeding with each other. **2** a kind.

specific adjective **1** clearly defined or identified. **2** precise and clear. **3** (specific to) belonging or relating only to. noun (specifics) precise details. ■ **specifically** adverb.

specification noun **1** the action of specifying. **2** (usu. specifications) a detailed description of the design and materials used to make something. **3** the standard of workmanship and materials in a piece of work.

specify verb (specifies, specifying, specified) state, identify, or require clearly and definitely.

specimen noun **1** an example of an animal, plant, object, etc. used for study or display. **2** a sample for med-

ical testing. **3** a typical example of something. **4** informal a person of a specific type: *a sorry specimen.*

specious /spee-shuhss/ adjective **1** seeming reasonable, but actually wrong. **2** misleading in appearance.

speck noun a tiny spot or particle. verb mark with small spots.

speckle noun a small spot or patch of colour. verb (speckles, speckling, speckled) mark with speckles.

specs plural noun informal spectacles.

spectacle noun a visually striking performance or display.

spectacles plural noun Brit. a pair of glasses.

spectacular adjective very impressive, striking, or dramatic. noun a spectacular performance or event. ■ **spectacularly** adverb.

spectate verb (spectates, spectating, spectated) be a spectator.

spectator noun a person who watches at a show, game, etc.

spectral adjective **1** like a spectre. **2** having to do with the spectrum.

spectre (US spelling **specter**) noun **1** a ghost. **2** a possible unpleasant or dangerous occurrence.

spectrum noun (plural **spectra**) **1** a band of colours produced by separating light into elements with different wavelengths, e.g. in a rainbow. **2** the entire range of wavelengths of light. **3** a range of sound waves or different types of wave. **4** a scale extending between two points: *the political spectrum.*

speculate verb (speculates, speculating, speculated) **1** form a theory without firm evidence. **2** invest in stocks, property, etc. in the hope of gain but with the risk of loss. ■ **speculation** noun **speculator** noun.

speculative adjective **1** based on theory or guesswork rather than knowledge. **2** (of an investment) risky. ■ **speculatively** adverb.

speech noun **1** the expression of thoughts and feelings using spoken language. **2** a formal address delivered to an audience. **3** a sequence of lines written for one character in a play. □ **speech therapy** treatment to help people with speech problems.

speechify verb (**speechifies, speechifying, speechified**) deliver a speech in a boring or pompous way.

speechless adjective unable to speak due to shock or strong emotion.

speed noun **1** the rate at which someone or something moves or operates. **2** a fast rate of movement or action. **3** each of the possible gear ratios of a vehicle or bicycle. **4** the sensitivity of photographic film to light. **5** informal an amphetamine drug. verb (**speeds, speeding, speeded** or **sped**) **1** move quickly. **2** (**speed up**) move or work more quickly. **3** travel at a speed greater than the legal limit. **4** old use make prosperous or successful.

speedboat noun a motor boat designed for high speed.

speedometer noun an instrument that indicates a vehicle's speed.

speedway noun a form of motorcycle racing in which the riders race around an oval dirt track.

speedy adjective (**speedier, speediest**) done, occurring, or moving quickly. ■ **speedily** adverb.

spell[1] verb (**spells, spelling, spelled** or chiefly Brit. **spelt**) **1** write or name the letters that form a word in correct sequence. **2** (of letters) form a word. **3** be a sign of. **4** (**spell out**) explain clearly and in detail.

spell[2] noun **1** a form of words with magical power. **2** a state of enchantment caused by a spell. **3** an ability to control or influence others.

spell[3] noun a short period of time.

spellbind verb (**spellbinds, spellbinding, spellbound**) hold the complete attention of someone.

spellchecker noun a computer program which checks the spelling of words in text.

spelling noun **1** the process of spelling a word. **2** the way in which a word is spelled.

spend verb (**spends, spending,** spent) **1** pay out money to buy or hire goods or services. **2** use up completely. **3** pass time in a specified way. □ **spend a penny** Brit. a polite way of saying 'urinate'. ■ **spender** noun.

spendthrift noun a person who spends money irresponsibly.

sperm noun (plural **sperm** or **sperms**) **1** semen. **2** a spermatozoon. □ **sperm whale** a toothed whale that feeds largely on squid.

spermatozoon /sper-muh-tuh-**zoh**-on/ noun (plural **spermatozoa** /sper-muh-tuh-**zoh**-uh/) the male sex cell of an animal, that fertilizes the egg.

spermicide noun a contraceptive substance that kills spermatozoa.

spew verb **1** pour out in large quantities. **2** informal vomit. noun informal vomit.

sphagnum /**sfag**-nuhm/ noun a kind of moss that grows in boggy areas.

sphere noun **1** a round solid figure in which every point on the surface is at an equal distance from the centre. **2** an area of activity or interest.

spherical adjective shaped like a sphere. ■ **spherically** adverb.

sphincter noun a ring of muscle surrounding an opening such as the anus.

sphinx noun an ancient Egyptian stone figure having a lion's body and a human or animal head.

spice noun **1** a strong-tasting substance used to flavour food. **2** an element that provides interest and excitement. verb (**spices, spicing, spiced**) **1** flavour with spice. **2** (**spice up**) make more exciting or interesting.

spick and span adjective neat, clean, and well looked after.

spicy adjective (**spicier, spiciest**) **1** strongly flavoured with spice. **2** mildly indecent. ■ **spiciness** noun.

spider noun a small insect-like creature (an arachnid) with eight legs. ■ **spidery** adjective.

spiel /shpeel, speel/ noun informal an elaborate and insincere speech made in attempt to persuade someone.

spiffing adjective Brit. informal, dated excellent; splendid.

spigot noun **1** a small peg or plug. **2** the end of a section of a pipe that fits into the socket of the next one.

spike noun **1** a thin, pointed piece of metal or wood. **2** each of several metal points set into the sole of a sports shoe to prevent slipping. **3** a cluster of flower heads attached directly to a long stem. verb **(spikes, spiking, spiked) 1** impale on or pierce with a spike. **2** cover with sharp points. **3** informal secretly add alcohol or a drug to drink or food. ■ **spiky** adjective.

spill[1] verb **(spills, spilling, spilt** or **spilled) 1** flow, or allow to flow, over the edge of a container. **2** move or empty out from a place. noun **1** a quantity of liquid spilt. **2** informal a fall from a horse or bicycle. □ **spill the beans** informal reveal confidential information. **spill blood** kill or wound people. ■ **spillage** noun.

spill[2] noun a thin strip of wood or paper used for lighting a fire.

spin verb **(spins, spinning, spun) 1** turn round quickly. **2** (of a person's head) have a dizzy sensation. **3** (of a ball) move through the air with a revolving motion. **4** draw out and twist the fibres of wool, cotton, etc. to convert them into yarn. **5** (of a spider, silkworm, etc.) produce silk or a web by forcing out a fine thread from a special gland. **6 (spin out)** make something last as long as possible. noun **1** a spinning motion. **2** informal a brief trip in a vehicle for pleasure. **3** a favourable slant given to a news story. □ **flat spin** Brit. informal a state of agitation. **spin doctor** informal a person employed by a political party to give a favourable interpretation of events to the media. **spin dryer** a machine that dries washed clothes by spinning them in a drum. **spinning wheel** an apparatus for spinning yarn or thread with a spindle driven by a wheel operated by hand or foot. **spin-off** something unexpected but useful

resulting from an activity. ■ **spinner** adjective.

spina bifida /spy-nuh **bi**-fi-duh/ noun a condition in which part of the spinal cord is exposed, sometimes causing paralysis.

spinach noun a plant with large dark green leaves which are eaten as a vegetable.

spinal adjective relating to the spine. □ **spinal column** the spine. **spinal cord** the nerve fibres enclosed in the spine and connected to the brain.

spindle noun **1** a slender rod with tapered ends used for spinning wool, flax, etc. by hand. **2** a rod around which something revolves.

spindly adjective long or tall and thin.

spindrift noun spray blown from the sea by the wind.

spine noun **1** a series of bones extending from the skull to the small of the back, enclosing the spinal cord; the backbone. **2** the part of a book that encloses the inner edges of the pages. **3** a hard pointed projection found on certain plants and animals. □ **spinechiller** a story or film that causes terror and excitement. ■ **spiny** adjective.

spineless adjective **1** having no spine. **2** lacking spines. **3** lacking courage and determination. •

spinet noun a kind of small harpsichord.

spinnaker noun a large three-cornered sail used on a racing yacht when the wind is coming from behind.

spinney noun (plural **spinneys**) Brit. a small area of trees and bushes.

spinster noun disapproving a single woman beyond the usual age for marriage. ■ **spinsterhood** noun.

spiral adjective winding in a continuous curve around a central point or axis. noun **1** a spiral curve, shape, or pattern. **2** a continuous rise or fall of prices, wages, etc. verb **(spirals, spiralling, spiralled;** US spelling **spirals, spiraling, spiraled) 1** follow a spiral course. **2** show a continuous increase or decrease. ■ **spirally** adverb.

spire noun a pointed structure on the top of a church tower.

spirit noun **1** the part of a person that consists of their character and feelings rather than their body. **2** a supernatural being. **3** typical character, quality, or mood. **4** (**spirits**) a person's mood. **5** courage, energy, and determination. **6** the real meaning of something as opposed to its strict interpretation. **7** (also **spirits**) chiefly Brit. strong alcoholic drink, e.g. rum. **8** purified distilled alcohol, e.g. methylated spirits. verb (**spirits, spiriting, spirited**) (**spirit away**) take away rapidly and secretly. □ **spirit level** a glass tube partially filled with a liquid, containing an air bubble whose position reveals whether a surface is perfectly level.

spirited adjective energetic and determined. ■ **spiritedly** adverb.

spiritual adjective **1** having to do with the human spirit as opposed to material or physical things. **2** having to do with religion or religious belief. noun a religious song of a kind associated with black Christians of the southern US. ■ **spirituality** noun **spiritually** adverb.

spiritualism noun the belief that the spirits of the dead can communicate with the living. ■ **spiritualist** noun.

spirogyra /spy-ruh-jy-ruh/ noun a type of algae consisting of long green threads.

spit¹ verb (**spits, spitting, spat** or **spit**) **1** forcibly eject saliva, or food, liquid, etc., from the mouth. **2** say in a hostile way. **3** give out small bursts of sparks or hot fat. **4** (**it spits, it is spitting**) Brit. light rain falls. noun **1** saliva. **2** an act of spitting. □ **be the spitting image of** informal look exactly like.

spit² noun **1** a metal rod pushed through meat in order to hold and turn it while it is roasted. **2** a narrow point of land projecting into the sea.

spite noun a desire to hurt, annoy, or offend. verb (**spites, spiting, spited**) deliberately hurt, annoy, or offend someone. □ **in spite of** without being affected by.

spiteful adjective deliberately hurtful; malicious. ■ **spitefully** adverb.

spitfire noun a person with a fierce temper.

spittle noun saliva.

spittoon noun a container for spitting into.

spiv noun Brit. informal a flashily dressed man who makes a living by dishonest business dealings.

splash verb **1** (of a liquid) fall in scattered drops. **2** make wet with scattered drops. **3** move around in water, causing it to fly about. **4** (**splash down**) (of a spacecraft) land on water. **5** prominently display a story or photograph in a newspaper or magazine. **6** (**splash out**) Brit. informal spend money freely. noun **1** an instance of splashing. **2** a small quantity of liquid splashed on to a surface. **3** a small quantity of liquid added to a drink. **4** a bright patch of colour. **5** informal a prominent news story. □ **make a splash** informal attract a lot of attention.

splatter verb (**splatters, splattering, splattered**) splash with a sticky or thick liquid. noun a splash of a sticky or thick liquid.

splay verb spread out wide apart.

spleen noun **1** an organ involved in producing and removing blood cells. **2** bad temper.

splendid adjective **1** magnificent; very impressive. **2** informal excellent. ■ **splendidly** adverb.

splendour (US spelling **splendor**) noun magnificent and impressive appearance.

splenetic adjective bad-tempered or spiteful.

splice verb (**splices, splicing, spliced**) **1** join ropes by weaving together the strands at the ends. **2** join pieces of film, tape, etc. at the ends. noun a spliced join.

spliff noun informal a cannabis cigarette.

splint noun a rigid support for a broken bone.

splinter noun a small, thin, sharp piece of wood, glass, etc. broken off from a larger piece. verb (**splinters**, **splintering**, **splintered**) break into splinters. □ **splinter group** a small breakaway group.

split verb (**splits**, **splitting**, **split**) **1** break into parts by force. **2** divide into parts or groups. **3** (often **split up**) end a marriage or other relationship. **4** (**be splitting**) informal (of the head) be suffering great pain from a headache. noun **1** a tear or crack. **2** an instance of splitting. **3** (**the splits**) a leap or seated position with the legs straight and at right angles to the body. □ **split infinitive** Grammar an infinitive construction in which an adverb or other word is placed between to and the verb (e.g. *she used to secretly admire him*), traditionally regarded as bad English. **split-level** (of a room or building) having the floor divided into two levels. **split second** a very brief moment of time.

splodge noun Brit. a spot, splash, or smear.

splosh informal verb make a soft splashing sound. noun a splashing sound.

splurge informal noun **1** a sudden burst of extravagance. **2** a large or excessive amount. verb (**splurges**, **splurging**, **splurged**) spend extravagantly.

splutter verb (**splutters**, **spluttering**, **spluttered**) **1** make a series of short explosive spitting or choking sounds. **2** say in a rapid, unclear way. noun a spluttering sound.

spoil verb (**spoils**, **spoiling**, past and past participle **spoilt** (chiefly Brit.) or **spoiled**) **1** make something less good or enjoyable. **2** (of food) become unfit for eating. **3** harm the character of a child by not being strict enough with it. **4** treat with great or excessive kindness. **5** (**be spoiling for**) be extremely eager for. noun (**spoils**) stolen goods.

spoiler noun **1** a flap on an aircraft wing which can be raised to create drag and slow it down. **2** a similar device on a car intended to improve road-holding at high speeds.

spoilsport noun a person who spoils the pleasure of others.

spoke[1] noun each of the rods connecting the centre of a wheel to its rim.

spoke[2] past of **SPEAK**.

spoken past participle of **SPEAK**. adjective speaking in a specified way: *a soft-spoken man*. □ **be spoken for** be already claimed.

spokesman or **spokeswoman** noun a person who makes statements on behalf of a group.

sponge noun **1** a simple sea creature with no backbone and a soft porous body. **2** a piece of a light, absorbent substance used for washing, as padding, etc. **3** a cake made with little or no fat. verb (**sponges**, **sponging** or **spongeing**, **sponged**) **1** wipe or clean with a wet sponge or cloth. **2** informal obtain money or food from others without giving anything in return. □ **sponge bag** Brit. a toilet bag. ■ **sponger** noun **spongy** adjective.

sponsor noun **1** a person or organization that helps pays for an event in return for advertising. **2** a person who promises to give money to a charity if another person completes a task or activity. **3** a person who proposes a new law. verb be a sponsor for. ■ **sponsorship** noun.

☑ -or, not -er: spons**or**.

spontaneous adjective **1** done or occurring as a result of an unplanned impulse. **2** open, natural, and relaxed. **3** occurring without apparent external cause. ■ **spontaneity** noun **spontaneously** adverb.

spoof noun informal a humorous imitation of something.

spook informal noun **1** a ghost. **2** N. Amer. a spy. verb frighten.

spooky adjective (**spookier**, **spookiest**) informal sinister or ghostly. ■ **spookily** adverb.

spool noun a cylindrical device on which thread, film, etc. can be wound.

verb wind on to a spool.

spoon noun an implement consisting of a small, shallow bowl on a long handle, used for eating and serving food. **verb** transfer with a spoon. □ **spoon-feed 1** feed with a spoon. **2** provide someone with so much help that they do not need to think for themselves. ■ **spoonful** noun.

spoonbill noun a tall wading bird having a long bill with a very broad flat tip.

spoonerism noun a mistake in speech in which the initial sounds or letters of two or more words are accidentally swapped around, as in *you have hissed the mystery lectures*.

sporadic adjective occurring at irregular intervals or only in a few places. ■ **sporadically** adverb.

spore noun a tiny reproductive cell produced by lower plants, fungi, etc.

sporran noun a small pouch worn around the waist as part of men's Scottish Highland dress.

sport noun **1** a competitive activity involving physical effort and skill. **2** informal a person who behaves well when teased or defeated. **verb 1** wear a distinctive item. **2** literary amuse yourself or play in a lively way. □ **sports car** a small, fast car. **sports jacket** a man's informal jacket resembling a suit jacket.

sporting adjective **1** connected with or interested in sport. **2** fair and generous. ■ **sportingly** adverb.

sportive adjective playful; light-hearted.

sportsman or **sportswoman** noun **1** a person who takes part in a sport. **2** a person who behaves sportingly.

sporty adjective (sportier, sportiest) informal **1** fond of or good at sport. **2** (of clothing) suitable for sport or casual wear. **3** (of a car) compact and fast.

spot noun **1** a small round mark on a surface. **2** a pimple. **3** a particular place, point, or position. **verb** (spots, spotting, spotted) **1** notice or recognize, especially with difficulty or effort. **2** mark with spots. **3** (it spots, it

is spotting, etc.) light rain falls. □ **on the spot 1** immediately. **2** at the scene of an action or event. **spot check** a test made without warning on a randomly selected subject. **spot on** completely accurate or accurately. ■ **spotted** adjective **spotter** noun **spotty** adjective.

spotless adjective absolutely clean or pure. ■ **spotlessly** adverb.

spotlight noun **1** a lamp projecting a narrow, strong beam of light directly on to a place or person. **2** (the spotlight) intense public attention. **verb** (spotlights, spotlighting, past and past participle spotlighted or spotlit) light up with a spotlight.

spouse noun formal a husband or wife.

spout noun **1** a projecting tube or lip through or over which liquid can be poured from a container. **2** a stream of liquid flowing out. **verb 1** send out or flow in a stream. **2** express views in a lengthy or emphatic way. □ **up the spout** Brit. informal useless or ruined.

sprain verb wrench a joint violently so as to cause pain and swelling. **noun** an instance of wrenching a joint.

sprang past of **SPRING**.

sprat noun a small sea fish of the herring family.

sprawl verb **1** sit, lie, or fall with your arms and legs spread out awkwardly. **2** spread out irregularly over a large area. **noun 1** a sprawling position or movement. **2** the disorganized expansion of a town or city.

spray noun **1** liquid sent through the air in tiny drops. **2** a liquid which can be forced out of an aerosol or other container in a spray. **3** a stem or small branch bearing flowers and leaves. **4** a small bunch of cut flowers worn on clothing. **verb 1** apply liquid in a spray. **2** cover or treat with a spray. **3** (of liquid) be sent through the air in a spray. **4** scatter over an area with force.

spread verb (spreads, spreading, spread) **1** open out fully. **2** stretch out hands, fingers, wings, etc. **3** extend over a wide area or a specified period of time. **4** apply a substance in an even layer. **noun 1** the process of spreading. **2** the extent, width, or area covered by something. **3** the range of something. **4** a soft paste that can be spread on bread. **5** an article covering several pages of a newspaper or magazine. **6** informal a large and elaborate meal. ■ **spreader** noun.

spreadeagle verb (**be spreadeagled**) be stretched out with the arms and legs extended.

spreadsheet noun a computer program in which figures are arranged in a grid and used in calculations.

spree noun a spell of unrestrained activity: *a shopping spree.*

sprig noun a small stem bearing leaves or flowers.

sprightly adjective (**sprightlier, sprightliest**) (of an old person) lively; energetic.

spring verb (**springs, springing, sprang** or **sprung**; past participle **sprung**) **1** move suddenly upwards or forwards. **2** operate suddenly by the action of a spring. **3** (**spring from**) come or appear from. **4** (**spring up**) suddenly develop or appear. **5** (**sprung**) having springs. **noun 1** the season after winter and before summer. **2** a spiral metal coil that returns to its former shape after being pressed or pulled. **3** a sudden jump upwards or forwards. **4** a place where water wells up from an underground source. **5** the quality of being elastic. □ **spring-clean** clean a house or building thoroughly. **spring-loaded** containing a spring that presses one part against another. **spring onion** Brit. an onion taken from the ground before the bulb has formed. ■ **springy** adjective.

springboard noun **1** a flexible board from which a diver or gymnast jumps in order to push off more powerfully. **2** something that gives driving force to an action or enterprise.

springbok noun a southern African gazelle which leaps when disturbed.

sprinkle verb (**sprinkles, sprinkling, sprinkled**) **1** scatter or pour small drops or particles over an object or surface. **2** distribute something randomly throughout. **noun** a small amount that is sprinkled.

sprinkler noun **1** a device for watering lawns. **2** an automatic fire extinguisher installed in a ceiling.

sprint verb run at full speed over a short distance. **noun 1** a spell of sprinting. **2** a short, fast race.

sprite noun an elf or fairy.

spritzer noun a mixture of wine and soda water.

sprocket noun each of several projections on the rim of a wheel that engage with the links of a chain or with holes in film, paper, etc.

sprout verb **1** produce shoots. **2** grow plant shoots or hair. **noun 1** a shoot of a plant. **2** a Brussels sprout.

spruce[1] adjective neat and smart. verb (**spruces, sprucing, spruced**) (**spruce up**) make smarter.

spruce[2] noun an evergreen tree with hanging cones.

sprung past and past participle of SPRING.

spry adjective (of an old person) lively.

spud noun informal a potato.

spume noun literary froth or foam.

spun past and past participle of SPIN.

spunk noun **1** informal courage and determination. **2** Brit. vulgar semen. ■ **spunky** adjective.

spur noun **1** a spiked device worn on a rider's heel for urging a horse forward. **2** an encouragement. **3** a projection from a mountain. **4** a short branch road or railway line. verb (**spurs, spurring, spurred**) **1** urge a horse forward with spurs. **2** encourage. □ **on the spur of the moment** on a momentary impulse.

spurious /rhymes with curious/ adjective **1** false or fake. **2** (of reasoning) apparently but not actually correct. ■ **spuriously** adverb.

spurn verb reject with contempt.

spurt verb **1** gush out in a stream. **2** move with a sudden burst of speed. noun **1** a gushing stream. **2** a sudden burst of activity or speed.

sputter verb (**sputters, sputtering, sputtered**) make a series of soft explosive sounds. noun a sputtering sound.

sputum noun saliva and mucus that is coughed up.

spy noun (plural **spies**) a person who secretly collects information on an enemy or competitor. verb (**spies, spying, spied**) **1** be a spy. **2** (**spy on**) watch secretly. **3** see or notice.

spyglass noun a small telescope.

spyhole noun Brit. a peephole.

sq abbreviation square.

squab noun a young pigeon that has not yet left the nest.

squabble noun a noisy quarrel about something unimportant. verb (**squabbles, squabbling, squabbled**) engage in a squabble.

squad noun **1** a small group of soldiers. **2** a group of sports players from which a team is chosen. **3** a division of a police force.

squaddie noun (plural **squaddies**) Brit. informal a private soldier.

squadron noun **1** a unit of an air force. **2** a group of warships.

squalid adjective **1** extremely dirty and unpleasant. **2** very immoral or dishonest. ■ **squalidly** adverb.

squall noun **1** a sudden violent gust of wind. **2** a loud cry. verb (of a baby) cry noisily and continuously.

squalor noun the state of being squalid.

squander verb (**squanders, squandering, squandered**) waste in a reckless or foolish manner.

square noun **1** a flat shape with four equal straight sides and four right angles. **2** an open area surrounded by buildings. **3** the product of a number multiplied by itself. **4** an L-shaped or T-shaped instrument used for obtaining or testing right angles. **5** informal an old-fashioned or boring person. adjec-

tive **1** having the shape of a square. **2** having or forming a right angle. **3** (of a unit of measurement) equal to the area of a square whose side is of the unit specified: *2,000 square feet*. **4** referring to the length of each side of a square shape or object: *ten metres square*. **5** level or parallel. **6** broad and solid in shape. **7** fair or honest. **8** informal old-fashioned or boringly conventional. adverb directly; straight. verb (**squares, squaring, squared**) **1** make something square or rectangular. **2** (**squared**) marked out in squares. **3** multiply a number by itself. **4** (**square with**) make or be compatible with. **5** settle a bill or debt. **6** make the score of a game even. **7** (**square up**) take up the position of a person about to fight. □ **square dance** a country dance that starts with four couples facing one another in a square. **square meal** a large and balanced meal. ■ **squarely** adverb.

squash[1] verb **1** crush or squeeze something so that it becomes flat or distorted. **2** force into a restricted space. **3** suppress or inhibit. noun **1** a state of being squashed. **2** Brit. a concentrated liquid diluted to make a fruit-flavoured drink. **3** (also **squash rackets**) a game in which two players use rackets to hit a small rubber ball against the walls of a closed court. ■ **squashy** adjective.

squash[2] noun a gourd with flesh that can be cooked and eaten as a vegetable.

squat verb (**squats, squatting, squatted**) **1** crouch or sit with the knees bent and the heels close to the thighs. **2** unlawfully occupy an uninhabited building or area of land. adjective short or low and wide. noun **1** a squatting position. **2** a building occupied by squatters. ■ **squatter** noun.

squaw noun offensive an American Indian woman or wife.

squawk verb **1** (of a bird) make a loud, harsh noise. **2** say something in a loud, ugly tone. noun a squawking sound.

squeak noun a short, high-pitched

squeal sound or cry. **verb 1** make a squeak. **2** say something in a high-pitched tone. □ **squeaky clean** informal **1** completely clean. **2** very good or morally correct. ■ **squeaky** adjective

squeal noun a long, high-pitched cry or noise. **verb 1** make a squeal. **2** say something in a high-pitched tone. **3** (**squeal on**) informal inform on.

squeamish adjective **1** easily disgusted or made to feel sick. **2** having very strong moral views.

squeegee noun a scraping tool with a rubber-edged blade, used for cleaning windows.

squeeze verb (**squeezes, squeezing, squeezed**) **1** firmly press from opposite sides. **2** extract liquid from something by squeezing. **3** manage to get into or through a restricted space. **noun 1** an act of squeezing. **2** a hug. **3** a small amount of liquid extracted by squeezing. **4** a strong financial demand or pressure. ■ **squeezy** adjective.

squelch verb make a soft sucking sound, e.g. by treading in thick mud. **noun** a squelching sound. ■ **squelchy** adjective.

squib noun a small firework.

squid noun (plural **squid** or **squids**) a sea creature with a long body, eight arms, and two long tentacles.

squiffy adjective Brit. informal slightly drunk.

squiggle noun a short line that curls and loops irregularly. ■ **squiggly** adjective.

squint verb **1** look with partly closed eyes. **2** partly close your eyes. **3** have a squint affecting one eye. **noun 1** a condition in which one eye looks in a different direction from the other. **2** informal a quick or casual look.

squire noun **1** a country gentleman. **2** (in the past) a young nobleman who acted as an attendant to a knight.

squirm verb **1** wriggle or twist the body from side to side. **2** be embarrassed or ashamed. **noun** a wriggling movement.

squirrel noun a bushy-tailed rodent which lives in trees. **verb** (**squirrels,**

squirrelling, squirrelled; US spelling **squirrels, squirreling, squirreled**) (**squirrel away**) hide money or valuables in a safe place.

squirt verb **1** force liquid out in a thin jet from a small opening. **2** wet with a jet of liquid. **noun 1** a thin jet of liquid. **2** informal a weak or insignificant person.

squish verb **1** make a soft squelching sound. **2** informal squash. **noun** a soft squelching sound.

SS abbreviation **1** Saints. **2** steamship. **noun** the Nazi special police force.

St abbreviation **1** Saint. **2** Street. **3** (**st**) stone (in weight).

stab verb (**stabs, stabbing, stabbed**) **1** thrust a knife or other pointed weapon into. **2** thrust a pointed object at. **3** (of a pain) cause a sudden sharp feeling. **noun 1** an act of stabbing. **2** a sudden sharp feeling or pain. **3** (a **stab at**) informal an attempt to do.

stability noun the state of being stable.

stabilize or **stabilise** verb (**stabilizes, stabilizing, stabilized**) make or become stable. ■ **stabilization** noun **stabilizer** noun.

stable¹ adjective **1** not likely to give way or overturn; firmly fixed. **2** not worsening in health after an injury or operation. **3** emotionally well balanced. **4** not likely to change or fail. ■ **stably** adverb.

stable² noun **1** a building for housing horses. **2** an establishment where racehorses are kept and trained. **verb** (**stables, stabling, stabled**) put or keep a horse in a stable.

stablemate noun a horse from the same stable as another.

staccato /stuh-**kah**-toh/ adjective Music with each sound or note sharply separated from the others.

stack noun **1** a neat pile of objects. **2** a rectangular or cylindrical pile of hay, straw, etc. **3** informal a large quantity. **4** a chimney. **verb 1** arrange in a stack. **2** fill or cover with stacks of things. **3** cause aircraft to fly at different altitudes while waiting to land. **4** arrange a pack of cards dishonestly.

stadium noun (plural **stadiums** or **stadia**) an athletic or sports ground with rows of seats for spectators.

staff noun **1** the employees of an organization. **2** a group of military officers assisting an officer in command. **3** a long stick used as a support or weapon. **4** a rod or sceptre held as a sign of office or authority. **5** Music a stave. verb provide with staff. □ **staff nurse** Brit. an experienced nurse less senior than a sister.

stag noun a fully adult male deer. □ **stag night** an all-male celebration held for a man about to be married.

stage noun **1** a point or step in a process or development. **2** a raised platform on which actors, entertainers, or speakers perform. **3** (the stage) the acting profession. **4** a platform on to which passengers or cargo can be landed from a boat. verb (**stages, staging, staged**) **1** present a performance of a play. **2** organize an event. □ **stage fright** nervousness before or during a performance. **stage-manage** arrange carefully to create a certain effect. **stage manager** the person responsible for lighting and other technical arrangements for a play. **stage whisper** a loud whisper by an actor on stage, intended to be heard by the audience. **staging post** a regular stop on a journey.

stagecoach noun a horse-drawn vehicle formerly used to carry passengers along a regular route.

stagehand noun a person who deals with scenery or props for a play.

stagger verb (**staggers, staggering, staggered**) **1** walk or move unsteadily. **2** astonish. **3** spread over a period of time. **4** arrange objects or parts so that they are not in line. noun an act of staggering.

stagnant adjective **1** (of water or air) not moving and having an unpleasant smell. **2** showing little activity.

stagnate verb (**stagnates, stagnating, stagnated**) become stagnant. ■ **stagnation** noun.

stagy or **stagey** adjective excessively theatrical or exaggerated.

staid adjective respectable and unadventurous.

stain verb **1** mark or discolour with something that is not easily removed. **2** damage someone's reputation. **3** colour with a dye or chemical. noun **1** a discoloured patch or mark. **2** a thing that damages someone's reputation. **3** a dye or chemical used to colour materials. □ **stained glass** coloured glass used to form pictures or designs. **stainless steel** a form of steel containing chromium, resistant to tarnishing and rust. ■ **stainless** adjective.

stair noun **1** each of a set of fixed steps. **2** (stairs) a set of steps leading from one floor of a building to another.

staircase or **stairway** noun a set of stairs and its surrounding structure.

stairwell noun a shaft in which a staircase is built.

stake[1] noun a strong post driven into the ground to support a tree, form part of a fence, etc. verb (**stakes, staking, staked**) **1** support with a stake. **2** (stake out) mark an area with stakes to claim ownership. **3** (stake out) informal keep a place or person under observation.

stake[2] noun **1** a sum of money gambled. **2** a share or interest in a business or situation. **3** (stakes) prize money. **4** (stakes) a competitive situation. verb (**stakes, staking, staked**) gamble money or valuables. □ **at stake 1** at risk. **2** in question.

stalactite noun a tapering structure hanging from the roof of a cave, formed of calcium salts deposited by dripping water.

stalagmite noun a tapering column rising from the floor of a cave.

stale adjective **1** (of food) no longer fresh. **2** no longer new and interesting. **3** no longer interested or motivated. ■ **staleness** adjective.

stalemate noun **1** Chess a position in which a player is not in check but can only move into check. **2** a situation in which further progress by opposing parties seems impossible.

stalk[1] **noun 1** the stem of a plant or support of a leaf, flower, or fruit. **2** a slender support or stem.

stalk[2] **verb 1** follow or approach stealthily. **2** harass someone with unwanted and obsessive attention. **3** walk in a proud, stiff, or angry manner. ■ **stalker** noun.

stall noun **1** a stand or booth where goods are sold in a market. **2** a compartment for an animal in a stable or cowshed. **3** a compartment in which a horse is held before the start of a race. **4** a compartment in a set of toilets. **5** (**stalls**) Brit. the ground-floor seats in a theatre. **6** a seat in the choir or chancel of a church. **verb 1** (of a vehicle's engine) suddenly stop running. **2** (of an aircraft) be moving too slowly to be controlled effectively. **3** stop making progress. **4** delay by putting something off until later.

stallion noun an adult male horse that has not been castrated.

stalwart adjective loyal, reliable, and hard-working. noun a stalwart supporter or member of an organization.

stamen /stay-muhn/ noun a male fertilizing organ of a flower.

stamina noun the ability to keep up effort over a long period.

stammer verb (**stammers, stammering, stammered**) speak or say with difficulty, making sudden pauses and repeating the first letters of words. noun a tendency to stammer.

stamp verb **1** bring down your foot heavily. **2** walk with heavy, forceful steps. **3** (**stamp out**) decisively put an end to. **4** press with a device that leaves a mark or pattern. noun **1** a small piece of paper stuck to a letter or parcel to record payment of postage. **2** an instrument for stamping a pattern or mark. **3** a mark or pattern made by a stamp. **4** a characteristic impression or quality. **5** an act of stamping the foot. □ **stamp duty** a tax on some legal documents. **stamping**

ground a place you regularly visit or spend time in.

stampede noun **1** a sudden panicked rush of a number of horses, cattle, etc. **2** a sudden mass movement or reaction due to interest or panic. **verb** (**stampedes, stampeding, stampeded**) take part in a stampede.

stance noun **1** the way in which someone stands. **2** an attitude or standpoint.

stanch US spelling of **STAUNCH**[2].

stanchion noun an upright bar, post, or frame forming a support or barrier.

stand verb (**stands, standing, stood**) **1** be or become upright, supported by the feet. **2** place or be situated in a particular position. **3** remain stationary, undisturbed, or unchanged. **4** be in a specified state or condition. **5** tolerate or like. **6** Brit. be a candidate in an election. noun **1** an attitude towards an issue. **2** a determined effort to hold your ground or resist something. **3** a stopping of motion or progress. **4** a large structure for spectators to sit or stand in. **5** a raised platform for a band, orchestra, or speaker. **6** a structure for holding or displaying something. **7** a stall from which goods are sold or displayed. **8** (**the stand**) the witness box in a law court. □ **stand by 1** look on without becoming involved. **2** support or remain loyal to. **3** be ready to take action if needed. **stand down** (or **aside**) resign from a position or office. **stand for 1** be an abbreviation of or symbol for. **2** endure or put up with. **stand in** deputize. **stand-off** a deadlock between two opponents. **stand-offish** informal distant and cold in manner. **stand out 1** stick out or be easily noticeable. **2** be clearly better. **stand up** informal fail to keep a date with. **stand up for** speak or act in support of.

> 🛈 use **standing** rather than **stood** with the verb 'to be': say *we were standing in a line for hours* rather than *we were stood in a line for hours*.

standard noun **1** a level of quality or achievement. **2** a measure or model used to make comparisons. **3** (**standards**) principles of good behaviour. **4** a military or ceremonial flag. **adjective** used or accepted as normal or average. □ **standard-bearer 1** a soldier who carries a military or ceremonial flag. **2** a leading figure in a cause or movement. **standard English** the dialect of English used by most educated English speakers. **standard lamp** a tall lamp that is placed on the floor. **standard of living** the degree of comfort that a person or community has.

standardize or **standardise** verb (**standardizes, standardizing, standardized**) make something fit in with a standard. ■ **standardization** noun.

standby noun (plural **standbys**) **1** readiness for duty or action. **2** a person or thing ready to be used in an emergency. **adjective** (of tickets) sold only at the last minute.

standing noun **1** position, status, or reputation. **2** duration or length. **adjective 1** existing permanently. **2** remaining in force or use. □ **standing joke** something that regularly causes amusement or provokes ridicule. **standing order** Brit. an instruction to a bank to make regular fixed payments to someone. **standing ovation** a long period of applause during which the audience rise to their feet.

standpoint noun an attitude towards a particular issue.

standstill noun a situation or condition without movement or activity.

stank past of **STINK**.

stanza noun a group of lines forming the basic unit in a poem.

staple[1] noun **1** a small piece of wire used to fasten papers together. **2** a small U-shaped metal bar driven into wood to hold things in place. **verb** (**staples, stapling, stapled**) secure with a staple or staples. ■ **stapler** noun.

staple[2] noun **1** a main item of trade or production. **2** a main or important element. **adjective** main or important.

star noun **1** a large ball of burning gas which appears as a glowing point in the night sky. **2** a simplified representation of a star with five or six points. **3** a famous entertainer or sports player. **verb** (**stars, starring, starred**) **1** have someone as a leading performer. **2** have a leading role in a film, play, etc. □ **Stars and Stripes** the national flag of the US. **star sign** a sign of the zodiac. ■ **stardom** noun.

starboard noun the side of a ship or aircraft that is on the right when you are facing forward.

starch noun **1** a carbohydrate which is obtained from cereals and potatoes and is an important part of the human diet. **2** powder or spray used to stiffen fabric. **verb** stiffen with starch.

starchy adjective (**starchier, starchiest**) **1** containing a lot of starch. **2** stiff and formal in manner.

stare verb (**stares, staring, stared**) look with concentration and the eyes wide open. **noun** an act of staring.

starfish noun a sea creature having five or more arms extending from a central point.

stark adjective **1** severe or bare in appearance. **2** unpleasantly or sharply clear. **3** complete; sheer: *stark terror.* □ **stark naked** completely naked. ■ **starkly** adverb.

starkers adjective Brit. informal completely naked.

starlet noun informal a promising young actress or performer.

starling noun a bird with dark shining or iridescent plumage.

starry adjective (**starrier, starriest**) **1** full of or lit by stars. **2** informal relating to stars in entertainment. □ **starry-eyed** naively enthusiastic or idealistic.

starship noun (in science fiction) a spaceship for travel between stars.

start verb **1** begin to do or happen. **2** begin to operate or work. **3** make something happen or operate. **4** begin to move or travel. **5** (**start out** or **up**) begin a venture or undertaking. **6** jump or jerk from surprise. noun **1** an act of beginning. **2** the point at which something begins. **3** an advantage given to a competitor at the beginning of a race. **4** a sudden movement of surprise.

starter noun **1** a person or thing that starts. **2** the first course of a meal.

startle verb (**startles**, **startling**, **startled**) make someone feel sudden shock or alarm. ■ **startled** adjective.

startling adjective **1** alarming. **2** very surprising. ■ **startlingly** adverb.

starve verb (**starves**, **starving**, **starved**) **1** suffer or die from hunger. **2** make someone starve. **3** (**be starving** or **starved**) informal feel very hungry. **4** (**be starved of**) be deprived of. ■ **starvation** noun.

stash informal verb store safely in a secret place. noun a secret store.

stasis /stay-sis/ noun formal a period or state when there is no activity or change.

state noun **1** the condition of someone or something at a particular time. **2** a country considered as an organized political community. **3** an area forming part of a federal republic. **4** (**the States**) the United States of America. **5** the government of a country. **6** ceremony associated with monarchy or government. **7** (**a state**) informal an agitated, untidy, or dirty condition. verb (**states**, **stating**, **stated**) express definitely in speech or writing. □ **state-of-the-art** very up to date. ■ **stateless** adjective.

stately adjective (**statelier**, **stateliest**) dignified, imposing, or grand. □ **stately home** Brit. a large and fine house occupied or formerly occupied by an aristocratic family.

statement noun **1** a clear expression of something in speech or writing. **2** an account of events given to the police or in court. **3** a list of amounts paid into and out of a bank account.

statesman or **stateswoman** noun an experienced and respected political leader.

static adjective **1** not moving, acting, or changing. **2** (of an electric charge) acquired by objects that cannot conduct a current. noun **1** static electricity. **2** crackling or hissing on a telephone, radio, etc. ■ **statically** adverb.

station noun **1** a place where passenger trains stop on a railway line. **2** a place where an activity or service is based. **3** a broadcasting company. **4** the place where someone or something stands or is placed. **5** dated a person's social rank or position. verb assign to a station. □ **station wagon** N. Amer. & Austral./NZ an estate car.

stationary adjective not moving.

> **i** don't confuse **stationary** and **stationery**: **stationary** means 'not moving or changing', whereas **stationery** means 'paper and other writing materials'.

stationer noun a person who sells stationery.

stationery noun paper and other materials needed for writing.

stationmaster noun a person in charge of a railway station.

statistic noun **1** (**statistics**) the collection and analysis of large amounts of information shown in numbers. **2** a fact or piece of data obtained from a study of statistics. ■ **statistician** noun.

statistical adjective having to do with statistics. ■ **statistically** adverb.

statuary noun statues.

statue noun a carved or cast figure of a person or animal.

statuesque adjective (of a woman) attractively tall and dignified.

statuette noun a small statue.

stature noun **1** a person's height when they are standing. **2** importance or reputation.

status noun **1** the social or professional position of someone. **2** high rank or social standing. **3** the position of affairs at a particular time. □ **status symbol** a possession intended to show a person's wealth or high status.

status quo /stay-tuhss **kwoh**/ noun the existing state of affairs.

statute noun 1 a written law. 2 a rule of an organization or institution.

statutory adjective 1 required or permitted by law. 2 done or happening regularly and so expected.

staunch¹ adjective very loyal and committed. ■ **staunchly** adverb.

staunch² (US spelling **stanch**) verb stop or slow down a flow of blood.

stave noun 1 any of the lengths of wood fixed side by side to make a barrel, bucket, etc. 2 a strong stick, post, or pole. 3 (also **staff**) Music a set of five parallel lines which notes are written on or between. verb (**staves, staving**, past and past participle **staved** or **stove**) 1 (**stave in**) break something by forcing it inwards. 2 (past and past participle **staved**) (**stave off**) stop or delay something bad or dangerous.

stay verb 1 remain in the same place. 2 remain in a specified state or position. 3 live somewhere temporarily as a visitor or guest. 4 stop, delay, or prevent. noun 1 a period of staying somewhere. 2 a brace or support. 3 (**stays**) historical a corset stiffened by strips of whalebone. □ **staying power** informal endurance or stamina. **stay of execution** a delay in carrying out the orders of a law court.

stead noun (**in someone's** or **something's stead**) instead of someone or something. □ **stand in good stead** be useful to someone over time.

steadfast adjective determined and unwavering. ■ **steadfastly** adverb.

steady adjective (**steadier, steadiest**) 1 firmly fixed, supported, or balanced. 2 not faltering or wavering. 3 sensible and reliable. 4 regular, even, and continuous. verb (**steadies, steadying, steadied**) make steady. ■ **steadily** adverb **steadiness** noun.

steak noun 1 high-quality beef cut into thick slices for grilling or frying. 2 a thick slice of other meat or fish. 3 poorer-quality beef for stewing.

steal verb (**steals, stealing, stole**; past participle **stolen**) 1 take something

without permission and without intending to return it. 2 move quietly or secretively. noun informal a bargain. □ **steal the show** attract the most attention and praise.

stealth noun cautious and secretive action or movement.

stealthy adjective (**stealthier, stealthiest**) cautious and secretive. ■ **stealthily** adverb.

steam noun 1 the hot vapour into which water is converted when heated. 2 power derived from steam under pressure. 3 momentum. verb 1 give off or produce steam. 2 (**steam up**) mist over with steam. 3 cook food by heating it in steam from boiling water. 4 clean with steam. 5 (of a ship or train) travel under steam power. 6 informal move quickly or forcefully. ■ **steamer** noun.

steamroller noun a heavy, slow vehicle with a roller, used to flatten the surfaces of roads. verb (**steamrollers, steamrollering, steamrollered**) 1 forcibly pass a law. 2 force into doing or accepting something.

steamy adjective (**steamier, steamiest**) 1 producing or filled with steam. 2 informal involving passionate sexual activity.

steed noun literary a horse.

steel noun 1 a hard, strong metal that is a mixture of iron and carbon. 2 strength and determination. verb mentally prepare yourself for something difficult. □ **steel band** a band that plays music on drums made from empty oil containers.

steelworks plural noun a factory where steel is produced.

steely adjective (**steelier, steeliest**) 1 like steel. 2 coldly determined.

steep¹ adjective 1 rising or falling sharply. 2 (of a rise or fall in an amount) very large or rapid. 3 informal (of a price or demand) excessive. ■ **steepen** verb **steeply** adverb.

steep² verb 1 soak in water or other liquid. 2 (**be steeped in**) have a lot of a particular quality or atmosphere.

steeple noun a church tower and spire.

steeplechase noun **1** a horse race with ditches and hedges as jumps. **2** a race in which runners must clear hurdles and water jumps. ▪ **steeplechaser** noun.

steeplejack noun a person who climbs tall structures such as chimneys and steeples to repair them.

steer[1] verb **1** guide or control the movement of a vehicle, ship, etc. **2** direct or guide. □ **steer clear of** take care to avoid. **steering wheel** a wheel that a driver turns in order to steer a vehicle.

steer[2] noun a bullock.

steerage noun (in the past) the cheapest accommodation in a ship.

steersman noun a person who steers a boat or ship.

stegosaurus noun a plant-eating dinosaur with large bony plates along the back.

stellar adjective having to do with a star or stars.

stem[1] noun **1** the long, thin main part of a plant or shrub, or support of a fruit, flower, or leaf. **2** a long, thin supporting part of a wine glass, tobacco pipe, etc. **3** a vertical stroke in a letter or musical note. **4** the root or main part of a word. verb (**stems, stemming, stemmed**) (**stem from**) come from or be caused by.

stem[2] verb (**stems, stemming, stemmed**) stop or slow down the flow or progress of something.

stench noun a strong and very unpleasant smell.

stencil noun a thin sheet with a pattern or letters cut out of it, used to produce a design by the application of ink or paint through the holes. verb (**stencils, stencilling, stencilled; US** spelling **stencils, stenciling, stenciled**) decorate or form something with a stencil.

stenographer /sti-**nog**-ruh-fuhr/ noun N. Amer. a shorthand typist.

stentorian adjective (of a person's voice) loud and powerful.

step noun **1** an act of lifting and putting down the foot or feet in walking. **2** the distance covered by a step. **3** a flat surface on which to place the feet when moving from one level to another. **4** a position or grade in a scale or ranking. **5** a measure or action taken to deal with something. verb (**steps, stepping, stepped**) lift and put down your foot or feet. □ **step down** resign from a position or office. **step in** become involved in a difficult situation. **stepping stone 1** a raised stone which you can step on when crossing a stream. **2** something that helps you make progress towards a goal. **step up** increase the amount, speed, or strength of.

stepbrother noun a son of your stepfather or stepmother.

stepchild noun a child of your husband or wife by a previous marriage.

stepdaughter noun a daughter of your husband or wife by a previous marriage.

stepfather noun a man who is married to your mother but is not your father.

stepladder noun a short free-standing folding ladder.

stepmother noun a woman who is married to your father but is not your mother.

steppe noun a large area of flat unforested grassland in SE Europe and Siberia.

stepsister noun a daughter of your stepfather or stepmother.

stepson noun a son of your husband or wife by a previous marriage.

stereo noun (plural **stereos**) **1** stereophonic sound. **2** a stereophonic CD player, record player, etc. adjective stereophonic.

stereophonic adjective (of sound reproduction) using two or more channels so that the sound seems to come from more than one source.

stereotype noun an oversimplified idea of the typical characteristics of a person or thing. verb (**stereotypes, stereotyping, stereotyped**) represent as a stereotype. ■ **stereotypical** adjective.

sterile adjective **1** not able to produce children, young, crops, or fruit. **2** not imaginative, creative, or exciting. **3** free from bacteria. ■ **sterility** noun.

sterilize or **sterilise** verb (**sterilizes, sterilizing, sterilized**) make sterile. ■ **sterilization** noun.

sterling noun British money. adjective **1** excellent. **2** (of silver) of at least 92¼ per cent purity.

stern[1] adjective **1** grimly serious or strict. **2** severe. ■ **sternly** adverb.

stern[2] noun the rear end of a ship or boat.

sternum noun the breastbone.

steroid /ste-royd, steer-oyd/ noun **1** any of a class of substances, e.g. certain hormones and vitamins, produced in the body. **2** an anabolic steroid.

stertorous /ster-tuh-ruhss/ adjective (of breathing) noisy and laboured.

stethoscope noun a device used by doctors for listening to the sound of a person's heart or breathing.

Stetson noun (trademark in the US) a hat with a high crown and a very wide brim, worn by cowboys and ranchers in the US.

stevedore noun a person employed at a dock to load and unload ships.

stew noun **1** a dish of meat and vegetables cooked slowly in a closed dish. **2** informal a state of anxiety or agitation. verb **1** cook slowly in a closed dish. **2** Brit. (of tea) become strong and bitter with prolonged brewing. **3** informal be in a stifling atmosphere. **4** informal be anxious or agitated.

steward noun **1** a person who looks after the passengers on a ship or aircraft. **2** a person responsible for supplies of food to a college, club, etc. **3** an official who supervises arrangements at a large public event. **4** a person employed to manage a large house or estate. ■ **stewardship** noun.

stewardess noun a woman who looks after the passengers on a ship or aircraft.

stick[1] noun **1** a thin piece of wood that has fallen or been cut from a tree. **2** a piece of wood used for support in walking or as a weapon. **3** a long, thin implement used in hockey, polo, etc. to hit the ball or puck. **4** a long, thin object or piece. **6** the threat of punishment as a means of persuasion. **7** Brit. informal severe criticism or treatment. **8** (**the sticks**) informal remote country areas. □ **stick insect** a long, slender insect that resembles a twig.

stick[2] verb (**sticks, sticking, stuck**) **1** push something pointed into or through something. **2** be fixed with its point embedded in something. **3** protrude or extend. **4** informal put somewhere in a quick or careless way. **5** cling firmly to a surface; adhere. **6** (**be stuck**) be fixed or unable to move. **7** (**be stuck**) be unable to complete a task. **8** (**be stuck with**) informal be unable to get rid of or escape from. **9** (**stick around**) informal remain in or near a place. **10** (**stick to**) continue doing or using. **11** (**stick up for**) informal support.

sticker noun a sticky label or notice.

stickleback noun a small fish with sharp spines along its back.

stickler noun a person who insists on people behaving in a particular way.

sticky adjective (**stickier, stickiest**) **1** tending or designed to stick. **2** like glue in texture. **3** (of the weather) hot and humid.

stiff adjective **1** not easily bent. **2** difficult to turn or operate. **3** unable to move easily and without pain. **4** not relaxed or friendly. **5** severe or strong. noun informal a dead body. □ **stiff upper lip** the tendency to hide your feelings and not complain. ■ **stiffly** adverb **stiffness** noun.

stiffen verb **1** make or become stiff. **2** make or become stronger.

stifle verb (**stifles, stifling, stifled**) **1** prevent from breathing freely; suffocate. **2** smother or suppress.

stifling adjective unpleasantly hot and stuffy. ■ **stiflingly** adverb.

stigma noun (plural **stigmas** or **stig-**

mata) **1** a mark or sign of disgrace. **2** (**stigmata**) marks on a person's body believed by some Christians to correspond to those left on Jesus Christ's body by the Crucifixion. **3** the part of a plant that receives the pollen during pollination.

stigmatize or **stigmatise** verb (**stigmatizes, stigmatizing, stigmatized**) regard or treat as shameful.

stile noun an arrangement of steps in a fence or wall that allows people to climb over.

stiletto noun (plural **stilettos**) **1** a thin, high heel on a woman's shoe. **2** a short dagger with a tapering blade.

still adjective **1** not moving. **2** (of a drink) not fizzy. noun **1** deep, quiet calm. **2** a photograph or a single shot from a cinema film. **3** an apparatus for distilling alcoholic drinks such as whisky. adverb **1** even now or at a particular time. **2** nevertheless. **3** even. verb make or become still. □ **still life** a painting or drawing of an arrangement of objects such as flowers or fruit. ■ **stillness** noun.

stillborn adjective (of an infant) born dead. ■ **stillbirth** noun.

stilt noun **1** either of a pair of upright poles that are used to walk raised above the ground. **2** each of a set of posts supporting a building.

stilted adjective (of speech or writing) stiff and unnatural.

Stilton noun trademark a kind of strong, rich blue cheese.

stimulant noun something that stimulates.

stimulate verb (**stimulates, stimulating, stimulated**) **1** cause or provoke a reaction in the body. **2** make more active or interested. ■ **stimulation** noun.

stimulus noun (plural **stimuli**) something that stimulates.

sting noun **1** a sharp-pointed part of an insect, capable of inflicting a wound by injecting poison. **2** a wound from a sting. **3** a sharp tingling sensation. verb (**stings, stinging, stung**) **1** wound with a sting. **2** produce a stinging sensation. **3** hurt; upset.

stingray noun a ray (fish) with a poisonous spine at the base of the tail.

stingy /stin-ji/ adjective (**stingier, stingiest**) informal mean.

stink verb (**stinks, stinking, stank** or **stunk**; past participle **stunk**) **1** have a strong, unpleasant smell. **2** informal be scandalous or very bad. noun **1** a strong, unpleasant smell. **2** informal a row or fuss. ■ **stinker** noun.

stinking adjective **1** foul-smelling. **2** informal very unpleasant or bad. adverb informal extremely: *stinking rich*.

stint verb (**stint on**) restrict how much someone can have of something. noun a period of work.

stipend /sty-pend/ noun a fixed regular sum paid as a salary to a priest, teacher, or official.

stipendiary adjective receiving a stipend; working for pay.

stipple verb (**stipples, stippling, stippled**) mark a surface with many small dots or specks.

stipulate verb (**stipulates, stipulating, stipulated**) demand or specify as part of an agreement. ■ **stipulation** noun.

stir verb (**stirs, stirring, stirred**) **1** move an implement round and round in a liquid or soft substance to mix it. **2** move slightly. **3** wake or get up. **4** (often **stir up**) arouse a strong feeling in someone. **5** Brit. informal deliberately cause trouble by spreading rumours or gossip. noun **1** an act of stirring. **2** a disturbance or commotion. **3** informal prison. □ **stir-fry** fry quickly over a high heat while stirring. ■ **stirrer** noun.

stirring adjective causing great excitement or strong emotion.

stirrup noun each of a pair of loops attached to a horse's saddle to support the rider's foot.

stitch noun **1** a loop of thread made by a single pass of the needle in sewing or knitting. **2** a method of sewing or knitting that produces a particular pattern. **3** a sudden sharp pain in the side of the body, caused by strenuous exercise. verb make or mend with stitches. □ **in stitches** informal laughing uncontrollably. **stitch up** Brit. informal make someone appear to be guilty of something that they did not do.

stoat noun a small meat-eating mammal of the weasel family.

stock noun **1** a supply of goods or materials available for sale or use. **2** farm animals; livestock. **3** money raised by selling shares in a company. **4** (**stocks**) shares in a company. **5** water in which bones, meat, fish, or vegetables have been simmered. **6** a person's ancestry. **7** a breed, variety, or population of an animal or plant. **8** the trunk or stem of a tree or shrub. **9** a plant with fragrant lilac, pink, or white flowers. **10** (**the stocks**) a wooden structure in which criminals used to be locked as a public punishment. adjective common or conventional: *stock characters.* verb **1** have or keep a stock of. **2** provide or fill with a stock of something. **3** (**stock up**) collect stocks of something. □ **stock car** a car used in a type of racing in which cars collide with each other. **stock exchange** (or **stock market**) a place where stocks and shares are bought and sold. **stock-in-trade** the typical thing a person or company uses or deals in. **stock-still** completely still. **take stock** assess your situation.

stockade noun a barrier or enclosure formed from wooden posts.

stockbroker noun a person who buys and sells stocks and shares on behalf of clients.

stocking noun **1** either of a pair of women's close-fitting nylon garments covering the foot and leg. **2** US or old use a long sock. ■ **stockinged** adjective.

stockist noun Brit. a retailer that sells goods of a particular type.

stockpile noun a large stock of goods or materials. verb (**stockpiles**, **stockpiling**, **stockpiled**) gather together a large stock of.

stocktaking noun the process of listing all the stock held by a business.

stocky adjective (**stockier**, **stockiest**) (of a person) short and sturdy.

stodge noun Brit. informal food that is heavy and filling. ■ **stodgy** adjective.

stoic /stoh-ik/ noun a stoical person. adjective stoical.

stoical adjective enduring pain and hardship without complaining. ■ **stoically** adverb **stoicism** noun.

stoke verb (**stokes**, **stoking**, **stoked**) **1** add coal to a fire, furnace, etc. **2** encourage a strong emotion. ■ **stoker** noun.

stole¹ noun a woman's long scarf or shawl.

stole² past of **STEAL**.

stolen past participle of **STEAL**.

stolid adjective calm, dependable, and unemotional. ■ **stolidly** adverb.

stomach noun **1** the internal organ in which the first part of digestion occurs. **2** the front part of the body below the chest; the belly. **3** appetite or desire. verb consume or accept something without ill effects.

stomp verb **1** tread heavily and noisily. **2** dance with stamping steps.

stone noun **1** the hard material that rock is made of. **2** a small piece of stone found on the ground. **3** a piece of stone shaped as a memorial, a boundary marker, etc. **4** a gem. **5** the hard seed of certain fruits. **6** (plural **stone**) Brit. a unit of weight equal to 14 lb (6.35 kg). verb (**stones**, **stoning**, **stoned**) **1** throw stones at. **2** remove the stone from a fruit. adverb extremely or totally: *stone cold.* □ **leave no stone unturned** do everything possible to achieve something. **Stone Age** the prehistoric period when tools were made of stone. **a stone's throw** a short distance.

stoned adjective informal strongly affected by drugs or alcohol.

stonewall verb **1** refuse to answer questions, or give evasive replies. **2** Cricket bat very defensively.

stony adjective (**stonier**, **stoniest**) **1** full of stones. **2** of or like stone. **3** cold and unfeeling. ■ **stonily** adverb.

stood past and past participle of **STAND**.

stooge noun **1** disapproving a less important person used by someone to do routine or unpleasant work. **2** a performer whose act involves being the butt of a comedian's jokes.

stool noun **1** a seat without a back or arms. **2** Medicine a piece of faeces. □ **fall between two stools** Brit. fail to be either of two satisfactory alternatives.
stool pigeon a police informer.

stoop verb **1** bend the head or body forwards and downwards. **2** lower your standards to do something wrong. noun a stooping posture.

stop verb (**stops, stopping, stopped**) **1** come or bring to an end. **2** prevent from happening or from doing something. **3** no longer move or operate. **4** (of a bus or train) call at a place to pick up or let off passengers. **5** block up a hole or leak. noun **1** an act of stopping. **2** a place for a bus or train to stop at. **3** an object or part of a mechanism which prevents movement. **4** a set of organ pipes. □ **pull out all the stops** make a very great effort to achieve something. **stop press** Brit. news added to a newspaper at the last minute.

stopcock noun a valve which controls the flow of a liquid or gas through a pipe.

stopgap noun a temporary solution or substitute.

stoppage noun **1** an instance of being stopped. **2** an instance of industrial action. **3** a blockage. **4** (**stoppages**) Brit. deductions from wages for tax, National Insurance, etc.

stopper noun a plug for sealing a hole. verb (**stoppers, stoppering, stoppered**) seal with a stopper.

stopwatch noun a watch with buttons that start and stop the display, used to time races.

storage noun **1** the action of storing. **2** space available for storing. □ **storage heater** Brit. an electric heater that stores up heat during the night and releases it during the day.

store noun **1** an amount or supply kept to be used when needed. **2** (**stores**) equipment and food kept for use by an army, navy, etc. **3** a place where things are kept for future use or sale. **4** Brit. a large shop selling different types of goods. **5** N. Amer. a shop. verb (**stores, storing, stored**) **1** keep for future use. **2** enter information in the memory of a computer. □ **in store** about to happen. **set store by** consider to be important.

storey (US spelling **story**) noun (plural **storeys** or **stories**) a particular level of a building.

stork noun a tall long-legged bird with a long, heavy bill.

storm noun **1** a violent disturbance of the atmosphere with strong winds and rain, thunder, etc. **2** an uproar or controversy. verb **1** move angrily or forcefully. **2** (of troops) suddenly attack and capture a place. **3** shout angrily. □ **a storm in a teacup** Brit. great anger or excitement about a trivial matter. **storm troops** shock troops.

stormy adjective (**stormier, stormiest**) **1** affected by a storm. **2** full of angry or violent outbursts of feeling.

story[1] noun (plural **stories**) **1** an account of imaginary or real events told for entertainment. **2** an item of news. **3** (also **storyline**) the plot of a novel, film, etc. **4** informal a lie.

story[2] US spelling of **STOREY**.

stoup /stoop/ noun a basin for holy water in a church.

stout adjective **1** rather fat or heavily built. **2** sturdy and thick. **3** brave and determined. noun a kind of strong, dark beer. ■ **stoutly** adverb.

stove[1] noun a device for cooking or heating.

stove[2] past and past participle of **STAVE**.

stow verb **1** pack or store an object tidily. **2** (**stow away**) hide on a ship, aircraft, etc. to travel secretly.

stowaway noun a person who stows away.

straddle verb (**straddles, straddling, straddled**) **1** sit or stand with one leg on either side of. **2** extend across both sides of.

strafe /strahf, strayf/ **verb** (**strafes**, **strafing**, **strafed**) attack with gunfire or bombs from a low-flying aircraft.

straggle **verb** (**straggles**, **straggling**, **straggled**) **1** trail slowly behind the person or people in front. **2** grow or spread out in an untidy way. ■ **straggler** noun **straggly** adjective.

straight **adjective** **1** extending uniformly in one direction only; without a curve or bend. **2** level, upright, or symmetrical. **3** in proper order or condition. **4** honest and direct. **5** (of thinking) clear and logical. **6** in continuous succession. **7** (of an alcoholic drink) undiluted. **8** informal conventional or respectable. **9** informal heterosexual. **adverb 1** in a straight line or in a straight manner. **2** without delay or diversion. □ **straight away** immediately. **straight-laced** ⇒ **STRAIT-LACED**.

straighten **verb** make or become straight.

straightforward **adjective** **1** easy to do or understand. **2** honest and open. ■ **straightforwardly** adverb.

straightjacket ⇒ **STRAITJACKET**.

strain¹ **verb** **1** make an unusually great effort. **2** injure a muscle, limb, etc. by making it work too hard. **3** make great or excessive demands on. **4** pour a mainly liquid substance through a sieve to separate out solid matter. **noun 1** a force tending to strain something to an extreme degree. **2** an injury caused by straining a muscle, limb, etc. **3** a severe demand on strength or resources. **4** a state of tension or exhaustion. **5** the sound of a piece of music. ■ **strainer** noun.

strain² **noun 1** a breed or variety of an animal or plant. **2** a tendency in a person's character.

strained **adjective** **1** not relaxed or comfortable; showing signs of strain. **2** produced by deliberate effort; not graceful or spontaneous.

strait **noun 1** (also **straits**) a narrow passage of water connecting two other large areas of water. **2** (**straits**) trouble or difficulty: *in dire straits.*

straitened **adjective** **1** characterized by poverty; poor. **2** restricted or limited.

straitjacket or **straightjacket** **noun** a strong garment with long sleeves which can be tied together to confine the arms of a violent person.

strait-laced or **straight-laced** **adjective** very strictly moral and conventional.

strand¹ **verb** **1** drive or leave a ship, whale, etc. aground on a shore. **2** leave someone unable to move from a place. **noun** literary a beach or shore.

strand² **noun 1** a single thin length of thread, wire, etc. **2** an element that forms part of a complex whole.

strange **adjective** **1** unusual or surprising. **2** not previously visited or encountered. ■ **strangely** adverb.

stranger **noun 1** a person that you do not know. **2** a person who does not know a particular place.

strangle **verb** (**strangles**, **strangling**, **strangled**) **1** kill or injure someone by squeezing their neck. **2** prevent from developing. ■ **strangler** noun.

stranglehold **noun 1** a firm grip around a person's neck that deprives them of oxygen. **2** complete or overwhelming control.

strangulation **noun** the action of strangling.

strap **noun 1** a strip of flexible material used for fastening, carrying, or holding on to. **2** (**the strap**) punishment by beating with a leather strap. **verb** (**straps**, **strapping**, **strapped**) fasten or secure with a strap. ■ **strapless** adjective **strappy** adjective.

strapping **adjective** (of a person) big and strong.

stratagem **noun** a plan or scheme intended to outwit an opponent.

strategic **adjective** **1** forming part of a long-term plan to achieve something. **2** relating to the gaining of long-term military advantage. **3** (of weapons) for use against enemy territory rather than in battle. ■ **strategically** adverb.

strategy noun (plural **strategies**) **1** a plan designed to achieve a long-term aim. **2** the planning and directing of military activity in a war or battle. ■ **strategist** noun.

stratify verb (**stratifies, stratifying, stratified**) form or arrange into strata. ■ **stratification** noun.

stratosphere noun **1** the layer of the earth's atmosphere above the lowest layer, at a height of about 10–50 km. **2** informal the very highest levels of something. ■ **stratospheric** adjective.

stratum noun (plural **strata**) **1** a layer or series of layers of rock. **2** a level or class of society.

straw noun **1** dried stalks of grain. **2** a single dried stalk of grain. **3** a thin hollow tube used for sucking drink from a container. **4** a pale yellow colour. □ **clutch at straws** turn to something in desperation. **draw the short straw** be chosen to do something unpleasant. **the last** (or **final**) **straw** the final difficulty that makes a situation unbearable. **straw poll** an unofficial test of opinion.

strawberry noun a sweet red fruit with seeds on the surface. □ **strawberry blonde** (of hair) light reddish-blonde.

stray verb move away aimlessly from a group or from the right course or place. adjective **1** not in the right place; separated from a group. **2** (of a domestic animal) having no home or having wandered away from home. noun a stray person or thing.

streak noun **1** a long, thin mark. **2** an element in someone's character: *a ruthless streak*. **3** a spell of specified success or luck: *a winning streak*. verb **1** mark with streaks. **2** move very fast. **3** informal run naked in a public place to shock or amuse people. ■ **streaker** noun **streaky** adjective.

stream noun **1** a small, narrow river. **2** a continuous flow of liquid, air, people, etc. **3** Brit. a group in which schoolchildren of the same age and

ability are taught. verb **1** move in a continuous flow. **2** run with tears, sweat, etc. **3** float out in the wind. **4** Brit. put schoolchildren in streams. □ **on stream** in operation or existence.

streamer noun a long, narrow flag or strip of decorative material.

streamline verb (**streamlines, streamlining, streamlined**) **1** (**be streamlined**) have a shape that allows quick, easy movement through air or water. **2** make an organization or system more efficient.

street noun a public road in a city, town, or village. □ **street value** the price something, especially drugs, would fetch if sold illegally.

streetcar noun N. Amer. a tram.

streetwalker noun a prostitute who seeks clients in the street.

streetwise adjective informal able to deal well with modern urban life.

strength noun **1** the quality or state of being strong. **2** a good or useful quality or attribute. **3** the number of people making up a group. □ **go from strength to strength** progress with increasing success. **on the strength of** on the basis of.

strengthen verb make or become stronger.

strenuous adjective requiring or using great exertion. ■ **strenuously** adverb.

stress noun **1** pressure or tension exerted on an object. **2** mental or emotional strain or tension. **3** particular emphasis. **4** emphasis given to a syllable or word in speech. verb **1** emphasize. **2** subject to pressure, tension, or strain.

stressful adjective causing mental or emotional stress. ■ **stressfully** adverb.

stretch verb **1** be able to be made longer or wider without tearing or breaking. **2** extend something without tearing or breaking it. **3** extend part of the body to its full length. **4** extend over an area or period of time. **5** make demands on. noun **1** an act of stretching. **2** the capacity to stretch or be stretched; elasticity. **3** a continuous expanse or period. ■ **stretchy** adjective.

stretcher noun a long framework covered with canvas, used for carrying sick, injured, or dead people. verb (**stretchers, stretchering, stretchered**) carry on a stretcher.

strew verb (**strews, strewing,** past participle **strewn** or **strewed**) **1** scatter untidily over a surface or area. **2** (**be strewn with**) be covered with untidily scattered things.

striated adjective marked with ridges or furrows. ■ **striation** noun.

stricken North American or archaic past participle of **STRIKE**. adjective **1** seriously affected by something unpleasant. **2** showing great distress.

strict adjective **1** demanding that rules are obeyed. **2** following rules or beliefs exactly. ■ **strictly** adverb **strictness** noun.

stricture noun **1** a rule restricting behaviour or action. **2** a sternly critical remark.

stride verb (**strides, striding, strode;** past participle **stridden**) walk with long, decisive steps. noun **1** a long, decisive step. **2** a step made towards an aim. □ **take in your stride** deal calmly with something difficult.

strident adjective **1** loud and harsh. **2** excessively forceful. ■ **stridency** noun **stridently** adverb.

strife noun angry or bitter disagreement.

strike verb (**strikes, striking, struck**) **1** deliver a blow to. **2** make forcible contact with. **3** (in sport) hit or kick the ball. **4** light a match by rubbing it against an abrasive surface. **5** attack suddenly. **6** (**strike into**) cause a strong emotion in. **7** suddenly cause to become: *he was struck dumb.* **8** refuse to work as a form of organized protest. **9** unexpectedly discover. **10** (**strike off**) officially expel from a professional group. **11** (**strike out**) start out on a new course. **12** reach an agreement. **13** (of a clock) show the time by sounding a chime or stroke. noun **1** an act of striking by employees. **2** a sudden attack. **3** an act of striking a ball. □ **strike up 1** begin to play a piece of music. **2** begin a friendship or conversation with someone.

striker noun **1** an employee who is on strike. **2** (in soccer) a forward.

striking adjective **1** noticeable. **2** dramatically good-looking. ■ **strikingly** adverb.

string noun **1** material consisting of threads twisted together to form a thin length. **2** a length of catgut or wire on a musical instrument, producing a note by vibration. **3** (**strings**) the stringed instruments in an orchestra. **4** a sequence of similar items or events. verb (**strings, stringing, strung**) **1** thread things together on a string. **2** (**be strung** or **be strung out**) be arranged in a long line. **3** fit strings to a musical instrument, bow, etc. □ **with no strings attached** informal with no special conditions or restrictions. **string bean** any of various beans eaten in their pods. **string quartet** a chamber music group consisting of two violinists and a viola and cello player. ■ **stringed** adjective.

stringent adjective (of regulations or requirements) strict and precise. ■ **stringency** noun **stringently** adverb.

stringy adjective **1** resembling string. **2** (of food) tough and fibrous.

strip¹ verb (**strips, stripping, stripped**) **1** remove all coverings or clothes from. **2** take off your clothes. **3** leave a room, vehicle, etc. bare of accessories or fittings. **4** remove paint from a surface. **5** (**strip of**) deprive of rank, power, or property. noun **1** an act of undressing. **2** Brit. the identifying outfit worn by a sports team.

strip² noun **1** a long, narrow piece of cloth, paper, etc. **2** a long, narrow area of land. □ **strip light** Brit. a fluorescent lamp in the shape of a tube.

stripe noun a long, narrow band or strip of a different colour or texture from its surrounds. verb (**stripes, striping, striped**) mark with stripes. ■ **stripy** (or **stripey**) adjective.

stripling noun old use a young man.

stripper noun **1** a device or substance for stripping paint, varnish, etc. off a surface. **2** a striptease performer.

striptease noun a form of entertainment in which a performer gradually undresses to music in an erotic way.

strive verb (**strives, striving, strove** or **strived**; past participle **striven** or **strived**) **1** make great efforts. **2** (**strive against**) fight vigorously against.

strobe noun a bright light which shines at rapid intervals.

strode past of **STRIDE**.

stroke noun **1** an act of hitting. **2** a sound made by a striking clock. **3** an act of stroking with the hand. **4** a mark made by drawing a pen, pencil, etc. across paper or canvas. **5** a short diagonal line separating characters or figures. **6** each of a series of repeated movements. **7** a style of moving the arms and legs in swimming. **8** a sudden disabling attack caused by an interruption in the flow of blood to the brain. verb (**strokes, stroking, stroked**) gently move your hand over.

stroll verb walk in a leisurely way. noun a short leisurely walk.

strong adjective (**stronger, strongest**) **1** physically powerful. **2** done with or supplying great force. **3** able to withstand great force or pressure. **4** secure or stable. **5** great in power, influence, or ability. **6** great in intensity or degree. **7** (of something seen or heard) not soft or muted. **8** pungent and full-flavoured. **9** (of a solution or drink) containing a large proportion of a substance. **10** used after a number to indicate the size of a group. □ **going strong** informal continuing to be healthy, vigorous, or successful. ■ **strongly** adverb.

strongbox noun a small metal box in which valuables are kept.

stronghold noun **1** a place that has been strengthened against attack. **2** a place of strong support for a cause or political party.

strongroom noun a room designed to protect valuable things against fire and theft.

strontium noun a soft silver-white metallic element.

stroppy adjective Brit. informal bad-tempered or argumentative.

strove past of **STRIVE**.

struck past and past participle of **STRIKE**.

structural adjective relating to or forming part of a structure. ■ **structurally** adverb.

structure noun **1** the putting together of different parts to form a whole. **2** a building or other object constructed from several parts. **3** good organization. verb (**structures, structuring, structured**) put parts together to form a whole.

strudel /stroo-duhl/ noun a dessert of thin pastry rolled up round a fruit filling and baked.

struggle verb (**struggles, struggling, struggled**) **1** make great efforts to get free. **2** try hard to do something. **3** make your way with difficulty. noun **1** an act of struggling. **2** a very difficult task. ■ **struggler** noun.

strum verb (**strums, strumming, strummed**) play a guitar or similar instrument by sweeping the thumb or a plectrum up or down the strings. noun an instance of strumming.

strumpet noun old use a woman who has a lot of sexual partners.

strung past and past participle of **STRING**.

strut noun **1** a bar used to support or strengthen a structure. **2** a proud, confident walk. verb (**struts, strutting, strutted**) walk in a proud and confident way.

strychnine /strik-neen/ noun a bitter and highly poisonous substance obtained from an Asian tree.

stub noun **1** the remaining part of a pencil, cigarette, etc. after use. **2** a shortened or unusually short thing. **3** the counterfoil of a cheque, ticket, etc. verb (**stubs, stubbing, stubbed**) **1** accidentally strike your toe against something. **2** (often **stub out**) put out a cigarette by pressing the lighted end against something. ■ **stubby** adjective.

stubble noun **1** the cut stalks of cereal plants left in the ground after harvesting. **2** short, stiff hairs growing on a man's face when he has not shaved for a while. ■ **stubbly** adjective.

stubborn adjective **1** determined not to change your attitude or position. **2** difficult to move or remove. ■ **stubbornly** adverb **stubbornness** noun.

stucco noun plaster used for coating wall surfaces or moulding into decoration. ■ **stuccoed** adjective.

stuck past participle of **STICK**². □ **stuck-up** informal having snobbish views and thinking that you are better than other people.

stud¹ noun **1** a piece of metal with a large head that projects from a surface. **2** a small projection fixed to the base of a shoe or boot to provide better grip. **3** a small piece of jewellery which is pushed through a pierced ear or nostril. **4** a fastener consisting of two buttons joined with a bar. verb (**studs, studding, studded**) decorate with studs or similar small objects.

stud² noun **1** an establishment where horses are kept for breeding. **2** a stallion. **3** informal a man who is very active sexually.

student noun **1** a person studying at a university or college. **2** a school pupil.

studio noun (plural **studios**) **1** a room where an artist works or where dancers practise. **2** a room from which television or radio programmes are broadcast. **3** a place where film or sound recordings are made. □ **studio flat** Brit. a flat containing one main room.

studious adjective **1** spending a lot of time studying or reading. **2** done with careful effort. ■ **studiously** adverb.

study noun (plural **studies**) **1** the reading of books or examination of other materials to gain knowledge. **2** a detailed investigation into a subject or situation. **3** a room used for reading and writing. **4** a piece of work done for practice or as an experiment. verb (**studies, studying, studied**) **1** make a study of. **2** apply yourself to study. **3** look at something closely in order to observe or read it. **4** (**studied**) done with careful effort.

stuff noun **1** material, articles, or activities of a particular kind, or of a mixed or unspecified kind. **2** basic characteristics. **3** (**your stuff**) informal the things that you are good at or responsible for. verb **1** fill something tightly with a filling. **2** force something tightly or hastily into a container or space. **3** fill out the skin of a dead animal or bird with material to restore the original appearance.

stuffing noun **1** a mixture used to stuff poultry or meat before cooking. **2** padding used to stuff cushions, furniture, or soft toys.

stuffy adjective (**stuffier, stuffiest**) **1** lacking fresh air or ventilation. **2** conventional and narrow-minded. **3** (of a person's nose) blocked up.

stultify verb (**stultifies, stultifying, stultified**) make someone feel bored or drained of energy.

stumble verb (**stumbles, stumbling, stumbled**) **1** trip and momentarily lose your balance. **2** walk unsteadily. **3** make a mistake in speaking. **4** (**stumble across** or **on**) find by chance. noun an act of stumbling. □ **stumbling block** an obstacle.

stump noun **1** the part of a tree trunk left sticking out of the ground after the rest has fallen or been cut down. **2** a remaining piece. **3** Cricket each of the three upright pieces of wood which form a wicket. verb baffle.

stumpy adjective (**stumpier, stumpiest**) short and thick; squat.

stun verb (**stuns, stunning, stunned**) **1** knock someone into a dazed or unconscious state. **2** greatly astonish or shock someone.

stung past and past participle of **STING**.

stunk past and past participle of **STINK**.

stunner noun informal a strikingly attractive or impressive person or thing.

stunning adjective extremely impressive or attractive. ■ **stunningly** adverb.

stunt¹ verb slow down the growth or development of.

stunt² noun **1** an action displaying spectacular skill and daring. **2** something unusual done to attract attention.

stuntman noun a person taking an actor's place in performing dangerous stunts.

stupefy verb (stupefies, stupefying, stupefied) make someone unable to think properly. ■ **stupefaction** noun.

stupendous adjective extremely impressive. ■ **stupendously** adverb.

stupid adjective **1** lacking intelligence or common sense. **2** dazed and unable to think clearly. ■ **stupidity** noun **stupidly** adverb.

stupor noun a state of being very dazed or nearly unconscious.

sturdy adjective (sturdier, sturdiest) **1** strong and solidly built or made. **2** confident and determined. ■ **sturdily** adverb **sturdiness** noun.

sturgeon /ster-juhn/ noun a very large fish with bony plates on the body, from whose roe caviar is made.

stutter verb (stutters, stuttering, stuttered) **1** have difficulty talking because you are sometimes unable to stop repeating the first sounds of a word. **2** (of a machine or gun) produce a series of short, sharp sounds. noun a tendency to stutter while speaking. ■ **stutterer** noun.

sty¹ noun (plural sties) a pigsty.

sty² or **stye** noun (plural sties or styes) an inflamed swelling on the edge of an eyelid.

Stygian /sti-ji-iuhn/ adjective literary very dark.

style noun **1** a way of doing something. **2** a particular appearance, design, or arrangement. **3** a way of painting, writing, etc. characteristic of a particular period or person. **4** elegance and sophistication. **5** Botany a narrow extension of the ovary, bearing the stigma. verb (styles, styling, styled) **1** design, make, or arrange in a particular form. **2** give a particular name, description, or title to.

stylish adjective **1** having or displaying a good sense of style. **2** fashionably elegant. ■ **stylishly** adverb.

stylist noun a person who designs fashionable clothes or cuts hair.

stylistic adjective of or concerning style. ■ **stylistically** adverb.

stylized or **stylised** adjective represented in an artificial style.

stylus noun (plural styli /sty-ly/) **1** a pointed implement used for scratching or tracing letters or engraving. **2** a hard point that follows a groove in a gramophone record and transmits the recorded sound for reproduction.

stymie verb (stymies, stymying or stymieing, stymied) informal prevent or slow down the progress of.

styptic /stip-tik/ adjective able to make bleeding stop.

suave /swahv/ adjective (of a man) charming, confident, and elegant. ■ **suavely** adverb **suavity** noun.

sub informal noun **1** a submarine. **2** a subscription. **3** a substitute in a sporting team. verb (subs, subbing, subbed) act as a substitute.

subaltern /sub-uhl-tern/ noun an officer in the British army below the rank of captain.

subatomic adjective smaller than or occurring within an atom.

subconscious adjective concerning the part of the mind which you are not aware of but which influences your actions and feelings. noun this part of the mind. ■ **subconsciously** adverb.

subcontinent noun a large part of a continent considered as a particular area, such as North America or southern Africa.

subcontract verb employ a firm or person outside your company to do

---

WORD FORMATION   [i]

sub-

The main meanings of the prefix **sub-** are:

- at, to, or from a lower level or position, as in *subconscious* | *sub-zero*
- lower in rank or importance; subordinate: *subculture* | *sub-heading*
- secondary or subsequent: *subdivision* | *sublet*
- somewhat; nearly; more or less: *sub-Saharan*.

---

work. ■ **subcontractor** noun.

subculture noun the distinct culture of a group existing within a larger culture.

subcutaneous adjective situated or applied under the skin.

subdivide verb (**subdivides, subdividing, subdivided**) divide a part into smaller parts. ■ **subdivision** noun.

subdue verb (**subdues, subduing, subdued**) **1** overcome, quieten, or control. **2** bring a group or country under control by force.

subdued adjective **1** quiet and thoughtful or depressed. **2** (of colour or lighting) soft; muted.

subedit verb (**subedits, subediting, subedited**) check and correct newspaper or magazine text before printing. ■ **subeditor** noun.

subhuman adjective not worthy of a human being; depraved.

subject noun /sub-jikt/ **1** a person or thing that is being discussed, studied, or dealt with. **2** a branch of knowledge that is studied or taught. **3** Grammar the word or words in a sentence that name who or what carries out the action of the verb. **4** each of the people in a population ruled by a king or queen. adjective /sub-jikt/ (**subject to**) **1** able to be affected by. **2** dependent or conditional on. **3** under the control or authority of. adverb /sub-jikt/ (**subject to**) conditionally on. verb /suhb-jekt/ (**subject to**) **1** make someone undergo something bad. **2** bring someone under your control or authority. ■ **subjection** noun.

subjective adjective based on or influenced by personal opinions. ■ **subjectively** adverb **subjectivity** noun.

sub judice /sub joo-di-si/ adjective being considered by a court of law and therefore not to be publicly discussed elsewhere.

subjugate verb (**subjugates, subjugating, subjugated**) bring someone under your control by force. ■ **subjugation** noun.

subjunctive adjective Grammar (of a verb) expressing what is imagined or wished or possible.

sublet verb (**sublets, subletting, sublet**) let a property or part of a property that you are already renting to someone else.

sublimate verb **1** transform something into a purer or idealized form. **2** Chemistry = **SUBLIME**. ■ **sublimation** noun.

sublime adjective **1** of great beauty or excellence. **2** extreme or unparalleled. verb (**sublimes, subliming, sublimed**) Chemistry (of a solid substance) change directly into vapour when heated. ■ **sublimely** adverb.

subliminal adjective affecting your mind without your being aware of it. ■ **subliminally** adverb.

sub-machine gun noun a hand-held lightweight machine gun.

submarine noun a streamlined warship designed to operate completely submerged in the sea. adjective existing, occurring, or used under the surface of the sea. ■ **submariner** noun.

submerge verb (**submerges, submerging, submerged**) **1** push or hold something under water. **2** go down below the surface of water. **3** completely cover or hide.

submerse verb submerge. ■ **submersion** noun.

GRAMMAR

Subject

The subject of a sentence is the person or thing that carries out the action of the verb. It can be found by asking the question 'who or what?' before the verb, e.g.

The goalkeeper *made a stunning save*

Thousands of books *are now available on CD-ROM*.

The examples above have *active* verbs. In a *passive* construction the subject of the sentence is the person or thing to which the action of the verb is done, e.g.

I *was hit by a ball*

Has the programme *been broadcast yet?*

---

submersible adjective designed to operate while submerged.

submicroscopic adjective too small to be seen by a microscope.

submission noun **1** the submitting of something. **2** a proposal or application submitted for consideration.

submissive adjective very obedient or passive. ■ **submissively** adverb.

submit verb (**submits, submitting, submitted**) **1** give in to the authority, control, or greater strength of someone or something. **2** subject to a particular process. **3** present a proposal or application for consideration.

subordinate adjective /suh-**bor**-di-nuht/ **1** lower in rank or position. **2** of less importance. noun /suh-**bor**-di-nuht/ a person who is under the authority of someone else. verb /suh-**bor**-di-nayt/ (**subordinates, subordinating, subordinated**) treat someone or something as less important than another. ■ **subordination** noun.

sub-plot noun a secondary plot in a play, novel, etc.

subpoena /suhb-**pee**-nuh/ Law noun a written order instructing someone to attend a court. verb (**subpoenas, subpoenaing, subpoenaed**) summon someone with a subpoena.

subscribe verb (**subscribes, subscribing, subscribed**) **1** (often **subscribe to**) arrange to receive something regularly by paying in advance. **2** (**subscribe to**) contribute a

sum of money to a project or cause. **3** (**subscribe to**) say you agree with an idea or proposal. ■ **subscriber** noun.

subscript adjective (of a letter, figure, or symbol) printed below the line.

subscription noun **1** the action of subscribing. **2** a payment to subscribe to something.

subsection noun a division of a section.

subsequent adjective coming after something. ■ **subsequently** adverb.

subservient adjective **1** obeying others unquestioningly. **2** less important. ■ **subservience** noun.

subside verb (**subsides, subsiding, subsided**) **1** become less strong, violent, or severe. **2** (of water) go down to a lower level. **3** (of a building) sink lower into the ground. **4** (of the ground) cave in; sink. **5** (**subside into**) give way to a strong feeling.

subsidence noun the gradual caving in or sinking of an area of land.

subsidiary adjective **1** related but less important. **2** (of a company) controlled by another company. noun (plural **subsidiaries**) a subsidiary company.

subsidize or **subsidise** verb (**subsidizes, subsidizing, subsidized**) **1** support an organization or activity financially. **2** pay part of the cost of producing something to reduce its price. ■ **subsidization** noun.

subsidy noun (plural **subsidies**) a sum

of money given to help keep the price of a product or service low.

subsist verb maintain or support yourself at a basic level.

subsistence noun the action or fact of subsisting. **adjective** (of production) at a level which is enough only for your own use, without any surplus for trade.

subsoil noun soil lying under the surface soil.

subsonic adjective relating to or flying at a speed less than that of sound.

substance noun 1 a particular kind of matter. 2 the real physical matter of which a person or thing consists. 3 solid basis in reality or fact. 4 the quality of being important, valid, or significant. 5 the most important or essential part or meaning.

substandard adjective below the usual or required standard.

substantial adjective 1 of considerable importance, size, or value. 2 strongly built or made. 3 concerning the essentials of something.

substantially adverb 1 to a great extent. 2 for the most part; essentially.

substantiate verb (substantiates, substantiating, substantiated) provide evidence to support or prove the truth of.

substantive adjective real and meaningful. ■ substantively adverb.

substitute noun a person or thing that does something in place of someone or something else. **verb** (substitutes, substituting, substituted) make someone or something act as a substitute for. ■ substitution noun.

subsume verb (subsumes, subsuming, subsumed) include or absorb something in something else.

subterfuge noun secretive or dishonest actions.

subterranean adjective existing or happening under the earth's surface.

subtext noun an underlying theme in a piece of writing or speech.

subtitle noun 1 (subtitles) words displayed at the bottom of a cinema or television screen that translate what is being said. 2 a secondary title of a published work. **verb** (subtitles, subtitling, subtitled) provide something with a subtitle or subtitles.

subtle adjective (subtler, subtlest) 1 so delicate or precise as to be difficult to analyse or describe. 2 capable of making fine distinctions. 3 making use of clever and indirect methods to achieve something. ■ subtlety noun subtly adverb.

subtotal noun the total of one set within a larger set of figures.

subtract verb take away a number or amount from another to calculate the difference. ■ subtraction noun.

suburb noun an outlying residential district of a city. ■ suburban adjective.

suburbia noun suburbs, and the way of life of their inhabitants.

subversive adjective trying to undermine the power of an established system or institution. **noun** a subversive person. ■ subversively adverb.

subvert verb undermine the power of an established system or institution. ■ subversion noun.

subway noun 1 Brit. a passage under a road for use by pedestrians. 2 N. Amer. an underground railway.

sub-zero adjective (of temperature) lower than zero; below freezing.

succeed verb 1 achieve an aim or purpose. 2 achieve wealth or status. 3 take over a job, role, or title from someone else. 4 come after and take the place of.

success noun 1 the achievement of an aim or purpose. 2 the gaining of wealth or status. 3 a person or thing that achieves success.

successful adjective 1 having achieved an aim or purpose. 2 having achieved wealth or status. ■ successfully adverb.

✓ double c, double s, one l: successful.

succession noun 1 a number of people or things following one after the other. **2** the action, process, or right of inheriting a position or title.

☑ double *c* and double *s*: succession.

successive **adjective** following one another or following others. ■ **successively** adverb.

☑ double *c*, double *s*: successive.

successor **noun** a person or thing that succeeds another.

succinct /suhk-**singkt**/ **adjective** briefly and clearly expressed. ■ **succinctly** adverb.

succour /**suk**-ker/ (US spelling **succor**) **noun** help and support in difficult times. **verb** give help to.

succulent **adjective** **1** (of food) tender, juicy, and tasty. **2** (of a plant) having thick fleshy leaves or stems that store water. **noun** a succulent plant. ■ **succulence** noun.

succumb **verb** **1** give in to pressure or temptation. **2** die from the effect of a disease or injury.

such **determiner & pronoun** **1** of the type previously mentioned or about to be mentioned. **2** to so high a degree; so great. □ **such as 1** for example. **2** of a kind; like.

suchlike **pronoun** things of the type mentioned. **determiner** of the type mentioned.

suck **verb** **1** draw something into your mouth by tightening your lip muscles to make a partial vacuum. **2** hold something in your mouth and draw at it by tightening your lip and cheek muscles. **3** draw something in a particular direction by creating a vacuum. **4** (**suck in** or **into**) involve someone in something without them being able to choose or resist it. **5** (**suck up to**) informal do things to please someone in authority in order to gain advantage for yourself. **6** N. Amer. informal be very bad or disagreeable. **noun** an act of sucking.

sucker **noun** **1** a rubber cup that sticks to a surface by suction. **2** an organ that allows an animal to cling

to a surface by suction. **3** informal a person who is easily fooled. **4** (**a sucker for**) informal a person who is very fond of a particular thing. **5** a shoot springing from the base of a tree or other plant.

suckle **verb** (**suckles, suckling, suckled**) feed at the breast or a teat.

suckling **noun** a young child or animal that is still feeding on its mother's milk.

sucrose /**soo**-krohz/ **noun** the main substance in cane or beet sugar.

suction **noun** the force produced when a partial vacuum is created by the removal of air.

sudden **adjective** occurring or done quickly and unexpectedly. ■ **suddenly** adverb **suddenness** noun.

suds **plural noun** froth made from soap and water.

sue **verb** (**sues, suing, sued**) **1** start legal proceedings against someone that you claim has harmed you. **2** (**sue for**) formal appeal formally to a person for.

suede **noun** leather with the flesh side rubbed to make a velvety nap.

suet **noun** hard white fat obtained from cattle, sheep, and other animals, used in cooking.

suffer **verb** (**suffers, suffering, suffered**) **1** experience something bad. **2** (**suffer from**) be affected by an ailment. **3** become worse in quality. **4** old use tolerate. ■ **sufferer** noun.

sufferance ■ **noun** toleration, rather than genuine approval.

suffice **verb** (**suffices, sufficing, sufficed**) **1** be enough or adequate. **2** meet the needs of.

sufficiency **noun** (plural **sufficiencies**) **1** the quality of being enough or adequate. **2** an adequate amount.

sufficient **adjective** enough; adequate. ■ **sufficiently** adverb.

suffix **noun** a part added on to the end of a word (e.g. -*ly*, -*ation*).

suffocate **verb** (**suffocates, suffocating, suffocated**) die or cause to die from lack of air or being unable to breathe. ■ **suffocation** noun.

suffrage /suf-frij/ noun the right to vote in political elections.

suffragette /suf-fruh-**jet**/ noun (in the past, when only men could vote) a woman who campaigned for the right to vote in an election.

suffuse verb (**suffuses**, **suffusing**, **suffused**) gradually spread through or over. ■ **suffusion** noun.

sugar noun **1** a sweet substance obtained from sugar cane or sugar beet. **2** a type of sweet, soluble carbohydrate found in plant and animal tissue. **verb** sweeten, sprinkle, or coat with sugar. □ **sugar beet** a type of beet from which sugar is extracted. **sugar cane** a tropical grass with tall thick stems from which sugar is extracted. **sugar daddy** informal a rich older man who gives presents and money to a much younger woman. ■ **sugary** adjective.

suggest verb **1** put forward an idea or plan for people to consider. **2** make you think that something exists or is the case. **3** say or indicate something indirectly. **4** (**suggest itself**) (of an idea) come into your mind.

suggestible adjective quick to accept other people's ideas or suggestions.

suggestion noun **1** an idea or plan put forward for people to consider. **2** a thing that suggests that something is the case. **3** a slight trace or indication.

suggestive adjective **1** making you think of a particular thing. **2** hinting at sexual matters. ■ **suggestively** adverb.

suicide noun **1** the action of killing yourself intentionally. **2** a person who commits suicide. ■ **suicidal** adjective **suicidally** adverb.

suit noun **1** a set of clothes made of the same fabric, consisting of a jacket and trousers or a skirt. **2** a set of clothes for a particular activity. **3** any of the sets into which a pack of playing cards is divided (spades, hearts, diamonds, and clubs). **4** a lawsuit. **verb 1** be right or good for. **2** (of clothes, colours, etc.) be right for someone's features or figure. **3** (**suit yourself**) do as you wish.

suitable adjective right or good for a particular person or situation. ■ **suitability** noun **suitably** adverb.

suitcase noun a case with a handle and a hinged lid, used for carrying clothes and other possessions.

suite noun **1** a set of rooms. **2** a set of furniture. **3** (in music) a set of instrumental compositions to be played one after the other.

suitor noun old use a man who pays attention to a woman because he wants to marry her.

sulfur US spelling of **SULPHUR**.

sulk verb be quietly bad-tempered and resentful because you are annoyed. noun a period of sulking.

sulky adjective quietly bad-tempered and resentful. ■ **sulkily** adverb.

sullen adjective silent and bad-tempered. ■ **sullenly** adverb.

sully verb (**sullies**, **sullying**, **sullied**) spoil the purity or cleanness of something.

sulphur (US spelling **sulfur**) noun a chemical element in the form of yellow crystals, which easily catches fire. □ **sulphur dioxide** a poisonous gas formed by burning sulphur.

sulphuric (US spelling **sulfuric**) adjective containing sulphur. □ **sulphuric acid** a strong corrosive acid.

sulphurous (US spelling **sulfurous**) adjective containing or derived from sulphur.

sultan noun a Muslim king or ruler.

sultana noun **1** a light brown seedless raisin. **2** the wife of a sultan.

sultry adjective **1** (of the weather) hot and humid. **2** suggesting sexual passion.

sum noun **1** a particular amount of money. **2** (also **sum total**) the total amount resulting from the addition of two or more numbers or amounts. **3** a calculation in arithmetic. **verb** (**sums**, **summing**, **summed**) (**sum up**) **1** concisely describe the nature or character of. **2** summarize briefly.

summarize or **summarise** verb (summarizes, summarizing, summarized) give a summary of.

summary noun (plural summaries) a brief statement of the main points of something. adjective **1** dispensing with unnecessary details or formalities. **2** (of a legal process or judgement) done or made immediately and without following the normal procedures. ■ **summarily** adverb.

summation noun **1** the process of adding things together. **2** the action of summing up. **3** a summary.

summer noun the season after spring and before autumn. verb (summers, summering, summered) spend the summer in a particular place. □ **summer house** a small building in a garden, used for relaxing in in hot weather. ■ **summery** adjective.

summit noun **1** the highest point of a hill or mountain. **2** the highest possible level of achievement. **3** a meeting between heads of government.

summon verb **1** instruct someone to be present. **2** urgently ask for help. **3** call people to attend a meeting. **4** make a desirable quality or reaction emerge from within yourself.

summons noun (plural summonses) **1** an order to appear in a law court. **2** an act of summoning.

sumo /**soo**-moh/ noun (plural sumos) a Japanese form of wrestling.

sump noun the base of an internal-combustion engine, in which a reserve of oil is stored.

sumptuous adjective splendid and expensive-looking. ■ **sumptuously** adverb.

sun noun **1** (also **Sun**) the star round which the earth orbits. **2** any similar star. **3** the light or warmth received from the sun. verb (suns, sunning, sunned) (sun yourself) sit or lie outside in the heat of the sun.

sunbathe verb (sunbathes, sunbathing, sunbathed) sit or lie outside in the sun to get a suntan.

sunbeam noun a ray of sunlight.

sunbed noun Brit. **1** a long chair that you lie on when sunbathing. **2** a bed between two banks of sunlamps, which you lie on to get an artificial tan.

sunblock noun a cream or lotion used on the skin for complete protection from sunburn.

sunburn noun inflammation of the skin caused by too much exposure to the ultraviolet rays of the sun. ■ **sunburned** (or **sunburnt**) adjective.

sundae noun a dish of ice cream with added fruit and syrup.

 -ae, not -ay: sundae.

Sunday noun the day of the week before Monday and following Saturday, observed by Christians as a day of worship. □ **Sunday school** a class held on Sundays to teach children about Christianity.

sunder verb (sunders, sundering, sundered) literary split apart.

sundial noun an instrument showing the time by the shadow cast by a pointer.

sundry adjective of various kinds. noun (sundries) various items not important enough to be mentioned individually.

sunflower noun a tall plant with very large yellow flowers.

sung past participle of **SING**.

sunglasses plural noun glasses tinted to protect the eyes from sunlight.

sunk past and past participle of **SINK**.

sunken adjective **1** having sunk. **2** at a lower level than the surrounding area.

sunlamp noun a lamp giving off ultraviolet rays, under which you lie to get an artificial suntan.

sunlight noun light from the sun. ■ **sunlit** adjective.

sunny adjective (sunnier, sunniest) **1** bright with or receiving much sunlight. **2** cheerful.

sunrise noun **1** the time when the sun

WORD FORMATION   i

super-

Words beginning with **super-** mean:
- above; over; beyond, as in *superstructure*
- to a great or extreme degree, e.g. *supercool*
- extra large or powerful of its kind: *superpower.*

---

rises. **2** the colours and light visible in the sky at sunrise.

sunroof noun a panel in the roof of a car that can be opened for extra ventilation.

sunscreen noun a cream or lotion rubbed on to the skin to protect it from the sun.

sunset noun **1** the time when the sun sets. **2** the colours and light visible in the sky at sunset.

sunshade noun an umbrella or awning giving protection from the sun.

sunshine noun sunlight unbroken by cloud.

sunspot noun a temporary darker and cooler patch on the sun's surface.

sunstroke noun heatstroke brought about by staying too long in the sun.

suntan noun a golden-brown colouring of the skin caused by exposure to the sun. ■ **suntanned** adjective.

sup[1] verb (**sups**, **supping**, **supped**) dated or N. English take drink or liquid food by sips or spoonfuls. noun a sip.

sup[2] verb (**sups**, **supping**, **supped**) old use eat supper.

super adjective informal excellent.

superannuate verb (**superannuates**, **superannuating**, **superannuated**) **1** arrange for someone to retire with a pension. **2** (**superannuated**) humorous too old to be effective or useful.

superannuation noun regular payment made by an employee into a fund from which a future pension will be paid.

superb adjective **1** very good; excellent. **2** magnificent or splendid. ■ **superbly** adverb.

supercharger noun a device that makes an engine more efficient by forcing extra air or fuel into it. ■ **supercharged** adjective.

supercilious adjective having a manner that shows you think you are better than other people.

superficial adjective **1** existing or happening at or on the surface. **2** apparent rather than real. **3** not thorough. **4** lacking the ability to think deeply about things. ■ **superficiality** noun **superficially** adverb.

superfluous adjective more than what is needed.

superglue noun a very strong quick-setting glue.

supergrass noun Brit. informal a person who secretly gives the police information about the criminal activities of a large number of people.

superhuman adjective having exceptional ability or powers.

superimpose verb (**superimposes**, **superimposing**, **superimposed**) lay one thing over another. ■ **superimposition** noun.

superintend verb manage or oversee.

superintendent noun **1** a person who supervises and controls a group or activity. **2** a senior police officer.

superior adjective **1** higher in status, quality, or power. **2** of high quality. **3** arrogant and conceited. noun a person of higher rank or status.

superiority noun the state of being superior.

superlative adjective **1** of the highest quality or degree. **2** (of an adjective or adverb) expressing the highest degree of a quality (e.g. *bravest*). noun an exaggerated expression of praise.

superman noun informal a man who is unusually strong or intelligent.

supermarket noun a large self-service shop selling foods and household goods.

supermodel noun a very successful and famous fashion model.

supernatural adjective not able to be explained by the laws of nature. noun **(the supernatural)** supernatural events. ■ **supernaturally** adverb.

supernova noun (plural **supernovae** /soo-per-**noh**-vee/ or **supernovas**) a star that undergoes a catastrophic explosion, becoming suddenly very much brighter.

supernumerary adjective **1** present in more than the required number. **2** not belonging to a regular staff but engaged for extra work.

superpower noun any of the few most powerful nations of the world.

superscript adjective (of a letter, figure, or symbol) printed above the line.

supersede verb (**supersedes, superseding, superseded**) take the place of.

 -*sede*, not -*cede*: super*sede*.

supersonic adjective involving or flying at a speed greater than that of sound.

superstar noun an extremely famous and successful performer or sports player.

superstition noun a belief in the supernatural, especially that particular things bring good or bad luck.

superstitious adjective believing in the supernatural and in the power of particular things to bring good or bad luck. ■ **superstitiously** adverb.

superstore noun a very large out-of-town supermarket.

superstructure noun **1** a structure built on top of something else. **2** the part of a structure that is built above a supporting base or foundation.

supervene verb occur as an interruption or change to an existing situation.

supervise verb watch and direct the performance of a task or the work of a person. ■ **supervision** noun **supervisor** noun **supervisory** adjective.

supine adjective **1** lying face upwards. **2** passive or lazy.

supper noun a light or informal evening meal.

supplant verb take the place of.

supple adjective (**suppler, supplest**) able to bend and move parts of your body easily; flexible.

supplement noun **1** a thing added to something else to improve or complete it. **2** a separate section added to a newspaper or periodical. **3** an additional charge payable for an extra service or facility. verb provide a supplement for. ■ **supplemental** adjective.

supplementary adjective completing or improving something.

suppliant /**sup**-pli-uhnt/ noun a person who makes a humble request. adjective making a humble request.

supplicate verb (**supplicates, supplicating, supplicated**) humbly ask for something. ■ **supplicant** adjective & noun **supplication** noun.

supply verb (**supplies, supplying, supplied**) **1** make something available to someone. **2** provide someone with something. noun (plural **supplies**) **1** a stock or amount of something supplied or available. **2** the action of supplying. **3** (**supplies**) provisions and equipment necessary for a large group of people or for an expedition. ■ **supplier** noun.

support verb **1** bear all or part of the weight of. **2** give help, encouragement, or approval to. **3** favour and attend the matches of a particular sports team. **4** provide someone with a home and the necessities of life. **5** be capable of sustaining life. **6** confirm or back up. noun **1** a person or thing that supports. **2** the action of supporting. **3** help, encouragement, or approval. ■ **supporter** noun.

supportive adjective providing encouragement or emotional help.

suppose verb (supposes, supposing, supposed) **1** think that something is true or likely, but lack proof. **2** (of a theory or argument) require that something is the case as a necessary condition. **3** (be supposed to do) be required or expected to do.

supposedly adverb according to what is generally believed.

supposition noun a belief that something is likely to be true.

suppository noun (plural suppositories) a solid medical preparation designed to dissolve after being inserted into the rectum or vagina.

suppress verb **1** forcibly put an end to. **2** prevent or inhibit. **3** stop something from being stated or published. ■ **suppressant** noun **suppression** noun.

> ☑ two *p*'s: su**pp**ress.

suppurate verb (suppurates, suppurating, suppurated) form pus. ■ **suppuration** noun.

supremacist noun a person who believes that a particular group is superior to all others.

supremacy noun the state of being superior to all others.

supreme adjective **1** highest in authority or rank. **2** very great or greatest; most important. □ **supreme court** the highest law court in a country or state. ■ **supremely** adverb.

supremo noun (plural supremos) Brit. informal a person in overall charge.

surcharge noun an extra charge or payment.

surd noun Mathematics a number which cannot be expressed as a ratio of two whole numbers.

sure adjective **1** completely confident that you are right. **2** (sure of or to do) certain to receive, acquire, or do. **3** undoubtedly true. **4** steady and confident. adverb informal certainly. □ **surefire** informal certain to succeed. ■ **sureness** noun.

surely adverb **1** it must be true that. **2** certainly.

surety noun (plural sureties) **1** a person who guarantees that somebody else will do something or pay a debt. **2** money given as a guarantee that someone will do something.

surf noun the breaking of large waves on a seashore or reef. verb **1** stand or lie on a surfboard and ride on the crest of a wave towards the shore. **2** move from site to site on the Internet. ■ **surfer** noun **surfing** noun.

surface noun **1** the outside or top layer of something. **2** the upper limit of a body of liquid. **3** outward appearance. verb (surfaces, surfacing, surfaced) **1** rise to the surface. **2** become apparent. **3** provide a road, floor, etc. with a top layer.

surfboard noun a long, narrow board used in surfing.

surfeit noun an amount that is more than is needed or wanted.

surge noun **1** a sudden powerful movement forwards or upwards. **2** a sudden increase. **3** a powerful rush of an emotion or feeling. verb (surges, surging, surged) **1** move in a surge. **2** increase suddenly and powerfully.

surgeon noun **1** a medical practitioner who is qualified to practise surgery. **2** a doctor in the navy.

surgery noun (plural surgeries) **1** medical treatment that involves cutting open the body and repairing or removing parts. **2** Brit. a place where a doctor or nurse sees patients.

surgical adjective **1** relating to or used in surgery. **2** worn to correct or relieve an injury or ailment. **3** done with great precision. □ **surgical spirit** Brit. methylated spirit used for cleaning the skin before injections or surgery. ■ **surgically** adverb.

surly adjective (surlier, surliest) bad-tempered and unfriendly.

surmise verb (surmises, surmising, surmised) suppose something without having evidence. noun a guess.

surmount verb **1** overcome a difficulty or obstacle. **2** stand or be placed on top of.

surname noun an inherited name used by all the members of a family.

surpass verb be greater or better than.

surplice noun a white robe worn over a cassock by Christian ministers and people singing in church choirs.

surplus noun an amount left over. **adjective** more than what is needed or used.

surprise noun **1** a feeling of mild astonishment or shock caused by something unexpected. **2** an unexpected or astonishing thing. verb (**surprises, surprising, surprised**) **1** make someone feel surprise. **2** attack or discover suddenly and unexpectedly.

☑ don't forget the first *r*, and note also that **surprise** can't be spelled with an *-ize* ending: sur**prise**.

surreal adjective strange and having the qualities of a dream. ■ **surreally** adverb.

surrealism noun an artistic movement which combined normally unrelated images in a bizarre way. ■ **surrealist** noun & adjective.

surrender verb (**surrenders, surrendering, surrendered**) **1** give in to an opponent. **2** give up a right or possession. **3** (**surrender to**) abandon yourself to a powerful emotion or influence. noun an act of surrendering.

surreptitious adjective done secretly. ■ **surreptitiously** adverb.

surrogate noun a person who stands in for someone else. ▫ **surrogate mother** a woman who bears a child on behalf of another woman. ■ **surrogacy** noun.

surround verb **1** be all round something; encircle. **2** be associated with. noun **1** a border or edging. **2** (**surrounds** or **surroundings**) the conditions or area around a person or thing.

surtax noun an extra tax on something already taxed.

surtitle noun a caption projected on a screen above the stage in an opera, translating the text being sung.

surveillance /ser-**vay**-luhnss/ noun close observation, especially of a suspected spy or criminal.

survey verb (**surveys, surveying, surveyed**) **1** look carefully and thoroughly at. **2** examine and record the features of an area of land in order to produce a map or description. **3** Brit. examine and report on the condition of a building. **4** conduct a survey among a group of people. noun **1** a general view, examination, or description. **2** an investigation into the opinions or experience of a group of people, based on a series of questions. **3** an act of surveying. **4** a map or report obtained by surveying. ■ **surveyor** noun.

survival noun **1** the state or fact of surviving. **2** an object or practice that has survived from an earlier time.

survive verb (**survives, surviving, survived**) **1** continue to live or exist. **2** continue to live in spite of an accident or ordeal. **3** remain alive after the death of. ■ **survivor** noun.

susceptibility noun (plural **susceptibilities**) **1** the quality of being easily influenced or hurt. **2** (**susceptibilities**) sensitive feelings.

susceptible adjective **1** (**susceptible to**) likely to be influenced or harmed by. **2** easily influenced by feelings or emotions.

sushi /**soo**-shi/ noun a Japanese dish consisting of balls of cold rice with raw seafood, vegetables, etc.

suspect verb **1** believe something to be likely or possible. **2** believe that someone is guilty of a crime or offence, without having definite proof. **3** feel that something may not be genuine or true. noun a person suspected of a crime or offence. adjective possibly dangerous or false.

suspend verb **1** temporarily bring a stop to something. **2** temporarily stop someone from doing their job or attending school, as a punishment or during investigation. **3** postpone or delay an action, event, or judgement. **4 (suspended)** (of a sentence given by a court) not enforced as long as no further offence is committed. **5** hang something in the air.

suspender noun **1** Brit. an elastic strap attached to a belt or garter and fastened to the top of a stocking to hold it up. **2 (suspenders)** N. Amer. braces for holding up trousers.

suspense noun a state or feeling of excited or anxious uncertainty about what may happen.

suspension noun **1** the suspending of something. **2** a system of springs and shock absorbers which supports a vehicle on its wheels and makes it more comfortable to ride in. **3** a mixture in which particles are spread throughout a fluid. □ **suspension bridge** a bridge which is suspended from cables running between towers.

suspicion noun **1** an idea that something is possible or likely or that someone has done something wrong. **2** a feeling of distrust. **3** a very slight trace.

suspicious adjective **1** having a feeling that someone has done something wrong. **2** making you feel that something is wrong. **3** not able to trust others. ■ **suspiciously** adverb.

suss verb (**susses, sussing, sussed**) (often **suss out**) Brit. informal realize or understand the true character or nature of.

sustain verb **1** strengthen or support someone physically or mentally. **2** bear the weight of an object. **3** put up with something unpleasant. **4** keep something going over time or continuously.

sustainable adjective **1** able to be sustained. **2** (of industry, development, or agriculture) avoiding using up natural resources. ■ **sustainability** noun **sustainably** adverb.

sustenance noun **1** the food needed to keep someone alive. **2** the process of keeping something going.

suture noun **1** a stitch holding together the edges of a wound or surgical cut. **2** a thread used for this. verb (**sutures, suturing, sutured**) stitch up a wound or cut.

suzerainty /soo-zuh-rayn-ty/ noun the right of one country to rule over another country which has its own ruler but is not fully independent.

svelte adjective slender and elegant.

SW abbreviation south-west or south-western.

swab noun **1** a pad used for cleaning a wound or taking liquid from the body for testing. **2** a sample of liquid taken with a swab. verb (**swabs, swabbing, swabbed**) **1** clean or take liquid from a wound or part of the body with a swab. **2** wash down a surface with water and a cloth or mop.

swaddle verb (**swaddles, swaddling, swaddled**) wrap in garments or a cloth. □ **swaddling clothes** (in the past) strips of cloth wrapped round a baby to calm it.

swag noun **1** a curtain hanging in a drooping curve. **2** informal property stolen by a burglar.

swagger verb (**swaggers, swaggering, swaggered**) walk or behave in a very confident or arrogant manner. noun a swaggering walk or manner.

swain noun old use a young man.

swallow[1] verb **1** contract the muscles of the mouth and throat so that food, drink, or saliva pass down the throat. **2 (swallow up)** surround or absorb something so that it disappears. **3** believe an untrue statement unquestioningly. noun an act of swallowing.

swallow[2] noun a fast-flying bird with a forked tail.

swam past of **SWIM**.

swamp noun an area of boggy or marshy land. verb **1** flood an area with water. **2** overwhelm with too much of something. ■ **swampy** adjective.

swan noun a large white waterbird with a long flexible neck. verb (**swans, swanning, swanned**) Brit. informal go around in a casual, irresponsible, or flamboyant way.

swank informal verb show off your

achievements, knowledge, or wealth. **noun** the act of showing off.

swanky adjective (swankier, swankiest) informal **1** stylishly luxurious and expensive. **2** inclined to show off.

swansong noun the final performance or activity of a person's career.

swap or **swop** verb (swaps, swapping, swapped) exchange or substitute something for something else. **noun** an act of swapping.

sward noun an expanse of grass.

swarm noun **1** a dense group of flying insects. **2** a large number of honeybees that leave a hive with a queen in order to establish a new colony. **3** a large group of people or things. **verb 1** move in or form a swarm. **2** (**swarm with**) be crowded or overrun with. **3** (**swarm up**) climb something rapidly by gripping with your hands and feet.

swarthy adjective (swarthier, swarthiest) having a dark skin.

swashbuckling adjective having many daring and romantic adventures. ∎ **swashbuckler** noun.

swastika /swoss-ti-kuh/ noun an ancient symbol in the form of a cross with its arms bent at a right angle, used in the 20th century as the emblem of the Nazi party.

swat verb (swats, swatting, swatted) hit or crush something with a sharp blow from a flat object.

swatch noun a piece of fabric used as a sample.

swathe[1] /sway*th*/ (US spelling **swath** /swawth/) noun (plural **swathes** or **swaths**) **1** a row or line of grass, corn, etc. as it falls when cut down. **2** a broad strip or area.

swathe[2] /sway*th*/ verb wrap in several layers of fabric. **noun** a strip of material in which something is wrapped.

sway verb **1** move slowly and rhythmically backwards and forwards or from side to side. **2** make someone change their opinion. **noun 1** a swaying movement. **2** influence or control over people. ☐ **hold sway** have power or influence.

swear verb (swears, swearing, swore; past participle sworn) **1** promise something solemnly or on oath. **2** use offensive or obscene language. ☐ **swear by** informal have or express great confidence in. **swear in** admit someone to a position by directing them to take a formal oath. **swear word** an offensive or obscene word.

sweat noun moisture that comes out through the pores of the skin when you are hot, making a physical effort, or anxious. **verb** (sweats, sweating, past and past participle sweated or N. Amer. sweat) **1** give off sweat. **2** (**sweat over**) make a great deal of effort in doing. **3** be very anxious. **4** cook vegetables very slowly. ∎ **sweaty** adjective.

sweatband noun a band of absorbent material worn round the head or wrists to soak up sweat.

sweater noun a pullover with long sleeves.

sweatshirt noun a loose, warm cotton sweater.

sweatshop noun a factory or workshop employing workers for long hours in poor conditions.

swede noun Brit. a round yellow-fleshed root vegetable.

sweep verb (sweeps, sweeping, swept) **1** clean an area by brushing away dirt or litter. **2** move swiftly or forcefully. **3** (**sweep away** or **aside**) remove or abolish something swiftly and suddenly. **4** search an area. **noun 1** an act of sweeping. **2** a long, swift, curving movement. **3** a long curved stretch of road, river, etc. **4** the range or scope of something. **5** (also **chimney sweep**) a person who cleans out the soot from chimneys. ∎ **sweeper** noun.

sweeping adjective **1** extending or performed in a long, continuous curve. **2** wide in range or effect. **3** (of a statement) too general.

sweepstake or **sweepstakes** noun a form of gambling in which all the stakes are divided among the winners.

sweet adjective **1** having the pleasant taste characteristic of sugar or honey. **2** having a pleasant smell. **3** (of air, water, etc.) fresh and pure. **4** pleasant and kind. **5** charming and endearing. **6** causing satisfaction. noun Brit. **1** a small piece of confectionery made with sugar. **2** a sweet dish forming a course of a meal. □ **sweet-and-sour** cooked with both sugar and vinegar. **sweet pea** a climbing plant of the pea family with colourful, sweet-smelling flowers. **sweet potato** the pinkish-orange tuber of a tropical climbing plant, eaten as a vegetable. **sweet-talk** informal use charming or flattering words to persuade someone to do something. **sweet tooth** a great liking for sweet-tasting foods. ■ **sweetly** adverb **sweetness** noun.

sweetbread noun the thymus gland or pancreas of an animal, used for food.

sweetcorn noun a kind of maize with sweet-tasting yellow kernels which are eaten as a vegetable.

sweeten verb **1** make or become sweet or sweeter. **2** make something more agreeable or acceptable.

sweetener noun **1** a substance used to sweeten food or drink. **2** informal a bribe.

sweetheart noun a person you are in love with.

sweetmeat noun old use an item of confectionery or sweet food.

swell verb (**swells**, **swelling**, **swelled**; past participle **swollen** or **swelled**) **1** become larger or more rounded. **2** increase in strength or amount. noun **1** a full or gently rounded form. **2** a gradual increase in strength or amount. **3** a slow, regular, rolling movement of the sea. adjective N. Amer. informal, dated excellent.

swelling noun an abnormal enlargement of a part of the body as a result of an accumulation of fluid.

swelter verb (**swelters**, **sweltering**, **sweltered**) be uncomfortably hot.

swept past and past participle of **SWEEP**.

swerve verb (**swerves**, **swerving**, **swerved**) abruptly go off from a straight course. noun an abrupt change of course.

swift adjective **1** happening quickly or promptly. **2** moving or able to move at high speed. noun a fast-flying bird with long, slender wings. ■ **swiftly** adverb **swiftness** noun.

swig verb (**swigs**, **swigging**, **swigged**) drink deeply and quickly. noun a quick, deep drink.

swill verb Brit. **1** rinse something out with large amounts of water. **2** (of liquid) swirl round in a container or cavity. noun food waste mixed with water for feeding to pigs.

swim verb (**swims**, **swimming**, **swam**; past participle **swum**) **1** move through water using your arms and legs. **2** be immersed in liquid. **3** experience a dizzily confusing feeling. noun a period of swimming. ■ **swimmer** noun.

swimmingly adverb informal smoothly and satisfactorily.

swimsuit noun a woman's one-piece garment for swimming.

swindle verb (**swindles**, **swindling**, **swindled**) cheat someone in order to get money from them. noun a dishonest scheme to get money from someone. ■ **swindler** noun.

swine noun **1** (plural **swine**) a pig. **2** (plural **swine** or **swines**) informal a contemptible person. ■ **swinish** adjective.

swing verb (**swings**, **swinging**, **swung**) **1** move backwards and forwards or from side to side while suspended. **2** move by grasping a support and leaping. **3** move in a smooth, curving line. **4** (**swing at**) attempt to hit. **5** change from one opinion, mood, or state of affairs to another. **6** have a decisive influence on a vote or opinion. **7** informal succeed in bringing something about. noun **1** a seat suspended by ropes or chains, on which you can sit and swing backwards and forwards. **2** an act of swinging. **3** a clear change in public opinion. **4** a style of jazz or dance music with an easy flowing rhythm.

swingeing adjective chiefly Brit. extreme or severe.

swinging adjective informal lively, exciting, and fashionable.

swipe informal **verb** (swipes, swiping, swiped) **1** hit or try to hit something with a swinging blow. **2** steal. **3** pass a swipe card through an electronic reader. **noun 1** a sweeping blow. **2** an attack or criticism. □ **swipe card** a plastic card carrying coded information which is read when the card is slid through an electronic device.

swirl verb move in a twisting or spiralling pattern. **noun** a swirling movement or pattern. ■ **swirly** adjective.

swish verb move with a soft rushing sound. **noun** a soft rushing sound or movement. **adjective** Brit. informal impressively smart.

Swiss adjective relating to Switzerland. □ **Swiss roll** Brit. a thin sponge cake spread with jam or cream and rolled up.

switch noun **1** a device for making and breaking an electrical connection. **2** a change or exchange. **3** a flexible shoot cut from a tree. **verb 1** change in position, direction, or focus. **2** exchange for something else. **3** (switch off or on) turn an electrical device off or on. **4** (switch off) informal stop paying attention.

switchback noun Brit. a road with alternate sharp ascents and descents.

switchblade noun N. Amer. a flick knife.

switchboard noun a board with which incoming phone calls can be redirected within an organization.

swivel noun a connecting device between two parts enabling one to revolve without turning the other. **verb** (swivels, swivelling, swivelled; US spelling swivels, swiveling, swiveled) turn on a swivel or central point.

swizz noun Brit. informal an instance of

being mildly cheated or disappointed.

swollen past participle of **SWELL**.

swoon verb faint, especially from extreme emotion. **noun** an instance of swooning.

swoop verb **1** move rapidly downwards through the air. **2** carry out a sudden raid. **noun** an act of swooping.

swop ⇒ **SWAP**.

sword noun a weapon with a long, sharp metal blade.

swordfish noun a large sea fish with a sword-like snout.

swore past of **SWEAR**.

sworn past participle of **SWEAR**. **adjective** bound by an oath.

swot Brit. informal **verb** (swots, swotting, swotted) study hard. **noun** a person who spends a lot of time studying.

swum past participle of **SWIM**.

swung past and past participle of **SWING**.

sybarite /si-buh-ryt/ noun a person who is very fond of luxury. ■ **sybaritic** adjective.

sycamore noun **1** a large maple native to central and southern Europe. **2** N. Amer. a plane tree.

sycophant /si-kuh-fant/ noun a person who tries to gain favour with someone important by saying flattering things to them. ■ **sycophancy** noun **sycophantic** adjective.

syllable noun a unit of pronunciation having one vowel sound and forming all or part of a word. ■ **syllabic** adjective.

syllabus noun (plural syllabuses or syllabi /sil-luh-by/) all the things covered in a course of study or teaching.

syllogism /sil-luh-ji-z'm/ noun a form of reasoning in which a conclusion is drawn from two propositions.

sylph noun **1** an imaginary spirit of the air. **2** a slender woman or girl. ■ **sylphlike** adjective.

sylvan adjective literary having to do with woods; wooded.

symbiosis /sim-by-oh-siss/ noun

GRAMMAR

Syllable

A syllable is the smallest unit of speech that can normally occur alone, such as *a*, *at*, *ta*, or *tat*. A word can be made up of one or more syllables:

- *cat*, *fought*, and *twinge* each have one syllable;
- *rating*, *deny*, and *collapse* each have two syllables;
- *excitement*, *superman*, and *telephoned* each have three syllables;
- *American* and *complicated* each have four syllables;
- *examination* and *uncontrollable* each have five syllables.

(plural **symbioses** /sim-by-**oh**-seez/) Biology a situation in which two living things are connected with and dependent on each other to the advantage of both. ■ **symbiotic** adjective.

symbol noun **1** an object, person, or event that represents something else. **2** a letter, mark, or character used as a representation of something.

symbolic adjective **1** serving as a symbol. **2** involving the use of symbols or symbolism. ■ **symbolically** adverb.

symbolism noun the use of symbols to represent ideas or qualities. ■ **symbolist** noun & adjective.

symbolize or **symbolise** verb (**symbolizes**, **symbolizing**, **symbolized**) **1** be a symbol of. **2** represent something by means of symbols.

symmetrical adjective exactly the same on each side. ■ **symmetrically** adverb.

symmetry noun (plural **symmetries**) **1** the exact match in size or shape between two halves, parts, or sides of something. **2** the quality of being exactly the same or very similar.

sympathetic adjective **1** feeling or showing sympathy. **2** showing approval of an idea or action. **3** pleasing or likeable. ■ **sympathetically** adverb.

sympathize or **sympathise** verb (**sympathizes**, **sympathizing**, **sympathized**) **1** feel or express sympathy. **2** agree with an opinion.

sympathy noun (plural **sympathies**) **1** the feeling of being sorry for someone. **2** understanding between people. **3** support for or approval of something. □ **in sympathy** fitting in; in keeping.

> ℹ️ strictly, **sympathy** does not mean the same thing as **empathy**: if you have **sympathy** for someone you feel sorry for them, whereas if you have **empathy** for them you understand and share their feelings.

symphonic adjective having the form or character of a symphony.

symphony noun (plural **symphonies**) an elaborate musical composition for a full orchestra.

symposium /sim-**poh**-zi-uhm/ noun (plural **symposia** /sim-**poh**-zi-uh/ or **symposiums**) a conference to discuss a particular academic subject.

symptom noun **1** a change in the body or mind which is the sign of a disease. **2** a sign of an undesirable situation. ■ **symptomatic** adjective.

synagogue /**sin**-uh-gog/ noun a building where Jews meet for worship and teaching.

synapse /**sy**-naps, **si**-naps/ noun a connection between two nerve cells. ■ **synaptic** adjective.

sync or **synch** informal noun synchronization. □ **in** (or **out of**) **sync** working well (or badly) together.

synchromesh noun a system of gear changing in which the gearwheels are made to revolve at the same speed during engagement.

synchronize or **synchronise** verb (**synchronizes**, **synchronizing**, **synchronized**) make things happen or operate at the same time or rate.

synchronous /**sing**-kruh-nuhss/ ad-

jective existing or occurring at the same time. ■ **synchronously** adverb.

syncopate verb (**syncopates**, **syncopating**, **syncopated**) alter the beats or accents of music so that strong beats become weak and vice versa. ■ **syncopation** noun.

syndicate noun /sin-di-kuht/ a group of individuals or organizations who get together to promote a common interest. verb /sin-di-kayt/ (**syndicates**, **syndicating**, **syndicated**) **1** control or manage an operation through a syndicate. **2** publish or broadcast something in a number of different ways at the same time. ■ **syndication** noun.

syndrome noun a set of medical symptoms which tend to occur together.

synergy noun the working together of two or more things to produce a combined effect which is greater than the sum of their separate effects.

synod noun an official meeting of Church ministers and members.

synonym /sin-uh-nim/ noun a word or phrase that means the same as another word or phrase in the same language.

synonymous /si-non-i-muhss/ adjective **1** (of a word or phrase) having the same meaning as another word or phrase in the same language. **2** closely associated.

synopsis noun (plural **synopses**) a brief summary or survey.

syntax noun the way in which words and phrases are put together to form sentences. ■ **syntactic** adjective **syntactical** adjective.

synthesis noun (plural **syntheses**) **1** the combination of parts to form a connected whole. **2** the production of chemical compounds from simpler materials.

synthesize or **synthesise** verb (**synthesizes**, **synthesizing**, **synthesized**) **1** make something by chemical synthesis. **2** combine parts into a whole. **3** produce sound with a synthesizer.

synthesizer or **synthesiser** noun an electronic musical instrument that produces sounds by generating and combining signals of different frequencies.

synthetic adjective **1** made by chemical synthesis, especially to imitate a natural product. **2** not genuine. noun a synthetic textile fibre. ■ **synthetically** adverb.

syphilis noun a disease caused by bacteria that are passed on during sex. ■ **syphilitic** adjective.

syphon ⇨ **SIPHON**.

syringe noun a tube with a nozzle and a piston that is fitted with a hollow needle for injecting drugs or withdrawing blood. verb (**syringes**, **syringing**, **syringed**) clean something by spraying it with liquid using a syringe.

syrup (US spelling **sirup**) noun **1** a thick sweet liquid made by dissolving sugar in boiling water. **2** a thick sweet liquid containing medicine or diluted to make a drink.

syrupy (US spelling **sirupy**) adjective **1** like syrup. **2** too sentimental.

system noun **1** a set of things that are connected or that work together. **2** an organized scheme or method. **3** orderliness. **4** (**the system**) the laws and rules that govern society.

systematic adjective done according to a system. ■ **systematically** adverb.

systematize or **systematise** verb (**systematizes**, **systematizing**, **systematized**) arrange things according to an organized system.

systemic /si-steem-ik/ adjective relating to a system as a whole.

Tt

T or **t** noun (plural **Ts** or **T's**) the twentieth letter of the alphabet. □ **to a T** informal to perfection. **T-bone** a large piece of steak containing a T-shaped bone. **T-shirt** a short-sleeved casual top. **T-square** a T-shaped instrument for drawing or testing right angles.

TA abbreviation Territorial Army.

ta exclamation Brit. informal thank you.

tab[1] noun **1** a small flap or strip of material attached to something. **2** informal, chiefly N. Amer. a restaurant bill. □ **keep tabs on** informal keep a watch on.

tab[2] = TABULATOR.

tab[3] noun informal a tablet containing an illicit drug.

tabby noun (plural **tabbies**) a grey or brownish cat with dark stripes.

tabernacle noun **1** (in the Bible) a tent used by the Israelites to house the Ark of the Covenant during the Exodus. **2** a place of worship for some religions.

table noun **1** a piece of furniture with a flat top and legs, for eating, writing, or working at. **2** a set of facts or figures arranged in rows and columns. **3** (**tables**) multiplication sums arranged in sets. verb (**tables**, **tabling**, **tabled**) Brit. present something for discussion at a meeting. □ **table tennis** a game played with small round bats and a small hollow ball which is hit across a table over a net. **turn the tables** reverse a situation.

tableau /**tab**-loh/ noun (plural **tableaux** /**tab**-lohz/) a group of models or motionless figures representing a scene.

tablecloth noun a cloth spread over a table.

table d'hôte /tah-bluh **doht**/ noun a restaurant menu or meal offered at a fixed price and with limited choices.

tablespoon noun a large spoon for serving food.

tablet noun **1** a slab of stone or other hard material on which an inscription is written. **2** a pill in the shape of a disc or cylinder.

tabloid noun a newspaper that has small pages and is written in a popular style.

taboo noun (plural **taboos**) a social custom that prevents people from doing or talking about something. adjective banned or restricted by social custom.

tabular adjective (of facts or figures) arranged in columns or tables.

tabulate verb (**tabulates**, **tabulating**, **tabulated**) arrange facts or figures in columns or tables. ■ **tabulation** noun.

tabulator noun a facility in a word-processing program, or a device on a typewriter, used in creating columns or tables.

tachograph noun a tachometer used in commercial road vehicles to provide a record of engine speeds.

tachometer /ta-**kom**-i-ter/ noun an instrument which measures the working speed of an engine.

tachycardia /taki-**kah**-di-uh/ noun an abnormally rapid heart rate.

tacit /**ta**-sit/ adjective understood or meant without being stated. ■ **tacitly** adverb.

taciturn /**ta**-si-tern/ adjective saying little. ■ **taciturnity** noun.

tack[1] noun **1** a small broad-headed nail. **2** N. Amer. a drawing pin. **3** a long stitch used to fasten fabrics together temporarily. **4** a course of action. **5** Sailing an act of tacking. verb **1** fasten or fix with tacks. **2** (**tack on**) casually add. **3** change course by turning a boat's head into and through the wind. **4** make a series of such changes of course while sailing.

tack[2] noun equipment used in horse riding.

tack³ **noun** informal cheap, shoddy, or tasteless material.

tackle **noun** **1** the equipment needed for a task or sport. **2** a mechanism consisting of ropes, pulley blocks, and hooks for lifting heavy objects. **3** (in sport) an act of tackling an opponent. **verb** (**tackles**, **tackling**, **tackled**) **1** start to deal with. **2** confront someone about a difficult issue. **3** (in soccer, hockey, rugby, etc.) try to take the ball from or prevent the movement of an opponent. ■ **tackler** noun.

tacky¹ **adjective** (**tackier**, **tackiest**) (of glue, paint, etc.) not fully dry.

tacky² **adjective** (**tackier**, **tackiest**) informal showing poor taste and quality.

tact **noun** sensitivity and skill in dealing with others.

tactful **adjective** having or showing tact. ■ **tactfully** adverb.

tactic **noun** **1** the method you use to achieve something. **2** (**tactics**) the art of organizing and directing the movement of soldiers and equipment during a war. ■ **tactician** noun.

tactical **adjective** **1** planned in order to achieve a particular end. **2** (of weapons) for use in direct support of military or naval operations. **3** (of voting) done to prevent the strongest candidate from winning, rather than indicating your true political choice. ■ **tactically** adverb.

tactile **adjective** **1** having to do with the sense of touch. **2** fond of touching others in a friendly way.

tactless **adjective** thoughtless and insensitive. ■ **tactlessly** adverb.

tad **adverb** (**a tad**) informal to a small extent.

tadpole **noun** the larva of a frog or toad, which lives in water and has gills, a large head, and a tail.

taffeta **noun** a crisp shiny fabric.

tag **noun** **1** a label giving information about something. **2** an electronic device attached to someone to monitor their movements. **3** a nickname or commonly used description. **4** a frequently repeated phrase. **5** a metal or plastic point at the end of a shoelace.

6 a chasing game played by children. **verb** (**tags**, **tagging**, **tagged**) **1** attach a tag to. **2** (**tag on**) add to as an afterthought. **3** (**tag along**) accompany someone without being invited.

tagliatelle /tal-yuh-**tel**-li/ **plural noun** pasta in narrow ribbons.

tail **noun** **1** the part at the rear of an animal that sticks out and can be moved. **2** the rear part of an aircraft, with the tailplane and rudder. **3** the final, more distant, or weaker part. **4** (**tails**) the side of a coin without the image of a head on it. **5** (**tails**) informal a tailcoat. **verb** **1** informal secretly follow and observe. **2** (**tail off** or **away**) gradually become smaller or weaker. **3** (**tail back**) Brit. (of traffic) become congested.

tailback **noun** Brit. a long queue of stationary traffic.

tailcoat **noun** Brit. a man's formal jacket with a long skirt divided at the back into tails and cut away in front.

tailgate **noun** **1** a hinged flap at the back of a truck. **2** the door at the back of an estate or hatchback car.

tailor **noun** a person who makes men's clothing for individual customers. **verb** **1** make clothes to fit individual customers. **2** make or adapt for a particular purpose or person. □ **tailor-made** made for a particular purpose.

tailored **adjective** (of clothes) smart, fitted, and well cut.

tailplane **noun** Brit. a small wing at the tail of an aircraft.

tailspin **noun** a spin by an aircraft.

tailwind **noun** a wind blowing from behind.

taint **verb** **1** make impure. **2** affect with an undesirable quality. **noun** a trace of something undesirable.

take **verb** (**takes**, **taking**, **took**; past participle **taken**) **1** reach for and hold. **2** occupy a place or position. **3** gain possession of by force. **4** carry or bring with you. **5** remove from a place. **6** subtract. **7** consume. **8** bring into a specified state. **9** experience or be affected by. **10** use as a route or a means of transport. **11** accept or receive. **12** require or use up. **13** act on an opportunity. **14** see or deal with in a specified way. **15** tolerate or endure. **16** learn or sit for examinations in a subject. noun **1** a sequence of sound or vision photographed or recorded continuously. **2** a particular approach to something. **3** an amount gained or acquired. □ **take after** resemble a parent or ancestor. **take as read** Brit. assume. **take for granted 1** be too familiar with something to appreciate it properly. **2** assume that something is true. **take-home pay** a person's wages after the tax and insurance have been taken out. **take in 1** cheat or deceive. **2** make a garment tighter by altering its seams. **3** encompass, understand, or absorb. **take off 1** become airborne. **2** remove clothing. **3** mimic someone. **4** depart hastily. **take-off** an instance of taking off. **take on 1** employ someone. **2** undertake a task. **3** acquire a meaning or quality. **take over** assume control of or responsibility for. **take to 1** get into the habit of. **2** start liking. **3** go to a place to escape danger. **take up 1** adopt a pursuit. **2** occupy time, space, or attention. **3** pursue a matter further.

takeaway noun Brit. **1** a restaurant or shop selling cooked food to be eaten elsewhere. **2** a meal of such food.

takeout noun N. Amer. a takeaway.

takeover noun an act of taking control of something from someone else.

takings noun money received by a shop for goods sold.

talc noun **1** talcum powder. **2** a soft mineral.

talcum powder noun a powder used to make the skin feel smooth and dry.

tale noun **1** a story. **2** a lie.

talent noun **1** natural ability or skill. **2** people possessing natural ability or skill. **3** informal people seen in terms of their sexual attractiveness. **4** an ancient weight and unit of currency.

talented adjective having a natural ability or skill for something.

talisman noun (plural **talismans**) an object thought to have magic powers and to bring good luck.

talk verb **1** speak in order to give information or express ideas or feelings. **2** have the power of speech. **3** (**talk over** or **through**) discuss thoroughly. **4** (**talk back**) reply defiantly or disrespectfully. **5** (**talk down to**) speak to in a superior way. **6** (**talk round**) persuade someone to accept or agree to something. **7** (**talk into** or **out of**) persuade to or dissuade from. noun **1** conversation. **2** an address or lecture. **3** (**talks**) formal discussions. □ **talking-to** informal a telling-off.

talkative adjective fond of talking.

tall adjective **1** of great or more than average height. **2** measuring a specified distance from top to bottom. **3** unlikely to be true: *a tall story.* □ a **tall order** a difficult challenge. **tall ship** a sailing ship with high masts.

tallow noun a hard substance made from animal fat, used in making candles and soap.

tally noun (plural **tallies**) **1** a current score or amount. **2** a record of a score or amount. verb (**tallies, tallying, tallied**) **1** agree or correspond. **2** calculate the total number of.

tally-ho exclamation a huntsman's cry to the hounds on sighting a fox.

talon noun a curved claw.

tamarind noun a fruit with sticky brown pulp used in Asian cookery.

tamarisk noun a small tree with tiny leaves on slender branches.

tambourine noun a shallow drum with metal discs around the edge, which you play by shaking or hitting with the hand.

tame adjective **1** (of an animal) not dangerous or frightened of people. **2** not exciting, adventurous, or controversial. verb (**tames, taming, tamed**) **1** make an animal tame. **2** make less powerful and easier to control. ■ **tamely** adverb.

tamp verb firmly ram or pack a substance into something.

tamper verb (**tampers tampering**

tampered) (**tamper with**) interfere with something without permission.

tampon noun a plug of soft material inserted into the vagina to absorb menstrual blood.

tan noun **1** a yellowish-brown colour. **2** a golden-brown shade of skin developed by pale-skinned people after exposure to the sun. verb (**tans, tanning, tanned**) **1** make or become golden-brown from exposure to the sun. **2** convert animal skin into leather.

tandem noun a bicycle for two riders, one sitting behind the other. adverb one behind another. □ **in tandem 1** alongside each other. **2** one behind another.

tandoori /tan-**door**-i/ adjective (of Indian food) cooked in a clay oven called a **tandoor**.

tang noun **1** a strong flavour or smell. **2** the projection on the blade of a tool that holds it firmly in the handle. ■ **tangy** adjective.

tangent noun **1** a straight line that touches a curve but does not cross it at that point. **2** Mathematics (in a right-angled triangle) the ratio of the sides opposite and adjacent to a particular angle. **3** a completely different line of thought or action.

tangential /tan-**jen**-sh'l/ adjective **1** relating to or along a tangent. **2** only slightly relevant.

tangerine noun a small citrus fruit with a loose skin.

tangible adjective **1** able to be perceived by touch. **2** real. ■ **tangibility** noun **tangibly** adverb.

tangle verb (**tangles, tangling, tangled**) **1** twist together into a knotted mass. **2** (**tangle with**) informal conflict with. noun **1** a twisted, knotted mass. **2** a muddle.

tango noun (plural **tangos**) a South American ballroom dance with abrupt pauses. verb (**tangoes, tangoing, tangoed**) dance the tango.

tank noun **1** a large container for liquid or gas. **2** the container holding the fuel supply in a vehicle. **3** a clear container for keeping pet fish. **4** a heavy armoured fighting vehicle that moves on a continuous metal track. □ **tank engine** a steam locomotive with integral fuel and water holders. **tank top** a sleeveless top worn over a shirt or blouse.

tankard noun a large beer mug, sometimes with a hinged lid.

tanker noun a ship, road vehicle, or aircraft for carrying liquids in bulk.

tannin noun a bitter-tasting substance present in tea, grapes, etc.

tannoy noun Brit. trademark a type of public address system.

tantalize or **tantalise** verb (**tantalizes, tantalizing, tantalized**) tease someone by showing or promising them something that they cannot have.

tantamount adjective (**tantamount to**) equivalent in seriousness to.

tantrum noun an uncontrolled outburst of anger and frustration.

Taoiseach /tee-**shuhkh**/ noun the Prime Minister of the Irish Republic.

tap¹ noun a device for controlling the flow of liquid or gas from a pipe or container. verb (**taps, tapping, tapped**) **1** draw liquid from a cask, barrel, etc. **2** draw sap from a tree by cutting into it. **3** take some of a supply. **4** informal obtain money or information from. **5** connect a device to a telephone so as to listen to conversations secretly. □ **on tap 1** ready to be poured from a tap. **2** informal freely available whenever needed.

tap² verb (**taps, tapping, tapped**) **1** strike with a quick, light blow. **2** strike lightly and repeatedly against something. noun a quick, light blow. □ **tap dancing** a style of dancing performed in shoes with metal pieces on the toes and heels.

tapas /**tap**-uhss/ plural noun small Spanish savoury dishes served with drinks at a bar.

tape noun **1** light, flexible material in a narrow strip, used to hold, fasten, or mark off something. **2** tape with magnetic properties, used for recording sound, pictures, or computer data. **3** a cassette or reel containing magnetic tape. **verb (tapes, taping, taped) 1** record sound or pictures on magnetic tape. **2** fasten, attach, or mark off with tape. □ **tape measure** a strip of tape marked for measuring the length of things. **tape recorder** an apparatus for recording and then re-producing sounds on magnetic tape.

taper **verb (tapers, tapering, tapered) 1** reduce in thickness towards one end. **2 (taper off)** gradually lessen. **noun** a slender candle.

tapestry **noun** (plural **tapestries**) a piece of thick fabric with a design woven or embroidered on it.

tapeworm **noun** a long ribbon-like worm which lives as a parasite in the intestines of a person or animal.

tapioca **noun** hard white grains of cassava, used for making puddings.

tapir /**tay**-peer/ **noun** a pig-like animal with a short flexible snout.

tappet **noun** a moving part in a ma-chine which transmits motion be-tween a cam and another part.

tar **noun 1** a dark, thick liquid distilled from wood or coal. **2** a similar sub-stance formed by burning tobacco. **verb (tars, tarring, tarred)** cover with tar.

taramasalata **noun** a dip made from the roe of certain fish.

tarantula **noun 1** a very large hairy spider found in warm parts of Amer-ica. **2** a large black spider of southern Europe.

tardy **adjective (tardier, tardiest)** formal **1** late. **2** slow to act or respond. ■ **tar-dily** adverb **tardiness** noun.

tare **noun** the weight of a vehicle with-out its fuel or load.

target **noun 1** a person, object, or place that is the aim of an attack. **2** a board marked with a series of circles that you aim at in archery or shoot-ing. **3** something that you aim to achieve. **verb (targets, targeting, tar-geted) 1** select as an object of atten-tion or attack. **2** aim or direct.

tariff **noun 1** a tax to be paid on a par-

ticular class of imports or exports. **2** a list of the charges made by a hotel, restaurant, etc.

tarmac **noun 1** (trademark in the UK) a mix-ture of broken stone and tar used for surfacing roads. **2 (the tarmac)** a runway or other area surfaced with tarmac. **verb (tarmacs, tarmacking, tarmacked)** surface with tarmac.

tarn **noun** a small mountain lake.

tarnish **verb 1** make metal lose its shine by exposure to air or damp. **2** make something less respected. **noun** a film or stain formed on the ex-posed surface of metal.

tarot /**ta**-roh/ **noun** a set of cards used for fortune telling.

tarpaulin **noun** a sheet of heavy waterproof cloth.

tarragon **noun** a herb with narrow sweet-smelling leaves.

tarry **verb (tarries, tarrying, tarried)** old use stay longer than intended.

tarsus **noun** (plural **tarsi** /**tar**-sy/) the group of small bones in the ankle and upper foot.

tart¹ **noun** an open pastry case con-taining a sweet or savoury filling. ■ **tartlet** noun.

tart² informal **noun** disapproving a woman who has many sexual partners. **verb** Brit. **1 (tart yourself up)** make yourself look attractive with clothes or make-up. **2 (tart up)** improve the appear-ance of. ■ **tarty** adjective.

tart³ **adjective 1** sharp or acid in taste. **2** (of a remark or tone of voice) sharp or hurtful. ■ **tartly** adverb

tartan **noun 1** a pattern of coloured checks and intersecting lines. **2** cloth with a tartan pattern.

tartar¹ **noun** a person who is fierce or difficult to deal with.

tartar² **noun 1** a hard deposit that forms on the teeth. **2** a deposit formed during the fermentation of wine.

tartare sauce **noun** a sauce consist-ing of mayonnaise mixed with chopped onions, gherkins, and ca-pers.

task noun a piece of work to be done. □ **task force 1** an armed force organized for a special operation. **2** a unit specially organized for a task. **take to task** criticize or tell off.

taskmaster noun a person who imposes a demanding workload on someone.

tassel noun a tuft of threads that are knotted together at one end.

taste noun **1** the way in which a particular substance is perceived when it comes into contact with the mouth. **2** the sense by which taste is perceived. **3** a small sample of food or drink. **4** a brief experience of something. **5** a liking for something. **6** the ability to pick out things that are of good quality or appropriate. verb (**tastes, tasting, tasted**) **1** perceive the flavour of. **2** have a specified flavour. **3** sample the flavour of. **4** have a brief experience of. □ **taste bud** any of the clusters of nerve endings on the tongue and in the mouth which provide the sense of taste. ■ **taster** noun.

tasteful adjective showing good judgement of quality, appearance, or appropriate behaviour. ■ **tastefully** adverb.

tasteless adjective **1** lacking flavour. **2** not showing good judgement of quality, appearance, or appropriate behaviour. ■ **tastelessly** adverb.

tasty adjective (**tastier, tastiest**) **1** (of food) having a pleasant flavour. **2** Brit. informal attractive; appealing.

tat noun Brit. informal tasteless or badly made articles.

tattered adjective old and torn.

tatters plural noun torn pieces of cloth, paper, etc. □ **in tatters 1** torn in many places. **2** destroyed; ruined.

tattle noun gossip. verb (**tattles, tattling, tattled**) engage in gossip.

tattoo[1] noun (plural **tattoos**) **1** a military display with music and marching. **2** a rhythmic tapping or drumming.

tattoo[2] noun (plural **tattoos**) a permanent design made on the skin with a needle and ink. verb (**tattoos, tattooing, tattooed**) give someone a tattoo.

■ **tattooist** noun.

tatty adjective (**tattier, tattiest**) informal worn and shabby.

taught past and past participle of **TEACH**.

taunt noun a remark made in order to anger or upset someone. verb anger or upset with taunts.

Taurus noun a sign of the zodiac (the Bull), 21 April–20 May.

taut adjective **1** stretched or pulled tight. **2** (of muscles or nerves) tense. ■ **tauten** verb **tautly** adverb.

tautology noun (plural **tautologies**) the saying of the same thing over again in different words. ■ **tautological** adjective **tautologous** adjective.

tavern noun old use an inn or pub.

tawdry adjective **1** showy but cheap and of poor quality. **2** sleazy or unpleasant. ■ **tawdriness** noun.

tawny adjective of an orange-brown or yellowish-brown colour.

tax noun money that must be paid to the state, charged as a proportion of income and profits or added to the cost of some goods and services. verb **1** impose a tax on. **2** pay tax on a vehicle. **3** make heavy demands on. **4** accuse someone of doing something wrong. □ **tax-deductible** allowed to be deducted from income before the amount of tax to be paid is calculated. **tax exile** a wealthy person who chooses to live somewhere with low rates of taxation. **tax haven** a country or independent area where low rates of taxes are charged. **tax return** a form on which a person states their income, used to assess how much tax they should pay. ■ **taxable** adjective.

taxation noun **1** the imposing of tax. **2** money paid as tax.

taxi noun (plural **taxis**) a motor vehicle which transports fare-paying passengers to the place of their choice. verb (**taxies, taxiing** or **taxying, taxied**) (of an aircraft) move slowly along the ground before take-off or after landing. □ **taxi rank** Brit. a place where taxis wait to be hired.

taxicab noun a taxi.

taxidermy noun the art of preparing and stuffing the skins of dead animals so that they look like living ones. ∎ **taxidermist** noun.

taxing adjective physically or mentally demanding.

taxonomy noun **1** the branch of science concerned with classification. **2** a system of classifying things. ∎ **taxonomic** adjective.

TB abbreviation tuberculosis.

tbsp or **tbs** abbreviation tablespoonful.

tea noun **1** the dried leaves of an evergreen Asian shrub or small tree. **2** a hot drink made by soaking tea in boiling water. **3** Brit. a light afternoon meal consisting of sandwiches, cakes, etc., with tea to drink. **4** Brit. a cooked evening meal. □ **tea bag** a sachet of tea leaves on to which boiling water is poured to make tea. **tea room** a cafe serving tea, cakes, etc. **tea towel** (or **tea cloth**) Brit. a cloth for drying washed crockery, cutlery, etc.

teacake noun Brit. a kind of bun containing currants.

teach verb (**teaches**, **teaching**, **taught**) **1** give lessons in a particular subject to a class or pupil. **2** show someone how to do something. **3** make someone realize or understand something. ∎ **teacher** noun.

teacup noun a cup from which you drink tea.

teak noun hard wood obtained from a tree native to India and SE Asia.

teal noun (plural **teal** or **teals**) a small freshwater duck.

team noun **1** a group of players forming one side in a game or sport. **2** two or more people working together. **3** two or more horses harnessed together to pull something. verb **1** (**team up**) work together to achieve a shared goal. **2** (**team with**) match with. □ **team spirit** trust and cooperation among the members of a team.

teammate noun a fellow member of a team.

teamwork noun organized effort as a group.

teapot noun a pot with a handle, spout, and lid, in which tea is made.

tear¹ verb (**tears**, **tearing**, **tore**; past participle **torn**) **1** rip a hole or split in. **2** (usu. **tear up**) pull apart or to pieces. **3** damage a muscle or ligament by overstretching it. **4** (usu. **tear down**) demolish or destroy. **5** (be **torn**) be unsure of which of two options to choose. **6** informal move very quickly. **7** (**tear into**) attack verbally. noun a hole or split caused by tearing.

tear² noun a drop of clear salty liquid produced in a person's eye when they are crying or when the eye is irritated. □ **tear gas** gas that causes severe irritation to the eyes, used in warfare and riot control. **tear-jerker** informal a very sad book, film, etc.

tearaway noun Brit. a person who behaves in a wild or reckless way.

teardrop noun a single tear.

tearful adjective **1** crying or about to cry. **2** causing tears. ∎ **tearfully** adverb.

tease verb (**teases**, **teasing**, **teased**) **1** playfully make fun of or attempt to provoke. **2** tempt sexually. **3** (**tease out**) find out by searching through a mass of information. **4** gently pull tangled wool, hair, etc. into separate strands. noun a person who teases. ∎ **teaser** noun.

teasel or **teazle** noun a tall prickly plant with spiny flower heads.

teaspoon noun a small spoon for adding sugar to hot drinks.

teat noun **1** a nipple on an animal's udder or similar organ. **2** Brit. a plastic nipple-shaped device for sucking milk from a bottle.

technical adjective **1** having to do with the techniques of a particular subject, art, or craft. **2** requiring specialized knowledge. **3** having to do with the use of machinery and methods in science and industry. **4** according to the law or rules when applied strictly. □ **technical college** a college specializing in applied sciences and other practical subjects. ∎ **technically** adverb.

technicality noun (plural **technicalities**) **1** a small formal detail in a set of rules. **2** (**technicalities**) small details of a particular field or activity. **3** the use of technical terms or methods.

technician noun **1** a person who looks after equipment or does practical work in a laboratory. **2** an expert in a particular science or craft.

Technicolor noun trademark a process of producing cinema films in colour.

technique noun **1** a particular way of carrying out a task. **2** a person's level of skill in doing something.

techno noun a style of fast, loud electronic dance music.

technology noun (plural **technologies**) **1** the application of scientific knowledge for practical purposes. **2** the branch of knowledge concerned with applied sciences. ■ **technological** adjective **technologically** adverb **technologist** noun.

tectonic adjective Geology having to do with the earth's crust.

teddy or **teddy bear** noun (plural **teddies**) a soft toy bear.

Teddy boy noun (in Britain during the 1950s) a young man of a group who had their hair slicked up in a quiff and liked rock-and-roll music.

tedious adjective too long, slow, or dull. ■ **tediously** adverb.

tedium noun the state of being tedious.

tee noun **1** a place on a golf course from which the ball is struck at the beginning of each hole. **2** a small peg placed in the ground to support a golf ball before it is struck from a tee. **3** a mark aimed at in bowls, quoits, etc. verb (**tees, teeing, teed**) Golf **1** (**tee up**) place the ball on a tee ready to begin a round or hole. **2** (**tee off**) begin a round or hole.

teem verb **1** (**teem with**) be swarming with. **2** (of rain) fall heavily.

teen informal adjective relating to teenagers. noun a teenager.

teenage adjective having to do with teenagers. ■ **teenaged** adjective.

teenager noun a person aged between 13 and 19 years.

teens plural noun the years of a person's age from 13 to 19.

teeny or **teensy** adjective (**teenier, teeniest**) informal tiny.

teepee ⇒ **TEPEE**.

tee shirt noun a T-shirt.

teeter verb (**teeters, teetering, teetered**) move or sway unsteadily.

teeth plural of **TOOTH**.

teethe verb (**teethes, teething, teethed**) (of a baby) develop first teeth. □ **teething troubles** problems that occur in the early stages of a new project.

teetotal adjective choosing not to drink alcohol. ■ **teetotaller** noun.

telecommunications noun the technology concerned with long-distance communication by means of cable, telephone, broadcasting, satellite, etc.

telegram noun a message sent by telegraph and delivered in written or printed form.

telegraph noun a system or device for transmitting messages from a distance along a wire. verb send a message to someone by telegraph. □ **telegraph pole** a tall pole used to carry telegraph or telephone wires. ■ **telegraphic** adjective.

telekinesis /te-li-ky-nee-siss/ noun the movement of objects supposedly as a result of mental power. ■ **telekinetic** adjective.

telepathy noun the supposed communication of thoughts or ideas by means other than the known senses. ■ **telepathic** adjective.

telephone noun **1** a system for transmitting voices over a distance using wire or radio. **2** an instrument used in a telephone system for speaking into. verb (**telephones, telephoning, telephoned**) contact someone by telephone. □ **telephone directory** a book listing the names, addresses, and telephone numbers of the people in a particular area.

telephonist noun Brit. an operator of a telephone switchboard.

telephony /ti-**lef**-fuh-ni/ noun the working or use of telephones.

telephoto lens noun a lens that produces a magnified image of a distant object.

teleprinter noun Brit. a device for transmitting telegraph messages as they are keyed.

telesales plural noun the selling of goods or services over the telephone.

telescope noun an instrument designed to make distant objects appear nearer. verb (telescopes, telescoping, telescoped) **1** (of an object made up of several tubes) slide into itself so as to become smaller. **2** condense or combine to occupy less space or time. ■ **telescopic** adjective.

teletext noun an information service transmitted to televisions.

telethon noun a long television programme broadcast to raise money for a charity.

televise verb (televises, televising, televised) show on television.

television noun **1** a system for transmitting visual images with sound and displaying them electronically on a screen. **2** (also **television set**) a device with a screen for receiving television signals. **3** the activity or medium of broadcasting on television. ■ **televisual** adjective.

telex noun **1** an international system in which printed messages are transmitted and received by teleprinters. **2** a device used for telex. **3** a message sent by telex. verb send a message to someone by telex.

tell verb (tells, telling, told) **1** communicate information to. **2** instruct someone to do something. **3** relate a story. **4** (**tell on**) informal inform on. **5** (**tell off**) reprimand. **6** determine or perceive. **7** have a noticeable effect on someone. □ **telling-off** (plural **tellings-off**) informal a reprimand.

teller noun **1** a person who deals with customers' transactions in a bank. **2** a person who counts votes. **3** a person who tells something.

telling adjective having a striking or revealing effect. ■ **tellingly** adverb.

telltale adjective revealing or betraying something. noun informal a person who reports things that other people have done wrong.

telly noun informal television.

temerity noun excessive confidence or boldness.

temp informal noun a person who is employed on a temporary basis. verb work as a temp.

temper noun **1** a person's state of mind. **2** a tendency to become angry easily. **3** an angry state of mind. **4** the degree of hardness of a metal. verb (tempers, tempering, tempered) **1** harden metal by heating it and then cooling it. **2** neutralize or counterbalance.

tempera noun a method of painting with powdered colours mixed with egg yolk.

temperament noun a person's nature in terms of the way it affects their behaviour.

temperamental adjective **1** relating to or caused by temperament. **2** tending to change mood in an unreasonable way. ■ **temperamentally** adverb.

temperance noun complete avoidance of alcohol.

temperate adjective **1** (of a region or

climate) having mild temperatures. **2** showing self-control.

temperature noun **1** the degree of heat in a place, substance, or object. **2** informal a body temperature above the normal.

tempest noun a violent windy storm.

tempestuous adjective **1** very stormy. **2** characterized by strong and changeable emotion.

template noun **1** a shaped piece of rigid material used as a pattern for cutting out, shaping, or drilling. **2** a model for others to copy.

temple[1] noun a building for the worship of a god or gods.

temple[2] noun the flat part either side of the head between the forehead and the ear.

tempo noun (plural **tempos** or **tempi** /**tem**-pi/) **1** the speed at which a passage of music is played. **2** the pace of an activity or process.

temporal adjective **1** relating to time. **2** having to do with the material or physical world. ■ **temporally** adverb.

temporary adjective lasting for only a limited period. ■ **temporarily** adverb.

temporize or **temporise** verb (**temporizes, temporizing, temporized**) delay making a decision.

tempt verb **1** try to persuade someone to do something appealing but wrong. **2** (**be tempted to do**) have an urge or inclination to do. **3** attract; charm. □ **tempt fate** (or **providence**) do something risky or dangerous. ■ **tempting** adjective **temptingly** adverb.

temptation noun **1** the action of tempting. **2** a tempting thing.

temptress noun a sexually alluring woman.

ten cardinal number one more than nine; 10. (Roman numeral: **x** or **X**.) □ **Ten Commandments** (in the Bible) the ten rules of conduct given by God to Moses. ■ **tenfold** adjective & adverb.

tenable adjective **1** able to be defended against attack or objection. **2** (of a post, grant, etc.) able to be held or used for a specified period.

tenacious adjective **1** firmly holding on to something. **2** continuing to exist or do something for longer than might be expected. ■ **tenaciously** adverb **tenacity** noun.

tenancy noun (plural **tenancies**) possession of land or property as a tenant.

tenant noun a person who rents land or property from a landlord. verb occupy property as a tenant.

tench noun (plural **tench**) a freshwater fish of the carp family.

tend[1] verb **1** frequently behave in a particular way or have certain characteristics. **2** go or move in a particular direction.

tend[2] verb care for or look after.

tendency noun (plural **tendencies**) an inclination to act in a particular way.

tendentious adjective formal expressing a strong opinion; opinionated.

tender[1] adjective (**tenderer, tenderest**) **1** gentle and sympathetic. **2** (of food) easy to cut or chew. **3** (of a part of the body) sensitive. **4** young and vulnerable. **5** requiring careful handling. ■ **tenderly** adverb **tenderness** noun.

tender[2] verb (**tenders, tendering, tendered**) **1** offer or present formally. **2** make a formal written offer to do work, supply goods, etc. for a stated fixed price. **3** offer money as payment. noun a tendered offer.

tender[3] noun **1** a vehicle used by a fire service or the armed forces for carrying supplies. **2** a wagon attached to a steam locomotive to carry fuel and water. **3** a boat used to ferry people and supplies to and from a ship.

tendon noun a strong band or cord of tissue attaching a muscle to a bone.

tendril noun **1** a thin curling stem of a climbing plant, which twines round a support. **2** a slender ringlet of hair.

tenebrous adjective literary dark; shadowy.

tenement noun a building divided into flats.

tenet noun a central principle or belief.

tenner noun Brit. informal a ten-pound note.

tennis noun a game in which players use rackets to strike a ball over a net stretched across a grass or clay court.
□ **tennis elbow** inflammation of the tendons of the elbow caused by overuse of the forearm muscles.

tenon noun a projecting piece of wood that fits into a slot in another piece of wood.

tenor[1] noun the male singing voice below alto or countertenor.

tenor[2] noun the general meaning or character of something.

tenpin bowling noun a game in which ten skittles are bowled down with hard balls.

tense[1] adjective **1** stretched tight or rigid. **2** feeling, causing, or showing anxiety and nervousness. verb (tenses, tensing, tensed) make or become tense. ■ tensely adverb.

tense[2] noun Grammar a set of forms of a verb that indicate the time or completeness of the action referred to.

tensile adjective **1** relating to tension. **2** capable of being drawn out or stretched.

tension noun **1** the state of being stretched tight. **2** mental or emotional strain. **3** a situation that is strained because of differing views or aims. **4** voltage of specified magnitude: high tension.

tent noun a portable shelter made of cloth and supported by poles and cords. ■ tented adjective.

tentacle noun a long, slender, flexible part extending from the body of an animal, used for grasping or moving about, or bearing sense organs.

tentative adjective **1** done without confidence. **2** not certain or fixed. ■ tentatively adverb.

tenterhook noun (on tenterhooks) in a state of nervous suspense.

tenth ordinal number **1** that is number ten in a sequence; 10th. **2** (a tenth or one tenth) each of ten equal parts into which something is divided.

tenuous adjective **1** very slight or weak. **2** very slender or fine. ■ tenuously adverb.

tenure noun **1** the conditions under which land or buildings are held or occupied. **2** the holding of an office.

tenured adjective having a permanent post.

tepee or **teepee** noun a cone-shaped tent used by American Indians.

tepid adjective **1** lukewarm. **2** unenthusiastic.

tequila /te-kee-luh/ noun a clear Mexican alcoholic spirit.

tercentenary noun (plural **tercentenaries**) a three-hundredth anniversary.

term noun **1** a word or phrase used to describe a thing or to express an idea. **2** (terms) requirements or conditions. **3** (terms) relations: we're on good terms. **4** a period for which something lasts. **5** each of the periods in the year during which teaching is given in a school or college. **6** (also **full term**) the completion of a normal length of pregnancy. **7** Mathematics each of the quantities in a ratio, equation, etc. verb call by a specified term. □ **come to terms with** become able to accept or deal with. ■ termly adjective & adverb.

termagant noun a bossy woman.

terminal adjective **1** having to do with or situated at the end. **2** (of a disease) predicted to lead to death. noun **1** the station at the end of a railway or bus route. **2** a departure and arrival building for passengers at an airport. **3** a point at which connection can be made in an electric circuit. **4** a keyboard and screen joined to a central computer system. ■ terminally adverb.

terminate verb (terminates, terminating, terminated) **1** bring or come to an end. **2** (of a train or bus service) end its journey.

termination noun **1** the ending of

something. **2** a medical procedure to end a pregnancy at an early stage.

terminology noun (plural **terminologies**) a set of terms relating to a subject. ■ **terminological** adjective.

terminus noun (plural **termini** or **terminuses**) **1** Brit. a railway or bus terminal. **2** a final point or end.

termite noun a small insect which eats wood and lives in colonies in large nests of earth.

tern noun a white seabird with long pointed wings and a forked tail.

ternary adjective composed of three parts.

terpsichorean /terp-si-kuh-**ree**-uhn/ adjective relating to dancing.

terrace noun **1** each of a series of flat areas on a slope, used for growing plants and crops. **2** a patio. **3** Brit. a row of houses built in one block. **4** Brit. a flight of wide, shallow steps for standing spectators in a stadium. verb (**terraces**, **terracing**, **terraced**) make or form into terraces. ■ **terraced** adjective **terracing** noun.

terracotta noun unglazed, brownish-red earthenware.

terra firma noun dry land; the ground.

terrain noun a stretch of land seen in terms of its physical features.

terrapin noun a small freshwater turtle.

terrestrial adjective **1** having to do with the earth or dry land. **2** (of an animal or plant) living on or in the ground. **3** (of television broadcasting) not using a satellite.

terrible adjective **1** extremely bad, serious, or unpleasant. **2** troubled or guilty. **3** causing terror.

terribly adverb **1** extremely. **2** very badly.

terrier noun a small, lively breed of dog.

terrific adjective **1** of great size, amount, or strength. **2** informal excellent. ■ **terrifically** adverb.

terrify verb (**terrifies**, **terrifying**, **terrified**) make someone feel terror.

terrine /tuh-**reen**/ noun a mixture of chopped savoury food that is pressed into a container and served cold.

territorial adjective **1** relating to a territory or area. **2** (of an animal) having a territory which it defends. □ **Territorial Army** (in the UK) a military reserve force of volunteers. ■ **territorially** adverb.

territory noun (plural **territories**) **1** an area controlled by a ruler or state. **2** a division of a country. **3** an area defended by an animal against others. **4** an area in which a person has special rights, responsibilities, or knowledge.

terror noun **1** extreme fear. **2** a cause of terror. **3** the use of terror to intimidate people. **4** informal a person causing trouble or annoyance.

terrorist noun a person who uses violence and intimidation in an attempt to achieve political aims. ■ **terrorism** noun.

terrorize or **terrorise** verb (**terrorizes**, **terrorizing**, **terrorized**) threaten and frighten over a period of time.

terry noun a towelling fabric.

terse adjective (**terser**, **tersest**) using few words. ■ **tersely** adverb.

tertiary /**ter**-shuh-ri/ adjective **1** third in order or level. **2** Brit. relating to university education.

tessellated adjective decorated with mosaics. ■ **tessellation** noun.

test noun **1** a procedure intended to establish how reliable or good something is, or whether something is present. **2** a short examination of skill or knowledge. **3** a means of testing something. **4** a difficult situation. **5** a medical examination of part of the body. **6** (also **test match**) an international cricket or rugby match. verb **1** subject to a test. **2** touch or taste something before proceeding further. **3** severely try someone's endurance or patience. □ **test case** Law a case that sets an example for future cases.

test tube a thin glass tube used to hold material in laboratory tests.

test-tube baby informal a baby con-

ceived by in vitro fertilization.
■ **tester** noun.

testament noun **1** a person's will.
2 evidence or proof. **3** (**Testament**)
each of the two divisions of the Bible.
■ **testamentary** adjective.

testate adjective having made a valid
will before dying.

testicle noun either of the two oval
organs that produce sperm in male
mammals, enclosed in the scrotum.
■ **testicular** adjective.

testify verb (**testifies, testifying,
testified**) **1** give evidence as a witness
in a law court. **2** (**testify to**) be evidence or proof of.

testimonial noun **1** a formal statement of a person's good character and
qualifications. **2** a public tribute to
someone.

testimony noun (plural **testimonies**)
1 a formal statement, especially one
given in a court of law. **2** (**testimony
to**) evidence or proof of.

testosterone noun a hormone that
stimulates the development of male
physical characteristics.

testy adjective easily irritated. ■ **testily** adverb.

tetanus noun a disease that causes
the muscles to stiffen and go into
spasms.

tetchy adjective bad-tempered and irritable. ■ **tetchily** adverb.

tête-à-tête /tet-ah-**tet**/ noun a private conversation between two
people. adjective & adverb happening
privately between two people.

tether noun a rope or chain used to tie
an animal to a post. verb (**tethers,
tethering, tethered**) tie with a
tether.

tetrahedron /tet-ruh-**hee**-druhn/
noun (plural **tetrahedra** or **tetrahedrons**) a solid figure with four triangular faces.

Teutonic /tyoo-**ton**-ik/ adjective often
disapproving German.

text noun **1** a written or printed work
in terms of its content rather than its
form. **2** the main body of a work as

distinct from illustrations, notes, etc.
3 written or printed words or computer data. verb send someone a text
message. □ **text message** an electronic communication sent and received via mobile phone. ■ **textual**
adjective.

textbook noun a book used for the
study of a subject. adjective done in
exactly the recommended way.

textile noun any type of woven, knitted, or felted fabric.

texture noun the feel, appearance, or
consistency of a surface, substance,
or fabric. verb (**textures, texturing,
textured**) give a rough or raised texture to. ■ **textural** adjective.

Thai /tʏ/ noun (plural same or **Thais**) **1** a
person from Thailand. **2** the official
language of Thailand.

thalidomide /thuh-**lid**-uh-myd/ noun
a sedative drug which was found to
cause malformation of the fetus when
taken by pregnant women.

than conjunction & preposition **1** used to
introduce the second part of a comparison. **2** used to introduce an exception or contrast. **3** used in
expressions indicating one thing happening immediately after another.

thane noun an Anglo-Saxon or medieval Scottish landowner or nobleman.

thank verb **1** express gratitude to.
2 ironic blame or hold responsible.
□ **thank you** a polite expression of
gratitude.

thankful adjective **1** pleased and relieved. **2** expressing gratitude.
■ **thankfulness** noun.

thankfully adverb **1** in a thankful
way. **2** fortunately.

thankless adjective **1** (of a job or
task) unpleasant and unlikely to be
appreciated by others. **2** not showing
or feeling gratitude.

thanks plural noun **1** an expression of
gratitude. **2** = *thank you.* □ **thanks to**
due to.

thanksgiving noun **1** the expression
of gratitude to God. **2** (**Thanksgiving**)
(in North America) a national holi-

day held in November in the US and October in Canada.

that pronoun & determiner 1 (plural those) used to refer to a person or thing seen or heard or already mentioned or known. 2 (plural those) referring to the more distant of two things. pronoun used instead of which, who, when, etc. to introduce a clause that defines or identifies something. adverb 1 to such a degree; so. 2 informal very. conjunction introducing a statement or suggestion.

> ℹ️ **that** or **which**? The general rule is that, when introducing clauses that define or identify something, you can use either **that** or **which**: *a book which aims to simplify scientific language* or *a book that aims to simplify scientific language*. You should use **which**, but never **that**, to introduce a clause giving additional information: *the book, which costs £15, has sold over a million copies* not *the book, that costs £15, has sold over a million copies.*

thatch noun a roof covering of straw, reeds, etc. verb cover with thatch. ■ thatcher noun.

thaw verb 1 make or become liquid or soft after being frozen. 2 make or become friendlier. noun 1 a period of warmer weather that thaws ice and snow. 2 an increase in friendliness.

the determiner 1 used to refer to one or more people or things already mentioned or easily understood; the definite article. 2 used to refer to someone or something that is the only one of its kind. 3 used to refer to something in a general rather than specific way.

theatre (US spelling theater) noun 1 a building in which plays are performed. 2 the writing and production of plays. 3 the dramatic quality of a play or event. 4 a room where specific things are done: *an operating theatre.* 5 the area in which something happens: *a theatre of war.*

theatrical adjective 1 having to do with acting or the theatre. 2 exaggerated and excessively dramatic. noun

(theatricals) theatrical performances or behaviour. ■ theatricality noun theatrically adverb.

theatrics noun theatricals.

thee archaic or dialect form of **you**, as the singular object of a verb or preposition.

theft noun the action or crime of stealing.

their possessive determiner 1 belonging to or associated with the people or things previously mentioned or easily identified. 2 belonging to or associated with a person whose sex is not specified.

> ✓ **their** is an exception to the usual rule of *i* before *e* except after *c*.

theirs possessive pronoun used to refer to something belonging to or associated with two or more people or things previously mentioned.

> ✓ no apostrophe: theirs.

them pronoun 1 used as the object of a verb or preposition to refer to two or more people or things previously mentioned or easily identified. 2 referring to a person whose sex is not specified.

thematic adjective arranged according to subject, or connected with a subject. ■ thematically adverb.

theme noun 1 a subject which a person speaks, writes, or thinks about. 2 a prominent or recurring melody in a musical composition. 3 an idea that is often repeated in a work of art or literature. 4 (also theme tune or music) a piece of music played at the beginning and end of a film or programme. ◻ theme park a large amusement park based around a particular idea. ■ themed adjective.

themself pronoun used instead of 'himself' or 'herself' to refer to a person whose sex is not specified.

themselves pronoun 1 used as the object of a verb or preposition to refer to a group of people or things previously mentioned as the subject of the clause. 2 they or them personally.

3 used instead of 'himself' or 'herself' to refer to a person of unspecified sex.

then adverb **1** at that time. **2** after that. **3** also. **4** therefore.

thence or **from thence** adverb formal **1** from a place or source previously mentioned. **2** as a consequence.

thenceforth or **thenceforward** adverb formal from that time, place, or point onward.

theocracy noun (plural **theocracies**) a system of government by priests. ■ **theocratic** adjective.

theodolite /thi-**od**-uh-lyt/ noun an instrument used in surveying for measuring horizontal and vertical angles.

theologian /thi-uh-**loh**-juhn/ noun a person who is an expert in or is studying theology.

theology noun (plural **theologies**) **1** the study of God and religious belief. **2** a system of religious beliefs and theory. ■ **theological** adjective **theologist** noun.

theorem noun a scientific or mathematical rule or proposition that can be proved by reasoning.

theoretical adjective **1** concerned with the theory of a subject rather than its practical application. **2** based on theory rather than experience or practice. ■ **theoretically** adverb.

theoretician noun a person who develops or studies the theoretical framework of a subject.

theorist noun a theoretician.

theorize or **theorise** verb (**theorizes**, **theorizing**, **theorized**) form a theory or theories about something.

theory noun (plural **theories**) **1** an idea or system of ideas intended to explain something. **2** a set of principles on which an activity is based.

therapeutic /the-ruh-**pyoo**-tik/ adjective **1** relating to the healing of disease. **2** having a good effect on the body or mind. ■ **therapeutically** adverb.

therapy noun (plural **therapies**) **1** treatment of a physical problem or illness.

2 treatment of mental or emotional problems using psychological methods. ■ **therapist** noun.

there adverb **1** in, at, or to that place or position. **2** on that issue. ☐ **there is** (or **there are**) used to indicate that something exists or is true.

 don't confuse **there** with **their**.

thereabouts adverb near that place, time, or amount.

thereafter adverb after that time.

thereby adverb by that means; as a result of that.

therefore adverb for that reason.

therein adverb old use or formal in that place, document, or respect.

thereof adverb formal of the thing just mentioned.

there's short form **1** there is. **2** there has.

thereupon adverb formal immediately or shortly after that.

therewith adverb old use or formal **1** with or in the thing mentioned. **2** soon or immediately after that.

thermal adjective **1** relating to heat. **2** (of a garment) designed to keep the body warm by stopping heat from escaping. noun **1** an upward current of warm air. **2** (**thermals**) thermal underwear. ■ **thermally** adverb.

thermionic adjective relating to the emission of electrons from substances heated to very high temperatures.

thermodynamics noun the study of the relationship between heat and other forms of energy. ■ **thermodynamic** adjective.

thermometer noun an instrument for measuring temperature, usually containing mercury or alcohol which expands when heated.

thermonuclear adjective relating to or using nuclear fusion reactions that occur at very high temperatures.

Thermos noun trademark a vacuum flask.

thermostat noun a device that automatically controls temperature or activates a device at a set temperature. ■ **thermostatic** adjective **thermostatically** adverb.

thesaurus /thi-saw-ruhss/ noun a book containing lists of words which have the same or a similar meaning.

these plural of **THIS**.

thesis noun (plural **theses**) **1** a statement or theory that is put forward to be supported or proved. **2** a long piece of work involving research, written as part of a university degree.

thespian adjective relating to drama and the theatre. noun an actor or actress.

theta /thee-tuh/ noun the eighth letter of the Greek alphabet (Θ, θ).

they pronoun **1** used to refer to two or more people or things previously mentioned or easily identified. **2** people in general. **3** used to refer to a person whose sex is not specified (in place of either 'he' or 'he or she').

i many people now think that the traditional use of **he** to refer to a person of either sex (as in *every child needs to know that he is loved*) is old-fashioned and sexist; **he or she** is clumsy, and **they** is now often used instead, as in *anyone can join if they are a resident* and *each to their own*.

they'd short form **1** they had. **2** they would.

they'll short form **1** they shall. **2** they will.

they're short form they are.

✓ don't confuse **they're**, meaning 'they are', with **their** (as in *they left their books behind*).

they've short form they have.

thiamine or **thiamin** noun vitamin B₁, found in unrefined cereals, beans, and liver.

thick adjective **1** with opposite sides or surfaces relatively far apart. **2** (of a garment or fabric) made of heavy material. **3** made up of a large number of things or people close together. **4** (**thick with**) densely filled or

covered with. **5** difficult to see through or breathe. **6** (of something liquid or semi-liquid) relatively firm in consistency. **7** informal stupid. **8** (of a voice) hoarse or husky. **9** (of an accent) strong and difficult to understand. **10** informal having a very close, friendly relationship. noun (**the thick**) the middle or the busiest part. □ **through thick and thin** under all circumstances. ■ **thickly** adverb.

thicken verb make or become thick or thicker.

thicket noun a dense group of bushes or trees.

thickness noun **1** the distance through an object, as distinct from width or height. **2** the state or quality of being thick. **3** a layer of material.

thickset adjective heavily built.

thief noun (plural **thieves**) a person who steals another person's property.

✓ *i* before *e* except after *c*: th**ie**f.

thieve verb (**thieves**, **thieving**, **thieved**) steal things. ■ **thievery** noun.

thigh noun the part of the leg between the hip and the knee.

thimble noun a small covering that you wear to protect the end of the finger and push the needle in sewing.

thin adjective (**thinner**, **thinnest**) **1** having opposite surfaces or sides close together. **2** (of a garment or fabric) made of light material. **3** having little flesh or fat on the body. **4** having few parts or members in relation to the area covered or filled. **5** not dense or heavy. **6** containing a lot of liquid and not much solid substance. **7** (of a sound) faint and high-pitched. **8** weak and inadequate. verb (**thins**, **thinning**, **thinned**) (often **thin out**) make or become less thick or dense. ■ **thinly** adverb **thinness** noun.

thine pronoun & possessive determiner old use your or yours.

thing noun **1** an inanimate object. **2** an unspecified object, action, activity, etc. **3** (**things**) personal belongings. **4** (**the thing**) informal what is needed or required. **5 (your thing)** informal your special interest.

think verb (thinks, thinking, thought) **1** have a particular opinion, belief, or idea. **2** use or direct your mind. **3 (think of** or **about)** take into account or consideration. **4** intend. **5 (think over)** consider carefully. **6 (think up)** informal invent or devise. noun an act of thinking. □**think better of** reconsider and decide not to do. **think tank** a body of experts providing advice and ideas. ■ **thinker** noun.

thinner noun a solvent used to thin paint or other solutions.

third ordinal number **1** that is number three in a sequence; 3rd. **2 (a third** or **one third)** each of three equal parts into which something is divided. **3** Brit. a place in the third grade in an examination for a degree. □**third-degree 1** (of burns) of the most severe kind, affecting tissue below the skin. **2** N. Amer. (of a crime) in the least serious category. **the third degree** lengthy and harsh questioning. **third party 1** a person besides the two main ones involved in a situation. **2** Brit. (of insurance) covering damage or injury suffered by a person other than the insured. **Third World** the developing countries of Asia, Africa, and Latin America. ■ **thirdly** adverb.

thirst noun **1** a feeling of needing or wanting to drink. **2** the state of not having enough water to drink. **3 (thirst for)** a strong desire for. verb **1** old use feel a need to drink. **2 (thirst for** or **after)** have a strong desire for.

thirsty adjective (thirstier, thirstiest) **1** feeling or causing thirst. **2 (thirsty for)** having a strong desire for. ■ **thirstily** adverb.

thirteen cardinal number one more than twelve; 13. (Roman numeral: **xiii** or **XIII**.) ■ **thirteenth** ordinal number.

thirty cardinal number (plural **thirties**) ten less than forty; 30. (Roman numeral: **xxx** or **XXX**.) ■ **thirtieth** ordinal number.

this pronoun & determiner (plural **these**) **1** used to identify a specific person or thing close at hand, just mentioned,

or being indicated or experienced. **2** referring to the nearer of two things close to the speaker. adverb to the degree or extent indicated.

thistle noun a plant with a prickly stem and leaves and purple flowers.

thistledown noun the light fluffy down of thistle seeds.

thither adverb old use to or towards that place.

tho' or **tho** informal spelling of **THOUGH**.

thong noun **1** a narrow strip used as a fastening or as the lash of a whip. **2** a pair of knickers like a G-string.

thorax noun (plural **thoraces** /thor-uh-seez/ or **thoraxes**) **1** the part of the body between the neck and the abdomen. **2** the middle section of an insect's body, bearing the legs and wings. ■ **thoracic** adjective.

thorn noun **1** a stiff, sharp-pointed projection on a plant. **2** a thorny bush, shrub, or tree. □**a thorn in someone's side** (or **flesh**) a source of continual annoyance or trouble.

thorny adjective (thornier, thorniest) **1** having many thorns. **2** causing difficulty.

thorough adjective **1** complete with regard to every detail. **2** very careful and complete. **3** absolute; utter. ■ **thoroughly** adverb.

thoroughbred adjective of pure breed. noun a thoroughbred animal.

thoroughfare noun a road or path between two places.

thoroughgoing adjective **1** thorough. **2** complete; absolute.

those plural of **THAT**.

thou pronoun old use you (as the singular subject of a verb).

though conjunction **1** despite the fact that; although. **2** however; but. adverb however.

thought[1] noun **1** an idea or opinion produced by thinking, or occurring suddenly in the mind. **2** the process of thinking. **3 (thought of)** intention, hope, or idea of. **4** the forming of opinions, or the opinions so formed.

thought² past and past participle of **THINK**.

thoughtful adjective **1** absorbed in thought. **2** showing careful consideration. **3** showing consideration for other people. ■ **thoughtfully** adverb.

thoughtless adjective **1** not showing consideration for other people. **2** without considering the consequences. ■ **thoughtlessly** adverb.

thousand cardinal number **1** the product of a hundred and ten; 1,000. (Roman numeral: m or M.) **2** (thousands) informal an unspecified large number. ■ **thousandth** ordinal number.

thrall noun the state of being in another's power.

thrash verb **1** beat repeatedly with a stick or whip. **2** move in a violent or uncontrolled way. **3** informal defeat heavily. **4** (**thrash out**) discuss frankly and thoroughly.

thread noun **1** a thin strand of cotton or other fibres used in sewing or weaving. **2** a spiral ridge on the outside of a screw or bolt or on the inside of a hole, to allow two parts to be screwed together. **3** a theme running through a situation or piece of writing. verb **1** pass a thread through. **2** weave in and out of obstacles.

threadbare adjective thin and tattered with age.

threat noun **1** a stated intention to inflict harm on someone. **2** a person or thing likely to cause harm. **3** the possibility of trouble or danger.

threaten verb **1** make a threat to. **2** put at risk. **3** seem likely to produce an unwelcome result. ■ **threatening** adjective **threateningly** adverb.

three cardinal number one more than two; 3. (Roman numeral: iii or III.) □ **three-dimensional** having or appearing to have length, breadth, and depth. ■ **threefold** adjective & adverb.

threepence /**thrup**-uhnss/ noun Brit. the sum of three old pence before decimalization (1971). ■ **threepenny** adjective.

threesome noun a group of three people.

threnody /**thren**-uh-di/ noun (plural **threnodies**) a song, piece of music, or poem expressing grief or regret.

thresh verb **1** separate grains of corn from the rest of the plant. **2** move in an uncontrolled way. ■ **thresher** noun.

threshold noun **1** a strip of wood or stone forming the bottom of a doorway. **2** a level or point marking the start of something.

☑ there is only one *h* in the middle: threshold.

threw past of **THROW**.

thrice adverb old use three times.

thrift noun carefulness and economy in the use of money and other resources. ■ **thrifty** adjective.

thrill noun **1** a sudden feeling of excitement and pleasure. **2** an exciting or pleasurable experience. **3** a nervous tremor of emotion or sensation. verb **1** give someone a thrill. **2** (**thrill to**) experience something exciting.

thriller noun a novel, play, or film with an exciting plot, typically involving crime or spying.

thrilling adjective extremely exciting. ■ **thrillingly** adverb.

thrive verb (**thrives, thriving, thrived** or **throve**; past participle **thrived** or **thriven**) **1** grow or develop well or vigorously. **2** prosper; flourish.

throat noun **1** the passage which leads from the back of the mouth to the lungs and stomach. **2** the front part of the neck.

throaty adjective (**throatier, throatiest**) (of a voice or other sound) deep and husky. ■ **throatily** adverb.

throb verb (**throbs, throbbing, throbbed**) **1** beat or sound with a strong, regular rhythm. **2** feel pain in a series of pulsations. noun a strong, regular beat or sound.

throes plural noun severe or violent pain and struggle. □ **in the throes of** struggling in the midst of.

thrombosis noun (plural **thromboses**) the formation of a blood clot in a blood vessel or the heart.

throne noun **1** a chair for a king or

queen, used during ceremonies. **2 (the throne)** the power or rank of a king or queen.

throng noun a large, densely packed crowd. **verb** gather somewhere in large numbers.

throttle noun a device controlling the flow of fuel or power to an engine. **verb** (**throttles, throttling, throttled**) **1** attack or kill by choking or strangling. **2** control an engine or vehicle with a throttle.

through preposition & adverb **1** in one side and out of the other side of an opening or place. **2** continuing in time towards. **3** from beginning to end. **4** by means of. **adjective 1** (of public transport) continuing to the final destination. **2** (of traffic, roads, etc.) passing straight through a place. **3** having successfully reached the next stage of a competition. **4** informal having finished an activity, relationship, etc.

throughout preposition & adverb all the way through.

throughput noun the amount of material or number of items passing through a process.

throve past of THRIVE.

throw verb (**throws, throwing, threw**; past participle **thrown**) **1** send through the air with a rapid movement of the arm and hand. **2** move or place hurriedly or roughly. **3** project, direct, or cast light, an expression, etc. in a particular direction. **4** send suddenly into a particular position or condition. **5** upset or confuse. noun **1** an act of throwing. **2** a small rug or light cover for furniture. **3 (a throw)** informal a single turn or item. □ **throw away** (or **out**) get rid of. **throw up** vomit.

throwaway adjective **1** intended to be thrown away after use. **2** (of a remark) said without careful thought.

throwback noun something that existed in the same or a similar form in the past.

thrum verb (**thrums, thrumming, thrummed**) make a continuous rhythmic humming sound. noun a thrum-

ming sound.

thrush[1] noun a bird with a brown back and spotted breast.

thrush[2] noun infection of the mouth and throat or the genitals by a yeast-like fungus.

thrust verb (**thrusts, thrusting, thrust**) **1** push suddenly or violently. **2** make your way forcibly. noun **1** a sudden or violent lunge or attack. **2** the main point of an argument. **3** the force produced by an engine to push forward a jet, rocket, etc.

thrusting adjective aggressively ambitious.

thud noun a dull, heavy sound. **verb** (**thuds, thudding, thudded**) move, fall, or strike with a thud.

thug noun a violent man. ■ **thuggery** noun **thuggish** adjective.

thumb noun the short, thick first digit of the hand. **verb 1** turn over pages with your thumb. **2** ask for a free ride in a passing vehicle by signalling with your thumb. □ **thumb index** lettered notches cut into the side of a book to help you find the section you want. **thumbs up** (or **down**) informal an indication of approval (or disapproval). **under someone's thumb** under someone's control.

thumbnail noun the nail of the thumb. □ **thumbnail sketch** a brief, concise description.

thumbscrew noun an instrument of torture that crushes the thumbs.

thump verb **1** hit heavily with your fist or a blunt object. **2** put down forcefully. **3** (of a person's heart) beat strongly. noun a heavy dull blow or noise.

thumping adjective **1** pounding; throbbing. **2** informal very big.

thunder noun **1** a loud rumbling or crashing noise heard after a lightning flash due to the expansion of rapidly heated air. **2** a resounding loud deep noise. **verb** (**it thunders, it is thundering, it thundered**) thunder is sounding. **2** move heavily and forcefully. **3** speak loudly and angrily.

thunderbolt noun a flash of lightning

with a crash of thunder at the same time.

thunderclap noun a sudden crash of thunder.

thundercloud noun a cloud charged with electricity and producing thunder and lightning.

thunderous adjective **1** very loud. **2** (of a person's expression) very angry or threatening.

thunderstorm noun a storm with thunder and lightning.

thunderstruck adjective extremely surprised or shocked.

Thursday noun the day of the week before Friday and following Wednesday.

thus adverb formal **1** as a result or consequence of this; therefore. **2** in this way. **3** to this point; so.

thwack verb hit with a sharp blow. noun a sharp blow.

thwart verb prevent someone from accomplishing something.

thy or (before a vowel) **thine** possessive determiner old use your.

thyme /rhymes with time/ noun a low-growing, sweet-smelling plant used in cooking.

thymus noun (plural **thymi**) a gland in the neck which produces white blood cells for the immune system.

thyroid noun a large gland in the neck which produces hormones regulating growth and development.

tiara noun a jewelled ornamental band worn above the forehead.

tibia noun (plural **tibiae** /**ti**-bi-ee/) the inner of the two bones between the knee and the ankle.

tic noun a recurring spasm in the muscles of the face.

tick[1] noun **1** a mark (✓) used to show that an item in a text is correct or has been chosen or checked. **2** a regular short, sharp sound. **3** Brit. informal a moment. verb **1** mark with a tick. **2** make regular ticking sounds. **3** (**tick away** or **by** or **past**) (of time) keep passing. **4** (**tick over**) (of an engine) run slowly in neutral. **5** (**tick off**) Brit. informal tell

off.

tick[2] noun **1** a tiny insect-like creature which attaches itself to the skin and sucks blood.

ticker noun **1** informal a person's heart. **2** N. Amer. a machine that prints out data on a strip of paper. □ **ticker tape** strips of paper on which data is printed by a machine.

ticket noun **1** a piece of paper or card giving you the right to travel on public transport or admitting you to a place or an event. **2** an official notice that you have committed a parking or driving offence. **3** a label attached to a product, giving its price, size, etc.

ticking noun a hard-wearing material used to cover mattresses.

tickle verb (**tickles, tickling, tickled**) **1** lightly touch in a way that causes itching or twitching and often laughter. **2** be appealing or amusing to. noun an act of tickling, or the sensation of being tickled. ■ **tickly** adjective

ticklish adjective **1** sensitive to being tickled. **2** requiring care and tact.

tidal adjective relating to or affected by tides. □ **tidal wave** an exceptionally large ocean wave. ■ **tidally** adverb.

tidbit US spelling of **TITBIT**.

tiddler noun Brit. informal **1** a small fish. **2** a young or small person or thing.

tiddly[1] adjective informal slightly drunk.

tiddly[2] adjective Brit. informal little; tiny.

tiddlywinks plural noun a game in which small plastic counters are flicked into a cup.

tide noun **1** the alternate rising and falling of the sea due to the attraction of the moon and sun. **2** a powerful surge of feeling or trend of events. verb (**tides, tiding, tided**) (**tide over**) help through a difficult period.

tidings plural noun literary news; information.

tidy adjective (**tidier, tidiest**) **1** arranged neatly and in order. **2** liking to keep yourself and your possessions neat and in order. **3** informal (of a sum of money) considerable. noun (plural tidies) **1** an act of tidying. **2** a container for holding small objects. **verb** (tidies, tidying, tidied) **1** (often tidy up) make a place tidy. **2** (tidy away) put away for the sake of tidiness. ■ **tidily** adverb **tidiness** noun.

tie verb (ties, tying, tied) **1** attach or fasten with string, cord, ribbon, etc. **2** form into a knot or bow. **3** restrict to a particular situation or place. **4** connect someone or something with. **5** achieve the same score or ranking as another competitor. **noun** (plural **ties**) **1** a thing that ties. **2** a strip of material worn beneath a collar and tied in a knot at the front. **3** a result in a game or match in which two or more competitors are equal. **4** Brit. a sports match in which the winners proceed to the next round. □ **tie-break** (or **tie-breaker**) a means of deciding a winner from competitors who have tied. **tie-dye** the tying of knots in a piece of fabric before dying it, in order to produce a pattern. **tie in** be or cause to be connected or in harmony. **tie up 1** restrict someone's movement by binding their arms or legs. **2** bring to a conclusion. **3** informal occupy someone so that they have no time for other activities.

tied adjective 1 Brit. (of accommodation) rented by someone on condition that they work for the owner. **2** (of a pub) owned and controlled by a brewery.

tiepin noun an ornamental pin for holding a tie in place.

tier noun one of a series of rows or levels placed one above and behind the other. ■ **tiered** adjective.

tiff noun informal a trivial quarrel.

tiger noun a large cat with a yellow coat striped with black, native to the forests of Asia.

tight adjective 1 firmly fixed, closed, or fastened. **2** (of clothes) fitting very closely. **3** well sealed against water or air. **4** (of a rope, fabric, or surface) stretched so as to leave no slack. **5** (of an area or space) allowing little room for movement. **6** closely packed together. **7** (of a form of control) very strict. **8** (of money or time) limited.

adverb very closely or firmly. □ **tight-fisted** informal not willing to spend or give away your money. **tight-knit** (or **tightly knit**) (of a group of people) closely connected to each other through family or social relationships. **tight-lipped** unwilling to give way to an emotion, or to tell someone something. ■ **tightly** adverb **tightness** noun.

tighten verb make or become tight or tighter.

tightrope noun a rope or wire stretched high above the ground, on which acrobats balance.

tights plural noun a close-fitting garment made of a knitted yarn, covering the hips, legs, and feet.

tigress noun a female tiger.

tilde /til-duh/ **noun** an accent (~) placed over the Spanish *n* or Portuguese *a* or *o* to change the way they are pronounced.

tile noun a thin square or rectangular piece of fired clay, concrete, cork, etc., used for covering roofs, floors, or walls. **verb** (tiles, tiling, tiled) cover with tiles. ■ **tiler** noun.

till¹ less formal way of saying **UNTIL**.

till² noun a cash register or drawer for money.

till³ verb prepare and cultivate land for crops.

tiller noun a horizontal bar fitted to a boat's rudder and used for steering.

tilt verb 1 slip or move into a sloping position. **2** (tilt at) (in the past, in jousting) thrust at someone with a lance. **noun 1** a tilting position or movement. **2** a leaning or bias. **3** (in the past) a joust. **4** (tilt at) an attempt at winning something. □ **(at) full tilt** with maximum speed or force.

tilth noun cultivated soil.

timber noun wood prepared for use in building and carpentry.

timbre /tam-ber/ **noun** the quality of the sound in a voice or piece of music.

time noun 1 the continuing and limitless progress of existence and events in the past, present, and future. **2** a point or period within this. **3** a point of time as measured in hours and minutes past midnight or noon. **4** the right or agreed moment to do something. **5** time as a resource to be used. **6** an instance of something happening or being done. **7** (times) (following a number) expressing multiplication. **8** the rhythmic pattern or tempo of a piece of music. verb (times, timing, timed) **1** arrange a time for. **2** do at a particular time. **3** measure the time taken by. □ behind the times not using the latest ideas or techniques. for the time being until some other arrangement is made. in time **1** not late. **2** eventually. on time punctual, or punctually. time capsule a container storing a selection of objects typical of the present time, buried for discovery in the future. time-honoured (of a custom or tradition) respected or valued because it has existed for a long time. time off time spent away from your usual work or studies. time out time for resting. time-server a person who makes little effort at work because they are waiting to leave or retire. time signature a sign at the start of a piece of music saying the number of beats in a bar.

timekeeper noun **1** a person who records the amount of time taken by a process or activity. **2** a person regarded in terms of their punctuality. ■ timekeeping noun.

timeless adjective not affected by the passing of time.

timely adjective done or occurring at a good or appropriate time.

timepiece noun an instrument for measuring time; a clock or watch.

timer noun **1** a device that records how long something is taking. **2** a device that stops or starts a machine at a preset time.

timescale noun the time allowed for or taken by a process or events.

timeshare noun an arrangement in which joint owners use a property as a holiday home at different times.

timetable noun a list or plan of times

at which events are scheduled to take place. verb (timetables, timetabling, timetabled) schedule events to take place at particular times.

timid adjective not brave or confident. ■ timidity noun timidly adverb.

timorous adjective easily frightened.

timpani or **tympani** /tim-puh-ni/ plural noun kettledrums.

tin noun **1** a silvery-white metal. **2** an airtight container with a lid, made of tinplate or aluminium. **3** Brit. a sealed tinplate or aluminium container for preserving food. **4** an open metal container for baking food. verb (tins, tinning, tinned) **1** cover another metal with a thin layer of tin. **2** (tinned) Brit. preserved in a tin. □ tin whistle a metal musical instrument like a small flute.

tincture noun **1** a medicine made by dissolving a drug in alcohol. **2** a slight trace.

tinder noun dry material used in lighting a fire.

tinderbox noun (in the past) a box containing tinder, flint, a steel, and other items for lighting fires.

tine noun a prong or sharp point.

tinfoil noun metal foil used for covering or wrapping food.

tinge noun a slight trace of a colour, feeling, or quality. verb (tinges, tingeing or tinging, tinged) (often be tinged) give a tinge to.

tingle noun a slight prickling or stinging sensation. verb (tingles, tingling, tingled) (of a part of the body) prickle or sting slightly. ■ tingly adjective.

tinker noun **1** a travelling mender of pots, kettles, etc. **2** an act of tinkering with something. verb (tinkers, tinkering, tinkered) (tinker with) casually try to repair or improve.

tinkle verb (tinkles, tinkling, tinkled) make or cause to make a light, clear ringing sound. noun a tinkling sound.

tinnitus /tin-ni-tuhss/ noun a ringing or buzzing in the ears.

tinny adjective **1** having a thin, metallic sound. **2** made of thin or poor-quality metal.

tinplate noun sheet steel or iron coated with tin.

tinpot adjective informal of poor quality.

tinsel noun thin strips of shiny metal foil attached to a length of thread, used to decorate a Christmas tree.

tint noun **1** a shade of a colour. **2** a dye for colouring the hair. verb **1** add light colour to. **2** dye hair with a tint.

tintinnabulation noun a ringing or tinkling sound.

tiny adjective (**tinier, tiniest**) very small.

tip¹ noun **1** the pointed or rounded end of something slender or tapering. **2** a small part fitted to the end of an object. □ **tip-top** of the very best quality. ■ **tipped** adjective.

tip² verb (**tips, tipping, tipped**) **1** overbalance so as to fall or turn over. **2** be or put in a sloping position. **3** empty out the contents of a container by holding it at an angle. noun **1** Brit. a place where rubbish is left. **2** informal a dirty or untidy place.

tip³ noun **1** a small extra amount of money that you give to someone for their good service in a restaurant, taxi, etc. **2** a piece of practical advice. **3** a prediction about the likely winner of a race or contest. verb (**tips, tipping, tipped**) **1** give a tip to. **2** Brit. predict that a particular horse, competitor, etc. is likely to win something. **3** (**tip off**) informal give secret information to.

tipple verb (**tipples, tippling, tippled**) drink alcohol regularly. noun informal an alcoholic drink. ■ **tippler** noun.

tipster noun a person who gives tips as to the likely winner of a race or contest.

tipsy adjective slightly drunk. ■ **tipsily** adverb.

tiptoe verb (**tiptoes, tiptoeing, tiptoed**) walk quietly and carefully with your heels raised. □ **on tiptoe** (or **tiptoes**) with your heels raised.

tirade noun a long angry speech.

tire¹ verb (**tires, tiring, tired**) **1** make or become in need of rest or sleep. **2** exhaust the patience or interest of. **3** (**tire of**) become impatient or bored with.

tire² US spelling of **TYRE**.

tired adjective **1** in need of sleep or rest. **2** (**tired of**) bored with. **3** (of a statement or idea) boring or uninteresting because it has been said or used too often. ■ **tiredness** noun.

tireless adjective having or showing great effort or energy. ■ **tirelessly** adverb.

tiresome adjective making you feel impatient or bored. ■ **tiresomely** adverb.

'tis short form literary it is.

tissue /ti-shoo/ noun **1** any of the distinct types of material of which animals or plants are made. **2** a disposable paper handkerchief. **3** delicate gauzy fabric. **4** a web-like structure. □ **tissue paper** a very thin, soft paper.

tit¹ or **titmouse** noun a small bird that searches for food among foliage and branches.

tit² noun **1** vulgar a woman's breast. **2** Brit. informal a foolish person.

tit³ noun (**tit for tat**) a situation in which you insult or hurt someone because they have done the same to you.

Titan noun **1** any of a family of giant gods in Greek mythology. **2** (**titan**) a person of very great strength, intelligence, or importance.

titanic adjective of exceptional strength, size, or power.

titanium noun a silver-grey metal used in making strong alloys.

titbit (US spelling **tidbit**) noun **1** a small piece of tasty food. **2** a small item of interesting information.

titch noun Brit. informal a small person. ■ **titchy** adjective.

tithe noun (in the past) one tenth of what people produced or earned in a year, taken as a tax to support the Church.

titillate verb (**titillates, titillating, titillated**) make someone feel interested or mildly excited, especially sexually. ■ **titillation** noun.

> ☑ one *t*, two *l*'s: ti**till**ate. Also, don't confuse **titillate** with **titivate**, which means 'make smarter or more attractive'.

titivate verb (**titivates, titivating, titivated**) informal make smarter or more attractive. ■ **titivation** noun.

title noun **1** the name of a book, musical composition, or other work. **2** a name that describes someone's position or job. **3** a word, such as *Dr*, *Mrs*, or *Lord*, used before or instead of someone's name to indicate their rank or profession. **4** a descriptive name that someone has earned or chosen. **5** the position of being the champion of a major sports competition. **6** a caption or credit in a film or broadcast. verb (**titles, titling, titled**) give a title to. □ **title deed** a legal document giving evidence of someone's right to own a property. **title music** music played at the beginning of a film or television programme. **title role** the part in a play or film from which the title is taken.

titled adjective having a title indicating nobility or rank.

titration noun the calculation of the amount of a substance in a solution by measuring the volume of a reagent required to react with it.

titter noun a short, quiet laugh. verb (**titters, tittering, tittered**) give a titter.

tittle noun a tiny amount or part. □ **tittle-tattle** gossip.

titular /tit-yuu-ler/ adjective **1** relating to a title. **2** holding a formal position or title without any real authority.

tizzy noun (plural **tizzies**) informal a state of nervous excitement or worry.

TNT abbreviation trinitrotoluene, a high explosive.

to preposition **1** expressing direction or position in relation to a particular location, point, or condition. **2** Brit. (in telling the time) before the hour mentioned. **3** identifying the person or thing affected by an action. **4** identifying a particular relationship between one person or thing and another. **5** indicating a rate of return on something: *ten miles to the gallon*. **6** indicating that two things are attached. **infinitive marker** used with the base form of a verb to indicate that the verb is in the infinitive. adverb so as to be closed or nearly closed. □ **to and fro** backwards and forwards or from side to side. **to-do** informal a commotion or fuss.

> ⓘ don't confuse **to** with **too** or **two**. **To** mainly means 'in the direction of' (as in *the next train to London*), while **too** means 'excessively' (as in *she was driving too fast*) or 'in addition', and **two** is the number meaning 'one less than three'.

toad noun a tailless amphibian with a short stout body and short legs.

toadstool noun a fungus with a rounded cap on a stalk.

toady noun (plural **toadies**) a person who is too polite and respectful to someone in order to gain their favour. verb (**toadies, toadying, toadied**) act in an excessively polite and respectful way.

toast noun **1** sliced bread that has been held against a fire or heated element until it is brown and crisp. **2** an act of raising glasses at a gathering and drinking together in honour of a person or thing. **3** a person who is toasted or held in high regard. verb **1** make bread brown and crisp by holding it against a fire or heated element. **2** drink a toast to.

toaster noun an electrical device for making toast.

tobacco noun (plural **tobaccos**) a preparation of the dried nicotine-rich leaves of an American plant, used for smoking or chewing.

tobacconist noun Brit. a shopkeeper who sells cigarettes and tobacco.

toboggan noun a light, narrow vehicle on runners, used for sliding downhill over snow or ice. ■ **tobog-ganist** noun.

toccata /tuh-**kah**-tuh/ noun a musical composition for a keyboard instrument designed to show the performer's touch and technique.

tod noun (**on your tod**) Brit. informal on your own.

today adverb **1** on or in the course of this present day. **2** at the present period of time. noun **1** this present day. **2** the present period of time.

toddle verb (**toddles, toddling, toddled**) **1** (of a young child) move with short unsteady steps while learning to walk. **2** informal walk or go about in a leisurely way. noun an act of toddling.

toddler noun a young child who is just beginning to walk.

toddy noun (plural **toddies**) a drink of spirits mixed with hot water.

toe noun **1** any of the five digits at the end of the foot. **2** the lower end, tip, or point of something. verb (**toes, toeing, toed**) push or touch with your toes. □ **on your toes** ready and alert. **toe the line** be obedient.

toecap noun a piece of steel or leather fitted over the front part of a boot or shoe.

toehold noun a small foothold.

toenail noun a nail on the upper surface of the tip of each toe.

toff noun Brit. informal, disapproving a rich, upper-class person.

toffee noun a kind of firm sweet which softens when sucked or chewed, made by boiling together sugar and butter. □ **toffee apple** Brit. an apple coated with a thin layer of toffee and fixed on a stick. **toffee-nosed** Brit. informal snobbish.

tofu /**toh**-foo/ noun a soft curd made from mashed soya beans.

tog¹ informal noun (**togs**) clothes. verb (**togs, togging, togged**) (**be togged up**) be fully dressed for a particular occasion or activity.

tog² noun Brit. a unit for measuring the insulating properties of clothes and quilts.

toga noun a loose outer garment made of a single piece of cloth, worn in ancient Rome.

together adverb **1** with or near to another person or people. **2** so as to touch, combine, or be united. **3** regarded as a whole. **4** (of two people) married or in a sexual relationship. **5** at the same time. **6** without interruption. adjective informal level-headed and well-organized. ■ **togetherness** noun.

toggle noun a narrow piece of wood or plastic attached to a garment, pushed through a loop to act as a fastener.

toil verb **1** work extremely hard. **2** move somewhere slowly and with difficulty. noun exhausting work.

toilet noun **1** a large bowl for urinating or defecating into. **2** old use the process of washing yourself and attending to your appearance. □ **toilet bag** Brit. a waterproof bag for toothpaste, soap, etc., used when travelling. **toilet-train** teach a young child to use the toilet. **toilet water** a dilute form of perfume.

toiletries plural noun articles used in washing and taking care of your body, such as soap and shampoo.

token noun **1** a thing that represents a feeling, fact, or quality. **2** a voucher that can be exchanged for goods or services. **3** a disc used to operate a machine. adjective involving little effort or commitment and done only for show.

told past and past participle of **TELL**.

tolerable adjective **1** able to be tolerated. **2** fairly good. ■ **tolerably** adverb.

tolerance noun **1** the ability to accept things you do not agree with. **2** an allowable amount of variation in the dimensions of a machine or part.

tolerant adjective **1** able to accept things you do not agree with. **2** able to cope with particular conditions.

tolerate verb (**tolerates, tolerating, tolerated**) **1** allow someone to do something you do not like or agree with. **2** patiently accept something unpleasant. **3** be capable of continued exposure to a drug, toxin, etc. without adverse reaction. ■ **toleration** noun.

toll¹ noun **1** a charge you have to pay for the use of certain roads or bridges. **2** the number of deaths or casualties arising from an accident, war, etc. **3** the cost or damage resulting from something.

toll² verb **1** (of a bell) sound with slow, even strokes. **2** announce the time, a church service, or a person's death in this way. noun a single ring of a bell.

tom or **tomcat** noun a male domestic cat.

tomahawk noun a light axe used in the past by American Indians.

tomato noun (plural **tomatoes**) a glossy red fruit eaten with salads and other savoury foods.

 no *e* on the end: tomato.

tomb noun **1** a burial place consisting of a stone structure built above ground or an underground vault. **2** a monument to a dead person, built over their burial place.

tombola noun Brit. a game in which tickets are drawn from a revolving drum to win prizes.

tomboy noun a girl who enjoys rough, noisy activities traditionally associated with boys. ■ **tomboyish** adjective.

tombstone noun a flat stone standing or laid over a grave.

tome noun a large, serious book.

tomfoolery noun foolish behaviour.

tomography /tuh-**mog**-ruh-fi/ noun a technique for seeing a cross section through a human body or other solid object using X-rays or ultrasound. ■ **tomographic** adjective.

tomorrow adverb on the day after today. noun **1** the day after today. **2** the future.

 one *m*, two *r*'s: tomorrow.

tomtit noun a tit or similar bird.

tom-tom noun a drum beaten with the hands.

ton /tun/ noun **1** (also **long ton**) a unit of weight equal to 2,240 lb avoirdupois (1016.05 kg). **2** (also **short ton**) N. Amer. a unit of weight equal to 2,000 lb avoirdupois (907.19 kg). **3** a metric ton. **4** a unit of measurement of a ship's weight equal to 2,240 lb or 35 cubic feet (0.99 cubic metres). **5** informal a large number or amount. **6** Brit. informal a speed of one hundred miles per hour.

tonal adjective **1** relating to tone. **2** (of music) written using traditional keys and harmony. ■ **tonality** noun **tonally** adverb.

tone noun **1** the quality of a musical sound. **2** the feeling or mood expressed in a person's voice. **3** general character. **4** a basic interval in classical Western music, equal to two semitones. **5** a particular brightness, deepness, or shade in a colour. **6** firmness in a resting muscle. verb (**tones, toning, toned**) **1** (often **tone up**) give greater strength or firmness to a part of your body. **2** (**tone down**) make a statement or piece of writing less harsh, extreme, or strong. □ **tone deaf** unable to hear differences in musical pitch.

toner noun **1** a liquid applied to the skin to reduce oiliness. **2** a type of powder or ink used in photocopiers.

tongs plural noun a tool with two arms that are joined at one end, used for picking up and holding things.

tongue noun **1** the fleshy organ in the mouth, used for tasting, licking, swallowing, and speaking. **2** a person's manner of speaking: *a sharp tongue*. **3** a language. **4** a strip of leather or fabric under the laces in a shoe. verb (**tongues, tonguing, tongued**) sound a note on a wind instrument by interrupting the air flow with your tongue. □ **tongue and groove** wooden boards which are joined by means of interlocking ridges and grooves down their sides. **tongue-tied** too shy or embarrassed to speak. **tongue-twister** a sequence of words that are difficult to pronounce. **with tongue in**

cheek not seriously meaning what you are saying.

tonic noun **1** a drink taken as a kind of medicine, to make you feel energetic and healthy. **2** something that makes you feel invigorated. **3** (also **tonic water**) a fizzy drink that is both bitter and sweet, often mixed with gin.

tonight adverb on the evening or night of the present day. noun the evening or night of the present day.

tonnage noun **1** weight in tons. **2** the size or carrying capacity of a ship measured in tons.

tonne /tun/ noun a metric ton.

tonsil noun each of two small masses of tissue in the throat.

tonsillectomy noun (plural **tonsillectomies**) an operation to remove the tonsils.

tonsillitis noun inflammation of the tonsils.

tonsure noun a circular area on a monk's or priest's head where the hair is shaved off.

too adverb **1** to a higher degree than is desirable, allowed, or possible. **2** in addition.

> ⓘ don't confuse **too** with **to** or **two**; see the note at **TO**.

took past of **TAKE**.

tool noun **1** an implement used to carry out a particular function. **2** a thing that helps you to do your job or achieve something. verb **1** impress a design on leather with a heated tool. **2** equip an organization with tools for industrial production.

toot noun a short sound made by a horn, trumpet, or similar instrument. verb make a toot.

tooth noun (plural **teeth**) **1** each of the hard white projections in the mouth, used for biting and chewing. **2** a projecting part such as a cog on a gearwheel or a point on a saw or comb. ■ **toothed** adjective **toothless** adjective.

toothache noun pain in a tooth.

toothbrush noun a small longhandled brush for cleaning your teeth.

toothpaste noun a paste for cleaning the teeth.

toothpick noun a thin, pointed piece of wood or plastic for removing bits of food from between your teeth.

toothsome adjective **1** (of food) temptingly tasty. **2** informal attractive.

toothy adjective having large or prominent teeth.

tootle verb (**tootles, tootling, tootled**) make a series of easy sounds on a horn, trumpet, etc. noun an act or sound of tootling.

top¹ noun **1** the highest or uppermost point, part, or surface. **2** a thing placed on, fitted to, or covering the upper part of something. **3** (**the top**) the highest or most important level or position. **4** the utmost degree. **5** a garment covering the upper part of the body. adjective highest in position, status, or degree. verb (**tops, topping, topped**) **1** be more, better, or taller than. **2** be at the highest place or rank in. **3** reach the top of a hill or rise. **4** provide with a topping. **5** informal kill. □ **on top of 1** so as to cover. **2** very near to. **3** in command or control of. **4** in addition to. **over the top** Brit. informal excessive or exaggerated.

top hat a man's tall formal black hat. **top-heavy** too heavy at the top and therefore likely to fall. **top up 1** add to a number or amount to bring it up to a certain level. **2** fill up a partly full container.

top² noun a toy shaped like a cone with a point at the base, that can be set to spin.

topaz noun a colourless, yellow, or pale blue precious stone.

topcoat noun **1** an overcoat. **2** an outer coat of paint.

topiary noun (plural **topiaries**) **1** the art of clipping evergreen shrubs into interesting shapes. **2** shrubs clipped in such a way.

topic noun a subject that you talk, write, or learn about.

topical adjective **1** relating to or dealing with current affairs. **2** relating to a particular subject. ■ **topicality** noun **topically** adverb.

topknot noun a knot of hair arranged on the top of the head.

topless adjective having the breasts uncovered.

topography noun **1** the arrangement of the physical features of an area of land. **2** the representation of these features on a map. ■ **topographical** (or **topographic**) adjective.

topple verb (**topples**, **toppling**, **toppled**) overbalance and fall down, or make something do this.

topsoil noun the top layer of soil.

topspin noun a fast forward spin given to a moving ball.

topsy-turvy adjective & adverb **1** upside down. **2** in a state of confusion.

tor noun a small steep hill or rocky peak.

torch noun **1** Brit. a portable lamp powered by a battery. **2** (in the past) a piece of wood or cloth soaked in fat and ignited. verb informal set fire to.

tore past of **TEAR**[1].

toreador noun a bullfighter.

torment noun /tor-ment/ **1** great suffering. **2** a cause of suffering. verb /tor-ment/ **1** make someone suffer greatly. **2** annoy or tease unkindly. ■ **tormentor** noun.

torn past participle of **TEAR**[1].

tornado noun (plural **tornadoes** or **tornados**) a violent , rotating wind storm.

torpedo noun (plural **torpedoes**) a long narrow underwater missile. verb (**torpedoes**, **torpedoing**, **torpedoed**) attack using torpedoes.

torpid adjective inactive and having no energy. ■ **torpidity** noun.

torpor noun the state of being inactive and having no energy.

torque /tork/ noun a force causing rotation.

torrent noun **1** a strong, fast-moving stream of water or other liquid. **2** a large outpouring.

torrential adjective (of rain) falling rapidly and heavily.

torrid adjective **1** very hot and dry. **2** full of sexual passion. **3** full of difficulty.

torsion noun the state of being twisted.

torso noun (plural **torsos**) the trunk of the human body.

tort noun Law a wrongful act or a violation of a right.

tortilla /tor-tee-yuh/ noun **1** (in Mexican cookery) a thin, flat maize pancake. **2** (in Spanish cookery) a thick omelette containing potato.

tortoise /tor-tuhss/ noun a slow-moving reptile with a hard, round shell into which it can draw its head and legs.

tortoiseshell noun **1** the translucent mottled yellow and brown shell of certain turtles, used to make jewellery or ornaments. **2** a domestic cat with markings resembling tortoiseshell. **3** a butterfly with mottled orange, yellow, and black markings.

tortuous adjective **1** full of twists and turns. **2** excessively lengthy and complex. ■ **tortuously** adverb.

torture noun **1** severe pain inflicted on someone, especially to make them say something. **2** great suffering or anxiety. verb (**tortures**, **torturing**, **tortured**) subject someone to torture. ■ **torturer** noun **torturous** adjective.

Tory noun (plural **Tories**) a member or supporter of the British Conservative Party.

toss verb **1** throw lightly or casually. **2** move something from side to side or backwards and forwards. **3** jerk your head or hair backwards. **4** throw a coin into the air and see which side is facing upwards when it lands, using this to help decide something. **5** shake or turn food in a liquid to coat it lightly. noun an act of tossing. □ **toss-up 1** the tossing of a coin to make a decision. **2** a situation in which any of two or more outcomes is equally possible.

tot[1] noun **1** a very young child. **2** Brit. a small drink of spirits.

tot² verb (tots, totting, totted) (tot up) Brit. **1** add up numbers or amounts. **2** accumulate over time.

total adjective **1** comprising the whole number or amount. **2** complete. noun a total number or amount. verb (totals, totalling, totalled; US spelling totals, totaling, totaled) **1** amount to a total number. **2** find the total of. ■ **totality** noun **totally** adverb.

totalitarian adjective (of a system of government) consisting of only one leader or party and having complete power and control over the people. ■ **totalitarianism** noun.

totalizator or **totalisator** noun **1** a device showing the number of bets and amount of money staked on a race. **2** the system of betting based on this; the tote.

tote¹ noun (the tote) informal a system of betting based on the use of the totalizator, in which winnings are calculated according to the amount staked rather than odds offered.

tote² verb (totes, toting, toted) informal carry.

totem noun a natural object or animal believed to have spiritual meaning and adopted as an emblem. □ **totem pole** a pole on which totems are hung or on which images of totems are carved. ■ **totemic** adjective.

totter verb (totters, tottering, tottered) **1** move in an unsteady way. **2** shake or rock as if about to collapse. noun a tottering walk.

toucan /too-kuhn/ noun a tropical bird with a massive bill and brightly coloured feathers.

touch verb **1** bring your fingers or another part of your body into contact with. **2** come into or be in physical contact with. **3** have an effect on. **4** (be touched) feel moved with gratitude or sympathy because of someone's actions or situation. **5** harm or interfere with. **6** use or consume. **7** (touched) informal mad. noun **1** an act or manner of touching. **2** the ability to become aware of something and learn what it is like

through physical contact, especially with the fingers. **3** a small amount. **4** a distinctive detail or feature. **5** a distinctive or skilful way of dealing with something. □ **in touch 1** in or into communication. **2** possessing up-to-date knowledge. **out of touch** lacking up-to-date knowledge or awareness. **touch-and-go** (of a particular outcome) possible but very uncertain. **touch down** (of an aircraft or spacecraft) land. **touch on** deal briefly with. **touch-type** type using all of your fingers and without needing to look at the keys. **touch up** make small improvements to.

touchdown noun **1** the moment at which an aircraft touches down. **2** (in rugby) an act of scoring by touching the ball down behind the opponents' goal line.

touché /too-shay/ exclamation used to acknowledge a good point made at your own expense.

touching adjective making you feel gratitude or sympathy; moving.

touchline noun (in football) the boundary line on each side of the field.

touchstone noun a standard by which something is judged.

touchy adjective **1** quick to take offence. **2** (of a situation or issue) needing careful treatment.

tough adjective **1** strong enough to withstand wear and tear. **2** able to deal with pain or difficulty. **3** strict. **4** involving problems or difficulties. **5** (of a person) rough or violent. noun informal a rough or violent man. ■ **toughness** noun.

toughen verb make or become tough.

toupee /too-pay/ noun a small wig or hairpiece worn to cover a bald spot.

tour noun **1** a journey for pleasure in which several different places are visited. **2** a short trip to view or inspect something. **3** a series of plays, matches, etc. performed in several different places. verb make a tour of.

tour de force /toor duh forss/ noun

(plural **tours de force** /toor duh **forss**/) a performance or achievement accomplished with great skill.

tourism noun the commercial organization and operation of holidays and visits to places of interest.

tourist noun 1 a person who travels for pleasure. 2 a member of a touring sports team. ■ **touristy** adjective.

tournament noun 1 a series of contests between a number of competitors. 2 a medieval sporting event in which knights jousted with blunted weapons for a prize.

tourney /**toor**-ni, **ter**-ni/ noun (plural **tourneys**) a joust or tournament.

tourniquet /**toor**-ni-kay, **tor**-ni-kay/ noun a cord or tight bandage tied around a limb to stop the flow of blood through an artery.

tousle verb (**tousles, tousling, tousled**) make someone's hair untidy.

tout /towt/ verb 1 try to sell. 2 try to persuade people of something's value. 3 Brit. resell a ticket for a popular event at a higher price than you paid for it. noun a person who buys up tickets for an event to resell them at a profit.

tow verb use a vehicle or boat to pull another vehicle or boat along. noun an act of towing. □ **in tow** (also on tow) being towed. 2 accompanying or following someone.

towards or **toward** preposition 1 in the direction of. 2 getting nearer to. 3 in relation to. 4 contributing to the cost of.

towel noun a piece of absorbent cloth used for drying. verb (**towels, towelling, towelled**; US spelling **towels, toweling, toweled**) dry something with a towel.

towelling (US spelling **toweling**) noun absorbent cloth used for towels.

tower noun 1 a tall, narrow building or part of a building, especially of a church or castle. 2 a tall structure that houses special equipment. 3 a tall structure used as a container or for storage. verb (**towers, towering, towered**) 1 rise to or reach a great

height. 2 (**towering**) very important or influential. 3 (**towering**) very strong: *a towering rage.* □ **tower block** Brit. a tall modern building containing many floors of offices or flats.

town noun 1 a settlement larger than a village and generally smaller than a city. 2 the central part of a town or city containing its shopping area. □ **go to town** informal do something thoroughly or enthusiastically. **on the town** informal out enjoying the nightlife of a city or town. **town crier** (in the past) a person employed to shout out public announcements in the streets. **town hall** the building where local government offices are located. **town planning** the planning and control of the development of a town or other urban area.

township noun (in South Africa) a suburb or city of mainly black occupation.

towpath noun a path beside a river or canal, originally used as a pathway for horses towing barges.

toxic adjective 1 poisonous. 2 relating to or caused by poison. ■ **toxicity** noun.

toxicology noun the branch of science concerned with how poisons work. ■ **toxicologist** noun.

toxin noun a poison caused by a germ, to which the body reacts by producing antibodies.

toy noun 1 an object for a child to play with. 2 a gadget or machine that provides amusement for an adult. verb (**toy with**) 1 fiddle with something carelessly or unenthusiastically. 2 casually consider an idea. adjective (of a breed of dog) very small. □ **toy boy** Brit. informal a male lover who is much younger than his partner.

trace verb (**traces, tracing, traced**) 1 find by careful investigation. 2 find or describe the origin or development of. 3 follow the course or position of with your eye or finger. 4 copy something by drawing over its lines on a piece of transparent paper placed on top of it. 5 draw a pattern or outline.

noun 1 a mark or other sign of the existence or passing of something. **2** a very small amount. **3** a barely noticeable indication. **4** a line or pattern on paper or a screen showing information recorded by a machine. □ **trace element** a chemical element that is present in tiny amounts.

tracer noun a bullet or shell whose course is made visible by a trail of flames or smoke.

tracery noun (plural **traceries**) **1** a pattern of holes and outlines in stone. **2** a delicate branching pattern.

trachea /truh-**kee**-uh/ **noun** (plural **tracheae** /truh-**kee**-ee/ or **tracheas**) the tube carrying air between the larynx and the lungs; the windpipe.

tracheotomy /tra-ki-**ot**-uh-mi/ or **tracheostomy** /tra-ki-**oss**-tuh-mi/ **noun** (plural **tracheotomies**) a surgical incision in the windpipe, made to enable someone to breathe when their windpipe is blocked.

track noun **1** a rough path or small road. **2** a course or circuit for racing. **3** a line of marks left on the ground by a person, animal, or vehicle as it moves along. **4** a continuous line of rails on a railway. **5** a section of a record, compact disc, or cassette tape containing one song or piece of music. **6** a strip or rail along which something may be moved. verb **1** follow the trail or movements of. **2** (**track down**) find after a thorough search. **3** follow a particular course. **4** (of a camera) move along with the subject being filmed. □ **keep** (or **lose**) **track of** keep (or fail to keep) fully aware of or informed about. **on the right** (or **wrong**) **track** following a course that is likely to result in success (or failure). **track events** athletic events that take place on a running track. **track record** someone's past achievements. ■ **tracker** noun.

tracksuit noun an outfit consisting of a sweatshirt and loose trousers.

tract[1] **noun 1** a large area of land. **2** a major passage in the body.

tract[2] **noun** a short piece of religious writing in the form of a pamphlet.

tractable adjective **1** (of a person) easy to control or influence. **2** (of a difficulty) easy to resolve.

traction noun **1** the action of pulling a thing along a surface. **2** the power used in pulling. **3** a way of treating a broken bone by gradually pulling it back into position. **4** the grip of a tyre on a road or a wheel on a rail. □ **traction engine** a steam or diesel-powered road vehicle used for pulling heavy loads.

tractor noun a powerful motor vehicle with large rear wheels, used for pulling farm machinery.

trad adjective informal traditional.

trade noun **1** the buying and selling of goods and services. **2** a particular area of commercial activity. **3** a job requiring special skills and training. verb (**trades**, **trading**, **traded**) **1** (**trade in**) buy and sell goods and services. **2** buy or sell a particular item. **3** exchange. **4** (**trade in**) exchange a used article as part of the payment for another. **5** (**trade on**) take advantage of. **6** (**trade off**) exchange something of value as part of a compromise. □ **trade union** (or Brit. **trades union**) an association formed within an industry or particular workplace to protect the rights of the workers. ■ **trader** noun.

trademark noun **1** a symbol, word, or words chosen to represent a company or product. **2** a distinctive characteristic.

tradesman noun a person who has a small shop, or who goes from house to house to sell goods or services.

tradition noun **1** the passing on of customs or beliefs from generation to generation. **2** a long-established custom or belief passed on in this way. **3** a method or style established by an artist, writer, or movement, and followed by others.

traditional adjective having to do with or following tradition. ■ **traditionally** adverb.

traditionalism noun the upholding of tradition, especially so as to resist change. ■ **traditionalist** noun & adjective.

traduce verb (**traduces, traducing, traduced**) formal say things about someone that are unpleasant or untrue.

traffic noun **1** vehicles moving on public roads. **2** the movement of ships or aircraft. **3** the commercial transportation of goods or passengers. **4** the messages or signals sent through a communications system. **5** the action of trading in something illegal. verb (**traffics, trafficking, trafficked**) deal or trade in something illegal. □ **traffic jam** a congestion in the flow of traffic so that it is at or almost at a standstill. **traffic lights** a set of automatically operated lights for controlling the flow of traffic. **traffic warden** Brit. an official who locates and reports on cars breaking parking regulations. ■ **trafficker** noun.

tragedian /truh-**jee**-di-uhn/ noun **1** a tragic actor. **2** a writer of tragedies.

tragedy noun (plural **tragedies**) **1** a very sad event or situation. **2** a serious play with an unhappy ending.

tragic adjective **1** extremely sad. **2** relating to tragedy in a literary work. ■ **tragically** adverb.

tragicomedy noun (plural **tragicomedies**) a play or novel containing elements of both comedy and tragedy. ■ **tragicomic** adjective.

trail noun **1** a line of marks or signs left behind by someone or something as it moves along. **2** a track or scent used in following someone or hunting an animal. **3** a long thin part stretching behind or hanging down from something. **4** a beaten path through rough country. **5** a route planned or followed for a particular purpose. verb **1** draw or be drawn along behind. **2** follow the trail of. **3** walk or move slowly or wearily. **4** (**trail away** or **off**) become gradually quieter and then stop. **5** be losing to an opponent in a contest. **6** (of a plant) grow along the ground or so as to hang down.

trailblazer noun **1** a person who finds a new way through wild country. **2** a person who is the first to do some-

thing new. ■ **trailblazing** adjective.

trailer noun **1** an unpowered vehicle pulled by another. **2** the rear section of an articulated truck. **3** N. Amer. a caravan. **4** an extract from a film or programme used to advertise it.

train verb **1** teach a person or animal a particular skill or type of behaviour. **2** be taught a particular skill. **3** make or become physically fit through a course of exercise. **4** (**train on**) point something at. **5** make a plant grow in a particular direction or into a required shape. noun **1** a series of railway carriages or wagons moved by a locomotive. **2** a number of vehicles or pack animals moving in a line. **3** a series of connected events, thoughts, etc. **4** a long piece of trailing material attached to the back of a formal dress or robe. □ **in train** in progress.

trainee noun a person undergoing training for a job or profession.

trainer noun **1** a person who trains people or animals. **2** Brit. a soft shoe for sports or casual wear.

trainspotter noun Brit. a person who collects locomotive numbers as a hobby. ■ **trainspotting** noun.

traipse verb (**traipses, traipsing, traipsed**) walk or move wearily or reluctantly. noun a tedious walk.

trait /tray, trayt/ noun a distinguishing quality or characteristic.

traitor noun a person who betrays their country, an organization, or a cause. ■ **traitorous** adjective.

trajectory noun (plural **trajectories**) the path followed by a moving object.

tram or **tramcar** noun Brit. a passenger vehicle powered by electricity and running on rails laid in a road.

tramlines plural noun Brit. rails for a tram.

trammel noun (**trammels**) literary curbs to someone's freedom; restrictions. verb (**trammels, trammelling, trammelled**, US spelling **trammels, trammeling, trammeled**) restrict or limit.

tramp verb **1** walk heavily or noisily.

2 walk over a long distance. noun **1** a homeless person who travels around and lives by begging or doing casual work. **2** the sound of heavy steps. **3** a long walk. **4** N. Amer. informal a woman who has many sexual partners.

trample verb (**tramples, trampling, trampled**) **1** tread on and crush. **2** (**trample on** or **over**) treat with contempt.

trampoline noun a strong fabric sheet connected by springs to a frame, used as a springboard and landing area in doing acrobatic or gymnastic exercises. ■ **trampolining** noun.

trance noun a half-conscious state in which someone does not respond to things happening around them.

tranche /rhymes with branch/ noun a portion, especially of money.

tranquil adjective free from disturbance; calm. ■ **tranquillity** (or **tranquility**) noun **tranquilly** adverb.

tranquillize or **tranquillise** (US spelling **tranquilize**) verb (**tranquillizes, tranquillizing, tranquillized**) give a calming or sedative drug to.

tranquillizer or **tranquilliser** (US spelling **tranquilizer**) noun a drug taken to reduce tension or anxiety.

transact verb conduct or carry out business.

transaction noun **1** an instance of buying or selling. **2** the action of conducting business.

transatlantic adjective **1** crossing the Atlantic. **2** concerning countries on either side of the Atlantic.

transcend verb **1** be or go beyond the range or limits of. **2** be superior to.

transcendent adjective **1** going beyond normal or physical human experience. **2** (of God) existing apart from the material world. ■ **transcendence** noun.

transcendental adjective going beyond the limits of human knowledge in a religious or spiritual context. ■ **transcendentally** adverb.

transcontinental adjective crossing or extending across a continent or continents.

transcribe verb (**transcribes, transcribing, transcribed**) **1** put thoughts, speech, or data into written form, or into a different written form. **2** arrange a piece of music for a different instrument or voice.

transcript noun a written or printed version of material that was originally spoken or presented in another form.

transcription noun **1** a transcript. **2** the process of transcribing. **3** a transcribed piece of music.

transept noun (in a cross-shaped church) either of the two parts extending at right angles from the nave.

transfer verb (**transfers, transferring, transferred**) **1** move someone or something from one place to another. **2** move to another department, job, etc. **3** change to another place, route, or means of transport during a journey. **4** pass a property, right, or responsibility to another person. noun **1** an act of transferring. **2** Brit. a small coloured picture or design on paper, which can be transferred to another surface by being pressed or heated. ■ **transference** noun.

transfigure verb (**transfigures, transfiguring, transfigured**) (**be transfigured**) be transformed into something more beautiful or spiritual. ■ **transfiguration** noun.

transfix verb **1** make motionless with horror, wonder, or astonishment. **2** pierce with a sharp object.

transform verb **1** change or be changed in nature, form, or appearance. **2** change the voltage of an electric current. ■ **transformation** noun.

transformer noun a device for changing the voltage of an electric current.

transfusion noun a medical process in which someone is given a supply of someone's else's blood.

transgress verb go beyond the limits set by a law or accepted standard. ■ **transgression** noun **transgressive**

adjective **transgressor** noun.

transient adjective **1** lasting only for a short time. **2** staying or working in a place for a short time only. noun a transient person. ■ **transience** noun **transiently** adverb.

transistor noun **1** a silicon-based device which is able to amplify or rectify electric currents. **2** (also **transistor radio**) a portable radio using circuits containing transistors.

transit noun **1** the carrying of people or things from one place to another. **2** an act of passing through or across a place.

transition noun **1** the process of changing from one state or condition to another. **2** a period of such change. ■ **transitional** adjective.

transitive adjective (of a verb) able to take a direct object, e.g. *saw* in *he saw the donkey*. ■ **transitivity** noun.

transitory adjective lasting for only a short time.

translate verb (translates, translating, translated) **1** express the sense of words or text in another language. **2** (translate into) convert or be converted into another form or medium.

translation noun **1** the action of translating. **2** a text or word that is translated.

translator noun a person who translates from one language into another.

transliterate verb (transliterates, transliterating, transliterated) write a letter or word using the corresponding letters of a different alphabet or language. ■ **transliteration** noun.

translucent adjective allowing light to pass through partially; semi-transparent. ■ **translucence** (or **translucency**) noun.

transmission noun **1** the passing of something from one place or person to another. **2** a transmitted programme or signal. **3** the mechanism by which power is passed from an engine to the axle in a motor vehicle.

transmit verb (transmits, transmitting, transmitted) **1** cause to pass from one place or person to another. **2** broadcast or send out an electrical signal or a radio or television programme. **3** allow heat, light, etc. to pass through a material.

transmitter noun a device used to produce and transmit electromagnetic waves carrying messages or signals, especially those of radio or television.

transmogrify verb (transmogrifies, transmogrifying, transmogrified) humorous change into something else.

transmute verb (transmutes, transmuting, transmuted) change in form, nature, or substance. ■ **transmutation** noun.

transom noun **1** the flat surface forming the stern of a boat. **2** a strengthening crossbar.

transparency noun (plural transparencies) **1** the condition of being transparent. **2** a positive transparent photograph printed on plastic or glass, and viewed using a slide projector.

transparent adjective **1** allowing light to pass through so that objects behind can be distinctly seen. **2** obvious or evident. ■ **transparently** adverb.

transpire verb (transpires, transpiring, transpired) **1** come to be true. **2** take place; happen. **3** (of a plant or leaf) give off water vapour through pores in the surface layer. ■ **transpiration** noun.

transplant verb **1** transfer to another place or situation. **2** take living tissue or an organ and implant it in another part of the body or in another body. noun **1** an operation in which an organ or tissue is transplanted. **2** a person or thing that has been transplanted. ■ **transplantation** noun.

transport verb **1** carry people or goods from one place to another by means of a vehicle, aircraft, or ship. **2** (be transported) be overwhelmed with a strong emotion. **3** (in the past) send someone to a distant place as a punishment. noun **1** a system or method of carrying people or goods from one place to another. **2** the action of transporting. **3** a large vehicle, ship, or aircraft for carrying troops or stores. **4** (transports) overwhelmingly strong emotions. ■ **transportation** noun **transporter** noun.

transpose verb (transposes, transposing, transposed) **1** cause two or more things to change places with each other. **2** move something to a different place or context. **3** write or play music in a different key from the original. ■ **transposition** noun.

transsexual or **transexual** noun a person who emotionally and psychologically feels that they belong to the opposite sex.

transubstantiation noun (in Christian thinking) the doctrine that the bread and wine served in the Eucharist become the actual body and blood of Jesus after they have been blessed.

transverse adjective placed or extending across something. ■ **transversely** adverb.

transvestite noun a person who likes to dress in clothes worn by the opposite sex. ■ **transvestism** noun.

trap noun **1** a device, pit, or enclosure designed to catch and hold animals. **2** an unpleasant situation from which you cannot escape. **3** a trick causing someone to say or do something which they do not intend. **4** a container or device used to collect a specified thing. **5** a light, two-wheeled carriage pulled by a horse or pony. verb (traps, trapping, trapped) **1** catch and hold in a trap. **2** trick into doing something.

trapdoor noun a hinged or removable panel in a floor, ceiling, or roof.

trapeze noun a horizontal bar hanging on two ropes high above the ground, used by acrobats in a circus.

trapezium noun (plural trapezia or trapeziums) (in geometry) a quadrilateral with one pair of sides parallel.

trapper noun a person who traps wild animals.

trappings plural noun **1** the signs or objects associated with a particular situation or role. **2** a horse's ornamental harness.

Trappist noun a monk belonging to an order that takes a vow of silence.

trash noun **1** N. Amer. waste material. **2** poor-quality writing, art, etc. **3** N. Amer. a person or people of very low social status. verb informal wreck or destroy. □ **trash can** N. Amer. a dustbin. ■ **trashy** adjective.

trauma /traw-muh, trow-muh/ noun (plural traumas) **1** a deeply disturbing experience. **2** (in medicine) physical injury. **3** emotional shock following a stressful event. ■ **traumatic** adjective.

traumatize or **traumatise** verb (be traumatized) suffer lasting shock as a result of a disturbing experience or injury.

travail or **travails** noun old use painful or laborious effort.

travel verb (travels, travelling, travelled; US spelling travels, traveling, traveled) **1** go from one place to another, especially over a long distance. **2** journey along a particular road or through a particular region. noun **1** the action of travelling. **2** (travels) journeys over a long distance. □ **travel agent** a person or agency that makes the necessary arrangements for travellers.

traveller (US spelling traveler) noun **1** a person who is travelling or who often travels. **2** a gypsy. □ **traveller's cheque** a cheque for a fixed amount that can be exchanged for cash in foreign countries.

travelogue noun a film, book, or talk about a person's travels.

traverse verb (traverses, traversing, traversed) travel or extend across or through.

travesty noun (plural travesties) an absurd or shocking misrepresentation.

trawl verb **1** catch fish with a trawl net or seine. **2** search through something thoroughly. noun **1** an act of trawling. **2** a large wide-mouthed fishing net dragged by a boat along the bottom of the sea.

trawler noun a fishing boat used for trawling.

tray noun a flat container with a raised rim, used for carrying plates, cups, etc.

treacherous adjective **1** guilty of or involving betrayal. **2** having hidden or unpredictable dangers. ■ **treacherously** adverb **treachery** noun.

treacle noun Brit. **1** molasses. **2** golden syrup. ■ **treacly** adjective.

tread verb (**treads**, **treading**, **trod**; past participle **trodden** or **trod**) **1** walk in a specified way. **2** press down or crush with your feet. **3** walk on or along. noun **1** a manner or the sound of walking. **2** the top surface of a step or stair. **3** the part of a vehicle tyre that grips the road. **4** the part of the sole of a shoe that touches the ground. □ **tread water** stay in an upright position in deep water by moving the feet with a walking movement.

treadle noun a lever which you work with your foot to operate a machine.

treadmill noun **1** a large wheel turned by the weight of people or animals treading on steps fitted into it, used in the past to drive machinery. **2** a device used for exercise consisting of a continuous moving belt on which you walk or run. **3** a job or situation that is tiring or boring.

treason or **high treason** noun the crime of betraying your country. ■ **treasonable** adjective.

treasure noun **1** a quantity of precious coins, gems, or other valuable objects. **2** a very valuable object. **3** informal a much loved or highly valued person. verb (**treasures**, **treasuring**, **treasured**) **1** look after carefully. **2** value highly. □ **treasure hunt** a game in which players search for hidden objects by following a trail of clues. **treasure trove** valuables found hidden, whose owner is unknown.

treasurer noun a person appointed to manage the finances of a society, company, etc.

treasury noun (plural **treasuries**) **1** the funds or revenue of a state, institution, or society. **2** (**Treasury**) (in some countries) the government department responsible for the overall management of the economy.

treat verb **1** behave towards or deal with in a certain way. **2** give medical care or attention to. **3** apply a process or a substance to. **4** present or discuss a subject. **5** (**treat to**) provide with food, drink, or entertainment that you have paid for. **6** (**treat yourself**) do or have something very pleasurable. noun a gift or event that gives someone great pleasure.

treatise /tree-tiss/ noun a formal piece of writing on a subject.

treatment noun **1** a way of behaving towards someone or dealing with something. **2** medical care for an illness or injury. **3** the use of a substance or process to preserve or give particular properties to something. **4** the presentation or discussion of a subject.

treaty noun (plural **treaties**) a formal agreement between states.

treble¹ adjective **1** consisting of three parts. **2** multiplied or occurring three times. pronoun an amount which is three times as large as usual. verb (**trebles**, **trebling**, **trebled**) make or become treble.

treble² noun **1** a high-pitched voice, especially a boy's singing voice. **2** the high-frequency output of a radio or audio system. □ **treble clef** (in music) a clef placing G above middle C on the second-lowest line of the stave.

tree noun a woody plant consisting of a main stem and a number of branches, that can grow to a considerable height and live for many years. □ **tree diagram** a diagram with a structure of branching lines. **tree house** a structure built in the branches of a tree for children to play in.

treeline noun a height up a mountain above which trees do not grow.

trefoil noun **1** a small plant with yellow flowers and clover-like leaves. **2** a shape or design in the form of three rounded lobes like a clover leaf.

trek noun a long difficult journey, especially one made on foot. **verb** (**treks**, **trekking**, **trekked**) go on a trek. ■ **trekker** noun.

trellis noun a framework of bars used as a support for climbing plants.

tremble verb (**trembles**, **trembling**, **trembled**) **1** shake in a way that you cannot control, usually as a result of fear, excitement, or weakness. **2** be in a state of great worry or fear. **3** (of something light, such as a leaf) shake slightly. noun a trembling feeling, movement, or sound.

tremendous adjective **1** very great in amount, scale, or intensity. **2** informal extremely good or impressive. ■ **tremendously** adverb.

tremolo noun (plural **tremolos**) a wavering effect in singing or created in certain musical instruments.

tremor noun **1** a quivering movement that cannot be controlled. **2** (also **earth tremor**) a slight earthquake. **3** a sudden feeling of fear or excitement.

tremulous adjective **1** shaking or quivering slightly. **2** nervous.

trench noun **1** a long, narrow ditch. **2** a ditch dug by troops to provide shelter from enemy fire. **3** (also **ocean trench**) a long, deep depression in the ocean bed. □ **trench coat** a belted, double-breasted raincoat.

trenchant adjective (of something said or written) expressed strongly and clearly. ■ **trenchantly** adverb.

trencher noun (in the past) a flat piece of wood from which food was served or eaten.

trend noun **1** a general direction in which something is developing or changing. **2** a fashion.

trendsetter noun a person who leads the way in fashion or ideas.

trendy adjective (**trendier**, **trendiest**) informal very fashionable or up to date.

trepan /tri-pan/ noun (in the past) a saw used by surgeons for making

holes in the skull. **verb** (**trepans**, **trepanning**, **trepanned**) make holes in a person's skull with a trepan.

trepidation noun a feeling of fear or nervousness.

trespass verb **1** enter someone's land or property without their permission. **2** (**trespass on**) make unfair use of someone's time, help, etc. **3** (**trespass against**) old use do wrong or harm to. noun **1** Law the entering of someone's land or property without their permission. **2** old use a bad or wrongful act. ■ **trespasser** noun.

tress noun literary a long lock of hair.

trestle noun a structure consisting of a horizontal bar on sloping legs, used in pairs to support a surface such as a table top.

triad noun a group of three people or things.

trial noun **1** a formal examination in a court of law to decide if someone is guilty of a crime. **2** a test of performance, qualities, or suitability. **3** (**trials**) an event in which horses or dogs compete or perform. **4** something that tests a person's endurance or patience. **verb** (**trials**, **trialling**, **trialled**; US spelling **trials**, **trialing**, **trialed**) test something to assess its suitability or performance. □ **on trial 1** being tried in a court of law. **2** undergoing tests. **trial and error** the process of trying out various methods until you find one that works well.

triangle noun **1** a figure with three straight sides and three angles. **2** a musical instrument consisting of a steel rod bent into a triangle, sounded with a rod. **3** an emotional relationship involving a couple and a third person. ■ **triangular** adjective.

triangulation noun the division of an area into a series of triangles in order to determine distances and relative positions.

triathlon noun an athletic contest involving three different events, typically swimming, cycling, and long-distance running. ■ **triathlete** noun.

tribalism noun behaviour and attitudes that result from a system in which people belong to tribes.

tribe noun **1** a group of people within a traditional society sharing customs and beliefs and led by a chief. **2 (tribes)** informal large numbers of people. ∎ **tribal** adjective.

tribesman noun a member of a tribe in a traditional society.

tribulation noun trouble, suffering, or difficulty.

tribunal noun **1** Brit. a group of people established to settle disputes. **2** a court of justice.

tribune noun (in ancient Rome) an official chosen by the ordinary people to protect their interests.

tributary noun (plural **tributaries**) a river or stream that flows into a larger river or lake.

tribute noun **1** an act, statement, or gift intended to show respect or admiration for someone. **2** a thing that indicates the value of something. **3** historical payment made by a state to a more powerful one.

trice noun **(in a trice)** in a moment.

tricentenary noun (plural **tricentenaries**) a three-hundredth anniversary.

triceps /**try**-seps/ noun (plural **triceps**) the large muscle at the back of the upper arm.

triceratops /try-**se**-ruh-tops/ noun a large plant-eating dinosaur with two large horns.

trichology /tri-**kol**-uh-ji/ noun the branch of medicine concerned with the hair and scalp. ∎ **trichologist** noun.

trick noun **1** something intended to deceive or outwit someone. **2** a skilful act performed to entertain people. **3** an illusion. **4** a habit or mannerism. **5** (in card games) a single round of play. verb deceive or outwit with cunning or skill. ∎ **trickery** noun.

trickle verb (**trickles, trickling, trickled**) **1** (of a liquid) flow in a small stream. **2** come or go slowly or gradually. noun **1** a small flow of liquid. **2** a small number of people or things moving slowly.

trickster noun a person who cheats or deceives people.

tricksy adjective clever or mischievous.

tricky adjective (**trickier, trickiest**) **1** difficult or awkward. **2** crafty or deceitful.

tricolour /**tri**-kuh-ler/ (US spelling **tricolor**) noun a flag with three bands of different colours, especially the French national flag.

tricycle noun a vehicle similar to a bicycle but having three wheels.

trident noun a three-pronged spear.

tried past and past participle of **TRY**.

triennial adjective lasting for or happening every three years.

trier noun a person who always tries hard.

trifle noun **1** something of little value or importance. **2** a small amount. **3** Brit. a cold dessert of sponge cake and fruit with layers of custard, jelly, and cream. verb (**trifles, trifling, trifled**) (**trifle with**) treat without seriousness or respect.

trifling adjective unimportant; trivial.

trigger noun **1** a small lever that sets off a gun or other mechanism when pulled. **2** an event that causes something to happen. verb (**triggers, triggering, triggered**) **1** cause a device to function. **2** make something happen. □ **trigger-happy** tending to fire a gun on the slightest provocation.

trigonometry noun the branch of mathematics concerned with the relationships between the sides and angles of triangles.

trilby noun (plural **trilbies**) Brit. a man's soft felt hat with a narrow brim.

trill noun a high warbling sound. verb make a high warbling sound.

trillion cardinal number **1** a million million (1,000,000,000,000 or 10^{12}). **2** Brit. dated a million million million (1,000,000,000,000,000,000 or 10^{18}). ∎ **trillionth** ordinal number.

trilobite /**try**-luh-byt/ noun a fossil

sea creature with a rear part divided into segments.

trilogy noun (plural **trilogies**) a group of three related novels, plays, or films.

trim verb (**trims, trimming, trimmed**) **1** cut away unwanted parts from something. **2** reduce the size, amount, or number of. **3** decorate something along its edges. **4** adjust a sail. noun **1** decoration along the edges of something. **2** the upholstery or interior lining of a car. **3** an act of trimming. **4** good condition. adjective (**trimmer, trimmest**) neat and smart. □ **in trim** slim and fit.

trimaran /try-muh-ran/ noun a yacht with three hulls side by side.

trimming noun **1** (**trimmings**) small pieces trimmed off. **2** decoration or accompaniment.

trinity noun (plural **trinities**) **1** (**the Trinity** or **the Holy Trinity**) (in Christian belief) the three persons (Father, Son, and Holy Spirit) that make up God. **2** a group of three people or things.

trinket noun a small inexpensive ornament or item of jewellery.

trio noun (plural **trios**) **1** a set or group of three. **2** a group of three musicians.

trip verb (**trips, tripping, tripped**) **1** catch your foot on something and stumble or fall. **2** (**trip up**) make a mistake. **3** walk, run, or dance with quick, light steps. **4** activate a mechanism. **5** informal experience hallucinations as a result of taking a drug such as LSD. noun **1** a journey or excursion. **2** an instance of tripping or falling. **3** informal a period of hallucinations caused by taking a drug. **4** a device that trips a mechanism. □ **trip the light fantastic** humorous dance.

tripartite adjective **1** consisting of three parts. **2** shared by or involving three parties.

tripe noun **1** the stomach of a cow or sheep used as food. **2** informal nonsense.

triplane noun an early type of aircraft with three pairs of wings, one above the other.

triple adjective **1** consisting of three parts, things, or people. **2** having three times the usual size, quality, or strength. noun a thing that is three times as large as usual or is made up of three parts. verb (**triples, tripling, tripled**) make or become triple. □ **triple jump** an athletic event in which competitors perform a hop, a step, and a jump from a running start. ∎ **triply** adverb.

triplet noun **1** each of three children born at the same birth. **2** a group of three musical notes to be performed in the time of two or four.

triplicate adjective /**trip**-li-kuht/ existing in three copies or examples. verb /**trip**-li-kayt/ (**triplicates, triplicating, triplicated**) **1** make three copies of. **2** multiply by three.

tripod noun a three-legged stand for a camera or other apparatus.

tripper noun Brit. informal a person who goes on a pleasure trip.

triptych /**trip**-tik/ noun a picture or carving on three panels.

tripwire noun a wire that is stretched close to the ground and sets off a trap or alarm when disturbed.

trite adjective (of a remark or idea) unoriginal and dull.

triumph noun **1** a great victory or achievement. **2** the state of being victorious or successful. **3** joy or satisfaction resulting from a success or victory. **4** a highly successful example. verb achieve a triumph. ∎ **triumphal** adjective.

triumphant adjective **1** having won a battle or contest. **2** joyful after a victory or achievement. ∎ **triumphantly** adverb.

triumvirate /try-**um**-vi-ruht/ noun a group of three powerful or important people or things.

trivet noun an iron stand for a cooking pot or kettle.

trivia plural noun unimportant details or pieces of information.

trivial adjective of little value or importance. ∎ **triviality** noun (plural **trivialities**) **trivially** adverb.

trivialize or **trivialise** verb (trivializes, trivializing, trivialized) make something seem less important or complex than it really is. ∎ **trivialization** noun.

trod past and past participle of **TREAD**.

trodden past participle of **TREAD**.

troglodyte noun a person who lives in a cave.

troika noun **1** a Russian vehicle pulled by a team of three horses side by side. **2** a group of three people working together.

Trojan noun an inhabitant of ancient Troy in Asia Minor. adjective relating to Troy. ◻ **Trojan Horse** something intended to weaken or defeat an enemy secretly. **work like a Trojan** work extremely hard.

troll[1] noun (in stories) an ugly giant or dwarf.

troll[2] verb fish by trailing a baited line along behind a boat.

trolley noun (plural **trolleys**) **1** Brit. a large metal basket with wheels, for transporting heavy or bulky items. **2** a small table on wheels. ◻ **off your trolley** Brit. informal mad.

trolleybus noun a bus powered by electricity obtained from overhead wires.

trollop noun dated or humorous a woman who has many sexual partners.

trombone noun a large brass wind instrument with a sliding tube which you move to produce different notes. ∎ **trombonist** noun.

troop noun **1** (**troops**) soldiers or armed forces. **2** a unit of troops. **3** a group of people or animals. verb come or go as a group.

trooper noun **1** a soldier in a cavalry or armoured unit. **2** US a state police officer.

trophy noun (plural **trophies**) **1** a cup or other object awarded as a prize. **2** a souvenir of an achievement.

tropic noun **1** the line of latitude 23°26′ north (**tropic of Cancer**) or south (**tropic of Capricorn**) of the equator. **2** (**the tropics**) the region between the tropics of Cancer and Capricorn.

tropical adjective **1** having to do with the tropics. **2** very hot and humid. ∎ **tropically** adverb.

trot verb (**trots, trotting, trotted**) **1** (of a horse) proceed at a pace faster than a walk. **2** run at a moderate pace with short steps. **3** (**trot out**) informal produce an account that has been produced many times before. noun **1** a trotting pace. **2** a period of trotting. ◻ **on the trot** Brit. informal one after another.

troth noun (**pledge** or **plight your troth**) old use promise to marry.

trotter noun a pig's foot.

troubadour /**troo**-buh-dor/ noun a travelling singer and poet in medieval France.

trouble noun **1** difficulty or problems. **2** effort that you make to do something. **3** a cause of worry or inconvenience. **4** a situation in which you can be punished or blamed. **5** public unrest or disorder. verb (**troubles, troubling, troubled**) **1** cause distress or inconvenience to. **2** (**troubled**) feeling anxious or experiencing problems. **3** (**trouble to do**) make the effort required to do.

troublemaker noun a person who regularly causes trouble.

troubleshooter noun a person who investigates and solves problems or faults. ∎ **troubleshooting** noun.

troublesome adjective causing difficulty or problems.

trough noun **1** a long, narrow open container for animals to eat or drink out of. **2** (in weather forecasting) a long region of low atmospheric pressure. **3** a point of low activity or achievement.

trounce verb (**trounces, trouncing, trounced**) defeat heavily.

troupe noun a touring group of entertainers.

trouper noun **1** an entertainer with long experience. **2** a reliable and uncomplaining person.

trousers plural noun an outer garment that covers the body from the waist down and has a separate part for each leg.

trousseau /troo-soh/ noun (plural **trousseaux** or **trousseaus** /troo-sohz/) clothes and other belongings collected by a bride for her marriage.

trout noun (plural **trout** or **trouts**) an edible fish of the salmon family.

trove noun a store of valuable things.

trowel noun **1** a small tool with a curved scoop for lifting plants or earth. **2** a small tool with a flat blade for applying mortar or plaster.

troy noun a system of weights used mainly for precious metals and gems, with a pound of 12 ounces.

truant noun a pupil who stays away from school without permission or explanation. adjective wandering; straying. verb (also **play truant**) stay away from school without permission or explanation. ■ **truancy** noun.

truce noun an agreement between enemies to stop fighting for a certain time.

truck[1] noun **1** a large road vehicle for carrying goods. **2** Brit. an open railway vehicle for carrying goods. ■ **trucker** noun.

truck[2] noun (**have no truck with**) wish to have no dealings with.

truculent /truk-yuu-luhnt/ adjective quick to argue or fight. ■ **truculence** noun **truculently** adverb.

trudge verb (**trudges**, **trudging**, **trudged**) walk slowly and with heavy steps. noun a difficult or long and tiring walk.

true adjective (**truer**, **truest**) **1** in accordance with fact or reality. **2** rightly so called. **3** real or actual. **4** accurate and exact. **5** upright or level. **6** loyal or faithful. **7** (**true to**) in keeping with what is usual or expected. ■ **truly** adverb.

truffle noun **1** an underground fungus that is eaten as a delicacy. **2** a soft chocolate sweet.

trug noun Brit. a wooden basket for carrying flowers, fruit, and vegetables.

truism noun a statement that is obviously true and says nothing new or interesting.

trump noun (in card games) a card of the suit chosen to rank above the others. verb **1** play a trump on a card of another suit. **2** beat by saying or doing something better. **3** (**trump up**) invent a false accusation or excuse. □ **come** (or **turn**) **up trumps** Brit. informal **1** unexpectedly do very well. **2** be especially generous or helpful.

trumpery adjective old use showy but worthless.

trumpet noun **1** a brass musical instrument with a flared end. **2** the loud cry of an elephant. verb (**trumpets**, **trumpeting**, **trumpeted**) **1** play a trumpet. **2** (of an elephant) make its characteristic loud cry. **3** proclaim widely or loudly. □ **blow your own trumpet** talk boastfully about your achievements. ■ **trumpeter** noun.

truncate verb (**truncates**, **truncating**, **truncated**) shorten by cutting off the top or end. ■ **truncation** noun.

truncheon noun Brit. a short, thick stick carried as a weapon by a police officer.

trundle verb (**trundles**, **trundling**, **trundled**) move or roll slowly and unevenly.

trunk noun **1** the main woody stem of a tree. **2** a person's or animal's body apart from the limbs and head. **3** the long nose of an elephant. **4** a large box for storing or transporting articles. **5** N. Amer. the boot of a car. □ **trunk call** Brit. dated a long-distance telephone call. **trunk road** an important main road.

trunks plural noun men's shorts worn for swimming or boxing.

truss noun **1** a framework which supports a roof, bridge, or other structure. **2** a padded belt worn to support a hernia. verb **1** bind or tie up tightly. **2** tie up the wings and legs of a bird before cooking.

trust noun **1** firm belief in the truth,

reliability, or ability of someone or something. **2** responsibility for someone or something. **3** an arrangement by which someone manages property for the benefit of others. **4** an organization or company managed by trustees. **verb 1** have trust in. **2 (trust with)** allow someone to have, use, or look after. **3 (trust to)** commit someone or something to be looked after by. **4 (trust to)** rely on luck, fate, etc. **5** have confidence; hope. □ **trust fund** a fund of money or property that is held for someone by a trust.

trustee noun a person who is given legal powers to manage property for the benefit of others.

trustful adjective having total trust in someone. ■ **trustfully** adverb.

trusting adjective tending to trust others; not suspicious. ■ **trustingly** adverb.

trustworthy adjective honest and reliable. ■ **trustworthiness** noun.

trusty adjective (trustier, trustiest) old use or humorous reliable or faithful.

truth noun (plural **truths**) **1** the quality or state of being true. **2** true facts. **3** a fact or belief that is accepted as true.

truthful adjective 1 telling or expressing the truth. **2** accurate; true to life. ■ **truthfully** adverb **truthfulness** noun.

try verb (tries, trying, tried) 1 make an attempt to do something. **2** (also **try out**) test something new or different. **3** attempt to open a door. **4 (try on)** put on an item of clothing to see if it fits or looks good. **5** make severe demands on. **6** put someone on trial. **noun** (plural **tries**) **1** an attempt. **2** an act of testing something new or different. **3** Rugby an act of touching the ball down behind the opposing goal line to score points.

| ℹ | when writing, it is better to use **try to** rather than **try and** (we should try to help them rather than we should try and help them). |

trying adjective difficult or annoying.

tryst /trist/ **noun** literary a private, romantic meeting between lovers.

tsar, czar, or **tzar** /zar/ **noun** an emperor of Russia before 1917. ■ **tsarist** adjective.

tsetse fly /tset-si/ **noun** an African bloodsucking fly which transmits diseases.

tsp abbreviation teaspoonful.

tsunami /tsoo-**nah**-mi/ **noun** a tidal wave caused by an earthquake or other disturbance.

tub noun 1 a low, wide, open container with a flat bottom. **2** a small plastic or cardboard container for food. **3** informal a small boat that handles awkwardly. □ **tub-thumping** informal loud, aggressive expression of opinions.

tuba noun a large low-pitched brass wind instrument.

tubby adjective (tubbier, tubbiest) informal (of a person) short and rather fat.

tube noun 1 a long, hollow cylinder for conveying or holding something. **2** a flexible container sealed at one end and having a cap at the other. **3 (the tube)** Brit. informal the underground railway system in London.

tuber noun a thick underground part of the stem or root of some plants, from which new plants grow.

tubercular adjective relating to, or affected with, tuberculosis.

tuberculosis /tyuu-ber-kyuu-**loh**-siss/ **noun** a serious infectious disease in which small swellings (**tubercles**) appear, especially in the lungs.

tubular adjective 1 long, round, and hollow like a tube. **2** made from a tube or tubes.

TUC abbreviation Trades Union Congress.

tuck verb 1 push, fold, or turn between two surfaces. **2** put neatly into a small space. **3 (tuck in** or **up)** settle someone in bed by pulling the edges of the bedclothes under the mattress. **4 (tuck in** or **into)** informal eat food heartily. **noun 1** a flattened, stitched fold in a garment or material. **2** Brit. informal, dated food eaten by children at school as a snack.

tucker noun Austral./NZ informal food.

Tudor adjective relating to the royal family which ruled England 1485–1603.

Tuesday noun the day of the week before Wednesday and following Monday.

tufa noun **1** rock formed as a deposit from mineral springs. **2** rock formed from volcanic ash.

tuffet noun **1** a tuft or clump. **2** a footstool or low seat.

tuft noun a bunch of threads, grass, or hair held or growing together at the base. ■ **tufted** adjective **tufty** adjective.

tug verb (**tugs, tugging, tugged**) pull hard or suddenly. noun **1** a hard or sudden pull. **2** (also **tugboat**) a small, powerful boat for towing larger boats and ships. □ **tug of war** a contest in which two teams pull at opposite ends of a rope.

tuition noun teaching or instruction.

tulip noun a plant with boldly coloured cup-shaped flowers.

tulle /tyool/ noun a soft, fine net material, used for making veils and dresses.

tumble verb (**tumbles, tumbling, tumbled**) **1** fall suddenly or clumsily. **2** move in a headlong way. **3** decrease rapidly in amount or value. noun **1** a sudden or clumsy fall. **2** an untidy or confused arrangement. □ **tumble-dryer** a machine that dries washed clothes by turning them in hot air inside a revolving drum.

tumbledown adjective (of a building) ruined or ramshackle.

tumbler noun **1** a drinking glass with straight sides and no handle or stem. **2** an acrobat. **3** a part of a lock that holds the bolt until lifted by a key.

tumbril noun an open cart of a kind used to take prisoners to the guillotine during the French Revolution.

tumescent /tyuu-mess-uhnt/ adjective swollen or becoming swollen.

tumid adjective (of a part of the body) swollen.

tummy noun (plural **tummies**) informal a person's stomach or abdomen.

□ **tummy button** the navel.

tumour (US spelling **tumor**) noun an abnormal growth of tissue in the body.

tumult noun **1** a loud, confused noise. **2** confusion or disorder.

tumultuous /tyuu-**mul**-tyuu-uhss/ adjective **1** very loud or uproarious. **2** excited, confused, or disorderly.

tumulus /**tyoo**-myuu-luhss/ noun (plural **tumuli** /**tyoo**-myuu-ly/) an ancient burial mound.

tun noun a large beer or wine cask.

tuna noun (plural **tuna** or **tunas**) a large edible fish of warm seas.

tundra noun the vast, flat, treeless regions of Europe, Asia, and North America in which the soil under the surface is permanently frozen.

tune noun **1** a sequence of notes that form a piece of music; a melody. **2** correct musical pitch. verb (**tunes, tuning, tuned**) **1** adjust a musical instrument to the correct pitch. **2** adjust a radio or television to a particular frequency. **3** adjust an engine so that it runs smoothly and efficiently. **4** adjust or adapt to a purpose or situation. □ **tuning fork** a two-pronged steel device which produces a specific note when hit against a surface.

tuneful adjective having a pleasing tune. ■ **tunefully** adverb.

tuneless adjective not having a pleasing tune. ■ **tunelessly** adverb.

tuner noun **1** a person or device that tunes musical instruments. **2** a part of a stereo system that receives radio broadcasts.

tungsten noun a hard grey metal used to make electric light filaments.

tunic noun **1** a loose sleeveless garment reaching to the thigh or knees. **2** a close-fitting short coat worn as part of a uniform.

tunnel noun a passage built underground for a road or railway or by a burrowing animal. verb (**tunnels, tunnelling, tunnelled**; US spelling **tunnels, tunneling, tunneled**) dig a tunnel. □ **tunnel vision 1** a condition in which things cannot be seen properly if they are not straight ahead. **2** informal the tendency to focus only on a single situation or aspect.

tunny noun (plural **tunny** or **tunnies**) a tuna.

tuppence ⇒ **TWOPENCE**.

turban noun a long length of material worn wound round the head by Muslim and Sikh men. ■ **turbaned** (or **turbanned**) adjective.

turbid adjective (of a liquid) cloudy or muddy; not clear.

turbine noun a machine in which a wheel or rotor is made to revolve by a fast-moving flow of water, air, etc.

turbo = **TURBOCHARGER**.

turbocharger noun a supercharger driven by a turbine powered by the engine's exhaust gases. ■ **turbocharged** adjective.

turbofan noun a jet engine in which a turbine-driven fan provides additional thrust.

turbojet noun a jet engine in which the exhaust gases also operate a device for compressing the air drawn into the engine.

turboprop noun a jet engine in which a turbine is used to drive a propeller.

turbot noun (plural **turbot** or **turbots**) an edible flatfish.

turbulence noun **1** violent or unsteady movement of air or water. **2** conflict or confusion.

turbulent adjective **1** characterized by conflict, disorder, or confusion. **2** (of air or water) moving unsteadily or violently. ■ **turbulently** adverb.

turd noun vulgar a lump of excrement.

tureen noun a deep covered dish from which soup is served.

turf noun (plural **turfs** or **turves**) **1** grass and earth held together by its roots. **2** a piece of turf cut from the ground. **3** (**the turf**) horse racing. **4** (**your turf**) informal your territory. verb **1** (**turf out**) Brit. informal force to leave. **2** cover with turf.

turgid adjective **1** swollen or full. **2** (of language) tediously pompous.

turkey noun (plural **turkeys**) a large game bird bred for food.

Turkish noun the language of Turkey. adjective relating to Turkey or its language. □ **Turkish bath** a period of sitting in a room filled with very hot air or steam, followed by washing and massage. **Turkish delight** a sweet consisting of flavoured gelatin coated in icing sugar.

turmeric /ter-muh-rik/ noun a bright yellow powder obtained from a plant, used in Asian cookery.

turmoil noun a state of great disturbance, confusion, or uncertainty.

turn verb **1** move around a central point. **2** move so as to face or go in a different direction. **3** make or become: *Emma turned pale.* **4** shape on a lathe. **5** twist or sprain an ankle. noun **1** an act of turning. **2** a bend in a road, river, etc. **3** a place where a road meets or branches off another. **4** the time when a member of a group must or is allowed to do something. **5** a time when one period of time ends and another begins. **6** a short walk or ride. **7** a brief feeling of illness. **8** a short performance. □ **do someone a good turn** do something that is helpful for someone. **to a turn** to exactly the right degree. **turn down** reject an offer. **turn in 1** hand over to the authorities. **2** informal go to bed in the evening. **turn off** switch off. **turn of mind** a particular way of thinking. **turn on 1** switch on. **2** suddenly attack. **3** informal excite sexually. **turn out 1** switch off an electric light. **2** prove to be the case. **3** be present at an event. **4** (**be turned out**) be dressed in a particular way. **turn over 1** (of an engine) start to run. **2** hand someone over to the control of someone else. **turn up 1** increase the volume or strength of a device. **2** be found. **3** put in an appearance. **4** reveal or discover. **turn-up** Brit. **1** the end of a trouser leg folded upwards on the outside. **2** informal an unusual or unexpected event.

turncoat noun a person who deserts one party or cause in order to join an opposing one.

turning noun a place where a road branches off another.

turnip noun a round root which is eaten as a vegetable.

turnkey noun (plural **turnkeys**) old use a jailer.

turnout noun the number of people attending or taking part in an event.

turnover noun **1** the amount of money taken by a business in a particular period. **2** the rate at which employees leave a workforce and are replaced. **3** the rate at which goods are sold and replaced in a shop. **4** a small pie made by folding a piece of pastry over on itself to enclose a filling.

turnpike noun US & historical a road on which a toll is charged.

turnstile noun a gate with revolving arms allowing only one person at a time to pass through.

turntable noun a circular revolving platform or support, e.g. for the record in a record player.

turpentine noun a liquid derived from certain trees, used to thin paint and clean brushes.

turpitude noun formal wickedness.

turps noun informal turpentine.

turquoise noun **1** a greenish-blue or sky-blue semi-precious stone. **2** a greenish-blue colour.

turret noun **1** a small tower at the corner of a building or wall. **2** an armoured tower for a gun in a ship, aircraft, or tank. ■ **turreted** adjective.

turtle noun a reptile with a bony or leathery shell, that lives in the sea. □ **turn turtle** (of a boat) turn upside down. **turtle dove** a small dove with a soft purring call.

turtleneck noun **1** Brit. a high, round, close-fitting neck on a garment. **2** N. Amer. a polo neck.

turves plural of **TURF**.

tusk noun a long, pointed tooth which protrudes from the closed mouth, as in the elephant, walrus, or wild boar.

tussle noun a vigorous struggle or scuffle. **verb** (**tussles**, **tussling**, **tussled**) engage in a tussle.

tussock noun a dense clump or tuft of grass.

tutelage /**tyoo**-ti-lij/ noun formal **1** protection or authority. **2** instruction.

tutelary /**tyoo**-ti-luh-ri/ adjective formal serving as a protector, guardian, or patron.

tutor noun **1** a person who teaches a single pupil or a very small group. **2** Brit. a university or college teacher with extra responsibility for students. **verb** act as a tutor to.

tutorial noun a period of teaching by a university or college tutor. **adjective** relating to a tutor.

tutu noun a female ballet dancer's very short, stiff skirt that sticks out from the waist.

tuxedo /tuk-**see**-doh/ noun (plural **tuxedos** or **tuxedoes**) chiefly N. Amer. a man's dinner jacket.

TV abbreviation television.

twaddle noun informal trivial or foolish speech or writing.

twain old-fashioned form of **TWO**.

twang noun **1** a strong ringing sound made by the plucked string of a musical instrument. **2** a distinctive nasal way of speaking. **verb** make a twang. ■ **twangy** adjective.

tweak verb **1** twist or pull with a small but sharp movement. **2** informal improve by making fine adjustments. **noun** an act of tweaking.

twee adjective Brit. quaint, pretty, or sentimental in a stylized way.

tweed noun a rough woollen cloth flecked with mixed colours. ■ **tweedy** adjective.

tweet noun the chirp of a small or young bird. **verb** make a chirping noise.

tweeter noun a loudspeaker that reproduces high frequencies.

tweezers plural noun a small pair of pincers for plucking out hairs and picking up small objects.

twelfth ordinal number being number twelve in a sequence; 12th.

twelve cardinal number two more than ten; 12. (Roman numeral: **xii** or **XII**.)

twenty cardinal number (plural **twenties**) ten less than thirty; 20. (Roman numeral: **xx** or **XX**.) □ **twenty-twenty vision** normal vision. ■ **twentieth** ordinal number.

twerp noun informal a silly person.

twice adverb **1** two times. **2** double in degree or quantity.

twiddle verb (**twiddles**, **twiddling**, **twiddled**) fiddle with something in an aimless or nervous way. noun an act of twiddling. □ **twiddle your thumbs** have nothing to do. ■ **twiddly** adjective.

twig[1] noun a slender woody shoot growing from a branch or stem of a tree or shrub.

twig[2] verb (**twigs**, **twigging**, **twigged**) Brit. informal come to understand.

twilight noun **1** the soft glowing light from the sky when the sun is below the horizon. **2** a period or state of gradual decline. ■ **twilit** adjective.

twill noun a fabric with a slightly ridged surface.

twin noun **1** each of two children born at the same time. **2** a thing that is exactly like another. adjective forming or being one of a pair of twins. verb (**twins**, **twinning**, **twinned**) link or combine as a pair.

twine noun strong string consisting of strands twisted together. verb (**twines**, **twining**, **twined**) wind round something.

twinge noun **1** a sudden, sharp pain. **2** a brief, sharp pang of emotion.

twinkle verb (**twinkles**, **twinkling**, **twinkled**) **1** shine with a gleam that changes constantly from bright to faint. **2** (of a person's eyes) sparkle with amusement or liveliness. noun a twinkling sparkle or gleam. □ **in a twinkling of an eye** in an instant. ■ **twinkly** adjective.

twinset noun a woman's matching cardigan and jumper.

twirl verb spin quickly and lightly round. noun an act of twirling. ■ **twirly** adjective.

twist verb **1** bend, curl, or distort. **2** force out of the natural position. **3** have a winding course. **4** (**twisted**)

unpleasantly or unhealthily abnormal. **5** dance the twist. noun **1** an act of twisting. **2** a thing with a spiral shape. **3** a new or unexpected development or treatment. **4** (**the twist**) a dance with a twisting movement of the body, popular in the 1960s. □ **round the twist** Brit. informal mad. □ **twist someone's arm** informal forcefully persuade someone to do something. ■ **twister** noun.

twit[1] noun Brit. informal a silly person.

twit[2] verb (**twits**, **twitting**, **twitted**) informal tease good-humouredly.

twitch verb make a short jerking movement. noun a twitching movement.

twitcher noun Brit. informal a keen bird-watcher.

twitchy adjective informal nervous.

twitter verb (**twitters**, **twittering**, **twittered**) **1** (of a bird) make a series of short high sounds. **2** talk rapidly in a nervous or trivial way. noun **1** a twittering sound. **2** informal an agitated or excited state.

two cardinal number one less than three; 2. (Roman numeral: **ii** or **II**.) □ **put two and two together** draw a conclusion from what is known or evident. **two-dimensional** having or appearing to have length and breadth but no depth. **two-faced** insincere and deceitful. **two-time** be unfaithful to a husband, wife, or lover. ■ **twofold** adjective & adverb.

| i | don't confuse **two** with **to** or **too**; see the note at **TO**. |

twopence or **tuppence** /tuppuhnss/ noun Brit. the sum of two pence before decimalization (1971). ■ **twopenny** (or **tuppenny**) adjective.

twosome noun a set of two people or things.

tycoon noun a wealthy, powerful person in business or industry.

tying present participle of **TIE**.

tyke or **tike** noun informal a mischievous child.

tympani ⇒ **TIMPANI**.

tympanum noun (plural **tympanums**

or tympana) the eardrum.

type noun **1** a category of people or things having common features. **2** a person or thing that sums up or embodies something. **3** informal a person of a specified nature: *a sporty type.* **4** printed characters or letters. verb (**types, typing, typed**) write using a typewriter or computer. ■ **typist** noun.

typecast verb (**be typecast**) (of an actor) always be cast in the same type of role.

typeface noun a particular design of printed type.

typescript noun a typed copy of a text.

typeset verb (**typeset, typesetting, typeset**) arrange the type for a text that is to be printed. ■ **typesetter** noun.

typewriter noun a machine with keys that are pressed to produce characters similar to printed ones. ■ **typewriting** noun **typewritten** adjective.

typhoid noun an infectious fever that causes red spots on the chest and severe irritation of the intestines.

typhoon noun a tropical storm with very high winds.

typhus noun an infectious disease that causes a purple rash, headaches, fever, and usually delirium.

typical adjective **1** having the distinctive qualities of a particular type of person or thing. **2** characteristic of a particular person or thing. ■ **typically** adverb.

typify verb (**typifies, typifying, typified**) be typical of.

typo noun (plural **typos**) informal a small error in a typed or printed text.

typography noun **1** the setting and arrangement of printed characters. **2** the style and appearance of printed material. ■ **typographer** noun **typographical** (or **typographic**) adjective.

tyrannical adjective using power in a cruel and oppressive way. ■ **tyrannically** adverb.

tyrannize or **tyrannise** verb (**tyrannizes, tyrannizing, tyrannized**) rule or dominate in a cruel and oppressive way.

tyrannosaurus rex noun a large meat-eating dinosaur that walked on its strong hind legs.

tyranny noun (plural **tyrannies**) cruel and oppressive government or rule. ■ **tyrannous** adjective.

> ✓ one *r*, two *n*s : tyra**nn**y.

tyrant noun a cruel and oppressive ruler.

tyre (US spelling **tire**) noun a rubber covering, usually inflated, that fits around a wheel.

tyro noun (plural **tyros**) a beginner or novice.

tzar ⇨ **TSAR**.

tzatziki /tsat-**see**-ki/ noun a Greek side dish of yogurt with cucumber and garlic.

Uu

U or **u** noun (plural **Us** or **U's**) the twenty-first letter of the alphabet. **abbreviation** Brit. (in film classification) universal. □**U-boat** a German submarine of the First or Second World War. **U-turn 1** the turning of a vehicle in a U-shaped course so as to face the opposite way. **2** a complete change in policy.

ubiquitous /yoo-bi-kwi-tuhss/ **adjective** appearing or found everywhere. ■ **ubiquitously** adverb **ubiquity** noun.

udder noun the bag-like milk-producing organ of female cattle, sheep, horses, etc.

UFO noun (plural **UFOs**) a mysterious object seen in the sky that some people believe is carrying beings from outer space.

> ℹ️ short for *unidentified flying object*.

ugly adjective (**uglier**, **ugliest**) **1** unpleasant or unattractive in appearance. **2** hostile or threatening. □**ugly duckling** a person who unexpectedly turns out to be beautiful or talented. ■ **ugliness** noun.

UK abbreviation United Kingdom.

ukulele /yoo-kuh-**lay**-li/ noun a small four-stringed guitar.

> ✓ *uku*-, not *uke*-: ukulele.

ulcer noun an open sore on the body or on an internal organ. ■ **ulcerated** adjective **ulceration** noun.

ulna noun (plural **ulnae** /**ul**-nee/ or **ulnas**) the thinner and longer of the two bones in the human forearm.

ulterior adjective other than what is obvious or admitted: *she had an ulterior motive.*

ultimate adjective **1** happening at the end of a process. **2** being the best or most extreme example of its kind. **3** basic or fundamental. noun (**the ul-**timate) the best of its kind that is imaginable. ■ **ultimately** adverb.

ultimatum noun (plural **ultimatums** or **ultimata**) a final warning that action will be taken against you if you do not agree to another party's demands.

ultramarine noun a brilliant deep blue colour or pigment.

ultramicroscopic adjective too small to be seen by an ordinary optical microscope.

ultrasonic adjective involving sound waves with a frequency above the upper limit of human hearing.

ultrasound noun sound or other vibrations with an ultrasonic frequency, used in medical scans.

ultraviolet adjective (of electromagnetic radiation) having a wavelength just shorter than that of violet light.

ululate verb (**ululates**, **ululating**, **ululated**) howl or wail. ■ **ululation** noun.

umber noun a dark brown or yellowish-brown colour.

umbilical adjective relating to the navel or umbilical cord. □**umbilical cord** a flexible tube by which a fetus is nourished while it is in the womb.

umbilicus noun Anatomy the navel.

umbra noun (plural **umbras** or **umbrae** /**um**-bree/) the shadow cast by the earth or the moon in an eclipse.

umbrage noun (**take umbrage**) take offence; become annoyed.

umbrella noun **1** a folding dome-shaped device used as protection against rain. **2** a thing that includes or contains many different parts.

umlaut /**uum**-lowt/ noun a mark (¨) placed over a vowel in some languages to indicate how it should sound.

umpire noun (in certain sports) an official who supervises a game to ensure that players keep to the rules.

ultra-

Words beginning with **ultra-** mean:

- beyond or on the other side of, as in *ultramarine* and *ultraviolet*. *Ultramarine* comes from Latin *ultramarinus*, 'beyond the sea' (a reference to the fact that the pigment was imported); *ultraviolet* is so called because it refers to radiation with a wavelength shorter than that of violet light.
- extreme or extremely: *ultramicroscopic*.

ultra can also be used on its own as an adverb meaning 'very', as in *ultra modern furniture*. In Latin *ultra* means 'beyond'.

---

verb (**umpires, umpiring, umpired**) be the umpire of.

umpteen cardinal number informal very many. ■ **umpteenth** ordinal number.

UN abbreviation United Nations.

unabashed adjective not embarrassed or ashamed.

unabated adjective not reduced in intensity or strength.

unable adjective not able to do something.

unacceptable adjective not satisfactory or allowable. ■ **unacceptability** noun **unacceptably** adverb.

unaccountable adjective 1 unable to be explained. 2 not responsible for results or consequences. ■ **unaccountably** adverb.

unaccustomed adjective 1 not usual or customary. 2 (**unaccustomed to**) not familiar with or used to.

unacquainted adjective 1 (**unacquainted with**) having no experience of or familiarity with. 2 not having met before.

unadulterated adjective not mixed with any different or extra elements.

unadvisedly adverb in an unwise or rash way.

unaffected adjective 1 feeling or showing no effects. 2 sincere and genuine.

unaided adjective having no help.

unalloyed adjective 1 (of metal) not alloyed. 2 complete and unreserved.

unambiguous adjective not open to more than one interpretation. ■ **unambiguously** adverb.

unanimous adjective 1 fully in agreement. 2 (of an opinion, decision, or vote) held or carried by everyone involved. ■ **unanimity** noun **unanimously** adverb.

unannounced adjective without warning or notice.

unanswerable adjective 1 unable to be answered. 2 unable to be proved wrong.

unappetizing or **unappetising** adjective not inviting or attractive.

unapproachable adjective not welcoming or friendly.

unarguable adjective not able to be disagreed with. ■ **unarguably** adverb.

unarmed adjective not equipped with or carrying weapons.

unassailable adjective unable to be attacked, questioned, or defeated.

unassuming adjective not pretentious or arrogant.

unattached adjective without a husband or wife or established lover.

unattended adjective not being supervised or looked after.

unauthorized or **unauthorised** adjective not having official permission or approval.

unavailing adjective achieving little or nothing.

unavoidable adjective not able to be avoided or prevented. ■ **unavoidably** adverb.

WORD FORMATION

un-

un- can be divided into two categories:

1 it is used to form an almost limitless number of words that mean:
- not, as in *unabashed, unacademic, unrepeatable*
- a lack of, e.g. *unrest, untruth.*

2 it is added to verbs:
- referring to reversal or cancellation, e.g. *unsettle, undo, untie*
- referring to deprivation, separation, or change to a lesser state: *unmask.*

The prefixes **un-** and **non-** both have the meaning 'not', but tend to be used with a different emphasis, **non-** being weaker and more neutral than **un-**. For example, **unnatural** implies that something is not natural in a bad way, whereas **non-natural** is neutral.

---

unaware adjective having no knowledge of a situation or fact.

unawares adverb so as to surprise; unexpectedly.

unbalanced adjective emotionally or mentally disturbed.

unbearable adjective not able to be endured. ■ **unbearably** adverb.

unbeknown or **unbeknownst** adjective (**unbeknown to**) without the knowledge of.

unbelievable adjective **1** unlikely to be true. **2** extraordinary. ■ **unbelievably** adverb.

unbeliever noun a person without religious belief.

unbending adjective strict, severe, and inflexible.

unbiased or **unbiassed** adjective showing no prejudice.

unbidden adjective without having been invited.

unborn adjective not yet born.

unbounded adjective having no limits.

unbowed adjective not having given in or been defeated.

unbridgeable adjective (of a difference between people) not able to be closed or disregarded.

unbridled adjective uncontrolled: *unbridled lust.*

unburden verb (**unburden yourself**) confide in someone about your worries or problems.

uncalled adjective (**uncalled for**) undesirable and unnecessary.

uncanny adjective (**uncannier, uncanniest**) strange or mysterious. ■ **uncannily** adverb.

unceasing adjective not ceasing; continuous. ■ **unceasingly** adverb.

unceremonious adjective rude or abrupt. ■ **unceremoniously** adverb.

uncertain adjective **1** not known, reliable, or definite. **2** not completely confident or sure. □ **in no uncertain terms** clearly and forcefully. ■ **uncertainly** adverb **uncertainty** noun.

uncharitable adjective unkind or unsympathetic to others. ■ **uncharitably** adverb.

uncharted adjective (of an area of land or sea) not mapped or surveyed.

unchristian adjective **1** not in line with the teachings of Christianity. **2** ungenerous or unfair.

uncle noun the brother of your father or mother or the husband of your aunt. □ **Uncle Sam** the United States.

unclean adjective **1** dirty. **2** immoral. **3** (of food) forbidden by a religion.

uncomfortable adjective **1** not physically comfortable. **2** uneasy or awkward. ■ **uncomfortably** adverb.

uncommon adjective **1** out of the ordinary; unusual. **2** remarkably great. ■ **uncommonly** adverb.

uncomplimentary adjective negative or insulting.

uncomprehending adjective unable to understand something. ■ **uncomprehendingly** adverb.

uncompromising adjective **1** unwilling to compromise. **2** harsh or relentless. ■ **uncompromisingly** adverb.

unconcern noun a lack of worry or interest. ■ **unconcerned** adjective.

unconditional adjective not subject to any conditions. ■ **unconditionally** adverb.

unconfined adjective **1** not confined to a limited space. **2** (of joy or excitement) very great.

uncongenial adjective **1** not friendly or pleasant to be with. **2** not suitable or pleasing.

unconscionable /un-kon-shuh-nuh-b'l/ adjective formal not right or reasonable. ■ **unconscionably** adverb.

unconscious adjective **1** not awake and aware of your surroundings. **2** done or existing without you realizing. **3** (**unconscious of**) unaware of. noun the part of the mind which you are not aware of but which affects behaviour and emotions. ■ **unconsciously** adverb **unconsciousness** noun.

unconstitutional adjective not allowed by the constitution of a country or the rules of an organization. ■ **unconstitutionally** adverb.

unconstrained adjective not restricted or limited.

uncontrollable adjective not controllable. ■ **uncontrollably** adverb.

unconventional adjective not fitting in with what is generally done or believed. ■ **unconventionally** adverb.

unconvincing adjective failing to convince or impress. ■ **unconvincingly** adverb.

uncooperative adjective unwilling to help others or do what they ask.

uncoordinated adjective **1** badly organized. **2** clumsy.

uncouth adjective lacking good manners or refinement.

uncover verb (**uncovers, uncovering, uncovered**) **1** remove a cover or covering from. **2** discover something previously secret or unknown.

unction noun **1** formal the ceremonial smearing of someone with oil or ointment. **2** excessive politeness.

unctuous adjective excessively polite or flattering. ■ **unctuously** adverb.

undaunted adjective not discouraged by difficulty or danger.

undeceive verb tell someone that an idea or belief is mistaken.

undecided adjective **1** not having made a decision. **2** not yet settled or resolved.

undemonstrative adjective not tending to express feelings openly.

undeniable adjective unable to be denied or disputed. ■ **undeniably** adverb.

under preposition **1** extending or directly below. **2** at a lower level or grade than. **3** expressing control by another. **4** in accordance with rules. **5** used to express grouping or classification. **6** undergoing a process. adverb extending or directly below something. □ **under way 1** (of a boat) moving through the water. **2** having started and making progress.

underachieve verb (**underachieves, underachieving, underachieved**) do less well than is expected.

underarm adjective & adverb done with the arm or hand below shoulder level.

undercarriage noun the wheeled structure which supports an aircraft when it is on the ground.

underclass noun the lowest social class, consisting of very poor and unemployed people.

underclothes plural noun underwear.

undercoat noun a layer of paint applied before the top layer.

undercover adjective & adverb involving secret work for investigation or spying.

undercurrent noun an underlying feeling or influence.

undercut verb (undercuts, undercutting, undercut) **1** offer goods or services at a lower price than a competitor. **2** weaken; undermine.

underdog noun a competitor thought to have little chance of winning a fight or contest.

underdone adjective not cooked enough.

underdressed adjective dressed too plainly or informally.

underestimate verb (underestimates, underestimating, underestimated) **1** estimate something to be smaller or less important than it really is. **2** think of someone as less capable than they really are. noun an estimate that is too low. ■ **underestimation** noun.

underfoot adverb **1** on the ground. **2** constantly present and in the way.

undergarment noun an article of underwear.

undergo verb (undergoes, undergoing, underwent; past participle undergone) experience or sustain something unpleasant or difficult.

undergraduate noun a student at a university who has not yet taken a first degree.

underground adjective & adverb **1** beneath the surface of the ground. **2** in secrecy or hiding. noun **1** Brit. an underground railway. **2** a secret group working against the government or an enemy.

undergrowth noun dense shrubs and other plants.

underhand adjective done in a secret or dishonest way.

underlay noun material laid under a carpet.

underlie verb (underlies, underlying, underlay; past participle underlain) lie or be situated under.

underline verb (underlines, underlining, underlined) **1** draw a line

under. **2** emphasize.

underling noun disapproving a person of lower status.

undermine verb (undermines, undermining, undermined) **1** damage or weaken. **2** wear away the base or foundation of.

underneath preposition & adverb **1** situated directly below. **2** so as to be concealed by. noun the part or side facing towards the ground.

underpants plural noun an undergarment covering the lower part of the body and having two holes for the legs.

underpart noun a lower part.

underpass noun a road or tunnel passing under another road or a railway.

underpin verb (underpins, underpinning, underpinned) **1** support a structure from below. **2** support, justify, or form the basis for.

underplay verb represent something as being less important than it really is.

underprivileged adjective not having the same rights or standard of living as the majority.

underrated verb rated less highly than is deserved.

underscore verb underline.

undersea adjective found or situated below the surface of the sea.

undersecretary noun (plural undersecretaries) (in the UK) a junior minister or senior civil servant.

undersell verb (undersells, underselling, undersold) sell something at a lower price than a competitor.

underside noun the bottom or lower side or surface of something.

undersigned noun formal the person or people who have signed the document in question.

undersized or **undersize** adjective of less than the usual size.

underspend verb (underspends, underspending, underspent) spend too little or less than has been planned.

understaffed adjective having too few members of staff.

understand verb (understands, understanding, understood) **1** know or realize the real or intended meaning or cause of. **2** interpret or view in a particular way. **3** believe that something is the case because of information that you have received. **4** supply a missing word or phrase in your mind.

understandable adjective **1** able to be understood. **2** natural, reasonable, or forgivable. ■ **understandably** adverb.

understanding noun **1** the ability to understand something. **2** intellect. **3** the way an individual looks at a situation. **4** sympathetic awareness or tolerance. **5** an informal or unspoken agreement or arrangement. adjective sympathetically aware of other people's feelings. ■ **understandingly** adverb.

understate verb (understates, understating, understated) represent something as being smaller or less significant than it really is. ■ **understatement** noun.

understated adjective pleasingly subtle.

understudy noun (plural understudies) an actor who learns another's role in order to take their place if necessary. verb (understudies, understudying, understudied) be an understudy for.

undertake verb (undertakes, undertaking, undertook; past participle undertaken) **1** begin an activity. **2** formally guarantee or promise.

undertaker noun a person whose job is preparing dead bodies for burial or cremation and making arrangements for funerals.

undertaking noun **1** a formal promise to do something. **2** a task. **3** the business of an undertaker.

undertone noun **1** a subdued or muted tone. **2** an underlying quality or feeling.

undertow noun a current under the surface of water.

underuse verb (underuses, underusing, underused) not use something enough. noun insufficient use.

underwater adjective & adverb situated, occurring, or used beneath the surface of the water.

underwear noun clothing worn under other clothes next to the skin.

underweight adjective below a normal or desirable weight.

underwent past of **UNDERGO**.

underwhelmed verb humorous not very impressed.

underworld noun **1** the world of criminals or of organized crime. **2** the imaginary home of the dead, imagined as being under the earth.

underwrite verb (underwrites, underwriting, underwrote; past participle underwritten) **1** accept legal responsibility for an insurance policy. **2** accept financial responsibility for an undertaking. ■ **underwriter** noun.

undesirable adjective harmful, offensive, or unpleasant. noun an unpleasant or offensive person.

undeterred adjective persevering despite setbacks.

undeviating adjective constant and steady.

undies plural noun informal articles of underwear.

undisputed adjective not disputed or called into question.

undistinguished adjective not particularly good; unexceptional.

undivided adjective **1** not divided or broken into parts. **2** devoted completely to one thing.

undo verb (undoes, undoing, undid; past participle undone) **1** unfasten or loosen. **2** reverse the effects of something previously done. **3** formal cause the downfall or ruin of.

undoing noun formal a person's ruin or downfall.

undoubted adjective not questioned or doubted. ■ **undoubtedly** adverb.

undreamed or Brit. **undreamt** adjective (undreamed of) not previously thought to be possible.

undress verb **1** (also **get undressed**) take off your clothes. **2** take the clothes off someone else. noun formal the state of being naked or only partially clothed.

undue adjective excessive or unreasonably great. ■ **unduly** adverb.

undulate verb (**undulates, undulating, undulated**) **1** move with a smooth wave-like motion. **2** have a wavy form or outline. ■ **undulation** noun.

undying adjective lasting forever.

unearth verb **1** find in the ground by digging. **2** discover by investigation or searching.

unearthly adjective **1** unnatural or mysterious. **2** informal unreasonably early or inconvenient.

unease noun anxiety or discontent.

uneasy adjective (**uneasier, uneasiest**) troubled or uncomfortable. ■ **uneasily** adverb **uneasiness** noun.

unedifying adjective distasteful or unpleasant.

unemployable adjective not having enough skills or qualifications to get paid employment.

unemployed adjective without a paid job but available to work.

unemployment noun **1** the state of being unemployed. **2** the number or proportion of unemployed people.

unencumbered adjective not burdened or held back.

unending adjective seeming to last for ever.

unenviable adjective difficult, undesirable, or unpleasant.

unequal adjective **1** not equal. **2** not fair or even. **3** (**unequal to**) not having the ability to meet a challenge. ■ **unequally** adverb.

unequalled (US spelling **unequaled**) adjective better or greater than all others.

unequivocal adjective leaving no doubt; unambiguous. ■ **unequivocally** adverb.

unerring adjective always right or ac-

curate. ■ **unerringly** adverb.

uneven adjective **1** not level or smooth. **2** not regular or equal. ■ **unevenly** adverb **unevenness** noun.

uneventful adjective not marked by interesting or exciting events. ■ **uneventfully** adverb.

unexceptionable adjective not able to be objected to, but not particularly new or exciting.

unexceptional adjective not out of the ordinary; usual. ■ **unexceptionally** adverb.

unexpected adjective not expected or thought likely to happen. ■ **unexpectedly** adverb.

unexpurgated adjective (of a text) complete and containing all the original material.

unfailing adjective **1** without error. **2** reliable or constant. ■ **unfailingly** adverb.

unfair adjective not fair or just. ■ **unfairly** adverb **unfairness** noun.

unfaithful adjective **1** not faithful; disloyal. **2** having sex with someone who is not your husband, wife, or usual partner.

unfathomable adjective incapable of being fully understood.

unfavourable (US spelling **unfavorable**) adjective **1** not approving. **2** not good or likely to lead to success. ■ **unfavourably** adverb.

unfazed adjective informal not disconcerted or disturbed.

unfeasible adjective inconvenient or impractical. ■ **unfeasibly** adverb.

unfit adjective **1** unsuitable. **2** not in good physical condition.

unflagging adjective tireless or persistent.

unflappable adjective informal calm in a crisis.

unflinching adjective not afraid or hesitant. ■ **unflinchingly** adverb.

unfold verb **1** open or spread out from a folded position. **2** reveal or be revealed.

unforeseen adjective not anticipated

or predicted; unexpected. ∎ **unforeseeable** adjective.

unforgettable adjective highly memorable. ∎ **unforgettably** adverb.

unforgivable adjective so bad as to be unable to be forgiven. ∎ **unforgivably** adverb.

unforgiving adjective **1** not willing to forgive. **2** (of conditions) harsh.

unforthcoming adjective **1** not willing to give out information. **2** not available when needed.

unfortunate adjective **1** unlucky. **2** regrettable or inappropriate. noun a person who suffers bad luck. ∎ **unfortunately** adverb.

unfounded adjective having no basis in fact.

unfrequented adjective visited only rarely.

unfunny adjective (**unfunnier, unfunniest**) not amusing.

unfurl verb open something that is rolled or folded.

ungainly adjective clumsy; awkward. ∎ **ungainliness** noun.

ungodly adjective **1** immoral or disrespectful to God. **2** informal unreasonably early or inconvenient.

ungovernable adjective impossible to control or govern.

ungrateful adjective not grateful. ∎ **ungratefully** adverb.

unguarded adjective **1** without protection. **2** not well considered; careless: *an unguarded remark.*

unguent /ung-yuu-uhnt/ noun a soft greasy or thick substance used as ointment or for lubrication.

ungulate noun the name in zoology for a hoofed mammal.

unhappy adjective (**unhappier, unhappiest**) **1** not happy. **2** unfortunate. ∎ **unhappily** adverb **unhappiness** noun.

unharmed adjective not harmed.

unhealthy adjective (**unhealthier, unhealthiest**) **1** not having good health. **2** not good for your health. ∎ **unhealthily** adverb.

unheard adjective **1** not heard or listened to. **2** (**unheard of**) previously unknown.

unhelpful adjective not helpful. ∎ **unhelpfully** adverb.

unheralded adjective not previously announced, expected, or recognized.

unhesitating adjective without doubt or hesitation. ∎ **unhesitatingly** adverb.

unhinged adjective mentally ill or unbalanced.

unholy adjective **1** sinful; wicked. **2** unnatural and likely to be harmful. **3** informal dreadful.

unhurried adjective moving or doing things in a leisurely way. ∎ **unhurriedly** adverb.

unhurt adjective not hurt or harmed.

unhygienic adjective not hygienic.

unicameral adjective (of a parliament) consisting of only one main part. •

UNICEF abbreviation United Nations Children's Fund.

unicorn noun a mythical creature like a horse with a single long horn on its forehead.

unicycle noun a cycle with a single wheel. ∎ **unicyclist** noun.

unidentifiable adjective unable to be identified.

unidentified adjective not recognized or identified.

unification noun the process of uniting or of being united.

uniform adjective not varying in form or character; the same throughout. noun the distinctive clothing worn by members of the same organization or school. ∎ **uniformed** adjective **uniformity** noun **uniformly** adverb.

unify verb (**unifies, unifying, unified**) make or become united.

unilateral adjective done by or affecting only one person or group. ∎ **unilaterally** adverb.

unimaginable adjective impossible to imagine or understand. ∎ **unimaginably** adverb.

unimaginative adjective not using or showing imagination or new ideas;

dull. ■ **unimaginatively** adverb.

unimpeachable adjective not able to be doubted or criticized.

unimportant adjective lacking in importance. ■ **unimportance** noun.

uninhabited adjective having no people living there. ■ **uninhabitable** adjective.

uninhibited adjective saying or doing things without concern about what other people think.

uninitiated adjective without knowledge or experience of something.

uninspired adjective 1 not original or exciting; dull. 2 feeling no excitement. ■ **uninspiring** adjective.

unintelligible adjective impossible to understand. ■ **unintelligibility** noun **unintelligibly** adverb.

unintentional adjective not done on purpose. ■ **unintentionally** adverb.

uninterested adjective not interested or concerned.

> ℹ️ don't confuse **uninterested** and **disinterested**. Disinterested means 'impartial' , while **uninterested** means 'not interested'.

uninterrupted adjective not interrupted; continuous.

union noun 1 the act of uniting two or more things. 2 a state of harmony or agreement. 3 a marriage. 4 a club, society, or association. 5 a trade union. 6 (also **Union**) a political unit consisting of a number of states or provinces with the same central government. □ **Union Jack** (or **Union Flag**) the national flag of the United Kingdom.

unionist noun 1 a member of a trade union. 2 (**Unionist**) a person in Northern Ireland in favour of union with Great Britain.

unionize or **unionise** verb (**unionizes, unionizing, unionized**) make or become members of a trade union. ■ **unionization** noun.

unique adjective 1 being the only one of its kind. 2 (**unique to**) belonging or connected to one particular person, group, or place. 3 very special or unusual. ■ **uniquely** adverb.

unisex adjective designed to be suitable for both sexes.

unison noun the fact of two or more things being said or happening at the same time.

unit noun 1 a single thing or group that is complete in itself but can also form part of something larger. 2 a device, part, or item of furniture with a particular function: *a sink unit*. 3 a self-contained section of a building or group of buildings. 4 a subdivision of a larger military grouping. 5 a quantity used as a standard measure. □ **unit trust** Brit. a company that invests money in various different businesses on behalf of individuals, who can buy small units.

Unitarian noun a member of a Christian Church that believes that God is one being and rejects the idea of the Trinity. adjective relating to this Church or belief.

unitary adjective 1 single; uniform. 2 relating to a unit or units.

unite verb (**unites, uniting, united**) 1 join together with others in order to do something as a group. 2 bring together to form a unit or whole. ■ **united** adjective.

unity noun (plural **unities**) 1 the state of being united or forming a whole. 2 a thing forming a complex whole. 3 Mathematics the number one.

universal adjective 1 affecting or done by all people or things in the world or in a particular group. 2 true or right in all cases. ■ **universality** noun **universally** adverb.

universe noun the whole of space and everything in it.

university noun (plural **universities**) an institution where students study for a degree, and where academic research is done.

unjust adjective not just; unfair. ■ **unjustly** adverb.

unjustifiable adjective impossible to justify. ■ **unjustifiably** adverb.

unjustified adjective not justified; unfair.

unkempt adjective having an untidy appearance.

unkind adjective not caring or kind. ■ **unkindly** adverb **unkindness** noun.

unknowable adjective not able to be known.

unknowing adjective not knowing or aware. ■ **unknowingly** adverb.

unknown adjective not known or familiar. noun an unknown person or thing. □ **unknown quantity** a person or thing that is not known about and whose actions or effects are unpredictable. **Unknown Soldier** an unidentified member of a country's armed forces killed in war, buried in a national memorial to represent all those killed but unidentified.

unladylike adjective (of a woman or girl) not gracious, modest, or well mannered.

unlamented adjective not mourned or regretted.

unlawful adjective not obeying or allowed by law or rules. ■ **unlawfully** adverb.

> ℹ️ what is the difference between **unlawful** and **illegal**? Both can mean 'against the law', but **unlawful** has a broader meaning 'not permitted by rules': thus handball in soccer is **unlawful**, but not **illegal**.

unleaded adjective (of petrol) without added lead.

unleash verb release something from a leash or restraint; set free.

unleavened adjective (of bread) flat because made without yeast.

unless conjunction except when; if not.

unlicensed adjective not having a licence for the sale of alcoholic drinks.

unlike preposition **1** different from; not like. **2** in contrast to. **3** uncharacteristic of. adjective different from each other.

unlikely adjective (**unlikelier**, **unlikeliest**) **1** not likely to happen. **2** not what you would expect. ■ **unlikelihood** noun.

unlimited adjective not limited or restricted; infinite.

unload verb remove goods from a vehicle, ship, aircraft, or container.

unlock verb undo the lock of a door, container, etc. using a key.

unlooked adjective (**unlooked for**) not planned or expected.

unloose or **unloosen** verb (**unlooses**, **unloosing**, **unloosed**) release something.

unlovely adjective not attractive; ugly.

unlucky adjective (**unluckier**, **unluckiest**) having, bringing, or resulting from bad luck. ■ **unluckily** adverb.

unmade adjective Brit. (of a road) without a hard, smooth surface.

unmanageable adjective difficult or impossible to manage or control. ■ **unmanageably** adverb.

unmanned adjective not having or needing a crew or staff.

unmarked adjective **1** not marked. **2** not noticed.

unmarried adjective not married.

unmask verb reveal the true character of.

unmatched adjective not matched or equalled.

unmentionable adjective too embarrassing or offensive to be spoken about.

unmerciful adjective showing no mercy. ■ **unmercifully** adjective.

unmetalled adjective Brit. (of a road) not having a hard surface.

unmindful adjective (**unmindful of**) not conscious or aware of.

unmissable adjective that should not or cannot be missed.

unmistakable or **unmistakeable** adjective not able to be mistaken for anything else. ■ **unmistakably** adverb.

unmitigated adjective without any qualification; complete.

unmoved adjective not affected by emotion or excitement.

unnameable adjective too bad or frightening to mention.

unnatural adjective 1 different from what is found in nature or what is normal in society. 2 not spontaneous. ■ **unnaturally** adverb.

unnecessary adjective not necessary, or more than is necessary. ■ **unnecessarily** adverb.

unnerve verb (unnerves, unnerving, unnerved) make someone feel fearful or lacking in confidence.

unnoticeable adjective not easily seen or noticed.

unnoticed adjective not being or having been seen or noticed.

unobtainable adjective not able to be obtained.

unobtrusive adjective not conspicuous or attracting attention. ■ **unobtrusively** adverb.

unofficial adjective not officially authorized or confirmed. ■ **unofficially** adverb.

unopposed adjective not opposed; unchallenged.

unorthodox adjective different from what is usual, traditional, or accepted.

unpack verb take things out of a suitcase, bag, or package.

unpaid adjective 1 (of a debt) not yet paid. 2 done without payment. 3 not receiving payment for work done.

unpalatable adjective 1 not pleasant to taste. 2 difficult to accept.

unparalleled adjective having no equal; exceptional.

unpardonable adjective (of a fault or offence) unforgivable. ■ **unpardonably** adverb.

unperturbed adjective not concerned or worried about something.

unpick verb 1 undo the sewing of stitches or a garment. 2 carefully analyse the different elements of something.

unplanned adjective not planned.

unpleasant adjective 1 not pleasant or comfortable. 2 unfriendly; disagreeable. ■ **unpleasantly** adverb un-

pleasantness noun.

unplug verb (unplugs, unplugging, unplugged) 1 disconnect an electrical device from a socket. 2 remove a blockage from.

unpopular adjective not liked or popular. ■ **unpopularity** noun.

unprecedented adjective never done or known before.

unpredictable adjective not able to be predicted; changeable. ■ **unpredictability** noun **unpredictably** adverb.

unprejudiced adjective without prejudice; unbiased.

unpremeditated adjective not planned beforehand.

unprepared adjective not ready or able to deal with something.

unprepossessing adjective not attractive or interesting.

unpretentious adjective simple and straightforward and showing no pretension.

unprincipled adjective not acting in accordance with moral principles.

unprintable adjective (of words or comments) too offensive to be published.

unproductive adjective 1 not able to produce the required quantity of goods or crops. 2 not achieving much; not very useful.

unprofessional adjective not in accordance with professional standards or behaviour. ■ **unprofessionally** adverb.

unprofitable adjective 1 not yielding a profit. 2 not helpful or useful.

unpromising adjective not giving hope of success or good results in the future.

unprompted adjective without being prompted; spontaneous.

unpronounceable adjective too difficult to pronounce.

unproven or **unproved** adjective not proved or tested.

unprovoked adjective (of an attack or crime) not directly provoked.

unqualified adjective 1 not having

the necessary qualifications or requirements. **2** complete.

unquantifiable adjective impossible to express or measure.

unquestionable adjective not able to be denied or doubted. ■ **unquestionably** adverb.

unquestioned adjective not denied or doubted.

unravel verb (**unravels, unravelling, unravelled**; US spelling **unravels, unraveling, unraveled**) **1** undo twisted, knitted, or woven threads. **2** (of threads) become undone. **3** solve a mystery or puzzle.

unreadable adjective **1** not clear enough to read. **2** too dull or difficult to be worth reading.

unready adjective not prepared.

unreal adjective **1** strange and not seeming real. **2** not related to reality; unrealistic. ■ **unreality** noun.

unrealistic adjective **1** not showing things in a way that is accurate and true to life. **2** not having a sensible understanding of what can be achieved. ■ **unrealistically** adverb.

unreasonable adjective **1** not based on good sense. **2** beyond what is achievable or acceptable. ■ **unreasonably** adverb.

unrecognizable or **unrecognisable** adjective not able to be recognized.

unrelenting adjective **1** not stopping or becoming less severe. **2** not giving in to requests. ■ **unrelentingly** adverb.

unreliable adjective not able to be relied on. ■ **unreliability** noun **unreliably** adverb.

unrelieved adjective lacking variation or change.

unremarkable adjective not particularly interesting or surprising.

unremitting adjective never relaxing or slackening.

unrepeatable adjective **1** not able to be repeated. **2** too offensive or shocking to be said again.

unrepentant adjective showing no shame or regret for your actions.

unrequited adjective (of love) not given in return.

unreserved adjective **1** without any doubts or reservations. **2** honest and open. **3** not set apart or booked in advance. ■ **unreservedly** adverb.

unrest noun **1** a situation in which people are feeling discontented and rebellious. **2** a state of uneasiness.

unrivalled (US spelling **unrivaled**) adjective greater or better than all others.

unroll verb open out from a rolled-up state.

unruffled adjective calm and undisturbed.

unruly adjective (**unrulier, unruliest**) difficult to control; disorderly. ■ **unruliness** noun.

unsafe adjective **1** not safe; dangerous. **2** (of a decision in a court of law) not based on good evidence.

unsatisfactory adjective not good enough. ■ **unsatisfactorily** adverb.

unsaturated adjective Chemistry (of organic molecules) having double or triple bonds between carbon atoms and therefore containing fewer hydrogen atoms than the maximum possible.

unsavoury (US spelling **unsavory**) adjective **1** unpleasant to taste, smell, or look at. **2** not respectable.

unscathed adjective without suffering any injury, damage, or harm.

unschooled adjective lacking schooling or training.

unscientific adjective not done in accordance with proper scientific methods. ■ **unscientifically** adverb.

unscrew verb unfasten something by twisting or undoing screws.

unscrupulous adjective without moral scruples; dishonest or unfair. ■ **unscrupulously** adverb.

unseasonable adjective (of weather) unusual for the time of year. ■ **unseasonably** adverb.

unseasonal adjective unusual or inappropriate for the time of year.

unseat verb **1** cause someone to fall

from a saddle or seat. **2** remove someone from a position of power.

unseeing adjective having your eyes open but not noticing anything.

unseemly adjective (of behaviour or actions) not proper or appropriate.

unseen adjective **1** not seen or noticed. **2** (of a passage for translation in an examination) not previously read or prepared.

unselfconscious adjective not self-conscious; not shy or embarrassed. ■ **unselfconsciously** adverb.

unselfish adjective putting other people's needs before your own. ■ **unselfishly** adverb.

unserviceable adjective not in working order; unfit for use.

unsettle verb (unsettles, unsettling, unsettled) make someone anxious or uneasy.

unsettled adjective **1** frequently changing, or likely to change. **2** agitated; uneasy. **3** not yet resolved.

unshakeable or **unshakable** adjective (of a belief or feeling) firm and unable to be changed or disputed.

unshaven adjective not having shaved.

unsightly adjective unpleasant to look at; ugly.

unskilled adjective not having or needing special skill or training.

unsociable adjective not enjoying the company of others.

unsocial adjective (of hours of work) not falling within the normal working day.

unsolicited adjective not asked for.

unsophisticated adjective **1** lacking experience of cultured or refined society. **2** not complicated or highly developed; basic.

unsound adjective **1** not safe or strong; in poor condition. **2** not based on reliable evidence or reasoning.

unsparing adjective **1** merciless; severe. **2** giving generously.

unspeakable adjective too bad or horrific to express in words. ■ **unspeakably** adverb.

unspoilt or **unspoiled** adjective (of a place) largely unaffected by building or development.

unstable adjective **1** likely to fall or collapse. **2** likely to change; unsettled. **3** prone to mental health problems or sudden changes of mood.

unsteady adjective **1** liable to fall or shake; not firm. **2** not uniform or regular. ■ **unsteadily** adverb.

unstick verb (unsticks, unsticking, unstuck) separate things that have been stuck together. □ **come unstuck** informal fail.

unstinting adjective given or giving freely or generously.

unsuccessful adjective not successful. ■ **unsuccessfully** adverb.

unsuitable adjective not right or appropriate for a particular purpose or occasion. ■ **unsuitability** noun **unsuitably** adverb.

unsung adjective not celebrated or praised.

unsure adjective having doubts about something; not certain.

unsurpassed adjective better or greater than any other.

unsurprising adjective expected and so not causing surprise. ■ **unsurprisingly** adverb.

unsuspecting adjective not aware of the presence of danger.

unsustainable adjective **1** not able to be maintained at the current level. **2** not able to be upheld or defended. **3** upsetting the ecological balance by using up natural resources.

unswerving adjective not changing or becoming weaker.

unsympathetic adjective **1** not sympathetic. **2** not showing approval of an idea or action. **3** not likeable. ■ **unsympathetically** adverb.

unsystematic adjective not done or acting according to a fixed plan. ■ **unsystematically** adverb.

untapped adjective (of a resource) available but not yet exploited.

untenable adjective not able to be

maintained or defended against criticism or attack.

unthinkable adjective impossible to imagine or accept.

unthinking adjective not thinking about the effects of what you do or say. ■ **unthinkingly** adverb.

untidy adjective (untidier, untidiest) **1** not arranged tidily. **2** not inclined to be neat. ■ **untidily** adverb **untidiness** noun.

untie verb (unties, untying, untied) undo or unfasten something that is tied.

until preposition & conjunction up to the time or event mentioned.

> ✓ just one *l* at the end: unti*l*.

untimely adjective **1** happening or done at an unsuitable time. **2** (of a death or end) happening too soon or sooner than normal.

unto preposition old use **1** to. **2** until.

untold adjective **1** too much or too many to be counted. **2** not narrated or recounted.

untouchable adjective **1** not able to be touched. **2** not able to be criticized or rivalled. **noun** offensive a member of the lowest Hindu caste (social class).

> ℹ the official term today for the lowest Hindu social class is **scheduled caste**.

untouched adjective **1** not handled, used, or consumed. **2** not affected, changed, or damaged.

untoward adjective unexpected and unwanted.

untrammelled (US spelling untrammeled) adjective not restricted or hampered.

untrue adjective **1** false. **2** not faithful or loyal.

untrustworthy adjective unable to be trusted.

unused adjective **1** not used. **2** (un-used to) not accustomed to.

unusual adjective **1** not often done or occurring. **2** exceptional. ■ **unusually** adverb.

unutterable adjective too great or bad to describe. ■ **unutterably** adverb.

unvarnished adjective **1** not varnished. **2** plain and straightforward.

unveil verb **1** remove a veil or covering from. **2** show or announce something publicly for the first time.

unversed adjective (unversed in) not experienced or skilled in.

unwaged adjective chiefly Brit. unemployed or doing unpaid work.

unwanted adjective not wanted.

unwarrantable adjective not reasonable or justifiable.

unwarranted adjective not justified.

unwavering adjective not changing or becoming weaker.

unwelcome adjective not wanted.

unwell adjective ill.

unwholesome adjective **1** harmful to health. **2** unpleasant or unnatural.

unwieldy adjective hard to move or manage because of its size, shape, or weight.

> ✓ *i* before *e*: unwi**el**dy.

unwilling adjective not willing. ■ **unwillingly** adverb **unwillingness** noun.

unwind verb (unwinds, unwinding, unwound) **1** undo something that has been wound or twisted. **2** relax after a period of work or tension.

unwise adjective lacking good judgement; foolish. ■ **unwisely** adverb.

unwitting adjective **1** not aware of the full facts. **2** unintentional. ■ **unwittingly** adverb.

unwonted /un-**wohn**-tid/ adjective not customary or usual.

unworldly adjective **1** having little awareness of the realities of life. **2** not seeming to belong to this world.

unworthy adjective not deserving effort, attention, or respect. ■ **unworthiness** noun.

unwrap verb (unwraps, unwrapping, unwrapped) remove the wrapping from.

unwritten adjective (of a rule or law) generally known about and accepted, although not made official.

unyielding adjective **1** not bending or breaking; firm. **2** (of a person) not changing their mind.

unzip verb (unzips, unzipping, unzipped) **1** unfasten the zip of. **2** Computing decompress a file.

up adverb **1** towards a higher place or position. **2** to the place where someone is. **3** at or to a higher level or value. **4** into the desired condition or position. **5** out of bed. **6** (of the sun) visible in the sky. preposition **1** from a lower to a higher point of. **2** from one end of a street to another. adjective **1** directed or moving towards a higher place or position. **2** at an end. verb (ups, upping, upped) increase a level or an amount. □ **up-and-coming** likely to be successful. **up to date** using or aware of the latest developments and trends.

upbeat adjective informal positive and cheerful or enthusiastic.

upbraid verb scold or criticize.

upbringing noun the way in which a person is taught and looked after as a child.

upcoming adjective forthcoming.

update verb (updates, updating, updated) **1** make something more modern. **2** give someone the latest information on something. noun an act of updating, or an updated version of something.

upend verb set something on its end or upside down.

upfront informal adverb (usu. up front) **1** at the front. **2** (of a payment) in advance. adjective **1** bold and frank. **2** (of a payment) made in advance.

upgrade verb (upgrades, upgrading, upgraded) raise something to a higher standard or rank. noun an act of upgrading, or an upgraded version of something.

upheaval noun a big change that causes a lot of upset or disruption.

uphill adverb towards the top of a slope. adjective **1** sloping upwards. **2** difficult: *an uphill struggle.*

uphold verb (upholds, upholding, upheld) **1** confirm or support something which has been questioned. **2** maintain a custom or practice.

upholster verb (upholsters, upholstering, upholstered) provide an armchair, sofa, etc. with a soft, padded covering. ■ **upholsterer** noun.

upholstery noun **1** the soft, padded covering on an armchair, sofa, etc. **2** the art of upholstering furniture.

upkeep noun the process or cost of keeping something in good condition or of supporting a person.

upland or **uplands** noun an area of high or hilly land.

uplift noun **1** an act of lifting something up. **2** support from a garment for a woman's bust. **3** a feeling of hope or happiness. verb make someone feel hope or happiness.

upmarket adjective chiefly Brit. expensive or of high quality.

upon more formal term for ON.

upper adjective **1** situated above another part. **2** higher in position or status. **3** situated on higher ground. noun the part of a boot or shoe above the sole. □ **have the upper hand** have an advantage or control over someone. **upper case** capital letters. **upper class** the social group with the highest status. **the Upper House** (in the UK) the House of Lords.

uppercut noun a punch delivered with an upwards motion and the arm bent.

uppermost adjective & adverb highest in place, rank, or importance.

uppity adjective informal behaving as if you feel you are important.

upright adjective **1** vertical; erect. **2** greater in height than breadth. **3** strictly honest and respectable. **4** (of a piano) having vertical strings. adverb in or into an upright position. noun a vertical post, structure, or line.

uprising noun a rebellion.

upriver ⇒ **UPSTREAM.**

uproar noun **1** a loud and emotional noise or disturbance. **2** a public expression of outrage.

uproarious adjective **1** very noisy

and lively. **2** very funny. ■ **uproariously** adverb.

uproot verb **1** pull a tree or other plant out of the ground. **2** move someone from their home or usual surroundings.

upscale adjective N. Amer. upmarket.

upset verb (**upsets, upsetting, upset**) **1** make someone unhappy, disappointed, or worried. **2** knock something over. **3** disrupt or disturb a situation or arrangement. noun **1** a state of being upset. **2** a difficult or unexpected result or situation. adjective **1** unhappy, disappointed, or worried. **2** (of a person's stomach) having disturbed digestion.

upshot noun the eventual outcome or conclusion of something.

upside noun the positive aspect of something. □ **upside down** with the upper part where the lower part should be.

upsilon /uhp-**sy**-luhn/ noun the twentieth letter of the Greek alphabet (Y, υ).

upstage adverb & adjective at or towards the back of a stage. verb (**upstages, upstaging, upstaged**) draw attention away from someone so that people notice you instead.

upstairs adverb & adjective on or to an upper floor. noun an upper floor.

upstanding adjective very respectable and responsible.

upstart noun disapproving a person who thinks they are more important than they really are.

upstate adjective & adverb US in or to a part of a state remote from its large cities.

upstream or **upriver** adverb & adjective at or to a point nearer the source of a stream or river.

upsurge noun an increase.

uptake noun the action of taking up or making use of something. □ **be quick** (or **slow**) **on the uptake** informal be quick (or slow) to understand something.

uptight adjective informal nervously tense or angry, and unable to express your feelings.

upturn noun an improvement or upward trend. verb (**be upturned**) be turned upwards or upside down.

upward adjective & adverb towards a higher level. ■ **upwards** adverb.

upwind adverb & adjective into the wind.

uranium /yuu-**ray**-ni-uhm/ noun a radioactive metallic element used as a fuel in nuclear reactors.

urban adjective having to do with a town or city.

urbane /er-**bayn**/ adjective (of a man) confident, polite, and refined. ■ **urbanity** noun.

urchin noun a poor, raggedly dressed child.

Urdu /**oor**-doo, **er**-doo/ noun a language of Pakistan and India.

ureter /yuu-**ree**-ter/ noun the duct by which urine passes from the kidney to the bladder.

urethra /yuu-**ree**-thruh/ noun the duct by which urine passes out of the body, and which in males also carries semen. ■ **urethral** adjective.

urge verb (**urges, urging, urged**) **1** encourage or earnestly ask someone to do something. **2** strongly recommend. noun a strong desire or impulse.

urgent adjective **1** requiring immediate action or attention. **2** earnest and insistent. ■ **urgency** noun **urgently** adverb.

urinal noun a container into which men urinate, attached to the wall in a public toilet.

urinate verb (**urinates, urinating, urinated**) pass urine out of the body. ■ **urination** noun.

urine /**yoo**-rin, **yoo**-ryn/ noun a yellowish liquid that is stored in the bladder and which contains waste substances that are passed with it out of the body. ■ **urinary** adjective.

URL abbreviation uniform (or universal) resource locator, the address of a World Wide Web page.

urn noun **1** a container for storing a cremated person's ashes. **2** a metal container with a tap, in which tea or coffee is made and kept hot.

ursine adjective having to do with bears.

US abbreviation United States.

us pronoun used by a speaker to refer to himself or herself and one or more other people as the object of a verb or preposition.

USA abbreviation United States of America.

usable or **useable** adjective able to be used. ■ **usability** noun.

usage noun the using of something.

use verb (**uses, using, used**) **1** do something with an object or adopt a method. **2** (**use up**) consume the whole of. **3** treat someone in a particular way. **4** exploit a person or situation unfairly. **5** (**used to**) did something repeatedly in the past, or existed or happened in the past. **6** (**be** or **get used to**) be or become familiar with something through experience. **7** (**used**) second-hand. noun **1** the using of something. **2** the ability to use a part of the body. **3** a purpose for something, or a way in which something can be used. **4** value.

useful adjective able to be used for a practical purpose or in several ways. ■ **usefully** adverb **usefulness** noun.

useless adjective **1** serving no purpose. **2** informal having little ability or skill. ■ **uselessly** adverb.

user noun a person who uses or operates something. □ **user-friendly** easy for people to use or understand.

usher noun **1** a person who shows people to their seats in a theatre or cinema or in church. **2** an official in a law court who directs people in the taking of oaths and generally keeps order. verb (**ushers, ushering, ushered**) guide someone somewhere.

usherette noun a woman who shows people to their seats in a cinema or theatre.

USSR abbreviation historical Union of Soviet Socialist Republics.

usual adjective happening or done typically, regularly, or frequently.

■ **usually** adverb.

usurp /yuu-**zerp**/ verb take over someone's position or power without having the right to do so. ■ **usurper** noun.

usury /**yoo**-zhuh-ri/ noun formal the practice of lending money at unreasonably high rates of interest. ■ **usurer** noun.

utensil noun a tool or container, especially for household use.

uterus /**yoo**-tuh-ruhss/ noun the womb. ■ **uterine** adjective.

utilitarian adjective useful or practical rather than attractive.

utilitarianism noun the doctrine that the greatest happiness of the greatest number should be the guiding principle of right behaviour.

utility noun (plural **utilities**) **1** the state of being useful or profitable. **2** an organization supplying electricity, gas, water, or sewerage to the public. □ **utility room** a room where a washing machine and other domestic equipment is kept.

utilize or **utilise** verb (**utilizes, utilizing, utilized**) make practical and effective use of. ■ **utilization** noun.

utmost adjective most extreme; greatest. noun (**the utmost**) the greatest or most extreme extent or amount.

Utopia /yoo-**toh**-pi-uh/ noun an imagined world where everything is perfect.

utopian adjective idealistic.

utter[1] adjective complete; absolute. ■ **utterly** adverb.

utter[2] verb (**utters, uttering, uttered**) make a sound, or say something.

utterance noun **1** a word, statement, or sound uttered. **2** the action of saying or uttering something.

uttermost = **UTMOST**.

uvula /**yoo**-vyuu-luh/ noun (plural **uvulae** /**yoo**-vyuu-lee/) a small piece of flesh that hangs down at the top of the throat.

uxorious /uk-**sor**-i-uhss/ adjective (of a man) very fond of his wife.

V or **v** noun (plural **Vs** or **V's**) **1** the twenty-second letter of the alphabet. **2** the Roman numeral for five. **abbreviation 1** volts. **2** (**v**) versus. □ **V-neck** a V-shaped neckline. **V-sign 1** an insulting gesture made with the first two fingers pointing up and the back of the hand facing outwards. **2** a similar sign made with the palm facing outwards, used as a symbol of victory.

vacancy noun (plural **vacancies**) **1** an unoccupied position or job. **2** an available room in a hotel, guest house, etc. **3** empty space.

vacant adjective **1** empty. **2** (of a position) not filled. **3** showing no intelligence or interest. ■ **vacantly** adverb.

vacate verb (**vacates, vacating, vacated**) **1** go out of a place, leaving it empty. **2** give up a position.

vacation noun **1** a period when universities, law courts, etc. are closed. **2** N. Amer. a holiday. **3** the action of vacating a place. verb N. Amer. take a holiday.

vaccinate verb (**vaccinates, vaccinating, vaccinated**) give a person or animal an injection of a vaccine to protect them against a disease. ■ **vaccination** noun.

vaccine /vak-seen/ noun a substance injected into the body that causes the production of antibodies and so provides immunity against a disease.

vacillate /va-si-layt/ verb (**vacillates, vacillating, vacillated**) keep changing your mind about something. ■ **vacillation** noun.

vacuous adjective showing a lack of thought or intelligence. ■ **vacuity** noun.

vacuum /vak-yuu-uhm/ noun (plural **vacuums** or **vacua** /vak-yuu-uh/) **1** a completely empty space in which there is no air or other matter. **2** a gap left by the loss of someone or something important. verb informal clean a surface using a vacuum cleaner. □ **vacuum cleaner** an electrical machine that collects dust by means of suction. **vacuum flask** a container with a double wall enclosing a vacuum, used for keeping drinks hot or cold.

vagabond noun a person who has no settled home or job.

vagary /vay-guh-ri/ noun (plural **vagaries**) a change that is difficult to predict or control.

vagina /vuh-jy-nuh/ noun (plural **vaginas**) (in a woman or girl) a tube leading from an outer opening to the womb. ■ **vaginal** adjective.

vagrant /vay-gruhnt/ noun a person who has no settled home or job. **adjective** living as a vagrant. ■ **vagrancy** noun.

vague adjective **1** not certain or definite. **2** saying things or thinking in an unfocused and imprecise way. ■ **vaguely** adverb **vagueness** noun.

vain adjective **1** having too high an opinion of yourself. **2** useless or meaningless. □ **in vain** without success. ■ **vainly** adverb.

vainglorious adjective literary boastful or vain. ■ **vainglory** noun.

valance /va-luhnss/ noun a length of fabric hanging from the canopy of a bed, or fitted over the base of the bed beneath the mattress.

vale noun literary a valley.

valediction /va-li-**dik**-sh'n/ noun **1** the action of saying farewell. **2** a farewell statement.

valedictory /va-li-**dik**-tuh-ri/ adjective serving as a farewell.

valency /**vay**-luhn-si/ or **valence** noun (plural **valencies**) Chemistry the combining power of an element, especially as measured by the number of hydrogen atoms it can displace or combine with.

valentine noun **1** a card that you send

to a person you love on St Valentine's Day (14 February). **2** a person to whom you send such a card.

valerian /vuh-**leer**-i-uhn/ noun **1** a plant with small pink, red, or white flowers. **2** a sedative drug obtained from a valerian root.

valet /**va**-lay, **va**-lit/ noun **1** a person who looks after a man's clothes and other personal needs. **2** a person employed to clean or park cars. verb (**valets, valeting, valeted**) **1** act as a valet to. **2** clean a car.

valetudinarian /va-li-tyoo-di-**nair**-i-uhn/ noun a person who is in poor health, or worries too much about their health.

valiant adjective showing courage or determination. ▪ **valiantly** adverb.

valid adjective **1** (of a reason, argument, etc.) sound or logical. **2** legally binding or acceptable. ▪ **validity** noun.

validate verb (**validates, validating, validated**) make valid, or show to be valid. ▪ **validation** noun.

valise /vuh-**leez**/ noun a small travelling bag or suitcase.

Valium noun trademark a tranquillizing drug used to relieve anxiety.

valley noun (plural **valleys**) a low area between hills or mountains.

valour (US spelling **valor**) noun great courage in the face of danger. ▪ **valorous** adjective.

valuable adjective **1** worth a great deal of money. **2** extremely useful or important. noun (**valuables**) valuable items.

valuation noun an estimation of how much something is worth.

value noun **1** the importance or usefulness of something. **2** the amount of money that something is worth. **3** (**values**) standards of behaviour. **4** the amount represented by a letter or symbol. **5** the relative length of the sound represented by a musical note. verb (**values, valuing, valued**) **1** estimate how much something is worth. **2** consider something to be important or useful. □ **value added tax** a tax on the amount by which goods rise in value at each stage of production.

valve noun **1** a device for controlling the flow of a liquid or gas through a pipe or duct. **2** a mechanism that varies the length of the tube in a brass musical instrument. **3** a structure in the heart or a vein which allows blood to flow in one direction only.

vamp[1] verb **1** (**vamp up**) informal improve something by adding something more interesting to it. **2** repeat a short, simple passage of music.

vamp[2] informal noun a woman who uses her sexual attractiveness to control men. ▪ **vampish** adjective.

vampire noun **1** (in stories) a dead person that leaves their grave at night to drink the blood of living people. **2** (also **vampire bat**) a blood-sucking bat found mainly in tropical America. ▪ **vampirism** noun.

van[1] noun **1** a motor vehicle used for moving goods or a group of people. **2** Brit. a railway carriage used for large luggage, mail, etc.

van[2] noun (**the van**) the leading part of an advancing group of people.

vanadium noun a hard grey metallic chemical element, used to make alloy steels.

vandal noun a person who deliberately destroys or damages property. ▪ **vandalism** noun.

vandalize or **vandalise** verb (**vandalizes, vandalizing, vandalized**) deliberately destroy or damage property.

vane noun a broad blade that is moved by wind or water, forming part of a windmill, propeller, or turbine.

vanguard noun **1** the leading part of an advancing army. **2** a group of people leading the way in new developments or ideas.

vanilla noun a substance obtained from the pods of a tropical plant, used as a flavouring or scent.

vanish verb **1** disappear suddenly and completely. **2** gradually cease to exist.

vanity noun (plural **vanities**) **1** too much pride in your own appearance or achievements. **2** pointlessness; futility. □ **vanity case** a small case fitted with a mirror and compartments for toiletries.

vanquish verb defeat thoroughly.

vantage or **vantage point** noun a place or position giving the best view.

vapid adjective offering no stimulation or challenge. ■ **vapidity** noun.

vaporize or **vaporise** verb (vaporizes, vaporizing, vaporized) convert something into vapour. ■ **vaporization** noun **vaporizer** noun.

vapour (US spelling **vapor**) noun **1** moisture suspended in the air. **2** Physics a gaseous substance that can be made into liquid by pressure alone.

variable adjective **1** not consistent or having a fixed pattern. **2** able to be changed or adapted. noun a variable element, feature, or quantity. ■ **variability** noun **variably** adverb.

variance noun **1** the fact or quality of being different or inconsistent. **2** the state of disagreeing or quarrelling.

variant noun a version that varies from other forms of the same thing.

variation noun **1** a change or slight difference in condition, amount, or level. **2** a different or distinct form or version. **3** a new but still recognizable version of a musical theme.

varicose adjective (of a vein) swollen, twisted, and lengthened, as a result of poor circulation.

varied adjective involving a number of different types or elements.

variegated /vair-i-gay-tid/ adjective having irregular patches or streaks of a different colour or colours. ■ **variegation** noun.

> ✓ remember the **e** in the middle:
> variegated.

variety noun (plural **varieties**) **1** the quality of being varied. **2** (**a variety of**) a number of things of the same type that are distinct in character. **3** a thing which differs in some way from others of the same general class. **4** a

form of entertainment involving singing, dancing, and comedy.

various adjective of different kinds or sorts. **determiner & pronoun** more than one; individual and separate. ■ **variously** adverb.

varnish noun a liquid applied to wood to give a hard, clear, shiny surface when dry. verb apply varnish to.

vary verb (**varies, varying, varied**) **1** differ in size, degree, or nature from something else of the same general class. **2** change from one form or state to another. **3** alter something to make it less uniform.

vascular adjective referring to the system of vessels for carrying blood or (in plants) the tissues carrying sap, water, and nutrients.

vas deferens /vass **def**-uh-renz/ noun (plural **vasa deferentia** /vay-suh def-uh-**ren**-shuh/) the duct carrying sperm from a testicle to the urethra.

vase noun a container for displaying cut flowers.

vasectomy /vuh-**sek**-tuh-mi/ noun (plural **vasectomies**) the surgical cutting and sealing of part of each vas deferens as a means of sterilization.

vaseline noun trademark a type of petroleum jelly used as an ointment and lubricant.

vassal noun (in the feudal system) a man who promised to support and fight for a king or lord in return for holding a piece of land.

vast adjective of very great extent or quantity; immense. ■ **vastly** adverb **vastness** noun.

VAT abbreviation value added tax.

vat noun a large tank or tub used to hold liquid.

Vatican noun the official residence of the Pope in Rome.

vaudeville /**vaw**-duh-vil/ noun a type of entertainment featuring a mixture of musical and comedy acts.

vault[1] noun **1** a roof in the form of an arch or a series of arches. **2** a large room used for storage. **3** a chamber beneath a church or in a graveyard used for burials. ■ **vaulted** adjective.

vault² verb leap or spring using your hands or a pole to push yourself. noun an act of vaulting.

vaunted adjective praised or boasted about.

VC abbreviation Victoria Cross.

VCR abbreviation video cassette recorder.

veal noun meat from a young calf.

vector noun **1** Mathematics a quantity having direction as well as magnitude. **2** the carrier of a disease or infection.

veer verb (**veers, veering, veered**) **1** change direction suddenly. **2** (of the wind) change direction clockwise around the points of the compass. noun a sudden change of direction.

vegan noun a person who does not eat or use any animal products.

vegetable noun **1** a plant used as food. **2** offensive a person who is incapable of normal mental or physical activity as a result of brain damage.

 vege-, not *vega-*: vegetable.

vegetal adjective relating to plants.

vegetarian noun a person who does not eat meat. adjective eating or including no meat. ■ **vegetarianism** noun.

vegetate verb (**vegetates, vegetating, vegetated**) spend time in an inactive and unchallenging way.

vegetation noun plants.

vegetative adjective **1** relating to vegetation or the growth of plants. **2** relating to reproduction or breeding by asexual means. **3** Medicine alive but showing no sign of brain activity or responsiveness.

vehement /vee-uh-muhnt/ adjective showing strong feeling. ■ **vehemence** noun **vehemently** adverb.

vehicle noun a car, lorry, or other thing used for transporting people or goods on land. ■ **vehicular** /vi-**hik**-yuu-ler/ adjective.

veil noun **1** a piece of fine material

worn to protect or hide the face. **2** the part of a nun's headdress that covers the head and shoulders. **3** a thing that hides or disguises. □ **draw a veil over** refrain from discussing. verb **1** cover with a veil. **2** (**veiled**) partially hidden or disguised.

vein noun **1** any of the tubes that carry blood from all parts of the body towards the heart. **2** a blood vessel. **3** (in plants) a thin rib running through a leaf. **4** (in insects) a hollow rib forming part of the supporting framework of a wing. **5** a streak of a different colour in wood, marble, cheese, etc. **6** a fracture in rock containing a deposit of minerals or ore. **7** a source of a particular quality: *a vein of humour.* ■ **veined** adjective.

Velcro noun trademark a fastener consisting of two strips of fabric covered with tiny hooks.

veld or **veldt** /velt/ noun open, uncultivated country or grassland in southern Africa.

vellum noun fine parchment made from animal skin.

velociraptor /vi-los-si-rap-ter/ noun a small meat-eating dinosaur.

velocity noun (plural **velocities**) speed in a particular direction.

velour /vuh-**loor**/ noun a thick, soft fabric resembling velvet.

velvet noun a fabric with a soft, short pile on one side. ■ **velvety** adjective.

velveteen noun a cotton fabric resembling a thin velvet.

venal /vee-n'l/ adjective open to bribery. ■ **venality** noun.

vend verb sell small items. □ **vending machine** a machine that dispenses small articles when you insert a coin.

vendetta noun a feud in which the family of a murdered person seeks vengeance on the murderer or the murderer's family.

vendor (US spelling **vender**) noun **1** a person selling small items. **2** Law a person who is selling a property.

veneer noun **1** a thin covering of fine wood applied to a cheaper wood or other material. **2** an outward appearance that hides the true nature of someone or something. ■ **veneered** adjective.

venerable adjective given great respect because of age, wisdom, or character.

venerate verb (venerates, venerating, venerated) respect someone highly. ■ **veneration** noun.

venereal disease noun a disease caught by having sex with an infected person.

Venetian adjective relating to Venice. noun a person from Venice. □ **venetian blind** a window blind consisting of horizontal slats which can be turned to control the amount of light that passes through.

vengeance noun an act of harming or punishing someone in return for what they have done to you or someone close to you. □ **with a vengeance** with great intensity.

vengeful adjective wanting to punish or harm someone in return for something they have done.

venial /vee-ni-uhl/ adjective (of a fault or offence) slight and pardonable.

venison noun meat from a deer.

Venn diagram noun a diagram representing mathematical sets as circles, with overlapping sections representing elements shared between sets.

venom noun **1** the poisonous liquid produced by some animals that bite or sting, such as snakes and scorpions. **2** a strong feeling of hatred or bitterness.

venomous adjective **1** producing venom. **2** full of hatred or bitterness. ■ **venomously** adverb.

venous /vee-nuhss/ adjective relating to a vein or the veins.

vent¹ noun an opening that allows air, gas, or liquid to pass out of or into a confined space. verb **1** allow yourself to express a strong emotion. **2** let air, gas, or liquid pass through a vent.

vent² noun a slit in a garment.

ventilate verb (ventilates, ventilat-

ing, ventilated) cause air to enter and circulate freely in a room or building. ■ **ventilation** noun.

ventilator noun **1** an opening or a machine for ventilating a room or building. **2** a machine that pumps air in and out of a person's lungs to help them to breathe.

ventral adjective having to do with the underside or abdomen.

ventricle noun each of the two larger and lower cavities of the heart.

ventriloquist /ven-**tril**-uh-kwist/ noun an entertainer who can make their voice seem to come from elsewhere. ■ **ventriloquism** noun.

venture noun **1** a risky or daring journey or undertaking. **2** a business enterprise involving considerable risk. verb (ventures, venturing, ventured) **1** dare to do something dangerous or risky. **2** dare to say something bold.

venturesome adjective willing to take on something risky or difficult.

venue noun the place where an event or meeting is held.

Venus flytrap noun a plant with hinged leaves that spring shut on and digest insects which land on them.

veracious adjective formal truthful.

veracity noun the quality of truthfulness and accuracy.

veranda or **verandah** noun a roofed structure with an open front along the outside of a house.

verb noun a word expressing an action or occurrence.

verbal adjective **1** relating to or in the form of words. **2** spoken rather than written. **3** relating to a verb. ■ **verbally** adverb.

verbalize or **verbalise** verb (verbalizes, verbalizing, verbalized) express something in words.

verbatim /ver-**bay**-tim/ adverb & adjective in exactly the same words as were used originally.

verbiage noun excessively long or detailed speech or writing.

verbose adjective using more words than are needed. ■ **verbosity** noun.

GRAMMAR

Verb

A verb says what a person or thing does, and can describe:

- an action, e.g. *run, hit*
- an event, e.g. *rain, happen*
- a state, e.g. *be, have, seem*
- a change, e.g. *become, grow.*

Verbs occur in different forms, usually in one or other of their tenses. The most common tenses are:

- the simple present tense: *the boy walks down the road*
- the continuous present tense: *the boy is walking down the road*
- the simple past tense: *the boy walked down the road*
- the continuous past tense: *the boy was walking down the road*
- the perfect tense: *the boy has walked down the road*
- the future tense: *the boy will walk down the road.*

Each of these forms is a finite verb, which means that it is in a particular tense and that it changes according to the number and person of the subject, as in

I am	*you walk*
we are	*he walks.*

An infinitive is the form of a verb that usually appears with 'to', e.g.

to wander   *to look*   *to sleep.*

---

verdant adjective green with grass or other lush vegetation.

verdict noun **1** a decision made by a jury in a court of law about whether someone is innocent or guilty. **2** an opinion or judgement formed after trying or testing something.

verdigris /ver-di-gree/ noun a bright bluish-green substance formed on copper or brass by oxidation.

verdure noun lush green vegetation.

verge noun **1** Brit. a grass edging by the side of a road or path. **2** an edge or limit beyond which a particular thing will happen. **verb** (**verges, verging, verged**) (**verge on**) be very close to or similar to.

verger noun an official in a church who acts as a caretaker and attendant.

verify verb (**verifies, verifying, verified**) make sure or show that something is true and accurate. ∎ **verifiable** adjective **verification** noun.

verily adverb old use truly; certainly.

verisimilitude noun the appearance of being true or real.

veritable adjective genuine. ∎ **veritably** adverb.

verity noun (plural **verities**) formal truthfulness, or a truth.

vermicelli /ver-mi-**chel**-li/ plural noun **1** pasta made in long thin threads. **2** Brit. shreds of chocolate used to decorate cakes.

vermilion or **vermillion** noun a bright red pigment or colour.

vermin noun wild animals or birds which carry disease or harm crops. ∎ **verminous** adjective.

vermouth /ver-muhth/ noun a red or white wine flavoured with herbs.

vernacular noun the language or dialect spoken by the ordinary people of a country or region.

vernal adjective relating to the season of spring.

verruca /vuh-roo-kuh/ noun a contagious wart on the sole of the foot.

versatile adjective able to adapt or be

adapted to many different functions or activities. ■ **versatility** noun.

verse noun **1** writing arranged with a metrical rhythm. **2** a group of lines that form a unit in a poem or song. **3** each of the short numbered divisions of a chapter in the Bible.

versed adjective (**versed in**) experienced or skilled in.

versify verb (**versifies, versifying, versified**) write verse, or turn a piece of writing into verse. ■ **versification** noun.

version noun **1** a particular form of something which differs from other forms of the same type of thing. **2** an account of something told from a particular person's point of view.

verso /ver-soh/ noun (plural **versos**) a left-hand page of an open book, or the back of a loose document.

versus preposition **1** against. **2** as opposed to.

vertebra /ver-ti-bruh/ noun (plural **vertebrae** /ver-ti-bray, ver-ti-bree/) each of the series of small bones forming the backbone.

vertebrate noun an animal having a backbone, e.g. a mammal, bird, reptile, amphibian, or fish.

vertex noun (plural **vertices** /ver-ti-seez/ or **vertexes**) **1** the highest point. **2** a meeting point of two lines that form an angle.

vertical adjective going straight up or down, at a right angle to a horizontal line or surface. noun a vertical line or surface. ■ **vertically** adverb.

vertiginous /ver-tij-i-nuhss/ adjective extremely high or steep.

vertigo /ver-ti-goh/ noun a feeling of giddiness caused by looking down from a great height.

verve noun vigour, spirit, and style.

very adverb in a high degree. adjective **1** actual; precise. **2** extreme. **3** mere.

vespers noun a service of evening prayer.

vessel noun **1** a ship or large boat. **2** a tube or duct carrying a liquid within the body, or within a plant. **3** old use a bowl, cup, or other container for liquids.

vest noun **1** Brit. a sleeveless garment or undergarment worn on the upper part of the body. **2** N. Amer. & Austral. a waistcoat or sleeveless jacket. verb (**vest in**) give someone power or property, or the legal right to hold power or own property. □ **vested interest 1** a personal reason for wanting something to happen. **2** Law land or property that is being held in trust for someone.

vestibule noun a room or hall just inside the outer door of a building.

vestige noun **1** a last remaining trace of something. **2** the smallest amount. ■ **vestigial** adjective.

vestment noun a robe worn by ministers or members of the choir during church services.

vestry noun (plural **vestries**) a small room in a church, used as an office and for changing into ceremonial robes.

vet noun a veterinary surgeon. verb (**vets, vetting, vetted**) find out about someone's background and past before employing them.

vetch noun a plant that grows as a wild flower and is also grown for silage or fodder.

veteran noun **1** a person who has had long experience in a particular field. **2** a person who used to serve in the armed forces.

veterinarian noun N. Amer. a vet.

veterinary /vet-uh-ri-nuh-ri, vet-uhn-ri/ adjective relating to the treatment of diseases and injuries in animals. □ **veterinary surgeon** a person qualified to treat diseased or injured animals.

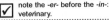

note the *-er-* before the *-in-*: veterinary.

veto /vee-toh/ noun (plural **vetoes**) **1** the right or power to reject a ruling or decision made by others. **2** such a rejection. verb (**vetoes, vetoing, vetoed**) exercise a veto against.

vex verb make someone annoyed or

worried. ■ **vexation** noun **vexatious** adjective.

vexed adjective **1** (of an issue) difficult to deal with and causing a lot of debate. **2** annoyed or worried.

VHF abbreviation very high frequency.

VHS abbreviation trademark video home system.

via preposition **1** travelling through a particular place on the way to a destination. **2** by way of; through. **3** by means of.

viable adjective **1** capable of working successfully. **2** (of a plant, animal, or cell) able to live. ■ **viability** noun.

viaduct noun a long bridge-like structure carrying a road or railway across a valley or other low ground.

vial noun a small container used for holding liquid medicines or potions.

viands plural noun old use food.

vibe or **vibes** noun informal the atmosphere of a place, or a feeling passing between people.

vibrant adjective **1** full of energy and enthusiasm. **2** (of sound) strong or resonant. **3** (of colour) bright. ■ **vibrancy** noun **vibrantly** adverb.

vibraphone noun an electrical percussion instrument giving a vibrato effect.

vibrate verb (**vibrates, vibrating, vibrated**) **1** move with rapid small movements to and fro. **2** (of a sound) resonate. ■ **vibration** noun.

vibrato /vi-**brah**-toh/ noun a rapid, slight variation in pitch in singing or playing some musical instruments.

vibrator noun a vibrating device used for massage or sexual stimulation.

vicar noun (in the Church of England) a minister in charge of a parish.

vicarage noun a vicar's house.

vicarious /vi-**kair**-i-uhss/ adjective experienced in the imagination rather than directly: *a vicarious thrill.* ■ **vicariously** adverb.

vice¹ noun **1** immoral or wicked behaviour. **2** criminal activities that involve sex or drugs. **3** a bad personal characteristic. **4** a bad habit.

vice² (US spelling **vise**) noun a metal tool with movable jaws which are used to hold an object firmly in place while work is done on it.

vice- combining form next in rank to; deputy: *vice-president.*

viceroy noun a person sent by a king or queen to govern a colony.

vice versa adverb reversing the order of the items just mentioned.

vicinity noun (plural **vicinities**) the area near or surrounding a place.

vicious adjective **1** cruel or violent. **2** (of an animal) wild and dangerous. □ **vicious circle** a situation in which one problem leads to another, which then makes the first one worse. ■ **viciously** adverb **viciousness** noun.

 no *s* in the middle: vi*c*ious.

vicissitudes /vi-**sis**-si-tyoodz/ plural noun the ups and downs and changes in your life.

victim noun a person who is harmed or killed as a result of a crime, injustice, or accident.

victimize or **victimise** verb (**victimizes, victimizing, victimized**) single someone out for cruel or unfair treatment. ■ **victimization** noun.

victor noun a person who defeats an opponent in a battle or contest.

Victorian adjective relating to the reign of Queen Victoria (1837–1901).

victorious adjective having won a victory. ■ **victoriously** adverb.

victory noun (plural **victories**) an act of defeating an opponent.

victuals /vi-**t'lz**/ plural noun old use food and provisions.

video noun (plural **videos**) **1** a system of recording and reproducing moving images using magnetic tape. **2** a film or other recording on magnetic tape. **3** Brit. a video recorder. verb (**videoes, videoing, videoed**) film or make a video recording of. □ **video game** a computer game played on a television screen. **video recorder** a machine used to record television programmes on to videotape, or to watch video films.

videotape noun **1** magnetic tape for recording and reproducing visual images and sound. **2** a cassette on which this magnetic tape is held. verb (**videotapes, videotaping, videotaped**) record on videotape.

vie verb (**vies, vying, vied**) compete eagerly with others in order to do or achieve something.

view noun **1** the ability to see something or to be seen from a particular position. **2** something seen from a particular position, especially natural scenery. **3** an attitude or opinion. verb **1** look at or inspect. **2** have a particular attitude towards. □ **in view of** because or as a result of. **with a view to** with the intention of. ■ **viewer** noun.

viewfinder noun a device on a camera that you look through to see what will appear in the picture.

viewpoint noun **1** a position giving a good view. **2** an opinion.

vigil /**vi**-jil/ noun a period of staying awake through the night to keep watch or pray.

vigilant adjective keeping careful watch for possible danger or difficulties. ■ **vigilance** noun **vigilantly** adverb.

vigilante /vi-ji-**lan**-ti/ noun a member of a group of people who take it on themselves to prevent crime or punish criminals without legal authority. ■ **vigilantism** noun.

vignette /vee-**nyet**/ noun **1** a brief, vivid description or episode. **2** a small illustration or photograph which fades into its background without a definite border.

vigorous adjective **1** strong, healthy, and full of energy. **2** involving physical strength, effort, or energy. ■ **vigorously** adverb.

vigour (US spelling **vigor**) noun **1** physical strength and good health. **2** effort, energy, and enthusiasm.

Viking noun a member of the Scandinavian people who settled in parts of Britain and elsewhere in NW Europe between the 8th and 11th centuries.

vile adjective **1** extremely unpleasant. **2** wicked. ■ **vilely** adverb.

vilify verb (**vilifies, vilifying, vilified**) speak or write about someone in a very unpleasant way. ■ **vilification** noun.

villa noun **1** a large house in ancient Rome. **2** Brit. a detached or semi-detached house. **3** a rented holiday home abroad.

village noun a small community of streets and houses in a rural area. ■ **villager** noun.

villain noun **1** a bad person. **2** a bad character in a novel or play whose actions are important to the plot. ■ **villainous** adjective **villainy** noun.

villein /**vil**-luhn, **vil**-layn/ noun (in medieval England) a poor man who had to work for a lord in return for a small piece of land on which to grow food.

vim noun informal energy; enthusiasm.

vinaigrette /vi-ni-**gret**, vi-nay-**gret**/ noun a salad dressing consisting of oil mixed with vinegar.

vindicate verb (**vindicates, vindicating, vindicated**) **1** clear someone of blame or suspicion. **2** show something to be right or justified. ■ **vindication** noun.

vindictive adjective having or showing a strong or inappropriate desire for revenge. ■ **vindictiveness** noun.

vine noun a climbing plant, especially one that bears grapes.

vinegar noun a sour-tasting liquid made from wine, cider, or beer, used as a seasoning or for pickling. ■ **vinegary** adjective.

vineyard noun a plantation of grapevines producing grapes used in winemaking.

vintage noun **1** the year or place in which wine was produced. **2** a wine of high quality made from the crop of a single identified district in a good year. **3** the harvesting of grapes for winemaking. **4** the grapes or wine of a particular season. **5** the time that something was produced. adjective

1 referring to vintage wine. **2** referring to something from the past of high quality.

vintner noun a wine merchant.

vinyl noun a strong flexible plastic or synthetic resin, used in making paints, gramophone records, etc.

viol /vy-uhl/ noun an early instrument like a violin, but with six strings.

viola[1] /vi-oh-luh/ noun an instrument of the violin family, larger than the violin and tuned to a lower pitch.

viola[2] /vy-uh-luh/ noun a flowering plant of a group that includes pansies and violets.

violate verb (violates, violating, violated) **1** break a rule or formal agreement. **2** treat something with disrespect. **3** rape or sexually assault. ■ violation noun.

violence noun **1** actions using physical force and intended to hurt or kill someone or to cause damage. **2** an unpleasant or destructive natural force. **3** strength of emotion.

violent adjective **1** using or involving violence. **2** very forceful or powerful. ■ violently adverb.

violet noun **1** a small plant with purple or blue five-petalled flowers. **2** a bluish-purple colour.

violin noun a musical instrument with four strings, that you play with a bow. ■ violinist noun.

violoncello /vy-uh-luhn-chel-loh/ formal term for CELLO.

VIP abbreviation very important person.

viper noun a poisonous snake with large fangs and a patterned body.

virago /vi-rah-goh/ noun (plural viragos or viragoes) a domineering, violent, or bad-tempered woman.

viral adjective having to do with a virus or viruses.

virgin noun **1** a person who has never had sex. **2** (the Virgin) the Virgin Mary, mother of Jesus. adjective **1** having had no sexual experience. **2** not yet used or exploited: *virgin forest*. **3** (of olive oil) made from the first

pressing of olives. ■ virginal adjective virginity noun.

Virgo noun a sign of the zodiac (the Virgin), 23 August–22 September.

virile adjective (of a man) having strength, energy, and a strong sex drive. ■ virility noun.

virtual adjective **1** almost or nearly the thing described, but not completely. **2** not existing in reality but made by computer software to appear to do so. □ virtual reality a system in which images that look like real objects are created by computer. ■ virtually adverb.

virtue noun **1** behaviour showing high moral standards. **2** a good or useful quality. **3** old use virginity or chastity. □ by virtue of because or as a result of.

virtuoso /ver-tyoo-oh-soh/ noun (plural virtuosi /ver-tyoo-oh-si/ or virtuosos) a person highly skilled in music or another art. ■ virtuosity noun.

virtuous adjective **1** having high moral standards. **2** old use chaste. ■ virtuously adverb.

virulent adjective **1** (of a disease or poison) extremely harmful in its effects. **2** bitterly hostile. ■ virulence noun virulently adverb.

virus noun **1** a submicroscopic organism which can cause disease. **2** informal an infection or disease caused by a virus. **3** a piece of code introduced secretly into a computer system in order to damage or destroy data.

visa noun a note on your passport indicating that you are allowed to enter, leave, or stay in a country.

visage noun literary a person's facial features or expression.

vis-à-vis /veez-ah-vee/ preposition in relation to.

viscera /vis-suh-ruh/ plural noun the internal organs of the body.

visceral adjective **1** relating to the viscera. **2** relating to deep inward feelings rather than to the intellect. ■ viscerally adverb.

viscose noun a smooth artificial fabric made from cellulose.

viscosity noun the state of being viscous.

viscount /**vy**-kownt/ noun a British nobleman ranking above a baron and below an earl. ■ **viscountess** noun.

viscous /**viss**-kuhss/ adjective having a thick, sticky consistency between solid and liquid.

vise US spelling of **VICE²**.

visibility noun **1** the state of being able to see or be seen. **2** the distance you can see, as determined by light and weather conditions.

visible adjective able to be seen or noticed. ■ **visibly** adverb.

vision noun **1** the ability to see. **2** the ability to think about the future with imagination or wisdom. **3** an experience of seeing something in a dream, trance, etc. **4** the images seen on a television screen. **5** a person or sight of unusual beauty.

visionary adjective **1** thinking about the future with imagination or wisdom. **2** relating to supernatural or dreamlike visions. noun (plural **visionaries**) a visionary person.

visit verb (**visits**, **visiting**, **visited**) **1** go to spend time with a person or in a place. **2** (**visit on** or **with**) literary inflict something harmful or unpleasant on someone. noun an act of visiting. ■ **visitor** noun.

visitation noun **1** an official or formal visit. **2** the appearance of a god, goddess, etc. **3** a disaster or difficulty seen as a punishment from God.

visor or **vizor** noun **1** a movable part of a helmet that can be pulled down to cover the face. **2** a screen for protecting the eyes from light.

vista noun a pleasing view.

visual adjective relating to seeing or sight. noun a picture, piece of film, or display used to illustrate or accompany something. □ **visual display unit** Brit. a device that displays information from a computer on a screen. ■ **visually** adverb.

visualize or **visualise** verb (**visualizes**, **visualizing**, **visualized**) form an image of something in the mind. ■ **visualization** noun.

vital adjective **1** absolutely necessary. **2** essential for life. **3** full of energy. noun (**vitals**) the body's important internal organs. □ **vital statistics** informal the measurements of a woman's bust, waist, and hips. ■ **vitally** adverb.

vitality noun the state of being strong and active.

vitalize or **vitalise** verb (**vitalizes**, **vitalizing**, **vitalized**) give strength and energy to.

vitamin noun any of a group of natural substances which are present in many foods and are essential for normal nutrition.

vitiate /**vi**-shi-ayt/ verb (**vitiates**, **vitiating**, **vitiated**) formal make something less good or effective.

viticulture noun the cultivation of grapevines.

vitreous adjective containing or resembling glass. □ **vitreous humour** the transparent jelly-like tissue that fills the eyeball.

vitrify verb (**vitrifies**, **vitrifying**, **vitrified**) convert into glass or a glass-like substance by exposure to heat.

vitriol noun **1** old use sulphuric acid. **2** extreme bitterness or malice. ■ **vitriolic** adjective.

vituperation noun bitter and abusive language. ■ **vituperative** adjective.

viva¹ /**vy**-vuh/ or **viva voce** /vy-vuh **voh**-chi/ noun Brit. an oral examination for an academic qualification.

viva² /**vee**-vuh/ exclamation long live!

vivacious adjective attractively lively. ■ **vivaciously** adverb **vivacity** noun.

vivarium noun (plural **vivaria**) a place for keeping animals in natural conditions for study or as pets.

vivid adjective **1** producing powerful feelings or strong, clear images in the mind. **2** (of a colour) very deep or bright. ■ **vividly** adverb **vividness** noun.

vivify verb (**vivifies**, **vivifying**, **vivified**) formal make more lively or interesting; enliven.

viviparous /vi-**vi**-puh-ruhss/ adjective

(of an animal) giving birth to live young.

vivisection noun the performance of operations on live animals for scientific research.

vixen noun 1 a female fox. 2 a spiteful or quarrelsome woman.

viz. adverb namely; in other words.

 short for Latin *videlicet*.

vizor ⇒ **VISOR**.

vocabulary noun (plural **vocabularies**) 1 all the words used in a particular language or activity. 2 all the words known to a person. 3 a list of words and their meanings, accompanying a text.

vocal adjective 1 relating to the human voice. 2 expressing opinions or feelings freely or loudly. 3 (of music) consisting of or including singing. noun (also **vocals**) a part of a piece of music that is sung. ◻ **vocal cords** strips of muscle in the throat that vibrate to produce the voice. ■ **vocally** adverb.

vocalist noun a singer.

vocalize or **vocalise** verb (**vocalizes, vocalizing, vocalized**) 1 utter a sound or word. 2 express with words.

vocation noun 1 a strong feeling that you ought to pursue a particular career or occupation. 2 a person's career or occupation. ■ **vocational** adjective.

vocative /vok-uh-tiv/ noun Grammar the case of nouns, pronouns, and adjectives used in addressing a person or thing.

vociferous /vuh-**sif**-uh-ruhss/ adjective vehement or loud. ■ **vociferously** adverb.

vodka noun a clear Russian alcoholic spirit.

vogue noun the fashion or style current at a particular time. ■ **voguish** adjective.

voice noun 1 the sound produced in a person's larynx and uttered through the mouth, as speech or song. 2 the ability to speak or sing. 3 a vocal part in a musical composition. 4 Grammar a form of a verb showing the relation of the subject to the action. verb (**voices, voicing, voiced**) express in words. ◻ **voice box** the larynx. **voice-over** a piece of speech in a film or broadcast not accompanied by an image of the speaker. ■ **voiceless** adjective.

voicemail noun an electronic system which can store messages from telephone callers.

void adjective 1 not valid or legally binding. 2 completely empty. 3 (**void of**) free from; lacking. noun a completely empty space. verb 1 declare to be not valid or legally binding. 2 discharge water, gases, etc.

voile /voyl, vwahl/ noun a thin, semi-transparent fabric.

volatile adjective 1 (of a substance) easily evaporated at normal temperatures. 2 liable to change rapidly and unpredictably. ■ **volatility** noun.

vol-au-vent /**vol**-oh-von/ noun a small round case of puff pastry filled with a savoury mixture.

volcanic adjective relating to or produced by a volcano or volcanoes.

volcano noun (plural **volcanoes** or **volcanos**) a mountain with an opening through which lava, rock, and gas are forced from the earth's crust.

vole noun a small mouse-like rodent.

volition noun a person's will or power of independent action.

volley noun (plural **volleys**) 1 a number of bullets, arrows, etc. fired at one time. 2 a series of questions, insults, etc. directed rapidly at someone. 3 (in sport) a strike of the ball made before it touches the ground. verb (**volleys, volleying, volleyed**) strike the ball before it touches the ground.

volleyball noun a team game in which a ball is hit by hand over a net and must be kept from touching the ground.

volt noun the basic unit of electric potential.

voltage noun an electrical force expressed in volts.

volte-face /volt-**fass**/ noun an abrupt

WORD FORMATION

-vorous

Words ending in **-vorous** mean 'eating a specified kind of food'. Some examples are:

carnivorous	eating meat
herbivorous	eating plants
insectivorous	eating insects
omnivorous	eating both plants and animals
piscivorous	eating fish.

The suffix **-vore** forms related nouns, e.g. *carnivore*, 'an animal that eats meat'. Both **-vorous** and **-vore** come from the Latin word *vorare*, 'to devour'.

and complete change of attitude or policy.

voluble adjective talking easily and at length. ■ **volubility** noun **volubly** adverb.

volume noun **1** a book, especially one forming part of a larger work or series. **2** the amount of space occupied by something or enclosed within a container. **3** the amount or quantity of something. **4** degree of loudness.

voluminous adjective **1** (of clothing) loose and full. **2** (of writing) very lengthy.

voluntary adjective **1** done or acting of your own free will. **2** working or done without payment. noun (plural **voluntaries**) an organ solo played before, during, or after a church service. ■ **voluntarily** adverb.

volunteer noun **1** a person who freely offers to do something. **2** a person who does work without being paid. **3** a person who freely joins the armed forces. verb (**volunteers, volunteering, volunteered**) **1** freely offer to do something. **2** say or suggest something without being asked. **3** freely join the armed forces.

voluptuary noun (plural **voluptuaries**) a person who loves luxury and pleasure.

voluptuous /vuh-**lup**-tyuu-uhss/ adjective **1** characterized by luxury and pleasure. **2** (of a woman) curvaceous and sexually attractive. ■ **voluptuously** adverb.

vomit verb (**vomits, vomiting, vomited**) **1** bring up food from the stomach through the mouth. **2** send out in an uncontrolled stream. noun food vomited from the stomach.

voodoo noun a religious cult practised in the Caribbean and the southern US and involving sorcery and possession by spirits.

voracious adjective **1** wanting or eating great quantities of food. **2** eagerly consuming something. ■ **voraciously** adverb **voracity** noun.

vortex noun (plural **vortexes** or **vortices** /**vor**-ti-seez/) a whirling mass of water or air.

votary noun (plural **votaries**) **1** a person who has dedicated themselves to God or religious service. **2** a devoted follower or supporter.

vote noun **1** a formal choice made between two or more candidates or courses of action. **2** (**the vote**) the right to participate in an election. verb (**votes, voting, voted**) give or register a vote. ■ **voter** noun.

votive adjective offered to a god as a sign of thanks.

vouch verb (**vouch for**) **1** state that something is true or accurate. **2** state that someone is who they claim to be, or that they are of good character.

voucher noun a piece of paper that entitles you to a discount, or that may be exchanged for goods or services.

vouchsafe verb (**vouchsafes, vouchsafing, vouchsafed**) formal give or say in a gracious or superior way.

vow noun a solemn promise. **verb** solemnly promise to do something.

vowel noun a letter of the alphabet representing a sound in which the mouth is open and the tongue is not touching the top of the mouth, the teeth, or the lips (in English *a*, *e*, *i*, *o*, and *u*).

voyage noun a long journey by sea or in space. **verb** (**voyages, voyaging, voyaged**) go on a voyage. ■ **voyager** noun.

voyeur /vwa-**yer**, voy-**er**/ noun **1** a person who gains sexual pleasure from watching others when they are naked or having sex. **2** a person who enjoys seeing the pain, problems, etc. of others. ■ **voyeurism** noun **voyeuristic** adjective.

vs abbreviation versus.

vulcanized or **vulcanised** adjective (of rubber) hardened by being treated with sulphur at a high temperature.

vulgar adjective **1** lacking sophistication or good taste. **2** referring inappropriately to sex or bodily functions; rude. □ **vulgar fraction** Brit. a fraction shown by numbers above and below a line, not decimally. ■ **vulgarity** noun **vulgarly** adverb.

vulgarize or **vulgarise** verb (**vulgarizes, vulgarizing, vulgarized**) spoil something by making it less refined or exclusive.

vulnerable adjective exposed to being attacked or harmed. ■ **vulnerability** noun **vulnerably** adverb.

vulpine adjective having to do with foxes, or like a fox.

vulture noun **1** a large bird of prey that feeds chiefly on dead animals. **2** a person who exploits others.

vulva noun the female external genitals.

vying present participle of VIE.

Ww

W or **w** noun (plural **Ws** or **W's**) the twenty-third letter of the alphabet. **abbreviation 1** watts. **2** West or Western.

wacky or **whacky** adjective (**wackier, wackiest**) informal funny or amusing in a slightly odd way.

wad noun **1** a lump or bundle of a soft material. **2** a bundle of paper or banknotes. **verb** (**wads, wadding, wadded**) **1** compress a soft material into a wad. **2** line or fill with soft material.

waddle verb (**waddles, waddling, waddled**) walk with short steps and a clumsy swaying motion. **noun** a waddling way of walking.

wade verb (**wades, wading, waded**) **1** walk through water or mud. **2** (**wade through**) read through a long piece of writing with effort. **3** (**wade in** or **into**) informal attack or intervene in a forceful way.

wader noun **1** a long-legged bird that feeds in shallow water. **2** (**waders**) high waterproof boots.

wafer noun **1** a very thin, light, crisp sweet biscuit. **2** a thin disc of unleavened bread used in the Christian ceremony of the Eucharist.

waffle[1] informal verb (**waffles, waffling, waffled**) speak or write at length in a vague or trivial way. **noun** lengthy but vague or trivial talk or writing.

waffle[2] noun a small, crisp batter cake, eaten hot with butter or syrup.

waft verb pass easily or gently through the air. **noun** a gentle movement of air.

wag verb (**wags, wagging, wagged**) move rapidly to and fro. **noun 1** a wagging movement. **2** informal a person who is fond of making jokes. ■ **waggish** adjective.

wage noun (also **wages**) a fixed regular payment for work. verb (**wages, waging, wages**) carry on a war or campaign.

wager more formal term for **BET**.

waggle verb (**waggles, waggling, waggled**) move with short, quick movements from side to side or up and down. noun an act of waggling.

wagon or Brit. **waggon** noun **1** a vehicle, especially a horse-drawn one, for transporting goods. **2** Brit. a railway vehicle for carrying goods in bulk. □ **on the wagon** informal not drinking any alcohol.

wagtail noun a slender bird with a long tail that it frequently wags up and down.

waif noun a poor, helpless person, especially a child.

wail noun **1** a long high-pitched cry of pain, grief, or anger. **2** a sound resembling this. verb give or utter a wail.

wain noun old use a wagon or cart.

wainscot /**wayn**-skuht/ noun an area of wooden panelling on the lower part of the walls of a room.

waist noun **1** the part of the human body below the ribs and above the hips. **2** a narrow part in the middle of something.

waistband noun a strip of cloth forming the waist of a skirt or pair of trousers.

waistcoat noun Brit. a waist-length garment with buttons down the front and no sleeves or collar.

waistline noun the measurement around a person's body at the waist.

wait verb **1** stay where you are or delay doing anything until a particular time or event. **2** be delayed or deferred. **3** (**wait on**) act as an attendant to. **4** act as a waiter or waitress. noun a period of waiting.

waiter or **waitress** noun a person whose job is to serve customers at their tables in a restaurant.

waive verb (**waives, waiving, waived**)

choose not to insist on a claim or right.

waiver noun an instance of waiving a right or claim, or a document recording this.

wake¹ verb (**wakes, waking, woke**; past participle **woken**) **1** (often **wake up**) stop sleeping. **2** bring to life, or make more alert. **3** (**wake up to**) become aware of. noun **1** a gathering held beside the body of someone who has died. **2** a party held after a funeral.

wake² noun a trail of disturbed water or air left by a ship or aircraft. □ **in the wake of** following as a result of.

wakeful adjective **1** not sleeping. **2** alert and aware of possible dangers. ■ **wakefulness** noun.

waken verb wake from sleep.

walk verb **1** move fairly slowly using the legs. **2** travel over a route or area on foot. **3** accompany someone on foot. **4** take a dog out for exercise. noun **1** a journey on foot. **2** an unhurried rate of movement on foot. **3** a person's way of walking. **4** a path for walking. □ **walking stick** a stick used for support when walking. **walk of life** the position in society that someone holds. **walk-on part** a small part in a play or film that does not involve any speaking. ■ **walker** noun.

walkie-talkie noun a portable two-way radio.

Walkman noun (plural **Walkmans** or **Walkmen**) trademark a personal stereo.

walkout noun a sudden angry departure as a protest or strike.

walkover noun an easy victory.

walkway noun a raised passageway or a wide path.

wall noun **1** a continuous upright structure forming a side of a building or room, or enclosing or dividing an area of land. **2** a barrier. **3** the outer layer or lining of an organ or cavity in the body. verb enclose or block with walls. □ **go to the wall** informal (of a business) fail. **off the wall** N. Amer. informal unconventional. **wall-eyed** informal having an eye that squints outwards.

wallaby noun (plural **wallabies**) an Australian animal resembling a small kangaroo.

wallet noun a small flat, folding holder for money and plastic cards.

wallflower noun 1 a plant with fragrant flowers that bloom in early spring. 2 informal a girl who has no one to dance with at a party.

wallop informal verb (**wallops, walloping, walloped**) 1 hit very hard. 2 heavily defeat. 3 (**walloping**) strikingly large. noun a heavy blow.

wallow verb 1 roll about or lie in mud or water. 2 (of a boat or aircraft) roll from side to side. 3 (**wallow in**) indulge in. noun 1 an act of wallowing. 2 an area of mud or shallow water where mammals go to wallow.

wallpaper noun 1 paper pasted in strips over the walls of a room as decoration. 2 a background pattern or picture on a computer screen. verb (**wallpapers, wallpapering, wallpapered**) apply wallpaper to.

wally noun (plural **wallies**) Brit. informal a silly or incompetent person.

walnut noun an edible nut with a wrinkled shell.

walrus noun a large sea mammal with downward-pointing tusks.

waltz noun a ballroom dance in triple time performed by a couple. verb 1 dance a waltz. 2 move in a casual or inconsiderate way.

waltzer noun a fairground ride in which cars are carried round a track that moves up and down.

wan /won/ adjective 1 (of a person) pale and appearing ill or exhausted. 2 (of light) pale; weak. 3 (of a smile) weak; strained. ■ **wanly** adverb.

wand noun 1 a rod used in casting magic spells or performing tricks. 2 a slender rod, especially one held as a symbol of office.

wander verb (**wanders, wandering, wandered**) 1 move in a leisurely, casual, or aimless way. 2 move slowly away from the correct place. noun a spell of wandering. ■ **wanderer** noun.

wanderlust noun a strong desire to travel.

wane verb (**wanes, waning, waned**) 1 (of the moon) appear to decrease in size day by day. 2 become weaker. □ **on the wane** becoming weaker.

wangle verb (**wangles, wangling, wangled**) informal obtain something by tricks or persuasion.

wank Brit. vulgar verb masturbate. noun an act of masturbating.

wanker noun Brit. vulgar a disliked or unpleasant man.

want verb 1 have a desire to possess or do. 2 feel sexual desire for. 3 (**be wanted**) (of a suspected criminal) be searched for by the police. 4 (also **want for**) lack or be short of. 5 informal need. noun 1 a desire for something. 2 lack or shortage. 3 poverty.

wanting adjective 1 not having something required or desired. 2 absent; not provided.

wanton adjective 1 (of a cruel or violent action) deliberate and unprovoked. 2 having many sexual partners. ■ **wantonly** adverb.

WAP abbreviation Wireless Application Protocol.

wapiti /wop-i-ti/ noun (plural **wapitis**) a large North American red deer.

war noun 1 a state of armed conflict between different nations, states, or groups. 2 a long contest between rivals or campaign against something. verb (**wars, warring, warred**) engage in a war. □ **be on the warpath** be very angry with someone. **war crime** an action that violates accepted international rules of war.

warble verb (**warbles, warbling, warbled**) sing in a trilling or quavering voice.

warbler noun a small songbird with a warbling song.

ward noun 1 a room in a hospital for one or more patients. 2 a division of a city or borough that is represented by a councillor or councillors. 3 a young person looked after by a guardian appointed by their parents or a court. 4 a ridge or bar in a lock that engages with grooves on a key. verb (**ward off**) keep from being harmful.

warden noun **1** a person supervising a place or procedure. **2** Brit. the head of certain schools, colleges, etc. **3** N. Amer. a prison governor.

warder noun (feminine **wardress**) Brit. a prison guard.

wardrobe noun **1** a large, tall cupboard for hanging clothes in. **2** a person's entire collection of clothes. **3** the costume department of a theatre or film company.

wardroom noun the room on a warship where the officers eat.

ware noun **1** pottery of a specified type. **2** manufactured articles. **3** (**wares**) articles offered for sale.

warehouse noun **1** a large building for storing raw materials or manufactured goods. **2** a large wholesale or retail store.

warfare noun the activity of fighting a war.

warhead noun the explosive head of a missile, torpedo, etc.

warhorse noun informal a very experienced soldier, politician, etc.

warlike adjective **1** hostile. **2** intended for war.

warlock noun a man who practises witchcraft.

warlord noun a military commander, especially one controlling a region.

warm adjective **1** at a fairly high temperature. **2** helping the body to stay warm. **3** enthusiastic, affectionate, or kind. **4** (of a colour) containing red, yellow, or orange tones. **5** (of a scent or trail) fresh; strong. verb **1** make or become warm. **2** (**warm to** or **towards**) become more interested in or enthusiastic about. noun (**the warm**) a warm place or area. □ **warm-blooded** (of animals) maintaining a constant body temperature by their body's chemical processes. **warm up 1** prepare for physical exertion by doing gentle stretches and exercises. **2** entertain an audience before the arrival of the main act. ■ **warmly** adverb.

warmonger noun a person who tries to bring about war.

warmth noun **1** the quality of being warm. **2** enthusiasm, affection, or kindness. **3** strength of emotion.

warn verb **1** tell someone of a possible danger or problem. **2** advise someone not to do something. **3** (**warn off**) order someone to keep away.

warning noun **1** a statement or event that indicates a possible danger or problem. **2** advice against wrong or foolish behaviour. **3** advance notice.

warp verb **1** make or become bent or twisted. **2** make abnormal or strange. noun **1** a distortion or twist in shape. **2** the lengthwise threads on a loom over and under which the weft threads are passed to make cloth.

warrant noun **1** an official authorization allowing police, soldiers, etc. to make an arrest, search premises, etc. **2** a document that entitles you to receive goods, money, or services. **3** justification or authority. verb **1** justify or make necessary. **2** officially state or guarantee. □ **warrant officer** a rank of military officer below the commissioned officers.

warranty noun (plural **warranties**) a written guarantee promising to repair or replace an article if necessary within a specified period.

warren noun **1** a network of interconnecting rabbit burrows. **2** a complex network of paths or passages.

warrior noun a brave or experienced soldier or fighter.

warship noun an armed ship designed to take part in warfare at sea.

wart noun a small, hard growth on the skin. □ **warts and all** informal including faults or unattractive qualities. ■ **warty** adjective.

warthog noun an African wild pig with warty lumps on the face.

wary adjective (**warier**, **wariest**) cautious about possible dangers or problems. ■ **warily** adverb **wariness** noun.

was 1st and 3rd person singular past of **BE**.

wash verb **1** clean with water and usually soap or detergent. **2** (of water) flow freely in a particular direction.

3 (wash over) occur all around without greatly affecting someone. **4** informal seem convincing or genuine. **noun 1** an act of washing. **2** a quantity of clothes needing to be washed. **3** the water or air disturbed by a moving boat or aircraft. **4** a medicinal or cleansing solution. **5** a thin coating of paint. □ **be washed out 1** be postponed or cancelled because of rain. **2 (washed out)** pale and tired. **wash your hands of** take no further responsibility for. **wash up 1** Brit. wash crockery and cutlery after use. **2 (washed up)** informal no longer effective or successful.

washbasin noun a basin for washing your hands and face.

washboard noun a ridged or corrugated board formerly used for scrubbing clothes when washing them.

washer noun **1** a person or device that washes. **2** a small flat ring fixed between a nut and bolt.

washing noun a quantity of clothes, bedlinen, etc. that needs washing or has just been washed. □ **washing machine** a machine for washing clothes, bedlinen, etc. **washing-up** Brit. crockery, cutlery, etc. that need washing.

washout noun informal a disappointing failure.

washroom noun N. Amer. a room with washing and toilet facilities.

washstand noun a piece of furniture formerly used to hold a bowl or basin for washing the hands and face.

wasn't short form was not.

wasp noun a stinging winged insect with a black and yellow striped body. □ **wasp waist** a very narrow waist.

waspish adjective sharply irritable. ■ **waspishly** adverb.

wassail /wos-sayl, wos-s'l/ old use noun lively festivities involving the drinking of a lot of alcohol. verb **1** celebrate with a lot of alcohol. **2** go carol-singing at Christmas.

wastage noun **1** the process of wasting. **2** an amount wasted. **3 (also natural wastage)** the reduction in the size of a workforce through people resigning or retiring.

waste verb **(wastes, wasting, wasted) 1** use carelessly or extravagantly. **2** fail to make good use of. **3 (be wasted on)** not be appreciated by. **4 (often waste away)** gradually become weaker and thinner. **5** N. Amer. informal kill. **6 (wasted)** informal under the influence of alcohol or illegal drugs. adjective **1** discarded because no longer useful or required. **2 (of land)** not used, cultivated, or built on. noun **1** an instance of wasting. **2** material that is not wanted or useful. **3** a large area of barren, uninhabited land. □ **lay waste to** completely destroy. ■ **waster** noun.

wasteful adjective using up something carelessly or extravagantly. ■ **wastefully** adverb.

wasteland noun a barren or empty area of land.

wastrel noun literary a wasteful or worthless person.

watch verb **1** look at attentively. **2** keep under careful observation. **3** be cautious about. **4 (watch for)** look out for. **5 (watch out)** be careful. noun **1** a small clock worn on a strap on your wrist. **2** an instance of watching. **3** a period of keeping watch during the night. **4** a shift worked by firefighters or police officers. □ **keep watch** be alert for danger or trouble. ■ **watchable** adjective **watcher** noun.

watchdog noun **1** a dog kept to guard property. **2** a person or group that monitors the practices of companies.

watchful adjective alert to possible difficulty or danger. ■ **watchfully** adverb **watchfulness** noun.

watchman noun a man employed to look after an empty building.

watchtower noun a tower built as a high observation point.

watchword noun a word or phrase expressing a central aim or belief.

water noun **1** the liquid which forms the seas, lakes, rivers, and rain. **2 (waters)** an area of sea under the authority of a particular country. **3 (waters)** fluid discharged shortly before a baby's birth. **verb** (**waters, watering, watered**) **1** pour water over a plant. **2** give a drink of water to an animal. **3** (of the eyes or mouth) produce tears or saliva. **4** dilute a drink with water. **5** (**water down**) make something less forceful or controversial. **6** (of a river) flow through an area. □ **hold water** (of a theory) appear sound. **water buffalo** a kind of Asian buffalo used for carrying heavy loads. **water cannon** a device that ejects a powerful jet of water, used to disperse a crowd. **water closet** dated a flush toilet. **water ice** a frozen dessert consisting of fruit juice or purée in a sugar syrup. **watering can** a portable container with a long spout, used for watering plants. **watering hole** informal a pub or bar. **water lily** a plant that grows in water, with large round floating leaves. **water meadow** a meadow that is periodically flooded by a stream or river. **water on the brain** informal hydrocephalus. **water polo** a game played by swimmers in a pool, who try to throw the ball into their opponents' net. **water table** the level below which the ground is saturated with water. **water tower** a tower that raises up a water tank to create enough pressure to distribute the water through pipes. ■ **waterless** adjective **watery** adjective.

waterbed noun a bed with a water-filled mattress.

watercolour (US spelling **watercolor**) noun **1** artists' paint that is thinned with water. **2** a picture painted with watercolours.

watercourse noun a stream or artificial water channel.

watercress noun a kind of cress which grows in running water.

waterfall noun a place where a stream of water falls from a height.

waterfowl plural noun ducks, geese, or other large birds living in water.

waterfront noun a part of a town or city alongside a body of water.

waterhole noun a water-filled hollow where animals drink.

waterline noun the level normally reached by the water on the side of a ship.

waterlogged adjective saturated with water.

watermark noun a faint design made in some paper that can be seen when held against the light.

watermelon noun a large melon-like fruit with smooth green skin, red pulp, and watery juice.

watermill noun a mill worked by a waterwheel.

waterproof adjective unable to be penetrated by water. **noun** Brit. a waterproof garment. **verb** make waterproof.

watershed noun **1** an area of land that separates waters flowing to different rivers, seas, etc. **2** a turning point in a state of affairs.

waterski noun (plural **waterskis**) each of a pair of skis that let you skim the surface of the water when towed by a motor boat. **verb** (**waterskis, waterskiing, waterskied**) travel on waterskis. ■ **waterskier** noun.

waterspout noun a column of water formed by a whirlwind over the sea.

watertight adjective **1** not allowing any water to pass through. **2** unable to be called into question.

waterway noun a river, canal, or other route for travel by water.

waterwheel noun a large wheel driven by flowing water, used to work machinery or to raise water to a higher level.

waterworks noun a place with equipment for managing a water supply.

watt noun the basic unit of power.

wattage noun an amount of electrical power expressed in watts.

wattle[1] noun rods interlaced with twigs or branches, used for making fences, walls, etc. □ **wattle and daub** wattle covered with mud or clay, formerly used in building walls.

wattle[2] noun a fleshy part hanging from the head or neck of the turkey and some other birds.

wave verb (**waves, waving, waved**) **1** move your hand, or something held in it, to and fro, especially when greeting someone. **2** move to and fro with a swaying motion. noun **1** a ridge of water moving along the surface of the sea or breaking on the shore. **2** a sudden increase in a phenomenon or emotion. **3** a gesture made by waving your hand. **4** a slightly curling lock of hair. **5** a regular to-and-fro motion of particles of matter involved in transmitting sound, light, heat, etc.

waveband noun a range of wavelengths used in radio transmission.

wavelength noun **1** the distance between successive crests of a wave of sound, light, radio, etc. **2** a person's way of thinking.

wavelet noun a small wave.

waver verb (**wavers, wavering, wavered**) **1** move in a quivering way; flicker. **2** begin to weaken; falter. **3** be indecisive.

wavy adjective (**wavier, waviest**) having a series of wave-like curves.

wax¹ noun **1** a substance produced by bees to make honeycombs; beeswax. **2** a soft solid substance used for making candles or polishes. verb polish or treat with wax. ■ **waxen** adjective **waxy** adjective.

wax² verb **1** (of the moon) gradually appear to increase in size. **2** literary become larger or stronger. **3** literary speak or write in the specified way: *they waxed lyrical.*

waxwork noun **1** a lifelike dummy made of wax. **2** (**waxworks**) an exhibition of waxworks.

way noun **1** a method, style, or manner of doing something. **2** a road, track, or path. **3** a route or means taken in order to reach, enter, or leave a place. **4** a direction. **5** the distance in space or time between two points. **6** condition or state. **7** (**ways**) parts into which something divides. **8** forward motion of a ship through water. adverb informal at or to a considerable distance or extent. □ **by the way** inci-

dentally. **give way 1** yield. **2** collapse or break under pressure. **3** (**give way to**) be replaced by. **in the way** obstructing someone's progress. **make way** allow room for someone or something else. **way-out** informal very unconventional.

wayfarer noun literary a person who travels on foot.

waylay verb (**waylays, waylaying, waylaid**) **1** intercept someone in order to attack them. **2** stop someone and talk to them.

wayside noun the edge of a road.

wayward adjective unpredictable and hard to control.

WC abbreviation Brit. water closet.

we pronoun **1** used by a speaker to refer to himself or herself and one or more other people considered together. **2** people in general.

weak adjective **1** lacking strength and energy. **2** likely to break or give way under pressure. **3** not secure or stable. **4** lacking power, influence, or ability. **5** (of a liquid or solution) heavily diluted. ■ **weakly** adverb.

weaken verb make or become weak.

weakling noun a weak person or animal.

weakness noun **1** the state of being weak. **2** a fault. **3** something that you cannot resist. **4** (**weakness for**) a self-indulgent liking for.

weal noun a red swollen mark left on flesh by a blow or pressure.

wealth noun **1** a large amount of money, property, or possessions. **2** the state of being rich. **3** a large amount of something desirable.

wealthy adjective (**wealthier, wealthiest**) rich.

wean verb **1** make a young mammal used to food other than its mother's milk. **2** (**wean off**) make someone give up a habit or addiction. **3** (**be weaned on**) be strongly influenced by something from an early age.

weapon noun **1** a thing used to cause physical harm or damage. **2** a means of gaining an advantage or defending yourself. ■ **weaponry** noun.

wear verb (**wears, wearing, wore;** past participle **worn**) **1** have something on your body as clothing, decoration, or protection. **2** display a particular facial expression. **3** damage by friction or use. **4** (**wear off**) stop being effective or strong. **5** (**wear down**) overcome by persistence. **6** (**wear out**) exhaust. **7** (**wearing**) mentally or physically tiring. **8** (**wear on**) (of time) pass slowly or tediously. noun **1** clothing of a particular type. **2** damage caused by continuous use. ■ **wearer** noun.

wearisome adjective causing you to feel tired or bored.

weary adjective (**wearier, weariest**) **1** tired. **2** causing tiredness. **3** (**weary of**) reluctant to experience any more of. verb (**wearies, wearying, wearied**) **1** make someone weary. **2** (**weary of**) grow tired of. ■ **wearily** adverb **weariness** noun.

weasel noun a small, slender meat-eating mammal with reddish-brown fur.

weather noun the state of the atmosphere in terms of temperature, wind, rain, etc. verb (**weathers, weathering, weathered**) **1** wear something away by long exposure to the weather. **2** come safely through. □ **keep a weather eye on** watch developments carefully. **make heavy weather of** informal have unnecessary difficulty in dealing with. **under the weather** informal slightly unwell.

weathercock noun a weathervane in the form of a cockerel.

weatherman noun a man who broadcasts a description and forecast of weather conditions.

weathervane noun a revolving pointer that shows the direction of the wind.

weave[1] verb (**weaves, weaving, wove;** past participle **woven** or **wove**) **1** form fabric by interlacing long threads with others. **2** (**weave into**) make facts, events, etc. into a story. noun a particular way in which fabric

is woven. ■ **weaver** noun.

weave[2] verb (**weaves, weaving, weaved**) move from side to side to get around obstructions.

web noun **1** a network of fine threads made by a spider to catch its prey. **2** a complex system of interconnected elements. **3** (**the Web**) the World Wide Web. **4** the skin between the toes of a bird or animal living in water. □ **web page** a document that can be accessed via the Internet.

webbed adjective (of an animal's feet) having the toes connected by a web.

webbing noun strong fabric used for making straps, belts, etc.

website noun a location on the Internet that maintains one or more web pages.

wed verb (**weds, wedding, wedded** or **wed**) **1** formal or literary marry. **2** (**wedded**) having to do with marriage. **3** combine two desirable factors or qualities. **4** (**be wedded to**) be entirely devoted to a particular activity or belief.

we'd short form **1** we had. **2** we should or we would.

wedding noun a marriage ceremony.

wedge noun **1** a piece of wood, metal, etc. with a thick end that tapers to a thin edge. **2** a golf club for hitting the ball as high as possible into the air. **3** a shoe with a fairly high heel forming a solid block with the sole. verb (**wedges, wedging, wedged**) **1** fix in position using a wedge. **2** force into a narrow space. □ **the thin end of the wedge** informal something unimportant in itself which is likely to lead to more serious developments.

wedlock noun old use or formal the state of being married.

Wednesday noun the day of the week before Thursday and following Tuesday.

wee[1] adjective Scottish little.

wee[2] informal, chiefly Brit. noun **1** an act of urinating. **2** urine. verb (**wees, weeing, weed**) urinate.

weed noun **1** a wild plant growing where it is not wanted. **2** informal can-

nabis. **3 (the weed)** informal tobacco.
4 informal a weak or skinny person.
5 (weeds) old use black clothes worn
by a widow in mourning for her husband. **verb 1** remove weeds from.
2 (weed out) remove unwanted
items.

weedkiller noun a substance used to
destroy weeds.

weedy adjective **(weedier, weediest)**
1 containing or covered with many
weeds. **2** informal thin and weak.

week noun **1** a period of seven days.
2 the five days from Monday to Friday, when many people work. **3** Brit. a
week after a specified day.

weekday noun a day of the week
other than Sunday or Saturday.

weekend noun Saturday and Sunday.
verb informal spend a weekend.

weekly adjective & adverb happening
or produced once a week.

weeny adjective **(weenier, weeniest)**
informal tiny.

weep verb **(weeps, weeping, wept)**
1 shed tears; cry. **2** discharge liquid.
noun a spell of shedding tears.

weepy adjective **(weepier, weepiest)**
informal **1** tearful. **2** sentimental.

weevil noun a small beetle which eats
crops or stored foodstuffs.

weft noun (in weaving) the threads
that are passed over and under the
warp threads to make cloth.

weigh verb **1** find out how heavy
someone or something is. **2** have a
specified weight. **3 (weigh out)** measure and take out a portion of a particular weight. **4 (weigh down)** be
heavy and troublesome to. **5 (weigh
on)** be depressing or worrying to.
6 (weigh in) (of a boxer or jockey) be
officially weighed before or after a
contest. **7** (often **weigh up**) assess the
nature or importance of. **8** (often
weigh against) influence a decision
or action. **9 (weigh in)** informal contribute forcefully.

weighbridge noun a machine on to
which vehicles are driven to be
weighed.

weight noun **1** the heaviness of a per-

son or thing. **2** the quality of being
heavy. **3** a unit used for expressing
how much something weighs. **4** a
piece of metal known to weigh a definite amount and used on scales to determine how heavy something is. **5** a
heavy object. **6** ability to influence decisions. **7** the importance attached to
something. **verb 1** make heavier or
keep in place with a weight. **2 (be
weighted)** be arranged so as to give
one party an advantage. ■ **weightless**
adjective.

weighting noun **1** adjustment made
to take account of special circumstances. **2** Brit. additional wages paid
to allow for a higher cost of living in a
particular area.

weightlifting noun the sport or activity of lifting heavy weights.
■ **weightlifter** noun.

weighty adjective **(weightier, weightiest)** **1** heavy. **2** very serious and important. **3** very influential.

weir noun a low dam built across a
river to control its flow.

weird adjective **1** strange in a frightening way; eerie. **2** informal very strange.
■ **weirdly** adverb **weirdness** noun.

> ☑ *weird* is an exception to the usual
> rule of *i* before *e* except after *c*.

weirdo noun (plural **weirdos**) informal a strange
and eccentric person.

welch ⇒ **WELSH**.

welcome noun **1** an instance or way
of greeting someone. **2** a pleased or
approving reaction. **verb (welcomes,
welcoming, welcomed) 1** greet someone in a polite or friendly way when
they arrive somewhere. **2** be glad to
receive or hear of. adjective **1** gladly received. **2** very pleasing because much
needed or desired. **3** allowed or invited to do a specified thing.

weld verb **1** join together metal parts
by heating the surfaces and pressing
or hammering them together. **2** make
two things combine into a whole. noun
a welded joint. ■ **welder** noun.

welfare noun **1** the health, happiness,
and fortunes of a person or group.

2 organized help given to people in need. □ **welfare state** a system under which the state provides pensions, health care, etc.

well[1] adverb **1** in a good way. **2** in prosperity or comfort. **3** thoroughly. **4** to a great extent or degree. **5** very probably; in all likelihood. **6** without difficulty. **7** with good reason. adjective **1** in good health. **2** in a satisfactory state or position. **3** sensible; advisable. exclamation used to express surprise, anger, resignation, etc. □ **as well 1** in addition. **2** with equal reason or an equally good result. **well advised** sensible; wise. **well appointed** having a high standard of equipment or furnishing. **well-being** the state of being comfortable, healthy, or happy. **well disposed** having a sympathetic or friendly attitude. **well heeled** informal wealthy. **well nigh** old use almost. **well off 1** wealthy. **2** in a good situation. **well spoken** having an educated and refined voice. **well-to-do** wealthy. **well-wisher** a person who wishes another well.

> ℹ **well** is often used with a past participle such as *known* or *dressed* to form adjectives such as **well known**, **well dressed**, etc. Write these adjectives without a hyphen when they come after a verb (*she is well known as a writer*) but with a hyphen when they come before a noun (*a well-known writer*).

well[2] noun **1** a shaft sunk into the ground to obtain water, oil, or gas. **2** a hollow made to hold liquid. **3** a plentiful source or supply. **4** a space in the middle of a building for stairs, a lift, etc. verb (often **well up**) **1** (of a liquid) rise up to the surface. **2** (of an emotion) arise and become stronger.

we'll short form we shall or we will.

wellington noun Brit. a knee-length waterproof rubber or plastic boot.

welly or **wellie** noun (plural **wellies**) Brit. informal **1** a wellington. **2** power or vigour.

Welsh noun the language of Wales. adjective relating to Wales. □ **Welsh rare-**

bit (or **Welsh rabbit**) a dish of melted cheese on toast. ■ **Welshness** noun.

welsh or **welch** verb (**welsh on**) fail to honour a debt or obligation.

welt noun **1** a leather rim to which the sole of a shoe is attached. **2** a weal.

welter noun a large disordered number of items.

welterweight noun a weight in boxing between lightweight and middleweight.

wench noun old use or humorous a girl or young woman.

wend verb (**wend your way**) go slowly or by an indirect route.

Wendy house noun Brit. a toy house large enough for children to play in.

went past of **GO**.

wept past and past participle of **WEEP**.

were 2nd person singular past, plural past, and past subjunctive of **BE**.

we're short form we are.

weren't short form were not.

werewolf /**wair**-wuulf/ noun (plural **werewolves**) (in stories) a person who periodically changes into a wolf, especially when there is a full moon.

west noun **1** the direction in which the sun sets. **2** the western part of a place. **3** (**the West**) Europe and North America. adjective & adverb **1** towards or facing the west. **2** (of a wind) blowing from the west. ■ **westward** adjective & adverb **westwards** adverb.

westerly adjective & adverb **1** facing or moving towards the west. **2** (of a wind) blowing from the west.

western adjective **1** situated in or facing the west. **2** (**Western**) having to do with the west, in particular Europe and North America. noun a film or novel about cowboys in western North America.

westerner noun a person from the west of a region.

westernize or **westernise** verb (**westernizes**, **westernizing**, **westernized**) bring under the influence of Europe and North America.

wet adjective (**wetter**, **wettest**)

1 covered or saturated with liquid. **2** (of the weather) rainy. **3** not yet having dried or hardened. **4** Brit. informal feeble. verb (**wets**, **wetting**, **wet** or **wetted**) **1** cover or touch with liquid. **2** urinate in or on. noun **1** liquid that makes something damp. **2** (**the wet**) rainy weather. **3** Brit. informal a feeble person. □ **wet blanket** informal a person who spoils other people's enjoyment with their disapproving or unenthusiastic manner. **wet nurse** a woman employed to breastfeed another woman's child. ■ **wetly** adverb **wetness** noun.

wether noun a castrated ram.

wetsuit noun a close-fitting rubber garment covering the entire body, worn in water sports or diving.

we've short form we have.

whack informal verb **1** hit forcefully. **2** defeat heavily. **3** place or insert roughly or carelessly. **4** (**whacked**) Brit. completely exhausted. **5** (**whacking**) Brit. very large. noun **1** a sharp blow. **2** Brit. a share or contribution.

whacky ⇒ **WACKY**.

whale noun (plural **whale** or **whales**) a very large sea mammal with a blowhole on top of the head for breathing. □ **have a whale of a time** informal enjoy yourself very much.

whalebone noun a hard substance growing in plates in the upper jaw of some whales, used by them to strain plankton from the seawater.

whaler noun **1** a whaling ship. **2** a sailor engaged in whaling.

whaling noun the practice of hunting and killing whales.

whammy noun (plural **whammies**) informal an event with a powerful and unpleasant effect.

wharf /worf/ noun (plural **wharves** or **wharfs**) a level area where ships are moored to load and unload.

what pronoun & determiner **1** asking for information about something. **2** whatever. **3** used to emphasize something surprising or remarkable. pronoun **1** asking someone to repeat something. **2** the thing or things that.

adverb to what extent?

whatever or **whatsoever** pronoun & determiner everything or anything that; no matter what. pronoun used for emphasis instead of 'what' in questions. adverb at all; of any kind.

whatnot noun informal an unidentified or unspecified item or items.

wheat noun a cereal crop whose grain is ground to make flour.

wheatear noun a small bird with a white rump.

wheatgerm noun a nutritious food consisting of the centre parts of grains of wheat.

wheatmeal noun flour made from wheat from which some of the bran and germ has been removed.

wheedle verb (**wheedles**, **wheedling**, **wheedled**) try to persuade someone to do something by flattering or being insincerely nice to them.

wheel noun **1** a revolving circular object that is fixed below a vehicle to enable it to move along or forms part of a machine. **2** (**the wheel**) a steering wheel. **3** a turn or rotation. verb **1** push or pull a vehicle with wheels. **2** carry on a vehicle with wheels. **3** fly or turn in a wide curve. **4** turn round quickly. **5** (**wheel out**) informal resort to something predictable or overused. □ **wheel and deal** take part in commercial or political scheming.

wheelbarrow noun a three-wheeled cart with two handles at the rear.

wheelbase noun the distance between the front and rear axles of a vehicle.

wheelchair noun a chair on wheels for an invalid or disabled person.

wheeler-dealer noun a person who wheels and deals.

wheeze verb (**wheezes**, **wheezing**, **wheezed**) **1** breathe with a whistling or rattling sound in the chest. **2** make a rattling or spluttering sound. noun **1** a sound of wheezing. **2** Brit. informal a clever or amusing scheme or trick. ■ **wheezy** adjective.

whelk noun a shellfish with a pointed spiral shell.

whelp noun old use **1** a puppy. **2** disapproving a boy or young man. verb give birth to a puppy.

when adverb **1** at what time? **2** in what circumstances? **3** at which time or in which situation. conjunction **1** at or during the time that. **2** at any time that; whenever. **3** in view of the fact that. **4** although; whereas.

whence or **from whence** adverb formal **1** from what place or source? **2** from which or from where. **3** to the place from which. **4** as a consequence of which.

whenever or formal **whensoever** conjunction **1** at whatever time or on whatever occasion. **2** every time that. adverb used for emphasis instead of 'when' in questions.

where adverb **1** in or to what place or position? **2** in what direction or respect? **3** at, in, or to which. **4** in or to a place or situation in which.

whereabouts adverb where or approximately where? noun the place where someone or something is.

whereas conjunction **1** in contrast or comparison with the fact that. **2** taking into consideration the fact that.

whereby adverb by which.

wherefore old use adverb for what reason? adverb & conjunction as a result of which.

wherein adverb formal **1** in which. **2** in what place or respect?

whereof adverb formal of what or which.

whereupon conjunction immediately after which.

wherever or formal **wheresoever** adverb **1** in or to whatever place. **2** used for emphasis instead of 'where' in questions. conjunction in every case when.

wherewithal noun the money or other resources needed for something.

wherry /rhymes with sherry/ noun (plural **wherries**) a light rowing boat or barge.

whet /wet/ verb (**whets, whetting,**

whetted) **1** sharpen a blade. **2** stimulate someone's interest or appetite.

whether conjunction **1** expressing a doubt or choice between alternatives. **2** indicating that a statement applies whichever of the alternatives mentioned is the case.

whetstone noun a stone used for sharpening cutting tools.

whey /way/ noun the watery part of milk that remains after curds have formed.

which pronoun & determiner **1** asking for information specifying one or more people or things from a set. **2** used to refer to something previously mentioned when introducing a clause giving further information.

whichever determiner & pronoun **1** any which; that or those which. **2** regardless of which.

whiff noun **1** a smell that is smelt only briefly or faintly. **2** Brit. informal an unpleasant smell. **3** a trace or hint of something bad or exciting. **4** a puff or breath of air or smoke.

Whig noun historical a member of a British political party that became the Liberal Party.

while noun **1** (**a while**) a period of time. **2** (**a while**) for some time. **3** (**the while**) meanwhile. conjunction **1** at the same time as. **2** whereas. **3** although. adverb during which. verb (**whiles, whiling, whiled**) (**while away**) pass time in a leisurely way. □ **worth while** (or **worth your while**) worth the time or effort spent.

whilst conjunction & adverb chiefly Brit. while.

whim noun a sudden desire or change of mind.

whimper verb (**whimpers, whimpering, whimpered**) make low, feeble sounds expressing fear, pain, or discontent. noun a whimpering sound.

whimsical adjective **1** playfully old-fashioned or fanciful. **2** showing sudden changes of mood or behaviour. ■ **whimsically** adverb.

whimsy noun (plural **whimsies**) **1** old-fashioned or fanciful behaviour or humour. **2** a fanciful or odd thing. **3** a whim.

whin noun chiefly N. English gorse.

whine noun **1** a long, high-pitched complaining cry. **2** a long, high-pitched sound. verb (**whines, whining, whined**) give or make a whine. ■ **whiny** adjective.

whinge Brit. informal verb (**whinges, whingeing, whinged**) complain persistently and irritably. noun an act of whingeing.

> remember the *h*: whinge.

whinny noun (plural **whinnies**) a gentle, high-pitched neigh. verb (**whinnies, whinnying, whinnied**) (of a horse) make a whinny.

whip noun **1** a length of leather or cord fastened to a handle, used for beating a person or urging on an animal. **2** an official of a political party appointed to maintain parliamentary discipline among its members. **3** a written notice from a party whip telling members how to vote in a debate. **4** a dessert made from cream or eggs beaten into a light fluffy mass. verb (**whips, whipping, whipped**) **1** strike with a whip. **2** beat or move violently. **3** move or take out fast or suddenly. **4** beat cream, eggs, etc. into a froth. □ **the whip hand** a position of power or control over someone. **whipping boy** a person who is blamed for or punished for the faults of others. **whipround** Brit. informal a collection of money. **whip up 1** make or prepare very quickly. **2** deliberately excite or provoke.

whiplash noun **1** the flexible part of a whip. **2** injury caused by a severe jerk to the head.

whippersnapper noun informal a young and inexperienced but over-confident person.

whippet noun a small, slender breed of dog.

whippoorwill /wip-per-wil/ noun an American bird with a distinctive call.

whirl verb **1** move rapidly round and round. **2** (of the head or mind) seem to spin round. noun **1** a rapid movement round and round. **2** busy or hurried activity.

whirligig noun **1** a toy that spins round. **2** a roundabout at a fair.

whirlpool noun a current of water that whirls in a circle.

whirlwind noun **1** a column of air moving rapidly round and round. **2** a very energetic or disorderly person or process. adjective very rapid and unexpected: *a whirlwind romance*.

whirr or **whir** verb (**whirs** or **whirrs, whirring, whirred**) (of something rapidly rotating or moving) make a low, continuous, regular sound. noun a whirring sound.

whisk verb **1** beat eggs, cream, etc. with a light, rapid movement. **2** move or take suddenly and quickly. noun **1** a utensil for whisking eggs, cream, etc. **2** a bunch of grass, twigs, etc. for flicking away dust or flies.

whisker noun **1** each of the long hairs or bristles growing from the face of an animal. **2** (**whiskers**) the hair growing on a man's face. **3** (**a whisker**) informal a very small amount.

whisky (Irish & US spelling **whiskey**) noun (plural **whiskies**) a strong alcoholic drink distilled from malted grain.

> Scotch whisky, but Irish whiskey.

whisper verb (**whispers, whispering, whispered**) **1** speak very softly. **2** literary rustle or murmur softly. noun **1** something whispered. **2** a very soft voice. **3** literary a soft rustling or murmuring. **4** a rumour or piece of gossip. **5** a slight trace.

whist noun a card game in which points are scored according to the number of tricks won.

whistle noun **1** a clear, high-pitched sound made by forcing breath between the lips or teeth. **2** any similar high-pitched sound. **3** a device used to produce a whistling sound. verb (**whistles, whistling, whistled**) **1** give out a whistle. **2** move rapidly with a whistling sound. **3** blow a whistle. □ **whistle-stop** very fast and with only brief pauses.

Whit noun Whitsun. □ **Whit Sunday** a Christian festival held on the seventh Sunday after Easter.

whit noun a very small part or amount.

white adjective **1** having the colour of milk or fresh snow. **2** very pale. **3** relating to people with light-coloured skin. **4** innocent and pure. **5** Brit. (of coffee or tea) with milk. **6** (of wine) yellowish in colour. noun **1** white colour or material. **2** the visible pale part of the eyeball around the iris. **3** the outer part which surrounds the yolk of an egg; the albumen. **4** a white person. □ **white-collar** relating to work in an office or other professional environment. **white elephant** a useless or troublesome possession. **white flag** a white flag waved as a symbol of surrender or truce. **white-hot** so hot that it glows white. **white lie** a harmless lie told to avoid hurting someone's feelings. **white magic** magic used only for good purposes. **White Paper** (in the UK) a government report giving information or proposals on an issue. **white sauce** a sauce made with flour, butter, and milk or stock. **white spirit** Brit. a colourless liquid distilled from petroleum, used as a paint thinner and solvent. ■ **whiteness** noun.

whitebait noun the young of various sea fish used as food.

whiten verb make or become white. ■ **whitener** noun.

whitewash noun **1** a solution of lime or chalk and water, used for painting walls white. **2** a deliberate concealment of mistakes or faults. verb **1** paint with whitewash. **2** conceal mistakes or faults.

whither adverb formal or old use **1** to what place or state. **2** what is the likely future of?

whiting noun (plural **whiting**) a sea fish with white flesh eaten as food.

Whitsun or **Whitsuntide** noun the weekend or week including Whit Sunday.

whittle verb (**whittles, whittling, whittled**) **1** carve wood by cutting small slices from it. **2** (**whittle away** or **down**) gradually reduce.

whizz verb (**whizzes, whizzing, whizzed**) **1** move quickly through the air. **2** move or go fast. noun informal a person who is extremely clever at something. □ **whizz-kid** informal a young person who is very successful or skilful.

who pronoun **1** what or which person or people? **2** introducing a clause giving further information about a person or people previously mentioned.

> ℹ the rule is that you should use **who** as the subject of a verb (*who decided this?*) and **whom** as the object of a verb or preposition (*whom do you think we should support?*). When speaking, however, it is acceptable to use **who** instead of **whom**, as in *who do you think we should support?*

whoa exclamation used as a command to a horse to stop or slow down.

who'd short form **1** who had. **2** who would.

whodunnit (US spelling **whodunit**) noun informal a crime story in which the identity of the murderer is not revealed until the end.

whoever or formal **whosoever** pronoun **1** the person or people who; any person who. **2** regardless of who. **3** used for emphasis instead of 'who' in questions.

whole adjective **1** complete; entire. **2** in one piece. noun **1** a thing that is complete in itself. **2** (**the whole**) all of something. □ **on the whole** taking everything into account; in general. ■ **wholeness** noun.

wholefood noun Brit. food that has been processed as little as possible and is free from additives.

wholehearted adjective completely

sincere and committed. ■ **whole-heartedly** adverb.

wholemeal adjective Brit. (of flour or bread) made from whole grains of wheat including the husk.

wholesale noun the selling of goods in large quantities to be sold to the public by others. **adjective & adverb 1** being sold in such a way. **2** on a large scale. verb (**wholesales, wholesaling, wholesaled**) sell goods wholesale. ■ **wholesaler** noun.

wholesome adjective **1** good for health or well-being. **2** morally good.

wholly adverb entirely; fully.

 two *l*s, no *e*: wholly, not *-ely*.

whom pronoun used instead of 'who' as the object of a verb or preposition.

whoop noun a loud cry of joy or excitement. verb **1** give or make a whoop. **2** (**whoop it up**) informal enjoy yourself in a lively way. □ **whooping cough** an illness chiefly affecting children, characterized by coughs followed by a rasping indrawn breath.

whoopee exclamation informal expressing excitement or joy. □ **make whoopee 1** celebrate wildly. **2** have sex.

whoops exclamation informal expressing mild dismay.

whoosh verb move quickly with a rushing sound. noun a whooshing movement.

whopper noun informal **1** something extremely large. **2** a blatant lie.

whopping adjective informal extremely large.

whore /rhymes with door/ noun **1** a prostitute. **2** disapproving a woman who has many sexual partners.

whorehouse noun informal a brothel.

whorl /worl, werl/ noun **1** each of the turns in a spiral or coil. **2** a spiral or coil. **3** a coil of leaves, flowers, or branches encircling a stem.

who's short form **1** who is. **2** who has.

ℹ️ don't confuse **who's** with **whose**. **Who's** is short for either **who is** or **who has**, as in *he has a son who's a doctor* or *who's done the reading?*, whereas **whose** means 'belonging to which person' or 'of whom or which', as in *whose is this?* or *he's a man whose opinion I respect*.

whose possessive determiner & pronoun **1** belonging to or associated with which person. **2** of whom or which.

why adverb **1** for what reason or purpose? **2** on account of which; the reason that. exclamation expressing surprise, annoyance, etc.

wick noun a length of cord in a candle, lamp, or lighter which carries liquid fuel to the flame. □ **get on someone's wick** Brit. informal annoy someone.

wicked adjective **1** very bad; evil. **2** playfully mischievous. **3** informal excellent; wonderful. ■ **wickedly** adverb **wickedness** noun.

wicker noun twigs plaited or woven to make items such as furniture and baskets. ■ **wickerwork** noun.

wicket noun **1** Cricket each of the two sets of three stumps with two bails across the top that are defended by a batsman. **2** a small door or gate.

wicketkeeper noun Cricket a fielder positioned close behind a batsman's wicket.

wide adjective (**wider, widest**) **1** of great or more than average width. **2** having a particular width. **3** open to the full extent. **4** including a great variety of people or things. **5** spread among a large number or over a large area. **6** at a distance from a point or mark. **7** (in football) at or near the side of the field. adverb **1** to the full extent. **2** far from the target. □ **wide awake** fully awake. **wide boy** Brit. informal a man involved in petty criminal activities. ■ **widely** adverb.

widen verb make or become wider.

widespread adjective spread among a large number or over a large area.

widgeon ⇒ **WIGEON**.

widget noun informal a small gadget or

mechanical device.

widow noun a woman whose husband has died and who has not married again. **verb (be widowed)** become a widow or widower.

widower noun a man whose wife has died and who has not married again.

width noun **1** the measurement or extent of something from side to side. **2** wide range or extent.

widthways or **widthwise** adverb in a direction parallel with a thing's width.

wield verb **1** hold and use a weapon or tool. **2** have power or influence.

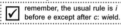

☑ remember, the usual rule is *i* before *e* except after *c*: w**ie**ld.

wife noun (plural **wives**) the woman a man is married to. ■ **wifely** adjective.

wig noun a covering for the head made of real or artificial hair.

wigeon or **widgeon** noun a duck with mainly reddish-brown and grey plumage.

wiggle verb (**wiggles**, **wiggling**, **wiggled**) move with short movements up and down or from side to side. noun a wiggling movement. ■ **wiggly** adjective.

wigwam noun a tent consisting of animal skins fixed over a framework of poles, formerly lived in by some North American Indian peoples.

wild adjective **1** (of animals or plants) living or growing in the natural environment. **2** (of scenery or a region) not cultivated or inhabited. **3** lacking discipline or control. **4** not based on reason or evidence. **5** informal very enthusiastic or excited. noun **1 (the wild)** a natural state. **2 (the wilds)** a remote area. □ **wild card 1** a playing card which can take on any value, suit, or colour that the player holding it needs. **2** a person or thing whose qualities are uncertain. **3** Computing a character that will match any character or sequence of characters in a search. **wild goose chase** a hopeless search for something that you will never find. ■ **wildly** adverb **wildness** noun.

wildcat adjective (of a strike) sudden and unofficial.

wildebeest /wil-duh-beest/ noun a gnu (a kind of antelope).

wilderness noun a wild, uninhabited, and unwelcoming region.

wildfire noun (**spread like wildfire**) spread with great speed.

wildfowl plural noun birds that are hunted as game.

wildlife noun all the animals, birds, and insects that naturally inhabit a particular region.

wiles plural noun cunning plans.

wilful (US spelling **willful**) adjective **1** deliberate. **2** stubborn and determined. ■ **wilfully** adverb **wilfulness** noun.

will¹ modal verb (3rd singular present **will**; past **would**) **1** expressing the future tense. **2** expressing a request. **3** expressing desire, consent, or willingness. **4** expressing facts about ability or capacity.

ℹ the traditional rule is that you should use **shall** when forming the future tense with **I** and **we** (*I shall be late*) and **will** with **you, he, she, it**, and **they** (*he will not be there*). Nowadays, people do not follow this rule so strictly and are more likely to use the shortened forms **I'll, she'll**, etc.

will² noun **1** the power you have to decide on something and take action. **2** (also **will power**) the ability to control your thoughts and actions in order to achieve something. **3** a desire or intention. **4** a legal document in which someone gives instructions about what should be done with their money and property after their death. verb **1** intend or desire that something should happen. **2** bring something about by using your mental powers. **3** leave money or property to someone in a will. □ **at will** whenever or in whatever way you like.

willies plural noun (**the willies**) informal a feeling of uneasiness or fear.

willing adjective **1** ready, eager, or prepared to do something. **2** given or done readily. ■ **willingly** adverb **willingness** noun.

will-o'-the-wisp noun a faint flickering light seen at night over marshy ground, thought to result from natural gases burning.

willow noun a tree which has narrow leaves and bears catkins.

willowy adjective tall and slim.

willy or **willie** noun (plural **willies**) Brit. informal a penis.

willy-nilly adverb **1** whether you like it or not. **2** without any direction or plan.

wilt verb **1** (of a plant) become limp through heat or lack of water. **2** feel tired and weak.

wily /rhymes with highly/ adjective cunningly clever.

wimp noun informal an unadventurous and timid person. ■ **wimpish** adjective **wimpy** adjective.

wimple noun a cloth headdress covering the head, neck, and sides of the face, worn in the past by women and still today by some nuns.

win verb (**wins**, **winning**, **won**) **1** be the most successful in a contest or conflict. **2** gain something as a result of success in a contest or conflict. **3** gain someone's attention, support, or love. **4** (**win over**) gain someone's agreement or support by persuading them that you are right. noun a victory in a game or contest.

wince verb (**winces**, **wincing**, **winced**) flinch slightly on feeling pain or distress. noun an act of wincing.

winceyette noun Brit. a soft brushed cotton fabric.

winch noun a hauling or lifting device consisting of a rope or chain winding around a rotating drum. verb hoist or haul something with a winch.

wind[1] noun **1** a natural movement of the air. **2** breath needed to play an instrument or do exercise. **3** wind or woodwind instruments forming a band or section of an orchestra. **4** Brit. air or gas in the stomach or intestines. verb **1** cause someone to have difficulty breathing because of exertion or a blow to the stomach. **2** Brit. pat a baby on its back to help it bring up air swallowed while feeding. □ **get wind of** informal hear a rumour of. **put the wind up** Brit. informal alarm or frighten. **wind instrument 1** a musical instrument which you play by blowing into it. **2** a woodwind instrument as distinct from a brass instrument. **wind tunnel** a tunnel-like structure in which a strong current of air is created, to test the effect of wind and air flow on vehicles. ■ **windy** adjective.

wind[2] verb (**winds**, **winding**, **wound**) **1** move in or take a twisting or spiral course. **2** pass something around a thing or person so as to encircle or enfold them. **3** (with reference to something long) twist or be twisted around itself or a core. **4** make a clockwork device work by turning a key or handle. **5** turn a key or handle repeatedly. **6** move an audio tape, videotape, or film backwards or forwards. □ **wind down 1** (of a clockwork mechanism) gradually lose power. **2** draw or bring gradually to an end. **3** informal relax. **wind up 1** gradually bring to an end. **2** informal end up in a particular situation or place. **3** Brit. informal tease or irritate.

windbag noun informal a person who talks trivially and at length.

windbreak noun a screen providing shelter from the wind.

windcheater noun a wind-resistant jacket with a close-fitting neck and cuffs.

windfall noun **1** an apple or other fruit blown from a tree by the wind. **2** a piece of unexpected good fortune.

windlass noun a winch used on a ship or in a harbour.

windmill noun a building with sails or vanes that turn in the wind and generate power to grind corn, generate electricity, or draw water.

window noun **1** an opening in a wall, fitted with glass to let in light and allow people to see out. **2** a framed area on a computer screen for viewing information. □**window dressing 1** the arrangement of a display in a shop window. **2** the presentation of something in a superficially attractive way to give a good impression. **window-shop** spend time looking at the goods displayed in shop windows. **window sill** a ledge or sill at the bottom of a window.

windowpane noun a pane of glass in a window.

windpipe noun the tube carrying air down the throat and into the lungs; the trachea.

windscreen noun Brit. a glass screen at the front of a motor vehicle.

windshield noun N. Amer. a windscreen.

windsock noun a light, flexible cone mounted on a mast to show the direction and strength of the wind.

windsurfing noun the sport of riding on a sailboard on water. ■ **windsurf** verb **windsurfer** noun.

windswept adjective · exposed to strong winds.

windward adjective & adverb facing the wind, or on the side facing the wind.

wine noun an alcoholic drink made from fermented grape juice. □**wine bar** a bar or small restaurant that specializes in serving wine. **wine cellar 1** a cellar for storing wine. **2** a stock of wine.

winery noun (plural **wineries**) an establishment where wine is made.

wing noun **1** a kind of limb used by a bird, bat, or insect for flying. **2** a rigid structure projecting from both sides of an aircraft and supporting it in the air. **3** a part of a large building. **4** a group or faction within an organization. **5** (**the wings**) the sides of a theatre stage out of view of the audience. **6** the part of a soccer or rugby field close to the sidelines. **7** Brit. the part of a car above and extending slightly over a wheel. **8** an air force unit of several squadrons. verb **1** fly, or move quickly as if flying. **2** shoot a bird so as to wound it in the wing. **3** (**wing it**)

informal speak or act without preparation. □**wing nut** a nut with a pair of projections for the fingers to turn it on a screw. ■ **winged** adjective.

winger noun an attacking player on the wing in soccer, hockey, etc.

wingspan noun the full extent from tip to tip of the wings of an aircraft, bird, etc.

wink verb **1** close and open one eye quickly as a private signal. **2** shine or flash intermittently. noun an act of winking.

winkle noun a small edible shellfish with a spiral shell. verb (**winkles, winkling, winkled**) (**winkle out**) Brit. **1** take something out from a tight or embedded position. **2** get information from someone who is reluctant to give it.

winning adjective attractive. noun (**winnings**) money won by gambling. ■ **winningly** adverb.

winnow verb blow air through grain in order to remove the chaff.

wino noun (plural **winos**) informal a person who sits all day in the streets drinking alcohol.

winsome adjective appealing.

winter noun the coldest season of the year, after autumn and before spring. verb (**winters, wintering, wintered**) spend the winter in a particular place.

wintry adjective cold or bleak.

wipe verb (**wipes, wiping, wiped**) **1** clean or dry something by rubbing it with a cloth or your hand. **2** remove something from a surface in this way. **3** erase data from a computer, video, etc. noun **1** an act of wiping. **2** an absorbent cleaning cloth. □**wipe out 1** remove or eliminate. **2** kill a large number of people. ■ **wiper** noun.

wire noun **1** metal in the form of a thin flexible strand. **2** a length of wire used for fencing, to carry an electric current, etc. **3** a concealed listening device. **4** informal a telegram. verb (**wires, wiring, wired**) **1** install electric circuits or wires in a room or building. **2** fasten or reinforce with wire. **3** informal send a telegram to.

wireless noun dated **1** a radio. **2** broadcasting using radio signals.

wiretapping noun the secret tapping of telephone lines in order to listen to other people's conversations.

wiring noun a system of wires providing electric circuits for a device or building.

wiry adjective 1 resembling wire. **2** lean, tough, and sinewy.

wisdom noun 1 the quality of being wise. **2** a body of knowledge and experience. □ **wisdom tooth** each of the four molars at the back of the mouth which usually appear at about the age of twenty.

wise¹ adjective 1 having or showing experience, knowledge, and good judgement. **2** (**wise to**) informal aware of. **verb** (**wises, wising, wised**) (**wise up**) informal become aware of something. ■ **wisely** adverb.

wise² noun old use the manner or extent of something.

wisecrack informal **noun** a witty remark or joke. **verb** make a wisecrack.

wish verb 1 feel a strong desire for something. **2** silently express a hope that something will happen. **3** say that you hope that someone will be happy, successful, etc. **noun 1** a desire or hope. **2** (**wishes**) an expression of hope that someone will be happy, successful, etc. **3** a thing wished for.

wishbone noun a forked bone between the neck and breast of a bird.

wishful adjective having or expressing a wish for something to happen. □ **wishful thinking** expectations that are based on impractical wishes rather than facts. ■ **wishfully** adverb.

wishy-washy adjective feeble or bland.

wisp noun a small, thin bunch or strand of something. ■ **wispy** adjective.

wisteria /wi-steer-i-uh/ or **wistaria** /wi-stair-i-uh/ **noun** a climbing plant with hanging clusters of bluish-lilac flowers.

wistful adjective having a feeling of vague or regretful longing. ■ **wistfully** adverb.

wit noun 1 (also **wits**) the capacity for inventive thought and quick understanding. **2** a natural talent for using words and ideas in a quick and funny way. **3** a quick, funny person.

witch noun a woman believed to have evil magic powers. □ **witch doctor** a person believed to have magic powers that cure illness. **witch hazel** a shrub whose bark and leaves are used to make a lotion that helps stop bleeding. **witch-hunt** a campaign against a person who holds unpopular views. ■ **witchery** noun.

witchcraft noun the use of evil magic powers.

with preposition 1 accompanied by. **2** in the same direction as. **3** possessing; having. **4** indicating the instrument used to perform an action or the material used for a purpose. **5** in opposition to or competition with. **6** indicating the manner or attitude in which a person does something. **7** in relation to. □ **with it** informal **1** up to date or fashionable. **2** alert and able to understand.

withdraw verb (**withdraws, withdrawing, withdrew**; past participle **withdrawn**) **1** remove or take away. **2** take money out of an account. **3** take back something you have said. **4** leave or cause to leave a place. **5** stop taking part in an activity. **6** go away to another place in search of quiet or privacy. **7** stop taking an addictive drug. **8** (**withdrawn**) very shy or reserved. ■ **withdrawal** noun.

wither verb (**withers, withering, withered**) **1** (of a plant) become dry and shrivelled. **2** become shrunken or wrinkled from age or disease. **3** become weaker; decline. **4** (**withering**) scornful.

withers plural noun the highest part of a horse's back, at the base of the neck.

withhold verb (**withholds, withholding, withheld**) **1** refuse to give. **2** hold back an emotion or reaction.

remember to double the *h*: with**hold**.

within preposition **1** inside. **2** inside the range or bounds of. **3** occurring inside a particular period of time. adverb **1** inside. **2** internally.

without preposition not accompanied by or having the use of. adverb old use outside.

withstand verb (**withstands**, **withstanding**, **withstood**) remain undamaged by; resist.

witless adjective foolish; stupid.

witness noun **1** a person who sees an event take place. **2** a person who gives evidence in a court of law. **3** a person who is present at the signing of a document and signs it themselves to confirm this. verb **1** be a witness to. **2** be the place, period, etc. in which an event takes place.

witter verb (**witters**, **wittering**, **wittered**) Brit. informal talk for a long time about unimportant things.

witticism noun a witty remark.

witty adjective (**wittier**, **wittiest**) able to say clever and amusing things. ■ **wittily** adverb.

wives plural of **WIFE**.

wizard noun **1** a man who has magical powers. **2** a person who is very skilled in something. ■ **wizardry** noun.

wizened adjective shrivelled or wrinkled with age.

woad noun a plant whose leaves were used in the past to make blue dye.

wobble verb (**wobbles**, **wobbling**, **wobbled**) **1** move unsteadily from side to side. **2** (of the voice) tremble. noun a wobbling movement or sound. ■ **wobbly** adjective.

woe noun literary **1** great sadness or distress. **2** (**woes**) troubles. □ **woe betide someone** a person will be in trouble if they do a particular thing.

woebegone /woh-bi-gon/ adjective looking sad or miserable.

woeful adjective **1** very sad. **2** very bad. ■ **woefully** adverb.

wok noun a bowl-shaped frying pan used in Chinese cookery.

woke past of **WAKE**[1].

woken past participle of **WAKE**[1].

wold noun an area of high, open land.

wolf noun (plural **wolves**) a wild animal of the dog family, that lives and hunts in packs. verb (**wolfs**, **wolfing**, **wolfed**) eat food quickly and greedily. □ **cry wolf** keep raising false alarms, so that when you really need help you are ignored. **wolf whistle** a whistle with a rising and falling note, addressed to a passer-by as a way of saying that they are sexually attractive. ■ **wolfish** adjective.

wolfhound noun a large breed of dog originally used to hunt wolves.

wolfram noun tungsten or its ore.

wolverine noun a heavily built meat-eating mammal found in cold northern areas.

woman noun (plural **women**) an adult human female. ■ **womanhood** noun **womanly** adjective.

womanize or **womanise** verb (**womanizes**, **womanizing**, **womanized**) (of a man) have a lot of casual affairs with women. ■ **womanizer** noun.

womankind noun women as a whole.

womb noun the organ in a woman's body in which a baby develops before it is born.

wombat noun an Australian animal resembling a small bear with short legs.

won past and past participle of **WIN**.

wonder noun **1** a feeling of amazement and admiration. **2** a person or thing that causes such a feeling. verb (**wonders**, **wondering**, **wondered**) **1** be interested to know about something. **2** feel doubt. **3** feel amazement and admiration. □ **no wonder** it is not surprising.

wonderful adjective extremely good or remarkable. ■ **wonderfully** adverb.

wonderland noun a place full of wonderful things.

wondrous adjective literary inspiring wonder.

wonky adjective informal **1** crooked. **2** unsteady or faulty.

wont /wohnt/ noun (your wont) formal your normal behaviour.

won't short form will not.

wonted /wohn-tid/ adjective old use or literary usual.

woo verb (woos, wooing, wooed) **1** (of a man) try to make a woman love him. **2** try to get someone's support or custom.

wood noun **1** the hard material forming the trunk and branches of a tree. **2** (also woods) a small forest. ◼ woody adjective.

woodcut noun a print made with a block of wood in which a design has been cut.

woodcutter noun a person who cuts down trees for wood.

wooded adjective (of land) covered with woods.

wooden adjective **1** made of wood. **2** acting or speaking in a stiff and awkward manner. ◼ woodenly adverb.

woodland or **woodlands** noun land covered with trees.

woodlouse noun (plural woodlice) a small insect-like creature with a grey segmented body.

woodpecker noun a bird with a strong bill that pecks at tree trunks to find insects.

woodturning noun the activity of shaping wood with a lathe. ◼ woodturner noun.

woodwind noun wind instruments other than brass instruments forming a section of an orchestra.

woodwork noun **1** the wooden parts of a room, building, or other structure. **2** the activity of making things from wood. ◼ woodworker noun.

woodworm noun the larva of a kind of beetle, that bores into wood.

woof[1] noun the barking sound made by a dog. verb bark.

woof[2] = WEFT.

woofer noun a loudspeaker that reproduces low frequencies.

wool noun the fine, soft hair forming the coat of a sheep.

woollen (US spelling **woolen**) adjective **1** made of wool. **2** relating to the production of wool. noun (woollens) woollen garments.

woolly adjective **1** made of wool. **2** covered with wool or hair resembling wool. **3** resembling wool. **4** confused or unclear. noun (plural woollies) informal a woollen jumper or cardigan.

woozy adjective informal unsteady, dizzy, or dazed. ◼ woozily adverb.

word noun **1** a unit of language which has meaning and is used with others to form sentences. **2** a remark or statement. **3** (words) angry talk. **4** (the word) a command, slogan, or signal. **5** (your word) your account of the truth of something that happened. **6** (your word) a thing that you promise. **7** news. verb express something in particular words. □ in a word briefly. **word of mouth** talking as a way of passing on information. **word processor** a computer or program for creating and printing a document or piece of text.

wording noun the way in which something is worded.

wordy adjective using too many words.

wore past of WEAR.

work noun **1** activity involving mental or physical effort done in order to achieve a result. **2** the activity or job that a person does in order to earn money. **3** a task or tasks to be done. **4** a thing or things done or made. **5** (works) a place where industrial or manufacturing processes are carried out. **6** (works) activities involving the construction or repair of something. **7** (works) the mechanism of a clock or other machine. verb **1** do work as your job. **2** make someone do work. **3** (of a machine or system) function properly. **4** (of a machine) be in operation. **5** have the desired result. **6** bring a material or mixture to a desired shape or consistency. **7** cultivate land, or extract materials from a mine or quarry. **8** move something gradually or with difficulty into another position. □ **get worked up** become stressed or angry. **have your work cut out** be faced with a hard or time-consuming task. **work out 1** solve something. **2** develop in the desired way. **3** plan something in detail. **4** engage in vigorous physical exercise. **work permit** an official document giving a foreigner permission to take a job in a country. **work-to-rule** a situation in which people refuse to do overtime or extra work, as a form of protest. **work up to** proceed gradually towards something more demanding or advanced.

workaday adjective ordinary.

workbench noun a bench at which carpentry and other work is done.

worker noun **1** a person who works. **2** a neuter or undeveloped female bee, wasp, ant, etc., large numbers of which perform the basic work of a colony.

workforce noun the people engaged in or available for work in a particular area, firm, or industry.

workhouse noun (in the past in the UK) a place where poor people were given accommodation and food in return for work.

working adjective **1** having paid employment. **2** doing manual work. **3** functioning or able to function. **4** used as a basis for everyday work or for discussion. noun **1** a mine from which minerals are being extracted. **2** (**workings**) the way in which a machine, organization, or system operates. □ **working class** the social group consisting largely of people who do manual or industrial work. **working party** a group set up to study and report on a particular question and make recommendations.

workload noun the amount of work to be done by someone or something.

workman noun a man employed to do manual work.

workmanlike adjective showing efficient skill.

workout noun a session of vigorous physical exercise.

workshop noun **1** a room or building in which things are made or repaired. **2** a meeting for discussion and activity on a particular subject or project.

workstation noun a desktop computer that is part of a network.

worktop noun Brit. a flat surface for working on in a kitchen.

world noun **1** (**the world**) the earth with all its countries and peoples. **2** all that belongs to a particular region, period, or area of activity. □ **world music** traditional music from around the world. **world power** a country that has great international influence. **world-weary** bored with or cynical about life. **World Wide Web** an information system on the Internet which allows documents to be connected to each other using hypertext links.

worldly adjective **1** of or concerned with material things rather than spiritual ones. **2** experienced and sophisticated. □ **worldly goods** everything that someone owns. **worldly-wise** having a lot of experience of life.

worldwide adjective & adverb throughout the world.

worm noun **1** an earthworm or other creeping or burrowing creature with a long, thin body and no limbs. **2** (**worms**) long, thin creatures that live as parasites in a person's or animal's intestines. verb **1** move by crawling or wriggling. **2** (**worm your way into**) gradually move into. **3** (**worm out of**) cleverly obtain information from someone who is reluctant to give it. □ **worm cast** a small spiral of earth or sand thrown up at the surface by a burrowing worm.

wormwood noun a plant with a bitter flavour, used in drinks such as vermouth.

worn past participle of **WEAR**. adjective thin or damaged as a result of wear. □ **worn out 1** exhausted. **2** damaged by wear, and no longer usable.

worried adjective feeling anxiety or concern. ■ **worriedly** adverb.

worrisome adjective causing anxiety or concern.

worry verb (worries, worrying, worried) **1** feel or cause to feel troubled over unwelcome things that have happened or may happen. **2** annoy or disturb. **3** (of a dog) repeatedly push at and bite something. **4** (of a dog) chase and attack livestock. noun (plural worries) **1** the state of being worried. **2** a source of anxiety. ■ **worrier** noun.

worse adjective **1** less good, satisfactory, or pleasing. **2** more serious or severe. **3** more ill or unhappy. adverb **1** less well. **2** more seriously or severely. noun a worse event or circumstance.

worsen verb make or become worse.

worship noun **1** the practice of praising and praying to a god or goddess. **2** religious rites and ceremonies. **3** a strong feeling of admiration and respect for someone. verb (worships, worshipping, worshipped; US spelling worships, worshiping, worshiped) **1** offer praise and prayers to a god or goddess. **2** feel great admiration and respect for. ■ **worshipper** noun.

worshipful adjective **1** feeling or showing great respect and admiration. **2** (Worshipful) Brit. a title given to justices of the peace.

worst adjective most bad, severe, or serious. adverb **1** most severely or seriously. **2** least well. noun the worst part, event, or circumstance.

worsted /wuus-tid/ noun a smooth woollen fabric of good quality.

worth adjective **1** equivalent in value to a particular sum or item. **2** deserving to be treated in a particular way. noun **1** the value of someone or something. **2** an amount of something that is equivalent to a particular sum of money.

worthless adjective **1** having no practical or financial value. **2** having no good qualities.

worthwhile adjective worth the time, money, or effort spent.

worthy adjective (worthier, worthiest) **1** deserving effort, attention, or respect. **2** (worthy of) deserving or good enough for. **3** well intended but too serious and dull. noun (plural worthies) humorous a person who is important in a particular sphere. ■ **worthily** adverb.

would modal verb (3rd singular present **would**) **1** past of **WILL**[1]. **2** indicating the consequence of an imagined event. **3** expressing a desire or inclination. **4** expressing a polite request. **5** expressing an opinion or assumption. **6** literary expressing a wish or regret. □ **would-be** wishing to be a particular type of person: *a would-be actress.*

wouldn't short form would not.

wound[1] noun **1** an injury to the body caused by a cut, blow, or bullet. **2** an injury to a person's feelings. verb **1** inflict a wound on. **2** injure someone's feelings.

wound[2] past and past participle of **WIND**[2].

wove past of **WEAVE**[1].

woven past participle of **WEAVE**[1].

wow informal exclamation expressing astonishment or admiration. noun a sensational success. verb greatly impress and excite.

WPC abbreviation woman police constable.

wrack[1] ⇨ **RACK**.

wrack[2] noun a coarse brown seaweed.

wraith /rayth/ noun a ghost.

wrangle noun a long dispute or argument. verb (wrangles, wrangling, wrangled) engage in a wrangle.

wrap verb (wraps, wrapping, wrapped) **1** enclose something in paper or soft material. **2** encircle or wind round. noun **1** a loose outer garment or piece of material. **2** paper or material used for wrapping. □ under wraps kept secret. wrap up **1** dress warmly. **2** bring a meeting or deal to a close. ■ **wrapper** noun.

wrasse /rass/ noun (plural wrasse or wrasses) a brightly coloured sea fish with thick lips and strong teeth.

wrath /roth, rawth/ **noun** extreme anger. ■ **wrathful** adjective.

wreak verb **1** cause a lot of damage or harm. **2** inflict vengeance.

wreath noun (plural **wreaths**) **1** an arrangement of flowers or leaves fastened in a ring. **2** a curl or ring of smoke or cloud.

wreathe verb (**wreathes**, **wreathing**, **wreathed**) **1** (**be wreathed**) be surrounded or encircled. **2** (of smoke) move with a curling motion.

wreck noun **1** the destruction of a ship at sea. **2** a ship destroyed at sea. **3** a building, vehicle, etc. that has been destroyed or badly damaged. **4** N. Amer. a road or rail crash. **5** a person in a very bad state. verb **1** cause a ship to sink or break up. **2** destroy or badly damage. **3** spoil a plan.

wreckage noun the remains of something that has been badly damaged.

wren noun **1** a very small bird with a cocked tail. **2** (in the UK) a member of the former Women's Royal Naval Service.

wrench verb **1** pull or twist something suddenly and violently. **2** twist and injure a part of the body. noun **1** a sudden violent twist or pull. **2** a feeling of sadness on leaving a place or person. **3** an adjustable tool used for gripping and turning nuts or bolts.

wrest verb **1** forcibly pull something from someone's grasp. **2** succeed in taking power or control from someone after a struggle.

wrestle verb (**wrestles**, **wrestling**, **wrestled**) **1** take part in a fight or contest that involves close grappling with your opponent. **2** struggle with a difficulty or problem. **3** struggle to move an object. noun **1** a wrestling bout or contest. **2** a hard struggle. ■ **wrestler** noun **wrestling** noun.

wretch noun **1** an unfortunate person. **2** informal a contemptible person.

wretched adjective **1** in a very unhappy or unfortunate state. **2** of poor quality. ■ **wretchedly** adverb.

wriggle verb (**wriggles**, **wriggling**, **wriggled**) **1** twist and turn with quick writhing movements. **2** (**wriggle out of**) use excuses to avoid doing something. noun a wriggling movement. ■ **wriggly** adjective.

wring verb (**wrings**, **wringing**, **wrung**) **1** squeeze and twist something to force water out of it. **2** twist and break an animal's neck. **3** squeeze someone's hand tightly. **4** (**wring from** or **out of**) obtain something from someone with difficulty.

wringer noun a machine with two rollers, used for squeezing water out of wet clothes or linen.

wringing adjective extremely wet.

wrinkle noun a slight line or fold, especially in fabric or a person's skin. verb (**wrinkles**, **wrinkling**, **wrinkled**) make or become covered with wrinkles. ■ **wrinkly** adjective.

wrist noun the joint connecting the hand with the lower part of the arm.

wristwatch noun a watch worn on a strap round the wrist.

writ[1] noun an official command issued by a court or other legal authority.

writ[2] archaic past participle of **WRITE**. □ **writ large** in an obvious or exaggerated form.

write verb (**writes**, **writing**, **wrote**; past participle **written**) **1** mark letters, words, or other symbols on a surface with a pen, pencil, etc. **2** write and send a letter to someone. **3** compose a text or musical work. **4** fill out a cheque or similar document. □ **write off 1** dismiss as insignificant. **2** decide not to pursue a debt. **write-off** a vehicle that is too badly damaged to be repaired. **write-up** a newspaper review of a recent event, performance, etc. ■ **writer** noun.

writhe /ry*th*/ verb (**writhes**, **writhing**, **writhed**) twist or squirm in pain or embarrassment.

writing noun **1** the activity or skill of writing. **2** a sequence of letters or symbols forming words. **3** (**writings**) books or other written works.

wrong adjective **1** not correct or true; mistaken or in error. **2** unjust, dishonest, or immoral. **3** in a bad or abnormal condition. **adverb 1** in a mistaken or unwelcome manner or direction. **2** with an incorrect result. **noun** an unjust, dishonest, or immoral action. **verb** treat someone unfairly. □**wrong-foot** (in a game) catch an opponent off balance. **2** place someone in a difficult situation by saying or doing something unexpected. **wrong-headed** having bad judgement. ■ **wrongly** adverb **wrongness** noun.

wrongdoing noun illegal or dishonest behaviour. ■ **wrongdoer** noun.

wrongful adjective not fair, just, or legal. ■ **wrongfully** adverb.

wrote past tense of **WRITE**.

wrought /rhymes with bought/ old-fashioned past and past participle of **WORK**. **adjective 1** (of metals) beaten

out or shaped by hammering. **2** made in a particular way: *well-wrought.* □**wrought iron** tough iron suitable for forging or rolling.

wrung past and past participle of **WRING**.

wry adjective (wryer, wryest or wrier, wriest) **1** using dry, mocking humour. **2** (of a person's face) twisted into an expression of disgust, disappointment, or annoyance. **3** bending or twisted to one side. ■ **wryly** adverb.

wunderkind /vuun-der-kind/ noun a person who is very successful at a young age.

Wurlitzer /wer-lit-ser/ noun trademark a large pipe organ or electric organ.

WWI abbreviation World War I.

WWII abbreviation World War II.

WWW abbreviation World Wide Web.

X or **x** noun (plural **Xs** or **X's**) **1** the twenty-fourth letter of the alphabet. **2** an X-shaped written symbol, used to indicate an incorrect answer or to symbolize a kiss. **3** the Roman numeral for ten. □**X chromosome** a sex chromosome, two of which are normally present in female cells and one in male cells. **X certificate** (in the past) a classification of a film as suitable for adults only. **x-rated** pornographic or indecent. **X-ray 1** an electromagnetic wave of very short wavelength, which is able to pass through many solids and so make it possible to see into or through them. **2** an image of the internal structure of an object produced by passing

X-rays through it.

xenon /zen-on/ noun an inert gaseous element, present in small amounts in the air.

xenophobia /zen-uh-foh-bi-uh/ noun dislike or fear of people from other countries. ■ **xenophobic** adjective.

Xerox /zeer-oks/ noun trademark **1** a process for copying documents using an electric charge and dry powder. **2** a copy made using such a process. **verb** (**xerox**) copy a document by such a process.

Xmas noun informal Christmas.

xylophone noun a musical instrument consisting of a row of bars which you strike with small beaters.

Yy

Y or **y** noun (plural **Ys** or **Y's**) the twenty-fifth letter of the alphabet. □ **Y chromosome** a sex chromosome which is normally present only in male cells. **Y-fronts** Brit. trademark men's or boys' underpants with a seam at the front in the shape of an upside-down Y. **Y2K** the year 2000.

yacht /yot/ noun **1** a medium-sized sailing boat. **2** a powered boat equipped for cruising. ■ **yachting** noun.

yahoo /yah-hoo/ noun informal a rude or coarse person.

yak[1] noun a large ox with shaggy hair and large horns, found in Tibet and central Asia.

yak[2] or **yack** verb (**yaks**, **yakking**, **yakked**) informal talk continuously about something trivial.

yam noun the tuber of a tropical plant, eaten as a vegetable.

yang noun (in Chinese philosophy) the active male force in the universe.

Yank noun informal an American.

yank informal verb pull quickly and hard. noun a sudden hard pull.

Yankee noun informal **1** an American. **2** US a person from New England or one of the northern states. **3** historical a Federal soldier in the Civil War.

yap verb (**yaps**, **yapping**, **yapped**) give a sharp, shrill bark. noun a sharp, shrill bark.

yard[1] noun **1** a unit of length equal to 3 feet (0.9144 metre). **2** a square or cubic yard. **3** a long piece of wood slung across a ship's mast for a sail to hang from.

yard[2] noun **1** Brit. a piece of enclosed ground next to a building. **2** an area of land used for a particular purpose. **3** N. Amer. the garden of a house.

yardarm noun either end of a ship's yard supporting a sail.

Yardie noun informal a member of a Jamaican gang of criminals.

yardstick noun a standard used for comparison.

yarmulke or **yarmulka** /yar-muul-kuh/ noun a skullcap worn by Jewish men.

yarn noun **1** spun thread used for knitting, weaving, or sewing. **2** informal a long story.

yashmak noun a veil concealing all of the face except the eyes, worn by some Muslim women.

yaw verb (of a moving ship or aircraft) turn unsteadily from side to side. noun yawing movement.

yawn verb **1** involuntarily open your mouth wide and take a deep breath, usually when tired or bored. **2** (**yawning**) wide open. noun **1** an act of yawning. **2** informal a tedious event.

yd abbreviation yard.

ye[1] plural of **THOU**.

ye[2] old use = **THE**.

yea adverb old use yes.

year noun **1** the period of 365 days (or 366 days in leap years) starting from January 1. **2** a period of this length starting at a different point. **3** the time taken by the earth to go around the sun. **4** (**your years**) your age or time of life. **5** (**years**) informal a very long time. **6** a set of students who enter and leave a school or college at the same time.

yearling noun an animal between one and two years old.

yearly adjective & adverb happening or produced once a year or every year.

yearn verb have a strong feeling of loss and longing for something.

yeast noun **1** a fungus capable of converting sugar into alcohol and carbon dioxide. **2** a substance formed from this, used to make bread dough rise and to ferment beer. ■ **yeasty** adjective.

yell noun a loud, sharp call or cry. **verb** shout loudly.

yellow adjective **1** of the colour of egg yolks or ripe lemons. **2** informal cowardly. noun a yellow colour. verb (of paper, fabric, etc.) become slightly yellow with age. ▢ **yellow card** (in soccer) a yellow card shown by the referee to a player being cautioned. **yellow fever** a tropical disease that causes fever and jaundice and often death. ■ **yellowish** adjective.

yellowhammer noun a bird with a yellow head, neck, and breast.

yelp noun a short, sharp cry. **verb** utter a yelp or yelps.

yen¹ noun (plural **yen**) the basic unit of money of Japan.

yen² noun informal a strong desire; a longing or yearning.

yeoman /yoh-muhn/ noun (in the past) a man having his own house and small area of farming land. ▢ **Yeoman of the Guard** a member of the British king or queen's ceremonial bodyguard.

yes exclamation **1** used to give a response in favour of something. **2** used to respond to someone who is addressing you. noun (plural **yeses** or **yesses**) a decision or vote in favour of something. ▢ **yes-man** a person who always agrees with people in authority.

yesterday adverb on the day before today. noun **1** the day before today. **2** the recent past.

yesteryear noun literary last year or the recent past.

yet adverb **1** up until now or then. **2** as soon as this. **3** from now into the future. **4** referring to something that will or may happen. **5** still; even. **6** in spite of that. **conjunction** but at the same time.

yeti noun a large hairy manlike creature said to live in the highest part of the Himalayas.

yew noun an evergreen tree with poisonous red fruit.

Yiddish noun a language used by Jews from central and eastern Eur-

ope. **adjective** relating to Yiddish.

yield verb **1** produce or provide a natural or industrial product. **2** produce a result or gain. **3** give way to demands or pressure. **4** give up possession of. **5** give way under force or pressure. noun an amount or result yielded.

> ✓ remember, *i* before *e* except after *c*: y*ie*ld.

yin noun (in Chinese philosophy) the passive female presence in the universe.

yob noun Brit. informal a rude and aggressive young man. ■ **yobbish** adjective.

yobbo noun (plural **yobbos** or **yobboes**) Brit. informal a yob.

yodel verb (**yodels**, **yodelling**, **yodelled**; US spelling **yodels**, **yodeling**, **yodeled**) sing or call in a style that alternates rapidly between a normal voice and a very high voice. noun a song or call of this type. ■ **yodeller** noun.

yoga noun a system involving breathing exercises and the holding of particular body positions, followed by fitness and relaxation and based on Hindu philosophy. ■ **yogic** adjective.

yogi noun (plural **yogis**) a person who is skilled in yoga.

yogurt, **yoghurt**, or **yoghourt** noun a semi-solid slightly sour food made from milk with bacteria added.

yoke noun **1** a piece of wood fastened over the necks of two animals and attached to a plough or cart in order for them to pull it. **2** a pair of yoked animals. **3** a frame fitting over the neck and shoulders of a person, used for carrying buckets or baskets. **4** a burden. **5** a part of a garment that fits over the shoulders and to which the main part of the garment is attached. verb (**yokes**, **yoking**, **yoked**) join together or attach to a yoke.

yokel noun an unsophisticated country person.

yolk noun the yellow part in the middle of an egg.

Yom Kippur /yom kip-**poor**/ noun an

important day in the Jewish religion in which people pray and fast.

yon old use or dialect **determiner & adverb** that. **pronoun** that person or thing.

yonder old use or dialect **adverb** over there. **determiner** that or those.

yonks plural noun Brit. informal a very long time.

yore noun (of yore) literary in the past; long ago.

you pronoun **1** used to refer to the person or people that the speaker is addressing. **2** used to refer to any person in general.

you'd short form **1** you had. **2** you would.

you'll short form you will or you shall.

young adjective (younger, youngest) **1** having lived or existed for only a short time. **2** relating to or characteristic of young people. **plural noun** young children or animals; offspring.

youngster noun a young person.

your possessive determiner **1** belonging to or associated with the person or people that the speaker is addressing. **2** belonging to or associated with any person in general.

> i don't confuse **your** meaning 'belonging to you' (as in *let me talk to your daughter*) with the form **you're**, which is short for **you are** (as in *you're a good cook*).

you're short form you are.

yours possessive pronoun used to refer to something belonging to or associated with the person or people that the speaker is addressing.

yourself pronoun (plural **yourselves**) **1** used as the object of a verb or preposition when this is the same as the

subject of the clause and the subject is the person or people being addressed. **2** you personally.

youth noun (plural **youths**) **1** the period between childhood and adult age. **2** the qualities of energy, immaturity, etc. associated with being young. **3** young people. **4** a young man. □ **youth club** a club where young people can meet and take part in various activities. **youth hostel** a place providing cheap overnight accommodation for young people.

youthful adjective **1** young or seeming young. **2** characteristic of young people. ■ **youthfully** adverb **youthfulness** noun.

you've short form you have.

yowl /*rhymes with* fowl/ **noun** a loud wailing cry of pain or distress. **verb** make such a cry.

yo-yo noun (plural **yo-yos**) (trademark in the UK) a toy consisting of a pair of joined discs with a groove between them in which string is attached and wound, which can be spun down and up as the string unwinds and rewinds. **verb** (**yo-yoes, yo-yoing, yo-yoed**) move up and down repeatedly.

yucca noun a plant with sword-like leaves, native to the southern US and Mexico.

yuck or **yuk** informal **exclamation** used to express disgust. ■ **yucky** adjective.

Yule or **Yuletide** noun old use Christmas.

yummy adjective (**yummier, yummiest**) informal delicious.

yuppie or **yuppy** noun (plural **yuppies**) informal a young middle-class professional person who earns a lot of money.

Zz

Z or **z** noun (plural **Zs** or **Z's**) the twenty-sixth letter of the alphabet.

zany adjective (**zanier**, **zaniest**) amusingly unconventional and individual.

zap informal verb (**zaps**, **zapping**, **zapped**) **1** destroy; obliterate. **2** move or propel suddenly and rapidly. **3** use a remote control to change television channels.

zeal noun great energy, enthusiasm, and commitment.

zealot /zel-uht/ noun a person who follows a religion, cause, or policy very strictly and enthusiastically. ■ **zealotry** noun.

zealous /zel-uhss/ adjective showing great energy or enthusiasm for a cause or aim. ■ **zealously** adverb.

zebra noun an African wild horse with black and white stripes. □ **zebra crossing** Brit. an area of road marked with broad white stripes, where pedestrians can cross.

zeitgeist /zyt-gysst/ noun the general spirit or mood of a particular period of history.

Zen noun a type of Buddhism that emphasizes the value of meditation and intuition.

zenith noun **1** the point in the sky directly overhead. **2** the highest point in the sky reached by the sun or moon. **3** the time at which something is most powerful or successful.

zephyr noun literary a soft, gentle breeze.

Zeppelin noun a large German airship of the early 20th century.

zero cardinal number (plural **zeros**) **1** the figure 0; nought. **2** a temperature of 0°C (32°F), marking the freezing point of water. verb (**zeroes**, **zeroing**, **zeroed**) **1** adjust an instrument to zero. **2** (**zero in on**) take aim at or focus attention on. □ **zero hour** the time at which a military operation or import-

ant event is set to begin.

zest noun **1** great enthusiasm and energy. **2** excitement or stimulation. **3** the outer coloured part of the peel of an orange or lemon.

zigzag noun a line having sharp alternate right and left turns. adjective & adverb veering to right and left alternately. verb (**zigzags**, **zigzagging**, **zigzagged**) take a zigzag course.

zilch pronoun informal nothing.

zillion cardinal number informal an extremely large number of people or things. ■ **zillionth** ordinal number.

Zimmer frame noun trademark a metal frame that people use to help them walk.

zinc noun a silvery-white metallic element used in making brass and to coat iron and steel.

zing informal noun energy, enthusiasm, or liveliness. verb move swiftly. ■ **zingy** adjective.

Zionism noun a movement for the development of a Jewish nation in Israel. ■ **Zionist** noun & adjective.

zip noun **1** Brit. a fastener consisting of two flexible interlocking strips of metal or plastic, closed or opened by pulling a slide along them. **2** informal energy; liveliness. verb (**zips**, **zipping**, **zipped**) **1** fasten with a zip. **2** informal move at high speed. **3** Computing compress a file so that it takes up less space. □ **zip code** US a postcode.

zipper chiefly N. Amer. noun a zip fastener. verb (**zippers**, **zippering**, **zippered**) fasten something with a zip.

zippy adjective informal **1** bright, fresh, or lively. **2** speedy.

zircon noun a brown or semi-transparent mineral.

zit noun informal a spot on the skin.

zither /zi-ther/ noun a musical instrument with numerous strings stretched across a flat box, which you